THE OXFORD HANDBOOK ON

THE UNITED NATIONS

THE OXFORD HANDBOOK ON

THE UNITED NATIONS

Edited by

THOMAS G. WEISS

AND

SAM DAWS

OXFORD

UNIVERSITY PRESS

OXFORD
UNIVERSITY PRESS

Great Clarendon Street, Oxford OX2 6DP

Oxford University Press is a department of the University of Oxford.
It furthers the University's objective of excellence in research, scholarship,
and education by publishing worldwide in

Oxford New York

Auckland Cape Town Dar es Salaam Hong Kong Karachi
Kuala Lumpur Madrid Melbourne Mexico City Nairobi
New Delhi Shanghai Taipei Toronto

With offices in

Argentina Austria Brazil Chile Czech Republic France Greece
Guatemala Hungary Italy Japan Poland Portugal Singapore
South Korea Switzerland Thailand Turkey Ukraine Vietnam

Oxford is a registered trade mark of Oxford University Press
in the UK and in certain other countries

Published in the United States
by Oxford University Press Inc., New York

First published 2007
First published in paperback 2008

British Library Cataloguing in Publication Data

Data available

Library of Congress Cataloging in Publication Data

The Oxford Handbook on the United Nations / edited by Thomas G. Weiss and Sam Daws.
p. cm.
1. United Nations–Handbooks, manuals, etc.   I. Weiss, Thomas George.   II. Daws, Sam.
JZ4970.093 2007
341.23–dc22   2006103221

Typeset by SPI Publisher Services, Pondicherry, India
Printed in Great Britain
on acid-free paper by
CPI Group (UK) Ltd, Croydon

ISBN 978–0–19–927951–7 (Hbk.)
978–0–19–956010–3 (Pbk.)

13

FOREWORD

by the UN SECRETARY-GENERAL

Much has been written over the past six decades about the United Nations and its work. Yet, since its establishment in 1945, there have been few comprehensive analyses of the structure and activities of the Organization as a whole. *The Oxford Handbook on the United Nations* fills a significant lacuna in scholarship.

Today's world of complex and global challenges is exactly the environment in which our United Nations thrives—because these are challenges that no country can resolve on its own. Whether we are speaking of peace and security, development, or human rights, demands on the Organization continue to grow. This *Handbook* offers a wide range of perspectives on the UN's work in those areas and brings alive the historical, legal, political, and administrative details of the Organization's multiple roles. It also explores how the international community can enhance the UN's capacity to fulfill its goals and foster global peace and progress.

These essays are diverse and strongly argued, and I may not agree with all of the views expressed in them. But they all share a deep conviction about the need for multilateral approaches to solving global problems, with the UN at the heart of the effort. I hope this *Handbook* will contribute to making our indispensable Organization better understood by experts, practitioners, and the public alike.

Ban Ki-moon
New York,
February 2007

ACKNOWLEDGMENTS

In the sixty-plus years since its establishment in 1945, the United Nations Organization, as well as the universal agencies that form part of the UN system, has been central to international relations. *The Oxford Handbook on the United Nations* fills a long-standing gap in the small library of distinguished guides to the humanities, sciences, and social sciences published by Oxford University Press (OUP). For libraries and research depositories worldwide, this book brings alive the historical, legal, political, and administrative details of the UN's many roles in well over a half-century.

Our task was to contextualize the world organization's role in helping to realize international achievements that, by the standards of previous centuries, have been unprecedented. Inevitably, the early hopes have wavered, especially when dashed by the bitter realities of international politics and conflicting economic interests. Even so, the vision and early ambitions have never been entirely lost—and the UN has continued to refashion its goals and objectives through the ups and downs of subsequent decades. We hope that we have captured the hopes and the despair, the triumphs and the tragedies, what has been achieved and especially what challenges remain.

One of the more agreeable tasks in writing a book is thanking the people who helped along the way. We begin with our editor at OUP, Dominic Byatt, who was not bashful about asking the two of us to assemble, between two covers, 400,000 words about the six-decade history of the present generation of global institutions. His confidence was reassuring, his astute advice invaluable, and his warm support unstinting. We would also like to express our gratitude to the OUP team who worked so efficiently with Dominic on this volume: Lizzy Suffling and Claire Croft for their administrative and organizational support, and Tom Chandler for his willingness to take on such a substantial copyediting task and complete it with such care and thoroughness.

The next round of appreciation goes to the forty-seven invited contributors whose analyses and prose grace these pages. When we agreed to edit this *Handbook* in June 2004, the task seemed daunting. Taking into account the commercial limits of what was a feasible project, we outlined what we thought every reader should know about the world organization but might be afraid to ask. After having decided upon the magic number of forty chapters, we then set about locating knowledgeable contributors. Using our respective multinational and multi-generational address books, along with those of colleagues, and searching libraries and our own book-shelves, we assembled what readers will agree is a world-class team. They have all either written extensively on the topic of their essays or been active practitioners in a related field—indeed, the vast majority have done both. Clearly, this *Handbook* reflects that collective wisdom.

It is no exaggeration to state that we could not have successfully completed a project of this magnitude and complexity without superb staff support at our two institutions. In the process of compiling the chapters, it suddenly dawned on us that we were actually trying to put together the equivalent of four edited books. The lion's share of the staff work was accomplished at the Ralph Bunche Institute for International Studies of The Graduate Center of The City University of New York. Five graduate students in particular should be singled out. First and foremost, we are extremely grateful to Ausama Abdelhadi who, from the very outset through June 2006, helped organize the logistics of this endeavor, chased down sources, and checked facts; and we relied on him for his critical eye in the logic of presentations. Quite simply, this volume would not have taken the shape it did without his help. Ian Jones and Zeynep Turan tidied up many of the early drafts and also checked citations and facts. Janet Reilly took over the relay in August 2006 and helped shepherd the manuscript through the queries, copy-editing, and page-proofs. Last but certainly anything except least, Danielle Zach Kalbacher's fastidious editing and attention to statistics improved the quality of many presentations, including our own; the care that she gives to every detail of a final product is exemplary, and in this case the very size of the manuscript made for an enormous number of details. And at the London headquarters of the United Nations Association of the United Kingdom, Veronica Lie exercised a meticulous eye to support the European side of the project, undertaking substantial research and the rewriting of several chapters. She was ably assisted by Tim Kellow, Mark Rusling and Natalie Samarasinghe. These nine individuals deserve a special round of applause from us and our readers.

We are also grateful for the financial and intellectual support that came from William Kelly, the president of The CUNY Graduate Center, and from the United Nations Intellectual History Project and our colleagues Richard Jolly and Louis Emmerij. The Graduate Center has been the home away from home for this entire undertaking.

The chapters here are totally independent examinations of the pluses and the minuses of many aspects of the world organization. Readers should keep in mind that this is a handbook *on* and not *of* the United Nations. We speak for all the contributors in saying plainly that the group as a whole consists of critical multilateralists. These are the voices of professionals who see the need for international cooperation to guarantee human survival with dignity, but no one is a card-carrying member of the UN fan club. The editors and the authors do not speak for the United Nations. The pages of this book represent our informed thinking, no more and (we hope) no less.

To all who participated and contributed with such dedication and skill, 'thanks' is really a pale reflection of our gratitude.

T.G.W and S.D.
New York and London
December 2006

Contents

List of Tables   xiii

List of Figures   xiv

Editors   xv

Contributors   xvi

List of Abbreviations   xxiv

PART I   INTRODUCTION

1. World Politics: Continuity and Change since 1945   3
   THOMAS G. WEISS AND SAM DAWS

PART II   THEORETICAL FRAMEWORKS

2. Political Approaches   41
   MICHAEL BARNETT AND MARTHA FINNEMORE

3. Legal Perspectives   58
   JOSÉ E. ALVAREZ

4. Evolution in Knowledge   82
   LEON GORDENKER AND CHRISTER JÖNSSON

PART III   PRINCIPAL ORGANS

5. General Assembly   97
   M. J. PETERSON

6. Security Council   117
   DAVID M. MALONE

7. Economic and Social Council   136
   GERT ROSENTHAL

8. Trusteeship Council   149
   RALPH WILDE

9. Secretariat: Independence and Reform   160
   JAMES O. C. JONAH

10. Secretary-General   175
    EDWARD NEWMAN

11. International Court of Justice   193
    JAMES CRAWFORD AND TOM GRANT

PART IV   RELATIONSHIPS WITH OTHER ACTORS

12. Regional Groups and Alliances   217
    WAHEGURU PAL SINGH SIDHU

13. Bretton Woods Institutions   233
    NGAIRE WOODS

14. Civil Society   254
    PAUL WAPNER

15. Private Sector   264
    CRAIG N. MURPHY

16. Media   275
    BARBARA CROSSETTE

PART V   INTERNATIONAL PEACE AND SECURITY

17. Disarmament   287
    KEITH KRAUSE

18. Peaceful Settlement of Disputes and Conflict Prevention   300
    RAMA MANI

19. Peacekeeping Operations   323
    MICHAEL W. DOYLE AND NICHOLAS SAMBANIS

20. Sanctions   349
    DAVID CORTRIGHT, GEORGE A. LOPEZ, AND
    LINDA GERBER-STELLINGWERF

21. Peace Enforcement 370
MICHAEL PUGH

22. Humanitarian Intervention 387
RAMESH THAKUR

23. Post-Conflict Peacebuilding 404
ROLAND PARIS

24. Terrorism 427
JANE BOULDEN

PART VI   HUMAN RIGHTS

25. Norms and Machinery 439
BERTRAND G. RAMCHARAN

26. International Criminal Court and Ad Hoc Tribunals 463
RICHARD GOLDSTONE

27. Humanitarian Action and Coordination 479
JEFF CRISP

28. Women and Gender 496
CHARLOTTE BUNCH

29. Children 511
YVES BEIGBEDER

30. Minorities and Indigenous Peoples 525
MAIVÂN CLECH LÂM

31. Human Security 539
FEN O. HAMPSON AND CHRISTOPHER K. PENNY

PART VII   DEVELOPMENT

32. Coordinating Economic and Social Affairs 561
JACQUES FOMERAND AND DENNIS DIJKZEUL

33. Health and Infectious Disease 582
GIAN LUCA BURCI

34. Natural Resource Management and Sustainable Development 592
NICO SCHRIJVER

35. Organized Crime 611
FRANK G. MADSEN

36. Democracy and Good Governance   620
    W. ANDY KNIGHT

37. Human Development   634
    RICHARD JOLLY

PART VIII   PROSPECTS FOR REFORM

38. Principal Organs   653
    EDWARD C. LUCK

39. Financing   675
    JEFFREY LAURENTI

40. Widening Participation   701
    CHADWICK F. ALGER

Appendices
  1. Suggested Further Reading   716
  2. The UN System   734
  3. The Charter of the United Nations   736
  4. Statute of the International Court of Justice   756
  5. Universal Declaration of Human Rights   767

Subject Index   773

Personal Name Index   807

LIST OF TABLES

5.1 Shifts in regional balance within the General Assembly, 1945–2005   106

6.1 Security Council statistics, Cold War and post-Cold War   121

7.1 Main subsidiary bodies of ECOSOC   137

12.1 UN peace operations involving regional actors after the Cold War   223

13.1 Voting-power allocations for the IMF and World Bank, 2006   244

19.1 Principal UN peacekeeping missions, 1947–2006   328

20.1 UN sanctions, 1990–2005   353

23.1 Major post-conflict peacebuilding operations, 1989–2005   407

25.1 Working groups of the former Commission on Human Rights and the
      Sub-Commission on the Promotion and Protection of Human Rights   448

25.2 System of special rapporteurs, independent experts, and
      representatives by country and theme, 2006   449

25.3 Human rights treaty bodies   452

35.1 Number of drugs and substances under international control,
      1912–1995   614

35.2 A nuclear glossary   617

37.1 Human development indicators for selected countries, 2003   639

39.1 Rates of assessment for selected countries   680

39.2 UN assessment adjustments for selected countries   682

39.3 UN peacekeeping and regular assessments for selected countries   686

List of Figures

19.1 Matching problem type and strategy type 336

19.2 The peacebuilding triangle 339

19.3 International capacities in 'hard' and 'easy' peacebuilding ecologies 342

23.1 Military and civilian police contributions to UN peacekeeping
operations, 1993–2005 408

23.2 UN peacekeeping costs, 1991–2001 409

23.3 The Peacebuilding Commission, Support Office, and Fund 421

39.1 United Nations Organization Regular Budget Appropriations 692

39.2 United Nations Organization voluntary contributions, 2002–2003 695

EDITORS

Thomas G. Weiss is Presidential Professor of Political Science at The CUNY Graduate Center and Director of the Ralph Bunche Institute for International Studies, where he is co-director of the United Nations Intellectual History Project. He is the president of the International Studies Association (2009–10) and chair of the Academic Council on the UN System (2006–9) and the former editor of its journal, *Global Governance*. He has written or edited some 35 books and 150 articles about multilateral approaches to international peace and security, humanitarian action, and sustainable development.

Sam Daws is Executive Director of the United Nations Association of the UK. He has served as a senior policy advisor on UN issues for 19 years, including three years as First Officer in the Executive Office of UN Secretary-General Kofi Annan. He previously directed a Geneva based international consultancy. He undertook doctoral studies on UN Security Council reform at New College, Oxford, and has been a visiting fellow at Cambridge and Yale Universities. He has co-authored or edited six books on the UN.

CONTRIBUTORS

Chadwick F. Alger is Mershon Professor of Political Science and Public Policy Emeritus, Ohio State University. He has published widely on his first-hand research on UN organizations in New York and Geneva, local communities, and peacebuilding. He is the author of *The UN System: A Reference Handbook* (2006) and editor of *The Future of the UN System* (1998). He was President of the International Studies Association and Secretary-General of the International Peace Research Association.

José E. Alvarez is Hamilton Fish Professor of International Law & Diplomacy and the Director of the Center on Global Legal Problems at Columbia Law School. He is President of the American Society of International Law (2006–2008), is a member of the Council on Foreign Relations and the US Department of State's Advisory Committee on Public International Law, and sits on the editorial boards of the *American Journal of International Law* and *Journal of International Criminal Justice*.

Michael Barnett is Harold Stassen Professor of International Affairs at the Humphrey Institute and Professor of Political Science at the University of Minnesota. He writes about international organizations, humanitarianism, international relations theory, and Middle Eastern politics. Among his books are *Dialogues in Arab Politics: Negotiations in Regional Order* (1998); *Security Communities* (1998, co-edited with Emanuel Adler); *Eyewitness to a Genocide: The United Nations and Rwanda* (2002); and *Rules for the World: International Organizations and World Politics* (2004, with Martha Finnemore).

Yves Beigbeder was for many years a human resources official in FAO and WHO. Since his retirement in 1984, he has given courses on international organization in universities in France, Switzerland, and North America, and lectures for UNITAR. He currently acts as Legal Counsel for international civil servants in Geneva, in complaints to internal boards and administrative tribunals. He has written eighteen books and many articles on international organizations, the international civil service, and international criminal justice.

Jane Boulden holds a Canada Research Chair in International Relations and Security Studies at the Royal Military College of Canada. From 2000 until 2003 she was a MacArthur Research Fellow at the Centre for International Studies, University of Oxford. Her recent edited books include *Terrorism and the UN: Before and After September 11th* (with Thomas G. Weiss, 2004) and *Dealing with Conflict in Africa: the United Nations and Regional Organizations* (2003); and she is the author of *Peace Enforcement* (2001).

Charlotte Bunch is Founder and Executive Director of the Center for Women's Global Leadership, Rutgers University, and has been an activist and organizer in the women's, civil, and human rights movements for four decades. She is Distinguished Professor in Women's and Gender Studies, author of numerous essays, and has written or edited ten books. Her contributions to conceptualizing and organizing for women's human rights have been recognized by many and include her induction into the National Women's Hall of Fame in the United States.

Gian Luca Burci is Legal Counsel of the World Health Organization. For a decade before arriving in Geneva, he was a legal officer in the Office of the Legal Counsel at UN headquarters in New York and also served in the International Atomic Energy Agency. A graduate of the School of Law of the University of Genoa, he is the author of *The World Health Organization* (2004) and more than twenty articles on United Nations issues, peacekeeping, and international health law.

David Cortright is President of the Fourth Freedom Forum and a research fellow at the Joan B. Kroc Institute for International Peace Studies at the University of Notre Dame. He has served as consultant or adviser to several UN organizations, the Carnegie Commission on Preventing Deadly Conflict, the International Peace Academy, and various governments. He has written widely on nuclear disarmament, nonviolent social change, and the use of incentives and sanctions as tools of international peacemaking.

James Crawford is Whewell Professor of International Law and Director of the Lauterpacht Centre for International Law, University of Cambridge. He was a member of the Australian Law Reform Commission and the UN International Law Commission. He was responsible for the ILC's Draft Statute for an International Criminal Court and the ILC's Articles on State Responsibility. As a member of Matrix Chambers, London, he practices before the International Court of Justice and other international tribunals and is active as an international arbitrator.

Jeff Crisp has held a number of senior positions with UNHCR, including head of the organization's Evaluation and Policy Analysis Unit. He also worked as Director of Policy and Research with the Global Commission on International Migration. He has published extensively on refugee, humanitarian and migration issues, and has first-hand experience of UN operations throughout the world.

Barbara Crossette was *The New York Times* United Nations bureau chief from 1994 to 2001, and earlier the paper's chief correspondent in Southeast Asia and South Asia. The author of several books on Asia, she is also a consulting editor at the United Nations Association of the United States of America, on advisory boards at the Foreign Policy Association and New York University's Center for Global Affairs, and a trustee of the Carnegie Council for Ethics in International Affairs.

Sam Daws is Executive Director of the United Nations Association of the UK. He has served as a senior policy advisor on UN issues for 19 years, including three years as First Officer in the Executive Office of UN Secretary-General Kofi Annan. He previously directed a Geneva based international consultancy. He undertook doctoral studies on UN Security Council reform at New College, Oxford, and has been a visiting fellow at Cambridge and Yale Universities. He has co-authored or edited six books on the UN.

Dennis Dijkzeul is Professor in the Management of Humanitarian Crises at the IFHV at Ruhr Universität Bochum and an adjunct professor at SIPA at Columbia University. His main interests concern the management of international organizations and the participation of local populations in humanitarian programs. He is the author of *Supporting Local Health Care in a Chronic Crisis* (2005), *Between Force and Mercy: Military Action and Humanitarian Aid* (2004), and *Rethinking International Organizations: Pathology and Promise* (2003).

Michael W. Doyle is Harold Brown Professor at Columbia University in the School of International and Public Affairs, Columbia Law School, and the Department of Political Science. His publications include *Ways of War and Peace* (1997), *Empires* (1986), *UN Peacekeeping in Cambodia* (1995), and *Making War and Building Peace* (2006). He was Assistant Secretary-General and Special Adviser to Kofi Annan and is the UN Secretary-General's representative on the Advisory Board of the UN Democracy Fund.

Martha Finnemore is Professor of Political Science and International Affairs at George Washington University in Washington, DC, and has written widely about global governance and international institutions. Her most recent book, *Rules for the World: International Organizations in Global Politics*, co-authored with Michael Barnett, won the International Studies Association's Best Book award in 2006. She is also the author of *National Interests in International Society* (1996) and *The Purpose of Intervention: Changing Beliefs about the Use of Force* (2003).

Jacques Fomerand joined the UN Secretariat in 1977 where he followed economic, social, and coordination questions in the Department of International Economic and Social Affairs, and from 1992 to 2003 he was Director of the UN University Office in North America. He now teaches at John Jay College of the City University of New York and has published widely on matters related to the UN. His latest book is a *Dictionary of the United Nations* (2007).

Linda Gerber-Stellingwerf is Research Director of the Fourth Freedom Forum. She is a participant in the joint Fourth Freedom Forum/Kroc Institute Sanctions and Security Project and the Counter-Terrorism Evaluation Project. She has helped research, write, and edit various reports and books produced by the Fourth Freedom Forum.

Richard Goldstone is a former Justice of the Constitutional Court of South Africa and former Chief Prosecutor of the UN International Criminal Tribunals for the former Yugoslavia and Rwanda. He was a member of the UN Independent Inquiry Committee into the Oil-for-Food Programme (the Volcker Committee) and is co-chair of the Human Rights Institute of the International Bar Association. He serves on the boards of a number of human rights organizations.

Leon Gordenker is Professor Emeritus of Politics at Princeton University. He has observed the United Nations system from its founding, including service in the UN Secretariat and as a consultant. His numerous publications include studies of the UN Secretary-General, NGOs, international responses to AIDS, treatment of refugees, economic development projects, and other multilateral efforts.

Tom Grant is Research Associate of the Lauterpacht Centre for International Law, University of Cambridge. He has been a Humboldt scholar and visitor of the Max-Planck-Institute for Public International Law in Heidelberg and a junior research fellow of St. Anne's College, University of Oxford. He teaches and does research in international law, and is a practicing lawyer.

Fen O. Hampson is Director of Carleton University's Norman Paterson School of International Affairs. He is the author of seven books and editor of more than twenty volumes. He is a member of the board of directors of the Pearson Peacekeeping Centre, served as chair of the Human Security Track of the Helsinki Process on Globalization and Democracy and of the Working Group on International Institutions, and was International Cooperation Oversight Coordinator for the International Summit on Democracy, Terrorism, and Security.

Richard Jolly is Honorary Professor at the Institute of Development Studies, Sussex University, and Senior Research Fellow and Co-director of the UN Intellectual History Project at the Ralph Bunche Institute for International Studies, The CUNY Graduate Center. For fifteen years, he was UNICEF's deputy executive director and for five years, UNDP's principal coordinator of the *Human Development Report*. He has co-authored many books, including *Ahead of the Curve?* (2001) and *UN Contributions to Development Thinking and Practice* (2004).

James O, C. Jonah is Senior Fellow at the Ralph Bunche Institute for International Studies of The CUNY Graduate Center, where he received a Carnegie Corporation of New York Scholar Grant to prepare his memoirs. He served Sierra Leone as Minister of Finance, Development, and Economic Planning and as Permanent Representative to the United Nations. He was a member of the UN Secretariat from 1963 to 1994 in a variety of capacities and retired as Under-Secretary-General for Political Affairs.

Christer Jönsson is Professor of Political Science at Lund University, Sweden, and served as President of the Nordic International Studies Association (NISA) 1996–99. In addition to international organization, his research interests include international negotiation, diplomacy, and the role of transnational networks in international cooperation. He has published numerous books, articles, and book chapters and is the co-author of *International Cooperation in Response to AIDS* (1995) and *Essence of Diplomacy* (2005).

W. Andy Knight is Professor of International Relations at the University of Alberta. He co-edited the journal, *Global Governance*, from 2000 to 2005 and is past Vice Chair of the Academic Council on the United Nations System. He has written and edited several books and numerous book chapters and articles on various aspects of multilateral governance and UN reform. His most recent book is the second edition of the edited volume *Adapting the United Nations to a Postmodern Era* (2001).

Keith Krause is Professor of International Politics at the Graduate Institute of International Studies in Geneva and Director of its Programme for Strategic and International Security Studies. He is the founder and Programme Director of the Small Arms Survey project and has jointly edited its annual yearbook since 2001. He has written or edited four other books, and published more than thirty articles in journals and edited volumes. He was a Rhodes scholar at Balliol College.

Maivân Clech Lâm is Professor of International Law and Associate Director of the Ralph Bunche Institute for International Studies at The City University of New York's Graduate Center. She serves as academic counsel to the American Indian Law Alliance and has worked on the Draft Declaration of the Rights of Indigenous Peoples and in the Permanent Forum on Indigenous Issues. Her book on the subject is entitled *At the Edge of the State: Indigenous Peoples and Self-Determination* (2000).

Jeffrey Laurenti is Senior Fellow in international affairs at The Century Foundation. He previously was Deputy Director of the United Nations and Global Security Initiative of the United Nations Foundation and Executive Director of policy studies at the United Nations Association of the United States of America. He has written numerous articles and book chapters on international politics and global policy in their UN dimensions. He served for six years as Executive Director of the New Jersey Senate and worked in numerous political campaigns, including his own.

George A. Lopez is Senior Fellow at the Kroc Institute for International Peace Studies at the University of Notre Dame. Since 1992, he has written more than twenty articles, book chapters, and five books on economic sanctions, with special reference to UN sanctions on Iraq. Recent research detailing the unlikely presence of WMDs in Iraq was published in 'Disarming Iraq,' *Arms Control Today* (2002) and 'Containing Iraq: the Sanctions Worked,' *Foreign Affairs* (2004).

Edward C. Luck is Director of the Center on International Organization and Professor of Practice in International and Public Affairs at Columbia University. He was President of the United Nations Association of the United States of America (1984–1994) and one of the architects of the UN reform efforts from 1995 to 1997. His books include *Mixed Messages: American Politics and International Organization, 1919–1999* (1999), *International Law and Organization: Closing the Compliance Gap* (2004), and *The UN Security Council: Practice and Promise* (2006).

Frank G. Madsen is Research Fellow at the Centre d'Etudes Diplomatiques et Stratégiques, Paris, France. He previously served in the UN's CIVPOL in Cyprus, headed criminal intelligence in Interpol, and directed international corporate security for a major multinational company. He has been visiting fellow at the Cambridge University Lauterpacht Research Centre for International Law and visiting researcher at Georgetown University Law Center. He is the author of *Compendium* (1981) and co-author of *The Intelligence Function* (1991).

David M. Malone is Canada's High Commissioner to India. A former Ambassador to the UN and President of the International Peace Academy, he has written extensively about international organizations, the political economy of civil wars, the causes of conflict and conflict prevention, and US foreign policy. He is author of *The UN Security Council: From the Cold War to the 21st Century* (2004) and *The International Struggle for Iraq: Politics in the UN Security Council, 1980–2005* (2006).

Rama Mani is the Executive Director of ICES—the International Centre for Ethnic Studies—in Colombo, Sri Lanka. She was Director of the New Issues in Security Course at the Geneva Centre for Security Policy, senior strategy adviser to the Centre for Humanitarian Dialogue, Africa strategy manager and regional policy coordinator for conflict for Oxfam in Ethiopia and Uganda, and senior external relations adviser to the Commission on Global Governance. She is the author of *Beyond Retribution: Seeking Justice in the Shadows of War* (2002) and numerous articles on peacebuilding and conflict prevention, peace, and justice.

Craig N. Murphy is M. Margaret Ball Professor of International Relations at Wellesley College. He is a former President of the International Studies Association, former Chair of the Academic Council on the UN System, and founding editor of *Global Governance: A Review of Multilateralism and International Organization*. He completed a two-year project for the UN Development Programme researching and writing a critical history of the organization and its predecessors, *The United Nations Development Programme: A Better Way? (2006)*.

Edward Newman is Director of Studies on Conflict and Security in the Peace and Governance Programme of the UN University. He has taught at or been associated with Shumei University, Aoyama Gakuin University, Tokyo University, and Institut d'Etudes Politiques de Paris (Sciences Po). He is the author of *The UN Secretary-General from the Cold War to the New Era: A Global Peace and Security Mandate?* (1998) as well as numerous articles and edited volumes.

Roland Paris is Associate Professor of Public and International Affairs at the University of Ottawa and author of *At War's End: Building Peace After Civil Conflict* (2004). Previously, he served as a foreign policy adviser in the Privy Council Office of the Canadian government, Director of Research at The Conference Board of Canada, and Assistant Professor at the University of Colorado, Boulder.

Christopher K. Penny is Assistant Professor of International Law, and Deputy Director, Centre for Security and Defence Studies, at the Norman Paterson School of International Affairs, Carleton University, located in Ottawa, Canada. His teaching and research focus on international law and conflict, addressing state and organizational decisions to use force, including the role of the Security Council and the 'responsibility to protect,' as well as the legal regime governing the conduct of resulting hostilities.

M. J. Peterson is Professor of Political Science at the University of Massachusetts Amherst. She has been a member of the editorial committee of *Global Governance* since 1994, was the editor of *Polity* in 1994–1999, and was a member of the Council of the American Society of International Law in 1998–2001. She is the author of books on the

UN General Assembly, multilateral management of Antarctica, and regimes for outer space, and of several journal articles on international institutions or multilateral resource management.

Michael Pugh is Professor of Peace and Conflict Studies, Peace Studies Department, University of Bradford, where he leads a research program on the transformation of war economies. He co-authored *War Economies in a Regional Context* (2004) and has written extensively on peacekeeping and peacebuilding. He founded and continues to edit the refereed journal *International Peacekeeping*, and the Cass Peacekeeping book series.

Bertrand G. Ramcharan is Professor of International Human Rights Law at the Geneva Graduate Institute of International Studies and Chancellor of the University of Guyana. He was Deputy and then Acting UN High Commissioner for Human Rights before retiring. He was Political Adviser with the international peacemakers and peacekeepers in the former Yugoslavia, Director of DPA's Africa Division, and head speech-writer for the Secretary-General. He is the author of several books on international law and human rights and is currently writing a volume on UN preventive diplomacy.

Gert Rosenthal is an economist who became Guatemala's Foreign Minister in mid-2006. He held cabinet-level posts in his government before joining the United Nations Secretariat, where he rose to become Executive Secretary of the Economic Commission for Latin America and the Caribbean between 1988 and 1997. He also dealt with the United Nations from the intergovernmental side as Guatemala's Permanent Representative from 1999 to 2004. He was President of ECOSOC in 2003. He has written numerous articles on development issues and on the UN.

Nicholas Sambanis is Associate Professor of Political Science at Yale University. He is the co-author of *Making War and Building Peace* (2006) and co-editor of *Understanding Civil War: Evidence and Analysis* (2005), case studies published by the World Bank. His articles have appeared in the *American Political Science Review, World Politics, Journal of Conflict Resolution, Perspectives on Politics*, and *Journal of African Economies*. He is currently working on a book on the causes of self-determination movements and secessionist civil war.

Nico Schrijver is Professor of International Law at Leiden University and the academic director of the Grotius Centre for International Legal Studies at its Campus in The Hague. He is President of the Netherlands Society of International Law and former Chair of the Academic Council on the UN System. He appeared as Counsel before the International Court of Justice and other international tribunals. He has co-authored or edited five books on the United Nations.

Waheguru Pal Singh Sidhu is Director of the New Issues in Security Course at the Geneva Centre for Security Policy. He was formerly Senior Associate at the International Peace Academy and co-editor of *International Peacekeeping*. He has written extensively on regionalism and the UN as well as arms control and Asian politics. He is the co-editor of *The Iraq Crisis and World Order: Structural, Institutional and Normative*

Challenges (2006), *Arms Control after Iraq: Normative and Operational Challenges* (2006), and *The United Nations and Regional Security: Europe and Beyond* (2003).

Ramesh Thakur is Senior Vice-Rector of the United Nations University and Assistant Secretary-General of the United Nations. Born in India, he has held full-time academic appointments in Fiji, New Zealand, and Australia and visiting appointments elsewhere. He was a commissioner on the International Commission on Intervention and State Sovereignty and principal writer of the UN Secretary-General's second reform report. He is the author/editor of over twenty books and also writes regularly for the national and international quality press.

Paul Wapner is Director of the Global Environmental Politics Program and Associate Professor in the School of International Service at American University in Washington, DC. He is the author of *Environmental Activism and World Civic Politics* (1996, winner of the Harold and Margaret Sprout Award) and co-editor of *Principled World Politics: The Challenge of Normative International Relations* (2000). He is presently at work on a book focusing on the concept of nature in environmental politics.

Thomas G. Weiss is Presidential Professor of Political Science at The CUNY Graduate Center and Director of the Ralph Bunche Institute for International Studies, where he is co-director of the United Nations Intellectual History Project. He is the president of the International Studies Association (2009–10) and chair of the Academic Council on the UN System (2006–9) and the former editor of its journal, *Global Governance*. He has written or edited some 35 books and 150 articles about multilateral approaches to international peace and security, humanitarian action, and sustainable development.

Ralph Wilde is Reader in Laws at University College London and a specialist in international law. His current research focuses on territorial administration by foreign actors, and his book on the subject is *International Territorial Administration* (2007). He is Joint Secretary of the British branch of the International Law Association, and a member of the Executive Councils of the ILA and the American Society of International Law.

Ngaire Woods is Director of the Global Economic Governance Programme at University College, Oxford University where she is also Dean of Graduates. Her most recent book is *The Globalizers: The IMF, the World Bank, and their Borrowers* (2006). She has served as Adviser to the UNDP's *Human Development Report*, and more recently as External Evaluator of the IMF's Independent Evaluation Office. She has published extensively on international institutions, globalization, and governance.

LIST OF ABBREVIATIONS

ACABQ	Advisory Committee on Administrative and Budgetary Questions
ACC	Administrative Committee on Coordination
ACP	African, Caribbean, and Pacific states
ACUNS	Academic Council on the United Nations System
ASEAN	Association of Southeast Asian Nations
ASP	Assembly of States Parties
AU	African Union
BTWC	Biological and Toxin Weapons Convention
CARICOM	Caribbean Community and Common Market
CCA	Common Country Assessment
CD	Conference on Disarmament
CEB	Chief Executives Board of Coordination
CEDAW	Committee on the Elimination of Discrimination Against Women
CERD	Committee on the Elimination of Racial Discrimination
CHR	Commission on Human Rights (became HRC in 2006)
CIS	Commonwealth of Independent States
CITES	Convention on International Trade in Endangered Species of Wild Fauna and Flora
CONGO	Conference of Non-Governmental Organizations in Consultative Relationship with the United Nations
CSD	Commission on Sustainable Development
CSW	Commission on the Status of Women
CTC	Counter-Terrorism Committee
CTED	Counter-Terrorism Committee Executive Directorate
CWC	Chemical Weapons Convention
DAW	Division (of the UN Secretariat) for the Advancement of Women
DDR	disarmament, demobilization, and reintegration
DESA	Department of Economic and Social Affairs
DHA	Department of Humanitarian Affairs
DPA	Department of Political Affairs
DPI	Department of Public Information
DPKO	Department of Peacekeeping Operations
DRC	Democratic Republic of the Congo

DSG	Deputy Secretary-General
EAD	Electoral Assistance Division
ECA	Economic Commission for Africa
ECE	Economic Commission for Europe
ECLAC	Economic Commission for Latin America and the Caribbean
ECOMOG	Monitoring Group of ECOWAS
ECOSOC	Economic and Social Council
ECOWAS	Economic Community of West African States
EEZ	Exclusive Economic Zone
ERC	Emergency Relief Coordinator
ESCAP	Economic and Social Commission for Asia and the Pacific
ESCWA	Economic and Social Commission for Western Asia
EU	European Union
FAO	Food and Agriculture Organization
G-7/G-8	Group of Seven/Group of Eight
G-77	Group of 77
GATT	General Agreement on Tariffs and Trade
GDI	Gender Development-Related Index
GEM	Gender Empowerment Measure
Habitat	see UNCHS
HDI	Human Development Index
HDR	Human Development Report
HFA	Health For All
HIPC	Heavily Indebted Poor Countries initiative
HLP	High-level Panel on Threats, Challenges and Change
HPI	Human Poverty Index
HRC	Human Rights Council
HRR	Humanitarian Response Review
IAEA	International Atomic Energy Agency
IASC	Inter-Agency Standing Committee
IBRD	International Bank for Reconstruction and Development
ICAO	International Civil Aviation Organization
ICC	International Criminal Court
ICCPR	International Covenant on Civil and Political Rights
ICESCR	International Covenant on Economic, Social and Cultural Rights
ICISS	International Commission on Intervention and State Sovereignty
ICJ	International Court of Justice
ICRC	International Committee of the Red Cross
ICSC	International Civil Service Commission

ICSID	International Centre for Settlement of Investment Disputes [World Bank Group]
ICT	International Criminal Tribunal (ICTY for the former Yugoslavia; ICTR for Rwanda)
IDA	International Development Association
IDP	internally displaced person
IEG	Independent Evaluation Group
IEO	Independent Evaluation Office
IFAD	International Fund for Agricultural Development
IFI	international financial institution
IFOR	Implementation Force [for the former Yugoslavia]
IGO	intergovernmental organization
IHL	international humanitarian law
IHR	international health regulations
IJP	international judges and prosecutors
ILC	International Law Commission
ILO	International Labour Organization
ILP	international legal process
IMF	International Monetary Fund
IMO	International Maritime Organization
INSTRAW	International Research and Training Institute for the Advancement of Women
INTERFET	International Force for East Timor
IO	international organization
IR	international relations
IRC	International Rescue Committee
ISAF	International Security Assistance Force
ISO	International Organization for Standardization
ITO	International Trade Organization
ITU	International Telecommunications Union
IWY	International Women's Year
MDG	Millennium Development Goal
MOP	meeting of the parties
MSC	Military Staff Committee
NAFTA	North American Free Trade Agreement
NAM	Non-Aligned Movement
NATO	North Atlantic Treaty Organization
NGO	nongovernmental organization
NIEO	New International Economic Order
NPT	Nuclear Non-Proliferation Treaty
OAS	Organization of American States

OAU	Organization of African Unity (now AU)
OCHA	Office for the Coordination of Humanitarian Affairs
ODA	Official development assistance
OECD	Organisation for Economic Co-operation and Development
OEOA	Office for Emergency Operations in Africa
OHCHR	Office of the High Commissioner for Human Rights
OHRM	Office of Human Resources Management
OIC	Organization of the Islamic Conference
OIOS	Office of Internal Oversight Services
OPEC	Organization of the Petroleum Exporting Countries
OSAGI	Office of the Special Adviser on Gender Issues and Advancement of Women
OSCE	Organization for Security and Co-operation in Europe
P-5	five permanent members of the Security Council
PBC	Peacebuilding Commission
PBSO	Peacebuilding Support Office
PCA	Permanent Court of Arbitration
PCIJ	Permanent Court of International Justice
PHEIC	public health emergencies of international concern
PKO	peacekeeping operation
PRSP	poverty reduction strategy paper
PWG	Policy Working Group
RUF	Revolutionary United Front
SAARC	South Asian Association for Regional Cooperation
SAM	Sanctions Assistance Mission
SAMCOMM	Sanctions Assistance Missions Communications Center
SFOR	Stabilization Force in Bosnia and Herzegovina
SPS	sanitary and phyto-sanitary measures
SRSG	Special Representative of the Secretary-General
TBT	technical barriers to trade
TCN	troop-contributing nations
TNC	transnational corporation
TWAIL	Third World Approaches to International Law
UDHR	Universal Declaration of Human Rights
UfP	Uniting for Peace
UK	United Kingdom of Great Britain and Northern Ireland
UN	United Nations
UNAEC	United Nations Atomic Energy Commission
UNAMIR	United Nations Assistance Mission for Rwanda
UNAMSIL	United Nations Mission in Sierra Leone

UNASOG	United Nations Aouzou Strip Observer Group
UNCED	United Nations Conference on Environment and Development
UNCHE	United Nations Conference on the Human Environment
UNCHS	United Nations Centre for Human Settlements [Habitat]
UNCITRAL	United Nations Commission on International Trade Law
UNCLOS	United Nations Conference on the Law of the Sea
UNCTAD	United Nations Conference on Trade and Development
UNDAF	United Nations Development Assistance Framework
UNDP	United Nations Development Programme
UNDRO	United Nations Disaster Relief Coordinator (Office of the)
UNEF	United Nations Emergency Force
UNEP	United Nations Environment Programme
UNESCO	United Nations Educational, Scientific and Cultural Organization
UNFCCC	United Nations Framework Convention on Climate Change
UNFPA	United Nations Population Fund
UNHCR	United Nations High Commissioner for Refugees
UNICEF	United Nations Children's Fund
UNIDO	United Nations Industrial Development Organization
UNIFEM	United Nations Development Fund for Women
UNIO	United Nations Information Office
UNITA	União Nacional para a Independência Total de Angola (National Union for the Total Independence of Angola)
UNITAF	Unified Task Force
UNITAR	United Nations Institute for Training and Research
UNMIK	United Nations Interim Administration Mission in Kosovo
UNMOGIP	United Nations Military Observer Group in India and Pakistan
UNOSOM	United Nations Operation in Somalia
UNRWA	United Nations Relief and Works Agency for Palestine Refugees in the Near East
UNSCOM	United Nations Special Commission
UNTAES	United Nations Transitional Authority in Eastern Slavonia, Baranja and Western Sirmium
UNTAET	United Nations Transitional Administration in East Timor
UNTSO	United Nations Truce Supervision Organization
UNU	United Nations University
UPU	Universal Postal Union
US	United States of America
USSR	Union of Soviet Socialist Republics
VAW	violence against women
WFP	World Food Programme
WHA	World Health Assembly

WHO	World Health Organization
WIPO	World Intellectual Property Organization
WMD	weapon of mass destruction
WMO	World Meteorological Organization
WTO	World Trade Organization
WWF	World Wide Fund for Nature

PART I

INTRODUCTION

CHAPTER 1

....

WORLD POLITICS
CONTINUITY AND
CHANGE SINCE 1945

....

THOMAS G. WEISS
SAM DAWS

SINCE its establishment in 1945, the United Nations Organization, as well as the universal agencies that form part of the UN system, has been central to international relations. The main story is one of continuity and change—the UN is over sixty years old and sixty years young. It faced specific opportunities and difficulties during the Cold War; and these were followed with a radically different set of interpretations, fears, hopes, and policies in the confusion of the post-Cold War era. That same description could again be used to characterize the briefer period since 11 September 2001.

But behind these macro-political changes lies a startling reality that was very much in evidence at the largest-ever global summit at UN headquarters in September 2005. Over 150 presidents, prime ministers, and princes encountered the same problems that have restricted international cooperation since the launching of the current generation of global institutions that replaced the defunct League of Nations—indeed since the beginning of modern experiments with multilateral cooperation in the nineteenth century.[1]

New challenges to international peace and security and human survival have arisen. New nonstate actors have appeared on the world stage, and older ones have occasionally been transformed. New conventions and norms have proliferated. New intergovernmental initiatives and institutions have been established. Yet, despite these challenges, decision-making in world politics and international organizations remains dominated by states.

Hence, nothing has altered the validity of Adam Roberts and Benedict Kingsbury's evaluation in *United Nations, Divided World*: 'international society has been modified, but not totally transformed.'[2] The UN does not exist in isolation from the world that it is attempting to serve. Many scholars and practitioners resist the notion that there has been a fundamental change in world politics. Essentially, they are right in claiming that the more things change the more they stay the same. Certainly the fundamental units of the system—sovereign states—are here to stay. They are still organized to pursue their perceived national interests in a world without any meaningful overall authority.

The world thus still reflects what Hedley Bull and virtually all political scientists call 'anarchy,'[3] or the absence of a central global authority. In spite of the construction of a seemingly ever-denser web of international institutions, there is nothing like a world government in the offing. Although it would be inaccurate to ignore the extremes—ranging from fractious political authority in failed states to the supranational integration of the European Union—it still is accurate to point to a fundamental continuity: state sovereignty remains the core of international relations.

CHANGE AND CONTINUITY

The clear recognition of this fundamental continuity pervades the chapters in *The Oxford Handbook on the United Nations*, as it does world politics; but it would be hard to argue that substantial change has not also marked the world organization since 1945. This *Handbook* is thus a contribution to greater analytical precision and historical reflection about the balance between change and continuity within the United Nations. The most pertinent changes can be conveniently grouped under four headings: the emergence of new threats; the increasing role of nonstate actors; the reformulation of state sovereignty; and the emergence of a single 'hyper-power.' What follows is an overview of the nature and role of each of these in today's international system.

The Rise of New Threats?

The first category of change consists in the proliferation of new threats and challenges to the well-being of states and their citizens that surpass the ability of individual states, however powerful, to address on their own. Some readers may find it hard to imagine that many of the problems central to this *Handbook* were not even on the international radar screen in 1945. For instance, environmental degradation, population growth, urbanization, and women's rights came onto the international agenda during the global conferences of the 1970s,[4] and the AIDS pandemic and the need for human development and human security appeared in the 1980s and 1990s. Moreover, other challenges that have long languished on the agenda—terrorism and self-determination come immediately to mind—have taken on a different urgency with the proliferation of weapons of mass destruction (WMDs).

In short, war, human rights abuse, and poverty have persisted throughout the last six decades. Judgments about the relative success or failure of the UN in addressing such perennial blights on the human condition can only be made with the recognition that many of these 'old' threats have themselves changed in nature over time, and that praise for success or criticism for failure cannot simply be placed at the door of the organization.

The threat of armed conflict was foremost in the minds of the architects of the UN Charter, the Preamble to which pledged members 'to save succeeding generations from the scourge of war.' This threat endures or, to paraphrase Inis Claude's classic early UN textbook, too few swords have been turned into ploughshares.[5] There has been, however, a significant change in the patterns of political violence. While interstate war is not yet a thing of the past—as demonstrated by the decision of the US and UK to go to war against Iraq in 2003—the UN's original focus on war between states has largely given way to the dominant reality of intrastate warfare.

Intrastate—or 'civil' or 'non-international'—wars (i.e., taking place primarily within the borders of a state and involving indigenous armed factions) accounted for over 90 percent of all armed conflicts in the 1990s that resulted in more than 1,000 deaths.[6] It is conventional wisdom that civilians have become the main victims in such civil wars—estimated at 90 percent in the turbulent 1990s, itself a notable reversal from the early twentieth century when soldiers accounted for that percentage.[7] However, new evidence raises questions about such statistics. Direct killing of civilians through armed conflict may have in fact declined significantly in the early 2000s although it remains difficult to calculate the indirect effects of war-exacerbated disease and malnutrition.[8] Whether or not these wars are truly 'new' is debatable, but clearly many of the usual dynamics have altered or been exaggerated. 'Changed' is probably a more accurate characterization of the transformation at hand as history demonstrates comparable dynamics.[9]

The woes of our planet are obvious. Egregious human rights violations have continued over six decades, and many of the moves towards national independence have ended in brutal dictatorship. Despite economic growth, the world has been left, at the opening of the new millennium, with widening gaps in wealth distribution (the world's 500 richest individuals' combined wealth is greater than that of the poorest 416 million), and almost half the global population (some 2.5 billion) survive on incomes equivalent to less than two dollars a day. These problems too have been with us for some time, but their magnitude continues to grow as does our real-time exposure to the plight of those who suffer.

The Importance of New Actors?

The second type of substantial change that is reflected in many of this *Handbook's* chapters is the burgeoning role of actors other than states. The proliferation of 'uncivil' actors—from belligerents and warlords to 'spoilers' and criminals whose interests are served by continued armed conflict[10]—is certainly a factor behind the ugly reality of civil war. However, the UN as an arena has also traditionally provided space for what is increasingly called 'global civil society' to interact with states, articulate demands and solutions, and pursue their own interests.

Charter Article 71 carved out space for nongovernmental organizations (NGOs) to engage with the United Nations. But during the Cold War, the Soviet bloc and many developing countries with totalitarian regimes resisted the intrusion of independent and dissident voices. Since the thawing of East–West relations in the mid-1980s, however, human rights advocates, gender activists, developmentalists, and groups of indigenous peoples have become ever more vocal, operational, and important in contexts that were once thought to be the exclusive preserve of states.

The sheer growth in NGO numbers has been nothing short of remarkable. The Union of International Associations estimates the number of international NGOs (operating in more than two countries) at about 25,000.[11] A more cautious estimate is 13,000, all but one-quarter of which have been created since 1990.[12] National NGOs have grown faster still in the South than in the North. Throughout the Third World, grassroots organizations are said to number in the millions.

For-profit businesses and the media are key nongovernmental sectors that relate directly to the United Nations. Corporations have always been an important lobbying presence. In addition, their potential contribution to the UN's work—as well as their labor, social, and environmental obligations—have been recognized in Kofi Annan's Global Compact initiative. The media's influence is widely acknowledged. Indeed, Secretary-General Boutros-Ghali suggested that they effectively constitute a '16th member of the Security Council' for some decisions.

Hence, it is no longer disputed that NGOs play a prominent role on the world stage and that we are unable to fully understand contemporary international relations without looking at such nonstate actors. What is insufficiently known is that their rate of growth has surpassed intergovernmental organizations (IGOs). By 2006, IGOs had shrunk to 238 (down from a peak of over 300 at the outset of the 1980s), which means that a quarter of a century ago, 'the ratio of NGOs to IGOs stood at 15:1, whereas today the relation is 28:1.'[13] The presence of alternative voices has become integral to the UN system's processes of deliberation[14] and to world politics more generally. International discussions are more pluralistic, and international decisions necessarily reflect a wider array of perspectives.

Indeed, and as a result, the term 'international community' can be confusing when it is used in relationship to the UN system and multilateralism more broadly. While international lawyers continue to use it to refer narrowly to the 'community of peace-loving states,' other observers frequently employ it far more loosely and expansively. Some include not merely states but also their creations in the form of intergovernmental bodies, while still other observers also use the term to embrace some of the nonstate actors that are contributing to the resolution of global problems. In these pages, we restrict the use of the term to the narrow legal sense, but the expanded cast playing roles on the UN's stage is a crucial part of the analysis in virtually every chapter in this volume.

Reinforced or Reduced State Sovereignty?

Reflecting the proliferation of threats and actors is the third dominant element of change—the reformulation of state sovereignty. Paradoxically, the UN has been responsible for both the triumph *and* the erosion of state sovereignty. There are almost four times as many member states at the outset of the twenty-first century as signed the Charter in June 1945. The Charter emphasized self-determination in response to colonialism, and decolonization is virtually complete. And since the collapse of the USSR in 1991 and the implosion of the former Yugoslavia the following year, the idea of the sovereign state has attained virtually universal resonance.

At the same time, however, sovereignty has never been as sacrosanct and unchangeable as many believe. Stephen Krasner went so far as to describe it as 'organized hypocrisy.'[15] The recasting of state sovereignty over the UN's lifetime is rooted in three factors.

The first is that technology and communications have remolded the nature of the global economy and economic aspirations.[16] There is great controversy over the oft-used and confused term 'globalization.'[17] Some observers argue that it has been occurring since the earliest trade expeditions (e.g., the Silk Road); and despite the current obsession, the process itself is not fundamentally new. Others suggest that the current era of globalization is unique in the rapidity of its spread and the intensity of the interactions that result. It is difficult to deny the processes of increased interconnectivity across the planet and the worldwide dimensions of human, financial, commercial, and cultural flows that require no passport. For the latter, the UN's normative efforts have been combined with technology to produce what one analyst called 'the end of geography.'[18]

Wherever one stands in the debate about globalization's reach, pace, and impact on state sovereignty, it is clear that definitions of vital national interests—often called *raisons d'état*—are expanding and being continually redefined. Their pursuit is not exclusive because sometimes state actors are playing in a non-zero-sum game; the European Union is often cited as an example of sovereignty being recast if not transcended, a process long-ago described by Ernst Haas as moving 'beyond the nation-state.'[19] Globalization creates losers as well as winners, and it entails risks as well as opportunities. The rapid growth of global markets has not seen the parallel development of social and economic institutions to ensure their smooth and efficient functioning, and the global rules on trade and finance produce asymmetric effects on rich and poor countries, very often to the detriment of the latter. This too means that some states are more or less 'sovereign' than others.

The second factor explaining the paradox is that the content of sovereignty itself has expanded to accommodate human rights. Underlying this is an unresolved tension in the Charter between respect for the domestic jurisdiction of states and the imperatives of individual rights. In his 1992 *An Agenda for Peace*, Secretary-General Boutros Boutros-Ghali summarized: 'The time for absolute and exclusive sovereignty, however, has passed; its theory was never matched by reality.'[20] Of course, for some time states have chosen to shed bits of sovereignty in signing international conventions or trade pacts—some 1,500 multilateral treaties were in existence in 1995 when a prominent legal group made the effort to count them.[21] But for human rights in particular, the trade-off is not always a conscious choice but rather involves a blurring of domestic and international jurisdictions over time. This became particularly clear with the willingness to override sovereignty by using military force for humanitarian purposes in the 1990s. The rationale came from Frances M. Deng and Roberta Cohen's notion of 'sovereignty as responsibility,' which they developed to protect internally displaced persons; from Secretary-General Annan's articulation of 'two sovereignties'; and from the norm of the 'responsibility to protect', elaborated and advocated by the International Commission on Intervention and State Sovereignty (ICISS).[22]

As a result, the four characteristics of a sovereign—territory, authority, population, and independence—spelled out in the 1934 Montevideo Convention on the Rights and Duties of States have been complemented by another, a modicum of respect for human rights. Sovereignty has become contractual or conditional rather than absolute. Indeed, with the possible exception of the prevention of genocide in the first years after World War II, no idea has moved faster in the international normative arena than 'the responsibility to protect.' The basic idea is that human beings should count more than the rigid sovereignty enshrined in Charter Article 2 (7) with its emphasis on nonintervention in the internal affairs of states. Or, as Kofi Annan graphically told a 1998 audience at Ditchley Park, 'state frontiers . . . should no longer be seen as a watertight protection for war criminals or mass murderers.'[23]

The third part of an explanation for the paradox of the UN's contribution to both strengthening and weakening sovereignty is that experience, beginning in the 1990s, suggests that states can be born *and* die—sovereign entities can, in the popular language of the day, 'fail.'[24] A number of other euphemisms have arisen—for instance, 'weak' and 'fragile'—while the 'on-the-ground' reality varies from the situation in Somalia,[25] where there has been no effective central authority since 1992, to the former Yugoslavia, which no longer exists as a unitary state. Charter Article 2 (1) is clear: 'The Organization is based on the principle of the sovereign equality of all its Members.' This essentially means that all states have equal sovereignty, but not that they are equal in nature. Fictions abound in world politics, including the pretence within the UN of treating member states that are not de facto sovereign as equal to functioning members, and treating China and Chad or Venezuela and Vanuatu on a par in the General Assembly despite their vast inequalities in size and power.

In short, the notion of state sovereignty seems considerably less sacrosanct today than in 1945. Borders still are crucial considerations in international relations, but their significance is very different than at the outset of the United Nations.

US Hegemony?

The fourth remarkable disjuncture is the pre-eminence of the United States—what former French foreign minister Hubert Védrine dubbed the *hyper-puissance*. On the one hand, major power politics have always dominated the deliberations of the world organization. The bitter East–West divide of the Cold War and the North–South clashes of the 1960s and the 1970s provide extensive evidence of this reality. On the other hand, there is no modern precedent for America's current military, economic, and cultural preponderance. Much of contemporary UN debate could be compared with the Roman Senate's effort to control the emperor.

Scholars speculate about the nuances of economic and cultural leverage in the international system resulting from US soft power,[26] but the hard currency of international politics undoubtedly remains military might. Before the war on Iraq, the 'hyper-power' was already spending more on its military than the 15–25 next highest-spending countries combined (depending on who was counting). With additional appropriations for Afghanistan and Iraq, Washington began spending more than the rest of the world's militaries combined. And even in the domain of soft power, the US remains without challenge on the world stage for the foreseeable future although some analysts see the hegemony as more Western than American.[27]

Yet at this moment, there are two world 'organizations.' The United Nations is global in membership, and the United States is global in reach and power. While many observers emphasize the peculiarly 'go-it-alone' character of the George W. Bush administration, American unilateralism is not new.[28] This reality creates acute difficulties for card-carrying multilateralists. For example, UN-led or UN-approved operations with substantial military requirements take place only when Washington approves or at least acquiesces. In other issue areas, moving ahead without the United States is problematic, although experiments are underway—for example, the 1998 Rome Statute establishing the International Criminal Court and the 1997 Convention on the Prohibition of the Use, Stockpiling, Production and Transfer of Anti-Personnel Mines and on Their Destruction.

Whether the US presence and power are overrated and will wane in the coming decade remains to be seen. Even if, as Joseph Nye claims, 'the world's only superpower can't go it alone,'[29] US power and Washington's willingness to resort to unilateralism may well dominate, for some years, every level of UN affairs—normative, legal, and operational.[30]

GLOBAL GOVERNANCE

The confluence among these four types of change along with the dominant continuity of an anarchical international system is such that very few contemporary UN watchers can imagine anything like a world government emerging in their lifetimes. We should nonetheless recall that such a notion was at least at the back of the minds of not only world federalists but many of the framers of the UN Charter. While pointing to the rise of 'networks of interdependence,' an earlier formulation of global governance, the late Harold Jacobson noted a fitting image for the older view of world government in the tapestries in the Palais des Nations in Geneva—the headquarters of the League of Nations and now the UN's European Office. He noted that they 'picture the process of humanity combining into ever larger and more stable units for the purpose of governance—first the family, then the tribe, then the city-state, and then the nation—a process which presumably would eventually culminate in the entire world being combined in one political unit.'[31]

That dream—Alexander Wendt still argues that 'a world state is inevitable'[32]—of a world government has been replaced by the contemporary idea of global governance.[33] Even the most enthusiastic proponents of national interests or those least sympathetic toward the United Nations are cognizant of the need for multilateral efforts in some sectors to address problems that spill beyond borders. 'Governance' refers to purposeful systems and rules or norms that ensure order beyond what occurs 'naturally.' In the domestic context, governance is usually more than government, implying shared purpose and goal orientation as well as formal authority or police powers.

The origins of this idea in the 1990s reflect an interesting marriage between academic and policy concerns. James Rosenau and Ernst Czempiel's theoretical *Governance without Government* was published in 1992, and the policy-oriented Commission on Global Governance's *Our Global Neighbourhood* was published three years later.[34] The first issue of the journal *Global Governance*, whose subscribers are both scholars and practitioners, also appeared in 1995. And the literature has burgeoned since that time.

Distinctions are not always made between the species of national and global governance. For example, UNDP's *Human Development Report 1999* argued that 'Governance does not mean mere government.'[35] In a national context, this is perfectly correct because governance is government plus additional nongovernmental mechanisms that contribute to order and predictability in problem-solving. For the planet, however, governance essentially is close to the whole story because there is no world government—hence, the sum of nongovernmental mechanisms but minus an input from a central authority because there is none. In many instances, the network of institutions and rules at the global level provides the appearance of partially effective governance, but normally without the actual desired effects.

So global governance is not a supplement to global government but rather a *faute de mieux*. It is a surrogate for transnational authority and enforcement in the contemporary world. However useful as a heuristic device to explain some kinds of complex multilateral cooperation and transnational interactions, the basic question remains: can global governance without a global government adequately address the range of problems faced by humanity in the new millennium?

EVALUATING UN EFFORTS
AT PROBLEM-SOLVING

Our point of departure in this *Handbook* is neither defensive nor celebratory—the UN's record should be viewed and analyzed empirically but in context.[36] The need to avoid repetition of two world wars and the massive global recession of the 1930s—as well as the failure of the League of Nations—sharply focused the thoughts of those who created the United Nations. In particular, they had very much in mind what the father of the international relations approach later dubbed 'realism.' E. H. Carr's sweeping interwar analysis of the catastrophic results of ill-considered idealism led to a very different generation of international organizations.[37] The basic structures, sketched during World War II and in the first decade or two afterwards, were all directed toward pragmatic ends.

But what made the UN's design and establishment so remarkable was its broader ambitions—for human rights on a global scale, for sovereign independence and freedom and democracy in all parts of the world, for improvements in standards of living worldwide. While such lofty idealism is often derided, more of that original vision has been achieved than is often recognized. No period in human history has seen so many people benefiting from advances in life expectancy, health, education, and living standards as in the UN's lifetime. The organization cannot claim credit for all the progress that has been made, any more than it can be blamed for the lack thereof.

At the same time, the UN's contribution is far from negligible. The globe undoubtedly would have been in a sadder state of affairs without the world organization's efforts. Successes have arguably surpassed the initial hopes and expectations of the delegates who first gathered at the San Francisco Conference on International Organization in April 1945, and of those attending the opening session of the first General Assembly in London in January 1946. For instance, there has been no world war. Although military spending has broken all records and tens of thousands of nuclear weapons still threaten the survival of the human race, deaths from war since 1945 have been markedly fewer than those in the first half of the twentieth century. In spite of the Cold War, indeed because it was mostly cold rather than hot, barely a fifth of the twentieth century's 110 million war-related deaths took place in the fifty-five years after the UN's creation, compared with some 85 million prior.

The *Human Security Report 2005* suggests that the surge of international activities after the end of the Cold War, aimed at stopping ongoing wars and preventing new ones, actually achieved considerable success. Spearheaded by the United Nations, these activities included a sixfold increase in the world body's preventive diplomacy missions and a fourfold increase in its peacemaking missions. This upsurge in international activism coincided with a decrease in crises and wars, despite the real and much publicized failures. While the UN did not act alone, the report asserts that there is evidence from a number of sources that the UN's initiatives were directly linked to quantifiable progress in the reduction and resolution of conflicts. This is, at the very least, a plausible proposition.

The end of colonization and the achievement of sovereign independence came within a decade or two, whereas in 1945 many observers expected that the decolonization process might well take a century. Today 192 countries are members of the UN, compared with the initial fifty-one. About two-thirds of them now have governments chosen through multiparty elections, a substantial shift from the situation in the early 1960s in the immediate aftermath of decolonization and throughout the Cold War when the vast majority of governments were anything except democratically elected.

Economic and social development has been impressive in many instances. In developing countries, average life expectancy has increased to double the estimated level of the late 1930s. Child mortality has been lowered by more than three-quarters. Nearly three-quarters of the world's population over the age of 18 are now literate, and some 85 percent of the world's children benefit from education. Malnutrition has been reduced in all regions of the world except Africa. Smallpox has been eradicated; and yaws, guinea worm, and polio—a worldwide scourge in the early postwar world—virtually eliminated. UNDP's 2005 edition of its annual *Human Development Report* noted that, since the first such report was issued in 1990, 'On average, people in developing countries are healthier, better educated and less impoverished—and they are more likely to live in a multiparty democracy.'[38]

Progress in human rights has also been nothing short of extraordinary, starting with the 1948 approval of the Universal Declaration of Human Rights. Beginning in the 1980s, a surge of ratifications of human rights conventions occurred along with increasing implementation of many measures and greater public outrage over abuses. While ratification and implementation are not always correlated as closely as we would like, it nonetheless is significant that almost a hundred countries, over half of UN member states, have now ratified six of the seven major human rights instruments, each of which has a committee of experts to monitor implementation; and some of which are supplemented by optional protocols. Moreover, about three-quarters of member states have ratified the International Covenants on Civil and Political Rights and on Economic, Social and Cultural Rights, and over 80 percent of countries the International Convention on the Elimination of All Forms of Racial Discrimination as well as the Convention on the Elimination of All Forms of Discrimination Against Women (CEDAW), a kind of international bill of rights for women.

THREE ANALYTICAL PROBLEMS

The preceding rapid summary is fleshed out in far greater detail in the chapters of this *Handbook*. In weighing elements of continuity and change and evaluating the UN's efforts to solve problems in spite of the obvious constraints on its operations, our authors adopt a variety of perspectives. In examining the evidence in each chapter, we urge readers to keep in mind three distinct analytical problems: defining the nature of change; determining the nature of success and failure; and tracking the ups and downs of world politics.

Defining 'Change'

The first analytical concern regards defining what constitutes 'change.' Kalevi Holsti's *Taming the Sovereigns* probes the concept of change and ways of measuring it: 'These include change as novelty or replacement, change as addition or subtraction, increased complexity, transformation, reversion, and obsolescence.'[39]

Change thus can be analyzed in quantitative or qualitative ways. If we think simply in terms of the growing scale and scope of international secretariats and staff or their budgets, there would be no debate. If change can be additive or subtractive and thus measured quantitatively, on any conceivable measure, the UN system has expanded exponentially.

We have already noted some of the data, such as the near quadrupling of the world body's membership. When the United Nations was born in 1945, there were fifty-one members, comprised mostly of European and Latin American countries. By 1975, the number of states sitting in the General Assembly had nearly tripled, as decolonization proceeded rapidly in the wake of the mass destruction wrought by World War II, in conjunction with the tide of nationalist independence movements that rippled across what became known as the Third World. Less than two decades later, the implosion of the Soviet Union (or formally the Union of Soviet Socialist Republics, USSR) and Yugoslavia gave birth to twenty new states. As of early 2007, the world body is comprised of 192 members. The number of democracies has quintupled.[40]

Other figures help illustrate quantitative change, such as the number of peacekeeping operations, also briefly discussed above. From the launch of the first peacekeeping operation in 1948 until 1978, only thirteen missions were deployed. For almost a decade thereafter, the Security Council approved no new operations with UN blue helmets. The political realities of the East–West split rendered launching such operations politically impossible. New operations resumed in 1988, when the Soviet Union dramatically altered its foreign policy position toward the world body. Since the thawing of the Cold War, the UN has undertaken fortyseven peacekeeping operations. In late 2006, for instance, the world body had boots on the ground in more than fifteen countries and some 100,000 troops deployed, collectively a larger overseas military presence than any country except the United States. In August, when it authorized hybrid operations in Lebanon and the Darfur region of Sudan, the Security Council approved, in principle, a 50 percent increase in the number of UN soldiers and total peacekeeping expenditures.

Change in the intensity of UN activity can also be illustrated with figures pertaining to the number of resolutions passed in the Security Council. During the Cold War, from 1946 to 1986, the Council passed 593 resolutions; in less than half the length of time, between 1987 and 2005, this figure amounted to 1,010.[41]

Another indication of change in multilateral cooperation more broadly can be illustrated with the number of treaties regulating state conduct. Between 1946 and 1975, the number of international treaties in force more than doubled from 6,351 to 14,061.[42] They span a broad gamut of issues—genocide, human rights, terrorism, the environment, and narcotics.[43]

Along with the greater extensiveness of its reach and membership, the UN's budget has grown to meet the ever increasing demands of a more interdependent and complex world. In 1946, the regular budget was $21.5 million;[44] some three decades later, the resources at the disposal of the world body amounted to $307 million,[45] while in 2006 the regular budget reached $1.8 billion. This regular budget, which is debated endlessly because of its significance for the control and direction of the United Nations, represents only 20 percent of total spending. In 2005, the peacekeeping budget alone amounted to another $5 billion, and extra-budgetary contributions another $2.8 billion.

In addition to financial wherewithal, the human resources on which the daily operations of the UN depend also have increased substantially. In 1945, the UN Secretariat itself was a small family while the entire system had some 1,500 people. Early in the millennium, the UN with its global reach relies on some 15,000 employees (7,500 are paid from the regular budget) from approximately 170 countries. The UN system as a whole—including the World Bank and International Monetary Fund—employs some 61,000 staff.

These quantitative indicators of growth, however, should be placed in context. Measured in comparison with the challenges to be overcome or in relationship to national expenditures, the UN's statistics could be considered almost trivial. Over the sixty-year period, the regular budget appears to have increased eighty-eight times; however, when the figures are adjusted for inflation, the increase corresponds approximately to sixteen times the 1946 budget. This amounts to an allocation of about $0.30 per human being alive in 2006; even with the peacekeeping budget included, this figure is only about $1.07.

Total global procurement by the UN, about 85 percent of which arises from peacekeeping, grew from about $400 million in 1997 to $1.6 billion in 2005. However, even the record-breaking expenditure on UN peacekeeping operations worldwide in 2005 was the equivalent of only one month of US expenditures in Iraq in that same year.

Writing in the mid-1990s, Erskine Childers and Brian Urquhart pointed out a number of relevant comparisons to challenge the commonplace impression of a 'vast, sprawling bureaucracy.' They wrote: 'The entire UN system world-wide, serving the interests of some 5,500,000,000 people in 184 countries [now 6.5 billion in 192 countries], employs no more workers than the civil service in the American state of Wyoming, population 545,000 . . . and less than the combined civil services of the Canadian Province of Manitoba and its capital city of Winnipeg.' They further noted that the budgets for the whole system's regular activities ($6.5 billion) amounted to about the same that US citizens spent annually on cut flowers and potted plants, while the total worldwide expenditure of the UN system—$10.5 billion—was three-and-a-half times *less* than the amount that UK citizens spend on alcoholic beverages per year. Moreover, the total budgetary portion allocated to the UN proper (some $4.1 billion) was no more than the budgets of the New York City fire and police departments together. In another quantitative comparison, Childers and Urquhart noted that the UN's 'giant paper factory' producing documents in six languages is also a myth in that 'the *New York Times* consumes more paper in one single Sunday edition than the United Nations consumes in all its documents in a whole year.'[46]

However, the more intriguing and perhaps controversial questions relate to qualitative change. And here too the UN has changed dramatically since 1945. One qualitative means is to conduct a historical analysis and trace great events. International relations scholars typically trace movements from one historical period to another in terms of wars in general and great power wars in particular. World War II and the founding of the UN itself followed by the Cold War qualify as do many of the crises over the last sixty years in which the world organization has been involved—in security ones from the division of Palestine to the Cuban Missile Crisis and the implosion of the Balkans; in human rights from McCarthyism to Rwanda's genocide; and in development from the influx of newly independent countries to the Asian financial crisis of 1997–1998. By commission or omission, many such events are viewed as seminal for the UN and defining moments for international cooperation.

Qualitative change can be defined as difference in kind. Novelty and replacement are types of qualitative change. The presumption is of rupture, or a clear break between what once was and what currently is.[47] To that extent, we are looking for discontinuities, when new forms replace old ones, which is pretty much the story of the United Nations—including, for instance, the creation of peacekeeping and the return to peace enforcement; the introduction of gender and other types of human rights mainstreaming; the change from protecting the environment to sustainable development.

Holsti notes that change is quite different for someone playing today's stock market or for those of us trying to understand it in international relations where recent events are not of interest unless they have a demonstrable effect on how diplomatic, military, or humanitarian work is actually done. 'This is the Hegelian and Marxist problem: at what point,' he asks, 'does quantitative change lead to qualitative consequences?'[48] In other words, we can also characterize as 'new' a tipping point[49] at which quantitative change is so substantial that it constitutes something qualitatively 'new.'

Many of the arguments about the shifts that have occurred over the last twenty years about the nature of humanitarian agencies, for example, are claims that the environment, the relationships among actors, and the process of delivery of relief itself have become more complex.[50] In many respects, the sum of such changes in quantitative trends have combined in such a way as to have 'system effects,'[51] the equivalent of qualitative change. The growing involvement of states, for instance, has had a series of important consequences on the organization of humanitarian action. The use of the military for human protection purposes is undoubtedly the clearest example.[52]

In many instances, the contemporary international order is in turmoil. The mere quantity of developments may strike readers—it certainly does the editors—as the equivalent of qualitative change. In presenting his reform proposals to the General Assembly in March 2006, Secretary-General Annan summarized: 'Today's United Nations is vastly different from the Organization that emerged from the San Francisco conference more than 60 years ago.'[53] In short, he was pointing to the obvious, namely a significant shake-up in the way that the UN does business is essential to keep pace with the significantly altered circumstances six decades after its founding.

Determining 'Success' and 'Failure'

A similar complication arises and constitutes a second analytical problem for readers who may be struggling to decide whether international cooperation through particular institutions has been a 'success' or a 'failure.' In this effort, they should keep in mind the often-ignored distinction between the 'two United Nations'[54]—one being the forum in which states make decisions and the other being the international civil service. Which UN is behind what is viewed as a success or failure, and to what extent? Both of these United Nations are woven throughout this *Handbook* as in most commentaries on the organization.

The success or failure of the 'first' UN, of course, depends upon governments' perceptions of their vital interests and the accompanying political will, or lack thereof, to move ahead within a multilateral framework. It is this United Nations that is most often the locus of evaluation by the public and scholars alike. But throughout the pages of this *Handbook* we show that the 'second' UN is capable, under certain circumstances, of leadership and influence that alter international outcomes. We maintain that individuals matter—for international secretariats as for all human endeavors. Success or failure in implementing policy is, of course, not independent of governments, resources, and political support. Yet there is more room for maneuver and autonomy for members of the international civil service, particularly in the intellectual and advocacy realms, than is often supposed.

The old adage comes to mind here—success has numerous parents, but failure is an orphan. States are often unwilling to dilute their sovereignty through multilateral cooperation and diplomacy, but they rarely are willing to blame themselves for breakdowns in international order and society. The 'first' UN has a convenient scapegoat in the 'second' UN, and vice versa. Conor Cruise O'Brien described the 'sacred drama' of these two entities whose creation was designed to appeal to the imagination. As such, he undoubtedly is correct in noting that 'its truths are not literal truths, and its power not a material power.'[55]

The stage for the drama by these two United Nations has, over the last six decades, become increasingly crowded with a diversity of other actors.[56] States are still the dominant players in the UN, and national interests have not receded as the basis for making decisions; and secretariats sometimes make a difference. However, there is substantial evidence that what might be called the 'third' UN—or perhaps the 'complementary' UN—is becoming increasingly salient. This consists in a host of important players who are part of a parallel world of independent experts and consultants whose job descriptions include research, policy analysis, and idea-mongering. They work along with NGOs, the private sector, and other nonstate actors. These voices too appear in many of our chapters because they are playing more prominent roles in the United Nations. Thus, deciding who is responsible for what portion of the blame for failure or what contribution to success is an increasingly complex task—for our readers as for our authors.

The UN's Changing Fortunes in World Politics

The third variety of analytical problem reflects a common oversight: too many observers forget the ebb and flow of world politics. In trying to wrap their minds around the previous two problems, an additional complicating factor is a pattern of reactions to experiments with international organization—high hopes followed by disillusionment, which in turn has an impact on the performance of the United Nations.[57] In the past, however, the disappointment often set in after a war or major cataclysm accompanied by the collapse of institutions—for example, the Concert of Europe or the League of Nations. Even without US participation in the latter, for example, the defections by important states took place over a decade and a half.

In the post-Cold War era, however, the disillusionment/euphoria roller coaster seems to be accelerating, with highs and lows exchanged with greater frequency. Because often the UN's business is tied to this morning's headlines, maintaining some perspective is a challenge. National and international reactions to the performance of the world organization follow an up-and-down pattern. The changing fortunes of the UN are continual—sometimes it is viewed as an essential player in international society, and then suddenly it is marginalized.

It is essential, for instance, in evaluating the debate of the 1990s about humanitarian intervention and multilateralism to search for historical baselines, even in the recent past, against which subsequent changes can be gauged. Shortly after the 1991 Gulf War and the allied efforts in Iraqi Kurdistan, the word 'renaissance' was ubiquitous. Apparently, there was nothing that the organization could not do. However, by 1994 there was nothing that it could do to halt the murder of 800,000 people in Rwanda's nightmare. From that nadir, 1999 was then either an *annus mirabilis* or *horribilis* for the UN, depending on one's views, with interventions in East Timor and Kosovo. And then following Washington and London's decision in

March 2003 to wage war in Iraq without explicit Security Council approval, the world organization was once again headed toward the 'dark ages' and confronted widespread disillusionment—there was nothing it could do to halt US hegemony, or there was nothing it could do to enforce decisions against the rogue regime of Saddam Hussein. Even seasoned observers of UN affairs seemed out of breath in attempting to gauge exactly the nature of the world organization's standing—not just in the United States but in 'new' and 'old' Europe, and virtually everywhere.

We would characterize the lead-up to the sixtieth anniversary of the UN, for example, as a reflection of a distinctly ahistorical perspective. A good place to begin is the dramatic imagery of the Secretary-General's famous 'fork in the road' speech,[58] which formed the basis for convening the High-level Panel on Threats, Challenges and Change (HLP).[59] The Secretary-General urged that 'the UN must undergo the most sweeping overhaul in its 60-year history.'[60] The outcome of the September 2005 UN World Summit inevitably failed to live up to such high expectations. But neither were the cynics who predicted a dismal failure proved entirely right. The World Summit's outcome and the initial follow-up indicated the tenacity of the organization with its ability to survive, grow, and adapt, but also that it achieves progress only through historical cycles of modest adaptation and change.

Its member states, throughout this process, continue to cling to the prerogatives of sovereignty while pursuing a predictable pattern. They find reasons to characterize the most incremental reforms in radiant hues, but they then begin again to bemoan the state of the world organization and assert that profound changes in the planet's situation necessitate sweeping structural renovations.

Despite these rhetorical sleights of hand, the UN's advances, while sometimes checkered, continue. Whether we consider more abstract advances in norm setting or concrete gains in the areas of conflict resolution, poverty alleviation, and human rights and democratization, the world organization—the first, second, and third United Nations—struggles to make the planet at least a little more habitable and hospitable.

We are reminded of a cautionary quip attributed to Dag Hammarskjöld: 'The UN was not created to take humanity to heaven, but to save it from hell.' Our view, which is reflected throughout the chapters in this *Handbook*, is that the relatively feeble power of the UN system will have to be augmented if many of the current threats to human survival and human dignity are to be adequately addressed. One reason that we are not in the netherworld already is the existence of the United Nations.

ABOUT THIS BOOK

With this overview now squarely before readers and in the interest of truth in packaging, we wish to make our own normative agenda clear. In putting together this collection of essays, we seek a better understanding of the origins, history, problems, and contributions of the world organization and the UN system as a whole. This, we hope, could result in improved strategies and tactics in the first decades of the turbulent twenty-first century. A better comprehension of the deficiencies of the current generation of international organizations could lead to the identification of appropriate remedies.

When we agreed to edit this *Handbook*, our initial task was to find a knowledgeable group of authors to write the thirty-nine chapters that follow. Brief biographies are found in the list of contributors at the beginning of this book. Adding to the value of this collection is the fact that all of the contributors have written extensively about the subject matter of their chapters or worked in a related field; many have done both.

Also at the outset of this *Handbook*, readers will find a lengthy list of abbreviations. The UN's discourse—like that of its member governments and the bevy of NGOs that follows its deliberations—is bedevilled with acronyms and abbreviations. Institutions and parts of them, along with individual peace operations, are almost always referred to by their initials. This alphabet soup may be off-putting, but it is a linguistic reality. In order to save space, contributors use these short-hand forms extensively, and so readers may need to consult the list with some frequency. In order to understand better the complicated interagency relationships that are present in every chapter, the reader may wish to consult the organizational diagram of the UN system in Appendix 2.

Also, in order to maximize space for analysis, illustrations, and appendices, we decided against a comprehensive bibliography, which would have duplicated the key references in each chapter. Hence, readers looking to pursue in-depth additional reading and research will find a solid intellectual resource in the endnotes. Contributors have emphasized published rather than electronic sources because of our fear that many of the websites in use when the chapters were finalized early in 2007 might not be available over the shelf-life of this volume.

However, in order to facilitate a novice's additional reading on every topic covered in this *Handbook*, we have exercised our collective editorial judgment and listed a handful of useful published works for each chapter. These sources are found in Appendix 1. With few exceptions, we have listed only recent books, which should be readily available in most research libraries.

Readers who wish to consult the texts of the UN Charter, the Statute of the International Court of Justice (ICJ), or the Universal Declaration of Human Rights will find them in Appendices 3, 4, and 5. Resolutions of the UN's principal organs are cited by number and date. Such texts along with many primary documents are readily available at www.un.org (a domain that will *not* change).

In designing this book, we obviously had to make decisions on what would be included and what would not. Reasonable people may disagree with our choices. In the pages that follow, we explain the logic of that selection and briefly examine the contents of each chapter as they pertain to our theme of continuity and change.

Part II: Theoretical Frameworks

The *Handbook* begins with overviews of the ways that international relations scholars and public international lawyers view the United Nations. Political and legal approaches provide the two main disciplinary tools for analyses of international organization. The two approaches are undoubtedly present in the educational backgrounds of many readers of this *Handbook*. They also provide the main vehicles for teaching in university classrooms where the United Nations is a core subject matter. Combining both of these approaches offers a sense of how knowledge about the UN system has grown since 1945. As one would expect, the ways of thinking about the world organization have changed almost as much as the institution itself and global politics over the last six decades.

In Chapter 2, 'Political Approaches,' Michael Barnett and Martha Finnemore draw on their own substantial writing and teaching in order to provide a *tour d'horizon* of theoretical approaches that have dominated the study of international organization, including the UN, over the last half century. New threats, new actors, and new norms are directly reflected in the theories used by international relations scholars to generalize about what makes the world go round. Barnett and Finnemore explore how analysts have conceived the ways that the UN not only regulates the existing activities of states but also helps to weave the fabric of international society. For them, the world organization makes a difference to member states—large and small, powerful and weak. The chapter makes clear the various schools of thought developed throughout the twentieth century to understand the behavior and misbehavior of international institutions. Barnett and Finnemore conclude by making a plea for scholars to work harder to understand the nuts and bolts of influence within intergovernmental organizations—what we earlier described as the first, second, and third United Nations.

In Chapter 3, 'Legal Perspectives,' José E. Alvarez presents readers with a succinct summary of his own substantial writing and teaching at several prominent law schools. He addresses how international organizations with a global reach have changed the mechanisms and reasoning behind the making, implementation, and enforcement of international law. While the 1990s were declared the United Nations Decade of International Law, the overwhelming tradition of positivism among international lawyers, in his view, does not do justice to the complex and largely beneficial changes resulting from the components of the UN system and their increased importance as 'lawmakers' since World War II. Alvarez is not among the international lawyers who are skeptical about the value of the United Nations in creating both 'hard' and 'soft' law. At the same time, he notes the disappearance of what had been an almost religious faith in law and multilateral approaches characteristic of the legal culture among those who helped design the world organization in the 1940s.

In Chapter 4, 'Evolution in Knowledge,' Leon Gordenker and Christer Jönsson bring to bear their combined three-quarters of a century in classrooms around the world to explore what has constituted new 'knowledge' about international organization in general and the UN in particular since World War II. Gordenker and

Jönsson examine the impact on the classroom and scholarship of the dominant approaches that emanate from Anglo-Saxon academia and think-tanks and that are reinforced by the preeminence of publishers and journals in North America and Europe. They also try to examine how the proverbial woman in the street has responded to different levels of knowledge over the years; they see little evidence that there is any in-depth knowledge of common UN concepts among the public or policymakers outside of specialist circles. They argue for unpacking the influences of both the UN of states and the UN of secretariats as a key research challenge, and also for communicating with larger publics as a main civic challenge.

Part III: Principal Organs

The next part of the *Handbook* provides a basic introduction to the six principal organs and to the 'secular pope,' the Secretary-General. The contents of this part are what many people understand as the United Nations. The main building blocks for the arenas where member states interact and make decisions and the people who constitute the second UN are spelled out.

M. J. Peterson's Chapter 5, 'General Assembly,' puts before readers the in-depth knowledge that she has accumulated in writing two often-cited books on this topic and in three decades of teaching UN studies. Many praise it as the 'world's parliament,' and others lambaste it as an ineffectual 'talk shop.' The Assembly is, of course, the forum where the sovereign equality of member states is taken very seriously. Indeed, the most prominent change in international relations in the second half of the twentieth century was the liberation of colonized peoples who now are the citizens of the overwhelming majority of member states. As there is no issue that is not on the Assembly's agenda, Peterson argues for a better division of labor with other principal organs and also an opening up of the General Assembly to other, nongovernmental voices.

In Chapter 6, 'Security Council,' David M. Malone brings to bear his edited and authored volumes on the UN's most powerful principal organ, which is responsible for determining what constitutes a threat to international peace and security, and often what international responses will result. This organ's first forty-five years are an essential part of the story, but the four issues that we outlined earlier as elements in a substantially changed landscape—new threats, new actors, new notions of sovereignty, and a single superpower—are all very much present in Malone's discussion of a post-Cold War Security Council. The extent to which decisions during the turbulent 1990s led to success or failure underlie the discussion, which includes the drama of the war in Iraq and its aftermath as essential challenges for the twenty-first century. In essence, the Council still functions as a club of great powers—and some would argue that the P-5 has effectively become the P-1 because of the US's preponderant power.

In Chapter 7, 'Economic and Social Council,' Gert Rosenthal relies on his research into this organ as well as his own stint as its president in examining the workings of what may be the most criticized principal organ. Besides twice increasing its size, the current fifty-four-member ECOSOC has, as Rosenthal notes, been criticized from the outset for its inability to pull together the various moving parts of an increasingly dispersed and complex UN system. It is unclear how the international system should respond to an increasingly complicated set of challenges to global survival and human dignity. However, ECOSOC's main weaknesses—an ambiguous relationship with the General Assembly, a lack of focus, an incapacity to attract high-level policymakers to its meetings, and the non-binding nature of its decisions—are unlikely to change in the near future. The proposal put forward by numerous groups to create an economic and social equivalent of the Security Council remains on the drawing boards of diplomatic architects rather than under construction.

In Chapter 8, 'Trusteeship Council,' Ralph Wilde examines a principal organ whose work was essential to the settlement arising from World War II, which involved establishing procedures for the independence of the defeated powers' colonies. This body accomplished its work so well that it should have been dismantled in 1994 when the last UN trusteeship, Palau, became independent. The difficulties of reforming the world organization are partially captured by that reality: this moribund organ continues to exist despite the 2005 World Summit's decision to put it to rest because implementation requires modifying the Charter, a non-starter. Wilde details the UN's pioneering efforts at facilitating the decolonization of trust territories, one part of the story of the world organization's contribution to the processes of self-determination for peoples in Africa, Asia, Latin America, the Caribbean, and the Middle East. The work of the Trusteeship Council was linked to what arguably may have been the most important political change of the twentieth century. Paradoxically, the UN thus has contributed to strengthening the traditional notion of sovereignty around newly constituted states at the same time that it has contributed to its erosion, or at least redefinition, in other ways.

In Chapter 9, 'Secretariat: Independence and Reform,' James O. C. Jonah's three decades as a senior international civil servant suffuse the analysis of the staff members who are recruited to constitute what we have referred to as the 'second UN.' Taking as a point of departure the Nobelmaire principles formulated under the League of Nations and repeated by its successor, Jonah stresses the critical importance of independent and competent staff and the efforts championed especially by Secretary-General Dag Hammarskjöld. He points out that politicians often blame government bureaucracies for failures and inadequacies, and that diplomats have a convenient scapegoat and can point a finger at the UN bureaucracy instead of a lack of political will. Nonetheless, Jonah sees the restoration and reinvigoration of the international civil service as the *sine qua non* of a strengthened United Nations in the new millennium.

Edward Newman's Chapter 10, 'Secretary-General,' puts before readers his own analytical experience and writing about the Secretariat's most senior official, what the

Charter calls its 'Chief Administrative Officer.' In the wake of the most serious and well-documented scandal in UN history, the Oil-for-Food Programme, Newman explores the intricacies of trying to perform what is not an exaggeration to describe—in the words of the first Secretary-General, Trygve Lie—as 'the most impossible job in the world.' While the Secretary-General is not a principal organ, a separate chapter in this part is devoted to this topic because dealing with the new challenges of the contemporary world is in the small print in the job description of the UN's head. Shortly before this book went into production, the General Assembly upon the recommendation of the Security Council made a decision to appoint Ban Ki-moon as the eighth person to hold the position.

In Chapter 11, 'International Court of Justice,' James Crawford and Tom Grant explore what journalists commonly call the 'World Court.' Crawford's writing and teaching about the UN's principal juridical organ is also infused with his practical experience before that body. Examining in detail the slow but steady growth of the global rule of law, Crawford and Grant begin with the juridical experiment of the League of Nations, the inaccurately labeled Permanent Court of International Justice. Charter Article 93 is clear that 'All Members of the United Nations are *ipso facto* parties to the Statute of the International Court of Justice.' As they point out, the Court in many ways goes against the grain of contemporary international relations and the proliferation of actors because Article 34 of its Statute specifies that 'Only states may be parties in cases before the Court.' While the ICJ's caseload has increased—until the 1990s, the fifteen judges handed down a ruling on only about a case and a half a year—there is little prospect that the 'rule of law' will be implemented soon by this body.

Part IV: Relationships with Other Actors

The fourth part of the *Handbook* provides an overview of how the world organization relates to the selected other actors whose activities are critically important to the actual functioning and performance of the UN system itself. The logic here is that it is impossible to understand the workings of the two United Nations without being familiar with the other institutions that often work in tandem with the world body.

In moving beyond the UN proper, in Chapter 12, 'Regional Groups and Alliances,' Waheguru Pal Singh Sidhu draws on his own substantial writing about regional security and begins his analysis with the provisions of the Charter's Chapter VIII, 'Regional Arrangements.' The actual implementation of many Security Council decisions would have been a dead letter without subcontracting to these institutions—indeed, all of the more robust peace operations in the post-Cold War world have included some form of involvement by regional arrangements. Sidhu clearly delineates their pluses and minuses in comparison with the universal United Nations. Of especial importance in thinking about the future resort to regional entities is the distinct difference in capacities between such regions as Europe with well-financed and well-equipped institutions and Africa, the continent with the most demand and perhaps the least capacity.

In Chapter 13, 'Bretton Woods Institutions,' Ngaire Woods's intimate knowledge of the Washington-based international financial institutions (IFIs) is very much in evidence as she spells out the contributions and power of these institutions that are *de jure* part of the UN system but de facto not. The power and procedures of the IFIs form a theme that creeps into all of the historical and actual depictions of the UN's efforts to foster economic and social development. Criticism is not in short supply. The far greater resources of the IFIs are one element, but the more distinguishing characteristic consists of the weighted voting procedures that differ from the principle of sovereign equality of such UN bodies as the General Assembly. In Washington, the voice of the 'haves' (the main financial backers) is much louder and more influential than the 'have nots' (the recipients of World Bank and IMF financial resources). And the voice of the United States is the loudest of all, enjoying the same kind of effective veto in the Bretton Woods institutions that it possesses in the Security Council.

In Chapter 14, 'Civil Society,' Paul Wapner's extensive research on nonstate actors is obvious as he spells out how the UN's approaches to NGOs and civil society have evolved. The appearance of this important element in what we above called the 'third UN' began with the vision of Charter Article 71, an early effort to reflect in the organization's deliberations the reality of the Charter's opening lines, 'We the Peoples of the United Nations.' He points out that there have always been tensions between the world organization's state-centered character and its aspiration to represent all the citizens of the globe. Many other chapters point to specific instances of inputs from NGOs—in global conferences, as executing agents for projects, as monitors and advocates—but Wapner's main concern is the enhanced legitimacy and accountability that come from involving civil society in intergovernmental deliberations and programs.

Craig N. Murphy's Chapter 15, 'Private Sector,' brings to the fore his lifelong teaching and analytical preoccupations with international political economy. He provides an extensive discussion of the for-profit sector's growing involvement— after being held at arm's length for much of the UN's first half century—not only as a lobby but as an active partner in international cooperation. He begins with the irony that intergovernmental organizations arose largely in response to problems and opportunities created by capitalist industrialism, what we now call 'economic globalization.' In seeing both the benefits and costs of capitalism's foot in the UN door, Murphy explores the complement to non-profit civil society in the for-profit business world. As part of globalization's continuing march, the growth of transnational corporations (TNCs) has been at least as dramatic as that of civil society.

In Chapter 16, 'Media,' Barbara Crossette's career as a working journalist is evident in her treatment of a surprisingly understudied part of the puzzle of UN affairs, namely how it interacts with and is reflected in the treatment by print and visual media. While it is commonplace to point to the 'CNN effect' (or the 'BBC effect'), Crossette is less impressed by evidence of such influence. She is more concerned to parse the various parts of the UN's public relations machinery and explore what makes 'news' for reporters covering the world organization. Here she is careful to trace the substantial changes over time—part technological, part political—that for a time rendered the UN of little news value. That, of course, changed with the end of the Cold War and the escalating number of crises on the world organization's daily agenda. She suggests that the UN itself try to set agendas rather than reacting to events as it has in the past.

Part V: International Peace and Security

Reflecting the UN's birth amidst the smoldering ashes of World War II, the fifth part of the *Handbook* is designed to provide the essential details—in addition to the dynamics of the principal organs discussed previously—of the organization's original *raison d'être*. The delegates from the fifty-one states gathered in San Francisco had in mind the tragedies of interstate war and the memory that World War I had supposedly been 'the war to end all wars.' They were responding to future threats of aggression and were seeking to maintain international peace and security in what can only be, with any historical perspective, a Sisyphean task to 'save succeeding generations from the scourge of war.'

This part begins with Chapter 17, 'Disarmament,' by Keith Krause whose own research and teaching has focused over the years on the control of various types of arms. The failure of the League of Nations did not preclude UN work in this area—indeed, after Hiroshima and Nagasaki, it seemed imperative. This unheralded part of the world organization's work has in many ways represented a profound adaptation of UN structures, and Krause points to disarmament efforts (including the Conference on Disarmament and the International Atomic Energy Agency), the Nuclear Non-Proliferation Treaty, the Chemical Weapons Convention, the UN Special Commission in Iraq, and more recent efforts to tackle the problems of antipersonnel land mines and small arms. While he does not downplay the interests of major powers as circumscribing the UN's possible contributions, nonetheless Krause sees intergovernmental institutions as possessing a limited but valuable autonomy to shape these interests as well as to frame the normative structures within which these interests are pursued.

In Chapter 18, 'Peaceful Settlement of Disputes and Conflict Prevention,' Rama Mani brings her own practical and analytical experience to bear on the issues spelled out or implicit in Charter Chapter VI, 'Pacific Settlement of Disputes.' Continuity and change come together in an unusual way. She examines the array of arrows that traditionally have been in the UN Secretary-General's quiver—negotiations, fact-finding, mediation, good offices, conciliation, and arbitration—along with some more recent inventions, including international tribunals and regional arrangements. As a result of leadership by Secretaries-General Boutros-Ghali and Annan, the 'culture of prevention' has become one of the world organization's main rhetorical emphases—an important contemporary interpretation of Chapter VI.

In Chapter 19, 'Peacekeeping Operations,' Michael W. Doyle and Nicholas Sambanis put before readers the essential dimensions of this UN 'invention.' 'Chapter VI and a half' is a term often used to describe the peculiar military efforts that go beyond the peaceful resolution of disputes in Chapter VI but fall short of the war-fighting enforcement in Chapter VII, 'Action with Respect to Threats to the Peace, Breaches of the Peace, and Acts of Aggression.' Most of the chapter is devoted to analyzing the effectiveness of contemporary UN peacekeeping as part of a comprehensive strategy to achieve sustainable peace. Here, 'success' and 'failure' are really in the eye of the beholder, or a subjective judgment from the evaluator. For Doyle and Sambanis the emphasis is on how and when peace is 'sustainable.' The authors examine peacekeeping as it interacts with peacemaking, peace enforcement, and post-conflict reconstruction—indeed, the standard character of second-generation operations was multifunctionality, a novelty in comparison with traditional peace-keeping during the Cold War era. Drawing upon their own empirical work, they see participation, rather than a mere cessation of violence, as the key variable in success, which is more likely after non-ethnic wars, in countries with relatively high development levels, and when UN peace operations and substantial financial assistance are available. Unfortunately, these conditions rarely characterize UN operations starting in the dramatically turbulent years of the 1990s.

In Chapter 20, 'Sanctions,' David Cortright, George A. Lopez, and Linda Gerber-Stellingwerf begin our consideration of enforcement with the least forceful provisions of Chapter VII. No other names are more intimately associated with this topic, on which the two senior authors have collaborated since sanctions became a favored tool of statecraft in the 1990s. This is certainly one area where substantial task expansion has occurred. During the UN's first forty-five years, the Security Council employed sanctions only twice—against Southern Rhodesia in 1966 and South Africa in 1977. During the next fifteen years, however, the Council adopted dozens of sanctions resolutions levied against sixteen distinct targets, including states and nonstate actors. Partially as a result of the experience—and certainly the negative humanitarian consequences of sanctions in Iraq—we have witnessed selective and targeted sanctions that bear little resemblance to the poorly-monitored, often blunt measures imposed in the early 1990s which often were manipulated by regimes to get their populations to 'rally around the flag'. There is, however, little evidence that these less-than-comprehensive sanctions actually alter policy by the targeted political authorities.

In Chapter 21, 'Peace Enforcement,' Michael Pugh continues the discussion of Chapter VII with the ultimate enforcement measure, the use of military force to back up Security Council decisions. Bringing to the essay his own experience as an author, teacher, and journal editor on these matters, he contests the notion that there has been a significant change in the underlying determinants of UN enforcement. He begins by parsing the elastic definitions that surround this topic. He does not believe that enforcement is based either on fixed rights or on an evolving norm but rather on traditional power politics. Pugh concisely surveys the key cases after the UN's renaissance in the 1990s and documents the extent to which subcontracting to major powers and regional organizations was the only feasible way to project military force to back up international decisions. The predominant military power of the United States is a main theme. Pugh hesitates to characterize as an unqualified success any use of the blunt instrument of military enforcement—with or without a UN blessing. Pugh's chapter, as well as others, makes clear that UN peace operations are remarkably cheap—in 2005, for example, the combined cost of all UN peace operations was $5 billion, approximately 5 percent of annual US costs in Iraq and Afghanistan. And in spite of many criticisms, the numbers of soldiers in UN operations outnumber the foreign military deployments of any country other than the United States. In the first five years of the twenty-first century, UN peacekeepers increased by nearly 500 percent. And during this same time, peacekeepers from regional organizations (often seen as the wave of the future) fell by half.

In Chapter 22, 'Humanitarian Intervention,' Ramesh Thakur applies his own broad-gauged analytical experience to one of the most controversial topics of the 1990s—the use of military force to protect human beings. Humanitarian intervention is the extension of fourth-century arguments by St. Augustine and seventeenth-century ones by Hugo Grotius. But the current manifestation of 'the responsibility to protect' provides an interesting distinction for Thakur because the so-called right to humanitarian intervention has been so controversial for so many developing countries. He thus begins his essay with an examination of humanitarian interventions by colonial powers in the nineteenth century. He then proceeds to what may be the fastest-moving normative development of our times—namely that the rights of human beings sometimes trump those of the states in which they live. In spite of Charter Article 2 (7) and basic continuities in the Westphalian system, the redefinition of sovereignty—to include conditions of respect for human rights and of the principle of nonintervention when a state is unable or unwilling to protect its citizens from mass murder and war crimes—is a fundamental alteration in UN decision-making and international relations.

In Chapter 23, 'Post-Conflict Peacebuilding,' Roland Paris's extensive writing and teaching on the topic are obvious in his treatment of the UN's efforts to move beyond violence once peace finally breaks out. The proliferation of civil wars has presented a substantial challenge to the UN system in trying to rebuild state capacity in countries ripped apart by the new threats and actors described earlier. Paris describes the trial-and-error experiments of helping mend war-torn countries in the 1990s. He sees a process of learning by which market democracy is no longer, if it ever was, seen as a miracle cure. There are no quick fixes because peacebuilding requires long-lasting and intrusive forms of international involvement in post-conflict countries, the kinds of commitment that are rare among donors. Among the more significant other lessons from UN efforts are the importance of building effective domestic institutions as well as the requirement for more effective coordination among the diverse array of international actors. The establishment of the Peacebuilding Commission in December 2005 as a result of the World Summit may be a step in the right direction.

Jane Boulden's Chapter 24, 'Terrorism,' provides readers with a *tour d'horizon* of UN efforts that began decades before that now fateful date, 11 September 2001, which many observers view as having fundamentally altered many international security calculations—certainly those of the United States. UN deliberations have assumed increased importance since that moment when a different type of possibility— namely the possibility of WMDs in the hands of a rogue state—has upped the international ante. Boulden discusses the two main sticking points in UN discussions, which ironically have led to several important treaties but to no definition. The first is captured by the expression 'your terrorist is my freedom fighter'—that is, many countries view as legitimate armed violence by those fighting for national liberation. The second is whether 'state terrorism' should be included in any definition agreed by the vast majority of member states—the use of force by Israeli and more recently US forces, for some, is mentioned in the same breath as suicide bombers. Among the many new threats on the UN's current agenda, those described in this chapter stand out as unsettling future challenges.

Part VI: Human Rights

The sixth part of the *Handbook* aims to put before our readers insights into what many believe to be the most 'revolutionary' of UN ideas, the international measures to enhance the protection of human rights. The tension—some would say contradiction—is obvious between the respect for fundamental human rights and the Charter's call in Article 2 (7): 'Nothing contained in the present Charter shall authorize the United Nations to intervene in matters which are essentially within the domestic jurisdiction of any state.' Much of the recent debate revolves around the possible interpretations of 'essentially.'

In Chapter 25, 'Norms and Machinery,' Bertrand G. Ramcharan's active thirty-year UN career in the human rights arena is obvious as is his own extensive writing on the topic. His point of departure is the revolutionary implications of taking human rights seriously, which leads him to discuss two possible analytical lenses through which to examine the UN's story. On the one hand, there are the all too evident failures, with the massive violations of the rights of large groups of humankind frequently ignored. On the other hand, Ramcharan highlights the struggle to move forward with the standard that societies should be governed by a basic respect for human rights and without discrimination on grounds of race, sex, language, or religion. He examines the acute difficulties of the UN's using the bully pulpit while being mindful of the principles of respect and confidence-building. The transformation of the Commission on Human Rights into the Human Rights Council as a result of the 2005 World Summit was the latest manifestation of clashing views between the West and many developing countries; but most observers viewed the

March 2006 General Assembly decision to move ahead as a step in the right direction.

The experience and wisdom of Justice Richard Goldstone are clear from Chapter 26, 'International Criminal Court and Ad Hoc Tribunals.' His point of departure is a relatively longer-run perspective of the last century and a half, which for him represents the relatively 'recent' experience in formulating a truly global rule of law. This chapter focuses on contemporary international efforts to consolidate and codify significant portions of existing customary international law through decisions rendered by the ad hoc UN tribunals for a number of countries and the passage of the Rome Statute of the International Criminal Court. In spite of the demonstrated reluctance and hostility from major powers, Goldstone sees as much change as continuity in that the ICC is an especially vital development in the emergence of a single model for international criminal justice, a substantial building block for the twenty-first century.

In Chapter 27, 'Humanitarian Action and Coordination,' readers find substantial evidence of Jeff Crisp's intimate exposure to civilian intergovernmental and non-governmental organizations that work to protect and assist human beings caught in the throes of war. This 'growth industry' of the 1990s—expenditures went from $2 billion to $6 billion over the turbulent 1990s and in 2005 were close to $10 billion—is illuminated by his discussion of a network of institutions struggling to respond to the spate of what became known as 'complex humanitarian emergencies.' Crisp analyzes the history of UN humanitarian action, in both natural and human-made disasters, as a way to argue that, while many contemporary problems have existed since 1945, they have become more acute with the dramatic growth in the humanitarian enterprise in the post-Cold War period. The tensions over jurisdiction and turf present in other chapters come to the surface most clearly in Crisp's examination of the bevy of UN institutions, and their NGO partners, that flock to the scene of contemporary humanitarian emergencies.

Charlotte Bunch's Chapter 28, 'Women and Gender,' draws upon her teaching and research into this issue as well as her own active participation in many of the UN's more recent normative efforts in this arena. The UN's visible efforts for women began to be noticed with the preparation for the World Conference of the International Women's Year in Mexico City in 1975, but they actually started with earlier endeavors to quantify women's contributions to economic development. After discussing the differences between women and gender, Bunch critically examines the norms and their institutional manifestations as well as selected UN system efforts to promote women's rights in development, health, human rights, and peace and security. Bunch balances her evaluation of how much things have changed for women and girls over the last six decades with a criticism of the world organization itself whose moral authority is weakened by failing to live up to its own high standards in the recruitment and promotion of women.

Yves Beigbeder's World Health Organization (WHO) and UN career in headquarters and the field provides a background for Chapter 29, 'Children.' A host of international meetings, resolutions, movements, and reports have increased the interest of leaders and public opinion in the international protection of children's rights, the preoccupation of one of the UN's most popular units since its inception. UNICEF is the focus for Beigbeder's examination, but other UN organizations also enter into the diplomatic promotion of children's rights and into associated operational issues. The emphasis on children is hardly new—the League of Nations had a program, and many NGOs have been working on the issue for decades. The Convention on the Rights of the Child broke all records in terms of its rapid entry into force. And while in many ways nothing should be easier and less politically sensitive than protecting the next generation, the international protection of children's rights remains a twenty-first century challenge.

In Chapter 30, 'Minorities and Indigenous Peoples,' Maivân Clech Lâm begins her essay by reminding readers of World War II and the catastrophic results of having ignored minority rights during the interwar years. Her own writing and teaching about critical race theory provide an excellent vantage point for her clear delineation of the nature of the two nascent regimes of international human rights law that respond to both personal and collective vulnerabilities. UN efforts here have aimed to ensure that minorities are protected and can participate in the dominant societies in which they live, while the cultures of indigenous peoples require protection from the societies around them which, in all too many cases, have almost obliterated them. For the latter, globalization has both threatened their existence and made it possible for others to be aware of their plight.

In Chapter 31, 'Human Security,' Fen O. Hampson and Christopher K. Penny provide not only a fitting introduction to this crucial and increasingly salient policy topic but also a transition to the next part of the *Handbook*. They draw on their own substantial work on this topic, from the point of view of international relations and law respectively, to spell out the benefits of recalibrating the definition of 'security' to emphasize human beings instead of states. Indeed, human security is firmly entrenched in today's language of world politics and reflects the UN's role in advancing and sometimes enforcing new international norms that place the individual—and not member states—at the core of modern understandings of international security. However individual human security is defined, it has certainly been enhanced by the work of the United Nations. But Hampson and Penny do not shy away from pointing to some of the analytical and policy costs arising from casting the net widely, which was the dominant characteristic of the 2005 World Summit and has become an increasingly popular framing for many agencies and governments.

Part VII: Development

The purpose of the seventh part of the *Handbook* is to introduce briefly some of the more essential and pertinent aspects of the UN's efforts to foster economic and social development. While the maintenance of international peace and security was clearly the raison d'être for the world organization's founding, the emphases and the actual work have changed substantially over time. While development was originally framed essentially as a way to ensure peace, the rapid pace of decolonization resulted in a change in priorities for the world organization—development was an essential objective in and of itself for newly independent countries. The contributions of the UN to development thinking and practice are seriously understudied.[61] Indeed, economic and social development—for example, the activities in such sectors as food, industry, and education—could be the subject of an entire handbook. Here, however, we have to content ourselves with an overview of several essential current topics that have clear transnational dimensions and also are part of the challenge of development. Readers should, of course, be mindful that many other chapters in the *Handbook* deal with important aspects of economic and social advancement.

Jacques Fomerand's long UN career and experience as an analyst and instructor is complemented by Dennis Dijkzeul's in Chapter 32, 'Coordinating Economic and Social Affairs.' Their chapter explores the historical and ongoing intricacies of cooperation across the various specialized agencies as well as special programs and funds of the UN's extended development system. They point to structural difficulties—separate funding and governing structures in institutions located across the globe—that are mixed with conventional bureaucratic politics and turf-consciousness. Moreover, the authors highlight the autonomy of the World Bank and the IMF—whose resources and annual disbursements dwarf those of the entire UN system—that make the Bretton Woods institutions distinct from the UN system even if the organizational chart includes them as linked components. In thinking through the challenges of the Charter's connection between economic and social development and the fundamental purpose of saving future generations from the scourge of war, they trace the reasons why development became *the* work of the world organization with the influx of almost 150 countries since 1945. The oft-heard criticism is of sclerosis in the UN system, but its evolution is actually never-ending. In February 2006, for example, the Secretary-General set up a fifteen-member High-level Panel on UN System-wide Coherence in the areas of development, humanitarian aid, and the environment. Whether this effort—co-chaired by the prime ministers of Mozambique, Norway, and Pakistan—will result in tinkering or actually lead to a substantial rationalization of the system remains to be seen.[62]

Gian Luca Burci's analytical and practical familiarity provides the basis for Chapter 33, 'Health and Infectious Disease.' There is continuity between UN efforts and those by states in the nineteenth and early twentieth centuries. The control of infectious diseases has an inherently international dimension because national boundaries do not halt pathogens; and the international movement of persons, animals, and goods makes every country vulnerable. Still, the dawn of new threats—HIV/AIDS, Ebola, SARs, and avian flu to name just a few from the last decades—suggests new vulnerabilities as well as new possibilities for international cooperation through the WHO and other UN organizations. The major achievement to date which suggests the effectiveness of a multilateral attack on infectious diseases was the eradication of smallpox in 1980—moreover, poliomyelitis probably will be eradicated within the next few years. At the same time, any exploration of these successes has been tempered by failed campaigns to control malaria and tuberculosis along with the seemingly futile fight against the HIV/AIDS pandemic. Whether framing diseases and bio-terrorism as threats to international peace and security will foster multilateral or unilateral responses remains an open question.

In Chapter 34, 'Natural Resource Management and Sustainable Development,' Nico Schrijver's exposure not only as an author and teacher but also as a legal practitioner is in evidence in his authoritative treatment of another quintessentially modern challenge that does not respect national boundaries, the effective management of the world's natural resources. While in 1945 the new world organization was conceived to maintain or restore international peace and security, Schrijver points out that throughout its existence the UN has had a profound impact on natural resource management, both conceptually and operationally. In many ways the UN's two blockbuster conferences on the topic of the human environment—in Stockholm in 1972 and in Rio de Janeiro in 1992—are markers of the efforts by state and especially nonstate actors to reframe the human relationship with the natural environment and development. As Schrijver points out, the initial clash between conservation and development has been reframed as 'sustainable development,' a useful analytical framework to bridge the North–South divide. The disconnect between the size of environmental challenges and the relatively feeble international machinery for addressing them—for example, the UN Environment Programme and the World Bank—is stark.

In Chapter 35, 'Organized Crime,' Frank G. Madsen probes a little-known but growing role of the UN, namely the world organization's contribution to combating transnational organized crime, including illicit traffic in drugs and in human beings. On the one hand, UN efforts in this arena are based on the Charter and the Universal Declaration of Human Rights and thus are not new. On the other hand, reinterpretations of older conventions are crucial in today's world where rapid communications, global financial systems, and ease of transportation increasingly place national authorities at a disadvantage in fighting such illicit activity. Even the prosecution of criminal cases assumes extreme complexity when dealing with different criminal laws and different legal systems. As Madsen points out, eradicating terrorism and money laundering is like putting a stop to the trafficking of illicit drugs and humans in that these should be intrinsic and not additional UN activities.

In Chapter 36, 'Democracy and Good Governance,' W. Andy Knight's long-standing research and teaching is very much in evidence as he examines what emerged in the 1990s as the overriding priority in approaches to development assistance and investment. Only a few states that signed the Charter in 1945 had democratically elected governments; but that number increased gradually to about forty in the 1970s and then dramatically after the end of the Cold War to around 120 countries today. Because of the intrusions into the so-called domestic prerogatives of recipient states, the UN has had limited success in addressing the need for better national policies—liberalization and democratization are the essence of 'good governance.'

At the same time, the UN system has struggled to go beyond organizing elections as the only component of 'democratization.' Pointing out that the terms do not figure in the Charter or the Universal Declaration of Human Rights, Knight nonetheless shows how much of the UN's normative and operational work has been devoted to these areas. The gap between rhetoric and reality constitutes a substantial democratic deficit—in member states and in the Secretariat.

In Chapter 37, 'Human Development,' Richard Jolly not only provides an overview of the approach of human development that has characterized much of UN development thinking since the early 1990s, but also helps highlight the importance of numerous institutions in the UN development system that are not singled out for separate treatment in this *Handbook*. Based on a long and distinguished career as a development practitioner and theorist, Jolly puts before readers the concern with accelerated economic and social development that has been a hallmark of the UN's efforts on behalf of developing countries from the outset. Arguing that the world organization and its component parts have followed a multidisciplinary approach to development—in contrast with the primarily economic framework championed by the World Bank and the IMF—Jolly concentrates on the conceptual approach that has been continually refined with the annual publication, beginning in 1990, of UNDP's *Human Development Report*. He also sees the Millennium Development Goals (MDGs) as a possible bridge between the UN system and the Bretton Woods institutions.

Part VIII: Prospects for Reform

The final part of the *Handbook* returns explicitly to our main theme but looks more toward the future than the present or past. The ongoing struggle to update the world organization in light of the new threats and new actors that figure prominently in these pages was most obvious in the September 2005 World Summit in New York. Here, three authors put squarely before readers the constraints inhibiting radical structural alteration in the United Nations—those working against substantial reform, more flexibility in financing, and wider participation—but with a sensitivity to what may be possible in the next decade. All point to considerable evidence of adaptation and change over the last sixty years while indicating that no such impression is widely shared by even the intelligent reading public.

No one is better qualified than Edward C. Luck to write Chapter 38, 'Principal Organs.' A lifelong student of the UN's processes, policies, and practices as well as of what may be the most important national dimension, US–UN relations, he focuses on the proposals on the negotiating tables at the World Summit dealing with four of the principal organs (the Security Council, the General Assembly, ECOSOC, and the suspended Trusteeship Council) whose characteristics raise similar reform conundrums. As in all his writing, however, Luck is careful to situate these ambitious reform possibilities in a proper historical context. In fact, the world organization has evolved in so many ways that its founders might not recognize many of its activities on the contemporary stage. Reform and change have been a constant refrain. At the same time, Luck examines the intricacies and the politics of the peculiar moment that was the sixtieth anniversary. The world organization is no stranger to controversy and criticism, but attempts to solve political problems by procedural changes are bound to fall short. He reminds readers of the oft-cited comment that reform is a process—not an event—and that the UN adapts to changing circumstances far more rapidly than it adopts structural reform.

In Chapter 39, 'Financing,' Jeffrey Laurenti's in-depth familiarity—gathered in a number of capacities with private organizations working to foster multilateral cooperation—is obvious as he spells out the proverbial bottom line of the world organization's ability to act. Resources are one concrete way to measure political will and commitment. Moreover, while the topic of UN financing would appear to some as mere housekeeping and the details of administration as boring and of little interest, in fact some of the most contentious political struggles that have wracked and at times imperiled the world organization have centered on its financing. Because financial resources are a fundamental metric of power, Laurenti outlines why it is hardly surprising that the major donors want their preferences to be heard. That the UN is not a world government is perhaps most obvious here because it levies no taxes and has no independent sources of finance, but must rely on the assessed and voluntary contributions of its member governments. The clash between the realities of power, especially of the United States as the main contributor, and Charter values are reflected in the recurrent battles over the state of the UN's financial health.

In Chapter 40, 'Widening Participation,' Chadwick F. Alger provides an appropriate book end with his examination of the changing face of multilateralism. He emphasizes the need for pluralizing the voices heard in UN deliberations, for taking more seriously the Charter Preamble's clarion call, 'We the Peoples of the United Nations.' His starting point resembles that of other chapters in this volume, namely that multilateralism has undergone continual change throughout the history of the United Nations; and he suggests that this dynamic process will continue. With the proliferation of actors and technologies, Alger observes the increasing involvement by nonstate actors in addition to the traditional foreign policy bureaucracies of member state governments. In the past, many observers saw the logical conclusion of UN efforts as a world government, modeled on those of existing states. But increasingly, the messier notion of global governance is the rubric under which many members of civil society attempt to improve international order. Alger calls upon readers to get involved in civil society organizations, business groups, and local groups and thereby change from unconscious to conscious participants in international society.

We wish readers *bon voyage* as they embark on their journey through the history of continuity and change in the United Nations since 1945.

NOTES

1. Craig Murphy, *International Organization and Industrial Change: Global Governance since 1850* (Cambridge: Polity, 1994).

2. Adam Roberts and Benedict Kingsbury, 'Introduction: The UN's Roles in International Society since 1945,' in *United Nations: Divided World*, 2nd edn., ed. Adam Roberts and Benedict Kingsbury (Oxford: Oxford University Press, 1993), 1.

3. Hedley Bull, *The Anarchical Society: A Study* (New York: Columbia University Press, 1977). A more recent treatment is Robert Jackson, *The Global Covenant: Human Conduct in a World of States* (Oxford: Oxford University Press, 2000).

4. Michael G. Schechter, *United Nations Global Conferences* (London: Routledge, 2005).

5. Inis L. Claude, Jr., *Swords into Plowshares: The Problems and Prospects of International Organization* (New York: Random House, 1956).

6. This is the definition used to determine whether a particular war was tabulated. Peter Wallensteen and Margareta Sollenberg, 'Armed Conflict, 1989–2000,' *Journal of Peace Research* 38, no. 5 (2001), 632. Some have argued that there has been an upswing in the number, intensity, and duration of civil wars, particularly since 1989. However, data indicate that the quantity of overall conflicts decreased while negotiated settlements increased over the 1990s. See Swedish International Peace Research Institute, *SIPRI Yearbook 1998: Armaments, Disarmament, and International Security* (Oxford: Oxford University Press, 1998), 17. This SIPRI data is shortened and updated annually by Wallensteen and Sollenberg in the *Journal of Peace Research*.

7. UNDP, *Human Development Report 2002: Deepening Democracy in a Fragmented World* (New York: Oxford University Press, 2002), 85.

8. Andrew Mack et al., *Human Security Report 2005: War and Peace in the 21st Century* (Oxford: Oxford University Press, 2005).

9. Mary Kaldor, *New & Old Wars: Organized Violence in a Global Era* (Palo Alto, Calif.: Stanford University Press, 1999); Mark Duffield, *Global Governance and the New Wars: The Merging of Development and Security* (London: Zed Books, 2001); and Peter J. Hoffman and Thomas G. Weiss, *Sword & Salve: Confronting New Wars and Humanitarian Crises* (Lanham, Md.: Rowman & Littlefield, 2006).

10. Stephen John Stedman, 'Spoiler Problems in Peace Processes,' *International Security* 22, no. 2 (1997): 5–53.

11. See Union of International Associations, 'International Organizations by Type (Table 1),' in *Yearbook of International Organizations* (Brussels: Union of International Associations, 2006).

12. Helmut Anheier, Marlies Glasius, and Mary Kaldor, 'Introducing Global Civil Society,' in *Global Civil Society 2001*, ed. Helmut Anheier, Marlies Glasius, and Mary Kaldor (Oxford: Oxford University Press, 2001), 4.

13. Kerstin Martens, *NGOs and the United Nations: Institutionalization, Professionalization and Adaptation* (Houndmills, Basingstoke, UK: Palgrave Macmillan, 2005), 2.

14. See Johan Kaufmann, *United Nations Decision Making* (Alphen aan den Rijn, Netherlands: Sijthoff & Noordhoff, 1980).

15. Stephen Krasner, *Sovereignty: Organized Hypocrisy* (Princeton, NJ: Princeton University Press, 1999).

16. Andrew Chadwick, *Internet Politics: States, Citizens, and New Communication Technologies* (New York: Oxford University Press, 2006).

17. For example, see David Held and Anthony McGrew, with David Goldblatt and Jonathan Perraton, *Global Transformations: Politics, Economics, and Culture* (Palo Alto, Calif.: Stanford University Press, 1999).

18. Richard O'Brien, *Global Financial Integration: The End of Geography* (London: Pinter, 1992).
19. Ernst B. Haas, *Beyond the Nation-State: Functionalism and International Organization* (Palo Alto, Calif.: Stanford University Press, 1964).
20. Boutros Boutros-Ghali, *An Agenda for Peace* (New York: UN, 1992), para. 17.
21. Paul Szasz, 'General Law Making Processes,' in *United Nations Legal Order*, ed. Oscar Schachter and Christopher Joyner (Washington, DC: American Society of International Law, 1995), 35 and 59.
22. See, for example, Frances M. Deng et al., *Sovereignty as Responsibility: Conflict Management in Africa* (Washington, DC: Brookings, 1996); Kofi A. Annan, *'We the Peoples': The United Nations in the 21st Century* (New York: UN, 2000); and International Commission on Intervention and State Sovereignty (ICISS), *The Responsibility to Protect* (Ottawa: ICISS, 2001).
23. Kofi A. Annan, *The Question of Intervention: Statements by the Secretary-General* (New York: UN, 1999), 7.
24. Gerald B. Helman and Steven R. Ratner, 'Saving Failed States,' *Foreign Policy*, no. 89 (1992–1993): 3–20.
25. Martin Meredith, *The State of Africa: A History of Fifty Years of Independence* (London: Free Press, 2005).
26. See Joseph E. Nye, Jr., *The Paradox of American Power: Why the World's Only Superpower Can't Go It Alone* (New York: Oxford University Press, 2002).
27. Donald J. Puchala, 'The United Nations and Hegemony,' *International Studies Review* 7, no. 4 (2005): 571–584.
28. Edward C. Luck, *Mixed Messages: American Politics and International Organization 1919–1999* (Washington, DC: Brookings, 1999).
29. Nye, *The Paradox of American Power*.
30. For a variety of interpretations, see Rosemary Foot, S. Neil MacFarlane, and Michael Mastanduno, eds., *US Hegemony and International Organizations: The United States and Multilateral Institutions* (Oxford: Oxford University Press, 2003); Steward Patrick and Shepard Forman, eds., *Multilateralism & US Foreign Policy: Ambivalent Engagement* (Boulder, Colo.: Lynne Rienner, 2002); David M. Malone and Yuen Foong Khong, eds., *Unilateralism & US Foreign Policy: International Perspectives* (Boulder, Colo.: Lynne Rienner, 2003); and Michael Byers and Georg Nolte, eds., *United States Hegemony and the Foundations of International Law* (Cambridge: Cambridge University Press, 2003).
31. Harold K. Jacobson, *Networks of Interdependence: International Organizations and the Global Political System*, 2nd edn. (New York: Knopf, 1984), 84.
32. Quoted by J. Martin Rochester, *Between Peril and Promise: The Politics of International Law* (Washington, DC: CQ Press, 2006), 27.
33. See Ramesh Thakur and Thomas G. Weiss, *The UN and Global Governance: An Idea and its Prospects* (Bloomington: Indiana University Press, forthcoming), ch. 1. See also Michael Barnett and Martha Finnemore, *Rules for the World: International Organizations in Global Politics* (Ithaca, NY: Cornell University Press, 2004); and Margaret P. Karns and Karen A. Mingst, *International Organizations: The Politics and Processes of Global Governance* (Boulder, Colo.: Lynne Rienner, 2004).
34. James N. Rosenau and Ernst-Otto Czempiel, *Governance Without Government: Order and Change in World Politics* (Cambridge: Cambridge University Press, 1992); and Commission on Global Governance, *Our Global Neighbourhood* (Oxford: Oxford University Press, 1995).
35. UNDP, *Human Development Report 1999: Globalization with a Human Face* (New York: Oxford University Press, 1999), 8.

36. The following draws on Louis Emmerij, Richard Jolly, and Thomas G. Weiss, *Ahead of the Curve? UN Ideas and Global Challenges* (Bloomington: Indiana University Press, 2001), 17–19; and *The Power of UN Ideas: Lessons from the First 60 Years* (New York: United Nations Intellectual History Project, 2005), 3–4.

37. Edward Hallett Carr, *The Twenty Years' Crisis, 1919–1939: An Introduction to the Study of International Relations* (London: Macmillan, 1939).

38. UNDP, *Human Development Report 2005: International Cooperation at a Crossroads: Aid, Trade and Security in an Unequal World* (Oxford: Oxford University Press, 2005), 3.

39. Kalevi J. Holsti, *Taming the Sovereigns: Institutional Change in International Politics* (Cambridge: Cambridge University Press, 2004), 12–13.

40. Freedom House, *Democracy's Century: A Survey of Global Political Change in the 20th Century* (New York: Freedom House, 1999).

41. This information is updated from David M. Malone, ed., *The UN Security Council: From the Cold War to the 21st Century* (Boulder, Colo.: Lynne Rienner, 2004).

42. David Held and Anthony McGrew, David Goldblatt, and Jonathan Perraton, *Global Transformations: Politics, Economics and Culture* (Palo Alto, Calif.: Stanford University Press, 1999), 53.

43. José E. Alvarez, *International Organizations as Lawmakers* (Oxford: Oxford University Press, 2005), 273–337.

44. Erskine Childers with Brian Urquhart, *Renewing the United Nations System* (Uppsala, Sweden: Dag Hammarskjöld Foundation, 1994), 143.

45. This figure represents approximately half of the biennial 1974–1975 budget. See UN General Assembly resolution 3551, 17 December 1975.

46. Childers and Urquhart, *Renewing the United Nations System*, 28–30, 143.

47. The related distinction between evolutionary and revolutionary change also is germane, as is the analytical distinction between punctuated equilibrium and evolution. See John Campbell, *Institutional Change and Globalization* (Princeton, NJ: Princeton University Press, 2004), 34.

48. Holsti, *Taming the Sovereigns*, 8.

49. Malcolm Gladwell, *The Tipping Point: How Little Things Can Make a Big Difference* (Boston: Little, Brown & Co., 2002).

50. See Michael Barnett and Thomas G. Weiss, eds., *Humanitarianism in Question: Politics, Power, Ethics* (Ithaca, NY: Cornell University Press, 2008 forthcoming).

51. Robert Jervis, *System Effects: Complexity in Political and Social Life* (Princeton, NJ: Princeton University Press, 1999).

52. Thomas G. Weiss, *Military–Civilian Interactions: Humanitarian Crises and the Responsibility to Protect*, 2nd edn. (Lanham, Md.: Rowman & Littlefield, 2004).

53. Kofi A. Annan, *Investing in the United Nations: For a Stronger Organization Worldwide*, UN document A/60/692, 7 March 2006, 1.

54. Inis L. Claude, Jr., 'Peace and Security: Prospective Roles for the Two United Nations,' *Global Governance* 2, no. 3 (1996): 289–298.

55. Conor Cruise O'Brien, *The United Nations: Sacred Drama* (London: Hutchinson, 1968), book jacket.

56. See Robert W. Cox and Harold K. Jacobson, eds., *The Anatomy of Influence: Decision Making in International Organization* (New Haven, Conn.: Yale University Press, 1973).

57. Francis. H. Hinsley, *Power and the Pursuit of Peace* (Cambridge: Cambridge University Press, 1963).

58. The UN Secretary-General's Address to the General Assembly, as delivered on 23 September 2003, available at: www.un.org.

59. High-level Panel on Threats, Challenges and Change, *A More Secure World: Our Shared Responsibility* (New York: UN, 2004).

60. Kofi A. Annan, 'In Larger Freedom: Decision Time at the UN,' *Foreign Affairs* 84, no. 3 (2005): 66. This is the title of his own summary document for the summit: *In Larger Freedom: Towards Development, Security and Human Rights for All*, UN document A/59/2005, 21 March 2005.

61. The independent United Nations Intellectual History Project began a remedial effort in 1999. For information, see www.unhistory.org.

62. United Nations High-level Panel on UN System-wide Coherence in the Areas of Development, Humanitarian Assistance, and the Environment, *Delivering as One* (New York: UN, 2006).

PART II

THEORETICAL FRAMEWORKS

CHAPTER 2

··

POLITICAL
APPROACHES

··

MICHAEL BARNETT
MARTHA FINNEMORE

DESPITE its sixty-year existence, efforts to theorize the United Nations have been scattered at best. Historically, scholars in the two major academic fields of study concerned with the UN, international relations and international law, have developed theories that largely sidelined the organization. Theories of international relations tend to be theories of states in which international organizations like the UN are mere stages on which others (mostly states) act. International legal scholarship has been dominated by a related stance—legal positivism, which has been highly influential in that field and has largely understood law to be solely the product of explicit contracts among states. The consequence in both fields was scholarly neglect. National capitals, not New York, were seen as the place policies are made. The UN might provide a convenient site for state representatives to bargain and negotiate, but the organization itself was not seen as causally consequential on more than minor matters. Without conceptual equipment that allowed them to conceive of the UN as an independent actor in its own right, scholars had little reason to study the organization.

This situation has changed. World events, notably the end of the Cold War, have led to a resurgence of activity in and around the UN. During the 1990s, the UN became not only a site for, but also a leader of, initiatives in global governance in many areas. The expansion of peacekeeping operations, both quantitatively and qualitatively, and the deployment of peace enforcement operations made the UN a consequential player in the security field. Some of these efforts brought the organization new acclaim, as in El Salvador, Namibia, and Cambodia, but even when they went horribly wrong, as in Bosnia and Rwanda, it was widely understood that, for better or worse, the world organization as an institution was shaping outcomes. The UN developed criteria for what kinds of states would be built after conflicts. It set standards for and successfully implemented free and fair elections in far-flung places under difficult conditions. With the Millennium Development Goals it set an ambitious new development agenda for not only itself but also the World Bank, the International Monetary Fund (IMF), bilateral aid organizations, and the host of nongovernmental organizations (NGOs) involved in development work. Even the Sisyphus-like efforts to reform the institution underscore not only the UN's short-comings but also the range of actors that believe the world organization makes a difference. If the UN matters to both state and nonstate actors, it should matter to scholars.

Indeed, scholars have been paying more attention, in part because of the UN's expanded activity but also because of changes in theoretical fashion and the devel-opment of new theoretical tools. After the Cold War, scholars began to think about the UN as more than a simple arena for state action. They also began to look for more varied effects that the world body might have than simply forcing reluctant states to conform to resolutions and the Charter. Certainly there are moments when the UN can frustrate the plans of strong states, but scholars are now exploring a much broader array of sometimes indirect ways in which the UN influences events. UN action can enhance prospects for international cooperation. It can legitimate policies and stabilize world order. It can create and diffuse international norms, policies, and models of political organization around the globe. With new and more varied theoretical tools, scholars are exploring ways in which the UN not only regulates the existing activities of states but also helps to constitute the very fabric of world politics and international order.

This chapter examines how prominent theories capture different kinds of effects of the UN on world politics. Different theories of international relations (IR) cast the UN in distinctive roles, which logically lead scholars to identify distinctive kinds of effects. We identify five roles that the UN might have: as an agent of great powers doing their bidding; as a mechanism for interstate cooperation; as a governor of international society of states; as a constructor of the social world; and as a legitim-ation forum. Each role has roots in a well-known theory of international politics.

In many, perhaps most, real-world political situations the UN plays more than one of these roles, but these stylized theoretical arguments about the world body's influence help discipline our thinking. They force us to be explicit about which effects of the world organization we think are important, what is causing those effects, and why. This is obviously crucial for scholars but it is also important for the United Nations itself. The organization and other analysts have generated innu-merable assessments of peacekeeping, for example, and while these identify successes and moments when peacekeepers made a difference, they rarely identify and untan-gle the often many causal mechanisms by which these outcomes were created. These theoretical arguments also force us to be conscious of inconsistency in our thinking or explain why contradictions exist. If, for example, one thinks the UN is primarily a tool of its most powerful members one needs some explanation for the (many) occasions when the United States and others are displeased with the organization. By making our assumptions and logical reasoning more clear, we can better detect flaws in our understanding and correct them.

Attention to the mechanisms by which the UN produces its effects has the added advantage of focusing our attention on the internal workings of the organization. These have been little theorized. After all, if our understandings of world politics tell us that the UN is little more than an instrument of states or an epiphenomenon of global structures, there is little reason to spend time thinking about what makes the UN tick. As scholars begin to recognize the importance of the UN as an autonomous actor, they must also begin to theorize that actor more fully and develop better understandings of its internal operations. Connecting internal workings with external effects is a promising avenue for both theorists and empirical researchers.

THE DIFFERENCE THE UN MAKES

Most scholars who study the UN do so because they think it makes a difference in the world. This is by no means a consensus view. Indeed, one of the most influential theories of international politics, realism, has long been skeptical about the UN's consequence. Rather than marching through myriad theories, we organize our discussion around five roles that the UN might play and the effects it is claimed to have in each. We pay particular attention to the mechanisms by which effects are thought to be produced. As will become apparent, scholars may agree that the UN creates some particular effect but offer different explanations about the way it does this. Since explanatory clarity is a primary goal of theory, we highlight these different mechanisms of influence in our discussion.

The UN as a Tool of Great Powers

In this view, the UN is a creature of the world's strongest states. They created the organization and designed it to serve their interests. Rhetoric about 'international community' and the equality of members is just window dressing. The formal structures of the world organization recognize that all members are not equal. Five are given vetoes in the Security Council, and a very small percentage of the members pay the lion's share of the bills. That these few should have disproportionate say in decision-making is hardly surprising. As a consequence, if someone wants to know what the UN will do, the place to look is not New York but Washington, London, Paris, Beijing, and Moscow. Foreign ministries in strong state capitals are where the consequential decisions about UN action are taken.

The well-known theory underlying this view of the UN's influence is realism.[1] In this view, the defining feature of the international system is anarchy, meaning no higher authority exists to protect states or create order among them. Anarchy thus creates a self-help system in which states must be concerned, first and foremost, with their own security and survival. International order, to the extent it exists, is order imposed by those with the power to do so. This does not mean that a realist world will be devoid of institutions or rules. It has them, but these rules and institutions are designed and run by the strong. International organizations, including the UN, exist because strong states create them and find their continued existence serves their interests.

Realists have staked out various positions on how to understand the UN. For some, the UN is largely irrelevant. Strong states determine world political outcomes, not the UN. Indeed, the tiresome phrase that inhabits many post-mortem discussions of the UN's failure, 'the lack of political will,' only serves to highlight how the most powerful states determine whether the world organization succeeds or fails. Others argue that it is irrelevant—unless states and peoples are foolish enough to believe in the UN's promises. The policy prescriptions of realism are prudence, preparedness, and self-help, and it is downright dangerous for people to be distracted by the high-sounding principles of the UN. Those looking for proof need go no further than the Bosnians at Srebrenica. Reliance on the UN encourages unrealistic, misguided, and destructive policies.[2]

Other realists allow the UN some relevance, but tend to see it as a tool of the strong that serves their interests. Scholars who argue that multilateralism in different forms can help secure US interests and create an international order consistent with those interests hold this view. International organizations, including the UN, can help legitimate a world of law and rules largely devised by strong states for their own benefit.[3] The International Monetary Fund is a useful tool for managing the global capitalist financial system, and dealing with poor, bankrupt countries so that the US does not have to do so. The World Bank is a handy place to off-load poverty issues. The UN's peacekeeping and peacebuilding operations relieve the United States and others of the need to deal with collapsing but strategically insignificant states and provide mechanisms to share the burden of managing these places more broadly.

From a realist perspective, the UN's influence in the world is dependent on what powerful states are willing to do. Without the support of strong states, the UN's ability to mediate disputes or mount a peacekeeping mission would be negligible. Without the financial contributions of strong states, the UN's ability to do any of the development assistance, human rights work, or technical assistance of specialized agencies would be hobbled. Further, strong states can stop the UN from doing anything they do not like by using the veto and/or withholding financial support. This dependence means that strong states call the shots at the UN. The organization's autonomy is severely circumscribed.

Realism usefully draws attention to the huge power disparities that underlie the UN's formal structure of sovereign equality and the crucial role played by the strongest members. Yet for all its insights, it does not tell us everything that we need or want to know. It provides little help in understanding why great powers often have trouble getting what they want out of the UN. The US's failure to get approval for a war against Iraq in March 2003 is only one of the most obvious and recent examples of a great power disappointed. It provides no help in understanding UN goals that might diverge from those of great powers. There is little indication that the great powers were keen to see the world organization take on the issue of humanitarian intervention after their bombing campaign against the Federal Republic of Yugoslavia in 1999, and many of the 'universal' values the UN strongly promotes, for example as embodied in the Millennium Development Goals (MDGs), are the agenda of the global South and not of the global North.

UN as Facilitator of Interstate Cooperation

In this view, the UN's influence and importance lies chiefly in its ability to facilitate cooperation among its state members. In a world where states compete and often have conflicting interests, the UN can help overcome distrust and foster jointly beneficial action by serving as an impartial broker, setting standards for behavior, creating transparency, and monitoring compliance with agreements. Thus, while states may have some conflicting interests, these theorists see a less zero-sum world than realists. Strong states may benefit disproportionately from UN action, but the emphasis here is on states' shared interests and the UN's ability to find cooperative solutions to problems that make everyone, big and small, better off.

The roots of this line of theorizing lie in microeconomics which has been embraced most influentially by a school of (mostly American) IR scholars calling themselves 'neoliberal institutionalists' or more recently and broadly, 'rationalist.'[4] Implicitly, and often explicitly, the international system is treated as a market in which states, like firms, vie for advantage but with the goal of welfare-improvement for themselves, not superiority to others. Thus, like realists, they take anarchy as their starting point; however, the problematic is not survival but rather endemic cheating. International organizations like the UN are created by states to deal with transaction costs, incomplete information, and other 'market failures.' By manipulating information, creating transparency, exposing non-compliance, and imposing sanctions, organizations like the UN can help enforce international agreements that states have designed to benefit themselves.[5] Importantly, international institutions in this view are endogenous but not epiphenomenal.[6] They are endogenous to state interaction because states create them in order to pursue mutual interests, but they are not epiphenomenal because, without some independent role, international institutions could not help states achieve their goals. This view suggests that international institutions must have some independence to be effective and that states will incorporate this independence into the design of these organizations and respect their autonomy to at least some degree.

Unlike most realists, scholars working with this theoretical apparatus have paid a great deal of attention not just to the UN but to a variety of international organizations, particularly ones dealing with economic and environmental matters. They have done extensive work to uncover the conditions under which states will agree to set up governance structures (like those in the UN, IMF, or World Bank) and offer detailed investigation of the kinds of mechanisms states have devised to overcome barriers to improving Pareto optimality. In order to increase credible information, states have given international organizations (IOs) the task of collecting data and publicizing information about both shared problems and state policies. For example, the IMF routinely collects and publicizes information on both the world economy and national economic policies of members. In order to increase trust that states will comply with their agreements, states have given IOs monitoring capacity and the ability to publicize defections. The International Atomic Energy Agency (IAEA) monitors and collects data on states' nuclear programs for exactly these reasons. Similarly, the UN's most famous tool for international peace and security, peacekeeping, is an expression of this logic. Peacekeepers were originally created to monitor a cease-fire between two combatant states in order to encourage compliance with the agreement. They encouraged compliance not through enforcement mechanisms but rather through information-gathering capacities. Their tasks include monitoring troop movements, investigating charges of violations, and publicizing violations in order to encourage states to comply with their existing agreements.

A related approach that is being applied to international organizations in recent years is principal–agent analysis, a form of rational choice analysis applied to the dynamics of institutions. Also derived from microeconomics and 'rationalist' in character, these theories understand international organizations like the UN to be 'agents' and their member states to be 'principals.' Principals, in this case states, delegate tasks to agents, like the UN, because they believe the agent has particular knowledge or capabilities that will help the principal achieve its goals. Problems inevitably arise when states delegate tasks to IOs. IOs as agents may have different preferences than their state masters and so have reasons to shirk their assigned tasks. Most IOs also serve multiple principals (in the UN's case, 192 member states) and disagreement among principals may hamper efforts to control the agent. Much of this scholarship is focused on identifying these various problems and constructing mechanisms that will ensure that agents (IOs) are faithful servants of their principals (states).[7]

Rationalist theory of this kind usefully draws our attention to both the importance of interstate bargaining inside the UN and to the organization's role as a facilitator trying to broker agreements among members. Particularly helpful is its attention to the specific mechanisms for bringing states to agreement—the way the UN (and other IOs) can use information or monitoring to create cooperation and trust. These scholars also give an important role to international law as a crucial medium of interstate cooperation and have been much engaged in bridge-building with that field.[8] Principal–agent analysis enhances our understanding of institutional design by focusing attention on mechanisms of state control that do (or perhaps should) exist in IOs. It also has the virtue of focusing attention specifically on problems in organizational performance—episodes when the UN did not do what states wanted.

These theories are less helpful on other points, however. While they are structured around state interests, they have little to say about where these interests come from and, crucially, how they change. Unlike some of the other theories that we examine, there is little room for persuasion of any kind in these theories or any notion that state interests might be changed by the UN or other actors. Indeed, in both realist and rationalist accounts, state interests are exogenous to these theoretical models in that they are defined a priori. These arguments are also strongly state-centric. They say little about the role of nonstate actors (NGOs, activists, transnational movements etc.) in politics.[9]

UN as Governor of Society of States

Another body of theory that emphasizes the UN's facilitating role comes out of the 'English School,' so-called because of its roots in the British Committee on the Theory of International Politics.[10] In this view, the world organization promotes cooperation but through very different means than the rationalist scholars identify. Rather than conceiving of the world as a market in which utility-maximizing states compete, English School scholars see it as an 'international society' held together by 'shared norms and values which the UN both reflects and projects.'[11] The UN operates in this 'society of states' as a guardian of the principles embodied in its Charter and agreed to by all its member states. Its role is not to be a tool of great powers but to help govern an international order. That order may have been created by great powers, but it rests on a set of norms and principles, and it is those that the UN embodies and uses to guide its work. It thus helps develop the rules, standards, laws, and institutions that make orderly social life possible at the international level. By acting to uphold agreed-upon norms and values, the UN helps states not simply to cooperate but to realize a stronger, better international community of the type they proclaimed they wanted in 1945.

The UN's role is not only to regulate the society of states but also to help spread the basic values of this society. In earlier eras, colonialism and imperialism did much of this work.[12] However, in the twentieth century, international organizations took over much of this role. One prominent example is the UN's work in spreading norms of sovereignty and self-determination. By overseeing much of the decolonization process, it helped to ensure that this process respected the principle of sovereignty and territorial integrity.[13] Since then the UN has been highly involved in diffusing other norms that are assumed to help regulate and stabilize the society of states, including the use of force and basic human rights.[14]

The UN's tools to facilitate cooperation in this view are quite different from those emphasized by microeconomic, neoliberal institutionalists and principal–agent analyses. For neoliberals, narrow self-interest is the driver of state behavior. In the society of states view, by contrast, principles and values are powerful tools for the UN. Appeals to principles, elaboration of standards of acceptable behavior, and moral censure are powerful tools to which states can and do respond, albeit imperfectly and inconsistently. States value membership in the international community and view the UN as a legitimate spokesman for community interests against opportunistic self-seekers. This gives the world organization important standing to promote its goals. States recognize it as a legitimate arbiter of disagreements. They recognize it as a standard-setter for good human rights behavior. They recognize it as an impartial monitor of elections. Thus, similar to the neoliberals, the UN in this view is a powerful creator of norms and regulator of state behavior, but it does its work primarily with legitimacy, principle, and impartiality, not transparency, monitoring, and information. For all its imperfections, action by the world organization is still widely perceived by states as being more legitimate and more likely to be impartial than that of individual member states, driven by Charter principles rather than narrow self-seeking.

Society of states arguments usefully highlight the importance of norms, principles, and moral suasion as tools for the UN. Far from being empty talk, appeals of this kind can have powerful effects in diplomacy. These principles provide common ground on which members agree and around which community action can be structured. Like the neoliberals, English School scholars see an important role for international law and institutions that flows from their normative character and moral force—very different mechanisms than those emphasized by neoliberals.[15] The English School's extensive historical work also invites us to think about the UN's role in the diffusion of international norms and law around the globe, a theme central to another school of thought.[16] Society of states scholars are less helpful on other issues, however. While they accept, indeed expect, normative persuasion to happen, they tell us little about how, why, and under what conditions states will be swayed by UN appeals. As with realists and neoliberals, these arguments are strongly state-centric. They say little about the role of nonstate actors in the politics of various issues. They also provide little guidance to understanding politics within the UN itself—its agenda, its actions, and, most of all, its dysfunctions.

UN as a Constructor of the Social World

Like the English School, this body of theory sees the UN's role in diffusing international norms as central to its influence in the world. These scholars differ, though, in that they see the UN as powerfully shaped by an emerging world culture that transcends national boundaries and permeates action from the transnational level down through the micro level of individuals. The laws and norms governing international society are not artifacts of autonomous states, as they are in theories discussed previously. Rather, they are the product of (and a producer of) a global culture that permeates states, nonstate actors, and individuals, all of whom play a role in creating the norms and laws that shape global life.[17]

One distinctive feature of this perspective is its emphasis on the way in which the UN does more than regulate or govern the actions of others. These scholars emphasize the organization's generative powers: its ability to constitute or construct new actors in world politics, create new interests for actors, and define shared international tasks. Peacekeepers, election monitors, and human rights observers are all types of international actors who are created or authorized by the UN. Redefinitions of state interests, like the redefinition of state security to include 'human security,' have been accomplished and entrenched through IOs, including the United Nations.[18] Shared tasks like 'development' and 'good governance' have been defined, institutionalized, and disseminated to states and other actors through the UN, World Bank, and other international organizations.[19] Without autonomous action by the UN and other IOs—all busily constructing these new actors, interests, and tasks—the world would be a very different, and worse, place.[20]

This line of theorizing draws from insights in sociology, anthropology, and the branch of international relations theory called 'constructivism,' so-called because it is attentive to the way the social world is constructed. 'Constructivism is about human consciousness and its role in international life.'[21] It understands the world as defined by both material and ideational forces, but emphasizes the social character of ideas. Ideas are not simply mental beliefs or psychological states that reside inside our heads. Our mental maps are shaped by knowledge, symbols, language, and rules that we hold collectively with others. One person's belief that a piece of paper is a $100 bill does not make it so. Only the shared belief among many (indeed virtually all) people that the piece of paper symbolizes or 'is' $100 of value makes that belief a reality in the world. Similarly, sovereign states exist because of the widespread recognition of territorially bounded jurisdiction and borders. In this way, constructivism also accepts some form of holism or structuralism. The world is irreducibly social and cannot be decomposed to the properties of atomized, pre-existing actors.

Shared ideas, then, shape reality and world politics. The emphasis on ideas does not mean a rejection of material reality. Rather, constructivism recognizes that the meaning and construction of material reality is dependent on ideas and interpretation. Nor does the emphasis on holism and ideational structure deny agency. Instead, this approach recognizes that agents have some autonomy and their practices and interactions help to construct, reproduce, and transform those structures. The emphasis on both agency and structure, therefore, directs our attention to how ideas become institutionalized, and how, once institutionalized, they shape the way we see the world.

Unlike the other theories that we have examined, constructivism does not see the world in state-centric terms. Powerful ideas about sovereignty, human rights, and markets might constitute actors—including states, activist NGOs, and global corporations. Thus, rather than simply assuming that states are the only actors that matter in the UN and imputing interests to them, constructivists problematize these building blocks of other theories. They investigate a range of nonstate actors, including NGOs and transnational social movements. They explore changes in interests in states and other actors. In this respect, they are interested in how international organizations such as the UN might help to socialize actors.[22] They also emphasize the role of ideas in changing the world. The UN has not had great material power with which it can coerce or induce states, but to the extent that the

UN has been a locus for the creation and dissemination of new ideas and values it can have significant effects in the world by changing the purposes to which material power is put by others.

More than approaches discussed previously, this one sees a world in which the UN is more than just a servant of states or reflection of their interests. As a source of ideas and a creator of new rules and norms, the UN has significant autonomy and can create effects in the world independent of states. Its effects may be indirect and incremental. Achieving decolonization and self-determination for most of the world's people took many decades.[23] As with any actor, the effects created are not always the effects intended. The creators of peacekeeping, for example, certainly did not envision the wholesale state-creation activities that have evolved from those early cease-fire monitoring tasks in the 1950s.

This approach usefully draws our attention to the ways in which the UN can be a creative agent of change in the world. The mechanisms of change here are ideas, norms, and values, and the myriad actors, including the world organization, who use them to create new actors, interests, and tasks. Creative, strategic, and sometimes accidental uses of framing, shaming, and debating by international organizations have been shown to transform beliefs and perceptions of interest, create new actors, and propagate new norms of behavior. Transnational networks of human rights activists have worked both with and through the UN to establish human rights as a core concern of, not only states, but all actors in the world. Development experts, anti-poverty activists, and developing country governments have similarly used the UN as a focal point for creating new expectations about national antipoverty policies, most recently in the MDGs. These perspectives tell us less, however, about which ideas or values will resonate in the UN and with the states or NGOs to whom the UN might proselytize. Persuasion and socialization often fail but we know little about the conditions under which failure (or, conversely, success) is likely. Force is also a powerful tool of social construction, but has been little explored from this perspective.

UN as a Structure of Legitimation

In this view, one of the primary functions of the UN is to legitimate *specific* decisions, values, and principles governing international order, some of which might be a reflection of the views of the strong, and some of which might be a reflection of more universal sentiments. The central insight here is that all international political orders cannot survive if they are enforced and reproduced through coercion alone. Instead, they require some kind of mechanism of legitimation, a role usually per-formed by a forum, body, or institution. The world organization, in this view, serves to legitimate an existing international order. International order can be underpinned by any number of norms or principles. Which ones define a particular order, and consequently what is legitimate, can be debated, contested, and revised by the actors involved. The UN, because it is viewed as a universal organization, becomes the locus for such debates.[24] Three different theoretical traditions have offered views on this matter, views that differ in part because of divergent understandings about what underpins international order.

One strand of realism, as already discussed, has long recognized that international orders are not produced and reproduced by material power alone. Power relations between states inherently involve conflict and competition, but these tensions can be minimized or stabilized if states believe that the overall international order has some degree of legitimacy and accept it as necessary, if not always entirely desirable.[25] While the legitimation of an international order will not level the playing field between inherently unequal states, it might generate something approximating consent. The UN can play a central role in this legitimation process. Inis Claude was one of the earliest and most influential scholars to argue that a principal political function of the UN was the collective legitimation of the international order. The UN, in large measure because of its inclusiveness and open processes of deliberations that allow all states to participate as legal equals, provides this essential function in world politics.[26]

Another perspective on the legitimation function of the UN is offered by various constructivist-inspired statements. Constructivists treat the international structure as both material and normative and thus recognize that states are central actors but also incorporate the role of laws, norms, and rules in constituting and constraining these states and in defining what is appropriate (that is, legitimate) behavior. Constructivists identify legitimacy as an essential component of political order since it provides states with reasons to comply with existing rules and standards of behavior. In contrast to realist and neoliberal theory, which focus on power and information, constructivists argue that compliance with rules is motivated not only by self-interest but also by a sense of moral correctness and social appropriateness— complying is the right thing to do.

These rules, norms, and principles that define what counts as a legitimate international order are not fixed in stone but rather are subject to debate. This debate can occur in various locales, but because of the UN's lofty symbolic standing in world politics—many venerate its status as almost a religious entity—it most centrally serves this function. Consequently, we can expect that many of the most important debates regarding what should be the rules and standards of behavior that guide the conduct of states will take place at the UN and will be most intense when there is a shift, shock, or challenge in world politics that potentially destabilizes the existing standards.[27] In a series of important articles on the debate over Kosovo and how to interpret legal norms at the Security Council, Ian Johnstone traces the role of legal discourse and politics in decision about the use of force.[28]

A third perspective on the relationship between the UN and international legitimacy is offered by those influenced by the political thought of Antonio Gramsci, a twentieth-century Italian Marxist philosopher. In their view, global life is structured primarily by global capitalism, not global anarchy. The structure of capitalist production shapes both the capacities and resources of actors, and the ideology that informs their interests and desires. This ideology constituted by capitalism is hegemonic; it serves the objective interests of capitalists and overshadows the real (but unrecognized) interests of the world's producing classes.[29] International organizations, such as the UN itself and other organizations in the UN system, can play a critical role in generating 'consent' for a world capitalist order that is stacked against the poor and the have-nots.[30] However, Gramscian thought also draws attention to sites of resistance to this ideological hegemony. While some of these sites exist outside (sometimes quite literally) established forums, for instance, the public protests that occur periodically outside World Bank, IMF, and Group of 8 meetings, at other times resistance is waged within the halls of international organizations. Perhaps the most famous example is the demand by developing states for the establishment of a New International Economic Order launched in the 1970s and institutionalized in various corners of the UN structure, notably the UN Conference on Trade and Development.[31]

OPENING UP THE UN

International relations scholars have primarily been interested in the effects of actors in the world. In the UN's case, this has been particularly true, and lack of perceived effects has led to its neglect. After all, why worry about what goes on *inside* the UN when it is not clear that the organization has significant impact on world events? As research piles up, amply demonstrating the UN's diverse effects, however, it is time for scholars to think more seriously about the internal politics producing these external results. Mechanisms at work producing the effects we have identified suggest a number of research questions about the internal features of the organization that scholars could fruitfully explore.

One thing that we do not understand well is the relationship between state power in the world at large and its exercise as influence inside the UN. Externally-oriented theories often assume or imply that state power translates directly into influence in the world body. Certainly state strength matters enormously and the strong have some very visible tools of influence. The United States can withhold dues and has done so. The permanent five members of the Security Council can exercise their vetoes and have done so. But it is not hard to think of confounding episodes that suggest a more complex relationship. Chronic resistance to US agendas for management reform of the UN is one prominent example. Conversely, smaller countries, such as Canada and the Nordics, often exercise influence in the UN disproportionate to their power in the world.[32]

What might account for this variation? Several possibilities are worth exploring. Reputation might be relevant. National reputations, particularly reputations for respecting UN principles and norms in one's own foreign policy, might increase trust of or respect for that country and its nationals inside the organization, making others more willing to follow their proposals. Nordic states and Canada, along with some other middle powers, often go out of their way to ensure that their own foreign policies accord with UN principles and emphasize connections between their foreign policy actions and the world organization's goals and directives. Thus, states that create a match between their external actions and the UN's agenda are more likely to be credible as leaders inside the institution.

An alternative conjecture might emphasize the structure of voting blocs and alliance patterns inside the organization.[33] Countries whose policy preferences fall in between or outside of large competing blocs may find themselves empowered, much as smaller third parties can find themselves as 'kingmakers' in forming coalition governments domestically. One can envision application of a wide variety of techniques developed to analyze other voting bodies (notably national legislatures) that might provide insights here. A third possibility might be that some foreign ministries simply invest more personnel and time in learning the ropes at the United Nations. Their nationals may have longer tenures in the UN and accumulate institutional knowledge that makes them both effective at accomplishing goals within the world organization and respected by others for their experience and abilities. How countries deploy personnel to the UN and how long they stay might shed some light on some of these discrepancies between external power and internal influence.

A second important research agenda concerns the UN's autonomy. A variety of theories are skeptical that it has any. They understand the UN to be a puppet or servant of some other more central power—strong states, global capitalism, and world culture. Empirical exploration of the conditions under which the UN acts autonomously from these various drivers and the mechanisms by which that autonomy is established would be important contributions. Moreover, understanding what the UN does with its autonomy and why might open doors to better understandings of the internal workings of the organization. Principal–agent analysis is organized around a clear assumption that organizational 'agents' like the UN can be autonomous from their state principals and will use this autonomy to pursue their own agendas. However, these theories say little about what those agendas might be. Constructivists have argued that the bureaucratic culture inside the UN, professional norms, and moral principles all provide direction to the UN's use of autonomy, but the surface of this research agenda has only been scratched.[34]

Better understanding of what UN staff—as opposed to member-state delegations—do would also improve our ability to link internal workings to external behavior. States might negotiate painstakingly over resolutions, the design of programs, or the structure of a new UN agency, but whether and how states' agreements have influence on the ground depends on how individual members of the international civil service interpret and implement member state agreements. The UN as an organization often serves its members very imperfectly, producing inefficient, ineffective, or even counterproductive outcomes that are supposedly not what member states want.

Rich theoretical literatures exist to explain organizational behavior in a variety of disciplines but few have been applied to the UN. Principal–agent problems, bureaucratic culture, institutional rivalry, and very specialized types of expertise and professional norms strongly shape particular UN activities in powerful ways that we are only beginning to understand. For example, principal–agent problems arise in an organization when the interests of staff (the agents in this case) do not coincide with those of the principal (in this case, the organization that employs them.) Staff incentives often do not accord with organizational goals. International civil servants may also have some unique behavioral incentives. In writing about the World Bank, Moises Naim has argued that staff are less likely to 'rock the boat' and seriously challenge superiors because losing their job at the Bank often means leaving the United States. Staff visas, and hence those of family members, depend on their employment at the organization. Unwillingness to speak freely or challenge superiors obviously diminishes the organization's ability to recognize and correct errors or to learn from varied professional opinions—both essential to mission success. An exploration of whether such arguments hold true for the UN would be well worth exploring.[35]

A fourth set of questions might involve the extent of the UN's being embedded in larger social networks of diplomats and specialized professionals. Many UN staff and field personnel have varied careers and move back and forth between UN appointments, jobs within their own governments at home, and positions in the private sector, universities, and NGOs. Analyses of other organizations conducted by sociologists, anthropologists, and scholars of organizational behavior suggest that these histories and relationships will profoundly influence the flow of information and even people inside the world organization. But we have few systematic studies of these connections. Good network analysis and good ethnographic work on the UN would contribute greatly to our understanding of its behavior.

These examples are offered only to suggest the wide range of important research questions that one could pursue by applying existing theoretical tools to the UN's internal workings. Robust and well-elaborated frameworks for studying organizations generally have been developed in disciplines ranging from sociology to economics, business, anthropology, and public policy. Few have been applied to the world organization, which presents rich potential opportunities for those of us interested in understanding it. Reasoning backward from the substantial and growing body of research on the UN's external effects in the world, we can hypothesize intelligently about the kinds of internal workings that might be causing them. Presumably, too, as we better theorize and research the UN's internal operations, we will be able to offer better understandings of its overall influence and importance.

Notes

1. Like many theories of world politics, realism comes in many flavors. For an analysis of these variations see Stephen G. Brooks, 'Dueling Realisms,' *International Organization* 51, no. 3 (1997): 445–447; Gideon Rose, 'Neoclassical Realism and Theories of Foreign Policy,' *World Politics* 51, no. 1 (1998): 144–172; Michael Doyle, *Ways of War and Peace* (New York: Norton, 1999), part one; and Benjamin Frankel, ed., *Roots of Realism* (Portland, Ore.: Frank Cass, 1996).

2. John Mearsheimer, 'The False Promise of International Institutions,' *International Security* 19, no. 3 (1994–1995): 5–49. For a particularly painful example, see David Rieff, 'We Hate You,' *New Yorker*, 4 September 1995, 41–48.

3. See, e.g., G. John Ikenberry, *After Victory: Institutions, Strategic Restraint, and the Rebuilding of Order after Major Wars* (Princeton, NJ: Princeton University Press, 2001).

4. Neoliberal institutionalism was the early term for this line of theory when its principal opponent was Kenneth Waltz's neorealism in the 1980s. With the rise of constructivist arguments in IR, the shared microeconomic roots of both theories eclipsed their differences and the two were bundled together under the umbrella term 'rationalist' and collectively distinguished from constructivist arguments. For discussions of the relationship between these two schools, Peter Katzenstein, Robert O. Keohane, and Stephen D. Krasner, eds., 'International Organization and the Study of World Politics,' *International Organization* 52, no. 4 (1998): 645–685; and James Fearon and Alexander Wendt, 'Rationalism v. Constructivism: A Skeptical View,' in *Handbook of International Relations*, eds. Walter Carlsnaes, Thomas Risse, and Beth Simmons (London: Sage Publications, 2002), 52–72.

5. Seminal works in this vein include Robert O. Keohane, *After Hegemony: Cooperation and Discord in the World Political Economy* (Princeton, NJ: Princeton University Press, 1984) and many of the essays in Stephen D. Krasner, ed., *International Regimes* (Ithaca, NY: Cornell University Press, 1983). For overviews of some subsequent work see Lisa Martin and Beth Simons, 'Theories and Empirical Studies of International Organizations,' and Helen V. Milner, 'Rationalizing Politics: The Emerging Synthesis Among International, American, and Comparative Politics' in *International Organization* 52, no. 4 (1998): 729–758 and 759–786; and Kenneth W. Abbott and Duncan Snidal, 'Why States Act Through Formal International Organizations,' *Journal of Conflict Resolution* 42, no. 1 (1998): 3–32.

6. Robert Keohane and Lisa Martin, 'Institutional Theory as a Research Program,' in *Progress in International Relations Theory: Appraising the Field*, ed. Colin Elman and Miriam Elman (Cambridge, Mass.: MIT Press, 2003), 71–107.

7. For principal–agent approaches, see Daniel Nielson and Michael Tierney, 'Principals and Interests: Agency Theory and World Bank Environmental Reform,' *International Organization* 57 (Spring 2003): 241–276; Darren Hawkins, David Lake, Dan Nielson, and Mike Tierney, *Delegation and Agency in International Organizations* (New York: Cambridge University Press, 2006).

8. See, e.g., the special issue of *International Organization* 54, no. 3 (2000) devoted to 'Legalization and World Politics.'

9. Some scholars working in this vein have, however, been attentive to domestic politics and interest group influence within states. See, for example, Helen Milner, *Interests, Institutions, and Information: Domestic Politics and International Relations* (Princeton, NJ: Princeton University Press, 1997); and Jeffrey Frieden, 'Real Sources of European Currency Policy: Sectoral Interests and European Monetary Integration,' *International Organization* 56, no. 4 (2002): 831–860.

10. Seminal works here include Hedley Bull, *The Anarchical Society* (New York: Columbia University Press, 1977); and Hedley Bull and Adam Watson, eds., *The Expansion of International Society* (Oxford: Clarendon Press, 1984).

11. Adam Roberts and Benedict Kingsbury, 'Introduction: The UN's Roles in International Society since 1945,' in *United Nations, Divided World: The UN's Role in International Relations*, 2nd edn., eds. Adam Roberts and Benedict Kingsbury (Oxford: Clarendon Press, 1993), 1–62; Robert Jackson, *The Global Covenant: Human Conduct in a World of States* (New York: Oxford University Press, 2000).

12. Bull and Watson, eds., *The Expansion of International Society.*

13. See Robert Jackson, *Quasi-States: Sovereignty, International Relations, and the Third World* (New York: Cambridge University Press, 1992), ch. 4.

14. See the contributions in Roberts and Kingsbury, eds., *United Nations, Divided World.* See also Louis Emmerij, Richard Jolly, and Thomas G. Weiss, *Ahead of the Curve? UN Ideas and Global Challenges* (Bloomington: Indiana University Press, 2001).

15. See Christian Reus-Smit, *Moral Purpose of the State* (Princeton, NJ: Princeton University Press, 1999) for a view of law's role from a perspective inspired by English School thinking that differs markedly from the role outlined by neoliberals in 'Legalization and World Politics,' special issue of *International Organization.*

16. In addition to Reus-Smit's *Moral Purpose of the State*, see Bull and Watson, eds., *The Expansion of International Society*, and Gerrit Gong, *The Standard of 'Civilization' in International Society* (New York: Oxford University Press, 1984).

17. Work influenced by the world polity model that deals specifically with international organizations includes: John Boli and George Thomas, eds., *Constructing World Culture: International Nongovernmental Organizations since 1875* (Palo Alto, Calif.: Stanford University Press, 1999); Connie McNeely, *Constructing the Nation-State: International Organization and Prescriptive Action* (Westport, Conn.: Greenwood Press, 1995); James Hawdon, *Emerging Organizational Forms: The Proliferation of Intergovernmental Regional Organizations in the Modern World-System* (Westport, Conn.: Greenwood Press, 1996); and Robert Kahn and Mayer Zald, eds., *Organizations and Nation-States: New Perspectives on Conflict and Cooperation* (San Francisco, Calif.: Jossey-Bass, 1990). For a review of this work see, Martha Finnemore, 'Norms, Culture, and World Politics: Insights from Sociology's Institutionalism,' *International Organization* 50, no. 2 (1996): 325–347.

18. Roland Paris, 'Human Security: Paradigm Shift or Hot Air?', *International Security* 26, no. 2 (2001): 87–102.

19. Arturo Escobar, *Encountering Development: The Making and Unmaking of the Third World* (Princeton, NJ: Princeton University Press, 1995); and Martha Finnemore, *National Interests in International Society* (Ithaca, NY: Cornell University Press 1996), ch. 3.

20. Not all of these scholars ascribe autonomy to international organizations. One strand of this work is strongly structural and sees the UN and other actors as non-autonomous accretions of an expanding world culture and the discourses associated with it. See, for example, Escobar, *Encountering Development*, and George M. Thomas, et al., *Institutional Structure: Constituting State, Society, and the Individual* (Newbury Park, Calif.: Sage, 1987). We focus here on theories that ascribe some agency to the UN.

21. John G. Ruggie, *Constructing the World Polity* (New York: Routledge, 1998), 856.

22. For the case of the EU, see Jeffrey T. Checkel, 'International Institutions and Socialization in Europe: Introduction and Framework,' *International Organization* 59, no. 4 (2005), 801–826.

23. See, e.g., Neta Crawford, *Argument and Change in World Politics: Ethics, Decolonization and Humanitarian Intervention* (New York: Cambridge University Press, 2002); and Michael Barnett, 'The New United Nations Politics of Peace: From Juridical Sovereignty to Empirical Sovereignty,' *Global Governance* 1, no. 1 (1995): 79–97.

24. Oran Young, 'The United Nations and the International System,' *International Organization* 22 (Autumn 1968): 902–922; Fritz Kratochwil and John Ruggie, 'International Organization: A State of the Art on an Art of the State,' *International Organization* 40, no. 4 (1995): 753–775.

25. See, e.g., Henry Kissinger, *A World Restored: Metternich, Castlereagh, and the Problems of Peace, 1812–1822* (Boston: Houghton Mifflin, 1957).

26. Inis L. Claude, 'Collective Legitimization as a Political Function of the United Nations,' *International Organization* 20, no. 3 (1966): 367–379.

27. Michael Barnett, 'Bringing in the New World Order: Legitimacy, Liberalism, and the United Nations,' *World Politics* 49, no. 4 (1997): 526–551. For an application see Ian Hurd, 'The Strategic Use of Liberal Internationalism: Libya and the UN Sanctions, 1992–2003,' *International Organization* 59, no. 3 (2005): 495.

28. Ian Johnstone, 'Security Council Deliberations: The Power of the Better Argument,' *European Journal of International Law* 14, no. 3 (2003): 437–480.

29. Robert Cox, 'Multilateralism and World Order,' *Review of International Studies* 18, no. 2 (1992): 161–180; and Mark Rupert, *Ideologies of Globalization: Contending Visions of a New World Order* (New York: Routledge, 2000).

30. Craig Murphy, *International Organization and Industrial Change: Global Governance since 1850* (Cambridge: Polity, 1994.)

31. See John Toye and Richard Toye, *The UN and Global Political Economy: Trade, Finance, and Development* (Bloomington: Indiana University Press, 2004); Mark Rupert, 'Class Power and the Politics of Global Governance,' in *Power and Global Governance*, ed. Michael Barnett and Raymond Duvall (New York: Cambridge University Press, 2004), 205–228; and B. S. Chimni, 'International Institutions Today: An Imperial Global State in the Making,' *European Journal of International Law*, 15, no. 1 (2004): 1–37.

32. For an early and still important contribution, see Robert Cox and Harold Jacobson, *The Anatomy of Influence* (New Haven, Conn.: Yale University Press, 1971); and also Hadewych Hazelzet, 'The Decision-Making Approach to International Organizations: Cox and Jacobson's Anatomic Lesson Revisited,' in *Autonomous Policy Making by International Organizations*, ed. Bob Reinalda and Bertjan Verbeek (London: Routledge, 1998), 27–41.

33. Work in this vein has already begun. See, e.g., Erik Voeten, 'Clashes in the Assembly,' *International Organization* 54, no. 2 (2000): 185–215.

34. Michael Barnett and Martha Finnemore, *Rules for the World: International Institutions in Global Politics* (Ithaca, NY: Cornell University Press, 2005).

35. Moises Naim, 'The World Bank: Its Role, Governance, and Organizational Culture,' in *Bretton Woods: Looking to the Future*, ed. Bretton Woods Commission (Washington, DC: Bretton Woods Commission, 1994), 273–287.

CHAPTER 3

LEGAL PERSPECTIVES

JOSÉ E. ALVAREZ

THE UN Charter was not intended to be an instrument for governing the world. The war-weary negotiators who hammered out its text were intent only on improving the mechanisms for collective security contained in the League of Nations Covenant. They were seeking to protect sovereignty, not to undermine it by interfering with states' ability to govern themselves, especially with respect to matters essentially within their 'domestic jurisdiction' under Charter Article 2 (7). The principal purposes of the UN were, after all, to better protect existing sovereigns from aggression and to usher into full fledged sovereignty those that expressed their preference for self-determination, as spelled out in Article 2 (1) and in Chapter XI.

Although the drafters of the Charter included one clear substantive legal obligation (Article 2 (4)'s ban on the use of force except in cases of self-defense as recognized under Article 51) and a few institutional legal obligations (most significantly, to respect the Security Council's decisions as binding under Articles 25 and 48), they firmly rejected proposals to emulate the tripartite structure of governments by making the General Assembly a global parliament, the International Court of Justice (ICJ) an organ of judicial review, or UN officials anything other than passive instruments of the collective will of the states that made up the organization.

Unlike, for example, the US Constitution, the UN Charter does not seek to establish a 'union' and does not establish three branches delegated with plenary powers. Articles 10–13 of the Charter authorize the General Assembly only to 'discuss' questions and matters within the scope of the Charter and to make non-binding 'recommendations.' A proposal to authorize the ICJ to judicially review the legality of the organization's acts was rejected and the Court's jurisdiction to issue legally binding judgments was specifically limited to instances in which states had consented to its jurisdiction (Article 36).

Neither the UN Secretariat nor the Security Council was constituted as a global enforcer of general law, as is routine for national executives and administrative agencies. The Secretary-General's powers were limited to sparse reporting functions in Article 99. Even the relatively powerful Security Council was authorized, under Article 36, only to 'recommend' that states refer their disputes to peaceful modes of settlement and, while that body was authorized to take action under Chapter VII, these measures were to be taken only after a determination of a threat to the international peace—a trigger that was presumably limited to rare occasions of interstate aggression. Any military force authorized by the Council, in any case, would be drawn from those previously volunteered by states through the consensual military agreements of Article 43.

There is nothing in the text of the Charter—or indeed in the constitutive instruments of other global international organizations (IOs) formed at that time—that challenges the fundamental tenets of legal positivism to which most international lawyers subscribed in 1945. As is suggested by Article 38 of the ICJ's Statute, which limited the sources of legal obligation that the Court could consider to treaties, custom, and general principles, these positivist tenets included the following propositions: that all international obligations result from the explicit consent of states freely given; that the most significant source of international obligations is interstate compacts strictly interpreted in accordance with their terms; that the charters establishing organizations like the UN are just another type of treaty compact subject to the same traditional rules of treaty interpretation; and that, since the powers to make international law are limited to international legal persons, namely states, and states have not generally delegated sovereign lawmaking powers to the UN (or to other global intergovernmental organizations), multilateral mechanisms for the making of global law do not exist. For the foregoing reasons, it was also assumed that the establishment of the UN did not change or add to the traditional threefold forms of international legal obligation. Indeed, the Charter did not indicate that, the UN was to be considered an 'international legal person' entitled to make international law.[1]

Yet, notwithstanding all of this, the components of the UN system have become significant lawmakers. Indeed, what is interesting about the ostensible limits on the UN's legal powers enumerated above is how few of them remain operative. The UN, and IOs generally, have transformed the three traditional sources of international law and generated a multitude of forms of 'soft law' that are difficult to fit within those traditional sources. IO-generated law is today challenging the tenets of legal positivism. Despite the text of the Charter, the UN's principal organs have had an impact on international law, and the interaction between the UN's political organs and a number of international courts has resulted in teleological interpretations of the Charter at odds with its plain text or its original intent. Increasingly, the Charter is regarded as a kind of 'constitution' for the world or at least the basis for a system of hierarchically superior legal norms and values. Its long shadow over all aspects of international law is very much at odds with the proposition that it is just another treaty.

This chapter will first survey how the role of the UN as a lawmaker has changed the sources of international law, their content, and the lawmaking actors. Subsequent sections will show, more generally, how the post-World War II turn to IOs has helped inspire theoretical frameworks for understanding international law that transcend or supplement legal positivism. New forms of positivism, a policy-oriented jurisprudence associated with the Yale School, international legal process, critical and 'Third World' perspectives, feminist critiques, law and economics, and approaches inspired by international relations now provide organizationally grounded ways for understanding how international law emerges and is enforced. The turn to organizations like the UN has resulted in interdisciplinary work at the international level that resembles that engaged in by those who study the impact of national lawmaking institutions. Lawyers are now joining forces with those from other disciplines to examine, for example, the impact of organizational bureaucracies and epistemic communities on law, the relevance of game theory or principal–agent approaches to understanding treaty negotiations convened under UN auspices, and constructivist explanations for why states comply with organizationally generated rules. In a post-Cold War age characterized by the dominance of a single state, lawyers are also revisiting, inevitably, realism—to consider how powerful states deploy their power by 'laundering' it through IOs—as well as Gramscian and Marxist approaches—to better understand how ideology is disseminated and collaborators encouraged through organizations.[2]

The considerable success of IOs as generators of legal rules has lent a considerably darker edge to many international lawyers' perspectives on international organizations. While those international lawyers 'present at the creation' generally shared a messianic, quasi-religious faith in institutionalized multilateralism, today's international lawyers are more skeptical of its value and the law that IOs produce.[3]

THE UNITED NATIONS AS LAWMAKER

The story of how the UN has transformed itself into a relevant lawmaking actor is the subject of a vast literature that can only be briefly surveyed here.[4] A glimmer of how this transformation occurred is suggested by the ICJ's advisory opinion in the Reparation for Injuries Case.[5] In 1949, after a UN mediator was killed in Israel, the General Assembly asked the ICJ for its views on whether the organization could bring an international claim to recover its own damages as well as those owed to the mediator's family against the state of Israel, at that time not yet a member of the UN. The ICJ answered in the affirmative, indicating that while the UN was not a 'super state,' it enjoyed sufficient international legal personality to fulfill its purposes, and these purposes, it could be assumed, included bringing both types of claims even against a non-member state. The Secretary-General thereafter recommended that the

Assembly accept the ICJ's opinion, the Assembly complied, and the Secretary-General sought relief from Israel. The incident indicates how the interaction of an advisory opinion of the ICJ, the actions of the Secretary-General and the Assembly, along with the subsequent acquiescence of member states, may produce a general change in the law applicable to all. In this instance, the actions of these UN organs yielded the principle, nowhere stated in the Charter, that the UN enjoys objective legal personality and is capable of not only bringing claims but also concluding treaties not specifically mentioned in the Charter.[6]

That the UN is an international legal person has also suggested to lawyers that it also owes duties, like other legal persons, even if these are also not specifically assumed via treaty.[7] The reparation precedent also helped to establish the proposition that other IOs are also international legal persons capable of taking many actions that states are entitled to take (such as concluding treaties) so long as these are necessary to fulfill their purposes. More broadly, it suggests the expansive, teleological interpretations of IOs' constituent instruments that have sometimes occurred, as well as the inference of implied powers. The reparation case is only one example among many in which entities whose legitimacy is premised on either their claim to universal representation (such as the General Assembly) or their impartiality or independence (such as the UN Secretariat, the ICJ, or UN bodies of experts) generate new law or reinterpretations of old law (including of the Charter itself), even though they are not explicitly accorded such power.

The UN's political organs' reinterpretations of their own powers over time have changed the meaning of the Charter. For example, the Assembly's power to create subsidiary bodies now includes the power to convene treaty negotiations capable of producing some of the most ambitious multilateral treaties the world has ever known. It includes the power to create an administrative tribunal capable of settling, with finality, some disputes, and some of the Assembly's 'recommendations' (as with respect to human rights) are now routinely cited, including by national courts, as establishing general legal principles or interpretations of treaties. The Assembly also seems to enjoy the 'power of the purse' and can require members to pay for expenses for activities nowhere formally authorized by the Charter (as for peacekeeping).[8]

The Security Council's practice over time has dramatically transformed Chapters VI and VII of the Charter. We now know that the Council can take action neither authorized by Chapter VI nor anticipated in Chapter VII, including: 'contracting out' the use of force without relying on either the Military Staff Committee of Article 47 or Article 43 agreements; creating other institutional bodies capable of taking direct legally binding action on states or individuals (such as ad hoc independent war crimes tribunals, a UN Compensation Commission, or a boundary demarcation body); imposing 'smart sanctions' directly on individuals and organizations; or requiring states to limit their access to weapons without recourse to treaty.[9] Even the Secretary-General has generated new law—as a mediator or arbitrator, in his capacity to engage in 'good offices,' as enforcer of UN privileges and immunities, and by assuming public leadership through the 'bully pulpit.'[10] While the UN's political organs have made a widely recognized contribution to the law of human rights,[11] their normative contribution has extended to many other matters as well, including the contemporary legal rules governing humanitarian intervention, the laws of war, or the modern rules governing occupation.[12]

The significance of legal interpretations offered and accepted within the organization often extends to matters of general public international law which are not relevant merely to the 'internal' life of the organization. The interaction of UN organs has helped to define such vague concepts referenced in the Charter as the right of self-determination, members' pledges to respect human rights or each other's domestic jurisdiction, and what constitutes a breach (or threat) to 'international peace and security.'[13] Because UN organizations have largely achieved universal membership, the practice of their organs often short-circuits the need to evaluate the disparate views and actions of states over time. If, for example, it is no longer acceptable for states to claim that scrutiny over how they treat their own nationals interferes with their 'sovereignty,' this has been established, at least in part, by innumerable examples of the rejection of such arguments by the General Assembly. Indeed, even powerful states are subject to diplomatic complaints and internal criticism, premised on, for example, the precise meaning given to the international ban on torture by UN actors, including the Assembly (through its many resolutions concerning torture and cruel, inhuman and degrading treatment), the UN Human Rights Committee (in its various views or general comments on the subject), or the UN Special Rapporteur on Torture. Views issued by such ostensible representatives of the international community are today being used to challenge US actions in its 'war' on terror. The views of such UN bodies and officials are also cited in other legal forums, including by regional human rights courts in Europe and the Americas, to interpret relevant national law or specific treaty provisions.

These and other forms of organizational lawmaking challenge the aforementioned basic tenets of nineteenth-century legal positivism. The first positivist premise—that states' consent is the basis for all international obligations—now seems artificial amidst an ever-rising number of organizationally generated legal norms produced decades after states manifested their consent to more limited organizational charters. The second proposition—that the most significant source of international rules remains the treaty—ignores phenomena as varied as de facto lawmaking by the now nearly forty institutionalized international dispute settlers or global rules enacted by Security Council decision, as with respect to its Chapter VII actions directed at counter-terrorism or states seeking to acquire weapons of mass destruction. And the third proposition—that all treaties are subject to strict interpretation intended to respect residual national sovereignty—is belied by the expansive ways IO charters have been interpreted. The activities of UN bodies and officials also challenge the fourth premise that states retain an absolute monopoly on the making of international law or that only the 'practice of (states) parties' to a treaty is relevant to its subsequent interpretation. Although the practice of collective bodies (such as the Assembly) and organs of selective membership (such as the Council) is not equivalent to practice of states, such practice is nonetheless accorded legal significance (as is suggested by the reparation case itself).[14] The age of IOs has also produced new legal actors—such as Secretaries-General, UN lawyers, and 'independent' experts—whose actions now need to be taken into account in the lawmaking process.

The UN's challenge to the fifth positivist premise—to the traditional sources of international obligation—merits greater discussion. The turn to institutions like the UN has transformed how most multilateral treaties are made, how custom is generated, and even when general principles drawn from national law are cited at the international level.

Most multilateral treaties today are negotiated in UN venues: in IO-authorized conferences, after initial consideration by expert bodies (such as the UN Commission on International Trade Law (UNCITRAL), the International Law Commission (ILC), or more specialized expert groups in the International Civil Aviation Organization (ICAO) or the International Labour Organization (ILO)), or through established IO procedures that may require states to report on what they have done to ratify, or later to implement, the treaty in question (as in the ILO). These institutional connections have dramatically affected the negotiation of contemporary treaties. Today, unlike in the nineteenth century, most multilateral treaty negotiations necessarily involve all or most states since it is inconceivable for UN venues to do anything less. Treaty negotiations under UN auspices typically come with set timetables intended to encourage agreement (such as the five weeks that the General Assembly gave the negotiators of the Rome Statute for the International Criminal Court (ICC)) and a neutral central registry (namely the Secretariat under Charter Article 102) to record subsequent ratifications and reservations.

The negotiating room states enjoy may be narrowed by prior draft provisions generated by IO experts (as in the case of the ICC, where negotiators at Rome began with a bracketed text provided by the ILC) or by a prior commitment to established negotiating rules and procedures (such that, as with the ICC, states are compelled to negotiate in a context that is open to group pressures and information generated by nongovernmental organizations (NGOs), belong to established regional groupings, and usually operate on the basis of informal consensus). IO lawyers are also normally involved in supplying compromise formulations (as in the case of the ICC where UN lawyers reportedly were responsible for 'final' provisions on reservations and entry into force). More generally, treaty negotiations under IO auspices encourage agreement through iteration (e.g., of issues and participants), the reduction of transaction costs, self-enforcing behavior, and reliance on sunk costs, including by increasing access to information and encouraging issue linkage and package deals.[15] Such venues also facilitate institutional mechanisms to monitor compliance or to mediate (or arbitrate) treaty disputes.

These institutional realities, and not merely the rising functional needs of states, may help to explain the ever-rising number of multilateral treaties successfully concluded as well as the relatively high numbers of ratifications achieved with respect to many of them. The fact that the underlying organizations centralize the resources of almost all states on the planet and establish neutral mechanisms for dealing with states' diverse claims may also help to explain why many such treaties are so ample in scope and aspiration for global participation. They help to explain the ambition, as well as the relatively rapid rates of ratification, for such global compacts as those governing landmines and certain arms, establishing the ICC, or governing the global commons (from the oceans to climate change).

The organizational mechanisms used to construct modern treaties also have had an impact on their content. Neither the Landmines Convention nor the Rome Statute would have ended up in the same place but for the efforts of the NGOs, ILC experts, and UN lawyers that interceded in these efforts.[16] The Tobacco Framework Convention, to cite another example, owes much to the joint efforts of the particular institutionally based epistemic communities that encouraged its adoption and helped form its provisions, involving alliances between states' health ministries and international health experts associated with the World Health Organization (WHO), and even economists at the World Bank.

It is also likely that the package deals encouraged by UN treaty-making forums help to explain the relative lack of precision of some of the provisions in those treaties. But while some have suggested that UN forums encourage vague common denominator solutions that reflect only states' agreement to disagree,[17] the lack of precision of some modern treaty provisions is not necessarily a handicap—not if the treaty in question also relies on institutional mechanisms to fill interpretative or enforcement gaps over time. Thus, each of the principal UN human rights treaties relies on an expert committee to mediate interpretative disputes, and even the 'independent' ICC relies, at least in part, on the Security Council (as was made clear in Security Council resolution 1593 on Darfur). Many modern multilateral treaties are not just the product of organizational venues; they continue to rely on the organization (or some organizational substitute such as periodic Meetings of the Parties (MOPs)) for ongoing interpretation, elaboration, or enforcement.

The turn to IOs also helps to explain why, although the traditional sources of law enumerated in Article 38 of the ICJ Statute are not premised on a normative hierarchy, presume that states are free to consent to any changes in pre-existing rules, and posit that international obligations exist only as between those states that freely consent to them, international lawyers today sometimes rely on hierarchically superior norms (including *jus cogens*) as well as the concept that some legal duties are owed by all states (that is *erga omnes* obligations). Such rules are the quintessential products of institutions that purport to represent 'the international community.' The proposition that some rules cannot be trumped by later agreement and reflect non-negotiable values of all the 'peoples' of the world—such as the right to life or the right to be free from torture—is, after all, implicit in the UN Charter, including in its Preamble and Articles 1, 55–56, and 103. The idea that there exist *erga omnes* obligations owed by all states whether or not specially established via treaty is a concept endorsed by the ICJ and encouraged by Charter Article 2 (6). Like the principle that states have a duty to negotiate multilaterally prior to taking unilateral action (affirmed by, among others, the Appellate Body of the World Trade Organization (WTO)), this too is a by-product of modern representatives of the 'international community' to which such duties are owed.[18]

Other attempts at hierarchy result from the sheer proliferation of IO-generated treaties. That the ILO has proven to be such an effective treaty machine helps to explain that organization's recent effort to elevate certain 'core' ILO treaties to a higher status; it also helps to explain ongoing attempts to devise priority rules to settle conflicts among IOs or their dispute settlers (e.g., as between the treaty rules established under the ILO and the WTO, the decisions reached by the Tribunal for the Law of the Sea and other dispute settlers, or decisions reached by the WTO Appellate Body and environmental regimes). Of course, the need to solve these problems at the 'joints' of IOs with ever-expanding (and therefore partly overlapping) institutional mandates only encourages the negotiation of yet more treaties, including relationship or joint participation agreements between IOs.[19]

But the turn to organizational forms of treaty-making does not invariably produce more widely ratified or 'better' treaties. The selection of some IO forums for negotiation may doom some negotiations or make the result unattractive to significant groups of states. Many scholars also note the significance of choosing among organizational venues for treaty negotiations (or 'forum-shifting'), particularly as a tool for powerful states to channel treaty negotiations that they favor (or disapprove of) to organizations that will produce the results that they want.[20] While forum-shifting does not always work, when it does, it may produce, over time, global rules that may favor the interests of certain states.[21]

The vaunted benefit of UN forums—their claim to universal participation—may undermine those negotiations that would have had a better chance if undertaken among a smaller group of like-minded states. The wide North–South divide that prevailed in global forums during the heyday of enthusiasm for a 'New International Economic Order,' for example, effectively killed most of the normative efforts of the UN Conference on Trade and Development (UNCTAD) or the UN Centre on Transnational Corporations, including a proposed Code of Conduct for Multilateral Corporations. Agreement may sometimes be precluded by the institutional bureaucracies involved. Like bureaucracies within governments, IO secretariats, UN lawyers, or UN designated experts may be inefficient or ineffective, or seek to promote agendas at odds with those of their collective principals, namely states.[22]

The 'path dependencies' that characterize organizational forums may rely on historical practices or biases that preclude innovation or compromise; the epistemic communities that characterize some UN bodies may have been 'captured' by the very interests sought to be regulated. Those involved in drafting treaties or other legal rules may be more intent on winning institutional turf battles than in achieving global benefits. Even experts in international law, such as those in the ILC, may undertake projects of dubious real world importance or encourage the conclusion of flawed treaties not likely to achieve their intended purpose. And, while the imprecision of some UN-generated treaties may be 'cured' by subsequent institutional interpretation, many such efforts are of dubious effectiveness, particularly when those charged with subsequent interpretation, such as human rights treaty bodies, are not given the authority to issue legally binding opinions.[23] For these reasons, even if it is true that the age of IOs has helped to produce higher numbers of treaties, it is not at all clear that such treaties are 'better' than those produced in the nineteenth century.

Custom, the second traditional source of international law, has also been transformed in the age of IOs. Today, national and international courts, as well as diplomats, UN lawyers and scholars, rely much more often on institutional short-cuts, including General Assembly resolutions, widely ratified multilateral treaties (that, as noted, are usually the products of IO processes), or other organizational work products (from model rules to normative 'declarations').[24] As is suggested by the reparation incident discussed above, new forms of customary law also emerge from the interaction of the UN's political organs as well as the pronouncements of an ever-rising number of institutional dispute settlers.

New custom differs from the old in the speed with which the rules form or evolve, the degree of state participation claimed, and, often, the extent to which its rules substantively intrude on previously sacrosanct sovereign domains. The last is particularly evident with respect to the growing body of IO-generated human rights customary law. Some scholars have suggested that these qualities, including the fact that new custom owes its origin and scope to forums that purport to represent the entire planet, have yielded an entirely new species of legal obligation that ought to be designated by a special term, such as 'supranational,' 'world,' 'declaratory,' or 'universal' law.[25] Debates over whether, in principle, pronouncements by the General Assembly can ever be relevant to determining what legal obligations states generally owe to one another have given way to general recognition that no other forum in the world has the unique status of the Assembly, albeit amidst continuing disputes over which Assembly resolutions have legal significance. Not even those states that were once most resistant to this kind of Assembly empowerment, such as the US, have been able to resist using some Assembly resolutions when convenient to prove a point of contested law, and indeed even the relatively conservative Restatement on Foreign Relations of the United States, widely cited by US courts, acknowledges the legal value of some Assembly resolutions, particularly when these attempt to interpret a Charter provision.[26]

The last traditional source of international law, general principles drawn from national law, has gained a new lease of life thanks to organizational venues, such as international courts and tribunals. Institutionalized dispute settlers, operating under the principles that they have 'competence to determine their own competence' and should never dismiss a case on the basis of a gap in the law (that is, on the basis of *non-liquet*) have drawn on general principles of law to settle the ever-rising number of international disputes submitted to them. Inevitably, their gap-filling efforts have been cited as relevant precedent subsequently by others, including other courts.

But the most evident change in international obligations—the turn to various forms of 'soft law' that, by definition, do not have a pedigree sanctioned by the ICJ's Article 38—is also, at least in part, a by-product of the turn to IOs. Perhaps the largest body of so-called soft law today consists of the judgments, advisory opinions, views, and general comments issued by a substantial number of institutionalized dispute settlers, including judges on ad hoc war crimes tribunals, UN human rights treaty bodies, UN rapporteurs, regional human rights courts, the ICJ, WTO panels and Appellate Body, and arbitrators of the International Centre for Settlement of Investment Disputes (ICSID). These judicialized, or at least reasoned, opinions, some formally binding (but only as to parties to the underlying dispute) and many purely advisory, do much more than settle discrete disputes among states, between them and IOs, or between states and private parties. They are usually treated as quasi-binding precedents by the bodies issuing them in ways analogous to how common law courts handle prior opinions by a hierarchically superior court (*stare decisis*). Moreover, irrespective of their formally non-binding status (at least with respect to non-parties to the disputes), these opinions are often routinely used by international lawyers and diplomats in ways that suggest that they are at least as much a subsidiary source of international obligation as any other identified in Article 38 of the ICJ's Statute.

Much the same can be said for many other institutional products—from presidential statements issued within the Security Council to formal declarations adopted at the end of UN summits or other UN conferences. Although these 'political' proclamations do not have the formally binding quality of a treaty (nor evince state agreement to be bound), some such pronouncements—such as the precautionary principle included as part of the Stockholm Declaration—have gained legal traction nonetheless as a result of invocations by states, NGOs, multinational corporations, judges, or international secretariats, in the course of settling disputes, lobbying, or attempting to interpret other law, both international and national. While traditional positivists have bemoaned such realities—with some objecting even to the term 'soft law'—recourse to such informal sources is characteristic of other social settings characterized by iterative interactions among repeat players.[27] Other institutions, from those of the administrative state to the modern corporation, also develop and enforce social norms in ways that are sometimes hard to distinguish from law. And even corporate lawyers, at least those that do not wish to be accused of malpractice by their clients, cannot afford to ignore such IO-generated forms of 'soft law' as, for example, the norms promoted under the UN's Global Compact or the OECD's (Organisation for Economic Co-operation and Development) Guidelines for Multinational Enterprises.[28]

Institutional soft law enjoys the benefits of other forms of informal or political agreements. States find arrangements like the original Helsinki Accords or the Universal Declaration of Human Rights attractive precisely because they are not legally binding and do not require either approval or implementation by national legislatures.[29] But, as those two examples suggest, if such 'soft' codes of conduct are embedded in institutions, they may 'harden' over time, whether or not they are displaced by formally binding sources of law such as a treaty or custom. Consider the example of the Articles of State Responsibility released by the ILC in August 2001.[30] These Articles, which purport to resolve critical issues concerning when and which state actors are to be deemed responsible for internationally wrongful acts, and enumerate permissible excuses from responsibility, such as the defenses of necessity or duress, were released by the ILC with no clear expectation or demand that the Articles be negotiated as a multilateral treaty—indeed, to date, the Assembly has not recommended that path. In the meantime, the ILC's Articles have proven to be extremely (and instantly) influential and have been widely cited, as have the ILC's extensive commentaries, by litigants and international and national judges, including in North American Free Trade Agreement (NAFTA) investor–state disputes, the ICJ, the WTO, and ICSID arbitrations.[31] In some respects, these Articles are the greatest success the ILC has achieved in a number of years precisely because the ILC did not risk that its work would be disturbed by subsequent interstate negotiations. In this instance, the ILC, which was originally conceived primarily as a body of academics that would recommend treaties to states for their adoption, adapted itself to an age that no longer requires its international rules to be codified in treaty form.

IOs have also changed the law-givers and law-enforcers. The most evident change, of course, is the addition of IOs themselves as relevant actors, a change that continues apace as IOs reproduce themselves or generate a proliferation of subsidiary organs.[32] But the expansion of legally relevant actors has extended beyond IOs. UN system organizations have 'democratized' international lawmaking not only by inviting all states, not merely the 'civilized,' to participate in most forms of organizational lawmaking, but also by empowering nonstate actors, especially NGOs, by granting them consultative or observer status, citing their reports, or, in cases of certain dispute settlers, permitting them to participate as *amici*.

There is a symbiotic relationship between NGOs and UN system organizations. Each needs the other for legitimacy. While many have noted how much NGOs are involved in the de facto enforcement of many treaty obligations, as with respect to human rights, most such opportunities for influence have involved UN forums where their voices can be heard, such as the Human Rights Committee.[33] IOs have also empowered (or in some cases disempowered) other nonstate actors, including business associations, multilateral corporations, and trade unions, by permitting (or denying) access to the inner sanctums of IO lawmaking, such as expert bodies or treaty negotiations.

The existence of IOs has also changed states themselves, by requiring establishment of national departments capable of implementing the efforts of UN specialized agencies like the UN Educational, Scientific, and Cultural Organization (UNESCO), WHO, or ICAO, or by empowering independent courts and law enforcement agencies capable of enforcing the myriad rights and duties contained in UN workproducts, such as Security Council resolutions. States' participation in UN system organizations has, in turn, empowered and legitimized specific groups within states, from particular ministries within the executive branch (e.g., health ministries empowered by the WHO or education departments under UNESCO) to labor unions and business associations (as through the ILO's tripartite membership).[34] Such participation has had an impact on the internal politics of states—as is suggested by some European states' national legislation requiring Security Council approval prior to the deployment of military force against another state.

As is discussed below, the changes in sources of law and its agents noted above have had ripple effects on international legal scholarship.

POSITIVISM LITE

Organizational realities have helped to change what remains the 'lingua franca of most international lawyers,'[35] namely legal positivism. As two leading European positivists, Bruno Simma (now a judge on the ICJ) and Andreas L. Paulus concede, the realities of organizationally-generated law have produced a new, lighter form of enlightened legal positivism that: accepts that law is 'not independent of context, as extreme positivism might suggest;' recognizes that, while states remain the principal lawmaking actors, IOs and NGOs are assuming 'growing importance;' acknowledges that the traditional ICJ Article 38 sources of international law are changing thanks to the actions of the ILC, 'voting records' or 'proclamations' in international forums, and the decisions of international tribunals; and recognizes that 'so-called soft law is an important device for the attribution of meaning to rules and for the perception of legal change.'[36]

While these authors do not renounce the five positivist tenets summarized at the beginning of this chapter, and while others, particularly Europeans, still adhere to more traditional versions of positivism,[37] the considerably tamer version of positivism that Simma and Paulus defend recognizes the possibility that law develops, at least in part, through organizational processes.

THE YALE SCHOOL

By contrast to positivism and its focus on rules, the legal approach pioneered by Harold Lasswell and Myres McDougal of Yale Law School in the mid-1940s is more open to looking to institutions from the outset since it views 'international law as a process of decision making by which various actors in the world community clarify and implement their common interests in accordance with their expectations of appropriate processes and of effectiveness in controlling behavior.'[38] Yale School adherents stress certain policy goals that are proclaimed to be in the interests of the entire international community, and suggest that the rules contained in that instrument as well as the institution thereby established should, above all else, be used to further these goals. They see jurisprudence as a 'policy-oriented' exercise driven by the need to further eight fundamental or universal human values: power, enlightenment, wealth, well-being, skill, affection, respect, and rectitude.[39]

By contrast to traditional positivists, Yale School adherents eagerly go beyond the plain meaning of treaty texts, including the Charter, to further interpretations they regard as more consistent with furthering these underlying values. They reconceive law as an 'ongoing process of authoritative and controlling decision' among 'politically relevant actors' (not just states), that is less a body of rules that enforce themselves but a series of 'communications with policy, or prescriptive, content, that are taken from communitywide perspectives of authority and backed up by control intent.' They recognize that this lawmaking process occurs within 'established structures of authority, with sufficient bases in effective power to secure consequential control, and by authorized procedures,' in which compliance is associated with significant benefits. Moreover, since 'noncompliance is sanctioned by the threat and/or imposition of severe deprivations,' their account of law provides a ready mold for explaining, for example, how the Security Council has emerged today as an entity capable, at least in some circumstances, of declaring, interpreting, promoting, or enforcing the law.

The Yale School approach readily accepts the dynamic forms of lawmaking produced by organizational processes. Indeed, its advocates stress that, unlike positivism which 'remains fixated on the past,' the New Haven approach to law adapts itself to the changing context in which law is made today, as well as its changing lawmakers.

INTERNATIONAL LEGAL PROCESS

The international legal process (ILP) school was first developed by Abram Chayes, Thomas Ehrlich, and Andreas Lowenfeld at Harvard Law School in the 1960s. It puts institutional processes, including those within the UN, at the center of discussion and seeks to answer realist complaints that international law has no effect on states by showing just how institutional processes constrain states and other actors.[40] At the same time, ILP does not presume the existence of certain universal values like the Yale School. It complements positivism by going beyond (but not ignoring) the significance of rules and their texts, by looking at how institutions—from international courts to the legitimating actions of organizations like the Organization of American States (OAS) during the Cuban Missile Crisis—are used by policymakers and in turn affect states' options.

ILP readily accepts the reality of soft law, as well as the premise that a variety of methods, beyond the classically binding judicial forms of adjudication or enforceable sanctions traditionally associated with law—such as the reporting obligations and other forms of discourse that exist within most UN forums—need to be considered by international lawyers. It also accepts that such organizational processes may be changing the very idea of what 'sovereignty' is. The ILP approach to explaining international law is associated with a 'managerial' approach to explaining why states comply with international law. Abram and Antonia Chayes have suggested that the turn to IOs has changed sovereignty into a 'status' consideration, wherein states measure their power and prestige less by their degree of autonomy than by the extent they participate in IOs.[41]

LAW AND ECONOMICS

Inspired by a movement within the US legal academy that purports to explain existing US laws and institutions as reflecting the most economically efficient outcome, and often proposes legal reforms designed to better maximize wealth, adherents of law and economics have begun to address international law. Because, like the Yale School, law and economics emphasizes comparative institutional analysis, rejects state-centered positivism, and does not presume that all legal rules have the equivalent legal force, the popularity of economic tools of analysis has taken off in the age of IOs and the ever-rising forms of international regulation produced in their wake.

Grounded in the premise that individual actors, such as states, seek to maximize their preferences ('rational choice'), law and economics deploys various tools of analysis: price theory (e.g., evaluating when supply and demand will be in stable equilibrium), transaction cost economics (e.g., evaluating the additional costs of negotiating and enforcing an agreement), game theory (e.g., evaluating how others will behave in reaction to one's strategic choice), and public choice (e.g., applying economic tools to decision-making in non-market settings such as a political lawmaking processes).[42] There is now a growing body of work that applies all of these tools to IO lawmaking processes and to the judgments issued by international tribunals. Thus, the judgments issued by WTO dispute settlers, and even by the ICJ and the ad hoc war crimes tribunals, have been evaluated on the basis of economic efficiency.[43] Analysis of the transaction costs of negotiating ex ante precise treaty terms—as opposed to determining these ex post through institutionalized mechanisms—have been used to explain states' resort to particular schemes for institutionalized dispute settlement, or alternatively, to explain why states fail to include such mechanisms.[44] Game theoretical models have been used to explain the likelihood that states will successfully reach agreement in institutional settings or will comply with the results reached.[45] Public choice critiques of organizational lawmaking processes question the quality of the products reached by bureaucrats or experts charged with drafting treaties or other normative products, as in the UN Commission on International Trade Law or the ILC.[46]

Economic analyses have raised significant questions about whether the establishment of particular institutional regimes—such as war crimes tribunals—is likely to be efficient or to work as predicted to deter the commission of international crimes.[47] Like the other jurisprudential approaches mentioned, economic analyses of international law have gone beyond the arid consideration of rules and provisions for justiciable methods for enforcing sanctions in cases of breach, to consider a variety of non-judicial, but institutionally grounded mechanisms for making law and inducing compliance.

INTERNATIONAL LAW AND INTERNATIONAL RELATIONS

Like law and economics, scholarship that blends insights from both international law and international relations (IR) is defined by its interdisciplinarity. It too has taken off in the age of IOs, even though some of the schools of thought within international relations upon which it draws its insights, most prominently variations on realism, pre-date the establishment of modern IOs like the UN. Realist critiques of institutions like the UN, including by lawyers, abound; there is no scarcity of legal scholarship concluding that, for example, the only effective IOs (or organs within them) are those that reflect the power of its most powerful member(s), as Hans Morgenthau suggested.[48] Thus, the degree of state compliance with the dictates of the Security Council, the IMF, or the WTO are routinely analyzed in terms of their congruence with the needs of the powerful states that dominate those bodies or the willingness of those states to enforce these edicts; when such institutions fail to satisfy the needs of their most powerful patrons, some realist lawyers are apt to predict their demise.[49]

But institutionalist theories of international relations—which purport to explain why states cooperate multilaterally and establish IOs—have understandably proven the most influential among modern international lawyers. Kenneth Abbott and Duncan Snidal's account of the 'centralization' and 'independence' needs fulfilled by IOs provides a useful explanation for many of the legal developments described in the first half of this chapter, that is, for why UN system organizations encourage treaty-making or recourse to new forms of custom, facilitate the pooling of resources that drives compliance, or encourage the peaceful settling of disputes through legal methods. [50] Institutionalists provide lawyers with explanations, grounded in political science, for developments as distinct as the evolution of peacekeeping and the establishment of an independent international civil service.

Liberal IR theory, which sees individuals, groups, and sub-units of governments as the fundamental actors, has proven useful for those seeking a political explanation of why states would be willing to cede normative and enforcement authority to certain IOs, including human rights regimes, or why nonstate actors have become enforcers of such law.[51] Some liberal scholars have speculated that liberal, democratic states might be more amenable to certain institutions, such as supranational courts capable of issuing binding decisions or regimes capable of generating intrusive regulations that reflect genuinely deep forms of cooperation.[52] International lawyers intent on explaining when states comply with institutionally generated rules, even when these are not enforced by credible sticks or carrots, have turned to theories inspired by constructivist theories of international relations. Constructivist international lawyers have built upon the work of Chayes and Chayes redefining sovereignty to contend that states' preferences, and even their very identities, may be changed as a result of the 'socialization' effects of participating in IOs.[53]

FIRST WORLD AND THIRD WORLD CRITICAL VOICES

A disparate group of legal scholars have, largely in reaction to the leading schools described above, focused on the 'contradictions, hypocrisies and failings of international legal discourse.'[54] These critical voices, whether designated as part of a 'new stream' of writing within the US and Europe or part of Third World Approaches to International Law ('TWAIL'), generally involve scholars writing in or about the 'Global South' who have argued that the various methods for analyzing international law above are not 'apolitical' or 'neutral' tools of analysis but mechanisms 'of inclusion and exclusion' that are normatively tinged.[55]

'Crits' (a convenient, if simplistic, label for these critical voices) focus on how international institutions and the resulting rules, as well as underlying jurisprudential approaches such as liberalism, conceal or ignore the deployment of power. Many crits contend that leading theoretical frameworks, including the Yale School and IR/IL theory, are, consciously or not, tools to promote particular ideologies, especially that associated with Western free market states.[56] Although a leading 'crit,' Martti Koskenniemi, has contended that legal styles of argument are merely forms of 'linguistic expression' that do not 'reflect' realities as much as create them,[57] the turn to institutions like the UN has provided crits with ample ammunition with which to launch their attacks on traditional international lawyers. Martti Koskenniemi, David Kennedy, and Tony Anghie, among others, have written ironic accounts of the role of international lawyers in constructing modern IOs like the UN.[58] These historical accounts serve to highlight the bias and blindspots of those Europeans and Americans 'present at the creation,' as well as the ways their institutions and approaches to law have served the needs of their rich states of origin, and may even be perpetuating the colonist project through institutions with a global reach. Other critical writers have sought to rectify the historical record by suggesting how IOs, including UN system organizations, have been affected by the participation of developing states or Third World social movements.[59]

The existence (and increased normative powers) of institutions characterized by weighted voting schemes (such as the Security Council or the IMF) have made it easier for some to detect organizational forms of 'hegemonic' international law.[60] But the contention that IOs serve the ideological and other needs of the powerful has not been limited to such organizations. Critical analyses suggesting that international forms of dispute settlement, like the WTO Appellate Body, ICSID (World Bank) arbitrations, and even the ICJ and the ad hoc war crimes tribunals, do not provide disputants with 'level playing fields' have cast a pall over hopes for an ever more institutionalized 'international judiciary.'[61]

FEMINIST THEORY

Feminist international legal scholars, who examine gender biases and blind-spots, have critiqued the UN and UN-generated law. Insofar as such critiques begin by noting the extent to which the structures of national governance remain dominated by men, it should scarcely surprise that the point has been plausibly extended to interstate institutions like the UN. The leading book-length feminist critique of international law, by Christine Chinkin and Hilary Charlesworth, includes an entire chapter devoted to showing the many ways the UN has fallen short in achieving the gender equality endorsed by the Charter, not only in terms of the level of women in high-level UN posts, or in such legally relevant positions as judges on the ICJ or experts in the ILC, but also in its activities with legally normative effects, such as the rules governing the conduct of peacekeepers, the privileges and immunities of staff engaged in sexual harassment, or the norms governing the organization's humanitarian efforts (as with respect to rules governing UN refugee camps).[62]

Feminist legal scholars contend that IOs replicate the patriarchy evident within most national institutions of governance (from national courts to legislatures). They argue that all too often the structures for global governance and their rules fall into the same problematic public/private dichotomies evident within national law. At both the international and national levels, the law all too often provides no help to those victimized by female infanticide, bride burning, genital mutilation, sexual trafficking, or 'private' violence in the home. Both inside nations and inside organizations like the UN, these critics charge, sex discrimination claims seem harder to bring than other claims for denial of equal treatment. As do the crits, feminists question the claim that international law and its institutions—including those charged with enforcing international criminal law—are 'objective' or 'neutral.' Like crits, they look to the silences of international institutions—such as the failure of international criminal courts until very recently to recognize and prosecute rape as a war crime, a method of committing genocide, or a crime against humanity—or the failure of international appointing bodies to consider gender and not just regional representation in appointing experts or judges.

Feminists suggest, at a deeper level, the gendered and sexed nature of basic concepts of international law embedded in the UN Charter itself, including the concepts of self-determination and statehood, international peace and security, and basic human rights. Feminist critics provide additional fodder for those who question whether UN organs, such as the General Assembly, are truly 'representative' of the 'peoples' of the world invoked in the Charter's opening words; they provide additional ammunition to those who would open the UN system more to 'representatives of civil society,' and to those who would deploy UN forms of lawmaking to intrude even further into formerly sacrosanct realms of 'domestic jurisdiction.'

DEMOCRATIC DEFICITS AND FUTURE DIRECTIONS

While several of the jurisprudential approaches enumerated above began at the national level (often within the US legal academy) and preceded the rise of post-World War II international organizations, at least some of these, to borrow an insight from the constructivists, were themselves changed in fundamental respects because international institutions emerged. While, for example, economic perspectives on international law would have been possible without considering the role of IOs, today's game theoretic and public choice insights are very much dependent on these institutional settings. In other instances, it is hard to say with assurance what came first—the theory or the organization(s).

While it is possible that a critical approach to international law could have emerged in 1945, prior to the establishment of the UN, a crucial critical insight—the critique of the notion of state consent as a real *grundnorm*—was made all the easier by the rise of post-organizational forms of norm-making, which made reliance on state consent all the more artificial. Similarly, although feminist critiques of international law could have arisen as a natural outgrowth of gendered criticisms of national law, the creation of interstate institutions that purport to affect law made the internationalization of theories that commented on national lawmaking institutions inevitable. Other contemporary approaches premised in whole or in part on the legal products of IOs—positivism lite, international legal process, or institutional IR/IL—are even more evidently the product of the move to institutions.

Many of the jurisprudential approaches surveyed here raise graver challenges to the UN system than those that confronted those who were 'present at the creation' of the League of Nations or the UN. Whereas earlier generations of lawyers faced realist skepticism about whether multilateral institutions or the law that they produce would truly affect the behavior of states, today's lawyers face not only continued neorealist critiques of this kind, but a growing backlash stemming from the ways IOs, including the UN, have departed from the strictures of traditional legal positivism and have become de facto lawmakers. Both the successes as well as the failures of IOs to engage with international law are now under scrutiny as never before. The developments described at the beginning of this chapter have generated myriad complaints, from both the political right and left, that these institutions are too constraining on states (or at least some states) and may not be producing legal rules that truly enhance global welfare.

Some critics, especially from developing nations, complain that the law produced or enforced by IOs, either because of weighted voting schemes or because of other power differentials, does not reflect in practice sovereign equality but suffers from a 'democratic deficit' at odds with interstate equity or the 'level playing field' promised by the recourse to law.[63] The ability of powerful states to manipulate who gets to participate in institutional lawmaking and to what end—as through 'forum-shifting' tactics with respect to which IO is entitled to engage in treaty-making, choosing which interest group has a say in institutional settings, selective condemnations of 'rogue' states (as by the International Atomic Energy Authority or the Security Council), or unequal access to or participation in institutionalized dispute resolution—casts doubt on whether the new conception of sovereignty as 'status' or of compliance as 'socialization' really constitutes progress or a 'progressive' development. Others, especially within the US, argue that UN system organs—like the General Assembly, the former Commission on Human Rights, expert bodies like those drafting treaties in the ILC or UN specialized agencies, or international tribunals like the ICC or the ICJ—are 'democratically deficient' because their agents are not accountable in the ways that the executive, legislative and judicial branches within democratic states are made accountable—namely through regular elections subject to proportional representation of national polities, constitutional doctrines protecting the 'separation of powers,' or other legal 'checks and balances.'[64]

To these democratic 'sovereignists,' the universality that was once regarded as a principal virtue of UN system organizations—because it appeared to mark significant progress from nineteenth-century Euro-American concepts of exclusion that limited international law's domain to only 'civilized nations'—is part of the problem. UN organizations are criticized for attempting to pronounce on law because they include, among their members, undemocratic states with no legitimacy to make legal claims upon the peoples of democratic nations.[65] Although their complaints usually address different problems and distinct IO organs, the new critics of IOs, from the right or the left, defend traditional sovereignty, albeit for different reasons.[66]

The chorus of second thoughts concerning IO lawmaking may help to explain why the pace of establishing new, independent IOs appears to be slowing down as well as the continuing appeal of regional, bilateral, or even unilateral alternatives to global forms of lawmaking.[67] It may also explain the growing recourse to less institutionalized alternatives for lawmaking, such as non-institutionalized but transnational government networks and hybrid, not-quite-international models for international adjudication (such as the tribunals for East Timor and Sierra Leone).[68] It may explain why some international lawyers now defend some retreats from institutionalized multilateralism, such as the use of force or deployment of economic sanctions without UN approval, refusals to negotiate or to ratify multilateral treaties produced by IO processes, the assertion of extraterritorial jurisdiction of one's law as an alternative to attempting multilateral regulation, or the rejection of some institutional forms for dispute settlement.[69]

CONCLUSION

Unlike those 'present at the creation' who tended to measure progress by whether more IOs (and more international rules) were being produced, today's international lawyers are more guarded about the virtues of institutionalized multilateralism—or at least more worried about quality control.[70] Indeed, some urge that the legislative, regulatory, or adjudicatory prowess of IOs needs to be reined in by returning to the virtues of positivism, including a stricter, non-teleological reading of their charters. This may mean refusing to find implied powers where none are explicitly provided, narrowing the scope of powers regarded as being 'delegated' to institutional organs like UN secretariats, or restricting the interpretative gap-filling power of international judges. Others argue, in addition, that legal limits need to be found, through a strict reading of the UN Charter, that would constrain the Security Council's power over states and individuals; some urge that national and international judges enforce such limits and that, if they do not, member states should ignore the Council's *ultra vires* edicts as a 'last resort.'[71]

For these reasons, the next generation of international lawyers is likely to remain engaged in delineating the consequences and the limits of the reparation case's finding that the UN is a legal person capable of affecting international law. As is suggested by the ongoing efforts of the ILC and other legal scholars, much work remains to be done on whether the solution to the UN's various 'democratic deficits' lies in making the UN subject to rules of responsibility like those to which states are subject, in institutional reforms intended to make the organization more accountable (in a representational sense) to the peoples of the world, in developing at the international level analogues of those that seek to promote accountability for national administrative law, or in improving its internal administration and structures for transparency (or all of these).[72] Solving these issues, while simultaneously not discouraging the UN from taking necessary action, will keep lawyers occupied for decades to come.

Notes

1. Indeed, the drafters of the Charter rejected a proposal to include an express provision recognizing international legal personality and opted instead for the far more hedged terms of Articles 104 and 105. See Louis B. Sohn, ed., *Cases on United Nations Law*, 2nd edn. (Brooklyn, NY: Foundation Press, 1967), 32–33.
2. See Martti Koskenniemi, 'What Should International Lawyers Learn from Karl Marx?' *Leiden Journal of International Law* 17 (2004): 229–246. See also Michael Barnett and Raymond Duvall, eds., *Power in Global Governance* (Cambridge: Cambridge University Press, 2005); and Lloyd Gruber, *Ruling the World: Power Politics and the Rise of Supranational Institutions* (Princeton, NJ: Princeton University Press, 2000).
3. See Martti Koskenniemi, *The Gentle Civilizer of Nations: The Rise and Fall of International Law 1870–1960* (Cambridge: Cambridge University Press, 2001); and David Kennedy, 'The Move to Institutions,' *Cardozo Law Review* 8, no. 5 (1987): 841–988.
4. For a book-length treatment of the themes outlined in this chapter, see José E. Alvarez, *International Organizations as Law-makers* (Oxford: Oxford University Press, 2005).
5. International Court of Justice, *Reparation for Injuries Suffered in the Service of the United Nations*, Advisory Opinion, 1949, 174.
6. See Philippe Sands and Pierre Klein, *Bowett's Law of International Institutions* (London: Sweet & Maxwell, 2001), 470–476; and Frederic C. Kirgis, *International Organizations in Their Legal Setting*, 2nd edn. (St. Paul, Minn.: West, 1993), 7–16.

7. See Sands and Klein, *Bowett's Law*, 512–526.

8. Ibid., 27–55; International Court of Justice, *Certain Expenses of the United Nations*, Advisory Opinion, 1962, 151.

9. See Erika De Wet, *The Chapter VII Powers of the United Nations Security Council* (Oxford: Hart Publishing, 2004); and David M. Malone, ed., *The UN Security Council: From the Cold War to the 21st Century* (Boulder, Colo.: Lynne Rienner, 2004).

10. See Marrack Goulding, 'The UN Secretary-General,' in Malone, *The UN Security Council*, 267–280.

11. See Philip Alston and Frederic Megret, eds., *The United Nations and Human Rights: A Critical Appraisal*, 2nd edn. (Oxford: Oxford University Press, 2005).

12. See Steven R. Ratner, 'The Security Council and International Law,' in Malone, *The UN Security Council*, 591–605.

13. See Rosalyn Higgins, *The Development of the International Law Through the Political Organs of the United Nations* (Oxford: Oxford University Press, 1963).

14. Compare Separate Opinion of Judge Sir Percy Spender, International Court of Justice, *Certain Expenses of the United Nations*, Advisory Opinion, 1962, 184–197.

15. See William J. Aceves, 'Institutionalist Theory and International Legal Scholarship,' *American University Journal of International Law and Politics* 12, no. 2 (1997): 227–266.

16. See Kenneth Anderson, 'The Ottawa Convention Banning Landmines, the Role of International Non-governmental Organizations and the Idea of International Civil Society,' *European Journal of International Law* 11, no 1 (2000): 91–120.

17. See Bruno Simma, 'Consent: Strains in the Treaty System,' in *The Structure and Process of International Law: Essays in Legal Philosophy, Doctrine and Theory*, ed. Ronald St. J. Macdonald and Douglas M. Johnston (Boston: Martinus Nijhoff, 1983), 487 and 494.

18. See Pierre-Marie Dupuy, 'The Place and Role of Unilateralism in Contemporary International Law,' *European Journal of International Law* 11, no. 1 (2000): 19–29; and Antonio Cassese, *International Law in a Divided World* (New York: Oxford University Press, 1987), 185.

19. See Kal Raustiala and David G. Victor, 'The Regime Complex for Plant Genetic Resources,' *International Organization* 58, no. 2 (2004): 277–309.

20. See Laurence R. Helfer, 'Forum Shopping for Human Rights,' *University of Pennsylvania Law Review* 148 (December 1999): 285–400; and Laurence R. Helfer, 'Regime Shifting: The TRIPS Agreement and the New Dynamics of International Property Lawmaking,' *Yale Journal of International Law* 29 (Winter 2004): 1–83.

21. See Kenneth W. Abbott, 'Rule-Making in the WTO: Lessons from the Case of Bribery and Corruption,' *Journal of International Economic Law* 4, no. 2 (2001): 275–296.

22. See Michael N. Barnett and Martha Finnemore, 'The Politics, Power, and Pathologies of International Organizations,' *International Organization* 53, no. 4 (1999): 699–732.

23. See Oona Hathaway, 'Do Human Rights Treaties Make a Difference?,' *Yale Law Journal* 111, no. 8 (2002): 1935–2042.

24. Compare 'The Paquete Habana,' 175 US 677 (US Supreme Court 1900) to 'Filartiga v. Pena-Irala,' 630 F.2d 876 (Second Circuit Court of the United States 1980).

25. See John W. Head, 'Supranational Law: How the Move toward Multilateral Solutions is Changing the Character of International Law,' *University of Kansas Law Review* 42, (Spring 1994): 605–666; Jost Delbruck, 'Prospects for a "World (Internal) Law"?,' *Indiana Journal of Global Legal Studies* 9 (Spring 2002): 401–431; and Jonathan I. Charney, 'Universal International Law,' *American Journal of International Law* 87, no. 4 (1993): 529–551.

26. See 'Restatement of the Law (Third),' *Foreign Relations Law of the United States* (American Law Institute, 1986), section 103, Reporters' Note 2.

27. Compare Prosper Weil, 'Towards Relative Normativity in International Law,' *American Journal of International Law* 77, no. 3 (1983): 413–442, to Martha Finnemore and Kathryn Sikkink, 'International Norm Dynamics and Political Change,' *International Organization* 52, no. 4 (1998): 887–917.

28. See Dinah Shelton, ed., *Commitment and Compliance: The Role of Non-Binding Norms in the International Legal System* (New York: Oxford University Press, 2000).

29. See Kenneth W. Abbott and Duncan Snidal, 'Hard and Soft Law in International Governance,' *International Organization* 54, no. 3 (2000): 421–456; and Charles Lipson, 'Why Are Some International Agreements Informal?' *International Organization* 45, no. 4 (1991): 495–538.

30. 'Draft Articles on Responsibility of States for Internationally Wrongful Acts,' in *Report of the International Law Commission on the Work of its Fifty-third Session*, UN document A/56/10, 10 August 2001, 43, para. 76.

31. See David Caron, 'The ILC Articles on State Responsibility: The Paradoxical Relationship Between Form and Authority,' *American Journal of International Law* 96, no. 4 (2002): 857–873.

32. See Paul Szasz, 'The Complexification of the United Nations System,' in *Max Planck Yearbook of United Nations Law* 3, ed. Jochen A. Forwein and Rüdiger Wolfrum (Leiden, Netherlands: Martinus Nijhoff Publishers, 1999): 1–57.

33. See Margaret E. Keck and Kathryn Sikkink, *Activists Beyond Borders: Advocacy Networks in International Politics* (Ithaca, NY: Cornell University Press, 1998).

34. See Martha Finnemore, *National Interests in International Society* (Ithaca, NY: Cornell University Press, 1996), 34–66; and David Wirth, 'Trade Union Rights in the Worker's State: Poland and the ILO,' *Denver Journal of International Law & Policy* 13, no. 2 and 3 (1984): 269–282.

35. Steven R. Ratner and Anne-Marie Slaughter, 'Appraising the Methods of International Law: A Prospectus for Readers,' *American Journal of International Law* 93, no. 2 (1999): 293.

36. Bruno Simma and Andreas L. Paulus, 'The Responsibility of Individuals for Human Rights Abuses in Internal Conflicts: A Positivist View,' *American Journal of International Law* 93, no. 2 (1999): 302 and 306–308.

37. See José E. Alvarez, 'Positivism Regained, Nihilism Postponed,' Review Essay of G. M. Danilenko's *Law-making in the International Community, Michigan Journal of International Law* 15, no. 3 (1994): 747–784.

38. Ratner and Slaughter, 'Appraising the Methods,' 294

39. Seigfried Wiessner and Andrew R. Willard, 'Policy-Oriented Jurisprudence and Human Rights Abuses in Internal Conflict: Toward a World Public Order of Human Dignity,' *American Journal of International Law* 93, no. 2 (1999): 316 and 318; see also Myres S. McDougal, Harold D. Lasswell, and W. Michael Reisman, 'Theories About International Law: Prologue to a Configurative Jurisprudence,' *Virginia Journal of International Law* 8, no. 2 (1968): 188–299.

40. See Mary Ellen O'Connell, 'New International Legal Process,' *American Journal of International Law* 93, no. 2 (1999): 334–351; and Abram Chayes, Thomas Ehrlich and Andreas F. Lowenfeld, *International Legal Process: Materials for an Introductory Course* (Boston: Little, Brown, & Co., 1968).

41. See Abram Chayes and Antonia Chayes, *The New Sovereignty: Compliance with International Regulatory Arrangements* (Cambridge, Mass.: Harvard University Press, 1995), 27.

42. Jeffrey L. Dunoff and Joel P. Trachtman, 'The Law and Economics of Humanitarian Law Violations in Internal Conflict,' *American Journal of International Law* 93, no. 2 (1999): 394–396.

43. See Jeffrey Dunoff and Joel P. Trachtman, 'The Law and Economics of International Law,' *Yale Journal of International Law* 24, no. 1 (1999): 1–55.
44. See Andrew T. Guzman, 'The Design of International Agreements,' *European Journal of International Law* 16, no. 4 (2005): 579–612.
45. See Kenneth W. Abbott, 'International Relations Theory: A Prospectus for International Lawyers,' *Yale Journal of International Law* 14, no. 2 (1989): 335–411.
46. See Paul Stephan, 'Accountability and International Lawmaking: Rules, Rents, and Legitimacy,' *Northwestern Journal of International Law and Business* 17 (Winter–Spring 1996–97): 681–735.
47. See Dunoff and Trachtman, 'The Law and Economics of Humanitarian Law,' 400–401.
48. See Richard H. Steinberg and Jonathan M. Zasloff, 'Power and International Law,' *American Journal of International Law* 100, no. 1 (2006): 64–87. See also Hans Morgenthau, 'Political Limitations of the United Nations,' in *Law and Politics in the World Community: Essays on Hans Kelsen's Pure Theory and Related Problems in International Law*, ed. George A. Lipsky (Berkeley: University of California Press, 1953), 143 and 150.
49. See Michael Glennon, 'Why the Security Council Failed,' *Foreign Affairs* 82, no. 3 (2003): 16–35; and John Mearsheimer, 'The False Promise of International Institutions,' *International Security* 19, no. 3 (1994/95): 5–49.
50. See Kenneth W. Abbott and Duncan Snidal, 'Why States Act Through Formal International Organizations,' *Journal of Conflict Resolution* 42, no. 1 (1998): 3–32. For a bibliography of the IR/IL literature, see Anne-Marie Slaughter, 'International Law and International Relations Theory: A Dual Agenda,' *American Journal of International Law* 87, no. 2 (1993): 205–239. For examples of IR/IL applied in specific contexts, see Kenneth W. Abbott, 'International Relations Theory, International Law, and the Regime Governing Atrocities in Internal Conflict,' *American Journal of International Law* 93, no. 2 (1999): 361–379; and 'Symposium: Legalization and World Politics,' *International Organization* 54, no. 3 (2000): 385–703.
51. See Andrew Moravscik, 'The Origins of Human Rights Regimes: Democratic Delegation in Postwar Europe,' *International Organization* 54, no. 2 (2000): 253–252.
52. Compare Anne-Marie Slaughter, 'International Law in a World of Liberal States,' *European Journal of International Law* 6, no. 4 (1995): 503–538, to José E. Alvarez, 'Do Liberal States Behave Better?,' *European Journal of International Law* 12, no. 2 (2001): 183–246.
53. See Ryan Goodman and Derek Jinks, 'How to Influence States: Socialization and International Human Rights Law,' *Duke Law Review* 54 (December 2004): 621–702; Jutta Brunnée and Stephen J. Toope, 'Persuasion and Enforcement: Explaining Compliance with International Law,' *Finnish Yearbook of International Law* XIII (2002): 273–295.
54. Ratner and Slaughter, 'Appraising the Methods of International Law,' 294
55. Martti Koskenniemi, 'Letter to the Editors of the Symposium,' *American Journal of International Law* 93, no. 2 (1999): 351–352. See also Makau Mutua, 'What is TWAIL?' ASIL, *Proceedings of the 94th Annual Meeting* (1999), 31.
56. See, e.g., Koskenniemi, 'Letter to the Editors of the Symposium,' 352–353.
57. Ibid. 359.
58. Koskenniemi, *The Gentle Civilizer of Nations*; Kennedy, 'The Move to Institutions'; and Antony Anghie, 'Time Present and Time Past: Globalization, International Financial Institutions, and the Third World,' *NYU Journal of International Law and Politics* 32, no. 2 (2000): 243–290.
59. See Balakrishnan Rajagopal, *International Law from Below* (Cambridge: Cambridge University Press, 2003).

60. See Nico Krisch, *Imperial International Law*, NYU Global Law Working Paper 01/04, www.nyulawglobal.org; José E. Alvarez, 'Hegemonic International Law Revisited,' *American Journal of International Law* 97, no. 4 (2003): 873–888; Gruber, *Ruling the World*; Ugo Mattei, 'Globalization and Empire: A Theory of Imperial Law,' *Indiana Journal of Global Legal Studies* 10 (Winter 2003): 383–447; and B. S. Chimni, 'International Institutions Today: An Imperial Global State in the Making,' *European Journal of International Law* 15 (February 2004): 1–37.

61. See Andrew T. Guzman and Beth A. Simmons, 'Power Plays and Capacity Constraints: The Selection of Defendants in World Trade Organization Disputes,' *Journal of Legal Studies.* 34, no. 2 (2005): 557–598; and José E. Alvarez, 'The New Dispute Settlers: (Half) Truths and Consequences,' *Texas International Law Journal* 38, no. 3 (2003): 405–444.

62. Hilary Charlesworth and Christine Chinkin, *The Boundaries of International Law: A Feminist Analysis*, (Manchester: Manchester University Press, 2000), 171–200.

63. See Eric Stein, 'International Integration and Democracy: No Love at First Sight,' *American Journal of International Law* 95, no. 3 (2001): 489–534.

64. See Paul B. Stephan, 'International Governance and American Democracy,' *Chicago Journal of International Law* 1 (Fall 2000): 237–256; Jeb Rubenfeld, 'The Two World Orders,' *Wilson Quarterly* (Autumn 2003): 22–26; and Ruth W. Grant and Robert O. Keohane, *Accountability and Abuses of Power in World Politics*, NYU School of Law, Institute for International Law and Justice, Working Paper 2004/7, Global Administrative Law Series.

65. See Jeremy A. Rabkin, *The Case for Sovereignty* (Washington, DC: American Enterprise Institute, 2004); and John R. Bolton, 'Should We Take Global Governance Seriously?' *Chicago Journal of International* Law 1 (Fall 2000): 205–221.

66. Compare Benedict Kingsbury, 'Sovereignty and Inequality,' *European Journal of International Law* 9, no. 4 (1998): 599–625, to Rabkin, *The Case for Sovereignty*, and Bolton 'Should We Take Global Governance Seriously?'

67. See Dan Bodansky, 'What's So Bad about Unilateral Action to Protect the Environment?' *European Journal of International Law* 11, no. 2 (2000): 339–348; Allan Gerson, 'Multilateralism à la Carte: The Consequences of Unilateral "Pick and Pay" Approaches,' *European Journal of International Law* 11, no. 1 (2000): 61–66; and John R. Bolton, 'The Risks and Weaknesses of the International Criminal Court from America's Perspective,' *Law and Contemporary Problems* 64, no. 1 (2001): 167–180.

68. See Anne-Marie Slaughter, *The New World Order* (Princeton, NJ: Princeton University Press, 2004).

69. See generally Jack Goldsmith and Eric Posner, *The Limits of International Law* (New York: Oxford University Press, 2005); and Laurence R. Helfer, 'Exiting Treaties,' *Virginia Law Review* 91, no. 7 (2005): 1579–1648.

70. See generally José E. Alvarez, 'Multilateralism and its Discontents,' *European Journal of International Law* 11, no. 2, (2000): 393–412. See also Joel P. Trachtman, 'Bananas, Direct Effect and Compliance,' *European Journal of International Law* 10, no. 4 (1999): 655–678.

71. De Wet, *The Chapter VII Powers*, 375–86.

72. Compare the proposals to promote international organization accountability by the International Law Commission in *Second report on responsibility of international organizations*, UN document A/CN.4/541, 2 April 2004, by the Committee on Accountability of International Organizations of the International Law Association in *Final Report* from the Berlin Conference (2004), and by Benedict Kingsbury, Nico Krisch, and Richard B. Stewart, 'The Emergence of Global Administrative Law,' *Law and Contemporary Problems* 68, nos. 3 and 4 (2005): 15–61. See also Richard Falk and Andrew Strauss, 'Toward Global Parliament,' *Foreign Affairs* 80, no. 1 (2001): 212–220.

CHAPTER 4

....

EVOLUTION IN KNOWLEDGE

....

LEON GORDENKER
CHRISTER JÖNSSON

As a basis for knowledge, information needs intellectual focusing by the use of specific approaches, perspectives, or conceptual lenses. Such processes mainly take place in research, learning, and administrative facilities that assemble, package, and distribute information in forms relevant for policy decisions and further learning. These knowledge packages are offered to recipients, some of whom make use of them in affecting policies, furthering research, or transmitting to others.

This chapter sketches the assembling of knowledge about the United Nations by treating the ways in which information is handled and readied for transmission and use. As some of the knowledge flows into channels of mass communication, the chapter points to evidence about its relevance to broad publics. In an increasingly globalizing world, information about the organization's agenda and operations has become more readily accessible and available.

ACCESS TO PUBLIC DIPLOMACY

....

Given his deep distrust of secret diplomacy, one of US president Woodrow Wilson's aims during World War I[1] and visions for postwar relations within the League of Nations was to establish a more transparent negotiating environment. With the failure of the League, the founders of the next experiment in international organization assumed the task. From the outset in 1945, delegates at the United Nations Conference on International Organization in San Francisco deliberated in largely open chambers under close observation by an unprecedented corps of journalists and observers from nongovernmental organizations (NGOs).[2]

These precedents for openness were broadened and applied throughout the UN system. Almost all formal meetings of the principal UN organs—the General Assembly, Security Council, the Economic and Social Council (ECOSOC), the suspended Trusteeship Council, and the International Court of Justice (ICJ)—take place in public. Decisive voting by member states is recorded, and visitors can even watch from the galleries. Media representatives enjoy a range of special facilities, bringing them closer to formal meetings as well as informal sources and behind-the-scenes consultations. Most of the subsidiary committees of the main organs and advisory bodies are also open to observation.

Transparency relates to the democratic notion expressed in the opening of the Charter's preamble—'We the Peoples.' Decision-making among governments of widely different characters and competences requires an information and knowledge base. The UN offers essential data for creating knowledge that feeds into formulating norms, making recommendations, and designing programs. Its staff has contributed to the development of knowledge by standardizing ways to collate and use data.[3] The UN's normative purposes are threaded through information and condition its uses in research and the formation of policy.

All formal UN meetings are documented with verbatim or summary records, lists of decisions, periodic and special reports from the Secretariat and, increasingly, by electronic recordings and images, as well as film. The written records of the principal organs, including the public arguments relating to recommendations and conclusions, are eventually published in Chinese, English, French, Russian, Spanish, and Arabic. These many volumes are available in a chain of depository libraries that, in principle, are maintained in all of the 192 member countries as well as in universities and research institutes.

The official records are continually supplemented by products emanating from the UN Department of Public Information (DPI).[4] These range from summary press releases and informational statements to an annual comprehensive yearbook, and from specialized books to pamphlets and periodicals intended for consumption by various publics that range from elementary to scholarly. For the mass media, DPI offers film materials, recordings of proceedings, and broadcast-ready radio and television programs. Extensive archives of photographs and films are maintained. Beyond such materials intended for wide audiences, a vast list of specialized publications, which notably include a wide range of statistics pertaining to various UN concerns, streams from the presses.[5] With the expansion of electronic communications in the closing decades of the twentieth century, the UN began to offer steadily more facilities for remote electronic access to information. Practically all of the contemporary official documentation and much of the output of the public information department can now be accessed through the UN website (www.un.org). Other members of the UN system similarly offer electronic access to information. Thus, an unprecedented volume of original source material is available for widespread consumption. This is a substantial change from the limited information flows that characterized the organization's first forty-five years.

At the same time, journalists, NGOs, and researchers probe beyond the formal meetings and documents, because not all—indeed, not even some of the most important—decisions in the UN universe are made in public. Even though diplomats often prefer confidentiality, advocates and researchers try to put UN processes and results in the public domain. Thus, information about informal contacts and negotiations among representatives of UN member states and the participation of the Secretary-General and his staff usually does not long remain secret. Much of this informally obtained output gives special attention to the concerns of the countries and policy-oriented groups where the publications and broadcasters are based. Headline journalism, however, tends to focus on dramatic debates, strong resolutions, and field operations that produce dramatic pictures.

Largely neglected in official documents is what many observers consider a major UN asset: diplomats from most countries in the world are permanently located in the same place, can immediately retrieve information, and can confer informally at any time, on any issues no matter how sensitive and in any constellation of participants. Journalists, NGO representatives, and some academics report some details of the dealing and jousting that crises and the effects of advocacy inspire.

APPROACHES AND PERSPECTIVES

Access to UN information may indeed provide a basis for advancing knowledge about the United Nations, international organization in general, and beyond that global politics, international conflict and cooperation, and the development of law. But access does not guarantee that what is available will be used or that its use will reach the multiple publics that may wish to consume it. It is difficult to generalize about what happens to that information, how it is processed by those who have obtained it, and how it is distributed and absorbed by different publics. But judging from the output of independent researchers, it is clear the results vary substantially in approach and form. Some broad trends in developing knowledge about the UN system can be inferred.

In the early years of the United Nations, many publications destined for both expert audiences, as well as mass publics, concentrated on the constitutional bases, structures, and parliamentary practices of the world body.[6] The rapid creation of new multilateral institutions following World War II encouraged scholarship, much of which was linked with growing attention to international relations as a subject of study. Especially in the United States, this stimulated scholarship about the United Nations as well as publications such as the journal *International Organization*. Since that time, the dominant language for publishing research has been English, and a large proportion of it emanates from North America.

Along with familiar contextual approaches, a predilection for numeric data soon led to an interest in studies of voting and coalitions in the General Assembly.[7] While this emphasis has become less popular since, research along contextual and institutional lines continues and reflects a still-growing accumulation of data about procedures, precedent, and adaptations. The continuing work of the UN also provides a focus for publications of legal treatises and commentaries in many specialized international law journals. International law textbooks invariably contain at least a chapter describing the United Nations and related institutions.[8] A long debate as to the legal significance of resolutions of the Security Council took a new turn with the adoption of resolutions 1373 and 1540 that are intended to counter terrorism. These resolutions for the first time imposed political obligations on UN members that were neither aimed only at a particular state nor subjected to temporal limitations.[9]

Revived institutional analysis has given rise to two complementary analytical lines. Neoliberal institutionalism emphasizes appropriate behavior of participants in institutions; historical institutionalism stresses path dependence. Studies inspired by the former approach focus on the emergence of a specific organizational culture and 'UN-speak,' the jargon employed by participants as shorthand.[10] Historical institutionalists emphasize how choices influence subsequent options.[11] Specifically, students of the UN system have estimated the adaptation of UN bodies to changing circumstances, mostly by incremental growth and adding new tasks, rather than revaluating their original purpose.

A second trend has accompanied but deemphasized the institutional approach. Explicitly and implicitly, relying partly on the experience of the origins of the two world wars, theorists and practicioners use realism as a lens to trace the emergence of global policy and the operation of the United Nations.[12] Especially during the Cold War, realism was a popular analytical tool.[13] Such an approach views UN politics as a competitive struggle for persuasiveness and influence. As realism probably still is the customary analytical tool in the portfolios of national diplomats, debates on issues in UN chambers provide rhetoric and arguments for its supposed utility. It also insistently emphasizes national interest and encourages attention to a normative balance sheet of gains and losses by individual governments in UN processes. Some neorealist scholars question whether international institutions, especially the UN with its limited ability to coerce, matter at all, while some assert that at best they only serve the interests of the most powerful states.[14]

A third trend, which is closer to idealism and strives for global policy, has affinity with the widely recognized favorable experiences of the League of Nations. Broad cooperation on such so-called technical issues as health, control of narcotics, the status of refugees, and—in the context of the International Labour Organization, a cousin of the League—conditions and welfare of labor led to a theory of international politics called 'functionalism.' It also emphasizes transnational cooperation among the experts on technical matters in national ministries, who offer services rather than engage in formal diplomacy.[15] Cooperation in one specific subject area, according to this reasoning, would 'spill over' into other sectors. Functionalism would provide the kind of discipline that conventional diplomacy alone could not accomplish, even in matters of peace and security.

If it does nothing else, functionalism demands attention to issues that have very wide salience and cannot be treated on a solely national basis. In this sense, it encouraged attention to factors that later would be understood as globalization of technology and social change. It also served as a rationale for constructing the extensive system of operating organizations that report to ECOSOC.

A fourth trend treats the UN system as a device to express, cope with, promote, and regulate interdependence among states.[16] This approach sets out in theoretical form one of the fundamental institutional assumptions of the world organization and of functionalism: all governments are linked by common concerns and agree to promote the general welfare. But it also tries to account for the ways in which decisions on global policies and national measures to implement them have differential repercussions on various countries. It incorporates attention to the transnational linking of government policies and practices.

Regimes theory, which could be described as a sequel of neofunctionalism and interdependence studies, constitutes a fifth trend with a basis in both political economy and in the experience of governments.[17] From the 1970s, the regimes approach has engaged a wide segment of North American and European scholarship.

This approach focuses on issue-specific normative frameworks that serve as vehicles for facilitating and executing substantial agreements among states. These agreements may be based on written legal documents or on tacit, informal understandings. Regimes may originate or be anchored in existing international organizations but need not be. Regimes theory necessarily involves attention to the role of the UN organizations in the creation, evolution, and administration of normative frameworks.

In many respects, the regimes concept resembles the idea of legal institutions (not organizations) familiar in international jurisprudence. The extent to which regimes influence, or are merely a reflection of, state interests is a bone of contention between realist and liberal proponents.

Relationships among the specialized service and regulatory bureaucracies of national governments clearly entail cross-border communication among national functionaries. These communications could be both formal and informal but depend on the perception of common concern and the willingness to promote similar conclusions.[18]

Related to regimes and networks, described below, is the analytical approach of constructivism. It emphasizes the growing influence of multilateral decision-making, diversification in the actors involved in program operations, and the broadening of participation as the outcome of the practices of the UN system.[19]

Such relationships and communications among organizations and individuals engaged in UN processes and operations form the basis for a sixth broad research trend. While this trend comprises a variety of studies that speak of networks,[20] it also bears a close relationship to aspects of other trends that seek to understand the mechanism and outcomes of global governance.[21] It involves institutions, transnational links, and power relationships. Studies that concentrate on the nature of transnational political campaigns and structures that regulate or encourage business relationships can rely on the concept of social networks. Others use the term 'networks' to point to the non-formal relationships that develop among state-organized sectors of society, such as the judiciary, the police, or labor unions.[22] Such analytical work on transactions among individuals is relatively new and undeveloped, but scholars are beginning to generate information about the links among UN organizations, member states, NGOs, enterprises, and individual governmental agencies.

Beyond these analytical trends, conventional memoirs and biographies touch on the work of the United Nations. However, in relation to the output of national political figures, few memoirs have come from UN officials. Of these, a small number stand out for the level of their information, mature judgment, and insightful treatment of material that lies beyond public view.[23] Five of the former Secretaries-General have written memoirs of varying quality but all with an institutional or contextual focus.[24] They emphasize peace and security and diplomatic negotiations and give secondary attention to policy leadership and management issues.

National political leaders, including a few heads of government and many former foreign ministers, write about their encounters with the United Nations. These memoirs almost invariably base their remarks on the application of national policy in the framework of international institutions. Their remarks about such international processes as leadership, management, and financing usually are not the focus of the narratives. Their comments specifically about the UN and multilateral diplomacy, while sometimes insightful, are hardly systematic.[25]

The sixtieth anniversary of the UN system was an occasion, like other anniversaries, for recommendations for reforms. It was preceded by the report of a High-level Panel on Threats, Challenges and Change and an action report by its convener, Secretary-General Kofi Annan. Its sweeping recommendations were coolly received, and only a few were adopted by the sixtieth UN General Assembly in 2005, which was the largest-ever gathering of national leaders.[26]

Scholars and others have only recently begun to compile oral history archives to tap and preserve the memories of participants. The oral history archive at Columbia University contains interviews with a few participants who were active in the founding and development of the United Nations.[27] A more recently established archive that extended a short-lived attempt with the Secretariat to compile oral history interviews is based at Yale University; copies are deposited in the UN's Dag Hammarskjöld Library.[28] The intellectual history project at The City University of New York's Graduate Center has interviewed some of the surviving leaders and others associated with economic and social development.[29]

Broad scope historical studies of the United Nations are relatively much rarer than the analytical scholarship noted above. Rather the organization gets incidental attention in historical treatments of international relations or in specialized volumes on such topics as arms control, peacekeeping, human rights, refugees, or the status of women.

The emphasis on economic development theories and programs, a UN preoccupation almost from the outset, has also inspired a body of serious study.[30] In the earlier years, this included influential theoretical explorations by Secretariat members and expert advisory panels. The creation of an enterprising statistical service—whose publications still provide basic empirical data for economists as well as scholars of regimes and political economy—complemented the Secretariat's work in this area. Beyond the headquarters, the studies and reports of UN regional economic and social commissions followed local issues, sometimes very creatively.[31] While theories of economic development added to knowledge, related radical approaches led to the creation of the UN Conference on Trade and Development (UNCTAD) and contributed to the attempt in the 1970s to reorganize global economic relations under the title of the New International Economic Order (NIEO).[32]

Such exploration opened the way to the publication of frequent (oftentimes annual) thematic studies by many UN organizations with titles referring among other subjects to human development, children, refugees, trade, and world development. Such volumes reflect the accretion of knowledge employing the informational resources of the UN system, as well as increasing conceptual sophistication. Not incidentally, many are published commercially, reflecting a growing market for such knowledge.

In sum, the formation, existence, and operation of the UN system have thus offered basic researchers, policy experts, participants, and pressure groups access to observation and data for dealing with specific issues. In this way, the UN's normal work has acted as a catalyst in advancing knowledge, not only of itself, but also the state of the world.

EVOLUTION AND SPONSORSHIP OF RESEARCH

Probably most of the profound research on the United Nations emanates from universities and learned societies. It continues to be published mainly in North America and Western Europe in scholarly publications, in journals and books for consumption primarily by highly-informed publics; sometimes this literature is adapted for advocacy campaigns and programs of NGOs and interest groups.

In the United States, the notion that the UN would be an integral factor in foreign policy attracted support initially from foundations. For example, the Carnegie Endowment for International Peace actively followed and promoted research on the new organization. It operated via offices in New York and Geneva from where it actively organized conferences, convened small, sometimes dispute-focused diplomatic gatherings, and supported research publications. In 1970, it changed its focus, moved its headquarters to Washington and by 1983 had closed its Geneva and New York offices to concentrate on American foreign policy with an occasional excursion into UN affairs. No other well-financed, large-scale research center of this sort took its place or was founded elsewhere until in 1997, when American businessman Ted Turner donated $1 billion to create the UN Foundation. It primarily sponsors research and development projects, carried out by other organizations, which are consonant with UN programs.

Several less sizeable institutions continued the Carnegie Endowment's efforts to gather governmental representatives, members of the Secretariat, and university scholars in occasional conference settings to discuss UN issues. These organizations include the Stanley Foundation, which produces conference summary documents, and the International Peace Academy, which sponsors policy research and training. The Academic Council on United Nations System (ACUNS) organizes analogous research services.

The General Assembly created a UN 'think tank' in 1965 and has chartered two universities with a focus on its agenda. The first of these establishments, the UN Institute for Training and Research (UNITAR)—always precariously funded— produced research on both policy issues and institutional developments during the UN's early years. Later, lacking funding for its full mandate, it perforce concentrated on training, especially directed at members of governmental delegations in the UN context.

Of the two UN-chartered universities, the United Nations University (UNU) centered in Tokyo and the University for Peace in Costa Rica, the former has concentrated on research on global issues that the UN system takes up. It does not offer degree programs and decentralizes its research through connections with universities and through a chain of thirteen government-supported research and training centers in Europe, Africa, the Americas, and Asia. It concentrates on developing countries through its conferences and commissioned research as well as short-term specialized training for governmental and organization functionaries. It has produced research publications, ranging from conference proceedings to monographs. The Costa Rica-based university has encountered obstacles in its development and has had a mainly local effect in Central America.

Other research institutions, contract-research agencies, and philanthropic foundations sometimes give concerted attention to UN issues, but few have made the UN system a central, continuing focus. In some cases, their output has deliberately concentrated on the failure of programs and the alleged inappropriateness of international organization. In other instances, the reflection of UN decisions and preoccupations in domestic politics has been the main interest. In the 1980s, for instance, highly critical studies of the UN system emanated from the Heritage Foundation in Washington, DC. This conservative think-tank had a marked effect on foreign policy in the United States. In the university world, a large number of relatively small research centers give attention to the UN, usually in the context of a broader focus on international organization and politics or national foreign policy.

On occasion, the UN sponsors an independent inquiry regarding internal issues that produces information and contributes to knowledge of otherwise obscured processes. A striking example is the investigation of the Oil-for-Food Programme in the 1990s after the first Iraq war. In 2004, a special commission probed deeply into the management process and disclosed the ramifications of the program's mismanagement by both the Secretary-General and the Security Council.[33]

POPULAR KNOWLEDGE OF THE UNITED NATIONS

It is impossible to measure accurately how much academic and policy research has been absorbed into mass consciousness. As the reactions of mass publics link directly to the UN's normative purposes in shaping public policy, knowledge can have political relevance.

Some inferences can be made from the occasional public opinion polls that touch on issues on UN agendas. Such material includes mainly surveys that reflect such questions as national foreign policy, elections, and particular conflict situations (e.g., the two wars in Iraq or the conflicts around Israel). A few polls, however, focus on UN actions and expectations about its processes. In these, much attention goes to issues of maintaining peace, rather than to economic and social activities or human rights. The most extensive sampling emanates from US sources, but similar surveys and a very few deliberately transnational efforts provide additional, perhaps more relevant, data. It is probably fair to conclude that broad publics have only vague knowledge of UN institutional structures, powers, and procedures.[34]

Surveys commissioned by pressure groups, such as the United Nations Association of the United States of America as well as independent survey research contractors, show that the UN as an institution evokes a high degree of general support, reaching 70 percent or more in some samples. This finding alone does not, however, necessarily indicate anything more than fleeting acquaintance with the institution.[35] Rather more detailed questions, such as those that touch on the financial support given by Western governments to the UN system, show answers that overestimate the sums involved by factors of at least ten and even much more. Moreover, it can be inferred that conclusions in mass opinion about UN ventures to keep the peace usually reflect issues of national foreign policy rather than of presumed global interests.

Reporters for mass media at UN headquarters in New York and at the European office in Geneva were once a corps numbering in the hundreds, but they have sharply declined over the years.[36] So did the quantity of reporting in 'newspapers of record.' While they once tried to offer comprehensive coverage of what the increasingly complex UN system did, they mainly cover the international reflection of violent crises and subsequent peace-maintenance. Exceptions to routine treatment come when especially large numbers, or controversial, national leaders attend UN meetings.

While the change in editorial focus doubtless reflects the growth of television as a news medium and the decline of print journalism, especially in developed countries, the conflict-oriented reporting on the UN on the whole remains the same. If anything, increasing emphasis on dramatic graphic material encouraged even more treatment on television of violent situations involving the world organization. The editorial definitions of 'news-worthiness' therefore tended to exclude the long-term, necessarily abstract, development of global policies related to socioeconomic issues. National governmental supervision of news media in many member states and preference for reporting on national foreign policies as promoted by the UN system further marginalized such concerns.

These trends suggest that only some member states and some publics have substantial knowledge of what the organization does. Within specialist groups, such as NGOs and commercial associations and some enterprises, as well as academic researchers, such knowledge certainly was available and often used in advocating policy options.

Whether deep or shallow, some knowledge of the UN system lends itself to domestic political maneuvering, especially where intense nationalistic feelings or normative preferences lend support to interest groups and parties. This was often apparent in the United States with regard to contributions to UN budgets. In contrast, opponents of the Iraq war in 2003 in many countries demanded that their governments act only on the basis of UN decisions. In both cases, public political debates often reflected only superficial understanding of UN processes and of the legal significance of decisions.

CONCLUSION: BLURRED FOCUS

Information about the United Nations as an institution and its operations flows in both torrents and drips. It has been transformed into knowledge that governments, researchers, and interest groups use daily, but it remains fragmented and not well balanced in geographical origin and focus. Moreover, close-up descriptions of the multinational processes engaging the United Nations institutions remain scattered and sometimes only incidental.[37]

NOTES

1. In a speech to the US Congress on 8 January 1918. A standard account of the League of Nations is Francis P. Walters, *A History of the League of Nations*, 2 vols. (London: Oxford University Press, 1950).
2. For accounts of the San Francisco conference, see Ruth B. Russell, *A History of the United Nations Charter: The Role of the United States, 1940–1945* (Washington, DC: Brookings

Institution, 1958); and Stephen C. Schlesinger, *Act of Creation: The Founding of the United Nations* (Boulder, Colo.: Westview Press, 2003).

3. Michael Ward, *Quantifying the World: UN Ideas and Statistics* (Bloomington: Indiana University Press, 2004).

4. See Mark D. Alleyne, *Global Lies? Propaganda, the UN and World Order* (Houndmills, Basingstoke, UK: Palgrave Macmillan, 2003).

5. Among the useful specialized bibliographies is Peter I. Hajnal, ed., *International Information: Documents, Publications and Electronic Information of International Governmental Organizations*, 2 vols. (Engelwood, Colo.: Libraries Unlimited, 1997–2001). See also Peter I. Hajnal, *Directory of United Nations Documentary and Archival Sources* (New York: United Nations, ACUNS, and Kraus International, 1991).

6. An influential example is Leland M. Goodrich, Edvard Hambro, and Anne Patricia Simons, *Charter of the United Nations: Commentary and Document*, 3rd edn. (New York: Columbia University Press, 1969), whose two leading authors were in San Francisco. A more recent, legally-oriented analysis is Bruno Simma, ed., *The Charter of the United Nations: A Commentary*, 2nd edn. (Oxford: Oxford University Press, 2002). A manual favored by diplomats is the *United Nations Handbook* (Wellington: New Zealand Ministry of Foreign Affairs, annual). From 1945 onwards, a large number of now at least partially outdated textbooks appeared. An exceptionally influential example that introduced seminal concepts is Inis L. Claude, Jr., *Swords into Plowshares: The Problems and Progress of International Organization* (New York: Random House, 1956). Other widely used textbooks of more recent origin are Paul Reuter, *Institutions Internationales* (Paris: Presses universitaires de France, 1969); H. G. Nicholas, *The United Nations as a Political Institution*, 5th edn. (London: Oxford University Press, 1975); Adam Roberts and Benedict Kingsbury, eds., *United Nations, Divided World: The UN's Roles in International Relations*, 2nd edn. (Oxford: Clarendon Press, 1993); Thomas G. Weiss, David P. Forsythe, Roger A. Coate, and Kelly-Kate Pease, *The United Nations and Changing World Politics*, 5th edn. (Boulder, Colo.: Westview Press, 2007); and Peter R. Baehr and Leon Gordenker, *The United Nations: Reality and Ideal*, 4th edn. (Houndmills, Basingstoke, UK: Palgrave Macmillan, 2005).

7. Hayward R. Alker, Jr. and Bruce M. Russett, *World Politics and the General Assembly* (New Haven, Conn.: Yale University Press, 1965); Arend Lijphart, 'The Analysis of Bloc Voting in the General Assembly,' *American Political Science Review* 57 (1963): 902–917; and Bruce M. Russett, 'Discovering Voting Groups in the United Nations,' *American Political Science Review* 60 (1966): 327–339.

8. See, for examples, Philippe Sands and Pierre Klein, eds., *Bowett's Law of International Institutions*, 5th edn. (London: Sweet & Maxwell, 2001); and Harry G. Schermers, *International Institutional Law*, 3 vols. (Leiden, Netherlands: Sijthoff, 1972). More general treatments can be found, for example, in Antonio Cassese, *International Law* (Oxford: Oxford University Press, 2001); and Michael Akehurst, *Akehurst's Introduction to International Law*, 8th edn. (London: Routledge, 2004).

9. For details, see Paul C. Szasz, 'The Security Council States Legislating,' *American Journal of International Law* 96 (2002): 901–905; Matthew Happold, 'Security Council Resolution 1373 and the Constitutions of the United Nations,' *Leiden Journal of International Law* 16 (2003): 593–610; and Roberto Lavalle, 'A Novel, If Awkward, Exercise in International Law-Making: Security Council Resolution 1540 (2004),' *Netherlands International Law Review* 51 (2004): 411–437.

10. For an argument that the bureaucratic culture of the United Nations shaped views and perceptions of the genocide in Rwanda, see Michael Barnett, *Eyewitness to a Genocide* (Ithaca, NY: Cornell University Press, 2002).

11. Ernst B. Haas, *When Knowledge Is Power: Three Models of Change in International Organization* (Los Angeles: University of California Press, 1990) provides an illustration of this approach by distinguishing adaptation and learning.

12. Still influential on this line of thought is E. H. Carr, *The Twenty Years' Crisis, 1919–1939* (London: Macmillan and Co., 1939).

13. Hans J. Morgenthau, *Politics Among Nations: The Struggle for Power and Peace* (New York: Alfred A. Knopf, 1960), many editions; F. H. Hinsley, *Power and the Pursuit of Peace* (Cambridge: Cambridge University Press, 1976); and Lawrence S. Finkelstein, ed., *Politics in the United Nations System* (Durham, NC: Duke University Press, 1988).

14. Robert O. Keohane, ed., *Neorealism and Its Critics* (New York: Columbia University Press, 1986).

15. David Mitrany, *A Working Peace System* (Chicago: University of Chicago Press, 1966); and Ernst B. Haas, *Beyond the Nation-State* (Stanford, Calif.: Stanford University Press, 1964).

16. Robert O. Keohane and Joseph S. Nye, *Power and Interdependence* (Boston: Little, Brown & Co., 1977).

17. Steven Krasner, ed., *International Regimes* (Ithaca, NY: Cornell University Press, 1983); and Robert O. Keohane, *After Hegemony: Cooperation and Discord in the World Political Economy* (Princeton, NJ: Princeton University Press, 1984).

18. Robert O. Keohane and Joseph S. Nye, Jr., eds., *Transnational Relations and World Politics* (Cambridge: Harvard University Press, 1972).

19. See John G. Ruggie, ed., *Multilateralism Matters* (New York: Columbia University Press, 1993); and Alexander Wendt, *Social Theory of International Politics* (Cambridge, Cambridge University Press, 1999).

20. Leon Gordenker, Christer Jönsson, Roger A. Coate, and Peter Söderholm, *International Cooperation in Response to AIDS* (London: Pinter, 1995); and Margaret E. Keck and Kathryn Sikkink, *Activists Beyond Borders: Advocacy Networks in International Politics* (Ithaca, NY: Cornell University Press, 1998).

21. The journal, *Global Governance*, explicitly concentrates on this line since it began publication in 1993.

22. See Anne-Marie Slaughter, *A New World Order* (Princeton, NJ: Princeton University Press, 2004); and Harold K. Jacobson, *Networks of Interdependence: International Organizations and the Global Political System,* 2nd edn. (New York: Knopf, 1984).

23. Among the best are Marrack Goulding, *Peacemonger* (London: John Murray, 2002); Benjamin Rivlin, ed., *Ralph Bunche, The Man and His Times* (New York: Holmes & Meier, 1990); and Brian Urquhart, *Hammarskjöld* (New York: Harper & Row, 1972); Urquhart, *A Life in Peace and War* (New York: Harper & Row, 1987); and Urquhart, *Ralph Bunche—An American Life* (New York: W.W. Norton, 1993).

24. Trygve Lie, *In the Cause of Peace* (New York: Macmillan, 1954); U Thant, *View from the UN* (Newton Abbot, UK: David & Charles, 1997); Kurt Waldheim, *In the Eye of the Storm: A Memoir* (Bethesda, Md.: Adler & Adler, 1986); Javier Pérez de Cuéllar, *Pilgrimage for Peace: A Secretary-General's Memoir* (New York: St. Martin's Press, 1997); and Boutros Boutros-Ghali, *The Unvanquished: A U.S.-U.N. Saga* (New York: Random House, 1999).

25. See, e.g., Henry Kissinger, *White House Years* (Boston: Little, Brown, & Co., 1979), and Harold Macmillan, *At the End of the Day, 1961–1963* (New York: Harper and Row, 1973).

26. See report of the High-level Panel on Threats, Challenges and Change, *A More Secure World: Our Shared Responsibility* (New York: UN, 2004), and Kofi A. Annan, *In Larger Freedom: Towards Development, Security and Human Rights for All* (New York: UN, 2005).

27. The Oral History Research Office at Columbia University maintains these files. See Columbia University Libraries, Oral History Research Office, www.columbia.edu/cu/lweb/indiv/oral/index.html.

28. See Yale University Library, United Nations Scholars' Workstation Homepage, Guide to the United Nations Oral History Project, www.library.yale.edu/un/un2g1a.htm.

29. The UN Intellectual History Project at The CUNY Graduate Center has collected a large number of oral interviews with persons who have contributed to the development of the United Nations, especially with regard to economic and social thought. For a selection, see Thomas G. Weiss, Tatiana Carayannis, Louis Emmerij, and Richard Jolly, *UN Voices: The Struggle for Development and Social Justice* (Bloomington: Indiana University Press, 2005).

30. Louis Emmerij, Richard Jolly, and Thomas G. Weiss, *Ahead of the Curve? UN Ideas and Global Challenges* (Bloomington: Indiana University Press, 2001).

31. See Yves Berthelot, ed., *Unity and Diversity in Development Ideas: Perspectives from the UN Regional Commissions* (Bloomington: Indiana University Press, 2004).

32. See John Toye and Richard Toye, *The UN and Global Political Economy: Trade, Finance, and Development* (Bloomington: Indiana University Press, 2004).

33. Reports of the Independent Inquiry Commission on the United Nations Oil-for-Food Programme, better known as the Volcker Commission, provides insight into the top-level program management at the United Nations. See especially its report of 7 September 2005, *The Management of the United Nations Oil-for-Food Programme*, available at: www.iic-offp.org.

34. See Edward C. Luck, *Mixed Messages: American Politics and International Organization 1919–1999* (Washington, DC: Brookings Institution, 1999).

35. While collected, comparative analyses of opinion survey findings on questions about the United Nations appear to be rather rare, summaries of many findings in broader polls can be found at www.pollingreport.com. For specific poll data involving publics in many countries, the extensive surveys conducted by the Pew Research Center for the People & the Press are available at www.people-press.org. The British Broadcasting Corporation World Service has worked with commercial and academic organizations to conduct transnational opinion surveys, including one in 2005 in twenty-three countries on UN reform. The Gallup Poll also publishes results of a transnational survey that touches on UN subjects. For an analytic study, see Ph. P. Everts, 'Ontwikkelingen in de publieke opinie,' annual in the *Jaarboek Vrede en Veiligheid* (Nijmegen, Netherlands: Centrum voor Internationaal Conflict-Analyse & Management, 2003).

36. The General Assembly frequently discusses public information on the basis of reports from the Secretary-General and its own sub-organs. These detailed treatments of the issues of public information as seen from the UN vantage point lay out a gradual evolution in attention by the media which is also reflected in mission statements presented by the Secretariat and reports made to the General Assembly in connection with the permanent preoccupation with organizational reform. For a recent example of the basis of intergovernmental discussion, see *Questions relating to information, Report of the Secretary-General*, General Assembly, 60th session, UN document A/60/173, 1 Aug. 2005.

37. An exception in its focus specifically on UN organizations and operations is the Routledge Global Institutions Series, which is edited by Thomas G. Weiss and Rorden Wilkinson. Ten volumes appeared in 2005–6, and another 30 have been commissioned.

PART III

PRINCIPAL ORGANS

CHAPTER 5

GENERAL ASSEMBLY

M. J. PETERSON

THE Charter establishes the General Assembly as one of the six 'principal organs' of the United Nations, and the only one in which all member states are represented with equal votes. It has two primary functions: a forum for deliberation among member governments providing collective legitimation (or de-legitimation) of norms, rules, and actions; and a provider of some administrative oversight of the UN system.[1] When the Assembly first met in London in January 1946 and for several years afterward, it enjoyed considerable attention as a war-weary world looked to the newly-founded UN for a more durable peace, but public attention waned in succeeding decades. Particular proceedings, such as the heated general debate at the 15th session in 1960, consideration of the Arab–Israeli conflict in 1967, and the special sessions on a New International Economic Order (NIEO) in the 1970s, attracted considerable notice, but these were exceptions to a steady trend of decreased attention indicative of institutional decline.[2]

The General Assembly's proceedings have inspired four streams of writing. Memoirs by current or former participants provide descriptions of views and reflections on particular events. A more extensive advocacy literature seeks to persuade governments and attentive members of the public to support a particular policy on some current issue. A third stream of writing examines the institutional features of and interaction dynamics in the Assembly, providing lessons in multilateral diplomacy for practitioners and students of intergovernmental organizations. A more diffuse fourth strand uses the Assembly's proceedings to illuminate the broader dynamics of world politics as they are refracted through intergovernmental forums.

An Overview of the Institution

The General Assembly functions as a standing international conference in which any UN member state can raise any international issue it regards as deserving global attention. An examination of the Assembly's basic character, methods of work, authority, and voting patterns provide a point of departure for the remainder of the chapter.

Basic Character

The General Assembly is an elaboration on both the long series of nineteenth-century international conferences on particular issues and the League of Nations Assembly, drawing on long traditions of multilateral diplomacy. Like the League Assembly, it was also intended as a public forum and therefore drew very heavily on the traditions of parliamentary procedure used to assure the orderly conduct of public debates in national legislatures. These multilateral and parliamentary practices were developed first among European states, but spread to other parts of the world as states on other continents were included in conferences, the League of Nations, and the United Nations.

The General Assembly expresses and reinforces the Westphalian norm of sovereign equality of states in three ways. It includes all UN member states, gives each of their delegations one vote, and adopts resolutions by majority—a simple majority for most resolutions and a two-thirds majority for those issues listed in Article 18 of the Charter or identified by the members as addressing 'important questions.'[3] The equal vote and majoritarian decision rules mean the Assembly has always been dominated by the many relatively weak states, though this was partially hidden during the UN's first decade by the cohesiveness of the US-led majority. Hence, it has always been easy to rally large majorities for asserting and reasserting sovereign equality and the related principles of territorial integrity, political independence, and nonintervention in the affairs of other states.

The Charter also defines the relations between the General Assembly and each of the other principal organs. The Assembly provides a partial counterpoise to the Security Council through its authority to discuss general conditions of peace and comment on particular conflicts. Many member governments thus regard the Assembly as a forum where 'the masses' can rally to counterbalance 'the aristocracy' of the permanent five (P-5)[4] as the Council fulfills its tasks of assuring the maintenance of international peace and security. The Assembly also functions as supervisor of work in the Economic and Social Council (ECOSOC) and the formerly active Trusteeship Council. Each of these councils has a defined membership and a particular mandate—respectively coordinating international cooperation in economic and social fields, and supervising the administration of UN Trust Territories (certain colonies). Though defined as principal organs of the UN, Articles 60 and 85 of the

Charter specify that these councils operate 'under the authority of the General Assembly.' This provides the Assembly with authority not only to comment on but also to provide instructions about their work. The General Assembly relates to a fourth principal organ, the International Court of Justice, mainly through its role in selecting the judges. The Court is an autonomous legal body which elucidates and applies international law in contentious cases between states or in advisory opinions requested by other UN organs. The Assembly exercises broad supervision over the fifth principal organ, the Secretariat, by approving the budget, staff regulations, and bureaucratic structure within which the Secretary-General appoints and leads the other individuals serving in it. The Secretariat performs the staff functions of the organization, has become responsible for implementing an increasing number of decisions and programs, and provides the Assembly with information and background studies on various issues. The more active Secretaries-General have used their office to mediate conflicts and offer wide-ranging proposals for reorganizing UN activity.[5]

The Assembly at Work

Most Assembly work is accomplished at regular sessions. These extend from approximately mid-September to mid-December each autumn, resume briefly in June to elect the officers for the next regular session, and can be resumed for longer periods in the spring when the members desire. The Assembly also can meet in special sessions to consider particular matters or in emergency special sessions to deal with conflicts between states that have resulted or are likely to result in armed conflict.

Charter Article 10 gives the Assembly a potentially unlimited agenda by specifying that it may discuss 'any questions or any matters within the scope of the present Charter or relating to the powers and functions of any organs provided for in the present Charter.' Assembly authority to adopt resolutions is limited only by the Article 12 provision that it should not make recommendations relating to conflicts being handled in the Security Council and the Article 2, paragraph 7 provision banning intervention in matters 'essentially within the domestic jurisdiction' of states. In practice neither provision has imposed any significant limitation on Assembly discussions. The Assembly has always commented on conflicts-in-progress, whether or not the Security Council was also addressing them at that moment. Even under the controversial definitions of 'intervention' that extend its meaning to include the application of economic pressure as well as the threat or use of armed force, Assembly majorities have always maintained that debates and resolutions do not amount to intervention even though they are intended to exert moral pressure on governments.

The Assembly's dual function as deliberative forum and organizational overseer, combined with its egalitarian practices, creates serious time pressures. The need to accommodate the smallest delegations by never having more than three main committees meet simultaneously and to report draft resolutions to the plenary by early December keep the busiest main committees from having extended discussion of every item before them. The some fourteen weeks of a regular session can be used best when governments know in advance what will be discussed and select a limited number of significant matters to address at length. The formal rules encourage advance notice by favoring items suggested in time to make the 'provisional list' proposed at least sixty days ahead of the start of a regular session or the 'supplementary list' of items proposed at least thirty days in advance. Though the formal rules specify that 'additional items' proposed less than thirty days before the session begins or after it has started should be of an 'urgent and serious nature,' the Assembly has routinely included all additional items proposed by member governments.[6] Conversely, it is hard to remove from the agenda any topic on which a resolution was adopted at an earlier session; the Assembly has been unwilling to de-list an item that any member state wants kept on the agenda.

The Assembly's rules give the General Committee—consisting of the president, the twenty-one vice-presidents, and the six main committee chairs—authority to propose deleting items from the agenda. The General Committee has never used that authority, though it has become active in suggesting which items should be considered only every other or every third year. The real allocations of time occur in the main committees as they set their own schedules of work. The few items that elicit little interest are quietly dropped; items on which there is insufficient agreement to draft a resolution are strung along by commissioning Secretariat studies or deferring consideration to a later session. The recent shift to listing agenda items under broad thematic headings highlights the substantive connections among items, but the continuing increase in their number encourages outsiders to conclude that the Assembly remains unable to define priorities.

The open agenda and large membership also shape the Assembly's deliberative process. The plenary first undertakes the wide-ranging annual General Debate in which delegations present their country's view of the state of the world, and then takes up the particularly salient topics of the day. Most agenda items are debated in one of the six (seven between 1947 and 1994) main committees. Lacking a party system or any other agreed way to divide up committee assignments among states, the main committees were established as and remain committees of the whole membership. Yet, like committees in national legislatures, each specializes in a particular issue. Today, their respective areas are:

First Committee—Disarmament and International Security
Second Committee—Economic and Financial
Third Committee—Social, Humanitarian, and Cultural
Fourth Committee—Special Political and Decolonization
Fifth Committee—Administrative and Budgetary (organizational concerns)
Sixth Committee—Legal (development of international law)

Even at their original membership of fifty-one, the plenary and the main committees were too unwieldy to proceed informally; they needed explicit and fairly elaborate rules of procedure. Assembly rules organize deliberations on any particular item into three phases: broad debate, detailed consideration of proposed resolutions, and voting on proposals. They also provide guidelines for presiding officer and delegate conduct during meetings intended to assure all an opportunity to be heard.

In the late 1940s the plenary and the main committees worked through their agendas item by item, not taking up the next item until consideration of the one under discussion had been completed. The most effective delegates were those who could steer deliberations through procedural motions, submission of amendments or alternate draft resolutions, or attempts to transform others' drafts through motions to delete particular pieces of a draft. Lengthy procedural wrangles were a regular part of delegations' efforts to secure General Assembly endorsement of principles or positions that advanced their state's or bloc's interests.

As membership grew from 51 to 192, and agendas lengthened from 108 items in 1946 to 158 in 2005 (or from 120 to 261 if counting by sub-items),[7] the Assembly sought to conserve time by streamlining proceedings in several ways. Modest changes included placing time limits on speeches, scheduling two or more items for the same meeting so that if discussions on one were bogged down another could be taken up, and staggering consideration of particular items. The greatest change resulted from substituting informal consultations for detailed public discussions of drafts. Informal consultations saved considerable time compared to the early public discussions, reinforced the development of regional and other caucuses of member states, and both depended on and fostered personal connections among delegates.

Use of informal consultations did not necessarily lead to increased agreement. During the first session in 1946, the Assembly adopted three-fourths of its resolutions without taking a vote because matters had been worked out in advance. The proportion dropped to less than one-third at the height of the Cold War between 1949 and 1954 when informal consultations were few. Despite increasing use of informal consultations after 1955, the proportion of resolutions adopted without a vote did not rise to three-quarters again until the 46th session in 1991.

Delegates and their home governments agree that the political influence of a resolution varies directly with both the breadth and the depth of support it attracts. The process of securing wide support begins with floating preliminary ideas by other delegations likely to be sympathetic, most often delegations of states belonging to the same regional or sub-regional caucus. If those delegations are receptive, the originators then expand their search for support, often modifying their proposal along the way. African, Asian, or Latin American delegations typically approach members of the other two Third World regional clusters; delegations from industrialized countries approach members of their own region and delegations of Third World countries with which their country has close associations because of alliances, trade agreements, or other ties. In most cases, delegations seek consensus, but there are times when a substantial majority decides against further concessions and presses for the adoption of some resolution even over vehement objections because of the importance it attaches to the issue being addressed.[8]

Having two sets of decision-making rules—the majoritarian rules established in the Charter and the consensual rules established through consistent practice—permits the Assembly to tailor its proceedings to the level of political contention inspired by some issue or proposal. However, there is no clear and linear relation between the degree of consensus on a resolution and the depth of support for what it says. Broad consensus may have been attained or preserved with a weak, lowest common denominator text or with one so ambiguous that it can be interpreted differently by various groups of governments. Taking a vote reveals more about the breadth of support, but even votes have to be interpreted with care. When the Assembly votes, each delegation may vote in favor, vote against, or abstain. A 'no' vote clearly reflects opposition, but many governments do not like getting into an isolated position and will abstain if few others are willing to vote against. Thus an abstention can indicate anything from indifference to fairly strong opposition. Delegations under pressure from different sources (for instance, their regional caucus and one or more of their country's non-regional patrons) often use abstentions to avoid taking sides.

Political calculations of support were complicated in the late 1990s by a shift in the ranking of the modes of adoption. Until then, a 'unanimous vote'—one in which all delegations that vote cast 'yes' votes—was regarded as the strongest endorsement, with adoption 'by consensus' a close second since it suggests a degree of positive endorsement by all delegations. Adoption 'without a vote' or 'without objection' came third because they indicate that some delegations are unenthusiastic but not seriously opposed. In the late 1990s 'consensus' came to be viewed as the stronger endorsement, and delegations no longer requested formal votes to demonstrate unanimity. Now requests for votes typically come from delegations desiring to register opposition by abstaining or voting no. These votes reveal more clearly whether opposition is confined to an isolated state or a few isolated states, or has spread to a more substantial group.[9]

Assessing the depth of support requires more subtle analysis. This begins with a close reading of the resolution to see whether support has been won by adopting vague or lowest common denominator statements. It also includes paying attention to statements made in debate or during the interval when delegations may offer explanations of their vote. The explanations permit individual delegations or groups of delegations to specify what they like or dislike about the particular terms of the resolution, and everyone looks to them for signals about how Assembly sentiments on the issue are likely to develop in the future.

The Assembly's Authority

In its relations with other UN bodies, the General Assembly's position resembles that of the legislature within a national government. Except when the Charter already specifies, the Assembly determines which states will serve on the Security Council, the Economic and Social Council, and the Trusteeship Council; and, acting on nominations by the Security Council, the Assembly selects the Secretary-General and the judges of the International Court of Justice.

The Assembly also can authorize the creation of new UN bodies, select the states or individuals to serve on those bodies, approve the UN budget, allocate the expenses among member states, and create 'external administrative rules' regulating relations between the UN organization and its member states.[10] Such rules include decisions about who should be accepted as representing a member state (the authority to decide is shared with the Security Council). Though normally a routine clerical function, the process of checking delegation credentials can be used to choose among rival delegations claiming to represent the same state. Even when only one delegation presents itself, the credentials process can be used to deny a member state its right to participate in the Assembly by failing to seat any delegation from that state.

The resemblance to a national legislature does not extend to the Assembly's relations with member states. Charter Article 10 defines the resolutions addressed to states as recommendations, and few governments have taken up international lawyers' suggestions that the Assembly has actually acquired some degree of legislative authority over states.[11] Yet even without direct legislative authority, the General Assembly's egalitarian treatment of members and open agenda should have assured its place as the preeminent global deliberative body. Latin American members actively promoted the Assembly's preeminence from the start; their efforts were reinforced in the 1960s because the 'new states' emerging from colonialism in Africa and Asia also shared a strong preference for taking up major world issues in forums open to all UN member states.

This dynamic was felt even on issues of peace and security. Though Article 24 gives the Security Council 'primary responsibility for the maintenance of international peace and security,' the General Assembly, on its own authority or at the request of any state involved, may consider disputes likely to lead to war. The possession of vetoes by the P-5 increases the likelihood that stalemate will prevent action by the Security Council, and on such occasions Assembly majorities can use the Assembly's parallel authority to address the conflict themselves. Even when the powers (the superpowers during the Cold War, the P-5 afterward) are managing conflicts through the Security Council, the rest of the membership has used the Assembly to comment on Security Council proceedings or make its own suggestions about resolving the situation.

This pattern of parallel handling of conflicts by the Council and Assembly developed in the late 1940s when the latter rather than the former was asked to deal with tensions in the Balkans and the future of Palestine. A combination of the US bloc's desire to bypass Soviet vetoes in the Security Council and small state delegates' determination to have the Assembly play a larger role in peace and security matters inspired establishment of an 'Interim Committee' in 1947 that would meet in the periods between regular Assembly sessions. Approved initially for a year and then extended, the Interim Committee was a committee of the whole created to address matters referred to it by the Assembly for further study, handle disputes referred to the Assembly when it was not in session, and develop suggestions for enhancing cooperation among member states. The Soviet bloc never accepted it, and it ceased meeting after completing a study of General Assembly working methods in mid-1950.

It was not long before another, more lasting, effort to facilitate Assembly consideration of acute conflict situations began. In June 1950, the US-led majority had been able to get Security Council endorsement of action to repel North Korea's invasion of South Korea because China was still represented by the Nationalist government (already in exile on Taiwan) and the USSR (Union of Soviet Socialist Republics) was boycotting all UN meetings to protest failure to allow the Communist government controlling the mainland to take up China's seat. When Soviet delegates returned to the Security Council, the US-led majority's desire to keep the UN operation going inspired the adoption of Assembly resolution 377 (V) on 'Uniting for Peace.' It established procedures by which a simple majority of the Security Council on a procedural vote (not subject to veto) or a majority of UN member states can convene the Assembly in 'emergency special session' on twenty-four hours' notice to consider and develop collective responses to a crisis when the Security Council has been unable to act.

Although bitterly opposed to resolution 377 in 1950, the Soviet bloc initiated the Security Council decision to transfer consideration of British and French intervention in the Suez Affair in 1956 to the Assembly and joined Third World members in having the Security Council convene Assembly discussion of the 1967 Arab–Israeli War. Resolution 377 thus became an enduring institutional feature. Yet the Security Council still retains two advantages over the Assembly: smaller size and authority to invoke Chapter VII of the Charter requiring member states' participation in sanctions or joint military action. The Assembly cannot invoke Chapter VII, though its resolutions do provide willing members with a UN endorsement of their actions in conflict situations.

The Assembly has let the Security Council take the lead in the renewed peace-keeping and 'peace enforcement' actions of the 1990s; there is general agreement that the 192-member Assembly is too unwieldy for that task. However, it has maintained its practice of commenting on Council proceedings and succeeded in moving the Council towards greater consultation not only with delegations of states contributing troops to UN missions but with the whole membership through frequent informal briefings. Assembly resolutions continue to address ongoing conflicts, and periodic continuations of the tenth emergency special session (first convened in 1997) supplement discussions of the Palestinian–Israeli conflict at each regular session.

The Assembly's efforts to assert its centrality have also marked its interactions with the other two Councils. The success of decolonization has rendered the Trusteeship Council irrelevant today, but the economic and social sides of UN activity remain hindered by ongoing confusion about the respective roles of the Assembly and ECOSOC.

Relations with the Trusteeship Council were shaped by strong Assembly assertiveness on colonial issues. This had two main sources: colonial powers' refusal to place under UN trusteeship any colony that had not been administered under a League of Nations Mandate or acquired from an Axis state at the end of World War II, and newly independent states' strong desire to have the rest of their continents freed from colonial rule. Assembly majorities reacted to the colonial powers' decision by invoking Chapter XI, the Declaration regarding Non-Self-Governing Territories, as the basis for Assembly discussion of all colonial affairs. Through the mid-1970s, the Fourth Committee (whose mandate was then limited to colonial affairs) was the most active main committee. It devoted many meetings to hearing from inhabitants and others with information about conditions in each colony, constantly urged an early end of colonial rule, and commented in detail on conditions and progress toward independence in individual colonies.

The pressure to end colonialism intensified in 1960 when the just-congealing Third World majority secured adoption of Assembly resolution 1514, the Declaration on the Granting of Independence to Colonial Countries and Peoples. Besides urging a faster pace, it also established a standing committee[12] to oversee implementation of the declaration, which became an important adjunct to Fourth Committee affairs.

Reasons for ECOSOC's eclipse are more complex, but also stem partly from the dynamics of the Third World majority. ECOSOC makes all of its decisions by majority vote, and enlargements in 1965 and 1973 assured Third World states control over its decisions.[13] Even so, most Third World governments continued to prefer presenting their main proposals on economic and social issues to the General Assembly. The creation of the UN Conference on Trade and Development (UNCTAD) in 1964, another forum of the whole membership, facilitated Third World efforts to bypass other parts of the UN system. Most obviously, it became a negotiating alternative to the International Monetary Fund, World Bank, and the General Agreement on Tariffs and Trade (GATT). All three have voting rules giving industrialized states control, and the economic radicals then leading the Group of 77 sought to avoid them as much as possible. Less obviously, UNCTAD weakened ECOSOC by taking over broad discussion of the development issues dominating the economic side of the UN's agenda.

While all of these choices reinforced General Assembly prominence within the UN system, expanded activities added to an already very long agenda. The resulting problem of time management was intensified by member states' collective refusal to adopt either of two frequently-suggested remedies: having the Assembly remain in session year-round or cutting back sharply on the number of individual items the Assembly considers each year. No member, but particularly the smaller ones straining to field four- or five-person delegations, was keen on year-round sessions. Pruning the agenda came up against political realities in the Third World coalition, which, even in the 1960s, often maintained cohesion only by aggregating items and drafting resolutions in ways that provided something for every important sub-cluster of members. This pattern was reinforced as the political preferences and economic performances of particular Third World states diverged further. Thus, the coalition could not agree to drop very many issues or to cut back on the number of resolutions adopted on the few issues where there was strong cohesion: outlines for a less market-oriented 'New International Economic Order' and condemnation of South Africa, Israel, and imperialism.

In the broader realm of world politics, the Assembly—like the rest of the UN—was overshadowed by the interactions between the superpower blocs, the later-developing

Sino–Soviet competition for leadership of the world Leninist movement, efforts to promote regional integration in Western Europe and elsewhere, and leading industrial states' discussions of economic affairs in the Organisation for Economic Co-operation and Development or Group of 7 (later 8) summits. Although the Security Council regained prominence after 1990 as a forum for managing international conflict, the General Assembly's inability to break with its mind-numbing routine of debating and adopting resolutions (often multiple resolutions) on the same long list of topics contributes greatly to its continued obscurity. Today it is overshadowed even within the UN not only by the more active Security Council but also by the series of UN global conferences and summits on particular issues. This overshadowing is so deep that recent efforts to renew Assembly prominence involve organizing global summits to coincide with or become the early part of the Assembly's regular fall session.[14]

Changing Majorities, Changing Priorities

As colonial empires were dissolved and the Soviet Union collapsed, the Assembly was transformed. Not only did the number of UN member states increase from fifty-one at the first session to 191 at the sixtieth, but the cultural diversity among them also broadened. The Assembly was transformed from a largely European and western hemisphere body to one with a majority of members drawn from the cultures of Africa and Asia. The extent and pace of change can be traced through shifts in the regional balance of the Assembly's membership in Table 5.1.

Politics in the General Assembly has never been entirely formless; no politics can be if the participants are to mutually comprehend one another and engage in useful deliberation. Building on experience in the League of Nations Assembly, the General

Table 5.1 Shifts in regional balance within the General Assembly, 1945–2005

Year	Total	African	Asian	Latin American	Eastern European	Western European and Other
1945	51	3	9	20	6	13
1955	76	4	20	20	10	22
1965	117	37	26	22	10	22
1975	144	47	36	27	11	23
1985	159	51	41	33	11	23
1995	185	53	50	33	20	26
2005	191	53	55	33	21	27

Source: M. J. Peterson, *The UN General Assembly* (London: Routledge, 2005), Table 3.1.

Assembly operates through regional and other caucusing groups of similarly-minded states that fulfill some of the organizing and vote-aggregating functions played by political parties in national legislatures. In early Assembly sessions, the main group-ings were the twenty-strong Latin American caucus, the Soviet bloc, the Western bloc, the Asian and Mid-East 5, and the cross-regional British Commonwealth. The main caucusing groups have been regional in character since the redefinition of electoral clusters in 1962–1963 when former British colonies in Africa and Asia chose to join the Afro-Asian group while the others were added to the Western Europeans to form the current Western European and Other group. As their numbers continued to grow, the Afro-Asian group split in two, and the larger regional groups divided along sub-regional or issue-oriented lines.[15]

The main regional groups have corresponded with the main political cleavages of world politics for much of the UN's history. 'Eastern Europe' was the USSR and the core of its bloc, 'Western European and Others' was the core of the US bloc, while the vast majorities of 'Africa,' 'Asia,' and 'Latin America' were developing states. Most developing states also belonged to either or both the Non-Aligned Movement (NAM), pursuing a 'third way' in the politics of the Cold War, or the Group of 77, using UN forums to promote changes in the rules for international economic relations. Today, 'Eastern Europe' is less distant from 'Western European and Others,' while the NAM has redefined its purpose as promoting open multilateral diplomacy and encouraging strong states (particularly the US) to act with restraint. The regional caucuses are increasingly supplemented by smaller clusters of states with similar interests on particular matters. These vary from issue to issue, but keep the Assembly from freezing entirely into the pattern of 'Rest versus West' that some have discerned in the roll-call votes.[16]

In most years Assembly proceedings have been guided by a coalition possessing a two-thirds majority of the votes and thus able to set the direction of deliberations on a wide range of issues. However, neither the US-led majority nor the Third World majority ever attained the cohesiveness of a national-level political party. There have always been cleavages within majorities, and delegates devote much effort to bridging or widening them depending on whether their government is inside or outside the current majority.

From the late 1940s through the late 1950s, the US, along with its North Atlantic Treaty Organization allies and other associates, formed a comfortable two-thirds majority. While allowing the Third World to voice concerns and constrained by procedural rules to accept vigorous Soviet bloc participation, the US-led majority was able to set the tone of resolutions. Having shaped the basic terms of the post-1945 international system, the US was a reformist power, preferring gradual change. It supported decolonization at a measured pace, the promotion of civil and political rights, and increased attention to the problems of development (once postwar reconstruction was well advanced) but was content with the fundamentals of the states system and the international market economy. Neither the revolutionary Soviet bloc nor revisionist Third World radicals had sufficient votes to set the tone; at most they could raise concerns and secure a few concessions.

The simultaneous admission of sixteen newly-independent African states in 1960 cemented a shift in the balance of the Assembly. Together with the Asian and Middle Eastern states that had been asserting a new, distinct 'nonaligned' identity since the 1955 Asian–African Conference held in Bandung, Indonesia, the new African members brought a greater degree of revisionism into the General Assembly. This showed most quickly on the issue of decolonization. Though rejecting Soviet proposals for the immediate independence of all colonies, the Afro-Asian group increased pressure for a more rapid end to colonialism. The new majority also pressed for much greater involvement of whole-membership UN bodies in formulating and financing economic development.

Coinciding with a period of relative liberalism in US domestic politics,[17] and benefiting from the pressures imposed by ideological competition with the USSR, these early Third World efforts attained some successes. Western powers other than Portugal picked up the pace of decolonization, and responded with support for the first UN Development Decade and an increase in financial and technical aid.

The reformism of the early 1960s was soon swamped by demands for greater change. By 1970 there was widespread confidence that only central planning or other forms of extensive state direction could assure economic development. Marxian, structuralist, and world-systems analyses also suggested that Third World countries would escape their subordination to the industrial West only through a fundamental restructuring of the international economy. Though varying in detail, these analyses pointed to the necessity of replacing the prevailing market economy and private enterprise oriented system with larger transfers of financial resources from industrialized to developing states, explicit structuring of world trade through intergovernmental agreements, and greater government coordination of production and distribution. Emergence of a 'counterculture' in the West, rising domestic and international criticism of US involvement in the Vietnam War, leftwing movements' successes there and in other Third World countries, and the success of the 1973 Organization of the Petroleum Exporting Countries oil embargo all raised the hopes of revolutionary and revisionist forces around the world. The Soviet bloc, believing that the 'correlation of forces' had shifted in favor of Leninist revolution, stepped up its support for leftist movements on other continents. Radicals everywhere expected that the New International Economic Order formulated by the NAM in the early 1970s would become reality.

The 6th and 7th Special Sessions of the General Assembly on Raw Materials and on Establishment of the NIEO held in 1974 and 1975 marked the high point of this optimism. Yet even then the public disagreements among Western governments about how much change to accept were paralleled by less visible fissures within the Third World majority. East and Southeast Asian developing countries were already using global markets to pursue policies of state-encouraged export-led growth that put them into the 'newly industrializing' tier within a decade. Oil exporters enjoyed a far more favorable financial situation than oil importers, and better export earnings than countries depending on other raw materials or agricultural commodities for their export earnings. Only by repeating the generalities of structuralist economic analyses and focusing on commonly viewed political conflicts were their leaders able to keep the NAM and the Group of 77 together.

While the Third World majority kept the General Assembly focused primarily on their concerns—economic development, decolonization, and elimination of racist regimes—superpower tensions flared again in 1979–1981 as the US under an initially reluctant Carter administration and then under the much more assertive Reagan administration began to counter Soviet initiatives. The Reagan administration, following the advice of several vocal 'neoconservatives' appointed to leading foreign policy positions, also adopted a different approach to the General Assembly. Rather than looking for areas of possible compromise with the majority, or simply ignoring the heated rhetoric coming from Third World radicals, the Reagan administration moved into confrontation. This took several forms: more explicit linking of US aid to votes in the Assembly, sharp opposition to any increase in the UN budget, and readiness to stand in isolated opposition on a wide range of issues. While the UK under Margaret Thatcher was sympathetic to many of these initiatives, other Western governments believed that continuing dialogue with the Third World majority would be more fruitful than confronting it.

The collapse of the Soviet bloc in 1989, and then of the USSR itself in 1991, did not fundamentally change the political balance within the General Assembly because Third World states remained in the vast majority. Yet it did have a significant impact on how that majority defined its goals by comprehensively discrediting central planning. Market economics prevailed, and policy arguments now focused on how and to what extent markets should be regulated to protect the less wealthy and less organized groups within societies. The shape of political conflict was also transformed as inter-bloc ideological tension was replaced by ethnic conflict and religious reassertion. The Third World radical–Leninist combination that had dominated rhetoric in the Assembly in the 1970s and early 1980s was replaced by a new combination of Third World 'moderates' or 'pragmatists' and European welfare states. It has been using the Assembly to advance conceptions of development stressing the distinct but related responsibilities of both industrialized and developing states and critiquing the excesses of the highly laissez-faire 'neoliberal' economics they perceive as emanating from 'Washington'—the US government and the Bretton Woods institutions.

The political realignments of the 1990s have set the stage for an improvement in the Assembly's fortunes. The full impact of Assembly resolutions has always depended upon the relation between the ability to muster votes inside the Assembly and the control of resources for taking effective action outside. The Assembly looked more effective during the era of the US-led majority not only because the Security Council was often stalemated but also because control of votes inside was matched by possession of ample resources for action outside. The Third World majority was hobbled by a serious disjuncture between its control of votes inside and lack of resources for action outside, exposing all the weaknesses of a deliberative body that commands no effective administrative and coercive institutions. The emerging coalition of European and Third World pragmatist governments possesses more resources for action than did the old Third World majority. Particularly if it is joined, or at least not actively opposed, by Russia, Japan, and China, the Assembly could reacquire the political weight that comes with having resolutions implemented. Whether this happens depends on the cohesiveness of the coalition, the attitudes of other influential states, and the ability of delegates in the Assembly to make the body more relevant to the twenty-first century.

Scholarship about the Assembly

Most writing about the General Assembly has one of three purposes: to describe its current workings, to provide immediate policy advice, or to use its votes and debates as indicators of patterns in world politics.

The largest number of writings about the Assembly summarize its proceedings, occasionally also offering suggestions on how to react to developments. The world organization itself publicizes Assembly proceedings through press releases, the *UN Monthly Chronicle*, the *Yearbook of the United Nations*, and its website.[18] Research centers and private organizations interested in United Nations affairs offer studies and summaries of their own. Former and current participants also tell of their activity in the Assembly.

The foreign policy advice carried in specialist and wide circulation journals includes commentary on Assembly proceedings and suggestions about how individual countries or groups of countries should define and pursue policy goals in it. Both governments and outside policy analysts are inspired to pay attention to the Assembly by the simple fact that it is going to meet each year to discuss a set of issues known in advance. Nowhere has the debate over whether and how to participate in the General Assembly (or the UN system generally) been as intense as in the United States. Unlike members of the Third World majority or such 'middle powers' as Canada, which can pursue a global policy only as part of a group, the United States has global reach and can act on its own. Yet the intensity is not simply a result of a great power's wider range of choice. The USSR also had global reach while Russia, China, a more coherent European Union, Brazil, and Japan have potential to develop global reach in coming decades. Yet in none of them has the domestic debate about participation in the Assembly or the UN more generally been as vehement as in the United States.

The intensity of debate in the United States reflects the depth of disagreement among contenders for influence over foreign policy. Even in the 1940s, US opinion was divided into at least three groups: advocates of world government viewed the General Assembly as a proto world legislature and concentrated on how to prepare it for that task; advocates of reviving isolationism regarded the General Assembly as part of a plot to dilute US independence and were already advocating withdrawal from the UN; the bipartisan foreign policy mainstream regarded the Assembly as a venue for a form of public diplomacy that appealed simultaneously to other governments through their delegates and to foreign publics through news reports of the Assembly's activities. The current US debates began to take shape in the 1970s when a new set of 'neoconservatives' argued that the foreign policy establishment's willingness to ignore Assembly debates and resolutions as 'mere words' needlessly ceded an important arena to the ideological pretensions of Leninists and other totalitarians.[19] They guided the US into a confrontational stance that has been moderated on occasion but has not disappeared. By the 1990s the original neocon-servatives had split into two groups, one preferring to work multilaterally,[20] and the other intensifying the unilateralism and dismissiveness of the UN that marked the Reagan administration. This group maintained a strong hold over Congressional leaders' opinion throughout the 1990s, and returned to positions in the executive branch with George W. Bush in 2001.

Scholarly writing on the General Assembly has reflected developments in the disciplines of international law, political science/politics, and international relations, the home disciplines of most scholars who study the Assembly as an institution. Given the different starting points of their analyses, the trajectories of these bodies of work have been quite distinct.

International lawyers concerned with explaining and developing the law of inter-national institutions—rules governing the relations among intergovernmental organizations as separate legal entities, the governments of their member states, and their secretariats—have continued to pay attention to the General Assembly because of its role in shaping the main parts of the UN system.[21] The Assembly has also been central to lawyers' debates about the UN's place in the making of international law.

In the 1940s and 1950s international lawyers could be found on both sides of the federalist–functionalist debate about whether formal centralization of authority or expanding the areas of administrative and technical collaboration would be the surer path to world government.[22] Different parts of the UN system figured in each path, with the General Assembly most relevant to the federalists. Both approaches were overtaken by events; the Cold War discouraged notions of world government, and the challenges of regional integration in Europe and globalization revealed the overly mechanical nature of the functionalist vision. International lawyers continue to project visions of improved global order, but disagree vigorously on the details and on how that better order would be institutionalized.

Political scientists and international relations specialists, distinct groups engaged in overlapping academic debates, have paid varying degrees of attention to intergov-ernmental organizations, the UN, and the General Assembly. In the late 1940s and early 1950s, studying the formal rules and informal workings of the Assembly fit well with the descriptive orientation of much scholarship. However, this emphasis on formal and informal institutional processes gave way in the 1950s to analyses seeking to explain the actual or potential roles of international organizations in maintaining or altering the international system. The debates inspired by successive theories of political integration tended to focus more on the European Common Market and other regional organizations; while those inspired by changes in conceptions of economic development paid more attention to the Bretton Woods institutions, GATT, and other international financial institutions.

Participants in the major academic debates about the broad contours of international relations theory seldom referred to either the UN as a whole or the General Assembly. The much heralded 'return to institutions' of the 1980s and 'return to norms' of the 1990s produced new interest in the UN, but not in the General Assembly. While international lawyers continued to use Assembly debates and resolutions as a source of information on government attitudes regarding various legal issues, most political scientists and international relations specialists looked elsewhere for the data that they needed.

Some quantitatively-oriented scholars have used General Assembly roll call votes on contentious issues (typically defined as those in which less than 90 percent of the votes are cast in favor) as a source of analyzable data. Roll calls have several advantages: they are available, they are repeated from year to year on many issues, and they cover most of the countries of the world. Early roll call studies tended to focus on what the voting patterns revealed about politics within the Assembly itself.[23] However, roll call analysis has also been used to trace more general foreign policy alignments among states,[24] to probe hypotheses about the relation of domestic regime or position in the global economy to foreign policy orientation,[25] or to assess the impact of intergovernmental organizations on state behavior.[26]

General Assembly debates also provide information about governments' attitudes, but are more difficult to use than roll calls. The sheer volume of material and the problem of sifting through the mix of sincere and strategic communications involved pose daunting analytical challenges. Computer-based methods of statement coding and textual analysis may become sufficiently robust to permit dealing with the volume of material, but the challenge of distinguishing between sincere and strategic communications and interpreting statements correctly will remain. Increasingly thin record keeping may also limit the debates' usefulness.

A REFORMED ASSEMBLY AND GLOBAL DEMOCRATIC GOVERNANCE

The future of the General Assembly depends on how the international system develops. In the nightmare scenarios of ecological collapse, global pandemic, nuclear winter, or spread of political disorder to large areas of the world, most nation-states collapse, people combine in smaller units, and neither the UN nor the General Assembly remain relevant. The future of the General Assembly in less pessimistic scenarios depends on how global level political organization develops. Three possibilities seem most plausible: a continued world of states marked by greater cooperation among governments to cope with the challenges of increased interconnection among societies, a shift of authority upward to world government, and a shift of authority sideways into a world of governance through trans-governmental and transnational networks. Each would be institutionalized in a distinct way, but face similar demands from articulate publics for the sorts of openness, transparency, and accountability summed up in the contemporary demand for democratic governance.

In a continued world of states, the UN system would continue as a mechanism for coordination among autonomous members and the General Assembly as a forum for deliberation among all members. With primary loyalties remaining at the state or regional level, the 'democratic deficits' resulting from the lack of direct election of delegates or a second 'people's chamber' might not be perceived as particularly important. The General Assembly could instead enhance the current systems for UN cooperation with individuals and organizations from various sectors of society.

In a world government, the UN might be supplanted by new institutions or might be the core from which a world government develops. To remain stable, a world government would need to avoid serious 'democratic deficits' in its legislative body. If the Assembly evolved into the legislature, it would either shift to popular election of national delegates or add an elected 'chamber of the peoples' to the current 'chamber of governments.' With a population ratio of some 122,000 to 1 between the most populous and the least populous UN member state, the democratic emphasis on the moral value of individuals would also create strong pressures to weight Assembly votes in proportion to population.[27]

In a world of network governance, the UN would flourish to the extent it provided institutions that help members of networks connect, communicate, and coalesce around agreed norms and policies. The General Assembly would not be part of any network, but could facilitate their operation though its ability to call global conferences and create new UN bodies to become loci of network activity. The Assembly would also promote transparency and accountability by reviewing network activity and opening the substantive results to public scrutiny.

CONCLUSION

As long as the United Nations exists in some form, the General Assembly will continue to perform its tasks of global deliberation and organizational oversight. However, it will perform those tasks effectively only if the members reconsider how they use the Assembly and focus on a more manageable agenda of questions that require global agreement for resolution and are not adequately addressed elsewhere. This will require more than pruning the agenda of a few items and further condensing the time devoted to formal speeches; it will require working out a new allocation of activity among the Assembly, other principal organs, and other parts of the UN system.

NOTES

1. Pointed out with particular clarity by Inis L. Claude, Jr., *The Changing United Nations* (New York: Random House, 1967), 73–103.
2. See, e.g., Marie-Claude Smouts, 'The General Assembly: Grandeur and Decadence,' in *The United Nations at the Millennium*, ed. Paul Taylor and A. J. R. Groom (London: Continuum, 2000), 21–60.
3. Article 18 defines recommendations on maintaining peace and security, electing the non-permanent members of the Security Council and of the Trusteeship Council, admitting new member states, suspending membership rights, expelling member states, operating the Trusteeship System, determining the budget and setting member assessments as 'important questions.'
4. The 'masses' versus 'aristocracy' phrasing of this view is used by Singaporean diplomat Kishore Mahbubani, 'The United Nations and the United States: An Indispensable Partnership,' in *Unilateralism and US Foreign Policy: International Perspectives*, ed. David Malone and Yuen Foong Khong (Boulder, Colo.: Lynne Reinner, 2003), 139–152.
5. Such as Boutros Boutros-Ghali's *An Agenda for Peace*, UN document A/47/277-S/24111, 17 June 1992, or Kofi Annan's *In Larger Freedom*, UN document A/59/2005, 21 March 2005.
6. *Rules of Procedure of the General Assembly (embodying amendments and additions adopted by the General Assembly up to 31 December 1984)*, UN document A/520/Rev.15, September 1986, Rule 15.
7. Compare *General Assembly Official Records, First Session*, part 1, 33–34 and part 2, L-LII (1946) and A/BUR/60/1, para. 54, 12 September 2005.
8. Good discussions of this process include John Hadwen and Johan Kaufmann, *How United Nations Decisions Are Made* (Leiden, Netherlands: A. W. Sijhoff, 1962); and Johan Kaufmann, *Conference Diplomacy: An Introductory Analysis*, 2nd rev. edn. (Leiden, Netherlands: Brill Academic Publishers, 1988).
9. The significance attached to these various ways of adopting resolutions is discussed in more detail in Hervé Cassin, 'Le consensus dans la pratique des Nations Unies,' *Annuaire française de droit international*, 1977, 456–85; and M. J. Peterson, *The United Nations General Assembly* (London: Routledge, 2005), 73–79.
10. The term comes from Ingrid Detter, *Law Making by International Organizations* (Stockholm: P. A. Norstedt & Söners Frölag, 1965), ch. 1, sections 4–5.
11. The international lawyers' discussion started almost as soon as the Assembly was established. Good recent summaries are Bruno Simma, ed., *Charta der Vereinten Nationen: Kommantar* (Munich: C. H. Beck, 1991) and English language version *Charter of the United Nations: A Commentary*, 2nd edn. (Oxford: Oxford University Press, 2002); and R. Y. Jennings and Arthur D. Watts, *Oppenheim's International Law*, 9th edn. (Harlow, Essex: Longman Group, 1992).
12. The Special Committee on the Implementation of the Declaration on the Granting of Independence to Colonial Countries and Peoples, usually known as the Committee of 24 from its size.
13. Seventeen of the 27 seats (63%) in 1963 and 37 of the 54 seats (69%) in 1971.
14. Such as the Millennium Summit and Millennium Assembly of September 2000 and the September 2005 High-level Meeting on Implementation of the Millennium Development Goals.
15. Recent discussions of groups include Sally Morphet, 'States groups at the United Nations,' in *The United Nations at the Millennium: The Principal Organs*, ed. Paul Taylor and A. J. R. Groom (London: Continuum International Publishing Group, 2001); and Sam

Daws, 'The Origins and Development of UN Electoral Groups,' in *What is Equitable Geographical Representation in the 21st Century?*, ed. Ramesh Thakur (Tokyo: UN University Press, 1999).

16. Stephen K. Holloway and Rodney Tomlinson, 'The New World Order and the General Assembly: Block Realignment at the UN in the Post-Cold War World,' *Canadian Journal of Political Science* 28, no. 2 (1995): 227–254.

17. The Democratic Party, committed to the New Deal legacy on welfare, Keynesian economic policy, and ending racial discrimination at home held the presidency in 1961–1969.

18. General Assembly information appears on www.un.org maintained at UN headquarters in New York.

19. A view succinctly conveyed in two early expositions, Abe Yeselson and Anthony Gaglione, *A Dangerous Place: The United Nations in World Politics* (New York: Grossman, 1974); and Daniel Patrick Moynihan, *A Dangerous Place* (Boston: Little, Brown & Co., 1978).

20. See Daniel Patrick Moynihan, *On the Law of Nations* (Cambridge, Mass.: Harvard University Press, 1990). Elements of this stance also come through in Pedro Sanjuan, *The UN Gang: A Memoir of Incompetence, Corruption, Espionage, Anti-Semitism and Islamic Extremism at the UN Secretariat* (New York: Doubleday, 2005).

21. Such as D. W. Bowett, *The Law of International Institutions* (London: Stevens & Sons, 1963 and later editions); C. F. Amerasinghe, *Principles of the International Law of International Institutions*, 2nd edn. (Cambridge: Cambridge University Press, 2005); and Jan Klabbers, *An Introduction to International Institutional Law* (Cambridge: Cambridge University Press, 2002).

22. Contrast the federalist vision of Grenville Clark and Louis Sohn, *World Peace through World Law* (Cambridge, Mass.: Harvard University Press, 1958), with the functionalist one of David Mitrany, *A Working Peace System* (London: Royal Institute of International Affairs, 1943).

23. Including M. Margaret Ball, 'Bloc voting in the General Assembly,' *International Organization* 5, no. 1 (February 1951): 3–35; Bruce M. Russett, 'Discovering voting groups in the United Nations,' *American Political Science Review* 60, no. 2 (June 1966): 327–39; and Frans N. Stokman, *Roll Calls and Sponsorship: a methodological analysis of Third World group formation in the United Nations*, (Leiden, Netherlands: Sijthoff, 1977).

24. Such as Hayward R. Alker, Jr., 'Dimensions of conflict in the General Assembly,' *American Political Science Review* 58, no. 3 (September 1964): 642–657; A. van Staden and Frans N. Stokman, 'Niet-gebonden landen en oost-west tagenstellingen; een poging tot positiebepaling' (with English summary), *Acta Politica* 5, no. 2 (1970): 133–164; Steven Holloway, 'Forty Years of United Nations General Assembly Voting,' *Canadian Journal of Political Science* 23, no. 2 (1990): 279–296; Keisuke Iida, 'Third World Solidarity: The Group of 77 in the United Nations General Assembly,' *International Organization* 42, no. 2 (Spring 1988): 375–395; Soo Yeon Kim and Bruce Russett, 'The new politics of voting alignments in the UN General Assembly,' *International Organization* 50, no. 4 (Autumn 1996): 629–652; and Eric Voeten, 'Clashes in the Assembly,' *International Organization* 54, no. 2 (2000): 185–215.

25. Including Eugene Wittkopf, 'Foreign aid and United Nations votes: A comparative study,' *American Political Science Review* 67, no. 3 (1973): 868–888; Neil R. Richardson and Charles W. Kegley, Jr., 'Trade dependence and foreign policy compliance: A longitudinal analysis,' *International Studies Quarterly* 24, no. 2 (June 1980): 191–222; Bruce E. Moon, 'Consensus or compliance? Foreign-policy change and external dependence,' *International Organization* 39, no. 2 (1985): 297–328; Joe D. Hagen, 'Domestic political regime changes and Third World voting realignments in the United Nations, 1946–84,' *International Organization* 43,

no. 3 (1989): 505–541; and T. Y. Wang, 'US foreign aid and UN voting: an analysis of important issues,' *International Studies Quarterly* 43, no. 1 (1999): 199–210.

26. Charles Boehmer, Erik Gartzke and Timothy Nordstrom, 'Do intergovernmental organizations promote peace?' *World Politics* 57, no. 1 (October 2004): 1–38.

27. The 2002 ratio of China's to Tuvalu's population. See Joseph E. Schwartzberg, *Revitalizing the United Nations: Reform Through Weighted Voting* (New York: Institute for Global Policy, World Federalist Union, 2004).

CHAPTER 6

....

SECURITY COUNCIL

....

DAVID M. MALONE

THE Security Council, while formally equal to other principal organs of the UN, bears 'primary responsibility for the maintenance of international peace and security' (Article 24), and has evolved into the UN's most powerful (and mediagenic) forum. Unlike the General Assembly, with which it has had a sometimes tense relationship, its decisions can be binding on all member states, and to a degree on other states as well when adopted under Chapter VII of the Charter. As the Council's membership is limited (including five permanent members—known collectively as the P-5—that have veto power over decisions) competition for the ten elected seats has been increasingly vigorous.[1]

The Council's history to date can be divided into two general periods: that of the Cold War, during which it was not so much paralyzed as operating on the margins of the major conflicts of its time, often intervening to encourage negotiation, to strengthen cease-fires and to deploy monitors and impartial peacekeeping forces. In the post-Cold War era, which arguably began at the UN with the Council's bold move to offer a settlement plan for the murderous Iran–Iraq war in 1987, the Council began more fully exploring its own potential under the ambitious terms the Charter laid out for it, greatly intensifying its work, largely free of the ideological and operational shackles of the superpower confrontation that marked the years 1948–1987.

Since that time, through its decisions—largely improvised and inconsistent though they may be—the Council has more deeply influenced international relations and, for good or ill, eroded the foundations of absolute conceptions of state sovereignty as defined in Article 2 (7), fundamentally altering the way in which many see the relationship between state and citizen. Interpretation of what developments may constitute 'threats to the peace,' and the practice, form, and frequency of Chapter VII measures have all evolved significantly in the post-Cold War era without Charter amendment or a clear break with earlier interpretations.

The organizing framework for this chapter is the division in the practice and legacy of the Council between the Cold War and post-Cold War periods. The narrative aims to highlight significant changes in the Council's decision-making, motivations and institutional preoccupations since the late 1980s, but first examines briefly the Council's relations with other UN principal organs.[2]

THE COUNCIL AND OTHER
UN PRINCIPAL ORGANS

The Council's relations with the General Assembly have been at times contentious. The Council shares responsibility for peace and security issues at the UN with the Assembly, but the latter is enjoined by the Charter from addressing such questions while they are being considered by the Council. In practice, however, this stipulation has often been ignored, primarily via the 'Uniting for Peace' (UfP) General Assembly resolution of 1950 aimed at short-circuiting Soviet veto power in the Council. Under this resolution, the Assembly can make recommendations to the Council if the latter fails to discharge its duties, normally as the result of a veto. UfP was invoked most famously to resolve the 1956 Suez Canal Crisis.[3] Routinely, the General Assembly addresses Middle East issues that the Security Council has failed to move forward (sometimes due to a veto). The other primary link between the Assembly and the Council is that the Assembly elects the latter's non-permanent members.

Council ties with the generally ineffective Economic and Social Council (ECO-SOC) have been limited. An attempt was made in 1998–1999 to pass responsibility from the Security Council to ECOSOC for oversight of UN peacebuilding activities in Haiti, but ECOSOC failed to rise to the challenge.[4] A modest joint Security Council–ECOSOC working-group was established on Guinea-Bissau.[5] Such initiatives, however, proved unconvincing, leading to a recommendation from the High-level Panel on Threats, Challenges and Change (HLP) for a Peacebuilding Commission,[6] which the General Assembly and the Security Council approved in concurrent resolutions 60/80 and 1645 in late 2005.

The now dormant Trusteeship Council was closely linked to the Security Council, not least through overlapping membership, but its role expired with the end of the UN's responsibility for the trust territories when Palau attained independence (and UN membership) in 1994. The most contentious issue that the Council addressed was South Africa's disputed trusteeship over what became Namibia, resolved with the latter's independence in 1990 (after a year of intensive UN involvement in the territory). The Transitional Administrations in Kosovo and East Timor have created interest in the possibility of UN 'virtual trusteeship.'[7] But the Trusteeship Council is unlikely to revive under any circumstances, particularly after the creation of the Peacebuilding Commission.

The Secretary-General entertains deep, complex and sometimes difficult relations with the Council, both as the UN's chief administrative officer and as an increasingly independent actor, for whom successive incumbents (notably Dag Hammarskjöld, Javier Pérez de Cuéllar, Boutros Boutros-Ghali, and Kofi Annan) have carved out a leading role in peace and security over the years. Under cover of Article 99 of the Charter, successive Secretaries-General, generally with Council encouragement, have expanded their initiative and remit on security challenges. The Secretary-General can often complement Council efforts to resolve disputes by proposing good offices or dispatching fact-finding missions, for example. He oversees an expanding network of agents representing him (often under Council mandate) who engage in diplomacy and sometimes also oversee UN peacekeeping operations, many of them designated as special representative of the Secretary-General (SRSG), who report to the Council through him.[8]

The Council's relations with the UN's judicial branch, the International Court of Justice (ICJ), have been modest but generally fruitful. Jointly with the General Assembly the Council elects the judges of the Court. In the security realm, the Council may request the Court to give an advisory opinion on any legal question, and can also recommend that disputants avail themselves of the Court in conflict resolution, which it has done on occasion. Additionally, appellants to the Court may refer their cases to the Council if Court decisions are not implemented by the opposing party.[9] The Council assisted in implementing an ICJ decision on the evacuation of Chad's Aouzou Strip by Libya in 1994 by deploying a small UN verification team (UN Aouzou Strip Observer Group, UNASOG). However, a Court decision undermining American policy in Nicaragua in 1985, a 2004 decision on an Israeli barrier erected in part within the West Bank, and growing US reservations over the jurisdiction of international courts and tribunals have introduced a degree of tension between that permanent member and several international judicial bodies (explored below), intensified by the fast-moving development of international criminal law from 1994.[10]

As the Council's agenda grew busier, its decisions more sweeping, and its interpretation of the Charter more free-wheeling, calls grew for judicial review of its decisions by the ICJ.[11] Pressure for judicial review, as well as for access to advisory opinions from the Court on peace and security issues by the Secretary-General (a proposal advanced by Boutros Boutros-Ghali in An Agenda for Democratization), was resisted by the P-5, but growing involvement of the Court in the Council's institutional life is likely in the longer term.

Relations with external bodies were conducted at arm's length, at least during the Cold War. Chapter VIII of the UN Charter is devoted to regional organizations, seen through the prism of their ability to contribute to the maintenance of international peace and security. Indeed, the Charter suggests a degree of subsidiarity, under which regional organizations might first help to settle disputes before the UN tries to do so.

The Charter is clear in Article 53 that no enforcement action may be undertaken by regional organizations 'without the authorization of the Security Council.' During the Cold War years, regional organizations occasionally sought Council endorsement for their initiatives, but overall they had little meaningful engagement with the Council and vice versa. All of that was to change in the post-Cold War era as we shall see below.

The Council also has significant but informal links with the international financial institutions (IFIs), particularly the World Bank, with security and development seen as interconnected. Occasionally, a ticklish question arises between them, such as whether the IFIs needed Council cover to engage in Iraqi reconstruction in 2003.

SOME HISTORY

With few exceptions, the Council was marginalized by the Cold War. With both blocs heavily dug in and backed up by the veto, key challenges to international peace and security, such as the Berlin Blockade, Cuban Missile Crisis, Prague Spring, and Vietnam War, were managed entirely or largely beyond the UN. Indeed, two exceptions to this pattern have clear explanations. Council authorization of the use of force in Korea in 1950 was possible due to a Soviet boycott of the Council in protest against Taiwan's occupancy of the Chinese seat. This was a running sore for the Council until 1971, when the People's Republic of China assumed the Chinese position on the Council. In the second case of Council activism, the Council's relatively bold approach to the problems of the Congo in 1960—although eventually provoking the ire of both Moscow and Paris—was perhaps due to the lack of immediate threat to either bloc's interests in that far-off outpost.

The Council was, however, able to carve out a niche in monitoring and peace-keeping, a product of necessity rather than design. The first such UN mission, the UN Truce Supervision Organization (UNTSO), deployed to Jerusalem in 1948, aimed to reinforce the cease-fire between belligerents pursuant to Israel's war of independence. This was followed in 1949 by military observers for the Kashmir region, in the forerunner to the UN Military Observer Group in India and Pakistan (UNMOGIP). However, the 'classic' form of monitoring and peacekeeping, in which larger numbers of lightly armed, blue-helmeted guardians of the status quo are deployed in order to bolster diplomatic efforts, cease-fires, and peace processes, took further shape in the 1950s. The first UN Emergency Force (UNEF I), deployed subsequent to the Suez Canal Crisis, was the grandfather of this era, with further examples including Cyprus (1964), the Dominican Republic (1965), and Lebanon (1978), among others. These 'Chapter VI and a half' peacekeeping operations (PKOs) required, in principle, an invitation or consent on the part of the recipient state(s).

As the pattern of direct confrontation between the blocs settled into latent conflict, the Council explored 'new' security challenges such as those of racism and apartheid in Southern Rhodesia and South Africa, invoking Chapter VII to declare them threats to international peace and security and permitting sanctions, arms embargoes, and a naval blockade. This interpretation foreshadowed much greater Council creativity in the post-Cold War era.

With the accession of Mikhail Gorbachev to power in Moscow in 1985, and his subsequent abandonment of the superpower confrontation, the climate among the P-5 improved markedly. Perceptive to the winds of change, Secretary-General Pérez de Cuéllar in January 1987 publicly challenged the Council to reach a 'meeting of the minds' to settle the internecine Iran–Iraq war.[12] In response, the Council passed resolution 598 and proceeded to address other wreckage of the Cold War era. Between 1988 and late 1989, the Security Council authorized an additional four PKOs to assist settlement of the Afghan, Angolan, and Namibian crises and inter-linked conflicts in Central America.

The post-Cold War era has been marked by the Council's disposition to tackle more numerous and diverse conflicts than it had been able to earlier, when it was stymied by the plethora of vetoes (cast and threatened) by the permanent members. Since 1990 there has been a sharp drop in the use of the veto, accompanying the introduction of a culture of accommodation among the P-5, and major shifts in the Council's approach to conflict and its resolution (see Table 6.1). Situations held by the Council to constitute threats to international peace expanded to include a coup against a democratically elected regime (in Haiti); a range of humanitarian cata-strophes, particularly those generating large exoduses of displaced persons, internally and internationally; and acts of terrorism.

This, in turn, allowed the Council to address a range of conflicts, mostly internal in nature, that it most likely would have avoided when Cold War antagonists played out

Table 6.1 Security Council statistics, Cold War and post-Cold War

Type	1946–1986	1987–2005
Resolutions	593	1010
Percentage of total	37	63
Vetoes	212	38
Percentage of total	85	15
Vetoes by country		
USSR/Russia	114	3
USA	54	26
UK	25	5
France	16	2
China	3	2

Note: As multiple countries may exercise the veto on any single draft resolution, the actual number of vetoed resolutions is 210, versus 250 vetoes cast.

their hostility through regional proxies and frustrated Council involvement. The Council's decisions in the 1990s proved highly innovative in shaping the normative framework for international relations, decisively reshaping notions of sovereignty.

SHIFTS IN THE NATURE OF THE COUNCIL'S DECISIONS

Freed from the shackles of the Cold War, the Council moved boldly to address both an ageing and a new generation of internal conflicts. Often frustrated in its aims, it experimented and improvised with much greater resort to coercive measures (sanctions, sanctions enforcement and outright use of force, by UN troops and coalitions of the willing). With the UN more ambitious and very much overextended, it entered into many partnerships, both political and operational, with regional organizations.

The Council's willingness to involve itself in a broad range of internal conflicts—encompassing intercommunal strife; crises of democracy; natural resource wars; and several other precipitating causes or incentives for continuation of war—forced it to confront hostilities of a much more complex nature (e.g., in Angola, Mozambique, Somalia, Bosnia, Kosovo, and East Timor) than the interstate disputes with which it had greater experience. International efforts to mitigate and resolve these conflicts required complex mandates significantly more ambitious than the modalities of 'classic' peacekeeping were designed to meet.[13] The most striking features of 'new generation' peacekeeping operations launched by the Council in the 1990s were not so much the large numbers of military personnel involved—earlier iterations in Sinai and Cyprus had featured large deployments of blue helmets—as the important role and substantive diversity of their civilian and police components.[14]

The new generation of multidisciplinary UN field missions and the need for rapid decision-making in areas of considerable political sensitivity necessitated the deployment of civilian SRSGs, to whom both military and civilian components reported. The civilian functions particularly specific to civil war circumstances mandated by the Council included civil administration (most notably in Namibia, Cambodia, the former Yugoslavia, East Timor, and Kosovo); humanitarian assistance; human rights monitoring and training; police and judicial support, training, and reform; political management often leading to elections; and even a degree of leadership on economic revival and development.[15]

However, the ambitious objectives served by these activities proved difficult to attain in many circumstances. Even Council-mandated military activities encountered significant resistance by shadowy belligerents, leading to incidents involving heavy casualties among peacekeepers and those they were charged to protect (as in Rwanda, Somalia, and the former Yugoslavia). The Council's inability to induce compliance with its decisions fueled two apparently contradictory, but all too frequently complementary, responses: on the one hand, it moved to enforce decisions that had failed to generate consent in the field, notably in the former Yugoslavia, Somalia, and Haiti; on the other, in the face of significant casualties, it cut and ran, as in Somalia and at the outset of genocide in Rwanda.[16]

Enforcement was another field that experienced quantum leaps in thinking and application. Resort to the provisions of Chapter VII of the UN Charter and to the enforcement of Council decisions was not new (e.g., Korea and the Congo). Nevertheless, the extent to which the Council adopted decisions under Chapter VII since 1990 has been wholly unprecedented.

The turning point for the post-Cold War era occurred in the Council's response to the Iraqi invasion of Kuwait in August 1990. The lack of a UN standing army and the scale of the challenge rendered UN peacekeepers inappropriate to the task—peace first had to be enforced—and paved the way for a mandate authorizing the use of force by a coalition of member states after sanctions had failed to induce Iraq's withdrawal from Kuwait. The success of the US-led UN-mandated Operation Desert Storm in January–February 1991, which expelled Iraqi forces from Kuwait, led to an era of euphoria for the Council during which—until reversals in Somalia, Bosnia, and Rwanda sobered it up—it experimented freely with innovative approaches to conflict-resolution, adopting myriad decisions. These included increasingly intrusive and forceful measures in northern Iraq and Somalia, adopted on humanitarian grounds, with far-ranging and long-lasting repercussions.

Thus, from March 1991 and October 1993 (when the deaths of eighteen US soldiers in Somalia seriously undermined prospects for the sustainability of the second UN Operation in Somalia, UNOSOM II), the Council accelerated the pace of its work (185 resolutions, as against 685 over the preceding forty-six years), and launched fifteen new peacekeeping and observer missions (as compared to seventeen in the previous forty-six years of UN history). Even after this 'golden era,' the number of new resolutions and PKOs continued to climb, dwarfing the Cold War period. Contrasting 1946–1986 and 1987–2006 shows that thirteen operations began in the earlier period whereas forty-seven started in the latter.

Through the UN's reversals in Somalia and Bosnia, it became clear to member states that, for the Council, transition from peacekeeping to peace enforcement represented more than 'mission creep.' The two types of operations were fundamentally different, one requiring consent and impartiality, the other requiring international personnel to confront one or several belligerent groups, even if in defense of a Council mandate conceived as neutral relative to the conflicting parties.

Boutros-Ghali concluded by 1994 that the UN should not itself seek to conduct large-scale enforcement activities. Consequently, the Security Council increasingly resorted to 'coalitions of the willing,' such as Operation Uphold Democracy in Haiti (1994), Implementation Force (IFOR) and then Stabilisation Force (SFOR) in Bosnia (1995), the Inter-African Mission to Monitor the Bangui Agreements (MISAB) in the Central African Republic (1997), the International Force for East Timor (INTERFET, 1999), the Kosovo Force (KFOR, 1999), and the International Security Assistance Force (ISAF) in Afghanistan (2002).[17] The Council also alternately both worried about and supported enforcement activities by regional bodies, notably ECOMOG, the Military Observer Group of the Economic Community of West African States, in Liberia and Sierra Leone. One enforcement technique, employed only once previously by the Council, against Rhodesia, was the resort to naval blockades to control access of prohibited goods to regions of conflict. Such blockades were mandated and occurred with varying success against Saddam Hussein's Iraq, various parties in the former Yugoslavia, and the military regime in Haiti.[18]

Council authorization for the use of force continued to be a lightning rod for the international community into the twenty-first century. The Council's refusal to endorse the use of force against Hussein's regime in March 2003 precipitated a crisis of confidence in the policies of those intervening militarily in Iraq, but also in the ability of the Council to manage decisions of war and peace.[19]

Mandatory economic (and, increasingly, diplomatic) sanctions under Chapter VII of the Charter also followed an exponential upward trend, so much so that it came to be known as the 'sanctions decade.'[20] While arms embargoes remained in vogue, imposition of comprehensive trade and other economic sanctions—initially seen as more gentle than the resort to force—faded noticeably once the humanitarian costs of sanctions regimes against Haiti and Iraq became widely known in the late 1990s. The ability of sanctioned governments to enrich themselves by controlling black markets in prohibited products took some time to become apparent. By then, Council members favored more targeted sanctions—such as the ban on air flights to and from Libya aimed at inducing the country's cooperation to address several terrorist aircraft bombings, and diplomatic sanctions, such as those applied against Sudan further to an assassination attempt against Egyptian president Hosni Mubarak.[21]

The difficulty of designing and implementing effective financial sanctions was brought to light by a useful Swiss-sponsored research and dialog initiative, the Interlaken process, in 1998–1999. Canada, while chairing the Council's Sanctions Committee for Angola, pressed for more rigorous application of the committee's mandate to suffocate UNITA's (National Union for the Total Independence of Angola) capacity to fund its war effort through the sale of diamonds. In a related initiative, a commission of experts on sanctions in Angola published a report in March 2000 that was groundbreaking in 'naming and shaming' third countries as 'sanction busters.'[22]

The Council's most famed sanctions committee (established by Council resolution 661 shortly after Iraq's invasion of Kuwait in 1990) illustrates the difficulties of calibrating sweeping sanctions regimes and mitigating their worst humanitarian consequences. The 661 committee had a poor track record in supervising the Oil-for-Food Programme it initiated in Iraq, the failings of which eventually led to the hard-hitting Independent Inquiry Committee chaired by Paul Volcker, which throughout 2005 reported serious shortcomings of the UN Secretariat and of the Council.[23]

A combination of 'systems overload' at the UN in coping with the Council's ambitious agenda in the early 1990s, and the need for meaningful political and operational partners, led the Council to work more closely with regional organizations. In Bosnia, the UN was operating alongside an alphabet soup of European organizations, including the Council of Europe, the Organization for Security and Co-operation in Europe (OSCE), the European Union (EU), and that ultimate military alliance, the North Atlantic Treaty Organization (NATO), a constellation that was largely to form again in Kosovo some years later.

In the Americas, the Council had normally yielded on security challenges to the Organization of American States (OAS).[24] Nevertheless, in circumstances in which the OAS proved incapable of achieving a negotiated settlement alone or in which conflicting parties and affected regional powers displayed greater confidence in the United Nations, such as in Guatemala or Haiti, the Council, sometimes reluctantly, did move to center stage, generally continuing to reserve a place for the OAS in its strategies.[25]

The over-stretched Organization of African Unity (OAU) largely met its Waterloo in the early post-Cold War years, with Africa awash in conflicts. The primary factor precluding effectiveness was a reticence on the part of member states to intrude in the affairs of other states, although the organization itself was prepared to do so.[26] Its relations with the UN were characterized by resentment over its own lack of resources and by justifiable demands that the world body not slough off responsibility for some of the worst conflicts onto an under-resourced and divided regional body. The organization's metamorphosis into the African Union and the formation of a Peace and Security Council have resulted in more robust engagement in Côte d'Ivoire and Darfur, but political will and resources remain inconsistent, underscored by its refusal to address gross human rights violations in Zimbabwe.[27] Many experts believe that subregional organizations such as the Economic Community of West African States (ECOWAS), the Southern African Development Community, and the Intergovernmental Authority on Development hold out more hope for Africa in the security field. They are seen as potentially more cohesive and effective, sometimes benefiting from the leadership of a regional hegemon, such as Nigeria within ECOWAS.[28] The Council has engaged extensively with ECOWAS over Sierra Leone, Liberia, and the Côte d'Ivoire, designing operational partnerships with its military arm, ECOMOG, in each.

In some conflicts, such as those in Georgia and in West Africa, Council-mandated UN missions monitored the activities of regional organizations purportedly keeping or promoting the peace.[29] This proved particularly delicate in Georgia, where peacekeeping forces of the Commonwealth of Independent States (CIS) were seen by a number of Western powers as neither markedly impartial nor deserving treatment that might imply or confer recognition on the CIS as a respectable regional organization.

For the projection of military power, the UN has increasingly turned to partnerships with the two best resourced regional actors, the EU and NATO. Their UN-mandated missions eventually evolved beyond their own geographical spheres, as in the EU-led Opération Artémis in the Bunia province of the Democratic Republic of the Congo in 2003, and the NATO-led ISAF in Afghanistan since 2003.

With the exception of the EU and NATO, regional bodies generally offer even more limited capacities than the United Nations. The Security Council's authority, even if respected too often in the breach, remains important in encouraging regional action.

SHIFTS IN THE DRIVERS OF COUNCIL DECISION-MAKING

During the Cold War, humanitarian concerns (particularly relating to human rights) were often invoked rhetorically in the Council, but they did not much influence the Council's decisions. However, détente among the P-5 coincided with the emergence of the so-called 'CNN Effect' of intense—if highly selective—media scrutiny of horrendous conditions endured by victims of war, impelling populations worldwide to press their governments to alleviate extreme suffering arising from a variety of conflicts. These images, and the reluctance of governments individually to take the lead in addressing these humanitarian crises, led the UN into Bosnia, Somalia, and a range of other conflicts.

The Council's initial rationale for involvement was not only the plight of war-induced refugees but also their impact on neighboring countries.[30] Council preoccupation with refugee issues has a long lineage in UN security annals, not least in the Middle East.[31] However, the widespread acceptance that refugee flows could actually be a major catalyst to conflict, rather than merely an outcome of it, was new.

In the early 1990s, at the peak of media and public fervor for humanitarian initiative, a lively debate unfolded over not only the international right to intervene in the internal affairs of countries to save civilian lives, but also a purported duty to do so. The movement was given scholarly and policy impetus by the findings of the International Commission on Intervention and State Sovereignty (ICISS), whose members inverted the traditional state right to protection from external interference to an internal responsibility for states to protect their own civilians.[32]

Human rights, long cloistered within intergovernmental machinery and Secretariat bureaucracy in part to quarantine the topic from those responsible for international peace and security at the United Nations, burst onto the Security Council's agenda instrumentally with the realization that civil strife was not amenable to negotiated solutions as long as human rights continued to be massively violated. For this reason, the protection, promotion, and monitoring of human rights formed an important part of the mandates of several UN peacekeeping operations, notably in El Salvador and Guatemala.[33] Where this was not the case, as in Rwanda, the UN General Assembly, as part of the broader UN strategy, deployed parallel human rights missions, as it did in Haiti in partnership with the OAS. This tendency to address human rights objectives in Security Council strategies was reinforced by the appointment of activist UN High Commissioners for Human Rights (notably Mary Robinson, Sergio Vieira de Mello, and Louise Arbour).

The quandaries faced in factoring human rights considerations into Council decisions were highlighted when the parties to Sierra Leone's civil war reached a peace agreement in mid-1999 that included sweeping amnesty provisions. Robinson sharply protested (and the UN Secretary-General's representative at the peace pact's signing ceremony registered a formal reservation). On the one hand, Sierra Leone's population was clearly eager for peace on virtually any terms; on the other, the agreement's amnesty provisions patently ran against long-standing and emerging human rights norms. Sierra Leone ultimately convened a Special Court along the lines of those established in Rwanda and Bosnia to prosecute war criminals and salve the national psyche.

The Council's focus on facilitating new and more stable political dispensations in countries emerging from internal violence, *inter alia* by mandating the organization and monitoring of elections, also created an instrumental focus on democratization in the Council's work.[34] Cambodia and Bosnia starkly illustrate that a single election rarely allows a democratic culture to take root. The Council increasingly recognizes that political change requires intensive long-term international support for post-conflict peacebuilding.[35]

The mushrooming of UN electoral activities presented a range of risks for the organization. Countries in need of electoral assistance once were likely to require it again, due to their high level of political tension and the limited degree of administrative and security capacity. In addition, many of the elections observed by UN teams were conducted in adverse circumstances, rendering it difficult to deem them free and fair. Short of massive fraud, UN electoral missions were loath to risk igniting or reigniting civil strife by contesting the results of polling and, consequently, were seen as willing to compromise on principle and as being less than impartial arbiters. Losers were rarely gracious, and the United Nations was little thanked for its prominent role in such electoral processes, frequently alongside regional organizations and nongovernmental teams of eminent persons, such as those associated with former US president Jimmy Carter.[36] And, as demonstrated by the experience of East Timor, where the outcome of a UN-implemented referendum on independence led to a sanguinary rampage by militias in 1999, the United Nations should be careful not to promote elections and referenda in the absence of adequate measures to protect the civilian population against the wrath of those discontent with the results.[37] While the learning curve has been steep, the UN did contribute to the success of Iraqi elections in January 2005, which were critical to the country's painful progress towards self-rule.

The Council has been active longer in addressing terrorism than is widely known.[38] At the conclusion of their first heads-of-state summit meeting on 31 January 1992, leaders 'express[ed] their deep concern over acts of international terrorism and emphasize[d] the need for the international community to deal effectively with all such acts.'[39] Soon thereafter, the Council adopted sanctions against Libya because of its non-cooperation with an investigation into two airline-bombing incidents, a course of action that ultimately led to a trial of Libyan suspects by a Scottish tribunal in the Netherlands. Following an assassination attempt against Egyptian President Mubarak in Ethiopia, diplomatic sanctions against Sudan also were somewhat effective. The Taliban regime was already under Council sanctions at the time of the 11 September 2001 Al Qaeda attacks against US targets because of devastating bombings at US embassies in Kenya and Tanzania.

The 9/11 attacks reinforced the Council's focus on terrorist threats. It adopted sweeping, legislative decisions binding all member states to combat the financing of terrorism and safe havens for terrorists in resolution 1373 immediately after those events. It also created a Counter-Terrorism Committee (CTC) to monitor compliance of all states with its terrorism-related decisions, although the performance of this body has been uneven.

INSTITUTIONAL DEVELOPMENTS
AND PRESSURES

The Council evolved little during the Cold War, with expansion from eleven to fifteen members in 1965. Given the remarkable shifts in international relations since the end of the Cold War, however, the Council has needed to adapt and engage in institutional change, gradually reducing the opacity of its working methods and improving upon its administration and relations with other bodies.

Under intense pressure from member states not serving on the Council—particularly the 'Troop Contributing Nations' (TCNs), which provided personnel and materiel to UN peacekeeping operations, and which were intensely irritated by the Council's working methods—the Council, quite reluctantly, allowed some transparency into its autocratic proceedings in the early 1990s.[40] As a result, a number of measures were adopted to introduce greater clarity into the Council's program of work, and meetings between the Council and TCNs (long resisted by the P-5, which preferred TCNs to meet merely with the Secretariat) started occurring in 1994. The Council also engaged with a number of individuals and organizations through the Arria formula, named for the Venezuelan ambassador who introduced it, of informal meetings to discuss specific issues. More generally, as of the mid-1990s, the Council reached out to a greater extent to non-members and made itself more accessible to observers of various sorts.

A somewhat related development was the emergence of 'groups of friends,' composed of countries influential in a given crisis.[41] Some of these groups, such as that on Haiti, were convened at the invitation of the Secretary-General, while others constituted themselves, with several hybrid varieties emerging. They generally featured one or several permanent members, either formally or in the wings (as was the case with the United States vis-à-vis the group on El Salvador). Their purpose was not only to advise the Secretary-General and Council on strategies to promote settlement of the conflict and implementation of a peace agreement, but also to serve as a potent lobby group vis-à-vis parties to the conflict, regional actors, and the General Assembly. Often, representatives of such groups in the field, or of Security Council members, helped support locally the efforts of the Secretary-General's special representatives, as was the case in Cambodia, Mozambique, and Haiti.

Complaints were sometimes registered that such groups usurped the role of the full Council, and the Secretariat occasionally voiced concern that the Secretary-General was sometimes unhelpfully constrained by them. However, given the vastly increased Council work load, most members saw groups of friends as a useful clearing house.

While early Secretaries-General were fettered by Cold War politics, their successors, starting with Pérez de Cuéllar (whose efforts to end the Iran–Iraq war were brave and productive), have displayed a more activist streak, often spurring the Council into action. Boutros Boutros-Ghali, who took office in early 1992, proved himself a passionate and well-reasoned advocate of a stronger UN role in conflict resolution and post-conflict peacebuilding, launching his seminal *An Agenda for Peace* in mid-1992. However, he was damaged by UN shortcomings in the former Yugoslavia and Somalia. His brittle personality and tone-deafness relative to the US domestic political scene brought him into conflict with several Security Council members, notably the United States, which ultimately vetoed his re-election bid.

Kofi Annan, the first career UN official to hold the position, staked out new ground in championing human rights and concern for civilians in war as key themes, both highly relevant to the Council's agenda at the turn of the century. His advocacy of humanitarian intervention was articulated most unambiguously in a speech to the UN General Assembly on 20 September 1999.[42] He was hailed early on by many as the second coming of Hammarskjöld, but Washington clashed with him over Kosovo in 1999, and more seriously over Iraq from 1998 onwards. Management shortcomings, peacekeeping sex scandals, and the Oil-for-Food debacle—which implicated his son—have taken their toll and proved a challenge for his unassuming, non-confrontational approach.[43]

The Council's impact on the development of international criminal law has been dramatic, notably through its creation of ad hoc international criminal tribunals for the former Yugoslavia in 1993 and Rwanda in 1994 to bring to justice those responsible for war crimes, crimes against humanity, and genocide. The foremost champion of these tribunals was the United States (possibly because of frustration over its own inability at the time to influence the course of events on the ground in the former Yugoslavia due to sharp policy differences with European allies and guilt over its refusal to confront genocide in Rwanda). In a similar mold, as previously noted, the Special Court for Sierra Leone, a joint Sierra Leone–UN enterprise, was convened in 2002, and a hybrid tribunal was agreed between the UN and the government in Phnom Penh in 2005 to try leaders of the former Khmer Rouge regime in Cambodia.

The creation of tribunals greatly intensified pressures for a permanent International Criminal Court with universal jurisdiction, but when a statute for this court was adopted in Rome in 1998, many of the P-5 balked.[44] While the UK and France have become states parties, Russia has yet to ratify, and the US and China largely oppose the Court. Its statute envisages a complex relationship with the Security Council. An illustration of the links between the two institutions arose in March 2005, when the Security Council referred to the ICC the situation in Darfur, notably individual responsibility for war crimes. US efforts to exempt Americans from ICC jurisdiction, initially successful, collapsed in 2004 amidst controversy over treatment of Iraqi prisoners in Baghdad's Abu Ghraib prison.[45]

During much of the Cold War, nongovernmental organizations (NGOs) operated on the periphery of the UN system, and few dealt specifically with security matters. NGOs have for many years been accredited by the lesser-known ECOSOC to monitor and contribute to UN activity in a broad range of fields, including on environmental, human rights, humanitarian, health, labor, education, and population issues.

The role and interaction of NGOs with respect to the Security Council both grew significantly and evolved in nature during the 1990s.[46] Increasingly, conflicts, particularly of an internal nature, were seen as featuring economic and social causes as well as effects. For this reason, *inter alia*, relevant NGOs clamored for access to the Council. The role of NGOs as major partners for the United Nations in humanitarian operations, the success of many NGO programs in the field, the mandate of the Secretariat's Department of Humanitarian Affairs to offer coordination services to NGOs as well as official agencies, the mediagenic nature of NGO activity, and a rapidly developing interest of governments in interaction with civil society all conspired to encourage the Council to display greater openness to NGO views and more generous recognition of their achievements.

In 1996, the Chilean president of the Council noted that the body recognized 'that those who are keeping overall stability and security in Somalia are the humanitarian organizations.'[47] Since the mid-1990s, the Council members have been interacting intensively, if informally, with an NGO Working Group comprised of roughly thirty institutions focused on varying issues.[48] While some question the sincerity of Council members in engaging in these exchanges, the achievement of genuine access and the growing recognition of NGOs as significant and mostly constructive contributors to international peace and security marked a new departure for the Council in its relations with actors beyond governments and intergovernmental bodies.

While the dichotomy between East and West has largely disappeared at the UN (at least in a structural sense), North–South divisions color many transactions and have occasionally undermined the UN's effectiveness. Neither camp is monolithic, however: the rich Northern countries liaise and assemble informally in ad hoc, mutable, and often fragile groupings, often with the United States or the European Union at the helm. The developing South organized in the 1960s into two formal bodies, the trade-oriented Group of 77 (G-77) (now with 132 members) and the more geopolitical Non-Aligned Movement (NAM), with leading countries in Cuba, Algeria, Egypt, and Pakistan (India and China play subtler, often independent games). Solidarity with G-77 and NAM positions wavers, as the challenges and dilemmas facing Chile or Malaysia are hardly the same as those for Mali.

The increased activism of the Security Council in the 1990s—its willingness to intrude on the internal affairs of member states and the broader range of issues that it deemed threats to international peace and security—created a degree of nervousness within the NAM. For instance, the Security Council-endorsed *Report of the Panel on United Nations Peace Operations* (the Brahimi report) of 2000, which recommended more robust peacekeeping mandates and a strategic analysis unit, was viewed with suspicion by some countries of the South, fearful of UN espionage. In another example, Western countries clearly felt justified in the NATO campaign over Kosovo in 1999, a position implicitly endorsed by Annan, but emphatically rejected by the president of Algeria, Abdelaziz Bouteflika, who reiterated the view that sovereignty remained the most prized possession of often defenseless developing countries.[49]

Industrialized countries, particularly the United States, have often clashed in the Security Council with NAM members over the Middle East, accounting for the majority of vetoes since 1990. However, the North–South dynamic can also be cooperative, as on security issues pertaining to Sierra Leone, Haiti, and Afghanistan. Overall, the North–South divide at the UN is less evident in the Security Council than in any other major UN deliberative or decision-making body, one factor in the Council's (relative) effectiveness compared to that of the General Assembly or ECOSOC.

REFORM OF THE SECURITY COUNCIL

Reform of the Security Council has long been an issue, and pressure for reform has sprung from several sources.[50] The Council's activism in the early 1990s made it a more valuable place to sit. The hermetic nature of its working methods drew greater attention at a time when its decisions were proving genuinely important. In an era marked by P-5 cooperation and a tendency to impose decisions on the remainder of the Council, resentment of the permanent members grew. However, widespread envy over their veto power was somewhat paradoxical since the veto was so little used during the 1990s (see Table 6.1).

In 1993, key member states launched consultations on how to proceed with a reform agenda encompassing working methods, the veto, and composition of the Council. As outlined above, working methods and relations with non-Council members (including NGOs) subsequently evolved considerably. Discussion of the veto revealed not only broad understanding of why it had been necessary during the Cold War, but also confirmation that it was now widely disliked. It was clear, however, that the existing P-5 members would not willingly give up their vetoes and could not be compelled to do so under Charter provisions. For this reason, debate focused more on whether new permanent seats should be created and, if so, whether they should be granted vetoes. In 2005, drawing on the report of the HLP, this debate eventually revolved around an attempt by Germany, Japan, India, and Brazil to secure permanent seats for themselves, which failed given strong opposition from China and a number of other member states and, to a lesser extent, from the United States and Russia. The debate proved highly contentious, crystallizing a view that a seat in the Security Council can be a proxy for global influence on peace and security issues.[51]

THE UNITED STATES AND THE COUNCIL

The major challenge facing the Council by 2005 was the parlous state of relations between the United States and the United Nations. US complaints against the UN's activism and apathy, cumbersome bureaucracy, lack of accountability, corruption, and mismanagement, primarily when manifested in opposition to the realization of American interests, have become a given in international relations, whichever party controls the White House and Congress.

The Clinton administration, initially keen on Madeleine Albright's idea of 'assertive multilateralism,' soon displayed an instinctive penchant for UN-bashing whenever in a tight spot, notably following the death of US troops in Mogadishu on 4 October 1993. Washington further attacked the UN for purported appeasement of the Iraqi regime in 1998. Failures in Rwanda and Bosnia resulted in disaffection with the UN's abilities, and hold-backs on US financial contributions to the UN throughout the mid- and late-1990s hobbled US–UN relations. The rhetoric of displeasure intensified after the Security Council withheld approval of the Bush administration's plan for military action against Saddam Hussein in March 2003. By mid-2005, Washington was again threatening to withhold US dues to the UN.[52]

Nevertheless, the Council remains useful to Washington in its advancement of American interests as its joint action with France on both Lebanon and Haiti in 2004 illustrated. Further, where US interests are little engaged, the UN is best placed from Washington's perspective to address 'orphan' conflicts, such as those of Sierra Leone, Liberia, and Côte d'Ivoire. Ultimately it is the view that only the Security Council can authorize the use of force that grates on many in Washington. Had the United States been able to secure a Council mandate for military intervention in Iraq in 2003, there is little doubt that the financial and military costs would have been shared much more broadly internationally, something American policymakers will want to bear in mind in the future.

CONCLUSION

The Council's withholding of approval for Operation Iraqi Freedom in March 2003, and the subsequent marginalization of the UN's role in Iraq, compounded by the bombing of UN headquarters in Baghdad in August 2003, generated a crisis of confidence in the UN, both internal and in terms of its global credibility. The deadlock in the Security Council over Iraq was, as Michael Doyle notes, both

a massive disappointment and a surprising relief. It disappointed all hopes that this essential international forum for multilateral policy could achieve a viable policy. At the same time, it demonstrated to the surprise of many that it would not let itself be bullied or bribed by any power, permanent or even hyper. The so far unanswered question is: Can it meet the challenge of keeping intact its integrity while improving its effectiveness?[53]

The Council has played an important role in confronting crises in Africa and in mobilizing resources to address them. It has also helped develop political strategies for Kosovo, East Timor, and Afghanistan that contained potentially dangerous crises and avoided excessive polarization among regional and global powers. But it has yet to demonstrate that, in Jeremy Greenstock's words, it can be 'effective on the hardest issues.'[54] The failure of the 2005 UN World Summit to produce any meaningful agreement among UN member states on values and principles to guide future UN action on security challenges, and the stinging Volcker report into oversight failures regarding the Oil-for-Food Programme in Iraq, leaves the Council's future clouded by an insufficient degree of common purpose, a growing sense of international disenchantment with its decisions, and doubt over its political legitimacy.

Nonetheless, while the future is uncertain, cumulatively the Council's decisions in the post-Cold War era have proved immensely influential, indeed transformative, on a normative level. By asserting the UN's responsibility to intervene, even in internal conflicts—where human rights and the humanitarian interests of populations are severely affected—Council decisions, arising from evolving interpretations of the Charter, have deeply affected the meaning of sovereignty at the international level. This is no small legacy for the Council in the post-Cold War era.

Notes

1. David M. Malone, 'Eyes on the Prize,' *Global Governance* 6, no. 1 (2000), 3–23.
2. For an excellent, concise analysis of the Council's functions and prospects, see Edward C. Luck, *The UN Security Council: Practice and Promise* (New York: Routledge, 2006).
3. Sydney D. Bailey and Sam Daws, *The Procedure of the UN Security Council*, 3rd edn. (Oxford: Clarendon Press, 1998), 296.
4. Edith M. Lederer, 'U.N. Launches Initiative on Economic Rehabilitation for Haiti,' *Associated Press Newswires*, 13 May 1999.
5. *Report of the Ad Hoc Advisory Group on Guinea-Bissau*, UN Document E/2003/8, 10 January 2003.
6. *A More Secure World: Our Shared Responsibility: Report of the High-level Panel on Threats, Challenges and Change*, UN document A/59/565, 2 December 2004.
7. Simon Chesterman, 'Virtual Trusteeship: Security Council Authorizations of Transitional Administrations,' in *The UN Security Council: From the Cold War to the 21st Century*, ed. David M. Malone (Boulder, Colo.: Lynne Rienner, 2004), 219–233.
8. Bailey and Daws, *The Procedure of the UN Security Council*, 110–111, 113, 114–116.
9. Ibid., 307.

10. Paul Lewis, 'World Court Supports Nicaragua After US Rejected Judges' Role,' *New York Times*, 28 June 1986, 1. See also S/18250 (1986) and Bailey and Daws, *The Procedure of the UN Security Council*, 317. On Libya, see David Ott, 'Libya and the ICJ: Clipping the Security Council's Wings,' *Middle East International*, 13 March 1998, 18.

11. Dapo Akande, 'The International Court of Justice and the Security Council: Is There Room for Judicial Control of Decisions of the Political Organs of the United Nations?' *International and Comparative Law Quarterly* 46 (1997): 309–343.

12. UN Press Release SG/SM/3956, 13 January 1987.

13. Thomas G. Weiss, David P. Forsythe, Roger A. Coate and Kelly-Kate Pease, *The United Nations and Changing World Politics*, 5th edn. (Boulder, Colo.: Westview Press, 2007), chs. 1–4.

14. Michael C. Williams, *Civil–Military Relations and Peacekeeping* (Adelphi Papers, No. 321, 1998).

15. Steven R. Ratner, *The New UN Peacekeeping: Building Peace in Lands of Conflict After the Cold War* (New York: St. Martin's Press, 1995).

16. Adam Roberts, 'Communal Conflict as a Challenge to International Organization: The Case of Former Yugoslavia,' *Review Of International Studies* 21 (1995): 389–410; John L. Hirsch and Robert B. Oakley, *Somalia and Operation Restore Hope: Reflections on Peacemaking and Peacekeeping* (Washington, DC: United States Institute of Peace Press, 1995), 111, 116–117; David M. Malone, *Decision-Making in the Security Council: The Case of Haiti, 1990–1997* (Oxford: Clarendon Press, 1998); Gérard Prunier, *The Rwanda Crisis: History of a Genocide* (New York: Columbia University Press, 1995).

17. For an excellent reference work, see Oliver Ramsbotham and Tom Woodhouse, *Encyclopedia of International Peacekeeping Operations* (Santa Barbara, Calif.: ABC-CLIO, 1999).

18. UN Department of Political Affairs, *A Brief Overview of Security Council Applied Sanctions–Smart Sanctions, The Next Step: Arms Embargoes and Travel Sanctions*, Second Expert Seminar, Berlin, 3–5 December 2000.

19. David M. Malone, *The International Struggle for Iraq: Politics in the UN Security Council, 1980–2005* (Oxford: Oxford University Press, 2006), 185–221.

20. David Cortright and George A. Lopez, *The Sanctions Decade: Assessing UN Strategies in the 1990s* (Boulder, Colo.: Lynne Rienner, 2000); see also their *Sanctions and the Search for Security: Challenges to UN Action* (Boulder, Colo.: Lynne Rienner, 2002).

21. Daniel W. Drezner, *The Sanctions Paradox: Economic Statecraft and International Relations* (Cambridge: Cambridge University Press, 1999), 4–6.

22. *Report of the Panel of Experts on Violations of Security Council Sanctions Against UNITA*, UN document S/2000/203, 10 March 2000.

23. UN document SG/A/871, 21 April 2004. For the Independent Inquiry Committee's findings, see www.iic-offp.org.

24. David M. Malone, 'Haiti and the International Community: A Case Study,' *Survival* (Summer 1997): 126, 129.

25. William G. O'Neill, 'Human Rights Monitoring vs. Political Expediency: The Experience of the OAS/UN Mission in Haiti,' *Harvard Human Rights Journal* 8 (1995): 101, 104.

26. Salim Ahmed Salim, 'The OAU Role in Conflict Management,' in *Peacemaking and Peacekeeping for the New Century*, ed. Olara A. Otunnu and Michael W. Doyle (Lanham, Md.: Rowman & Littlefield Publishers, 1998).

27. 'Africa rejects action on Zimbabwe,' *BBC News*, 24 June 2005.

28. Adekeye Adebajo and Ismail Rashid, eds., *West Africa's Security Challenges: Building Peace in a Troubled Region* (Boulder, Colo.: Lynne Rienner Publishers, 2004).

29. Shepard Forman and Andrew Grene, 'Collaborating with Regional Organizations,' in *The UN Security Council: From the Cold War to the 21st Century*, ed. David M. Malone (Boulder, Colo.: Lynne Rienner, 2004), 295–310.

30. UN Document S/23069, 25 September 1991.

31. Weiss et al., *The United Nations and Changing World Politics*, 188.

32. Jonathan Moore, ed., *Hard Choices: Moral Dilemmas in Humanitarian Intervention* (Lanham, Md.: Rowman & Littlefield, 1998); and *The Responsibility to Protect: Report of the International Commission on Intervention and State Sovereignty* (Ottawa: International Development Research Centre, 2001).

33. Ian Johnstone, 'Rights and Reconciliation in El Salvador,' in *Keeping The Peace: Multidimensional UN Operations In Cambodia And El Salvador*, ed. Michael W. Doyle et al. (New York: Cambridge University Press, 1997), 312.

34. Ratner, *The New UN Peacekeeping*, 117–134.

35. Unexpected fresh outbreaks of violence in East Timor in 2006, after the UN's presence there was reduced, served as a reminder to the Council of the need for long-term engagement with post-conflict countries.

36. Krishna Kumar, ed., *Postconflict Elections, Democratization, and International Assistance* (Boulder, Colo.: Lynne Rienner, 1998).

37. Ian Martin, *Self-Determination in East Timor: The United Nations, the Ballot, and International Intervention* (Boulder, Colo.: Lynne Rienner Publishers, 2001), 87–102.

38. Chantal de Jonge Oudraat, 'The UN and Terrorism: The Role of the UN Security Council,' in *Terrorism and the UN: Before and After September 11*, ed. Jane Boulden and Thomas G. Weiss (Bloomington: Indiana University Press, 2004), 151–172.

39. UN document S/23500, 31 January 1992, 3.

40. Bailey and Daws, *The Procedure of the UN Security Council*; see also Susan C. Hulton, 'Council Working Methods and Procedures,' in *The UN Security Council: From the Cold War to the 21st Century*, ed. David M. Malone (Boulder, Colo.: Lynne Rienner, 2004), 237–252.

41. Teresa Whitfield, 'Groups of Friends,' in *The UN Security Council: From the Cold War to the 21st Century*, ed. David M. Malone (Boulder, Colo.: Lynne Rienner, 2004), 311–324.

42. Kofi Annan, 'Two Concepts of Sovereignty,' *Economist*, 18 September 1999, 49.

43. See James Traub's fine *The Best Intentions: Kofi Annan and the UN in the Era of American World Power* (New York: Farrar, Strauss, and Giroux, 2006).

44. Alessandra Stanley, 'US Dissents, but Accord Is Reached on War-Crime Court,' *New York Times*, 18 July 1998, 3.

45. Warren Hoge, 'US Drops Plan to Exempt G.I.s from U.N. Court,' *New York Times*, 24 June 2004, 1.

46. See James A. Paul, 'Working with Nongovernmental Organizations,' in *The UN Security Council: From the Cold War to the 21st Century*, ed. David M. Malone (Boulder, Colo.: Lynne Rienner, 2004), 373–390.

47. Juan Somavía, 'Civil Society and the Security Council,' Remarks to the NGO Working Group on the Security Council, Global Policy Forum, 29 April 1996, www.globalpolicy.org/security/docs/somavia.htm.

48. See James A. Paul, 'A Short History of the NGO Working Group on the Security Council,' Global Policy Forum, April 2001, www.globalpolicy.org.

49. UN document A/54/PV.4, 20 September 1999.

50. Bardo Fassbender, 'Pressure for Security Council Reform,' in *The UN Security Council: From the Cold War to the 21st Century*, ed. David M. Malone (Boulder, Colo.: Lynne Rienner, 2004), 341–56; see also Thomas G. Weiss and Karen E. Young, 'Security Council Reform?' *Security Dialogue* 36, no. 2 (2005): 131–154.

51. David M. Malone, 'The High-level Panel and Security Council Reform,' *Security Dialogue* 36, no. 3 (2005): 370–372; *American Interests and UN Reform: Report of the Task Force on the United Nations* (Washington, DC: United States Institute of Peace, 2005).

52. Caroline Daniel and Scott Heiserin, 'House votes to cut dues to UN over reforms,' *Financial Times Online*, 17 June 2005.

53. David M. Malone, 'Conclusion,' in *The UN Security Council: From the Cold War to the 21st Century*, ed. David M. Malone (Boulder, Colo.: Lynne Rienner, 2004), 644.

54. Interview with the author, 25 January 2003.

CHAPTER 7

ECONOMIC AND SOCIAL COUNCIL

GERT ROSENTHAL

THE Economic and Social Council (ECOSOC) is one of the six principal organs of the United Nations. Charter Article 62 gives ECOSOC a remit in two broad areas: economic and social matters ('international economic, social, cultural, educational, health and related matters') and human rights ('human rights and fundamental freedoms for all').[1]

In economic and social matters, the Charter assigns several functions to ECOSOC as a forum: reflection on issues ('make or initiate studies and reports'); advocacy and policy formulation ('make recommendations'); normative purposes ('prepare draft conventions'); and combinations of these functions, among other means, by convening conferences.

Under Charter Articles 57, 58, 63, and 64, ECOSOC is charged with the coordination of the activities of the specialized agencies, presumably—although it is not spelled out explicitly—to bring greater coherence to the work of the United Nations system as a whole. This role is to be carried out through consulting with specialized agencies and making recommendations to the General Assembly and to member states as well as through the receipt of regular reports from the specialized agencies. Article 66 also gives member states the ability to task ECOSOC with other general functions under its remit.

A final and important ECOSOC function consists of interacting with representatives of nongovernmental organizations (NGOs), in its role as their main 'portal of entry' to the United Nations.[2] Over the years the mandate contained in Article 71—the Council 'may make suitable arrangements for consultation with nongovernmental organizations'—has embraced a wide spectrum of nongovernmental entities, including the business sector.

ECOSOC has an array of subsidiary bodies, which primarily deal with specialized matters. The authority to create these bodies is contained in Article 68 of the Charter, but most of the relevant legislation appears in the Rules of Procedure, especially 24–27. Thus, an additional function is to offer oversight and coordinate its wide-ranging subsidiary machinery—some of the subsidiary bodies in turn have their own ancillary bodies—offering policy guidance and making use of the considerable expertise under its general purview. Table 7.1 lists the main subsidiary bodies, most of which are made

Table 7.1 Main subsidiary bodies of ECOSOC

Subsidiary bodies	Year established	Membership	Ancillary bodies
Functional commissions			
Statistical Commission	1946	24	No
Population and Development	1946	47	No
Social Development	1946	46	No
On the Status of Women	1946	45	No
Narcotic Drugs	1946	53	Yes
Crime Prevention and Criminal Justice	1991	40	No
Science and Technology for Development	1992	33	Yes
Sustainable Development	1993	53	Yes
Forum on Forests	2000	universal	
Ad hoc open-ended working groups			
Intergovernmental Group of Experts on Energy and Sustainable Development	2001	universal	No
Working Group on Informatics	2000	universal	
Expert bodies composed of governmental experts			
Committee on the Transport of Dangerous Goods and on the Globally Harmonized System of Classification and Labeling of Chemicals	1999	33	Yes
Group on Geographical Names	1959	22	No
Expert bodies composed of experts in their personal capacity			
Committee for Development Policy	1996	34	No
Committee on Public Administration	1967	24	No
Ad Hoc Group on International Cooperation in Tax Matters	1967	25	No
Committee on Economic, Social and Cultural Rights	1976	18	No
Permanent Forum on Indigenous Issues	2000	16	No
ECOSOC standing committees			
Programme and Coordination	1962	34	No
On Non-Governmental Organizations	1946	19	No
Negotiations with Intergovernmental Agencies	1946	ad hoc	No
Other related bodies			
Intl. Narcotics Control Board	1966	13	No
Board of Trustees INSTRAW	1983	11	No

up of member states elected by ECOSOC (that being the case for the functional commissions and the standing committees), but some of which are made up of independent or government-appointed experts. In addition, the five regional commissions also fall under ECOSOC's purview,[3] as do several ad hoc working groups, including groups on African countries emerging from conflict.[4]

ECOSOC traditionally addressed its second major area of remit, human rights, through interactions with one of its subsidiary bodies, the Commission on Human Rights (CHR), whose functions were transferred to the Human Rights Council in June 2006 after the General Assembly's March 2006 decision in resolution 60/251. From its establishment in 1946 until its abolition in 2006, ECOSOC had elected the CHR's members and received and acted upon its reports.

Since the 1990s, ECOSOC has assumed a complementary role to the General Assembly in the follow-up to major UN conferences in the economic and social spheres,[5] and particularly in the follow-up to the 2002 International Conference on Financing for Development. ECOSOC's yearly spring meeting with the Bretton Woods institutions and the Word Trade Organization was designated in the 'Monterrey Consensus'—the declaration produced by the conference—as part of the follow-up process devoted to moving the Monterrey process forward.[6]

ECOSOC has a membership of fifty-four member states, elected by the General Assembly for three-year terms. The members elect their own bureau every year, comprising a president and four vice-presidents.[7] Formal actions are taken through either decisions or resolutions, most of which are approved by consensus, but some of which are submitted to a vote, where a simple majority according to Charter Article 67 is needed for approval. ECOSOC's decisions and resolutions are not binding on member states, or even on the specialized agencies. Thus, all the functions outlined are indicative of its powerlessness. Still, many of the deliberations—which have an intrinsic value for those that participate in them—and formal decisions and resolutions have helped raise public awareness of emerging development issues and have influenced policymaking within the UN system and at the national level.[8]

A difficulty in characterizing ECOSOC's functions is found in its ambiguous relationship with the General Assembly. Chapter IX of the Charter, which spells out the role of the UN in 'International Economic and Social Co-operation', indicates in Article 60 that 'Responsibility for the discharge of the functions of the Organization set forth in this Chapter shall be vested in the General Assembly and, under the authority of the General Assembly, in the Economic and Social Council.' This raises the vexing problem of the respective responsibilities of these two principal organs in the economic and social sectors. ECOSOC's relationship with the Security Council is spelled out in Article 65: ECOSOC 'may furnish information to the Security Council and shall assist the Security Council upon its request.' Similarly sparse references are made to its relations with the other principal organs: the Trusteeship Council (Article 91), the International Court of Justice (Article 96 (2)), and the Secretariat (Articles 98 and 101).

ECOSOC's working methods have been shaped by its Rules of Procedure and by a series of important resolutions adopted by the General Assembly.[9] Since 1990

ECOSOC's own initiatives include improving the organization of its work, into high-level, coordination, operational activities, and humanitarian segments. Innovations have included organizing round tables of experts and nongovernmental organizations prior to the high-level and coordination segments to help inform intergovernmental deliberations.

Typically, an ECOSOC organizational session is held at the beginning of the year, and a substantive session in late summer. The substantive session normally begins with a review of the current status and trends in the international economy, and is then followed by an agenda divided into five segments: high-level, coordination, operational activities, humanitarian, and general. The analytical and advocacy functions come to the fore during the high-level segment, while the other segments are a mix of coordination and oversight functions. Normally, ECOSOC is convened for several resumed substantive sessions in the late autumn. In addition, there is a second organizational session to elect the members of the subsidiary bodies, and a joint meeting in the spring with the Bretton Woods institutions and the WTO, to which the UN Conference on Trade and Development (UNCTAD) was subsequently added. The meeting with the Bretton Woods institutions was initiated in 1998 as a dialogue between the attending institutions (at both the intergovernmental and management levels), but has now also become a centerpiece of follow-up activities of the International Conference on Financing for Development.

Most of the Secretariat's support to ECOSOC is provided by the Office of ECOSOC Support and Coordination, which is part of the Department of Economic and Social Affairs (DESA). However, part of the substantive backstopping originates in other divisions of DESA, the secretariats of the regional commissions, and even UNCTAD.

History and Development of ECOSOC

The Dumbarton Oaks proposals drafted in 1944 by the Allies emerging from World War II embraced the idea that the United Nations should be involved in economic and social cooperation. The UN's role was to be part of a wider international machinery including the International Bank for Reconstruction and Development (IBRD), the International Monetary Fund (IMF), and an International Trade Organization (which never came to fruition but negotiations led to the General Agreement on Trade and Tariffs, GATT). Dumbarton Oaks also recognized the conceptual link between peace and security and economic well-being. Although the proposals posited the creation of a UN economic and social council as a subsidiary body of the General Assembly, ECOSOC later emerged from the 1945 United Nations Conference on International Organization in San Francisco as a principal organ, in recognition of the importance of economic and social cooperation and the priority attached to economic reconstruction.[10]

However, the original intention of making the Council a subsidiary body of the General Assembly endured in parts of the Charter, introducing ambiguities that have affected the Council's work ever since. For example, Article 13 not only assigns the General Assembly certain functions that virtually duplicate those that Article 62 assigns to ECOSOC, but also, together with Article 60, clearly places the Council under the authority of the General Assembly. On the other hand, Article 7 elevates ECOSOC to the category of a principal organ, which suggests that it is not subject to the authority of any other UN organ (unless, of course, the Charter expressly provides otherwise).

Another issue that has further complicated the relations between the two organs is that the General Assembly (and its Second and Third Committees) are universal bodies, whose legitimacy tends to be viewed by many states as superior to that of the intergovernmental bodies with a more limited membership. Perhaps for this reason, the trend in ECOSOC has been toward a larger membership with frequent calls to 'universalize' its membership. Indeed, ECOSOC was originally composed of eighteen members; a number that was expanded to twenty-seven in 1965, and to the present fifty-four in 1973.[11]

Some UN observers hold that ECOSOC was established to provide a global policy coordination framework, arguing, for example, that the 'founding governments [of the United Nations] intended ECOSOC to be the 'economic security council' that is now mooted, fifty years later, as some sort of additional body.' This observation is based on an interpretation of the responsibilities assigned to some of ECOSOC's subsidiary bodies, and particularly to the now defunct Economic and Employment Commission. However, the same observers recognized that 'within a few years full employment ceased to be a regular Council agenda item. In the same years the separation of the Bretton Woods institutions was consolidated. The long process of diverting the United Nations away from macro-economic policy formulation and into development assistance had begun.'[12]

A close reading of the Charter suggests that ECOSOC was never intended to be the center of global policy coordination. Rather, the main powers emerging from World War II preferred to concentrate global policymaking in organizations that reflected their weight in world affairs. The right to exert a veto in the Security Council provided such a UN mechanism in the area of peace and security, while in the area of economic policymaking the weighted voting arrangements at the Bretton Woods institutions made the World Bank and the IMF far more attractive alternatives to the UN General Assembly and ECOSOC, where each sovereign state has one vote.

Some observers have suggested that ECOSOC's influence has waned over time.[13] Others point out that the forum never exercised much influence. For example, Walter R. Sharp undertook an in-depth study on the work of ECOSOC during its thirty-sixth session in 1963 and its forty-third session in 1967. He explored the various activities of ECOSOC and reached the conclusion that 'it is only too easy to be pessimistic concerning the Council's future utility.'[14] However, there is little doubt that the enthusiasm— even the mystique—of ECOSOC's early years (the late 1940s and early 1950s), combined with a manageable membership of eighteen members, made its proceedings more agile and less bureaucratic than has been the case in more recent times.[15]

ECOSOC, at least up to 2005, has changed little since the 1950s and 1960s. Similarities can be found in the agendas, the level of representation, the tone of the discussion reflected in the official records, the capacity to engage with the specialized agencies, the degree of participation of NGOs, the quality of coordination of ECOSOC's subsidiary bodies, and the content of the decisions and resolutions adopted. Thus, the official records suggest that an idealized ECOSOC that offered clear policy guidance and coordinated the many fractious parts of the United Nations never existed. While it has had successes over the years, the Council has not been able either to resolve its ambiguous relationship with the General Assembly or to consistently put its role and functions into clearer focus.[16]

Equally, ECOSOC has had difficulty in fulfilling its role in coordinating the specialized agencies, or even in offering oversight to its subsidiary bodies. This is due, in part, to the interests of the framers of the Charter that the structure of the UN system be decentralized. Consequently, many parts of the system have their own intergovernmental machinery, their own constituency, their own institutional agenda, and their own bureaucratic culture. The specialized agencies and ECOSOC's subsidiary bodies tend to give lip service to the goal of coordination under the banner of the United Nations while fiercely resisting subordinating their own agendas for the greater good of the organization.

ECOSOC has thus been beset with some serious problems since its inception. The General Assembly encroaches on its role of fostering policy debate, while the Security Council encroaches on its role in the development aspects of post-conflict peace-building. This leaves ECOSOC occupying an ill-defined 'middle-ground' where its most important single mandate has been fostering coordination and cooperation of the component parts of the UN system that strongly resist being the objects of such coordination.

STRENGTHS AND WEAKNESSES

The Economic and Social Council is the principal organ that has most frequently come under criticism for a perceived lack of effectiveness. ECOSOC is further weakened by virtue of the fact that the key domestic actors in member states in the economic policymaking arena tend to gravitate towards the international financial institutions (IFIs) rather than the United Nations. There is, therefore, a 'disconnect' between ECOSOC's policy prescriptions and those actors at the national level to whom those prescriptions are presumably addressed. The situation is less stark in the arena of social policy and certain specialized areas, such as statistics, the environment, the advancement of women, and demographic issues, where the United Nations shows considerable capacity to convene national actors.

ECOSOC's shortcomings are enumerated in the reports of a number of independent panels. In 1988 the United Nations Association of the United States sponsored a blue-ribbon panel to identify ways of improving the UN's effectiveness. A familiar diagnosis appears in the report when it states that 'a comparison of the agendas of ECOSOC, the Second Committee of the General Assembly and the Trade and Development Board shows that very often the same topics are addressed without any real difference of approach.' To address this matter, a 'vision for change' was proposed, which included defining common objectives, streamlining the existing machinery, and searching for a common approach at the intergovernmental level.[17]

A new wave of reports appeared in the 1990s. First, in the UN Development Programme's (UNDP's) *Human Development Report 1992*, Mahbub ul Haq proposed replacing ECOSOC, which he deemed 'too large and unwieldy,'[18] with a Development Security Council tasked with designing a global policy framework in all key economic and social areas, providing a policy coordination framework, and preparing a global budget of development resource flows. Second, an independent working group sponsored by the Ford Foundation observed that 'over time, the membership of ECOSOC has become too large to be effective. It has never been able to perform its coordinating role.... There has been no lack of proposed remedies, but none has improved matters.'[19] Consequently, the abolition of ECOSOC and its replacement by two smaller and more authoritative bodies—an Economic Council and a Social Council—was proposed.

Third, the Commission on Global Governance allocated a chapter of its report to reforming the United Nations, with a special section dedicated to the Economic and Social Council. Commission members stated, 'the UN, and in particular ECOSOC, has fallen far short of its envisaged role of co-ordination and overall direction in the economic and social fields. This is partly because this role is still being contested nearly fifty years after San Francisco, despite the clear intent of the Charter.' Under the heading 'The time has come to retire ECOSOC,' the commission recommended the creation of a new Economic Security Council and, in effect, the universalization of ECOSOC so that it could be merged with the Second and Third Committees of the General Assembly. The commission ended its analysis with this lapidary statement: 'Fifty years is long enough to know what works and what does not work within any system. ECOSOC has not worked.'[20]

Fourth, in 1991 the Nordic Countries published a series of reports between 1991 and 1996 offering a 'Nordic Perspective on UN Reform Issues in the Economic and Social Sectors.' Far from proposing ECOSOC's demise, the second report proposed strengthening its role as a coordinator (of the various parts of the system and of its subsidiary bodies) and suggested a significant role in the coordinated follow-up of global conferences. It also suggested convening ECOSOC whenever necessary to address 'urgent developments in the economic, social and related fields that may require guidance and coordination by the Council.' However, for the sake of a better division of labor between the various governing bodies, the report recommended concentrating the role of policymaking and guidance in the General Assembly.[21]

Fifth, in 1996 the South Centre prepared a proposal on UN reform, which argued for a strong economic role for the United Nations:

The United Nations must be allowed to assume the full range of powers and functions provided for it in the UN Charter, enabling all members of the world community to participate and to defend their interest in the field of socio-economic affairs. . . . In particular, ECOSOC and UNCTAD require protection against forced erosion from within, as well as from demands for their outright abolition. Their stature at the intergovernmental and secretariat levels must be enhanced through a series of concrete measures aimed at boosting their policy-making, negotiating and research functions.[22]

Finally, Erskine Childers and Brian Urquhart prepared a series of studies between 1991 and 1994, in which they supported the notion of enhancing ECOSOC as a forum for policymaking and orientation. They argued, 'the lack of engagement of agencies in the work of the UN as a centerpiece of the system is perennially reinforced by the fact that Ministers of Agriculture only talk to each other in Rome, Ministers of Health in Geneva, Ministers of Industry in Vienna, Ministers of Finance in Washington, Ministers of Foreign Affairs in New York, and so on.' They went on to propose that the General Assembly should recommend to ECOSOC that it include in its agenda each year a high-level theme meeting at which the delegations to the Council should be led by their governments' ministers of the relevant sector.[23]

In spite of the abundant criticisms, many of ECOSOC's activities over the years have been reasonably effective. These include efforts to streamline and improve ECOSOC's working methods, introduce greater coherence in the activities of the different intergovernmental bodies, and adapt its agenda to changing circumstances. For example, the scope of ECOSOC's subsidiary bodies has changed over the years— albeit slowly—to reflect emerging and waning issues.[24] Other useful innovations mentioned above include ECOSOC meetings with the IFIs and its interactions with the Security Council.

Equally important, the United Nations, in part through its Economic and Social Council, has had successes in promoting the development debate, identifying emerging issues, and offering guidelines for policymakers. Many states have viewed ECOSOC as an impartial and objective meeting place where different positions and approaches can be contrasted, and implications of alternative policy prescriptions can be analyzed. It could even be argued that the non-binding nature of decisions and resolutions has been an asset in furthering the policy debate, and has contributed to the organization's considerable achievements in the development of ideas, in its advocacy role, and in its ability to shape public awareness.[25]

RECURRING EFFORTS AT REFORM

Since the early years of the UN, there have been calls to reform ECOSOC and more generally in UN parlance for the 'restructuring and revitalization of the United Nations in the economic, social and related fields.' In 1950 ECOSOC considered 'a number of matters relating to the question of increasing the effectiveness of the organization and operation of the Council and its commissions' and 'examined the question of establishing an ad hoc committee to undertake a comprehensive review of the organization and operation of the Council and all of its commissions.'[26]

Recurring efforts to increase ECOSOC's relevance have run the gamut of changes in its rules of procedure, working methods, agenda, role, and membership. There have been three major reform reviews, each stemming from ad hoc committees or panels of experts, which led to decisions by the General Assembly.

In 1975 a special session of the General Assembly was held to discuss development and international economic cooperation. The member states asked the Secretary-General 'to appoint a group of high-level experts to propose structural changes within the United Nations system so as to make it fully capable of dealing with problems of international economic co-operation in a comprehensive manner.'[27] The resulting report recommended new responsibilities for ECOSOC in the area of operational activities, and sought to clarify the responsibilities of ECOSOC vis-à-vis the General Assembly. Among other recommendations, the report suggests, 'The General Assembly... should reaffirm the Council's central role with respect to global policy formulation.'[28] The report also recommended reforms of some of ECOSOC's subsidiary bodies and the regional economic commissions, and strengthening of Secretariat support of the Council.[29]

The General Assembly finally acted on the report in December 1977 through resolution 32/197. This contained a watered-down version of the report's recommendations but nevertheless was a significant step. The resolution prescribed that ECOSOC undertake the following functions:

(*a*) to serve as the central forum for the discussion of international economic and social issues of a global or interdisciplinary nature; (*b*) to monitor and evaluate the implementation of overall strategies, policies and priorities established by the General Assembly in the economic, social and related fields; (*c*) to ensure the over-all coordination of the activities of the United Nations system in the economic, social and related fields and, to that end, the implementation of the priorities established by the GA for the system as a whole; (*d*) to carry out comprehensive policy reviews of the operational activities throughout the United Nations System.

The second major reform took place in 1986, following a report from the Group of High-level Intergovernmental Experts to Review the Efficiency of the Administrative and Financial Functioning of the United Nations (the 'Group of 18'). Though resolution 32/197 had been adopted only a few years prior, the report contained a recommendation that asked for 'a careful and in-depth study of the intergovernmental structure in the economic and social fields.'[30] The General Assembly tasked ECOSOC with undertaking this study, and ECOSOC, in turn, established a Special Commission for this purpose, which presented its report in June 1988.[31]

The conclusions and recommendations of the Special Commission[32] put more emphasis on coordination and less on policy formulation than those in resolution 32/197, but the differences are nuanced.[33] The report was submitted to the General Assembly, and some but not all of its recommendations have been reflected in subsequent Assembly resolutions. In particular, resolution 50/227 expressly assigns the policy-guidance role to the General Assembly and emphasizes ECOSOC's coordination role.

The third reform initiative originated in the Secretary-General's statement to the General Assembly on 23 September 2003, when he proclaimed that the United Nations had come to 'a fork in the road.'[34] He announced the establishment of the High-level Panel on Threats, Challenges and Change to propose new directions for international cooperation and the UN. The panel presented its report in December 2004.[35] Among many other topics, the report addressed the need to reform ECOSOC. This was then reflected in the Secretary-General's own UN reform proposals contained in the report *In Larger Freedom*.[36] Subsequently, the General Assembly, at its summit meeting in September 2005 included a call 'for a more effective ECOSOC' in the 2005 World Summit Outcome and Assembly resolution 60/1.[37]

These documents all underline the importance of building on ECOSOC's existing functions while emphasizing its role in linking peace and development, fostering the policy debate, and providing follow-up in the achievement of key development objectives as well as undertaking its more traditional role of coordination. However, while the previous two documents do not clarify whether the accent in future activities should be placed on coordination or policy guidance, the World Summit Outcome did suggest that equal weight be given to the functions of policy review and dialogue, on the one hand, and the function of coordination, on the other hand.

CURRENT AND EMERGING ISSUES

Does the World Summit Outcome spell 'more of the same' for ECOSOC, as much of its ritualistic drafting suggests, or does it offer the seeds of possible new directions? At the Secretariat level, much has been made of the 'new functions' assigned by the Summit to ECOSOC.[38] Indeed, while the Council has dedicated increasing attention to the follow-up of major UN conferences, resolution 60/1 went a step further in calling for yearly ministerial substantive reviews to track and assess progress in the implementation of the Millennium Development Goals. Innovation was also found in the mandated biennial high-level Development Cooperation Forum to review trends in international development cooperation. This was intended to introduce greater focus to ECOSOC's work, to enhance its convening power, and to promote greater coherence among the development activities of different multilateral and bilateral partners. Partnership with the Bretton Woods institutions would also be strengthened as a result of the World Summit's directives, especially in the area of Monterrey follow-up activities. In addition, the resolution emphasized the link between humanitarian assistance and development by assigning ECOSOC a role in addressing humanitarian emergencies. In November 2006, the General Assembly passed resolution 61/16, signifying agreement on a number of the World Summit's recommendations, but falling short of a radical transformation of ECOSOC.

The World Summit also took two additional decisions that the General Assembly subsequently acted upon. First, a new Peacebuilding Commission was created through Assembly resolution 60/180; this may provide ECOSOC with a new channel to institutionalize the links between peace and development, and between ECOSOC and the Security Council. Second, the Assembly's decision in resolution 60/251 to replace the Commission on Human Rights with the Human Rights Council transferred an important function from ECOSOC to the General Assembly; however, this should allow ECOSOC to concentrate on development and humanitarian issues.

In spite of these innovations, the World Summit did not directly address some of the major historical weaknesses of ECOSOC, such as its ambiguous relationship with the General Assembly, the non-binding nature of its decisions, or its composition. It is not clear whether the yearly ministerial reviews and the global Development Cooperation Forum will do much to alter ECOSOC's inability to attract high-level policymakers to its meetings. It is equally unclear whether the renewed call for overall coordination in the activities of funds, programs, and agencies in order to gain greater coherence and avoid overlap and duplication will be any more successful than previous attempts. Perhaps the Millennium Development Goals and the Common Country Assessments will facilitate this task.

Finally, the presence and role of NGOs in the UN's work may well increase. This could provide ECOSOC with an enhanced opportunity to enlarge its role as the 'portal of entry' of civil society to the United Nations.[39]

NOTES

1. Information about ECOSOC is available at: www.un.org/docs/ecosoc.
2. In order for NGOs to be granted formal consultative status, they must go through a screening procedure conducted by the Committee on Non-Governmental Organizations, in accordance with rules 80–84 of ECOSOC's *Rules of Procedure*.
3. ECA (headquarters, Addis Ababa), ECE (Geneva), ESCAP (Bangkok), ECLAC (Santiago), and ESCWA (Beirut).
4. ECOSOC resolution 2002/1 of 15 July 2002 established the mechanism to deal with African Countries emerging from conflict, while resolutions 2002/304 and 2003/16 created the Ad Hoc Groups on Guinea-Bissau and Burundi, respectively.
5. See resolution 57/270B of 23 June 2003.
6. United Nations, *Report of the International Conference on Financing for Development*, UN document A/Conf.198/11, 22 March 2002, Monterrey Consensus, Art. 69 (a) and (b), 16.
7. The functions of the Bureau are spelled out in rules 18 to 21 of the *Rules of Procedure*.
8. An example can be found in the Ministerial Declaration on the role of information technology in the context of a knowledge-based global economy, adopted on 7 July 2000, UN document E/2000/L.9, which not only raised awareness of the importance of information technologies for development, but led, in March of 2001, to the creation of the Information and Communication Technologies Task Force. See www. unicttaskforce.org.

9. Notably, resolution 45/177 of 19 December, 1990; resolution 45/264 of 13 May 1991; resolution 46/235 of 13 April 1992; resolution 48/162 of 20 December 1993; and resolution 50/227 of 24 May 1996.

10. Decision II/3, see *Yearbook of the United Nations 1946–1947*, 28.

11. Resolution 1991 (XVIII) came into effect on 31 August 1965, and resolution 2847 (XXVI) came into effect on 14 September 1973.

12. Erskine Childers and Brian Urquhart, *Renewing the United Nations System* (Uppsala, Sweden: Dag Hammarskjöld Foundation, 1994), 57–58.

13. Sidney Dell, 'The Bertrand Critique of the Role of the United Nations in the Economic and Social Fields,' *World Development* 19, no. 6 (1991): 735–740.

14. Walter R. Sharp, *The United Nations Economic and Social Council* (New York: Columbia University Press, 1969), 245.

15. For a first-hand account of ECOSOC's work in the 1950s, see H. Santa Cruz, *Cooperar o Perecer* (Buenos Aires: Grupo Editor Latinoamericano 1984), Tomo 1, especially 95–96 and 118–128.

16. See Bruno Simma, ed., The *Charter of the United Nations: A Commentary*, 2nd edn., vol. 2 (Oxford: Oxford University Press, 2002), which contains allusions such as 'the persistent unimportance of ECOSOC' (984) and 'The Reasons for the Decreasing Importance of ECOSOC' (1009–1010). Also see Tim Arnold, *Reforming the UN: Its Economic Role* (London: The Royal Institute of International Affairs, 1995), which states on p. 26: 'the UN's central economic body, ECOSOC, has been largely ineffective, having long ago become just another part of the labyrinthine institutional structure of the United Nations.'

17. Peter Fromuth, ed., *A Successor Vision: The United Nations of Tomorrow* (Lanham, Md.: University Press of America, Inc., 1988), esp. ch. 8. Quotes from 138–140 and 150–153.

18. UNDP, *Human Development Report 1992* (New York: United Nations, 1992), 82.

19. The Independent Working Group on the Future of the United Nations, *Agenda for Change: New Tasks for the United Nations* (New York: Ford Foundation, 1995), 292.

20. Commission on Global Governance, *Our Global Neighbourhood* (Oxford: Oxford University Press, 1995), ch. 5, 236–302. Quotes from 275–278.

21. The Nordic UN Reform Project, *The United Nations in Development: Strengthening the UN Through Change: Fulfilling its Economic and Social Mandate* (Stockholm: The Nordic UN Reform Project, 1996), 11 and 32–35.

22. The South Centre, *For a Strong and Democratic United Nations* (Geneva: The South Centre, 1996), 226–227.

23. Childers and Urquhart, *Renewing the United Nations System*, 63.

24. See, e.g., resolution 50/227, resolution 51/240, and resolution 52/12B; ECOSOC resolution 1997/61, ECOSOC resolution 1998/46, ECOSOC resolution 1999/51, and ECOSOC resolution 2001/27.

25. See Richard Jolly, Louis Emmerij, Dharam Ghai, and Frédéric Lapeyre, *UN Contributions to Development Thinking and Practice* (Bloomington: Indiana University Press, 2004).

26. *Yearbook of the United Nations, 1950*, 68.

27. General Assembly resolution 3343 (XXIX) adopted on 17 December 1974, para. 5.

28. Group of Experts on the Structure of the United Nations System, *A New United Nations Structure for Global Economic Co-operation*, UN document E/AC.82/9, 28 May 1975. The group proposed clustering of the agenda of the Second Committee and prior consultation of ECOSOC about said agenda, 12.

29. For an assessment of the report, see Ronald I. Meltzer, 'Restructuring the United Nations System: Institutional Reform Efforts in the Context of North–South Relations,' *International Organization* 32, no. 4 (1978): 993–1018.

30. *Official Records of the Forty-First Session of the General Assembly, Supplement No. 49*, UN document A/41/49, 1986, recommendation 8.

31. *Report of the Special Commission of ECOSOC on the In-Depth Study of the United Nations Intergovernmental Structure and Functions in the Economic and Social Fields* (New York: E/1988/75).

32. UN document E/SCN.1/CRP.1, May 1988.

33. Where 32/197 states that one of the main functions ECOSOC should concentrate on is 'to serve as the central forum for the discussion of international economic and social issues of a global or interdisciplinary nature,' the Special Commission states: 'to serve as the central forum for the substantive co-ordination of international economic and social issues of a global or interdisciplinary nature and for the formulation of policy recommendations thereon addressed to Member States and to the United Nations system as a whole.'

34. Address by the Secretary-General to the General Assembly, New York, 23 September 2003.

35. High-level Panel on Threats, Challenges and Change, *A More Secure World: Our Shared Responsibility* (New York: UN, 2004), para. 274–281.

36. Kofi Annan, *In Larger Freedom: Towards Development, Security and Human Rights for All* (New York: UN, 2005), especially para. 171–180.

37. *2005 World Summit Outcome*, UN document A/RES/60/1, passed on 16 September 2005, para. 136.

38. *Implementation of decisions from the 2005 World Summit Outcome for action by the Secretary-General*, UN document A/60/430, 25 October 2005, 7.

39. See the Report of the Panel of Eminent Persons on United Nations—Civil Society Relations, *We the People: Civil Society, the United Nations and Global Governance*, UN document A/58/817, 11 June 2004, and the *Secretary-General's Report in Response to the Panel's Report*, UN document: A/59/354, 13 September 2004.

CHAPTER 8

....

TRUSTEESHIP COUNCIL

....

RALPH WILDE

THE Trusteeship Council is a UN principal organ. Under Chapters XII and XIII of the Charter, it has special responsibility for the Trusteeship System, an institution-alized form of colonial administration broadly following the League of Nations Mandates arrangements. This system came to be repudiated, alongside other forms of colonialism, by the external self-determination entitlement that emerged in international law after the creation of the UN in 1945.[1] No Trust Territories now exist and the Trusteeship Council has not operated since its suspension in 1994, with the granting of independence to Palau.

The trusteeship provisions have not, however, been removed from the Charter, and proposals have been made to reactivate the Council or some other body to perform equivalent or related functions, for example supervising complex UN peace missions involved in so-called 'state-building.' The experience and operation of the Trusteeship Council, therefore, may be relevant to any future international structures created to supervise activities with trusteeship characteristics.

This chapter details the concept of 'trust' in international policy; the central features of the League of Nations and United Nations trust arrangements; the territories covered; the objectives and duration of the arrangements; the structure of administration and supervision; the historical controversy over South West Africa/Namibia; the self-determination entitlement; the revival of trusteeship; reform pro-posals; and the new Peacebuilding Commission.

The Concept of 'Trust'

The concept of 'trust' denotes a relationship of 'care' between one actor deemed incapable of looking after itself, and another actor who as 'trustee' takes over some responsibility for the first actor, performing this role not on its own behalf, but on behalf of the 'ward.' Internationally this concept was invoked to underpin certain colonial arrangements, mainly through the racist notion of civilizational differences whereby certain people were designated 'uncivilized' for lacking organized societies along Western European lines, thereby requiring the colonial 'guardian' to provide 'civilized' governance and, sometimes, also 'tutelage' in order to improve local conditions.[2] The idea of colonial trusteeship is reflected in the following comment by Jan Smuts about South Africa, as reported by H. G. Wells: 'I remember Cecil Rhodes used to say that the proper relation between Whites and Blacks in this country was the relation between guardian and ward. This is the basis of trusteeship.'[3]

The Mandates and Trusteeship Arrangements

After the two world wars, it was decided by the victorious allies that the defeated powers should lose some of their territories, including colonies. Some of the victorious powers after World War I wanted to annex these territories as their own, but this policy of formal re-colonization was rejected.[4] At the same time, the Allies did not wish to grant independence: most of the territories were regarded as failing their test for 'civilized' and organized societies, thereby lacking the necessary structures for statehood; in the words of Article 22 of the League's Covenant, their people were 'not yet able to stand by themselves.' Some type of foreign administration without formal annexation was therefore deemed necessary, and the League's Mandates System was created as a means of institutionalizing this arrangement, operating, in the words of the International Court of Justice, 'in the interests of the inhabitants of the territory, and of humanity in general, as an international institution with an international object—a sacred trust of civilization.'[5]

Some within the Allies wanted the League to take on the role of the administering authority within each Mandate,[6] but because of concerns about the capacity of the new international organization to take on such an ambitious role, and as a sop to the annexation ambitions of some of the victorious powers, these states were allowed to administer the territories that they had captured from the defeated states. The notion of 'trust' was formalized as the international legal basis for the arrangements, and

Mandate administration was subject to an overarching regime of control and supervision operating through the League of Nations.

At the end of World War II, the League precedent was followed and again the victorious states took on the role of administering authorities, with the UN performing the control and supervision role.[7] Under Charter Article 81, the 'administering authority' could be one or more states or the UN itself. In practice, however, the organization did not take on this role, although, as explained below, such a role was conceived but not implemented for South West Africa (later Namibia), and outside the formal Trusteeship System the UN did, in fact, become involved in the administration of territory.

TERRITORIES COVERED

Under Charter Article 77 the Trusteeship System was intended to cover existing mandated territories from the League era and territories detached from the defeated states of World War II. There was also the possibility that other territories could be voluntarily placed under the system by the states responsible for their administration, but this was never utilized.[8] According to Charter Article 78, UN member states could not be made subject to the system.

In some cases, Mandates were not transferred to the Trusteeship System. Some territories became independent or were subject to another form of occupation: Iraq, Syria, Lebanon, and Palestine (what is now Israel, Jordan, and the Palestinian territories). Finally, as discussed further below, South Africa's Mandate in South West Africa was not transferred into the Trusteeship System.

The following eleven Trust Territories were created: Togoland (the former Mandate of British Togoland, administered by the United Kingdom); Togoland (the former Mandate of French Togoland, by France); Somaliland (by Italy); Cameroons (the former Mandate of French Cameroons, by France); Cameroons (the former Mandate of British Cameroons, by the UK); Tanganyika (by the UK); Ruanda-Urundi (by Belgium); Western Samoa (by New Zealand); Nauru (by Australia on behalf of Australia, New Zealand, and the UK); New Guinea (by Australia); and the Strategic Trust Territory of the Pacific Islands (the former Japanese Mandates, by the United States).

OBJECTIVES AND DURATION

When the idea of trusteeship became associated with colonial arrangements, the suggestion of eventual self-administration through local improvements was occasionally made. For the League Mandates, despite the word 'yet' in the phrase 'not yet able to stand by themselves' in the Covenant—suggesting that in all cases conditions might improve, thereby obviating the need for foreign administration—such an assumption was not made for most of the territories involved. Instead, the territories were arranged into three categories, classes 'A', 'B', and 'C'.[9] For the latter class, administration was not understood as remedying local incapacities, and there was no suggestion of improvement in such capacities and the eventual end of foreign rule.[10] For 'B' Mandates, foreign administration was introduced because of the 'stage' that they had reached, but there was no suggestion that this condition might improve.[11] Only with 'A' Mandates was foreign administration to operate 'until such time as they are able to stand alone.'[12]

In contrast to this variegated approach, the UN's Trusteeship System adopted a simple, uniform approach echoing certain aspects of the formula adopted for the League's 'A' Mandates. Foreign administration in Trust Territories was, according to Charter Article 76, to 'promote the political, economic, social and educational advancement of the inhabitants...and their progressive development towards self-government or independence.'

Whereas with certain classes of Mandates the level of development was invoked as the basis for introducing external administration (classes 'A' and 'B'), and the reason for removing it (class 'A'), in the Trusteeship System it was invoked in a third sense: a positive alteration in the developmental level was set as one of the objectives for administration. Not only was administration introduced because of the idea of a poor developmental level; it was also supposed to be aimed at improving this situation, an objective that was missing from the League's class 'A' arrangements. This implied that foreign administration in Trust Territories might come to an end if the developmental level improved.

As far as their legal status was concerned, Trust Territories ceased to be the sovereign territory of the defeated powers from which they had been detached. Equally, they did not form part of the territory of the administering powers.[13] As Sir Arnold McNair remarked about the Mandates system in his separate opinion in the 1950 *South West Africa Advisory Opinion* of the International Court of Justice:

[t]he doctrine of sovereignty has no application to this new system. Sovereignty...is in abeyance; if and when the inhabitants of the Territory obtain recognition as an independent state...sovereignty will revive and vest in the new State.[14]

ADMINISTRATION AND SUPERVISION

The League Covenant's Article 22 specified that mandated territories were to be subject to the 'tutelage' of an individual state 'exercised...on behalf of the League.' In practical terms, this amounted to varying degrees of administrative control exercised over the territory by the foreign state involved, supervised by the League Mandates Commission and by the League Council.

According to the Charter, administration of Trust Territories was exercised under the UN's authority (Article 75), and the terms by which administration took place, as well as the designation of the state or states responsible for carrying it out, were specified in agreements approved by the General Assembly or, in the case of the 'strategic areas' (the Pacific Islands), by the Security Council (Articles 79, 81, 83, and 85). Overall responsibility for supervising the administration of Trust Territories was given to the Assembly or, in the case of 'strategic areas,' the Security Council, in both cases assisted by the Trusteeship Council (Articles 83 and 85). The Trusteeship Council was authorized by Article 87 to examine and discuss reports from the administering authority on the political, economic, social, and educational advancement of the peoples of the Trust Territories and, in consultation with the administering authority, to examine petitions from inhabitants of the territories. In addition, it was authorized to undertake periodic visits and other special missions to Trust Territories.

THE SOUTH WEST AFRICA/NAMIBIA CONTROVERSY

By the 1960s, when all other states administering territories that had been Mandates had either granted the territories independence or registered them under the Trusteeship System, South Africa continued to refuse to make such moves in respect of its Mandate of South West Africa, despite repeated requests by the General Assembly,[15] and purported to assimilate the territory as part of its sovereign territory.[16] In 1966, the General Assembly terminated South Africa's Mandate over South West Africa in resolution 2145 (XXI), and placed the territory under the direct responsibility of the UN, even though no explicit power to take such action with respect to League Mandates had been granted to it under the Charter. Although South Africa challenged the UN's legal competence to do this, in its *Namibia Advisory Opinion* of 1971, the International Court of Justice held that the General Assembly had succeeded the League in its competence over Mandates, enjoyed a power to terminate Mandates, and in this instance had exercised the power lawfully.[17]

General Assembly resolution 2248 (S-V) of 1967 established the 'United Nations Council for South West Africa' in order 'to administer South West Africa until independence,' and provided for South Africa's withdrawal. In resolution 2372 (XXII) of 1968 the Assembly changed the name of South West Africa and the Council for South West Africa to Namibia and the Council for Namibia respectively. However, the latter body never took up its administrative role due to South Africa's continued occupation of the territory, despite the Security Council calling for a withdrawal in resolution 264 of 1969.[18]

After twenty years of unlawful occupation, South Africa finally agreed to Namibian independence, implementing in 1989 a plan originally conceived in 1978, whereby the UN supervised and controlled elections for the first government of an independent state of Namibia through the United Nations Transition Assistance Group (UNTAG), rather than taking over full administrative control as originally intended with the Council for Namibia and as specified in Security Council resolutions 435 (1978) and 632 (1989). Once the result of the elections had been obtained, South Africa withdrew and independence was proclaimed.

SELF-DETERMINATION AND THE REPUDIATION OF TRUSTEESHIP

The self-determination entitlement that emerged after World War II repudiated the legitimacy of foreign territorial administration, including colonialism and state administration under the Trusteeship System. Such activity was to be brought to an end through independence or voluntary association with another entity, unless its continuance was agreed to by the local population through a free and fair popular vote.[19] Thus, the normative tenor of international trusteeship radically shifted; it was now presumed to be invalid, unless a particular type of consent for it was forthcoming from the local population.

The idea that for Trust Territories independence would come about progressively, depending on the 'advancement' of the societies involved, was dropped in favor of an instant entitlement. General Assembly resolution 1514 of 1960 stated that '[i]nadequacy of political, economic, social or educational preparedness should never serve as a pretext for delaying independence.' The eleven Trust Territories exercised their right to self-determination by either becoming independent states or associating themselves with other states or territories to form new states.[20]

The territory of Togoland under UK administration united with the Gold Coast, a UK colony, in 1957 to become Ghana, while the territory under French administration became independent as Togo in 1960. Somaliland united with British Somaliland, previously a UK protectorate, in 1960, to form Somalia. The territory of the Cameroons under French administration became independent as Cameroon in 1960; the northern territory of the Cameroons administered by the UK joined Nigeria in 1961, while the southern territory of the UK-administered Cameroons joined Cameroon in the same year. Tanganyika became independent in 1961; in 1964 it united with the former UK protectorate of Zanzibar to form the United Republic of Tanzania. Ruanda-Urundi was divided into two states, Rwanda and Burundi, in 1962. Western Samoa became independent as Samoa in 1962, and Nauru became independent in 1968. New Guinea united with the colony of Papua, to become the independent state of Papua New Guinea in 1975. Three components of the Trust

Territory of the Pacific Islands became fully self-governing in free association with the United States (the Federated States of Micronesia and the Republic of the Marshall Islands in 1990, Palau in 1994). The Commonwealth of the Northern Mariana Islands became fully self-governing as a Commonwealth of the United States in 1990.

REVIVAL—'FAILED STATES,' TRUSTEESHIP PROPOSALS, INTERNATIONAL AND FOREIGN STATE TERRITORIAL ADMINISTRATION

International concern about local incapacities for territorial governance endured in the post-decolonization era. Despite the self-determination entitlement, the idea of foreign administration on a trusteeship basis was revived within international public policy discourse and implemented though administration by the United Nations and, in Iraq, by the United States, the United Kingdom and their allies.

Policy proposals emerged alongside the idea of the 'failed state,' an objectionable term used to describe a state where organized government has collapsed.[21] Gerald Helman and Steven Ratner proposed 'United Nations Conservatorship,' whereby the organization would be responsible for managing the affairs of the state concerned, possibly involving partial or even plenary administration. With African states the frequent focus of attention, proposals by either the UN or individual states were made by a number of commentators, with one arguing that 'benign colonialism' should be reintroduced in parts of Africa.[22] Many of these proposals included a Trusteeship Council-type supervisory role for an international institution, whether the Trustee-ship Council itself, other UN bodies, or regional organizations.

Trusteeship through foreign administration did take place, but on an ad hoc basis without a dedicated, institutionalized system of international organization involvement in constitution and oversight. Whereas the Trusteeship Council remained limited to the original trusteeship territories (despite being open to new territories being placed under it) and, when these were no more, suspended its operation, the activity of trusteeship continued elsewhere, carried out chiefly by international organizations. For instance, UN missions exercised partial administrative functions in Somalia (1993–1995) and Cambodia (1992–1993); the UN High Commissioner for Refugees (UNHCR) runs camps housing forced migrants and aid programs in many countries; the UN exercised plenary administration in Eastern Slavonia (1996–1998) and East Timor (1999–2002), and has administered Kosovo since 1999; the EU administered Mostar in Bosnia and Herzegovina (1994–1996); the Organization for Security and Co-operation in Europe (OSCE) ran the electoral system in Bosnia and Herzegovina (1996–2003) and in Kosovo (1999–2004); and the Office of the High Representative (OHR) has exercised partial administrative powers (e.g., imposing legislation) in Bosnia and Herzegovina since 1996.[23]

When the United States and its allies invaded Iraq in 2003 and removed the existing government, they remained as occupying authorities, acting as the government of Iraq through the Coalition Provisional Authority (CPA) for a twelve-month period before the transfer of formal civil administrative competence to a CPA-appointed transitional body.[24]

A degree of supervision for these projects has operated through regular reporting to the Security Council. However, the narrowness of this function and the elite membership of the body performing it, when compared with the functions and composition of the bodies involved in the earlier Trusteeship System, represent a retrograde move as far as the idea of a legitimate and effective system of international scrutiny and control is concerned.

Although Charter amendment would have been necessary to allow territories of member states to be placed under the Trusteeship System, even in instances of nonstate territories—for example, East Timor in 1999—the Trusteeship Council remained dormant. This perhaps reflected a reluctance on the part of member states, especially former colonial states, to legitimize international trusteeship in this manner, even if they were prepared to see it reintroduced in particular places on an ad hoc basis when administration was conducted by the UN.[25]

REFORM PROPOSALS FOR THE TRUSTEESHIP COUNCIL

Within the debate on UN reform, the future of the Trusteeship Council has been addressed by the Special Committee on the Charter of the United Nations and on the Strengthening of the Role of the Organization.[26] In 1994, Boutros Boutros-Ghali recommended that the Trusteeship Council be eliminated through a Charter amendment. In 1995, following a proposal by Malta,[27] Trusteeship Council reform was included in the agenda of the General Assembly by resolution 50/55. The Maltese proposal envisaged a new role for the Council as 'guardian and trustee of the global commons and the common concerns.'[28] Whilst the proposal appeared to receive tentative approval by newly-elected Secretary-General Kofi Annan in his 1997 reform proposals, it received a less enthusiastic response from member states.[29]

INTO THE FUTURE, THE PEACEBUILDING COMMISSION

More recently, consensus seems to have settled on the abolition of the Trusteeship Council. In his 2005 *In Larger Freedom* report, Secretary-General Kofi Annan proposed the elimination of the Trusteeship Council. This proposal was endorsed by member states at the 2005 World Summit, where the General Assembly recognized that 'the Trusteeship Council no longer meets and has no remaining functions,' and that the Charter should be amended to delete Chapter XIII, and to eliminate references to the Trusteeship Council elsewhere.[30]

Although the idea of reforming the Trusteeship Council to make it responsible for supervising and coordinating international administration in cases where local actors are considered to be incapable or unwilling to perform governance seems to have been abandoned, there remains an acknowledgment that, in the words of Secretary-General Kofi Annan, 'a gaping hole in the United Nations institutional machinery' exists with respect to 'the challenge of helping countries with the transition from war to lasting peace.'[31]

The High-level Panel on Threats, Challenges and Change proposed creating a Peacebuilding Commission;[32] this was subsequently endorsed by the Secretary-General,[33] and by member states at 2005 World Summit.[34] In December 2005, the Security Council approved resolution 1645 and, concurrently, the General Assembly adopted resolution 60/180 that established this 'dedicated institutional mechanism to address the special needs of countries emerging from conflict towards recovery, reintegration and reconstruction and to assist them in laying the foundation for sustainable development.' The main purpose of the Commission will be to coordinate, and, to a certain extent, supervise, the activities of actors involved in post-conflict peacebuilding and reconstruction.

Whatever the constitutional status of the Trusteeship Council, the idea of international trusteeship and the role of international organizations in relation to it remain key components of international public policy.

NOTES

1. On the Trusteeship System, see, e.g., Ramendra N. Chowdhuri, *International Mandates and Trusteeship Systems, A Comparative Study* (The Hague: Martinus Nijhoff, 1955); H. Duncan Hall, *Mandates, Dependencies and Trusteeship* (Dordrecht: Martinus Nijhoff, 1948); Robert Y. Jennings and Arthur Watts, eds., *Oppenheim's International Law*, vol. 1, *Peace*, 9th edn. (London: Longman, 1992), 89–95 and sources cited at 308; C. L. V. Narayan, *United Nations' Trusteeship of Non-Self-Governing Territories* (Paris: Imprimeries Populaires, 1951); Christopher Weeramantry, *Nauru: Environmental Damage Under International Trusteeship* (Melbourne: Oxford University Press, 1992); Catherine Redgwell, *Intergenerational Trusts and Environmental Protection* (Manchester, UK: Manchester University Press, 1999), 149–154; and H. Duncan Hall, 'The Trusteeship System,' *British Yearbook of International Law* 24, (1947): 33.
2. Bill Ashcroft, Gareth Griffiths, and Helen Tiffin, *Post-Colonial Studies: The Key Concepts* (London: Routledge, 2000), 47; A. W. Brian Simpson, *Human Rights and the End of Empire: Britain and the Genesis of the European Convention* (Oxford: Oxford University Press, 2001), 291–295; Simon Schama, *A History of Britain*, vol. 3: *The Fate of Empire 1776–2000* (New York: Miramax Books, 2002), 269–270; Ruth Gordon, 'Saving Failed States: Sometimes a Neocolonialist Notion,' *American University Journal of International Law and Policy* 12 (1997): 903, 926; Anthony Anghie, 'Finding the Peripheries: Sovereignty and Colonialism

in Nineteenth-Century International Law,' *Harvard International Law Journal* 40, no. 1 (1999): 62–65 and sources cited therein.

3. Herbert G. Wells, *'42 to '44: A Contemporary Memoir Upon Human Behaviour During the Crisis of the World Revolution* (London: Secker & Warburg, 1944), 71.

4. Quincy Wright, *Mandates Under the League of Nations* (Chicago: University of Chicago Press, 1930), 26–34.

5. *International Status of South West Africa, Advisory Opinion*, ICJ Reports 1950, 128 (hereafter 'South West Africa Opinion 1950'), 132. On the Mandates arrangements, see, e.g., Sydney H. Olivier, *The League of Nations and Primitive Peoples* (Oxford: Oxford University Press, 1918); Aaron M. Margalith, *The International Mandates* (Oxford: Oxford University Press, 1930); Wright, *Mandates*; Hall, *Mandates, Dependencies and Trusteeship*; Oppenheim's *International Law*, 86 and sources cited, 295; and Redgwell, *Intergenerational Trusts*, 147–149.

6. Wright, *Mandates*, 26–34.

7. On the commonality of the two systems see, e.g., Jennings and Watts, eds., *Oppenheim's International Law*, 89 and 308. Harris states that the Trusteeship System was 'inspired by the same problem and the same objective'; and David J. Harris, *Cases and Materials on International Law*, 6th edn. (London: Sweet & Maxwell, 2004), 130. For collective treatment of the two institutions, see Chowdhuri, *International Mandates*; Hall, *Mandates, Dependencies and Trusteeship*; and Redgwell, *Intergenerational Trusts*, 146–163 (as 'international trusteeship').

8. For details of Mandates and Trust Territories, see James Crawford, *The Creation of States in International Law*, 2nd edn. (Oxford: Oxford University Press, 2006), Appendix 2.

9. League Covenant Article 22, paras. 4–6 cover classes A, B, and C respectively but without mentioning the letters, which were adopted by the League to denote the different classes of territory set out therein.

10. League Covenant Article 22, para. 6 applied to 'territories, such as South West Africa and certain of the South Pacific Islands.'

11. League Covenant Article 22, para. 5 applied to 'other peoples, especially those of Central Africa.'

12. League Covenant Article 22, para. 4 applied to 'certain communities formerly belonging to the Turkish Empire.'

13. This point in relation to mandated territories is made by the International Court of Justice in the *South West Africa Opinion 1950*, 131–132. On the legal status of Mandates and Trust Territories see, e.g., *South West Africa Opinion 1950* and separate opinion of Judge McNair; Crawford, *The Creation of States*, 568–574 and sources cited therein; Percy E. Corbett, 'What is the League of Nations?' *British Yearbook of International Law* 5 (1924): 119, 128–136 (on the Mandates); and Wright, *Mandates*, 90–92.

14. *South West Africa Opinion 1950*, separate opinion of Lord McNair, 150.

15. See the discussion in *Legal Consequences for States of the Continued Presence of South Africa in Namibia (South West Africa) Notwithstanding Security Council Resolution 276 (1970), Advisory Opinion of 21 June 1971*, International Court of Justice Reports 1971, 16 (hereafter 'Namibia Advisory Opinion 1971'), paras. 84–86, and in the *South West Africa Opinion 1950*, 141–143.

16. On the claims of title see, e.g., *Namibia Advisory Opinion 1971*, paras. 82–83.

17. *Namibia Advisory Opinion 1971*.

18. On South Africa's refusal see, e.g., John Dugard, ed., *The South West Africa/Namibia Dispute: Documents and Scholarly Writings on the Controversy between South Africa and the United Nations* (Berkeley: University of California Press, 1973), 436, 440.

19. *Western Sahara, Advisory Opinion*, ICJ Reports 1975, 12.

20. See United Nations, Decolonization Unit, Department of Political Affairs, 'Trust Territories that have achieved self-determination', available at www.un.org.
21. Gerald B. Helman and Steven R. Ratner, 'Saving Failed States,' *Foreign Policy* 89 (1992): 3. For a critique, see Ralph Wilde, 'Representing International Territorial Administration: A Critique of Some Approaches,' *European Journal of International Law* 15, no. 1 (2004): 89–91.
22. Charles Krauthammer, 'Trusteeship for Somalia: An Old Colonial Idea whose Time Has Come Again,' *Washington Post*, 9 October 1992; William Pfaff, 'A New Colonialism? Europe Must Go Back Into Africa,' *Foreign Affairs* 74, no. 1 (1995): 2; and Ali A. Mazrui, 'Decaying Parts of Africa Need Benign Colonization,' *International Herald Tribune*, 4 August 1994.
23. On the establishment and mandate of these administration missions see, in general, Ralph Wilde, 'From Danzig to East Timor and Beyond: The Role of International Territorial Administration,' *American Journal of International Law* 95 (2001): 583–606.
24. On the CPA, see 'Letter dated 8 May 2003 from the Permanent Representatives of the United Kingdom of Great Britain and Northern Ireland and the United States of America to the United Nations addressed to the President of the Security Council,' UN document S/2003/538, 8 May 2003; see also Security Council resolution 1483 (2003), UN document S/RES/1483, 22 May 2003, and Security Council resolution 1546 (2004), UN document S/RES/1546, 18 September 2004.
25. For a further discussion of this, see Ralph Wilde, 'The Post-colonial Use of International Territorial Administration and Issues of Legitimacy,' American Society of International Law, *Proceedings of the 99th Annual Meeting* (2005), 38.
26. Report of the Special Committee on the Charter of the United Nations and on the Strengthening of the Role of the Organizations, UN document A/60/33, 23 March 2005, Chapter V, 'Proposals Concerning the Trusteeship Council,' para. 61.
27. On the proposal before the Assembly, see 'Request for the inclusion of an item in the provisional agenda of the 50th session: Review of the role of the Trusteeship Council, *Letter dated 2 June 1995 from the Permanent Representative of Malta addressed to the Secretary-General*,' UN document A/50/142, 16 June 1995. The proposal has been reiterated in 1999 before the Special Committee in the *Report of the Special Committee on the Charter of the United Nations and on the Strengthening the Role of the Organization*, UN document A/54/33, 12 May 1999, Chapter V, paras. 123–124.
28. See Appendix: 'Transforming the Role of the Trusteeship Council *Pro memoria* on the proposal launched by the Deputy Prime Minister and Minister of Foreign Affairs of Malta, Prof. Guido de Marco, during his tenure of the Presidency of the General Assembly at its forty-fifth session,' UN document A/50/142, 16 June 1995. A similar proposal was made by the Commission on Global Governance in *Our Global Neighbourhood: The Report of the Commission on Global Governance* (Oxford: Oxford University Press, 1995).
29. See *Renewing the United Nations: A Programme for Reform, Report of the Secretary-General*, UN document A/51/950, 14 July 1997.
30. *Resolution adopted by the General Assembly, 60/1. 2005 World Summit Outcome*, A/RES/60/1, 24 October 2005, para. 176.
31. *In Larger Freedom: Towards Development, Security and Human Rights for All, Report of the Secretary-General*, UN document A/59/2005, 21 March 2005, (hereafter 'Annan, *In Larger Freedom*'), para. 114.
32. High-level Panel on Threats, Challenges and Change, *A More Secure World: Our Shared Responsibility*, UN document A/59/565, 2 December 2004, section XV.
33. See Annan, *In Larger Freedom*, paras. 114–118.
34. *2005 World Summit Outcome*, para. 97.

CHAPTER 9

SECRETARIAT
INDEPENDENCE
AND REFORM

JAMES O. C. JONAH

THIS chapter focuses on twin themes that have run through the entire life of the UN Secretariat: a battle over its independent nature and an almost constant restructuring accompanied by calls for its reform. These struggles have been primarily political and have often related to disagreements over the direction of the United Nations, the setting of policy priorities, and the consequent allocation of resources.

The chapter is divided into four main sections. The first examines the origins of the concept of an independent international civil service. The second section addresses human resources management polices including staff recruitment, the geographical distribution of staff members, the International Civil Service Commission, and administrative justice. The final two sections examine the oil-for-food and peace-keeping procurement scandals and the selection of the Secretary-General.

HISTORY OF AN INTERNATIONAL
CIVIL SERVICE

The concept of an independent international civil service had early origins. Divergent views on the nature and structure of the Secretariat were evident in the creation of the League of Nations. During the planning stage for the first international secretariat, distinct from the earlier practice of allowing the host government of conferences to set up an ad hoc conference secretariat, some vigorously opposed the setting up of a permanent secretariat and rejected the notion that it should be established on the model of the British civil service.[1]

The views of Sir Eric Drummond prevailed and he became the first Secretary-General of the League of Nations. He laid the firm foundation of an independent international civil service. His tenure lasted until 1933, during which time it was proven that an international civil service—composed of men and women from different nations, nationalities, ideologies, and cultures but devoted to a common international cause—was a realistic proposition. Sadly, his successor in 1933, Joseph Avenol of France, who had served as deputy to Drummond, did not live up to expectations. In fact, Drummond had opposed Avenol's appointments on these grounds but was ignored.[2] Avenol's conduct as the second Secretary-General of the League of Nations was arguably a contributory factor to the break-down of the League system.[3]

When the time came to make arrangements for a new international organization as the successor to the League of Nations at Dumbarton Oaks, the lessons learned in the League Secretariat under both Drummond and Avenol were applied in formulating proposals for the Secretariat of the future United Nations. What one observer called 'a great experiment in international administration' became the model.[4] The League's Staff Regulations and Rules obligated staff members to be independent of governments and to observe scrupulously the international character of the Secretariat. However by 1936 the League Secretariat had become politicized to the extent that staff members of certain nationalities openly sided with their governments.[5] With this experience in mind, the staff rules and regulations in the new United Nations organization were reformulated to require Charter obligations on both member states and the staff. Those proposals were finally embodied in Charter Articles 100 and 101.

During the San Francisco United Nations Conference on International Organization in June 1945 and at the Preparatory Commission of the United Nations that met in London in November–December 1945, further efforts were made to derogate from the independence and the international character of the Secretariat. The Soviet Union favored an intergovernmental secretariat with staff members representing national views. The majority of delegates firmly opposed that concept and opted to maintain an independent and international secretariat. Later, when the Secretariat initially commenced its activities in New York, Moscow made another attempt to dilute the international character of the Secretariat. It argued that each department of the Secretariat should operate autonomously. That idea too was rejected.

The Secretary-General is the fulcrum of the organization and wears two hats: he or she is the 'chief administrative officer of the Organization' and head of the Secretariat, which is one of the six principal organs of the United Nations.[6] The first Secretary-General of the United Nations, Trygve Lie, was a Norwegian labor leader who had no known record as a diplomat. He presided over a Secretariat governed by the terms of a 'gentleman's agreement' reached in London in 1946.[7] By that agreement the five permanent members were assigned the major departments of the Secretariat. The directors of these departments were expected to manage their respective departments, and the heads of the departments acted as links to their governments. In essence, they were diplomatic representatives.

Upon assumption of the office of Secretary-General in 1953, Dag Hammarskjöld instituted major changes in policy and direction. The practice had developed by which many governments established at New York headquarters permanent diplomatic missions accredited to the United Nations. That clearly meant that there was a direct channel of communication between the Secretary-General and the member states. The diplomatic role of the Assistant Secretaries-General as heads of departments became unnecessary.

In his 1954 reforms, Hammarskjöld abolished the echelon of Assistant Secretary-General and replaced it with the position of Under-Secretaries with which he was familiar from Sweden's system of government. Although some of the senior officials rejected his changes and therefore resigned,[8] Hammarskjöld pressed on. In addition, while Lie had succumbed to US pressure during the McCarthy period by compromising the independence of the Secretariat and its international character, Hammarskjöld reminded the US of its obligations under the Charter to respect the independence of the international civil service. By dint of his forceful representation, Hammarskjöld was able to secure the removal from UN premises of the Federal Bureau of Investigation the presence of which Lie had allowed. Hammarskjöld was thereby able to lift the sinking morale of the staff.[9]

Throughout his term of office, Hammarskjöld was tireless in promoting the independence of the international civil service as the *sine qua non* of a vibrant and credible staff to conduct the work of the organization. Significantly, Hammarskjöld's last major speech—at Oxford University on 30 May 1961—before his death in a plane crash in Ndola, Northern Rhodesia was his strong defense of the concept of an independent civil service.[10] Hammarskjöld correctly observed that many governments, even in Western democratic countries, were wary about having an international civil service. Many had thought that only the Soviet Union and its allies were opposed to the concept.[11] In the light of current growing doubts about that concept, it would be instructive to revisit Hammarskjöld's Oxford speech, which continues to be relevant.

When Premier Khrushchev proposed the Soviet *Troika* plan[12] during the Congo crisis, Hammarskjöld understood that its implementation would result in the destruction of the independence of the international civil service by having the direction of the world organization under the leadership of three individuals—the proposal was one Soviet, one American, and one person from the Non-Aligned Movement (NAM). He felt so strongly that he became inflexible in considering any compromise towards the *Troika* proposal. The developing countries in the General Assembly saved the day when they sided with Hammarskjöld despite Khrushchev's energetic campaign to win them to his side. When Hammarskjöld died suddenly, there was serious concern that the Soviet Union would insist on a *Troika* as a condition for agreeing to the appointment of a new Secretary-General, but Khrushchev did not press his case after the death of Hammarskjöld.

Burma's U Thant followed Hammarskjöld, initially as Acting Secretary-General and then Secretary-General. By and large, U Thant maintained the health and viability of the international civil service. He was assisted in this effort by the continuing service of the first generation of international civil servants, such as Ralph Bunche. However, in his own reform proposals in 1968,[13] U Thant abandoned Hammarskjöld's top tier of Under-Secretaries and replaced them with two top echelons with the ranks of Under-Secretary-General and Assistant Secretary-General. As a result of the turmoil during the Congo crisis, it was considered prudent to recruit nationals of developing countries to the top ranks of the Secretariat. It may be true to say that some token representations were made with respect to nationals of the developing world. It is important to note that U Thant made no compromises with regard to the independence of the international civil service; nor did he accept the *Trioka* system in his office in the form of a cabinet system as proposed by the Soviet Union.

Except for minor changes, the two top echelons introduced by U Thant have remained in force. However, in 1975 the General Assembly, on the recommendation of Secretary-General Kurt Waldheim—the fourth Secretary-General—established the new post of Director-General for Development and International Economic Co-operation.[14] Subsequently, Secretary-General Boutros Boutros-Ghali—the sixth Secretary-General—abolished this post in 1992, as part of an institutional reform (which also amalgamated disparate political offices and departments into just two— DPKO and DPA). On the recommendation of his successor Secretary-General Kofi Annan—the seventh Secretary-General—the General Assembly approved the establishment of the post of Deputy Secretary-General.[15] Prior to the 1991 election of Boutros-Ghali, a study undertaken by Brian Urquhart and Erskine Childers, under the joint auspices of the Ford Foundation and the Dag Hammarskjöld Foundation, proposed the establishment of four sector Deputy Secretaries-General.[16] Although the proposal had wide support among member states, Boutros-Ghali did not endorse it on the ground that it might undermine the authority of his office.

HUMAN RESOURCES MANAGEMENT

The Secretariat has been undergoing reforms since its establishment, accompanied by ceaseless calls for further reforms, reflecting an ongoing divergence of views among member states as to how best to restructure the nature of the international staff working for the world organization. While the majority of member states had opted for a permanent international secretariat with a career civil service, symbolized by permanent contracts to ensure independence, the then Soviet Union and its allies rejected that concept and instead instructed their nationals to accept only two- to five-year, fixed-term contracts. Hammarskjöld struggled with the problem and finally reached a compromise by proposing that the Secretariat should have 75 percent permanent contract staff and 25 percent fixed-term contracts. He further accepted that Soviet nationals and those of its allies could join the Secretariat on the basis of secondment, which involves joint agreements between staff, governments, and the United Nations.

Over the years, many governments have criticized permanent contracts as well as secondments. There remains a widespread perception that permanent contracts result in 'dead wood,' and under Kofi Annan's two terms, permanent contracts were increasingly phased out. The preferred options were outlined by the Secretary-General in 2004. New contractual arrangements were to be of three types:

- Short-term—up to a maximum of six months to meet work loads and specific short-term requirements.
- Fixed-term—renewable up to a maximum of five years.
- Continuing—to be granted to staff who served on fixed term for five years and met the highest standards of efficiency, competence and integrity.[17]

Annan made clear that continuing contracts could have the same status as current permanent contracts, but could also be terminated 'in the interest of the Organization.' Probationary and permanent contracts would no longer be used in the future.

UN staff union representatives have strongly resisted the phasing out of permanent contracts.[18] Unions have claimed that the introduction of the notion of 'continuing contracts' is intended to make it easier to terminate staff, and expressed fears that this might be abused. Under the League system, both Drummond and Avenol had considerable flexibility in the termination of staff on the ground of 'service reorganization.' In particular, Avenol used this provision to dismiss staff whom he personally disliked. Advocates of permanent contracts stress the importance of their 'psychological' significance as a symbol of a vibrant, independent, and international civil service and argue that the Secretariat is not a public corporation and should not be treated as such.[19] Under the system of permanent contracts, as originally conceived, the Staff Regulations and Rules provide for five-year periodic reviews to determine whether a staff member should retain the status of permanent contract in the international civil service. The problem has long been the unwillingness of program managers to prepare honest periodic reviews and to make requests for periodic reviews. What happens to institutional memory once permanent contracts have been abandoned?

A report of the Panel on the Strengthening of the International Civil Service stressed both independence and high standards as the benchmarks for any reform or modernization of the Secretariat:

[The] basic principles on which the Charter of the United Nations is based not only retain all their validity but acquire even greater relevance in the new international environment in which the UN system is presently operating. Indeed, in relation to the international civil service, the Charter principles of independence (Article 100) and of the 'highest standards of efficiency, competence and integrity' (Article 101) should be the overriding values to which all efforts at advancing a modern international civil service, responsive to the changing demands and requirements of the new century, should be geared.[20]

Recruitment

Current methods and procedures for the recruitment of staff have changed significantly from the more idealistic earlier years.[21] For instance, in Dag Hammarskjöld's efforts to strengthen the international civil service, he underlined the critical importance of the office of Personnel Services—now renamed the Office of Human Resources Management (OHRM)—and made the office directly responsible to him. That arrangement was necessary to ensure uniformity of standards in the recruitment process. However, with the growing politicization of the Secretariat over the years, the Office of Personnel Services began to lose some of its authority. It was not helpful when, under the reform of U Thant, the Office of Personnel was placed in a subordinate position within the Department of Administration and Finance. One immediate consequence was the emergence of fiefdoms within the Secretariat and the weakening of common standards in the recruitment and promotion of staff. The process was cushioned somewhat by the retention of staff participation in independent central bodies, such as the Appointment and Promotion Boards, Committee and Panels.[22]

In 2002, the Secretary-General introduced a new staff selection system. It integrated recruitment, placement, managed mobility and promotion; it placed the responsibility for selection decisions in the hands of heads of departments who are responsible for program delivery. The role and responsibilities of the Department of Peacekeeping Operations (DPKO) was also expanded and given significant additional staffing resources,[23] delegating to it authority in the recruitment of peacekeeping staff in order to improve speed and direct management of staff in the field.

There is a wide divergence of views among member states as to whether the new system has strengthened or weakened the overall management of the Secretariat.[24] A widespread view within the Secretariat was that these reforms had not yet adequately addressed deeper problems of poor management, lack of accountability, and cronyism. When the Secretariat conducted an extensive 'Integrity Survey' during 2004, it showed that the majority of staff had no confidence in the integrity of senior management. Commenting on the 2004 integrity perception survey, and the crisis of confidence caused by the oil-for-food scandal, the Secretary-General remarked, 'In addition recent events have created the imperative to establish new mechanisms to improve ethics in the Organization.'[25]

The United States used the budgetary lever to move reform ahead in late 2005—for the first time a biennium budget was approved on an interim basis to be reviewed in June 2006 in light of actual reform efforts. A number of states, though not the majority of the Group of 77 and China, were hesitant during the September 2005 World Summit about giving the Secretary-General more management authority along the lines of a corporate chief executive officer. Attempts by the Secretary-General in April 2006 to break the log-jam on management reform were rejected by developing countries in a General Assembly resolution. Many developing countries regarded managment reform as a subterfuge. They argued that, if more discretionary authority and power of the purse were placed in the senior UN administration, it would be more subject to Western (and especially American) influence.

To many UN veterans, the low level of staff morale, linked to the integrity of senior managers and the corruption revealed, particularly in peacekeeping procurement, would have been inconceivable in the first few decades of the UN. It is questionable whether the mere establishment of a new Ethics Office with independent status, or the full financial disclosure program, outlined as part of the current management reform, will help matters significantly.[26] What is urgently required is to return to basics and make certain that as far as possible only men and women who meet the standard of integrity mentioned in the Charter are recruited into the Secretariat and promoted on the basis of merit.

Geographical Distribution

At the sixtieth session of the General Assembly when management reform was being discussed, a number of delegations voiced criticism about the current composition of the Secretariat. The main focus was on professional staff which, unlike the general service category, is subject to recruitment by geographical distribution. According to the Charter, the Secretariat should be recruited, among other things, on a wide geographical basis. To achieve this goal, the General Assembly has approved what is referred to as 'desirable ranges for the geographical distribution of staff.' Three factors—membership, geography, and level of financial contributions—are used to set the desirable range of staff members from all member states.[27]

Desirable ranges have been interpreted over the years as a form of quota, which they are not. Critics have maintained that geographical distribution has lowered standards in the Secretariat. This issue is complicated by the fact that the number of posts used to determine desirable range in the Secretariat is actually very small, when compared with the total size of the Secretariat. Only 3,000 professional posts are used to determine desirable range, but as of mid-2005 the UN Secretariat's global staff numbered just over 14,000 persons—this figure includes the large number of general service staff and project personnel.[28]

Concerns have been expressed by the G-77 and China over the perceived dominance of nationals from Europe and North America, particularly at the most senior policy levels in the Secretariat, and that this might lead the Office of the Secretary-General to reflect more the concerns of industrialized countries than those of the majority of states.[29]

The practice of secondment, or borrowing officials from governments, raised particular concerns among developing country governments in the late 1990s. With the rapid expansion of peacekeeping in the 1990s, the DPKO had become one of the largest Secretariat departments and increasingly reliant on 'gratis personnel' officers seconded by member states, almost all from industrialized countries, to back-stop new field operations.[30] These were staff placed at the disposition of DPKO, but were paid by their own governments.[31] The General Assembly terminated this practice on the grounds that it was contrary to the cardinal principles of an independent international civil service.

The overarching goal of ongoing reform proposals relating to the Secretariat is to ensure greater policy coherence and operational effectiveness. At the end of the day, the UN system should work and deliver, and should be perceived to do so. The Secretary-General has recognized that human management reform involves a change of culture and takes time. Indeed, the G-77 and China remain skeptical about the scope and effectiveness of management reforms. While they support reform of the United Nations, they are wary of reform measures that may weaken the role of the General Assembly where they are in the majority. Member states of the European Union (EU) and the United States strongly support the management reform proposals put on the table by the Secretary-General, and the very fact that these proposals are supported by the West has raised suspicions among the G-77 and China. This perception may partially account for the enormous difficulties in reaching a consensus on management reform.

Member states have welcomed the whistle-blower program established by the Secretary-General within the Secretariat with the aim of encouraging staff members to come forward to report evidence of corruption without jeopardizing their careers.[32] But the proposal on the framework for one-time staff buy-outs has encountered difficulties, resulting in part from a fear about how the senior managers of the organization would implement this policy. Some member states have been inconsistent with respect to management reform. For example, the United States is a major supporter of granting the Secretary-General the authority to decide on the modalities for staff buy-out but has also made statements that appear to qualify other aspects of support for an independent civil service.[33]

The International Civil Service Commission

In its December 1974 resolution 3357 (XXIX), the General Assembly approved the statute of the International Civil Service Commission (ICSC) and its mandate and functions in respect of the UN and those specialized agencies and other international organizations which participate in the common system and accept the ICSC statute. Currently there are thirteen organizations that adhere to the statute. The ICSC itself has fifteen members. Neither the International Monetary Fund (IMF) nor the World Bank is a member of the common system as they have established their own rules for appointments and remuneration. The ICSC makes recommendations to the General Assembly regarding salaries and other conditions of employment of staff in the professional and higher categories of the Secretariat. Salary scales are determined in accordance with the Noblemaire principles, which established as the point of reference those applicable in the civil service of the country with the highest pay levels. The US federal civil service has been used as the basis of comparison since the inception of the United Nations although other Western European government salary levels may have over time become better remunerated.

In previous years the major contributors to the UN budget have criticized what they considered the high pay scale of UN staff and have successfully pressed for freezes in salary increases. However, views are changing, as reflected in the statement of the UK representative speaking on behalf of the EU. He remarked:

The EU attaches great importance to the effective functioning of the common system which is the sole instrument for establishing the pay and benefits package for UN employees system wide. In this regard, the EU further attaches importance to the Nobelmaire principle. We acknowledge that the staff of the UN constitute its most important asset. As such, fair remuneration for UN staff, which often performs their duties in difficult and dangerous circumstances, is key to the functioning of the United Nations.[34]

Administrative Justice in the Secretariat

For many years staff members have complained about the dysfunctional nature of the administration of justice in the Secretariat.[35] The act of seeking remedies in the Secretariat is often protracted and cumbersome. When the cost of administrative decisions taken by the Secretary-General increases, the member states become concerned. Accordingly, in a decision taken by the General Assembly in April 2003, the Secretary-General was requested to develop, as a matter of priority, an effective system of personal accountability, including the issuance of an administrative instruction, to recover losses to the world organization caused by management irregularities, and to ensure that a department or program manager, whose decision is challenged by an appellant, cooperates fully with and is accountable to the internal system of justice.[36]

In compliance with this request, the Secretary-General requested the Office of Internal Oversight Services (OIOS) to conduct a management review of the appeals process.[37] The OIOS made eighteen recommendations with the aim of making the process more effective through the provision of additional resources and the strict use of time limits, as well as through improved training, communication and case management. The review further touched on a major concern of staff: the UN's recourse system. The system depends on volunteers, and often faces significant difficulties in identifying a sufficient pool of staff to serve on the Joint Appeals Board and the Joint Disciplinary Committee, given that volunteer staff members also serve on other specialized advisory bodies. Many delays have resulted from these difficulties. The OIOS also made remarks about the potential for conflicts of interest since all elements of the internal justice system—other than the independent Administrative Tribunal—are under the authority of the Secretary-General.

The overall conclusion was that the delays and backlogs in the justice process are for the most part the result of inadequate resources. To tackle this problem, the Secretary-General recommended a full-time presiding officer at the New York Joint Appeals Board and the increase in targeted training to be offered to all participants in the process. These changes should improve the quality of the advice given by the Panels to the Secretary-General, which would result in his increasing acceptance of such advice. In the circumstances, that would address another recurrent concern of the Joint Appeals Board members and staff representatives, namely that their unanimous recommendations are sometimes not accepted by the Secretary-General.

The establishment of the Office of the Ombudsman in the Secretariat was calculated to reduce the resort to the appeals procedure. However, on the basis of growing demands on the Panel of Counsel, the situation has not improved as quickly as was hoped, although a positive sign is that, of the 211 new cases in 2003, over half were dealt with informally.[38]

The General Assembly, through resolution 59/283 of April 2005, requested the Secretary-General to appoint a panel of external and independent experts to explore ways to redesign the system of administration of justice. In accordance with the resolution and as part of the reform process, in January 2006 the Secretary-General appointed a six-member panel of experts to undertake the study.[39] The UN Staff Council, which had misgivings about this official panel, in September 2005 appointed its own panel to make recommendations about reforming the administration of justice in the Secretariat.

Disciplinary measures available to the Secretary-General may trigger the appeal process. Staff rule 110.3 provides that disciplinary measures can take one or more of the following forms, not excluding more than one measure being imposed in each case: written censure by the Secretary-General; loss of one or more steps in grade; deferment, for a special period, of eligibility from within-grade increment; suspension without pay; fine; and demotion. The Secretary-General can also take other measures, such as withholding of salary increments and non-renewal of contracts or termination of appointments, to uphold standards of proper conduct and to promote accountability. Over the years, disciplinary actions by the Secretary-General have been warranted on the account of the following: theft and misappropriation; fraud and misrepresentation; assault; and sexual exploitation and sexual abuse. Staff members seeking remedies in the justice system of the Secretariat have the following bodies available to them: Joint Appeals Board and Panel; Panel of Counsel; Administrative Law Unit; Secretariats of the Joint Appeals Board in New York, Geneva, Vienna and Nairobi; Joint Disciplinary Committees; and the Administrative Tribunal, which acts as the final adjudication stage of employment disputes.

OIL-FOR-FOOD AND PEACEKEEPING PROCUREMENT SCANDALS

The issue of Secretariat reform was also given prominence in the wake of the oil-for-food scandal which came to light in 2004–2005. Secretary-General Kofi Annan established an Independent Inquiry Committee, often referred to as the Volcker

Committee after its chair, the former head of the Federal Reserve Bank, Paul A. Volcker.[40] The five reports of the committee contained direct criticism of the Secretary-General and his deputy for their failures to adequately manage the Oil-for-Food Programme. The reports also highlighted a number of wider management deficiencies in the Secretariat, especially in the areas of procurement and audit. But after exhaustive investigation, it found only isolated evidence of staff members who gained financially from the scandal. However, the reports showed evidence of cronyism and questionable behavior by senior officials. Moreover, the publications of the final two reports of the Volcker Committee apportioned equal blame for the failings of the Programme to UN member states and private companies, which were complicit in paying bribes to the Saddam Hussein regime, and in bypassing UN sanctions.

The UN's own investigations into peacekeeping procurement in 2005–2006 through the OIOS uncovered further evidence of mismanagement, inadequate management controls, and individual corruption. In response to Volcker and the findings of successive OIOS reports, the General Assembly, on the basis of proposals put forward by the Secretary-General, supported the creation of a new Ethics Office, an independent audit committee, and a better resourced and more independent OIOS.

SELECTION OF THE CHIEF ADMINISTRATIVE OFFICER

Key to the success of the Secretariat is its leadership. Commentators and students of the UN system have often expressed surprise at the Byzantine manner by which the Security Council goes about making its recommendation to the General Assembly for the appointment of the Secretary-General. Under the Charter the Secretary-General serves as the chief administrative officer of the world organization.[41] Given the fact that the competence, capability, and general character of any Secretary-General have an impact on the effectiveness of the Secretariat, one would think that the procedure for selection to the position would be more rational and above-board. The permanent members of the Security Council are keen to maintain their influence over the selection process and loath to recommend as Secretary-General any candidate that is strong and independent. In referring to Boutros Boutros-Ghali, then US permanent representative Madeleine Albright is reported to have said: 'We want a secretary and not a general.' The prospects are not bright that the P-5's views will change.

The contradiction is that they have shied away from selecting a strong and independent Secretary-General while maintaining the expectation that he or she will perform miracles. But they also have been proved wrong, and twice previously the permanent members miscalculated. In 1953 Dag Hammarskjöld was chosen with the expectation that he would be a quiet and safe technician. He turned out to be the most imaginative and innovative of Secretaries-General who gave flesh to key articles of the Charter, such as Articles 98 and 99.[42] Boutros-Ghali was selected among five African candidates because he was considered less troublesome and more malleable than the others. Instead he became very independent, which often annoyed some of the permanent members. For that reason he was denied a second term.[43] If what is desired is an effective and forward-looking Secretariat, as conceived under the Charter, then what is needed is a strong, imaginative and independent individual as Secretary-General.

CONCLUSION

It is a common practice of politicians to blame the civil service for their failures and inadequacies. More often than not, their citizens join them in complaining about the evils and sloppiness of bloated bureaucracies. The UN Secretariat is not immune to such criticisms, and over the years all and sundry have decried its waste and ineffectiveness. Despite these complaints about perceived defects, it would be inconceivable for member states to contemplate the dismantling of the Secretariat or parts of it. Surely they would not abolish their own civil services despite their dissatisfaction?

What then are the prospects for reviving a strong, dependable, and credible Secretariat? In the first place there should be the recognition of what Dag Hammarskjöld made his central belief. Speaking at the University of California at Berkeley in the summer of 1955, he made a pertinent observation:

It has rightly been said that the United Nations is what the Member nations make it. But it may likewise be said that, within the limits set by government action and government cooperation, much depends on what the Secretariat makes it. That is our pride in the Secretariat and that is the challenge we have to face.[44]

The oil-for-food scandal and deficiencies in peacekeeping procurement have damaged the reputation of the Secretariat. Critics of the world organization have lost no time in exploiting this weakness. Efforts at management reform undertaken since the World Summit's call for change are vital to rehabilitating the stature and standing of the Secretariat. However, the confrontation about management reform at the sixtieth session between the Group of 77 and China, on the one hand, and the Western powers, on the other, made clear the need for historical perspective. The lack of trust by the majority of member states with respect to the independence and impartiality of the Secretariat can have a negative impact on the effectiveness of the Secretary-General and international cooperation. No one questioned Dag Hammarskjöld's independence and integrity, and the overwhelming majority of member states had no difficulty in giving him much flexibility in the management of the Secretariat.

The strengthening of the international civil service should be given special emphasis by Ban Ki-moon, the eighth Secretary-General. The career civil service, which has been the foundation of the Secretariat, should be respected and reinvigorated. Above all, member states should keep faith with their obligations under Articles 100 and 101 of the Charter by honoring both the independence of the Secretariat and its international character.

NOTES

1. For a view of the legislative history pertaining to the Secretariat, see Theodor Meron, *The United Nations Secretariat* (Lanham, Md.: Lexington Books, 1977), 1–9.
2. James Barros, *Betrayal from Within—Joseph Avenol, Secretary-General of the League 1933–1940* (New Haven, Conn.: Yale University Press, 1969), 2.
3. Ibid., 206–265.
4. Egon Ranshofen-Wertheimer, *The International Secretariat: A Great Experiment in International Administration* (Washington, DC: Carnegie Endowment, 1945). For other historical treatments of the League and the United Nations, see also Thomas G. Weiss, *International Bureaucracy: An Analysis of Functional and Global International Secretariats* (Lexington, Mass.: DC Heath, 1975); Robert S. Jordan, ed., *International Administration: Its Evolution and Contemporary Applications* (New York: Oxford University Press, 1971).
5. Ibid., 145.
6. Charles Winchmore, 'The Secretariat: Retrospect and Prospect,' *International Organization* XIX, no. 3 (1965): 629.
7. The 1946 London 'gentleman's agreement' allocated five of the Assistant Secretary-General posts to the five permanent members of the Security Council. In accordance with this understanding a Soviet national was to be Assistant Secretary-General for Political and Security Council Affairs, and an American for Administrative and Financial Services, Brian Urquhart, *Hammarskjöld* (New York: Alfred A. Knopf, 1972), 72.
8. Joseph P. Lash, *Dag Hammarskjöld, Custodian of the Brushfire Peace* (Garden City, NY: Doubleday and Company, Inc, 1961), 53–54, 76; and Urquhart, *Hammarskjöld*, 76.
9. Urquhart, *Hammarskjöld*, 59–64.
10. For a complete text of Hammarskjold's speech, 'The International Civil Servant in Law and in Fact,' delivered to a congregation at Oxford University, 30 May 1961, see 'The International Civil Servant in Law and in Fact,' in *Servant of Peace—A Selection of the Speeches and Statements of Dag Hammarskjöld*, ed. Wilder Foote (New York: Harper and Row, Publishers, 1962), 329–349.
11. Meron, *The United Nations Secretariat*, p. xiii.
12. On the *Troika* and its implications for the Secretariat see Urquhart, *Hammarskjöld*, 460–462.
13. *The Report of the Committee on the Re-Organization of the United Nations Secretariat*, UN document A/7359, 27 November 1968, and UN document A/C.5/SR.1128, 12 December 1968.

14. On the recommendation of an Expert Group appointed by Kurt Waldheim, a new structure was established in the Secretariat. By its resolution 32/197, the General Assembly established the new post of Director-General for Development and International Economic Co-operation, UN document E/A.C.62/9, 28 May 1975.

15. 'Renewing the United Nations: A Programme for Reform, *Report of the Secretary General—Addendum: Establishment of the Post of Deputy Secretary-General*,' UN document A/51/950/Add.1, 7 October 1997.

16. Brian Urquhart and Erskine Childers, *A World in Need of Leadership: Tomorrow's United Nations* (Uppsala: Hammarskjöld Foundation, 1990).

17. *Human Resources Management Reform: Report of the Secretary General—Addendum: contractual arrangements*, UN document A/59/263/Add.1, 9 September 2004.

18. 'Statement by Rosemary Waters, President of the United Nations Staff Union, New York, to the Advisory Committee for Administrative and Budgetary Questions,' (ACABQ), 7 October 2004. See also 'Statement by the President of the United Nations Staff Union, Ms Waters, to the Fifth Committee of the 59th UN General Assembly,' 28 October 2004 (Internal United Nations Staff Union communications).

19. At one time, the Secretariat sought the service of a company called Russell Reynolds Associates to help define the duties and qualification of a Special Adviser on Senior Appointments.

20. *Report of the Panel on the Strengthening of the International Civil Service, note by the Secretary-General*, UN document A/59/399, 1 October 2004, and *Report of the Panel on the Strengthening of the International Civil Service*, UN document A/59/153, 25 June 2004.

21. Seymour Maxwell Finger and John Mugno, 'The Politics of Staffing the United Nations Secretariat,' *ORBIS* 19, no. 1 (1975): 117; and Seymour Maxwell Finger and Nina Hanan, 'The United Nations Secretariat Revisited,' *ORBIS* 25, no. 1 (1981): 205.

22. James O. C. Jonah, 'Independence and Integrity of the International Civil Service: The Role of the Executive Heads and the Role of States,' *New York Journal of International Law and Politics* 14, no. 4 (1982): 844.

23. *Criteria used for recruitment to support account posts*, UN document A/58/767, 8 April 2004.

24. *Human resources management reform*, UN documents A/59/263, 13 August 2004, and *Impact of the human resources management reform*, UN document A/59/253, 24 September 2004.

25. *Implementation of decisions from the 2005 World Summit—Outcome for action by the General Assembly, Ethics office; comprehensive review of governance arrangements, including an independent external evaluation of the auditing and oversight system; and the independent audit advisory committee: Report of the Secretary-General*, UN document A/60/568, 28 November 2005. See resolution No. 63 adopted at special meeting of the 41st Staff Council on 4 October 2005.

26. *Amendments to the staff regulations: Report of the Secretary-General*, UN document A/60/365, 20 September 2005.

27. *Composition of the Secretariat: Report of the Secretary-General*, UN document A/60/310, 29 August 2005.

28. Ibid.

29. Letter dated 6 October 2005 addressed to the Secretary-General by the current Chairman of the Group of 77 and China.

30. *Criteria used for recruitment to support account posts: Report of the Secretary-General*, UN document A/58/767, 8 April 2004.

31. *Administrative and budgetary aspects of the financing of the United Nations peacekeeping operations: Financing of the United Nations peacekeeping operations, support account for*

peacekeeping operations: Note by the Secretary-General, UN documents A/C.5/51/52, 27 March 1997, and 'Resolution Adopted by the General Assembly on the Report of the Fifth Committee (A/51/922/Add.2)–51/243. 'Gratis personnel provided by Governments,' (A/Res/51/243), 10 October 1997 (reissued for technical reasons).

32. *Secretary-General's bulletin: Protection against retaliation for reporting misconduct and cooperating with duly authorized audits or investigations,* UN document ST/SGB/2005/21, 19 December 2005.

33. Statement by Ann W. Patterson, Deputy United States Representative to the United Nations, On Agenda Item 124: Proposed Program Budget for the Biennium 2006–2007 (A/60/6), in the Fifth Committee, October 27, 2005. USUN Press Release #188 (05), October 27, 2005, www.usunnewyork.usmission.gov.

34. Statement made by UK Representative in the Fifth Committee, 20 October 2005, on Agenda Item 131.

35. Meron, *The United Nations Secretariat,* 159–171.

36. 'Resolution adopted by the General Assembly on the Report of the Fifth Committee (A/57/768)–57/307. Administration of justice in the Secretariat,' UN document A/Res/57/307, 15 April 2003 and 'Resolution adopted by the General Assembly on the report of the Fifth Committee (A/59/650)–59/266. Human resources management,' UN document A/Res/59/266, 23 December 2004.

37. Ibid.

38. Ibid.

39. Press Release SG/A/971 and ORG/1458, 12 January 2006.

40. The committee was composed of Paul A. Volcker, Richard J. Goldstone, and Mark Pieth. The reports are available at www.iic-offp.org.

41. Urquhart and Childers, *A World in Need of Leadership,* 23–30.

42. See, Hans J. Morgenthau, 'The UN of Dag Hammarskjold is dead,' *New York Times Magazine,* 14 March 1965.

43. For his side of the story, see Boutros Boutros-Ghali, *Unvanquished* (New York: Random House, 1999).

44. Foote, ed., *Servant of Peace,* 93.

C H A P T E R   1 0

SECRETARY-
GENERAL

EDWARD NEWMAN

IN the early years of the United Nations the international civil service was still a novel, even revolutionary, concept. The 'great experiment' had survived the League of Nations, and there was a renewal of the pioneer spirit.[1] On the basis of independence, impartiality and public service this 'new human category' would underpin an international society of rules, justice, progress, and institutions.[2] At the pinnacle of this would be the 'international leadership' of the UN Secretary-General.[3] In the aftermath of World War II there was a wide hope that the UN would pave the way to a better world; in the words of one commentator in 1945, 'May the International Civil Service now to be set up prepare the way!'[4]

The reality has usually been quite different from this idealist vision. In a world of power politics, the Secretary-General occupies 'the most impossible job in the world,' as the first holder of the position observed. As the UN administrative head and guardian of the Charter, the Secretary-General can be a significant force in promoting the principles and objectives of the organization, and mediating between powerful and sometimes conflicting interests in international politics. Without the traditional levers of power, the Secretary-General can nevertheless wield real influence in international politics through the use of moral suasion and his authority as the embodiment of the 'international community'. However, this is always within the context of an organization controlled by member states which have as their primary concern their national interests. The role of the Secretary-General is conditioned by a number of factors, particularly the Charter provisions and evolving rules of procedure of the office, the personal attributes of the office holder, and the extent to which the world organization is supported (or obstructed or sidelined) by leading member states. The opportunities and constraints of the Secretary-General result from an interaction amongst these variables, in varying ways and with mixed results, according to different circumstances. The Charter provisions form a procedural base which the Secretary-General can maximize according to his personal skills, but always within parameters set by a political environment which is essentially beyond his control. A true understanding of the Secretary-General, therefore, requires an analysis which weighs personality and systemic factors within the historical context in which the Secretary-General finds himself.

This chapter describes the evolution of the roles of the Office of Secretary-General in the context of international politics. It outlines the articles of the Charter relating to the Secretary-General, the evolution of the office during the Cold War, and how the office has encountered challenges in the 'new era.'

THE OFFICE

The articles of the Charter relating directly to the Secretary-General are 7 and 97–101. The office can also derive indirect authority from other articles, such as Article 33 on the peaceful settlement of conflict and Article 96 relating to the International Court of Justice (ICJ). Article 7 states that the Secretariat (with the Secretary-General as its head) is a principal organ of the United Nations. Whilst this does not imply equality with the other principal organs, it does endow the office with a certain independent authority and the responsibility to uphold the aims and purposes of the Charter; Javier Pérez de Cuéllar referred to the Secretary-General's 'independent responsibilities of "a principal organ."'[5]

Article 97 relates to the appointment of the Secretary-General 'by the General Assembly upon the recommendation of the Security Council' and his status as 'chief administrative officer.' This means that the five permanent members of the Council (P-5) have a veto over the choice of Secretary-General. As a result, the selection process has developed into a dubious political and geographic great power trade-off where practical qualifications seem to be of secondary concern. Years of experience led Brian Urquhart to lament that 'political differences dictate a search for a candidate who will not exert any troubling degree of leadership, commitment, originality, or independence.'[6] A number of norms have emerged in connection with the process: the Secretary-General has as yet not been a citizen of a P-5 country, he is generally appointed to serve two five-year terms,[7] and a rather unscientific geographical rotation occurs in terms of his background.

There have been proposals to rationalize the appointment process and make it more transparent and meritocratic, including the idea of an open search committee. In addition, a single seven- or ten-year incumbency—instead of two terms of five years—might give the Secretary-General greater independence from national pressures. Proposals such as these have not resulted in any change to the appointment and extension of the term of office. The appointment of Ban Ki-moon in 2006, whilst relatively transparent, demonstrated that the process remained totally controlled by the P-5. In any case, the scope of the Secretary-General's role will always be circumscribed by the realities of power politics and the dominance of the most powerful member states; changing the rules of procedure within which the Secretary-General works will unfortunately not change this. Moreover, none of the major initiatives of the reform process of 2004–2005—including the High-level Panel on Threats, Challenges and Change, the Secretary-General's report *In Larger Freedom*, and the September 2005 World Summit declaration—gave any significant attention to the office of Secretary-General.

The substantive elements of Article 98 spell out that the Secretary-General must perform functions that are entrusted to him by the General Assembly, Security Council, or other principal organs, and that the office holder will make an annual report on the work of the organization. It may seem rather obvious that the Secretary-General would be given instructions by other organs, but it is worth noting that this has been a significant instrument for delegating authority and tasks to the Secretary-General; anything from routine requests for reports to the most sensitive delegations of responsibility. And once delegated, important responsibilities—such as organizing peacekeeping missions and assessing the security or human rights situation in member states—have become routine. The annual report is also more than a mere administrative chore. The reports of the League Secretaries-General were not framed as a major instrument of policy. Under Eric Drummond, the reports were little more than a factual account of the work of the organization. However, with the United Nations the practice of presenting an expressive and creative annual report was almost immediately established. Some hold a special place in UN history, for example Dag Hammarskjöld's 1960 treatise which outlined his conception of the 'choice' which faced the organization, and the first report of Pérez de Cuéllar in 1982, outlining the crisis of multilateralism and asserting the need for a greater role for the Secretary-General in preventing conflict. More recent reports have not received as much attention; perhaps the custom of the Secretary-General presenting personal political opinions has become accepted and is no longer controversial.

Article 99 states that the Secretary-General 'may bring to the attention of the Security Council any matter which in his opinion may threaten the maintenance of international peace and security.' According to Hammarskjöld, this 'was considered by the drafters of the Charter to have transformed the Secretary-General of the United Nations from a purely administrative official to one with an explicit political responsibility.'[8] Article 99 forms the basis for much of the Secretary-General's political status and activities; the report of the Charter Preparatory Commission stated that with this mandate 'he has been given a quite special right which goes beyond any power previously accorded to the head of an international organization.'[9]

The drafting of Article 99 involved debates which reflected different attitudes toward the role and status of the Secretary-General. There were discussions as to whether Article 99 should be an obligation or a right, whether the right should also be applied to the Secretary-General's relationship with the General Assembly as well as the Security Council, and whether the Secretary-General should be required to bring violations of the Charter (and not only threats to international peace and security) to the attention of the Council.[10] The final formulation was more limited. Nevertheless, the article retains a great deal of discretion on the part of the Secretary-General, providing that the office holder *may* bring to the Council *any matter* which *in his opinion may* threaten the maintenance of international peace and security.

The real influence of this article has not so much derived from its formal invocation but from the legal implications that derive from it and the political responsibility that it invests in the Secretary-General. This article can give, in Hammarskjöld's words, 'by necessary implication, a broad discretion to conduct inquiries and to engage in informal diplomatic activity in regard to matters which may threaten the maintenance of international peace and security.'[11] In this sense a broad interpretation of Article 99 can endow the Secretary-General with a wide responsibility for activity and initiative in the field of conflict prevention and early warning. Boutros-Ghali stated that '[t]he Charter recognizes, through Article 99, that preventive diplomacy is a particular responsibility of the Secretary-General. Early warning, fact-finding, confidence-building measures, personal contacts, and good offices, all are instruments of this.'[12]

A number of scholars have drawn a distinction between the formal invocation of Article 99 and the informal authority it gives to the Secretary-General. Stephen Schwebel observed the 'shadow' of this article and the difference between 'invoking' and 'employing' it;[13] Leon Gordenker wrote of 'overt invocation' and 'use by implication.'[14] The extent to which a Secretary-General has been able to apply Article 99 has clearly depended upon a number of circumstances. Overuse or ill-timing, in either the formal or informal use of Article 99, can prove counterproductive. If the Secretary-General placed an issue on the agenda which embarrassed or alienated a permanent member of the Security Council, for example, he would risk ostracism.

Article 100, which seeks to ensure the independence and impartiality of the Secretary-General, underpins the political basis of the office. As Hammarskjöld observed, 'Article 98, as well as 99, would be unthinkable without the complement of Article 100 strictly observed both in letter and spirit.'[15]

The constitutional basis was merely a loose framework within which the development of the Secretary-General has occurred in practice, depending on a number of factors. It also represented a compromise amongst different opinions regarding the role of the Secretary-General, requiring the office holder 'to be a politician, diplomat and international civil servant all rolled into one.'[16] A varying room for maneuver exists for the Secretary-General, depending upon the specific circumstances of every situation in which he is engaged. Inis Claude wrote that 'the secretary-general of the United Nations has a constitutional license to be as big a man as he can.'[17] While this might be an exaggeration, it is true that circumstances have allowed a considerable development and expansion of the bounds within which the office works.

It is not possible to identify, let alone evaluate in a comparative sense, all the factors and variables which influence this development. In particular, it is difficult to evaluate the impact of personality in relation to other variables. Clearly personalities do shape political processes and history. Yet the Secretary-General is constrained by a multitude of environmental factors over which he has little or no control. The office is not merely an adjunct of the personality of the Secretary-General, and this is evident in the memoirs of the office holders themselves.[18] The Secretary-General has resources which come with the office—such as political and moral authority and legitimacy—and personal qualities are relevant to how successfully he optimizes and applies these resources. It is not possible to construct a clear equation which accounts for these many factors, but Gordenker's proposition is still useful: 'the Secretary-General can act within narrow but undefined and shifting limits, and his independent actions influence the course of international politics but never at a constant level. The configuration of international politics always modulates his actions and his influence. So do his character, energy, intelligence, and style.'[19]

In 1945 many observers hoped that the Secretary-General would become a figurehead for the international community, a force for liberal internationalism. According to Egon Ranshofen-Wertheimer:

The head of an international agency should be an international leader. He must be a statesman, a man of public affairs rather than a civil servant. . . . The international leader should be given a rank unmistakably suggesting equality of status with the top governmental delegates of the organs that shape the policies of his agency.[20]

At odds with this, the realist school argues that international civil servants will inevitably find themselves in an untenable position if they act against the interests of states. According to James Barros, the idea that any Secretary-General can lead states to a goal that they do not support is pure fiction; 'the desire for a Secretary-General who takes public initiatives is an escape from reality.'[21] This conservative approach to the international civil service advocates the administrative, behind-the-scenes model of the Secretary-General.

The development of the office of Secretary-General has reflected both the realist and liberal international worldviews. When Secretaries-General have been in confrontation with major powers, their position—and usefulness—has been undermined. And yet the office has also accrued an aura of leadership as the embodiment of international community, and in promoting collective efforts towards addressing common problems. The Secretary-General has also proven effective in agenda setting and influencing policy at the United Nations and at the national level. Power may be the final arbiter in international politics, but authority and legitimacy—the resources of the Secretary-General—can exist without power and have an impact upon political outcomes.

THE COLD WAR

In the decades following the UN's establishment, the Secretary-General's role evolved through practice. This was conditioned by international political trends that were reflected in the politics of the UN, such as the Cold War and détente, decolonization and conflict in the developing world, and the burgeoning North–South friction. This environment often constrained the Secretary-General; countless issues were excluded from the UN agenda because of the political conflict which pervaded the Security Council. Yet the failure of collective security, somewhat paradoxically, also elevated the office when it was delegated mandates which the Council could not deal with. Within this context, the office developed a tradition of mediation, directing peace-keeping operations, early warning and prevention of conflict, and diplomatic 'face-saving.'

The first Secretary-General, Trygve Lie (1946 to his resignation in 1952), felt that his office should be active in pursuit of the interests of the UN despite the constraints imposed by the Cold War. His style was vocal and assertive, and as such he established a number of norms for the office. He asserted the Secretary-General's investigatory and conflict prevention responsibilities, and fought a successful but 'bitter fight' to gain rights of communication in the General Assembly and Security Council.[22] Lie established the practice of expressing forthright political opinions, such as his support of communist Chinese representation and his 'Twenty-Year Program for Achieving Peace Through the United Nations.'[23] However, in addition to contributing to the development of the political role of his office, this assertive approach antagonized powerful UN members. In the end, Lie's stance on the Korean War—in support of UN collective security against North Korea—won him the hostility of the Soviet Union and his position became untenable. Ostracized by the Soviet Union, Lie realized that it was impossible to fulfill his responsibilities as Secretary-General and resigned. Ultimately, the results of his activism demonstrated the limitations of the Secretary-General's political role.

Dag Hammarskjöld (Secretary-General from 1953 until his death in Africa in September 1961) built upon this political tradition to develop roles in providing mediation and conflict prevention, and by asserting a political personality for the office of Secretary-General. This was the idea of 'creative administration': Hammarskjöld sought to fill the gap left by Security Council deadlock, 'filling any vacuum which may appear in the systems which the Charter and traditional diplomacy provide for the safeguard of peace and security.' The first issue that displayed Hammarskjöld's diplomatic skills and indicated a further procedural development of the office concerned the American prisoners of war in China left over from the Korean War. In December 1954, General Assembly resolution 906 (IX) asked him to make 'continuing and unremitting efforts' to secure the release of the airmen 'by the means most appropriate in his judgement.' This put Hammarskjöld in a rather shaky position, asking China to recognize the Secretary-General and a mandate from a UN organ when it was itself barred from membership. Hammarskjöld's approach, which eventually contributed to the release of the Americans, was the 'Peking Formula': discussions were not held on the basis of the Assembly resolution but on the authority the Secretary-General could derive from the Charter, as a representative of the international community, in the knowledge that China sought international recognition. He made a distinction between his responsibilities as an agent of the General Assembly and Security Council under Article 98, and his status as an officer of the organization under Article 7. This gave him a certain amount of independence. The 'Peking Formula' also involved the Secretary-General filling the vacuum left as a result of disagreement amongst UN member states and the vagueness of some mandates handed down by the other UN organs, so that freedom of action could be assumed by the Secretary-General if not explicitly prohibited.

Hammarskjöld's tenure hinged on an historic improvisation: the collective security mechanisms of the UN were flawed, and so the Secretary-General worked within Chapter VI of the Charter in providing mediation and in developing peacekeeping. In particular in the Middle East and Africa he adopted a forthright and creative approach towards conflicts in which the superpowers had an interest in order to prevent them from escalating into direct confrontation between the US and the Soviet Union. He took advantage of a margin of freedom on a number of occasions; Jordan wrote that in the first peacekeeping operation in Egypt, Hammarskjöld was 'a commander-in-chief of his own army.'[24]

However, this element of independence was to propel him into controversy in the Congo where he antagonized Cold War sensitivities and aroused suspicion toward the concept of creative administration. One popular theme holds that 'in the end he carried this implicit challenge to national sovereignty further than some of the more powerful states were prepared to tolerate.'[25] At that time, the Soviet Union recommended the reform of the Secretary-General's office on the presumption that, 'whilst there are neutral countries, there are no neutral men.'[26] They claimed that a single executive officer could not hope to represent the divisions of the world, and therefore proposed a *troika* of three Secretaries-General, representing East, West, and neutral countries. Hammarskjöld resisted this and helped to maintain the integrity of the international civil service. However, on 18 September 1961 he died in a plane crash while on a peace mission in the Congo. While most historians agree that it was an accident, suspicions and conspiracy theories persist.[27] Nevertheless, had he not died so tragically, his political fate may have resembled that of Lie. It is unlikely that he could have continued effectively in office due to the confrontation with the USSR.

Following Hammarskjöld, the office of Secretary-General experienced a less active period—even something of a slump—as a result of the office holders and the overall condition of the United Nations. U Thant (1961 to 1971) favored a more low-profile focus on issues of economic development. After the Congo crisis, the UN was reluctant to take on major peacekeeping operations. In fact, from the 1970s the organization suffered from a broader malaise. A number of historical processes were transforming the organization into something quite different from that which was created in 1945 and something increasingly at odds with key actors in international politics. The influx of new members as former colonial territories became independent alienated the organization from its principal sponsors as the organization became embroiled in North–South tensions and revisionist 'Third World' campaigns. Disillusionment with multilateral organizations on the part of much of the West, and in particular the United States, meant that the UN was often peripheral to the foreign policy of major powers. The Vietnam War, the maintenance and balances of superpower détente, arms control, the Middle East peace process, and many crises of decolonization are examples of critical issues pursued or left outside the UN.

Secretary-General Kurt Waldheim (1972 to 1981) could not make a major impact within this difficult political environment, as a result of both the lack of support for the UN by major powers in general, and the involvement of Security Council members in many of the regional conflicts. As a result, they often obstructed the UN from playing a significant role in such regional conflicts. Kurt Waldheim was also a controversial figure as a result of his war-time activities and the extent to which they were known to various parties during and even before his appointment. In his first book of memoirs, Waldheim claims he was wounded on the Russian front late in 1941 and left the army to resume his law studies in early 1942.[28] However, evidence came to light that Waldheim had been an intelligence officer with German army units involved in war crimes in Yugoslavia and Greece, including the execution of British soldiers, attacks on civilians, and the deportation of Jews to concentration camps. A study by Finger and Saltzman concluded that there is 'no conclusive evidence to date that Waldheim ordered or personally committed a war crime, but he was definitely a bureaucratic accessory.'[29]

The political environment of multilateral malaise continued into the first half of Javier Pérez de Cuéllar's incumbency (1982 to 1991) and led him to write of a 'crisis in the multilateral approach.'[30] The United Nations was often marginalized within a general climate of political ill-will, and beset by financial crises. On many issues—especially regional conflicts in which the superpowers were directly or indirectly involved—the Secretary-General was either powerless or excluded.

THE NEW ERA

From 1987 the organization's activities flourished. With the decline of Cold War hostility the UN and the Secretary-General played a major role in facilitating the settlement of a number of conflicts in which the superpowers had been involved. The climate of cooperation was manifested in the Security Council with the application of collective leverage upon conflicts such as those in El Salvador, Nicaragua, Afghanistan, Iran–Iraq, Western Sahara, and Cambodia. These were addressed by the P-5 in tandem with, and often under the auspices of, Pérez de Cuéllar. Thus, after years of frustration and in some cases even irrelevance, the Secretary-General came to represent an organ of authority and facilitation in the roles of creative mediation and conflict settlement. The changing international political environment was the key to this transformation.

This was not entirely positive. After the post-Cold War honeymoon, the UN was confronted with issues which raised a fundamental challenge to the political and legal bases of the organization. As former Under-Secretary-General Marrack Goulding put it, there had been a 'meltdown' of the world order which led to conflicts in which the UN became overreached—with 'disastrous results.'[31] The Secretary-General was embroiled in this and was a focal point of post-Cold War multilateral turbulence as the UN struggled to adapt to rapidly evolving circumstances. The United Nations, and its Secretary-General, therefore reflected systemic volatility, forcing the member states and the Secretariat to reconsider the roles and limitations of the organization. The condition of the organization in the peace and security field was particularly unstable in the new era, often reflecting the political and material constraints of multilateral malaise and widely divergent views of what the UN's role should and should not be.

A number of trends characterized the office of Secretary-General in the decade following the end of the Cold War. The profile of the office—especially in the peace and security field—increased as a result of the expansion of the UN's activities, offering opportunities for leadership and activism. The enhanced role was evident in the activities of the Secretary-General in peace operations and conflict prevention, in exerting pressure upon the Security Council, in influencing policy, and in expressing normative opinions as well as in the involvement of the Secretary-General in the use of force or coercion.

At the same time, there was sometimes a narrowing of the Secretary-General's scope for independent action as a result of Security Council cohesion and US predominance. During the Cold War the paralysis of the Security Council and the balance of power that existed between Washington and Moscow at times allowed the Secretary-General to take up important responsibilities which the Council could not fulfill, for example in peacekeeping and mediation. As a corollary, with the new found effectiveness of the Security Council in the post-Cold War world, and the formidable influence of the United States, the independence of the Secretary-General in important situations was sometimes less significant. The Secretary-General was not, for example, a major actor in the decision to go to war against Iraq in 1991, or in the implementation of the 1991 Gulf War settlement, or yet again in the 2003 war against Iraq. According to a former permanent representative of Britain to the United Nations,

the more the cooperation between the Great Powers, the less the room for political maneuver for the Secretary-General. If you regard the P-5 as the Board of Directors, the Secretary-General will always be the Company Secretary. When the Board is unanimous, the Company Secretary should have clear instructions, his job being to carry them out efficiently.[32]

A further trend, especially in the immediate post-Cold War period, concerned issues—such as civil war—where the organization had not developed a coherent doctrine and the Secretary-General was plunged into precarious and volatile situations. A number of operations, such as those in the former Yugoslavia, demonstrated this.

These processes were reflected in the turbulent experiences of the Secretary-General under Boutros Boutros-Ghali (1992 to 1996) and Kofi Annan (1997 to 2006). With the end of the Cold War many people looked to the Secretary-General to harness and channel opportunities for progress in multilateralism and demonstrate leadership based upon a revival of liberal internationalism. The landmark Security Council summit meeting of heads of state in January 1992 pledged its commitment to the Secretary-General and invited him to recommend ways of strengthening the UN's capacity for preventive diplomacy, peacekeeping, and peacemaking.

Boutros-Ghali had a vision of the Secretary-General as 'an impartial figure with a global mandate.'[33] According to this vision, there was a pressing normative agenda for his office: the Secretary-General must lead the UN towards a broader vision of peace and security which reflects the shifting values of state sovereignty and evolving human rights norms. For example, Boutros-Ghali developed a doctrine of democracy and democratization that led the way for the UN to take a significant role in electoral assistance and democracy promotion.[34] However, as a result of experimentation, overreach and even crisis, both the organization's and Boutros-Ghali's reputations were tarnished from around 1993. Earlier pledges of support by many member states were forgotten as the cost—in human and material terms—of the 'new' agenda, and especially peacekeeping, became apparent.

The limitations of the UN were learned the hard way, most pointedly in Bosnia and Somalia, where outmoded and unrealistic peacekeeping norms proved to be disastrous. Not so long after President George H. W. Bush had proclaimed the 'new world order' and his commitment to the UN 'mission,' many political leaders in the US and elsewhere became wary of collective internationalism as the 'slippery slope' and a 'recipe for chaos.' Ideas of nation-building were abandoned and an environment of cautious realism and multilateral fatigue subsequently pervaded the organization.

Boutros-Ghali's reappointment was forcefully obstructed by the United States in 1996, as a result of the problems of the UN in the early 1990s and Boutros-Ghali's association with them. In addition, he had made enemies in the US administration as a result of his personal approach to the job. When Boutros-Ghali wrote of the 'global leadership' of the Secretary-General in 1996, he aroused skepticism, suspicion, and even hostility.[35] What had gone wrong?

It is difficult to judge if Boutros-Ghali personally went 'too far' in assuming a political role, or if he was simply unfortunate in having been encumbered with a series of unmanageable tasks during his tenure. He confronted politically charged situations in the field of peace and security as the UN launched operations in volatile situations such as Bosnia and Somalia. But he also courted controversy by taking on personal responsibility for the new activism and articulating a grand vision of the world organization and his position.

Washington claimed that it had obstructed Boutros-Ghali's reappointment because he had failed to make enough progress in reforming the UN and that he initially had committed himself to a single term of office. There also was a strong element of US domestic politics in the decision. However, behind these motivations was a fundamental divergence of ideology between the cautious new thinking on multilateralism in the US administration and the internationalist rhetoric of

Boutros-Ghali. He was tainted—irrespective of whether he deserved it—by the miscalculations of UN experimentation, assertive multilateralism and the over-extension of the organization in the early 1990s.

Boutros-Ghali was also an easy target for unilateralist and isolationist conservatives in the United States, a country that was essential to the UN's functioning. He was unable to defend himself against attacks because he failed to communicate with, or fully understand, the US political system. For example, after Washington had made clear its opposition to his reappointment, he campaigned globally for support and appeared to believe that the US would change its mind when he returned with some form of 'global mandate.' To believe that he could continue to work with Washington under such circumstances, and to campaign to win reappointment despite the public objection of the US, was to fail to understand the lessons of history—most obviously the fate of Trygve Lie. Boutros-Ghali's memoir, if anything, strengthens this impression. Whilst he realized that the organization had been engulfed by 'the fire of realism'[36] he did not want to accept that he had been made a sacrifice to this conflagration.

In relation to Somalia, Boutros-Ghali promoted nation-building in the belief that the Security Council—and particularly the US—would continue to support 'assertive multilateralism.' He played a key role in the escalation of the UN operation in Somalia (UNOSOM), first to the US-led Unified Task Force and then UNOSOM II. In UNOSOM II he held significant powers under Chapter VII at an operational and coordination level with the use of peace enforcement methods. The Secretary-General was directing the use of force in a stark departure from the classical model of the international civil service (Hammarskjöld assumed comparable duties in the Congo, but not with the explicit Security Council backing which existed for Boutros-Ghali in Somalia). However, it transpired that this position of authority—perhaps even power—was precarious. With the disastrous culmination of the attempt to pacify Somalia's warlords—resulting in the deaths of eighteen American soldiers—the political backlash in Washington was largely directed against the UN and its Secretary-General.

The former Yugoslavia also epitomized the complexities and the hazards of multifaceted peace operations in situations of civil conflict. Beginning with an effort to assist the distribution of humanitarian relief, the mandate of the UN Protection Force snowballed with the passing of endless resolutions—many under or alluding to Chapter VII—which had little practical effect on the ground. This credibility gap between the resolutions and the will to support them frustrated and imperiled the efforts of the UN operations. As the ultimate field director, this reflected upon the Secretary-General and was an example of the office burdened with an unrealistic mandate as a result of exaggerated expectations and shortsightedness in New York. Still, the Secretary-General showed determination to be involved in policymaking, and not only in its execution. On a number of occasions modifications to the UN's mandate were made on the basis of the Secretary-General's assessments and reports. As David Owen recalled, the Secretary-General 'prodded' the Security Council when he felt that it could be worthwhile.[37] For example, in 1995 Boutros-Ghali suggested that the organization faced a defining moment with regard to Bosnia and set out four options: withdrawal, greater use of force, a continuation as before, and a revision of the mandate to include only realistic tasks. Although he presented the report as a proposal of options, Boutros-Ghali was clearly also advocating a course of action. Yet the negative perceptions of Boutros-Ghali's performance in the former Yugoslavia still prevail. He attempted to make the political point that equally dire conflicts in the developing world were being neglected, comparing Bosnia with 'worse off' situations in Africa. Perhaps most damaging, the Secretary-General was associated with the UN's lame stance towards some of the atrocities committed in Bosnia.

The mediation and conflict prevention roles of the United Nations and specifically of the Secretary-General burgeoned in addressing post-Cold War civil strife. The third-party activities of the office in areas formerly considered to be the spheres of influence of great powers within Africa, Central America, and the former Soviet Union have been particularly important. The Secretary-General experienced more room for maneuver compared to during the Cold War, when political sensitivities precluded the office from a role in resolving many regional conflicts.

Normative developments also encouraged a greater use by the Secretary-General of the public declaratory pulpit: the 'moral responsibility' to draw the world's attention to issues and conflicts which might otherwise be neglected.[38] Under the constraints of post-Somalia multilateral fatigue, Boutros-Ghali attempted to exert moral leverage in the face of political constraints in a number of cases. During the genocide in Rwanda he told the Security Council that 'we have failed in our response to the agony of Rwanda, and thus have acquiesced in the continued loss of lives.'[39]

In the following years Boutros-Ghali continued to draw attention to the time-bomb which existed around the borders of Rwanda—in the form of refugee camps containing former *génocidaires*—after the media and the Security Council had largely lost interest. He called upon the Security Council either to back an international force to police the refugee camps or to support the efforts of countries in the region to restore law and order. Similarly, in Somalia, after the withdrawal of the UN and with it the interest of the world's media, Boutros-Ghali endeavored to maintain a UN presence in the region to keep alive hopes for reconciliation. Boutros-Ghali's declaratory activism was also demonstrated in relation to Israel, with doubtful results. He wrote of 'the plight of the Palestinian people living under occupation' and the 'particularly grave incident' of Israel deporting over 400 Palestinians—who Israel claimed had terrorist connections—to south Lebanon in December 1992. The Secretary-General was also clear, on occasions, in condemning Israeli bombing of south Lebanon, suggesting that it was intended to displace the civilian population. After Israel's bombardment of southern Lebanon in April 1996 when approximately 100 civilians died, Boutros-Ghali made public a UN report that implied that Israeli forces might have deliberately targeted a UN camp where refugees were sheltering. The decision to issue this report was a bold step but it could not have helped the UN's relationship with Israel or the US. Indeed, it is probable that it was this act which won Boutros-Ghali unswerving opposition in Washington.

Angola was a further example where the Secretary-General was engaged in a peace process thrown into disarray, in this case by the failure of the peace process after the 1992 elections. Moreover, there have been criticisms that, by acting as a neutral arbiter, the UN strengthened UNITA's (National Union for Total Independence of Angola) claim to equal status and therefore inadvertently emboldened UNITA's decision to return to war. It is a reflection of the 'new era' of UN activities that the Secretary-General had to deal with people like the warlord Jonas Savimbi, and give legitimacy to UNITA, before Savimbi had irreversibly committed himself to the peace process. Few peace and security situations in the post-Cold War world—and particularly those of a domestic nature—are 'black and white' and the Secretary-General must be seen in this light. The international civil service has to engage the local strongmen—whether in Angola, Bosnia or Haiti—however risky or distasteful this may at times appear.

Boutros-Ghali's embrace of activism and his proximity to the use of force or coercion represented a major step for the office. The association between the Secretary-General and the use of force or coercion grew out of the burgeoning activity of the UN in civil war, an unprecedented level of mandatory sanctions, the increasingly interventionist agenda of multilateralism, and the freedom of opinion enjoyed by Boutros-Ghali. The third-party role of the Secretary-General, which has achieved some independence from the other organs of the UN in the past, was partially jeopardized under Boutros-Ghali. This classical, impartial role does not sit comfortably with UN coercion, especially as the political dynamics of the P-5 largely determine how and when the organization addresses issues. Moreover, Boutros-Ghali appeared to have a thirst for political activism, sometimes without much consideration for the cumulative implications for the Secretary-General's image.

In one example, Boutros-Ghali called, on a number of occasions, for the deployment of a military force under UN authority in Burundi to stem the escalation of violence in that country, despite the opposition of the government of Burundi. He believed that he had a responsibility to encourage 'a major initiative to prevent another tragedy.'[40] In the context of post-Cold War wariness amongst many states in the developing world towards interventionist multilateral trends, the last thing they wanted was the Secretary-General of the UN proposing an unwelcome military force. In addition, the leading members of the Council did not want to be pressed into such action or to be embarrassed by the public statements of the Secretary-General. Again, Boutros-Ghali appeared to be stretching his responsibilities as 'chief administrative officer.'

The post-Cold War era demonstrated that the idealist model of the Secretary-General promoted by Hammarskjöld—and perhaps Lie—was not feasible and would not return. Boutros-Ghali's tenure as Secretary-General saw the office plunged into controversy as the result of a collision of a number of factors: a volatile international political environment that thrust the UN into largely uncharted territory; a shifting international power balance; and the activist—some might say confrontational—personality of Boutros-Ghali. A tumultuous historical period

combined with personality factors to force the office into often controversial—
sometimes untenable—situations.

Boutros-Ghali became entangled in the political turbulence of the immediate
post-Cold War period at the UN, to which his personal style contributed. Kofi
Annan, in contrast, took a quieter approach to mediating between the pressures of
this environment, and in particular between the US and the wider international
community. He was appointed, in part, as a healer and a quiet insider after Boutros-
Ghali and as someone who could take advantage of the learning process of the
immediate post-Cold War period. Kofi Annan was progressive and assertive, at the
same time as being sensitive to political realities. He carefully castigated member
states for ignoring particular types of crises and certain geographical areas. He
challenged the concept that sovereignty and borders are inviolable, arguing for a
norm of humanitarian intervention which has fueled a necessary and overdue debate
on the issue. While Annan did not seek controversy, he was not afraid to raise issues
at the heart of the UN's mission, however uncomfortable these might be. For
example, he presided over the publication of frank and self-critical reports on the
UN's involvement in Rwanda and Srebrenica.

Much of Annan's work has been characterized by his mediating between
Washington and the rest of the membership. This involved keeping the United
States engaged, but trying to maintain his own and the organization's independ-
ence; mediating between hegemony and the universal aspirations of the United
Nations. On some occasions, this meant taking positions at odds with those of
Washington. He expressed concern about the suffering of the Iraqi population
under the UN sanctions regime. After the contentious 2003 war in Iraq, he
effectively described the intervention as illegal. He was also frank and direct with
African leaders concerning their own responsibility in their countries' development
and governance.

Kofi Annan was instrumental in harnessing emerging norms and seeking to give
them policy relevance; indeed he promoted creative and often controversial thinking.
His ideas on human rights, human security, and the international responsibility to
protect civilians—including the possible use of military force for human protection
purposes—led the way in international policy and academic discussions. Most
pointedly, the international civil service has moved away from the stance of moral
neutrality and impartiality. After the experiences of Rwanda and Srebrenica—among
others—the United Nations and its staff cannot be neutral in the face of egregious
suffering. This ethical stance as personified by Annan is a fundamental step forward
for the international civil service. The oil-for-food scandal tainted this reputation in
some quarters, but this legacy is likely to remain intact.

The oil-for-food scandal implicated some UN officials—along with private companies and some national officials—in financial impropriety in connection with the
UN program which allowed Iraq to export a certain amount of oil in the 1990s
in return for food and other supplies to mitigate the terrible humanitarian impact
of the sanctions. While Kofi Annan was himself not guilty of fraud, the independent
inquiry into the scandal headed by Paul Volcker pointed to serious management

failures in the UN Secretariat, including by the Secretary-General and the Deputy Secretary-General.[41]

Others criticized Annan's for hesitating to take clear sides in particular situations. It was somewhat difficult to gauge if he supported the 1999 NATO military action against Serbia in connection with Kosovo. The Secretary-General generally supported the norm of humanitarian intervention in dire circumstances, and effectively endorsed the NATO air strikes against Serbia. At the same time Kofi Annan implicitly reprimanded NATO for having acted without Security Council authorization.

CONCLUSION

The fundamental question is whether the Secretary-General is a mere appendage of the intergovernmental political structure or part of a wider process of global governance that transcends state interests. The Secretary-General works for an international—and some might say inherently conservative—organization. Given the structural constraints within which the office works—depending upon an intergovernmental system for mandates and support—there are limits to what the Secretary-General can do. This is a function of the broader reality of international politics. All countries depend upon multilateralism and the maintenance of regularity, reciprocity, and public goods in the international system. But the international system is nevertheless basically anarchical. States vary in power, political outlook, and interests. They are formally sovereign, and generally driven by self-interests which are frequently in conflict. Powerful states can work outside established multilateral channels if they wish although there are costs. Leaders and hegemons—invariably the chief sponsors of international organizations—decline or increase in relative power and perceive negative changes in cost–benefit equations related to multilateralism.

Thus, international organizations are largely a reflection of the dynamics and processes of international power. This does not mean that formal or informal multilateral institutions are not effective or important, or cease to be effective in changing circumstances. It does, however, suggest that they are conditioned by changing international power configurations, and by conflicts that exist within the broader international system. In this environment, the activism of Trygve Lie, Dag Hammarskjöld, and Boutros Boutros-Ghali went beyond what powerful states were prepared to accept.

Despite this fact of political life, the office of Secretary-General has often been at the forefront of forward-looking UN activities and normative ideas. Indeed, issues formerly considered to be within the domestic jurisdiction of states, such as democratization and the promotion of human rights, are undoubtedly being internationalized; and the Secretary-General's office has made a contribution to these developments. The Secretary-General has pushed the Security Council to commit itself to areas of activity that otherwise may have been considered outside its remit, or outside the narrow interests of the individual members states. In agenda-setting, proposing institutional reform, and taking proactive steps, the Secretary-General has promoted new ways of thinking—and sometimes new ways of acting—at the United Nations. While the results of this are never easy to measure and always open to debate, the practice itself is no longer controversial; the Secretary-General is accepted as much more than the 'chief administrative officer'.

The office of Secretary-General is not totally constrained by conservative statist norms and does not only respond to issues. Indeed, it can be seen to be displaying clearly proactive tendencies, taking initiatives, and influencing policies. Yet, as Robert Jordan observed, 'the international civil service, caught between "global" responsibilities and national constraints . . . can only muddle along, performing in an imperfect way according to admittedly imperfect criteria of accomplishment.'[42] The eighth Secretary-General, Ban Ki-moon, still confronts these basic constraints in exercising leadership.

Notes

1. Egon F. Ranshofen-Wertheimer, *The International Secretariat: A Great Experiment in International Administration* (Washington, DC: Carnegie Endowment for International Peace, 1945).
2. George S. Langrod, *The International Civil Service: Its Origins, its Nature, its Evolution* (New York: Oceana Publications Inc., 1963), 24.
3. Ranshofen-Wertheimer, *The International Secretariat*, 435.
4. Archibald A. Evans, 'The International Secretariat of the Future,' *Public Administration* 43 (Spring 1945). On the evolution of the international civil service, see also Thomas G. Weiss, *International Bureaucracy: An Analysis of the Operation of Functional and Global International Secretariats* (Lexington, Mass.: Lexington Books, 1975).
5. Javier Pérez de Cuéllar, 'The Role of the Secretary General,' in *United Nations, Divided World: The UN's Roles in International Relations*, ed., Adam Roberts and Benedict Kingsbury (Oxford: Oxford University Press, 1993), 63.
6. Brian Urquhart, *A Life in Peace and War* (New York: Harper & Row Publishers, 1987), 227–228.
7. There were two exceptions: Trygve Lie whose second term was only for three years during which he resigned; and Boutros Boutros-Ghali who was not appointed to a second term. In addition, Dag Hammarskjöld was appointed to a second term but died before completing it.
8. Dag Hammarskjöld, 'The International Civil Servant in Law and in Fact,' Oxford Lecture, 30 May 1961, in *The Servant of Peace: A Selection of the Speeches and Statements of Dag Hammarskjöld, Secretary-General of the United Nations 1953–1961*, ed., Wilder Foote (London: The Bodley Head, 1962), 335.
9. Report of the Preparatory Commission on the United Nations, para. 16.
10. See Stephen M. Schwebel, 'The Origins and Development of Article 99 of the Charter: The Powers of the Secretary-General of the U.N.,' *The British Yearbook of International Law* 28 (1951): 372–376.

11. Hammarskjöld, 'The International Civil Servant,' 335.
12. Boutros Boutros-Ghali, 'An Agenda for Peace: One Year Later,' *Orbis: A Journal of World Affairs* 37, no. 3 (1993): 324.
13. Stephen M. Schwebel, *The Secretary-General of the United Nations: His Political Powers and Practice* (Cambridge, Mass.: Harvard University Press, 1952), 84 and 87.
14. Leon Gordenker, *The UN Secretary-General and the Maintenance of Peace* (New York: Columbia University Press, 1967), 139 and 143.
15. Hammarskjöld, 'The International Civil Servant,' 337–338.
16. Ramesh Thakur, *The United Nations, Peace and Security: From Collective Security to the Responsibility to Protect* (Cambridge: Cambridge University Press, 2006), 321.
17. Inis L. Claude, Jr., *Swords into Plowshares: The Problems and Progress of International Organization*, 4th edn. (New York: Random House, 1984), 211.
18. Trygve Lie, *In the Cause of Peace: Seven Years with the United Nations* (New York: Macmillan, 1954); U Thant, *View from the UN: The Memoirs of U Thant* (Garden City, NY: Doubleday, 1978); Kurt Waldheim, *The Challenge of Peace* (London: Weidenfeld and Nicolson, 1980); Kurt Waldheim, *In the Eye of the Storm* (London: Weidenfeld and Nicolson, 1985); Javier Pérez de Cuéllar, *Pilgrimage for Peace: A Secretary General's Memoir* (New York: St. Martin's Press, 1997); and Boutros Boutros-Ghali, *Unvanquished: A US–UN Saga* (New York: Random House, 1999).
19. Gordenker, *The UN Secretary-General*, xiii. See also Leon Gordenker, *The UN Secretary-General and Secretariat* (London: Routledge, 2005).
20. Ranshofen-Wertheimer, *The International Secretariat*, 435.
21. James Barros, *Office Without Power: Secretary-General Sir Eric Drummond 1919–1933* (Oxford: Clarendon Press, 1979), 402.
22. Schwebel, 'The Origin and Development of Article 99,' 86.
23. Lie, *In the Cause of Peace*, 277.
24. Robert S. Jordan, 'Prologue: The Legacy which Dag Hammarskjöld Inherited and his Imprint on it,' in Robert S. Jordan, ed., *Dag Hammarskjöld Revisited: The UN Secretary-General as a Force in World Politics* (Durham, NC: Carolina Academic Press, 1983), 8.
25. Brian Urquhart, *Hammarskjöld* (London: Bodley Head, 1973), 596.
26. Statement by Premier Khrushchev according to Walter Lippmann, *New York Herald Tribune* (European edition), 17 April 1961.
27. Matthew Hughes, 'The Strange Death of Dag Hammarskjöld,' *History Today* 51, no.10, (October 2001).
28. Waldheim, *The Challenge of Peace*, 24.
29. Seymour Maxwell Finger and Arnold A Saltzman, *Bending with the Winds: Kurt Waldheim and the United Nations* (New York: Praeger Publishers, 1990), 9–10. There are also various conspiracy theories that Waldheim was being controlled or blackmailed whilst at the UN as a result of his shady past, see Shirley Hazzard, *The Countenance of Truth: The United Nations and the Waldheim Case* (New York: Viking, 1990), 59–65.
30. Javier Pérez de Cuéllar, *Report of the Secretary-General on the Work of the Organization*, UN document A/37/1, 7 September 1982.
31. Marrack Goulding, 'The UN Secretary-General,' in *The UN Security Council: From the Cold War to the 21st Century*, ed. David M. Malone (Boulder, Colo.: Lynne Rienner Publishers, 2004), 267–268.
32. Personal correspondence to the author, 12 August 1995.
33. Boutros Boutros-Ghali, 'The diplomatic role of the United Nations Secretary-General,' Cyril Foster Lecture, Oxford University, 15 January 1996.

34. Boutros Boutros-Ghali, *Support by the United Nations System of the Efforts of Governments to Promote and Consolidate New or Restored Democracies*, UN document A/51/761, 20 December 1996. More commonly known as 'An Agenda for Democratization.'

35. Boutros Boutros-Ghali, 'Global Leadership after the Cold War,' *Foreign Affairs* 75, no.2 (1996): 86–98.

36. Boutros Boutros-Ghali, 'United Nations must find its truth in fire of realism, Secretary-General says, on eve of General Assembly's Fifty-First Session,' UN Press Release SG/SM/6053, 16 September 1996.

37. David Owen, *Balkan Odyssey*, (London: Victor Gollancz, 1995), 68.

38. Boutros Boutros-Ghali, Cyril Foster Lecture.

39. Raymond Bonner, 'Shattered Nation: A special report. Rwanda Now Faces Painful Ordeal of Rebirth,' *The New York Times*, 29 December 1994.

40. 'Letter dated 16 January 1996 from the Secretary-General to the President of the Security Council,' UN document S/1996/36, 17 January 1996.

41. Paul A. Volcker along with Richard J. Goldstone and Mark Pieth constituted the Independent Inquiry Committee into the United Nations Oil-for-Food Programme whose five-volume report is available at www.iic-offp.org.

42. Robert S. Jordan, 'Truly International Bureaucracies: Real or Imagined?', in *Politics in the United Nations System*, ed. Lawrence S. Finkelstein (Durham, NC: Duke University Press, 1988), 441.

CHAPTER 11

INTERNATIONAL COURT OF JUSTICE

JAMES CRAWFORD

TOM GRANT

THE International Court of Justice (ICJ) is one of six principal organs of the United Nations and the main judicial organ. Its Statute is annexed to the Charter, Article 93 of which specifies that 'All Members of the United Nations are *ipso facto* parties.' This chapter examines the origins and development of the Court, provides an overview of its main dimensions, and assesses its work.

ORIGINS AND DEVELOPMENT

Before the establishment of a permanent international court, states used ad hoc arbitration where necessary to resolve international disputes between them. The *Alabama Claims* arbitration of 1872[1] is frequently identified as a key nineteenth-century example, though it was by no means the earliest.

The Permanent Court of Arbitration (PCA) was established by the First Hague Convention for the Peaceful Settlement of International Disputes in 1899 (and revised in 1907). It was not a court as distinct from a framework for the establishment of ad hoc panels, but it had a distinct caseload, in particular until the 1920s. Although it was characterized as evanescent,[2] it continues to exist and in recent years even to flourish.

By contrast the Permanent Court of International Justice (PCIJ) was established in 1922 as a permanent court with its own full-time judges. Though institutionally distinct from the League of Nations, there were close links between the two. Article XIV of the League Covenant provided for the establishment of a court; the League Council decided on conditions of access for non-member states; League organs elected the judges; the League bore the costs of the court; and under Article 14 (3) of the Covenant, the court had an advisory jurisdiction on a request of the League Council or Assembly. The PCIJ delivered 32 judgments and 27 advisory opinions in the interwar period, laying down a jurisprudence regularly applied by the ICJ after 1945.[3]

The PCIJ was wound up in 1946 at the same time as the League. But its Statute was closely followed in the Statute of the International Court of Justice, adopted at San Francisco in 1945. Textually, there were only a few differences: most importantly, the ICJ became part of the United Nations, its 'principal judicial organ' (Charter Article 7; Statute Article 1).[4] But, as with the PCIJ Statute, the Charter stopped short of conferring any general contentious jurisdiction on the Court. Under Chapter VI the Security Council 'should . . . take into consideration that legal disputes should as a general rule be referred by the parties to the International Court of Justice in accordance with the provisions of the Statute of the Court' (Article 36 (3)). This makes it clear that, while the Security Council may exhort states to have recourse to the Court, it may not actually confer jurisdiction over disputes between states.[5] In fact, the Security Council has only used this provision twice—once after the incident in the Corfu Channel; and once in connection with the multiple questions in dispute between Greece and Turkey. The United Kingdom instituted proceedings against Albania; at that time neither Greece nor Turkey did so.[6]

In the interwar period it was sometimes suggested that the court should stay proceedings when the League was seized of a dispute,[7] but there was no practice to that effect. Similarly since 1945 the ICJ has consistently upheld its jurisdiction faced with the plea that the same matter was pending before the Security Council or some other political organ. Its function is to determine legal disputes, leaving to the Security Council the task of dealing with political issues. Thus the two bodies operate in parallel, if not quite in isolation.[8]

OVERVIEW

Like the constitutional courts of a number of states (e.g., Canada, Germany, and India), the International Court of Justice may hear both contentious and advisory cases.

Contentious Cases

Only states may be parties to contentious cases before the ICJ (Statute Article 34), and only if they have consented to its jurisdiction in accordance with the Statute.[9] There are now two steps before a contentious case can be brought. First, each state concerned either must be a UN member or separately a party to the Statute or must have been permitted to have recourse to the Court, pursuant to October 1946 Security Council resolution 9.[10] Second, each state party to the proceeding must have consented to jurisdiction over the dispute.

Consent to jurisdiction may be given generally in advance, pursuant to the 'optional clause,' Article 36 (2) of the Statute; or by treaty with respect to a defined class of cases (the usual formula is 'disputes concerning the interpretation or application' of the treaty); or by special agreement in relation to a dispute which has already arisen; or by ad hoc consent.

Under Statute Article 36 (1), the Court's jurisdiction extends to 'all cases which the parties refer to it and all matters specially provided for in the Charter of the United Nations or in treaties and conventions in force.' The Court has competence to decide its own jurisdiction 'in the event of a dispute as to whether the Court has jurisdiction' (Article 36 (6)). It is also for the Court to determine whether a justiciable dispute has been submitted.[11]

While the consent of the parties is always necessary, jurisdiction has been described as 'quasi-compulsory,' when it derives from one of the numerous treaties providing in general terms for submission of disputes to the Court or from the acceptance of compulsory jurisdiction under Article 36 (2). This provides that member states may

recognize as compulsory *ipso facto* and without special agreement in relation to any other state accepting the same obligation, the jurisdiction of the Court in all legal disputes concerning (a) the interpretation of a treaty, (b) any question of international law, (c) the existence of any fact which, if established, would constitute a breach of an international obligation, (d) the nature or extent of the reparation to be made for the breach of an international obligation.

Article 36 (3) makes clear that compulsory jurisdiction is not an all-or-nothing proposition: a state making a declaration accepting the Court's jurisdiction in advance may do so 'unconditionally or on condition of reciprocity on the part of several or certain States, or for a certain time.'[12] Most states accepting compulsory jurisdiction have elected to include the condition of reciprocity;[13] time limits on acceptance are not uncommon; and, in some cases, further qualifications have been attached.[14] Though Article 36 (3) specifies reciprocity and time limits as matters in relation to which a state may make a reservation, the Statute does not say that only these matters are the proper object of a reservation, and in practice a wide range of reservations have been made,[15] including some clearly directed at specific pending disputes.[16]

There has been, relatively, a decline in the number of optional clause declarations. A number of states have allowed their declarations to lapse or have actually terminated them. Bolivia, Brazil, Guatemala, Thailand, and Turkey had accepted compulsory jurisdiction with time limits and did not renew acceptance after the limits had run. South Africa terminated its acceptance in 1967; France in 1974; and the United States and Israel in 1985. China stated in December 1972 that it did not recognize the acceptance of compulsory jurisdiction that the Nationalist government had communicated in 1946. Thus, apart from the United Kingdom, no permanent member of the Security Council currently accepts the Court's compulsory jurisdiction.[17] Currently only some sixty-four of the UN's 192 member states accept it at all; and 'special reservations' are widespread. Suriname, for example, reserves 'disputes, which have arisen or may arise with respect to or in relation with the borders of the Republic of Suriname';[18] India, disputes concerning, *inter alia*, 'zones of national maritime jurisdiction including for the regulation and control of marine pollution and the conduct of scientific research by foreign vessels.'[19] Even where a reservation excludes compulsory jurisdiction or no declaration is in force, it is still open to states to accept, by way of *compromis*, the Court's jurisdiction for a particular dispute. The compromissory clauses of various treaties—for example, the Genocide Convention—also furnish a basis for jurisdiction.[20] At present, there are some 300 treaties in force containing compromissory clauses, varying in form and extent.[21]

Since jurisdiction in a dispute between two states depends on nothing but their own consent, the Court will leave it to them to raise any objection. But there may be questions of admissibility which depend, for example, on considerations of mootness or non-justiciability, and these may be raised by the Court of its own motion.[22] Where the states parties to a case before it do not include some third state whose legal interests are at stake, the Court may decline jurisdiction, as for example in the *Monetary Gold* case.[23] In effect, the case as presented to the Court is artificial and does not coincide with the real underlying dispute.[24] The *Monetary Gold* principle was revisited in *East Timor*, where Portugal sought a decision as to the legality of a maritime boundary agreement between Australia and Indonesia concerning the Timor Gap. Indonesia (not being a party to the optional clause) had not been sued; the Court found that the decision sought by Portugal directly concerned Indonesia's claims to sovereignty over East Timor and could not be given in the absence of Indonesia.[25]

Advisory Opinions

The Court's advisory jurisdiction derives from Charter Article 96, under which the General Assembly or the Security Council may request the Court 'to give an advisory opinion on any legal question.' Specialized agencies or subsidiary organs of the UN may also request advisory opinions respecting 'legal questions arising within the scope of their activities,' where the General Assembly has authorized them to do so. In *Legality of the Use by a State of Nuclear Weapons in Armed Conflict*, the Court held that a request did not fall within the scope of the activities of the specialized agency making the request, the World Health Organization, and thus could not be answered.[26] Thus the purpose of a specialized agency, as set out in its constitution, is a constraint on authority to request advisory opinions.

Most often it has been the General Assembly which has requested advisory opinions,[27] and here the problem of scope of activities hardly arises, given the wide range of matters that can interest it under the Charter.[28] Nor has the Court been sympathetic to the argument that the Security Council's priority under the Charter in matters of international peace and security precludes the Assembly from seeking legal advice on such matters: generally speaking the subject matter competence of the two principal organs overlaps, even if only the Council can pass binding resolutions and impose sanctions.[29]

The Court is not obliged to give an advisory opinion, though it has repeatedly said that 'a reply to a request for an opinion should not in principle be refused.'[30] It has sometimes been suggested that the Court should adopt a 'political question doctrine,' and should decline to deal with questions not 'purely legal.' Early on, however, in connection with the interpretation of Charter Article 4, the Court made clear that it would not decline requests for advisory opinions simply because there were political implications underlying the legal questions it was asked to address.[31] This was made clear again in the *Nuclear Weapons* and *Wall* advisory opinions.[32] Indeed, to say that cases before the Court have a political aspect is to say nothing at all; there always will be. The issue is whether there are available legal standards for the resolution of the question asked, whatever the political implications may be of the answer given.

A concern of the Court in deciding whether to exercise advisory jurisdiction has been to avoid adjudication of a dispute the parties to which have not consented to jurisdiction. In the *Eastern Carelia* case, the League Council had requested an opinion as to the obligations of Russia under the Treaty of Dorpat, acting at the request of Finland which had a dispute with Russia on the matter. Russia refused to participate, and the PCIJ rejected jurisdiction as inconsistent with 'the essential rules guiding their activity as a Court': the request was a straightforward attempt to evade the express requirements of Article 17 of the Covenant in relation to an existing interstate dispute—moreover Russia was not then a party to the Covenant.[33] But *Eastern Carelia* has been narrowly construed, and indeed has never been applied. In most situations that might call for an advisory opinion, there exists some dispute between states, and the non-consent of a state to ICJ jurisdiction has not prevented the Court from giving an advisory opinion provided the requesting organ has its own valid interest in receiving legal guidance on the question asked. The *Interpretation of Peace Treaties*, *Western Sahara*, and *Wall* cases illustrate this consistent approach.[34]

Law Applied by the ICJ

Article 38 of the Statute sets out the sources of law to which the Court may have reference in reaching decisions. These are

(a) international conventions, whether general or particular, establishing rules
    expressly recognized by the contesting states;
(b) international custom, as evidence of a general practice accepted as law;
(c) the general principles of law recognized by civilized nations;
(d) subject to the provisions of Article 59, judicial decisions and the teachings of the
    most highly qualified publicists of the various nations, as subsidiary means for
    the determination of rules of law.

With the agreement of the parties, the Court also may decide *ex aequo et bono* (Article
38 (2)), though it has never had to do so. Article 59 limits the binding effect of a
decision of the Court to the parties and case with respect to which it was adopted.

Standing before the ICJ

Any state party to the Statute of the Court may institute proceedings. All UN members
are, under Charter Article 93 (1), '*ipso facto* parties to the Statute.' The Security Council
has authority under Charter Article 93 (2) and Statute Article 35 (2) to authorize states
not party to the Statute to participate in proceedings. Under this provision, a number
of states that were not members became parties to the Statute. Since the achievement of
virtually universal UN membership, this provision has ceased to operate in practice.

Composition of the Court

The Court consists of 'a body of independent judges, elected regardless of their
nationality from among persons of high moral character, who possess the qualifications required in their respective countries for appointment to the highest judicial
offices, or are jurisconsults of recognized competence in international law' (Statute
Article 2). There are fifteen judges, no two of whom may be nationals of the same state.
Elections take place every three years, five judges being chosen at each election (Article
13). Judges serve a term of nine years and may be re-elected. The Court's president and
vice-president serve terms of three years and are elected by the Court (Article 21).

Election is by absolute majority of the General Assembly and the Security Council,
voting independently from a list of nominees. The Security Council veto does not
apply; thus permanent members are not guaranteed a seat, though so far no
candidate of a permanent member has been defeated. A complex procedure
addresses the situation in which the Council and the Assembly have not voted for
the same fifteen candidates. The Court itself, in the event the political organs cannot
agree, may choose judges to fill vacancies, though this has not yet been necessary.
Removal of a judge before expiration of his term is by unanimous agreement of the
other members of the Court: in fact no judge has been removed in this way.

A judge of the nationality of a party to a case before the Court retains the right to
sit. A state party, if it does not have a national judge of the Court, may designate a

judge ad hoc. Thus, in some cases, as many as seventeen judges may comprise the Court. A number of judges have served earlier as judges ad hoc, and since practitioners before the Court cannot also act as ad hoc judges, retired judges are natural candidates for the role.

Nominations for election are made by the national groups of the Permanent Court of Arbitration (Article 4 (1)) and, for countries not represented on it, from national groups appointed for this purpose by their governments, under the same conditions as prescribed for members of the PCA by Article 44 of the 1907 Hague Convention. Each national group may nominate up to four candidates, no more than two of whom may share the nationality of the nominators.[35]

Article 9 of the Statute states the general principle guiding the composition of the Court:

At every election, the electors shall bear in mind not only that the persons to be elected should individually posses the qualifications required, but also that in the body as a whole the representation of the main forms of civilization and of the principal legal systems of the world should be assured.

In conformity with Article 9, the Court consists of judges from the world's major regions and has reflected the major legal traditions. There are conventions of long standing as to regional representation on the Court, which have not changed despite the end of the Cold War and of the division of Europe.

Procedure

Chapter III of the Statute (Articles 39–64) sets out the basic elements of procedure. Cases are heard publicly, unless the parties request or the Court requires a closed hearing (Article 46). French and English are the Court's languages; others may be authorized by the Court (Article 39). Decisions are binding only between the parties which have submitted their dispute to the Court (Article 59). This does not mean that precedent has no role. Indeed the Court has rarely departed explicitly from its earlier decisions, and reference to its own case law 'has become one of the most conspicuous features of the Judgments and Opinions of the Court.'[36]

Under Article 41, the Court may indicate provisional measures 'which ought to be taken to preserve the respective rights of either party.' Despite this language, provisional measures have been held to be binding on the parties.[37] The Court deals with provisional measures requests with commendable speed—unlike its general caseload which is currently being dealt with only after long delays.[38]

Under Charter Article 94, member states undertake to comply with decisions of the Court, and provision is made for the Security Council to take action in the event of non-compliance ('decide upon measures to be taken to give effect to the judgment'). Generally the record of voluntary compliance is a good one; in some cases the Security Council has assisted in the implementation process.[39]

A case is presented to the Court both in writing (with two, three, or occasionally even four rounds of written pleadings) and orally. In oral proceedings the Court may hear witnesses, factual and expert—but usually cases are presented by the agents and counsel based on the documentary record.[40] The Court is competent to select individuals or bodies to give an expert opinion or to carry out an inquiry (Article 50), something it did to effect in *Corfu Channel*.[41]

The Court sits at the Peace Palace in The Hague, a building completed in 1913 as a sort of full-frontal false-Gothic emporium: more recent additions, funded largely by the Dutch government, have improved functionality to a degree.[42] Not all the judges are resident in The Hague, but the Court is formally fixed there. In the *Gabčíkovo–Nagymaros* case, the Court visited parts of the Danube River affected by the project. An invitation by South Africa to do the same in connection with the *South West Africa* cases was declined,[43] and the Court has shown no disposition to visit disputed locations farther afield than Budapest or Bratislava.

Some of the matters organized under the procedural provisions of the Statute might equally be seen as matters of substance—for example, Article 53 concerning non-appearance, under which the Court may reach a decision on the merits in the event that one of the parties fails to appear. Article 53 requires that, before the Court reaches a decision on the merits, it 'satisfy itself . . . that the claim is well founded in fact and law': this raises a question as to the extent of the examination incumbent on the Court in such a case. In practice it has conducted as full an inquiry as possible, giving no hint of a default judgment. For example in *Diplomatic and Consular Staff in Tehran*, though the United States was 'unable to furnish detailed factual evidence' relating to events in Iran after a certain date,[44] the key facts were clear and the Court decided in its favor.[45] In the *Nicaragua* case the United States, having lost on jurisdiction, declined to contest the merits—and lost badly.[46] The posture of non-appearance has not been much repeated since.[47]

There is no appeal from a decision, whether given by a full Court or a Chamber (Article 60), but an application for revision of judgment may be made on the basis of 'the discovery of some fact of such a nature as to be a decisive factor, which fact was, when the judgment was given, unknown to the Court and also to the party claiming revision' (Article 61 (1)). Applications for revision have sometimes been brought but they face major obstacles and none have yet succeeded.[48]

Pursuant to Article 30 (1), the Court is to 'frame rules for carrying out its functions.' The procedure of the Court is developed in detail in the Rules of Court adopted on 14 April 1978 and amended periodically; the Court has been more active in seeking interstitial reform through the use of its rule-making power.

Reflecting the view that its advisory jurisdiction involves equally an exercise of a judicial function, the Court applies a broadly similar procedure in both contentious and advisory cases. According to Article 102 (2) of the Rules of Court,

The Court shall also be guided by the provisions of the Statute and of these Rules which apply in contentious cases to the extent to which it recognizes them to be applicable. For this purpose, it shall above all consider whether the request for the advisory opinion relates to a legal question actually pending between two or more States.

All parties with an interest in a question under review by way of advisory request are given the opportunity to plead, a practice established in *Administrative Tribunal of the ILO* : 'The judicial character of the Court requires that both sides directly affected by these proceedings should be in a position to submit their views and their arguments to the Court.'[49] The Court in later advisory proceedings similarly received submissions from states with an interest in the question: in the two *Nuclear Weapons* opinions, forty-three states appeared;[50] in the *Wall* case, forty-four states[51] (despite an attempted Western boycott).

Under Statute Article 26 (1), the Court may form 'one or more chambers... for dealing with particular categories of cases; for example, labour cases and cases relating to transit and communications.' Under Article 26 (2), a chamber may be formed to hear a particular case. The formation and functioning of chambers is elaborated in Articles 15–18 of the Rules. In the *Gulf of Maine* case, the parties (the United States and Canada) effectively designated the judges to comprise the Chamber, under threat of a reference to arbitration otherwise. Chambers have been convened in a few cases since; since they depend on the consent of the parties, they are in practice only used in special agreement cases, and often not then.[52]

Internal Deliberations and Delivery of Opinions

How the Court is to reach a decision is sketched only in general outline in the Statute. Article 54 (3) provides that deliberations of the Court are to take place in private and remain secret. 'All questions shall be decided by a majority of the judges present' (Article 55 (1)), with the president having a casting vote (Article 55 (2)). Judgments shall state the reasons on which they are based (Article 56 (1)), and provision is made for any judge to deliver a separate opinion (Article 57). Article 19 of the Rules of Court authorizes the Court to adopt resolutions respecting its internal procedure, and, under this authority, procedures for deliberations have been elaborated.

Preference has been expressed for avoiding tie-breaking votes in the interests of maintaining the collegial basis of the Court's decisions,[53] but casting votes have occurred in a number of cases. It also has been said that separate voting has been a difficulty for the Court, in particular as concerns defining which issues are to be open to a separate vote. It is a matter for the Court whether to hold separate votes at all.[54] Petrén has suggested that the written notes submitted by the members of the Court after the first deliberation on a case are required too early and, because they tend to settle judges' views, contribute to the adoption of individual and dissenting opinions, whose number and prolixity have been criticized.[55] However, such opinions can provide important insight into the issues and can develop points in which the judgment itself is summary or even silent. According to Gerald Fitzmaurice:

the separate or dissenting opinions of individual Judges... play a valuable part in the functioning of the Court, and to ignore them would be to give but an incomplete portrayal of its work as a whole, as well as to disregard material of primary importance from the standpoint of the present study; for although dissenting Judges differ from the Court as to the actual conclusion, they may well, in the course of so doing, make general statements or explanations of principle which are in themselves not in any way inconsistent with the views of the Court, but merely differently applied to the facts...[E]ven where the views of an individual Judge are definitely contrary to those of the Court, on matters of principle, it may be desirable to quote them, because it is often the case, particularly with difficult or controversial questions, that a decision can only properly be appreciated in the light of a contrary view.[56]

At the same time, some judges (e.g., Gilbert Guillaume) who have dissented rarely may have been more effective in contributing to decision-making as a publicly silent member of the majority.

Finance

The expenses of the Court, pursuant to Statute Article 33, are 'borne by the United Nations in such a manner as shall be decided by the General Assembly.' Unless otherwise decided, parties bear their own costs (Article 64): in practice costs orders against the losing party are not made.

ASSESSING THE ICJ AND ITS WORK

Quite apart from its role in addressing (and sometimes settling) individual disputes, the Court has contributed in a significant way to the development of international law in a variety of areas and fields. It has been described as 'filling many gaps in international legislation'[57] but this is an understatement: many areas of the law— concerning for example international organizations, the law of treaties, international claims, territorial issues, the law of the sea—have been fundamentally influenced by the ICJ and its predecessor. Less tangibly the two courts have established a continuity of law and process between states and have contributed to creating a canon of judicial method at the international level which was previously embryonic. According to Robert Jennings:

That Court is a permanent court and its constituency is the world. Consequently it is crucially, intimately and inescapably concerned with the development and shaping of international law to a far higher degree than ad hoc tribunals which are, certainly not wholly, yet undoubtedly primarily concerned with the satisfactory disposal of particular disputes.[58]

Despite its organizational continuity, however, the Court has gone through periods of inactivity. In the period 1965–1985, relatively few cases were brought to it, and the debacle of the *South West Africa* cases (1966) harmed its reputation not only in the Third World. Various remedies were suggested. It was proposed, for example, to extend advisory jurisdiction to allow national courts to request opinions on matters of international law, on the analogy of references to the European Court of Justice;[59] that the UN Secretary-General be authorized to request advisory opinions[60] and that there be introduced 'binding advisory opinions' on matters involving international organizations.[61] Most of the Court's docket then concerned land and maritime boundary disputes, which led some to suggest that such cases were the natural task of the Court and, perhaps, should be its exclusive focus.

But gradually in the 1980s and then with some persistence after 1990 the Court's caseload revived and widened. New cases were brought by a range of states from Central Europe (formerly a no-go area), Africa, Central America, and even Asia. Starting mainly with maritime boundary cases in the 1980s, the subject matter of the Court's caseload expanded—military and paramilitary activities, compensation for the environmental effects of colonial mining operations, disputes about dam projects on rivers and bridge projects across straits, questions of land and insular sovereignty, diplomatic and consular immunities, international criminal law and so on. Thus President Guillaume's succinct description of the Court as 'la seule Cour [de] caractère universel ayant une compétence générale' became broadly true in fact and not merely in form.[62]

The conception of the Court as the 'principal judicial organ' of the United Nations has to take into account certain features of the international system as it currently exists. One is that many disputes at the international level are not simply bilateral. There is for various reasons a multilateralization of disputes, yet the Court's dominant mode is bilateral. A second and associated point is that in many respects international disputes are dealt with in the context of collective actions of international organizations or ad hoc coalitions. This raises serious questions about the accountability of those organizations or entities in a situation where there is contentious jurisdiction only as between a minority of states. The United States and the United Kingdom may instigate the Security Council to take action against Libya, but any action taken is arguably that of the Council and not of the major proponents.[63] An informal coalition may coordinate action against a state such as the Federal Republic of Yugoslavia without any Security Council mandate; there may be patently no jurisdiction over the major proponents,[64] leaving minor participants carrying the forensic can.[65]

One of the Court's standard responses—understandably in jurisdictional terms—has been to characterize such disputes as bilateral. It did so, for example, in *Nicaragua*, even to the point of refusing El Salvador permission to intervene.[66] It did so again in *Nauru*, in the context of action taken by an 'administering authority' consisting not of the respondent state alone but of three states, two of them not parties to the case.

Developments in the Court's approach to third-state intervention may help address the situation in which a case is genuinely multilateral. Following *Nicaragua*, there was a real risk that it would become almost impossible to intervene before the Court. The Court's decision to allow Nicaragua to intervene in the *El Salvador v. Honduras* case, albeit in a qualified way, was welcome.[67] The adoption of the Chamber's reasoning by the full Court in *Cameroon v. Nigeria*, as regards the application by Equatorial Guinea to intervene, further consolidated the position (though there the application was not opposed by either party).[68] In this context, no criticism is to be made of the Court's handling of the various interventions in the revived *Nuclear Tests* case in 1995.[69] The interveners made no claim to intervene as to the essential point about jurisdiction, which the Court quite properly chose to take first. Nonetheless that was an illustration of the more basic point. Those four small states, none of which had previously attempted to appear before the Court, felt strongly about French actions and were as affected by them as the principal Applicant, New Zealand. This is so far the only case of an attempted collective intervention, but it suggests that there may be an increasing number of cases in which some form of intervention is appropriate. To address this, the Court might conduct a review of its rules with respect to intervention. In the first place, it should enable parties with a bona fide interest in intervening to see the pleadings, and not to have to rely on covert cooperation from a party to the case. A legitimate intervener may have interests adverse to both the parties in a case, so that such cooperation is not always forthcoming. The Rules of Court might also be amended so as to require better specification of grounds of intervention, and in particular to require the intervener to make clear in advance whether it is seeking to intervene as a party or is limiting itself to third-party intervention.[70]

At least with intervention the matter is largely dealt with by the Rules, which are much easier to amend than the Statute.[71] In respect of disputes involving international organizations the position is quite different. The essential problem here is that, whereas states acting alone or in small groups will each be accountable for their own acts, there is no regular system of accountability when states choose to act under the aegis of an international organization created by them, and this seems to be true whether the action is taken against a member of the organization or a third state. In *Nicaragua*, the Court held very firmly that if two or more states are acting together in a collective self-defense situation, nonetheless the principle of individual responsibility applies and the *Monetary Gold* principle does not prevent proceedings being brought against one of them. In *Nauru*, it held that the fact that three states acted through what one might call an 'unincorporated association'—the administering authority—did not preclude action being brought against any one of them in respect of its own conduct.[72]

But states may be able to avoid the problem by acting under the aegis of an international organization with separate legal personality. In that situation, it will usually be the international organization which is responsible—at least if it is acting *intra vires* and possibly even if it is not. The international organization is a separate legal entity in accordance with the *Reparation* principle.[73] The principle was indeed important for 'reduc[ing] ... to their true proportions' the doctrines of the exclusiveness of states as subjects of international law and of nationality of claims.[74] But in accordance with the Institute of International Law's distillation of the principles arising from the *Tin Council* dispute, only the organization, and not its member states, will be responsible for its acts.[75] In neither the discussions of the Institute nor in the *Tin Council* debate itself was there much support for an automatic principle of attribution to the members of the acts of an international organization. However there is—or ought to be—a corollary. The Court operates at the public international level and so do international organizations. Yet, as Article 34 of the Statute makes quite clear, only states can be parties to contentious proceedings before the Court. Thus states, if they act through the medium of international organizations, and notwithstanding that they are acting wholly in the public sector, can act unaccountably from the perspective of the jurisdictional system of the Court. If the chance was presented in the *Lockerbie* case for the Court to review Security Council practice, it did not take it.[76]

It should be stressed that Statute Article 34 is, legally speaking, beyond the possibility of interpretation: an international organization is not a state, notwithstanding that it is entirely composed of states and operates solely under their influence and collective control. Moreover the question whether an international organization can sue or be sued (to which international law now gives a firm positive answer) is not the same question as whether it should be regarded as a state. That it is necessary, in the context of the World Trade Organization (WTO)[77] or the Law of the Sea Convention of 1982 and associated instruments,[78] to equate the European Union (EU) with a state party does not mean that it is a state, even though it has state-like qualities.[79] The truth is that the Security Council in doing certain things—such as creating criminal courts—has state-like qualities. But the distinction between states and international organizations remains, as the Court long ago pointed out.[80]

This raises a serious problem with regard to the rule of law at the international level.[81] If international organizations are subject to the rule of law there should be some ultimate process by which accountability to and between member states can be maintained. This is the case, for example, with the EU for the purposes of EU law, and for some international purposes, including fisheries under the law of the sea and interstate trade disputes under the WTO. In the classic mode of federal relations, the EU's exclusive external competence can be expected to expand even as its membership expands,[82] and a side-effect is to sideline the Court.

There are no doubt many reasons for distinguishing the European institutions, with their 'spirit of integration' and elaborate institutional structure, from institutions at the universal level such as the United Nations and its various organs. But the point remains that there is a serious underlying problem of the accountability of international organizations, including the UN itself. The problem is not to be resolved by binding advisory opinions, and it was a sensible decision to abolish the Court's jurisdiction in staff cases.[83] Binding advisory opinions are a device—in the nature of a legal fiction—and are undesirable for a variety of reasons.[84]

It is useful to compare, however, the problem in the *Lockerbie* cases.[85] There, although remedies were sought against individual states, and although it can be argued that those remedies or some of them ought to have been available, in substance what Libya sought was a decision in relation to action taken by the requisite majority of the Security Council under the Charter. The fact that one state or another may have acted as a protagonist in that regard is of little relevance. National experience suggests that it is difficult to sue the individual members of a deliberative body in their capacity as members of that body. For example, how can one have a situation in which some members of a deliberative body are prevented from acting by judicial procedure when other members are not? Thus there are difficulties in seeking to subvert the Security Council umbrella by proceeding against individual members of the Council.

Whatever the prospects for Statute amendment, the point of principle in relation to public international organizations remains. And, in the longer term, unless the Court becomes an available forum in relation to the whole range of public international law matters, its claims to universality will fade,[86] and its correlative task of developing international law as a coherent body of norms will be more difficult to achieve.

A related issue presented by globalization is the fact that many disputes and situations concern nonstate actors (NSAs) as well as states. Peace and security may be threatened by NSAs both internally (as in the Sudan and Liberia) and beyond the state (as with sundry terrorist groups). The Court has tended to focus on the interstate aspects of the use of force,[87] but this is unrealistic. Outside the field of use of force, too, the state has no monopoly of responsibility. For example, both foreign direct investment and international human rights matters are now usually presented as mixed disputes, distinct in various ways from the old system of diplomatic protection in which the interests of private parties were notionally aggregated in the state.[88] Thus, the Court is excluded from the major growth areas of international dispute resolution.[89]

It may be said, however, that such broader issues are utopian when the Court cannot deal expeditiously with its existing case-load. Even in the field of maritime delimitation—where it had been the principal forum since 1969—there is an issue of comparative performance. Arbitration under the 1982 Law of the Sea Convention can be expected to take two to three years from commencement through to award; on current performance the Court may take twice as long.[90] Concerns about delay combine with other factors to create a new preference for ad hoc adjudication or the creation of new institutions.[91]

CONCLUSION

Despite the difficulties, the Court has made a considerable contribution to the development of international law and to the resolution of deputes over sixty years, building on the work after 1922 of its predecessor, the PCIJ. By no means are all international disputes suitable for judicial resolution, and there has been a proliferation of other forums for dealing with specific categories (e.g., in the field of world trade), sometimes with great success. At the same time, the settlement of interstate disputes is not a zero-sum game. Given the increasing number of international forums, there are signs that more states are exposed to litigation and see it as an available option for addressing otherwise intractable conflicts. In this evolving situation, the International Court of Justice retains a distinctive place as the UN's principal judicial organ.

Notes

1. John Bassett Moore, *History and Digest of the Arbitrations to which the United States has been a Party* (Buffalo, NY: Hein, 1995), i. 653.
2. Friedrich Martens described it some years after its founding as 'only a shadow which, from time to time, materialises, only to fade away once again:' League of Nations, Permanent Court of International Justice, *Advisory Committee of Jurists* (1922), 22.
3. See, e.g., Hersch Lauterpacht, *The Development of International Law by the International Court* (Cambridge: Cambridge University Press, 1958), 11–13. On the transfer of PCIJ records to the ICJ in 1946, see Shabtai Rosenne, *Documents on the International Court of Justice* (1991), 493–497. Generally on the PCIJ, see Ole Spiermann, *International Legal Argument in the Permanent Court of International Justice: The Rise of the International Judiciary* (Cambridge: Cambridge University Press, 2005).
4. On the relation of the ICJ to other organs of the United Nations, see Bruno Simma, ed., *The Charter of the United Nations: A Commentary*, 2nd edn. (Oxford: Oxford University Press, 2002), 1139.
5. *Corfu Channel*, joint separate opinion, Judgment on Preliminary Objections (ICJ Rep 1947–1948), 17.
6. See Sydney Bailey and Sam Daws, *The Procedure of the UN Security Council*, 3rd edn. (Oxford: Oxford University Press, 1998), 314–316. A later application to the Court by Greece failed for want of jurisdiction: *Aegean Sea Continental Shelf Case (Greece v. Turkey)*, ICJ Rep 1978, 3, 45 (para. 109).
7. Shigeru Oda, 'Reservations in the Declarations of Acceptance of the Optional Clause and the Period of Validity of those Declarations: The Effect of the Shultz Letters,' *British Yearbook of International Law* 59 (1988): 6–7.
8. *Armed Activities on the Territory of the Congo (Democratic Republic of the Congo v. Uganda)*, Provisional Measures, ICJ Rep 2000, 111 and 126 (para. 36). Cf. *Armed Activities on the Territory of the Congo (Democratic Republic of the Congo v. Rwanda)*, Provisional Measures, ICJ Rep 2002, 219, 258–259 (para. 6), Declaration of Judge Thomas Buergenthal. On the relation between the Security Council and the Court generally, see Shabtai Rosenne, *The Law and Practice of the International Court 1920–2005*, 4th edn. (Leiden, Netherlands: Martinus Nijhoff, 2006), 128–140; and Derek Bowett, 'Judicial and Political Functions of the Security Council and the International Court of Justice,' in *The Changing Constitution of the United Nations*, ed. James Fox (London: British Institute of International and Comparative Law, 1997), 73.
9. See generally Pierre-Marie Dupuy, 'Competence of the Court: Article 34,' in *The Statute of the International Court of Justice: A Commentary*, ed. Andreas Zimmermann, Christian Tomuschat, and Karin Oellers-Frahm (Oxford: Oxford University Press, 2006), 545.
10. Statute Article 35 (2) appears to allow states generally to have access to the Court pursuant to 'the special provisions contained in treaties in force' but this provision has been (without any textual warrant) limited to treaties in force in 1945, reducing this possibility to insignificance.

See Kosovo case: *Case concerning Legality of Use of Force (Serbia and Montenegro v. Belgium)*, Preliminary Objections, ICJ Rep 2004, (para. 114). See Andreas Zimmermann, 'Article 35' in *The Statute of the International Court of Justice*, 568–575 and 577–587; and Rosenne, *Law and Practice*, 609–614.

11. See, e.g., *Applicability of the Obligation to Arbitrate under Section 21 of the United Nations Headquarters Agreement of 26 June 1947*, Advisory Opinion, ICJ Rep 1988, 27.

12. See Rosenne, *Law and Practice*, 701–802.

13. About which see *Aegean Sea Continental Shelf case*, Judgment, ICJ Rep 1978, 3, 17, and 20.

14. For examples of such 'special reservations,' see Rosenne, *Law and Practice*, 769–776.

15. *Aerial Incident of 10 August 1999 (Pakistan v. India)*, ICJ Rep 2000, 12 and 29 (para. 37).

16. See *Case concerning Fisheries Jurisdiction (Spain v. Canada)*, ICJ Rep 1998, 432, 438–439, 452–467 (paras. 14, 42–87), and see also Rosenne, *Law and Practice*, 739–740, n. 98.

17. The United Kingdom, by declaration of 5 July 2004, amended its acceptance of compulsory jurisdiction to read as follows:

1. The Government of the United Kingdom of Great Britain and Northern Ireland accept as compulsory ipso facto and without special convention, on condition of reciprocity, the jurisdiction of the International Court of Justice, in conformity with paragraph 2 of Article 36 of the Statute of the Court, until such time as notice may be given to terminate the acceptance, over all disputes arising after 1 January 1974, with regard to situations or facts subsequent to the same date, other than:

(i) any dispute which the United Kingdom has agreed with the other Party or Parties thereto to settle by some other method of peaceful settlement;

(ii) any dispute with the government of any other country which is or has been a Member of the Commonwealth;

(iii) any dispute in respect of which any other Party to the dispute has accepted the compulsory jurisdiction of the International Court of Justice only in relation to or for the purpose of the dispute; or where the acceptance of the Court's compulsory jurisdiction on behalf of any other Party to the dispute was deposited or ratified less than twelve months prior to the filing of the application bringing the dispute before the Court.

2. The Government of the United Kingdom also reserve the right at any time, by means of a notification addressed to the Secretary-General of the United Nations, and with effect as from the moment of such notification, either to add to, amend or withdraw any of the foregoing reservations, or any that may hereafter be added.

This replaces the declaration of 1 January 1969: 654 UNTS 335.

18. Surinamese declaration of 31 August 1987.

19. Indian declaration of 18 September 1974.

20. See John Collier and Vaughan Lowe, *Settlement of Disputes in International Law* (Oxford: Oxford University Press, 1999), 133 n. 36.

21. For a list, see www.icj-cij.org.

22. See, e.g., *South West Africa* cases (Second Phase), ICJ Rep 1962, 319, 328; *Nuclear Tests* cases, ICJ Rep 1974, 253, 259–260 (para. 23), 271 (para. 57); Rosenne, *Law and Practice*, 898–901.

23. *Case of the Monetary Gold Removed from Rome in 1943 (Italy v. France, United Kingdom of Great Britain and Northern Ireland and United States of America)*, ICJ Rep 1954, 19 and 32: 'In the present case, Albania's legal interests would not only be affected by a decision, but would form the very subject-matter of the decision. In such a case, the Statute cannot be

regarded, by implication, as authorizing proceedings to be continued in the absence of Albania.'

24. Shabtai Rosenne, *Procedure in the International Court: A Commentary on the 1978 Rules of the International Court of Justice* (The Hague: Martinus Nijhoff, 1983), 12.

25. *Case Concerning East Timor (Portugal v. Australia)*, ICJ Rep 1995, 90, 104 (paras. 32–35). On 'essential parties,' see generally Rosenne, *Law and Practice*, 539–547.

26. *Legality of the Use by a State of Nuclear Weapons in Armed Conflict*, Advisory Opinion of 8 July 1996, ICJ Rep 1996, 66.

27. Simma, ed., *The Charter of the United Nations*, 1182–1183.

28. Cf. *Legality of the Threat or Use of Nuclear Weapons*, Advisory Opinion of 8 July 1996, ICJ Rep 1996, 226, 232–233 (paras. 11–2).

29. *Legal Consequences of the Construction of a Wall in the Occupied Palestinian Territory*, Advisory Opinion of 9 July 2004, ICJ Rep 2004, 136, 148–150 (paras. 24–28).

30. *Reservations to the Convention on the Prevention and Punishment of the Crime of Genocide*, Advisory Opinion of 28 May 1951, ICJ Rep 1951, 15, 19; and *Legal Consequences for States of the Continued Presence of South Africa in Namibia (South West Africa) Notwithstanding Security Council Resolution 276 (1970)*, Advisory Opinion of 21 June 1971, ICJ Rep 1971, 16 and 27 (para. 41). See also *Application for Review of Judgment No. 158 of the United Nations Administrative Tribunal*, Dissenting Opinion, Judge De Castro, ICJ Rep 1973, 166 and 280 (para. 13).

31. *Conditions of Admission of a State to Membership in the United Nations (Article 4 of the Charter)*, ICJ Rep 1947–48, 61; and *Competence of the General Assembly for the Admission of a State to the United Nations*, ICJ Rep 1950, 6.

32. *Legality of the Threat or Use of Nuclear Weapons*, Advisory Opinion of 8 July 1996, ICJ Rep 1996, 226, 233–234 (para. 13); and *Legal Consequences of the Construction of a Wall in the Occupied Palestinian Territory*, Advisory Opinion of 9 July 2004, ICJ Rep 2004, 136 and 155 (para. 41).

33. *Status of Eastern Carelia* (1923) PCIJ Series B, no. 5, 29.

34. *Interpretation of Peace Treaties with Bulgaria, Hungary and Romania*, Advisory Opinion of 18 July 1950, ICJ Rep 1950, 65, 70–72; *Western Sahara*, Advisory Opinion of 16 October 1975, ICJ Rep 1975, 5, 20 (para. 21); and *Legal Consequences of the Construction of a Wall in the Occupied Palestinian Territory*, Advisory Opinion of 9 July 2004, ICJ Rep 2004, 136 and 148–162 (paras. 24–58).

35. For details of practice respecting elections to the Court, see Bailey & Daws, *The Procedure of the UN Security Council*, 307–314.

36. Lauterpacht, *Development*, 8–9. On precedents, see Mohamed Shahabuddeen, *Precedent in the World Court* (Cambridge: Cambridge University Press, 1996).

37. *LaGrand case (Germany v. United States of America)*, (ICJ Rep 2001), 466 and 516 (para. 128).

38. Shabtai Rosenne, *Provisional Measures in International Law: The International Court of Justice and the International Tribunal for the Law of the Sea* (Oxford: Oxford University Press, 2005), 102–120.

39. *Agreement on the Peaceful Settlement of the Territorial Dispute between the Republic of Chad and Libya*, 31 August 1989, (1990) 29 ILM 15; and *Agreement on the Implementation of the ICJ Judgment Concerning the Territorial Dispute*, 4 April 1994, (1994) 33 ILM 619, S/1994/402, Annex, 13 April 1994. See also Security Council resolution 910 (S/RES/910), 14 April 1994 and Security Council resolution 915 (S/RES/915), 4 May 1994.

40. In the *Case concerning Gabčíkovo–Nagymaros Project (Hungary v. Slovakia)*, the most important dispute heard by the Court in which disputed issues of science and technology were raised, there were extensive presentations on both sides by scientific advocates, rather than the presentation of expert testimony (ICJ Reports 1997), 7.

41. *Corfu Channel Case (United Kingdom of Great Britain and Northern Ireland v. Albania)*, Merits, ICJ Rep 1949, 4; *Quantum*, ICJ Rep 1949, 244. Compare *Case Concerning Delimitation of the Maritime Boundary in the Gulf of Maine Area (Canada v. United States of America)*, ICJ Rep 1984, 165; and *Case Concerning the Frontier Dispute (Burkina Faso v. Republic of Mali)*, ICJ Rep 1986, 554, 587–588, and 648 (paras. 65 and 176), ICJ Rep 1987, 7, 8. See further Rosenne, *Law and Practice*, 1116–1117, 1325–1332.

42. About the premises, see Arthur Eyffinger, *The International Court of Justice 1946–1996* (The Hague: Kluwer Law International, 1996), 65–71.

43. *South West Africa cases (Ethiopia v. South Africa; Liberia v. South Africa)*, Order of 29 November 1965, ICJ Rep 1965, 9.

44. *United States Diplomatic and Consular Staff in Tehran (United States of America v. Iran)*, ICJ Rep 1980, 9 (para. 11).

45. On this and Article 53 generally, see Hugh W. A. Thirlway, *Non-Appearance before the International Court of Justice* (Cambridge: Cambridge University Press, 1985), 120–136.

46. Constanze Schulte, *Compliance with Decisions of the International Court of Justice* (Oxford: Oxford University Press, 2004), 403–404.

47. *Case Concerning Oil Platforms (Islamic Republic of Iran v. United States of America)*, ICJ Rep 2003, 161.

48. *Application for Revision of the Judgment of 11 July 1996 in the Case Concerning Application of the Convention on the Prevention and Punishment of the Crime of Genocide (Bosnia and Herzegovina v. Yugoslavia)*, Preliminary Objections, ICJ Rep 2003, 7 and 32 (para. 73): no 'facts' had been adduced for purposes of Article 61. See also *Application for Revision of the Judgment of 11 September 1992 in the Case Concerning the Land, Island, and Maritime Frontier Dispute (El Salvador v. Honduras: Nicaragua intervening)*, ICJ Rep 2003, 392.

49. *Judgments of the Administrative Tribunal of the ILO upon Complaints made against UNESCO*, ICJ Rep 1956, 77.

50. Though not all in both: *Legality of the Use of Nuclear Weapons by a State in Armed Conflict*, Advisory Opinion of 8 July 1996, ICJ Rep 1996, 66 (para. 6); *Legality of the Threat or Use of Nuclear Weapons*, Advisory Opinion of 8 July 1996, ICJ Rep 1996, 226 and 229 (para. 5).

51. And several international organizations: *Legal Consequences of the Construction of a Wall in the Occupied Palestinian Territory*, Advisory Opinion of 9 July 2004, ICJ Rep 2004, 136 and 142 (para. 9).

52. Further instances of ad hoc chambers proceedings have been *Case Concerning the Frontier Dispute (Burkina Faso v. Mali)*, ICJ Rep 1986, 554; *Case Concerning the Land, Island, and Maritime Frontier Dispute (El Salvador v. Honduras: Nicaragua intervening)*, ICJ Rep 1992, 351; *Case Concerning Elettronica Sicula SpA (ELSI) (United States of America v. Italy)*, ICJ Rep 1989, 15; *Case Concerning the Frontier Dispute (Benin v. Niger)*, ICJ Rep 2002, 613.

53. Rosenne, *Procedure*, 231.

54. Ibid., 231–232.

55. S. Petrén, 'Forms of Expression of Judicial Activity,' in *The Future of the International Court of Justice*, ed. Leo Gross (New York: Oceana Publications, 1976), 445, cited by Rosenne, *Procedure*, 232.

56. Gerald Fitzmaurice, 'The Law and Procedure of the International Court of Justice: General Principles and Substantive Law,' *British Yearbook of International Law* 27 (1950): 1–2, quoted in Robert Jennings, 'The Internal Judicial Practice of the International Court of Justice,' *British Yearbook of International Law* 59 (1988): 44.

57. Antonio Cassese, *International Law in a Divided World* (Oxford: Oxford University Press 1986), 63.

58. Jennings, 'Internal Judicial Practice,' 29.

59. Stephen M. Schwebel, 'Preliminary Rulings by the International Court of Justice at the Instance of National Courts,' *Virginia Journal of International Law* 28 (1988), 495; also in Stephen M. Schwebel, *Justice in International Law* (Cambridge: Cambridge University Press, 1994), 84; Shabtai Rosenne, 'Preliminary Rulings by the International Court of Justice at the Instance of National Courts; A Reply,' *Virginia Journal of International Law* 29 (1989): 401–12; and Gilbert Guillaume, 'La Cour Internationale de Justice. Quelques propositions concretes,' *Revue Generale du Droit International Public* 102 (1996): 332.

60. Hans Corell, 'The International Court of Justice at Fifty,' in *Increasing the Effectiveness of the International Court of Justice: Proceedings of the ICJ/UNITAR Colloquium to Celebrate the 50th Anniversary of the Court*, eds. Connie Peck and Roy S. Lee (The Hague: Martinus Nijhoff, 1997), 6 and 8–9; and Louis B. Sohn, 'Important Improvements in the Functioning of the Principal Organs of the United Nations that Can be Made Without Charter Revision,' *American Journal of International Law* 91, no. 4 (1997): 658–659.

61. Stephen M. Schwebel, 'Authorizing the Secretary-General of the United Nations to Request Advisory Opinions of the International Court of Justice,' *American Journal of International Law* 78, no. 4 (1984): 869–878; and Rosalyn Higgins, 'A Comment on the Current Health of Advisory Opinions,' in *Fifty Years of the International Court of Justice: Essays in honour of Sir Robert Jennings*, ed. Vaughan Lowe and Malgosia Fitzmaurice (Cambridge: Cambridge University Press, 1996), 567.

62. Guillaume, 'La Cour Internationale de Justice,' 332 ['the only Court with a universal jurisdiction having a general competence'].

63. See *Lockerbie* cases: (ICJ Rep 1998), 115 and 128–129 (para. 36).

64. *Case Concerning Legality of Use of Force (Yugoslavia v. United States of America)*, ICJ Rep 1999, 916.

65. See *Case Concerning Legality of Use of Force (Yugoslavia v. Belgium)*, Request for the Indication of Provisional Measures, ICJ Rep 1999, 124.

66. *Military and Paramilitary Activities in and against Nicaragua (Nicaragua v. United States of America)*, ICJ Rep 1984, 392 and 429–431.

67. This point was made by the Study Group (Derek Bowett, James Crawford, Ian Sinclair, and Arthur Watts) established by the British Institute of International and Comparative Law in connection with the UN Decade of International Law. J. P. Gardner and Chanaka Wickremasinghe, eds., *The International Court of Justice: Process, Practice and Procedure* (London: British Institute of International and Comparative Law, 1997).

68. *Case Concerning the Land and Maritime Boundary Between Cameroon and Nigeria (Cameroon v. Nigeria)*, Application by Equatorial Guinea for Permission to Intervene, ICJ Rep 1999, 1029, 1034–1035 (para. 14). See *Case concerning Sovereignty over Pulau Ligitan and Pulau Sipadan (Indonesia v. Malaysia)*, Application by the Philippines for Permission to Intervene, ICJ Rep 2001, 575, where the Philippines' attempt to intervene concerned a collateral issue (the 'Sabah claim') having no particular relevance to the two islands in dispute between the parties.

69. *Request for an Examination of the Situation in Accordance with Paragraph 63 of the Court's Judgement of 20 December 1974 in the Nuclear Tests (New Zealand v. France) Case*, ICJ Rep 1995, 288.

70. On intervention generally, see José María Ruda, 'Intervention before the International Court of Justice' in *Fifty Years of the International Court of Justice: Essays in honour of Sir Robert Jennings*, eds. Vaughan Lowe and Malgosia Fitzmaurice (Cambridge: Cambridge University Press, 1996), 487.

71. The procedure for amending the Statute is effectively the same as for the UN Charter: Charter Article 108. It requires ratification by two-thirds of the membership including all the permanent members.

72. *Certain Phosphate Lands in Nauru (Nauru v. Australia)*, ICJ Rep 1992, 240. It was not contested that the 'administering authority' under the Trusteeship Agreement for Nauru was not a separate legal entity but was simply the three states concerned (Australia, New Zealand, and the United Kingdom) acting in the context of the various agreements for the administration of Nauru. The Court expressly left open the implications of these arrangements in terms of the extent of Australia's liability: ibid., 262 (para. 56). In the first instance Nauru sought only a declaratory judgment.

73. *Reparation for Injuries Suffered in the Service of the United Nations*, Advisory Opinion of 11 April 1949, ICJ Rep 1949, 174. It is true that the Court articulated the principle only in respect of a limited class of international organizations. But in subsequent practice, the general legal personality of international organizations has been conceded without limitation.

74. Hersch Lauterpacht, *The Development of International Law by the International Court* (Cambridge: Cambridge University Press, 1958), 45.

75. 'Organisations internationales,' *Annuaire de l'Institut* 66/I (1995), 251–427.

76. *Questions of Interpretation and Application of the 1971 Montreal Convention arising from the Aerial Incident at Lockerbie (Libyan Arab Jamahiriya v. United States of America)*, ICJ Rep 1998, 115 and 128–130 (paras. 36, 40).

77. Under Articles XI and XIV of the Marrakesh Agreement establishing the World Trade Organization, of 15 April 1994, the European Communities are entitled to, and did in fact become, an original member of the WTO; its voting rights are regulated by Article IX (1), which makes clear that EC member states are also members of the WTO. The WTO Agreement and its associated instruments refer throughout to 'Members' of the WTO, which may include certain autonomous customs territories (Article XII (1)). The EC may be a party vis-à-vis other WTO members to the dispute settlement procedures under Annex 2 of the Agreement. De facto, however, the EC, though never formally a party to GATT 1947, exercised the rights of its members states before 1994, including in relation to dispute settlement: see Jacques Bourgeois, 'The Uruguay Round of GATT: Some General Comments from an EC Standpoint,' in *The European Union and World Trade Law*, ed. Nicholas Emiliou and David O'Keeffe (Chichester, UK: John Wiley & Sons, 1996), 81 and 85.

78. UNCLOS art 305(1)(e) & Annex XI; cf. Straddling Fish Stocks Convention, 8 September 1995, (1995) 34 ILM 1547, Articles 1 (2) (b) and 47.

79. See James Crawford, *The Creation of States in International Law*, 2nd edn. (Oxford: Oxford University Press, 2006), 495–499.

80. *Reparation for Injuries Suffered in the Service of the United Nations*, ICJ Rep 1949, 174. The distinction between a state and an international organization is also clearly made in Article 66 (2) of the Statute.

81. About which see generally James Crawford, 'International Law and the Rule of Law,' *Adelaide Law Review* 24, (2003): 3–12; and Arthur Watts, 'The International Rule of Law,' *German Yearbook of International Law* 36 (1993): 15–45.

82. *MOX Plant case (Ireland v. United Kingdom)*, Order no. 3, 24 June 2003, 42 ILM 1187, 1190–1191 (paras. 21–28).

83. 'Review of the procedure provided for under article 11 of the statute of the Administrative Tribunal of the United Nations,' UN document A/RES/50/54, 29 January 1996; see Higgins, 'A Comment,' 580–581.

84. See the proposal to use advisory jurisdiction to resolve divergences that might arise amongst various international tribunals: Tullio Treves, 'Advisory Opinions of the Inter-

national Court of Justice on Questions Raised by Other International Tribunals,' *Max-Planck Yearbook of United Nations Law* 4 (2000): 215–231; and Karin Oellers-Frahm, 'Multiplication of International Courts and Tribunals and Conflicting Jurisdiction—Problems and Possible Solution,' *Max-Planck Yearbook of United Nations Law* 5 (2001): 67–104.

85. ICJ Rep 1992, 3 (*Libya v. UK*), 114 (*Libya v. US*).

86. The suggestion that states hold the organization accountable before their own courts has been rejected on these grounds: divergent rules inevitably will result and the law will lose any coherence at international level. See Dan Sarooshi, *International Organizations and Their Exercise of Sovereign Powers* (Oxford: Oxford University Press, 2005), 120.

87. *Legal Consequences of the Construction of a Wall in the Occupied Palestinian Territory*, Advisory Opinion of 9 July 2004, ICJ Rep 2004, 136 and 171 (para. 87).

88. On investment disputes see Zachary Douglas, 'The Hybrid Foundations of Investment Treaty Arbitration,' *British Yearbook of International Law* 74 (2003): 151–289. On the systems of human rights adjudication, see Roger Masterman, 'Taking the Strasbourg Jurisprudence into Account: Developing a 'Municipal Law' of Human Rights under the Human Rights Act,' *International and Comparative Law Quarterly* 54, no. 4 (2005): 907–931; Conor Gearty, *Principles of Human Rights Adjudication* (Oxford: Oxford University Press, 2004); Manfred Nowak, *Introduction to the International Human Rights Regime* (Leiden, Netherlands: Brill, 2003); and Yuval Shany, *The Competing Jurisdictions of International Courts and Tribunals* (Oxford: Oxford University Press, 2004), 59–66.

89. See further Dinah Shelton, 'The Participation of Non-Governmental Organizations in International Judicial Proceedings,' *American Journal of International Law* 88, no. 4 (1994): 623.

90. For example the *Nicaragua v. Honduras* case was commenced before the Court in 1999; pleadings have been closed since 2003; yet a merits hearing is not in sight. By contrast *Barbados v. Trinidad and Tobago*, commenced in 16 February 2004, was decided on 11 April 2006, i.e., within twenty-six months: www.pca-cpa.org.

91. Martti Koskenniemi, International Law Commission Study Group on Fragmentation, Topic (a): The Function and Scope of the Lex Specialis Rule and the Question of 'Self-Contained Regimes' (2003); Shany, *The Competing Jurisdictions*; and Martti Koskenniemi & Paivi Leino, 'Fragmentation of International Law: Postmodern Anxieties,' *Leiden Journal of International Law* 15, no. 3 (2002): 553–579. See also 'Fragmentation of International Law: Difficulties Arising from the Diversification and Expansion of International Law,' 'Report of the International Law Commission,' Chapter X, UN document A/59/10, Supp. 10, 16 September 2004.

PART IV

RELATIONSHIPS WITH
OTHER ACTORS

CHAPTER 12

REGIONAL GROUPS AND ALLIANCES

WAHEGURU PAL SINGH SIDHU

THE UN Charter provides for a prominent role for 'regional agencies or arrangements' under Chapters VI and VIII. In past practice, the potential of regional groups in resolving disputes or maintaining peace and security remained largely unrealized. Subsequently, partly due to the largely successful process of decolonization and partly on account of the end of the Cold War, regional agencies and arrangements began to play a more assertive role in global politics. This new role was most evident in the sphere of peace and security and was increasingly conducted under Chapter VII of the Charter, at times without the explicit authorization of the Security Council. This regionalization of peace operations came about in an improvised way and in response to specific situations.[1]

Scholars have used two distinct approaches to study and explain the regionalization of peace operations. The first is the so-called 'managerialist or "problem solving" approach,' which 'takes the world as it finds it' and seeks to improve peace operations by making existing relationships and institutions 'work smoothly by dealing with particular sources of trouble' within contemporary political structures without seeking to address the structural issues themselves.[2] The second is the 'critical theory' approach, which 'questions existing institutions and structures of the prevailing world order' and, in the field of peace operations, 'seeks to investigate who benefits from certain types of practices, what linkages exist between local actors and global structures, and why certain voices and experiences are marginalized in policy debates.'[3] This chapter argues that neither approach by itself adequately provides a satisfactory explanation of the challenges posed by the regionalization of peace

The author is grateful to Katja Flückiger for her indispensable research assistance.

operations. The chapter begins with an historical overview of the role of regional groups and alliances as well as their relationship to the UN structure in the Cold War period; it takes note not only of the different types of regional groups and alliances but also of their changing role in maintaining peace and security—sometimes in cooperation with and sometimes in opposition to the world organization. The second section on missed opportunities after the Cold War notes that most of the robust peace operations in the post-Cold War world have included some form of involvement by regional arrangements, and identifies and examines the different types of roles that regional groups and alliances have played in the enforcement and maintenance of international peace and security both within and outside the UN structure. These include subcontracting; bridging operations; joint operations; integrated operations; and evolving operations. The section also notes the nonmilitary operations involving regional actors and how they are likely to evolve. The chapter highlights the benefits and risks of the regionalization of peace operations and concludes that the rise of regional groups and alliances both within their own regions and beyond is a double-edged sword: it has the potential to make the UN more effective in conducting peace operations *and* simultaneously to weaken the capacity and capability of the world body in leading effective peace operations. The challenge remains to enhance the former potential while guarding against the latter.

Historical Overview

At the founding conference of the UN in San Francisco in summer 1945, the issue of the role of 'regional agencies or arrangements' in maintaining international peace and security was fiercely debated, even though there were only two 'regional agencies,' the Pan-American Union and the League of Arab States, represented at the conference. In all probability, this debate was instigated by the mother of all 'regional arrangements' present at San Francisco—the three victorious powers (Great Britain, the Soviet Union, and the United States) and France—who by the time of the signing of the UN Charter on 26 June had already defeated and occupied Germany and were weeks away from inflicting a similar fate on Japan. One indication of this was Winston Churchill's vision of a UN based on 'several regional councils . . . [which] should form the massive pillars upon which the world organisation would be founded in majesty and calm.'[4]

In the dying days of World War II only the United States and the Soviet Union, along with the British (Commonwealth) and, perhaps, the French colonial empires, were in a position to provide the bases for such 'pillars.' The big three (London, Moscow, and Washington) in particular were keen to maintain their autonomy of action in their respective regional groups and did not want to be accountable to the Security Council.[5] In light of these developments, it was very likely that the Arab League would have sought similar exceptionality for its actions from the Security Council. Thus, the 'theoretical preference for universalism and the political pressure for regionalism . . . produced an ambiguous compromise,' which provided a role for regional groups in the UN Charter but 'contained provisions . . . making them serve as adjuncts to the UN' and under the firm direction of the Security Council, at least on paper.[6]

However, this 'ambiguous compromise' was further compromised by the presence of the five permanent, unelected, veto-wielding members in the Security Council. The veto arrangement ensured that regional groupings which included one or more of the five veto holders as members were often able to act independently and without UN authorization and could also neutralize the ability of the Security Council to act against them. In contrast, other regional groups that did not include veto-wielding states as members had far less autonomy of action and were often subject to the *diktats* of a united Security Council. Thus, while in theory Chapter VIII was designed to treat all regional groups and alliances on an equal footing, in practice some regional actors were, clearly, more equal than others.

This became apparent during the course of the Cold War when the Security Council was effectively incapacitated by the persistent use of the veto by the two superpowers. During this period the US 'resisted efforts to subordinate the OAS (Organization of American States) to the UN' and carried out a series of so-called peace operations under the OAS banner without UN authorization in Guatemala (1954), the Dominican Republic (in 1960 and 1965), and Cuba (between 1960 and 1962).[7] Similarly, the Soviet Union, which intervened in Hungary (1956) and Czechoslovakia (1968), claimed that its actions were within the Warsaw Pact region and, therefore, that the regional group had precedence over the UN. Earlier, even the Arab League argued in 1948 that its forces had entered Palestine in the wake of Israel's declaration of independence in order to uphold the UN Charter. This argument was rejected by the Security Council which, although its resolution called for all parties to 'abstain from any military action,' lacked the necessary consensus to enforce the decision.[8]

Thus, during the Cold War three distinct trends, which were to have an impact on the future of the UN's relations with regional actors, became evident. First, the actions of the superpowers in bypassing the paralyzed Security Council and sometimes using regional groups instead not only weakened the primacy of the UN over regional organizations but also established a two-tier system of regional groups, which was precisely what the drafters of the Charter had tried so hard to avoid.

Second, by acting though the regional organizations, the superpowers also established a precedent for regional groups to take action, including the use of force, often without the consent of or even in opposition to Security Council mandates to ostensibly maintain peace and security. The fact that such initiatives were rare during the Cold War might have more to do with the *absence* of such regional and subregional groups than with the respect for the primacy of the UN among such groups.[9]

Third, in 1951, barely two years after the creation of the North Atlantic Treaty Organization (NATO), and in line with Article 53 of the UN Charter, some officials within the UN and the US gave serious consideration to the possibility that a 'regional agency like NATO might serve as the UN's military component whenever circumstances require.'[10] Although such a prospect was out of the question during the Cold War, it was, perhaps, to be one of the factors that prompted the UN to consider military-capable regional groups beyond NATO for its operations in the post-Cold War era.[11] However, in the Cold War, without access to the enforcement capabilities of regional groups, the UN had no choice but to invent peacekeeping which was 'creatively crafted "Chapter VI ½"' and take on the burden itself.[12] These early peacekeeping operations were based on the 'so-called "holy-trinity" of consent, impartiality and the minimum use of force.'[13] Significantly, as the pace of decolonization picked up during the latter part of the Cold War, the recently decolonized countries, particularly from Asia and Africa, also emerged as the biggest troop-contributing countries to UN operations.

MISSED OPPORTUNITIES AFTER THE COLD WAR

The end of the Cold War witnessed a dramatic spurt in the UN's peacekeeping operations: compared to the mere thirteen operations launched between 1945 and 1987 (an average of one operation every three years), the world body initiated an equal number in the next four years alone (an average of one new operation every three months).[14] The end of the Cold War also saw the intervention in August 1990 in Liberia by the Economic Community of West African States (ECOWAS)—the first of many peace operations launched by regional and subregional groups during the decade without Security Council authorization.[15] There were several factors behind this new wave of peacekeeping. The most prominent was the P-5 concord, which finally activated the Security Council after nearly four decades of debilitating paralysis.[16] In many ways the end of the Cold War provided an ideal opportunity not only to redefine peace operations but also to reconsider the role of regional groups in this new era.

The UN seized this opportunity, evidenced by two key developments—first, the publication of *An Agenda for Peace* and, second, the establishment of the Department of Peacekeeping Operations (DPKO) in 1992. But the world organization failed to capitalize on building links with regional actors on account of its flip-flop approach as well as internal turf battles within the Secretariat.

With the mid-June 1992 publication of *An Agenda for Peace*, Secretary-General Boutros Boutros-Ghali acknowledged the important role of regional organizations in preventive diplomacy, peacekeeping, peacemaking, and post-conflict peacebuilding. While admitting that the 'Charter deliberately provides no precise definition of regional arrangements and agencies,' he argued that this ambiguity allows 'useful flexibility for undertakings by a group of States to deal with a matter appropriate for regional action which also could contribute to the maintenance of international peace and security.'[17]

In addition, he spelled out three key principles for the future relationship between the UN and regional actors. First, the relationship needed to be governed by the primacy of the Security Council in authorizing the actions of regional actors, which should be designed to support the UN's own efforts. Second, while recognizing that no two regional groups were alike, there was a tacit acknowledgement that all regional groups were to be treated on an equal footing. Third, there should not be 'any formal pattern of relationship between regional organisations and the United Nations, or... any specific division of labour.'[18] However, barely two-and-a-half years later in January 1995 in the tragic aftermath of the 1994 Rwanda massacres, the *Supplement to An Agenda for Peace: Position Paper of the Secretary-General on the Occasion of the Fiftieth Anniversary of the United Nations* effectively renounced all three principles.[19]

The *Supplement* argued that that while the UN had developed 'a range of instruments for controlling and resolving conflicts between and within States'—specifically preventive diplomacy, peacemaking, peacekeeping, peacebuilding, disarmament, and peace enforcement—the world body 'does not have or claim a monopoly of any of these instruments' and acknowledges that other actors can employ and have employed these instruments. Simultaneously the *Supplement* argued that the primacy of the UN must be respected and that 'regional organisations should not enter into arrangements that assume a level of United Nations support not yet submitted to or approved by its Member States.' The *Supplement* also retracted the principle that all regional groups should be dealt with equally and claimed that 'it would not be appropriate to try and establish a universal model for their relationship' with the UN. Finally, in a clear reversal of the *Agenda*'s policy not to seek a division of labor between the UN and regional actors, the *Supplement* categorically insisted that the 'division of labour must be clearly defined and agreed in order to avoid overlap and institutional rivalry where the United Nations and regional organizations are both working on the same conflict.'[20]

While both *An Agenda for Peace* and the *Supplement* sought to define and improve relations between the UN and regional actors, there was very little effort to improve this cooperation on a practical basis. Indeed, the only effort in this sphere during this period was a meeting convened in New York in August 1994 between Secretary-General Boutros-Ghali and the heads of a number of regional organizations. While a useful first step, the proceedings of this meeting, according to one participant, 'resembled more an academic seminar than a forum for operational planning.'[21] Besides, as this meeting was led by the Department of Political Affairs (DPA), and not the nascent DPKO, which was already working with regional actors in peace operations, there was an institutional disconnect. Although around half-a-dozen high-level meetings have taken place since 1994, the institutional disconnect prevails.[22]

The missed opportunity to improve relations between the UN and regional actors continued with the *Report of the Panel on United Nations Peace Operations* (2000) chaired by veteran Algerian diplomat and UN observer, Lakhdar Brahimi. The so-called Brahimi report, which focused specifically on the UN's peace operations, did a commendable job of highlighting the limitations of the existing UN structure, including the lack of communication and coordination between DPA and DPKO, and made significant, practical recommendations on improving the conduct of UN peace operations. The report acknowledged that the Charter encourages cooperation with regional and subregional organizations, but it advised caution because:

military resources and capabilities are unevenly distributed around the world, and troops in the most crisis-prone areas are often less prepared for the demands of modern peacekeeping than is the case elsewhere. Providing training, equipment, logistical support and other resources to regional and subregional organizations could enable peacekeepers from all regions to participate in a United Nations peace operation or to set up regional peacekeeping operations on the basis of a Security Council resolution.

In addition, while recognizing that 'coalitions of the willing' are best suited to conduct 'enforcement actions' because the UN 'does not wage war,' the report insisted that such action should be authorized under Chapter VII of the Charter by the Security Council.[23]

Thus, in a reversal of both the *Agenda for Peace* and the *Supplement*, the Brahimi panel's report actually puts the onus on the UN to ensure that potential peacekeepers in *all* regions have a minimum capacity to undertake modern peace operations in their respective regions, if necessary. The report, however, does not clarify or elaborate to any significant degree how the overstretched United Nations would ensure the necessary capacity-building of the various regional and subregional organizations.

The effectiveness of the Brahimi reforms have also suffered on account of the lack of progress in two areas also highlighted in the report: reform of Security Council mandates for operations; and better coordination between troop-contributing countries, DPKO, and the Security Council.[24]

Since 2003, the Security Council has met with heads of regional organizations (in April 2003, July 2004, October 2005, and September 2006) to discuss the role of regional organizations in the Council's work. In 2005, the Council passed resolution 1631, outlining concrete steps to enhance cooperation between the UN and regional organizations. Progress, however, remains to be seen.

In contrast to these initiatives, confined largely to UN headquarters, the fifteen years between 1990 and 2005 saw multifaceted practical and operational cooperation between the UN and a variety regional actors in the field. Indeed, of the forty-two UN peace operations launched after 1990, as many as thirty-two have had a regional actor involved in them.[25] These missions dealt with nineteen intrastate conflicts and the involvement of regional actors has ranged from preventive diplomacy to peace-making, and from peacekeeping to peacebuilding and disarmament. However, the engagement has been most dramatic and significant in the area of peace enforcement and the use of force as indicated in Table 12.1.

All of the ten ongoing operations launched after the end of the Cold War involve regional actors. Of the ten, seven (Western Sahara, Congo, Ethiopia–Eritrea, Liberia, Côte d'Ivoire, Burundi and Sudan) are in Africa; whereas Europe (Kosovo), the Caucasus (Georgia) and the Americas (Haiti) each have one. At present there are no peace operations in Asia involving regional actors, although the EU Aceh Monitoring Mission and Humanitarian Dialogue, the Geneva-based nongovernmental organization, are still engaged in Aceh. The UN peace operations involving regional actors are usually divided into five categories.[26] First, military subcontracting operations are those where several newly deployed or existing UN operations have 'outsourced,' or in more legal terms 'subcontracted,' the task of providing military

Table 12.1 UN peace operations involving regional actors after the Cold War

UN Peace Operation	Location	Established	Regional Involvement
United Nations Iraq–Kuwait Observation Mission (UNIKOM)	Iraq–Kuwait border	Apr 1991	Established after US-led coalition
United Nations Advance Mission in Cambodia (UNAMIC) & United Nations Transitional Authority in Cambodia (UNTAC)	Cambodia	Oct 1991 & Mar 1992	ASEAN diplomacy
United Nations Protection Force (UNPROFOR)	Former Yugoslavia	Feb 1992	NATO peace enforcement
United Nations Operation in Somalia (UNOSOM I & II)	Somalia	Apr 1992 & Mar 1993	US-led Unified Task Force (UNITAF) humanitarian assistance and disarmament; US Quick Reaction Force
United Nations Operation in Mozambique (ONUMOZ)	Mozambique	Dec 1992	OAU diplomacy and broader Supervisory and Monitoring Commission role
United Nations Observer Mission Uganda–Rwanda (UNOMUR) & United Nations Assistance Mission for Rwanda (UNAMIR)	Uganda–Rwanda border & Rwanda	June 1993 & Oct 1993	OAU Neutral Military Observers Group (NMOG) I & II; French-led multinational force
United Nations Observer Mission in Georgia (UNOMIG)	Georgia (Abkhazia)	Aug 1993	CIS cease-fire monitoring; CSCE diplomacy
United Nations Observer Mission in Liberia (UNOMIL)[a] & United Nations Mission in Liberia (UNMIL)	Liberia	Sep 1993 & Sep 2003	ECOWAS (ECOMOG) cease-fire monitoring; ECOWAS (ECOMIL) early entry, cease-fire monitoring, and bridging[b]
International Civilian Mission in Haiti (MICIVIH)[c], United Nations Mission in Haiti (UNMIH), United Nations Support Mission in Haiti (UNSMIH), United Nations Transition Mission in Haiti (UNTMIH), United Nations Civilian Police Mission in Haiti (MIPONUH), & United Nations Stabilization Mission in Haiti (MINUSTAH)	Haiti	Feb 1993, Sep 1993, Jul 1996, Aug 1997, Dec 1997, & Jun 2004	OAS/UN joint mission (MICIVIH); US-led multinational force & Multinational Interim Force (MIF); OAS & CARICOM diplomacy; MINUSTAH force led by Brazil and included troops from other MERCOSUR countries[d]

(Continued)

Table 12.1 (*Continued*)

UN Peace Operation	Location	Established	Regional Involvement
United Nations Mission of Observers in Tajikistan (UNMOT)	Tajikistan	Dec 1994	CIS Collective Peacekeeping Force cooperation and support; OSCE electoral monitoring and diplomacy
United Nations Preventive Deployment Force (UNPREDEP), United Nations Mission in Bosnia and Herzegovina (UNMIBH), United Nations Transitional Authority in Eastern Slavonia, Baranja and Western Sirmium (UNTAES), United Nations Mission of Observers in Prevlaka (UNMOP)	Macedonia, Bosnia and Herzegovina, Eastern Slavonia, Baranja and Western Sirmium (Croatia) & Prevlaka peninsula	Mar 1995, Dec 1995, Jan 1996 & Feb 1996	OSCE monitoring; NATO (SFOR, IFOR); EU (EUPM) police training; OSCE & COE election monitoring
United Nations Verification Mission in Guatemala (MINUGUA)	Guatemala	Jan 1997	EU & OAS demobilization support
United Nations Mission in the Central African Republic (MINURCA)	Central African Republic	Apr 1998	Inter-African Force (MISAB); France logistics support
United Nations Observer Mission in Sierra Leone (UNOMSIL) & United Nations Mission in Sierra Leone (UNAMSIL)	Sierra Leone	Jul 1998, Oct 1999	ECOWAS (ECOMOG) cease-fire monitoring and enforcement
United Nations Interim Administration Mission in Kosovo (UNMIK)	Kosovo	Jun 1999	NATO (KFOR) security for peacebuilding; OSCE institution building; EU reconstruction
United Nations Mission in East Timor (UNAMET), United Nations Transitional Administration in East Timor (UNTAET), & United Nations Mission of Support in East Timor (UNMISET)	East Timor/Timor-Leste	Jun 1999, Oct 1999, & May 2002	INTERFET early entry, cease-fire monitoring, and bridging (from UNAMET to UNTAET)
United Nations Organization Mission in the Democratic Republic of the Congo (MONUC)	Democratic Republic of the Congo	Nov 1999	EU (Artemis) bridging
United Nations Mission in Ethiopia and Eritrea (UNMEE)	Ethiopia–Eritrea	Jul 2000	OAU mediation[e]

United Nations Assistance Mission in Afghanistan (UNAMA)[f]	Afghanistan	Mar 2002	NATO (ISAF) security for peacebuilding
United Nations Mission in Côte d'Ivoire (MINUCI)[g] & United Nations Operation in Côte d'Ivoire (UNOCI)	Côte d'Ivoire	May 2003 Apr 2004	ECOWAS (ECOFORCE) cease-fire monitoring;[h] French forces assisted implementation
United Nations Operation in Burundi (ONUB)	Burundi	Jun 2004	AU (AMIB) forces incorporated into ONUB
United Nations Mission in the Sudan (UNMIS)	Sudan	Mar 2005	IGAD diplomacy; AU (AMIS) forces incorporated into UNMIS; NATO training and logistics support

Source: Updated and modified version of Cyrus Samii with Harold Rodriguez, *The UN and Euro-Atlantic Organizations: Evolving Approaches to Peace Operations Beyond Europe*, (New York: International Peace Academy, 2004), 4.

[a] UNOMIL was the first UN peacekeeping operation undertaken in cooperation with a peacekeeping operation already established by another organization, in this case, ECOWAS/ECOMOG.

[b] ECOMIL/UNMIL deployments involved the contributions of SHIRBRIG in early entry and headquarters set-up.

[c] MICIVIH is technically a political mission and was the first joint mission between the UN and a regional organization (OAS).

[d] Troop-contributing countries from the region included: Argentina, Bolivia, Brazil, Canada, Chile, Guantemala, Paraguay, Peru, the United States, and Uruguay.

[e] UNMEE deployments involved the contributions of SHIRBRIG in early entry and headquarters set-up.

[f] UNAMA is technically a political mission but is directed and supported by DPKO.

[g] MINUCI is technically a political mission but is directed and supported by DPKO.

[h] In February 2003, French forces were activated to monitor and enforce a cease-fire in the run-up to the ECOFORCE deployment.

cover to regional organizations, coalitions of the willing, or individual countries for a limited time. Such examples include the Implementation Force (IFOR) support for the UN Protection Force (UNPROFOR), as well as the US-led Unified Task Force (UNI-TAF) support and preparation for the first UN Operation in Somalia (UNOSOM I). Second, bridging or hand-over operations include those in which the UN precedes or follows a regional group or coalition of the willing or even an individual country operation. The transfer from ECOWAS to the UN Observer Mission in Sierra Leone (UNOMSIL) and the Australian-led International Force for East Timor (INTERFET), which bridged the gap between the UN Mission in East Timor (UNAMET) and the UN Transitional Administration in East Timor (UNTAET), are examples. Third, joint operations are those in which a mission has a joint operational approach that reflects a civil–military division between the UN and regional actors. Such examples include the military support provided by NATO to the United Nations Interim Administration Mission in Kosovo (UNMIK), as well as the relationship between the UN Assistance Mission in Afghanistan (UNAMA) and the International Security Assistance Force (ISAF) in Afghanistan. Fourth, integrated operations are designed to include the UN and other non-UN actors right from the planning stage to ensure better collective effort and coordination. The best examples of such operations are the UN–OAS human rights operation in Haiti as well as the three-pillar (the UN, the Organization for Security and Co-operation in Europe (OSCE), and the European Union (EU)) UNMIK operation in Kosovo. And fifth, evolving operations include nonmilitary models such as the Quartet (the United States, Russia, the UN, and the EU) in the Middle East.

Peace operations have been assessed on the basis of legitimacy, mandates, and effectiveness in providing stable peace, as well as their costs. With the exception of costs, none of the other criteria is uncontested and poses a challenge in determining whether a particular operation could be considered successful or not.[27] What is evident is that irrespective of the type of peace operation—UN only, regional only or mixed—the results have varied and appear to depend on the specificity of the situation rather than the legitimacy, mandate, capacity or even efficiency of the operation. However, on the cost front, it would appear that UN-led operations are presently, perhaps, the most economical. For instance, a study conducted by the US Government Accountability Office revealed that a US peacekeeping operation in Haiti would cost twice that of a UN operation.[28]

Yet the UN is unlikely to be able to conduct significantly more operations, partly because of external political constraints and partly because of internal structural limitations. In 2006 there were as many as 85,000 UN peacekeepers worldwide, making them the second biggest deployment of personnel under arms in the world. Only the United States had more troops deployed globally. According to a DPKO inter-office memo, the Brahimi reforms were intended to give the department the capacity to launch one large peace operation a year; in 2004 alone, DPKO began four. The present headquarters to field ratio of 1:135 simply would not allow DPKO to deploy many more operations. Clearly, the UN's capacity is overstretched.[29] While there might be several good reasons for structural changes to be made in the UN to give DPKO the capacity to handle more peace operations, such changes are unlikely in the short term, on account of the present state of US–UN relations, as well as the desire of some regional organizations to build up their own peacekeeping capabilities for a variety of political reasons.

The Benefits and Risks of Regional Involvement in UN Peace Operations

There are particular benefits of engaging regional actors in peace operations: some intrastate conflicts have regional causes;[30] there are often shared cultural values and experiences within the region; regional stability might also be in the national interest of states located in the troubled region; regional actors know their region and spoiler/aggressors better than outsiders; proximity also allows for quicker mobilization of a peacekeeping force; through local operations regional organizations can 'socialize "new peacekeepers"' and thus also contribute to the UN's peacekeeping capacity;[31] and subsequent peacebuilding might be easier, especially if membership of the regional organization is coveted. Conflict prevention (and particularly early warning) as well as the analysis of root causes and options to address them might also be best addressed at the regional level. Some regional organizations are also perceived to have contributed to creating 'security communities' by 'eliminating the risk of conflict between their members.'[32] The EU, NATO, and the Association of Southeast Asian Nations (ASEAN) are good examples.

Despite these advantages, there are, however, two concerns regarding the conduct of, in particular, robust peacekeeping by some regional organizations. First, according to Michael Pugh, 'regionalization carries the risk of ghettoizing "undisciplined" parts of the world,' in which the proponents of 'liberal peace will simply continue to exert clout regionally and to keep the unruly parts of the world at arm's length by subsidizing regional initiatives.'[33] This is especially true for those regions that do not have a well-endowed regional organization of their own (such as Afghanistan/Central Asia); or have ineffective regional organizations (such as the Commonwealth of Independent States (CIS) or the South Asian Association for Regional Cooperation (SAARC)); or do not yet possess their own established regional peacekeeping capacity (such as the AU); or for those regions (such as Darfur) that are not the beneficiaries of the out-of-area operations of the Western regional organizations because they are not of strategic interest. Here the possibility is that these regions are likely to remain in a perpetual state of conflict or will be attended to infrequently and ineffectively by the already overstretched UN peacekeeping capacity.

Second, there is the prospect of the emergence of 'peacekeeping apartheid,' or first-class and second-class peacekeeping where better trained and equipped troops will be increasingly unwilling to operate alongside the relatively poorly equipped UN troops from the traditional peacekeeping nations.[34] This would result in differentiated missions, command structures, equipment and, possibly, outcomes between the two groups of troops. For instance, NATO and the UN are estimated to have spent an average of US $3.5 billion per year between 1995 and 2003 on Bosnia-Herzegovina alone while, in contrast, a mere US $2.38 billion was available for all the seven UN missions in Africa in 2004.[35] A related concern is that of the commitment gap: would regional organizations, such as the EU and NATO give priority to EU and NATO-led missions over the UN missions further afield? The EU currently provides for less than 10 percent of the total UN peacekeeping force. Thus, there is a genuine concern that by pouring resources into regional arrangements and organizations some developed countries are 'diverting resources which could otherwise have assisted the UN capacity to undertake complex peace operations, and thereby enhance its credibility.'[36]

THE WAY FORWARD

Given the missed opportunities during the first decade of the post-Cold War era, what are the prospects of improving relations between the UN and various regional groups and alliances? In this context, it is inevitable that, while the role of regional actors is likely to increase in future peace operations, this involvement is unlikely to be evenly applied in every region. Some, notably Africa, are likely to see the greatest involvement while Asia is likely to see the least. Similarly, while some regional organizations are likely to enhance their capacity to conduct peace operations, including possibly out of their geographical areas, others are likely to disappoint similar expectations. These differences underline one salient fact: regional organizations are deliberately different and, perhaps, unequal and should be treated accordingly.

So, on what grounds should regional organizations be differentiated? According to a recent study there are three distinctions that are likely to condition the interaction of regional arrangements with the UN as well as other regional groups. The first is whether the regional or subregional group mandates itself 'a role in conflict management within or among its member states.' Based on their norms and constitutions, the OAS, the OSCE, the AU, ECOWAS, the EU, the Arab League, and to some extent ASEAN meet this criterion. In contrast, SAARC deliberately does not. The second is whether the group 'possesses, or intends to endow itself with, a peace-keeping capability.' Again, NATO, the EU, the Arab League, and the AU meet this criterion while SAARC and ASEAN do not. The third relates to the 'geographical scope of the regional arrangement's mandate and activities.' Here, with the exception of the EU and NATO, none of the other regional actors has a desire 'to become active outside the perimeter of their membership.'[37] From the perspective of the UN, it would be logical to build operational relationships with groups that meet at least the first two criteria if not all three.

However, given the disparity in the size, budget and capacity of different regional organizations it is again evident that the UN will have to set up different kinds of relations with different groups. For instance, there is widespread agreement that the UN and wealthier regional organizations should support capacity-building of the AU; an idea first suggested in the Brahimi report. This reflects the realization that Africa remains the locus of most peace operations—whether UN, regional, or mixed. In 2006 at least 60,000 peacekeepers under various hats were deployed in Africa. Moreover, the AU has very limited capacity to deal with the variety of crises in its region and needs to be bolstered. For instance, the AU launched its Darfur mission with Type-2 preparedness although, according to its own classification, it required a Type-6 deployment. Similarly, there is also an understanding that the development of rapid deployment and standby arrangements by regional entities like the EU would also benefit the United Nations.[38]

In this context the UN appears to have launched a two-pronged approach. The first builds directly on the Brahimi reforms augmenting them with recommendations from *A More Secure World*, the report from the UN's independent High-level Panel on Threats, Challenges and Change, and the Secretary-General's own report *In Larger Freedom*, which culminated in the World Summit Outcome of September 2005.[39] This approach was further endorsed by Security Council resolution 1631 in October 2005, which invited regional organizations to participate in the UN standby peacekeeping arrangements.[40] The second approach seeks to build on the creation of the Peacebuilding Commission (PBC) and Peacebuilding Support Office (PBSO).

On the one hand, the Summit Outcome generally calls for 'formalized agreements between respective secretariats' and the 'involvement of regional organizations in the work of the Security Council' as well as for the capacity of regional organizations to prevent armed conflict to be 'placed in the framework of the United Nations Standby Arrangements System.' In particular, the Summit document calls for support for the development and implementation of a ten-year plan for capacity-building with the AU, which was finalized in 2007, as well as support for the EU's desire to develop capacities for rapid deployment and standby arrangements.[41] On the other hand, it provides scope for improving the operational cooperation between the UN and regional actors.[42] At a minimum the UN, led by DPKO, could seek to establish common standard operating procedures for military forces, compatible logistics concepts, and conditions of engagement.[43] A promising step has been taken in this direction with the development of the *Handbook on Multidimensional Peace Operations*, sample rules of engagement, and standard training modules. However, there is now a need to ensure appropriate training both at the national and regional levels of these procedures as well as joint pre-deployment training.

At a more maximal level, the UN is seriously considering financing regional operations authorized by the Security Council on a case-by-case basis. This would not only provide a monetary incentive for seeking Council authorization for operations but would also impose a minimum standard of accountability and reporting on the regional organizations.

In the long run, the world organization could also pursue the ambitious prospect of setting up a strategic reserve for peace operations, which would go beyond the existing proposal for a UN Standby Arrangements System. 'In principle, such a reserve force could be drawn from regional formations and might include either the continental or regional elements of the African Standby Force, one or more EU Battlegroups, or elements of the NATO Response Force' as well as other troop-contributing nations.[44] In practice, while the 2005 Summit did not adopt the recommendation to set up a strategic reserve for peacekeeping, it did call for 'enhanced rapidly deployable capacities to reinforce peacekeeping operations in times of crisis.'[45] This recommendation is likely to be dependent, within the UN, on the successful development of the PBC and the PBSO as well as the institutional integration of the new commission with DPKO, among others. Progress towards this long-term goal will also depend on other key external actors, such as the African Union, the European Union, and NATO, as well as the operational coordination between them and the United Nations.

These long-term developments will be possible only if there is significant structural change in the existing world order and a strengthening of marginalized actors, such as the AU and other key troop-contributing countries. It would also alleviate, to a large degree, concerns about peacekeeping apartheid and ghettoized parts of the world. Until this happens, the effectiveness of peace operations is likely to remain uncertain.

Notes

1. Here the term 'peace operations' is used in the broadest possible sense to include the political, economic, and social dimensions of conflict prevention and peacemaking, peacekeeping, and peacebuilding. This definition is based on the *Report of the Panel on United Nations Peace Operations*. See 'Defining the elements of peace operations,' in the chapter on 'Doctrine, strategy and decision-making for peace operations,' available at www.un.org.
2. Alex J. Bellamy and Paul Williams, 'Introduction: Thinking Anew about Peace Operations,' in *Peace Operations and Global Order*, ed. Alex J. Bellamy and Paul Williams (London: Routledge, 2005), 6. See also Robert W. Cox, 'Social Forces, States and World Order: Beyond International Relations Theory,' *Millennium* 10, no. 2 (1981): 126–155.
3. Bellamy and Williams, 'Introduction,' 6 See also Michael Pugh, 'Peacekeeping and Critical Theory,' in *Peace Operations and Global Order*, ed. Bellamy and Williams, 39–58; and Roland Paris, 'Peace-building and the Limits of Liberal Internationalism,' *International Security* 22, no. 2 (1997): 54–89. See also Cox, 'Social Forces, States and World Order.'
4. Cited in Inis L. Claude, Jr., *Swords into Ploughshares: The Problems and Progress of International Organizations* (New York: McGraw Hill, 1984), 113.
5. See Stephen C. Schlesinger, *Act of Creation: The Founding of the United Nations: A Story of Superpowers, Secret Agents, Wartime Allies and Enemies and their Quest for a Peaceful World*, (Boulder, Colo.: Westview, 2003), 175–192. Although there was some debate within the US and UK delegations whether they wanted one or two regional groups to be excluded from the purview of the Security Council, the Soviets keenly sought such an exclusion for themselves and their region.
6. Claude, *Swords*, 114.
7. Ibid., 116.

8. Alex J. Bellamy and Paul Williams, 'Who's Keeping the Peace? Regionalization and Contemporary Peace Operations', *International Security* 29, no. 4 (2005): 162.

9. Indeed, most of today's regional and subregional organizations, particularly in the global South, emerged only after the process of decolonization, independence, or even democratization was well underway. For instance, the OAU was established in 1963, ASEAN was founded in 1967, OIC was created in 1969, CARICOM was born in 1973, ECOWAS was established in 1975, the Community for Security and Co-operation in Europe (CSCE, later OSCE) emerged in 1975, SAARC came into being in 1985, CIS was created in 1991, and the EU came into being only in 1992 (preceded by the European Community (EC), established with the Treaty of Rome in 1957).

10. See Claude, *Swords*, 116.

11. See, e.g., Boutros Boutros-Ghali, *An Agenda for Peace—Preventive Diplomacy, Peacemaking and Peacekeeping: Report of the Secretary-General pursuant to the statement adopted by the Summit meeting of the Security Council on 21 January 1992*, UN document A/47/277-S/24111, 17 June 1992, particularly para. 43–44.

12. For the origins and evolution of 'peacekeeping,' see James Cockayne and David M. Malone, 'The Ralph Bunche Centennial: Peace Operations Then and Now,' *Global Governance* 11, no. 3 (2005): 332–333. See also Michael Barnett, 'Partners in Peace? The UN, Regional Organizations and Peacekeeping,' *Review of International Studies* 21, no.4 (1995): 415; and Brian Urquhart, 'The United Nations and International Security After the Cold War,' in *United Nations, Divided World: The UN's Role in International Relations*, ed. Adam Roberts and Benedict Kingsbury (Oxford: Clarendon Press, 1994), 91–92.

13. Bellamy and Williams, 'Introduction,' 3

14. Boutros-Ghali, *An Agenda for Peace*, para. 47. For the structural and operational reasons behind this dramatic spurt, see Cyrus Samii and Waheguru Pal Singh Sidhu, 'Strengthening Regional Approaches to Peace Operations,' in *The United Nations and Regional Security: Europe and Beyond*, ed. Michael Pugh and Waheguru Pal Singh Sidhu (Boulder, Colo.: Lynne Rienner, 2003), 255–269. See also Bruce Jones and Feryal Cherif, *Evolving Models of Peacekeeping: Policy Implications and Responses*, September 2003, an external Study done for the Peacekeeping Best Practices Unit of the United Nations Department of Peacekeeping Operations, www.un.org.

15. See Funmi Olonisakin and Comfort Ero, 'Africa and the Regionalization of Peace Operations: the UN and ECOWAS,' in *The United Nations and Regional Security*, ed. Pugh and Sidhu, 233.

16. See Cockayne and Malone, 'The Ralph Bunche Centennial,' 334–335; and Boutros-Ghali, *An Agenda for Peace*, para. 14. According to the latter, the UN was rendered powerless on account of the staggering 279 vetoes cast in the Security Council between 1945 and mid-1990.

17. Boutros-Ghali, *An Agenda for Peace*, para. 61.

18. Ibid., para. 64.

19. Boutros Boutros-Ghali, *Supplement to An Agenda for Peace: Position Paper of the Secretary-General on the Occasion of the Fiftieth Anniversary of the United Nations*, UN document A/50/60-S/1995/1, 3 January 1995.

20. Quotes from *Supplement*, paras. 23–24 and 87–88.

21. Presentation by David Hannay, 'The UN's Relationship with Regional Organisations in Crisis Management and Peacekeeping: How Should It be Developed to Mutual Advantage?', 21–23 April 2005, Wilton Park, UK. He was a member of the High-level Panel on Threats, Challenges and Change.

22. *Security Council Report*, no. 3, 18 September 2006, 'The United Nations and Regional Organizations'.

23. *Report of the Panel on United Nations Peace Operations*, UN document A/55/305-S/2000/809, 17 August 2000, paras. 53–54.

24. Bellamy and Williams, 'Conclusion: What Future for Peace Operations? Brahimi and Beyond,' in *Peace Operations and Global Order*, ed. Bellamy and Williams, 186.
25. The list of UN peacekeeping operations can be found at www.un.org.
26. For the challenges of categorizing peace operations, see Jones and Cherif, *Evolving Models of Peacekeeping*.
27. Bellamy and Williams, 'Who's Keeping the Peace?' 171–179.
28. Mark Turner, 'US peace mission to Haiti would cost twice that of UN,' *Financial Times*, 24 February 2006.
29. Inter-office memorandum on 'Peace Operations 2010' from the Under-Secretary-General of DPKO, Jean-Marie Guéhenno, to all DPKO headquarters and mission staff, 30 November 2005. See also his remarks to the Fourth Committee of the General Assembly, 20 October 2005.
30. For an early discussion, see S. Neil MacFarlane and Thomas G. Weiss, 'Regional Organizations and Regional Security,' *Security Studies* 2, no. 1 (1992): 6–37.
31. Bellamy and Williams, 'Conclusion: What Future for Peace Operations?', 195. See also The Challenges of Peace Operations Project, National Defence College (Sweden), *Challenges of Peace Operations: Into the 21st Century* (Stockholm: Elanders Gotab, 2002), 53–54.
32. John Roper, 'The Contribution of Regional Organizations in Europe,' in *Peacemaking and Peacekeeping for the New Century*, ed. Olara A. Otunnu and Michael W. Doyle (Lanham, Md.: Rowman & Littlefield, 1998), 262.
33. See Michael Pugh, 'The World Order Politics of Regionalization,' in *The United Nations and Regional Security*, 33 and 42.
34. Ramesh Thakur and David M. Malone, 'Tribes within the UN,' *The Hindustan Times*, 20 November 2000.
35. Cyrus Samii, 'Peace Operations in Africa: Capacity, Operations and Implications,' Final Report of the 34th IPA Vienna Seminar, July 2004, www.ipacademy.org.
36. The Challenges Project, *Challenges of Peace Operations*, 52. See also Thierry Tardy, 'EU–UN cooperation in peacekeeping: a promising relationship in a constrained environment', in Martin Ortega, ed., *The European Union and the United Nations: Partners in Effective Multilateralism, Chaillot Paper*, no. 78, European Union Institute or Security Studies, June 2005, 49–68.
37. Ibid., 57–58.
38. Tardy, 'EU–UN cooperation in peacekeeping,' 60–68.
39. High-level Panel on Threats, Challenges and Change, *A More Secure World: Our Shared Responsibility*, UN document A/59/565, 1 December 2004; Kofi Annan, *In Larger Freedom: Towards Development, Security and Human Rights for All—Report of the Secretary-General*, UN document A/59/2005, 21 March 2005; and the *2005 World Summit Outcome*, UN document A/60/L.1, 15 September 2005.
40. UN Security Council 1631, 17 October 2005.
41. See Ian Johnstone, 'Dilemmas of Robust Peace Operations,' in A Project of the Center on International Cooperation, *Annual Review of Global Peace Operations 2006* (Boulder, Colo.: Lynne Rienner, 2006), 6.
42. *2005 World Summit Outcome*, para. 170.
43. UN DPKO Peacekeeping Best Practices Unit, *Lessons Learned from the United Nations Peacekeeping Experience in Sierra Leone*, September 2003, www.un.org.
44. The Challenges of Peace Operations Project, *Meeting the Challenges of Peace Operations: Cooperation and Coordination—Challenges Project, Phase II Concluding Report 2003–2006* (Stockholm: Elanders Gotab, 2005), 80.
45. Johnstone, 'Dilemmas of Robust Peace Operations,' 6.

CHAPTER 13

BRETTON WOODS INSTITUTIONS

NGAIRE WOODS

THE Bretton Woods institutions are often described as the 'sister institutions' of the United Nations. Of all the specialized agencies, the World Bank and the International Monetary Fund (IMF) have generated particularly heated debate and criticism, especially over the past two decades. This chapter explains how that has come about, what the institutions do, why it has become contentious, and how this relates to the activities of other UN organizations.

AN OVERVIEW

What do the World Bank and the IMF do?[1] They were born to fulfil distinct roles, as detailed below. But by the end of the twentieth century, their work had changed dramatically. The World Bank's core task is development assistance. The IMF's core task is to promote international monetary cooperation through surveillance and lending to countries with short-term balance of payments difficulties. In the latter role, the Fund's work overlaps heavily with that of the Bank in three areas. First, both institutions are involved in managing financial crises, such as in East Asia and Latin America in the late 1990s where the Fund took a lead, but the World Bank played a key back-up role. Second, they both lend for development in the poorest, often war-torn parts of the world. Here the World Bank has taken the lead, but with the IMF ever-present in setting down the macroeconomic framework for assisted countries.

Finally, both institutions have been involved in transition economies such as Russia and the former Soviet republics where they have been expected to help foster transition from centrally planned to market-oriented economies.

The work of the Fund and Bank deeply affects that of other UN organizations, not least because the Fund and Bank set the economic parameters within which virtually all other assistance to a country and aid programming must fit. That said, there is little effective coordination among the Fund and Bank and other UN bodies either at headquarters or on the ground. This is surprising given that all members of these organizations have agreed global objectives such as the Millennium Development Goals (MDGs). However, there are few if any incentives for agencies such as the Fund or Bank actively to cooperate with other organizations or to alter their behavior to achieve goals set by others. In practice, each international agency is driven by its own discrete bureaucratic pressures, incentives, and standards of success. And in this the IMF and World Bank have some special characteristics.

Several features distinguish the IMF and World Bank from other UN organizations. First, membership of the Fund and Bank is conditional. Countries must belong to the IMF in order to be members of the World Bank. In turn, membership of the IMF requires countries to accept specific terms and responsibilities—such as surveillance of their exchange rate arrangements by the IMF. A second difference is that the core budgets of the Fund and Bank do not depend on regular contributions from member states. Each organization derives income from lending operations and investments they have made with prior income. This gives them scope for independence from member countries.

Governance in the Fund and the Bank is different from other UN agencies. Neither has a one-country, one-vote system. Voting is weighted according to the size and openness of each member's economy as reflected in a series of formulae (which are not immune from political manipulation). There is also a difference in the nature of the board which runs each institution. The day-to-day work of the Fund and the Bank is governed by a Board of Directors who represent member countries but are paid by the institution and directed to work as officers of the organization.

For countries that work with the Bank and Fund, there is also a great difference in the staff. IMF and World Bank personnel are not hired according to formal or informal quotas to ensure that all countries are represented. The institutions pride themselves on having a meritocracy of non-nationality-based appointments that attract highly trained graduates from the world's top economics and finance departments. The exception is the senior management in each organization. The heads are political appointees (a European in the case of the IMF, an American in the case of the Bank), and so too senior management appointments are influenced by powerful shareholders.

Unlike other UN institutions, the Fund and Bank are situated in the capital of the US government in Washington, DC, and work exclusively in English. This, combined with the fact that they draw a large proportion of their staff from graduate programs in North America makes the Fund and Bank the most 'Anglo-Saxon' of the current generation of international organizations.

Their working relationship with the UN system is a very loose one. Although they are specialized agencies, in fact they are more like distant cousins than sisters. The lack of any real coordination between them and other UN organizations is repeatedly cited across the literature on development assistance. For this reason, UN Secretary-General Kofi Annan convened two High-level Panels to propose ways of making the UN system more coherent and effective: both the High-level Panel on Threats, Challenges and Change (2004) and that on UN System-wide Coherence (2006) recommended strengthened coordination among different UN organizations and the IMF and World Bank.[2] These aspirations are worthy but face a significant obstacle—namely, that while the governance, funding, and operations of the Fund and Bank are separate to those of the UN system, there are few incentives for real coordination.

The financing and governance structure of the IMF and World Bank give them a degree of potential autonomy from member governments which other UN agencies do not enjoy. Yet this has not insulated them from political influence, nor from public criticism. Left-wing groups denounce the Fund and Bank as tools of US imperialism. Anti-globalization websites accuse them of enforcing global capitalism. Meanwhile, right-wing think-tanks accuse the Fund and Bank of supporting corrupt elites and governments which 'cripple their economies, maul their environments, and oppress their people' and criticize them as part of the evil of over-weaning government projected into the world economy. Somewhere between these extremes the IMF and World Bank work in scores of countries across the world—reaping both some successes and some failures. Their sixty-year evolution helps to explain how and why.[3]

THE CREATION

The IMF and the World Bank were founded while World War II was still raging. In 1944 at Bretton Woods, New Hampshire, a global conference of 'one and a half' parties took place.[4] The goal was to establish global economic rules which would prevent a replay of the Great Depression and its aftermath. The United States, which was already emerging from the war with a clear military, technological, and economic superiority over its Western allies, led the negotiations. The United Kingdom constituted the other 'half' party, due not just to its position in the alliance at the time but also to the fact that it was represented at Bretton Woods by the internationally renowned economist John Maynard Keynes. The contribution of the other forty-three countries at the conference has been memorably described by Harold James as weaving consensus, harmony, and agreement in an atmosphere of cordial cacophony as if under the spell of a magician.[5]

The new system planned at Bretton Woods put the IMF at the heart of a new monetary system, managing a system of fixed but adjustable exchange rates and lending on a strictly short-term basis to countries facing short-term balance of payments crises. Investment in the postwar economy would be facilitated by the

International Bank for Reconstruction and Development (IBRD, but more commonly known as the World Bank) which would raise capital in money markets and lend it at advantageous rates to war-torn and developing countries.

The original Bretton Woods plan was at first subsumed by the Cold War. The Marshall Plan announced in 1947 provided the United States with a more immediate bilateral way to ensure stabilization, investment, and reconstruction in Western Europe. Nevertheless, by the 1950s both the IMF and the World Bank were modestly assuming a place in the international economy. The IMF was managing a fixed exchange rate system and making short-term loans to assist countries with balance of payments deficits. The World Bank was channelling funds from private capital markets to developing countries by issuing top-rated bonds on world financial markets and lending on the money for specific development projects.

In ensuing decades, the role of both institutions changed dramatically. The World Bank expanded its resources and moved steadily away from pure project lending into more policy-based lending. Over time the institution acquired three new arms. In 1956 the International Finance Corporation (IFC) was founded to mobilize private investment through syndications, underwritings and co-financing. In 1960 the International Development Association (IDA) was established to provide long-term credits at concessional rates to the poorest country members of the World Bank. In 1988 the Multilateral Investment Guarantee Agency (MIGA) was formed to stimulate foreign direct investment by providing guarantees against political risk, armed conflict, civil unrest and so forth. Meanwhile in the 1970s under the presidency of Robert McNamara, the Bank began to express its core objectives in terms of redistribution with growth and basic human needs. Rural development projects were added into the overarching modernization and growth-promoting priorities of the institution.

Over this period, the IMF's fortunes fluctuated. In the 1960s, concerns about global liquidity led members to create a new virtual reserve asset managed by the IMF and called the Special Drawing Right (SDR). It never took off. The move was soon superseded by an opposite problem—the excess of dollars in the international financial system. Unable to back a surplus of dollars with its gold reserves, on 15 August 1971 the United States suspended the gold-convertibility of the dollar. In one swoop the IMF's central role as manager of a fixed exchange rate system disappeared. The IMF then attempted unsuccessfully to take a lead role in negotiations over what kind of exchange rate regime would replace the Bretton Woods system. By 1973 major industrialized countries together embarked on a new system in which countries could opt to float their currencies, relying on demand and supply in the foreign exchange market to determine the value. It was not until 1978 that the new system was formally recognized by an amendment to the IMF's Articles of Agreement.

The events of the early 1970s have limited the Fund's subsequent role in respect of non-borrowing members to surveillance. This entails monitoring and reporting on the exchange rate policies of member states and thereby helping to assure a stable international exchange rate system. In practice the IMF staff work with their own information as well as the economic data provided by member countries, to compile reports on each member's economic policy and performance. These reports are then presented to the Board of Governors. They rarely have an impact on the stronger, wealthier members of the institution.

Changes in Mission since the 1970s

Several challenges have altered the work of the IMF and World Bank since the 1970s. The four highlighted below are the debt crisis of the 1980s, the challenge of transition in centrally planned economies, the new financial crises of the 1990s, and the long-term challenge of facilitating development in some of the poorest, most conflict-ridden countries of the world.

The Debt Crisis of the 1980s

The IMF and the World Bank underwent further change in the 1980s. The debt crisis, which began in Latin America in the early 1980s, drew them into a new role. Throughout the 1970s they had been marginalized as lenders to countries who could instead borrow from commercial banks anxious to recycle the massive surpluses of the Organization of the Petroleum Exporting Countries (OPEC) and the new excess of liquidity within international capital markets. The IMF initially responded by expanding access to its resources, particularly to countries with no access to commercial finance. The Bank undertook more policy-based lending and expanded its focus to include rural development.

The festival of lending ended when the US Federal Reserve increased interest rates in 1979. Suddenly indebted governments found that their creditors would not roll over their loans. The borrowers could not meet their debt repayment obligations. Several large commercial banks were on the brink of failure. The IMF and World Bank were called upon to make loans to the debtors to ensure that they would repay their over-exposed creditors and therefore avert an international banking crisis. The conditional loans required borrowers to undertake stringent measures to stabilize and ensure adjustment in their economies in order to access credit from the Bretton Woods institutions.

Conditionality in the first phase of the debt crisis emphasized stabilization. This meant that governments were required to reduce inflation, to rationalize and stabilize the exchange rate, to increase interest rates, to reduce public sector expenditure and investment, to increase taxation, and to eliminate subsidies. These are the staple requirements of IMF conditionality. They are reinforced by requirements made by the World Bank in its structural adjustment loans which require governments to liberalize trade and minimize tariffs, to privatize state-owned industries, to encourage foreign investment, and to deregulate their economies. Taken together the conditionality of the IMF and World Bank came to be labeled the 'Washington consensus.'[6]

Facilitating Transition at the End of the Cold War

In the early 1990s the institutions took on a new challenge: transforming the former Eastern bloc economies. The end of the Cold War left Western policymakers attempting to secure both economic and security goals in what had been the Soviet sphere of influence. These 'transition economies' posed significant new challenges to both institutions and led to a rethinking of the role of institutions in the process and goals of policy reform. Privatization, for example, had long been pushed by both the Fund and Bank as a way to reinvigorate investment and production in formerly state-managed sectors. In Russia, it became apparent that transparency and an effective rule of law were necessary prerequisites for privatization to produce the hoped-for results.

Criticized by borrowing countries as well as their major industrialized country members for the inadequacy of their efforts in Russia and elsewhere to promote transition and economic growth, the 'conditionality' of the Bretton Woods institutions became broader. A wide raft of good governance measures were included which aimed at strengthening and modernizing the institutions of government, rooting out corruption, and bolstering the rule of law within countries. The expanded set of activities has elsewhere been described as 'mission creep,' highlighting the way that the complexity of transition pushed each agency into new tasks beyond their core competency.[7]

Coping with Financial Crises in Emerging Economies in the 1990s

By the end of the 1990s, both the Fund and the Bank were being called upon to manage a slew of new financial crises. In 1995 the Mexican peso went into free fall catalyzing a crisis in Mexico in spite of its extraordinary decade-long program of economic reform. In 1997 the dangers of contagion were highlighted when a crisis in Thailand soon spread even to the relatively sound and prospering economy of South Korea. The East Asian financial crisis was followed in 1998 by Russia, then Brazil, Turkey, and Argentina. Common to each country's plight was an initial liberalization which had permitted a very substantial inflow of short-term investment, often into a very poorly regulated banking sector. When market confidence teetered, short-term capital fled the country, leaving a massive repayments crisis for the government.

The first resort in managing the financial crises of the 1990s was for the IMF to make large loans to try to stem the crisis of confidence in a country. The World Bank was subsequently deployed to make longer-term loans and to try to ensure that social safety-nets were put in place to protect the most vulnerable from the harsh adjustment resulting from the first round of crisis management. The experience of the crises led to a very public questioning of the role of the institutions and the down-side of liberalization and globalization. The starkest reminder of this was the massive anti-globalization street demonstrations which came to accompany the Annual Meetings of the IMF and World Bank from the late 1990s onwards.

In the wake of the financial crises of the 1990s, by 2002 the most powerful members of the IMF were forced to discuss in earnest a more robust and rule-based mechanism for dealing with financial crises which would more deeply involve the private sector. Several officials and commentators were calling for some form of international bankruptcy or standstill provision.[8] However, as the crises receded, so too did any official resolve to identify or rectify gaps in the international financial architecture.

The street protests of the late 1990s highlighted not just the plight of emerging economies. One of the most powerful motivating factors behind public engagement in the work of the IMF and the World Bank was their perceived failure to assist the poorest and most heavily indebted countries within the world economy.

The Debts of the Poorest and Most Heavily Indebted Countries

Throughout the 1980s and 1990s, both the Fund and the Bank had become deeply embroiled in lending to the poorest and most highly indebted countries in the world economy. The unrepayable debts of these countries had been rescheduled throughout the period leaving the lion's share owing to the Fund and Bank. Both institutions were concerned to prevent members going into arrears on their loans and thereby eroding the institutions' own resources. This was one push toward a new strategy.

By the late 1990s there was considerable public and political pressure for the IMF and the World Bank to do more to alleviate suffering in the world's poorest and most heavily indebted countries. The political pressure was intensified by the activities of nongovernmental organizations such as the umbrella group Jubilee 2000, which campaigned for debt relief. The result was a succession of official debt relief announcements made within the framework of the Heavily Indebted Poor Countries initiative (HIPC) based in the Bretton Woods institutions.

The debt strategy aimed to reduce the debts of the poorest countries as well as to alleviate poverty within them. Traditionally the latter task had been more part of the mission of the World Bank than that of the IMF. By the late 1990s, both institutions were linking new forms of debt relief to poverty alleviation. HIPCs wishing to avail themselves of greater debt relief were required to submit to the IMF and World Bank poverty reduction strategy papers (PRSPs) formulated through a process of national consultation and participation.

The new poverty reduction strategy requirement brought to bear the lessons both institutions had learnt from their experience with good governance conditionality. Ownership and participation had to be at the core of any reform process for it to be effective. In other words, to increase the effectiveness of reforms you had to engage, consult, and devolve responsibility to key groups within the society or country undertaking reform. For each of the IMF and the World Bank such a lesson was a deep challenge to their traditional ways of thinking and working, requiring them to spend more time in the field, deploying staff more as facilitators rather than as policy experts. This brought the Bretton Woods twins into closer than ever contact with counterparts from other UN organizations. Yet coordination among agencies has been very slow to emerge. This is amply illustrated in the area of post-conflict development assistance.

Post-conflict Reconstruction

In the wake of conflicts such as that in Iraq, Afghanistan, Bosnia-Herzegovina, and the West Bank and Gaza, the Fund and Bank have found themselves thrust into a coordinating role, conducting needs assessments, auditing aid efforts, and advising on post-conflict economic policy. This role has brought new challenges to each institution and has brought them into yet closer contact with other UN agencies.[9] Coordination among international agencies has always been a thankless task. In spite of good intentions, formal agreements and much rhetoric about working better together, the group of important actors—UN agencies, the Bretton Woods institutions, and bilateral donors—have found effective coordination nigh impossible. For example, even in Bosnia-Herzegovina where the major donors (themselves overlapping groups)—the World Bank, the European Community, most of the G-7, and the Netherlands—agreed with the government to have an externally appointed 'aid coordination board' and a small, specialist 'reconstruction task force' within Bosnia-Herzegovina, actual coordination proved extremely difficult.

The United States had played the most important political role in the peace negotiations, and developed its own coordination mechanism that would include a political Steering Board of the Peace Implementation Council and an Economic Task Force (ETF) comprising the donors. Eventually Washington and the UN Office of the High Representative succeeded in having their structure accepted. However, fifteen Islamic countries also formed the Assistance Mobilization Group under the Organization of the Islamic Conference (AMG/OIC) but they were not made part of the ETF. As a result their contributions to the multilateral aid programmes declined. Finally, while the Bosnia-Herzegovina government created a Reconstruction Cabinet, its coordination efforts suffered from political disputes over the state structure with ministers from Republika Srpska (RS) refusing to participate in donor meetings and Bosnians and Croats in the federal government unable to find consensus on the coordination mechanisms.[10]

Coordination is an area in which the Bretton Woods institutions have special roles. The IMF has long de facto coordinated conditionality—mostly because it sets down terms in the absence of which most other agencies will not lend. Lacking has been any correlate coordination of the delivery of assistance, including even basic coordination among donors and lenders on the reporting requirements to which a country must conform. The World Bank's Comprehensive Development Framework announced in 1999 sought to enhance coherence across sectors (economic and social policies) as well as inclusion and coordination among the various actors involved in any one country's development strategy—under the leadership of the recipient government. The joint IMF and World Bank PRSPs are another attempt to formulate a wider development strategy through a more inclusive process, as have been Sector-Wide Approaches (SWAPS).

The work of the Bretton Woods institutions in post-conflict situations highlights a common problem within the UN system. Effective coordination among international organizations rarely occurs. This is not an accident nor the deliberate strategy of the international organizations themselves. It reflects powerful interests in non-coordination. These include: competing interests at the national level (between government agencies, private companies, nongovernmental organizations, and inter-est groups, and the desire to gain public support for highly visible aid efforts); public accountability concerns (including budget pressures to disburse, national auditing requirements of donors and so forth); disagreements among donors about goals as well as policies (such as the recent disavowal by the UK's Department for Inter-national Development of the conditionality of the IMF and World Bank); and the desire of powerful states to expand the number of goals or policy mechanisms that are available in order to reduce the reliance on any over-arching institutional arrangements.

MEASURING SUCCESS AND FAILURE

There are several yardsticks for measuring the success or failure of the Bretton Woods institutions. The narrowest yardstick is that used by the institutions themselves—their internal and independent evaluations. A broader yardstick is offered by the strategic objectives laid out in each institution's Articles of Agreement.

The IMF's Independent Evaluation Office (IEO) has documented mistakes made in process or analysis by the IMF as well as by governments with which the organization has worked. One reason for failure is poor advice. In reports published in 2002 and 2003 the IEO highlighted problems in programs designed by the IMF.[11] Another reason for failure is political. Borrowing governments prove either unwilling or unable to implement conditions to which they have signed up. The Fund has attempted to overcome this problem by bolstering the ownership and participation of borrowing governments in the design of conditionality.

Reviews of the World Bank's lending are conducted in an ongoing fashion by the Bank's Independent Evaluation Group (IEG), which produces an Annual Report on Development Effectiveness (ARDE) as well as a large number of evaluations covering most of the Bank's activities. These reports highlight failures to achieve major relevant goals, institutional development, and sustainability in Bank-sponsored policies or projects. Critics of the Bank point to the percentage of loans that register unsatisfactory on one, two, or three of these criteria, and a high-level review commissioned by the Bank itself reported in 1992 that nearly 40 percent of borrowing countries had 'major problems' with at least 25 percent of their projects.

A much broader yardstick for measuring the success or failure of the Bretton Woods institutions is provided by their Articles of Agreement. Both are charged with enhancing stability and growth in the world economy. The Fund's contribution to this has been as a forum for cooperation among states, as a framework for surveillance over exchange rate systems, and as a short- to medium-term lender to countries with debt problems so as to prevent international financial crises. The Fund's success in these broader goals has been hailed in several studies and in its own histories. Fund critics allege that it has pursued these objectives in ways which have consistently ignored or further impoverished the poorest and most vulnerable members of developing countries.

The Bank has contributed to global growth and stability by lending to developing countries at rates and in quantities permitted only because the Bank pools the credit-ratings of all of its members. Poorer countries thus gain from sharing the strong credit ratings of other non-borrowing World Bank members. The Bank's critics allege that Bank lending has had adverse effects on poverty, the environment, and human rights.

CONTEMPORARY DEBATES

In 2006 the IMF and World Bank faced a new challenge. Each has come to depend upon income earned by lending money. But in 2006 their largest borrowers were looking elsewhere for finance. If the trend continues, fewer clients and less lending means that each institution must reconsider what they do, for whom, and at whose expense. These questions touch on key contemporary debates about the institutions.

Governance

Since the Bretton Woods Conference in 1944, the governance structure of the IMF and World Bank has been contentious. Back then the United Kingdom and United States wrestled not just over how much power different countries should have and where the headquarters should be located, but also over whether a full-time resident board should oversee the work of each organization. In recent years the debate about the governance of the institutions has focused on whether the voting power of developing countries should be increased,[12] and how to insulate the Boards from direct political pressures applied by major shareholders.[13]

At present each organization has an Executive Board on which all members are represented. The Executive Board sits in almost continuous session and makes decisions on the day-to-day work of each institution. It is composed of officials from economic agencies within member states. They are called executive directors. Their bosses—the ministers of finance and central bank governors from each country—meet only once a year as the Board of Governors.

Representation on the Executive Board is not equal. Only the largest shareholders in each organization—the United States, Japan, Germany, France, and the United Kingdom—along with China, Russia, and Saudi Arabia, have their own seats on the Board. The other sixteen executive directors are elected for two-year terms by groups of countries, known as constituencies represented by just one executive director. For example, twenty-one African countries are represented by one executive director in the IMF, and twenty-two African countries by one executive director in the World Bank. This has led to calls for increasing the voice of African countries such as by increasing the staff in their offices or giving them another seat on the Board.

A second contentious issue is voting power and how it is allocated. Even though the Boards work by consensus, all of their work and indeed, the work of the staff, is underpinned by an awareness of voting power. Each country has a weighted number of votes which depends on their 'quota,' which is determined by formulae which translate relative weight in the world economy into a share of contributions and votes (and in the IMF, access to resources). Although the notion of a formula implies a technical allocation of votes, this is not strictly the case.

The allocation of quotas has always been deeply political. Raymond Mikesell was the man who was asked in 1943 to determine the very first allocation of quotas within the IMF. He describes how he was simply told by the US Secretary of the Treasury to give the United States a quota of approximately $2.9 billion; the United Kingdom (including its colonies) about half the US quota; the Soviet Union an amount just under that of the United Kingdom; and China somewhat less. The US's major concern was to ensure that military allies (President Franklin D. Roosevelt's Big Four) should have the largest quotas, with a ranking on which the president and the secretary of state had agreed.[14]

Quota allocations continue to be deeply political with Asian countries particularly aggrieved that voting power has been slow to reflect changes in their economic weight in the global economy. The current voting power is found in Table 13.1.

Only one member state has an individual veto power over major decisions. While most decisions require a simple majority, there is a special category of decisions that requires an 85-percent majority. What this means, in effect, is that the United States has a veto over those decisions because it is the only member with more than 15 percent of votes. Even as the US share of votes in the organization has declined, it has preserved this veto right by increasing the 'special' majority required and by increasing the number of decisions requiring that majority. Although on occasion other countries have grouped together to veto decisions, they rarely do so. EU

Table 13.1 Voting–power allocations for the IMF and World Bank (2006)

Country	IMF Voting power (%)	IBRD Voting power (%)
United States	17.08	16.39
Japan	6.13	7.86
Germany	5.99	4.49
France	4.95	4.30
United Kingdom	4.95	4.30
Italy	3.25	2.78
Saudi Arabia	3.22	2.78
China	2.94	2.78
Canada	2.94	2.78
Russia	2.74	2.78
The Netherlands	2.38	2.21

countries have a caucus within the institutions but they seldom coordinate their positions. Similarly, developing countries only rarely act collectively. As a result, the United States remains the only member with an effective and practiced veto power.

Power and influence within the Bretton Woods institutions also derive from the way that members exercise their voice. Washington is not only the largest single vote-holder in the Fund and Bank, it is also the most vocal member of the Boards of both institutions. To cite a senior Treasury official's testimony to a Congressional Committee examining the IMF: 'Representing the largest, most influential member, the US representatives speak on virtually every issue coming before the Board.'[15]

Focusing further on the IMF, the US capacity to speak on all issues in the institution derives from the considerable resources which lie behind US representation. While many countries have one or two officials at the Fund, Washington has at least three dozen US Treasury officials regularly involved in working with, thinking about, and offering advice concerning the IMF, as well as officials within the US Federal Reserve. Such officials make frequent direct contacts with the management, staff, and the offices of executive directors within the Fund, either individually or in groups, also using bilateral relations, the G-7 framework, and other multilateral forums to garner support for positions within the IMF. This behind-the-scenes work means that when Washington does raise an issue within the Fund's Board it can do so 'without triggering counterproductive reactions and a hardening of positions.'[16]

In respect of the World Bank, the United States has a similar structure with an executive director's office within the Bank supported by the Office of International Development, Debt and Environmental Policy within the Treasury, with input from the US Agency for International Development (USAID) and the State Department. The US Department of Commerce also maintains a liaison office at the World Bank to inform and advise US companies on bidding for contracts arising out of World Bank loans. It is supported in this by at least eight other government agencies including: the US Trade and Development Agency; the US Trade Representative; the Departments of State, Homeland Security and Transportation; the Export-Import Bank of the United States; the Overseas Private Investment Corporation; and the Foreign Agricultural Service.

Finally it bears noting that whilst the Executive Boards are supposed to be the political masters of the Fund and Bank, controlling the work and policies of the organizations, in practice, this formal control is very light-handed. Board members face a heavy workload and therefore many issues are barely touched by the directors. This leaves issues such as the administration and organization of the institutions very much in the hands of the management or senior bureaucrats. This does not, however, mean that political influence is averted.

The staff who prepare everything that comes to the Board are overseen by the head and senior management of each organization. In theory the whole Executive Board decides the head of each organization. In practice, however, the World Bank always gets a president nominated by the United States, a tradition dating back to early days when it was thought vital if the institution were successfully to float bond issues within the US markets. The IMF always gets a managing-director nominated by Western Europe. In recent years, these conventions concerning headships have attracted increasing critical attention. Lower down the chain of command, however, similar conventions also continue in force. The first deputy managing director of the IMF is always an American and most senior appointments in both organizations are made after the US view is ascertained. All that said, this informal power of appointment does not necessarily confer control.

Political appointments in each organization have not always produced obedient servants. Certainly, the overall perspective of any successful candidate is never incongruent with the views of the major appointing shareholders. However, individuals in these jobs can wield influence based on their charisma, ideological legitimacy, administrative competence, expert knowledge, previous association with the organization, negotiating ability, and ability to persist. Their formal powers derive from the fact that the head of each of the IMF and World Bank chairs Executive Board meetings, sets the agenda, directs the discussion, and sums up at the end. They also have the power to appoint and dismiss officers and staff. Perhaps the most significant constraint and mechanism for overt and covert political influence within each of the IMF and the World Bank concerns resources.

Funding the Budget

The issue of who pays for the IMF and World Bank has long concerned all of its members. In the current context, when it looks as though income earned from lending may decrease, the issue is spotlighted yet more.

Many walking past the large prestigious-looking offices of the IMF and World Bank in the heart of Washington, DC, wrongly believe that the US government is paying for their air-conditioning, economists, car-parks, and overall running costs. On the contrary, however, the overheads and running costs of the institutions are paid for out of income which derives mainly from payments by developing and transition country members who borrow money from the institutions. Each institution earns income from lending in any year, as well as income from the investment of income earned in previous years.

Unlike the United Nations and other members of the UN system, the Bretton Woods institutions do not depend upon annual subscriptions or levies from member states. As a result, in theory they should be more independent of direct political pressures exerted by those with the power to withhold contributions. However, each institution has some funds which do rely on contributions. In the World Bank these include the International Development Association (IDA), which is the soft-loan facility of the World Bank, and the special Bank trust funds such as that created for debt relief in the 1990s. In the IMF any increase in general resources or quotas require political agreement from members, as do special agreements called the general arrangements to borrow (GAB) and the new arrangements to borrow (NAB).

The IMF's Resources

It is often assumed that there is a simple congruence between funding for the IMF and the largest say in the organization. This is misleading. The largest shareholders in the IMF enjoy the lion's share of the votes but the actual expenses of running the institution are not paid for from contributions by the wealthiest countries, but largely from the charges it levies on borrowers and from investment income.

The largest shareholders are so called because they contribute subscriptions of capital which form the IMF's core assets. Each country contributes according to their 'quota' which roughly reflects the size of their economy relative to others (as discussed above). For this reason, the United States is often described as the largest shareholder. It contributes 17.67 percent of the capital subscriptions in the IMF. Since 1968 it bears noting that Washington and all other creditors have been remunerated for providing this credit and indeed this is a serious expense for the Fund. Furthermore, the US benefits from the fact that all countries have to provide 25 percent of their quota in 'reserve assets,' gold or the US dollar, and this makes it easier and cheaper for the United States than for other countries.

The 'quota system' directly links money and votes. It determines how much a country contributes to the Fund's core assets as well as that country's voting power and credit limits. The Unites States contributes 17.67 percent of capital subscriptions and enjoys 17.33 percent of votes on the Executive Board. It is this symmetry that leads some to think that the United States contributes most of the IMF's resources. This perception ignores, as detailed above, the fact that the Fund's operational income accrues from its lending to transitional and developing countries, not to mention the fact that creditor countries are remunerated for providing credits.

At least every five years, there is a review of the Fund's quotas, which inevitably results in the US Congress demanding changes in the IMF. How does this come about? Normally, each year member countries pay an automatic subscription to the Fund, which does not require political approval or debate within any member country, including the US Congress. However, an increase in subscriptions does require political approval. Hence, it offers members an opportunity to express their views on the direction and work of the institution.

In practice, the US voice (or better said, voices) in quota increase debates is always the loudest. In part this is because any increase in quota requires an 85 percent majority, and so Washington enjoys a veto. Normally the US government agency in charge of looking after the IMF is the Treasury Department (with input from other departments and the Federal Reserve). However, a quota increase requires the approval of the US Congress, which, once engaged, leads inevitably toward a much broader debate. For example, over the 1990s the Congress attempted to influence Fund conditionality over issues such as worker rights, the role of the private sector, human rights, and military spending. In 1998 in negotiations over the US share of a 45 percent increase in Fund quota, the US Congress established an International Financial Institution Advisory Commission (the 'Meltzer Commission') to recommend future American policy towards the IMF, as well as the World Bank and other multilateral economic organizations. The resulting report proposed deep changes in each of the IMF and World Bank.

The World Bank's Resources

The International Bank for Reconstruction and Development is the main arm of the World Bank Group and lends to developing countries at market-related interest rates. This main body has extraordinary independence in its financial structure. It does not require regular contributions from members. It does not need to ask the US Congress for 'top-ups.' With the backing of paid-in capital subscriptions from member countries, the Bank raises its lending resources on the financial markets. It sells AAA-rated bonds and other debt securities to pension funds, insurance companies, corporations, other banks, and individuals around the world. The Bank's paid-in capital subscriptions, which are essentially guarantees provided by governments, have never been called upon. Furthermore, they amount to less than 5 percent of the Bank's funds, a proportion which is diminishing over time.

However, it is important not to underestimate the capital subscriptions which are the core assets of the Bank. The members' subscriptions are a prerequisite for the Bank's activities. They permit the Bank to borrow at the lowest market rates available applying the sovereign credit of its rich shareholders—in the form of their capital guarantees. Like a credit club, the Bank disperses the risks of lending, whilst aggregating its capacity to borrow money.

The United States contributes 16.9 percent of the paid-in capital subscriptions. The flipside of this contribution is that the US enjoys 16.52 percent of votes on the Bank's Board and a veto over all decisions requiring an 85-percent majority. Yet US influence within the Bank extends well beyond the picture these facts depict. This is because of what occurs in another arm of the World Bank Group.

The International Development Association was created in 1960 to make concessional loans to the poorest developing countries. The IDA's finances are different to the IBRD. Specifically, it relies upon governments agreeing and providing it with periodic replenishments. As a result, the funding of the IDA opens up political negotiations within and among member governments each time it needs replenishment.

The US contributes 20.86 percent of IDA funds, with the next largest contributors being Japan at 18.7 percent, and the United Kingdom and France at 7.3 percent. As provider of a fifth of the funds of the association, the United States doubtless has great influence within the IDA. However, its actual influence reflects more than its level of contribution. Specifically, a US exit or reduction in commitment to the IDA would affect other contributors and therefore have a devastating effect. This was further magnified during negotiations on the IDA's fifth replenishment (IDA 5) when it was agreed then that all other members could reduce their own contributions pro rata by any shortfall in US contributions. This pro rata provision ensured an evenly shared burden across contributors. However, it has also enhanced the impact of any threat by Washington to diminish its contribution. For if the United States does so, all other contributors can follow suit. For these reasons, Washington has long enjoyed a disproportionate degree of influence within the IDA.

This influence in IDA replenishment negotiations has been used to leverage influence across the Bank as a whole. Even though the IDA itself accounts for only about 25 percent of IBRD/IDA total lending, there have been several instances in which Washington has used threats to reduce or withhold contributions to the IDA in order to demand changes in policy in the World Bank as a whole. For instance, during the late 1970s, the Bank was forced to promise not to lend to Vietnam in order to prevent the defeat of IDA 6, and in 1993 under pressure from Congress, the United States linked the creation of an Independent Inspection Panel in the World Bank to IDA 10. In effect, the Unites States has used its grip on the IDA to shake the whole of the Bank—literally the 'tail' has been used to wag the dog.

Finally, there is a new way in which the finances of the Bank are introducing political influence. Increasingly it is using co-financing and trust funds arrangements. By the financial year 1999, disbursements under these arrangements had increased by 17 percent to account for nearly half of all World Bank disbursements. Both trust funds and other forms of co-financing give a much more direct control over the use of resources to donors whose Trust Fund Administration Agreement with the Bank governs how the funds are used. It bears noting, however, that this does not mean that trust funds have become a conduit of exclusively American

influence. Indeed the US's contribution in 1999 was less than that of the Netherlands and Japan, and for a period it was not a contributor to the HIPC Trust Fund
(the Bank's largest) which meant it did not exercise direct influence over that fund.
More generally, the growth of trust funds and co-financing arrangements signals
the potential for increased bilateral and selectively multilateral control over Bank
lending, but not necessarily an enhancement of Washington's influence.

By far the most politically influential work of both the IMF and the World Bank
lies in their loans and policy advice to developing countries. It is worth investigating
the degree to which the political influence so far discussed translates into control over
the decisions of either institution in this regard.

The Beneficiaries and Conditions Governing Grants and Loans

A final issue of debate concerns what the Bretton Woods institutions should do and
at whose behest. In theory the surveillance, advice, lending practices and policies of
the IMF and World Bank are a strictly technical affair. The Articles of Agreement of
each institution declare that politics should play no role in their lending. Any
member country can propose a loan for the Bank or Fund to consider. The staff
carefully prepare the proposal in close negotiations with the borrower. A detailed
proposal goes to the Board and a successful proposal requires a simple majority of
votes. No one country can veto a loan. Ostensibly all cases are decided on technical
and economic grounds. Indeed, the Articles of Agreement of both the Fund and the
Bank set out deliberately to curb potential political influence.

The Articles of Agreement of the IBRD state clearly in the first article the apolitical
character of the undertaking:

The Bank and its officers shall not interfere in the political affairs of any member; nor shall they
be influenced in their decisions by the political character of the member or members
concerned. Only economic considerations shall be relevant to their decisions, and these
considerations shall be weighed impartially in order to achieve the purposes stated in Article I.

Likewise staff owe their duty entirely to the Bank or the Fund and to no other
authority. Member states must refrain from all attempts to influence any of the staff
in the discharge of their functions.

Does all this mean that the lending of the IMF and World Bank is not subject to
political considerations? In reality, the Executive Boards are influenced by political
considerations in making their lending decisions. Furthermore, the staff and management of the institutions in working with members to propose loans do so with an
eye to the political possibilities and constraints awaiting them in Washington, DC.
Indeed, studies demonstrate that the lending record of both the Fund and the Bank
during the Cold War clearly reflects the desire at the time of Western allies to shore
up sympathetic regimes and to limit Soviet influence in the Third World.[17]

That said, in order to do their job, Fund and Bank staff rely on good relations forged with sympathetic interlocutors in lending countries. Powerful shareholders may well push and shove on the Executive Board and demand or block speedily disbursed loans. Over the longer term, however, any loan proposal must be negotiated and detailed by the staff and presented to the Board of the Fund or the Bank for approval. In preparing the loan, officials from the Bretton Woods institutions must persuade governments to share data and to enter into detailed negotiations on a wide range of areas. The conditionality which results is not usually the result of overt political pressures (although a case such as the IMF's agreement with South Korea in 1997 in which US political pressures played a key role in shaping the details of the agreement presents an obvious exception). More usually the content of conditionality agreements is shaped by the staff and management of the Fund or Bank, and in particular by the prevailing economic theories, beliefs and orthodoxies within those institutions. This requires us to examine more deeply the nature of expertise and knowledge within the Bretton Woods institutions.

Several thousand economists sit in offices in the headquarters of the IMF and World Bank, all within a couple of hundred meters from each other. All this collective brain power, applied to a wealth of information about most economies in the world, and state-of-the-art theorizing about economics cannot fail to have a dynamism of its own. For some the so-called Washington consensus on policy reforms forged by the IMF and World Bank throughout the 1980s and 1990s demonstrates the way their technical capacity can be brought to bear on key questions of economic policy. Others argue that this 'expertise' is itself based not just on research but equally on political interests and influences.

Subtle forms of political influence are exercised in a number of ways. It has long been the case that countries wishing to influence a project or loan make their views known to senior management and let them percolate down to staff working with a country. In the early days of the IMF, it was said that 'the US voice in the Fund was decisive. . . . The practical question in those years, in any prospective large use of Fund resources, was whether the United States would agree—and the answer was usually obtained by direct inquiry.'[18] Direct inquiries still occur, or at least informal soundings among powerful Board members with direct interests in a particular loan or country. This behind-the-scenes politics within the IMF and World Bank reverberate throughout the institutions. When staff know that their senior managers will be unwilling to take particular kinds of recommendations to the Board, they will naturally not want to waste their time preparing such recommendations. The work of the institutions becomes invisibly bounded by the known preferences of powerful members. That said, the staff and experts of the IMF and World Bank do not do all of their work directly under the gaze of US officials.

The staff of the Bretton Woods institutions often work far away from Washington, DC, gathering information and negotiating deals with governments in the capital cities of borrowing countries. The nature of their work takes them not just physically but also mentally out of reach of the Executive Board and their most powerful government members. As experts, they can only do their job of collecting confidential data from governments if they succeed in persuading or coercing governments to trust them and give them access. This sometimes even means that senior staff have to promise confidentiality to government officials, keeping secrets either from other staff members or from the Executive Board. The result is that the staff and management gain control over information which the Executive Board does not have. Furthermore, once the staff put a proposal to the Board, it is rarely if ever amended. Rather the Board will simply say 'yes' or 'no', for any amendment would unpick long and careful negotiations between the staff and government officials in a borrowing country. In this way, control of the details of loan proposals remains in the hand of the staff and management of the organizations.

CONCLUSION

As critics have become steadily more powerful, the Bretton Woods institutions have had to confront a widespread perception that they lack legitimacy and effectiveness. Critics certainly differ—from left to right, from globalists to localists, from modernizers to anti-globalizers. That said, from the US Congress-appointed Meltzer Commission to local grassroots organizations, they all tend to share a couple of core premises, such as that the Bank and the Fund do not effectively alleviate poverty and that they are not accountable enough.

The effectiveness of the institutions in the twenty-first century is limited by two key factors. First, their resources, however large they appear in comparison with those of other UN organizations, look increasingly meagre when compared to burgeoning global capital markets. This strictly limits their capacity to affect or influence those markets through their own lending behavior or actions. Small surprise then that, in 2002, the IMF tried to establish a new form of sovereign debt resolution mechanism, and the Bank is making much of its capacities as a knowledge bank rather than a lending bank. Second, both institutions have encountered profound difficulties in trying to implement deeper sets of conditions for their borrowers. In both institutions this has led to a new rhetoric highlighting the need for participation and ownership in borrowing countries. They are still searching for ways to translate this into a workable modus operandi.

The legitimacy of the Bretton Woods institutions has been placed under scrutiny by its developed and developing country members alike. At the behest of their members, both institutions have become more accountable. The Fund and the Bank now each have a more-or-less independent evaluation unit assessing how well their programs are working. There is much greater access to documents about what they do and how they are doing it. The World Bank has an Inspection Panel that can adjudicate claims that Bank staff have acted outside of the Bank's rules and guidelines. The Fund's member countries have yet to consider establishing such an oversight mechanism.

Yet both institutions still face the accusation that they are insufficiently account-able. This is largely because the voices of those they most profoundly affect—poorer countries and poor people within those countries—remain marginal and without influence within the respective decision-making processes. These groups have long argued that they need a greater voice in institutions which so profoundly and asymmetrically affect them. Their call for reform remains unheeded by the powerful industrialized countries that would need to step aside—or at least back a little—in order to make this possible.

Notes

1. Official documentation from the organizations is available on their websites www.imf.org and www.worldbank.org.
2. High-level Panel on Threats, Challenges and Change, *A More Secure World: Our Shared Responsibility* (New York: UN, 2004), paras. 277–278; and the High-level Panel on UN System-wide Coherence in the Areas of Development, Humanitarian Assistance and the Environment, *Delivering as One* (New York: UN, 2006), paras. 70–71.
3. The material draws from Ngaire Woods, 'The World Bank and IMF', in Mary Hawkesworth and Maurice Kogan, eds., *The Routledge Encyclopedia of Government and Politics*, 2nd edn. (London: Routledge, 2003).
4. This early history is recounted in Harold James, *International Monetary Cooperation since Bretton Woods* (Oxford: Oxford University Press 1996); Richard N. Gardner, *In Pursuit of World Order: US Foreign Policy and International Organizations* (New York: Praeger, 1964); and Devesh Kapur, John P. Lewis, and Richard Webb, *The World Bank: Its First Half Century*, 2 vols. (Washington, DC: Brookings Institution, 1997); and Edward Mason and Robert Asher, *The World Bank since Bretton Woods* (Washington, DC: Brookings Institutions, 1973).
5. James, *International Monetary Cooperation*, 53.
6. See John Williamson, ed., *Latin America Adjustment: How Much Has Happened?* (Washington, DC: Institute for International Economics, 1990); and John Williamson, 'The Washington Consensus Revisited,' in *Economic and Social Development into the XXI Century* ed. Louis Emmerij (Baltimore, Md.: Johns Hopkins University Press, 1997), 48–61.
7. See Ngaire Woods, *The Globalizers: The IMF, the World Bank, and their Borrowers* (Ithaca, NY: Cornell University Press, 2006), ch. 5.
8. See, e.g., Anne Krueger, 'International Financial Architecture for 2002: A New Approach to Sovereign Debt Restructuring,' speech to the National Economists Club Annual Members' Dinner at the American Enterprise Institute, Washington, DC, 26 November 2001.
9. See Adele Harmer and Joanna Macrae, eds., *Beyond the Continuum: The Changing Role of Aid Policy in Protracted Crises*, Humanitarian Policy Group Report 18 (London: Overseas Development Institute, 2004).
10. Elizabeth Cousens, 'From Missed Opportunities to Overcompensation: Implementing the Dayton Agreement on Bosnia,' in *Ending Civil Wars: The Implementation of Peace Agreements*, ed. Stephen John Stedman, Donald Rothchild, and Elizabeth Cousens (Boulder, Colo.: Lynne Rienner, 2002), 531–566.

11. Independent Evaluation Office, *Evaluation of Prolonged Use of IMF Resources* (Washington, DC: IMF/Independent Evaluation Office, 2002), and *Fiscal Adjustment in IMF-Supported Programs* (Washington, DC: IMF/Independent Evaluation Office, 2003).

12. Ariel Buira, ed., *Reforming the Governance of the IMF and World Bank* (London: Anthem Press, 2005).

13. Centre for Economic Policy Research, *Independent and Accountable: A New Mandate for the Bank of England*, CEPR Reports (London: Centre for Economic Policy Research, 1993), or more recently Mervyn King, 'Reform of the International Monetary Fund,' speech given at the Indian Council for Research on International Economic Relations, New Delhi, India, 20 February 2006.

14. Raymond Mikesell, *The Bretton Woods Debates: A Memoir* (Princeton, NJ: Princeton University, 1994).

15. Timothy Geithner, under-secretary of treasury for international finance, 'Treasury Assistant Secretary (International Affairs) Timoth F. Geithner Testimony before the House Banking Sub-Committee on General Oversight and Investigations,' 21 April 1998, www.treasury.gov.

16. Ibid.

17. Strom Thacker, 'The High Politics of IMF Lending,' *World Politics* 52, no. 1 (1999): 38–75.

18. Frank A Southard, *The Evolution of the International Monetary Fund*, Essays in International Finance, no. 135 (Princeton, NJ: Princeton University, 1979), 19–20.

CHAPTER 14

CIVIL SOCIETY

PAUL WAPNER

WHAT is the relationship between the United Nations and civil society? How does the world organization perceive and work with civil society and vice versa? Has the relationship changed over time? What kind of future will the two realms of global life have with each other? These questions are not simply circumscribed empirical inquiries but ask about the nature of global governance itself. Since its inception, the UN has struggled to gain legitimacy, assert its authority, and carry out its missions. Its relationship with civil society has been key to these efforts. Similarly, civil society has routinely worked to garner credibility, support, and governing authority. It has engaged the UN in its struggles to do so. Given the reciprocal needs of both the UN and civil society, relations between the two can serve as a window into the challenges of global governance. This chapter explains the changing relationship between the UN and civil society with an eye toward learning about what these challenges are about.

There has always been a tension between the UN's state-centered character and its aspiration to represent 'We the peoples of the United Nations,' the opening words of the organization's Charter. States established the UN, and member states, for the most part, constituted the organization as a governing body. States enjoy the exclusive privilege of voting in the General Assembly and in the vast majority of UN organizations and, to the degree that the most significant decisions must be approved by the Security Council, the institution is clearly statist in design, orientation, and practice. States are, of course, partially representative of their people— this is especially the case with liberal democracies. The problem is that states *qua* states, whether democratic or autocratic, have short-term and geographically circumscribed interests that often conflict with longer-term, more globalized social

The author thanks Eve Bratman, Katherine Grover, and Meredith Van Horn for research assistance on this chapter.

goods. To the degree that the authors of the UN Charter saw themselves as representing 'peoples' of the world and thereby committed to advancing the good of humanity, the world organization's statist character has always been a sticky point. Put another way, the limitations that statism has imposed on the UN is the reason why the organization has turned to civil society.

For better or worse, many see civil society as a stand-in for the people of the world. This is especially the case with global civil society, a realm in which people voluntarily come together to form relationships, develop identities, and work to further shared interests across state boundaries. As such, it offers a domain in which people can organize themselves outside their roles as citizens of a particular state and thus engender a sense of transnational and possibly global solidarity. Political activist groups, academic associations, religious organizations, and clubs of all sorts populate civil society and many of these have worked to advance quasi-universalist goals such as human rights, environmental protection, humanitarian aid, and gender equality. Civil society groups are, to use James Rosenau's phrase, 'sovereignty-free actors.'[1] Unaffiliated with any given territory, civil society groups appear to represent people's interests to the degree that these interests are unattached to a particular state. This is what makes them attractive as seemingly genuine representatives of humanity itself.

There is, of course, no such thing as a genuine representative of the world's peoples. Both states and civil society can make different kinds of claims on this. These differing claims help explain the dynamic between the UN and civil society. The chapter explores this dynamic through the UN's ongoing efforts to establish itself as a legitimate, authoritative, and effective institution of global governance and the attempts by civil society actors to become more influential and credible players in world affairs. The first section clarifies the meaning of civil society and identifies its key components. The second describes the interactions between civil society and the UN. The third section explains how problems of representation continue to dog the UN as it seeks to deepen its relationship with civil society and bolster itself as the preeminent governing body at the global level and how these same dilemmas challenge civil society. The chapter concludes by reflecting on the nature of global governance as seen through UN–civil society relations.

CIVIL SOCIETY

The idea of civil society goes back at least to ancient Rome and the notion of a community of citizens whose lives are regulated by a system of law.[2] In the political thought of the seventeenth and eighteenth centuries, thinkers employed it more specifically to disaggregate various sectors of collective life and describe a realm in which citizens could relate to each other independent of, and at times in opposition to, the state.[3] The distinction between civil society and the state has remained key to all subsequent understandings of the term.

Early thinkers conceptualized civil society as a sphere above the family but below the state wherein free association could take place between individuals and corporate groups.[4] This notion of civil society embraced all kinds of horizontal relations, including commercial as well as social interactions. Many observers still include the economy in their understanding of civil society—and, at times, the UN seems to do so. Indeed, the Global Compact looks specifically to businesses and market forces as part of civil society to assist in implementing certain policies. Moreover, many international business associations have been accepted and enjoy consultative status within the world organization. But, for the most part, theorists these days distinguish civil society from both the state and the economy,[5] a practice followed in this chapter.

Accordingly, civil society refers to a domain in which actors voluntarily associate with each other outside both their identities as citizens of a particular state and their roles as consumers or producers. When analyzing the relationship between civil society and the UN, it is useful to talk about *global* civil society, which refers to voluntary associations occurring across state boundaries. It is analytically separate from both the state system and the world economy and stands as a realm for transnational collective action. As mentioned, nongovernmental organizations (NGOs) such as international scientific bodies, transnational political activist groups, religious associations, and various clubs comprise global civil society.

The robustness of global civil society has varied over time. For the most part, however, it continues to grow in terms of numbers of actors and their increasing importance in world affairs. In 2003, analysts estimated that there were more than 250,000 NGOs working deliberately across state boundaries. This represented an increase of 43 percent since 1993.[6] Additionally, there are hundreds of thousands, and perhaps more than a million, NGOs working in various domestic settings on issues that have global relevance.[7] Some of these, like Amnesty International and the Nature Conservancy, have budgets that rival those of small states and possess memberships in the millions. Furthermore, they enjoy synergistic power insofar as many networks overlap with each other. Global civil society thus represents a seemingly important realm within contemporary world affairs.

Civil society assumes political relevance when those within it deliberately work for social change. Activist organizations, social movements, and interest groups realize that both governmental institutions and nonstate mechanisms shape widespread thought and behavior. Consequently, civil society groups work not only to change government policies but also shift standards of good conduct, economic incentives and cultural understandings.[8] At the global level, this entails targeting states, the world economy, global norms and international organizations. The United Nations represents the only recognized worldwide governance body mandated to address global issues. To the degree that global civil society actors wish to change world affairs, it makes sense for them to target the UN as a main player—both as an arena where states make decisions and as a semi-autonomous secretariat carrying out operations.

CIVIL SOCIETY AND THE UN

The relationship between civil society and the UN might best be described in terms of reciprocity. The UN works with civil society to boost the organization's legitimacy, support UN authority, and partner in undertaking specific operations. Civil society groups, in turn, engage the UN so as to enhance their own legitimacy, gain a greater foothold in global governance efforts, and offer their expertise in the delivery of on-the-ground services. The marriage between them, however, has not always been harmonious. At times, the UN has tried to shut its doors to certain NGOs, and NGOs have had to claw their way in. For example, the International Gay and Lesbian Association was expelled in 1994 under pressure from the United States and Arab countries. It successfully fought to be re-accredited three years later. Notwithstanding such dynamics, UN–civil society relations have been mostly beneficial even if they haven't always found their most workable form. One can see this by looking at the relationship between the UN and civil society through the organization's main governing activities.

The most important role the UN plays in global governance is to serve as a forum for the development of intergovernmental policy. It plays this role by providing leadership and an arena for international deliberation. Over its history, the organization has initiated and convened many international conferences, framework conventions, and formal treaties. In addition to its deliberative role, the United Nations also serves an implementing body which tries to put into practice specific political, social, and economic goals. It staffs secretariats that oversee treaties and other international agreements, and often supplies the muscle to carry out global programs. It is useful to conceptualize the reciprocal relationship between the UN and civil society through these two types of activities.

Global Deliberations

The UN has included civil society actors in its deliberative activities since its inception. Article 71 of the Charter empowers the Economic and Social Council (ECOSOC) to make arrangements for NGOs to act as consultants to the UN on issues in which these groups have competence. The formal arrangements for this consultative relationship have been refined at least three times since then: ECOSOC resolution 1296 (XLIV) in 1968; ECOSOC resolution 1996/31 in 1996; and the 2004 Cardoso report titled, *We the Peoples: Civil Society, the United Nations and Global Governance.* These successive efforts have expanded the role of NGOs and have acknowledged how significant this expansion is to global governance. As the Cardoso report—named after its chair, Brazil's former president Fernando Henrique Cardoso—put it, 'The rise of civil society is indeed one of the landmark events of our times. Global governance is no longer the sole domain of Governments. The growing participation and influence of nonstate actors is enhancing democracy and reshaping multilateralism.'[9]

Civil society groups generally gain access to the UN as recognized NGOs acting in a consultative role. As such, they perform numerous functions. They gather information, offer advice, educate member states, help draft treaties, mobilize governmental and citizen support for UN policies, provide data about on-the-ground conditions relevant to the organization's operations, and generally supply a specialized knowledge-base for UN deliberations and interstate negotiations. They offer these services at a range of United Nations forums, including conferences, ECOSOC, and subsidiary body meetings, secretariat offices, the Department of Public Information (DPI), and conferences of the parties to various international agreements. Resolution 1996/31 created three types of consultative status—general, special and roster—specifying how NGOs can participate in these settings. NGOs may achieve a formal place within the UN by playing these consultative roles. NGOs of all three types can attend conferences and meetings but only those with general status can propose agenda items. Only groups with general or special status can circulate and make statements at ECOSOC and subsidiary body meetings.[10]

The number of NGOs with consultative status has grown tremendously since the UN's inception. In 1948, there were 41; in 2005, more than 2,613 were accredited by ECOSOC, another 400 were accredited to the Commission on Sustainable Development, and an additional 1,500 enjoyed consultative status with DPI.[11] Consultative status has enabled NGOs to make significant contributions to international policymaking. NGOs with expertise on disability issues, for instance, participated in drafting a treaty on the rights of persons with disabilities. NGOs offered advice, drafted treaty language, and were central in promoting the effort as a human rights issue.[12] Likewise, consultative NGOs have played a key role in communicating the scientific basis and sense of urgency for various environmental treaties. This was the case with NGO participation in the Ozone Trends Panel that led to the 1987 Montreal Protocol on Substances that Deplete the Ozone Layer and with meetings leading up to the UN Framework Convention on Climate Change (UNFCCC).[13]

These instances are not rare. Since NGO participation in the UN burgeoned in the 1990s, accredited NGOs have left their signatures, as it were, on almost all significant UN policymaking.

Not all NGOs enjoy consultative status. Many choose not to apply for accreditation and some would not qualify if they did so. Such organizations still try to influence UN deliberations. Even without consultative status, NGOs may officially participate by registering at UN conferences. For example, some 1,400 NGOs registered at the United Nations Conference on Environment and Development (UNCED) in Rio de Janeiro, of which only a minority had consultative status.[14] These groups tried to influence delegates and UN personnel in the halls of the convention center, in hotel rooms, and on the street.

NGOs may work to influence the organization from *outside* in multiple ways. NGOs play a particularly useful role in educating UN personnel, state representatives, and the general public about emerging crises or other broad transnational concerns. They pressure states and the UN to address such dilemmas through media campaigns, lobbying efforts, citizen mobilization, or protest. Indeed, the repertoire of such efforts spans those of social movements in general.[15] In 2005, an effort by a coalition of some 1,000 scientists, representing 230 environmental groups, asked the UN to ban commercial long-line fishing—a technique that kills 4.4 million animals a year, many of which are endangered species. The activists wrote letters and organized meetings with UN personnel and state representatives, aiming at persuading the General Assembly to use its authority under the Law of the Sea Treaty to adopt a resolution halting the practice.[16]

At a more general level, civil society groups hold parallel meetings at large UN conferences in an attempt to influence deliberations. Such gatherings began at the Stockholm Conference on the Human Environment in 1972 and have become a regular feature since that time. They took place, for instance, at the 1992 Earth Summit, 1995 World Conference on Women, 2000 World Summit for Social Development (+5), and the 2002 World Summit on Sustainable Development, and provided opportunities for civil society groups to network, share information, celebrate their participation in global governance, and coordinate political strategies. Many such efforts are aimed at influencing UN deliberations and policies.[17] To be sure, such events are often held many miles from the official conference center and this reduces direct encounters between NGOs, on the one hand, and state delegates, UN personnel, and others intimately involved in the formal proceedings, on the other. Nonetheless, parallel conferences serve as a meeting place and networking forum for NGOs at a time when many such organizations are trying to influence the UN.

A final form of influence involves side events at UN conferences. Here, NGOs work with certain governments and international organizations to stage information meetings about salient issues relevant to ongoing negotiations. These meetings take place at the official conference site, in nearby hotels and other venues, and at the parallel NGO conference. They have a semi-official quality insofar as the UN Secretariat often helps organize them and provides logistical assistance.

This complex combination of consultative and advocacy roles aimed at UN deliberative processes suggests the mutualities between the UN and civil society. The United Nations turns to civil society for expert advice, consultation, and so forth, and global civil society actors engage the UN to win support for issues they believe are important. At times, the relationship is complementary and supportive; at other times, it is adversarial. In both cases, however, the UN and civil society engage each other.

Global Partnerships

In addition to its deliberative and facilitating activities, the UN also assumes an operational role, and civil society is crucial to assisting with this type of undertaking. Civil society actors partner with the UN to help implement its mandates and support its humanitarian, developmental, and environmental work. Inputs include such diverse activities as electoral assistance, famine relief, post-conflict reconstruction, de-mining operations, and monitoring treaty compliance.

Partnerships have long been part of UN operations. For example, in the 1970s, the world organization turned to the World Wide Fund for Nature (WWF) to help enforce the Convention on International Trade in Endangered Species of Wild Fauna and Flora (CITES). Tracking trade and overseeing transportation through ports around the world is a huge challenge. The United Nations turned to WWF for help and together they created TRAFFIC, a network of offices throughout the world that monitor and enhance compliance with CITES.[18] Since then, the UN has partnered with many civil society actors. For example, it consistently works with humanitarian NGOs, such as the International Rescue Committee (IRC) and Oxfam, to provide relief services for people affected by violent conflict—in places like Rwanda and Darfur—or natural catastrophes—like the Asian tsunami.[19] The United Nations essentially contracts with these NGOs because these organizations have the expertise, equipment, and personnel to address humanitarian crises and thus are best positioned to further the UN's goals.

Another type of partnership involves advancing certain educational and health campaigns. For example, since 1988, the World Health Organization (WHO) and the UN Children's Fund (UNICEF) have worked with Rotary International, the US Centers for Disease Control and Prevention, and other NGOs to advance the Global Polio Eradication Initiative. This effort, aimed at wiping out polio, has been particularly successful; the disease has been eliminated from all but six countries. Such partnerships have included raising funds, disseminating information and facilitating vaccination programs.[20]

In terms of field operations, another type of partnership occurs in both the development and humanitarian arenas where UN organizations frequently contract to NGOs for the delivery of funds from multilateral budgets. The Office of the UN High Commissioner for Refugees (UNHCR), for instance, relies on private agencies for the delivery of the vast majority of its program dollars. And more and more NGOs are delivering such money, along with equipment and technical assistance, for UN Development Programme (UNDP) projects.[21]

In 1999 Secretary-General Kofi Annan sought to expand civil society partnerships to include the business community through the Global Compact, which aims to harness the power of the market and corporations in the service of global governance. It calls on businesses to work with UN agencies and civil society actors to advance a set of universal environmental and social principles. Since its inception, the Global Compact has included hundreds of companies and NGOs from around the world. While the UN itself and most political theorists have often thought about civil society as excluding business—indeed, many people criticized Annan's initiative for blurring such distinctions—the Global Compact represents an important moment in UN governance. By turning to the business community and trying to integrate it with global civil society, the compact recognized the power of the world economy and the general insight that effective governance requires utilizing multiple mechanisms for shaping widespread thought and behavior.

CIVIL SOCIETY AND UN RELATIONS: LEGITIMACY, ACCOUNTABILITY, AND GOOD GOVERNANCE

Civil society actors are increasingly central players in UN governance, and this raises questions of legitimacy, accountability, and public-minded authority. Established 'to save succeeding generations from the scourge of war,' the UN aspires to actualize the highest ideals of international society. As such, the world organization must present itself as a fair, legitimate authority that is answerable to world opinion and concerned about the well-being of all humanity. This is where the UN's struggle between its statist and public character becomes most intense, and where civil society's role is most pertinent.

As a statist organization, the United Nations represents and is accountable to the community of states. This provides a modicum of legitimacy and authenticity to the organization's governing capacity. As mentioned, however, states *qua* states are not always themselves genuine representatives of their peoples nor can one count on states to care about global well-being. This is what inspires many to look to NGOs for a more globalist and nonsectarian orientation to world problems. NGOs, however, have their own problems.

While scholars and others initially looked to NGOs as the paradigmatic expression of global civil society and thus representative of humanity as a whole, this has been changing. Since the mid-1990s, many scholars (as well as governments) have begun to question the representative character, legitimacy, integrity, public-mindedness, and accountability of civil society actors themselves. Rather than assuming that their inputs were positive, this criticism has problematized a set of questions revolving around governing authority and accountability at the global level.[22] As their critics often point out, NGOs are unelected groups, operate free from systematic scrutiny, and at times advance self-serving interests. Furthermore, since many civil society organizations have headquarters in the global North, many observers regard civil society organizations as promoting the agenda of industrialized countries. In short, while some see civil society as representing the interests of humanity, serious questions have been raised about its ability to play this role. These criticisms of NGOs place the UN in a quandary, since it wishes to maintain its own claims to good governance and simultaneously depends on NGOs to help it establish this reputation.

Recent criticisms of NGOs are insightful and extremely important. NGOs should not be free from harsh scrutiny and critiques simply because they inhabit global civil society, of which many have an overly romantic understanding. But neither should the criticisms themselves dismiss the contributions that NGOs make to UN legitimacy, authority, and public-mindedness. All institutional forms of political expression fail as ideal types of genuinely democratic, legitimate, and globalist bodies. Thus, it should come as no surprise that civil society has its share of governing deficits.[23]

What is essential is that the United Nations and NGOs look to each other to compensate for their own failings and work together to address global collective action problems. To be sure, there are no easy or singular answers to such problems. But, as long as we live in an interdependent world with pressing collective issues, and as long as we need strong, legitimate and effective governing mechanisms to coordinate global political life, we will need the UN to act with authority and credibility. It garners some of this capacity by working with global civil society. Likewise, as long as we live in a world in which government power is unable to monopolize and instrumentalize all mechanisms of governance, and as long as we need to coordinate widespread behavior across innumerable domains of collective life, we will need global civil society. Civil society boosts its own claim to good governance, legitimacy, effectiveness, and so forth by working with the United Nations. Together, they deepen the prospects for global governance.

Conclusion

UN–civil society relations are longstanding. The history of these relations has been rocky at times, and they are constantly being reassessed by both parties as well as the world organization's member states. A key dimension informing such reassessments has been the relative legitimacy, authority, credibility, and public-mindedness that either the UN or civil society believes can be gained from sustained interactions. The UN's main challenge in this arena has been squaring its commitment to govern at the behest of the world's people, on the one hand, and the organization's statist institutional character, on the other. The challenge for civil society actors has been to play a relevant role in world affairs and to boost their own legitimate and efficacious claims to governance.

These challenges will not disappear, nor should they. They represent that perennial dilemma inherent in political life itself: how to govern in ways that advance the well-being of humanity. This is not a puzzle in search of a single solution but a constant challenge that each generation and every governing body must confront anew. Thus, while there are innumerable problems plaguing UN–civil society relations, we can look to those relations as a dynamic interplay in which efforts toward good governance are slowly but significantly being worked out.

Notes

1. James Rosenau, *United Nations in a Turbulent World* (Boulder, Colo.: Lynne Rienner, 1992).
2. Jean L. Cohen and Andrew Arato, *Civil Society and Political Theory* (Cambridge, Mass.: MIT Press, 1992); and Krishnan Kumar, 'Civil Society: An Inquiry into the Usefulness of an Historical Term,' *British Journal of Sociology* 44, no.3 (1993): 375–395.

3. John Keane, 'Despotism and Democracy: The Origins and Development of the Distinction between Civil Society and the State, 1750–1850,' in *Civil Society and the State: New European Perspectives*, ed. John Keane (London: Verso, 1988), 35–71.
4. G. W. F. Hegel, *Hegel's Philosophy of Right* (Oxford: Clarendon Press, 1942).
5. Don E. Eberly, ed., *The Essential Civil Society Reader: Classic Essays in the American Civil Society Debate* (Lanham, Md.: Rowman & Littlefield, 2000).
6. Centre for the Study of Global Governance, *Global Civil Society 2004/5*, ed. Helmut Anheier, Marlies Glasius, and Mary Kaldor (Oxford: Oxford University Press, 2004). Data were collected from Union of International Associations, *Yearbook of International Organizations: Guide to Civil Society Networks, 1994* and *2004*.
7. Earthtrends, 'Technical And Source Notes: Environmental Governance and Institutions—Civil Society: Number of international non-governmental organizations (INGOs),' www.earthtrends.wri.org.
8. Paul K. Wapner, *Environmental Activism and World Civic Politics* (Albany, NY: State University of New York Press, 1996).
9. 'We the Peoples': Civil Society, The United Nations and Global Governance: Report of the Panel of Eminent Persons on United Nations–Civil Society Relations*, UN document A/58.817, 7 June 2004.
10. United Nations Association of the United States and the Business Council for the United Nations, 'UN and Civil Society,' www.unausa.org.
11. For a complete list, see: www.un.org.
12. Julie Mertus, *Bait and Switch: Human Rights and US Foreign Policy* (New York: Routledge, 2004); United Nations Programme on Disability, 'NGO Comments on the Draft Text United Nations Programme on Disability, 2003–2004' (2005).
13. David Hunter, James Salzman, and Durwood Zaelke, *International Environmental Law and Policy*, 2nd edn. (New York: Foundation Press, 2002), 241.
14. Leon Gordenker and Thomas G. Weiss, 'Pluralizing Global Governance: Analytical Approaches and Dimensions,' in *NGOs, the UN and Global Governance*, ed. Thomas G. Weiss and Leon Gordenker (Boulder, Colo.: Lynne Rienner, 1996), 17–47.
15. Sidney G. Tarrow, *Power in Movement: Social Movements and Contentious Politics* (Cambridge: Cambridge University Press, 1998).
16. 'Findings: Environmental Groups Seek Ban on Long-Line Fishing,' *Washington Post*, 7 June 2005.
17. Michael G. Schechter, *United Nations Global Conferences* (London: Routledge, 2005).
18. www.traffic.org.
19. www.theirc.org.
20. See 'Sixty Ways the United Nations Makes a Difference,' point #20, available at: www.undpi.org.
21. See Thomas G. Weiss, ed., *Beyond UN Subcontracting: Task-Sharing with Regional Security Arrangements and Service-providing NGOs* (New York: St. Martin's Press, 1998), 30–45, 139–258.
22. Bob Clifford, *The Marketing of Rebellion: Insurgents, Media, and International Activism* (New York: Cambridge University Press 2005); Kenneth Anderson, 'The Limits of Pragmatism in American Foreign Policy: Unsolicited Advice to the Bush Administration on Relations with International Nongovernmental Organizations,' *Chicago Journal of International Law* 2 (Fall 2001): 371–388; Jan Aart Scholte, 'Civil Society and Democracy in Global Governance,' *Global Governance* 8, no.3 (2002): 281–304.
23. For a defense of NGOs, see Paul Wapner, 'Defending Accountability in NGOs,' *Chicago Journal of International Law* 3, no. 1 (2002): 197–205.

CHAPTER 15

PRIVATE SECTOR

CRAIG N. MURPHY

ONE of the great ironies in recent global affairs is that intergovernmental institutions arose largely in response to problems and opportunities created by capitalist industrialism, what we now call 'economic globalization.' Yet throughout much of the sixty-year history of the United Nations, the private sector was held at arm's length by almost all parts of the UN system. This began to change in the late 1970s, initially as specific UN agencies responded to the calls of nongovernmental organizations (NGOs) for more aggressive forms of regulation of some practices of multinational firms that were poorly controlled, especially in the developing world. Shortly afterward, efforts began from a very different direction: in the wake of the widespread failure of two decades of internationally supported, government-directed development policies and the advent of Thatcher/Reagan-era conservatism, some UN development organizations began to change long-standing ideas and practices. By 1992, with the Rio conference on environment and development, active engagement with business organizations that supported UN-promoted norms had become significant enough to affect major intergovernmental agreements.

Over the last decade, especially throughout the tenure of Kofi Annan as Secretary-General, partnerships with the private sector have deepened. Kofi Annan, a management school graduate with close personal connections to corporate leaders around the world, relied on those networks to help establish initiatives to bring businesses more directly into the work of the UN, e.g., the Global Compact, and even to fund parts of the work of the UN system.

By the beginning of the twenty-first century, some observers were pointing to the close collaboration between the UN system and particular segments of international capital as a sign of a transformation of the global political economy, a kind of end point of economic globalization, marked by the emergence of a 'global ruling class' that was better served by the 'global governance' embodied within the UN system than by the national policies of the various countries of origin of that class's members. Be that as it may, there is undoubtedly growing tension between the coalition of businesses and the Secretariat, which supports an unusually cosmopolitan agenda, and the UN's traditional role as a reflection of the interests of its member states, especially its most powerful members, many of whom have not embraced the cosmopolitan goals.

BUSINESS AND INTERNATIONAL ORGANIZATION BEFORE THE UN AND ITS EARLY YEARS

Capitalist industrialism's internal logic constantly pushes it beyond the political boundaries of the moment. Thus, the 'globalizing' industrial economies have always fit poorly with the political system of separate, geographically limited sovereign states that we inherited from the agricultural age. Governments, in fact, created many of the nineteenth-century predecessors of today's 'standard-setting' UN specialized agencies to facilitate the expansion of economies across borders (removing barriers to the creation of transnational communication and transportation networks) and to mitigate the negative consequences of economic internationalization (e.g., the disempowerment of traditional agricultural sectors, the potential ratcheting-down of conditions of industrial labor to those in the newest and poorest of the industrial countries).[1]

Business organizations and individual businessmen played central roles in the foundation of many of these institutions. National chambers of commerce and, eventually, the International Chamber of Commerce (ICC) lobbied governments to create the new institutions.[2] Men such as David Lubin, the California clothing magnate at the center of the process that created the predecessor to the Food and Agriculture Organization (FAO), both came up with organizational designs and acted as critical benefactors of new institutions, while 'The Businessman's Peace Movement' lobbied for a general purpose international organization, a 'League of Nations,' at the Hague conference in 1899 and 1907 and throughout the First World War.[3] In this historical context, the 'tripartite' structure of the early institutions for 'international labor legislation' (with separate representation of businessmen, labor organizations, and governments) was less remarkable than the International Labour Organization's (ILO) structure may appear today.

Private businesses continued to play a role under the League. The Boston haberdasher Edward Filene paid for the first experiments in simultaneous translation that were further developed by Thomas J. Watson of IBM.[4] The foundation set up by John D. Rockefeller underwrote much of the early international health work, which governments were especially reluctant to support.[5] Filene and Britain's Quaker chocolate manufacturers sponsored an extension of the ILO, an International Management Institute (an ancestor of today's World Economic Forum in Davos), to teach the most progressive 'scientific management' principles to the world.[6] In fact, the job of establishing the regulatory structure of the post-First World War economy was largely handed over to business at the (almost forgotten) 1916 Atlantic City Conference, the precedent for the well-remembered, and very different, post-Second World War conference at Bretton Woods.[7]

The failure of the interwar economic 'system'—or, more correctly, the 'non-system'—that the businessmen at Atlantic City agreed upon had a great deal to do with the UN's original lack of involvement with the private sector. The non-system *was* the '*laissez-faire* utopia' upon which E. H. Carr heaped so much scorn in *The Twenty Years' Crisis*.[8] The UN's founders believed that 'utopia' was implicated in the outbreak of the Great Depression, helped assure the rise of fascism, and had to be at the center of any explanation of World War II.

The designers and the first operators of the UN system, including John Maynard Keynes and Harry Dexter White, the key figures at Bretton Woods, largely shared Carr's view that the twentieth-century tide of history was shifting from laissez-faire to planning. Carr's friend, the accomplished British diplomat, David Owen, was the first person hired by the Secretariat. He became the UN's first chief of economic policy issues, the man who coordinated the economic development funding of the 1950s and early 1960s that was funneled through the specialized agencies and allowed them to grow, and the person with the greatest influence over the composition of the UN's development staff until well into the 1970s, or later.[9]

One of Owens's formative experiences was working with Hans Singer (Keynes's student and later Owens's 'economic brain' within the Secretariat) on a multi-year field study of impoverished families across Britain at the height of the Great Depression. It is not surprising that he surrounded himself with a global staff deeply committed to planning. It is perhaps more surprising that the other key person in the establishment of the UN's global economic network, Paul Hoffman, the former Studebaker executive and Eisenhower fundraiser who had headed the Marshall Plan, had the same commitments. He remained in charge of the UN Development Programme (UNDP) until 1971.[10]

Hoffman's close connections to the private sector were the exception in the early UN—not the rule. In the UN's early years, both the Secretariat in New York and the specialized agencies were dumbfounded and could not respond when many East Asian governments asked for UN technical assistance experts to teach about managing private firms, marketing, and entrepreneurship.[11] Most of Singapore's leadership credits their Owen-and-Hoffman-era UN economic adviser, Albert Winsemius, with convincing the country's democratic socialist party to adopt the business-oriented development strategy that proved so successful, but Winsemius was definitely an odd duck among his UN colleagues. Even Hoffman's deputy and later Nobel laureate W. Arthur Lewis found resistance when he argued that the female entrepreneurs around whom much of Africa's agricultural production and trade revolved should be at the center of the UN's development work. This was despite the fact that his Fabian pamphlet on planning in the underdeveloped countries was widely cited by his colleagues and it emphasized the centrality of private sector in the developing world rather the grand schemes of government investment that the UN favored in the 1950s and 1960s.[12] Even the World Bank, which Eisenhower's Republicans had convinced to open a window that provided financing to private companies operating in the developing world, the International Finance Corporation, did not see the private sector as having a particular 'comparative advantage' in the developing countries until the 1980s.[13]

Nonetheless, even in the 1950s and 1960s, the earlier tradition of enlisting 'progressive' corporations in the task of building international governance never completely disappeared. Paul Hoffman considered one of his great triumphs to have been enlisting the Xerox Corporation in sponsoring a series of films that used the conventions of the Hollywood blockbuster (and big stars, including Grace Kelly and Edward G. Robinson) to tell the story of the UN's work in promoting human rights, encouraging development, confronting the drug trade, and the like. Some of the film's titles—'Once Upon a Tractor' and 'The Poppy is also a Flower'—give some sense of why they did not become part of the cinematic canon.[14]

CONTESTS OVER REGULATION

Even while the secretariats of most organizations within the UN system remained at a relative arm's length from the private sector, the scope of truly international regulation of business was growing. John Braithwaite and Peter Drahos's comprehensive study summarizes the mechanisms: laws of property and contract (and food regulations) converged through the reciprocal adjustment of national (and European Community) law.[15] The most powerful states tended to dictate the shifting regimes of global finance. The US and British markets shaped global regimes for corporations and securities. A snowballing deregulatory movement, beginning in the United States in the 1950s, gave us today's global communications regimes. Private regulatory institutions (insurers) were central to changes in the shipping regime. The US government and US companies shaped global civil aviation regimes,[16] and drug policy became world drug policy.[17]

The UN system was rarely involved. The old tripartite labor standards regime 'ha[d] fallen on hard times.'[18] Nevertheless, 'Most of the important globalizations of trade regulation have occurred since 1950 under the auspices of the GATT [General Agreement on Tariffs and Trade].' However, the GATT was only a forum, a place where the US government had an unusual power to influence the regulatory schemes designed by 'a small number of major US companies.' Yet, even in the GATT, the companies remained at arm's length from the secretariat.[19]

The one institution that followed a different strategy was the International Organization for Standardization (ISO), whose relationship to the UN system has always been a bit ambiguous. At the moment, ISO calls itself a 'nongovernmental organization,' although, in the past, it was 'the UN's standards organization.' It is a federation of what were originally the *industrial* standards bodies of 149 countries.[20] These days ISO is not just concerned with standardizing physical things like screw threads or lumber sizes. It also works on business practices, environmental standards, and even social issues. The basic 'standard setting' model involves negotiations among the companies that are the primary players in any field as well as active harmonization of standards promulgated within a particular country.

The North–South conflict of the mid-1970s began to expand the UN's engagement with business, especially the New International Economic Order (NIEO) advocated by the Third World. The NIEO rapidly evolved along with scholarship on international political economy, one part of which focused on the negative effects of multinational corporations in the developing world. This work had a great deal of impact on Northern social movement organizations concerned with the developing world. In 1973, the Oxford-based independent *New Internationalist* magazine— which began as a house organ for Oxfam, but later severed the relationship (at least formally) in order to take more political stances—published an article criticizing the strategies for marketing milk formula in the developing world adopted by the Swiss firm, Nestlé, and others.[21] The article accused the firms of giving free formula to mothers immediately after birth, often in hospitals, ensuring that the mothers' breasts ceased to produce milk, with the result that many mothers became dependent on a product that they could not afford to purchase. NGOs then mounted an international boycott and called for a global marketing code, which was rapidly developed under the auspices of the World Health Organization (WHO) and the UN Children's Fund (UNICEF) and adopted by the World Health Assembly in 1981.[22]

Almost simultaneously, beginning in 1972, the Economic and Social Council (ECOSOC) engaged in discussions aimed at creating a Commission and a Centre on Transnational Corporations, which were formed in 1975. Throughout the rest of the decade and through the 1980s these groups held hearings and seminars that helped build the capacity of governments to deal with transnational firms and attempted to develop codes of conduct for a range of issues from accounting practices to paying kickbacks on government contracts. Unlike most national bodies that regulate corporations, the UN bodies rarely engaged directly with major companies. Moreover, throughout their history, the UN bodies were widely seen as policy instruments of the South. In 1993, after years of waning support by the countries that provide most of the UN's budget, the responsibilities of the commission were moved to the UNCTAD Commission on Investment, Technology, and Enterprise Development, and much of the staff on permanent contracts was sent there as well.[23]

The Organisation for Economic Co-operation and Development (OECD), largely a club of the industrialized countries of the West, increasingly became the primary locus of the development of comprehensive codes of conduct for multinational firms. The OECD's work goes back to 1977 when it passed a declaration that responded to one of the first proposals of the UN Commission on Transnational Corporations with a set of principles that favored the position taken by many firms.

In the same year, the ILO passed a similar declaration that listed a set of key ILO conventions and declarations that should apply to transnational investors. The ILO declaration has been updated a number of times to take into account additional agreements made since 1977.

A New Direction

In 1986, the UN began a fundamentally new kind of engagement with private firms. In place of the arm's length relationships that had characterized most of the UN's interactions, and the adversarial, regulatory approach of the relatively successful infant formula campaigns, as well as the unsuccessful attempt to enforce a code of conduct on transnational corporations, the UN began to view private firms as major allies in some of its core work. The change began when William A. Draper, III took over as UNDP's Administrator, the title of the organization's most senior official, the role that Paul Hoffman had filled until 1971. Draper was an extremely successful American venture capitalist who had served a short term as head of the US Import–Export Bank, after having been appointed by Ronald Reagan, who also nominated him for the job at UNDP.

UNDP was the UN's major development program as well as the coordinator of the UN system's field presence throughout the developing world. In most countries the UNDP's resident representative, whose official role is simply 'the first among equals' in the group of heads of UN organizations in a particular country, is in fact treated as the personal embodiment of the United Nations—the exception being those crisis countries where a special representative or envoy of the Secretary-General heads a military and/or civilian team.

UNDP's corporate self-image was long that of the servant of each developing country in which it was resident, but Draper decided to change that by adding a 'second track' of work: advocating (but not requiring) a set of policies that the program was convinced would contribute to development. These included the protection of the environment and the promotion of women, NGOs, and the private sector. Initially, Draper's focus on the private sector was treated with derision by many UNDP staffers, but the conjuncture of Draper's 'second track' with his embrace and commitment to the egalitarian principles of 'human development' articulated by the thinker on whom he most relied, Mahbub ul Haq, eventually endeared him to the 'Fabian' culture within the organization. By the early 1990s, after the fall of the Leninist regimes in Eastern Europe and the Soviet Union, UNDP was actively promoting the private sector in almost all parts of the world, building direct links to some of the major corporate giants in the developing world such as Packages Limited in Pakistan, Iran Khodro (the largest manufacturing firm in the Middle East), and Ghana Aluminum Products.[24]

The same cultural change that influenced UNDP's engagements in the Third World helped shift UN secretariat views as well. Maurice Strong, the extremely successful Canadian businessman who was at the center of the UN's work on the environment beginning in the early 1970s, started to marshal environmental 'first movers'—companies that make significant investments in cleaner technologies and who, therefore, have an interest in assuring that their competitors bear the same costs—in support of a host of global regulatory campaigns beginning in the 1980s. While these campaigns led to the creation of a creative development financing facility to be used by Third World governments to achieve better environmental outcomes,[25] arguably only one of the many proposed regimes has been successful—the Montreal Protocol on Substances that Deplete the Ozone Layer of 1987 (with major revisions in 1990 and 1992). In that case, one key to the negotiations was a single company with a long (if complex and sometimes mixed) history of social responsibility, which had an interest in creating large markets for its new, proprietary alternative to ozone depleting gases.[26]

Nonetheless, this one case revived a model of how to achieve effective international regulation.[27] It also catalyzed business groups such as the Business Council for Sustainable Development (BCSD) made up of 'first movers' ready to work with governments and UN system secretariats to promote the next generation of international regulation.[28] Beginning with the 1992 Rio summit on the environment and development, the BCSD and other groups became major nongovernmental players in the field of 'civil society' lobbyists working the global intergovernmental conferences, a field long dominated by non-corporate NGOs.

THE ANNAN ERA

When Kofi Annan became the UN's seventh Secretary-General in January 1997 and brought in Strong as a key advisor, the global system of intergovernmental organizations returned to an era of deep partnership with private companies similar to those that existed in the interwar years. Then in 1998, the US media magnate, Ted Turner, gave US$ 1 billion to a foundation 'to support UN causes and activities.'[29] Over the subsequent decade, Turner's example was followed by other US corporate leaders, including Microsoft's Bill Gates, whose foundation has become a major supporter of the WHO's work on HIV/AIDS.

In 1999, Annan turned even more directly to corporate leaders, asking them to enforce a 'Global Compact' between labor and capital, North and South, and humanity and the rest of the living world. The Global Compact has private firms signing on to the UN's core labor, environmental, anti-corruption and human rights standards. It does not establish a strict monitoring regime or sanctions for violations, but it does create a complex process by which companies each year report exemplary 'best practices' and a host of NGOs evaluate those reports and help compile what will be, essentially, a continuously updated process handbook of the practices of first movers companies in each of these fields.[30]

The idea of some sort of 'compact' went back to the 1995 Social Summit in Copenhagen, where the focus had been on getting commitments from states. Northern states would commit to meeting the never-achieved aid targets that had been affirmed for more than fifty years. Those targets originated before the creation of the world organization, in the wartime anti-fascist alliance. Southern states would commit to higher budgets for human development. Everyone would commit to enforcing widely agreed upon human rights and other standards. The Copenhagen summit was followed by year-after-year of decreasing aid budgets, continuing a trend that began at the end of the Cold War. If governments could not be reliable partners in such an effort, perhaps corporations could be.

The Global Compact is supported by a group of six UN organizations. Perhaps the most significant involvement has come from UNDP because firms headquartered in the developing world seem to have most embraced the idea as something more than an exercise in public relations. There is some evidence, for example, that in Brazil the Compact has led to a kind of virtuous circle of firms competing to prove their adherence to the various principles, and in many countries providing exemplary models to the global process handbook has become a sign of membership in a global community of the leading corporations.[31]

Annan followed the Global Compact initiative with a more ambitious 'Commission on the Private Sector and Development' headed by the then Prime Minister of Canada, Paul Martin, and the former President of Mexico, Ernesto Zedillo. The Commission included some of the most well-known advocates of the role of business in economic development, including former US Treasury Secretary Robert Rubin, Jannik Lindbaek, who had served as head of the IFC and of Norway's STATOIL, and Kwame Pianim, perhaps the leading private management consultant in sub-Saharan Africa. The Commission issued a report in a dozen languages. It urged developed countries to create a more conducive international trade and macroeconomic environment for development, as developing countries strengthened the rule of law and were urged to become more open to inviting the private sector into the policy process.[32] At this point, it is too early to see if the Commission has marshaled significant support behind this different 'Global Compact.' It is certainly clear that this agenda has influenced UN policymakers. When then UNDP Administrator Mark Malloch Brown left in 2005, to become Annan's chief of staff and then deputy, he told his successor that creating a 'practice area' focusing on this private sector compact would have been his top priority had he stayed at UNDP.[33]

Annan's UN was a very different world than what went before. It was one in which corporate leaders had privileged access into the inner circles of the Secretariat not only in New York, but also in most of the country offices where the UN's work is coordinated by a strong special representative or by a dynamic UNDP resident representative. At a country level, it can mean the establishment of partnerships such as those between the Soros Foundation and UNDP to set up 'Freenets' across much of the former Soviet space, something that did play a role in Ukraine's Orange Revolution of 2004, although such partnerships are perhaps not quite the conspiratorial US hegemonic project that one can read about on the internet.[34] Nonetheless, the Secretariat's increasing ties to the private sector and to private foundations have led to understandable questions about whether such actions are appropriate for a body that is supposed to report to the General Assembly—i.e., a body constituted to serve the interests of states, not the interests of some segment of capitalist enterprise.

Many governments' complaints about the new closeness between the Secretariat (along with organizations such as UNDP) and the private sector were put in terms of Annan or other staffers reflecting the interests of the United States.[35] This misses much of the point of much of the cooperation. By deciding to fund the development and distribution of vaccines for a host of the most destructive infectious diseases, the Gates Foundation accomplished with a few strokes of a pen something that activists within the WHO had been struggling to achieve for decades, but could not achieve due to the lack of support from the legislatures of the industrialized world. Social scientists who see the new closeness between the UN and one part of the private sector as the development of a form of global governance reflecting the interest of an emergent 'global ruling class' not tied to the government of any particular state, including the most powerful, have an explanation of the phenomena that is more consistent with the facts.[36]

Yet, the explanation may be even simpler. During World War II, analysts who tried to understand the failures of the League in order that they would not be repeated under the new organization pointed to the reliance that the League's Secretariat developed upon private enterprise in order to fund its social and economic work. The turn to businessmen had been, they argued, a creative bureaucratic expedient seized upon by officials who recognized that the League *could not* ask for sufficient support from its members because it had lost most of its legitimacy. Looking back at 1925 from the vantage point of 1945, the turn to men like Filene, Rockefeller, Rowntree, and Watson should have been a warning sign—a canary in the coal mine—something that future generations should look to recognize in case it were to happen again.[37]

Notes

1. Craig N. Murphy, *International Organization and Industrial Change: Global Governance since 1850* (Cambridge: Polity Press, 1994), 46–81.
2. George L. Ridgeway, *Merchants of Peace: The History of the International Chamber of Commerce*, 2nd edn. (Boston: Little, Brown & Co., 1959).
3. Olivia R. Agresti, *David Lubin: A Study in Practical Idealism*, 2nd edn. (Berkeley: University of California Press, 1941), 193–245; and World Peace Foundation, *75th Anniversary Report* (Boston: World Peace Foundation, 1985), 9.

4. Ridgeway, *Merchants of Peace*, 115.

5. Egon-Ferdinand Ranshofen-Wertheimer, *The International Secretariat* (New York: Carnegie Endowment Studies in the Administration of International Law and Organizations, 1945), 158.

6. Charles D. Wrege, Ronald G. Greenwood, and Sakae Hata, 'The International Management Institute and Political Opposition to Its Efforts in Europe, 1925–1934,' Paper presented at the Business History Conference, Wilmington, Del., 12–14 March 1987.

7. Murphy, *International Organization and Industrial Change*, 160–161, 172.

8. Edward Hallett Carr, *The Twenty Years' Crisis: 1919–1939*, 2nd edn. (London: Macmillan, 1946), 51.

9. John Toye and Richard Toye, *The UN and Global Political Economy: Trade, Finance, and Development* (Bloomington: Indiana University Press, 2004), 61.

10. Craig N. Murphy, *The United Nations Development Programme: A Better Way?* (Cambridge: Cambridge University Press, 2006), 62–63; and Alan R. Raucher, *Paul G. Hoffman: Architect of Foreign Aid*, (Lexington: University of Kentucky Press, 1985), 133–154.

11. Murphy, *The United Nations Development Programme*, 108; and United Nations Commission for Asia and the Far East, *Fields of Economic Development Handicapped by Lack of Trained Personnel in Certain Countries of Asia and the Far East* (Bangkok: United Nations, 1951).

12. Murphy, *The United Nations Development Programme*, 105–106; and W. Arthur Lewis, *Principles of Economic Planning: A Study Prepared for the Fabian Society* (London: D. Dobson, 1949).

13. Devesh Kapur, John B. Lewis, and Richard Webb, *The World Bank: Its First Half-Century* (Washington, DC: Brookings Institution Press, 1997), 23.

14. Mark D. Alleyne, *Global Lies? Propaganda, the UN and World Order* (Houndmills, Basingstoke, UK: Palgrave Macmillan, 2003), 84–86.

15. John Braithwaite and Peter Drahos, *Global Business Regulation* (Cambridge: Cambridge University Press, 2000), 84 and 417.

16. Braithwaite and Drahos, *Global Business Regulation*, 138–142, 173–173, 356–357, 435–437, and 469–470.

17. Ibid., 397–398.

18. Ibid., 253.

19. Ibid., 218–219. Compare to Rorden Wilkinson, *The WTO, Crisis and the Governance of Global Trade* (London: Routledge, 2006).

20. Compare 'Who ISO Is,' www.iso.org, with the cover of ISO Information Centre, *Information Transfer* (Geneva: ISO, 1977).

21. See entire issue of 'The Baby Food Tragedy,' *New Internationalist*, no. 6 (August 1973).

22. Lee E. Preston and Duane Windsor, *The Rules of the Game in the Global Economy: Policy Regimes for International Business*, 2nd edn. (Dordrecht, Netherlands: Kluwer Academic Publishers, 1997), 74–79.

23. See John H. Dunning, 'In Search of a Global Moral Architecture,' in *Making Globalization Good: The Moral Challenge of Global Capitalism*, ed., John H. Dunning (Oxford: Oxford University Press, 2003), 363–65; UNCTAD, 'The United Nations Centre on Transnational Corporations: Origin, Evolution, and Contribution,' www.unctad.org and Torbjörn Fredricksson, 'Forty Years of UNCTAD Research on FDI,' *Transnational Corporations* 12, no. 3 (2003): 1–39.

24. Murphy, *The United Nations Development Programme*.

25. Helen Sjoberg, *From Idea to Reality: The Creation of the Global Environment Facility*, GEF Working Paper no. 10, Washington, DC, October 1994, 4–5.

26. Dale D. Murphy, *The Structure of Regulatory Competition: Corporations and Public Policy in a Global Economy* (Oxford: Oxford University Press, 2004), 125.

27. Craig N. Murphy, *Global Institutions, Marginalization, and Development* (London: Routledge, 2005), 165–174.

28. Stephan Schmidheiny, *Changing Course: A Global Perspective on Business and the Environment* (Cambridge, Mass.: MIT Press, 1992).

29. United Nations Foundation, *About Us*, www.unfoundation.org.

30. See John Gerard Ruggie, 'Global_Governance.net: The Global Compact as Learning Network,' *Global Governance* 7, no 4 (2001): 371–378; and Steve Hughes and Rorden Wilkinson, 'The Global Compact: Promoting Corporate Responsibility?,' *Environmental Politics* 10, no. 1 (2001): 155–159.

31. *UNDP and the Global Compact*, www.undp.org/business/undp_gc.html.

32. Commission on the Private Sector and Development, *Unleashing Entrepreneurship: Making Business Work for the Poor* (New York: UNDP, March 2004), 1–5.

33. Memorandum report, UNDP 1999–2005—Accomplishments and Remaining Challenges, from Mark Malloch Brown to Kemal Dervis, August 2005.

34. Murphy, *The United Nations Development Programme*, 280–281.

35. For example, in a heated exchange of letters among the Secretariat, the Group of 77, and the US House of Representatives at the beginning of 2006, Thalif Deen, 'US Legislators Cross Swords with UN Bloc,' *Inter Press Service News Agency*, 16 February 2006, www.ipsnews.net.

36. For example, William I. Robinson, *A Theory of Global Capitalism: Production, Class, and the State in a Transnational World* (Baltimore, Md.: Johns Hopkins University Press, 2004).

37. Ranshofen-Wertheimer, *The International Secretariat*, 158.

CHAPTER 16

....

MEDIA

....

BARBARA CROSSETTE

THE relationship between the United Nations and the world's media organizations is unusual in a number of ways, and this affects not only how the global institution is portrayed worldwide but also how the UN, in all its complexity, deals with an equally diverse world of journalism: in print, broadcasting, and online—and in an age when personalities outrank institutions in the eyes of editors.

There are about 600 correspondents accredited full time to UN headquarters in New York, with up to 2,500 more given temporary passes for annual General Assembly sessions or when there is a major event such as a summit of world leaders or an important conference. Security concerns and a lack of workspace increasingly circumscribe the activities of visiting journalists, who roam around the corridors of the world organization, often confused by a multifaceted information system. But even for those reporters who classify as 'resident correspondents' and work at headquarters more or less full time, there is neither the imposed discipline nor the intense focus of the highly regulated press corps found around, for example, presidential offices and government ministries in most national capitals. At the UN, the interests of reporters and their media organizations are much more diffuse, and attitudes toward the gathering and use of information are varied.

The UN by its nature does not produce a uniform message or a singular story every day. The Secretary-General is not, like a president, always at the center of events, and there are many issues in play and many other focal points vying for coverage, not least among them the Security Council and the General Assembly. Correspondents often pursue different stories, or report the same events from differing angles. The answer to the question 'What happened at the UN today?' would depend on any one of many individual perspectives. All this contributes to the erratic and episodic way that the UN tends to get reported around the world—and to the varied impressions of it held by people from country to country.

The international news agencies are the most comprehensive and consistent in their coverage. Both in New York and in Geneva, the UN's second-largest media center, the core journalists are those from major news services such as Agence France-Presse, the Associated Press, Reuters, Xinhua, the Press Trust of India, EFE (the Spanish-language agency) and Inter Press Service, with its emphasis on reporting for the developing world. Wire service reporters send out thousands of words virtually around the clock every day on a range of subjects, and to a wide world audience. A few leading international broadcast networks with large viewing and listening publics—including CNN, the BBC, Japan's NHK, the Voice of America, and Al Jazeera—maintain radio and/or television studios in the Secretariat building, though they do not provide blanket coverage. Some leading newspapers, with smaller but often very influential audiences, also have permanent news bureaus, among them *The New York Times*, *The Washington Post*, *Le Monde*, *Al Hayat*, a variety of British papers, and a few Latin American publications.

Many more media organizations cover the UN part time with correspondents based in New York or Washington who also report on many other subjects. Additionally, there are representatives of government-owned or controlled national news agencies in the mix, plus an assortment of freelance correspondents who may have other occupations unrelated to news gathering. Finally, there are visiting specialists: medical reporters, for example, who follow the HIV/AIDS pandemic, writers on disarmament or international law, environmental specialists and so on. In such a heterogeneous and polyglot press corps, opinions, perspectives, methods, and ethical considerations differ vastly. This can either enrich the work of reporters enormously or make cooperation among journalists impossible when there is an issue of importance—such as access to officials or documents—to take up with UN officials.

What do reporters around UN headquarters—and countless other journalists who may interact only sporadically with the UN in offices far beyond New York and Geneva, or in crisis areas in the field—tell the world? How do the UN's own information services contribute to media work and public awareness? This chapter examines how media relations have evolved over the UN's history and the contemporary media environment in which the UN must work. It outlines the structure of UN information operations and considers the important influence of UN officials beginning with the Secretary-General, while taking account of the political tensions inherent in an institution with member nations that may or may not support the free flow of information.

THE DEPARTMENT OF PUBLIC INFORMATION

At the center of all UN media outreach efforts is the Department of Public Information (DPI), whose antecedent was the United Nations Information Organization (UNIO). Formed during World War II to disseminate news about proposals to create a world organization, UNIO was run by a former British colonial administrator, with the help of two experienced journalists, and that small team went on to direct media relations during the organization's start-up years.

In 1946, a year after the UN was formally established, the General Assembly called for the creation of a department to provide 'the fullest possible direct access to the activities and official documentation of the Organization.' DPI was to work with print publications, radio, film, graphics, and exhibitions, while also serving as a liaison to the public and as a reference center. Sir Brian Urquhart, who began his long career with the UN in its earliest days and was still writing about the organization in his eighties, has said that DPI was modeled in large part on the US Office of War Information, which dealt in propaganda and control of news—the wrong template for the UN. In some ways, the tension between two operational poles—a managed flow of mostly positive information versus free access for reporters to rummage on their own, for better or worse—has never gone away.

After 1950, many of the most important media outlets established bureaus in the new UN headquarters overlooking the East River in Manhattan. The UN was one of the biggest international stories of the postwar era, and some of the most famous names in journalism wanted to be there. Free office space was provided for reporters, a practice that continues. During the Cold War, the press corps dropped in numbers and prestige, as East–West rivalries often paralyzed the organization, and real news was scarce. Media interest returned somewhat in the 1990s after the end of the Cold War, when the Security Council, free of crippling vetoes, became much more active. Peacekeeping and nation-building operations burgeoned in the Balkans, Africa, and Southeast Asia.[1] Reporting interest continued into the twenty-first century as reform of the organization became a hot political topic—coincident with a rash of scandals involving some UN operations.

The DPI, now headed by an Under-Secretary-General and employing hundreds of information specialists, reaches an international audience in the UN's six official languages—Arabic, Chinese, English, French, Russian, and Spanish. The UN News Center website, www.un.org/News, provides daily reports from across the UN system, along with transcripts of press briefings, texts of speeches, documents and formal and informal remarks by the Secretary-General. Its free email news alert service is available to anyone. The companion multimedia center is a source of video news footage, web casts and special programming through www.un.org. Photographs of UN events and personalities are also readily available and in the public domain.

The main UN website was still cumbersome to navigate in 2005, especially for those unfamiliar with UN acronyms and terminology. Reporters frequently use commercial search engines such as Google for a quicker route to specific reports, documents, or events. But UN agencies, funds, and programs have their own, more user-friendly, sites—for example, www.unicef.org, www.who.org, www.unfpa.org, or www.undp.org. Reporters working in crises not only use these websites but also gravitate to agencies in the field as sources. Journalists sometimes travel into dangerous territory with UN staff to provide the kind of on-the-scene reports demanded by news organizations. In the process, these correspondents in the field see the UN in a different light from those reporters based at headquarters. Humanitarian agencies encourage reporters on the scene to tell their stories most dramatically.[2]

UN Radio, also part of DPI, broadcasts programs on UN activities and offers free audio downloads on its website, www.un.org/radio. In 2005, UN Radio began making its daily broadcasts available to the American public though the internet and local radio stations through a program called UN Radio News/USA, www.un.org/radio/newsusa. UN radio experts have contributed enormously to the success of peacekeeping by establishing local networks in areas where missions are operating, to inform and reassure battered populations who may never have known credible media.

UNTV, in addition to running an internal network at UN headquarters to cover daily events and archive footage, produces documentaries, videos, and webcasts. Its website, in a choice of languages, is www.un.org/av/tv.

A report in September 2005 by the Secretary-General on upgrading DPI to keep up with rapidly changing technologies noted that 40,000 subscribers were receiving the free daily email updates from UN News and that a daily ten-minute TV broadcast was being sent to over 500 Associated Press TV subscribers worldwide.[3] In 2004 alone, UN webcasts attracted 3.3 million views, the Secretary-General reported. Partnerships were also being formed with commercial companies, among them Bloomberg News in New York for UN public service feeds to Asia and Latin America, and the Dutch multimedia agency Novum Nieuws for distribution in Europe.

For both the media and the general public, DPI maintains a global network of more than fifty United Nations Information Centres (UNIC) from Washington to Windhoek to Sydney and many points along the way, including a major new center in Brussels serving the European Union, a much-debated move that led to the closing of offices in other European cities. DPI uses teleconference and video links to give reporters in, for example, Mexico, a chance to interview crime experts in Vienna.

Such services, and the spread of the internet worldwide, make it much easier for reporters and editors in even the remotest regions to follow and write about international topics, helping to break down the great disparities between media organizations in the global North and South. Nongovernmental organizations (NGOs), which have their own extensive information networks and online newsletters on topics related to the UN's work, also use UN sites globally. A DPI liaison office serves more than 1,500 NGOs accredited to the UN and holds a large annual conference for their representatives.

In New York, DPI manages the Dag Hammarskjöld Library, the most important repository of UN-related publications and documents and a research center with data on a range of material from UN member voting records to copies of international treaties. Much of this material is accessible on the library's website, www.un.org/Depts/dhl.

SPEAKING FOR THE UN: ONE VOICE OR MANY?

DPI has another important function. It provides member states and others in the UN community with a daily journal of events, copies of documents, and summaries of meetings. This service is much appreciated and heavily relied on by diplomats, especially in smaller missions. This function accounts for a significant portion of DPI's work and is often criticized by budget-cutters as unjustifiably expensive in personnel and the sheer volume of paper produced. Journalists grumble that DPI's extensive diplomatic tasks detract from its ability to serve the press, broadcasting and, more recently, online news services. For quicker results, and from a staff dedicated solely to the media, reporters turn to the Office of the Spokesman of the Secretary-General, a part of DPI that is recognized unofficially as a near-independent operation (the president of the General Assembly also has a spokesman, a one-year assignment).

Tensions have arisen at times between DPI and the Secretary-General's spokesman's office, often over turf. Frederic Eckhard, spokesman for Secretary-General Kofi Annan from 1997 to 2005, recommended that the Office of the Spokesman be finally de-linked from DPI and made a part of the Secretary-General's office to give it a clearer mandate, with more autonomy and authority as the UN's voice and not part of its public relations or general information arm. Global media coverage emanating from New York has made the Secretary-General's team of spokesmen (including women who use that title) the spokesmen for the UN system as a whole. Not that speaking for the organization is easy, or even possible. The UN's satellite agencies, funds, and programs, as well as overseas operations of various kinds, maintain their own media and communications staffs, which focus only on their agencies' or missions' work. Agencies employ professional public relations companies or consultants to run campaigns around important reports or initiatives. Within the Secretariat, various departments also have specialists in media relations.

Increasingly, part of the job of the Secretary-General's spokesman and his or her office team is to follow closely (if not actually manage or coordinate) the many voices speaking for the organization so that reporters, and thus the public, get as coherent a picture as possible. The release of major reports or other news takes place in the main Secretariat news conference room, where daily noon briefings are held—room 226, on the second floor, near the Security Council. Some agencies also release reports in other major cities such as London, Nairobi, Paris, or Tokyo to avoid the appearance of being too New York-centric and to give reporters abroad the opportunity to ask questions.

FROM THE TOP DOWN

Secretary-General Kofi Annan, who introduced new guidelines opening the UN more widely to the media, told a roundtable of former UN spokesmen in April 2005 of his frustration at seeing a too-often silent organization get hammered repeatedly by critics, particularly in the United States. 'How do we defend ourselves?' he asked. 'We are outgunned. We are out-manned. They have resources that we don't have, and they are relentless, and they are organized.'[4] He faulted a UN culture, at least in part. 'There's a sort of auto-sanction on ourselves: These things are confidential, they are secret and we cannot reveal it to the press,' he said. 'In the end, we get battered.' Not coincidentally amid several bad years, Annan named Mark Malloch Brown, the former UN Development Programme (UNDP) Administrator and a media-savvy communications expert who earlier had been at the World Bank, as his chief of staff in late 2004, and then Deputy Secretary-General in 2006.

Every Secretary-General influences the relationship between the UN and the media. Over several decades before Annan's tenure, the UN was led by men with little interest in the media, or who even harbored a clear contempt for journalists. When reporters were brushed aside rather than accommodated, there was less coverage and fewer headlines for the organization. The story did not begin this way. The first Secretary-General, Trygve Lie of Norway, who served from 1946 until 1953, surrounded himself with experienced, mostly American, advisers and journalists to handle press relations. Lie would occasionally invite a few correspondents to his office at the end of the day for drinks and informal discussions.

U Thant of Burma, the third Secretary-General, whose term ran from 1961 to 1971, had been a journalist himself, and this made him very accessible to reporters, according to his grandson, Thant Myint-U.[5] 'That self-identity as a journalist was something which infused his attitude towards the media here,' he said. Under U Thant's spokesman, Ramses Nassif of Egypt, weekday daily press briefings were instituted, and Nassif became the first UN official to have the formal title of Spokesman for the Secretary-General. It was during this period in the 1960s that the membership of the UN began to grow rapidly as a result of decolonization, though most new, relatively poor countries were not able to afford the cost of keeping correspondents in New York, and many still cannot.

Between Trygve Lie and U Thant was the Dag Hammarskjöld era, from 1953 until his death in a plane crash in Africa in 1961. While Hammarskjöld is widely hailed as a great Secretary-General, he was never comfortable with journalists. Sir Brian Urquhart, who worked closely with Hammarskjöld, described him as a shy man who did not like backslapping or socializing, and was not a good speaker. A reluctance to interact with the media also characterized the terms of Kurt Waldheim of Austria, 1972–1981; Javier Pérez de Cuéllar of Peru, 1982–1991; and Boutros Boutros-Ghali of Egypt, 1992–1996. Joe Sills, who was a spokesman for both Pérez de Cuéllar and Boutros-Ghali, said that neither kept the spokesman 'in the loop.' This has been a perennial problem for most UN spokesmen, who often have had to face tough questions not knowing much about how any given issue was being handled at the top.

A REFLECTION OF THE WORLD

When Madeleine Albright was permanent representative of the United States at the United Nations in the mid-1990s, she remarked that it was like working for a company with 189 directors on the board. Now, with 192 member states and various observer delegations represented in New York, the world's diplomatic capital, there is no uniform, shared 'information culture' among either diplomats or officials of the Secretariat. The UN spokesman's office frequently has to cajole officials into meeting reporters. When in the 1990s some Security Council presidents, who rotate monthly, decided to hold open press briefings, they met initial resistance from fellow Council members. Member governments can block press conferences by people whose message they want to silence—as China has done in barring Taiwanese or Tibetans (including the Dalai Lama) from headquarters.

Member countries where the press and broadcasting are free and protected by law tend to be open to journalists at the UN. Those diplomats are often good sources for the media when, for example, official information on Security Council consultations or key meetings in the Secretariat is scarce. That allows for 'spin' from one nation's point of view, as media-friendly diplomats use their skills in news conferences, in smaller 'background' briefings or over private lunches for selected journalists. At the other extreme are member countries where the press is completely controlled or at best heavily circumscribed, and this is reflected in more negative attitudes toward UN reporters. When advocates of secrecy or obfuscation win, the UN suffers because it loses ground in the information marketplace. The urge to corral the media within certain guidelines was a factor in the ill-fated attempt by the UN Educational, Scientific and Cultural Organization (UNESCO) to organize a 'New International Information Order' in the mid to late 1970s, which the Western media vigorously opposed and ultimately killed, seeing it as an attempt to regulate the world's press to the satisfaction of governments.[6]

One of Annan's innovations was to allow officials of varying ranks to speak to reporters in areas of their competence and not wait for permission from above, which invited delay. Joseph Chamie, former head of the UN's Population Division, which collects and analyzes the world's statistics, had already broken down some of those barriers. Encountering an entrenched fear of the media, even in his own office, he told his staff: 'If someone is calling from the *Financial Times*, take the call. Cancel your meeting. Do not say, 'I'll call you back in ten minutes.' Take the call if it's a big paper, or a small paper in Djibouti or Kuwait. Give them whatever they want. Send them material as fast as you can. The bus is coming by; it's not going to stop again.'[7] Chamie's division attracted wide media coverage by being the first to publicize statistics on, for example, the seriousness of population aging in Europe and Japan, and the need for immigrant labor to rectify workforce imbalances. He also documented a noticeable trend toward falling fertility rates in some large developing countries. The UN got a lot of attention, but Chamie also came under fire when Europeans complained that the UN's figures would inflame anti-immigration lobbies, and family planning organizations accused him of appearing to undercut their campaigns and give ammunition to those who said there was no global population problem.

Editors and Producers Call the Shots

For all the work done by DPI and the crew of professionals in the Office of the Secretary-General's Spokesman, what gets written, broadcast, and posted on blogs is mostly out of the UN's hands. Editors, publishers, and television producers in scores of countries, many of them surprisingly unfamiliar with the organization, make the decisions about what to tell the public. When important global issues go unreported it is not because they are ignored by journalists at UN headquarters or in the field, but because they have not risen to the attention of those people journalism professors call 'gatekeepers.' This leads to considerable frustration within the UN, where DPI, under Shashi Tharoor, the Under-Secretary-General for Communications and Public Information in 2005, devised an annual list of '10 stories the world should hear more about.'[8] Tharoor, who had been a close colleague of Secretary-General Annan for several decades and the first Director of Communications in his office, established a communications strategy group there to discuss outreach, a job later taken on by Edward Mortimer, a former foreign editor of the *Financial Times*, who was also Annan's speech writer.

Making matters worse for the UN, by the end of the last century leading media organizations everywhere had moved away from covering institutions and wanted reporters to focus on 'human interest' or celebrity-focused stories. The UN has a growing phalanx of celebrities drawn from the entertainment or sports industries who volunteer to promote projects, and they are making some inroads into the media, albeit sporadically and usually in crises. The problem remains that some important issues—the development of international criminal law and disarmament are two—do not lend themselves easily to human interest or feature treatment.

In developing countries, where the UN and its agencies are often partners in efforts to speed development, the world organization gets more media attention than in Europe and North America, where development issues are rarely covered. Thalif Deen, UN bureau chief for the Inter Press Service (IPS) news agency, tells the story of an African diplomat who once approached Tarzie Vittachi, a Sri Lankan newspaper editor who had become deputy executive director of the UN Children's Fund (UNICEF), to ask how best to get mainstream media attention in New York for his prime minister, who was about to make an important speech on poverty and child mortality. 'Shoot him,' said Vittachi, 'and you will get front page coverage.'

Deen, whose reporting has a much higher global readership than many other journalists at the UN, said in an exchange of emails in early 2006:

In contrast to the Western news media, newspapers and radio in most developing nations tend to focus primarily on UN issues relating to their own national socio-economic problems, including poverty alleviation, reproductive health, gender empowerment, development aid and globalization. But these are considered "unsexy" in most American and European newspapers. Newspapers in developing countries also provide considerable space to regional political and economic issues. African newspapers, for example, will usually pick up UN stories relating to AIDS in Uganda, desertification in the Sahel or child soldiers in the Democratic Republic of the Congo.[9]

Meeting these interests has been the strength of IPS, which fills a global niche, Deen added: 'IPS has over the last 40 years covered UN issues primarily from a third-world perspective. Since most newspapers and radio in the developing world still depend on mainstream news agencies for political coverage of the UN, IPS has continued to provide in-depth coverage of socio-economic issues, holding a near-monopoly in this field.'

Among powerful industrialized countries of the global North, editors and correspondents looking at the UN tend to focus mostly on the politics of Security Council, really only an extension of national foreign policy debates. In the developing world, the Millennium Development Goals (MDGs) and how countries are faring in their efforts to meet targets in such areas as poverty reduction, gender-equal education, and better health services to push back diseases by 2015 have been a continuing story. It would be hard to find Americans who have heard of the MDGs, even though President George W. Bush endorsed them in his September 2005 speech to the World Summit.[10] Foreign policy reporters do not use the UN to collect information or solicit opinions from diplomats or officials—a situation that contributed to significant reporting mistakes before the 2003 war in Iraq. UN weapons experts, with a decade of Iraqi experience and a mountain of archives, would have painted a different picture of Saddam Hussein's arsenal than that promoted by Washington and London.

Conclusion

In an age of fast-moving technological and commercial developments in global communications, and the flow of virtually unlimited information and opinion online, the UN can make use of new opportunities, as some of its agencies have discovered. There is already a gap between the slow-moving UN Secretariat and the media-savvy, action-oriented agencies in dealing with information and with journalists. The Secretariat will probably always be hobbled by politics, but its technological advances and the phenomenal expertise might be put to better use with more professionals in DPI who understand and follow media trends. A team of professionals has reshaped the spokesman's office where, at this writing, the spokesman, Stéphane Dujarric, and his deputy, Marie Okabe, are both veterans of mainstream media work. The competition for world media attention is fierce. The UN should make news and set agendas. Reacting to events (or brickbats) is not enough.

Notes

1. For a discussion of the media treatment of UN peace operations, see Ingrid A. Lehmann, *Peacekeeping and Public Information: Caught in the Crossfire*, Cass Series on Peacekeeping 5 (London: Frank Cass, 1999).
2. For a discussion, see Nik Gowing, *Real-time Television Coverage of Armed Conflicts and Diplomatic Crises: Does It Pressure or Distort Foreign Policy Decisions?* Press, Politics and Public Policy Working Papers 94–1 (Cambridge, Mass.: Harvard University, 1994); Johanna Neuman, *Lights, Camera, War* (New York: St. Martin's Press, 1996); and Larry Minear, Colin Scott, and Thomas G. Weiss, *The News Media, Civil War, & Humanitarian Action* (Boulder, Colo.: Lynne Rienner, 1996).
3. *Report of the Secretary-General to the General Assembly on 'Questions relating to information,'* UN documentA/60/173, 1 August 2005.
4. Quoted by Frederic Eckhard, ed., *Speaking for the Secretary-General—A History of the UN Spokesman's Office* (New York: United Nations, 2005).
5. Eckhard, ed., *Speaking for the Secretary-General*, 22.
6. International Commission for the Study of Communication Problems, *Many Voices, One World: Towards a New More Just and More Efficient World Information and Communication Order* (Paris: UNESCO, 1980). For a discussion, see C. Edwin Baker, *Media, Markets and Democracy* (New York: Cambridge University Press, 2002) and Daya Kishan Thussu, *International Communication: Continuity and Change* (New York: Oxford University Press, 2000).
7. Interview with the author, June 2005.
8. www.un.org/events/tenstories.
9. Interview with the author, January 2006.
10. 'Statement of H. E. George W. Bush, President of the United States of America, 2005 World Summit, High-level Plenary Meeting, September 14, 2005,' www.un.org or www.whitehouse.gov.

PART V

INTERNATIONAL PEACE
AND SECURITY

CHAPTER 17

....

DISARMAMENT

....

KEITH KRAUSE

THE failure of the League of Nations to achieve progress towards comprehensive disarmament did not deter the framers of the UN system from including disarmament and regulation of armaments as one of the key missions for the new world organization. Although framed in conventional terms in the Charter, in the months after Hiroshima and Nagasaki, disarmament took on an entirely new and more pressing meaning: ridding the world of nuclear weapons, and indeed of all weapons of mass destruction.

Conceiving the United Nations as a focal point for disarmament efforts was a natural and logical step at the end of World War II. The underlying belief in multilateral maintenance of 'international peace and security,' via a robust collective security system and enforced by the great powers, was coherent with the rest of the architecture and philosophy of the post-1945 multilateral system. Like many aspects of the UN's institutional architecture, however, the premises on which the system was built did not accord with the reality of world politics during the Cold War. The UN's role in global disarmament efforts illustrates well the tension between a purely realist vision that sees the success or failure of multilateral institutions as resting solely on the configuration of interests of great powers, and a vision that sees institutions as possessing some (limited) autonomy, both to shape these interests and to frame the normative context within which these interests are defined and pursued.

As in many other domains, the UN system proved to be adaptable in the field of disarmament, assuming roles and facilitating activities beyond what the Charter's framers had imagined. This does not make the UN a central player in the past sixty years of arms control and disarmament efforts—far from it—but neither has the UN been a prisoner of a realist institutional logic. This chapter evaluates the achievements and limitations of the world organization in the field of disarmament, emphasizing the UN's role as part of the broader tapestry of efforts to control arms as a means to achieve international peace and security. It looks beyond the current stalemate in major UN disarmament mechanisms, to highlight the areas in which the organization has played a positive or relatively autonomous role.

In addition to presenting an overview of the textual and institutional foundations for UN disarmament efforts (including the Conference on Disarmament (CD)), the chapter notes specific cases where progress was achieved or not, such as the Nuclear Non-Proliferation Treaty (NPT), the Chemical Weapons Convention (CWC), and more recent efforts to tackle the problems of anti-personnel land mines and small arms and light weapons. It does *not* include a discussion of concrete disarmament initiatives, such as the coercive disarmament undertaken by the UN's Special Commission (UNSCOM) that was responsible for overseeing the destruction of Iraq's weapons of mass destruction after the 1991 Gulf War, or the practical disarmament, demobilization, and reintegration (DDR) measures conducted in numerous post-conflict zones under UN auspices.[1]

Finally, it draws out some of the broader implications for international relations of the UN experience with formal multilateral arms control, disarmament and security-building processes by evaluating the role of the UN as a negotiating forum, a norm setter, an implementing agency, or an instrument of great power security governance.

TEXTUAL GENESIS

Institutions and practices are anchored in internationally agreed texts. And for the United Nations, in the beginning is the Charter, which points to a general understanding, but with several cautionary notes, that *disarmament* was to be a central topic of the new organization. Article 11 noted that 'the General Assembly may consider the general principles of co-operation in the maintenance of international peace and security, including the principles governing disarmament and the regulation of armaments.' Article 26 made the Security Council 'responsible for formulating... plans to be submitted to the Members of the United Nations for the establishment of a system for the regulation of armaments.' And Article 47 empowered the Military Staff Committee 'to advise and assist the Security Council on questions relating to... the regulation of armaments, and possible disarmament.'

The caution that is sounded here is evident, especially with the idea of *possible* disarmament, the equal emphasis on *regulation* of armaments (which does not necessarily imply reductions), and the tentative language of the role for the Security Council: *submitting plans* to member states rather than a more active role. This caution was both understandable and justified, given the failure of the League of Nations to achieve tangible progress in the interwar period towards its goal of 'reduc[ing] national armaments to the lowest point consistent with national safety and the enforcement by common action of international obligations.'[2] The accelerating nuclear arms race and the Cold War between East and West also ensured that any practical discussions of disarmament or regulation of armaments would be difficult, either within or outside the UN system.

Nevertheless, the world organization rapidly emerged as a focal point for those voices that wanted to promote general and complete, and especially nuclear, disarmament. The first resolution of the first session of the General Assembly in 1946—supported with the encouragement of the US, UK, and USSR—established an Atomic Energy Commission (UNAEC), which had as one of its terms of reference to make proposals 'for the elimination from national armaments of atomic weapons and of all other major weapons adaptable to mass destruction.' Later that year, General Assembly resolution 41 (I) reiterated the need to eliminate weapons of mass destruction and also drew attention to what was rapidly being thought of as the 'conventional' side of the equation, recommending that the Security Council 'give prompt consideration to formulating the practical measures...which are essential to provide for the general regulation and reduction of armaments and armed forces.'

These two resolutions expressed clearly the key assumptions or constraints of multilateral disarmament diplomacy: it was to focus on nuclear weapons and weapons of mass destruction, and it emphasized the efforts and responsibilities of the Security Council. Given the rapidly worsening climate of the Cold War, it was not surprising that the early institutional expressions of UN involvement in disarmament were either weak, or slow to emerge.

INSTITUTIONAL EXPRESSIONS WITHIN THE UN SYSTEM

The UNAEC was the site for the articulation of the first concrete plan to control nuclear technology. The American-sponsored Baruch Plan, presented to the UNAEC in 1946, was an ambitious and radical proposal to put the control of *all* nuclear technology in the hands of an International Atomic Development Authority, which would control or manage the exploitation of nuclear energy, from the mining of raw materials, to the activities of production plants, to the sole 'right to conduct research in the field of atomic explosives.' It would also have had rights of inspection and free access, as well as a system of sanctions for non-compliance. This initiative, according to the Soviets, placed the problem of 'control' before the problem of 'disarmament,' which, since only the United States possessed nuclear weapons at the time, was unacceptable.[3] No other practical initiative emerged from the UNAEC, and after meeting for more than 200 sessions, it was disbanded in 1949 having achieved nothing.

On the conventional side, the Security Council established in 1947 a Commission for Conventional Armaments, which was the concrete follow-up to the 1946 General Assembly resolutions. It made no progress either, and there matters stood until 1952, when General Assembly resolution 502 disbanded the UNAEC (and proposed disbanding the commission) and created a successor eleven-member Disarmament Commission. It was given the ambitious task of 'preparing proposals to be embodied in a draft treaty... for the regulation, limitation and balanced reduction of all armed forces and all armaments, [and] for the elimination of all major weapons adaptable to destruction.' The Disarmament Commission suffered the same fate as previous efforts. It remained deadlocked, and was enlarged to twenty-five members in 1957, and then enlarged again in 1959 to include all member states. It met only once after that (in 1965) and produced no practical results.[4]

None of these early institutional efforts produced concrete results; and the reason was simple: Washington and Moscow did not agree on how (or even if) to proceed with concrete arms control and disarmament. They did, however, establish that the UN system would be a focal point for the development of *multilateral* disarmament initiatives and would embody and reflect the normative framework or consensus against which disarmament and arms control efforts would be measured. The importance of the normative framework for disarmament established within the UN cannot be underestimated. Indeed, it remains the main, and sometimes sole, vehicle for the expression of positions on disarmament issues by the overwhelming majority of the world's states. The norms were, at least on paper, simple: to achieve complete nuclear disarmament and the elimination of weapons of mass destruction, and to reduce conventional weapons to the lowest possible levels consistent with the maintenance of internal order and international peace and security. A full discussion of the development and crystallization of these norms is beyond this chapter, but they have been consistently reflected in all major UN documents and resolutions, and have also been generally accepted—at different points and to different degrees—by the nuclear powers.

OVERCOMING THE STALEMATE: DISARMAMENT COMMISSION AND THE CONFERENCE ON DISARMAMENT

Functioning institutions, concrete treaties, and practical measures for arms control and disarmament only emerged in the early 1960s, when the United States and the Soviet Union overcame their nuclear deadlock and embarked on a wide-ranging series of bilateral and multilateral arms control agreements. That great power agreement was the key was illustrated by the Joint Statement of Agreed Principles of Disarmament Negotiations, submitted by the two governments to the General Assembly in 1961.[5] Its principles included: general and complete disarmament; reduction of non-nuclear weapons; a sequential, balanced, time-limited and verifiable disarmament process;

and international control under an International Disarmament Organization within the UN framework.

Although progress towards these goals has been slow, and sometimes painfully so, three specific developments (two of which are significant) can trace their origins to this joint statement. The first is the (re)creation in 1978 of the Disarmament Commission, and the second is the emergence of the Conference on Disarmament; both are discussed in this section. And the third is the negotiation and entry into force of the Nuclear Non-Proliferation Treaty.

A recognition of the delicate balance between 'political will' (meaning agreement by the nuclear and/or major powers) and 'normative consensus' (meaning the universal role of the UN system) led the General Assembly in its Special Session on Disarmament in 1978 to advocate the creation of both a *deliberative* (norm-setting) and a *negotiating* body on disarmament. The Disarmament commission, which meets annually in New York for three weeks, and which includes all UN member states, was established to fill the former role, as a successor to the stillborn 1952 commission. Its role is to 'consider and make recommendations on various problems in the field of disarmament.'[6] In practice, it has not been a forum for concrete action, but has been the focus of efforts by different groups of states (such as the Non-Aligned Movement) to reinforce the normative commitment of general and complete nuclear disarmament.

Parallel to the effort to establish a universal deliberative body within the UN system went efforts to create a permanent *negotiating* body on disarmament. Even before the 1961 US–USSR declaration, the seed of such a body had been planted. In 1960 already the two governments along with the United Kingdom had agreed to establish the 'Ten Nation Committee on Disarmament,' a body essentially balanced equally with five representatives from each bloc. Expanded to eighteen states in 1962 (to include neutral or nonaligned states), after 1969 it grew to twenty-six members and became the Conference of the Committee on Disarmament (CCD). Throughout this process, the group received instructions from and reported back to the General Assembly, and was jointly chaired by the United States and Soviet Union.[7]

After the General Assembly Special Session on Disarmament in 1978, the CCD was expanded to thirty members, and it became formally known as the Conference on Disarmament in 1984. By 2005, it had grown to sixty-six members. The Geneva-based CD is—unlike the Disarmament Commission—a hybrid body autonomous from, but closely linked to, the United Nations. It meets at the world organization's European headquarters in Geneva, its costs are part of the regular UN budget, and its work is facilitated by UN staff. It takes into account General Assembly resolutions on disarmament, but is not bound to act on them. It reports to the UN and by tradition the texts of any agreements or treaties that it negotiates are forwarded to the General Assembly for adoption and subsequent ratification.

It also operates by consensus, which in practice means every one of the sixty-six participating states has a veto—a situation somewhat more rigid than the machinery of the UN itself. Its agenda, known as the Decalogue, was more or less fixed by the 1978 special session and placed a high priority on disarmament of nuclear and other weapons of mass destruction, within a ten-item agenda.[8] Subsequent attempts to renegotiate this work program have failed. These constraints and features of the CD's organization and work reflect the realities of disarmament negotiations, which implicate the intense sensitivity of national security issues.

FROM INSTITUTIONS TO PRACTICAL ACCOMPLISHMENTS

Despite these high politics considerations, the CD or its predecessors can point to some major accomplishments, including in particular the Chemical Weapons Convention (opened for signature 1993, entered into force 1997), the Biological and Toxin Weapons Convention (BTWC, opened for signature 1972, entered into force 1975), the Partial Test Ban (1963) and Comprehensive Test Ban Treaties (CTBT, opened for signature 1996, not entered into force), and the Nuclear Non-Proliferation Treaty (opened for signature 1968, entered into force 1970). These are discussed below. Since 1996, however, it has not moved forward on any element of its work program—having recently marked what NGOs and other observers have called 'the decade of inaction.'

The NPT

The Nuclear Non-Proliferation Treaty is the capstone of multilateral disarmament efforts. A treaty regulating nuclear weapons was first proposed by Ireland in 1959 and reflected in General Assembly resolution 1380. A series of resolutions (and negotiations) followed, and by 1965 the United States and the Soviet Union both submitted drafts of such treaties to what was then the Eighteen-Nation Committee on Disarmament in Geneva. Subsequent negotiations resulted in a final treaty being adopted by the General Assembly in 1968 and signed that year. The NPT entered into force in 1970, and was indefinitely extended in 1995.[9]

The NPT 'bargain' rests on three pillars: preventing the spread of nuclear weapons beyond the five recognized nuclear weapons states (the US, Russia, the UK, France, and China); progressive nuclear disarmament by these states; and access, under appropriate safeguards, to nuclear technology for peaceful uses. These three pillars are interlinked—the forswearing of nuclear weapons by those thirty or so states that could, in principle, have built nuclear weapons was only possible because nuclear weapons states undertook to reduce and ultimately eliminate their arsenals.[10] Similarly, access to nuclear technology for civilian purposes was a quid pro quo for agreeing to intrusive oversight over nuclear activities to prevent diversion to military purposes. Unlike most other nuclear arms control treaties, therefore, its success depended on both 'haves' and 'have nots' being included.

While an impressive achievement, the NPT is not an unqualified success. Although 187 states are members, most of the exceptions—India, Pakistan, Israel, and (perhaps) North Korea (which withdrew from the NPT in 2003)—are geopolitically important; Cuba is also a non-member, but not a major proliferation concern. India and Pakistan are declared nuclear weapons states, Israel is undeclared but widely believed to have nuclear weapons, and North Korea has conducted a range of suspect activities that point towards an ongoing nuclear weapons program.[11] Other states, most notably Iran, while in formal compliance with their treaty obligations, are suspected of conducting activities that go beyond narrow civilian nuclear programs.[12] Finally, critics have argued that the five declared nuclear weapons states, and in particular the United States and Russia, have not taken seriously their Article 6 treaty commitments (reaffirmed in 1995 in order to win the indefinite extension of the treaty) to pursue 'progressive efforts to reduce nuclear weapons globally, with the ultimate goal of eliminating those weapons.'[13]

Ultimately, determining whether or not the NPT is a success depends on responding to two counterfactual questions: Would nuclear proliferation have proceeded beyond the eight or nine current nuclear weapons states in the absence of the NPT? And has the treaty provided a critical lever with which steps towards nuclear disarmament have been advanced? Most scholars would respond 'yes' to both of these questions, meaning that despite its limitations the NPT can be considered a significant success for disarmament and arms control, both in practical and norm-setting terms.

The CWC

By contrast, the Convention on the Prohibition of the Development, Production, Stockpiling and Use of Chemical Weapons can be considered an unalloyed success for multilateral disarmament. Opened for signature in 1993, after years of negotiations in the Conference on Disarmament, it entered into force in 1997. It bans the production, acquisition, transfer, possession, and use of chemical weapons, and obligates states to destroy existing chemical weapons stocks on a clear timetable. The CWC has been ratified by 176 states—enjoying the same near-universal status as the NPT, and only eight states have neither signed nor ratified the treaty. Several of these, including North Korea, Egypt, and Syria, can be considered potential chemical weapons proliferators.

There are several noteworthy aspects to the CWC.[14] First, it bans weapons that are technologically within the reach of any state with a moderate industrial capacity—a vastly larger number of states than for nuclear weapons. Second, and because of this, it includes robust and intrusive verification and compliance monitoring mechanisms. These include both routine inspections of factories and production facilities that produce chemicals of concern (some of which have limited civilian uses), and 'challenge inspections' that give 'each State Party ... the right to request an on-site challenge inspection of any facility or location in the territory or in any other place under the jurisdiction or control of any other State Party for the sole purpose of clarifying and resolving any questions concerning possible non-compliance with the provisions of this Convention.' The open-ended and comprehensive nature of this verification procedure is a significant development in disarmament, and a clear step beyond traditional notions of sovereignty and national security. Finally, the CWC is implemented by the Organisation for the Prohibition of Chemical Weapons (OPCW), which is one of the few standing formal disarmament organizations.

The BTWC

By contrast, international efforts to deal with the potential threat of biological weapons are somewhat weaker. The 1975 Biological and Toxin Weapons Convention was negotiated also in the Conference on Disarmament. It followed from the 1925 Geneva Protocol that banned not only the use of biological weapons but also the development, stockpiling, acquisition, production or transfer of biological agents and toxins beyond the limited quantities needed for protective or peaceful (research) purposes. It has been ratified by 150 states, but again, some states of proliferation concern remain outside of the treaty. More importantly, however, the treaty has no verification provisions, and efforts to negotiate a robust verification regime failed in 2001, when the United States declared its unwillingness to accept an additional verification protocol to the treaty.

What explains the difference in strength between the chemical, nuclear and biological weapons regimes? One factor explaining the bans on chemical and biological weapons is that they have proven to have (or are thought to have) only a limited military utility, and therefore states have found it relatively easy to ban that which they did not need. Nuclear weapons, while perhaps also not 'useful' in the narrow sense of the term, have a certain 'utility in non-use' as a deterrent, and as a means of expressing ultimate or existential state power. A second factor, which helps explain the difference between the chemical and biological weapons regimes, is that states have found it more difficult to establish verification regimes on biological agents, because of the larger number of potential harmful agents, the uncertain nature of rapidly changing biotechnologies (including genetic engineering), and the economic or commercial implications of intrusive verification on cutting-edge technologies within the biotech industry.[15]

Partial and Comprehensive Test Ban Treaties

The clash between national interests and multilateral disarmament norms is nowhere clearer than in efforts to ban the testing of nuclear weapons. This is a step that was seen as early as the 1960s as one means of halting the arms race by preventing the development of new nuclear weapons.[16] The first step towards this goal, the Partial Test Ban Treaty, was driven mainly by environmental concerns, and banned the atmospheric, underwater, and space testing of nuclear weapons. Underground testing was still permitted and continued until the 1990s, when negotiations for a comprehensive test ban treaty got underway.[17]

The Comprehensive Nuclear Test Ban Treaty was agreed in 1996 in the Conference on Disarmament, but it remains in a paradoxical limbo. It has been signed by 176 states and ratified by 129, and has established the infrastructure for monitoring and verification of the test ban. However, it has not entered into force due to the requirement that a specified list of forty-four states (with nuclear weapons and/or nuclear reactors) must ratify the treaty.[18] Eleven of these states have not ratified the treaty, including the United States, China, Iran, and Egypt, as well as India, Pakistan, and North Korea, which have neither signed nor ratified the treaty. Although all of the signatory states are adhering to the formal provisions of the treaty, the nuclear tests conducted by India and Pakistan in 1998, and by North Korea in 2006, mean that the future of the CTBT remains uncertain.

BEYOND WEAPONS OF MASS DESTRUCTION

The UN's original disarmament brief included not only weapons of mass destruction (WMDs) but all weapons, including what we now consider conventional weapons. Yet UN efforts in the area of conventional weapons disarmament have been extremely limited. The only UN initiative dealing with major weapons systems (aircraft, tanks, military vehicles, etc.) has been the establishment of a Register of Conventional Arms, a non-binding reporting mechanism for arms imports and exports.[19] With respect to small arms and light weapons, states negotiated in 2001 a politically binding 'Programme of Action to Prevent, Combat and Eradicate the Illicit Trade in Small Arms and Light Weapons in All Its Aspects,' but this too has not resulted in any legally binding treaties to deal with the proliferation and misuse of small arms.[20] The complexity of the issues involved, the number of actors with strong and legitimate security and economic interests, and the difficulty in finding any obvious 'focal points' for negotiation or agreement all make conventional weapons particularly problematic within a global multilateral organization. Third World states see attempts to control the conventional arms trade as imposing restrictions on their inherent right of self-defense because arms producing countries would not be affected.

One result has been that efforts at conventional arms control have been either regionally-based, where the military–strategic context is clear, or based on technology denial by supplier states. The only major conventional disarmament treaty, the Treaty on Conventional Armed Forces in Europe (CFE), is geographically limited, and the most prominent technology denial regime, the Wassenaar arrangement, is limited to thirty-nine states.[21]

The most significant global conventional disarmament initiative has been the treaty banning the production, use, stockpiling and transfer of anti-personnel land mines. The Ottawa Convention, as it is generally known, was signed in 1997, entered into force in 1999, and has been subsequently ratified by 149 states. Not surprisingly, among the forty states outside of the convention, one finds many of the 'usual suspects': Egypt, Iran, India, Pakistan, China, Russia, North Korea, and the United States.[22] What is distinctive about the landmines treaty, however, is that it was negotiated outside of the Conference on Disarmament, and *not* subject to a consensus decision-making procedure, since the states leading the struggle to ban land mines concluded that the CD was not going to address landmines in a comprehensive and adequate way.

This effort reflects the 'new multilateralism' in which states, NGOs, and international organizations worked in flexible and sometimes complex coalitions to achieve practical results.[23] The Ottawa Convention thus includes extensive provisions for de-mining and mine destruction programs, and for assistance to landmine victims and survivors. Even some nonsignatories, such as the United States, contribute financially to the goals of the convention.

Conclusion: The UN, Disarmament, and Adaptive Multilateralism

This brief survey of UN disarmament efforts highlights several tensions that characterize the role of multilateral institutions in security issues. These concern mainly the different roles that multilateral institutions can play, including as a negotiating forum, a norm setter, an implementing agency, or an instrument of great power security governance. In the field of disarmament, the UN has clearly played a significant role as a negotiating forum; but even here, the need to distinguish between *deliberative* and *negotiating* bodies led to a split between the (universal) Disarmament Commission and the hybrid minilateral institution of the Conference on Disarmament.

With respect to norm setting, it seems that the UN system often crystallizes norms that have emerged (concerning, for example, the chemical weapons taboo, or the emerging norms regarding the excessive accumulation and spread of small arms and light weapons), but does not often play a leading or autonomous role in the development of new norms, except as a site for their negotiation. It remains, however, the only reliable ongoing forum in which lesser powers can voice their international security concerns. As recent debates around the authorized use of force have shown, the UN can constrain, at least to some extent, the freedom of action of major powers or pass judgement on the legitimacy of their acts.

As an implementing agency, the UN record in disarmament is weak, with only the OPCW enjoying a strong institutional existence. Other agencies, such as the International Atomic Energy Agency (IAEA), are part of the UN system, but they have dual or multiple roles that do not put disarmament at the center of their mandates. It should be noted, however, that in the field of coercive disarmament UNSCOM in Iraq stands out as a success, in light of the failure to find weapons of mass destruction in Iraq after the 2003 invasion.[24]

All of these roles are conditioned and constrained by the central fact of great power security governance. In the field of disarmament, no concrete action by the UN was possible until Washington and Moscow agreed in the early 1960s to move forward on arms control discussions. All major achievements—the NPT, CWC, and BTWC—required great power consensus; when it did not exist, such as in the Comprehensive Test Ban Treaty, disarmament efforts stalled. Only the Ottawa Convention provides an illustration of the ability of states to work around great powers, and this was done deliberately and consciously outside the UN system. Hence the world organization's experience confirms the dual lesson, that shortcomings of the UN system are the result of a lack of political will among great powers, but that the UN system possesses some relative autonomy in norm setting, negotiation and implementation that attenuates the harshest aspects of great power security governance.

Some progress undoubtedly has been made in suffocating, if not extinguishing, the nuclear arms race, and the NPT stands as the major achievement of multilateral disarmament. The threat of chemical and biological weapons is also either wholly or partly contained. At the same time, global military expenditures in 2006 exceeded $1 trillion; the nuclear powers held more than 16,000 warheads of enormous destructive power in their arsenals; tens of thousands of tanks, armoured vehicles, and military aircraft are in the world's armed forces; and more than 600 million small arms and light weapons are held worldwide. The day of comprehensive and general disarmament remains distant.

NOTES

1. On UNSCOM, see 'Iraq: The UNSCOM Experience,' *SIPRI Fact Sheet* (Stockholm: Stockholm International Peace Research Institute, 1998), www.sipri.org; on Disarmament, Demobilization and Reintegration, see *Small Arms Survey 2005: Weapons at War* (Oxford: Oxford University Press, 2005), 266–301; and Mats Berdal, 'Disarmament and Demobilization after Civil Wars: Arms, Soldiers and the Termination of Armed Conflict,' *Adelphi Paper* no. 303 (Oxford: Oxford University Press, 1996).
2. For an overview of interwar efforts, see Richard Dean Burns, ed., *Encyclopedia of Arms Control and Disarmament*, vol. 2 (New York: Charles Scribner's Sons, 1993). Article 8 of the League Covenant requested the League Council to formulate plans for arms reductions and to oversee national armaments programs and required states to exchange information on arms acquisitions and levels. Article 9 established a permanent commission to oversee this work.

3. For a concise overview of this early history see David Fischer, *History of the International Atomic Energy Agency: The First Forty Years* (Vienna: International Atomic Energy Agency, 1997), 17–23, and the Baruch Plan, www.atomicarchive.com.

4. See 'Arms Regulation and Disarmament: Initial Efforts,' www.nationsencyclopedia.com.

5. These are commonly called the 'McCloy–Zorin principles.' For the text of the statement and a full list of proposals see: www.nuclearfiles.org.

6. General Assembly resolution A/S-10/2, para. 118 adopted on the report of the ad hoc committee of the Tenth Special Session (1978).

7. For an overview of the history of the CD see www.reachingcriticalwill.org. The CCD added five more members in 1975.

8. The eleven-point agenda includes: nuclear weapons in all aspects; chemical weapons (removed from the agenda in 1993 after the Chemical Weapons Convention was agreed); other weapons of mass destruction; conventional weapons; reduction of military budgets; reduction of armed forces; disarmament and development; disarmament and international security; collateral measures; confidence building measures; effective verification methods in relation to appropriate disarmament measures, acceptable to all parties; and comprehensive program of disarmament leading to general and complete disarmament under effective international control.

9. For a good overview of the NPT regime, see George Bunn, 'The Nuclear Nonproliferation Treaty: History and Current Problems,' *Arms Control Today* 33 (December 2003): 4–10; also see other articles in this issue.

10. There are some who argue that this linkage is not integral to the success of the treaty, and that it was in the interest of the non-nuclear states *themselves* to agree to forego a costly and dangerous nuclear arms race, regardless of what the nuclear powers did.

11. See Bong-Guen Jun, 'North Korean Nuclear Crises: An End in Sight?' *Arms Control Today* 36, no. 1 (2006): 6–10.

12. See www.iranwatch.org for details.

13. Quoted in Bunn, 'The Nuclear Nonproliferation Treaty,' 9.

14. The best academic treatment of chemical weapons remains Richard Price, *The Chemical Weapons Taboo* (Ithaca, NY: Cornell University Press, 1997).

15. For comparison, the Australia Group of states that harmonize export controls on agents of proliferation concern includes about seventy items in its list of viruses, bacteria and toxins of concern, while only forty-three chemical agents figure on the lists of the CWC. See www.australiagroup.net and the Organisation for the Prohibition of Chemical Weapons, www.opcw.org.

16. Another, which is not discussed here, is a ban on the production of fissile material, negotiations on which have been stalled in the Conference on Disarmament since 1995.

17. For a detailed overview of the obstacles to the CTBT, see Keith A. Hansen, *The Comprehensive Nuclear Test Ban Treaty: An Insider's Perspective* (Palo Alto, Calif.: Stanford University Press, 2006). See also David Mutimer, 'Testing Times: Of Nuclear Tests, Test Bans and the Framing of Proliferation,' *Contemporary Security Policy* 21, no. 1 (2000): 1–22.

18. The CTBT even has an organization, the Preparatory Commission for the Comprehensive Nuclear Test Ban Treaty Organization, that existed before its treaty came into force! See www.ctbto.org.

19. For overviews of the UN arms register, see Malcolm Chalmers and Owen Greene, *The United Nations Register of Conventional Arms: An Initial Examination of the First Report*, Bradford Arms Register Studies no. 2 (Bradford, UK: Bradford University, 1993); and Malcolm Chalmers et al., eds., *Developing the UN Register of Conventional Arms*, Bradford

Arms Register Studies no. 4 (Bradford, UK: Bradford University, 1994). The register also includes the possibility of reporting on arms holdings, but few states do so.

20. However, the UN Convention against Transnational Organized Crime includes a protocol against the Illicit Manufacturing of and Trafficking in Firearms, Their Parts and Components and Ammunition, which entered into force in 2005. Similarly, a politically binding instrument on the marking and tracking of illicit arms was successfully negotiated in 2005, but has not yet been practically implemented.

21. See www.wassenaar.org, and James A. Lewis, 'Multilateral Arms Transfer Restraint: The Limits of Cooperation,' *Arms Control Today* 35, no. 9 (2005): 45–48.

22. For a complete and updated list, see www.icbl.org.

23. See Maxwell Cameron et al., eds., *To Walk Without Fear: The Global Movement to Ban Landmines* (New York: Oxford University Press, 1998).

24. See Jessica Tuchman Matthews, 'Weapons of Mass Destruction and the United Nations,' *Global Governance* 10, no. 3 (2004): 265–271.

CHAPTER 18

PEACEFUL SETTLEMENT OF DISPUTES AND CONFLICT PREVENTION

RAMA MANI

IN the aftermath of the Second World War and the Holocaust, the founders of the United Nations focused on reorienting international affairs away from aggression and unilateralism toward cooperation and multilateralism. Article 1 of the Charter concisely states the organization's principal objective—'to maintain international peace and security'—and the ways in which that goal is to be attained—collectively, peacefully, and preventively. At the dawn of the twenty-first century, the peaceful settlement of disputes is widely considered essential, not only in the interest of avoiding deadly armed conflict, but also for a host of corollary reasons:

So long as States cannot rely on the peaceful resolution of their disputes, there can be no genuine reversal of world-wide arms competition; no adequate resources for the eradication of poverty; no proper respect for human rights or the environment; nor sufficient funds for health, education, the arts and humanities.[1]

As a means of safeguarding international peace and security, Article 1 identifies two complementary aims: 'to take effective collective measures for the prevention

The author is indebted to Katja Flückiger for her invaluable research assistance and editorial support, and grateful to Katya Shadrina for early research assistance.

and removal of threats to the peace, and for the suppression of acts of aggression or other breaches of the peace'; and 'to bring about by peaceful means, and in conformity with the principles of justice and international law, adjustment or settlement of international disputes or situations which might lead to a breach of the peace.' Thus, both preventing conflict and resolving disputes through peaceful means can be viewed as twin pillars in the foundations of the world organization.

The peaceful settlement of disputes and conflict prevention are closely interconnected. Conflict prevention takes the peaceful settlement of disputes one step farther by attempting to address both the immediate and the deeper causes of conflict. Contemporary approaches to conflict prevention also emphasize the linkage between security and development, a salient theme at the September 2005 UN World Summit—the occasion of the organization's sixtieth anniversary.

Since the early 1950s a considerable body of literature has emerged around the concept and practice of the peaceful settlement of disputes, particularly in the UN context. While most of this literature is legalistic—tending to concentrate on the elaboration of Article 33 and its modalities—there now also exists a substantial pool of case studies examining the practical application of these techniques.

Since 1990, analysis and advocacy of conflict prevention have effectively burgeoned, as successive Secretaries-General have seized upon the removal of the Cold War yoke to adopt a more activist approach to conflict prevention. *An Agenda for Peace*, Boutros Boutros-Ghali's response to the General Assembly's appeal for a revitalized UN role in this area, found resounding approval among member states. His successor, Kofi Annan, went further still, calling for the inculcation of a 'culture of prevention' within the UN, and elsewhere.[2]

This chapter addresses in turn the two components of the core UN objective. The peaceful settlement of disputes is dealt with in Part One, which traces the development of pacific dispute settlement and examines the provisions under Article 2 (3) and Article 33 of the UN Charter. It then names the key actors and organs within dispute settlement, as well as the tools available for this purpose. Part Two turns to conflict prevention, delineating its underlying principles and outlining the evolution of the UN's approach to this issue. The chapter concludes by raising some critical issues and questions about the future of both the peaceful settlement of disputes and conflict prevention.

PART ONE: PEACEFUL SETTLEMENT OF DISPUTES

With a view to replacing aggression with cooperation in international relations, the United Nations has championed both the norm and practice of the peaceful settlement of disputes. Article 2 of the Charter lays out the principles under which the UN and its members are required to pursue the aims of Article 1. Article 2 (3) states that 'all members shall settle their international disputes by peaceful means in such a manner that international peace and security, and justice, are not endangered.'

As noted by Bruno Simma, 'the principle of the peaceful settlement of disputes occupies a pivotal position within a world order whose hallmark is the ban on force and coercion.'[3] This principle therefore creates certain obligations for member states and responsibilities for the UN's principal organs. States themselves bear primary responsibility for the pacific settlement of disputes, while the Charter enumerates institutional arrangements to facilitate the pursuit of this principle.

The Charter's emphasis on the peaceful settlement of disputes has been echoed and elaborated in a number of subsequent declarations and resolutions. The 'Friendly Relations Declaration,' set out in General Assembly resolution 2625 (XXV) of October 1970, attempted to specify the scope and content of the principle of the peaceful settlement of disputes. The Manila Declaration on the Peaceful Settlement of International Disputes of 1982 (approved in General Assembly resolution 37/10 of November 1982) provided a more detailed exposition, as it defined the substantive duties of states in peaceful dispute settlement as well as the competencies of relevant UN organs. In resolution 40/9 of November 1985, the General Assembly appealed solemnly to all states to resolve conflicts and disputes by peaceful means.

Of particular significance is the December 1988 General Assembly resolution 43/51, 'Declaration on the Prevention and Removal of Disputes and Situations Which May Threaten International Peace and Security and on the Role of the United Nations in this Field,' featuring preventive measures. This resolution thus represents a departure from the more restricted scope of Article 2 (3), which addresses only existing disputes, not potential ones. Similarly, Boutros-Ghali's recommendations in *An Agenda for Peace*, reaffirmed in General Assembly resolution 47/120 of December 1992, highlighted within the pacific settlement of disputes the importance of preventive diplomacy, fact-finding, and involvement of the General Assembly, and urged states to find early solutions to disputes through peaceful means. The 2005 World Summit Outcome document devoted four paragraphs to the 'Pacific Settlement of Disputes,' underlining its salient importance in intergovernmental practice today.[4]

The Scope of Article 2 (3)

The state obligation to settle disputes peacefully, enshrined in Article 2 (3) of the Charter, applies only to international disputes; indeed, at the founding 1945 United Nations Conference on International Organization held in San Francisco, the Four Powers (China, the Soviet Union, the United Kingdom, and the United States) saw to it that the word 'international' was added to the article, explicitly limiting the injunction to disputes of a trans-border nature, in deference to the principle of sovereignty.

'International' disputes, however, are not restricted to those between states: also applicable are those disputes involving other entities, including international organizations, 'de facto regimes, ethnic communities enjoying a particular kind of status under international law, national liberation movements,' and 'peoples who are holders of the right of self-determination.'[5] This does not imply that a government is obliged to stand by as an insurgency movement grows or to initiate steps towards a peaceful resolution, unless the group has a legitimate right to self-determination.[6] Nonstate actors are also required to resolve disputes peacefully. Charges brought by an individual against a state for non-compliance with human rights obligations do not create an international dispute. Only when one party to a human rights treaty requires a second party to comply with its legal obligations might an international dispute arise.

A controversial question is whether reprisals and counter-measures can legitimately be used in instances where the dispute arose as a result of an unlawful act by one party. There is in general no prohibition on counter-measures provided these do not entail the use of force and do not contravene *ius cogens*, or widely accepted norms codified in international law.[7]

Article 33: Intent and Scope

Article 33 (1) catalogs various methods to be employed by states to settle disputes pacifically:

The parties to any dispute, the continuance of which is likely to endanger the maintenance of international peace and security, shall, first of all, seek a solution by negotiation, enquiry, mediation, conciliation, arbitration, judicial settlement, resort to regional agencies or arrangements, or other peaceful means of their own choice.

Although usually interpreted as an elaboration of Article 2 (3), Article 33 (1) speaks more broadly of 'any dispute' without making any stipulations about its international scope. Further, it hints that internal disputes can jeopardize international peace and security. One explanation for this difference is that Article 33 was intended to address disputes in their incipient stages, prior to the activation of the UN. Article 33 also clarifies that, while it is the obligation of all states to resolve systematically and regularly all disputes through peaceful means, the UN organs are obliged to act only when international peace and security is in danger.

Article 33 (2) continues: 'The Security Council shall, when it deems necessary, call upon parties to settle their disputes by such means' (i.e., negotiation, enquiry, mediation, etc.). This article, therefore, also aims to demarcate the responsibilities of the parties to the conflict from those of the UN. First, indeed 'first of all,' it is the responsibility of parties to seek peaceful resolution; thereafter, the provisions of Chapter VI or Chapter VII are applicable.

The responsibility to seek means of settling disputes peacefully extends not only to the states directly involved in conflict but also to third party states that have the right to bring any issue to the Security Council or the General Assembly. Likewise, it applies to all entities that enjoy the protection of the ban on the use of force, such as national liberation movements and de facto regimes. Their responsibility continues even after armed hostilities may have begun. Nevertheless, states are not obliged to exhaust diplomatic options before approaching the International Court of Justice

(ICJ) for legal remedy. Also, their responsibility continues even after they have referred the matter to a UN body or the matter has been seized by one.

Measures for the Peaceful Settlement of Disputes

The Charter is very precise about the ways and means by which all member states must seek the peaceful settlement of disputes, with the use of force permitted only in self-defense. Despite the injunction to use exclusively peaceful means, states may resort to such counter-measures as are acceptable under international law and the principles of the Charter. However, that counter-measures are in some instances permitted does not negate the fundamental obligation to refrain from the threat or use of force.

The list in Article 33 (1) is not a prescriptive register of priorities but rather a set of options for realizing the peaceful settlement of disputes—indeed, as Simma observes, '[many] of these procedures are rarely resorted to or are even waiting for their first test of practice.'[8] Several legal texts explain in detail each of the mechanisms put forward; particularly detailed is the manual developed by the UN's Legal Office, which provides comprehensive descriptions of each procedure. For the purposes of this chapter, a brief overview of the eight main categories is in order—negotiation, enquiry, mediation, conciliation, arbitration, international tribunals, regional organizations, and 'other peaceful means.'[9]

Negotiation

The tool of negotiation enjoys a special place among the pacific measures listed in Article 33 (1)—not least because negotiations are a universally accepted method of dispute resolution and possess several advantages. One important feature is flexibility: negotiations can be applied to conflicts of a political, legal, or technical nature. Moreover, since only the concerned states are involved, negotiation empowers the parties themselves to steer the process and shape its outcome to deliver a mutually accepted settlement. A key disadvantage of negotiation is its inherent basis in compromise between the parties, a drawback which often leads to the imposition of a solution by the stronger over the weaker party.[10]

The UN Legal Office manual provides a step-by-step guide to the different types of negotiation as well as the phases, methods, and outcomes of each.[11] In 1998 the General Assembly adopted resolution 53/101, 'principles and guidelines for international negotiations,' which underlines the duty of states to act in good faith in negotiations. A vast body of literature addresses negotiation processes, styles, and outcomes.[12]

Inquiry or Fact-Finding

Two parties to a dispute may initiate a commission of inquiry or fact-finding in order to establish the basic information about the case, to see if the claimed infraction was indeed committed, to ascertain what obligations or treaties may have been violated, and to suggest remedies or actions to be undertaken by the parties. These findings and recommendations are not legally binding, and the parties ultimately decide what action to take. A commission of inquiry may usefully be employed in parallel with other methods of dispute resolution—for instance, negotiation, mediation, or conciliation—as factual clarity is an important factor in any dispute resolution strategy. In 1991, the General Assembly adopted resolution 46/59, which contains detailed rules for fact-finding by organs of the UN, and the UN Legal Office manual explains in detail the process and phases of inquiry.[13] It is worth noting that such commissions precede the UN, having already been provided for in the Hague Conventions for the Pacific Settlement of International Disputes of 1899 and 1907.[14]

Mediation and Good Offices

Mediation refers to the offer by a third party of its good offices to the parties to a dispute in the interest of seeking a resolution and preventing an escalation of the conflict. The third party mediator may be an individual, a state or group of states, or an international or regional organization. The function of the mediator is to encourage the parties to undertake or resume negotiations. The mediator may also proffer proposals to help the parties identify a mutually acceptable outcome. The good offices of the third party mediator may be offered on the initiative of the mediator, or solicited by one or both of the parties to the conflict. A fundamental prerequisite is that the mediator is accepted by all parties.

A central actor within mediation, the UN Secretary-General has been traditionally called upon to provide his good offices to mediate between conflicting parties, and a number of his special envoys have played critical roles as mediators in acute conflicts, including in El Salvador and Guatemala. However, other types of mediators—with nongovernmental and independent backgrounds—have appeared in many contexts, which often cause confusion among the parties when several options are on the table.[15]

Mediation, like negotiation, has generated a vast analytical literature.[16] It is perhaps the principal form of dispute settlement and has a long history, having featured in the Hague Conventions of 1899 and 1907.

Although Article 33 does not specifically use the term in its list of measures, 'good offices' is listed in the UN Legal Office manual, as well in other studies of dispute settlement, as a separate method. However, the manual also notes that 'mediation' and 'good offices' can be substituted for each other.

Conciliation

Conciliation combines fact-finding and mediation. A conciliation commission functions not only to engage in enquiry—to set out clearly the facts of the case—but also to act as a mediator, to propose solutions mutually acceptable to the parties to the dispute. Such a commission may be a permanent body or it may be established by the parties to a particular dispute. The commission's proposals are not binding, but each party has the option of declaring unilaterally that it will adopt the recommendations. Several international treaties feature provisions for the systematic referral of disputes for compulsory conciliation. Often provisions include the requirement that the parties first exhaust negotiation before broaching conciliation, and that, in turn, conciliation is attempted before taking up arbitration or approaching an international tribunal.[17]

Conciliation commissions, frequently used in the interwar period, subsequently fell into desuetude, to be revived somewhat in recent decades.[18] The 1969 Vienna Convention on the Law of Treaties articulated a procedure for the submission by states of requests to the UN Secretary-General for the initiation of conciliation. On 11 December 1995, the General Assembly adopted resolution 50/50, containing the UN Model Rules for the Conciliation of Disputes between States, which substantiates and clarifies conciliation procedures.[19]

Arbitration

The precedent for arbitration emerges from the 1899 and 1907 Hague Conventions, which state that the objective of international arbitration is the settlement of disputes between states by judges of their choice based on respect of the law. Arbitration represents a 'qualitative leap' over the other measures, as it necessitates the settlement of the dispute in accordance with existing international legal standards.[20] The parties agree to submit the dispute to arbitration, and thereby commit to respect in good faith the outcome, which is binding.

Arbitration has features similar to aspects of international tribunals; however, the former gives greater control to the parties, empowering them, for example, to appoint judges. Each party may appoint an equal number of judges, with one judge chosen by mutual agreement of the parties, with a view to guaranteeing parity in the proceedings. Arbitration is used particularly in disputes arising over territory and over differing interpretations of bilateral or multilateral treaties.

The most concrete achievement of the 1899 Hague Peace Conference was the establishment of the Permanent Court of Arbitration (PCA), located in the Peace Palace in The Hague. The PCA, which is accessible at all times, has competence in all arbitration cases submitted to it by agreement of the parties involved. The PCA provides a list of arbitrators, appointed by the states parties to the Hague Convention, from which parties wishing to submit a dispute to arbitration can choose.[21]

International Tribunals

The term 'international tribunals' refers to the International Court of Justice and other courts with international jurisdiction. Depending on the definition employed, there are currently between seventeen and forty international courts and tribunals.[22] Normally, the decisions of an international tribunal are definitive and cannot be appealed—see, for example, Article 60 of the Statute of the ICJ.[23]

The advantage of permanent international tribunals over arbitral courts is that they are better situated than an ad hoc tribunal to become seized of a matter since they already exist.[24] Normally, the cases brought to the ICJ tend to hinge upon the interpretation and application of treaties; sovereignty over territory and border disputes; maritime borders and other matters related to the law of the sea; diplomatic protection afforded to foreigners; the use of force; violations of contracts; and principles of customary international law.[25]

Regional Agencies or Arrangements

Article 33 leaves scope for the referral of a dispute to 'regional agencies or arrangements,' which refers to both regional treaties and regional organizations. Chapter VIII is devoted to 'regional arrangements,' and their role in dispute settlement is addressed specifically in Article 52.

The UN's dispute settlement manual describes the resolution mechanisms and procedures of the Arab League, the Organization of American States, the Organization of African Unity (now reconstituted as the African Union), the Council of Europe, the Conference on Security and Co-operation in Europe (now the Organization for Security and Co-operation in Europe, or OSCE), the European Communities (now the EU), and ECOWAS (the Economic Community of West African States). Also mentioned are the European and American human rights systems, as well as the African Charter on Human and Peoples' Rights. In sum, the UN envisages an important role for regional organizations within dispute settlement.

Yet a key question is how to harmonize the work of regional organizations with the efforts of the UN. Normally, local disputes are addressed in the first instance to the appropriate regional body. If a satisfactory agreement is successfully brokered by the regional body, action by the UN is rendered unnecessary. However, should there be dissatisfaction with the terms proposed, the dispute may be referred to the Security Council whose practice is in such cases to note the issue on its agenda. If the Council judges that the dispute does not pose a threat to international peace and security, it will refer the case back to the regional body while keeping a close watching brief on the situation for potential future action in the event that the conflict escalates.

'Other Peaceful Means'

Notwithstanding the extensive menu of measures listed in Article 33, the last item— 'other peaceful means'—effectively lifts any bar on options for action. It gives parties the freedom to identify for themselves the most appropriate way of resolving their disputes.

The UN's dispute settlement manual describes three categories of measures that have been employed by states to this end. The first category includes entirely original measures, based neither on an adaptation nor on a combination of the listed measures. Examples include consultations and conferences, and the referral of a dispute to a political organ or non-judicial organ of an international organization.

The second category features those cases in which states have adapted the methods named in Article 33. For example, the parties may agree in advance that the report of a conciliation commission will be binding rather than non-binding.

The third category contains the instances in which a single organ employs two or more of the listed measures. For example, a treaty may provide for the progressive application of a range of methods. Also, a single organ may be entrusted with both conciliation and arbitration.

Responsible Actors and Organs

Several actors and organs within the UN system have responsibilities in the area of peaceful settlement of disputes. Although Chapters VI and VII of the Charter focus on the role of the Security Council, the Council is by no means the sole agent in the peaceful settlements of disputes. In fact, the principal responsibility lies first with the parties to the conflict who may settle the dispute themselves or refer it to any of the mandated international institutions. The secondary responsibility falls on the Security Council to call upon the parties to settle their disputes, including by those means set out in Chapter VI. Thereafter, the General Assembly may, under Articles 11 and 12, bring issues to the attention of the Security Council. Article 99 then empowers the Secretary-General to act to secure the peaceful settlement of disputes. Finally, the ICJ provides recourse to judicial remedy. The respective roles of the major actors and organs are discussed below.

Parties to the Conflict

Article 2 (3) creates an obligation 'primarily incumbent' on all UN member states that applies to all disputes, 'whether they are connected with the UN Charter or rooted in other subject-matters.'[26] Since this principle has become an established part of customary law, states have at any time the right to bring any dispute to the attention of the General Assembly or the Security Council.

As such, the principle of peaceful means is not optional, and states have a legal obligation to endeavor to settle their disputes through pacific means. However, while the principle obliges states to pursue peaceful outcomes in good faith, it does not oblige them to arrive at a particular result. Thus, a violation of the principle occurs when a state is proved to have worked against a peaceful outcome—not if states do not agree a resolution.

Security Council

As the principal UN organ with—in the words of Article 24 (1)—'the primary responsibility for the maintenance of international peace and security,' the Security Council has a central role in peaceful dispute resolution, once the parties themselves have proved unable or unwilling to negotiate a settlement. The Council's responsibilities are specified not only under Chapter VI but also under both Chapter VII, applicable in more acute situations requiring enforcement, and Chapter VIII, applicable to regional arrangements.

It is only since the end of the Cold War that the Security Council has been able to devote greater attention and resources to the task of dispute settlement, doing so with growing effectiveness, despite criticisms of its inconsistency.[27] This increased activity has manifested itself most visibly in the surge in the number of peacekeeping missions mandated by the Council since 1989. Another development has been the expansion of the Security Council's purview to include—in addition to conflict prevention—humanitarianism, human rights, democratization, terrorism, and armed nonstate actors.[28]

General Assembly

Although Chapter VI makes only passing reference to the General Assembly's role in the peaceful settlement of disputes, during the Cold War the Assembly filled the gap in Council capacity to address conflicts. Most notably, during the Korean War, the General Assembly was able to offset the gridlock among the permanent five arising from the end to the Soviet Union's boycott of the Security Council and the latter's subsequent incapacitation. 'Uniting for Peace,' instituted in November 1950 by General Assembly resolution 377 (V), specifically authorized continued UN enforcement in Korea. According to that resolution,

if the Security Council, because of lack of unanimity of the permanent members, fails to exercise its primary responsibility for the maintenance of international peace and security in any case where there appears to be a threat to the peace, breach of the peace, or act of aggression, the General Assembly shall consider the matter immediately with a view to making appropriate recommendations to members for collective measures, including in the case of a breach of peace or act of aggression the use of armed force when necessary, to maintain or restore international peace and security.

Uniting for Peace, which has been invoked ten times, therefore allows the General Assembly to assume the mantle of the Security Council when it fails to act. However, with the post-Cold War revitalization of the Security Council, the Assembly has been marginalized in dispute settlement, despite several calls from the Secretary-General and others for a more active role. During the 2003 deadlock over Iraq, several NGOs appealed on the basis of Uniting for Peace for authority to be shifted from the Security Council to the General Assembly.[29]

Secretary-General

Charter Article 99 makes provision for the role of the Secretary-General within the pacific settlement of disputes. Successive Secretaries-General have taken an activist approach to this mandate, making valuable contributions to dispute resolution, and to preventive diplomacy and conflict prevention, more broadly. The good offices of the Secretary-General are particularly important, as is the Secretary-General's contribution through mediation. Indeed the legacies of Secretaries-General are often evaluated against their success as mediators, and by extension against the degree of influence they enjoy, their political acceptability, and perceived neutrality.[30]

Each of the seven Secretaries-General has sought to play a decisive role in the key conflicts of their respective tenures, albeit with varied degrees of success.[31] This mandate has been exercised personally, but also through staff in the Secretariat and ad hoc appointments—in particular special envoys and special representatives.[32]

The first to occupy the post, Norway's Trygve Lie, demonstrated the Secretary-General's dispute settlement function. A high profile figure, he sought to exercise his authority in the Korean War. His assertiveness incurred the hostility of the Soviet Union and brought about his eventual resignation in 1952.

Continuing his predecessor's activism, Sweden's Dag Hammarskjöld developed a unique and skillful approach of 'combined public and private multilateral diplomacy.'[33] He advocated preventive rather than corrective action and was active particularly in the Congo conflict. However, Hammarskjöld also alienated Moscow. Had he not died in a tragic accident in 1961, he likely would have struggled to pursue his mandate in the face of Soviet opposition.

The third Secretary-General, U Thant of Burma, was soft-spoken and given to quiet diplomacy. Having successfully steered the Congo operation to completion, Thant came under criticism for his 1967 withdrawal of the peacekeeping operation from the Sinai, under pressure from President Gamal Abdel Nasser of Egypt. Nevertheless, he has been named a 'courageous and skillful' Secretary-General who 'salvaged the prestige, independence and effectiveness of his office.'[34]

Kurt Waldheim, of Austria, has been judged overly deferent to the major powers and too anxious about his reelection.[35] His efforts, however, in Cyprus, the Middle East, Southern Africa, and elsewhere, have been deemed noteworthy.

It was with Javier Pérez de Cuéllar of Peru that the UN Secretary-General's potential in conflict mediation and resolution reemerged, although he attracted less publicity than his predecessors. His achievements are notable: the end of the Iran–Iraq war, the Soviet withdrawal from Afghanistan, Namibian independence, and Salvadoran peace agreements following arduous negotiations.

Egypt's Boutros Boutros-Ghali was highly active, and *An Agenda for Peace* served to revitalize debate at the UN on the world body's capacity to maintain international security. However, his outspoken positions, often counter to the view of some permanent five members, made him unpopular in some circles, and led eventually to the non-renewal of his tenure.

Kofi Annan, a career UN official from Ghana, worked vigorously to foster a culture of prevention. In 2001, in recognition of these efforts, the Nobel Peace Prize was awarded to Kofi Annan and the UN.

It remains to be seen how Ban Ki-moon will use Article 99 to further the Secretary-General's role in conflict prevention.

Special Envoys and Special Representatives of the Secretary-General

Many of the successes attributed to particular Secretaries-General are in fact owed to the meticulous work and perspicacity of their special envoys and representatives. Though the latter now are mainly deployed in support of post-conflict peacebuilding, several outstanding individuals have been nominated by the Secretary-General to represent him personally as mediators in conflicts. Several studies have examined their contributions to conflict resolution.[36]

At the 2005 World Summit, member states endorsed the Secretary-General's proposals to strengthen his capacity to bring his 'good offices' to bear in conflict prevention and resolution. The Department of Political Affairs (DPA) is charged with creating a Mediation Support Unit for UN peace envoys in the field.[37]

International Court of Justice

Established in 1945, the ICJ represents the last rung in the ladder of dispute settlement, providing for judicial remedy when enquiry, consultation, negotiation, and mediation have failed. The settlements of the ICJ are binding upon states parties; however, member states submit to the Court voluntarily, even if they have ratified its Statute.

The differences between the ICJ and other international courts have been the subject of many scholarly examinations,[38] as have the proliferation of other international and ad hoc tribunals and the implications of this for the ICJ's authority.[39] The ICJ has been criticized for not pulling its full weight, and there is a tendency to condemn the ICJ to irrelevance because of a supposedly habitual noncompliance with its judgments. However, there are indications that, in fact, the ICJ generally enjoys a high degree of compliance. One review concluded that, of the judgments on fourteen contentious cases occurring after the Cold War, 'five have met with less compliance than the others, although no state has been directly defiant.'[40]

PART TWO: CONFLICT PREVENTION

Part One of this chapter has discussed the principle of peaceful dispute resolution, the sources and scope of this principle, some of the mechanisms available, and the key actors involved. This section considers the next step following the peaceful settlement of disputes—conflict prevention, an enhanced focus for the United Nations since the mid-1990s.

Conflict prevention is implicitly the core business of the world organization. Yet it was only after the Cold War, in fact, that the term entered UN parlance and practice. *An Agenda for Peace* signaled the beginning of this shift, and thereafter the focus on conflict prevention intensified, particularly following the international community's inaction in the face of the 1994 Rwandan genocide.

Under the leadership of Secretary-General Kofi Annan conflict prevention moved to the top of the UN's agenda. In June of 2001, he presented to the General Assembly and the Security Council a report entitled *Prevention of Armed Conflict*, in which he set out his pledge 'to move the United Nations from a culture of reaction to a culture of prevention.'[41] This report reviewed the development of the UN's mandate in conflict prevention and proposed several system-wide measures to enhance its capacity in this field. Strong emphasis was given to the need for preventive strategies to address the underlying reasons for conflict: 'one of the principal aims of preventive action should be to address the deep-rooted socio-economic, cultural, environmental, institutional and other structural causes that often underlie the immediate political symptoms of conflicts.'[42] In July 2006, Annan produced another report on conflict prevention, which introduced the concept of 'systemic prevention,' defined as 'measures to address global risks of conflict that transcend particular states.' Such efforts would include the curbing of trade in conflict goods and illicit small arms.

With this report, Annan was building on the work of the previous decade. Since the late 1980s, the General Assembly and Security Council had been toiling to strengthen the organization's conflict prevention mandate. Crucially, *An Agenda for Peace* distinguished preventive diplomacy—undertaken before the outbreak of violent conflict—from the key tasks of peacemaking, peacekeeping, and peacebuilding, and prescribed for the UN a signal role in all four tasks.

Several external events and initiatives have had an important impact on the UN's approach to conflict prevention. The effect of the Rwandan genocide was catalytic, throwing into stark relief the devastating consequences of failing to act preventively. The 1997 report of the Carnegie Commission on Preventing Deadly Conflict defined, conceptualized, and operationalized conflict prevention and injected some rigor to thinking and policy in this area.[43] Gareth Evans, former foreign minister of Australia, has made several notable contributions to promoting the concepts of prevention and cooperative security: through his book *Cooperating for Peace: The Global Agenda for 1990s and Beyond*;[44] through his co-chairmanship of the International Commission on Intervention and State Sovereignty;[45] and through his leadership of the International Crisis Group.

In November 1999 and July 2000, the Security Council held open debates on conflict prevention. This exercise highlighted that, although conflict prevention was a concern shared by member states, priorities and approaches to the issue varied widely, with some states emphasizing socio-economic causes, others human rights and governance. The continuity, interdependence and linkages between conflict prevention and peacebuilding formed a key theme in the Council's debate on peacebuilding in February 2001. In August 2001, the Security Council, in resolution 1366, responded to the Secretary-General's report on conflict prevention and noted 'the importance of a comprehensive strategy comprising operational and structural measures for prevention of armed conflict.' Resolution 1366 also focused on conflict prevention—noting that it was driven by 'overriding political, humanitarian and moral imperatives' and would confer 'the economic advantages of preventing the outbreak and escalation of conflicts.' The Secretary-General's 2001 report made it onto the agenda for the 56th session of the General Assembly, but was overshadowed by the terrorist attacks of 11 September 2001—even though many observers noted that prevention and addressing root causes in 'bad neighborhoods' such as Afghanistan were integral to winning the war on terror.[46]

While the emphasis on conflict prevention has slackened somewhat, there have been a few highlights since 2001. In 2002, the Rome Statute of the International Criminal Court (ICC) entered into force. By prosecuting war criminals and countering impunity, the ICC can be expected to have a deterrent effect and aid in preventing violent conflict and abuses. In 2003, the Secretary-General presented his follow-up to his 2001 report, an *Interim Report on the Prevention of Armed Conflict*, and the General Assembly adopted decisions which put in place relevant institutional arrangements.[47] In 2004, to mark the tenth anniversary of the Rwandan genocide, the Secretary-General appointed a special adviser on genocide prevention. In July 2005, the Global Partnership for Conflict Prevention responded to the Secretary-General's earlier call for a greater role for civil society by convening a large meeting of NGOs to discuss their contribution to the UN's work in this area. In September of that same year, the 2005 UN World Summit approved the Secretary-General's proposals to strengthen his good offices and mediation capacities, as noted above. This development was accompanied by two other decisions of potentially considerable importance to conflict prevention: agreement on the principle of the responsibility to protect and agreement on the establishment of a Peacebuilding Commission.

Though the UN's role in conflict prevention is widely recognized, the development of its preventive mandate and its various attempts at operationalizing it since 1989 have attracted controversy. Some analysts have gone so far as to compare the UN's efforts in this area to alchemy or opium use.[48] Connie Peck summarized some of the key sources of this resistance.[49] First, the conceptual confusion in *An Agenda for Peace* between preventive deployment and preventive diplomacy suggested that the latter could entail the use of force; this naturally provoked opposition. Second, with the 1989 renaissance of the Security Council following its impotence during the Cold War, many envisaged that the Council would apply itself to challenging tasks, such as peacekeeping and peace-enforcement, rather than the seemingly softer option of prevention. It was also often the case that issues were brought to the Security Council's attention only when a crisis had already erupted and the time for prevention had passed. Third, the Council's new activism worried smaller and developing countries who suspected that prevention was a façade for interventionism. Fourth, developing countries viewed the UN's focus on peace and security as an unhelpful diversion of resources and attention away from their acute social and developmental needs. Fifth, there was confusion as to what prevention constituted in operational terms, and this uncertainty made practical progress difficult.

To some extent, this apprehension towards prevention still persists. For example, the original proposal for the Peacebuilding Commission, put forward by the High-level Panel on Threats, Challenges and Change, had envisaged a preventive function for the commission alongside its role in post-conflict peacebuilding.[50] However, some states resisted, and resolutions 1645 and 1646, which formally established the Peacebuilding Commission, do not give the body a preventive role.

Sources of the UN's Conflict Prevention Mandate

In his 2001 report the Secretary-General outlined the basis of the UN's conflict prevention mandate. He began with Article 1 (1), which lays out member states' commitment 'to take effective collective measures for the prevention and removal of threats to the peace.' He also referred to Article 2 (3) (discussed in detail above) as providing one of the 'defining elements of the philosophy underlying the collective security system.'[51]

Also highlighted in the Secretary-General's report as a source of the UN's mandate for conflict prevention is Article 55, from Chapter IX on 'International Economic and Social Co-operation.' The 2001 report echoes Article 55's central point: economic and social standards of life—such as employment, health, and education—are important in and of themselves. These factors, however, are also prerequisites for creating 'conditions of stability and well-being which are necessary for peaceful and friendly relations among nations.'[52] The Secretary-General's proposed conflict prevention strategy is accordingly comprehensive and multi-faceted; its main aspects are described further below.

Key Principles Underlying UN Conflict Prevention

The Secretary-General structured his report on six premises.[53] First, the obligation of member states to prevent conflict derives from the Charter, with which all preventive action must be consistent. Second, national governments ultimately bear primary responsibility for conflict prevention, with a supportive role for the UN. Third, preventive action is most effective when executed at the earliest possible stage, and when it addresses structural root causes. Fourth, approaches need to be comprehensive, looking at the short and the long term and encompassing a range of perspectives, from the political and humanitarian to human rights and development. Fifth, investments in conflict prevention and sustainable and equitable development are mutually reinforcing. Sixth, the success of prevention relies on the cooperation of multiple actors and bodies across the UN system, as well as the input of member states, regional organizations, the private sector, and civil society.

Prevention in UN Practice: Approaches and Tools

The Secretary-General's report incorporated the two categories of preventive action identified by the Carnegie Commission on Preventing Deadly Conflict report: the first category—operational prevention—refers to those 'measures applicable in the face of immediate crisis'; and the second—structural prevention—includes 'measures to ensure that crises do not arise or, if they do, that they do not recur.'[54]

The academic literature distinguishes under the umbrella of operational prevention two types of activities. The first is cooperative management, which includes problem-solving, training, dialog, fact-finding, negotiation, and preventive diplomacy by the Secretary-General. The second is coercion or inducement, which consists of using 'sticks and carrots,' sanctions, and the deployment of observers.[55]

Structural prevention seeks to transform the underlying 'characteristics of groups, states, and regions that increase their risk of violent conflict,' and therefore often entails programs aimed at enhancing development and improving governance. Despite the theoretical distinction between operational and structural prevention, these categories should be seen in context: 'An integrated strategy for long-term structural prevention would combine policies for growth, targeted programs to reduce sources of conflict, and support for governance to "strengthen the capacity of a society to manage conflict without violence." '[56]

Operational Prevention

For obvious reasons, the UN organs responsible for operational prevention—that is, when a crisis is already looming or hostilities have actually broken out—largely mirror those entrusted with the peaceful settlement of disputes: the General Assembly, the Security Council, the Secretary-General, and the ICJ. The Secretary-General's first recommendation, which deals in fact with the General Assembly and not the Security Council, calls on the Assembly to 'consider a more active use of its powers, in accordance with Articles 10, 11, and 14 of the Charter of the United Nations, in the prevention of armed conflict.'[57] The Assembly is also urged to enhance its interaction with the Security Council, especially in the areas of long-term prevention and peacebuilding. The Security Council is encouraged to adopt innovative mechanisms to regularize discussions on prevention to facilitate early action, while member states are urged to submit disputes to the ICJ 'earlier and more often.'[58]

The Secretary-General's report considers at some length his own role within conflict prevention, which again, as in dispute settlement, emerges as central. His proposals focus on enhancing his traditional preventive diplomacy role in several ways: more fact-finding and confidence-building missions; the establishment of an informal network of eminent persons to advise and support him; better cooperation with regional organizations; and strengthened capacity within the Secretariat.

The Department of Political Affairs plays an important role in operational prevention as the appointed lead for both conflict prevention and peacemaking. It describes its own functions in this area as follows:

The Department of Political Affairs plays a central role in these efforts: monitoring and assessing global political developments; advising the UN Secretary-General on actions that could advance the cause of peace; providing support and guidance to UN peace envoys and political missions in the field; and serving Member States directly through electoral assistance and through the support of DPA staff to the work of the Security Council and other U.N. bodies.[59]

DPA convenes the Executive Committee on Peace and Security, established in 1997 as part of the organization's restructuring. The committee has a broad membership from across the UN system, covering political, peacekeeping, humanitarian, legal, economic, and social issues, and it meets twice a month. It also creates task forces to address specific issues or contribute to the Secretary-General's reports.

Other bodies within the UN system also coordinate work on conflict prevention. Set up in 1995, the UN Interdepartmental Framework Team for Coordination on Early Warning and Conflict Prevention brings together various parts of the world organization to formulate strategies to consolidate peace which are rooted in field-based national and civil society efforts. The chair of this body rotates among its members, who are derived from fourteen agencies, departments, and programs.

Structural Prevention

An innovation in the Secretary-General's 2001 report on conflict prevention was the emphasis on structural prevention and, based on this, the recommendation that conflict prevention be incorporated into the work of all UN agencies, programs, and departments. The report also called upon the Economic and Social Council (ECOSOC) to address structural prevention, and specifically proposed that it devote a high-level segment of one of its annual meetings to considering the root causes of conflict and how development might promote prevention.

The Secretary-General's 2003 interim report stated that all UN development programs were in the process of instituting new methodologies that would subject them to a 'conflict prevention lens.'[60] The Secretary-General reported, for example, that the risk of conflict was being integrated into the Common Country Assessment/ UN Development Assistance Framework Guidelines. He acknowledged, however, that addressing the root causes of conflict, including structural ones, remained an unmet challenge.

CONCLUSION: THE CHALLENGES AND PROSPECTS OF THE UN's ROLE IN DISPUTE SETTLEMENT AND CONFLICT PREVENTION

The September 2005 World Summit, the largest-ever gathering of heads of state and government, underscored the importance of peaceful dispute settlement and noted the central role of the Secretary-General in peacemaking as well as in conflict prevention. However, there remain several challenges to achieving progress in both pacific dispute settlement and conflict prevention as pursued by the United Nations.

Regarding the peaceful settlement of disputes, three challenges are worth highlighting. First, whereas Article 2 (3) creates a clear and binding obligation on member states to *seek* to resolve their disputes peacefully, the wording is such that there is no obligation to *find* a particular solution. In actual practice, therefore, a belligerent's lack of good faith could scupper efforts to arrive at a peaceful outcome. Article 2 (3) also opens up the possibility for a dispute to be dragged out, as parties exhaust all options in the ladder of means.

Second, recourse to the ICJ, as a judicial avenue for settling disputes, faces obstacles. The emergence of international criminal tribunals and other courts may be undermining the world court's authority; and, in symbolically important cases, either the ICJ is not appealed to, or its final judgments or advisory opinions are overlooked. For instance, the ICJ's 2004 advisory opinion on the *Legal Consequences of the Construction of a Wall in the Occupied Palestinian Territory* was partly rejected by an Israeli High Court of Justice ruling.[61]

Third, while the office of the Secretary-General plays a critically important role in dispute settlement, its success is contingent upon the aptitude of the incumbent and is hostage to the vagaries of world politics. The tendency of powerful member states to eschew assertive leaders is particularly damaging. Although leaders agreed at the 2005 World Summit to strengthen the capacity of the Secretary-General for preventive diplomacy, it is not yet clear what fruit this will bear.

Conflict prevention by the UN, while rhetorically prominent, also faces major challenges and criticism on the ground.[62] A generic problem facing conflict prevention is its 'invisibility.' Successful prevention is not seen or heard; without a crisis, the media are not interested. As it is intrinsically impossible to measure something that was prevented, the political pay-off of undertaking preventive action is often judged insufficient, however easy the rhetoric may flow from politicians. This certainly affects all UN organizations involved in conflict prevention, particularly the Security Council, whose actions are highly visible. However, it poses a particular conundrum for the Secretary-General. Drawing attention to 'successful' prevention could backfire because parties to such conflicts usually wish to avoid publicity about their compromises and weaknesses; yet without demonstrating the tangible benefits of active conflict prevention it will be difficult for the Secretary-General to rally the requisite support or resources.

A second major challenge lies in the UN's division of conflict prevention into the two categories of operational and structural prevention. While the simultaneous emphasis on peace and security and social and economic development tallies with the UN's expansive and multifaceted mandate, this classification does not easily transfer from theory into practice. Structural prevention has proven the most nebulous to conceive and to implement. Despite efforts on paper and practices such as systematic conflict assessment, there is little evidence that these are the most effective ways to prevent conflict structurally.

The third and most important challenge, however, is for the UN to focus more on the issue of systemic prevention, which was largely ignored by the world body until Kofi Annan's 2006 report.[63] Simply stated, 'violent conflicts are embedded in an international system that often provokes them.'[64] According to Michael Lund, 'all post-Cold War conflicts, peaceful or otherwise, are not ethnic, self-determination or Islamic fundamentalist conflicts. They are fundamentally *liberalization conflicts*.'[65] He alludes to the dilemma that the very institutions and practices of market liberalization and political democratization that might be desirable in the long term provoke conflicts that could turn violent in the short term, as in Croatia, Bosnia, and Burundi. The dangers of growing inequality, long known to conflict researchers, are now being publicly recognized by economists—for example, the World Bank's 2006 annual *World Development Report* whose subtitle was *Equity and Development*.[66] The UN's prevention efforts have mostly focused narrowly on factors within a conflictual society, with only scant attention paid to the glaring factors within the global system. The world organization has also ignored the fact that the UN itself is a major actor and decision-maker in this system. As starkly expressed by Rubin:

Unless we confront the way in which our own institutions and practices foment violence, we beneficiaries of this global economy engaged in the work of international prevention are no more than half-heartedly patching up damage we have an interest in perpetuating. A global economy needs a global social policy and a global politics.[67]

What do these challenges presage for the future of UN practice in the interlinked areas of dispute settlement and conflict prevention? While the General Assembly, the only fully representative and hence quasi-democratic organ of the UN, has been repeatedly urged to assume a larger role in dispute settlement and conflict prevention. However, it has so far failed to do so and shows few signs of change, as demonstrated during the Iraq crisis in 2003. As a consequence, the Security Council has amassed greater executive powers in all aspects of conflict management, from prevention to resolution to post-conflict peacebuilding. Yet, its actions remain weighted toward the more visible, forceful, and reactive rather than the invisible, quiet, and proactive initiatives required for dispute settlement and conflict prevention. Further, it is not clear whether either the General Assembly or the Security Council is ideally suited to undertake the fine-tuned, sensitive tasks of dispute settlement and conflict prevention in practice, the former being too unwieldy and the latter too unrepresentative. Nor is it clear that the Secretary-General and Secretariat, notwithstanding persistent efforts over the last decade, have yet gained the necessary expertise, resources, and mechanisms to deploy effectively and consistently.

However, the ultimate power to settle disputes peacefully and to prevent them from turning violent lies with states. The effectiveness of the UN in this area depends upon the political will of its member states and upon their active support for the central principle of the nonuse of force. Yet, as illustrated by the contrast between the collective security reaction in the Gulf War in 1991, on the one hand, and the preemptive war in Iraq in 2003, on the other, there is no longer a clear consensus on the place of multilateralism and the nonuse of force in dispute settlement.

The future for UN practice in the areas of dispute settlement and conflict prevention sits squarely, therefore, in the hands of member states. They are required to act upon their declarations at the 2005 World Summit and to entrust to the UN, particularly the Secretary-General, a more forceful mandate and enhanced resources. Even more crucially it will require member states to exercise restraint in their own conduct in the use of force *in all circumstances*. It will equally depend on the recognition by member states, and especially the richest and most powerful, that the greatest potential source of violent conflict stems from deepening economic inequality and political marginalization, and that the most effective way to prevent conflict—though not the most popular politically—would be to redress these immediately.

Notes

1. Julie Dahlitz, 'Introduction,' in *Peaceful Resolution of Major International Disputes*, ed. Dahlitz (New York: United Nations, 1999), 5.
2. See Kofi Annan, *Facing the Humanitarian Challenge: Towards a Culture of Prevention* (New York: UN, 1999). The same text appears as the introduction to *Report of the Secretary-General on the Work of the Organization*, UN document A/54/1, Supplement no. 1, 31 August 1999; and *Prevention of Armed Conflict: Report of the Secretary-General*, UN document A/55/985–S/2001/574, 7 June 2001.

3. Bruno Simma, ed., *The Charter of the United Nations: A Commentary*, 2nd edn., vol. 1 (Oxford: Oxford University Press, 2002), 103. This section draws heavily upon his authoritative commentary.

4. *2005 World Summit Outcome*, UN document A/60/L.1, 15 September 2005, paras. 73–76.

5. Simma, *The Charter of the United Nations*, 108.

6. On the right to self-determination, see General Assembly resolutions 1514 (XV), 14 December 1960 and 1541 (XV), 15 December 1960.

7. See 'Responsibility of States for internationally wrongful acts,' General Assembly resolution A/RES/56/83, 28 January 2002, which takes note of, and commends to the attention of governments, the draft articles on responsibility of states for internationally wrongful acts by the International Law Commission. Draft articles 22 and 49–54 deal with countermeasures. The draft articles can be consulted at www.ilsa.org.

8. Simma, *The Charter of the United Nations*, 588.

9. UN Legal Affairs Office, Codification Division, *Handbook on the Peaceful Settlement of Disputes between States* (New York: UN, 1992). This section draws on this source. J. G. Merrills, *International Dispute Settlement*, 4th edn. (Cambridge: Cambridge University Press, 2005) provides a detailed and very up-to-date survey of peaceful dispute settlement. For a useful reading list (case accounts, treaties, resolutions, and comments) covering good offices, mediation, conciliation, and fact-finding/commissions, see Vaughan Lowe, *International Dispute Settlement 2003–2004, handout 3 (Alternative Dispute Resolution)*, University of Oxford, Faculty of Law.

10. Antonio Cassese, *International Law in a Divided World* (Oxford: Clarendon Press, 1986), 202.

11. UN Legal Affairs Office, *Handbook*, 9–24.

12. See, e.g., I. William Zartman, ed., *The Negotiation Process: Theories and Applications* (Beverly Hills, Calif.: Sage, 1978); Fred Charles Iklé, *How Nations Negotiate* (New York: Praeger, 1964); and P. Terence Hopmann, *The Negotiation Process and the Resolution of International Conflicts* (Columbia: University of South Carolina Press, 1996).

13. UN, Legal Affairs Office, *Handbook*, 24–32.

14. Conventions for the Pacific Settlement of International Disputes of 29 July 1899 (Articles 9–14) and of 18 October 1907 (Articles 9–36). Classic instances of the use of fact-finding or inquiry commissions include the Dogger Bank incident (enquiry agreement between Great Britain and Russia: Declaration of St. Petersburg of the 12th (25th) November 1904) and the Tavignano incident (enquiry agreement between France and Italy on 12 May 1912). For both, see James Brown Scott, ed., *The Hague Court Reports: Comprising the Awards, Accompanied by Syllabi, the Agreements for Arbitration, and Other Documents in Each Case Submitted to the Permanent Court of Arbitration* (Buffalo, NY: William S. Hein & Co., Inc., 2004), 404, 413, 616 (originally published in New York by Oxford University Press, 1916).

15. This is described well in Chester A. Crocker, Fen Osler Hampson, and Pamela R. Aall, eds., *Herding Cats: Multiparty Mediation in a Complex World* (Washington, DC: United States Institute for Peace Press, 1999).

16. See Hugh Miall, *The Peacemakers: Peaceful Settlement of Disputes since 1945* (New York: St. Martin's Press, 1992); Jacob Bercovitch and Jeffrey Z. Rubin, eds., *Mediation in International Relations: Multiple Approaches to Conflict Management* (Basingstoke, UK: Macmillan, 1992); Jacob Bercovitch, ed., *Resolving International Conflicts: The Theory and Practice of Mediation* (Boulder, Colo.: Lynne Rienner, 1996); and John Darby and Roger MacGinty, eds., *Contemporary Peacemaking: Conflict, Violence and Peace Processes* (Basingstoke, UK: Palgrave Macmillan, 2003).

17. UN Legal Affairs Office, *Handbook*, 45–47.
18. Examples of agreements during the interwar period include: Chile–Sweden, 26 March 1920 (Aprueba Convención celebrada con el Reino de Suecia, sobre establecimiento de una Comisión Permanente de Investigación y Conciliación); Switzerland–France, 3 December 1921 (Traité d'arbitrage et de conciliation du 3 décembre 1921 entre la Confédération suisse et le Reich allemand [avec protocole final]); and Switzerland–France (Traité de conciliation et d'arbitrage obligatoire du 6 avril 1925 entre la Suisse et la France), which functioned as a model for the Treaty of Mutual Guarantee between Germany, Belgium, France, Great Britain, and Italy of 16 October 1925 (The Locarno Pact, article 3 and special agreements signed the same day). A more recent example is the Jan Mayen Conciliation Commission between Iceland and Norway: Agreement on the Continental Shelf Between Iceland and Jan Mayen, 22 October 1981. Examples taken from Lowe, *International Dispute Settlement 2003–2004*.
19. Cassese, *International Law in a Divided World*, 211–212.
20. Ibid., 202.
21. For a list of arbitration websites and information, see Permanent Court of Arbitration, *Directory of Arbitration Websites and Information on Arbitration Available Online*, compiled by *Rosabel E. Goodman-Everard*, www.pca-cpa.org.
22. Robert O. Keohane, Andrew Moravcsik, and Anne-Marie Slaughter, 'Legalized Dispute Resolution: Interstate and Transnational,' *International Organization* 54, no. 3 (2000): 457; see Cesare P. R. Romano, 'The Proliferation of International Judicial Bodies: The Pieces of the Puzzle,' *New York University Journal of International Law and Politics* 31, no. 709 (1999): 723–728.
23. UN Legal Affairs Office, *Handbook*, 66.
24. For an examination of the role of arbitration and tribunals in international affairs and their advantages and disadvantages relative to other dispute settlement mechanisms, see also Richard Bilder, 'Adjudication: International Arbitral Tribunals and Courts,' in *Peacemaking in International Conflict: Methods and Techniques*, ed. I. William Zartman and J. Lewis Rasmussen (Washington, DC: United States Institute of Peace Press, 1997), 155–190.
25. UN Legal Affairs Office, *Handbook*, 68–69.
26. Simma, *The Charter of the United Nations*, 105.
27. See, e.g., David M. Malone, ed., *The UN Security Council: From the Cold War to the 21st Century* (Boulder, Colo.: Lynne Rienner, 2004).
28. See ibid., especially Part I: Security Council Decisionmaking: New Concerns, 37–132.
29. Thalif Deen, 'NGOs Lead Move to Use UN General Assembly to Stop War,' *Inter Press Service*, 31 January 2003, www.globalpolicy.org. For a list of General Assembly instruments in the field of conflict prevention and peaceful settlement of disputes adopted as the result of the Special Committee on the Charter of the United Nations and on the Strengthening of the Role of the Organization, see the latter's website at www.un.org/law/chartercomm.
30. Kjell Skjelsbaek and Gunnar Fermann, 'The UN Secretary-General and the Mediation of International Disputes,' in Jacob Bercovitch, ed., *Resolving International Conflicts*, 83.
31. Benjamin Rivlin and Leon Gordenker, eds., *The Challenging Role of the UN Secretary-General: Making 'The Most Impossible Job in the World' Possible* (Westport, Conn.: Praeger, 1993).
32. Skjelsbaek and Fermann, 'The UN Secretary-General,' 75–106.
33. Ibid., 80.
34. Ibid., 82.

35. Ibid.
36. Cyrus R. Vance and David A. Hamburg, *Pathfinders for Peace: A Report to the UN Secretary-General on the Role of Special Representatives and Personal Envoys* (Washington, DC: Carnegie Commission on Preventing Deadly Conflict, 1997); and Connie Peck, 'Special Representatives of the Secretary-General,' in David M. Malone, ed., *The UN Security Council, 325–340.*
37. *2005 World Summit Outcome*, para. 76
38. Connie Peck, *Sustainable Peace: The Role of the UN and Regional Organizations in Preventing Conflict* (Lanham, Md.: Rowman & Littlefield, 1998), 76–80; Colter Paulson, 'Compliance With Final Judgements of The International Court of Justice since 1987,' *The American Journal of International Law* 98, no. 3 (July 2004): 434–461; James A. R. Nafziger, 'Political Dispute Resolution by the World Court, with Reference to United States Courts,' *Denver Journal of International Law and Policy* 26, no. 5 (1998): 775–786; and Keohane, Moravcisk, and Slaughter, 'Legalized Dispute Resolution,' 457–488.
39. Pierre-Marie Dupuy, 'The Danger of Fragmentation or Unification of the International Legal System and the International Court of Justice,' *New York University Journal of International Law and Politics* 31, no. 4 (1999): 791–807; see also Keohane, Moravcisk, and Slaughter, 'Legalized Dispute Resolution.'
40. Colter Paulson, 'Compliance With Final Judgements of The International Court of Justice since 1987,' *The American Journal of International Law* 98, no. 3 (2004): 436–437.
41. *Prevention of Armed Conflict: Report of the Secretary-General*, opening line of the executive summary.
42. Ibid., executive summary, 2.
43. See, e.g., Carnegie Commission on the Prevention of Deadly Conflict, *Preventing Deadly Conflict, Final Report* (Washington, DC: Carnegie Commission on Preventing Deadly Conflict, 1997), and a host of research monographs and books resulting from this multi-year effort to place 'prevention' on the map, www.wilsoncenter.org.
44. Gareth Evans, *Cooperation for Peace: The Global Agenda for the 1990s and Beyond* (St. Leonards, Australia: Allen & Unwin, 1993).
45. International Commission on Intervention and State Sovereignty, *The Responsibility to Protect* (Ottawa: International Development Research Centre, 2001).
46. Michael Ignatieff, 'Nation-Building Lite,' *New York Times Magazine*, 28 July 2002, 26–31, 54–56.
47. *Interim Report of the Secretary-General on the Prevention of Armed Conflict*, UN document A/58/365-S/2003/888, 12 September 2003.
48. See Stephen John Stedman, 'Alchemy for a New World Order: Overselling "Preventive Diplomacy",' *Foreign Affairs* 74, no. 3 (1995): 14–20; and Thomas G. Weiss, 'The UN's Prevention Pipe-dream,' *Berkeley Journal of International Law* 14, no. 2 (1996): 423–437.
49. Peck, *Sustainable Peace*, 68–71.
50. High-level Panel on Threats, Challenges and Change, *A More Secure World: Our Shared Responsibility*, UN document A/59/565, 2 December 2004; and Kofi Annan, *In Larger Freedom: Towards Development, Security and Human Rights for All: Report of the Secretary-General*, UN document A/59/2005, 21 March 2005.
51. *Interim Report of the Secretary-General on the Prevention of Armed Conflict*, Part one, II, A, para. 17, 9.
52. Ibid., para. 20, 9.
53. *Prevention of Armed Conflict: Report of the Secretary-General*, executive summary.
54. Ibid., executive summary, para. 8.

55. Barnett R. Rubin, ed., *Cases and Strategies for Preventive Action*, Preventive Action Reports, vol. 2 (New York: The Century Foundation Press, 1998); Barnett R. Rubin, *Blood on the Doorstep: The Politics of Preventive Action* (New York: The Century Foundation Press, 2002); and Anne-Marie Gardner, 'Diagnosing Conflict: What Do We Know,' and Michael Lund, 'From Lessons to Action,' in *From Reaction to Conflict Prevention: Opportunities for the UN System*, ed. Fen Osler Hampson and David M. Malone (Boulder, Colo.: Lynne Rienner, 2002), 15–40 and 159–184.

56. Rubin, *Blood on the Doorstep*, quotes 168–175, partly quoted from UNDP, Emergency Response Division, *Governance and Conflict Prevention: Proceedings of Expert Group Meeting*, 7–8 March 2000.

57. *Prevention of Armed Conflict: Report of the Secretary-General*, Part III, A, Recommendation I, 11.

58. Ibid., Part III, D, Recommendation 5, 14.

59. UN, Department of Political Affairs, Introduction, www.un.org/Depts/dpa/intro.html.

60. *Interim report of the Secretary-General on the prevention of armed conflict*, UN document A/58/365-S/2003/888, 12 September 2003, para. 14, 5.

61. International Court of Justice, *Legal Consequences of the Construction of a Wall in the Occupied Palestinian Territories*, advisory opinion, 9 July 2004; *Advisory opinion of the International Court of Justice on the Legal Consequences of the Construction of a Wall in the Occupied Palestinian Territory, including in and around East Jerusalem*, General Assembly resolution 10/15, UN document A/RES/ES-10/15, 20 July 2004; and Israeli High Court of Justice, *International Legality of the Security Fence and Sections near Alfei Menashe*, Ruling Docket HCJ 7957/04, 15 September 2005.

62. Edward C. Luck, 'Prevention: Theory and Practice,' in *From Reaction to Conflict Prevention: Opportunities for the UN System*, ed. Fen Osler Hampson and David M. Malone (Boulder, Colo.: Lynne Rienner, 2002); and Chandra Lekha Sriram and Karin Wermester, eds., *From Promise to Practice: Strengthening UN Capacities for the Prevention of Violent Conflict* (Boulder, Colo.: Lynne Rienner, 2003).

63. See *Progress report on the prevention of armed conflict*, Report of the Secretary-General, UN document A/60/891, 18 July 2006. Here the Secretary-General adds systemic prevention, referring to illicit trade in resources, weapons, drugs, etc., and also global factors like HIV/AIDS and the environment, but without the radical meaning that Rubin and Lund intend here.

64. Rubin, *Blood on the Doorstep*, 151

65. Michael Lund, 'From Lessons to Action,' in Hampson and Malone, eds., *From Reaction to Conflict Prevention*, 159–183 (164).

66. World Bank, *World Development Report 2006: Equity and Development* (New York: Oxford University Press, 2005).

67. Rubin, *Blood on the Doorstep*, 151.

C H A P T E R   1 9

PEACEKEEPING OPERATIONS

MICHAEL W. DOYLE

NICHOLAS SAMBANIS

TODAY peacekeeping is the multidimensional management of a complex peace operation, usually in a post-civil war context, designed to provide interim security and assist parties to make those institutional, material, and ideational transformations that are essential to make a peace sustainable. It was not always this way. The record of UN peacekeeping began during the Cold War with a limited activity—monitoring the performance of a truce by two hostile parties.

This chapter traces the evolution of peacekeeping doctrine from 'first generation' monitoring through 'second' and 'third' generation multidimensional management and enforcement. Most of the chapter is devoted to an analysis of the effectiveness of contemporary UN peacekeeping as a comprehensive strategy to achieve sustainable peace. This is the perspective embodied in the UN's contemporary doctrine in the 2000 *Report of the Panel on United Nations Peace Operations* (known as the Brahimi report) and the 2001 *No Exit without Strategy* report, building upon Secretary-General Boutros-Ghali's 1992 report, *An Agenda for Peace*, and the 1995 *Supplement*.

'Sustainable peace' is the best measure of successful peacekeeping. Successful and unsuccessful efforts to resolve civil wars are influenced by three key variables that characterize the environment of the postwar civil peace: the degree of hostility of the factions, the extent of local capacities remaining after the war, and the amount of

This chapter draws on Michael W. Doyle and Nicholas Sambanis, *Making War and Building Peace: United Nations Peace Operations* (Princeton, NJ: Princeton University Press, 2006). The authors are grateful to Olena Jennings and Daniel Noble for editorial suggestions.

international assistance provided. Together, these factors constitute the interdependent logic of a 'peacebuilding triangle': the deeper the hostility, the more damaged local capacities, and the more international assistance necessary to succeed in establishing a stable peace.

GENERATIONS OF UN PEACE OPERATIONS

With the end of the Cold War in the early 1990s, the UN's agenda for peace and security rapidly expanded. At the request of the Security Council Summit of January 1992, Secretary-General Boutros Boutros-Ghali prepared the conceptual foundations of an ambitious UN role in peace and security in his seminal report, *An Agenda for Peace*.[1] In addition to preventive diplomacy designed to head off conflicts before they became violent, the Secretary-General outlined the four interconnected roles that he hoped the UN would play in the fast changing context of post-Cold War international politics.

- peace-enforcement: authorized to act with or without the consent of the parties in order to ensure compliance with a cease-fire mandated by the Security Council acting under the authority of Chapter VII of the Charter, these military forces are composed of heavily armed, national forces operating under the direction of the Secretary-General.
- peacemaking: designed 'to bring hostile parties to agreement' through peaceful means such as those found in Chapter VI. Drawing upon judicial settlement, mediation and other forms of negotiation, UN peacemaking initiatives would seek to persuade parties to arrive at a peaceful settlement of their differences.
- peacekeeping: established to deploy a 'United Nations presence in the field, hitherto with the consent of all the parties concerned,' as a confidence-building measure to monitor a truce between the parties while diplomats strive to negotiate a comprehensive peace or officials seek to implement an agreed peace.
- post-conflict reconstruction:[2] organized to foster economic and social cooperation with the purpose of building confidence among previously warring parties, developing the social, political and economic infrastructure to prevent future violence, and laying the foundations for a durable peace.

An Agenda for Peace is the culmination of an evolution of UN doctrine and an adjustment of the instruments used to maintain the peace since the organization was formed in 1945. It combines in a radical way instruments of war-like enforcement and peace-like negotiation that were once kept separate and that evolved separately. A unique vocabulary separates distinct strategies that fit within the generic UN doctrine of building peace. These strategies, evolving over time, have encompassed three generational paradigms of peacekeeping.[3] They include not only the early activities identified in Chapter VI (or so-called Chapter VI and a half)[4] *first generation* peacekeeping—which calls for the interposition of a force after a truce has been reached. They also encompass a far more ambitious group of *second generation* operations that rely on the consent of parties, but engage in activities once thought to be only within the scope of domestic jurisdiction, such as elections monitoring. Finally, they include an even more ambitious group of *third generation* operations that operate with Chapter VII mandates and without a comprehensive agreement reflecting the parties' acquiescence. In today's circumstances, these operations involve less interstate conflict and more factions in domestic civil wars, not all of whom are clearly identifiable and few of whom are stable negotiating parties. Current peace operations thus intrude into aspects of domestic sovereignty once thought to be beyond the purview of UN activity.

Indeed, the Charter emanated from World War II and can be seen as having been designed for interstate wars (e.g., Article 39's threats to 'international' peace); appropriately so, since from 1900 to 1941, 80 percent of all wars were interstate and fought by professional armies. But from 1945 to 1976, 85 percent of all wars were on the territory of one state and internally oriented—of course with proxies.[5]

Traditional peace operations, or first generation peacekeeping, were designed to respond to interstate crises by stationing unarmed or lightly armed UN forces between hostile parties to monitor a truce, troop withdrawal, or buffer zone while political negotiations went forward.[6] As the late F. T. Liu, an eminent UN peacekeeping official, noted: monitoring, consent, neutrality, nonuse of force, and unarmed peacekeeping—the principles and practices of first generation peacekeeping—constituted a stable and interdependent combination. These key principles were articulated by Secretary-General Dag Hammarskjöld and former Canadian prime minister Lester Pearson in conjunction with the creation of the first peacekeeping operation (PKO), the UN Emergency Force (UNEF) in the Sinai, which was sent to separate Israel and Egypt following the Franco–British–Israeli intervention in Suez in 1956.[7] The principle of neutrality referred to the national origin of UN troops and precluded the use of troops from the permanent five members of the Security Council (P-5) in order to quiet fears of superpower intervention. Impartiality implied that the UN would not take sides in the dispute and was a precondition for acquiring the consent of all the parties. Enjoying the consent of all factions in turn made it easier for monitors or peacekeepers not to have to use force except in self-defense.[8] Lastly, the Secretary-General exercised control of the force, and the Security Council authorized it (or, rarely, the General Assembly, under the auspices of the 'Uniting for Peace Resolution'[9]).

Impartiality and neutrality are frequently used interchangeably. Scholars and practitioners often speak of peacekeepers as 'neutral,' 'disinterested,' 'impartial,' or 'unbiased', and they tend to mistake the need for impartiality with a policy of 'strict neutrality' and a disposition of passivity. We define neutrality as a synonym for noninterference with respect to peacekeeping outcomes and impartiality as equal enforcement of unbiased rules. Good cops act impartially but not neutrally when they stop one individual from victimizing another. We argue that it is as important for peacekeepers to be *impartial* concerning, for example, which party in a freely conducted democratic election wins as it is for them to be *non-neutral* (i.e., not passive) with respect to violations of the peace and obstructions to their ability to implement their mandate.

This is closely related to the interpretation of the fourth principle of peacekeeping—the nonuse of force. Peacekeeping uses soldiers not to win wars, but rather to preserve the peace. But peacekeepers must also protect their right to discharge their functions in accordance with the spirit of the parties' consent as provided at the outset of the operation. Raising the costs of non-cooperation for the parties must, on occasion, allow the use of force in defense of the mandate. The limited use of force to protect a mandate authorized by a peace treaty or to enforce an agreed-upon cease-fire (as happened in Cyprus in 1974 or Namibia in 1989) does not equate peacekeeping with peace enforcement (that attempts to impose an overall settlement), but it does generate concerns with mission creep if the need to use force is extensive.

During the Cold War, the UN record included much success in interstate conflicts (little in intrastate), and in material and territorial settlement (little in value or identity conflicts).[10] The success of traditional peacekeeping was also dependent on successful *peacemaking*: a strategy designed 'to bring hostile parties to agreement' through peaceful means such as those found in Chapter VI of the UN Charter. Drawing upon judicial settlement, mediation, and other forms of negotiation, UN peacemaking initiatives would seek to persuade parties to arrive at a peaceful settlement of their differences. Traditional PKOs referred to a UN presence in the field, with the consent of all the parties concerned, as a confidence-building measure to monitor a truce while diplomats negotiated a comprehensive peace. Peacekeeping was therefore designed as an interim arrangement where there was no formal determination of aggression, and was frequently to monitor a truce, establish and police a buffer zone, and assist the negotiation of a peace. Monitoring or observer missions had several of the same objectives as traditional PKOs, though they were typically less well-armed (or unarmed) and focused on monitoring and reporting to the Security Council and the Secretary-General.

Both monitoring operations and traditional peacekeeping provided transparency—an impartial assurance that the other party was not violating the truce—and were supposed to raise the costs of defecting from an agreement by the threat of exposure and the potential (albeit unlikely) resistance of the peacekeeping force. The international legitimacy of UN mandates increased the parties' benefits of cooperation with the peacekeepers. The price of first generation peacekeeping, as in the long Cyprus operation, was sometimes paid in conflicts delayed rather than resolved. Today these monitoring activities continue to play an important role in the Golan Heights between Israel and Syria and, until recently, on the border between Kuwait and Iraq.

Monitoring and traditional PKOs were strictly bound by the principle of consent. Consent derives from the parties' 'perceptions of the peacekeepers' impartiality and moral authority.'[11] It reduces the risk to peacekeepers and preserves the sovereignty of the host state. Eroding consent can significantly diminish peacekeepers' ability to discharge their mandate, so peacekeepers have an incentive to enhance the parties' consent. Since eroding consent could turn PKOs into multibillion dollar 'obsolescing investments' that are easy hostages to insincere parties, it follows that the UN should develop strategies to enhance consent.[12] This flexibility is more easily provided in second generation, multidimensional operations that involve the implementation of complex, multidimensional peace agreements designed to build the foundations of a self-sustaining peace. These have been utilized primarily in post-civil war situations. In addition to the traditional military functions, peacekeepers are often engaged in various police and civilian tasks, the goal of which is a long-term settlement of the underlying conflict. These operations are based on consent of the parties, but the nature of consent and purposes for which it is granted are qualitatively different from traditional peacekeeping.

Beyond monitoring and traditional peacekeeping, the key strategy was to foster economic and social cooperation with the purpose of building confidence among previously warring parties; develop the social, political, and economic infrastructure to prevent future violence; and lay the foundations for a durable peace. Multidimensional peacekeeping is aimed at capacities-expansion (e.g., economic reconstruction) and institutional transformation (e.g., reform of the police, army, and judicial system, elections, civil society rebuilding). In these operations, the UN is typically involved in implementing peace agreements that go to the roots of the conflict, helping to build long-term foundations for stable, legitimate government. As Boutros-Ghali observed in *An Agenda for Peace*, 'peace-making and peace-keeping operations, to be truly successful, must come to include comprehensive efforts to identify and support structures which will tend to consolidate peace... [T]hese may include disarming the previously warring parties and the restoration of order, the custody and possible destruction of weapons, repatriating refugees, advisory and training support for security personnel, monitoring elections, advancing efforts to protect human rights, reforming or strengthening governmental institutions and promoting formal and informal processes of political participation.'[13]

The UN has a commendable record of success, ranging from mixed to transformative, in second generation, multidimensional peace operations as diverse as those in Namibia (UNTAG), El Salvador (ONUSAL), Cambodia (UNTAC), Mozambique (ONUMOZ), and Eastern Slavonia (UNTAES).[14] The UN's role in helping settle those conflicts has been four-fold: it served as a peacemaker facilitating a peace treaty among the parties; as a peacekeeper monitoring the cantonment and demobilization of military forces, resettling refugees, and supervising transitional civilian authorities; as a peacebuilder monitoring and in some cases organizing the implementation of human rights, national democratic elections, and economic rehabilitation; and in a very limited way as a peace enforcer when the agreements came unstuck.

In Boutros-Ghali's lexicon, 'peace-enforcing'—effectively war-making—missions are third generation operations, which extend from low-level military operations to protect the delivery of humanitarian assistance to the enforcement of cease-fires and, when necessary, authoritative assistance in the rebuilding of so-called failed states. Like Chapter VII enforcement action to roll back aggression in Korea in 1950 and against Iraq in the Gulf War, the defining characteristic of third generation

Table 19.1 Principal UN peacekeeping missions, 1947–2006

Mission	Date	Peak Force Size	Function
United Nations Special Committee on the Balkans (UNSCOB)	1947–52	36	Monitor violations of Greek border
United Nations Commission for Indonesia (UNCI)	1947–51	63	Observe Indonesian cease-fire and Dutch troop withdrawal
United Nations Truce Supervision Organization (UNTSO)	1948–present	572	Report on Arab–Israeli cease-fire and armistice violations
United Nations Military Observer Group in India and Pakistan (UNMOGIP)	1949–present	102	Observe Kashmir cease-fire
United Nations Emergency Force (UNEF I)	1956–67	6,073	Observe, supervise troop withdrawal and provide buffer between Israeli and Egyptian forces
United Nations Observer Group in Lebanon (UNOGIL)	1958	591	Check on clandestine aid from Syria to Lebanon rebels
United Nations Operation in the Congo (ONUC)	1960–64	19,828	Maintain order in the Congo, expel foreign forces, prevent secession and outside intervention
United Nations Security Force in West New Guinea (UNSF)	1962–63	1,576	Maintain order during transfer of authority in New Guinea from the Netherlands and Indonesia
United Nations Yemen Observation Mission (UNYOM)	1963–64	189	Supervise military disengagement in Yemen
United Nations Peacekeeping Force in Cyprus (UNFICYP)	1964–present	6,411	Prevent internal conflict in Cyprus, avert outside intervention
Mission of the Representative of the Secretary-General in the Dominican Republic (DOMREP)	1965–66	2	Report cease-fire between domestic factions
United Nations India–Pakistan Observation Mission (UNIPOM)	1965–66	96	Observe India–Pakistan border
United Nations Emergency Force (UNEF II)	1973–79	6,973	Supervise cease-fire and troop disengagement, control buffer zone between Egypt and Israel
United Nations Disengagement Observer Force (UNDOF)	1974–present	1,450	Patrol Syria–Israel border
United Nations Interim Force in Lebanon (UNIFIL)	1978–present	7,000	Supervise Israeli troop withdrawal, maintain order, help restore authority of Lebanese government

United Nations Good Offices Mission in Afghanistan and Pakistan (UNGOMAP)	1988–90	50	Monitor Geneva Accords on Afghanistan and supervise Soviet withdrawal
United Nations Iran–Iraq Military Observer Group (UNIIMOG)	1988–91	399	Supervise cease-fire and mutual withdrawal of forces by Iran and Iraq
United Nations Angola Verification Mission (UNAVEM I)	1989–91	70	Verify withdrawal of Cuban troops from Angola
United Nations Transition Assistance Group (UNTAG)	1989–90	4,493	Assist Namibia's transition to independence, ensure free and fair elections
United Nations Observer Mission for the Verification of Elections in Nicaragua (ONUVEN)	1989–90	120	Monitor Nicaraguan elections
United Nations Observer Group in Central America (ONUCA)	1989–92	1,098	Verify compliance by Costa Rica, El Salvador, Guatemala, Honduras, and Nicaragua with agreement to disarm and neutralize irregular forces in the area
United Nations Observer Mission for the Verification of Elections in Haiti (ONUVEH)	1990–91	260	Observe elections in Haiti
United Nations Iraq–Kuwait Observation Mission (UNIKOM)	1991–2003[a]	1,440	Monitor demilitarized zone between Kuwait and Iraq. Removed with the occupation of Iraq by an American-led coalition. (Small observer group remains, but technically nonfunctioning and awaiting Security Council action)
United Nations Angola Verification Mission (UNAVEM II)	1991–95	476	Verify compliance with Peace Accord to end civil strife in Angola
United Nations Observer Mission in El Salvador (ONUSAL)	1991–95	1,003	Monitor cease-fire and human rights agreements in El Salvador's civil war
United Nations Mission for the Referendum in Western Sahara (MINURSO)	1991–present	375	Conduct referendum in Western Sahara on independence or union with Morocco
United Nations Advance Mission in Cambodia (UNAMIC)	1991–92	380	Assist Cambodian factions to keep cease-fire agreement
United Nations Protection Force (UNPROFOR)	1992–95	21,980	Encourage cease-fire in Croatia and Bosnia-Herzegovina, protect relief programs

(Continued)

Table 19.1 (*Continued*)

Mission	Date	Peak Force Size	Function
United Nations Transitional Authority in Cambodia (UNTAC)	1992–93	19,500	Demobilize armed forces of Cambodian factions, supervise interim government, conduct free elections
United Nations Operation in Somalia (UNOSOM I)	1992–93	550	Monitor cease-fire between Somali parties, protect shipments of relief supplies
United Nations Operation in Mozambique (ONUMOZ)	1992–94	7,500	Supervise internal peace accord in Mozambique, disarm combatants, establish a non-partisan army, hold national elections, conduct humanitarian program
United Nations Observer Mission in Georgia (UNOMIG)	1993–present	120	Verify cease-fire agreement with Abkhazia, observe CIS peacekeeping force
United Nations Observer Mission Uganda–Rwanda (UNOMUR)	1993–94	100	Observer mission in Uganda–Rwanda, monitor arms shipments
United Nations Operation in Somalia (UNOSOM II)	1993–95		UN mission in Somalia, peacemaking operations
United Nations Assistance Mission for Rwanda (UNAMIR)	1993–96	5,500	Stop the massacre of the defenseless population of Rwanda, assist refugees, report atrocities
United Nations Mission in Haiti (UNMIH)	1993–96	900	Mission in Haiti, pacification and monitor elections
United Nations Observer Mission in Liberia (UNOMIL)	1993–97	91	Observer group in Liberia monitor OAU peacekeeping
United Nations Aouzou Strip Observer Group (UNASOG)	1994	25	Observer group in Aouzou Strip, Libya–Chad border
United Nations Mission of Observers in Tajikistan (UNMOT)	1994–2000	24	Investigate cease-fire violations and work with OSCE and CIS missions in Tajikistan
United Nations Mission in Bosnia and Herzegovina (UNMIBH)	1995–2002	1,584	Monitor law enforcement in Bosnia and Herzegovina
United Nations Preventive Deployment Force (UNPREDEP)	1995–99	1,150	Preventive deployment force in Former Yugoslav Republic of Macedonia
United Nations Confidence Restoration Operation (UNCRO)	1995–96	20	Confidence restoration in Croatia
United Nations Angola Verification Mission (UNAVEM III)	1995–97	5,560	Angola verification of the Peace Accords (1991),

			the Lusaka Protocol (1994), and relevant Security Council resolutions
United Nations Mission of Observers in Prevlaka (UNMOP)	1996–2002	28	Monitor demilitarization in Prevlaka Peninsula, Croatia
United Nations Transitional Authority for Eastern Slavonia, Baranja and Western Sirmium (UNTAES)	1996–98	5,257	Facilitate demilitarization in Eastern Slavonia (Croatia)
United Nations Support Mission in Haiti (UNSMIH)	1996–97	1,549	Support Mission in Haiti
United Nations Transition Mission in Haiti (UNTMIH)	1997	300	Transition Mission in Haiti
United Nations Verification Mission in Guatemala (MINUGUA)	1997	155	Verification Mission in Guatemala
United Nations Civilian Police Mission in Haiti (MIPONUH)	1997–2000	290	Civilian Police Mission in Haiti
UN Observer Mission in Angola (MONUA)	1997–99	5,560[b]	Observer Mission in Angola and a follow-on to UNAVEM III
United Nations Mission in the Central African Republic (MINURCA)	1998–2000	1,350	Help maintain and enhance security and stability in the Central African Republic
United Nations Mission in Sierra Leone (UNAMSIL)	1999–2005	109	To observe and report to the Security Council on military conditions in Sierra Leone
United Nations Organization Mission in the Democratic Republic of the Congo (MONUC)	1999–present	5,537	Monitor cease-fire agreement, provide humanitarian assistance to the Democratic Rep. of the Congo
United Nations Interim Administration Mission in Kosovo (UNMIK)	1999–present	40,000 (KFOR)	Combines effort in pacification of Kosovo with KFOR/NATO forces, essentially humanitarian assistance
United Nations Mission in Ethiopia and Eritrea (UNMEE)	2000–present	4,300	Monitor cessation of hostilities
United Nations Assistance Mission in Afghanistan (UNAMA)	2002–present[c]	450	Not technically a peacekeeping mission, works with International Security Assistance Force, provides humanitarian aid
United Nations Mission of Support in East Timor (UNMISET) Succeeded by UNMIT in 2006	2002–present	5,000	Transitional security for the new Timor-Leste government
United Nations Mission in Côte d'Ivoire (MINUCI) Replaced by UNOCI in 2004	2003–present	8,037	Oversee implementation of Linas-Marcoussis Agreeement with ECOWAS and French troops

(Continued)

Table 19.1 (*Continued*)

Mission	Date	Peak Force Size	Function
United Nations Mission in Liberia (UNMIL)	2003–present	15,000	Oversee implementation of the cease-fire and peace agreement, provide police training and assist in formation of a new restructured military
United Nations Stabilization Mission in Haiti (MINUSTA)	2004–present	6,684	Support the Transitional Government
United Nations Operation in Burundi (ONUB)	2004–2006	1,731	Support the implementation of the Arusha Agreement
United Nations Mission in the Sudan (UNMIS)	2005–present	9,326	Support implementation of the Comprehensive Peace Agreement

Source: Lawrence Ziring, Robert Riggs, and Jack Plano, *The United Nations* (Belmont, Calif.: Wadsworth, 2005), 216–219; United Nations Peacekeeping Operations, *Police, Troops and Military Observers—Contributors by Mission and Country*, UN Peacekeeping home page, December 2006; Center for International Relations, *Current UN Peace-Keeping Operations*, Zurich, Switzerland, PKO webmaster, Jan. 1998.

[a] Still in force by UN records.
[b] The force identified with UNAVEM III is the same force operating under MONUA.
[c] Not judged a UN peacekeeping force.

operations is the lack of consent by one or more of the parties to some or all of the UN mandate.[15] These operations have been of three types. In the first, international forces attempt to impose order without significant local consent, in the absence of a comprehensive peace agreement, and must, in effect, conquer the warring factions (as was attempted in Somalia). In the second, international forces do not have unanimous consent and choose to impose distinct arrangements on parties in the midst of an ongoing war (e.g., no-fly zones or humanitarian corridors of relief). In the third, international forces exercise force to implement the terms of a comprehensive peace agreement from which one or more of the parties has chosen to defect.

Enforcement operations draw upon the authority of Charter Article 42, which permits the Security Council to 'take such action by air, sea, or land forces as may be necessary to maintain or restore international peace and security'; Article 25 under which member states 'agree to accept and carry out the decisions of the Security Council'; and Article 43 in which they agree to 'make available to the Security Council, on its call . . . armed forces, assistance and facilities.'

Insightful doctrine for these peace-enforcing operations appeared just as Somalia and Bosnia exposed their practical limitations. Recent studies have thoughtfully mapped out the logic of the strategic terrain between traditional peacekeeping and enforcement action. Militarily, these operations seek to deter, dissuade, and deny.[16] By precluding an outcome based on the use of force by the parties, the UN instead uses collective force (if necessary) to persuade the parties to settle the conflict by negotiation. In the former

Yugoslavia, for example, the world organization following this strategy could have established strong points to deter attacks on key humanitarian corridors. (It actually did, but the Serbs bypassed them.) Or it could threaten air strikes, as was done successfully around Sarajevo in February 1994, to dissuade a continuation of the Serb shelling of the city. Or, it could have denied (but did not) the Serb forces their attack on Dubrovnik in 1992 by counter-shelling from the sea or bombing from the air the batteries in the hills above the city. Forcing a peace depends on achieving a complicated preponderance in which the forces (UN and local) supporting a settlement acceptable to the international community hold both a military predominance and a predominance of popular support, which together permit them to impose a peace on recalcitrant local military forces and their popular supporters.

Countries provide troops to UN peace operations in various ways. Troop-contributing countries negotiate in detail the terms of the participation of their forces under UN command and thus with the Secretary-General (as in El Salvador or Cambodia); with a delegated regional organization as authorized in Chapter VIII; or with the leader of a multinational 'coalition of the willing' authorized under Chapter VII (as was the case with US leadership of Unified Task Force in Somalia). Many operations draw on a combination of authorizations: peace treaties among factions, backed-up or supplemented by other measures (such as arms embargoes, no-fly zones) authorized under Chapter VII, as in the various UN Protection Force (UNPROFOR) and Implementation Force (IFOR) operations.[17] And, named in honor of its sponsors, 'Chinese Chapter VII' (employed to authorize the use of force for the UN Transitional Authority in Eastern Slavonia (UNTAES)) has emerged as a new way to signal firm intent to enforce a consent-based operation. In essence, however, Chinese Chapter VII reaffirms the 'Katanga Rule' of the UN Operation in the Congo (ONUC): the traditional principle that force can be used in self-defense both of peacekeeping troops and of the mission (mobility of the force).

The result of these three 'generations' operating together in the post-Cold War world was an unprecedented expansion of the UN's role in the protection of world order and in the promotion of basic human rights in countries that until recently had been torn by costly civil wars. Between 1987 and 1994, the Security Council quadrupled the number of resolutions it issued, tripled the peacekeeping operations it authorized, and multiplied by seven the number of economic sanctions it imposed per year. Military forces deployed in peacekeeping operations increased from fewer than 10,000 to more than 70,000. The annual peacekeeping budget skyrocketed correspondingly from $230 million to $3.6 billion in the same period, thus reaching to about three times the UN's regular operating budget of $1.2 billion.[18] In the process, self-determination and sovereignty were enhanced, and a modicum of peace, rehabilitation, and sustained self-determination was introduced in Namibia, Cambodia, El Salvador, Mozambique, and Eastern Slavonia. Tens—perhaps, even hundreds—of thousands of lives were saved in Somalia and the former Yugoslavia. But in 1993 and 1994, the more ambitious elements of 'third generation' peace enforcement exhibited many of the problems interventionist and imperial strategies have faced in the past, and encountered fresh problems peculiar to the UN's global character. Secretary-General Boutros Boutros-Ghali then famously called for a retrenchment of an over-extended UN commitment to peacekeeping in his *Supplement to an Agenda for Peace* report of January 1995.

The debacles in Somalia and Bosnia forced a radical rethinking of when and where the UN should get involved. Disingenuously, US President Bill Clinton told the General Assembly that it needed to learn when to say 'no.' Many came to believe that the UN was not well-suited to mounting effective peace operations—no more suited to make peace than the lobbyists who represented a trade group of hospitals would be to conduct surgery.[19] Others thought that such operations should be delegated to regional organizations, especially the North Atlantic Treaty Organization (NATO). This last group began calling for a 'fourth generation' of delegated peacekeeping.[20]

The lessons of the 1990s were embodied in an eloquent plea for strategic peace-keeping made in the *Report of the Panel on United Nations Peace Operations*[21] chaired by the experienced UN peacekeeper and former Algerian foreign minister, Lakhdar Brahimi. In reaction to a perceived passivity in traditional peacekeeping in the face of armed challenges, the panel advocated 'robust doctrines' and 'realistic mandates' together with improved capacities for headquarters management and rapid deployment. In the *No Exit without Strategy* report, the Secretary-General responded to a request from the Security Council for a comprehensive strategy to achieve a sustainable peace. The report drew on the Security Council's own deliberations to make a case for an ambitious, comprehensive, three-pronged strategy: 'consolidating internal and external security,' 'strengthening political institutions and good governance,' and 'promoting economic and social rehabilitation and transformation.'[22] The theme of both reports—the first operational, focusing on peacekeeping operations, and the second doctrinal, focusing on the role of the Security Council—was a plea for strategically matching missions to capabilities.

STRATEGIC PEACEKEEPING

What can political science literature tell us about how to plan for a sustainable peace? Is strategic peacekeeping in fact realizable? The peacekeepers' first concern in designing intervention strategies is to properly identify the type of conflict underlying a civil war. Political scientists have explored a wide range of theories about why and how parties enter into and resolve various kinds of conflicts. At the more abstract level, 'neoliberal' theories explore conflicts among rational actors over absolute goods valued for their own sakes. 'Neorealists' examine conflicts among rational actors that raise issues of security and relative gains, based on the assumption that relative power (dominance) alone provides security and that it is therefore the gains that truly matter. 'Constructivists' relax the assumption that perceived identities and interests are fixed and explore the circumstances in which conflicts and social relations more generally constitute and then reshape identities and interests.[23] We find aspects of each of these three factors in the peacekeeping record we examine. Factions and their leaders seek absolute advantages as well as relative advantages. Sometimes international actors assist the peace process by eliminating old actors (war criminals, factional armies), introducing new actors (domestic voters, political parties, international monitors, nongovernmental organizations) or fostering changes of identity (reconciliation)—or by all three together. But a more informative analytic lens portrays the peace process through two classic game situations, *coordination* and *cooperation*, each of which incorporates neoliberal, neorealist, and constructivist dynamics.

Thus, to simplify, conflicts can be over coordination or cooperation, depending on the structure of the parties' preferences over possible outcomes of the negotiations. Each preference structure characterizes a specific type of conflict, and different intervention strategies are optimal for different conflict types. Some conflicts are mixed, reflecting elements of both, and conflicts do change over time, evolving from one to the other and, sometimes, back again.[24] Well-chosen strategies can maximize the available space for peace, whereas strategies that are poorly matched to the conflict at a particular time can reduce the space for peace.

Coordination problems have a payoff structure that gives the parties no incentives to violate agreements.[25] A classic example is driving on the right side of the road (or on the left in Great Britain or India). The best strategy to resolve coordination problems is information provision and improvement of the level of communication between the parties.[26] Communication gives the parties the ability to form common conjectures about the likely outcomes of their actions.[27] By contrast, cooperation problems create incentives to renege on agreements, particularly if the parties discount the benefits of long-term cooperation in favor of short-run gain. In one-shot games of cooperation (of which the prisoner's dilemma is a well-known example), the parties will try to trick their adversaries into cooperating while they renege on their promises. In the prisoner's dilemma, for example, two accomplices in police custody are offered a chance to 'rat' on their partner. The first to rat gets off and the 'sucker' receives a very heavy sentence. If neither rats, both receive light sentences (based on circumstantial evidence); and, if both rat, both receive sentences (but less than the sucker's penalty). Even though they would be better off trusting each other by keeping silent, the temptation to get off and the fear of being the sucker make cooperation extremely difficult. These structural differences between cooperation and coordination problems imply that different peacekeeping strategies should be used in each case.

Figure 19.1 suggests that different strategies are needed to resolve different types of problems. Transformative intervention strategies, such as multidimensional peacekeeping or enforcement with considerable international authority, are needed to resolve *cooperation* problems, whereas facilitative peacekeeping strategies, such as monitoring and traditional peacekeeping, are sufficient to resolve *coordination* problems. Facilitative peacekeeping has no enforcement or deterrence function. Transformative peacekeeping through multidimensional operations can increase the costs of non-cooperation for the parties and provide positive inducements by helping rebuild the country and restructure institutions so that they can support the peace.

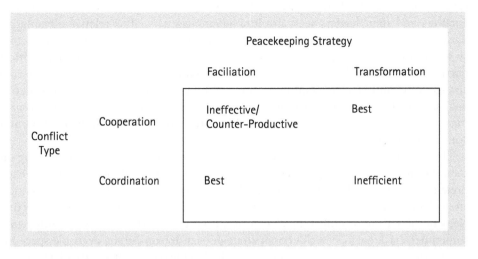

Fig. 19.1 Matching problem type and strategy type

Enforcement may be necessary to resolve the toughest cooperation problems.[28] Not all civil war transitions are plagued by cooperation problems. Some wars resemble coordination problems, whereas frequently we find both types of problems, in which case intervention strategies must be carefully combined or sequenced.

Can peacekeeping have an impact and how? The literature suggests that peace-keepers can change the costs and benefits of cooperation by virtue of the legitimacy of their UN mandate, which induces the parties to cooperate; by their ability to focus international attention on non-cooperative parties and condemn transgressions; by their monitoring of and reporting on the parties' compliance with agreements; and by their function as a trip-wire that would force aggressors to go through the UN troops to change the military status quo.[29]

Ultimate success, however, may depend less on changing incentives for existing parties within their preferences and more on transforming preferences—and even the parties themselves—and thus turning a cooperation problem into a coordination problem. In our book, we describe the institution-building aspects of peacekeeping as a revolutionary transformation in which voters and politicians replace soldiers and generals; armies become parties; war economies, peace economies. Reconciliation, when achieved, is a label for these changed preferences and capacities. To be sure, the difficulty of a trans-formative strategy cannot be overestimated. Most postwar societies look a great deal like they did prewar. But, for example, if those that have committed the worst war crimes can be prosecuted, locked up, and thus removed from power, the prospects of peace rise. The various factions can begin to individualize rather than collectivize their distrust and hostility and, at the minimum, the worst individuals are no longer in control.[30]

Therefore, even where enforcement is used at the outset, the peace must eventually become self-sustaining, and consent needs to be won if the peace enforcers are ever to exit with their work done. And consensual peace agreements can rapidly erode, forcing all the parties to adjust to the strategies of 'spoilers.' The success or lack of success of spoilers tends to be decisive in whether a sustainable peace follows.

How can the peacekeepers know which type of conflict they are facing? A first clue is the peace treaty. If a treaty has been signed that outlines a postwar settlement, then the parties' preferences have been revealed to some extent (though the fact that some peace treaties are quickly undermined also means that only by observing the parties' compliance with the treaty can we be more certain about their true preferences). Patterns of compliance with the treaty can help distinguish moderates from extremists. In other cases, such knowledge cannot be attained until the first (or several) encounters with the parties. Where a treaty is not in place, all parties can be assumed to be spoilers and strong peacekeeping must be used. Subsequent cooperation or conflict with peacekeepers can help distinguish those parties who respond to inducements from those who are committed to a strategy of war. This also means that UN missions must be flexible to adjust their mandate given observations of cooperation or conflict on the ground and based on the peacekeepers' changing assessments about the nature of the conflict.

A treaty is usually the outcome of a 'mutually hurting stalemate,' which is a necessary, but not sufficient, condition for successful peace.[31] Such a stalemate exists when the status quo is not the preferred option for any faction, while overturning the status quo through military action is unlikely to be successful. This condition pushes parties to the negotiating table, and their declared preferences for peace are more credible as a result of their inability to forcibly achieve a better outcome.[32]

However, the parties will not negotiate a settlement unless peace is likely to generate higher rewards than continued fighting. This condition becomes unattainable if 'spoilers' are present. Spoilers are leaders or parties whose vital interests are threatened by peace implementation.[33] These parties will undermine the agreement and reduce the expected utility of a negotiated settlement for all parties. In terms of our previous arguments, the presence of spoilers implies the 'payoff structure' of a prisoner's dilemma or an assurance game, as spoilers will not coordinate their strategies with moderates. Thus, if spoilers are present in a peace process, peacekeepers can only keep the peace if they can exercise some degree of enforcement by targeting the spoilers and preventing them from undermining the negotiations. The dynamics of spoiler problems deserve a closer look.

Spoiler problems were first systematically analyzed by Stephen Stedman, who identified three types—total, greedy, and limited spoiler—according to their strategies and likely impact on the peace implementation process. These are behavioral types, and Stedman defines them in terms of their preferences over the strategies they use to undermine the peace. However, all parties can act as total spoilers if conditions deteriorate markedly. But parties whose ultimate goals over the outcomes of the peace are more moderate will have incentives not to spoil the peace process if they can get a reasonable outcome. The difficulty facing the peacekeepers is to distinguish moderates from extremists, or total spoilers, when conditions are such as to encourage all parties to defect from agreements.

The principal gain of good UN peacekeeping will be to allow moderates—limited spoilers with specific stakes—and greedy opportunists to act like peacemakers in the peace process without fearing reprisals from total spoilers who are unalterably opposed to the peace settlement. Effective strategies must combine consent from those willing to coordinate and cooperate with coercive carrots and sticks directed at those who are not. We suggest that the record shows that, by strategically combining peacemaking, peacekeeping, post-conflict reconstruction, and peace enforcement, peace can be built from problematic and unpromising foundations.

A PEACEKEEPING TRIANGLE

International peacekeeping strategies should therefore be 'strategic' in the ordinary sense of that term, matching means to ends. Although a peacekeeping strategy must be designed to address a particular conflict, broad parameters that fit most conflicts can be identified. These strategies combine peacemaking, peacekeeping, post-conflict reconstruction, and (where needed) enforcement.

Effective transitional strategies must take into account levels of hostility and factional capacities, but whether they in fact do so depends on strategic design and international commitment. Designs for transitions incorporate a mix of legal and bureaucratic capacities that integrate in a variety of ways domestic and international commitments.

Important lessons can already be drawn from efforts to establish effective transitional authority.[34] First, a holistic approach is necessary to deal with the character of factional conflicts and civil wars. Successful exercises of authority require a coordinated approach that draws in elements of 'peacemaking' (negotiations), peacekeeping (monitoring), peacebuilding, reconstruction, and discrete acts of enforcement, when needed, to create a holistic strategy of reconciliation.[35]

Transitional strategies should first address the local causes of continuing conflict and, second, the local capacities for change. Effective transitional authority is the residual dimension that compensates for local deficiencies and the continuing hostility of the factions—the (net) specific degree of international commitment available to assist change. One can think of effective transitional authority as authority multiplied by resources multiplied by international institutional capacities.

Local root causes, domestic capacity, and effective transitional authority are three dimensions of a triangle, whose area is the effective capacity for building peace. This metaphor suggests that some quantum of positive support is needed along each dimension, but that the dimensions also substitute for each other—more of one substitutes for less of another (e.g., less deeply rooted causes of war substitute for weak local capacity or minor international commitment). In a world where each dimension is finite we can expect, first, that compromises will be necessary in order to achieve peacekeeping; second, that the international role must be designed to fit each case; and, third, that self-sustaining peace is not only the right aim—it is the practically necessary aim of building peace when the international community is not prepared to commit to long-term assistance.

Strategies should address the local sources of hostility; the local capacities for change; and the (net) specific degree of international commitment available to assist change. One can conceive of the three as the three dimensions of a triangle, whose area is the 'political space' needed for building peace (see Figure 19.2).

International peace operation mandates must take into account the characteristics of the factions and whether the parties are prepared to coordinate or must be persuaded or coerced into cooperation. These mandates operate not upon stable states but, instead, on unstable factions. These factions (to simplify) come in various dimensions of hostility. Hostility, in turn, is shaped by the number of factions, including the recognized state as one (if there is one). Numerous factions make it difficult for them to cooperate and engender suspicion. Two, few, or many factions complicate both coordination and cooperation. In addition, harm done—casualties and refugees generated—creates the resentment that makes jointly beneficial solutions to coordination and cooperation that much more difficult to envisage. The more hostile and numerous the factions, the more difficult the peace process will be and the more international assistance/authority will be needed if peace is to be established.[36]

In less hostile circumstances (with few factions, a hurting stalemate, or less harm done), international monitoring and facilitation might be sufficient to establish transparent trust and self-enforcing peace. Monitoring helps create transparency

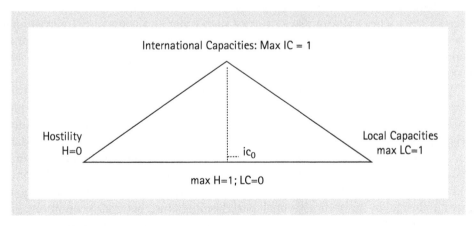

Fig. 19.2 The peacebuilding triangle

Note: The triangle is a metaphor for the peacebuilding space after civil war. Available space is determined by the interaction of the triangle's three sides: Local Capacities (LC), International Capacities (IC), and Hostility (H) level. The greater local and international capacities and the lower the hostility, the greater will be the space for peace. We assume a strictly positive level of IC, given the support and legitimacy offered sovereign states by international law and norms. This positive level of international support is denoted by the constant ic_0 which ensures that IC cannot be zero. All three variables, LC, IC, and H can be measured as indices, ranging from 0 to 1 (maximum).

among partners lacking trust but having compatible incentives favoring peace. Traditional peacekeeping assistance can also reduce tradeoffs (helping, for example, to fund and certify the cantonment, demobilization, and reintegration of former combatants). In these circumstances—with few players, some reconciliation, less damage—international coordination and assistance can be sufficient to overcome hostility and solve implementation problems. An international peacekeeping presence itself can deter defections from the peace treaty, because of the possible costs of violating international agreements and triggering further international involvement in an otherwise domestic conflict. International capacity-building—such as foreign aid, demobilization of military forces, institutional reform—will assist parties that favor the peace in meeting their commitments.

In more hostile circumstances, international enforcement can help solve commitment and cooperation problems by directly implementing or raising the costs of defection from peace agreements. International enforcement and long-term trusteeship will be required to overcome deep sources of distrust and powerful incentives to defect from agreed provisions of the peace. As in other conflict–cooperation situations such as prisoner's dilemma and mixed motive games,[37] the existence of deeply hostile or many factions, or factions that lack coherent leadership, complicate the problem of achieving self-enforcing cooperative peace. Instead, conscious direction and enforcement by an impartial international agent to guarantee the functions of effective sovereignty become necessary, and peacekeepers must include activities such as conducting a free and fair election, arresting war criminals, and policing and administering a collapsed state. The more difficult it is for the factions to cooperate, the greater the international authority and capacity the international peacekeepers must wield. In addition to large numbers of troops, extensive budgets for political reconstruction and substantial international authority need to be brought to bear because the parties are so unlikely to trust each other and cooperate. International mandates may need to run from monitoring to administration to executive authority and full sovereign trusteeship-like supervision if peace is going to be maintained and become eventually self-sustaining.

War-torn countries also vary in economic and social capacity. Some war-torn countries started out with considerable economic development (the former Yugoslavia) and retain levels of social capacity in an educated population. Others began poor and the war impoverished them further (Angola, Sudan, Cambodia). For both types of cases, reconstruction is vital; the more the social and economic devastation, the larger the multidimensional international role must become, whether consent-based multidimensional peacekeeping or non-consent enforcement followed by multidimensional peacekeeping. International economic relief and productive jobs are the first signs of peace that can persuade rival factions to truly disarm and take a chance on peaceful politics. Institutions must be rebuilt, including a unified army and police force and (even more challenging) a school system that can assist the reconciliation of future generations.[38] In countries with a low level of local capacities, competition over resources will be intense at the early stages of the peace process, which can further intensify the coordination and collaboration problems that the peacekeepers will be asked to resolve.

There thus should be a relation between the depth of hostility (harm and factions) and local capacities (institutional and economic collapse), on the one hand, and the extent of international assistance and effective authority, from monitoring to enforcing, needed to build peace, on the other. In a world where each dimension is finite, we can expect: first, that compromises will be necessary to achieve peacekeeping success; and, second, that the international role will be significant in general and will be successful when designed to fit the case. The extent of transitional authority that needs to be delegated to the international community will be a function of the level of postwar hostility and local capacities.

The relations among the three dimensions of the triangle are complicated. The availability and prospect of international assistance and the existence of extensive local capacities, for example, can, if poorly managed, both raise the gains from victory (spoils of war and rebuilding assistance) and reduce the costs of fighting (as the assistance serves to sustain the fighting). So, too, deep war-related hostilities can have dual effects. They increase rational incentives to end the conflict, but also make the peace harder to achieve.

We test our hypotheses about the positive impact of international capacities using an extensive data set for all peace processes after civil war from 1945 until the end of 1999. We identify 145 civil wars and estimate a statistical model that gives us the probability of 'participatory peace' success for conflicts that have just ended. Participatory peace implies an absence of war or lower-level armed conflict, undivided sovereignty, and a minimum degree of political participation. This model includes various measures of postwar hostility, local capacities, and international capacities. UN peace mandates are our key measure of international capacities. The model helps identify broad guidelines for peace strategies after civil war, given different levels of local capacities and hostility, as can be seen in the various parts of Figure 19.3.[39]

For simplicity, peace processes can be divided into difficult and easy cases. In a hypothetical difficult case, all the variables with a negative coefficient in our model (i.e., variables that reduce the probability of participatory peace success) would have high values (we set them at their 75th percentile) and all the variables with positive coefficients would have low values (we set them at their 25th percentile).[40] We can explore the impact of international capacities on the probability of success in hypothetical difficult and easy cases. Figures 19.3a and 19.3b represent two hypothetical difficult cases, whereas Figures 19.3c and 19.3d represent two hypothetical easy cases.

Figure 19.3a maps the probability of success in a difficult case across all levels of hostility (measured by the log of deaths and displacements) with and without a transformative UN operation and a treaty. The results are striking: a difficult case without a treaty or UN mission, even at the lowest level of hostility, has a very low likelihood of success, several times lower than with a transformative UN mission and a treaty. Peacekeeping does make a positive difference, and early intervention pays. But at very high levels of hostility, after massive civilian slaughter, the two probabilities decline, and the probability declines more rapidly in the case with a UN mission

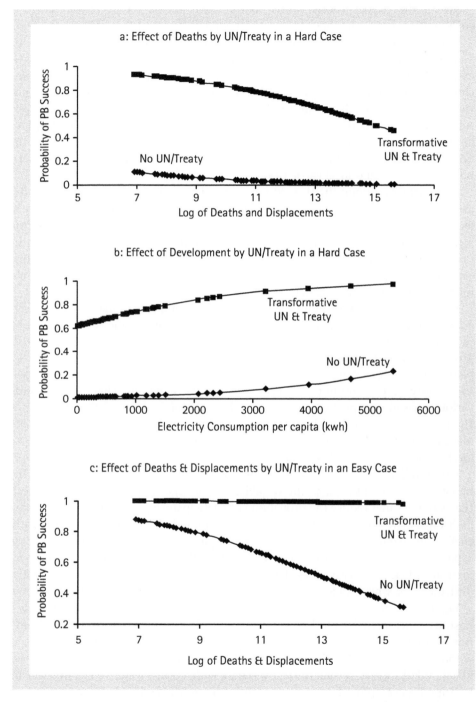

Fig. 19.3 International capacities in 'hard' and 'easy' peacebuilding ecologies

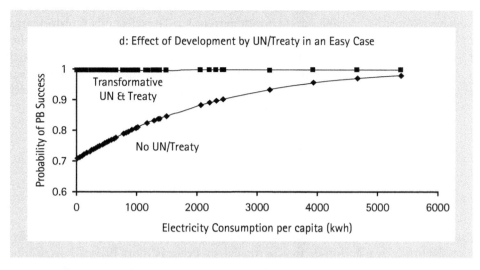

Fig. 19.3 (*Continued*)

and a treaty, although there is still a greater chance of success with a PKO and treaty. For example, a substantial multidimensional PKO made a positive difference in Cambodia, despite the massive killings and displacements that took place there; an equivalent effort might have been useful in Rwanda.

These results are almost the opposite of those for an easy case in Figure 19.3c. Here, the probability of success is quite high at low levels of hostility, even though it is still slightly higher if a transformative UN mission is deployed on the basis of a treaty among the parties. But the major effect of the treaty and the UN occurs at high levels of hostility, where they are crucial in maintaining the probability of success. Without a treaty and transformative UN mission, the likelihood of success drops substantially at extreme values of hostility. This appears, for example, to have mapped the situation in Bosnia during the late 1990s, one of the more developed countries among those that have had a civil war and suffered many casualties. Bosnia was only held together in peace by NATO, the UN, and a plethora of other international organizations.

Figure 19.3b maps the probability of successful participatory peace for a difficult case across all levels of electricity consumption per capita (which proxies the level of economic development, or local capacities) with and without UN mission and peace treaty (this is a difficult case because we have set hostility variables at their 75th percentile). We see that a treaty and UN mission are even more important for success since the slope of the curve with a transformative UN mission gets much steeper much sooner than the slope of the curve without a UN mission or treaty, and the resulting probability of success without a treaty and UN mission is very low even at extremely high levels of economic development.

By contrast, Figure 19.3d maps the probability of success across levels of local capacities (electricity consumption per capita) for a hypothetical easy case with and without a transformative UN mission and peace treaty (this is an easy case because we have set hostility variables at their 25th percentile). The effect of a transformative UN mission and a treaty is highest at very low levels of development, whereas neither a treaty nor a strong international presence seems necessary for success at very high levels of development. Developed countries that experience minor civil violence can put themselves back together. The UN is most needed elsewhere, in the less developed countries that have suffered extensive violence.

CONCLUSION

Our analysis identifies the critical determinants of the peacekeeping that results in a participatory peace and finds that participatory peace is more likely to occur after non-ethnic wars, in countries with relatively high development levels, and when UN peace operations and substantial financial assistance are available. Peaces without an element of participation—a simple end to the violence—are more dependent on muscular third-party intervention and on low-hostility levels rather than on the breadth of local capacities (although here, too, a rapidly improving economic situation will help create disincentives for renewed violence).

Peacemaking aimed at facilitating a negotiated settlement is potentially life-saving, since we find that treaties that stick and result in an end to the violence are highly correlated with success, at least in the short-term. The strategic logic underlying the peacekeeping triangle seems to work. Strategically designed peacekeeping combined with peace enforcement does make a difference. International capacities can foster peace by substituting for limited local capacities and alleviating factors that feed deep hostility. Such intervention improves the prospects for peace, but only if the peace operation is appropriately designed. Enforcement operations alone cannot create the conditions for a self-sustaining democratic peace. In the right circumstances, consent-based peacekeeping operations with civilian functions (multidimensional PKOs) are, by contrast, good not only in ending the violence, but also in assisting with the institutional and political reform that helps secure longer-term peace. Truly intractable conflicts, such as those in Bosnia, Kosovo, and East Timor, probably will require both enforcement and reconstruction activities, coordinated, and in the right order.

NOTES

1. Boutros Boutros-Ghali, *An Agenda for Peace: Preventive Diplomacy, Peacemaking and Peacekeeping: Report of the Secretary-General*, UN document A/47/277-S/24111, 17 June 1992. Quotes are from paras. 20–21 and 55–99.

2. The Secretary-General and the UN often refer to this as 'post-conflict peacebuilding.' To avoid confusion with the wider meaning of peacebuilding we use below, we refer to this as 'post-conflict reconstruction.'

3. The time-line of evolution has by no means been chronologically straightforward. One of the most extensive 'third generation' operations undertaken by the UN was ONUC in the then-Congo, from 1960 to 1964, which preceded the spate of 'second generation' operations that began with UNTAG in Namibia in 1989.

4. The 'six and a half' refers to the fact that peacekeeping per se is nowhere described in the Charter and thus falls between Chapter VI's peaceful settlement of disputes and Chapter VII's peace enforcement.

5. Ernst B. Haas, *The United Nations and Collective Management of International Conflict* (New York: United Nations Institute for Training and Research, 1986); and Henry Wiseman, 'The United Nations and International Peace,' in *The United Nations and the Management of International Peace and Security*, ed. UNITAR (Lancaster, UK: Martinus Nijhof, 1987), 219.

6. The first peacekeeping operation was the UN Emergency Force (UNEF) in Egypt, deployed in October 1956 to maintain a truce between the Egyptian army and Israel, England, and France during the Suez crisis. UNEF's experience helped define the four principles of traditional peacekeeping: consent, impartiality, neutrality, and use of force only in self-defense. The UN Treaty Supervision Organization (UNTSO) was deployed in 1948 in Palestine, but it was a limited observer mission.

7. United Nations, *The Blue Helmets: A Review of United Nations Peacekeeping*, 2nd edn. (New York: UN, 1990), 5–7; and Brian Urquhart, *A Life in Peace and War* (London: Weidenfeld and Nicolson, 1987), 133.

8. Traditional peacekeeping is a shorthand term that describes many but by no means all Cold War peacekeeping missions (the most notable exception being the Congo operation and possibly also the Cyprus operation, as we discuss later in our book). For cogent analyses of different types of peacekeeping, see Marrack Goulding, 'The Evolution of United Nations Peacekeeping,' *International Affairs* 69, no. 3 (1993): 451–464; F. T. Liu, *United Nations Peacekeeping and the Non-use of Force*, International Peace Academy Occasional Paper Series (Boulder, Colo.: Lynne Rienner, 1992); and Thomas G. Weiss, ed., *Collective Security in a Changing World* (Boulder, Colo.: Lynne Rienner, 1993).

9. This was a controversial resolution introduced in the context of the Korean War designed to circumvent the deadlock in the Security Council that resulted from the return of the Soviet Union to the Council, following the boycott that allowed, in Moscow's absence, the Council to authorize the US-led force in Korea in June 1950. The resolution was applied to authorize the Sinai peace force in 1956.

10. Hugh Miall, *The Peacemakers: Peaceful Settlement of Disputes Since 1945* (London: Palgrave Macmillan, 1992), 185, 112–113; and Paul Diehl, *International Peacekeeping* (Baltimore, Md.: Johns Hopkins University Press, 1993), 171.

11. William J. Durch, ed., *The Evolution of UN Peacekeeping: Case Studies and Comparative Analyses* (New York: St. Martin's Press, 1993), 12.

12. Michael W. Doyle, *UN Peacekeeping in Cambodia: UNTAC's Civil Mandate*, International Peace Academy Occasional Paper Series (Boulder, Colo.: Lynne Rienner Publishers, 1995), 85; and Steven R. Ratner, *The New UN Peacekeeping: Building Peace in Lands of Conflict After the Cold War* (New York: St. Martin's Press, 1995), 39.

13. Boutros-Ghali, *An Agenda for Peace*, para. 21.

14. Success is of course an ambiguous and contested term. We discuss its various meanings and how to measure it in *Making War and Building Peace* in both our data analysis and case studies.

15. Other recent categories include 'preventive deployments' fielded with the intention of deterring a possible attack, as in the Former Yugoslav Republic of Macedonia. There the credibility of the deterring force must ensure that the potential aggressor knows that there will be no easy victory. In the event of an armed challenge, the result will be an international war that involves costs so grave as to outweigh the temptations of conquest. Enforcement action against aggression (Korea or the Gulf), conversely, is a matter of achieving victory—'the decisive, comprehensive and synchronized application of preponderant military force to shock, disrupt, demoralize and defeat opponents'—the traditional zero sum terrain of military strategy. See John Mackinlay and Jarat Chopra, 'Second-Generation Multinational Operations,' *Washington Quarterly* 15, no. 3, (1992): 113–131. And for 'hybrid' operations that mix UN, regional, and unilateral, see *Annual Review of Global Peace Operations* (Boulder, Colo.: Lynne Rienner, 2006).

16. See John G. Ruggie, 'The United Nations Stuck in a Fog Between Peacekeeping and Peace Enforcement,' in *Peacekeeping: the way ahead?* (McNair Paper 25), ed. William H. Lewis (Washington, DC: Institute for National Strategic Studies, National Defense University, 1993) for these distinctions.

17. For a valuable discussion of the international law on the use of force and its bearing on authority for peace operations, see Karen Guttieri's 'Symptom of the Moment: A Juridical Gap for US Occupation Forces,' *International Insights* 13, Special Issue (Fall 1997): 131–155.

18. Boutros Boutros-Ghali, *Supplement to An Agenda for Peace: Position Paper of the Secretary-General on the Occasion of the Fiftieth Anniversary of the United Nations*, UN document A/50/60-S/1995/1, 25 January 1995, para. 11.

19. Michael Mandelbaum, 'The Reluctance to Intervene,' *Foreign Policy* 95 (Summer 1994): 3–18.

20. For an account of the various positions and factors, see Ramesh Thakur, 'UN Peace Operations and US Unilateralism and Multilateralism,' in *Unilateralism and US Foreign Policy: International Perspectives*, ed. David M. Malone and Yuen Foong Khong (Boulder, Colo.: Lynne Rienner, 2003), 153–179.

21. UN, *Report of the Panel on United Nations Peace Operations*, UN document A/55/305-S/2000/809, 21 August 2000.

22. UN, *No Exit without Strategy: Security-Council Decision-making and the Closure or Transition of United Nations Peacekeeping Operations: Report of the Secretary-General*, UN document S/2001/394, 20 April 2001, para. 20.

23. The literature expounding the three is vast, but for central differences see Robert Keohane, *After Hegemony: Cooperation and Discord in the World Political Economy* (Princeton, NJ: Princeton University Press, 1984); Joseph Grieco, 'Anarchy and the Limits of Cooperation: A Realist Critique of the Newest Liberal Institutionalism', *International Organization* 42, no. 3 (1988): 485–507; and Martha Finnemore and Kathryn Sikkink, 'Taking Stock: The Constructivist Research Program in International Relations and Comparative Politics,' *Annual Review of Political Science* 4, no. 1 (2001): 391–416.

24. For a theoretical discussion of the problem of providing assurance and building trust in conflicts that combine elements of both coordination and cooperation games, see Andrew Kydd, 'Trust, Reassurance, and Cooperation,' *International Organization* 54, no. 2 (2000): 325–357.

25. For a precise game-theoretic definition of coordination and collaboration games, refer to James D. Morrow, *Game Theory for Political Scientists* (Princeton, NJ: Princeton University Press, 1994); and David M. Kreps, *Game Theory and Economic Modeling* (Oxford: Clarendon Press, 1990).

26. A useful summary of the literature is Kenneth Oye, 'Introduction' and Robert Axelrod and Robert Keohane, 'Conclusion,' in *Cooperation Under Anarchy*, ed. Kenneth Oye (Princeton, NJ: Princeton University Press, 1986).

27. Morrow, *Game Theory*, 222.

28. Transformative peacekeeping is different from peace enforcement. The former can only deter or punish occasional violations. If the violations are systematic and large-scale, a no-consent enforcement operation might be necessary.

29. Two recent valuable contributions are Virginia Page Fortna, *Peace Time: Cease-fire Agreements and the Durability of Peace* (Princeton, NJ: Princeton University Press, 2004) and Kimberly Zisk Marten, *Enforcing the Peace: Learning from the Imperialist Past* (New York: Columbia University Press, 2004).

30. See Gary Bass, *Stay the Hand of Vengeance: the Politics of War Crimes Tribunals* (Princeton, NJ: Princeton University Press, 2000); and for the difficulties, Jack L. Snyder and Leslie Vinjamuri, 'Trials and Errors: Principle and Pragmatism in Strategies of International Justice,' *International Security* 28, no. 3 (2003/04): 5–44; and Chandra Lekha Sriram, *Confronting Past Human Rights Violations: Justice vs. Peace in Times of Transition* (London: Frank Cass, 2004).

31. The mutually hurting stalemate is from I. William Zartman, *Ripe for Resolution: Conflict and Intervention in Africa* (Oxford: Oxford University Press, 1985) where he discusses 'ripe' conflicts. Additional conditions for conflict 'ripeness' in Zartman's theory are: a sense of crisis; a deadline for negotiations; a reversal in the parties' relative strength; a leveraged external mediation; and a feasible settlement that can address all the parties' basic needs.

32. The settlement of El Salvador's civil war is a good example of a hurting stalemate.

33. Stephen John Stedman, 'Spoiler Problems in Peace Processes,' *International Security* 22, no. 2 (1997): 7.

34. See the chapter by Thomas Franck, 'A Holistic Approach to Peace-building,' in *Peace-making and Peacekeeping for the New Century*, ed. Olara Otunnu and Michael W. Doyle (Lanham, Md.: Rowman and Littlefield, 1998), 275–295; and Elizabeth M. Cousens, Chetan Kumar, and Karin Wermester, eds., *Peacebuilding as Politics: Cultivating Peace in Fragile Societies* (Boulder, Colo.: Lynne Rienner, 2000).

35. See Alvaro de Soto and Graciana del Castillo, 'Obstacles to Peacebuilding,' *Foreign Policy* 94 (1994): 69–83. This is the coordinating role that Japan, for example, played in Cambodia in organizing the Tokyo conference and the International Committee on the Reconstruction of Cambodia (ICORC).

36. 'Factions' refers to actual factions in a civil war. While the peacebuilding triangle measures hostility generated by these factions (e.g., it can measure the number of factions, whether or not they have signed a treaty, and the issues over which they are fighting a war), we cannot measure the factions' local capacities except at the national level. Thus, we use country-level indicators of local capacities in our empirical analysis. This is not inconsistent with our analysis, as national-level capacities are crucially important for economic construction after civil war. In some cases, only a small part of a country is affected by civil war and local capacities are lower in that part as compared to the rest of the country. But even in those cases, the capacity of the central government to rebuild the war-torn region by re-directing resources to it is critical for the peacebuilding process. Our measure of national-level capacities captures this fact.

37. See Oye, 'Introduction' and Axelrod and Keohane, 'Conclusion'; and Kenneth Oye, 'Explaining Cooperation Under Anarchy,' *World Politics* 38, no. 1 (1985): 1–24.

38. Having observed negotiations in El Salvador, Cambodia, Eastern Slavonia (Croatia), Brcko (Bosnia), and Cyprus, it is our opinion that establishing a unified army or multi-ethnic police force, though difficult, is easy compared to agreeing on an elementary school curriculum.

39. Figure 19.3 is based on regression results that we discuss at great length in our book and two supplements that are available online (see Doyle and Sambanis, *Making War*, ch. 3). These estimates were obtained with logistic regression. Our estimates of the effects of UN operations are statistically significant using several different model specifications and econometric assumptions. The effects of UN missions also persist in the longer-term, though they are felt more strongly in the first few years after the end of the civil war.

40. Easy cases imply a non-ethnic war, two factions, 75th percentile in net transfers per capita and electricity consumption per capita, and 25th percentile in primary exports as percent of GDP and deaths and displacements. Hard cases imply an ethnic war with four factions, electricity consumption and net current transfers at the 25th percentile of their ranges, and deaths and displacements and primary commodity exports at the 75th percentile of their ranges.

....

CHAPTER 20

SANCTIONS

....

DAVID CORTRIGHT
GEORGE A. LOPEZ
LINDA GERBER-STELLINGWERF

WITH the imposition of trade sanctions on Iraq in August 1990 in resolution 661, the Security Council opened a new era in the use of collective coercive economic measures as a means of responding to violations of international norms. In the previous forty-five years of UN experience, the Council employed sanctions only twice, in the cases of Southern Rhodesia in 1966 and South Africa in 1977. The next fifteen years witnessed an active phase of decision-making, with dozens of sanctions resolutions levied against sixteen distinct targets, including such nongovernmental entities as the National Union for the Total Independence of Angola (UNITA), Rwandan forces and local militias in eastern Congo, and Al Qaeda.

The legal authority for UN sanctions rests in Chapter VII of the Charter, which provides in Article 41 that the Council may call upon states to impose nonmilitary measures such as the interruption of economic and diplomatic relations to protect international peace and security.[1] The political logic of sanctions lies in the desire of policymakers to have options other than war for applying pressure on targeted states, entities, and individuals accused of violating international norms. Sanctions offer a middle course 'between words and wars.'[2] They avoid the costs of military action, yet they provide a more forceful option beyond diplomatic remonstrance. When employed effectively they can exert significant pressure on those targeted. When designed and applied astutely sanctions can serve as the basis for a bargaining dynamic in which the promise of lifting sanctions becomes an incentive to encourage political concessions and cooperation.[3]

Sanctions emerged as a preferred form of action by the Security Council for a number of reasons. First, the application of Chapter VII sanctions was an acceptable form of action that permitted big power cooperation as the UN entered the post-Cold War era. The fact that sanctions were being imposed mostly against states which were not critical allies of the rival superpowers made this cooperation feasible. Second, unlike earlier times in which the dynamics of international trade provided benefits—at least in the short term—to states subverting embargoes, the 1990s saw more rewards to nations who would join and support international economic coalitions. Finally, in a world where vocal domestic concerns and transnational advocacy networks push governments and the United Nations 'to do something' about war and human rights abuses, sanctions served as a public indicator that the Council was prepared to take action.[4]

The record of Security Council sanctions since 1990 is one of striking contrasts, if not contradictions. As it moved forcefully to use sanctions as a means for advancing the UN mandate to preserve peace and security, most particularly in Iraq, it found that the outcomes of these measures were undermining another pillar of its core mandate: to enhance the human condition. While sanctions provided the major powers with a powerful tool for collective action within the Council, the wide-ranging social impacts of these measures resulted in declining consensus on Iraq and disagreements on sanctions reform. After 1994, it had learned numerous lessons from these detrimental sanctions episodes, had adapted its measures to mitigate unanticipated consequences, and explored prospects for improving sanctions implementation. An era of sanctions reform ensued as the Security Council shifted its focus from comprehensive to more selective measures. Aided by a series of international processes sponsored by individual states—Switzerland, Germany, and Sweden—the Security Council abandoned the use of general trade sanctions and relied instead on targeted measures: financial assets freezes, travel bans, aviation sanctions, commodity boycotts, and arms embargoes. As the UN counter-terrorism program developed after September 2001, the Council mandated the application of these targeted tools to disable terrorist networks.[5]

IRAQ: THE MOST CONTESTED CASE

The United Nations sanctions against Iraq were the longest, most comprehensive, and most controversial in the history of the world body. Although sanctions were criticized for their harmful humanitarian impacts,[6] they were largely successful in achieving Iraq's disarmament by pressuring the regime to accept grudgingly the UN weapons monitoring mandate.[7] Sanctions also helped to extract concessions from Iraq on the border dispute with Kuwait and cemented the military containment of Iraq. The embargo on oil exports drastically reduced the revenues available to the Baghdad regime, prevented the rebuilding of Iraqi defenses after the Gulf War, and blocked the import of vital materials and technologies for producing weapons of mass destruction.[8]

Sanctions were less successful in encouraging greater Iraqi cooperation with the international community. In part, this was due to the truculent nature of the regime, but it also resulted from the unwillingness of the US to consider any lifting of UN sanctions in exchange for Iraqi concessions. As early as May 1991, the first president Bush stated, 'my view is we don't want to lift these sanctions as long as Saddam Hussein is in power.'[9] This policy continued under President Bill Clinton, who remarked in November 1997, 'sanctions will be there until the end of time, or as long as he [Hussein] lasts.'[10] This position was contrary to the 1991 Security Council resolution 687 that stated that sanctions were to be lifted when Iraq complied with UN disarmament obligations. This moving of the 'political goalposts' became an obstacle in diplomatic relations between Iraq and the UN.

According to the head of the UN disarmament commission, Rolf Ekéus, sanctions were crucial to the success of UN weapons inspection and dismantlement efforts in Iraq.[11] Sanctions supplied the pressure for Iraqi officials to accept UN weapons inspections, and they kept pressure on the regime once the disarmament process was underway. On several occasions UN officials used the leverage of sanctions, and the hope that the embargo might be lifted, to persuade the Baghdad government to cooperate. 'Sanctions were the way to convince Iraq to cooperate with inspectors,' said Ekéus. 'In this case it was a combined carrot-and-stick approach. Keeping the sanctions was the stick, and the carrot was that if Iraq cooperated with the elimination of its weapons of mass destruction, the Security Council would lift the sanctions. Sanctions were the backing for the inspections, and they were what sustained my operation almost for the whole time.'[12]

Beyond helping to drive the disarmament process, sanctions undermined Iraqi military capabilities by cutting off the regime's financial lifeblood. Sanctions kept the revenues from Iraq's vast oil wealth out of the hands of Saddam Hussein. Estimates of the total amount of oil revenue denied the Iraqi government range as high as $250 billion.[13] For the first six years of sanctions, Iraq sold no oil whatsoever, except for a small allowance to Jordan. After the Oil-for-Food Programme began in 1996, oil sales were permitted and eventually generated a total of $64.2 billion in revenue.[14] The proceeds were deposited in a UN escrow account, not the Central Bank of Iraq. While the Iraqi government used smuggling and kickback schemes to siphon hard currency out of the Oil-for-Food Programme, these funds were only a fraction of the total oil revenues being generated. The Independent Inquiry Committee into the United Nations Oil-for-Food Programme chaired by former US Federal Reserve chairman Paul A. Volcker investigating corruption in the program reported Iraqi earnings from oil smuggling outside the sanctions regime for the period 1991 to 2003 at about $11 billion. Total illicit income within the program from illegal surcharges and fees was approximately $1.8 billion.[15] These were enormous sums although less than 20 percent of total oil revenues generated through the program.

By denying financial resources to the Iraqi government, the sanctions prevented the regime from rebuilding its military capabilities. This was the stated goal of both the United States and the UN. According to US government figures, a precipitous drop in Iraqi military spending and arms imports occurred after 1990. Iraqi military expenditures dropped from over $15 billion in 1989 (constant 1999 dollars) to an average of approximately $1.4 billion per year through the 1990s.[16] Estimated Iraqi arms imports showed a similar steep decline, dropping from more than $3.5 billion in 1989 (constant 1999 dollars) to minimal levels through the 1990s.[17] Unfortunately, the achievement of the UN's goals in military terms did not equate with political success, as Saddam Hussein continued to undermine the inspection process.[18]

In the late 1990s political support for continued sanctions in Iraq began to erode. In response, the Security Council sought to reform the sanctions system by easing restrictions on civilian imports, while tightening pressure on weapons and military-related goods. The strategy became known as 'smart sanctions' and built on the sanctions reform processes noted above. It was intended to enable the rehabilitation of Iraq's civilian economy while maintaining restrictions on military goods and dual-use imports.[19] The Security Council came close to approving this approach a number of times in 2000 and 2001, and the next year adopted resolution 1409. The new plan restored political consensus in the Security Council and created an arms-denial system that could have been sustained indefinitely.

But a year later, the US government was unwilling to settle for the revived sanctions system. It also rejected the renewed weapons monitoring program that began a few months later. As analysts weigh the costs and consequences of the Iraq war, it will be important to remember that viable alternative means were available, and were functioning effectively, to contain the threat from Saddam Hussein without the use of military force.

UN SANCTIONS: AN OVERVIEW

The Iraq saga was only one of sixteen distinct cases of Security Council sanctions imposed between 1990 and 2005. The table below summarizes these cases which include two separate episodes each in former Yugoslavia (Bosnia, 1991–1995, and Kosovo, 1998–2000) and Sudan (Khartoum regime, 1996–2001, and Janjaweed and targeted Sudanese individuals and entities, 2004–).[20]

Of the sixteen cases under review, most involved targeted or selective measures. In only three cases—Iraq, Haiti, and Yugoslavia (1992–1995)—were comprehensive trade sanctions applied. In one other case, Angola, the combination of selective UN sanctions imposed over the years (arms and oil in 1993, travel and diplomatic in 1997, and diamonds in 1998) amounted to a nearly comprehensive trade embargo on territory controlled by UNITA. In all other cases, sanctions were partial and selective in nature: nine examples of financial restrictions (always in combination with other measures), six cases of commodity boycotts (most involving petroleum products;[21] three involving diamonds; and one on lumber products), ten uses of travel sanctions (also in combination with other measures), and fifteen cases of arms

Table 20.1 UN sanctions, 1990–2005

Sanctioned Country or Entity	Authorizing Resolutions	Type of Sanction	Comments
Iraq	S/RES/661, 6 August 1990	Comprehensive sanctions[1]	Significant impact. Aided the success of the UN disarmament mission; helped convince the regime to accept redrawn border with Kuwait; contributed to military containment of the Baghdad government.
	S/RES/1483, 22 May 2003	Sanctions lifted, but arms embargo continued, assets freeze imposed on former regime members	
Yugoslavia	S/RES/713, 25 September 1991	Arms embargo	Significant impact. Pressured the regime to negotiate and accept Dayton accords.
	S/RES/757, 30 May 1992 S/RES/1021, 22 November 1995	Comprehensive sanctions Terminated 713 arms embargo	
	S/RES/1022, 22 November 1995	Trade sanctions suspended indefinitely	
Yugoslavia	S/RES/1160, 31 March 1998	Arms embargo	Limited impact, but in combination with US and EU measures contributed to regime's isolation.
	S/RES/1367, 10 September 2001	Sanctions terminated	
Somalia	S/RES/733, 23 January 1992	Arms embargo	No impact. Poorly enforced.
Libya	S/RES/748, 31 March 1992	Aviation, arms embargo, travel, diplomatic	Significant impact. Convinced regime to extradite terrorist suspects and to reduce support for international terrorism.
	S/RES/883, 11 November 1993	Assets freeze, imports of oil-transporting equipment	
	S/RES/1506, 12 September 2003	Sanctions lifted	

(Continued)

Table 20.1 (*Continued*)

Sanctioned Country or Entity	Authorizing Resolutions	Type of Sanction	Comments
Liberia	S/RES/788, 19 November 1992 S/RES/1343, 7 March 2001	Arms embargo Terminated 788 arms embargo; Imposed arms embargo, assets freeze, travel/aviation ban, diamond embargo, called for certificate of origin scheme for diamonds	Some impact. Helped to weaken and isolate Charles Taylor regime.
	S/RES/1478, 6 May 2003 S/RES/1521, 22 December 2003	Timber embargo Terminated 1343 and 1478 sanctions. Imposed arms embargo, travel ban, diamond and timber exports from Liberia, called for certificate of origin scheme for diamonds	
	S/RES/1532, 12 March 2004	Assets freeze on Charles Taylor and other designated individuals	
Haiti	S/RES/841, 16 June 1993	Fuel and arms embargo, funds freeze	Considerable impact. Effective in convincing military junta to negotiate the return of civilian power, but the resulting Governors Island accord was not enforced and gave way to military intervention.
	S/RES/917, 6 May 1994 S/RES/944, 29 September 1994	Comprehensive sanctions Sanctions terminated upon Aristide's return to power	

Angola	S/RES/864, 15 September 1993	Arms embargo, petroleum embargo	Considerable impact. Initial limited sanctions replaced by more comprehensive and better enforced measures, which contributed to the isolation and weakening of UNITA.
	S/RES/1127, 28 August 1997	Travel, aviation, diplomatic	
	S/RES/1173, 12 June 1998	Assets freeze, financial, diamond imports not certified by Angolan government, travel	
	S/RES/1448, 9 December 2002	Lifted all sanctions	
Rwanda	S/RES/918, 17 May 1994	Arms embargo	No impact.
Sudan	S/RES/1054, 26 April 1996	Diplomatic, travel restrictions	Little direct impact, although Osama bin Laden was expelled from the country soon after sanctions were imposed, and the regime subsequently took steps to improve counter-terrorism cooperation with the West.
	S/RES/1070, 16 August 1996	Travel, aviation (never went into effect), terminated in September 2001	
	S/RES/1372, 28 September 2001	Terminated all 1054 and 1070 measures	
Sudan	S/RES/1556, 30 July 2004	Arms embargo on Janjaweed and other groups	Little impact.
	S/RES/1591, 29 March 2005	Arms embargo expanded to all parties in Darfur, travel restrictions, assets freeze on designated Sudanese and Janjaweed and other leaders	
Sierra Leone	S/RES/1132, 8 October 1997	Oil embargo, arms embargo, travel restrictions	Little impact, but contributed to the weakening of the Revolutionary United Front.
	S/RES/1156, 16 March 1998	Lifted the oil embargo	
	S/RES/1171, 5 June 1998	Arms embargo, travel ban	
	S/RES/1306, 5 July 2000	Diamond exports (expired 2003)	

(Continued)

Table 20.1 (*Continued*)

Sanctioned Country or Entity	Authorizing Resolutions	Type of Sanction	Comments
Afghanistan, Al Qaeda and the Taliban*	S/RES/1267, 15 October 1999	Aviation, financial	Little impact.
	S/RES/1333, 19 December 2000	Arms embargo, travel, assets freeze, diplomatic, aviation	
	S/RES/1390, 28 January 2002	Aviation ban lifted; financial, travel, arms measures against designated individuals	
	S/RES/1526, 30 January 2004	Assets, travel, arms embargo	
Ethiopia and Eritrea	S/RES/1298, 17 May 2000 S/PRST/2001/14, 15 May 2001	Arms embargo Arms embargo expired	Little impact.
DRC	S/RES/1493, 28 July 2003 S/RES/1596, 3 May 2005	Arms embargo Travel, assets freeze, aviation	Little impact. Arms embargo poorly enforced.
Côte d'Ivoire	S/RES/1572, 15 November 2004	Arms embargo, travel, assets freeze	Little impact.

* On 2 September 2003, the name of the committee was changed to 'Al-Qaida and Taliban Sanctions Committee.'

embargoes.²² Diplomatic sanctions or restrictions on international participation were also employed in several instances. The accompanying table summarizes the cases and types of sanctions employed and assesses general impact.

Sanctions did not produce immediate and full compliance in any of the cases examined. But in a number of cases they resulted in partial compliance and/or generated bargaining pressure. In Yugoslavia, sanctions exerted leverage on the Belgrade regime that led to the Dayton Accords. In Libya, sanctions were a central factor in the negotiations that eventually brought suspected terrorists to trial and convinced the regime to reduce its support of international terrorism. In Angola, sanctions that were initially ineffective became stronger over the years and combined with military and diplomatic pressures to weaken the UNITA rebel movement. In Liberia, sanctions denied legitimacy to the Charles Taylor regime. In most of these cases UN member states made at least some attempt to comply with Security Council sanctions. In the cases where the Council imposed only stand-alone arms embargoes—Sudan, Liberia (until 2001), Rwanda, Yugoslavia (after 1998), and Ethiopia/Eritrea—sanctions had little or no impact. The limited measures imposed in Afghanistan prior to 2001 also had no discernible effect on the Taliban regime. In the cases of the Democratic Republic of the Congo and Côte d'Ivoire, arms embargoes were not well enforced. In approximately one-third of the cases examined, therefore, Security Council sanctions had some impact. In these cases the pressure of sanctions was sufficient to produce at least partial progress in achieving Security Council objectives.²³

ADJUSTING TO HUMANITARIAN IMPACTS

Much of the debate about sanctions has centered on their humanitarian impacts. In the case of Iraq, sanctions contributed to severe humanitarian suffering among innocent and vulnerable populations. For the first six years of sanctions in Iraq, comprehensive sanctions cut off all trade and shut down oil exports, which shattered the country's economy. The combination of sanctions and Gulf War bombing damage caused a severe humanitarian crisis, resulting in hundreds of thousands of preventable deaths among children.²⁴ Infant and child mortality rates in south/central Iraq more than doubled, according to one study.²⁵ Relief from the humanitarian crisis did not come until after the Oil-for-Food Programme took effect. Although the program was plagued by corruption, substantial amounts of relief began to arrive in the late 1990s, gradually easing some of the hardships suffered by Iraqi civilians.

The desire to avoid humanitarian suffering from the imposition of economic sanctions became a dominant feature of Security Council policymaking during the 1990s. The ambassadors of the P-5 wrote to the president in 1995 that 'further collective actions in the Security Council within the context of any future sanctions regimes should be directed to minimize unintended adverse side-effects of sanctions on the most vulnerable segments of targeted countries.'[26] Efforts to assess and mitigate the humanitarian impacts of sanctions became a priority concern. In 1995 the Department of Humanitarian Affairs (DHA) commissioned a report on the impact of sanctions on humanitarian assistance efforts.[27]

In 1997 the DHA developed a methodology and series of specific indicators for assessing humanitarian impacts.[28] Many of the recommendations in these studies became the basis for an ongoing humanitarian assessment methodology developed by DHA's successor, the Office for the Coordination of Humanitarian Affairs (OCHA). Efforts to assess the humanitarian impact of particular sanctions cases became a regular feature of UN sanctions policy. In 2003 OCHA updated its indicators and methodology in light of recent cases and based on the success of the earlier venture.[29] Assessment reports and missions to examine the impact of sanctions are now a frequent feature of sanctions cases, and they provide the Security Council an opportunity to anticipate and prevent potential humanitarian problems.

LEARNING AND INNOVATION

The Security Council responded to the controversies surrounding the humanitarian impact of sanctions by altering the design of sanctions. General trade embargoes were abandoned in favor of more targeted sanctions. After the imposition of comprehensive sanctions on Haiti in 1994, all subsequent sanctions involved targeted measures. Targeted sanctions apply pressure on specific decision-making elites and the companies or entities they control. They also deny access to specific products or activities that are necessary for repression and war. Targeted sanctions are designed to reduce unintended humanitarian consequences by focusing coercive pressure on decision-making elites. By imposing costs specifically on those responsible for violations of international law, rather than on innocent bystanders, the Security Council thus seeks to serve its primary mission of enhancing peace and security without jeopardizing its parallel mission of improving the human condition.

In each of the categories of targeted sanctions—finance, travel, arms, and commodities—the Security Council introduced important innovations. In the area of financial sanctions, it moved beyond freezing the assets of governments alone. In the cases of Iraq, Libya, and Yugoslavia, it imposed financial sanctions only on government assets. Beginning in 1994, with action against the military junta in Haiti, the Security Council applied financial sanctions against designated individuals and entities as well. This pattern continued through the Angola and Afghanistan cases in the latter part of the decade. In the cases of the Democratic Republic of the Congo (DRC) and Côte d'Ivoire the Council was authorized to apply targeted measures on designated individuals. The counter-terrorism financial sanctions mandated in resolution 1390 were also directed against entities and individuals.

As the Security Council shifted toward imposing targeted sanctions in cooperation with member states, it developed the capacity to develop and publish lists of designated sanctions targets. The entities and individuals on these designation lists were subjected to asset freezes and travel bans. The Council was empowered to impose financial sanctions and travel bans on lists of designated targets in the cases of Angola, Sierra Leone, Afghanistan, Liberia, DRC, Sudan, and Côte d'Ivoire. This practice would later prove significant for the Council's approach to handling terrorism.

It also attempted to make improvements in the design and implementation of arms embargoes. Measures to halt the flow of weapons and military-related goods are the most frequently employed form of economic sanctions. In the fifteen years after 1990, the Security Council imposed arms embargoes in all but one of the sanctions cases. In theory, arms embargoes are an ideal form of targeted sanction. They deny aggressors or human rights abusers the tools of war and repression, while avoiding harm to vulnerable and innocent populations. Although frequently employed, arms embargoes have been the least effective form of sanction. In the four instances where arms embargoes were imposed as stand-alone measures—Somalia, Rwanda, Ethiopia/Eritrea, and Yugoslavia 1998–2001—the impact of these measures was minimal. Only in the case of Iraq, where the United States and other countries made a major commitment to enforcement, did the continuing restrictions on the supply of arms and dual-use technologies have a significant military-political impact.[30]

To overcome the problems resulting from inadequate implementation of arms embargoes, the Security Council adopted a number of policy innovations. The language and technical terms employed in the Council's arms embargo resolutions became more precise. Arms embargo resolutions included prohibitions not only against the supply of arms and ammunition, but also against training, military cooperation, and various support services, including air transportation. This refinement of terms and broadening of covered items helped to close loopholes and reduced the ambiguities that previously impeded enforcement. More vigorous efforts also were made to monitor compliance with arms embargoes. Efforts were made to encourage member states to criminalize violations of UN arms embargoes and strengthen export control laws and regulations. These initiatives helped to create a firmer foundation in the domestic law of member states for penalizing companies and individuals who supply arms and military-related goods in violation of UN arms embargoes. In 2004 the Security Council directed UN peacekeeping forces in the DRC and Côte d'Ivoire to assist with the monitoring of arms embargoes in these countries. This added significant new responsibilities to the mission of UN peacekeepers in these countries.

Commodity-specific boycotts were also imposed more frequently. Oil embargoes were imposed as part of the sanctions against Iraq, Yugoslavia, Haiti, UNITA in Angola, and the military junta in Sierra Leone. An embargo on the import of logs from Liberia was imposed in 2003. Diamond embargoes were introduced in 1998 with the case of Angola. As nongovernmental agencies and human rights groups documented the role of diamond smuggling in financing the armed rebellions in Angola and Sierra Leone, the Security Council took action to interdict the trade in so-called 'blood diamonds.' The Council imposed diamond embargoes against UNITA in 1998 by resolution 1173, in 2000 the Revolutionary United Front areas (RUF) of Sierra Leone by resolution 1306, and in 2001 the government of Liberia by resolution 1343.

As a means of enforcing these measures, the UN worked with diamond exporting countries, the diamond industry, and nongovernmental organizations to establish the Kimberley Process, an international agreement among dozens of countries to combat the trade in conflict-related diamonds. Governments created certificate-of-origin systems designed to protect the legitimate diamond trade by screening out blood diamonds. Targeted diamond sanctions became a tool for the Security Council to shrink the financial base sustaining armed conflict in Africa, and they became a model for commodity-focused embargoes of the future.[31]

SANCTIONS ASSISTANCE MISSIONS: THE CASE OF FORMER YUGOSLAVIA

One of the most important features of the 1991–1995 sanctions imposed on the Belgrade government was the introduction of an elaborate, multinational monitoring and enforcement system. A network of sanctions assistance missions (SAMs) was organized by the Conference on Security and Co-operation in Europe (CSCE) and the European Community (EC). The SAMs system represented a significant innovation in the implementation of Security Council sanctions.

Soon after sanctions were imposed, the CSCE and the EC formed a Sanctions Liaison Group to provide technical assistance for sanctions implementation, concentrating on the states immediately surrounding Yugoslavia. In October 1992 customs officials were dispatched to Bulgaria, Hungary, and Romania to form the first SAMs, which were also established in Albania, Croatia, the Former Yugoslav Republic of Macedonia (FYROM), and Ukraine. The EC established a Sanctions Assistance Missions Communications Center (SAMCOMM) at its headquarters in Brussels and created the post of sanctions coordinator. By March 1995, the SAMCOMM staff had grown to twenty-six people.[32] SAMCOMM developed a computerized satellite communications system linking its headquarters in Brussels with the UN sanctions committee in New York. This system, made available and maintained by the United States, enabled customs officers in the field to verify shipping documents and prevent the use of forged or falsified documents.[33] These measures established a substantial institutional capacity for monitoring and enforcing sanctions. It was the first time that major regional organizations stepped in to assist the UN in providing staff and financial resources.

Other European institutions also contributed to the enforcement of sanctions. In April 1993, the Western European Union (WEU) established a Danube Patrol Mission of eight patrol boats staffed with customs and police officers to inspect riparian traffic. The North Atlantic Treaty Organization (NATO) also joined the effort, teaming with WEU in June 1993 to establish a combined naval task force in the Adriatic Sea. Fourteen nations provided ships, crews, and resources to the Sharp Guard operation, which was responsible for checking all vessels entering or leaving the Adriatic and diverting ships to Italian harbors when necessary to inspect cargoes and documents.[34] According to a US State Department report, this international naval force 'prevented large merchant vessels from calling at Bar—Serbia's only significant port' and had a significant impact on trade.[35] According to the official UN report on SAMs, 'this unique and unprecedented formula of coordinated inter-institutional cooperation at the regional level . . . was identified as the main reason for the effectiveness of the sanctions in the case of the former Yugoslavia.'[36] The State Department report concluded, 'the presence of monitors bolsters frontline state enforcement by exerting pressure on the host government and its police, customs, and military to minimalize the violations.'[37] The main lesson of the Yugoslavia experience, according to the UN report, was that 'adequate arrangements for international cooperation and assistance can enhance sanctions effectiveness.'[38] It also illustrated that porous borders can be controlled even after a history of undermining sanctions by actors in frontline states.

IMPROVING SANCTIONS MONITORING AND IMPLEMENTATION

Beginning in the late 1990s, the Security Council developed a number of additional mechanisms for making sanctions more effective against law-violating regimes. As the situations in which sanctions were imposed—such as long-standing civil wars, or in failed economies characterized by extensive criminalization—increased in complexity, the Council recognized the need both for an expert view of the prospects for sanctions compliance in any particular case, and more precision in fashioning the sanctions process. The creation of special investigative and expert panels dealt with the former challenge, while specially convened and nationally sponsored 'processes' contributed to the latter.

To overcome the lack of monitoring capacity within the UN system, the Security Council appointed independent expert panels and monitoring mechanisms to provide support for sanctions implementation. The first panel was established in conjunction with the arms embargo against Rwandan Hutu rebels by resolution 1013 in 1995. The Council created the United Nations Independent Commission of Inquiry (UNICOI), which issued six reports from 1996 through 1998 documenting the illegal supply of arms to the rebel groups in eastern Zaire. UNICOI reports provided voluminous evidence of wholesale violations of the arms embargo and contained numerous recommendations for cracking down on arms smuggling in the region. A breakthrough toward more effective monitoring came in the case of Angola. In 1999, the Angola sanctions committee became more active in monitoring sanctions violations and encouraging greater implementation efforts. The Security Council also appointed a panel of experts and a subsequent monitoring mechanism to improve compliance with the Angola sanctions. The panel of experts and monitoring mechanism issued a series of reports that focused continuing attention on sanctions implementation efforts.[39]

The Angola panel of experts and the monitoring mechanism were followed by similar investigative panels for Sierra Leone, Afghanistan, Liberia, Somalia and the DRC. Panel reports were also commissioned in 2005 in the cases of Sudan and Côte d'Ivoire. In each of these settings, the investigative panels produced detailed reports on sanctions violations and smuggling activities. The Sierra Leone panel of experts focused on the link between arms trafficking and diamond smuggling and found a pattern of widespread violations of UN sanctions. The panel issued numerous policy recommendations, the most important of which was that sanctions be imposed on the government of Liberia for its role in undermining sanctions implementation and providing support for the rebels in Sierra Leone.[40] Sanctions on the Charles Taylor regime soon followed.

The Security Council created a monitoring mechanism for Afghanistan in July 2001 through resolution 1363 and established an associated Sanctions Enforcement Support Team, which never deployed, to strengthen the implementation of the arms embargo, travel sanctions, and targeted financial sanctions imposed against the Taliban regime. After the defeat of the Taliban the Council altered the mission of the monitoring group through resolution 1390 (2002). It later created a new Analytic Support and Sanctions Monitoring Team to investigate and provide support for the continued financial, travel, and arms sanctions on former Taliban leaders and members of Al Qaeda. The Liberia panel of experts reports confirmed allegations of the Monrovia government's extensive involvement with and support for the armed rebellion of the RUF in Sierra Leone. The panel recommended a series of measures for strengthening the enforcement of the arms embargo, diamond embargo, and travel sanctions against Liberia.[41]

In parallel with the emergence of the monitoring mechanisms and their many recommendations for improved implementation were a series of reform initiatives by individual member states to improve Security Council policymaking. The governments of Switzerland, Germany, and Sweden sponsored several working meetings and a series of research studies to increase the effectiveness of Security Council sanctions and strengthen the prospects for member state implementation and target state compliance. The first of these policy initiatives was the so-called Interlaken

Process in 1998–1999. The focus of the Swiss initiative was to enhance the effectiveness of targeted financial sanctions. The Interlaken process attempted to apply the methods utilized in combating money laundering to the challenge of implementing targeted financial sanctions. Participants in the Interlaken seminars examined the extent to which financial sanctions could achieve their goal of cutting off the financial support that is crucial to sustaining abusive regimes and the decision-making elites who control such regimes. As a part of the Swiss initiative, model legislation for governments was developed to strengthen their capacity to implement targeted financial sanctions.[42]

Building on the Interlaken Process, the German Ministry of Foreign Affairs initiated an effort to refine the implementation of travel bans and arms embargoes. Managed by the Bonn International Center for Conversion, the German initiative included meetings in Bonn in 1999 and Berlin in 2000. The so-called Bonn–Berlin Process considered ways of improving travel bans and arms embargoes. In the area of arms embargoes, the Bonn–Berlin process recommended the use of standardized lists of dual-use items drawn from the Wassenaar Arrangement, to assure common definitions of military-related technologies subject to restrictions. The recommendations emanating from the German initiative helped to advance the capacity of the Security Council to implement travel bans and arms embargoes. The final report of the German initiative provided rich detail of the monitoring and enforcement of future travel and arms sanctions.[43]

In 2001 the government of Sweden launched a new initiative to improve sanctions policymaking at the United Nations. The Swedish program brought together leading sanctions scholars, UN policymakers, and international legal experts for a series of meetings in Uppsala, Gimo, and Stockholm to develop recommendations for strengthening the monitoring and enforcement of Security Council sanctions. Known as the Stockholm Process on the Implementation of Targeted Sanctions, the Swedish initiative added to the work already achieved by the Swiss and German governments and helped to advance international understanding of the requirements for effectively implementing targeted sanctions.[44]

REFORM OPPORTUNITIES AND OBSTACLES

The enthusiasm of member states for improving Security Council sanctions oscillated. The 'sanctions fatigue' generated by humanitarian controversies and political differences over UN policy in Iraq, and impatience with less than effective arms embargoes, slowed the momentum for reform and made agreement on contentious issues more difficult. Power politics and the narrow national interests of the P-5 in the Security Council overshadowed the concern for improving the ability of the system to design and implement effective sanctions. In this atmosphere of competing agendas among the permanent five, it fell to middle powers such as Canada to champion the cause of more systematic upgrading of the UN's capacity to design and execute economic sanctions. In April 2000 Canadian foreign minister Lloyd Axworthy hosted a special session of the Security Council for the purpose of initiating a working group on sanctions reform. The Canadian initiative reflected widespread agreement among member states that improvements in Security Council sanctions were both possible and necessary. The Informal Working Group on General Issues of Sanctions was intended to complement the Swiss and German government initiatives, with the goal of designing a new structure and roadmap for Security Council sanctions.

Chaired by Ambassador Anwarul Chowdhury of Bangladesh, the sanctions working group initially made progress in recommending improvements in the administration, design, and monitoring of sanctions policies, but soon foundered over differences among Security Council members on the issue of time limits for sanctions. France and other members argued vigorously that all sanctions should be time limited, with a specified date for when sanctions would be lifted unless the Security Council took action to extend them. The demand for time limits was a direct outgrowth of the experience in Iraq, where sanctions continued indefinitely and some permanent members, especially the United States, would not consider easing the sanctions. The US and the UK were the most vigorous advocates of maintaining pressure on Iraq and resolutely opposed any recommendation that would require time limits. Washington and London argued that such limits would divert the attention of a targeted regime from meeting the necessary conditions for compliance to waiting until sanctions are lifted. France and others countered that the Security Council would always have the option of extending sanctions if a targeted regime failed to comply. They insisted on requiring an affirmative vote for the continuation of sanctions, rather than the present ability of a single permanent member to block the lifting of sanctions.

Although the US and UK opposed time limits as a general principle, primarily to avoid its application in the case of Iraq, in actual practice they readily accepted time limits in specific cases. In most sanctions episodes—the 2000 arms embargo against Ethiopia and Eritrea in resolution 1298, the arms embargo and further sanctions imposed the same year against Afghanistan in resolution 1333, the 2001 diamond embargo and other sanctions against Liberia in resolution 1343, and the various targeted measures imposed in the DRC and Côte d'Ivoire in 2004—Washington and London voted with other member states to accept time limits of generally one year for the duration of the imposed measures. In the cases of Afghanistan and Liberia, the Security Council readily agreed that the targeted regime had failed to comply with UN demands within the designated time limit, and the sanctions were extended. In the case of Ethiopia/Eritrea, the end of the war between the two states convinced a majority of the members of the Council that the arms embargo imposed the previous year was no longer relevant, and the sanctions were lifted.

Another contentious issue for the Security Council sanctions working group was the question of decision-making procedures within sanctions committees. The US and UK wanted to retain the existing consensus rule, while France, Russia, and other countries urged a majority vote procedure. At stake was the issue of whether a single state could impose its will on other members and block decisions that had the support of a majority of committee members. Once again the Iraq case cast a shadow over debate. The US and UK did not want to lose their ability to place holds on the import of dual-use goods into Iraq, while France and others argued that such decisions should be by majority vote, not the will of one or two members.

The Security Council sanctions working group was unable to reach consensus for issuing a final report, but it produced a 'Chairman's Proposed Outcome' paper in February 2001 that summarized the major agreements and proposals of the working group. Many of the working group proposals coincided with recommendations made by the various expert panels and monitoring mechanisms. Together, these two sources—the Security Council working group, and reports of the expert panels and monitoring mechanisms—produced a coherent agenda for reform to improve the effectiveness of sanctions. The most significant of the major recommendations for institutionalizing reform included:

- Strengthen the capacity of the UN Secretariat;
- Promote greater transparency and more effective communications, to inform member states and the public about sanctions requirements and purposes;
- Develop improved guidelines and standardized reporting procedures to assist member states in the implementation of sanctions;
- Clarify the conditions that must be met for sanctions to be lifted, and consider easing sanctions partially in response to partial compliance by targeted regimes;
- Standardize and improve procedures for providing humanitarian exemptions and assistance;
- Utilize expert panels and monitoring mechanisms for the investigation of sanctions compliance;
- Take action against those who are found to be deliberately violating sanctions (the expert panel reports recommended imposing sanctions against such violators);
- Provide technical assistance and expert advice to states needing help in the implementation of sanctions;
- Conduct periodic assessments of humanitarian impact, third party effects, and the progress of implementation efforts;
- Tighten the enforcement of arms embargoes through mandatory registration of arms brokers and intermediaries and the development of standardized end-use certificates for arms and military equipment;
- Improve air traffic control and interdiction capacity in zones of conflict, and revoke the aircraft registrations and licenses of those known to be violating sanctions;
- Develop a worldwide standardized system for certificates of origin for all diamond exports; and
- Improve the capacity of the UN system to maintain and update accurate lists of individuals and entities subject to travel bans and targeted financial sanctions.

Despite the resistance to reform, many of these policy recommendations were implemented in practice in Security Council resolutions adopted after 2002.

CONCLUSIONS

UN sanctions policy has matured significantly since 1990, as UN diplomats, expert investigators, academic scholars, nongovernmental analysts, and many others have contributed to a process of learning, adaptation, and reform. The result has been a substantial transformation of sanctions policymaking. The targeted, more selective sanctions of recent years, supported by humanitarian assessment missions and expert panel reports, bear little resemblance to the poorly-monitored, often blunt measures imposed in the early 1990s. Many problems remain in the implementation of Security Council sanctions, but substantial progress has been made.

Some of the obstacles to effective sanctions policy, such as power rivalries among the P-5, are endemic to the international system, and have been shown to be at play when sanctions episodes continue over time.[45] But other challenges, such as the development of greater member state capacity for sanctions implementation, can be addressed through specific forms of assistance and policy improvements. The UN system has shown remarkable capacity for adaptation and learning in recent years. With continued attention to and implementation of appropriate reform recommendations, the Security Council can take further steps in the years ahead to mold the sanctions instrument into a more effective tool for preserving peace and security.

NOTES

1. While some observers view the active use of Security Council sanctions as a fulfillment of functions envisioned by the founding members of the UN, skepticism regarding the legal basis of comprehensive UN sanctions and controversies regarding the reach of Chapter VII authorization have been a concern to a number of analysts. See Paul Conlon, *United Nations Sanctions Management: A Case Study of the Iraq Sanctions Committee, 1990–1994* (Ardsley, NY: Transnational Publishers, 2000); and Vera Growlland-Debbas, ed., *United Nations Sanctions and International Law. The Graduate Institute of International Studies*, vol. 1 (The Hague: Kluwer Law International, 2001).

2. Peter Wallensteen and Carina Staibano, eds., *International Sanctions: Between Words and Wars in the Global System* (New York: Frank Cass, 2005).

3. Our past research confirms this mix of coercion and the promise of its release as a bargaining tool that increases the likelihood of sanctions success. See David Cortright and George A. Lopez, *The Sanctions Decade: Assessing UN Security Council Sanctions in the 1990s* (Boulder, Colo.: Lynne Rienner, 2000), esp. ch. 2.

4. See David Cortright and George A. Lopez, 'Economic Sanctions in Contemporary Global Relations,' in eds. Cortright and Lopez, *Economic Sanctions: Panacea or Peacebuilding in a Post-Cold War World?* (Boulder, Colo.: Westview Press, 1995), 3–16.

5. For an overview of these targeted sanctions see David Cortright and George A. Lopez, eds., *Smart Sanctions: Targeting Economic Statecraft* (Lanham, Md.: Rowman & Littlefield, 2002); and Peter Wallensteen and Carina Staibano, eds., *International Sanctions: Between Words and Wars in the Global System* (New York: Frank Cass, 2005).

6. The most articulate analyst of humanitarian impact is Joy Gordon, 'A Peaceful, Silent, Deadly Remedy: The Ethics of Economic Sanctions,' *Ethics and International Affairs* 13, no.1 (1999): 123–142; and 'Cool War: Economic Sanctions as a Weapon of Mass Destruction,' *Harper's Magazine* (November 2002): 43–52. For a comparative analysis of the humanitarian impact of sanctions on Iraq and elsewhere, see Thomas G. Weiss et al., eds., *Political Gain and Civilian Pain: Humanitarian Impacts of Economic Sanctions* (Lanham, Md.: Rowman & Littlefield, 1997).

7. See George A. Lopez and David Cortright, 'Containing Iraq: Sanctions Worked,' *Foreign Affairs* 83, no. 4 (2004): 90–103.

8. Barton Gellman, 'Iraq's Arsenal Was Only on Paper: Since Gulf War, Nonconventional Weapons Never Got Past the Planning Stage,' *Washington Post*, 7 January 2004.

9. George H. W. Bush, 'The President's News Conference with Chancellor Helmut Kohl of Germany' (transcript, Washington, DC, 20 May 1991), http://bushlibrary.tamu.edu.

10. As quoted in Barbara Crossette, 'The World; For Iraq, A Dog House with Many Rooms,' *New York Times*, 23 November 1997.

11. Rolf Ekéus (speech, Conference on Nuclear Nonproliferation and the Millennium: Prospects and Initiatives, Carnegie Endowment for International Peace, Washington, DC, 13 February 1996).

12. Rolf Ekéus, 'Shifting Priorities: UNMOVIC and the Future of Inspections in Iraq: An Interview with Ambassador Rolf Ekéus,' *Arms Control Today* 30, no. 2 (March 2000): 6.

13. The estimate comes from Meghan O'Sullivan, *Shrewd Sanctions: Statecraft and State Sponsors of Terrorism* (Washington, DC: Brookings Institution Press, 2003), 139.

14. UN Office of the Iraq Programme: Oil-for-Food, 'Oil Exports (By Phase),' updated 21 March 2003, www.un.org.

15. The Independent Inquiry Committee into the United Nations Oil-for-Food Programme, *The Management of the United Nations Oil-for-Food Programme*, vol. 1: *The Report of the Committee*, (7 September 2005), 95; and The Independent Inquiry Committee into the United Nations Oil-for-Food Programme, *Manipulation of the Oil-for-Food Programme by the Iraqi Regime: Oil Transactions and Illicit Payments, Humanitarian Goods Transactions and Illicit Payments, The Escrow Bank and the Inspection Companies, Other UN-Related Issues* (27 October 2005), 1, www.iic-offp.org.

16. O'Sullivan, *Shrewd Sanctions*, 139.

17. US Department of State, Bureau of Verification and Compliance, *World Military Expenditures and Arms Transfers 1999–2000* (Washington, DC: US Government Printing Office, June 2002), 77 and 129, see www.state.gov/t/vci. In an earlier version of the same document, released by the Clinton administration, the amount given for the identical dataset is much higher. In it, Iraq's military expenditures (in constant 1997 dollars) for 1989 equal $25.5 billion, a difference of $10.4 billion from the 2002 version. See US Department of State, Bureau of Verification and Compliance, *World Military Expenditures and Arms Transfers 1998* (Washington, DC: US Government Printing Office, April 2000), 87, see www.state.gov.

18. George A. Lopez and David Cortright, 'Trouble in the Gulf: Pain and Promise,' *The Bulletin of the Atomic Scientists* 54, no. 3 (1998): 39–43.

19. Human Rights Watch developed early proposals along these lines. See Hanny Megally, Executive Director, Middle East and North Africa division, Human Rights Watch, 'Letter to United Nations Security Council,' 4 January 2000, www.hrw.org.

20. The assumptions underlying our categorization of sixteen distinct cases are as follows. Two separate sanctions cases are listed for former Yugoslavia and Sudan. The two episodes in each country were not continuous chronologically and were imposed in response to different crises. With regard to Iraq, Liberia, and Afghanistan, the sanctions cases are classified as a single continuous episode, although in each case sanctions were significantly altered at times, and previous sanctions were lifted or terminated and replaced with new measures. Nonetheless, in each case Security Council sanctions were continuously applied.

21. An oil embargo on Yugoslavia was not specified in the Security Council resolutions imposing sanctions but was implicit in the general ban on exports and imports.

22. The five stand-alone arms embargoes were Somalia, Rwanda, Yugoslavia (1998), Ethiopia/ Eritrea, and Liberia. In 2001 the Security Council adopted resolution 1343 (S/RES/1343, 7 March 2001) imposing diamond and travel sanctions on Liberia and reauthorizing the arms embargo originally established in 1992.

23. For a detailed assessment of these cases see David Cortright and George A. Lopez, *Sanctions and the Search for Security: Challenges to UN Action* (Boulder, Colo.: Lynne Rienner, 2002).

24. Richard Garfield, *Morbidity and Mortality Among Iraqi Children from 1990 to 1998: Assessing the Impact of Economic Sanctions* (Goshen, Ind.: Joan B. Kroc Institute for International Peace Studies at the University of Notre Dame and the Fourth Freedom Forum, March 1999), www.fourthfreedom.org.

25. Mohamed M. Ali and Iqbal H. Shah, 'Sanctions and Childhood Mortality in Iraq,' *The Lancet* 355, issue 9218 (May 2000): 1851–1857.

26. Security Council, *Annex: Humanitarian Impact of Sanctions*, UN document S/1995/300, 13 April 1995.

27. Claudia Von Braunmühl and Manfred Kulessa, *The Impact of UN Sanctions on Humanitarian Assistance Activities, Report on a Study Commissioned by the United Nations Department of Humanitarian Affairs* (Berlin: Gesellschaft für Communication Management Interkultur Training mbH, December 1995).

28. Larry Minear et al., *Toward More Humane and Effective Sanctions Management: Enhancing the Capacity of the United Nations System*, Occasional Paper 31 (Providence, RI: Thomas J. Watson Jr. Institute for International Studies, Brown University, 1998).

29. Manuel Bessler, Richard Garfield, and Gerard McHugh, *Sanctions Assessment Handbook: Assessing the Humanitarian Implications of Sanctions* (New York: UN Office for the Coordination of Humanitarian Affairs, 2004).

30. For more detailed analysis of arms embargoes, see Andy Knight, *The United Nations and Arms Embargoes Verification* (Lewiston, NY: Edwin Mellen Press, 1998); and Michael Brzoska and George A. Lopez, eds., *Putting Teeth in the Tiger* (forthcoming).

31. David Cortright, George A. Lopez, and Linda Gerber, 'The Viability of Commodity Sanctions: The Case of Diamonds,' in David Cortright and George A. Lopez, eds., *Sanctions and the Search for Security*: 181–200.

32. UN Security Council, *Letter Dated 24 September 1996 from the Chairman of the Security Council Committee Established Pursuant to Resolution 724 (1991) Concerning Yugoslavia Addressed to the President of the Security Council, Report of the Copenhagen Roundtable on United Nations Sanctions in the Case of the Former Yugoslavia, Held at Copenhagen on 24 and 25 June 1996*, UN document S/1996/776, 24 September 1996, paras. 33 and 34.

33. UN Security Council, *Letter Dated 15 November 1996 from the Chairman of the Security Council Committee Established Pursuant to Resolution 724 (1991) Concerning Yugoslavia*

Addressed to the President of the Security Council, UN document S/1996/946, 15 November 1996, para. 14.

34. UN Security Council, *Letter Dated 24 September 1996 from the Chairman of the Security Council Committee Established Pursuant to Resolution 724 (1991) Concerning Yugoslavia Addressed to the President of the Security Council, Report of the Copenhagen Roundtable on United Nations Sanctions in the Case of the Former Yugoslavia, Held at Copenhagen on 24 and 25 June 1996,* UN document S/1996/776, 24 September 1996, paras. 48 and 49.

35. US Department of State, *UN Sanctions against Belgrade: Lessons Learned for Future Regimes* (Washington, DC: US Department of State, 1996), 11. Paper presented by the Interagency Task Force on Serbian Sanctions, June 1996.

36. UN Security Council, *Letter Dated 24 September 1996 from the Chairman of the Security Council Committee Established Pursuant to Resolution 724 (1991) Concerning Yugoslavia Addressed to the President of the Security Council, Report of the Copenhagen Roundtable on United Nations Sanctions in the Case of the Former Yugoslavia, Held at Copenhagen on 24 and 25 June 1996,* UN document S/1996/776, 24 September 1996, para. 78.

37. *UN Sanctions against Belgrade,* 11.

38. UN Security Council, *Letter Dated 24 September 1996 from the Chairman of the Security Council Committee Established Pursuant to Resolution 724 (1991) Concerning Yugoslavia Addressed to the President of the Security Council, Report of the Copenhagen Roundtable on United Nations Sanctions in the Case of the Former Yugoslavia, Held at Copenhagen on 24 and 25 June 1996,* UN document S/1996/776, 24 September 1996, para. 78.

39. UN Security Council, *Report of the Panel of Experts on Violations of Security Council Sanctions Against UNITA,* UN document S/2000/203, 10 March 2000; *Interim Report of the Monitoring Mechanism on Angola Sanctions Established by the Security Council in Resolution 1295 (2000) of 18 April 2000,* UN document S/2000/1026, 25 October 2000; *Final Report of the Monitoring Mechanism on Angola Sanctions,* UN document S/2000/1225, 21 December 2000; *Addendum to the final report of the Monitoring Mechanism on Sanctions Against UNITA,* UN document S/2001/363, 11 April 2001; *Supplementary Report of the Monitoring Mechanism on Sanctions Against UNITA,* UN document S/2001/966, 12 October 2001; *Additional Report of the Monitoring Mechanism on Sanctions Against UNITA,* UN document S/2002/486, 26 April 2002; and *Additional Report of the Monitoring Mechanism on Sanctions Against UNITA,* UN document S/2002/1119, 16 October 2002.

40. UN Security Council, *Report of the Panel of Experts Appointed Pursuant to Security Resolution 1306 (2000), paragraph 19, in relation to Sierra Leone,* UN document S/2000/1195, 20 December 2000.

41. UN Security Council, *Report of the Panel of Experts Pursuant to Security Council Resolution 1343 (2001), paragraph 19, concerning Liberia,* UN document S/2001/1015, 26 October 2001.

42. The Swiss Confederation in association with the United Nations Secretariat, and the Watson Institute for International Studies at Brown University, *Targeted Financial Sanctions: A Manual for Design and Implementation—Contributions from the Interlaken Process* (Providence, RI: Thomas J. Watson Jr. Institute for International Studies, 2001).

43. Michael Brzoska, ed., *Design and Implementation of the Arms Embargoes and Travel and Aviation Related Sanctions: Results of the 'Bonn-Berlin Process'* (Bonn: Bonn International Center for Conversion, 2001).

44. Peter Wallensteen, Carina Staibano, and Mikael Eriksson, eds., *Making Targeted Sanctions Effective: Guidelines for the Implementation of UN Policy Options* (Uppsala, Sweden: Uppsala University Department of Peace and Conflict Research, 2003). The International Peace Academy (IPA) in New York played an important role in documenting the evolution of sanctions policy and highlighting the most significant sanctions reform issues.

45. See Lisa Martin, *Coercive Cooperation: Explaining Multilateral Economic Sanctions* (Princeton, NJ: Princeton University Press, 1992).

CHAPTER 21

....

PEACE ENFORCEMENT

....

MICHAEL PUGH

ONE of the most vexing and contentious issues confronting the United Nations is the use of forceful means to maintain international peace and security under Chapter VII of the Charter. The various meanings of peace enforcement are constructed with an eye to legal or moral legitimacy, and authoritative appeals to international practice. But the notion that there has been a shift in the underlying determinants of enforcement is highly contested and serves various purposes, as reflected in the production of different meanings and the quest by commentators and practitioners to blur the distinctions between Chapter VI and VII operations.

Although a particular peace enforcement operation may be portrayed as stabilizing a peace process or protecting people from abuse, and it can achieve immediate results in this respect (though the non-UN force in Iraq has been highly destabilizing), its underlying strategic function is generally to contribute to an international order that maintains a global hierarchy. The consistent norm in enforcement is its basis in interests as conceived by the ruling elites of intervening states. Governments have taken a close interest in the domestic order of other states when it has been consequential to them, but have otherwise tended to try to avoid commitments. The impetus for international peace enforcement mainly arises in the relatively powerful states in the world, or from regional hegemonic powers. It is no coincidence that the 'targets' of enforcement are overwhelmingly from poorer parts of the world, marginalized or excluded from core industrialized capitalism. Furthermore, in spite of potential opportunities that arose in the 1990s, the UN has not been accorded the necessary means to conduct peace enforcement except as part of a peacekeeping mandate. The Department of Peacekeeping Operations (DPKO) is not a ministry of defense, and peace enforcement has generally been reserved by, or delegated to, governments with interests in using force to obtain solutions to issues. 'Coalitions of the willing' are the standard operating procedure.

This chapter begins by surveying the meanings of peace enforcement and their evolution, particularly its crisis management role. It then surveys key developments in particular crises since 1992. The politics of peace enforcement, with an emphasis on delegation and decentralization, form the subsequent discussion, and this is followed by consideration of doctrine and operational issues.

The Meanings of Peace Enforcement

Peace enforcement has been broadly defined as 'operations that seek to impose the will of the Security Council by direct military or economic action.'[1] But analysis has been bedevilled by confusing use of the term to mean different things at different times and in different military cultures. It can have both collective security and conflict management meanings. The construction initially favored by American analysts and the US Army, was unalloyed coercion or force under Chapter VII against specific targets—or even more explicitly 'to expel an aggressor from occupied territory.'[2] This representation enveloped war in a cloak of peace and was based on the patently flawed idea that collective security and peace support operations were linked on a continuum of force. A more nuanced representation, favored by European militaries and the DPKO, characterizes peace enforcement as a distinctive, robust mutation of peace-keeping and a key element in the conflict management options available to the UN. It is predicated on the impartial threat or use of force in so-called 'gray area' situations, for example to protect relief supplies against bandits, to ensure force protection and freedom of movement, or to secure peace agreements against spoilers.

Collective Security against Specific Targets

In its collective security sense, peace enforcement is a permit to go to war with a designated enemy. NATO's definition refers to the employment of 'conventional combat operations.'[3] These may be designed to halt aggression, as in the Korean War, or to bring about a change in sovereign authority, as in the invasion of Afghanistan. It can include 'coercive acts,' such as aid conditionality, as well as combat. Indeed, the exertion of economic power may be just as fatal as military power. In Johan Galtung's formulation, there is an equivalence between military and nonmilitary coercion, such that nonmilitary control by powerful states, multi-national corporations, and international financial institutions over the have-nots brings death from poverty-related causes (in the order of 20,000 deaths a day) and amounts to 'structural violence.'⁴ Direct economic sanctions have also been backed by military force under Chapter VII. A UN mandate to blockade Southern Rhodesia in 1966 authorized the naval forces of member states to intercept oil tankers bound for the east African coast. This mandate was subsequently revisited for the Arabian Gulf in the Iraq–Kuwait conflict in 1990 and 1991, and for the Adriatic Sea from November when maritime patrols by NATO and the Western European Union enforced a blockade against parties in the Yugoslav wars.⁵

According to this representation, the first notable case to be conducted with a Chapter VII mandate was the coalition war against North Korea in 1950. This was possible because the Soviet Union was absent from the Security Council and could not exercise its veto. The UN flag flew in Korea, and the Security Council was kept informed of the progress of operations ex post facto. The General Assembly's legitimating function emerged through the Uniting for Peace Resolution of 1950, which reiterated the General Assembly's ability to recommend action in cases in which the Security Council could not act on a threat to, or breach of, the peace because of a veto. But the UN exercised no operational control, and the episode marks the success of the US and its allies in obtaining UN endorsement for the containment of communism during the Cold War rather than any conceptual development of collective security or any significant development of UN competence and authority. The Military Staff Committee was supposed to develop plans for implementing collective security under Article 47 of the Charter, but it effectively stopped work in the late 1940s. It was another forty years before another Korea arose. After Iraq's invasion of Kuwait the Security Council authorized the coalition war, Operation *Desert Storm*, against Iraq in 1991. A further ten years passed before another coalition war, Operation *Enduring Freedom*, was authorized by the Council against the Taliban in Afghanistan. Three UN-authorized coalition wars in fifty years do not signify a normative evolution.

The rewriting of the Korean War and the like as peace enforcement or a species of peace operation serves the cause of politico-military window-dressing by camouflaging militarism as pacification—a charge that has been leveled at UN operations more generally.⁶ Until the Somalia débâcle, US military doctrine tended to blur war, peace enforcement, and peacekeeping by locating them in a continuum of levels of force rather than in conceptually distinct categories for which impartiality and consent were key variables. The oxymoron in this representation of peace enforcement also obscures the particular value of collective self-defense protected in the Charter. Indeed, peace enforcement has been (mis)used to include operations that do not seek to impose the will of the Security Council at all, but only the will of some of its members and their allies.⁷ Two coalition wars, Operation *Allied Force* against the Federal Republic of Yugoslavia in 1999 and Operation *Iraqi Freedom* against Iraq in 2003, were 'illegal' (i.e., without explicit UN authorization) and in theory could have justified UN mobilization against the belligerents (or enforcers).

None of these wars entailed any operational leadership on the part of the UN or Security Council instructions as to how action could be taken. Operations were, in effect, delegated to a single state (the UK in the case of Rhodesia) and to coalitions on other occasions. Every single coalition war, though the term 'war' was consciously avoided in the case of Kosovo, had two features in common: overwhelming US political leadership, military deployment, command, and control; and virtually no UN material input or supervision. All except the Rhodesia example involved potent battle capabilities, with states devising their own standard operating procedures and rules of engagement (though often poorly coordinated between each other).

Crisis Management in Peace Operations

By contrast, in a crisis management sense, peace enforcement has been taken to mean overcoming resistance to compliance with a mandate but without a nominated enemy.[8] This representation assumes that civil wars are not clearly defined by battles between centrally orchestrated regular armed forces. These unstable and messy situations, referred to as 'gray areas,' when parties do not respect UN neutrality, are judged to require robust and combat-ready forces to facilitate the achievement or maintenance of cease-fires where internal conflict has been raging and where central authority is weak or has collapsed. This concept has been so closely associated with peace operations that it might be characterized as a 'militarization' of peacekeeping.

Traditionally, the blue berets were an arm of peaceful diplomacy, generally only mandated to return fire in self-defense. The UN's first Congo mission (1960–1964) had crossed over into military action but the peacekeepers were quite ill-prepared to enforce freedom of movement and to expel foreign troops and mercenaries. This, and a few low-profile instances, such as the UN Force in Cyprus protecting Nicosia airport from Turkish aggression in 1974,[9] were exceptional. The Congo proved so damaging to the political consensus for peacekeeping that member states insisted on six-month mandates which could only be renewed if they were not vetoed by the Security Council. Generally, peacekeepers under UN control make themselves highly conspicuous and inoffensive, and have negotiated rather than fought their way out of trouble. In Cambodia, a Chapter VI mission, there was no provision for enforcement and the blue berets relied on consent for their presence, or withdrawal when confronted by even minimal opposition.

However, the concept of peacekeeping underwent a transformation in the 1990s, and it was widely accepted that noncombatant peacekeepers in intrastate conflicts often faced situations in which consent could not be relied upon. Following the UN's inability to deal with civil war in Somalia (1992–1995), the former Yugoslavia (1992–1995) and Rwanda (1994), traditional peacekeeping was dismissed by many observers in the late 1990s as far too risky in the so-called new civil wars. In addition to other complications, peacekeepers were being attacked and killed.

KEY DEVELOPMENTS

The most significant event in this respect was the UN–US intervention in Somalia. It began with a peacekeeping operation (UNOSOM I) in 1992, but Secretary-General Boutros Boutros-Ghali soon had to request a heavily armed, partial occupation to provide security for humanitarian aid and allow time to prepare for a bigger UN mission. Operation *Restore Hope* was conducted by an American-led Unified Task Force (UNITAF) under a Chapter VII mandate. The Security Council's December 1992 resolution 794 did not envisage this as a precedent; the resolution contained cautious phrasing about: 'the unique character of the present situation...the complex and extraordinary nature...which requires an exceptional response.' Somalia was regarded as a state where sovereignty was no longer exercised and therefore could not be contravened. It was thought to be a case of confronting clan-bandits rather than negotiating among nationalists. In this case, states were acting on Security Council instructions to protect humanitarian relief and disarm factions (rather than merely gaining UN authorization to do what they would have done anyway). Robust disarmament and protection operations began even before UNOSOM II, another Chapter VII operation, replaced it in the summer of 1993. The United States completely dominated its command and control structure, and its military units remained independent, reporting directly to headquarters in the United States. Although claiming to be fulfilling a mandate impartially, this was fatally compromised when the mission targeted the United Somali Congress (and its leader Mohammed Farah Aideed), which was blamed for killing twenty-four Pakistanis of UNOSOM II. At the behest of the Secretary-General and the US Secretary of State, Madeleine Albright, the June 1993 resolution 837 called for Aideed's capture and trial. It was rushed through the Security Council to get a quick response. Rules of engagement were changed and the UN Special Representative for Somalia, former US admiral Jonathan Howe, also put a price on Aideed's head. In July a US missile attack on a clan meeting killed fifty Somalis and injured 170 and generated more local support for Aideed. Boutros-Ghali, Albright, Howe, and the commander of the US forces, Major-General Thomas Montgomery, had made a disastrous attempt to slide from peacekeeping into enforcement and back again.

Reluctance on the part of the UN Secretary-General and of member states to mix peacekeeping and enforcement became particularly evident during the crisis in the former Yugoslavia.[10] A peacekeeping operation, the UN Protection Force (UNPRO-FOR), was eventually injected into this war zone, but as consent disintegrated at the tactical level, and as the conflict spread, its mandate was frequently updated (and contradicted), so that it was expected to secure strategic areas and respond to violations of cease-fires. In June 1992 Security Council resolution 758 accorded UNPROFOR Chapter VII enforcement powers to take control of Sarajevo airport. But UNPROFOR lacked ground-force capacity to stop the conflict or subsequently to protect so-called safe areas from attack. Apart from a few occasions, such as the

Danish contingent in Tuzla silencing Serb guns with over seventy tank rounds, the dominant forceful response took the form of air power. NATO conducted air strikes against Bosnian Serb positions around Goražde in April 1994, against Serb controlled Udbina airport and positions in northern Bosnia in November 1994, against Pale the day after Serb forces took 350 peacekeepers hostage in May 1995, and against Bosnian Serb positions after a shell landed in Sarajevo market place in August 1995. The UN's failure to request NATO air strikes to support the Dutch in Srebrenica in July 1995 was, however, only one of the factors in the failure to hold the town. In the effort to break the siege of Sarajevo, the Bosniak leadership appears to have regarded Srebrenica as a potential trade-off for Serb suburbs of Sarajevo, withdrew commanders from the town and made no effort to relieve it.[11]

In mid-1995 a rapid reaction force with camouflaged tanks was organized by, and made answerable to, the United Kingdom and France. But it had no clear purpose, other than to avoid having to fight in white-painted vehicles. At one point French President Jacques Chirac proposed retaking Srebrenica, but the British demurred on the grounds that the force had insufficient capability and had no mandate 'to go to war.'[12] The effort to be impartial was manifested in Commander Michael Rose's threat in October 1994 to use air strikes against the Bosniak Army if it contravened the demilitarized zone on Mount Igman. But since this even-handedness was increasingly eroded by Serb artillery and growing US and NATO support for the Bosniaks this was an unlikely prospect. As enforcement was almost entirely used against the Serbs, UNPROFOR's impartiality was compromised. Moreover, although robust posturing may well have assisted in deterring attacks in particular areas, and in the negotiation of relief supplies and refugee safety, neither the rapid reaction force nor the air strikes played a pivotal role in bringing about a sustainable cease-fire, which was primarily the result of the US-backed Croatian offensive, Operation *Storm*, in 1995.

By contrast, after Somalia, the United States, the United Kingdom, and France not only denied the Security Council the means to rescue Rwandans from atrocities: they also denied the genocide. The reluctance of Western political elites to provide political and material support for the UN Assistance Mission for Rwanda (UNAMIR) meant that the UN Secretariat lacked the backing to undertake population protection and weapons raids. Members of the Secretariat adopted a defeatist approach to the UNAMIR commander's calls for a liberal interpretation of his mandate. Indeed French policy in Rwanda, under the direct control of the French president, actively supported the hard-line Hutus with whom France had strong political, economic, and military links. In June 1994 the Security Council invoked Chapter VII for resolution 929 to mandate France to end the massacres and prepare for a UN follow-on force. It provided *Opération Turquoise* with retrospective legitimacy after French troops had crossed into Rwanda. But far from protecting Tutsi civilians, French troops either turned a blind eye to the killing spree or actually assisted the Hutu *génocidaires*.[13]

There was no such queasiness about enforcement in the case of Haiti. The General Assembly and the Secretary-General's good offices had been mobilized to participate in election monitoring, and subsequently to back action by the Organization of American States. The Security Council did not get involved until 1993 when peace-keepers were sent to modernize Haiti's armed forces and police after a military coup had toppled an elected leader, Jean-Bertrand Aristide. They were denied disembark-ation by armed demonstrators. In contrast to the response to unrest in Rwanda, the US persuaded the Security Council that domestic turmoil in Haiti was a threat to international peace and security and required a Chapter VII enforcement to restore democracy. The Security Council passed resolution 940 in July 1994 authorizing a US military operation to pave the way for a peacekeeping mission. The Haitian govern-ment resigned and the enforcement was unopposed. The construction was contested as a smokescreen. The United States had long tolerated the vicious regimes of both the Duvaliers, father and son, and the Reagan administration had supported the abusive military dictatorship until President Bill Clinton ushered in a change of policy and planned a military invasion. The threat to 'international' peace and security presented by the Haitian military regime amounted to the preservation of US borders from an influx of large numbers of refugees and asylum seekers.[14]

A decade later, Haiti was still characterized by political instability and violence. The United Nations returned in 2004 in response to armed conflict between Aristide and his opponents, who after taking control of the northern part of the country threatened to march on the capital. After Aristide's flight into exile, and at the interim president's request, the Security Council authorized a Multinational Force led by the United States, which was followed-up by the 7,500-strong UN Stabilization Mission in Haiti (MINUSTAH), which continued the robustness with aggressive search and patrol operations.[15]

If Somalia and Bosnia had caused considerable angst in the DPKO and in national military institutions about the value of enforcement, Rwanda and Haiti demon-strated the P-5's destabilizing selectivity. But the shock of Rwanda did not prevent the Security Council from issuing further Chapter VII mandates to peacekeeping forces. For example, in February 2000, the mandate for peacekeepers in Sierra Leone was changed to allow them to afford protection to civilians. This is not to say, however, that peacekeepers were adequately furnished with the necessary personnel and capacity to conduct enforcement effectively. Sierra Leone had become another cause célèbre.

The United Nations Mission in Sierra Leone (UNAMSIL) was sent to monitor the Lomé Peace Accord between the rebels and the government in the spring of 1999. This accord was disastrously flawed in its demilitarization and demobilization provisions, for which the United States, United Kingdom, and UN were largely responsible. It soon collapsed. The Revolutionary United Front (RUF) took some 500 peacekeepers hostage in May 2000. Rather than strengthen UNAMSIL, the United Kingdom sent an independent combat force of paratroopers and marines offshore to secure Freetown and drive the RUF back. In July 2000, UNAMSIL also conducted counter-attacks, including an operation to release over 200 Indian hostages. The Security Council authorized UNAMSIL to 'decisively counter' any threat or actual hostility.

Although varied interpretations of the mandate led the Indians and Jordanians to withdraw, the DPKO's Best Practices Unit regarded the enforcement operation as a positive development.[16] In East Timor, also, the troops of the UN Transitional Administration (UNTAET) secured an interpretation of the rules of engagement to conduct enforcement operations against militias. In the Democratic Republic of the Congo, MONUC (the UN mission in the DRC) fought a pitched battle with militias in the Ituri area at the beginning of 2005 under a mandate to protect civilians and humanitarian workers.

However, the international response to events in Sudan (where, by some estimates, mass killings in Darfur numbered 300,000 and those forcibly displaced some 2 million by the middle of 2006) suggested that little had changed since Rwanda. Certainly, the DPKO had begun codifying operational standards to prevent a repeat of UN personnel standing aside during atrocities against civilians, and a special adviser on genocide was established in 2004 to make recommendations to the Security Council. But a sanctions regime and no-fly zone were poorly enforced, and neither the Security Council nor potential leaders such as the United Kingdom, France, and the United States would go beyond supporting a small and underfunded military operation by the African Union (AU). This mission in Sudan commenced in August 2004 with monitors and a protection force that protected a few locations rather than the population in general. The AU itself failed to invoke its own 2002 charter provision (Article 4h) to protect populations from egregious crimes. According to critics, both the UN and the African Union 'decided that respecting Sudanese sovereignty was more important than conducting a military response capable of protecting the civilian population.'[17]

These key developments indicate that member states were increasingly influenced by the discourses favoring enforcement. In practice, this was applied in particular to the military protection of peace processes involving international administrations charged with wielding legislative and executive authority, with establishing security and law and order, and with establishing government functions. In East Timor, Bosnia and Herzegovina, Kosovo, and Afghanistan the Security Council authorized Chapter VII operations where a cease-fire or peace agreement was fragile or local consent was untrustworthy. However, in many other cases, states wanted to be seen to be taking action, but did not have sufficient interests at stake to make the necessary commitments and risk soldiers' lives to ensure effective implementation.

THE POLITICS OF PEACE ENFORCEMENT

In spite of inconsistencies—about the rectitude of using Chapter VII on the one hand and the overuse of it on the other—cosmopolitan perspectives depict a normative shift that allows peace enforcers to challenge the sovereign right of domestic authorities to slaughter their own people. The protection of sovereignty and forcible humanitarian intervention are not contradictory; peace enforcement can liberate a 'people's sovereignty' from oppressive regimes.[18] Historically, states had rarely, if ever, claimed humanitarian motives as the grounds for enforcement, except ex post facto. But beginning with Somalia, a humanitarian justification has been an important ingredient in the discourse of peace enforcement. Initially, Boutros-Ghali insisted that in local conflicts 'when all semblance of state authority vanishes, as in Somalia, and when whole populations are singled out for genocide, as in Rwanda,' then the Security Council was acting under the Charter to maintain international peace and security and was not intervening in internal affairs.[19]

His successor, Kofi Annan, argued in his Annual Report to the General Assembly of September 1999 that the world was being transformed by a redefinition of state sovereignty and an emerging consciousness of the right of individuals to control their destiny. His appeal to a humanitarian ethic had been heightened by the genocide in Rwanda that, he argued, would 'define for our generation the consequences of inaction in the face of mass murder.' For cosmopolitans, Chapter VII resolutions from the 1990s indicate a shift towards recognizing cosmopolitan ethics and justice. Another proposition holds that conceptions of sovereignty are ever changing, and in the current era holding a membership card in the international system is contingent on the way domestic order is maintained. If a government flouts fundamental principles of justice, then enforcement can be a consequence.

This was basically the position of NATO leaders in justifying their evasion of existing international law in order to conduct an attack on Yugoslavia in 1999, the first occasion when a group of states claimed to be acting primarily on humanitarian grounds without UN authorization. They argued that NATO was legitimately pushing at the frontiers of humanitarianism—which according to an independent commission made the effort 'legitimate' if 'illegal.'[20] The idea of enforcement for the protection of populations within states has also been hailed as a normative development since the reports into Rwanda and Srebrenica and formulation of the principle of the responsibility to protect,[21] and is reflected in the outcome document of the 2005 World Summit as well as earlier preparatory reports from the UN High-level Panel on Threats, Challenges and Change (HLP), and from the Secretary-General.[22]

But critics doubt whether there has been any enforcement directly impelled by a high moral purpose without the accompaniment of self-interest.[23] In spite of the heralded shift in discourse, in practice, new norms of enforcement are not clearly defined or articulated. Moreover, it may be a sign of weakness that even the hegemonic power, the United States, has to bully and cajole allies to participate in enforcement. The UN membership is deeply divided over the desirability of challenging domestic jurisdiction through Chapter VII enforcement measures. In February 2000, the UN Special Committee on Peacekeeping Operations revealed perennial distrust of enforcement without invitation. Obviously, humanitarianism and human rights have become politicized issues, to the extent of provoking a (defensive) counter-reaction. But the analyst has to untangle the altruistic public packaging by governments from other agendas. A change in the way that enforcement is constructed and represented may amount to no more than a repackaging of imagined self-interest, and 'rewriting' the notion of sovereignty a matter of convenience.[24]

There has been no clear notion of the boundaries around peace enforcement. A particular representation of enforcing peace in a particular community is not considered relevant for all communities. The Kurdish 'safe haven' in northern Iraq was not a precedent for the general protection of oppressed people, and certainly did not extend to the protection of Kurds in Turkey, for example. It could be readily imposed through massive military superiority by the victors in the 1991 Gulf War, and it was essentially a measure to satisfy domestic public opinion, concerned that the war victory was proving detrimental to innocents. The representation of enforcement (in terms of cause, justification, and relationship to sovereignty) is thus highly flexible, and perhaps the customary practice of states has not changed so much as the idealistic rhetoric, imagery, and packaging of traditional power politics. The Italian-led coalition that arrived to secure humanitarian access in Albania in 1997 was essentially part of a broad policy to stem an outflow of refugees into Western Europe. The chief determinant in enforcing the peace in Kosovo appears to have been the US State Department's anxiety to preserve US leadership in European security through NATO as the primary instrument of Western defense. Overriding the military chiefs, who expressed doubts about the strategic wisdom and operational feasibility of the war, President Clinton revealed in a speech in March 1999 that it was essentially about a strong US-European partnership and NATO's credibility.[25]

Overriding determinants of peace enforcement, then, are government-defined interests and capabilities and the likelihood of being able to convey an image of success, plus the avoidance of financial burdens, loss of life and open-ended commitments. The Clinton administration was quite candid about this in Presidential Decision Directive 25 (PDD 25) of May 1994, which expressly argued that the US would continue to act unilaterally unless the UN could be captured to further US national interests. Critics have grounds therefore for suggesting that 'humanitarian' motives were a camouflage for hegemony.[26] The critique is supported by another discernible trend: decentralization of peace enforcement.

Delegation and Decentralization

The Security Council had given peacekeepers extended tasks that were beyond them, known as 'mission creep.' In 1992 Boutros-Ghali recommended in *An Agenda for Peace* that under Article 40 of the Charter the Security Council consider the option of using 'peace-enforcement units in clearly defined circumstances.' These would consist of volunteer units made available on call by member states, heavily armed and extensively trained by national forces, but like peacekeepers would come under the Secretary-General's tactical command during missions. The notion was stillborn. The most approximate mechanism has been a Standby High Readiness Brigade, sent to the Ethiopia–Eritrea border in 2000, which is a 'Chapter VI' arrangement. The P-5 have had no interest in equipping the UN with the means to conduct enforcement effectively.

Consequently, when the UN either failed to stretch peacekeeping into enforcement (in Rwanda) or authorized it without providing the means (Bosnia), or attempted it with the means provided by a partisan force (Somalia), it fulfilled the skeptics' prophesy that the UN could not lead and control forces for peace enforcement. This has been reflected in the acronyms and code names for these operations. They are not prefixed by 'United Nations'—the 'UN' in UNITAF stood for Unified Task Force. UN mandates for forces under DPKO auspices are usually short-term and extended at six-monthly intervals, irrespective of the situation itself, reflecting the political and financial constraints that the UN has to operate under. Delegated enforcement operations are much more open-ended.

In some situations non-UN enforcements have been endorsed retrospectively by the Security Council to give them legitimacy, e.g., the operations of the Economic Community of West African States (ECOWAS) in Liberia (from 1991). More commonly, the delegation of responsibilities has been an important trend in managing peace enforcement, a trend favored by the UN Secretary-General, the Brahimi report and the report of the HLP. Indeed, regional bodies are encouraged to tackle problems, under Chapter VIII of the Charter, provided the efforts are compatible with the spirit of the Charter. Sometimes referred to as subcontracting or burden sharing, it means that regional organizations, or groups of states, with a special interest in a crisis, are authorized to deal with it. Given that the UN is under resourced it can make practical sense to delegate responsibility to ad hoc coalitions.

New Zealand and Australia took on the burden of peace enforcement in Bougainville in 1998, and in 1999 an Australian-led coalition entered East Timor with a Chapter VII mandate for the International Force for East Timor (INTERFET). An International Security Assistance Force in Afghanistan was originally led by the UK in 2001 and was subsequently a NATO-led operation. Using NATO assets the EU conducted crisis management through Operation *Concordia* in Macedonia in March 2003 and an autonomous Operation *Artemis* in Ituri, DRC with limited tasks and limited timeframe in June 2003.

The 'impartial' enforcement of peace settlements was handed over to non-UN forces. In Bosnia, for example, the UN mission was confined to civilian tasks and the International Police Task Force (IPTF). Security Council resolution 1031 of December 1995 established a NATO-led coalition, the Implementation Force (IFOR), with 60,000 troops, which was superseded by the Stabilization Force (SFOR) and then European Union Force (EUFOR). Other manifestations of the trend are: 18,000 troops of the Russian-dominated Commonwealth of Independent States (CIS) in Georgia and Tajikistan and 7,500 West African troops in Liberia. After the war against Serbia, the military pillar of the UN Mission in Kosovo was left to NATO and then the EU. At the end of 1995 the number of UN peacekeepers was only 60,000 compared to over 80,000 other peace enforcement troops and half a million other conventional forces, mostly US, stationed around the world.

Regional and subregional organizations have been relied upon for two main reasons. First, the UN's management abilities depend on what the member states, especially the Security Council members, permit and what they are willing to fund. They have diluted UN management of enforcement measures by failing to provide the means to accomplish mandates and by denying authority to the UN. In particular, governments have been reluctant to furnish troops for risky enforcement operations under UN control. This has damaged the UN's credibility and paved the way for enforcement to be farmed out to other bodies. Second, the trend is welcomed by coalitions of states because they can justify greater selectivity about their UN contributions and because regional organizations may be more easily manipulated than the UN.

The development also raises three problematic issues. First, few regional organizations are adequately equipped in terms of managerial expertise and military capacity for balanced multilateral roles. This is especially so in sub-Saharan Africa. The OAU provided little leadership or management in the early 1990s, and ECOWAS took eight years to make an impact on the civil war in Liberia. The United States, France, and the United Kingdom have subsidized various capacity-building initiatives in Africa and the African Union has generated various initiatives. But regional competence is no greater than the UN's, as demonstrated in Darfur.

Second, decentralization promotes regional hegemony, licensing dominant states to promote their ambitions. Governments will consider that they continue to have carte blanche to police their own spheres of influence, as Russia did in Chechnya from the mid-1990s, South Africa in Lesotho in 1998–1999, and Nigeria in ECOMOG in Liberia and Sierra Leone. In Europe, the United States has a veto over the use of any NATO assets by the EU. Third, little thought has been given to the need to manage the relationship between the UN and regional organizations. If the UN delegates authority, it tends to lack control over an operation.

MILITARY DOCTRINE AND OPERATIONAL ISSUES

Although aiming to operate with 'active impartiality,' in practice peace enforcement disguises actual bias, or is perceived as bias, toward particular parties and can have a prejudicial impact on the outcomes of disputes. As a prominent authority on peace support operations comments:

the idea that a 'peace enforcement' or 'peace restoring' operation can clinically apply force to manipulate the behaviour of various parties on the ground *without* designating an enemy, while simultaneously assuming that such action will not influence the political dynamics of the conflict is to seriously underestimate the impact of outside military action on the balance of military, political and economic interests in . . . complex intra-state conflicts.[27]

The notion that impartiality can survive enforcement seems tenuous: military force is employed to influence an authority structure without the consistent consent of all parties. Indeed, Boutros-Ghali had a partisan role in encouraging the attack on Aideed.

Furthermore, competition in stabilization operations means a blurring not only in the perceptions of local communities between relief and enforcement operations, but between various components of a peace process. Thus the UN's legitimizing function is undermined by the operational practice of coalition forces beyond UN control. Its ambiguous role in authorizing or partnering enforcement operations risks making it a party to disputes, as France became in Côte d'Ivoire and the United States became in Afghanistan and Iraq. Any pretence at being an impartial intermediary is compromised in two respects. Local leaders manipulate the limitations of peacekeepers in order to get a forceful intervention that will act on their side (as the Bosniaks and Kosovo Liberation Army did). Local communities make little distinction on political grounds between one force and another, and more on which individuals within which organizations will provide the most to satisfy local needs or assist in political competition among the local oligarchs.[28]

For military cultures in which peacekeeping was historically a very marginal activity—notably in the United Kingdom, France, and the United States—doctrine writers were well-disposed to enforcement.[29] They searched for a 'middle ground' in which troops would be prepared to engage in limited combat short of war, by having the capability to escalate in the use of force. Thus the interveners could enforce a separation of warring parties (who were thought to be relatively easily deterred) or coerce them into respecting a peace agreement.[30] UNITAF and UNOSOM II had reflected US reliance on fire power to resolve the 'gap' in peacekeeping. Army doctrine, as in *FM 100-23: Peace Operations*, proposed a spectrum of force rather than discrete kinds of operation. After Somalia, the raw continuum in US Army doctrine was dropped (and UN-sponsored wars were dropped from the definition of peace enforcement). Bosnia had also highlighted the disparity between superior military power in the air, provided mainly by the US, and unarmed peacekeeping on land, provided by others who were vulnerable targets in the event of air power being threatened or used.

By 2000 peacekeeping and peace enforcement in US doctrine had become subcategories of peace operations which were a prominent feature of 'stability operations,' which in turn was a subcategory of 'Operations Other Than War.'[31] But peace enforcement in US doctrine still encompassed both consent-based operations, such as protection of relief supplies, and those that did not rely on consent, such as sanctions and arresting war criminals. Elsewhere, in Nordic countries for example, doctrine makes peacekeeping and peace enforcement the two main subspecies of peace support operations. There remains complete disagreement, also, as to whether peace enforcement can transition back to peacekeeping, US commentators claiming it can, and others claiming that enforcement compromises any attempt to return to consent-based operations.[32]

In addition to doctrinal disharmony among participating states, various operational issues also arise that have not been satisfactorily resolved:

- Where enforcement has been attempted some forces, particularly the US Army, have been preoccupied with force protection, but this hampers their responses and distances them from the population.

- Harmonization of the rules of engagement is more difficult in improvised peace enforcement coalitions, because of the greater likelihood of force being used. Since the Vietnam War, US military culture has allowed commanders on the spot considerable flexibility in changing rules of engagement, and the 'fire threshold' tends to be lower than in many other forces. It is also a critical issue because soldiers who use force may be held liable for deaths and casualties, depending on the writ of local laws and the existence of memoranda of understanding.

- The principles of humanitarian relief workers may be compromised and personnel placed at higher risk. There are also legal issues for other non-enforcement personnel (from military observers to private security companies), regarding their potential status as prisoners of war for example.

- Use of force to protect civilians is a specialized task, requiring extensive deployment and clear guidelines. Neither of these facets has been particularly evident in operations. There is a considerable deficit in capabilities to protect civilians (as in Darfur, for example), and in operational concepts (how to protect and whether it is primarily a task for police units). A mandate to protect civilians can give rise to false expectations and place non-protected civilians at greater risk of reprisals.

- Communities tend to discriminate between outsiders according to whether they can offer security, assistance, and respect. It is by no means clear that local communities have any understanding of the purposes of the mission, its rules of engagement or the distinctions between its components, let alone appreciate the niceties of doctrine.

CONCLUSION

Peace enforcement has been a particularly thorny issue for the UN. But the use of force to solve deep-seated and complex political issues is a blunt instrument whoever does it. One should remember that non-UN enterprises, as in Afghanistan and Iraq (where conflicts continue), have hardly been unqualified successes. And the fact that US allies have had to be cajoled into supporting enforcement suggests limits to both US hegemonic power and the notion of a normative shift.[33]

The increased use of Chapter VII and the widening of mandates to provide for civilian protection, reinforced by the Brahimi and HLP reports, have been written up as a significant normative shift. Autocratic governments have to contend with the prospect that their abuses might provide the trigger for a foreign intervention. But perhaps the end of the Cold War has not made a great difference to the way that enforcement works. The norms that govern implementation have not shifted in parallel. Tellingly, most UN mandates with protection in view have reflected the norm that governments are wary of enforcement unless it also serves an ulterior purpose. Accordingly, the phrase 'within capabilities and areas of deployment' accompanies the 'responsibility to protect.' The underlying political determinants of enforcement remain based on constructed perceptions of state power. Governments adapt their representations of enforcement to the discourse of ethics and justice. But they remain nervous about incurring casualties to uphold international peace and justice and weigh up a range of costs and benefits, including intangible factors such as credibility and prestige, before participating. Such governments may be under public pressure to do something when media reports reveal abuse of populations. But governing elites are the prime determinants of enforcement and its representation.

The debate about enforcement has also presented doctrine with the issue of how, if at all, it is distinctive from other kinds of peace support operation. As a South African expert comments: '[N]o-one really knows how to do peace enforcement operations. And no-one really wants to do these operations—unless, of course, there are strongly perceived own interests at stake. Hence, the concept of peace enforcement remains an extremely under-developed area of military doctrine—even though it is perhaps most needed.'[34]

Some analysts propose an international consensus on criteria for enforcement, on the lines of Just War doctrine, to provide a normative framework that will set standards of legitimacy and lead to consistent application. Without clear criteria about who might invoke enforcement, and in what circumstances, the alternatives are inaction on the part of the UN, or the ad hoc *posse comitatus* among self-selected governments. But even if such a normative framework were universally accepted, interpretation of the criteria and their application would be manipulated by states with the greatest sway in authorizing bodies. The risk is that perpetual interveners would enforce peace to promote strategic or ideological interests and act as the arbiters of what constitutes humanitarianism, domestic jurisdiction, last resort, legitimacy, and other qualifying criteria.

The deployment of multinational forces depends upon coincidences among state authorities with the means and interests. Enforcement only deals with the manifestations of social, economic, and political problems which are embedded in the state-oriented and capitalist structure of the international system. The construction and representation of peace enforcement is framed by the ideologies of the most dominant and formative actors. This point should not be construed as an argument in favor of leaving populations to the mercy of abuse by their own political elites. In international relations the nonintervention principle constructs a vision of hell as war inflicted on a people from outside the state, whereas the common experience of many people is that hell is on the inside inflicted by their own state or fellow citizens. Any ethical basis for a redistributive justice that mitigates, if not rejects, the disintegrative socioeconomic effects of the global economy ought to be reciprocated by respect for human security by public and private authorities in all states.

NOTES

1. Alex J. Bellamy, 'The "Next Stage" in Peace Operations Theory?' in *Peace Operations and Global Order*, ed. Alex J. Bellamy and Paul Williams (London: Frank Cass, 2004), 22.

2. Dick Zandee, 'Use of Force—is there a middle ground?' in *Challenges of Peace Support into the 21st Century*, ed. Bo Huldt, Annika Hilding, and Arita Eriksson (Stockholm: Försvarshögskolans ACTA B9, Strategic Institute, Swedish National Defence College, 1998), 62.

3. *NATO, Peacekeeping, and the United Nations* (London: British–American Security Information Council, 1994), 5.

4. Johan Galtung, 'Violence, Peace and Peace Research,' *Journal of Peace Research* 6, no. 3 (1969): 167–191.

5. For maritime enforcement see Michael Pugh, ed., *Maritime Security and Peacekeeping: A Framework for United Nations Operations* (Manchester, UK: Manchester University Press, 1994).

6. Francois Debrix, *(Re)Envisioning Peacekeeping: The United Nations and the Mobilization of Ideology* (Minneapolis: University of Minnesota Press Borderlines Series, 1997).

7. Frederick H. Fleitz, Jr., *Peacekeeping Fiascoes of the 1990s: Causes, Solutions, and US Interests* (New York: Praeger, 2002), 116, table 7.4.

8. Mats Berdal, 'Lessons Not Learned: The Use of Force in "Peace Operations" in the 1990s,' in *Managing Armed Conflicts in the 21st Century*, ed. Adekeye Adebajo and Chandra Lekha Sriram (London: Frank Cass, 2001), 56.

9. Francis Henn, 'The Nicosia Airport Incident of 1974: A Peacekeeping Gamble,' *International Peacekeeping* 1, no. 1 (1994): 80–98.

10. Marrack Goulding, *Peacemonger* (London: John Murray, 2002), 317, 319.

11. Marko Attila Hoare, 'Civil–Military Relations in Bosnia-Herzegovina 1992–1995,' in *The War in Croatia and Bosnian-Herzegovina 1991–1995*, ed. Branka Magaš and Ivo Žanić (London: Frank Cass, 2001), 196–197.

12. Laura Silber and Allan Little, *The Death of Yugoslavia*, 2nd edn. (London: Penguin, 1996), 351–352.

13. Roméo A. Dallaire, *Shake Hands with the Devil: The Failure of Humanity in Rwanda* (Toronto: Random House, 2003); and Philip Gourevitch, *We Wish To Inform You That Tomorrow We Will Be Killed With Our Families: Stories From Rwanda* (London: Picador, 1998).

14. Béatrice Pouligny, *Peace Operations Seen from Below: UN Missions and Local People* (London: Hurst, 2006), 19–20.

15. Ian Johnstone, 'Dilemmas of Robust Peace Operations,' in *Annual Review of Global Peace Operations 2006*, A Project of the Center on International Cooperation (Boulder Colo.: Lynne Rienner, 2006), 5.

16. Ibid., 3.

17. Paul D. Williams, 'Military Responses to Mass Killing: The African Union Mission in Sudan,' *International Peacekeeping* 13, no. 2 (2006): 168–183.

18. See, Tom Woodhouse and Oliver Ramsbotham, 'Cosmopolitan Peacekeeping and the Globalization of Security,' *International Peacekeeping* 12, no. 2 (2005): 139–156.

19. Boutros Boutros-Ghali, 'Beleaguered Are the Peacekeepers,' *New York Times*, 30 October 1994.

20. Independent International Commission on Kosovo, *Kosovo Report: Conflict, International Response, Lessons Learned* (Oxford: Oxford University Press, 2000), 4.

21. International Commission on Intervention and State Sovereignty, *The Responsibility to Protect* (Ottawa: ICISS, 2001).

22. See *2005 World Summit Outcome*, UN document A/60/L.1, 15 September 2005; *A More Secure World: Our Shared Responsibility*, Report of the High-level Panel on Threats, Challenges and Change (New York: UN, 2004); and Kofi Annan, *In Larger Freedom: Towards Development, Security and Human Rights for All*, UN document A/59/2005, 21 March 2005.

23. James Mayall, 'The Concept of Humanitarian Intervention Revisited,' in *Kosovo and the Challenge of Humanitarian Intervention*, ed. Albrecht Schnabel and Ramesh Thakur (Tokyo: United Nations University, 2000), 326.

24. Cynthia Weber, *Simulating Sovereignty: Intervention, the State and Symbolic Exchange* (Cambridge: Cambridge University Press, 1995).

25. Peter Gowan, 'The Euro-Atlantic Origins of NATO's Attack on Yugoslavia,' in *Masters of the Universe? NATO's Balkan Crusade*, ed. Tariq Ali (London: Verso, 2000), 3.

26. See, e.g., Noam Chomsky, *The New Military Humanism: Lessons from Kosovo* (London: Polity, 1999).

27. Berdal, 'Lessons Not Learned,' 67.

28. Pouligny, *Peace Operations Seen from Below*, 106.

29. Christopher Coker, 'Peace Support Flexibility and Different Military Cultures,' in *Challenges of Peace Support into the 21st Century*, 62.

30. Zandee, 'Use of Force' in ibid., 88.

31. Theo Farrell, 'Sliding into War: The Somalia Imbroglio and US Army Peace Operations Doctrine,' *International Peacekeeping* 2, no. 2 (1995): 194–214; and US Army, *FM 100–20/AFP 3–20: Military Operations in Low Intensity Conflicts* (Washington, DC: Departments of the Army and Air Force, 5 December 1990).

32. See George Oliver, 'Summary,' and Satish Nambiar, 'Risk Tolerances versus Mission Accomplishment,' in *Challenges of Peacekeeping and Peace Support: The Doctrinal Dimension*, ed. Daniel Miltenberger, report of seminar, US Army War College, Carlisle Barracks, 22–25 May 2000, 91 and 101.

33. See David P. Forsythe, Patrice C. McMahon, and Andrew Wedeman, eds., *American Foreign Policy in a Globalized World* (New York: Routledge, 2006).

34. Mark Malan, 'Peace Support Operations in Africa: Addressing the Doctrinal Deficit,' in *Challenges of Peacekeeping and Peace Support*, ed. Daniel Miltenberger, 65.

CHAPTER 22

HUMANITARIAN INTERVENTION

RAMESH THAKUR

UNDER what circumstances, if ever, is the use of force both lawful and legitimate to provide effective international humanitarian protection to at-risk populations without the consent of their own governments? Without consensus and clarity on this, the UN's performance will be measured against contradictory standards, exposing it to charges of ineffectiveness from some and irrelevance from others, increasing the probability of unauthorized interventions, and further eroding the UN's primacy in peace and security.

The debate over when and how force may be used lies at the intersection of law, politics, and norms. The United Nations is the forum of choice for debating and deciding on collective action requiring the use of military force. But is it the only appropriate forum? It also has been the principal forum for the progressive advancement of the human rights agenda in its totality, including group-based social, economic, and cultural rights as well as individual civil and political rights. The human rights movement grew as an effort to curb arbitrary excesses by states against the liberties and rights of their own citizens. International humanitarian law emerged as an effort to place limits on the behavior of belligerent forces during armed conflict. The convergence of the interests of human rights and humanitarian communities with respect to protecting victims of atrocity crimes (crimes against humanity, large-scale killings, ethnic cleansing, and genocide) is a logical extension of their original impulses. At the same time, it produces the paradox of humanitarianism—'an endless struggle to contain war in the name of civilization'[1]—encouraging, even demanding, the use of force.

The author is grateful to Edward Newman and Vesselin Popovski for their comments.

'Humanitarian intervention'—the use of military force on the territory of a state without its consent with the goal of protecting innocent victims of large-scale atrocities—is of long-standing interest to students of international affairs. Traditional warfare is the use of force by rival armies of enemy states fighting over a clash of interests: us against them. Collective security rests on the use of force by the international community of states to defeat or punish an aggressor: all against one. Traditional peacekeeping involved the insertion of neutral and unarmed or lightly armed third-party soldiers as a physical buffer between enemy combatants who had agreed to a cease-fire. It was not meant to check a warlike intent; rather, it helped to give effect to a new-found pacific intent. Peace enforcement accepted the use of force by better armed but still neutral international soldiers against spoilers and transgressors of a peace agreement. Humanitarian intervention differs from all these in that it refers to the use of military force by outsiders for the protection of victims of atrocities: us between perpetrators and victims.

While previously some restricted the concept of humanitarian intervention to those interventions not authorized by the world organization, the more recent practice has been to apply it to either UN or UN-authorized interventions as well. The distinction has a policy significance. The first debate, by pointing to possible justification for intervention outside the UN framework, concentrated on developing and amplifying the exception to the rule. The second seeks to elaborate a new rule that itself justifies and may require international intervention.[2] Both debates demonstrate that the controversy over humanitarian intervention arises from a conflict between different contemporary norms, producing normative incoherence, inconsistency, and contestation.[3]

The arguments against intervention hold up less easily in principle than in pragmatism. A perennial difficulty in trying to justify intervention is that 'The use of force as a sanction for a breach of an international obligation may do more harm than the breach of the international obligation; the cure is often worse than the disease.'[4] Yet a decision not to intervene can have grave consequences: 'The principle of non-interference in the internal affairs of sovereign states, while protecting them from the use of force from without, simply sanctifies the rule of force from within.'[5] Allied powers in effect, even if not in intention, helped the cause of Franco by refusing to intervene in the Spanish Civil War (1936–1939). More recently, the Kosovo crisis highlighted the need for guidelines for intervention in a world in which nonintervention is in practice impossible: guidelines for determining the nature and gravity of threats that would justify external military intervention, and for determining the conditions that would trigger economic and humanitarian intervention.[6]

This chapter introduces the *problématique* of so-called humanitarian intervention in a world of sovereign states, traces the major examples in practice of such interventions, and concludes with international efforts to come to terms with the conceptual and policy dilemmas and tensions through blue-ribbon commissions.

SOVEREIGNTY

The states system dates from the 1648 Peace of Westphalia. The core elements of that sovereignty-based system were codified in the 1933 Montevideo Convention on the Rights and Duties of States. The attributes of statehood include government, territory, and people. Sovereignty is the foundational principle on which contemporary world order rests, affirmed by the International Court of Justice (ICJ) and expressed in UN Charter Article 2 (1). Externally, sovereignty means the legal identity of the state in international law, an equality of status with all other states, and the claim to be the sole official agent acting in international relations on behalf of a society. The juridical equality of states can exist alongside extreme disparities in size, wealth, power and status. The principle of nonintervention is the most important embodiment of the notion that states are autonomous entities, and its ancestry also can be traced back to Westphalia.[7]

Sovereignty originated historically in the European search for a secular basis of state authority in the sixteenth and seventeenth centuries. It embodies the notion that in every system of government there must be some absolute power of final decision. The state's primary concern is with order. In order to discharge this function of government, the sovereign must be above the law.

Subsequently, sovereignty was redefined in terms of a social contract between citizens and rulers. Violations of the contract by rulers voided the duty of citizens to obey the commands of the sovereign. By the end of the nineteenth century a distinction was being drawn between legal sovereignty as vested in parliament and political sovereignty as vested in the electorate. In the twentieth century, the trend was taken further with the notion of popular sovereignty that was conceived initially as consent and subsequently as active choice of the citizens. Even while the absolute conception of sovereignty based on effective control over a defined territory continued to dominate the scholarly literature, the notion of popular sovereignty gained adherence in domestic political and legal theory in the Western democracies.

National sovereignty locates the state as the ultimate seat of power and authority, unconstrained by internal or external checks; constitutional sovereignty holds that the power and authority of the state are not absolute but contingent and constrained. Domestically, power sharing between the executive, legislature and judiciary, at federal and provincial levels, is regulated by constitutional arrangements and practices. Internationally, states are constrained by globally legitimated institutions and practices.

Modern international society is built around sovereign statehood as its bedrock organizing principle. The United Nations is the chief agent of the system of states for exercising international authority in their name. UN membership has typically been the final symbol of sovereign statehood for freshly independent countries and their seal of acceptance into the international community of states. Charter Article 2 (7) prohibits the organization from intervening in 'matters that are essentially within the domestic jurisdiction' of any member state.

Yet by signing the Charter a country accepts collective obligations and international scrutiny. The restrictions of Article 2 (7) can be set aside when the Security Council decides to act under the collective enforcement Chapter VII. The scope of what constitutes threats and breaches has steadily widened to include such matters as HIV/AIDS, terrorism, and atrocities. In any case, this article concerns matters 'essentially' within domestic jurisdiction. This implies that the issue is subject to judgment, which may differ from one competent authority to another and may evolve. Moreover, as shown in Somalia, the collapse of state authority means that there is no functioning government to fulfill an essential condition of sovereignty, on the one hand, and that the violence, instability, and disorder can spill over from that failed state to others, on the other. The Security Council thus dealt with Somalia under the coercive clauses of Chapter VII rather than the consensual Chapter VI. Applying this argument more broadly, some analysts have questioned just how many of today's states would meet the strict requirements of sovereign statehood, describing many as 'quasi-states.'[8] And finally, the norm of nonintervention has softened as that of human rights has hardened.

Sovereignty, far from being absolute, has thus generally been considered to be contingent. The more significant change of recent times is that it has been reconceived as being instrumental. Its validation rests not in a mystical reification of the state, but in its utility as a tool for the state serving the interests of the citizens. Internal forms and precepts of governance must conform to international norms and standards of state conduct. That is, sovereignty must be exercised with due responsibility. This crucial normative shift was articulated by Francis M. Deng, the Special Representative of the Secretary-General on Internally Displaced Persons.[9] States are responsible for providing life-protecting and life-sustaining services to the people. When unable to do so, as responsible members of the international community they must seek and accept international help. If they fail to seek—or if they obstruct—international assistance and put large numbers of people at risk of grave harm, the world has an international responsibility to respond.

CHANGING WORLD POLITICS AND EMERGING CHALLENGES

Going to war was once an acknowledged attribute of sovereignty, and war was an accepted institution of the international system with distinctive rules, etiquette, norms, and stable patterns of practices. Now there are significant restrictions on the authority of states to use force either domestically or internationally. It has become commonplace to note dramatic increases in political, social, commercial-economic, environmental, and technological influences across borders, while the proportion subject to control and regulation by governments has diminished.

The combined effect is to pose significant conceptual and policy challenges to the notion of state sovereignty.

A second challenge came with the adoption of new standards of conduct for states in the protection and advancement of international human rights. Over time, the chief threats to international security have come from violent eruptions of crises within states, including civil wars, while the goals of promoting human rights and democratic governance, protecting civilian victims of humanitarian atrocities, and punishing governmental perpetrators of mass crimes have become more important. Given the changing nature and victims of armed conflict, the need for clarity, consistency, and reliability in the use of armed force for civilian protection lies at the heart of the UN's credibility in the maintenance of peace and security.

The Charter contains an inherent tension between the intervention-proscribing principle of state sovereignty and the intervention-prescribing principle of human rights, which explains the controversy over humanitarian intervention. Individuals became subjects of international law as bearers of duties and holders of rights under a growing corpus of human rights and international humanitarian law treaties and conventions—especially the Charter, the Universal Declaration of Human Rights and the two covenants, the four Geneva Conventions and the two prohibiting torture and genocide. The cluster of norms inhibiting, if not prohibiting, humanitarian intervention includes, alongside the norm of nonintervention, state sovereignty, domestic jurisdiction, pacific settlement of disputes, nonuse of force and, in the case of UN-authorized use of force, impartiality.

In the first four decades, state sovereignty was privileged over human rights, with the significant exception of white-majority rule in Rhodesia and apartheid in South Africa. The balance tilted in the 1990s. In a number of cases, the Security Council endorsed the use of force with the primary goal of humanitarian protection and assistance: in the proclamation (no matter how ineffectually) of UN safe areas in Bosnia, the delivery of humanitarian relief in Somalia, the restoration of the democratically elected government of Haiti, and the deployment of the multinational Kosovo Force (KFOR) in Kosovo after the 1999 war.[10]

There was a second change. From 1945 to the end of the Cold War in 1989–1990, the preservation of peace was privileged over the protection of human rights. The Charter talks of both but provides concrete instruments for the maintenance of the former. The end of the Cold War lessened the fear that international action in defense of human rights would threaten the peace by cutting across the vital interests of Moscow or Washington vis-à-vis their allies. At the same time, the proliferation of complex humanitarian emergencies, and the inappropriateness of the classical tenets of UN peacekeeping for dealing with them,[11] highlighted the inherent tension between the neutrality of traditional peacekeeping and the partial consequences of peace enforcement. The dilemma was confronted squarely in the Brahimi report which concluded that political neutrality has often degenerated into military timidity and the abdication of the duty to protect civilians. Impartiality should not translate into complicity with evil. While striving to remain impartial, the UN should soften its principle of neutrality between belligerents in favor of 'adherence to the principles of the Charter and to the objectives of [the] mandate.'[12]

THE PRACTICE AND THEORY OF 'HUMANITARIAN' INTERVENTION UNTIL THE 1990S

'Humanitarian intervention' has a long history. Three European powers—England, France, and Russia—intervened in Greece in 1827 to stop massacres by Turkey, and France intervened again in Syria in 1860 to stop the killings of Maronite Christians. Various European powers intervened in defense of Christians also in Crete (1866–1868), the Balkans (1875–1878) and Macedonia (1903–1908). Doctrine followed to justify practice, with one analyst justifying humanitarian intervention as the use of force to protect victims of 'arbitrary and persistently abusive' treatment by their own governments.[13] At the same time, the growing anti-colonial narrative pointed to the underlying reality of commercial and geopolitical calculations cloaked in the language of humanitarian and religious motives, as well as the paternalism of the European colonial powers. As a result, 'humanitarian intervention' as a doctrine was discredited in large parts of the world gaining independence from colonial rule.

The theory and practice of military intervention was circumscribed also by the gathering effort to put increasingly strict limits on the right of states to wage war as unilateral policy. The fetters of the Covenant of the League of Nations were reinforced normatively by the 1928 Kellogg–Briand Pact outlawing war and followed by proscriptions in the UN Charter on the use of force except for self-defense or when authorized by the Security Council.

Developments that were inimical to intervention in the post-1945 period included the growth of will and capacity in former colonies to resist intervention, the erosion of the post-colonial Western will to intervene, the enhanced power of the Soviet Union, a general balance of power which worked in favor of the targets of intervention against interveners, and a new climate of international legitimacy unfavorable to intervention in general, and to Western intervention in particular.[14]

The supposed illegality of humanitarian intervention was neither uncontested in academic discourse nor abandoned in state practice. The ICJ ruled against humanitarian intervention, for example in the 1986 case *Nicaragua v. United States*. In practice, the legitimacy of intervention often turned on the answer to four questions on actor, act, target, and purpose. Who or what was the subject or intervening *agent*; what was the mode or *form* of intervention; who or what was the putative *object* of intervention, and what degree of legitimacy attached to the target; and what was the motive for or *goal* of intervention?

At least eleven justifications for intervention were used during the Cold War:

1. The Soviet Union argued in regard to Czechoslovakia in 1968 that relations within the socialist community could not be the subject of a legal order reflecting capitalist class relations, and that fraternal assistance to a fellow-socialist regime was not intervention (the so-called Brezhnev doctrine).

2. Chinese and Soviet assistance to North Vietnam was defended on the argument that counter-intervention to help the victim of original intervention is not proscribed by international law.

3. Several countries (Israel, the United States in Indochina, and South Africa) sought to justify short military incursions into land territories by invoking the principle of hot pursuit, even though the principle was developed in relation to the high seas—that is, areas where no sovereign exercises jurisdiction.

4. Israel also justified military action on the grounds of preemptive self-defense, as in June 1967. The same justification was adduced for the strikes on Iraqi nuclear facilities in 1981, and Israel reportedly offered help to India to conduct comparable raids on Pakistan's nuclear installations at Kahuta.[15]

5. Israel has felt no compunction about launching punitive raids in retaliation for guerrilla/terrorist attacks on it. Israel has repeatedly extended the right to self-defense to include the right to take military action inside the borders of its neighbors who are incapable of preventing their territories from being used as launching pads for attacks on Israel, for example Lebanon (1978, 1982, 2006). The United States used similar justification for its raids on Libya in 1986.

6. European countries and the United States intervened to protect their nationals in the nineteenth century.[16] Israel has repeatedly extended the right to self-defense to include the right to take military action anywhere in the world to secure the release of its citizens unlawfully held as hostages, for example the raid on Entebbe airport in 1976. The United States explicitly justified its invasion of Grenada in 1983 with reference to securing the safety of its nationals.

7. In Afghanistan in 1979 Moscow fell back on the argument used by Washington to justify its military presence in South Vietnam in the 1960s: namely, that it was a permissible response to an invitation of the legitimate government. The United States and the Organisation of Eastern Caribbean States that engaged in the Grenada intervention also asserted that their action was validated by the prior invitation of the governor-general, Sir Paul Scoon.

8. India sent troops into Bangladesh in order to protect Bengali-Pakistanis from the oppressive rule of a military dictatorship in West Pakistan in 1971; Tanzania intervened to overthrow Idi Amin in Uganda in 1979; and Vietnam sent its troops into Cambodia to get rid of Pol Pot. But because 'humanitarian intervention' was not an accepted doctrine, the actual justifications tended to be couched in the language of self-defense (the threat from regional instability caused by the civil war raging in East Pakistan in 1971) or demographic aggression (ten million refugees streaming into India in a desperate effort to escape from the civil war in East Pakistan).

9. Given the importance of self-determination in the contemporary normative order, this principle can be used to justify intervention. But the international community is not agreed, and is not likely to be agreed in the foreseeable future, on the appropriate unit of self-determination. The practical difficulties are such that 'the need for prudence overwhelms...the moral argument for intervention.'[17]

10. The question of intervention in a civil war, extensively debated during the Vietnam War,[18] is particularly vexing. The Charter draws an untenably sharp distinction between domestic and external affairs, and consequently fails to address the type of intervention which has been the most common since World War II, namely intervention on behalf of parties engaged in a civil war (Angola, Chad, Lebanon, and Vietnam).

11. The most immediately acceptable justification for intervention is the collectivist principle: not *why* intervention was undertaken, but *who* took the decision to intervene. Since 1945, the UN has been the most widely accepted legitimator of international action. But regional organizations might also be acceptable as authorizing agents for action within their area of jurisdiction—although the first point above highlights the risk of a hegemonic regional organization legitimizing the imperialism of the dominant power as in Hungary in 1956 and Czechoslovakia in 1968.

The history of interventions by South Africa in southern Africa is a cautionary tale about the troubling antecedents of interventions by the powerful against the weak. The United States has a long history of intervening in Latin America as its sphere of influence, and in the Middle East to effect regime change (Iran 1953, Lebanon 1958, Iraq 2003). At the same time, some of the iconic events in Latin America—Cuba in the 1960s, Chile in the 1970s, Nicaragua and Panama in the 1980s—show how difficult it is to pinpoint with precision just what constitutes military intervention, let alone 'humanitarian' intervention. Concerned to justify the moral legitimacy of US support for insurgencies under certain circumstances, the Reagan doctrine rejected 'the inviolability of sovereignty.' Legitimate government based on the consent of the governed and respect for human rights was entitled to expect and receive US support when subjected to armed attack or attempted subversion. Washington was entitled to reject majority opinion in the world organization or of the ICJ in favor of unilateral determinations.[19]

But in practice states have followed a restrictive view of the Charter's law on the use of force, with virtually every resort since World War II being condemned or arousing strong controversy. In the *Nicaragua* case, the ICJ interpreted Article 2 (4) broadly to impose strict limits on the use of force, and Article 51 narrowly to limit the use of force against another state to self-defense against armed attack from that state. Prior to the Reagan doctrine, US lapses from Charter proscriptions on the use of force were occasional and partial: the Bay of Pigs invasion of Cuba, the intervention in the Dominican Republic. The Reagan doctrine, in seeking to make it general and wholesale, was 'untenable in law.'[20]

Thus, the many examples of intervention in actual state practice throughout the twentieth century did not lead to an abandonment of the norm of nonintervention. Often the breaches provoked such fierce controversy and aroused so much nationalistic passion that their net effect was to reinforce the norm more than to negate it. The difficulty with justifying intervention is that the real world is characterized by moral ambiguity rather than clarity. Intervention may be self-serving from the start, or begin as humanitarian but be transformed into self-aggrandizement. Interventions by India into East Pakistan in 1971 and by Vietnam into Cambodia in 1978 removed two regimes that were clearly guilty of having committed gross humanitarian atrocities. But neither action was incompatible with the national security interests of the two intervening powers.

The UN is an organization dedicated to the territorial integrity, political independence, and national sovereignty of its member states and the maintenance of international peace and security on that basis. But the overwhelming majority of today's armed conflicts are intrastate and not interstate. Moreover, because the proportion of civilians killed increased from about one in ten at the start of the twentieth century to around seven to nine in ten by its close, the world organization confronts a major difficulty: how to reconcile its foundational principle of member states' sovereignty with the primary mandate to maintain international peace and security and the equally compelling mission to promote the interests and welfare of 'We the peoples of the United Nations.' Secretary-General Kofi Annan discussed the dilemma in the conceptual language of two sovereignties, of the state and of the people.[21]

The Charter is itself an example of an international obligation voluntarily accepted by member states. On the one hand, in being granted membership to the United Nations, a signatory state is welcomed as a responsible member of the international community. On the other hand, by signing the Charter the state accepts the responsibilities of membership. There is a de facto redefinition from sovereignty as right of exclusivity to sovereignty as responsibility in both internal functions and external duties. In today's world, political frontiers have become less salient both for international organizations, whose rights and duties can extend beyond borders, and for member states, whose responsibilities within borders can be subject to international scrutiny. The gradual erosion of the once sacrosanct principle of national sovereignty is rooted today in the reality of global interdependence.

FROM 'HUMANITARIAN INTERVENTION' TO 'THE RESPONSIBILITY TO PROTECT'

The 1990s were a challenging decade with regard to conscience-shocking atrocities in many parts of the world. With the end of the Cold War and a more activist Security Council, the UN de facto intervened in Iraq to protect the Kurds from the defeated

Saddam Hussein regime, and the UK and United States enforced no-fly zones in parts of Iraqi territory throughout the 1990s. The debate on intervention was ignited in particular by such humanitarian crises as Somalia, Rwanda, Srebrenica, and East Timor that revealed a dangerous gap between the codified best practice of international behavior as articulated in the UN Charter and actual state practice since the UN was founded. Rwanda in 1994 caused lasting damage to UN ideals and credibility when the organization failed to stop a three-month-long genocide; Kosovo in 1999 showed the damage to the UN's credibility and the sharp polarization of international opinion when NATO intervened militarily outside the UN framework.

In early 1994, as genocide unfolded in Rwanda and 800,000 people were butchered in a mere three months, the world bore silent and shameful witness to its own apathy. It was a failure of collective conscience and civic courage at the highest and most solemn levels of responsibility. The skill, speed, and logistical efficiency displayed by Belgium, France, and the United States in evacuating their soldiers and nationals during the early days of the genocide reinforced UN Force Commander General Roméo Dallaire's conviction that the rapid deployment of just 5,000 well-trained and well-armed professional troops in the first days of the genocide (6–22 April) would have stopped or substantially reduced the tragedy. He sadly concluded that serving the UN goals is not high on the foreign policy priority of most countries. Instead, 'What they want is a weak, beholden, indebted scapegoat of an organization, which they can blame for their failures or steal victories from.'[22] The question that champions of humanitarian intervention posed was: what if a coalition of the willing had been prepared to move in with military force, but the Security Council was deadlocked?

Against that backdrop, Western allies concluded that, for decisive and effective action against President Slobodan Milošević, the political solidarity and military cohesion of NATO was a more congenial multilateral framework for collective action than the Security Council. Sickened by Milošević's record of brutality in the Balkans and evasions and deceit in dealings with the Europeans and the UN, in 1999 the US decided on 'humanitarian intervention' in Kosovo through the multilateral framework of NATO without Security Council authorization. This set off a debate whose intensity and breadth failed to be appreciated by many Western commentators, because they do not habitually read the opinions expressed outside the dominant Anglo-US academic and serious media outlets, or 'the trans-Atlantic [policy] community.'[23] And it culminated with the conclusion of an international blue-ribbon commission that, although the intervention by NATO was illegal, it was nonetheless legitimate.[24]

Under the impact of the two contrasting experiences of Rwanda and Kosovo, Annan urged member states to come up with a new consensus on the competing visions of national and popular sovereignty and the resulting 'challenge of humanitarian intervention.'[25] States 'bent on criminal behaviour,' he declared, should know that frontiers are not an 'absolute defence.'[26]

The response from the developing countries was that sovereignty was their final defense against the rules of an unjust world.[27] The Non-Aligned Movement—with

113 members, the most representative group of countries outside the UN itself—three times rejected 'the right of humanitarian intervention,' demonstrating just how deeply divisive the issue was.[28] Even America's 'new sovereigntists' launched three lines of counter-attack: the emerging international legal order is vague and illegitimately intrusive on domestic affairs; the international lawmaking process is unaccountable and the resulting law unenforceable; and Washington can opt out of international regimes as a matter of power, legal right, and constitutional duty.[29]

The Canadian-sponsored International Commission on Intervention and State Sovereignty (ICISS) wrestled with the whole gamut of difficult and complex issues involved in the debate. Its report, entitled *The Responsibility to Protect*, sought to: change the conceptual language; pin the responsibility on state authorities at the national level and the Security Council at the international level; and ensure that interventions, when they do take place, are done properly.[30]

ICISS adapted sovereignty as responsibility and proceeded to replace the familiar 'humanitarian intervention' with 'the responsibility to protect.' Humanitarians had complained that 'humanitarian intervention' was as much an oxymoron as the 'humanitarian bombing' of Kosovo. It also conjures up in many non-Western minds memories of the strong imposing their will on the weak, from the civilizing mission of spreading Christianity to the cultivation and promotion of human rights. It focused attention on the claims, rights and prerogatives of the potentially intervening states much more so than on the urgent needs of the putative beneficiaries of the action. And the phrase is used to trump sovereignty with intervention at the outset of the debate: it loads the dice in favor of intervention before the argument has even begun, by labeling and delegitimizing dissent as anti-humanitarian.

By contrast the 'responsibility to protect' implies an evaluation of the issues from the point of view of those seeking or needing support and acknowledges that the primary responsibility to protect rests with the state concerned. Only if the state is unable or unwilling to fulfill this responsibility, or is itself the perpetrator, does it become the responsibility of others to act in its place. Thus, the responsibility to protect is more of a linking concept that bridges the divide between intervention and sovereignty, whereas the language of the right or duty to intervene is inherently more confrontational. Moreover, it incorporates the 'responsibility to prevent,' the 'responsibility to react,' and the 'responsibility to follow up.' It provides conceptual, normative and operational linkages between assistance, intervention and reconstruction.

Based on state practice, Security Council precedent, established and emerging norms, and evolving customary international law, ICISS held that the proscription against intervention is not absolute. The foundations of the international responsibility to protect lie in obligations inherent in the concept of sovereignty; the responsibility of the Council, under Article 24 of the Charter, for the maintenance of international peace and security; specific legal obligations under human rights and human protection declarations, covenants and treaties, international humanitarian law and national law; and the developing practice of states, regional organizations and the Council itself.

While the state whose people are directly affected has the default responsibility to protect, a residual responsibility also resides with the broader international community of states. This is activated when a particular state either is unwilling or unable to fulfill its responsibility to protect or is itself the perpetrator of crimes or atrocities; or where populations living outside a particular state are directly threatened by actions taking place there. The fallback responsibility requires that in some circumstances action must be taken by external parties to support populations that are in jeopardy or under serious threat. The goal of protective intervention is not to wage war on a state in order to destroy it and eliminate its statehood, but always to protect victims of atrocities inside the state, to embed the protection in reconstituted institutions after the intervention, and then to withdraw all foreign troops.

Military intervention, even for humanitarian purposes, is a nicer way of referring to the use of deadly force on a massive scale. Even when there is agreement that military intervention may sometimes be necessary and unavoidable in order to protect innocent people from life-threatening danger by interposing an outside force between actual and apprehended victims and perpetrators, key questions remain about agency, lawfulness, and legitimacy. ICISS argued that the UN is the principal institution for building, consolidating, and using the authority of the international community. Because of this, it is especially important that every effort be made to encourage the Security Council to exercise—and not abdicate—its responsibilities.

The High-level Panel on Threats, Challenges and Change (HLP) reaffirmed the importance of changing the terminology from the deeply divisive 'humanitarian intervention' to 'the responsibility to protect' if the international community is to forge a new consensus. It explicitly endorsed the ICISS argument that 'the issue is not the 'right to intervene' of any state, but the 'responsibility to protect' of *every* State.' And it proposed five criteria of legitimacy: seriousness of threat, proper purpose, last resort, proportional means, and balance of consequences.[31] In a significant breakthrough for the growing acceptance of the new norm, China's official paper on UN reform and the Gingrich–Mitchell task force in the US endorsed the responsibility to protect.[32] Annan made an explicit reference to ICISS and the responsibility to protect as well as to the HLP, endorsed the legitimacy criteria, and urged the Security Council to adopt a resolution 'setting out these principles and expressing its intention to be guided by them' when authorizing the use of force. This would 'add transparency to its deliberations and make its decisions more likely to be respected, by both Governments and world public opinion.'[33]

In the event, the 'responsibility to protect' was one of the few substantive items to survive the negotiations at the 2005 World Summit. The final outcome document contained clear, unambiguous acceptance of individual state responsibility to protect populations from genocide, war crimes, ethnic cleansing, and crimes against humanity. Member states further declared that they 'are prepared to take collective action, in a timely and decisive manner, through the Security Council...and in cooperation with relevant regional organizations as appropriate, should peaceful means be inadequate and national authorities are manifestly failing to protect their populations.' The concept was given its own subsection title.[34] But the legitimacy criteria—which would simultaneously make the Security Council more responsive to outbreaks of humanitarian atrocities than hitherto and make it more difficult for individual states or ad hoc 'coalitions of the willing' to appropriate the language of humanitarianism for geopolitical and unilateral interventions—were dropped.

'SOFT' INTERVENTION

Foreign aid and capital investment too constitute intervention of sorts. But because these occur with the consent of target governments, the pejorative label of 'intervention' is not usually attached to them. Yet withdrawal of aid and investment because of changes in certain circumstances in recipient countries can be ferociously attacked as intervention in internal affairs. This type of 'soft' intervention has become endemic rather than less pronounced since 1945 by becoming embedded in the structure of the international system.

Another form of international intervention, particularly in response to atrocity crimes, is international criminal prosecution. The world has made revolutionary advances in the criminalization of domestic and international violence by armed groups and their individual leaders.[35] The way to apprehend and punish the perpetrators of conscience-shocking crimes on a mass scale is through an international legal framework that establishes the notion of 'universal jurisdiction,' where jurisdiction in respect of such crimes depends not on the place where they are committed, but on the nature of the crime itself. 'Crimes against humanity' can be prosecuted before the courts of any country. The Geneva Convention of 1949 established a new category of war crimes called 'grave breaches' which could be prosecuted in the courts of all countries that have ratified the convention.

Nuremberg and Tokyo were instances of victors' justice. Yet by historical standards, both tribunals were remarkable for giving defeated leaders the opportunity to defend their actions in a court of law instead of being dispatched for summary execution. The ad hoc tribunals of the 1990s are important milestones in efforts to fill institutional gaps in the original central mission of the UN and to control group violence. They have been neither unqualified successes nor total failures. While they have helped to bring hope and justice to some victims, combat the impunity of some perpetrators and greatly enrich the jurisprudence of international criminal and humanitarian law, they have been expensive and time-consuming and have contributed little to sustainable national capacities for justice administration. The International Criminal Court (ICC) offers hope for a permanent reduction in the phenomenon of impunity. The landscape of international criminal justice has changed dramatically over the last fifteen years. In 1990, a tyrant could have been reasonably confident of the guarantee of sovereign impunity for his atrocities. Today, there is no guarantee of prosecution and accountability, but the certainty of impunity is gone.

CONCLUSION

Thomas G. Weiss and Don Hubert examined ten cases of intervention between 1945 and 1990 and came to some general conclusions for that forty-five-year period of the United Nations.[36] First, the rhetoric of humanitarianism was used most stridently in cases where the humanitarian motive was among the weakest, including protecting one's own nationals. The common refrain of humanitarian rhetoric masking other motivations is clear proof of the scope for abuse of such a right to intervention. Yet the same facts point to the illogic of the objection that granting such a right would encourage self-interested interventions: great powers have a history of intervening against weak states whether or not the right exists.

Second, those cases where interventions were justified on the basis of self-defense included some that could have made the strongest claim to being humanitarian. This is especially true of India's intervention in East Pakistan in 1971, Vietnam's in Cambodia in 1978, and Tanzania's in Uganda in 1979. Yet the intervening powers did not couch their justification in the emancipatory language of humanitarianism, and many others spoke out strongly against such a right existing in international law or accepted state practice. It is only retrospectively that the argument could be made that allowing the atrocities to have continued would have been the greater evil.

After the end of the Cold War the Security Council experienced a spurt of enforcement activity within civil war contexts to provide international relief and assistance to victims of large-scale atrocities or failing states.[37] From Liberia and the Balkans to Somalia, Kosovo, and East Timor, the conscience-shocking humanitarian catastrophes were explicitly recognized as threats to international peace and security requiring and justifying a forcible response by the international community. When the Security Council was unable to act due to lack of enforcement capacity, it subcontracted the military operation to UN-authorized coalitions. And if it proved unwilling to act, sometimes groups of countries forged 'coalitions of the willing' to act anyway even without Security Council authorization.

Humanitarianism provides us with a vocabulary and institutional machinery of emancipation. But it must be judged also against the pragmatism of intentions and consequences. For example, 'Far from being a defense of the individual against the state, human rights has become a standard part of the justification for the external use of force by the state against other states and individuals.'[38] In making up the rules of intervention 'on the fly'[39] in Kosovo, NATO put at peril the requirements for a lasting system of world order grounded in the rule of international law. The template of robust 'humanitarian intervention' and foreign-led 'regime change' proved too rusty to accomplish the task in Iraq in 2003.[40] The Iraq war drove home the lesson that the sense of moral outrage provoked by humanitarian atrocities must be tempered by an appreciation of the limits of power, a concern for international institution-building, and sensitivity to the law of perverse consequences.

Both Kosovo and Iraq show how norms are transmission mechanisms for embedding underlying ethical principles and values in legal instruments and conventions. The collision of different Charter norms that produced the heated and tense debates over 'humanitarian intervention' thus reflected a growing erosion of the sense of community among the different members of the family of nations. What are the values constituting a global society of states? How, and by whom, are the relative values of individual dignity and communitarian rights to be prioritized and enforced? These are questions that divide more than unite the international community six decades after they were seemingly settled in the Charter. As well as strongly held beliefs in contrary directions, states and peoples no longer share a common belief in the means and procedures by which their differences can be mediated and reconciled.

This suggests that the response of states—whether individually, in groups or collectively through the UN—will continue to be ad hoc and on a case-by-case basis, rather than principled and consistent. Those with capacity and with interests engaged might be sufficiently motivated to mobilize external sentiment in support of intervention to protect victims of atrocities inside supposedly sovereign states. Acceptance of the responsibility to protect norm no more guarantees 'humanitarian intervention' than its non-existence had foreclosed it as a tool of individual and collective statecraft. But, by shaping the calculation of the balance of interests, the norm makes it modestly more, rather than less, likely that victims will not be callously abandoned.

NOTES

1. David Kennedy, *The Dark Sides of Virtue: Reassessing International Humanitarianism* (Princeton, NJ: Princeton University Press, 2004), 323.
2. Barend ter Haar, *Peace or Human Rights? The Dilemma of Humanitarian Intervention*, Study 11 (The Hague: Clingendael Institute, 2000), 9.
3. This is developed in Ramesh Thakur, *The United Nations, Peace and Security: From Collective Security to The Responsibility to Protect* (Cambridge: Cambridge University Press, 2006), ch. 12.
4. Michael Akehurst, 'Humanitarian Intervention,' in *Intervention in World Politics*, ed. Hedley Bull (Oxford: Clarendon, 1984), 111. See also Shashi Tharoor and Sam Daws, 'Humanitarian Intervention: Getting Past the Reefs,' *World Policy Journal* 18, no. 2 (2001): 21–30.
5. W. F. Mackey quoted in Stephen Ryan, 'Explaining Ethnic Conflict: The Neglected International Dimension,' *Review of International Studies* 14 (July 1988): 171.
6. See Albrecht Schnabel and Ramesh Thakur, eds., *Kosovo and the Challenge of Humanitarian Intervention: Selective Indignation, Collective Action, and International Citizenship* (Tokyo: United Nations University Press, 2000).
7. See, e.g., Samuel Pufendorf, *De jure naturae et gentium, libri octo* (1688), trans. C. H. and W. A. Oldfather (Oxford: Clarendon, 1934); Emerich de Vattel, *The Law of Nations or the Principles of Natural Law* (1758), trans. Charles G. Fenwick (Washington, DC: Carnegie

Institution, 1916); and Christian Wolff, *Jus gentium methodo scientifica pertractatum* (1749), translated by Joseph H. Drake (Oxford: Clarendon, 1934).

8. Robert H. Jackson, *Quasi-States: Sovereignty, International Relations, and the Third World* (Cambridge: Cambridge University Press, 1990). See also Stephen D. Krasner, *Sovereignty: Organized Hypocrisy* (Princeton, NJ: Princeton University Press, 2001).

9. Francis M. Deng et al., *Sovereignty as Responsibility: Conflict Management in Africa* (Washington, DC: Brookings, 1996); and Francis M. Deng, 'Frontiers of Sovereignty,' *Leiden Journal of International Law* 8, no. 2 (1995): 249–286. See also, Thomas G. Weiss and David A. Korn, *Internal Displacement: Conceptualization and its Consequences* (London: Routledge, 2006).

10. See Brian D. Lepard, *Rethinking Humanitarian Intervention* (University Park, PA: Pennsylvania State University Press, 2002), 7–23.

11. See Ramesh Thakur and Carlyle A. Thayer, eds., *A Crisis of Expectations: UN Peacekeeping in the 1990s* (Boulder, Colo.: Westview, 1995).

12. *Report of the Panel on United Nations Peace Operations*, UN document A/55/305-S/2000/809, 21 August 2000, para. 50.

13. Ellery Stowell, *Intervention in International Law* (Washington DC: J. Byrne, 1921), 53, quoted in Thomas G. Weiss and Don Hubert et al., *The Responsibility to Protect: Research, Bibliography, Background* (Ottawa: International Development Research Centre, 2001), 17.

14. Hedley Bull, 'Intervention in the Third World,' in Bull, *Intervention in World Politics*.

15. Ramesh Thakur, *The Politics and Economics of India's Foreign Policy* (London: Hurst, 1994), 292.

16. See Natalino Ronzitti, *Rescuing Nationals Abroad Through Military Coercion and Intervention on Grounds of Humanity* (Leiden, Netherlands: Brill, 1985).

17. Stanley Hoffmann, 'The Problem of Intervention,' in Bull, *Intervention in World Politics*, 25.

18. See, in particular, Richard A. Falk, ed., *The Vietnam War and International Law* (Princeton, NJ: Princeton University Press, 1968).

19. Jeane J. Kirkpatrick and Allan Gerson, 'The Reagan Doctrine, Human Rights, and International Law,' in *Right v. Might: International Law and the Use of Force*, ed. Louis Henkin et al. (New York: Council on Foreign Relations, 1989), 19–36, especially 21 and 25.

20. Louis Henkin, 'Use of Force: Law and US Policy,' in *Right v. Might*, 37–69, especially 47 and 56.

21. Kofi A. Annan, 'Two Concepts of Sovereignty,' *The Economist*, 18 September 1999, 49–50.

22. Roméo Dallaire, *Shake Hands with the Devil: The Failure of Humanity in Rwanda* (Toronto: Random House Canada, 2003), 90.

23. Weiss and Hubert, *Responsibility to Protect*, 23.

24. The Independent International Commission on Kosovo, *Kosovo Report: Conflict, International Response, Lessons Learned* (Oxford: Oxford University Press, 2000). Other works that can be traced to the debate launched in the aftermath of the Kosovo crisis include *Humanitarian Intervention* (The Hague: Advisory Council on International Affairs, 2000); *Humanitarian Intervention: Legal and Political Aspects* (Copenhagen: Danish Institute of International Affairs, 1999); Alton Frye, *Humanitarian Intervention: Crafting a Workable Doctrine* (New York: Council on Foreign Relations, 2000); and Kofi A. Annan, *The Question of Intervention: Statements by the Secretary-General* (New York: UN, 1999).

25. Kofi A. Annan, *Facing the Humanitarian Challenge: Towards a Culture of Prevention* (New York: UN, 1999). See also Simon Chesterman, *Just War or Just Peace? Humanitarian Intervention and International Law* (Oxford: Oxford University Press, 2001); and Nicholas Wheeler, *Saving Strangers: Humanitarian Intervention in International Society* (Oxford: Oxford University Press, 2000).

26. Speech by the Secretary-General to the 54th session of the General Assembly, 20 September 1999.

27. Weiss and Hubert, *Responsibility to Protect*, 7.

28. Ibid., 162, 357. See also Philip Nel, 'South Africa: the demand for legitimate multilateralism,' in eds. Schabel and Thakur, *Kosovo and the Challenge of Humanitarian Intervention*, 245–259.

29. Peter J. Spiro, 'The New Sovereigntists,' *Foreign Affairs* 79, no. 6 (2000): 9–15.

30. International Commission on Intervention and State Sovereignty, *The Responsibility to Protect* (Ottawa: International Development Research Centre, 2001).

31. HLP, *A More Secure World: Our Shared Responsibility*, UN document A/59/565, December 2004, paras. 201 (emphasis in original) and 207.

32. *Position Paper of the People's Republic of China on the United Nations Reforms* (Beijing: 7 June 2005), Part III.1, 'Responsibility to Protect', http://news.xinhuanet.com; *American Interests and UN Reform: Report of the Task Force on the United Nations* (Washington, DC: US Institute of Peace, 2005), 15.

33. Kofi A. Annan, *In Larger Freedom: Towards Development, Security and Human Rights for All*, UN document A/59/2005, 21 March 2005, paras. 122–135.

34. *2005 World Summit Outcome*, adopted by UN General Assembly as resolution A/RES/60/1, (24 October 2005), paras. 138–140.

35. See Ramesh Thakur and Peter Malcontent, eds., *From Sovereign Impunity to International Accountability: The Search for Justice in a World of States* (Tokyo: United Nations University Press, 2004).

36. Weiss and Hubert, *Responsibility to Protect*, ch. 4, 'Interventions before 1990,' 49–77.

37. Ibid., 79–126.

38. Kennedy, *Dark Sides of Virtue*, 25.

39. Michael J. Glennon, 'The New Interventionism: The Search for a Just International Law,' *Foreign Affairs* 78, no. 3 (1999): 6.

40. See Ramesh Thakur and Waheguru Pal Singh Sidhu, eds., *The Iraq Crisis and World Order: Structural, Institutional and Normative Challenges* (Tokyo: United Nations University Press, 2006).

CHAPTER 23

....

POST-CONFLICT PEACEBUILDING

....

ROLAND PARIS

AT the end of the Cold War, the United Nations was called upon to oversee the implementation of peace agreements in several countries that were just emerging from civil conflicts. These operations were the first wave of what became the UN's principal security activity in the post-Cold War era: helping war-torn states to make the transition from civil violence to a durable peace, or post-conflict 'peacebuilding.' While peacebuilding was not entirely new—the UN had played a similar role in the Congo in the early 1960s and the United States and its allies had reorganized and rebuilt Germany and Japan after World War II—the post-Cold War flurry of peace-building operations was unprecedented. Never before had so many international actors been involved in such complex rehabilitation missions in so many troubled states. Faced with this challenge, and with little recent experience or knowledge of how to foster a stable and lasting peace in the aftermath of large-scale violence, international peacebuilders improvised new strategies and techniques. Through several years of trial and error, the practice of post-conflict peacebuilding has become more sophisticated, but it remains an uncertain science, prone to catastrophic failure. It is—and perhaps will always be—an enormous and ambitious experiment in societal rehabilitation.

Yet it is also an indispensable experiment, given the consequences of failing to address the problem of civil violence and collapsing states in many parts of the world. Research has shown that intrastate wars tend to destabilize neighboring countries, produce humanitarian crises and mass refugee flows, spread infectious diseases like malaria and HIV/AIDS, facilitate the production and international trafficking of illegal narcotics, and attract international criminal syndicates and terrorist groups.[1] Post-conflict peacebuilding is one of the avenues by which major countries and international organizations have sought to stabilize fragile, war-torn societies.

This chapter identifies the principal features of these operations, examines the record of peacebuilding since the end of the Cold War, and describes the main issues and controversies surrounding these missions.

THE EVOLUTION OF PEACEBUILDING

During the Cold War, the UN's main security activity was the 'traditional' version of peacekeeping, which typically involved deploying lightly-armed military forces to monitor cease-fires or patrol neutral buffer zones between former combatants. With rare exceptions, UN peacekeepers restricted themselves to the role of cease-fire observers, staying out of the domestic politics of their host states. Successive Secretaries-General held that international peacekeepers 'must not take on responsibilities which fall under the Government of the country' in which they were operating.[2]

But at the end of the Cold War the UN began to launch ambitious new missions, including some that aimed to help reconstruct the political, economic, and social foundations of countries that were just emerging from civil wars—a much more intrusive role than traditional peacekeeping. In 1989, the world organization sent a mission to Namibia to monitor the conduct of local police and disarm former fighters, while preparing the country for its first democratic election and assisting in the preparation of a new national constitution. In 1991, new missions began in Angola, El Salvador, Western Sahara, and Cambodia, involving the organization of elections, human rights training, and monitoring, and even (in Cambodia) temporarily taking over the administration of an entire country. In 1992, the UN also launched a mission in Mozambique with wide-ranging responsibilities paralleling those in Angola, El Salvador, and Cambodia, including the preparation and supervision of democratic elections. With this rapid proliferation of new operations and functions, the idea of peacekeeping seemed suddenly outmoded, giving rise to a new set of terms and concepts.

Defining 'Peacebuilding'

Secretary-General Boutros Boutros-Ghali's 1992 policy statement, *An Agenda for Peace*, presented a conceptual map of new mission types.[3] Peacekeeping was now defined as a subset of peace operations focusing on the traditional task of observing cease-fires. A second category of operations—*peace enforcement*—comprised more heavily armed missions authorized to use force to achieve purposes other than self-protection. A third category—*post-conflict peacebuilding*—comprised missions aiming 'to strengthen and solidify peace' in the aftermath of 'civil strife.' According to Boutros-Ghali, peacebuilding might include such functions as 'disarming the previously warring parties and the restoration of order, the custody and possible destruction of weapons, repatriating refugees, advisory and training support for security personnel, monitoring elections, advancing efforts to protect human rights, reforming or strengthening governmental institutions and promoting formal and informal processes of political participation.' In addition, Boutros-Ghali underlined the importance of *preventive diplomacy*, or efforts to ease tensions before they result in conflict, which might include the 'preventive deployment' of UN forces in order to avert violence.

The distinction between these different mission types was never absolute—nor could it be. The UN was moving in the direction of more complex 'multifunctional' operations that sometimes displayed elements of all the mission types combined. Indeed, in the years following publication of *An Agenda for Peace*, some actors broadened the idea of peacebuilding to include everything from preventive diplomacy to humanitarian aid and different types of civilian assistance, military operations, development activities, and post-conflict reconstruction.[4] By 2001, for example, the Security Council was using the concepts of peacebuilding and preventive diplomacy interchangeably. In some respects, this was understandable, since post-conflict peacebuilding aimed not only to consolidate peace after war, but to prevent renewed violence in countries that had recently experienced conflict. On the other hand, the rapidly expanding definition of peacebuilding risked deflecting attention away from the special challenges and circumstances of *post-conflict* reconstruction.

Growth of Peacebuilding through the 1990s

As it turned out, peacebuilding—in its post-conflict form—became the UN's principal peace and security activity in the 1990s. Between 1989 and 1993 alone, eight major missions were launched (Table 23.1). The apparent failure of peace-enforcement operations in Somalia and Bosnia in 1993–1994 had a chilling effect on all UN operations through the mid-1990s—although even in this relatively slow period three new missions were launched: in Bosnia (1995), Croatia (1995), and Guatemala (1997). By the end of the decade, demand for new post-conflict deployments was surging once again, with operations launched in East Timor, Kosovo, Sierra Leone, and the Democratic Republic of the Congo (DRC) in 1999. The number of personnel deployed on UN peace operations also peaked in 1993–1995, declined precipitously in the middle of the decade, and then began climbing again steeply by the late 1990s (Figure 23.1). Peacekeeping budgets followed a similar pattern (Figure 23.2).

Moreover, both the number and variety of international actors involved in peacebuilding also expanded during this period—including regional and subregional organizations.[5] While the Organization of American States was involved in the Central American peace processes in the early and mid-1990s, European and African

Table 23.1 Major post-conflict peacebuilding operations[a], 1989–2005

Location	Duration (military component)
Namibia	1989–1990
Nicaragua	1989–1992
Angola	1991–1997
Cambodia	1991–1993
El Salvador	1991–1995
Mozambique	1992–1994
Liberia	1993–1997
Rwanda	1993–1996
Bosnia	1995-present
Croatia (Eastern Slavonia)	1995–1998
Guatemala	1997
Congo (DRC)	1999-present
East Timor	1999–2002
Kosovo	1999-present
Sierra Leone	1999–2005
Ethiopia–Eritrea border	2000-present
Afghanistan	2002-present
Iraq	2003-present
Liberia	2003-present
Burundi	2004-present
Côte d'Ivoire	2004-present
Sudan	2005-present

[a] Excludes missions with fewer than 200 military personnel and those not following an armed conflict.

organizations became more active in peacebuilding in the latter part of the decade, including the North Atlantic Treaty Organization (NATO), the European Union (EU), and the Organization for Security and Co-operation in Europe (OSCE) in the Balkans; the Economic Community of West African States (ECOWAS) in West Africa; and the Organization of African Unity (OAU; now the African Union (AU)) in Burundi and the DRC. More controversially, private military companies were also employed by governments embroiled in internal conflict, including Military Professional Resources Incorporated in Croatia and Executive Outcomes in Sierra Leone. Meanwhile, as peacebuilding operations became more multifaceted and involved, the civilian aspects of these operations also multiplied—along with the number and variety of nongovernmental organizations (NGOs) present in the field, delivering humanitarian aid, promoting human rights and development, fostering

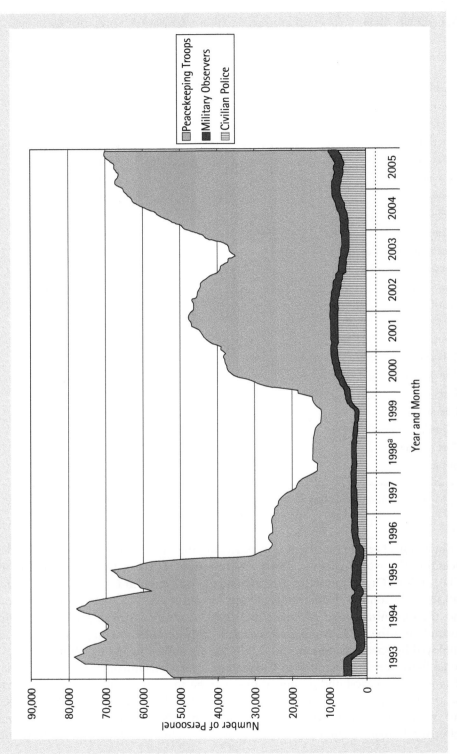

Fig. 23.1 Military and civilian police contributions to UN peacekeeping operations, 1993–2005

[a] Figure for December 1998 are estimates.

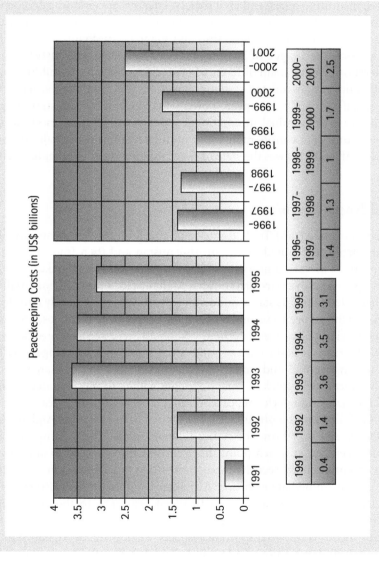

Fig. 23.2 UN peacekeeping costs 1991–2001

Source: United Nations website (www.un.org/Depts/dpko/dpko/pub/pub/pdf/7.pdf), accessed on 8 May 2006.

Peacekeeping Costs (in US$ billions)

1991	1992	1993	1994	1995
0.4	1.4	3.6	3.5	3.1

1996– 1997	1997– 1998	1998– 1999	1999– 2000	2000– 2001
1.4	1.3	1	1.7	2.5

intercommunal political dialogue, training judges and lawyers, and supporting the development of new political parties, among other things.

Thus, peacebuilding emerged from the decade of the 1990s as a vast, complex, and growing network of private and public agencies that provided a kind of 'life support' to fragile states just emerging from conflict—a decentralized (and at times chaotic) system for reconstituting a peaceful civil society, effective governance and economic life in war-torn states. In its most expansive and intrusive forms, peacebuilding could be viewed as a successor to the trusteeship and mandate mechanisms that the UN and its predecessor, the League of Nations, had established to administer 'non-self-governing' territories.[6] The main difference between 1990s-era peacebuilding and the earlier trusteeship and mandates systems, however, was that the earlier systems authorized specific, mainly European powers to continue administering certain former colonies under nominal international supervision, whereas modern peace-building operations were considerably more multilateral and decentralized—some-times to a fault. At least, this was the state of peacebuilding prior to 11 September 2001.

Peacebuilding after 9/11

The destruction of the World Trade Center and attack on the Pentagon provoked a fierce reaction from the United States: in Afghanistan and then Iraq. It also trans-formed the problem of state failure in eyes of many American policymakers. Al Qaeda had based its operations in a war-torn country, Afghanistan, and could potentially find refuge in other failed or fragile states. Suddenly, instability in strategically remote parts of the world, which had been a secondary issue for US policy in the 1990s, rose to near the top of the foreign policy agenda. The US *National Security Strategy* of September 2002 identified terrorists as the enemy—and 'weak states' as their refuge.[7] With this new focus on 'ungoverned and under-governed areas' as potential sanctuaries for terrorists,[8] American policymakers were no longer willing to rely on a decentralized, multilateral mechanism to perform peacebuilding tasks in key countries.

In late 2001, following the 9/11 attacks, the United States invaded Afghanistan to destroy Al Qaeda and overthrow the ruling Taliban regime. The fighting was largely over by mid-December, at which point the Security Council voted to authorize the deployment of a multilateral security force to maintain order in the country's capital city, Kabul, and its immediate environs. A civilian UN mission was also established to provide technical, humanitarian, and financial assistance to the newly formed Afghan government and to facilitate elections. This peacebuilding exercise differed from previous missions in two important respects. First, prior to Afghanistan all of the major peacebuilding missions had been deployed in the aftermath of a civil war, where local parties had negotiated cease-fires and invited international peacebuilders to oversee the implementation of these agreements, whereas in Afghanistan peace-building followed the conquest of a country by an external power. Second, although the UN played an important role in smoothing political negotiations leading to the formation of a new government, the main responsibility for the political and military aspects of the post-conflict operation initially fell to the United States—its soldiers, diplomats, and intelligence officials. This type of 'post-conquest peacebuilding' was even more apparent in Iraq, where Washington created its own occupation authority after invading the country in March 2003.

Some observers have expressed fear that the peacebuilding project is at risk of being 'overtaken by other agendas' in the post-9/11 environment, including 'the attempt to conflate peacebuilding with the narrowly-cast national security agendas of power- ful . . . states.'[9] This is a warranted concern. If peacebuilding is perceived as an imperial project, local actors in post-conflict countries that could benefit from international assistance might think twice about inviting or accepting this assistance, and the result might be more cease-fire collapses, renewed fighting and zones of chronic violence. On the other hand, the post-9/11 period has also witnessed the deployment of several new operations in the more multilateral, consensual mode that characterized the missions of the 1990s: in Liberia, Côte d'Ivoire, Burundi, and Sudan. Although these operations are authorized to use force, they were all deployed at the request of local parties in order to oversee the implementation of a peace agreement.

In sum, two distinct but overlapping styles or modes of peacebuilding were under way at the time of this writing: post-conquest peacebuilding in Afghanistan and Iraq, deeply connected to US national security objectives; and post-settlement peace- building, primarily in Africa, and considerably more multilateral in character than post-conquest peacebuilding. How these two approaches will evolve, and how they might influence each other, remains to be seen. In the light of difficulties in Iraq, American policymakers may be discouraged from launching new 'regime change' efforts that create the need for post-conquest peacebuilding. And in other parts of the world—Africa, in particular—the demand for post-civil war operations to imple- ment peace settlements is likely to remain strong.

EVALUATING THE PEACEBUILDING RECORD

By most accounts, the record of peacebuilding operations in fostering peace since 1989 has been mixed. Much depends, however, on how one defines and measures success. Before evaluating the outcomes of peacebuilding, therefore, we need to explore its purposes and strategies in greater depth, and to consider some of the technical problems in measuring outcomes.

Methodological Challenges

There are significant methodological challenges in evaluating mission outcomes. First, one must be conscious of the diversity of international actors engaged in a mission—and the fact that they may not all be pursuing the same goals. Second, distinguishing the effects of the peacebuilding actors from other local and international factors is made difficult by the different context for each case. Third, the uncertainties that arise from this variation are worsened by the relatively limited number of peacebuilding missions launched since the end of the Cold War. Fourth, not enough time has passed to reach definitive conclusions on the longer-term effects of peacebuilding missions launched since 1989, particularly those deployed in recent years. For all of these reasons, the evaluation of peacebuilding outcomes remains an inexact science.

Measurement difficulties are particularly pronounced in studies that define peacebuilding 'success' in broad rather than narrow terms. One of the narrowest definitions of success comes from George Downs and Stephen Stedman, who examine whether a cease-fire prevails in a host country at the moment when peacebuilding agencies depart.[10] This is a relatively straightforward yardstick, since large-scale killing (i.e., the opposite of a cease-fire) tends to be easily observable—indeed, incidents of major violence are recorded annually by groups such as the Stockholm International Peace Research Institute.[11] Virginia Page Fortna also employs this standard, but uses a longer timeframe to determine whether violence has reignited in the aftermath of a peace operation.[12] Fen Osler Hampson asks a broader question: did missions accomplish the goals of their formal mandates?[13] This approach adds a layer of complexity to the measurement challenge because mission mandates may include an array of tasks including demobilization and reintegration of former combatants, physical and economic reconstruction, and institutional rebuilding. Other analysts use even broader standards of evaluation, including the post-mission level of democracy in the host country, economic growth, and other indicators of success.[14]

It is tempting to define the purposes of peacebuilding in very narrow terms, thereby minimizing the methodological challenges outlined above. However, any full assessment of peacebuilding operations must consider whether the resulting peace is likely to be *durable*, which in turn requires some attention to the societal conditions that fueled conflict in the first place. This is what Boutros-Ghali called the 'essential goal' of peacebuilding—namely, the 'institutionalization of peace,' or what his successor, Kofi Annan, has called the 'consolidation of peace.'[15] 'We are no longer asked,' said Annan in 2004, 'just to 'keep the peace' by helping maintain a ceasefire.' Modern peacebuilding means tackling 'root causes' of violence in order to 'build a lasting peace.'[16] Studies such as the work of Downs and Stedman, which identifies a peacebuilding success as the absence of large-scale fighting at the end of an operation, are too narrow because they neglect to assess the prospects for peace over the longer term, which is central to the notion of constructing a durable, self-sustaining peace. Making such assessments is not easy, but doing so is necessary if peacebuilding is to be viewed as more than cease-fire observation.

A Mixed Record

If the test of peacebuilding success is whether large-scale violence has resumed in countries that have hosted peacebuilding missions, then the record of peacebuilding is a largely positive one. Only three of the countries listed in Table 23.1 slipped back into conflict: Angola, Rwanda, and Liberia. Indeed, there are good reasons to believe that the deployment of a peacebuilding mission reduces the danger of renewed conflict. Several studies have found that the presence of a multidimensional peace-building operation in a country just emerging from civil war increases the likelihood and duration of peace.[17] Some observers go further, speculating that the proliferation of peacebuilding missions in the post-Cold War period may help to explain the overall decline in the number of civil wars since the mid-1990s.[18]

If, however, we consider the broader question of whether peacebuilding missions have created the conditions for durable peace, the record is mixed.[19] Some cases still stand out as clear successes. Namibia hosted UN-supervised elections in 1989 and has emerged as one of the most peaceful societies in Africa. Mozambique held elections in 1994 and has since enjoyed relative peace and high rates of economic growth. Croatia hosted a peacebuilding mission beginning in 1995 that temporarily adminis-tered the government of its Eastern Slavonia region, as part of the implementation of the Dayton Peace Accords, and oversaw regional and local elections in 1997 before returning the territory to Croatian control. In all three of these cases, the prospects of renewed conflict appear to be remote. The world body also conducted a mission in East Timor, beginning in 1999, which included the creation of new governing structures for the country as part of the civil war settlement that included the end of Indonesian sovereignty over the territory. This mission appeared to be largely successful until early 2006, when violence erupted between competing factions of the East Timorese military and police.

It is worth noting that, in these four cases, the task of post-conflict reconciliation was made considerably easier by the fact that key belligerents effectively abandoned the territories at the end of the civil conflicts, thereby reducing the danger of resurgent violence. In Namibia, the South African army withdrew from the country under the auspices of the peace accord. South Africa had been a principal sponsor of the Renamo insurgency in Mozambique; indeed, Renamo was based in South Africa for much of the war. At the time of the peace settlement, however, South Africa cut off support to this group. In Croatia, much of the Serbian population abandoned the region of Eastern Slavonia in the latter stages of the war, and those who remained lost the support of their patron, the government of Yugoslavia. In East Timor, pro-Indonesian militias fled the newly independent country for the Indonesian-con-trolled western portion of the island. The disengagement of these belligerent parties almost certainly facilitated the consolidation of peace in these four cases—although in East Timor, as noted, new lines of violent conflict emerged after several years of relative tranquility.

The missions in Nicaragua, El Salvador, and Guatemala were largely successful in that they facilitated an end to long-standing political violence in these countries. Former guerrilla groups have been incorporated into peaceful and largely democratic political systems. In all three cases, however, the economic policies promoted as part of the peacebuilding missions, which mandated rapid market-oriented reforms and fiscal austerity policies, have widened distributional gaps between rich and poor.

Combined with escalating street crime and gang violence since the end of the war, which has produced among the highest homicide rates in the world, the living conditions for many ordinary citizens are as bad as, or worse than, during the war itself. Given that great inequalities in wealth and power are widely viewed as factors that have historically fueled bouts of revolutionary violence in these countries, it is reasonable to be concerned about the longer-term prospects of peace in Central America, and to doubt the degree to which peacebuilders addressed the 'root causes' of conflict in these countries.

Cambodia is another country that emerged from its peacebuilding mission much better off than it was before. Here, too, there are no signs of an imminent return of large-scale violence. The Khmer Rouge, which ruled the country under the brutal leadership of Pol Pot in the late 1970s and later fought a guerrilla campaign against the Vietnam-backed government of Hun Sen, has all but disappeared. Today, Cambodia is a relatively free and peaceful country which has held several elections since the peace settlement of the early 1990s. But there are also grounds for concern. The pattern of conflict in the country is marked by cycles of charismatic strongmen seeking absolute power, suppressing potential rivals, and engendering similarly intolerant and extreme forms of opposition. While holding periodic elections, Prime Minister Hun Sen has used a strategy of violence and intimidation to undermine the ability of his political opponents to challenge his authority, leaving only a veneer of democracy. Further, Cambodia's courts and parliament are incapable of acting independently to check Hun Sen's power. Peace prevails, but the peacebuilding mission arguably did little to prevent a return to de facto one-person rule, which raises doubts as to whether the pathological pattern of harsh repression and violent counter-reaction has been broken in Cambodia.

A similar pathology has defined the politics of Liberia, which gained independence in 1847 under the leadership of a community of freed American slaves. In a tragic irony of history, the former slaves themselves created a system of forced labor and subjugated the indigenous population of the territory. Indigenous army officers responded by overthrowing the regime and installing an equally severe dictator, Samuel Doe, who squashed all resistance and funneled state resources to his own minority ethnic group. This, in turn, gave rise to further rebellion led by another brutal autocrat, Charles Taylor. The first major peacebuilding operation in Liberia—led by ECOWAS but with UN participation—rushed forward with elections in 1997 from which Taylor emerged victorious. The peacebuilders declared their mission a success and departed. Shortly afterwards, however, Taylor began to reverse many of the democratic trappings of the new Liberian state, and reverted to old-style coercion and attacks on his opponents. The result was new rebellion and Taylor's overthrow. This led to a second peacebuilding mission in 2003—this time under the UN's authority, which oversaw the election of Liberia's first woman president in November 2005. Whether this mission will be more successful than the last remains to be seen, but previous experience suggests that the 'quick fix' of an election alone is not enough to break Liberia's long-standing conflict pathology.

Perhaps the two most obvious failures of peacebuilding were in Angola and Rwanda, both of which also illustrated the danger of relying on quick and superficial political reforms to establish the conditions for a consolidated peace. In Angola, the United Nations and other international agencies oversaw the implementation of a peace agreement that included elections in 1992 without first demobilizing or disarming the parties or establishing mechanisms to enforce the results of the election. Before the elections were completed, one of the two major candidates and leaders of the formerly warring parties, Jonas Savimbi, concluded that he would lose and resumed fighting. Over the two years that followed, an estimated 300,000 people died in the violence. A new peace agreement was reached in 1994 but failed to hold, and a frustrated UN withdrew its mission in 1999. It was not until Savimbi was killed in combat in 2002 that a new peace process could begin in earnest.

In Rwanda, the international community was similarly over-optimistic and under-prepared for the spasm of killing that ended the peace process in 1994. A peace settlement between the Hutu-led regime and the Tutsi opposition, negotiated under international auspices in Arusha, Tanzania in 1993, led to the deployment of a small UN force to oversee elections. But hard-line elements of the Hutu regime, determined to scuttle the peace agreement and destroy their ethnic adversaries, launched a genocide in April 1994 that left international peacebuilders helpless on the sidelines. Given that the country had experienced several waves of mass killing in the past, it seems unrealistic, at best, not to have made greater preparations to enforce the peace in the event of problems.

The outcome of the missions in Bosnia and Kosovo, by contrast, was considerably less bleak—although in both cases the operations are still ongoing at the time of this writing. Mass killing has ended in both places, thanks in part to the presence of tens of thousands of NATO troops. But the prospects for lasting or self-sustaining peace remain uncertain. In Bosnia, there has been little reconciliation or remixing of the Croat, Muslim, and Serbian communities, and the Bosnian government has done little to overcome these divisions—in part because the country's constitutional structure, established under the Dayton Accords, established a tripartite presidency that allowed voters to cast ballots only for one of the three presidents who represented their ethnic group. This created—and continues to create—an incentive for presidential candidates to seek support only from their own communities, rather than to reach across ethnic lines in order to build a cross-factional constituency. In Kosovo, there are, at the time of writing, uncertainties around the ultimate status of the territory, with the overwhelming majority of ethnic Albanians supporting outright independence for the territory, and a rump Serbian community, under the perpetual protection of NATO, wanting Kosovo to remain formally part of Yugoslavia.

Sierra Leone and Côte d'Ivoire are two more recent cases that offer some hope for success—although it is still too early to make more than preliminary observations. A peacebuilding operation began in Sierra Leone in 1999 but quickly lost control of the situation as fighting resumed and more than 500 UN troops were taken hostage in May 2000. The arrival of a British military task force restored stability, allowing elections to take place in May 2002 under relatively peaceful conditions. Over 75,000 combatants were disarmed and demobilized over the ensuing two years, and the last contingent of UN troops left Sierra Leone in December 2005, leaving behind a UN 'Integrated Office' to oversee political and economic assistance to the country. In Côte d'Ivoire, the UN and other international agencies agreed to assist in the implementation of a peace agreement negotiated in early 2003, backed up by a contingent of French troops. Presidential and legislative elections, originally planned for late 2005, were rescheduled for late 2006, pending the completion of disarmament efforts.

The outcome of recently launched missions in the Democratic Republic of the Congo, Burundi, and Sudan is also uncertain. Sporadic fighting continues in the DRC, the mission in the Darfur region of Sudan is too small to establish security, and the danger of intercommunal violence remains high in Burundi. The operation in Afghanistan is also a work in progress. It has focused primarily on establishing security in the capital city, Kabul, and some provincial centers, leaving de facto authority over much of the country in the hands of regional warlords who also control the thriving poppy trade. And in Iraq, which like Afghanistan is a case of post-conquest rather than post-settlement peacebuilding, the United States is struggling to suppress an insurgency while advancing a political democratization process. No one knows how that mission may turn out.

In sum, the record of peacebuilding since the end of the Cold War is varied. For those who focus narrowly on whether a cease-fire remains in force, the overall record is mixed but fairly positive, since most host states remain at peace today. For those who consider the broader question of whether peacebuilding has fostered the conditions for a stable and lasting peace, the record is also mixed but more problematic, due to doubts about the durability of today's cease-fires and the extent to which peacebuilders have altered the underlying dynamics of conflict in many of these countries.

LESSONS AND CONTROVERSIES

Although peacebuilding is still in its early days, several 'lessons' have emerged from the first decade-and-a-half of operations.[20] Some of these lessons have already been embraced by the international agencies involved in peacebuilding, while others remain unsettled or controversial. These lessons and issues are divided into eight themes below.

A Long-Term Commitment

Many countries just emerging from civil war remain teetering on the brink between war and peace, with their inhabitants divided by mutual animosities and fears. Often, too, there are large numbers of weapons in circulation, as well as ex-combatants proficient in using them. In addition, conditions of general economic distress, weak or nonexistent governmental institutions, few social services for the needy (including those displaced or dispossessed during the war), and damaged physical infrastructure combine to exacerbate local instability.[21]

For such countries, there is no simple and quick formula for lasting peace. In the early and mid-1990s, peacebuilders tended to underestimate the size of the commitment—both of time and resources—required to begin the political, economic, and social rebuilding process in these countries. Typically, missions were intended to last one to three years, with the first postwar election serving as the end goal, after which the operation could be terminated. In the case of Bosnia—amazingly, in hindsight— the mission was supposed to be over in twelve months, by the end of 1996. But it soon became apparent that this 'quick and dirty' approach to peacebuilding was problematic. Humanitarian aid could be distributed in weeks, and elections held within months or a few years, but establishing the institutional foundations for peace—the rule of law, effective security forces, functioning legislatures and at least a rudimentary legal system, including the legal foundation for a market economy—would require several years or longer. Accordingly, missions launched in the latter part of the 1990s and early 2000s were deployed for longer periods and with more realistic expectations of what could be accomplished in the short term.

The Importance of Security

Preventing new eruptions of violence must be the foremost goal of any peacebuilding mission. Without a reasonable assurance of physical security for the bulk of the population, there is little hope of achieving progress on institution-building, intercommunal reconciliation, reconstruction and development. International agencies learned tough lessons in Angola, Rwanda, and elsewhere about the importance of deploying a large enough international force to deter and, if necessary, suppress cease-fire violations. Disarmament and demobilization of former combatants are a top priority, and should generally be completed prior to holding elections. Planning should assume the worst, not the best—including the possibility that local spoilers might actively seek to reverse the peace process through organized violence.

Since the early 1990s, such enforcement functions have been increasingly performed by regional organizations (such as NATO in the Balkans, ECOWAS in West Africa, and the AU in Sudan), groups of states organized into 'coalitions of the willing' (such as the French-led force in the DRC or the Australian-led force in East Timor), individual states (such as Britain in Sierra Leone and France in Côte d'Ivoire), and to a lesser extent by private military companies (most notably in Iraq). Over the longer term, international peacebuilders must focus on creating indigenous security forces that are functionally capable and politically neutral (that is, beholden to the state rather than to any of the formerly warring factions).

As noted above, achieving these goals requires a substantial commitment of resources and time.

Careful Democratization

In spite of the diversity of international actors involved in peacebuilding and the relative lack of central coordination, one of the most interesting features of all the post-Cold War peacebuilding operations is that most international actors have subscribed to the strategy of promoting peace through democratization and marketization. There are good reasons for doing so: well-established democracies tend to be more peaceful both internally and in their relations with other states than non-democracies, and some form of market-oriented economic system appears to be a necessary (though not sufficient) condition for long-term economic growth.

However, the peacebuilding record also shows that rushing ahead with democratic reforms can exacerbate societal tensions and even, in some cases, provoke renewed fighting. Elections are moments of intensified political competition that can create incentives for candidates to exploit intercommunal hatreds and fan the flames of intolerance and hostility. Careful design of political institutions and voting rules can minimize these incentives and promote cross-factional constituencies—but devising these rules, and creating judicial and security mechanisms to uphold electoral results, takes time.[22] Peacebuilders should also use this pre-election period to promote the growth of new groupings and civil society organizations that embrace cross-communal dialogue and cooperation.

Pro-Peace Economic Liberalization Policies

Rapid economic liberalization can also undermine efforts to promote postwar political stability. 'Orthodox' structural adjustment programs, which have typically emphasized immediate privatization, deregulation, and reductions in public expenditures for macroeconomic balancing, tend to be politically and socially wrenching for countries undergoing these reforms—in part because certain segments of the population emerge as winners, and others as losers, when market forces are unleashed and government expenditures and interventions are reduced. While the purpose of these reforms is to establish the conditions for sustainable growth in the long term, in the short term they can impose considerable hardship, which can be very dangerous in the fragile circumstances of a society in which major groups have recently been killing each other. For these reasons, the World Bank and (to a lesser extent) the International Monetary Fund (IMF) have adopted more 'conflict sensitive adjustment policies' for such states since the late 1990s, emphasizing the importance of reducing hardship on key communities in postwar societies. These new approaches could be taken much further—for example, by multiplying investments in 'social adjustment' programs to mitigate the most disruptive effects of adjustment, and by expanding the use of targeted 'conditionalities' on the disbursement of certain aid funds in order to encourage aid recipients to implement and comply with peace accords.[23]

At least the rudimentary legal structures of a functioning market economy should be established as quickly as possible, including currency, customs and taxation systems, and commercial law and banking regulations. As liberal economic theorists from Adam Smith onward have observed, 'free' markets tend to go awry if they lack basic legal and regulatory frameworks. In Bosnia, for instance, privatization of state-owned enterprises took place before such structures were established and, as a result, proceeds from privatization were diverted into the hands of criminal networks, including those connected to the former combatants.[24] More generally, peacebuilders need to pay close attention to sources of finance for combatant groups and potential 'spoilers,' such as black marketeering in natural resources, in order to reduce the capacity of these groups to derail a peace process, and to ensure that proceeds from economic activity can be effectively taxed by legitimate governing authorities.[25]

Sensitivity to Regional and Local Conditions

Civil wars, by definition, are fought primarily within the boundaries of a single state, but they are rarely isolated from political and economic dynamics in the surrounding region. In some cases, violence in one country is part of a larger, regional constellation of conflicts. Even when civil unrest appears to be isolated, combatant groups may have informal alliances or supply lines in neighboring countries. In the case of Afghanistan, for example, it is nearly impossible to imagine an effective peacebuilding policy that does not seek to secure the Afghanistan–Pakistan border and the nearby areas of Pakistan.[26]

Strengthening regional peacebuilding capacities goes hand-in-hand with addressing the external sources of conflict in a civil war. As noted, regional organizations have become increasingly involved in peacebuilding since the early 1990s, particularly in Europe and Africa. The AU has taken on new peacebuilding roles—in Burundi and Sudan—but its capacity to mount and maintain military deployments is limited.[27] The organization (at the time of this writing) hopes to establish a permanent African security force of five or six brigades of 3,000–5,000 troops each by 2010.

Beyond the need for regional approaches to peacebuilding, perhaps the most common critique of peacebuilding to date has been that international agencies are not sufficiently sensitive to the unique characteristics of each host country.[28] External actors (and social scientists) have a tendency to categorize countries according to typologies—democratizing, fragile, failing, war-torn, and so on. Yet, as Nicole Ball points out, one should not assume that 'a particular institutional solution or sequencing of events is appropriate simply because it has been used with relative success in another conflict-affected country.'[29] Terms such as 'civil society' are misleadingly monolithic: countries have unique histories and traditions of social organization, which create different challenges and opportunities for conflict resolution.[30]

However, the degree of country-specific knowledge within most international organizations, including the UN, is limited.[31] Some action has been taken to make peacebuilding practices more context-sensitive. Donor agencies, for instance, have increasingly used conflict-sensitivity analyses to anticipate the impacts of their policies in particular environments.[32]

The Hard Nut of Coordination

One of the problems noted since the early days of post-Cold War peacebuilding is the difficulty of coordinating the activities of the myriad international agencies and actors involved in these operations. At times, peacebuilding agencies have worked at cross-purposes. In the early 1990s, for instance, observers noted that the UN was urging authorities in El Salvador, Mozambique, and Cambodia to increase spending on peacebuilding-related programs, while the IMF was pushing in the opposite direction, demanding fiscal restraint. In fact, the coordination problem existed at many levels: between major international bodies, within the UN itself, and among the various departments of national governments—defense, development, and foreign ministries—that were involved in particular missions.

The 2000 *Report of the Panel on United Nations Peacebuilding Operations* (known as the Brahimi report) made improved coordination in the field a focus of its recommendations. 'Collaboration across divisions, departments and agencies does occur,' the Brahimi panel wrote, 'but relies too heavily on personal networks and ad hoc support.'[33] In response, the UN implemented a new 'integrated mission' approach to bring the UN's resources and activities closer together, under the in-country leadership of the special representative of the Secretary-General, and to ensure that these are applied in a coherent way. The world organization and the international financial institutions are also working more closely together to conduct joint 'needs assessments' prior to deploying missions, along with other measures aimed at improving strategic planning within the UN Secretariat. Further, several national governments have pursued 'whole of government' approaches to cross-departmental cooperation for peacebuilding; and in December 2005 the General Assembly and Security Council voted to create a new Peacebuilding Commission in order to promote greater strategic coordination among UN bodies and major international donors, and to ensure more sustained attention to countries after the initial deployment of peacebuilding missions (Figure 23.3).

These initiatives are vitally important, given the disorganization and lack of communication that have hampered missions in the past. Several recent studies have highlighted the 'strategic deficit' in the planning and execution of peacebuilding, which has led to delayed, ad hoc, fragmented, and at times contradictory responses to crisis situations.[34] However, the effectiveness of these new measures remains to be seen, and the challenges are great. As Shepard Forman writes, 'the effectiveness of the UN response to complex crises continues to be weakened by incoherent and overlapping planning and funding appeals, and by competing

Two parallel resolutions in the General Assembly and Security Council set out the main purposes, composition and functioning of the Peacebuilding Commission.[a]

Purposes of the Commission:

- To bring together all relevant actors to marshal resources and to advise on and propose integrated strategies for post-conflict peacebuilding and recovery;
- To focus attention on the reconstruction and institution-building efforts necessary for recovery from conflict and to support the development of integrated strategies in order to lay the foundation for sustainable development; and
- To provide recommendations and information to improve the coordination of all relevant actors within and outside the United Nations, to develop best practices, to help to ensure predictable financing for early recovery activities and to extend the period of attention given by the international community to post-conflict recovery.

Composition:

- The main 'organizational committee' of the Peacebuilding Commission will be comprised of 35 members: seven from the Security Council; seven from the Economic and Social Council (giving particular consideration to those that have experienced post-conflict recovery); five out of the top 10 financial contributors to UN budgets; five out of the top 10 providers of military personnel and civilian police to UN missions; and seven additional members elected by the General Assembly.
- In addition, the Commission will meet in 'country specific' configurations to discuss particular cases. Such meetings will also include representatives of the country under consideration, key states in the region, major troop and financial contributors to the recovery effort, senior UN officials, and regional and international financial institutions 'as may be relevant.'

Functioning:

- The Commission will be a purely advisory body, providing recommendations and counsel upon the request of the Security Council, ECOSOC, the Secretary-General, and member states that are 'on the verge of lapsing or relapsing into conflict.'
- The Commission will operate on the basis of consensus among all its members.

Peacebuilding Support Office

- Comprised of 15 people (12 professional and three administrative assistants), housed within the UN Secretariat and funded out of the existing UN budget, the Peacebuilding Support Office will support the work of the Commission.[b]
- The functions of this office could include gathering and analyzing information relating to the availability of financial resources, relevant United Nations in-country planning activities, progress towards meeting short- and medium-term recovery goals and best practices with respect to cross-cutting peacebuilding issues.

Peacebuilding Fund

- The parallel resolutions also called for the creation of a standing Peacebuilding Fund to ensure 'the immediate release of resources needed to launch peacebuilding activities and the availability of appropriate financing for recovery,' to be funded through voluntary contributions from UN member states.

Fig. 23.3 The Peacebuilding Commission, Support Office, and Fund

[a] Security Council resolution 1645 (20 December 2005), and General Assembly resolution 60/180 (30 December 2005).
[b] General Assembly document A/60/694 (23 February 2006).

mandates and agendas of multiple agencies and programs.'³⁵ The lack of a clear institutional center for peacebuilding also makes it difficult to accumulate expertise and experience from one mission to the next. Because none of the agencies involved in these operations views peacebuilding as its *primary* task, the personnel, resources and knowledge necessary for such missions must be cobbled together each time. The planned creation of a Peacebuilding Support Office within the UN, serving the new Peacebuilding Commission, may provide such a locus.

Legitimacy, Accountability, and Participation

There is an inherent tension in any peacebuilding mission: while the goal is to create conditions for peaceful self-government, the means of achieving this goal involve the presence of foreign actors exercising varying levels of authority over the domestic affairs of the state. This disjuncture between goals and means raises a larger problem: how to ensure that peacebuilding missions are perceived as legitimate in the eyes of those they are trying to help. For longer-lasting state-building missions, the problem is even more acute. As Simon Chesterman puts it, 'how does one help a population prepare for democratic governance and the rule of law by imposing a form of benevolent autocracy?'³⁶

The deceptively simple answer to this question is to maximize 'local ownership' by involving populations as quickly and as extensively as possible in their own governance. But this can be very tricky to accomplish in practice—not least because local ownership can 'unintentionally come to mean ownership by conflict parties, or by the most powerful sectors of society.'³⁷ While it is undoubtedly a good idea to incorporate local perspectives into the planning and management of peacebuilding,³⁸ the challenge is to figure out exactly *whose* perspectives are to be included—and how.

In spite of these difficulties, an urgent rethinking of the relationship between peacebuilders and their host populations is now needed. The mission in Bosnia has come under increased criticism for failing to promote local ownership and for the operation's lack of accountability to the Bosnian populace.³⁹ If, as noted above, effective peacebuilding will require longer-term commitments and deployments, new strategies for promoting popular participation, accountability and legitimacy will be required to avoid perceptions of neocolonialism and a backlash against the institution of peacebuilding.

Peacebuilders should consider a four-part strategy. First, incorporate indigenous advisory groups into every major institution of peacebuilding—from local projects to the national administration, and even at the international level: in the Peacebuilding Commission itself. Second, even if conditions for national elections are not ripe, democratically constituted *local* government councils should be expeditiously established. Third, local actors should be recruited into leadership and middle-management positions in the governance and administration of the territory as quickly as possible. If no qualified candidates are available, then the most qualified should be recruited and provided with on-the-job training. Fourth, peacebuilders of all stripes should be expected to create systems facilitating and inviting individual complaints to the equivalent of an ombudsman in the field who is attached to each international agency.

Building Effective States

Peacebuilding missions need to focus on building functioning, self-sustaining state institutions capable of providing at least basic services, including security, to their citizens. Although some commentators have suggested that 'shared sovereignty' or joint international–local governance of fragile states is possible on a *permanent* basis, this prescription seems unwise and unfeasible, given post-colonial sensitivities to foreign rule. In most circumstances, lasting solutions must involve the eventual departure of peacebuilders and the construction of at least the foundations of an effective state. To be sure, the state's ability to fulfill its basic functions increases to the extent that it is seen as representing the main forces of society, and it decreases if the state is identified with the protagonists of war or is excessively authoritarian.[40] But democratic polities (and market-oriented economies) cannot be built on nothing: they presuppose the existence of public institutions to enforce rules and to structure political and economic competition. Thus, as the OECD's Development Co-operation Directorate recommended in 2005, 'The long-term vision for international engagement in fragile states is to help national reformers to build legitimate, effective and resilient state institutions.'[41]

CONCLUSION

After fifteen years and more than a dozen major operations, peacebuilding remains a vast, complex, and only partially successful experiment. Important lessons have been learned along the way, including the importance of building effective domestic institutions as a foundation for lasting peace, as well as the requirement for more effective coordination among the diverse array of international peacebuilding actors. Yet there is still much that we do not know about building the conditions for durable peace in war-torn states. Nor is it possible to predict how the US-led campaign against terrorism (including the post-conquest operations in Afghanistan and Iraq) may shape the future of the peacebuilding project.

Perhaps the most encouraging development in peacebuilding is the agreement to create the Peacebuilding Commission—one of the few proposals at the September 2005 World Summit to receive widespread support from both developing and developed countries. Although the new body will have no formal decision-making powers, it has the potential to become an important forum for the international coordination, planning and analysis of peacebuilding activities, which has been sorely lacking to date. The Commission's creation is a sign that the international community has not given up on trying to rehabilitate countries after war—despite all of the controversies, complexities and frustrations that accompany this task. Nor can we afford to give up, given the dangers that chronic civil violence poses to the inhabitants of failed and fragile states, to neighboring countries, and to global security.

NOTES

1. Paul Collier, Lani Elliot, Håvard Hegre, Anke Hoeffler, Marta Reynal-Querol, and Nicholas Sambanis, *Breaking the Conflict Trap: Civil War and Development Policy* (Washington, DC: World Bank, 2003).
2. *Report of the Secretary-General on the Implementation of Security Council Resolution 425*, UN document S/12611, 19 March 1978.
3. Boutros Boutros-Ghali, *An Agenda for Peace: Preventive Diplomacy, Peacemaking and Peace-keeping* (New York: UN, 1992).
4. Charles Call, 'Institutionalizing Peace: A Review of Post-Conflict Peacebuilding Concepts and Issues for DPA,' paper prepared for the UN Department of Political Affairs, 31 January 2005, 3–5; and Michael Lund, 'What Kind of Peace Is Being Built? Taking Stock of Post-Conflict Peacebuilding and Charting Future Directions,' paper prepared for the International Development Research Centre, January 2003, 26–27.
5. Bruce Jones with Faryal Cherif, 'Evolving Models of Peacekeeping: Policy Implications and Responses,' External Study, Peacekeeping Best Practices Unit, UN Department of Peacekeeping Operations, September 2003, www.pbpu.unlb.org.
6. Roland Paris, 'International Peacebuilding and the "Mission Civilisatrice",' *Review of International Studies* 28, no. 4 (2002): 637–656.
7. *The National Security Strategy of the United States of America* (Washington, DC: Office of the President of the United States, September 2002), www.whitehouse.gov/nsc/nss.pdf.
8. 'Prepared Statement before the House Armed Services Committee, as Prepared for Delivery for the House Armed Services Committee by Under Secretary of Defense for Policy Douglas J. Feith,' Washington, DC, 23 June 2004, www.pentagon.mil/speeches.
9. Neclâ Tschirgi, *Post-Conflict Peacebuilding Revisited: Achievements, Limitations, Challenges* (New York: International Peace Academy, 2004), 1.
10. George Downs and Stephen John Stedman, 'Evaluation Issues in Peace Implementation,' in *Ending Civil Wars: The Implementation of Peace Agreements*, ed. Stephen John Stedman, Donald Rothchild, and Elizabeth M. Cousens (Boulder, Colo.: Lynne Rienner, 2002), 43–69.
11. See the *SIPRI Yearbook* (New York: Oxford University Press, 2005).
12. Virginia Page Fortna, 'Does Peacekeeping Keep Peace? International Intervention and the Duration of Peace After Civil War,' *International Studies Quarterly* 48, no. 2 (2004): 269–292.
13. Fen Osler Hampson, *Nurturing Peace: Why Peace Settlements Succeed or Fail* (Washington, DC: United States Institute of Peace Press, 1996).

14. Michael W. Doyle and Nicholas Sambanis, 'International Peacebuilding: A Theoretical and Quantitative Analysis,' *American Political Science Review* 94, no. 4 (2000): 779–801; and James Dobbins, et al., *The UN's Role in Nation Building: From the Congo to Iraq* (Santa Monica, Calif.: RAND Corporation, 2005).

15. Boutros Boutros-Ghali, *Supplement to An Agenda for Peace*, UN document A/50/60, 3 January 1995; Kofi Annan, *The Causes of Conflict and the Promotion of Durable Peace and Sustainable Development in Africa*, UN document S/1998/318, 13 April 1998; and 'War Less Likely Between Mature Democracies, Says Secretary-General in Lecture at Oxford University,' UN document SG/SM/7850, 19 June 2001.

16. 'Secretary-General Outlines Key Lessons for Building Peace in War-Torn Societies, in Lecture at University of Ulster,' UN document SG/SM/9549, 19 October 2004.

17. Doyle and Sambanis, 'International Peacebuilding'; and Fortna, 'Does Peacekeeping Keep Peace?'.

18. *Human Security Report: War and Peace in the 21st Century* (Vancouver: Human Security Centre, University of British Columbia, 2005), 153–155.

19. Roland Paris, *At War's End: Building Peace After Civil Conflict* (Cambridge: Cambridge University Press, 2004).

20. See, e.g., Dennis A. Rondinelli and John D. Montgomery, 'Regime Change and Nation Building: Can Donors Restore Governance in Post-Conflict States?', *Public Administration and Development* 25 (2005): 15–23; and Sultan Barakat and Margaret Chard, 'Theories, Rhetoric and Practice: Recovering the Capacities of War-Torn Societies,' *Third World Quarterly* 23, no. 5 (2002): 817–835.

21. Matthias Stiefel, *Rebuilding After War: Lessons From WSP* (Geneva: War-torn Societies Project, 1999), www.idrc.ca.

22. See Andrew Reynolds, 'Constitutional Medicine,' *Journal of Democracy* 16, no. 1 (2005): 54–68.

23. On 'peace conditionalities,' see James K. Boyce, 'Aid, Conditionality and War Economies,' Working Paper no. 70 (Amherst: Political Economy Research Institute, University of Massachusetts, November 2003).

24. Timothy Donais, 'The Politics of Privatization in Post-Dayton Bosnia,' *Southeast European Politics* 3, no. 1 (2002): 3–19.

25. David M. Malone and Heiko Nitzschke, 'Economic Agendas in Civil Wars: What We Know, What We Need to Know,' Discussion paper no. 2005/07, (Helsinki: United Nations University-World Institute for Development Economics Research (UNU-WIDER), April 2005).

26. Haneef Atmar and Jonathan Goodhand, *Aid, Conflict and Peacebuilding in Afghanistan: What Lessons Can Be Learned?* (London: International Alert, February 2002).

27. Jane Boulden, ed., *Dealing With Conflict in Africa: The United Nations and Regional Organizations* (London: Palgrave, 2003).

28. For example, Charles T. Call and Susan E. Cook, 'On Democracy and Peacebuilding,' *Global Governance* 9, no. 2 (2003): 233–246; and Jarat Chopra and Tanja Hohe, 'Participatory Peacebuilding,' in *Building Sustainable Peace*, ed. Tom Keating and W. Andy Knight (Tokyo: United Nations University Press, 2004), 241–261.

29. Nicole Ball, 'Strengthening Democratic Governance of the Security Sector in Conflict-Affected Countries,' *Public Administration and Development* 25 (2005): 34.

30. Beatrice Pouligny, 'Civil Society and Post-Conflict Peacebuilding: Ambiguities of International Programmes Aimed at Building "New" Societies,' *Security Dialogue* 36, no. 4 (2004): 495–510.

31. Call, 'Institutionalizing Peace.'

32. Adam Barbolet et al., *The Utility and Dilemmas of Conflict Sensitivity* (Berlin: Berghof Research Center for Constructive Conflict Management, 2005), www.berghof-handbook.net.

33. *Report of the Panel on United Nations Peace Operations*, UN document A/55/305, 21 August 2000, para. 200, www.un.org/peace/reports/peace_operations.

34. Suzanne Verstegen, Luc van de Goor, and Jeroen de Veeuw, *The Stability Assessment Framework: Designing Integrated Responses for Security, Governance and Development*, prepared by the Clingendael Institute for the Netherlands Ministry of Foreign Affairs (The Hague: The Netherlands Ministry of Foreign Affairs, January 2005); and Dan Smith, *Towards a Strategic Framework for Peacebuilding: Getting Their Act Together*, Overview Report of the Joint Utstein Study of Peacebuilding (Brattvaag, Norway: Royal Norwegian Ministry of Foreign Affairs, April 2004).

35. Shepard Forman, 'Working Better Together: Implementing the High Level Panel's Recommendations on Peacebuilding,' in *Irrelevant or Indispensable? The United Nations in the 21st Century*, ed. Paul Heinbecker and Patricia Goff (Waterloo, Ont.: Wilfred Laurier University Press, 2005), 156.

36. Simon Chesterman, *You, the People: The United Nations, Transitional Administration and State Building* (New York: Oxford University Press, May 2004), 127.

37. Smith, *Towards a Strategic Framework for Peacebuilding*.

38. *A Review of Peace Operations: A Case for Change* (London: Conflict, Security and Development Group, King's College, 2003).

39. Richard Caplan, 'Who Guards the Guardians? International Accountability in Bosnia,' *International Peacekeeping* 12, no. 3 (2005): 463–476; and David Chandler, *Bosnia: Faking Democracy After Dayton* (London: Pluto, 1999).

40. Stiefel, *Rebuilding After War*.

41. OECD, *Principles for Good International Engagement in Fragile States: Learning and Advisory Process on Difficult Patnerships (LAP)*, DCD(2005)8/REV2, Unclassified (Paris: Organization for Economic Co-operation and Development, Development Co-operation Directorate (OECD/DCD), 7 April 2005).

CHAPTER 24

....

TERRORISM

....

JANE BOULDEN

TERRORISM was not on the minds of the framers of the Charter when they sat down to draft a blueprint for a general system of international peace and security in the midst of World War II. While intent on preventing a reoccurrence of the kind of interstate war that had generated such devastation in two world wars, they were also extremely mindful of the lessons associated with the failure of the League of Nations. The provisions of the resulting Charter, therefore, established an organization and a set of legal obligations whose scope was sufficiently flexible to encompass a whole range of activity packaged into the threats to international peace and security basket. That expansive nature has made it possible for the UN to address terrorism and to do so in a variety of ways and through a number of different channels. The Secretary-General, the Security Council, and the General Assembly have all sought to address the issue in one way or another. Associated UN bodies, ranging from the UN Commission on Crime Prevention and Criminal Justice to the UN Office on Drugs and Crime and the Department of Disarmament Affairs, are all in some fashion dealing with terrorism. This is the inherent problem of the issue. Terrorism is simultaneously everywhere and nowhere at the UN.

Its ubiquity reflects its multidimensional nature but also the dilemma it poses, in particular through the most recent incarnation of terrorism in the form of Al Qaeda. Loosely linked groups and individuals, global in location and reach, this form of terrorism poses a threat not just to the world organization's member states but ultimately to the organization itself. While this chapter argues that the UN's response to terrorism has been significant, it is difficult to argue that the world organization's counter-terrorism efforts are at the forefront of most member states' national counter-terrorism programs. The UN's response thus often runs in parallel to state efforts rather than as part and parcel of them.

The focus of this chapter is on the response of the three main UN actors in international peace and security: the General Assembly, Security Council, and

Secretary-General. It is not, therefore, an exhaustive portrayal of counter-terrorism efforts at the world organization, in that this chapter leaves out the many responses of other agencies and actors. It is also not exhaustive in that not every resolution or action is detailed here. Rather key themes, debates and decisions are used to highlight the nature of the response and the issues raised by it.

ROLE OF THE GENERAL ASSEMBLY

The General Assembly first began to deal with terrorism in 1972 in response to a request by the Secretary-General, Kurt Waldheim. His request reflected growing international concern about the upsurge in the number of high profile attacks, especially the attack on Israeli athletes at the Munich Olympics. The issue did not surface on the agenda of the Security Council. Given that the terrorist attacks of the time were primarily associated with the conflict and politics of the Middle East the permanent members had little appetite for overcoming the overlay of Cold War politics to consider a response. For almost thirty years, therefore, the General Assembly was the primary UN actor when it came to terrorism.[1]

Once it took on the issue, the General Assembly found itself in the midst of a divisive debate. Any effort to deal with terrorism raised the question as to how to define it: a question that touched on a number of sensitive issues. For some, a definition of terrorism must include state terrorism; that is, there must be some recognition that states engage in terror themselves. A second line of argument resists defining terrorism in any way that rules out the use of such methods in situations where individuals or groups have no other choice. For this group there are situations such as liberation struggles, where groups or individuals have no other recourse than to use terrorism to achieve their goals. In these instances, the argument goes, terrorism is justifiable, and efforts to define it should not rule out this possibility. Unable to overcome this obstacle, the General Assembly addressed the issue by tackling the question of method even while the debate as to motive continued.

In addition to annual resolutions condemning terrorism, the General Assembly, primarily through the work of the Sixth Committee, has negotiated and completed thirteen international legal conventions relating to terrorism. These establish prohibitions against, among other things, hijacking, crimes against internationally protected persons, the taking of hostages, terrorist bombings, and the use of nuclear material.[2] The most recent of these is the International Convention for the Suppression of Acts of Nuclear Terrorism, concluded in April 2005 in General Assembly resolution 290. Together, the General Assembly resolutions and the conventions work to establish a set of norms and legal requirements that seek to condition behavior and to encourage states to take measures to counter these activities. While they may not have reached agreement on the precise nature of terrorism, they have succeeded in establishing the boundaries of acceptable methods of behavior even in situations where some believe that the actors' motives may be considered justifiable.

In 1996, the General Assembly established an Ad Hoc Committee on Terrorism.[3] The initial mandate for the Committee was to develop a convention on terrorist bombings, and thereafter to work towards the establishment of a comprehensive treaty on terrorism by drawing together existing conventions and filling the gaps between them. The Committee continues to work towards this goal. While progress has been made, to date the main obstacle to a final document remains the question of definition. Nonetheless, the very fact that the Assembly is working on a comprehensive convention is symptomatic of the extent to which terrorism has remained a consistent and increasing source of concern to member states.[4]

THE SECURITY COUNCIL

The first mention of terrorism at the UN occurred in 1948 in Security Council resolution 57 condemning the 'criminal group of terrorists' who assassinated the UN mediator in Palestine, Count Bernadotte. The long hiatus that followed was a reflection of a variety of factors, chief among them the stalemating influence of the Cold War on Security Council action. A sharp increase in hijackings in the late 1960s generated sufficient agreement on the part of Council members that, in 1970, they passed resolution 286, calling on states to take measures to prevent them. It was not until the end of the Cold War, however, that the Council addressed terrorism again.

Beginning in the early 1990s, the Council began reacting to a new upsurge in activity that began with the bombings of Pan American flight 103 over Lockerbie and UTA flight 772 over Niger, as the 1980s drew to a close.[5] In contrast to the approach of the General Assembly, but in keeping with the general division of labor between them, the Council's response to terrorism was to deal with it on a case-by-case basis in the context of its role as custodian of international peace and security. The nature of its response was reactive and punitive, with sanctions being the main tool of choice. Thus, the Council imposed and then strengthened sanctions against Libya in order to pressure them to hand over suspects in the Lockerbie bombing, and did the same against Sudan in order to pressure them to extradite suspects in the 1995 assassination attempt against Egyptian president Hosni Mubarak.[6] The Security Council maintained this strategy in response to al Qaeda bombings of US embassies in East Africa in 1998. In a sequence of resolutions the Council condemned the bombings and imposed increasingly severe mandatory sanctions against the Taliban government in Afghanistan who were giving safe haven to Osama bin Laden and al Qaeda.[7]

In imposing sanctions in this instance the Council also moved to establish a committee, known as the 1267 Committee after its resolution number, to monitor the implementation of the sanctions. This committee is the forerunner of other terrorism committees that followed, and remains one of the most intensive, hands-on efforts of the Council to deal with terrorism.

In the midst of this response, however, the Security Council signaled a new approach by taking itself beyond the realm of case specifics for the first time. In resolution 1269, the Council 'unequivocally condemns all acts, methods, and practices of terrorism as criminal and unjustifiable, regardless of their motivation, in all their forms and manifestations, wherever and by whomever committed.' This 1999 resolution went on to call on member states to fully implement international conventions against terrorism, to work towards suppressing terrorist activity within their territory, to deny safe haven to those involved, and to guard against the abuse of asylum regulations by potential terrorists.

The resolution was important in a number of ways. Its focus on an overarching approach edged it towards the domain of the General Assembly and did so without any effort to define terrorism one way or the other. Indeed, the nature of the Council's condemnation moves beyond this question by explicitly denying any form of justification for such acts. And, the resolution sent a clear signal that terrorism was firmly on the agenda of the Security Council, not just by virtue of event-specific requirements but as an issue of international peace and security in and of itself.

By the time of the attacks in the United States on 11 September 2001, therefore, terrorism was not a new issue for the Security Council. Its immediate response was resolution 1368—passed unanimously the day after the attacks—which recognized the right to self-defense. Within a fortnight the Council moved, again unanimously, to establish a series of requirements for action by member states. Invoking Chapter VII the Security Council decided that 'all states shall' take the measures then listed. This language marks a shift from the usual use of 'calls on states' wording used by the Council. The resolution requires states to take extensive national measures to 'prevent and suppress the financing of terrorist acts' as well as measures to prevent the use of their territory by terrorists or those assisting terrorists. The resolution also calls on states to exchange information and cooperate with one another in working to counter terrorism. In order to ensure the requirements of the resolution are carried out, the Council created a committee to monitor its implementation and requires states to report to the committee on their progress on these measures.

Resolution 1373 moved the Security Council from the periphery of the General Assembly's orbit to well within it. Although established in the context of 9/11 the resolution addresses terrorism broadly and establishes binding requirements for all member states. In establishing a monitoring committee, known as the Counter-Terrorism Committee (CTC), the Council built on previous experience in using sanctions monitoring committees. The CTC is different, however, in that it is not punitive in nature and the measures in question are not specific to a particular situation. The CTC began its work very promptly and it soon became evident that the tasks involved required a degree of institutionalization not initially envisaged when the CTC was created. In March 2004, the Security Council approved resolution

1535 and the 'revitalization' of the committee through the creation of a Counter-Terrorism Executive Directorate (CTED). It was not until September 2005, however, that the CTED became officially operational.

Nonetheless, the CTC and CTED have made significant substantial progress. Dealing with reports from member states has proved to be a significant and time-consuming task in and of itself. Member states have generally responded strongly to the reporting requirements of 1373. By 30 September 2005, the CTC had received 622 reports from member states and other actors.[8] The CTC has established and continues to establish strong relationships with regional organizations and other international organizations, which are also developing counter-terrorism programs. It has established a program to facilitate the provision of technical support to those states who are in need of assistance to meet the requirements of resolution 1373, and has engaged in fifteen visits to states to meet with various officials there to discuss their implementation programs.

The combined effects of 9/11 and revelations of the existence and extent of A. Q. Khan's illicit network for transferring nuclear weapons related technology compounded to strengthen a preexisting concern about terrorists acquiring such a capability. To guard against that possibility the Security Council passed resolution 1540 in April 2004. As with resolution 1373, the Security Council invoked Chapter VII to establish binding obligations on member states. Resolution 1540 requires states to undertake a series of measures to ensure adequate laws, domestic accounting measures and controls on nuclear, chemical, and biological weapons and their means of delivery. Following the 1373 model the Council also established a committee to oversee the implementation of the resolution and calls on states to report to the committee on their efforts.

Shortly after the killings at the school in Beslan, Russia, during the first few days of September 2004, the Security Council moved to strengthen its efforts. Resolution 1566 established a working group to provide recommendations on 'practical measures' that could be imposed on individuals or groups linked to terrorism, and to consider the possibility of establishing a fund to compensate victims of terrorism. The following summer, in resolution 1624, the Council reacted to the July bombings in London by adding to the list of what it requires of states. The Council called on member states to take whatever legal measures might be necessary to prohibit incitement to commit terrorism, prevent such conduct, and deny safe haven to those guilty of it. As with previous Council-imposed requirements, states are also asked to report to the CTC on their implementation of these measures.

This burst of committee activity is an indication of the sustained level of interest the Council has maintained on terrorism. In addition to these efforts the Council has passed resolutions and issued Presidential Statements in response to terrorist attacks. All of the Council's work on this issue has been done unanimously, a further testament not just to the level of interest in this issue but the degree to which terrorism affects all states—permanent member or otherwise.

THE SECRETARY-GENERAL

Of the three main UN actors in international peace and security, the Secretary-General is the one with the greatest inherent ability to move beyond the realm of member state debate and negotiation to consider issues in a more comprehensive, longer-term, and less event-driven light. In highlighting key themes and strategies while also raising warning flags over potential problems, Secretary-General Kofi Annan played this role through the creation of a policy working group and the High-level Panel on Threats, Challenges and Change (HLP), through his repeated calls for state action and cooperation, and through his consistent reminder of the overriding need to ensure the protection of human rights in the struggle against what he has called one of the major threats of this century.

In the wake of the attacks of 9/11, the Secretary-General established a Policy Working Group (PWG), consisting of Secretariat staff members and outside experts, to examine the implications of terrorism for the world organization. The PWG's report proposed an overall strategy based on three elements: dissuading disaffected groups from embracing terrorism; denying groups or individuals the means to carry out terrorism; and sustaining broad-based international cooperation in countering terrorism.[9]

The crisis surrounding the failure of the Security Council to agree on a resolution authorizing the use of force in Iraq prompted the Secretary-General to establish the High-level Panel on Threats, Challenges and Change to consider the ways in which the organization might move ahead. The HLP incorporated the Secretary-General's ideas into its own recommendations for a comprehensive strategy while adding the need to counter extremism and intolerance and build state capacity. It also stepped squarely into the debate on how to define terrorism. Arguing that the lack of agreement on a definition was impeding progress and undermining the UN's ability to send a clear message against terrorism, the HLP argued that attacks specifically targeting civilians and noncombatants must be unequivocally condemned. The panel then outlined the basis for a definition of terrorism that, in its view, should include

any action, in addition to actions already specified by the existing conventions...that is intended to cause death or serious bodily harm to civilians or non-combatants, when the purpose of such an act...is to intimidate a population, or to compel a Government or an international organization to do or to abstain from doing any act.[10]

On the eve of the first anniversary of the bombings in Madrid the Secretary-General outlined a revised and updated strategy for combating terrorism. Building on his previous proposals, he put forward a strategy based on five 'Ds': dissuasion; denial of means; deterring state support; developing state capacity for prevention; and defending human rights in counter-terrorism efforts. He also announced the establishment of an implementation task force under the direction of his office, which would meet on a regular basis to review how terrorism was being addressed within the UN system.[11] Shortly thereafter, in laying out his proposals for the agenda of the upcoming World Summit, he reiterated this approach and also stated his belief that the HLP proposal on the question of a definition 'has clear moral force.'[12]

With the September 2005 World Summit in the offing, momentum seemed to be building towards a breakthrough on a definition. These hopes were unfulfilled. Existing beliefs on the part of a group of states that such methods may be justified in certain situations could not be overcome.

World leaders did, however, endorse the Secretary-General's proposals for a comprehensive strategy and, while they failed to agree on a definition as such, they did agree to a condemnation of terrorism 'in all its forms and manifestations, committed by whomever, wherever and for whatever purposes.'[13] The wording reflects the Security Council approach in its resolutions and the agreement is itself significant in that all member states joined together in the condemnation. Now, in addition to existing international conventions, which many states still have not signed, and Security Council resolutions, the international community has a universal condemnation.

In response to a request in the World Summit Outcome that he continue his work on developing a comprehensive UN strategy, in May 2006, the Secretary-General submitted a report titled *Uniting against terrorism: Recommendations for a global counter-terrorism strategy*, to the General Assembly. On the basis of this report, a plan of action was negotiated and adopted by the General Assembly on 8 September 2006. In doing so, the General Assembly established, for the first time, a comprehensive strategy intended to guide future action across the spectrum of prevention and response.

ISSUES AND QUESTIONS

The efforts of these three organs of the UN reveal an organization that clearly is seized of the issue of terrorism. Together they have developed innovative, significant, and sustained responses. The ongoing unanimity of the Security Council's response is particularly notable, continuing through many changes in the composition of nonpermanent members, and especially at a time when events surrounding the war in Iraq have created deep divisions. Council action has not been without missteps. The erroneous naming of the Basque dissident group Euskadi Ta Askatasuna as the perpetrators in its March 2004 resolution 1530 condemning the Madrid bombing is one such example. Overall, however, the Security Council has been both innovative and consistent in its prioritizing of terrorism.

There are a number of issues that arise, however, with respect to the nature of the UN's response. The first of these is the question of the use of force. The Council's reaffirmation of the right to self-defense in the immediate aftermath of the 9/11 attacks was much more a gesture of solidarity than it was a legal requirement. Article

51 of the Charter makes clear that self-defense is entirely acceptable—at least until the Security Council itself takes action. There are a number of relatively unexplored issues here. The first is the question of what exactly is meant by self-defense. Are there any constraints on the nature of the self-defense response? When does it begin and end?

Limitations of space in this chapter do not permit discussing the extent to which the Security Council has, over the years, criticized the use of force by some member states in response to terrorist acts, considered such criticism and failed to agree on it, or simply not addressed the issue at all.[14] If, as seems likely, terrorism and responses to it continue to be an issue of concern for the world organization, especially the Security Council, these questions are likely to move to the forefront of the debate. Left unaddressed the inconsistencies in the Council's response and the potentially open-ended nature of self-defense, as evidenced in the case of the US actions in Afghanistan, will raise questions about the nature and legitimacy of the response.

The second issue is that of human rights. The Secretary-General has taken the lead in arguing for the need to ensure that human rights standards are met in any national or international response to terrorism.[15] The detention center at Guantánamo Bay and the revelations of abuses at the Abu Ghraib prison in Iraq are the most high-profile examples of the types of problems that may arise, but there are many others, and the potential for problems exists in international as well as in national responses. In considering measures that require the naming of individuals, for example, the Security Council is moving into this realm. What recourse do individuals have if they are incorrectly listed? Beyond the specifics, an increasing awareness of the need to safeguard human rights in this process is evident in the consistency with which Security Council resolutions carry language requiring the maintenance of human rights commitments, and the high priority given to the issue by the General Assembly and the Secretary-General. As with the use of force, how human rights concerns are balanced with security imperatives is likely to be and should be a central theme in the consideration of terrorism responses.

As the forgoing indicates, one of the key themes in all of this remains the thorny question of definition. Between Security Council resolutions and the HLP's recommendations, one could argue that a definition is all but there. What is present is a Security Council definition, as articulated in various binding resolutions, especially resolution 1566. What is absent, however, is a definition agreed by all member states in the General Assembly rather than established by the Council. In practical terms the absence of an agreed definition detracts from the overall coherence of UN efforts, while also making it difficult to work towards comprehensive and comparable legislation at the state level. In political and normative terms, the absence of an agreed definition reflects concerns about motive, and links to the question of root causes. Are there, in fact, circumstances in which the use of terrorism is justified? And if so, should efforts to combat terrorism not focus on addressing those causes? The problematic trigger here is that, for states on the receiving end of terrorist attacks, any discussion of justification and root causes suggests, deliberately or otherwise, a shifting of some portion of the blame on to their shoulders—for them a completely unacceptable proposition. This reveals an interesting continuity in the UN's response. Motive and justification still matter even as the nature of the terrorist threat being addressed has expanded beyond the various well-defined and country-specific groups of the 1970s and 1980s to include more amorphous groups such as al Qaeda.

Once the possibility of justifying actions based on motivation is opened, there is no easy way to circumscribe the potential justifications. Context is everything in these situations. Many point to the fact that Nelson Mandela, now one of the world's most respected statesmen, was a member of the African National Congress (ANC), once branded a terrorist organization and now the governing party of South Africa, and something similar could be said of the Irish Republican Army and Gerry Adams in Northern Ireland. Similarly, the acceptance of the PLO as a legitimate voice for the Palestinian people was, not so long ago, a completely unacceptable outcome. While it may be some time before it is clear how the January 2006 election of Hamas will ultimately play out, the very fact of its success demonstrates how difficult it is to deal with clarity and certainty in the realm of terrorism and counter-terrorism.

The August 2003 attack on UN headquarters in Baghdad gave devastating symbolism to the fact that terrorism is a threat not just to the UN's member states but to the world organization itself. Terrorism, by virtue of the apparent power it gives nonstate actors and in its objectives, is ultimately an attack on order.[16] The UN's response, therefore, in which all three key actors have worked to deal with terrorism through the lens of the state, must be read as a reflection of the realities of its mandate as an organization of and for states, but also as a reaffirmation of the importance of the state in ensuring the order from which international peace and security can grow.

Notes

1. For more on the General Assembly role see M. J. Peterson, 'Using the General Assembly,' in *Terrorism and the UN, Before and After September 11,* ed. Jane Boulden and Thomas G. Weiss (Bloomington: Indiana University Press, 2004), 173–197.
2. A list of conventions is available at www.unodc.org.
3. General Assembly resolution 51/210, 17 December 1996.
4. The latest of its periodic reports is UN document A/60/37, April 2005.
5. The bombing of Pan Am flight 103 took place on 21 December 1988. UTA flight 772 went down over Niger en route from Brazzaville to Paris on 19 September 1989.
6. Against Libya: Security Council resolutions 731, 21 January 1992; 748, 31 March 1992; 883, 11 November 1993. Against Sudan: Security Council resolutions 1044, 31 January 1996; 1054, 26 April 1996; 1070, 16 August 1996.
7. For more on the role of the Security Council see Chantal de Jonge Oudraat, 'The Role of the Security Council,' in Jane Boulden and Thomas G. Weiss, *Terrorism and the UN,* 151–172.
8. UN document S/2005/663, 21 October 2005.
9. *Report of the Policy Working Group on the United Nations and Terrorism,* Annex to UN document A/57/273 and S/2002/875, 6 August 2002.

10. High-level Panel on Threats, Challenges and Change, *A More Secure World: Our Shared Responsibility* (New York: UN, 2004), para. 162.

11. 'Secretary-General Offers Global Strategy for Fighting Terrorism,' UN document SG/SM/9757, 10 March 2005.

12. Kofi Annan, *In Larger Freedom: Towards Development, Security and Human Rights for All*, UN document A/59/2005, 21 March 2005, para. 91.

13. *2005 World Summit Outcome*, UN document A/60/L.1, 15 September 2005, para. 81.

14. For more on this see de Jonge Oudraat, 'The Role of the Security Council.'

15. See Thomas G. Weiss, Margaret E. Crahan, and John Goering, eds., *Wars on Terrorism and Iraq: Human Rights, Unilateralism, and US Foreign Policy* (London: Routledge, 2004).

16. Nicholas Rostow also makes this point in 'Before and After: The Changed UN Response to Terrorism since September 11th,' *Cornell International Law Journal* 35, no. 3 (2002): 475–490.

PART VI

HUMAN RIGHTS

CHAPTER 25

NORMS AND MACHINERY

BERTRAND G. RAMCHARAN

THERE are different ways of looking at the evolution of human rights norms and machinery in the United Nations. Certainly the system is imperfect, and it is necessary to explore the impact of politics and politicization.[1] The record shows rights violations of large groups of humankind, and one could highlight these failures. Yet, the UN's history in this area is also a story of striving, in the midst of adversity, to take forward the idea that societies should be governed on the basis of respect for the human rights of all, without discrimination on grounds of race, sex, language, religion, or other prejudices. This narrative emphasizes the latter—the significant evolution that has taken place over the course of a half a century—but is intertwined with the sober recognition that political will is often absent, resulting in conscience-shocking violence in places such as Rwanda, Srebrenica, and Darfur. So while there has been significant normative progress, illustrated by the 1948 Convention against Genocide and the 'responsibility to protect,'[2] there have been clear failures—mass killings, rape, and ethnic cleansing—that inspire continued efforts to improve physical and legal protection.[3]

Whatever the imperfections of the Commission on Human Rights (CHR), the initial vision of an international bill of human rights—consisting of a declaration, one or more covenants, and measures of implementation—has inspired the human rights movement throughout the UN's history. While Cold War politics led the General Assembly to decide on two covenants—on civil and political rights, and on economic, social and cultural rights—the contemporary challenge remains ensuring that governments do not violate the basic rights of their peoples and national resources are used fairly to give everyone equitable life chances.

Another challenge is upholding the idea of international protection when gross violations of human rights occur, but governments plead non-interference in their internal affairs and try to hide behind Charter Article 2 (7). Many new states emerged from colonialism with arbitrary borders. The challenges of nation-building are many. During the Cold War, the major powers competed for influence in many developing countries, supporting one or another side in the local power struggle. With the end of that conflict, these fragile countries struggle with nation-building.

Moreover, market capitalism has emerged internationally as the dominant economic system, but many developing countries do not have the infrastructure or human capital to compete with more developed countries, or to withstand the onslaught of the major international corporations. How are they to uphold basic standards of economic, social, and cultural rights and civil and political rights in these circumstances? Many contend that the UN should strive to promote cooperation among countries rather than putting countries experiencing human rights problems in the dock.

These are thorny issues. On the one hand, in no circumstance should one tolerate gross violations of human rights, for example, the right not to be tortured. On the other hand, with leading developing countries arguing for cooperative instead of confrontational approaches in dealing with human rights problems, imagination is required to devise effective approaches to protection. Three principles should guide the international human rights movement: respect, confidence-building, and protection.

At a time when the challenges of protection have become intertwined with challenges of poverty and international political divisions between countries of the North and the South, the 2005 UN World Summit placed on the international agenda two issues that will influence future debate: the responsibility to protect, and transforming the Commission on Human Rights into a Human Rights Council. Despite resistance from some Southern countries, it was relatively easier to agree on the responsibility to protect, which embraces the idea that state sovereignty implies a responsibility on the part of governments to protect their populations. In the context of mass killing and ethnic cleansing, a government forfeits its sovereignty and the international community of states assumes the responsibility to protect the country's citizens from such atrocities. Some developing countries, however, remain wary that the responsibility to protect norm could lead to interventions by major powers in weaker countries.

The controversy over reforming the Commission on Human Rights was more acrimonious. Developing countries resent the fact that they are being demonized at a time when they are facing massive economic and social problems. Developed countries, with the Secretary-General leading them, argued that the commission should be rid of members that egregiously violate human rights. On the one side there was pride and numbers; on the other side, there was principle and power. Historians will judge whether the Secretary-General should have engaged in diplomacy to reform, strengthen, or change the CHR—particularly the commission's electoral system—instead of publicly denigrating and denouncing the organ, which was a

Charter-based body brought into being largely through the efforts of human rights activists present at the 1945 founding UN conference in San Francisco. Three decades later, a high-level expert group, headed by Richard N. Gardner, first championed the case for a Human Rights Council.

This chapter offers a brief historical overview and an outline of the principles governing human rights, the vision of the international bill of human rights, and the evolution of norms. It then introduces some of the essential institutional mechanisms before discussing implementation measures and strategies to halt abuse. It concludes with the essential task of the future—prevention.

SAN FRANCISCO CHOICES

At the 1945 United Nations Conference on International Organization in San Francisco, there was a groundswell of sentiment that the 'new world order' should be built on a foundation of human rights. Civil society organizations, leading academics, and governments developed blueprints for an international bill of human rights.[4] The leading powers assembled at San Francisco, however, were all violators of human rights. In the US South segregation and racial discrimination were rife. The United Kingdom and France perpetrated egregious abuses in their colonies. The Union of Soviet Socialist Republics (USSR) had gulags—forced labor camps. Despite the grand rhetoric, the leading powers were more concerned with the looming struggle for supremacy than with inspiring human rights choices.

Thanks largely to civil society pressure upon the delegates, particularly the American delegation, the Charter included several human rights provisions that would be significant in the future. First, there was the emphasis on the principle of self-determination as the bedrock for pursuing the independence of colonies and territories. While certainly one of the UN's achievements, it should be noted that this principle coincided with US interests to dismantle European empires and open up markets for its expanding productive base.[5] Second, the world organization would be based on the principle of nondiscrimination on grounds of race, sex, language, or religion among nations and peoples. This commitment has characterized the UN ever since its existence and would also be one of the great foundational principles of the new world order. Third, member states committed themselves to the pursuit of international cooperation for the promotion of human rights for all peoples. Fourth, member states pledged themselves to take measures jointly and separately for the achievement of universal respect for human rights and fundamental freedoms. This commitment, encapsulated in Charter Articles 55 and 56, was significant for the advancement of human welfare and for the universal realization of human rights.

Fifth, and crucially in institutional terms, Charter Article 68 called for a Commission on Human Rights to be established as a functional organ of the Economic and

Social Council (ECOSOC). This commission would be asked to consider proposals that had been submitted at the San Francisco conference for an international bill of human rights. While the Charter spoke of international cooperation and the promotion of human rights, the leading powers rejected the inclusion of language pertaining to protection.[6] Language pertaining to protection would mean that segregation in the United States, discrimination in the colonies, or mistreatment in the gulags, for example, could be scrutinized in efforts to protect people.

In San Francisco and subsequent debates in the General Assembly, the delegates of the major powers, including the much venerated Eleanor Roosevelt, argued that the UN could only act for the promotion of human rights, not their protection. This limitation would impede the development of robust human rights machinery. First, protection had to be tackled under the guise of promotion. Second, the protective capacity of the world organization would have to be built up gradually through practice.[7] The word 'protection' was rarely used in UN documents and parlance until 1993, when the General Assembly gave the newly established UN High Commissioner for Human Rights the competence to promote and protect human rights.[8]

The San Francisco choice for promotion over protection had major consequences throughout the Cold War. The CHR, with the former American first lady Eleanor Roosevelt herself at the helm, initially took the view that it had no competence to act on the thousands of petitions concerning gross violations of human rights in different parts of the world. It took great ingenuity to establish procedures to foster the human rights agenda, including annual debates to discuss gross violations. How this procedure will fare with the Human Rights Council remains to be seen.

With the wave of decolonization in the 1960s, newly independent states assumed seats at the UN and pushed for procedures to deal with gross violations of human rights in the remaining colonies and apartheid South Africa. Their efforts laid the foundation for the procedures and mechanisms subsequently developed. Ironically, those very developing countries now are arguing that the UN should not seek to condemn countries but should rather seek to assist them through cooperation rather than confrontation, promotion rather than protection. The way forward must be a judicious combination of promotion and protection. The key must surely lie in prevention through efforts to build an effective national protection system in each country that covers not only civil and political but also economic, social, and cultural rights. Articles 55 and 56 provide the platform for action.

The Vision of an International Bill of Human Rights

At San Francisco some governments, especially from Latin America, proposed that the Charter should contain an international bill of human rights. Partly because of controversy and partly because of shortage of time, the question was referred to the newly established Commission on Human Rights.

After the commission was formally constituted, it set forth the vision of an international bill that would contain three parts: a declaration of moral principles;

one or more treaties that, after ratification, would contain legally binding obligations; and measures of implementation. These three elements were developed over time and are commonly considered to constitute that bill of rights. The 1948 Universal Declaration of Human Rights and the Convention against Genocide of that same year; the International Convention on the Elimination of All Forms of Racial Discrimination in 1965; the International Covenant on Economic, Social and Cultural Rights and the International Covenant on Civil and Political Rights; and a series of human rights treaties provide a solid normative foundation. Measures of implementation proved more difficult to conceptualize and to establish. In 1947, the 'nuclear commission'—the predecessor of the larger CHR—even raised the idea of a separate UN agency to ensure compliance with human rights. Pending its establishment, the commission could advise the Security Council of problematic human rights situations that might endanger international peace and security. The challenge of implementation remains six decades later, but the idea of an international bill of human rights proved, from the outset, a rallying vision and remains so to this day.

THE DEVELOPMENT OF INTERNATIONAL HUMAN RIGHTS NORMS

The development of international human rights norms has been one of the UN's success stories.[9] Cumulatively, a veritable international code of human rights exists, governing practically every area of the relationship between the individual and the state. And the process of drafting new norms continues, with the adoption by the General Assembly of an International Convention for the Protection of All Persons from Enforced Disappearances in December 2006. This phenomenon was widespread in Latin America in the 1970s and 1980s and is still prevalent in many parts of the world.

The development of human rights norms has been influenced by many factors. First, concepts of human rights from different parts of the world were drawn upon in giving content to the Universal Declaration, including the historic English, French, and American declarations of human rights. Second, there was a strong push for an approach to human rights that recognized the interrelationship among civil and political rights and economic, social, and cultural rights. However, Western countries argued that civil and political rights were interdictions upon governments (so-called negative rights), whereas economic, social, and cultural rights were programmatic aspirations (so-called positive rights). The Cold War pitted the West as the champion of the former (also known as 'first generation rights') against the East as the advocate of the latter (also known as 'second generation rights').

This struggle resulted in two covenants instead of one. Western governments were reluctant to recognize equality of rights during an era in which the United Kingdom and France still had colonies and the United States had corrosive segregation in the South. The protection of minorities and indigenous populations was another difficult topic, especially as Latin American countries insisted that they did not have minority populations and were reluctant to recognize the rights of indigenous populations. Some of these difficulties still remain. For example, some Western countries, such as the United States, still deny that economic, social, and cultural rights are part of the human rights complex.

The developing countries, for their part, pressed hard for the recognition of the right to self-determination and the right to development.[10] These countries saw the development of human rights norms as having a role to play in consecrating as international public policy major aspirations of large parts of humanity for peace, self-determination, development, and justice. A tension between classical, restrictive approaches to human rights and more dynamic, public order approaches to human aspirations and rights continues to be felt in our time, particularly as regards the implementation of the right to development.

Whatever the difficulties, we are now the inheritors of great normative human rights instruments, with pride of place belonging to the Universal Declaration of Human Rights, the International Covenant on Civil and Political Rights and the International Covenant on Economic, Social and Cultural Rights. Views differ as to whether the Universal Declaration, in part or as a whole, is a legally binding document but most commentators agree that some parts of it represent binding international law.

In addition to the declaration, the main treaties are: the two international covenants and the conventions against racial discrimination, against torture, on the rights of the child, on the elimination of discrimination against women, and on the rights of migrant workers and their families. The covenants and the five conventions are widely ratified, with the Convention on the Rights of the Child being the one subscribed to by all but two states. The Convention on the Rights of Migrant Workers and their Families is the least ratified.

PRINCIPLES OF INTERNATIONAL HUMAN RIGHTS LAW

General principles of law found in the major legal systems of the world are a source of international law that international courts and tribunals may invoke.[11] General principles of law include: the rule of law (society shall be governed through laws and everyone is subject to the law); constitutionalism (governance that advances the rights of the people); democratic governance (the will of the people shall be the basis of the authority of governments); and the principle of responsibility for unlawful acts.

Principles of international public policy (*jus cogens*) have been recognized in international law. The International Court of Justice (ICJ) has asserted the existence of obligations of a state towards the international community of states as a whole: 'Such obligations derive, for example, in contemporary international law, from the outlawing of acts of aggression, and of genocide, as also from the principles and rules concerning the basic rights of the human person, including protection from slavery and racial discrimination.' Ian Brownlie contends that the least controversial examples of principles of international public policy are the prohibition of the use of force; the law of genocide; the principle of racial nondiscrimination; crimes against humanity; and the rules prohibiting trade in slaves and piracy.[12] The outlawing of torture is also widely accepted.

International humanitarian law seeks to uphold the principle of humanity in armed conflicts. The principles pervading international humanitarian law are, as classically developed in the Red Cross movement, the principles of humanity, impartiality, neutrality, independence, voluntary service, unity, and universality.

In the *Nicaragua* case the ICJ invoked general principles of humanitarian law based upon Article 3, common to the four Geneva Conventions on humanitarian law. Expounding on the general principles of humanitarian law, the Court held that the Geneva Conventions were in some respects a development and in other respects no more than the expression of such principles.[13] Common Article 3 of the four Geneva Conventions provides that, in the case of armed conflict not of an international character occurring in the territory of one of the high contracting parties, each party to the conflict shall be bound to apply, as a minimum, the rule that 'Persons taking no part in the hostilities, including members of armed forces who have laid down their arms and those placed *hors de combat* by sickness, wounds, detention, or any other cause, shall in all circumstances be treated humanely, without any adverse distinction founded on race, colour, religion or faith, sex, birth, or wealth, or any other similar criteria.' To this end, violence to life and person, hostage-taking, outrages on personal dignity, and sentencing or execution without judgment are prohibited at any time and in any place whatsoever. Furthermore, the wounded and sick must be collected and cared for.

Turning to principles of international human rights law, we may identify the principles of universality, democratic legitimacy, justice, protection, legality, respecting and ensuring the protection of human rights, equality and nondiscrimination, and remedy. In view of their importance these principles are presented summarily.

The 1993 World Conference on Human Rights succinctly expressed a consensus on the universality of human rights: 'The universality of these rights and freedoms is beyond question.' It went on to say, 'While the significance of national and regional particularities and various historical, cultural and religious backgrounds must be borne in mind, it is the duty of States, regardless of their political, economic and cultural systems, to promote and protect all human rights.' These pronouncements sought to end the controversy over cultural relativism.[14]

Article 21 (3) of the Universal Declaration of Human Rights provides that the will of the people shall be the basis of the authority of government through periodic and genuine elections which shall be by universal and equal suffrage and shall be held by secret vote or by equivalent free voting procedures. Article 25 of the International Covenant on Civil and Political Rights states that everyone shall have the rights and the opportunity—without any of the distinctions mentioned in Article 2 and without unreasonable restrictions to take part in the conduct of public affairs, directly or through freely chosen representatives—to vote and to be elected at genuine periodic elections, which shall be by universal and equal suffrage and shall be held by secret ballot, guaranteeing the free expression of the will of the electors; and to have access, on general terms of equality, to public service in his or her country.

The World Conference on Human Rights declared that democracy, development, and respect for human rights and fundamental freedoms are interdependent and mutually reinforcing. It emphasized: 'The international community should support the strengthening and promoting of democracy, development and respect for human rights and fundamental freedoms in the entire world.'

The principle of justice is at the heart of the human rights movement and has been taken forward with the establishment of institutions such as the International Criminal Court. In *A. v. Australia*, the Human Rights Committee recalled that the notion of 'arbitrariness' must not be equated with 'against the law' but be interpreted more broadly to include such elements as inappropriateness and injustice.[15]

The International Commission on Intervention and State Sovereignty elaborated the core principles of the responsibility to protect. This responsibility, according to the commission and later endorsed by the General Assembly in 2005, embraces three specific duties: 'the responsibility to prevent . . . to react . . . [and] to rebuild.'[16]

In General Comment No. 27,[17] the Human Rights Committee provides general principles applicable in the interpretation of restrictions or limitation clauses in human rights treaties. Where, for example, one finds the expression 'as provided by law,' the law itself has to establish the conditions under which the rights may be limited. Further, the restriction must not impair the essence of the right, should use precise criteria, and may not confer unfettered discretion on those charged with their execution.

In the same vein, a restriction must be legitimate and necessary:

Restrictive measures must conform to the principle of proportionality; they must be appropriate to achieve their protective function; they must be the least intrusive instrument amongst those which might achieve the desired result; and they must be proportionate to the interest to be protected.

The committee puts particular emphasis on the fundamental principles of equality and nondiscrimination whenever restrictions are made.

The principles of equality and nondiscrimination are hallowed principles of international human rights law. In its General Comment No. 18, the Human Rights Committee provided the following definition of discrimination:

'discrimination' as used in the Covenant should be understood to imply any distinction, exclusion, restriction or preference which is based on any ground such as race, colour, sex, language, religion, political or other opinion, national or social origin, property, birth or other status, and which has the purpose or effect of nullifying or impairing the recognition, enjoyment or exercise by all persons, on an equal footing, of all rights and freedoms.

In today's world of terrorist threats, the Human Rights Committee has provided invaluable guidance on the balance to be struck between security and human rights. Referring to Article 4 of the International Covenant on Civil and Political Rights, the Committee declared in General Comment No. 29:

Not every disturbance or catastrophe qualifies as a public emergency which threatens the life of the nation, as required by article 4, paragraph 1. During armed conflict, whether international or non-international, rules of international humanitarian law become applicable and help, in addition to the provisions in article 4 and article 5, paragraph l, of the Covenant, to prevent the abuse of a State's emergency powers. The Covenant requires that even during an armed conflict measures derogating from the Covenant are allowed only if and to the extent that the situation constitutes a threat to the life of the nation. If States parties consider invoking article 4 in other situations than an armed conflict, they should carefully consider the justification and why such a measure is necessary and legitimate in the circumstances.

Article 8 of the Universal Declaration of Human Rights states the fundamental principle: 'Everyone has the right to an effective remedy by the competent national tribunal.' The 1993 Vienna conference emphasized that 'Every State should provide an effective framework of remedies to redress human rights grievances or violations. In its views under the Optional Protocol the Human Rights Committee has consistently retained its position that, in a case where a violation of the Covenant has been established through the Optional Protocol procedure, the State Party in question has a legal obligation to provide an effective remedy.'[18]

HUMAN RIGHTS MACHINERY

Not only human rights norms have increased since 1945. The framers of the Charter would undoubtedly also be pleased to see the institutional machinery whose growing density and budgets reflect an increased importance attached by many states and individuals to enforcing human rights norms.

Commission on Human Rights

The CHR was established by ECOSOC in 1946. Its first session was in 1947, and its final session was in March 2006. It was abolished in June of that year and replaced

Table 25.1 Working Groups of the former Commission on Human Rights and the Sub-Commission on the Promotion and Protection of Human Rights

Working Groups of the Commission on Human Rights

Enforced or Involuntary Disappearances

The Right to Development

Arbitrary Detention

Human Rights Situations

Indigenous Peoples

Optional Protocol to the International Covenant on Economic, Social and Cultural Rights

Intergovernmental Working Group on the Effective Implementation of the Durban Declaration and Programme of Action

Working Group of Experts on People of African Descent

Group of Independent Eminent Experts

Working Groups of the Sub-Commission on the Promotion and Protection of Human Rights

Contemporary Forms of Slavery

Indigenous Populations

Administration of Justice

Communications

Minorities

by the Human Rights Council (HRC). The new council was directed to prepare recommendations and reports regarding several main themes including: the right to self-determination; racism; the right to development; the question of the violation of human rights and fundamental freedoms in any part of the world; economic, social, and cultural rights; and civil and political rights, including the questions of torture and detention.

The commission originally had eighteen members, but ECOSOC subsequently increased its membership several times. In its final session in 2006, it had fifty-three states elected by ECOSOC for three-year terms. Over the years, the commission established numerous working groups and the Sub-Commission on Prevention of Discrimination and Protection of Minorities—changed to the Sub-Commission on the Promotion and Protection of Human Rights in 1999—to carry out vital functions, which are listed in Table 25.1. It also entrusted designated special rapporteurs, experts, and representatives to examine and publicly report on specific human rights situations, which are found in Table 25.2.

Persistence was essential to develop the system of working groups and special rapporteurs who engage in fact-finding about allegations of gross violations of human rights—including, arbitrary or summary executions, enforced or involuntary disappearances, arbitrary detention, violence against women, trafficking in human

Table 25.2 System of Special Rapporteurs, Independent Experts, and Representatives by country and theme, 2006

Country Mandates

Special Rapporteur on the situation of human rights in *Belarus*

Independent Expert on the situation of human rights in *Burundi*

Special Representative of the Secretary-General for human rights in *Cambodia*

Personal Representative of the High Commissioner for Human Rights on the situation of human rights in *Cuba*

Special Rapporteur on the situation of human rights in the *Democratic People's Republic of Korea*

Independent Expert on the situation of human rights in the *Democratic Republic of the Congo*

Independent Expert appointed by the Secretary-General on the situation of human rights in *Haiti*

Independent Expert on the situation of human rights in *Liberia*

Special Rapporteur on the situation of human rights in *Myanmar*

Special Rapporteur on the situation of human rights in the *Palestinian territories occupied since 1967*

Independent Expert appointed by the Secretary-General on the situation of human rights in *Somalia*

Special Rapporteur on the situation on human rights in the *Sudan*

Independent Expert on the situation of human rights in *Uzbekistan* (1503 procedure)

Thematic Mandates

Special Rapporteur on *adequate housing* as a component of the right to an adequate standard of living

Special Rapporteur on the *sale of children*, child prostitution and child pornography

Special Rapporteur on the right to *education*

Special Rapporteur on *extrajudicial, summary or arbitrary executions*

Independent Expert on the question of human rights and *extreme poverty*

Special Rapporteur on the right to *food*

Special Rapporteur on the promotion and protection of the right to *freedom of opinion and expression*

Special Rapporteur on *freedom of religion or belief*

Special Rapporteur on the right of everyone to the enjoyment of the highest attainable standard of physical and mental *health*

Special Representative of the Secretary-General on the situation of *human rights defenders*

Special Rapporteur on the *independence of judges and lawyers*

Special Rapporteur on the situation of human rights and fundamental freedoms of *indigenous people*

Representative of the Secretary-General on the human rights of *internally displaced persons*

Special Rapporteur on the human rights of *migrants*

Independent Expert on *minority issues*

Special Rapporteur on contemporary forms of *racism*, racial discrimination, xenophobia and related intolerance

(Continued)

Table 25.2 (*Continued*)

Independent Expert on human rights and *international solidarity*

Independent Expert on the *effects of economic reform policies and foreign debt* on the full enjoyment of human rights, particularly economic, social and cultural rights

Special Rapporteur on the promotion and protection of human rights while countering *terrorism*

Special Rapporteur on *torture* and other cruel, inhuman or degrading treatment or punishment

Special Rapporteur on the adverse effects of the illicit movement and dumping of *toxic and dangerous products and wastes* on the enjoyment of human rights

Special Rapporteur on *trafficking in persons*, especially in women and children

Special Representative of the Secretary-General on human rights and *transnational corporations and other business enterprises*

Special Rapporteur on violence against *women*, its causes and consequences

Source: Office of the High Commissioner for Human Rights.

beings, persecution on grounds of religion or belief, or massive abuses in particular countries. This system began in the late 1960s but took off in the late 1970s.

Rapporteurs and working groups issue urgent appeals when people are at risk, make public statements denouncing violations, and submit annual reports to the CHR/HRC or the General Assembly. Their independent judgment is a key asset, although some have been judged to have links with their home governments. Precisely because of their independent character and their courage in denouncing human rights violations, they are often criticized. For developed as well as developing countries, self-protection is a priority. The human rights business at the United Nations is very much one of seeking to advance idealism in the midst of hard-nosed politics. Idealism without political understanding amounts to amateurism.

Human Rights Council

The 2005 World Summit, prodded by Secretary-General Kofi Annan, resolved to create a Human Rights Council to replace the much-criticized Commission on Human Rights. Negotiations on the establishment of the new council presented an opportunity to modernize the roles of the main UN human rights body and perhaps, one day, transform it into a principal UN organ.[19] However, the negotiations became protracted because of political differences. And it took until March 2006 for the General Assembly to decide finally about the new council's mandate and composition. The first members were elected by the General Assembly in May 2006, and the council convened in Geneva for the first time in mid-June.

Some were disgruntled because the mandate given to the new council was mainly promotional with no clear emphasis on the importance of a protection role. Some were displeased because the number of members of the new council had decreased to forty-seven, while others thought this perhaps still too large. There was criticism that membership was subject only to a simple majority vote instead of the more stringent two-thirds requirement proposed by the Secretary-General. However, the fact that membership entailed scrutiny was designed to discourage the worst human rights offenders, and the fact that the new council would meet at least three times a year for ten weeks was a step forward.

The performance of the Human Rights Council will require more time to evaluate, but we should keep in mind that other organs will continue to play their part, including the Security Council, General Assembly, and human rights treaty bodies established under the seven main human rights treaties. One is therefore looking to a leadership and spearheading orientation for the new council, as well as protection and coordination roles.

The emphasis within international debates is rightly placed these days on prevention,[20] and one should expect the HRC to focus on forestalling gross violations, a topic that is discussed below. Other priority tasks would include a leading role in the formulation of strategies and programs to combat discrimination and take the lead in encouraging human rights education in the schools, universities, and other educational institutions of every country, in local languages. The Human Rights Council could also make it a central part of its work to contribute to the strengthening of national protection systems; and on this issue, a peer review process can have an important role. The HRC can improve upon the system of special procedures—both rapporteurs and working groups working against torture, arbitrary executions, disappearances, arbitrary detention, violence against women and children, and other blots on civilization.

Finally, the new Human Rights Council should work in close partnership with all relevant actors, beginning with civil society, to ensure optimal participation. An effective partnership with human rights NGOs was an essential feature of the CHR and should remain with the new council. In this regard, the council should also work in close partnership with regional human rights bodies such as the African Commission on Human Rights, the European Court of Human Rights, and the Inter-American Commission and Court of Human Rights, as well as the UN's principal specialized agencies. The mainstreaming of human rights in all parts of the UN system should be the avenue for cooperation with the World Bank and the International Monetary Fund.

Human Rights Treaty Bodies

Of central importance, but with potential still to be tapped, are the seven human rights treaty bodies established under the main conventions, which have the same names and are listed in Table 25.3.[21] The human rights treaty bodies are committees of experts that monitor compliance with the core international human rights treaties. They are created by the provisions of the treaty that they oversee and (except for the Committee on the Elimination of Discrimination against Women, which is supported by the Division for the Advancement of Women) they receive secretariat support from the Treaties and Commission Branch of OHCHR (see below).

These committees consider reports from state parties to their particular convention; engage in a dialog with governments about their efforts to promote and protect

Table 25.3 Human rights treaty bodies

The *Human Rights Committee (HRC)* monitors implementation of the International Covenant on Civil and Political Rights and its Optional Protocols

The *Committee on Economic, Social and Cultural Rights (CESCR)* monitors implementation of the International Covenant on Economic, Social and Cultural Rights

The *Committee on the Elimination of Racial Discrimination (CERD)* monitors implementation of the International Convention on the Elimination of All Forms of Racial Discrimination

The *Committee on the Elimination of Discrimination Against Women (CEDAW)* monitors implementation of the Convention on the Elimination of All Forms of Discrimination against Women

The *Committee Against Torture (CAT)* monitors implementation of the Convention against Torture and Other Cruel, Inhuman or Degrading Treatment

The *Committee on the Rights of the Child (CRC)* monitors implementation of the Convention on the Rights of the Child and its Optional Protocols

The *Committee on Migrant Workers (CMW)* monitors implementation of the International Convention on the Protection of the Rights of All Migrant Workers and Members of Their Families

Source: Office of the United Nations High Commissioner for Human Rights.

human rights or about problems being encountered; make country-specific or general recommendations; react to situations of concern; in some instances travel to sites of concern; and, where they have this competence, consider individual or group petitions. The Human Rights Committee, operating under the International Covenant on Civil and Political Rights, is considered the premier treaty body because of the importance of its work.

The Office of High Commissioner for Human Rights

The 1993 World Conference on Human Rights recommended the creation of the post of High Commissioner for Human Rights, which the General Assembly established later that year (OHCHR). It began functioning in 1994 and absorbed other UN Secretariat human rights functions in 1998. The High Commissioner was called upon to fulfill contradictory roles—moral leadership, political sensitivity, and bureaucratic-managerial duties—which have been felt by successive commissioners: José Ayala Lasso (1994–1997); Mary Robinson (1998–2002); Sergio Vieira de Mello (2003); Bertrand G. Ramcharan (High Commissioner ad interim, 2003–2004); and Louise Arbour (2004–).

Their major contributions to the quest for measures of implementation and protection have been to provide a voice for victims, to exercise the initiative in launching investigations into gross violations of human rights, and to spearhead the human rights movement, interacting with bodies such as the Security Council and the ICC. Despite progress, the OHCHR is still in the early stages and receives meager allocations from the UN's regular budget supplemented by voluntary contributions. This reflects adversely on its staffing structure and on its ability to plan and act independently. As a result of the 2005 World Summit, a plan of action to double the OHCHR's regular budget in five years is under way, which also was a recommendation from both the High-level Panel on Threats, Challenges and Change and the Secretary-General in the lead-up to the summit.

MEASURES OF IMPLEMENTATION

As mentioned previously, the vision of the CHR for an international bill of human rights placed emphasis on measures of implementation to follow the adoption of the Universal Declaration and the two covenants. This third part would prove the hardest to achieve; and although some steps have been made, implementation remains problematic.

Shortly after the General Assembly adopted the Universal Declaration of Human Rights and the Convention against Genocide, it registered an important success on the route to implementation: India brought the issue of apartheid before the General Assembly. South Africa argued strenuously that this was a matter within its internal jurisdiction and that the Assembly lacked competence to consider it. The Assembly disagreed, which established the principle of international concern with situations of gross violations of human rights. Thereafter, the UN established a variety of investigative working groups and a Special Committee against Apartheid, and stayed the course until the end of white-minority rule.

The CHR, however, would fail in dealing with allegations of gross violations of human rights. As it drafted the covenants, it emphasized reporting procedures to be monitored by treaty-based organs such as the Human Rights Committee and the Committee on Economic, Social and Cultural Rights. But how would it respond to the thousands of petitions alleging gross violations in different parts of the world? The CHR declared, during the Cold War, that it lacked competence to deal with those petitions, a historic betrayal from which the commission only partially recovered.

With newly independent member states pressing for the UN to deal with allegations of gross human rights violations, the CHR, in 1967, decided that it would consider annually the question of violations of human rights and fundamental freedoms in any part of the world. This would lead to annual debates, to the establishment of working groups and rapporteurs, to the adoption of resolutions of concern and condemnation, to the generation of technical advice and assistance to countries, and to other approaches intended to deal with the problems of gross violations of human rights.

As developing countries pressed for action, NGOs and independent experts in the CHR's subcommission also pushed for a system to deal with the petitions. A confidential procedure was established in 1970 for a dialog with governments, the initiation of a study into the situation, or the provision of advice or assistance.

Since the establishment of this confidential petitions procedure, some one hundred countries were brought before the commission.

Meanwhile, under the principal human rights treaties, countries have been reporting on their efforts to implement those treaties, and treaty-monitoring bodies have been providing country-specific comments as well as general comments providing guidance on the implementation of the treaties. A few of these treaties also provide for individual petitions procedures. This is the case for the First Optional Protocol to the International Covenant on Civil and Political Rights, Article 14 of the International Convention on the Elimination of All Forms of Racial Discrimination, the Convention against Torture, and the Optional Protocol to the Convention on the Elimination of All Forms of Discrimination against Women (CEDAW). Under these petitions procedures jurisprudence has been developed of lasting value and global relevance.

Alongside the Charter-based machinery and the treaty-based human rights monitoring bodies, a modest implementation role is played by the General Assembly and an increasing one by the Security Council. The Assembly has been inconsistent. In the first place, under the pressure of the newly independent countries, it led the call for the UN to deal with gross violations of human rights. At times, it has provided important statements of principle on this matter, such as in 1979 when it adopted resolution 34/175 expressing its determination to deal with situations of mass and flagrant violations of human rights. More recently, it has underscored the responsibility to protect. But, under the counter-pressure of the very majority that had called for action to deal with gross violations of human rights, the majority in the General Assembly is more inclined presently to argue that the UN should not place countries in the dock when it comes to allegations of violations of human rights.

In this matter the General Assembly has echoed the voices of developing countries and others in the CHR to promote dialog and cooperation. The increasing tendency for countries accused of gross violations to secure election as one of the fifty-three members of the former commission for their self-protection resulted in a call by Secretary-General Kofi Annan for the CHR's abolition and its replacement by a smaller Human Rights Council,[22] although his High-level Panel on Threats, Challenges and Change had recommended that its membership become universal.[23]

The Security Council played, up until the end of the Cold War, a negligible role in the protection of human rights. Since then it has shown a greater readiness to invoke human rights provisions, and the Council's establishment of the ad hoc tribunals on the former Yugoslavia and Rwanda were important precedents on the road to strengthened protection of human rights. The Security Council remains, however, a political body, and its inconsistency in coming to the protection of people, as in the case of Darfur, is testimony to the ascendancy of politics over human rights.

The 1998 adoption in Rome of the Statute of the International Criminal Court and the commencement of the court in 2004 are important milestones in the quest for stronger protection of human rights. While a champion of human rights in other quarters, the US challenge to the ICC is a major hindrance. The quest to effectively protect human rights and counter egregious violations remains a pressing challenge of our times.

Strategies for Dealing with Gross Violations of Human Rights

What, it may be asked, are the main strategies that have been developed in international and regional bodies since 1948 to deal with situations of gross violations of human rights? Human rights strategies include the drafting of norms to deal with new problems, the conduct of research and studies into contemporary problems, the provision of advisory services and technical assistance to governments to help them strengthen national capacity for the protection of human rights, the consideration of state reports, the operation of some regional and international petitions procedures, the conduct of fact-finding into problem situations, naming and shaming governments and nonstate actors responsible for gross violations, the development of human rights education, and the dissemination of information about human rights.

The methods in use by international and regional human rights bodies deserve mention here because they are complements to the UN system. Reporting systems are in operation under the seven principal human rights treaties and in the African Commission on Human and Peoples' Rights. The Council of Europe's secretary-general may call for reports but has rarely done so. A reporting system is provided for under the Arab Charter on Human Rights but the charter has not yet come into force. The Inter-American Commission on Human Rights does not have a reporting system. A monitoring role of state reports is being carried out by the seven international treaty bodies and by the African Commission. A Peer Review Process has begun operations within the New Partnership for Africa's Development (NEPAD).

Country studies are carried out by the Inter-American Commission on Human Rights on its own initiative. The commission has a long-standing practice in conducting such studies.

Early warning, preventive procedures, strategies, or policies exist under some treaties and in some international or regional bodies. The Convention on the Prevention of Genocide, the European Convention for the Prevention of Torture, and the Inter-American Convention on the Prevention of Violence against Women are examples of treaties with a preventive orientation. The first Summit of the Americas, held in Miami, Florida, called for preventive capacity in the Inter-American human rights system. The OSCE high commissioner on national minorities has a preventive role as does the OSCE representative on freedom of the media. The UN Office of the High Commissioner for Human Rights has regional representatives in Africa, Asia and the Pacific, the Arab region, Central Africa, Central Asia, and in Latin America.

Petitions procedures are in operation in the African, European, and inter-American regional systems, in optional procedures established by the Convention on the Elimination of Racial Discrimination, the First Optional Protocol to the International Covenant on Civil and Political Rights, and the Convention against Torture, and under procedures established within the International Labour Organization (ILO) and the UN Educational, Scientific and Cultural Organization (UNESCO). There is a growing body of international and regional human rights case law. There are admissibility rules before petitions may be considered; these include that petitions should not be anonymous or abusive, and local remedies must have been exhausted where they exist. In the European Court of Human Rights petitioners participate in all stages. This is also the case in the Inter-American Court.

Regional human rights commissions are functioning under the African and inter-American systems. Previously there was a European Commission but its role has been taken over by the European Court of Human Rights. The Arab Charter provides for an Arab Commission, and the Commonwealth of Independent States established a human rights commission in 1993. The last two commissions are not yet functioning. The Asia-Pacific region does not have a regional commission, but the OHCHR organizes an annual Asia-Pacific Forum that concentrates on human rights education, national human rights plans of actions, economic and social rights, and the right to development.

Regional human rights courts are operational in the European and inter-American regional systems. An African Court of Human Rights has been agreed upon but is in the process of being merged with the African Court of Justice. There is, as yet, no international human rights court. The African, European, and inter-American courts may consider petitions referred to them under their respective procedures and may also give advisory opinions. The enforcement of judgments of the European Court of Human Rights is followed up by the Committee of Ministers of the Council of Europe. There is no similar arrangement in the African or inter-American systems or in the United Nations.

Fact-finding and thematic rapporteurs and groups function in the UN as well as in the African and Inter-American regional systems. These mechanisms are crucial for independent oversight against gross violations of human rights.

Targeted approaches have been used for dealing with the situations of particular sectors of the population. The rights of the child and the rights of women are cases in point. So are the rights of minorities, indigenous populations, and migrants. An Inter-American Commission of Women has been in existence since 1928. Its mission is to promote and protect women's rights, advancing equality of participation by women and men in all aspects of society.

The Right to Development and the MDGs

Based on the work of the CHR, the General Assembly declared a right to development in 1986 as a rallying concept to advance the development aspirations of every individual and country. Developing countries emphasize transfers of resources from industrialized countries, whereas the latter stress the totality of human rights—requiring efforts to implement all human rights, civil and political and economic, social, and cultural.

Variations notwithstanding, all countries should use their resources so as to advance the right to development for their peoples in an equitable manner, and all countries should cooperate for the mutual achievement of the right to development. The alternative to such a policy framework is a Darwinian world governed by market forces with no social or human rights safety nets.

The Millennium Development Goals (MDGs), adopted at the Millennium Summit of the General Assembly in 2000, bear direct relevance to the implementation of the right to development. The Millennium Summit's Declaration centralizes human dignity within strategies of governance and proceeds from the premise that everything must be done to achieve fundamental human rights for everyone as crystallized in the Universal Declaration and the two international covenants.

Historically, the human rights idea has contributed to development goals through norms articulating policy standards, advocacy, supervision, studies, and the activation of the international conscience. Will the human rights emphasis help in the implementation of the MDGs? The UN campaign for their achievement emphasizes human rights in broad terms and notes that injustice and discrimination of one kind or the other are increasingly seen as key determinants of poverty, and that it is not by coincidence that the very same determinants account for most human rights abuses. The campaign also presses the point that the human rights approach:

implies that we are talking not of welfare or charity, but of rights and entitlements. This means that taking action to achieve the goals is an obligation. And the approach also creates a framework for holding various actors, including governments, accountable. Moreover it is widely acknowledged that sustainable development requires the active involvement of the poor and civil society. Thus without respect and fulfillment of human rights such as nondiscrimination, right to participation, freedom of expression and assembly, achieving—and even more importantly—sustaining the Millennium Goals will not be possible.[24]

Human rights approaches can contribute to the achievement of the MDGs in six ways. The first relates to the national human rights protection system of each country and how it covers key economic, social, and cultural rights. There should be human rights focal points in key government ministries devoted to advancing a human rights approach and watching over the principle of equality and nondiscrimination. Courts should also play more of a role in protecting key economic, social, and cultural rights. Second, governments should bring to the fore the concept of preventable poverty; preventive human rights strategies are not given the attention they deserve. Third, there is an important role for the principle of nondiscrimination in the International Covenant on Economic, Social and Cultural Rights. State parties should be watching out for pockets of the population that are facing discrimination with regard to basic human rights and take steps to rectify the situation. Fourth, one needs to place the spotlight more on vulnerable groups such as minorities, indigenous populations, migrants, and historically disadvantaged communities. Placing the spotlight on them brings their plight to the fore and enables the forging of a national consensus to act for their relief and protection. Fifth, the UN could pay more attention to consistent patterns of gross violations of economic, social, and cultural rights alongside civil and political rights, as the CHR decided in 1975. There has been little follow-up to this decision. Sixth, there is a case for the periodic publication of a world report on economic, social, and cultural rights. Such a report would help show, through a human rights lens, what could be done to prevent and reduce poverty and act for the relief of the vulnerable and the poor.

The Responsibility to Protect

The heads of state and government gathered at UN headquarters in September 2005 underlined that states have the responsibility to protect their own populations from genocide, war crimes, ethnic cleansing, and crimes against humanity. This responsibility, they acknowledged, entailed the prevention of such crimes, including their incitement, through appropriate and necessary means.[25] They accepted that responsibility and not only pledged to act in accordance with it but also called upon the international community of states, when appropriate, to encourage and help weaker members to exercise this responsibility and to support UN early warning capabilities.

The heads of state and government also declared that the UN has the responsibility to use appropriate diplomatic, humanitarian, and other peaceful means, in accordance with Chapter VI of the Charter, to help protect populations from genocide, war crimes, ethnic cleansing, and crimes against humanity. In this context, they declared their preparedness to take collective action, in a timely and decisive manner, through the Security Council in accordance with Chapter VII in cooperation with regional organizations as appropriate, should peaceful means be inadequate and national authorities manifestly fail to protect their population from egregious human rights violations.

Preventive Strategies and Risk Assessment

Human rights in a country must be a central dimension of risk analysis—whether for the purposes of conflict prevention or assessing stability for foreign investment opportunities. However, the literature on risk assessment only marginally considers human rights, although a country's human rights infrastructure, record, and problems are authoritative indicators of stability. An essential undertaking in the future by the OHCHR, the Human Rights Council, and the UN system is prevention.

In UN human rights strategies, increasing emphasis is placed on the concept of the national protection system, which means looking at the constitution, laws, and courts of a country to see the extent to which they reflect international human rights norms. It is also necessary to examine whether the country has specialized human rights institutions such as a national human rights commission or an ombudsman, whether the country is providing for human rights education in primary and secondary schools in particular, and whether the country has monitoring arrangements to detect grievances on the part of a group or groups of the population with a view to resolving those grievances. If significant parts of the national protection system of a country are missing, then it is likely to be shaky and unstable and, depending on its configuration, could easily erupt into violence.

The role of the Universal Declaration of Human Rights and of the core international human rights conventions is to require states to live up to international minimum standards. If a country has not ratified the key conventions, then it is already an indicator that national consensus might be shaky because the country has not yet begun to internalize internationally agreed values that should guide nation-building and that should arbitrate relations between the government and its citizens. That a country has not ratified one or more of these conventions may not necessarily indicate potential instability. The United States, for example, largely because of the relations between the federal and state governments, has ratified very few international conventions but has announced its willingness to abide by them. Even in such instances, however, it would be fair to say that by staying outside of the conventions, a country is denying itself the opportunity of engaging in a dialog with the international community on how key values are faring within the country.

A democratically governed country is more likely to respect human rights than an authoritarian state. Hence, good indicators in risk assessment are genuine periodic elections and freely operating courts. If either of these conditions is absent, the level of grievances in the country will be high and the risk of instability, and even conflict, serious.

Another good indicator of the human rights health of a country is to ask whether one can point to a unifying vision embracing all parts of the population. In countries where there is the danger of ethnic or religious conflict, such a unifying national vision is vital and can only be constructed on the basis of the international human rights norms guaranteeing the principles of the rule of law, nondiscrimination, and respect for the rights of minorities, indigenous populations, migrants, and other such groups.

The national security doctrine of a government can often provide an indicator of a country's stability or equality in income distribution. A national security doctrine should be grounded in international human rights norms and must give priority to upholding human rights nationally, regionally, and internationally. In a world of terrorist threats and global mobilization against terrorism, it is particularly important that there be safeguards against trampling upon human rights in protecting national security or countering terrorism.[26]

A de facto or *de jure* state of emergency in a country indicates that the human rights situation needs to be closely examined. If a country is democratically governed under the rule of law, however, a state of emergency might not necessarily indicate instability.

If freedom of expression is being stifled and freedom of religion or belief is not respected, it would be fairly safe to say that there could be grievances lurking beneath the surface of the country that could erupt at any time. If people cannot practice their religion or give expression to their beliefs, they are often ready to fight for it, and, if necessary, to die.

Under the principal human rights conventions, states are required to submit reports on their actions to implement the conventions and these reports are considered by treaty monitoring bodies. The comments, conclusions, and recommendations of these treaty monitoring bodies can often be quite telling about the state of protection of human rights in the country and about whether there are seething problems. Those engaged in risk analysis should therefore take into consideration what the international human rights treaty bodies are saying about the state of human rights within a country.

An important question to ask in human rights risk assessment is whether the police and military are under civilian control. If this is not the case, they are likely to be engaging in excesses on the civilian population leading to potentially explosive situations. Even if there is civilian control of the police and military, it would be important to ask if there is abuse of power by either.

In April 2004, to mark the tenth anniversary of the Rwandan genocide, the Secretary-General announced the creation of a position for a special adviser on the prevention of genocide, ethnic cleansing, and mass killings. This innovation leads to the thought that in risk assessment, it would be necessary to ask about the danger of genocide, ethnic cleansing, or mass killing. A related indicator is whether there is torture, arbitrary detention or enforced disappearances in the country. If any evidence exists that such pernicious practices are taking place then it can be safely concluded that the country presents major risks of instability and possibly strife or conflict.

Conclusion

This chapter has traced the UN's steps in the intellectual, policy, political, legal, and operational human rights journey since 1945. It has highlighted the necessity of furthering the protection of human rights in a world of mass poverty, conflict, terrorism, inequality, state violence, and bad governance. The normative and institutional foundations have been laid, even if the latter will require strengthening and modernization. Politics and interests continue to trump principles and idealism.

If the UN is not perceived as faithful to the protection of human rights, it will lose legitimacy. Moreover, the world body must operate on the basis of the principles of respect and confidence-building. In order to be effective, UN organs must show respect for their interlocutors and seek to build confidence among member states and all peoples in the methods and approaches that it employs.

A high priority in ongoing diplomacy at the UN should thus be to foster understanding of and trust in these principles. While working at these principles, the world organization should emphasize universal human rights education, strengthen national protection systems, and implement the principal human rights treaties. The human rights treaty bodies provide an invaluable service through their human rights expertise. Using the international conventions as normative platforms on which to build strong national protection systems, creative policies, and strategies is necessary in a world of infinite variety and complexity.

NOTES

1. For general discussions see, e.g., David Forsythe, *The Internationalization of Human Rights* (Lexington, Mass.: Lexington Books, 1991); Jack Donnelly, *Universal Human Rights in Theory and Practice* (Ithaca, NY: Cornell University Press, 1989); Tim Dunne and Nicholas J. Wheeler, eds., *Human Rights in Global Politics* (Cambridge: Cambridge University Press, 1999); and Thomas Risse, Stephen C. Ropp, and Kathryn Sikkink, eds., *The Power of Human Rights: International Norms and Domestic Change* (Cambridge: Cambridge University Press, 1999).
2. International Commission on Intervention and State Sovereignty, *The Responsibility to Protect* (Ottawa: ICISS, 2001).
3. See Bertrand G. Ramcharan, ed., *Human Rights Protection in the Field* (Leiden, Netherlands: Martinus Nijhoff, 2006).
4. See, e.g., Hersch Lauterpacht, *The International Bill of Human Rights* (Paris: Librairie du Recueil Sirey, 1947; London: Stevens, 1950).
5. See Julie A. Mertus, *Bait and Switch: Human Rights and US Foreign Policy* (London: Routledge, 2004); and Sarah Zaidi and Roger Normand, *Human Rights Ideas at the United Nations: The Political History of Universal Justice* (Bloomington: Indiana University Press, 2008 forthcoming).
6. See on this Louis B. Sohn and Thomas Buergenthal, *International Protection of Human Rights* (Indianapolis: Bobbs-Merrill, 1973), 510–511.
7. See, Bertrand G. Ramcharan, *The Concept and Present Status of the International Protection of Human Rights: Forty Years After the Universal Declaration* (Dordrecht, Netherlands: Martinus Nijhoff, 1988).
8. See on this Bertrand G. Ramcharan, *The UN High Commissioner for Human Rights: The Challenges of International Protection* (Leiden, Netherlands: Martinus Nijhoff, 2002).
9. See Julie A. Mertus, *The United Nations and Human Rights: A Guide for a New Era* (London: Routledge, 2005); and Zaidi and Normand, *Human Rights Ideas*.
10. The concept of the right to development was launched by Kéba M'baye, chief justice of Senegal, in a lecture to the International Institute for Human Rights, Strasbourg, in 1975.
11. See Bin Cheng, *General Principles of Law, as applied by International Courts and Tribunals* (London: Stevens and Sons, 1953).
12. Ian Brownlie, *Principles of Public International Law*, 6th ed. (Oxford: Oxford University Press, 2003), 489.
13. Ibid. 538.
14. See Joanne R. Bauer and Daniel A. Bell, eds., *The East Asian Challenge for Human Rights* (New York: Cambridge University Press, 1999).
15. Raija Hanski and Martin Scheinin, *Leading Cases of the Human Rights Committee* (Turku, Finland: Åbo Academy, Institute for Human Rights, 2003), 121.
16. ICISS, *The Responsibility to Protect*.
17. See Manfred Novak, *U.N. Covenant on Civil and Political Rights: CCPR Commentary* (Kiel, Germany: N.P. Engel, 2005), 1134.
18. See Hanski and Scheinin, *Leading Cases*, 113.
19. For a discussion of the reasons for change, see Kenneth Roth, 'The UN Reform Agenda and Human Rights,' in *Irrelevant or Indispensable? The United Nations in the 21st Century*, ed. Paul Heinbecker and Patricia Goff (Waterloo, Ontario: Wilfred Laurier University Press, 2005), 131–139.
20. See Bertrand G. Ramcharan, *Preventive Diplomacy at the UN: The Journey of an Idea* (Bloomington: Indiana University Press, 2008 forthcoming).

21. The Committee on the Elimination of Racial Discrimination, the Committee on the Elimination of Discrimination Against Women, the Committee on the Rights of the Child, the Human Rights Committee, the Committee on Economic, Social and Cultural Rights, the Committee against Torture, and the Committee on the Rights of Migrant Workers.

22. See Kofi Annan, *In Larger Freedom: Towards Development, Security and Human Rights for All*, UN document A/59/2005, 21 March 2005, paras. 181–183.

23. High-level Panel on Threats, Challenges and Change, *A More Secure World: Our Shared Responsibility*, UN document A/59/565, 1 December 2004, paras. 282–291.

24. Millennium Development Goals Campaign, 'The Millennium Goals: A Rights Agenda,' 2004.

25. See Thomas G. Weiss, *Military–Civilian Interactions: Humanitarian Crises and the Responsibility to Protect*, 2nd edn. (Lanham, Md.: Rowman & Littlefield, 2005).

26. See Iain Cameron, *National Security and the European Convention on Human Rights* (The Hague: Kluwer Law International, 2000).

CHAPTER 26

INTERNATIONAL CRIMINAL COURT AND AD HOC TRIBUNALS

RICHARD GOLDSTONE

Though local rules and customs of war have been promulgated for millennia, the development of a truly global 'Law of War'—and the consequent evolution of international crimes and humanitarian law—is a comparatively recent phenomenon. It was not until the nineteenth century that a first body of written rules appeared. Beginning in the 1860s, the law developed briskly on many fronts, proceeding in North America with the Lieber Code (authored to guide the Union Army's actions in the American Civil War, 1861–1865),[1] the first Red Cross Treaty in 1864 (concerning the treatment of those wounded in the field),[2] and in 1868 the St. Petersburg Declaration,[3] which is arguably the first truly modern exposition of international humanitarian law (IHL). That document, a result of the first international convention on the laws of war that was convened by Czar Alexander II, included a set of principles closely resembling modern conceptions of IHL. In particular, they concentrated on limiting the use of specific weapons during war in order to limit 'needless suffering.' This declaration was expanded, in large part by elements in the Lieber Code, six years later and in 1880 the Institute of International Law brought various strands of development together under its 'Oxford Manual on the Laws of

The author wishes to acknowledge the research assistance of Adam M. Smith in the preparation of this chapter.

War on Land.'[4] While a significant accomplishment, the Manual suffered from many limits, not the least of which the fact that the 'laws of war' only dealt with interstate conflicts, leaving civil wars untouched by international law. Though many claimed that civil wars were covered under 'customary international law' (see below) this oversight would not explicitly be corrected until the adoption (by most, but not all, states) of the second Additional Protocol of the Geneva Conventions in 1977.[5]

The momentum of these developments led to the 1899 and 1907 Hague Conventions, concerning limits on the practice of war, and the 1929 and 1949 Geneva Conventions, addressing humanitarian principles during both war and peace. Together, 'Hague' and 'Geneva' form the foundation of IHL. While such 'treaty' law is critical, a major component in the development of IHL has been principles of 'customary international law' which consist of rules that have not been codified. For example, the Nuremberg defendants were accused of violating the 'laws or customs of war.' In IHL, custom is defined as 'a widespread practice accepted by states as law' (known as *opinio juris*),[6] or 'the principles of the law of nations, as they result from the usage established among civilized peoples, from the laws of humanity, and the dictates of the public conscience.'[7] Customary law is used in cases where there is either an absence of treaty law or only incomplete provisions, or to compensate for the inapplicability of treaty law to certain situations.

The difficulty with an unwritten rule is to establish its existence. Both the objective requirement of 'widespread practice' and the subjective requirement that the practice is followed *because* it is 'accepted by states as law' (rather than due to any other reason) have proven resistant to definition.[8] Despite this, customary principles have become critical elements in modern IHL. Customary principles include the central distinction between combatants and noncombatants (and the different rules applying to each), the principle of proportionality in military action and response, and prohibition on the use of weapons having indiscriminate effects and/or causing superfluous injury or unnecessary suffering.

Steps toward consolidating and codifying significant portions of existing customary international law are the subject of this chapter. The decisions rendered by the ad hoc UN tribunals for a number of countries and the passage of the Rome Statute of the International Criminal Court are preceded by a short discussion of the building blocks resulting from World War II.

WORLD WAR II: THE SLOW BIRTH
OF INTERNATIONAL JUSTICE

Though a lackluster war crimes tribunal followed the conclusion of World War I, it is widely recognized that the trials of Axis leaders in Nuremberg following World War II represented the first real multinational (though not technically 'international') trials. Following a contentious meeting in London between the four victorious allied powers, the London Charter of the International Military Tribunal, Article 1, called for the 'just and prompt trial and punishment of the major war criminals of the European Axis.' The tribunal claimed jurisdiction over three main crimes, each of which encompassed novel charges that, in many instances, had never before been charged, or, in some cases, even defined. The tripartite charges consisted of: (1) 'Crimes Against Peace,' which included the planning of, or participation in, a conspiracy for the planning/waging of, 'aggressive war'; (2) 'War Crimes,' which included the enslavement of civilian populations, the ill-treatment of prisoners of war, and the destruction of civilian property 'not justified by military necessity'; (3) 'Crimes Against Humanity'—a neologism that quickly entered the popular vernacular—which included 'inhumane acts' and 'persecutions on political, racial or religious grounds' regardless of whether such acts were 'in violation of the domestic law of the country where perpetrated.' Importantly, the Charter forbade as a defense that of superior responsibility.

The end of World War II, the start of Nuremberg, and the realization of the scope of Nazi crimes led to intense activity in initiating a global human rights code. The first step towards achieving such a goal was the 1948 passage of the Universal Declaration of Human Rights. Although not a binding instrument, the Universal Declaration looked ahead to the Genocide Convention, the updated Geneva Conventions of 1949, and the United Nations human rights covenants that followed in the 1960s. The law and procedure of the United Nations' ad hoc tribunals, and the more recent creation of the International Criminal Court (ICC), owe much to all of these agreements. In this context it is significant that, in its Article 6, the Genocide Convention foresaw the creation of an 'international penal tribunal' that would be empowered to prosecute such crimes on behalf of the world community. However, the creation of such an international court would be delayed for almost half a century by the onset of the Cold War.

THE UN'S AD HOC TRIBUNALS

Following the end of the Cold War and the severe violations of fundamental human rights in the Balkans and then in the African Great Lakes region, the international community, working through the UN Security Council, established two ad hoc tribunals: the International Criminal Tribunal for the former Yugoslavia (ICTY), established in May 1993 in The Hague, and the International Criminal Tribunal for Rwanda (ICTR), established in November 1994 in Arusha, Tanzania. They were established under the wide powers conferred on the Security Council by Chapter VII of the UN Charter, a fact which *inter alia* allowed the tribunals to claim primacy over the domestic courts in the two regions, as well as demanding legally cognizable cooperation from UN member states in the work of the courts. Interestingly, the UN

Charter makes no reference to international criminal courts; in its establishing of the courts it was assumed that the Chapter VII powers, conferred on the Security Council to forcibly remove threats to international peace and security, were sufficient warrant for the erection of such criminal courts, founded, at least in part, precisely to curb such threats to peace and security in the impacted regions. The legality of this assumption and the resulting establishment of both the ICTY and ICTR were challenged in early cases in both tribunals and rejected by their trial and appellate chambers.[9]

The two UN courts were structured very similarly, and share the same appellate chamber. Until August 2003, when the Security Council decided otherwise in resolution 1503, they also shared the same chief prosecutor. Under Resolution 808 (1993) the ICTY was empowered to try grave breaches of the Geneva Conventions, violations of the laws and customs of war (including those occurring in noninternational armed conflicts), genocide, and crimes against humanity committed on the territory of the former Yugoslavia since 1991. The court's temporal jurisdiction is unbounded until otherwise decided by the Security Council, and consequently the ICTY has prosecuted crimes that occurred after 1995 which marked the cessation of civil war hostilities. Notable in this regard are the charges against Milošević stemming from his 1999 incursion into Kosovo. Article 9 of the Statute of the ICTY granted the tribunal concurrent jurisdiction with domestic Yugoslav courts in the prosecution of war crimes, but provided it with the power to claim primacy over national courts due to concerns over the ability of domestic institutions to hear cases impartially.

The ICTR was established by Resolution 955 (1994) which provided the tribunal with jurisdiction over crimes of genocide, crimes against humanity, violations of 'Common Article Three' (a clause present in the Four Geneva Conventions of 1949 which addresses the conduct of military forces and humanitarian concerns in noninternational armed conflict) and of the 1977 Additional Protocol Two to the Geneva Conventions (which provides further protection to civilians in noninternational armed conflicts). Despite the wide scope of coverage—bringing into its purview crimes committed by anyone on the territory of Rwanda, or by Rwandans in neighboring countries—the ICTR is temporally limited to dealing only with infractions that occurred between 1 January 1994 and 31 December 1994. Due to similar concerns as expressed in the ICTY, Article 8 of the ICTR Statute also established its primacy over the domestic courts of Rwanda.

The tribunals were tested very soon after they began their work. As an initial matter, they faced uncooperative states—who, *inter alia*, refused prosecutors access to evidence, witnesses, and even to those indicted by the tribunals. The novelty of court and trial procedures also proved to be challenging. The Security Council resolutions did not mandate any particular rules of evidence and procedure for the tribunals, leaving it to the elected judges to devise appropriate regulations. Over the decade of their existence they have developed broad sets of regulations that, despite being frequently amended and at times representing an uneasy blend of common and civil law, have served as a solid foundation for court operations. Though there are slight differences between ICTR and ICTY rules and practices, they essentially mirror each other.

Successes and Failures of the ICTY and ICTR

The expense of the tribunals—at their height they accounted for more than 10 percent of the UN's annual budget—combined with their rather modest judicial output (after ten years of operation, the ICTY and ICTR had completed fewer than thirty cases each) have led critics to question the benefit of these institutions. Added to concerns regarding efficiency are even more central worries. One relates to unequal rights for defendants. The offices of the prosecutors are necessarily well resourced in respect of the quality of their staff and their facilities. Most of the lawyers who represent defendants before international tribunals are not similarly resourced. This inequality was one of the reasons that the Nuremberg trial of the major Nazi leaders was criticized as an example of 'victors' justice.' Although important steps have been taken by modern war crimes tribunals in an attempt to remedy this inequality of arms, the problem is an enduring one. Another concern relates to the politicization of justice. If the Security Council had remained the only power to establish international criminal courts, the politicization would have been complete. No ad hoc tribunals would have been established to investigate war crimes alleged to have been committed by any of the five permanent members or those nations they might have wished to protect.

There is a continuing debate about the relationship between peace and justice. In some situations a war crimes investigation and especially the issue of indictments and arrest warrants might retard peace negotiations. And, highly contentious and emotional evidence might create tensions impacting negatively on the promotion of reconciliation. This is the debate that accompanied the issue of indictments by the ICC against leaders of the Ugandan Lord's Resistance Army.

The inconclusive success of the tribunals in keeping the peace and promoting reconciliation and the fact that several senior figures from both the Balkans and Rwanda have yet to be captured and brought to trial have led many to question their utility. As of this writing, the ICTY's two primary fugitives, Radovan Karadžić and Ratko Mladić, as well as some of the most notorious of ICTR's indictees—including Charles Sikubwabo and Aloys Ndimbati—remain free.

Despite these difficulties, the tribunals have also had many successes, with their primary achievement being the broad-based furthering of the development and application of international criminal law. Some of the key cases[10] to have aided this success and development of the law include *Tadic* (*inter alia* establishing the legality of the tribunals),[11] *Blaskic* (defining culpability under command responsibility),[12]

Akayesu (finding rape to be a form of genocide),[13] *Musema* (extending command responsibility to civilian enterprises),[14] *Kambanda* (holding that one can be personally responsible for genocide),[15] and *Barayagwiza* (which was the first-ever verdict against members of the media for inciting genocide).[16] In addition to these cases, the tribunals have encouraged the growth of domestic war crimes legislation and prosecutions. Their presence and the publicity they have given to humanitarian law has likely deterred some war crimes in subsequent military campaigns in Kosovo, Afghanistan, and Iraq, and encouraged the movement towards a permanent ICC. Further, through the dissemination of evidence—such as the June 2005 release of the graphic video of several murders of Muslims by Bosnian Serb forces at Srebrenica— they have impeded the ability of both deniers and perpetrators to hide behind the 'unknown.'

Arguably, the tribunals' greatest challenge was the ill-fated prosecution of former Yugoslav president, Slobodan Milošević. He faced a sixty-six count indictment spread across the full scope of actions he commanded in Croatia, Bosnia and Herzegovina, and Kosovo. Even prior to the death of Milošević in March 2006 in the detention cells of the ICTY, the trial had proven to be very difficult for the tribunal. It was marked by close media scrutiny, the death of one of the trial judges, the defendant's continued refusal to recognize the legality of the court—and thus refusal to accept or appoint counsel—and the defendant's ill health which resulted in many postponements. The fact that the trial will not be brought to a conclusion is unfortunate both for the many victims of the alleged crimes for which Milošević stood trial but also for the ICTY. There are lessons to be learned. The most important relate to the wisdom of including sixty-six counts in the indictment, thereby making the trial cumbersome and unduly lengthy, and the leniency shown by the judges to Milošević thereby allowing him to effectively use the court as a political platform.

'COMPLETION STRATEGY' OF THE ICTY AND ICTR

From their inceptions, the ad hoc tribunals were designed to be temporary judicial institutions, and with the July 2004 release of their 'completion' strategies,[17] both bodies began the process of winding up operations. It is rare for judicial systems to intentionally terminate their operations and as such the tribunals are faced with a host of unique challenges in the process of completing their mandates. For both bodies, 'completion' comprises three stages. First, prosecutors ceased issuing any new indictments after 31 December 2004, with the goal of completing all trials by 31 December 2008, and all appeals by 31 December 2010. Second, the tribunals have begun to winnow their caseloads to focus their attention and resources on trying only the most senior level military and political leaders charged with violations of law.

Third, cases involving mid- and low-level perpetrators are to be transferred to national courts for prosecution. This transfer process has begun in both Arusha and The Hague.

Though the ICTY and ICTR have similar completion strategies and deadlines, the two tribunals have diverged in practice. At the ICTY, the transfer of responsibility to local courts has been one of the most controversial components of its completion strategy, engendering debate both within the tribunal and outside it. Internally, the strategy has required amendments in the Rules of Evidence and Procedure, providing for the transfer of cases (Rule '11 *bis*'[18]) and ensuring that only the most senior perpetrators are kept on the tribunal's dockets (Rule 28). The prosecutors balked at Rule 28, concerned about the limitations it posed on their investigatory autonomy. The transfer of cases is controversial for several procedural and practical reasons. Procedurally, in its writing—and operations thus far—it is not apparent what guides the decision to transfer. In particular, to what country are individuals to be transferred?

The importance of this question cannot be underestimated. Not only do there remain concerns about the ability of ethnic minorities to receive fair trials throughout the states of the former Yugoslavia, but also all Balkan states have constitutional prohibitions against extradition. If a defendant was arrested in Croatia, transferred to The Hague and then transferred to Bosnia, the extradition prohibition would be obviated, much to the displeasure of Croats throughout the Balkans. Secondly, due to concerns about judicial fairness and competence, new courts have been built throughout the Balkans specifically designed to handle war crimes trials. The scope of international involvement and oversight in these courts differs substantially, and remains in flux. The new courts vary from the body established in Belgrade, which is a 'pure' domestic court, to the new State Court of Bosnia and Herzegovina that is a domestic court that, for its first five years, will operate with international prosecutors, administrators, and judges serving alongside local counterparts.

The Rule 28 controversies stretch back to the so-called 1996 'Rules of the Road,' whereby the government of Bosnia and Herzegovina pledged to investigate war crimes and bring perpetrators to justice in their domestic courts.[19] However, the government agreed to allow the ICTY Prosecutor oversight of any indictment issued. The process of oversight has been domesticated in some states—for example, the State Court of Bosnia and Herzegovina was opened on 27 January 2003 and a War Crimes Chamber was added on 9 March 2005 (see below regarding 'mixed courts'). The separation of senior indictees (who are to be tried by the tribunals) and less senior defendants (who will be brought before domestic bodies) is emblematic of the larger tension between international and local systems of justice. Within the tribunals there is a similar tension between prosecutors and judges regarding which body has the power to decide on the seniority of particular defendants and the sufficiency of indictments.

The ICTR, meanwhile, faces numerous unique problems that have had an impact on its completion strategy. The key difference between it and the ICTY is based on the nature of the crimes over which the ICTR has jurisdiction. The slaughter of Tutsis and moderate Hutus during the genocide of 1994 was undertaken in a much more decentralized manner than were the crimes committed in the Balkans. Consequently, though there have been no definitive counts of perpetrators, and though, as of the middle of 2006, fewer than seventy indictees have ever been detained at the tribunal (with fewer than fifty incarcerated in Arusha), there are at least tens of thousands of perpetrators. The magnitude of the number of potential defendants, combined with its still-rudimentary judicial infrastructure, has threatened to overwhelm the Rwandan justice system. Despite this, very soon after the genocide was perpetrated, the country began vigorous prosecution against thousands of defendants. Though a similar process also occurred throughout the Balkans, the magnitude of the Rwandan domestic prosecution system has been unmatched. Thus far, approximately 6,500 individuals have been tried in Rwanda, and the government has another 80,000 people imprisoned and theoretically awaiting trial.[20] Meanwhile, the state has also paroled 30,000 others, many of whom have pledged to participate in a system of informal community dispute resolution, known as *gacaca*.[21]

In addition to the difficulties resulting from the types of crimes committed, the ICTR has suffered from a lack of governmental support. Again, the same problems have appeared in the ICTY context, but the extent of hostility toward the ICTR expressed by the Rwandan government and other states has been unequaled. Rwanda, which had one of the rotating seats on the Security Council during debates on the ICTR, actually voted against the creation of the body, and its support for the ICTR has been modest ever since. Consequently, the Rwandan government has welcomed the completion process. Despite the fact that many Rwandans continue to view their national court system with skepticism, the ICTR has also begun engaging in the transfer process under Rule 11 *bis*, with the first group of fifteen cases presented to Rwandan authorities in February 2005.

THE CREATION OF 'MIXED' COURTS

In the decade between the establishment of the ICTR and ICTY and the formation of the International Criminal Court (see below), the UN became aware that several other countries attempting to address past abuses could benefit from establishing similar tribunals. Managing these countries' needs proved challenging to the UN. The international community was eager to promote judicial tools for societal reconciliation and redress, and given that many post-conflict states lacked the judicial capacity to handle complex war crimes trials, the UN was cognizant that its assistance would be required in establishing any new tribunals. However, the financial and administrative burdens of the ICTY and ICTR made UN member states wary of setting up additional 'subsidiary' courts.

Consequently, the UN began developing a compromise judicial model, creating tribunals similar to the ICTY/ICTR, but based in and owned by local states. Thus were born the 'mixed' or 'hybrid' courts, so named because their jurisdictions, administrations, and compositions are partially locally derived and partially international. The hybrid courts have clear, domestic foundations but also have critical international components, inserted specifically to mitigate concerns about judicial capacity and trial fairness.

There are two broad classes of such courts; the first, as in East Timor (the 'Panels with Exclusive Jurisdiction Over Serious Criminal Offences'), Kosovo (the 'International Judges and Prosecutors' (IJP) system whereby international personnel are introduced into the domestic justice system on an ad hoc basis), and Bosnia and Herzegovina (the 'State Court of Bosnia and Herzegovina'), arose in regions under the actual or effective control of international administrators (the UN directly, as in East Timor and Kosovo, or UN-approved authorities, as in Bosnia and Herzegovina). As such these courts share the 'imposed' character of the ICTY and ICTR. Though local officials in each region may have welcomed their arrival and may have even been involved in their establishment, it was external pressure that implemented these hybrid court systems.

In East Timor, the 1999 Security Council resolution 1272 (passed under the Security Council's Chapter VII enforcement powers) required the UN Transitional Administration in East Timor (UNTAET) to bring to justice those responsible for violence in the country.[22] UNTAET established 'mixed panels'[23] of judges within the existing District Court and the Court of Appeals in East Timor's capital Dili.[24] Though the courts were 'existing' it is important to note that the end of Indonesian occupation left a devastated East Timorese justice system, requiring substantial initial construction by the UN and other international agencies. However, once implemented, the 'mixed panels' have proven resilient and maintain to this day. Each panel is composed of three judges, two international and one East Timorese. Prosecution is conducted by international lawyers, though under the overall authority of the local General Prosecutor. Though they have recorded some modest successes, the 'mixed panels' have been hampered by reluctant Indonesian cooperation, a UN that has intermittently distanced itself from its proceedings (as the UN did when the court issued a politically incendiary indictment against Indonesian General Wiranto), and persistent concerns regarding financial and administrative shortcomings.

Operating under the mandate of the 1999 Security Council resolution 1244, the UN Interim Administration Mission in Kosovo (UNMIK) initially attempted to establish a separate 'Kosovo War and Ethnic Crimes Court.' Following recognition of the costs and logistical difficulties of doing so, UNMIK opted to inject international judges and prosecutors into the existing Kosovar judicial system. Introduced in 2000, the IJP system gives UNMIK the power—upon a request by prosecutor, accused or defense counsel—to appoint an international prosecutor, an international judge, or a panel of three international judges, to proceedings throughout the region.[25] Depending upon the case, international judges may either operate alongside domestic colleagues, or completely supplant them. Though there have been concerns regarding the limited size of the IJP program, it is widely recognized both that the international presence has been critical to the re-establishment of the rule of law in Kosovo, and that internationalizing components of the domestic system has been, at least in this case, preferable to creating a separate, international tribunal system.

In Bosnia and Herzegovina a third kind of 'mixed' court has been established. Drawing its authority from Article V of Annex 10 to the 1995 Dayton Agreement (which ended the Bosnia/Croatian/Serbian part of the Yugoslav conflict), the new State Court officially opened in March 2005, and is linked directly to the completion strategy of the ICTY.[26] The court is explicitly designed to take on cases transferred to it from The Hague. As such, it is a manifestly domestic court, but one in which international judges, administrators and prosecutors work alongside locals. According to plan, the international presence is to deplete over the next five years, resulting in a fully domestic State Court. As of this writing, the new court has yet to be tested, with the first cases that the ICTY prosecutor has proposed for transfer under appeal by defendants in The Hague.

The second class of mixed courts, one established in 2002 in Sierra Leone (the 'Special Court for Sierra Leone') and the other soon to be in operation in Cambodia (the 'Extraordinary Chambers for Cambodia'), was formed in response to requests from independent governments for international assistance in establishing tribunals to deal with, respectively, the human rights abuses and war crimes perpetrated during the Sierra Leone civil war of the 1990s and the mass killings orchestrated during Cambodia's Khmer Rouge regime of the late 1970s. The independent status of the requesting states meant that the establishment of these hybrid courts proceeded from often tendentious negotiation between states, the UN, concerned third-party governments, and NGOs. In fact, the negotiations were so contentious that, at least regarding the Cambodian tribunal, the Secretary-General publicly stated his skepticism whether the negotiated structure of the court could produce robust trials conducted to international standards. The General Assembly, however, approved the agreement.[27]

The negotiated tribunals presented a host of difficulties, many of which were reflected in the tense nature of the discussions. The contentious issues included the question of whether domestic or international law would control (though unsettled and still largely untested in both courts, domestic law holds, but relevant international law is usually said to be 'incorporated' into domestic statutes as needed), the legal status of amnesties given to several perpetrators prior to the courts' establishments (the prosecutors are called upon to use their 'discretion' in issuing indictments), and several unique problems associated with the particular nature of the crimes at issue. For instance, despite the scope of killings in both states, 'genocide' in the strict, legal sense, did not occur in either country as killings were not ordered on an ethnic basis. In Sierra Leone an added complexity is the fact that many of the worst abuses were perpetrated by children who had been forcibly conscripted into various factions and often compelled to commit crimes.

While the Sierra Leone court has begun trials, it remains unclear how successful it will be at both securing justice for victims and mending the rifts created by the conflict. The death of Foday Sankoh, the leader of the main opposition group during the war and arguably the court's most important indictee, and the tense relationship that has developed between the Special Court and the Sierra Leone Truth and Reconciliation Commission (which is operating alongside the court and has markedly different—and perhaps incompatible—goals), have posed significant hurdles. The March 2006 arrest in Nigeria and appearance before the Special Court of Charles Taylor was a significant event for the court. Taylor, the former president of Liberia, was probably the court's second most important indictee. As of this writing, the Cambodia court has finally secured full funding and the government has chosen a site for its seat. However, local and international bureaucracy and politics have thus far stunted commencement of operations, making it uncertain exactly when (and potentially 'if') it will officially be launched.

The Emergence of a Single Model for International Criminal Justice: The International Criminal Court

Though it was doing so in the shadows of the UN ad hoc and hybrid courts, throughout the 1990s the process toward creating a permanent international criminal court progressed. Indeed, in some ways the difficulties encountered by the ad hocs and hybrids made the establishment of the court seem all the more urgent. Amongst other benefits, such a court would reduce the confusions produced by competitor ad hoc and mixed court models of tribunal operations, providing for a stable, uniform model of international criminal justice.

The 1998 Rome Conference and the treaty that led to the formation of the International Criminal Court were the culmination of a process that began in 1989 when the General Assembly asked the International Law Commission (ILC) to address the establishment of an international criminal court. In 1993 the General Assembly followed up on this request and asked the ILC to write a draft statute for such a court; one year later the Assembly established an ad hoc committee to review the major issues arising out of the draft. Annual Preparatory Committee meetings followed, laying the foundation for the Rome Conference in 1998. The United Nations Diplomatic Conference of Plenipotentiaries on the Establishment of an International Criminal Court took place in Rome from 15 June to 17 July 1998. 160 states, 33 intergovernmental organizations, and 236 NGOs participated in the deliberations. The conference concluded by adopting the Rome Statute of the International Criminal Court[28] by a vote of 120 in favor, 7 against, and 21 abstentions. The United States and China publicly indicated that they voted against the Statute, but other permanent members of the Security Council—France, the United Kingdom, and the Russian Federation—supported it.

The treaty, which codified much of the criminal law that had been developed at the ICTY and ICTR, was opened for ratification in July 1998 and came into force on 1 July 2002, following ratification by its sixtieth state party. The ICC borrows much from the ICTY and ICTR, with similarities in their basic structure and, as the ad hoc tribunals continue to wind up, a substantial number of personnel, with senior tribunal lawyers and other officials finding employment at the ICC.

The primary administrative body for the court is the Assembly of States Parties (ASP), made up of all member states. It meets annually and each state has one vote. Amongst other tasks, the ASP elects the court's judges, its prosecutor and deputy prosecutor, all of whom have nine-year terms. While selection of the prosecutor and deputy prosecutor is limited primarily by the requirement that they be of different nationalities, judicial selection is much more constrained. Judicial selection is governed by Article 36 (8) of the Rome Statute, with the choice of judges statutorily informed by the ASP taking into account the 'principal legal systems' of the world, equitable geographic representation and, for the first time in a statute of any international court, a fair representation of male and female judges.

Though the ICC is not a constituent body of the UN, the treaty provides for the establishment of a legal relationship between the two. Not only does the Rome Statute empower the UN, through the Security Council, to refer matters to the court and even to ask the ICC to defer investigation or prosecution, but also its Article 2 posits that the court and the UN will have a broad-based working partnership. The details of this partnership were elaborated in the ICC–UN Agreement, affirmed in September 2004.[29] The underlying principle of this agreement is 'mutual respect' between the two organizations with both parties pledging to closely cooperate so as to increase the effectiveness of the ICC and to limit any duplication of work. The agreement asks the UN, if requested, to provide the ICC with information or documents and to facilitate the giving of testimony by UN officials or agencies. The ICC, meanwhile, has the power to suggest certain items for the General Assembly or Security Council agenda.

The Rome Statute gives the ICC jurisdiction over four types of crimes: genocide, crimes against humanity, war crimes, and crimes of aggression. The first three crimes are defined in exhaustive detail by the treaty in Articles 5–8. The definition of the crime of aggression proved too contentious and thus, though it remains in the Statute, it remains undefined. The ASP has deferred further consideration of this issue until 2009. The Court's jurisdiction is constrained both in the means by which the ICC can begin a case and by the necessary characteristics for a crime to be included under its jurisdiction. Under Article 13, the ICC can open an investigation if a matter is referred to it by the Security Council or by states parties. There is also an opportunity for the prosecutor to begin a prosecution on his or her own initiative, though this has yet to occur. The ICC can exercise its jurisdiction only if the crime is alleged to have been committed in the territory of a member state, the alleged perpetrator is a national of a member state, or a non-member state formally accepts the court's jurisdiction.

As of mid-2006, the ICC had four cases.[30] Three of them have been referred to the court by states parties: in January 2004 Uganda referred crimes allegedly committed by the Lord's Resistance Army in Northern Uganda for investigation, in April 2004 the Democratic Republic of the Congo (DRC) asked for an examination of crimes in the Ituri region, and in January 2005 the Central African Republic requested investigation into alleged crimes committed throughout its territory. The prosecutor has thus far decided to proceed with investigations in Uganda and the Democratic Republic of the Congo. The DRC subsequently provided the ICC with its first defendant; following his indictment—which *inter alia* alleged that he had ordered the killing of nine Bangladeshi peacekeepers in February 2005—Thomas Lubanga was detained in the DRC and transferred to the ICC in March 2006. The Security Council referred the court's fourth matter, regarding the situation in Darfur, Sudan, to the ICC in March 2005. These investigations will result in trials only if a pre-trial judicial chamber is satisfied that the prosecutor has gathered sufficient evidence to issue a warrant for the arrest of alleged perpetrators.

It is in the wider issue of the relationship between the ICC and member and non-member states that the new court will likely be most challenged. Without a police force of its own, the ICC, like the ICTY and ICTR, requires the cooperation of states in fulfilling its duties, ranging from the collecting of evidence, to the arresting of those indicted and the housing of those convicted and serving sentences. The dynamics of the relationships between the court and states remains in flux, with the first real tests of the principle of complementarity—which underlies the Rome Statute in Article 18 and calls for the ICC to become involved in prosecutions only if a state fails to appropriately investigate their own alleged perpetrators—yet to come. Additionally, the lack of support rendered by the United States to the endeavor, which has resulted in its signing of dozens of mutual Bilateral Immunity Agreements with states by which the US and the co-signatory pledge not to surrender their nationals (civilian or military) to the court, is troubling. Although the US has brokered more than one hundred of these 'Article 98 Agreements'—named for the article in the Rome Statute under which they are purportedly allowed—they have yet to definitively impact the workings of the court, and it remains unclear how much they will alter its operations.

It is the US opposition to the ICC that presents the most serious concern to its officials and supporters. Without US political and economic support, the ad hoc tribunals, in all likelihood, would not have been able to operate successfully. For instance, US threats to deny financial assistance to Croatia and Serbia were the cause of their surrender of important alleged war criminals to the ICTY. The June 2001 transfer of Milošević to the ICTY by the government of Serbian prime minister Zoran Djindjic came in the face of the threatened denial of aid worth more than $1 billion from the Clinton Administration.

The US opposition to the ICC appears to be based upon fears, especially in its armed forces, that a runaway prosecutor or biased judge will launch politically motivated and unjustifiable prosecutions against American military personnel or political leaders. This seems an unlikely eventuality and one which is seemingly addressed by several safeguards built into the Rome Treaty. The first such safeguard is the requirement that judges on the ICC must receive the affirmative vote of two-thirds of all of the states parties, ensuring a broad level of support of states for those serving on the ICC bench. The second safeguard is the principle of complementarity referred to earlier. According to the treaty itself, the US could thwart an investigation by the ICC by launching its own bona fide investigation. The third safeguard is the requirement that the prosecutor requires the permission of a pre-trial chamber in order to proceed with an investigation or to issue an arrest warrant. This can be a serious hurdle as a nation whose citizen is sought to be investigated has standing to oppose the motion of the prosecutor. Moreover, the decision of the pre-trial chamber to investigate a given citizen may be taken on appeal to the Appeals Chamber of the ICC.

It is a matter for regret that these safeguards were not sufficient to persuade the US to join its traditional allies in ratifying the Rome Treaty. It is hoped that, if the ICC succeeds in its mission and its operations are handled professionally and with integrity, the US will take a leadership role in the ASP.

Since the time that the ad hoc tribunals began to issue indictments against high-profile political leaders, an issue that has arisen is the unclear, complex relationship between tribunal actions and peace and justice. Tribunals are not in a vacuum, and ICTY and ICTR actions have clearly had an impact on the situation on the ground in the Balkans and Rwanda; and the hybrid courts have similarly influenced the political environments of their home states. For instance, it was much debated at the time that a second indictment was issued by the ICTY against Karadžić and Mladić during the week that the Dayton peace talks were being held. The prosecutor was accused by some of using the indictment to ensure that the ICTY was not used as a 'bargaining chip' in the negotiations. Similar arguments were raised when the ICTY indicted Slobodan Milošević during the NATO bombing over Kosovo and at a time when talks were being held with Milošević designed to stop the war. Concerns are now being raised with regard to the issue of arrest warrants by the ICC against Ugandan leaders. Indeed, the principal mediator in Uganda's peace talks has threatened to resign if such warrants are issued.

The appropriate response might well be that the sole mandate and obligation of a prosecutor is to investigate serious war crimes and, if there is sufficient evidence, to issue arrest warrants. If there are political reasons for delaying or suspending investigations or indictments, it is for an appropriate political—rather than legal—body to consider. In the case of the ad hoc tribunals that body is the Security Council. It has the power to suspend the work of ad hoc tribunals by virtue of their being sub-organs of the Security Council. As mentioned earlier, in the case of the ICC, it is given the power by Article 16 of the Rome Statute to suspend an investigation or prosecution for a period of twelve months or for successive periods of twelve months.

Conclusion

The continuing growth of support for the ICC—manifest in the increasing number of ratifications, the passage of ICC-enabling laws in the domestic legislatures of many signatory states, and the growing attention to the court as it begins to address issues such as Darfur—suggests that the ICC will be very busy in the near term. Its first trials and indictments will provide the first real operational test for the body and the future of institutionalized, international criminal justice.

Since the establishment of the ICTY in May 1993, the advances in international humanitarian law and international criminal justice would have astounded their most optimistic supporters. An important dynamic has been created and exciting developments in the war crimes tribunals and courts are being reported with greater regularity. Impunity for war criminals is no longer the order of the day.

Notes

1. Richard Shelly Hartigan, ed., *Lieber's Code and the Law of War* (Chicago: Precedent, 1983).
2. 'Conditions for the Amelioration of the Condition of the Wounded in Armies in the Field,' 22 August 1864. (Known variously as the 'Geneva Convention of 1864' and the 'Red Cross Treaty of 1864').
3. Nicolas Borsinger, ed., *25th anniversary of the 1868 Declaration of St. Petersburg: International Symposium on the Law of War 1–2 December 1993: Summary of Proceedings* (Geneva: International Committee of the Red Cross, 1994).
4. James Brown Scott, ed., *Resolutions of the Institute of International Law Dealing with the Law of Nations* (New York: Oxford University Press, 1916).
5. Yves Sandoz et al., eds., *International Committee of the Red Cross Commentary on the Additional Protocols of 8 June 1977 to the Geneva Conventions of 12 August 1949* (Geneva: International Committee of the Red Cross, 1977). As of March 2006, 159 states were party to the Second Additional Protocol.
6. Shabtai Rosenne, *Practice and Methods of International Law* (New York: Oceana Publications, 1984), 55; and Antonio Cassese, 'A Follow-Up: Forcible Humanitarian Countermeasures and Opinio Necessitatis,' *European Journal of International Law* 10 (December 1999): 797.
7. *Convention on the Laws of War: Laws and Customs of War on Land*, (The Fourth Hague Convention); 18 October 1907, Preamble.
8. Theodor Meron, 'The Geneva Conventions as Customary Law,' *American Journal of International Law* 81 (April 1987): 367.
9. In *Prosecutor v. Tadic*, Case IT-94-1-AR72, the appellate chamber of the International Criminal Tribunal for the former Yugoslavia (ICTY) found that the tribunal had the power to determine the propriety of its own jurisdiction (the power of 'Competence de la Competence') and thus its finding that the tribunal was justly formed could stand.
10. All ICTY cases, indictments, etc. are available at: www.icty.org; all ICTR cases, indictments, etc. are available at www.ictr.org.
11. *Prosecutor v. Tadic*, Case No. IT-94-1-AR72.
12. *Prosecutor v. Blaskic*, Case No. IT-95-14.
13. *Prosecutor v. Akayesu*, Case No. ICTR-96-4-T.
14. *Prosecutor v. Museum*, Case No. ICTR-96-13-A.
15. *Prosecutor v. Kambanda*, Case No. ICTR-97-23-DP.
16. *Prosecutor v. Barayagwiza*, Case No. ICTR-97-19-I.
17. Security Council resolution 1534, 26 March 2004.

18. Rule 11 *bis* of this Tribunal's Rules allows referral for trial to be ordered to the authorities of (1) a State where the crime was committed, or (2) a State where the accused was arrested, or (3) a State which has jurisdiction and which is willing and adequately prepared to accept the case.

19. Mark S. Ellis, 'Bringing Justice to an Embattled Region: Creating and Implementing the "Rules of the Road" for Bosnia-Herzegovina,' *Berkeley Journal of International Law* 17 (1999): 1–25.

20. Mark A. Drumbl, 'Law and Atrocity: Settling Accounts in Rwanda,' *Ohio Northern Law Review* 31 (2005): 44.

21. Aneta Wierzynska, 'Consolidating Democracy Through Transitional Justice: Rwanda's Gacaca Courts,' *New York University Law Review* 79 (November 2004): 1934.

22. The formation of the tribunal was further recommended by a 2000 report of the Office of the UN High Commissioner for Human Rights. See 'Report of the International Commission of Enquiry on East Timor to the Secretary-General,' January 2000. Reference to the report can be found in Sylvia de Bertodano, 'Current Developments in Internationalized Courts,' *Journal of International Criminal Justice* 1, no. 1 (2003): 226–244, p. 229.

23. These panels are not to be confused with Indonesia's own trials concerning abuses perpetrated during the time of East Timor's independence. The now-concluded 'Jakarta Trials' were wholly domestic, Indonesian proceedings.

24. United Nations Transition Authority in East Timor (UNTAET), 'On the establishment of panels with exclusive jurisdiction over serious criminal offences,' Regulation No. 2000/15, UNTAET/REG/2000/15, 6 June 2000.

25. United Nations Interim Administration Mission In Kosovo (UNMIK), 'On the Appointment and Removal from Office of International Judges and International Prosecutors,' UNMIK Regulation No. 2000/64, 12 January 2001.

26. See the Statement by the President of the Security Council, S/PRST/2002/21, 2002.

27. General Assembly, 'Approval of Draft Agreement, A/57/806, Annex' 13 May 2003, 85th Plenary Session.

28. Rome Statute of the International Criminal Court, UN document A/CONF.183/9, 17 July 1998.

29. General Assembly, 'Cooperation between the United Nations and the International Criminal Court,' GAOR, 2004, 58th session, A/Res/58/318.

30. Up-to-date information about the ICC's current investigations, cases and other activities can be found at its website: www.icc-cpi.int.

CHAPTER 27

HUMANITARIAN ACTION AND COORDINATION

JEFF CRISP

HUMANITARIAN action has been defined as the task of 'saving lives, alleviating suffering and maintaining human dignity in the face of man-made crises and natural disasters.'[1] In the past two decades, such action has become central to the work and public image of the United Nations. When an emergency erupts and large numbers of people are placed at risk, the UN's role in that crisis is likely to be discussed in the Security Council, while the Secretary-General will call upon the governments and peoples of the world to support the organization's relief operations. On the ground, a host of different UN agencies move into action: UNICEF catering for the needs of women and children, UNHCR providing protection and assistance to refugees and other displaced people, WFP providing food to the hungry, and UNDP striving to ensure that such emergency activities are linked to longer-term rehabilitation efforts. In many instances, the UN's humanitarian actors find themselves working alongside other representatives of the UN system: peacekeeping forces, civilian police officers, human rights monitors, and representatives of the world body's political organs. While it may not have been anticipated at the time of the organization's establishment in 1945, the UN's involvement in humanitarian action now forms an uncontested component of its *raison d'être*.

This is not to suggest that the UN's role in humanitarian action has been unproblematic. On numerous occasions, the UN has been criticized for responding too slowly to the needs of disaster victims, functioning in a bureaucratic manner and using an excessive proportion of the funds at its disposal to meet staffing and administrative costs. Important questions have been raised as to whether the political and military activities of the UN compromise its ability to respect the traditional humanitarian principles of independence, neutrality and impartiality. And as this chapter explains, despite a succession of institutional reforms and rearrangements, it has proved very difficult to ensure that the different components of the UN's humanitarian machinery function as a coordinated system. This chapter begins by looking at the evolution of international humanitarian action prior to the establishment of the UN, and then goes on to chronicle the evolution of the system during the Cold War and the turbulent years thereafter.

INTERNATIONAL HUMANITARIAN ACTION PRIOR TO 1945

Throughout recorded history, individuals and communities have sought to provide assistance to people whose lives and welfare are at risk. At certain times and places, efforts have also been made to establish norms for the conduct of war and the treatment of people affected by armed conflict. But it was not until the second half of the nineteenth century, when the globalization process enabled international standards and institutions to be established in a growing number of areas, that the notion of humanitarian action began to be codified and expressed in an organizational form. The most significant development in this respect was the establishment of the International Committee of the Red Cross (ICRC) in 1864, and the subsequent development of the broader Red Cross movement.[2] A private Swiss organization, the ICRC quickly gained recognition from states, enabling it to undertake relief programs for wounded combatants, prisoners of war and civilians, and, by means of the Geneva Conventions, to establish rules for the protection of those people. At the same time, the Red Cross became progressively involved in peacetime and natural disaster relief, assisting people affected by earthquakes, floods, and epidemics.

The scale and significance of international humanitarian action was reinforced by the need to care for victims of the First World War.[3] In addition to the expansion of the Red Cross movement, this period witnessed the establishment of the Commission for Relief in Belgium, which was politically neutral and operationally independent, and was accorded special privileges and immunities by the parties to the conflict. In the post-war period, a more ambitious but ultimately unsuccessful initiative was launched, supported by the Red Cross and the League of Nations, to establish an International Relief Union (IRU) which would provide and coordinate assistance to populations 'afflicted by sudden calamity.'

The League of Nations itself made only a modest contribution to the institutionalization of emergency relief. The League's Covenant made a general reference to the organization's objective of promoting international cooperation and achieving international peace and security, but did not make any reference to the role of humanitarian action in attaining these ends. According to Covenant Article 25, national governments and the Red Cross movement continued to bear primary responsibility for such action: 'The Members of the League agree to encourage and promote the establishment and cooperation of duly authorised voluntary national Red Cross organizations, having as purposes the improvement of health, the prevention of disease and the mitigation of suffering throughout the world.'

The League of Nations assumed its most important humanitarian role in relation to refugee movements, where the advantages of international cooperation were more readily perceived by states.[4] Thus in 1921, the League appointed Fridtjof Nansen to the post of High Commissioner for Russian Refugees, whose mandate was subsequently extended to other displaced populations in the Balkans and Near East. Following Nansen's death in 1930, the League established a number of other mechanisms to provide assistance to refugees. As with the IRU, however, these initiatives were constrained by the global economic depression, the preoccupation of states with the welfare of their own citizens, and the growing turmoil provoked by the rise of fascism. By the time of the League's demise, the international humanitarian machinery remained in a rudimentary form.

THE EMERGING UN ROLE

When World War II came to an end, the international community was ready to address the issue of humanitarian action in a more concerted manner. The Charter of the newly established United Nations stated that a principal purpose of the world body was 'to achieve international cooperation in solving international problems of an economic, social, cultural, or humanitarian character' and 'to be a centre for harmonizing the actions of nations in the attainment of these common ends.'

In the late 1940s and early 1950s, such aspirations inspired the establishment of many new international organizations, all of which had a direct interest in the issue of emergency relief: the UN Relief and Rehabilitation Administration (UNRRA), the UN International Children's Emergency Fund (later better known by its acronym, UNICEF), the Food and Agriculture Organization (FAO), the World Health Organization (WHO), and the International Refugee Organization which subsequently become the Office of the UNHCR.[5] The same period also witnessed the creation of more than two hundred humanitarian nongovernmental organizations (NGOs), including influential organizations such as the US-based CARE and the International Rescue Committee, the UK-based Oxfam, and the Lutheran World Federation, founded in Sweden and later based in Geneva.

Despite these developments, the scope and scale of the UN's humanitarian activities were constrained in two important ways. On one hand, the immediate preoccupation of the Western powers in the early postwar years was to respond to the devastation, displacement, and human suffering that had taken place in Europe. Thus, the refugee definition adopted at the time of UNHCR's establishment in 1951 was restricted to people who had been uprooted 'by events occurring in Europe before 1 January 1951.' On the other hand, as the postwar decolonization process gathered pace and the newly independent states of Africa and Asia became UN members, primary attention was given to the role of the world body in promoting long-term development, rather than the provision of short-term relief. To the extent that emergency assistance was required, there was an assumption that it could be provided by national governments, by the Red Cross movement and NGOs, and by countries such as the United States, United Kingdom, and France, which maintained global spheres of interest.

The situation began to change in the course of the 1960s, when it became increasingly clear that many of the UN's new members were economically and politically weak, prone to environmental disasters and political crises, and unable to meet the needs of citizens who found themselves in distress, let alone destitute refugees arriving from neighboring states. It was in this context in 1974 that the new World Food Programme was established. In the same period, UNHCR became progressively involved in the provision of assistance to displaced populations in developing countries, and the geographical limitation on the refugee definition was finally lifted.

These events raised some important questions concerning the UN's prioritization of development over disaster relief. During the Biafra war of 1967–1970, for example, UN agencies were generally conspicuous by their absence, while the Red Cross and NGOs attracted an enormous amount of publicity for their efforts to assist victims of the conflict. Within the UN Secretariat, some senior officials continued to feel that the world body lacked the capacity to assume a major role in the field of humanitarian action. But the tide was now turning. When a major emergency, combining so-called natural and human-made elements, struck East Pakistan (later Bangladesh) in 1971, the Secretary-General designated UNHCR as the 'focal point' for all UN assistance. The same concept was employed the following year, when an Office of the UN Disaster Relief Coordinator (UNDRO) was established within the UN Secretariat and mandated to be 'the focal point in the United Nations system for disaster relief matters.'

THE UNDRO YEARS

In the years that followed the establishment of UNDRO, it became increasingly clear that disasters were as much the norm as under-development in many of the world's poorest countries. The early 1970s witnessed a growing number of environmental catastrophes, including a drought and famine in the Sahel that prompted experts to ask whether changing climatic and land-use patterns were rendering the planet more susceptible to such crises. At the same time, armed conflicts and political upheavals throughout Africa, Asia, and Latin America, many of them sustained by the principal protagonists in the Cold War, were destroying the lives and livelihoods of growing numbers of people. Thus the global number of refugees jumped from less than three million in 1971 to more than 10 million in 1981, while millions more were displaced within their own countries.

Humanitarian action (or 'disaster relief' as it was commonly referred to at the time) now began to assume a more prominent role in world affairs, attracting unprecedented amounts of publicity and resources. In response to these changing circumstances, and prompted by the modest role it had played in the Sahel emergency, UNDRO's budget and personnel were significantly strengthened in the mid-1970s. At the end of the decade, UNDRO also reached an agreement whereby UNDP's resident representatives assumed responsibility for coordinating the emergency activities of all UN agencies at country level.

In practice, however, these efforts to consolidate the UN's role in the provision and coordination of emergency relief met with very limited success. First, during this period of intense Cold War rivalries, the United States and other Western donors regarded such relief as a means of winning hearts, minds, and political influence in developing regions, and were therefore wary of according the world body greater authority in the allocation of their resources. Second, as individual UN agencies became more actively engaged in disaster relief, they also became competitors, anxious to raise their own profile, to attract additional funding, and to resist any form of centralized control. Third, those mechanisms that had been established to foster coordination within the UN system were not particularly effective. Despite its increased size and budget, UNDRO remained insignificant in comparison with an operational agency such as UNHCR, which in the course of the 1970s and early 1980s extended its presence to most parts of the world, increasing its annual budget from some $50 million to over $500 million. At country level, UNDP's resident representatives generally pursued a cautious line in relation to disaster relief, not least because emergency operations often bypassed official structures and raised sensitive political issues with government, especially when they took place in a context of armed conflict and human rights violations.

A final coordination conundrum facing the UN at this time derived from the rapid expansion of the nongovernmental sector in the provision of disaster relief. During and after the Biafra conflict, where the UN had played such a limited humanitarian role, many new NGOs came into existence, benefiting from the extensive media coverage given to the war—most notably Médecins sans Frontières (MSF). While regarded somewhat disdainfully by the UN's member states and agencies, where they were considered to be amateurish and politically naïve, the NGOs brought some important attributes to the field: speed, flexibility, efficiency, the ability to mobilize local resources and a skill in combining operational activities with public advocacy and fund-raising efforts. Like the Red Cross movement, the NGOs valued their independence. While they were prepared to work closely with the UN and even to act as 'implementing partners' (or 'sub-contractors') for organizations such as UNHCR, the NGOs were instinctively opposed to the notion that the UN should have a monopoly or a controlling interest in the growing humanitarian industry.[6]

In the early 1980s, almost a decade after the establishment of UNDRO, two UN reports revealed with unusual frankness the very limited extent to which the diverse parts of the world body's humanitarian machinery were capable of acting as a coordinated system. The first, prepared by the Joint Inspection Unit, stated that UNDRO had not acted as an effective focal point within the UN system, that its mandate in relation to man-made disasters was unclear, and that other UN agencies had obstructed its role in the mobilization and coordination of relief.[7] The second report, by a former UN under-secretary for administration and management, acknowledged that the emergency response capabilities of individual UN agencies had been strengthened significantly during the previous ten years, but concluded that far less progress had been made on the issue of coordination. Making his frustration evident, the report's author stated that 'if the components of the United Nations system and the cooperating inter-governmental and voluntary agencies are not to speak with 'one voice', the least that can be expected of them is that they perform as a harmonious chorus and not as a babble of dissonant and discordant voices.'[8] The continued difficulty of coordinating the different components of the UN's humanitarian machinery was underlined in the mid-1980s, when the Horn of Africa was struck by a catastrophic famine. The Office for Emergency Operations in Africa (OEOA) was established under the leadership of two highly respected and senior UN officials, Bradford Morse and Robert Jackson, with the task of 'ensuring the effective coordination of the assistance and support of the United Nations.' In their efforts to meet this objective the OEOA established coordinating mechanisms at the international, regional, and national levels, involving all of the agencies participating in the relief effort: FAO, UNDP, UNDRO, UNHCR, UNICEF, WFP, and WHO.

The OEOA is widely recognized to have been a UN success story, not least because it was able to raise an unprecedented level of funding—some $4.6 billion—in the two years of its existence.[9] In the specific area of interagency coordination, however, the qualities of the OEOA's leadership and the direct support which they received from the Secretary-General were not enough to overcome the centrifugal tendencies of the UN system. According to one assessment, the OEOA 'was never able to bring the separate operations of intergovernmental and nongovernmental organizations to an agreed assessment of need and requirements.' And 'Despite the UN's officially acknowledged coordinating role,' such organizations 'were disinclined to seek basic agreement on priority areas... Under the glare of international publicity, agencies sought to demonstrate their individual capabilities and undertook whatever measures they felt inclined to. The resources that were available to provide assistance made the operation attractive to a wide range of actors, and harmony of purpose was all too often forgotten in the rush to partake of the relief cake.'[10] Similar assessments of the UN's coordinating role in emergency relief were to be made throughout the next decade, when the issue of humanitarian action attained a much more prominent place on the organization's agenda.

THE END OF THE COLD WAR

When the Cold War came to an end at the close of the 1980s, there were widespread expectations that the armed conflicts, political upheavals, and humanitarian emergencies that had characterized much of the world during the period of superpower rivalry would finally come to end. With the collapse of the Soviet bloc, proxy wars would cease, and reductions in military spending would provide an unprecedented 'peace dividend' that could be devoted to development, while democracy and good governance would soon reign in countries where autocratic and kleptocratic regimes had been kept in power by either (and sometimes both) of the superpowers. Such expectations were not entirely confounded. In a number of regions—Central America, South-East Asia, and Southern Africa—longstanding conflicts were indeed concluded, enabling millions of refugees and displaced people to go back to their homes and to end their dependence on international relief. But the early 1990s also witnessed a spate of new conflicts just as devastating in terms of human suffering as those of the Cold War period, if not worse.

The Persian Gulf crisis of 1991, prompted by Iraq's invasion of Kuwait and the Baghdad regime's subsequent suppression of uprisings in the south and north of the country, created a humanitarian emergency of unusual speed and complexity. Large numbers of foreign workers from Arab, African, and Asian states had to be evacuated from the region. Displaced Iraqis fled into Iran, Jordan, and to the mountainous Turkish border, where most were refused entry by the authorities. The UN's relief agencies and a host of NGOs flocked to the region, many of them working inside Iraq and in close collaboration with US-led and UN-sanctioned military forces.

The Persian Gulf crisis, like the Biafra emergency some thirty years earlier, proved to be a turning point for the UN's humanitarian action and coordination. UNHCR, which was initially appointed 'lead agency' for the Iraq operation, had been unprepared for the crisis, both operationally and in terms of the key policy dilemmas arising from the emergency. As the operation progressed and coordination responsibilities passed to an Executive Delegate appointed by the Secretary-General, the limitations of the UN's response continued to be exposed. According to an independent evaluation concluded in 1992, the mandates of the major UN agencies involved in the crisis were overlapping and conflicting, while their emergency procedures were inconsistent.[11] Under the pressure of a fast-moving emergency, it had proved hard to maintain a coordinated division of labor. The evaluation also noted the absence of focused leadership from UN headquarters, a lack of clarity in the UN's formal lines of authority and accountability, and even, at the most practical level, the incompatibility of the communications systems employed by different UN agencies. Concluding its analysis, the evaluation asserted that 'the United Nations failed to coordinate humanitarian activities in the Gulf crisis effectively, either those of its own organizations or those carried out by governments and private relief groups.' At the same time, it pointed out that 'some of the lack of coordination

identified was largely beyond the UN's control,' underlining 'a contradiction between the heavy bilateralism of donor governments and their oft-stated insistence that the UN exercise a coordinating role.' Finally, the evaluation commented on the coordination problems created by the many voluntary agencies that had rushed to the scene of the crisis. 'The prevailing picture of NGOs in the Gulf crisis is thus one of energy and determination, mixed with confusion and disarray.' 'There was,' it concluded, 'little sense among NGOs of humanitarian principles shared with the UN or of mutuality with it.'

Recognizing the urgent need to restore the UN's credibility as a (if not *the*) leading factor in the humanitarian sector, the Secretariat and certain member states moved quickly to establish new standing arrangements for the coordination of emergency operations. The chosen approach was manifest in General Assembly resolution 46/182 of December 1991 that supposedly established a more centralized coordination system than that which had prevailed under UNDRO, while recognizing the need to solicit the cooperation of individual UN agencies, the Red Cross system, and the NGOs, all of which were determined to retain a high degree of autonomy. Seeking to meet these somewhat divergent objectives, the resolution affirmed the UN's 'unique and central role' in leading and coordinating international humanitarian action and paved the way for the appointment of an emergency relief coordinator (ERC) reporting directly to the Secretary-General and supported by a newly established Department of Humanitarian Affairs (DHA). The ERC was to coordinate and facilitate the UN's emergency response, manage a central emergency fund, negotiate access by humanitarian organizations to populations in need, process requests for assistance from states and make consolidated appeals for funding to donors. At the same time, an Inter-Agency Standing Committee (IASC) was established to facilitate cooperation and coordination amongst humanitarian actors. Chaired by the ERC, the new committee brought together all of the relevant UN agencies and actors, as well as representatives of the Red Cross movement, the International Organization for Migration (IOM) and the NGO community. Resolution 46/182 also confirmed the role of the UN resident coordinator (usually the UNDP resident representative) in coordinating humanitarian action at country level.

In addition to these institutional provisions, the December 1991 resolution set out certain norms and principles on which the UN's humanitarian activities would in future be based. Humanitarian assistance 'must be provided in accordance with the principles of humanity, neutrality and impartiality,' although it did not provide a definition of these terms, which had long formed the basis of the ICRC's work. More significantly, perhaps, while it affirmed that 'the sovereignty, territorial integrity and national unity of states must be fully respected,' the resolution did not go so far as to suggest that a state must request humanitarian assistance before it was provided. Mindful of recent experiences in Iraq, where the Baghdad regime had agreed to a UN presence under irresistible military and political pressure from the United States and its allies, the resolution stated that 'humanitarian assistance should be provided with the consent of the affected country, and in principle on the basis of an appeal by the affected country.' While the wording might have been deliberately ambiguous, the implication of the language used was clear enough: governments (or at least weaker governments) would no longer be able to use the principle of state sovereignty as a means of obstructing the provision of protection and assistance to vulnerable populations. In other words, 'humanitarian action' might sometimes necessitate 'humanitarian intervention.'

THE CHANGING HUMANITARIAN LANDSCAPE

The establishment of DHA took place at a time of intense UN activity. On one hand, the organization was expected to facilitate the transition from war to peace in conflict-affected countries such as Cambodia, El Salvador, and Mozambique. On the other hand, the UN was required to assume a leading role in the international response to a succession of new emergencies and a number of protracted crises, all of them characterized by intense violence, widespread human rights abuses, and large-scale population displacements: Afghanistan, Angola, Burundi, Liberia, Rwanda, Sierra Leone, Somalia, Sri Lanka, Sudan, parts of the former Soviet Union, and most of former Yugoslavia.

While the conflicts in these countries varied considerably in terms of their causes, consequences, and characteristics, it is possible to make some broad generalizations with respect to their implications for the international humanitarian system.[12] First, the emergencies of the post-Cold War period led to a massive new demand for 'humanitarian action'—a concept that now replaced the old notion of 'disaster relief.' The funding, personnel, and field presence of UN and other humanitarian agencies expanded very rapidly, as did the coverage that their activities received in the international media.[13] Indeed, press and public relations became an increasingly important priority for such organizations as they competed for visibility and resources.

Second, humanitarian agencies found themselves working in more difficult and dangerous conditions. In the past, UN organizations had worked primarily with refugees in the relative safety provided by countries of asylum, or in non-conflict but disaster-affected areas. In the 1990s, however, as new forms of armed conflict emerged, 'failed states' came into being and the incidence of humanitarian intervention increased, it became the norm for aid workers to be deployed in the heart of conflict zones, dealing with combatants and communities who were unwilling or unable to protect the security of humanitarian personnel.

Third, the crises of the early and mid-1990s were generally more complex and protracted than earlier emergencies. In many of the countries concerned, armed conflicts were inextricably linked to developmental and governance failures, economic collapse and environmental degradation, social and political violence, banditry and criminality. As a result of these circumstances, new questions were raised concerning the proper role of humanitarian agencies: should they confine themselves to relieve immediate suffering, or should they espouse a more ambitious and reformative agenda?[14]

Fourth, the 1990s witnessed a growth in the number of actors involved in what were now tellingly described as both 'complex humanitarian emergencies' and 'complex political emergencies.' As well as IASC members such as DHA, UNHCR, UNICEF, WFP, the Red Cross movement, and NGOs, emergency operations now frequently involved UN peacekeepers, other military forces, representatives of donor states and regional organizations, special envoys dispatched by the Secretary-General and the political organizations of the UN, as well as the international media.

Fifth, humanitarian action now moved into a much closer relationship with political and military action, a situation that the ICRC, the founder and guardian of humanitarian principles, had always strived to avert. As the Secretary-General indicated in his seminal 1992 report, *An Agenda for Peace*, the UN's primary function of maintaining international peace and security could not be dissociated from its task of solving international problems of an economic, social, cultural, or humanitarian character. 'Poverty, disease, famine, oppression and despair abound,' he explained, 'joining to produce 17 million refugees, 20 million displaced persons and massive migrations of peoples.... These are both sources and consequences of conflict that require the ceaseless attention and the highest priority in the efforts of the United Nations.' The same report famously observed that 'the time of absolute and exclusive sovereignty has passed,' reinforcing the suggestion in resolution 46/182 that the UN's involvement in an emergency was no longer contingent on a request from, or even the consent of, the state concerned.[15] In accordance with these sentiments, the Security Council became much more actively engaged in the issue of humanitarian action, the number and nature of the UN's peacekeeping operations changed significantly, and in a number of crises the world body found itself wearing both a military and a humanitarian hat.

Finally, the changing humanitarian landscape gave rise to a range of acute policy dilemmas for UN member states. How, for example, should the organization respond when a state such as Turkey closed its borders to desperate people who were fleeing from persecution? Was it acceptable for a certain proportion of the UN's humanitarian assistance to be given to the Serbian military, so that the organization could gain access to besieged populations in Bosnia? Could the UN accept the conditions imposed on it by the Taliban in Afghanistan, including the restrictions which they wished to place on female staff? Should the UN provide assistance to Rwandan refugee camps in Zaire, when those camps were known to harbor and be administered by the *génocidaires*? Should the UN continue to provide so much humanitarian assistance to Angola, when the country's massive oil revenues were largely unaccounted for? In many instances, different components of the UN system, and different members of the IASC, reached quite different conclusions with respect to such issues.

The rapidly changing international landscape of the 1990s lent a new degree of importance to the issue of humanitarian coordination, both operationally and in terms of policy. But those changes also made the task of humanitarian coordination more difficult, exposing the limitations of the arrangements ushered in by resolution

46/182.[16] DHA was widely recognized to be a more effective organization than UNDRO in terms of its coordination capacity. But it also shared some of UNDRO's constraints. Like its predecessor, DHA generally lacked the expertise, resources, field presence, and political muscle required to lead the UN system's humanitarian endeavors. And like its predecessor, DHA had few if any friends amongst the UN's humanitarian agencies, who were prone to dismiss it as 'another layer of bureaucracy' and who felt that its efforts to develop an operational role represented a threat to their interests. UNHCR, whose budget, reputation and influence had soared as a result of its high-profile role in former Yugoslavia, regarded DHA with particular suspicion and made little secret of its intention to prevent DHA from fulfilling its coordinating role. Compounding its problems, DHA was divided into two branches, one based in New York (where the political organs of the UN are located) and one based in Geneva (the world's 'humanitarian capital'). Far from being able to coordinate the whole of the UN system, the two branches of DHA often found it difficult to coordinate their own policies and priorities.

The issue of DHA's role and capacity came to a head in 1997, in the context of a broader initiative taken by the Secretary-General to reform the UN's structure and functions. In the course of this process, a proposal emerged to incorporate DHA in UNHCR, thereby giving the high commissioner and her agency a much broader and more powerful role in the coordination of the world body's humanitarian activities. While UNHCR was predictably content with such an arrangement, other agencies, especially UNICEF and WFP, were strongly opposed to the plan. The proposal was quickly withdrawn when the heads of the two agencies, both of them US citizens, were able to mobilize the support of key donors.[17]

Instead of the relatively radical UNHCR option, a less controversial decision was taken to replace DHA with a new Office for the Coordination of Humanitarian Affairs (OCHA), with a particular responsibility for humanitarian policy development, humanitarian advocacy and, like UNDRO and DHGA before it, the coordination of emergency response. At the same time, a new Executive Committee on Humanitarian Affairs (ECHA) was established, chaired by the head of OCHA and bringing together on a regular basis some fifteen UN agencies and departments. While the IASC continued to act as the principal mechanism for coordination between humanitarian actors within and outside of the UN, ECHA's primary role was to ensure better coordination between those parts of the UN system responsible for humanitarian action, human rights, peacekeeping, and political affairs.

RENEWED CALLS FOR REFORM

In comparison with the early and mid-1990s, the turn of the new millennium was a relatively quiet period for the UN's humanitarian actors. A number of the armed conflicts that had characterized the earlier period, most notably that in the former

Yugoslavia, had been brought to a formal end, while others had diminished significantly in intensity. While some new crises erupted (in East Timor and Kosovo, for example), and others (such as those in Colombia and northern Uganda) became more serious, the issues of humanitarian action and human security no longer occupied such a prominent place on the international agenda. Following the events of 9/11, the attention of UN member states turned overwhelmingly to the questions of international terrorism and state security.[18] When states attended the 2001 ECOSOC session, they declared themselves broadly satisfied with the organization's humanitarian coordination arrangements. While improvements might still be made, they did not believe that radical reform was required. It was to take another crisis in Africa, involving the displacement of up to two million people in the Sudanese province of Darfur, to prompt renewed calls for a reform of the UN's humanitarian machinery.

A persistent weakness in the UN's humanitarian activities throughout the 1980s and 1990s was to be found in the organization's response to the plight of internally displaced persons (IDPs), those who have been forced to abandon their homes, usually as a result of armed conflict and human rights violations, but who, unlike refugees, remain within the borders of their own country. Despite a rapid rise in the global number of IDPs, despite the terrible circumstances in which many were obliged to live, and despite vigorous advocacy on their behalf by a number of NGOs and human rights organizations, the international response to the plight of IDPs remained inadequate. While a number of different UN agencies regularly became involved in IDP situations, they did not do so in a predictable or well-coordinated manner.[19]

Several steps were taken to improve the UN's performance in this area. In 1992, the Secretary-General appointed a representative on internally displaced persons, while in 1997, the head of the newly established OCHA was designated as focal point for examining and addressing the needs of IDPs. In 2000, an Inter-Agency Senior Network on IDPs was created, leading subsequently to the establishment of a dedicated but nonoperational IDP Unit within OCHA. While such initiatives did something to meet the growing international clamor for UN action in relation to IDPs, they did little to ensure greater predictability or improved coordination. The UN agencies continued to establish IDP programs on a 'pick-and-choose basis,' while the IOM (an intergovernmental but non-UN agency) made determined efforts to expand into this area of humanitarian action. In these circumstances, the only coordinating arrangement that could be agreed upon by IASC members was a loosely defined 'Collaborative Approach,' which was to be worked out on a country-by-country basis.

Between 2000 and 2004, a number of different actors expressed their reservations about the effectiveness of the so-called collaborative approach, while other analysts warned that the UN's effectiveness in IDP situations would prove to be the litmus test of the organization's humanitarian capacities—especially because IDPs now outnumbered refugees by some 2.5 to 1.[20] But international attention had turned to other matters, and it was not until the middle of the decade, when the Darfur crisis slowly dawned on the world's consciousness and conscience that the spotlight was again focused on the UN's humanitarian machinery.

For political, geographical, and logistical reasons, Darfur presented the UN and other members of the international humanitarian system with enormous challenges. Providing protection to people who had been attacked and deliberately displaced by government-supported militia, and meeting the basic needs of these people in an isolated and almost infrastructure-free desert area were never going to be simple tasks. And yet as the Darfur crisis progressed, it became difficult to escape the conclusion that the UN's response to the emergency had been sorely lacking. Analyzing that response, one aid worker deployed in western Sudan observed that 'the current framework for responding to the humanitarian crisis in Darfur is the Collaborative Response.' 'Is it this methodology,' he asked, 'which is failing UNHCR, the relief agencies and ultimately the beneficiaries?' Answering that question in the affirmative, the author pointed out that OCHA's stated prerequisites for the effective implementation of the collaborative approach, 'effective leadership, effective communication and transparent decision-making,' had not been fulfilled in Darfur.[21] Writing earlier in the same journal, the Secretary-General's representative on IDPs had observed that 'the problem in Darfur was that the Collaborative Approach allowed agencies to say 'no' to playing specific roles, especially in the area of protection, and gave the government the possibility to opt for solutions that it found the least threatening.'[22]

Another critique of the UN's role in Darfur was provided by the UK's Parliamentary Committee on International Development. 'There have been and remain large coordination gaps,' it observed, 'particularly as regards specific issues: providing relief and protection to IDPs; and managing the huge camps which in Darfur are now home for 1.8 million people.' 'That conflicts cause the displacement of people within the borders of their own country should not come as a surprise,' it continued. 'That the international humanitarian system remains ill-equipped to deal with such people is shocking.' 'If the international community is to be able to fulfil its responsibility to protect,' it concluded, 'it must act now to ensure that it is able to deal effectively with crises involving IDPs. Ad hoc arrangements will not see duties adequately fulfilled. To respond to IDPs' needs with excuses about institutional mandates would be laughable if it did not have such tragic human consequences.'[23] Stinging criticism of this kind, coupled with the simultaneous need for the UN to mount an effective response to the Asian tsunami, prompted OCHA to initiate an urgent Humanitarian Response Review (HRR) in December 2004. On its completion the following year, OCHA concluded that 'the humanitarian response system was designed well over a decade ago. In general, it has stood the test of time well, and while there is no need for major reform we do need a 'system upgrade' that makes the tools that we developed in the 1990s work more effectively in the environment of 2006.'[24]

In practical terms, this 'system upgrade' was to comprise of three components: the establishment of an expanded and more flexible Central Emergency Revolving

Fund (now named the Central Emergency Response Fund); a reform of the way in which the UN's resident coordinators and humanitarian coordinators are selected and supported; and the introduction of a 'cluster approach,' establishing an agreed division of labor amongst the UN's humanitarian agencies in any new conflict-related and non-refugee emergency. In future, UNHCR would act as 'cluster lead' in relation to protection, shelter and camp coordination, while nutrition, water and sanitation activities would be the primary responsibility of UNICEF. The health cluster would be led by WHO, WFP would assume responsibility for logistics, while UNDP was allocated the cluster of 'early recovery.'

CONCLUSION

Since its establishment in 1945, the UN has played a vital role in humanitarian action, saving the lives and protecting the welfare and rights of millions of people across the world. In their efforts to deliver such assistance, UN humanitarian workers have on too many occasions been obliged to sacrifice their own lives and to jeopardize their personal welfare.

Despite these undoubted achievements and attributes, the UN's humanitarian machinery has encountered some persistent difficulties, not least in the area of interagency coordination. As this chapter has explained, the HRR represents the latest in a long line of initiatives intended to address this issue, and the obstacles that confront the effective implementation of this 'system upgrade' are formidable.[25] The proposed reforms will not guarantee the new and additional funding required to meet the growing needs of people affected by armed conflicts and natural disasters. And even if such funding is available, an earlier and more effective humanitarian response on the part of the UN system will not necessarily be the outcome. With regard to coordination, the different components of the UN's humanitarian machinery will retain their own financing mechanisms, their different mandates and their separate governing bodies. It seems highly likely that the UN agencies will continue to compete against each other and to resist increased levels of centralized control. Such agencies must also come to terms with the fact that they control a declining share of the world's humanitarian activities and resources, a situation that may well be reinforced by the emergence of new humanitarian donors and agencies. Finally, the reforms that emerged from the HRR are intentionally technical and managerial in nature, designed to make the current machinery work better, rather than to replace it with a radically new model.

Significantly, even before the HRR was initiated, a number of the world's leading experts on the UN's role in humanitarian action had reached the conclusion that a more fundamental approach to reform was required. Writing in 2002, Thomas G. Weiss gave strong backing to the proposal that had been rejected in 1997, namely to consolidate the UN's emergency activities in UNHCR which is 'almost totally oriented towards the delivery of protection and assistance.' 'The only practical solution,' he concluded, 'is more consolidation and centralization...Without such structuring, we will continue with the charade that a multi-headed non-system can somehow function as if it were a centrally organized system.'[26] Prior to his tragic death in a terrorist attack on the UN's Baghdad headquarters in August 2003, Arthur Helton stated that 'ultimately what is needed is a consolidated UN humanitarian agency with a fully integrated budget and programme.'[27] Most recently, Susan Martin has called for 'the consolidation of all protection and assistance responsibilities for all forced migrants in a single new organization,' an initiative that would address the problem associated with the cooperative and collaborative approaches associated with UNDRO, DHA and OCHA: that 'when everyone is responsible for a particular population or set of activities, no-one can be held accountable for failures.'[28]

Two final questions arise in relation to the consolidated and centralized approach advocated by these experts: is it likely to happen, and if not, why should the issue of fundamental humanitarian reform nevertheless be pursued? With regard to the first question, it is difficult to be optimistic. As Edward Luck has argued, 'power is anything but centralized in the UN system' and most components of the UN's humanitarian machinery have an interest in maintaining that status quo, especially at headquarters level. While 'strategic coordination' may be impossible, he concludes, the best we may be able to hope for is improved 'operational coordination,' involving field-level managers who 'are more cognizant of the pressing need to make the best of limited resources through rational burden-sharing arrangements.'[29] But field-level managers have to work in a broader organizational and hierarchical context, and it would be unrealistic to expect them to succeed where their superiors have been found wanting. If fundamental reforms rather than 'system upgrades' are required to improve the UN's ability to save lives, alleviate suffering and maintain human dignity, then such reforms should be vigorously pursued.

Notes

1. *Saving Lives, Relieving Suffering, Protecting Dignity: DfID's Humanitarian Policy—Draft for Comment* (London: Department for International Development (DfID), 17 January 2006).
2. The Red Cross movement incorporates the ICRC, the League of Red Cross, and Red Crescent Societies (LRCS), and national societies. See David P. Forsythe, *The Humanitarians: The International Committee of the Red Cross* (Cambridge: Cambridge University Press, 2005).
3. The early evolution of the international humanitarian system is examined in Peter Macalister-Smith, *International Humanitarian Assistance: Disaster Relief Actions in International Law and Organization* (Dordrecht, Netherlands: Martinus Nijhoff, 1985), 8–21; and Randolph C. Kent, *Anatomy of Disaster Relief: The International Network in Action* (London: Pinter, 1987), 33–67.

4. UNHCR, *The State of the World's Refugees: Fifty Years of Humanitarian Action* (Oxford: Oxford University Press, 2000), 15; and Gil Loescher, *The UNHCR and World Politics: A Perilous Path* (Oxford: Oxford University Press, 2001), 24–26.

5. In addition, the UN established two agencies with specific geographical mandates: the UN Relief and Works Agency for Palestine Refugees in the Near East (UNRWA), and the UN Korean Reconstruction Agency (UNKRA).

6. For a discussion, see Thomas G. Weiss, ed., *Beyond UN Subcontracting: Task-sharing with Regional Security Arrangements and Service-providing NGOs* (Houndmills, Basingstoke, UK: Palgrave Macmillan, 1998).

7. Joint Inspection Unit Report, *Evaluation of the Office of the United Nations Disaster Relief Coordinator,* Joint Inspection Unit Report No. 11, UN document A/36/73, October 1980.

8. George Davidson, quoted in Kent, *Anatomy,* 62.

9. For a positive appraisal of OEOA, see Susan Martin, *Forced Migration and the Evolving Humanitarian Regime,* New Issues in Refugee Research, Working Paper no. 20, (Geneva: UN Office of the High Commissioner for Refugees, July 2000), 25–26.

10. Kent, *Anatomy of Disaster Relief,* 63.

11. Larry Minear et al., *United Nations Coordination of the International Humanitarian Response to the Gulf Crisis, 1990–1992* (Providence, RI: Watson Institute for International Studies, 1992).

12. There is an extensive literature on the humanitarian dimensions of the armed conflicts of the 1990s produced under the aegis of the Humanitarianism and War Project available at http://hwproject.tufts.edu. See also Arthur C. Helton, *The Price of Indifference: Refugees and Humanitarian Action in the New Century* (New York: Oxford University Press, 2002); Sadako Ogata, *The Turbulent Decade: Confronting the Refugee Crises of the 1990s* (New York: W. W. Norton, 2005); and Adam Roberts, 'The Role of Humanitarian Issues in International Politics in the 1990s,' *International Review of the Red Cross* 81, no. 383 (1999): 19–42.

13. According to one estimate, international humanitarian expenditure increased from $2 billion in 1990 to $6 billion in 2000. Michael Barnett, 'Humanitarianism transformed,' *Perspectives on Politics* 3, no. 4 (December 2005): 723.

14. Antonio Donini, 'Humanitarianism in the 00s: Is Universality under Threat?', paper presented at the annual meeting of the International Studies Association, Honolulu, Hawaii, 2005.

15. *An Agenda for Peace—Preventive Diplomacy, Peacemaking and Peace-Keeping: Report of the Secretary-General pursuant to the statement adopted by the Summit Meeting of the Security Council on 31 January 1992,* UN document A/47/277-S/24111, 17 June 1992, paras. 4 and 17.

16. Antonio Donini, *The Policies of Mercy: UN Coordination in Afghanistan, Mozambique and Rwanda* (Providence, RI: Watson Institute for International Studies, 1996).

17. See Thomas G. Weiss, 'Humanitarian Shell Games: Whither UN Reform?' *Security Dialogue* 29, no. 1 (March 1998): 9–23.

18. For an analysis of the relationship between these issues, see Adele Harmer and Joanne Macrae, eds., *Humanitarian Action and the 'Global War on Terror': A Review of Trends and Issues,* Humanitarian Policy Group (HPG) Report no.14 (London: Overseas Development Institute, 2003).

19. See Thomas G. Weiss and David A. Korn, *Internal Displacement: Conceptualization and Its Consequences* (London: Routledge, 2006).

20. The reservations are summarized in Susan Martin et al., *The Uprooted: Improving Humanitarian Responses to Forced Migration* (Lanham, Md.: Lexington, 2005), 112–117. The highly prescient warning was issued by Nicola Reindorp in 'Trends and Challenges in

the UN Humanitarian System,' in *The New Humanitarianisms: A Review of Trends in Global Humanitarian Action*, HPG Report no.11, ed. Joanna Macrae (London: Overseas Development Institute, 2002), 29–38.

21. Daniel Turton, 'Darfur Dilemmas: The Need for Leadership,' *Forced Migration Review*, IDP Supplement (formerly no. 24) (October 2005): 31.

22. 'Interview with Walter Kälin,' *Forced Migration Review*, no. 23 (May 2005): 6.

23. House of Commons International Development Committee, *Darfur, Sudan: The Responsibility to Protect, Fifth Report of Session 2004–2005*, vol. 1 (London: House of Commons, The Stationery Office, 19 March 2005), 25.

24. See 'Humanitarian Response Reform,' in *OCHA in 2006: Activities and Extra-Budgetary Funding Requirements* (New York: United Nations Office for the Coordination of Humanitarian Affairs, 2006), 124.

25. These obstacles are summarized in 'The currency of humanitarian reform,' HPG Briefing Paper (London: Overseas Development Institute, November 2005); and 'Special Issue: Humanitarian Reforms,' *TALK BACK: The Newsletter of the International Council of Voluntary Agencies (ICVA)* 7, no. 3 (3 October 2005).

26. Thomas G. Weiss, 'UNHCR should lead the international humanitarian enterprise,' www.nira.go.jp.

27. Helton, *The Price of Indifference*, 225.

28. Martin et al., *The Uprooted*, 120.

29. Edward Luck, *Reforming the UN's Humanitarian Machinery: Sisyphus Revisited?* (New York: Columbia University, Center on International Organization, 4 February 2003), 2 and 14.

CHAPTER 28

WOMEN AND GENDER

CHARLOTTE BUNCH

THE principle of women's equality and nondiscrimination on the basis of sex was inscribed in the UN from the outset through the Charter and the 1948 Universal Declaration of Human Rights (UDHR). These unprecedented breakthroughs did not happen without struggle. A handful of women delegates (from Asia and North and South America) attending the San Francisco Conference worked together with forty nongovernmental organizations (NGOs) to ensure inclusion of sex in the antidiscrimination clause of the Charter as well as to change 'equal rights among men' to 'equal rights among men and women.' A similar effort had to be made in the drafting of the UDHR.[1]

This example of women working across geographic boundaries as well as across the lines of governmental delegations, NGOs, and UN staff to advance equality is repeated often in the history of women and the UN. Precisely because the numbers of women in governmental delegations have been small, women's organizations and movements have played an essential role in injecting the views of women into the world organization.

Even the terms to use in this discussion are under debate, but the distinction between women and gender is important—and often misunderstood. 'Women' are an identifiable group based on biological sex; and 'gender' refers to the ways in which roles, attitudes, privileges, and relationships regarding women and men are socially constructed—hence, gender shapes the experience of males as well as females. For example, one can speak of the need to empower women as a defined group and to increase their numbers in decision-making, while gender is more appropriately used to talk about how social attitudes shape perceptions of issues and of who gets invited to the table. Men as well as women can be (or not be) 'gender conscious.' To be aware of the impact of gender and committed to women's equality is at the core of a political perspective called 'feminism.' As used in this chapter, these terms are overlapping but not synonymous.[2]

One of the ongoing dilemmas in work on this issue has been whether to pursue women's equality through separate entities or through other UN organs. Some have argued that without women-specific units, these concerns would be neglected and women's efforts diluted, while others maintain that women will always be marginalized unless gender is mainstreamed into all areas of the UN. History indicates that both strategies are necessary, and indeed are mutually reinforcing. This chapter explores how both have evolved and influenced each other.

Another dilemma has been where to place women and gender in terms of the UN's division of work. The obvious answer is everywhere, as such a broad topic does not fall into only one box—social, political or economic, rights or development. As Devaki Jain points out, one of women's contributions to the UN has been questioning the knowledge base with its embedded hierarchies and 'critiquing ideas such as the dichotomies of development and rights, public and private, theory and practice, women's rights and human rights, home and workplace.'[3] The practical matter of where to place work on women/gender continues, but addressing the interrelatedness of this topic has fared better as the UN has grappled with the overlapping nature of its work in all arenas.

This chapter cannot cover everything about women and gender over six decades of UN history, much less reflect the vibrant work at the national and regional level, which has fed and been fed by the global. It does outline the major international institutions, standards, and trends as they have evolved: from the initial emphasis on political participation and citizenship to development/health in the 1970s–1980s, and then to human rights, peace and security, and gender integration, in the 1990s and beyond.

WOMEN-SPECIFIC INSTITUTIONS, CONFERENCES, AND STANDARD SETTING

Women-specific entities and events have primarily driven the agenda on this topic in the UN and have served as the incubator for ideas about women's equality and gender to develop, and then often move into the mainstream. Without these, it is hard to imagine how this work would have progressed. Yet, women-specific work has largely remained marginalized, and the miniscule resources and power invested in it have plagued efforts to achieve implementation of the high standards repeatedly espoused on this topic.[4]

The Commission on the Status of Women (CSW), the UN intergovernmental policy body on women, was established in 1946 as a subsidiary body of the

Commission on Human Rights. There was debate amongst supporters about where to place women's rights, but after pressure from NGOs and an appeal by the chair of the subcommission (Bodil Begtrup) not to make women dependent on another commission, where they would end up 'in the queue' competing with many other human rights issues, it was made an independent entity that first met in 1947.[5]

The mandate of the CSW is to prepare policy recommendations and reports to the Economic and Social Council (ECOSOC) on promoting women in political, economic, civil, social, and educational fields and on urgent problems of women's rights. The resources of the commission are meager, and before 1987 it met only every other year. But it draws upon the active engagement of NGOs, which have always been a significant presence at the CSW—averaging thirty to fifty in the 1950s and swelling by the 1990s to over 600 with the growth of civil society participation in the UN.[6]

The early years of the CSW laid the groundwork for legal equality with a primary focus on the political rights of women—including the right to vote and status in marriage, access to education and vocational training, and women's rights as workers. Several declarations and conventions were adopted, building in particular on the pioneering work of the International Labour Organization (ILO), in collaboration with the UN Educational, Scientific and Cultural Organization (UNESCO).[7] While weak on implementation, these documents began to set standards and were often accompanied by gathering statistics—the first real global data on women's status—a critical role that the UN has continued to play, illustrated by numerous reports, including a 2005 report on the state of data in this field.[8]

The work of the CSW was transformed by the four UN world conferences on women (in Mexico City in 1975, Copenhagen in 1980, Nairobi in 1985, and Beijing in 1995) discussed below. In 1987, it began to meet annually, as it was mandated to monitor implementation of the Nairobi Forward-looking Strategies from the 1985 conference. Much of its work since has focused on monitoring implementation of the platforms for action from the conferences and on five- and ten-year reviews of them.

The Division for the Advancement of Women (DAW) is the current name of the unit in the UN Secretariat that provides substantive servicing to the CSW. Based in New York within the Department of Economic and Social Affairs, it elaborates global policies and norms on women mandated by the CSW, ECOSOC, and the General Assembly and conducts research, prepares reports, and develops policy options as needed. It also promotes and supports the mainstreaming of gender perspectives within the UN system and provided substantive and technical servicing to the Committee on the Elimination of Discrimination against Women until 2007, when this function was transferred to the Office of the High Commissioner for Human Rights.[9]

A number of factors converged leading to the declaration of 1975 as International Women's Year (IWY) and of 1976–1985 as the UN Decade for Women: Equality, Development, and Peace. The world organization had designated several theme years, and the second UN Development Decade had just begun when the Women's International Democratic Federation suggested designating a women's year to the CSW.[10] Proposed by Eastern and Western European women concerned with peace during the Cold War, many women in North and South America in the midst of a feminist resurgence took it up with enthusiasm. Meanwhile women from newly independent states in the Third World saw it as an opportunity to address women's role in development and move the work of the CSW 'beyond the negotiating tables in New York and Geneva and into the fields and rice paddies of the developing world.'[11]

The first World Conference on Women held in Mexico City in 1975 was tumultuous and ground breaking in bringing global attention to a multitude of issues raised by the 8000+ people who attended the conference and the NGO parallel Tribune. Government delegations—73 percent female and primarily headed by women—brought many women into the UN's orbit for the first time; both events introduced activists to the potential of pursuing their interests through the world organization at a time when there were few international venues for women's rights. The conference developed a Plan of Action and, recognizing that a year was hardly enough, called for a UN Decade for Women. Further, over a hundred governments set up 'national institutions' dealing with policy, research and programs on women during IWY.[12]

Awareness-raising about women's status prevailed even amidst differences in Mexico, but the mid-decade Conference on Women in Copenhagen in 1980 brought out the cleavages in North–South debates as well as political divisions, especially around Israel. Nevertheless, especially at the NGO Forum, women listened and networked—a learning experience that prepared the groundwork for greater understanding of the enormous diversity of women and their needs.[13]

The Third World Conference on Women in Nairobi in 1985 ushered in the era of the international women's movement, with its multitude of diverse regional and global manifestations. Women's groups and feminist leaders had being emerging over the decade in all regions, and more Southern voices now took center stage. For example, DAWN (Development Alternatives with Women for a New Era)—a new Southern network of researchers—launched its feminist critique of development in Nairobi.[14] The vibrant NGO Forum embraced women's diversity as strength and reflected the growing consensus that all issues are women's issues and all would benefit from gender analysis. The 'Nairobi Forward-looking Strategies for the Advancement of Women Towards 2000' presented a detailed and sophisticated approach to achieving women's equality.

The UN Decade for Women proved to be an enormous catalyst for women's organizing, which provided resources, space, and legitimization for the issue nationally and brought women together regionally and globally. As Peggy Antrobus notes: 'It was within this context that women from around the world first encountered each other in a sustained and ever-deepening process . . . [that] was to nurture and expand this movement in a way that not even its strongest protagonists could have imagined.'[15]

The Fourth World Conference on Women in Beijing in 1995 showcased this movement and consolidated its gains on the UN agenda. The largest UN conference held to that time, it had delegations from 189 governments and 17,000 delegates (from governments, NGOs, the media, and UN organizations). Meanwhile some 35,000+ people attended the NGO Forum.[16] Beijing illustrated the enormous interest in this topic globally but also exposed its controversial aspects and the growing political strength of opponents to women's rights. The Beijing Platform for Action covers the human rights of women in twelve critical areas of concern, ranging from poverty and education to violence against women and armed conflict, and including the girl child—a topic that was advanced especially by African women.[17] Beijing was the last world conference on women to date, but the CSW has conducted two well-attended reviews of implementation of the Beijing Platform—in 2000 and 2005. Both events reaffirmed the platform and added to it in areas, such as HIV/AIDS; but they were less bold in spirit and reflected the impact that conservative forces have had on governments' attitudes toward women's issues, especially in areas such as sexual and reproductive rights.[18]

The UN Development Fund for Women (UNIFEM) began as the Voluntary Fund for the UN Decade for Women in 1976 to promote the decade and support implementation in developing countries of the Mexico City Plan of Action. As the only UN fund mandated solely to assist women, the Voluntary Fund was a catalyst both within the UN system and, through support to innovative activities, at the national level. In 1984, it became a separate operational entity (and was renamed UNIFEM) in association with UNDP. With headquarters in New York, it has fifteen regional offices and is linked to UN development activities at the country level. The scope of UNIFEM's work has expanded with a growing understanding of what is vital to development for women, and now includes programs on women and governance, peace, security and violence against women, and economic justice.[19]

The International Research and Training Institute for the Advancement of Women (INSTRAW) also came out of a recommendation in Mexico City and was created in 1976, but its headquarters moved to the Dominican Republic in 1983. INSTRAW carries out research programs related to gender and development in such areas as valuing women's household production, and it identifies gaps in order to promote further studies. It also conducts training seminars and has elaborated training materials and methodologies related to research on gender and development.

The Office of the Special Adviser to the Secretary-General on Gender Issues and Advancement of Women (OSAGI) resulted from a recommendation made at Beijing that there should be a higher-level official who reported directly to the Secretary-General. The office provides leadership for the work on gender mainstreaming and for the Inter-Agency Network on Women and Gender Equality, as well as for the Inter-Agency Task Force on Women, Peace, and Security. It also includes the Focal Point for Women in the Secretariat, which works to improve the status of women within the Secretariat.

The Convention on the Elimination of All Forms of Discrimination Against Women (CEDAW) was adopted in 1981 as part of the advances made during the Decade for Women. Commonly called the 'Women's Convention' because it is the key international legal instrument on women's rights, CEDAW incorporates the provisions on sex discrimination in previous UN conventions and spells out social and economic as well as political and civil rights for women in both the private and public sphere. It has been ratified by some 185 governments. However, CEDAW also has the largest number of reservations of any such treaty, reflecting the ambivalence of states about many of the provisions including the very concept of discrimination, especially with regard to culture, family, and reproductive rights.

CEDAW provides for a monitoring body that meets several times a year to hear and comment on governmental reports on their obligations under the treaty. The CEDAW Committee also receives information from NGOs about what governments have done (or not done), and many NGOs have produced 'shadow' or alternative reports which they use to pressure governments and call attention to issues nationally. In 2000, the convention was strengthened when an optional protocol was adopted that allows the Committee to hear and act on complaints from individuals on violations of the convention in countries that have ratified the protocol.

While some aspects of violence against women (VAW)—for instance, trafficking and harmful traditional practices—had been addressed by the world organization over the years, generally VAW was framed as a private matter and not placed firmly on the UN's agenda until the 1990s. For example, VAW was not mentioned in CEDAW; and UNIFEM had to commission a concept paper to justify funding projects on this topic as late as 1991.[20] However, work on VAW has advanced rapidly in the past decade, reflecting innovations in standard setting that cross over women specific/general lines, public/private, and demonstrate its cross-cutting nature.

The primary standard-setting, but non-binding, instrument is the Declaration on the Elimination of Violence against Women (DEVAW). Developed over several years by CSW/DAW, the General Assembly adopted it in 1993. DEVAW identifies violence in three spheres: family, community, and state. In 1992, the CEDAW Committee adopted a General Recommendation affirming that VAW is a form of sex discrimination, and thus, should be included in states' reports. UNIFEM initiated the Inter-Agency Trust Fund on the elimination of VAW in 1996, which provides resources in this area. The WHO has collected the most comprehensive cross-cultural data on VAW, and the Secretary-General reported on the topic during the 2006 General Assembly, illustrating how gender has moved somewhat onto the UN's mainstream agenda.[21]

GENDER INTEGRATION AND WOMEN'S ADVANCES ON UN AGENDAS

Women and gender perspectives have been propelled forward by women-specific entities, but they have influenced and been advanced in other areas of the UN as well. Gender integration received a big push from the international women's movement in the 1990s. Antrobus argues that feminists changed the terms and outcomes of global debates 'in ways that clarified linkages between social, cultural, economic, and political factors and pointed the way to more credible solutions to problems of environmental degradation, sustainable livelihoods, poverty, human rights and population.'[22] During this decade, the UN mandated 'gender mainstreaming,' which was described as 'a strategy for making women's as well as men's concerns and experiences an integral dimension of the design, implementation, monitoring and evaluation of policies and programmes...so that women and men benefit equally and inequality is not perpetuated.'[23] Most UN agencies created or expanded gender focal points and programs in this area. While some advances have been gained from mainstreaming, it is not a substitute for women-specific work, which pioneers new issues and makes women's rights a priority. Space does not permit covering the complexity of gender integration throughout the UN system, but we will highlight four major areas: development, health, human rights, and peace and security.

First, given the importance of development activities within the UN and during the Women's Decade, it has been addressed by women extensively for some time. Jain contends that women 'brought new ways of looking at the conceptualization of work; challenged the hierarchies of how economic and social contributions are valued; insisted that women have a right to development...and that the degree of access of women...was a measure of the stage of development of a nation.'[24] Initially labeled 'women in development (WID),' this work built upon Ester Boserup's 1970 study of women's work that provided evidence of their crucial (but often unrecognized) role in national economic activity and helped to legitimize looking at women's productive (and reproductive) roles in development processes.[25] The integration of women in development was recognized in the plans for the Second Development Decade (1970–1980) and became a focus not only of the CSW, but also of the Commission for Social Development (CSD) and of the UN's regional commissions.[26]

Planners began to recognize the importance of women to the success of development and the need to include them in design and country-level implementation. More attention focused on women's education as key to family improvement, and on microfinance for women's enterprises, through institutions such as Women's World Banking and the Grameen Bank, and other similar initiatives. But as the numbers of women in poverty did not decrease, a feminist critique emerged that went beyond women's inclusion to looking at how gender was inscribed in models of development in a way that disadvantaged women. This 'Gender and Development' (GAD rather than WID) approach put more emphasis on the need to change models of development.[27]

In the 1990s, as women organized to bring feminist critiques into mainstream UN World Conferences, the first to register this impact was the 1992 Earth Summit in Rio. Women held their own World Congress in advance of Rio, prepared a Women's Agenda 21, and then lobbied to ensure that their perspectives were included in the conference's analysis of environmental degradation—linking it to sustainable development and other 'economic, political, social and cultural factors.'[28] At the 1995 Social Summit in Copenhagen, women again brought their critiques of development—linking the feminization of poverty to the impact of structural adjustment and unfair trade policies. The Secretary-General concluded that Copenhagen 'was the international community's most forthright acknowledgement that the problems faced by women lie at the heart of the global agenda.'[29] Women's growing influence was also reflected in the focus on 'Gender and Human Development,' which launched the Gender-related Development Index (GDI) to measure women's status, as the theme of the *Human Development Report* in 1995.[30]

Yet, in 2000, women again found themselves marginalized at the Millennium Summit. Gender equality was one of the MDGs, but the only agreed concrete target set for it was equal access to education. Another MDG which focused on women—decreasing maternal mortality—only addresses women as child bearers. From 2000 to 2005, many feminists spent time with the MDG task forces, expanding the gender equality MDG into seven key target areas and seeking to bring gender perspectives into the others. Nevertheless, the first draft for the Millennium Summit +5 document again failed to address the centrality of women's rights to this process, containing only passing reference to gender equality. Once again, women mobilized to bring gender more fully onto the agenda, concluding after the summit that gains had been made but that governments and the UN still fell far short of both the development and the gender equality goals espoused.[31]

Second, gender has been raised as part of health concerns in a number of areas, such as WHO's work on VAW, attention to maternal mortality by WHO and the UN Population Fund (UNFPA), and greater consideration of sex discrimination in food and healthcare provided to girls by UNICEF and FAO. An increasingly important area where there is growing awareness within the UN of gendered dimensions is the HIV/AIDS epidemic. Females are the most vulnerable and fastest growing segment of those with HIV, especially in Africa. UNAIDS has begun to address this with initiatives like the UN/NGO partnership in the Global Coalition on Women and AIDS.

The most controversial aspects of health raised within the UN context concern sexual and reproductive health and rights. These issues were discussed as far back as the UN Conference on Human Rights in Teheran in 1968, the first World Population Conference in Bucharest in 1974, and the Women's Conference in 1975. In 1968, the CSW appointed Helvi Sipilä as a special rapporteur to study the interrelationship of the status of women and family planning. Sipilä also informally mobilized women in governments to ensure that women's status was on the Bucharest agenda.[32]

An understanding of the centrality of women's rights to issues of population evolved over two decades of debates, during which women's health movements made sharp critiques of family planning abuses and coercive practices. The paradigm shift was embodied in the Plan of Action from the 1994 International Conference on Population and Development in Cairo. Rosalind Petchesky describes the shift as one that 'moves firmly from an approach based on demographic targets . . . to a comprehensive reproductive health approach. . . . integrates women's empowerment into population and development strategies; and . . . recognizes reproductive rights as fundamental human rights.'[33] UNFPA, one of the strongest advocates for women's rights in the UN system, shepherded the Cairo agenda and its implementation, and subsequently suffered a withdrawal of financial support by the United States in 2001.

The discussion of sexual rights has arisen in the UN not only within the context of health but also of human rights. As a concept, it is implicit in the Vienna, Cairo, and

Beijing conference documents, in which reference is made to the right to control over one's sexuality. However, a number of governments have been repudiating the concept of sexual rights as well as seeking to limit reproductive rights in a highly vocal backlash at the UN.[34] One of the most controversial aspects of sexual rights is the assertion of the right to live free from violence and discrimination on the basis of sexual orientation—a concept that has been raised by a few special rapporteurs and discussed at the CHR.

Third, since the CSW is autonomous and separated from the human rights machinery in Geneva, women were primarily seen as part of the UN's social and economic work, and women's rights were only rarely addressed in the human rights arena before the 1990s. While some women had long argued for an understanding of their rights as human rights, the change in perception came most forcefully at the 1993 World Conference on Human Rights in Vienna. With the Cold War over and the issue of rape in war gaining media coverage in the Balkans, women seized the opportunity to demand attention to women's rights as human rights. They organized across the North–South divide and in all the regional preparatory processes to ensure that the Vienna Declaration and Program of Action included a strong affirmation of the rights of women as universal human rights and in particular the recognition that all forms of violence against women are a violation of human rights.[35]

One of the specific demands in Vienna was for a Special Rapporteur on Violence Against Women, its Causes and Consequences to report to the CHR. This rapporteur was appointed in 1994, and her annual reports have elaborated human rights standards on VAW and outlined governments' responsibilities to abide by those standards in concrete policy terms, following the parameters outlined in the UN Declaration on VAW.[36]

Another call from Vienna was for gender integration into all the work of the human rights machinery—the subject of a resolution each year at the CHR from 1994 to 2006. Vienna also resulted in the appointment of a High Commissioner for Human Rights, and the Office of the High Commissioner for Human Rights (OHCHR) has included a mandate for gender integration from its inception.

Moreover, a growing number of human rights treaty bodies and special procedures have given attention to the gendered aspects of their mandates. For example, the Human Rights Committee that monitors the International Convention on Civil and Political Rights (ICCPR) issued General Comment 28 on the equality of rights between men and women, which spells out how inequality violates the ICCPR.[37] Other treaty bodies are also addressing how gender affects their mandates on torture, racial discrimination, child rights, and economic and social rights. Considerable attention has been paid to gender integration and women in the work of a number of the special rapporteurs and representatives in such areas as internally displaced persons, migrants, housing, extra judicial and summary executions, and human rights defenders.[38]

Another gender-related issue addressed by several bodies in the UN over the years is trafficking in persons, especially women, involving both sexual and economic exploitation. This chapter cannot cover the extensive debates over trafficking that involve questions of prostitution, sex work, human rights, migration and immigration. The 1949 convention on this subject was prepared by the General Assembly's Social Committee, and trafficking is also covered in CEDAW and in the Beijing Platform. Different aspects of this topic are addressed by OHCHR, the ILO, UNESCO, UNICEF, and the UN Crime Commission. An operative definition is contained in the Palermo Protocol that supplements the UN Convention Against Transnational Organized Crime, adopted in 2000. In 2004, the CHR appointed a Special Rapporteur on Trafficking in Persons, especially in Women and Children.[39]

The ongoing tension within the UN between the principle of the universality of human rights and respect for cultural specificity, and between the responsibility of the international community to enforce respect for human rights and national sovereignty, comes up often when addressing the human rights of women. Many UN documents consistently state variations on the idea that while cultural and religious diversity is to be respected, it is not to be used as justification for violating human rights, including those of women. But the debate continues, and nowhere are the stakes of this debate clearer than in the resistance to the realization of women's human rights.[40]

Fourth, one of the first issues that women's NGOs addressed in the early days of the UN was peace; it was a prominent theme in the UN Decade for Women, and in 1974 the General Assembly adopted a Declaration on the Protection of Women and Children in Emergency and Armed Conflict. Nevertheless, not until the 1990s did real changes come to international law in this area, and efforts to alter the traditional approach to peacekeeping and security as essentially male terrain begin to get a hearing in UN circles.

By the early 1990s, women's groups had brought VAW to public attention. The recognition of rape as a systematic tool of war was spurred by the rapes in Bosnia, and by the Korean former 'comfort women,' who broke the silence about their subjugation through military sexual slavery by the Japanese in World War II. These situations were highlighted in women's organizing at Vienna in 1993, which helped bring global attention to VAW in armed conflict there, as well as at the Beijing Women's Conference. Soon after, the International Criminal Tribunal for the former Yugoslavia began to prosecute rape and sexual violence as war crimes, and the International Criminal Tribunal for Rwanda prosecuted rape as genocide.

When negotiations for the Rome Statute to create an International Criminal Court got underway, women organized the Women's Caucus for Gender Justice to ensure that sexual and gender-based crimes were included. As a founder of the Caucus explains: 'The Rome Statute names a broad range of sexual and reproductive violence crimes—rape, sexual slavery including trafficking, forced pregnancy, enforced prostitution, enforced sterilization . . . as among the gravest crimes of war. . . . and [as] crimes against humanity. . . . [It] also encompasses groundbreaking structures and processes to ensure that crimes will be prosecuted in a nondiscriminatory, respectful manner that minimizes the potential for retraumatization and overcomes women's reluctance to participate.'[41]

Another major advance was the unanimous passage in 2000 of Security Council Resolution 1325 on Women, Peace, and Security—the first Council resolution specifically addressing the impact of war on women and recognizing women's contributions to conflict resolution and sustainable peace. It adds to the growing attention to VAW in war, and also calls for involving greater numbers of women in both peacemaking and peacekeeping. In 2002, the Secretary-General issued a report on women, peace, and security; and work to implement this resolution is a focus of OSAGI and UNIFEM, as well as of many NGOs.[42]

Gender awareness has also grown in humanitarian assistance. For example, UNHCR began to recognize refugee women as a particular group and issued guidelines on the protection of refugee women in 1991, and for preventing and responding to sexual violence against refugees in 1995. Implementation of such guidelines on the ground by UN and NGO aid personnel continues to be a challenge, evidenced by the exposure of sexual exploitation and abuse by both UN peacekeepers and NGO personnel. The Secretary-General commissioned a report on strategies to eliminate abuses in UN peacekeeping, which has resulted in specialized units to address personnel conduct during UN field missions and strengthened mechanisms for investigation and sanction of such abuse.[43] Thus, the UN is seeking to address issues of women, peace and security, both internally and as the body the world hopes will prevent such human rights abuse around the world.

CONCLUSION

Assessment of the status of women's rights and gender equality in the United Nations after the 2005 World Summit is a matter of determining whether the proper perspective is a glass half full or half empty. On the one hand, there has been much progress since women first fought for their inclusion in the UN Charter; on the other hand, after sixty years of struggle, one could expect more from the world body, whose power depends on its moral authority. The UN should lead by example. However, a target of 50/50 males/females in positions of authority by 2000 was agreed upon at the Beijing Conference in 1995, but ten years later women still occupied fewer than 30 percent of higher-level professional posts—and the percentage gets lower the higher the level.[44] The continuing gender imbalance at the upper levels of the UN, and in the governments that make up its member states, points to the need for women and their male allies to bring such issues forward more forcefully.

As part of the UN reform process, considerable discussion took place in 2006 about the need to strengthen the UN's work on women's rights and its 'gender architecture.' A major proposal to consolidate DAW, OSAGI, and UNIFEM into one stronger women's agency with more resources was recommended by the Secretary-General's High-level Panel on UN System-wide Coherence in November 2006 and endorsed by Kofi Annan as well as by many women's NGOs. In 2007, the General Assembly will decide how to act on this proposal which could alter considerably the units described here. Both this decision and how vigorously the mandate for 'gender mainstreaming' is pursued under the new Secretary-General will be significant markers for the UN's work in this area in the future.

Other useful indicators of women's status will be how well governments and the Secretariat integrate gender and advance women in the newly created Peacebuilding Commission and the Human Rights Council, as well as in implementing the MDGs. The UN remains an important arena in women's pursuit of justice and human rights; progress globally has repercussions nationally and locally, and vice-versa. The world organization has provided a venue where high standards of gender equality and women's human rights have been elaborated, but the ongoing challenge is how to implement these lofty goals within the UN itself and in the everyday lives of women and girls around the world.

NOTES

1. For sources on women in the UN, see Division for the Advancement of Women, *Women Go Global: The United Nations and the International Women's Movement, 1945–2000*, CD-ROM developed with the National Council for Research on Women (New York: United Nations, 2002); and Hilkka Pietilä, *Engendering the Global Agenda: The Story of Women and the United Nations* (New York: United Nations Non-Governmental Organization Liaison Service, 2002).
2. For more useful discussion of these terms see UNIFEM, *Report of the Expert Group Meeting on the Development of Guidelines for the Integration of Gender Perspectives into United Nations Human Rights Activities and Programmes* (Geneva: United Nations Development Fund for Women, July 1995).
3. Devaki Jain, *Women, Development, and the UN: A Sixty Year Quest for Equality and Justice* (Bloomington: Indiana University Press, 2005), 8.
4. Lack of resources has long been a problem. See, e.g., John Mathiason, *The Long March to Beijing*, CD-ROM, 1998; and Stephen Lewis, *Race Against Time* (Toronto: House of Anansi Press, 2005), 109–144.
5. Pietilä, *Engendering the Global Agenda*, 13–14; Felice Gaer, 'And Never the Twain Shall Meet? The Struggle to Establish Women's Human Rights as International Human Rights,' in *The International Human Rights of Women: Instruments of Change*, ed. Carol Elizabeth Lockwood, Daniel Barstow Magraw, and S. I. Strong (New York: American Bar Association, 1998).
6. *Women Go Global*.
7. Pietilä, *Engendering the Global Agenda*, 19–20; Jain, *Women, Development, and the UN*, 11–42.; For conventions and declarations on women's rights, see *Women Go Global*; Center for the Study of Human Rights, *Women and Human Rights: The Basic Documents* (New York: Columbia University, 1996); and www.un.org/womenwatch.
8. UN, *The World's Women 2005: Progress in Statistics* (New York: United Nations Department of Economic and Social Affairs, Statistics Division, 2006).
9. For information on UN activities on women and gender specific websites in the UN see www.un.org/womenwatch.

10. Pietilä, *Engendering the Global Agenda*, 31.
11. Boutros Boutros-Ghali, 'Introduction,' *The United Nations and the Advancement of Women, 1945–1995*, The Secretary-General's Blue Book Series, vol. 5 (New York: United Nations, 1995), 27.
12. Jain, *Women, Development, and the UN*, 69; Virgina R. Allan, Margaret E. Galey, and Mildred E. Persinger, 'World Conference of International Women's Year,' in *Women, Politics, and the United Nations*, ed. Anne Winslow (Westport, Conn.: Greenwood Press, 1995), 29–44.
13. Charlotte Bunch, 'What Not to Expect From the UN Women's Conference in Copenhagen,' in *Ms. Magazine* (July 1980): 80–83; and Peggy Antrobus, *The Global Women's Movement: Origins, Issues and Strategies* (London: Zed Books, 2004), 49–52.
14. Gita Sen and Caren Grown, *Development, Crises, and Alternative Visions: Third World Women's Perspectives* (New York: Monthly Review Press, 1987); Devaki Jain, 'The DAWN Movement,' in *Routledge International Encyclopedia of Women: Global Women's Issues and Knowledge*, ed. Chris Kramarae and Dale Spender (New York: Routledge, 2000), 298–299.
15. Antrobus, *The Global Women's Movement*, 37.
16. Pietilä, *Engendering the Global Agenda*, 58.
17. Anita Anand with Gouri Salvi, eds., *Beijing: UN Fourth World Conference on Women* (New Delhi: Women's Feature Service, 1998); Amrita Basu, *The Challenge of Local Feminisms: Women's Movements in Global Perspectives* (Boulder, Colo.: Westview Press, 1995); and Charlotte Bunch, Mallika Dutt, and Susana Fried, 'Beijing 1995: A Global Referendum on the Human Rights of Women,' *Canadian Women's Studies* 16, no. 3 (June 1996): 7–12.
18. Cynthia Meillón with Charlotte Bunch, *Holding On to the Promise: Women's Human Rights and the Beijing +5 Review* (New Brunswick, NJ: Center for Women's Global Leadership, 2001); Women's Environment and Development Organization, *Mapping Progress: Assessing Implementation of the Beijing Platform 1998* (New York: Women's Environment and Development Organization, 1998); and Anna Grossman, *Beijing Betrayed: Women Worldwide Report that Governments Have Failed to Turn the Platform into Action* (New York: Women's Environment and Development Organization, 2005).
19. See Margaret Snyder, *Transforming Development: Women, Poverty, and Politics* (London: Intermediate Technology Publications, 1995).
20. Roxanna Carrillo, *Battered Dreams: Violence against Women as an Obstacle to Development* (New York: United Nations Development Fund for Women, 1992).
21. Claudia García-Moreno, *WHO Multi-country Study on Women's Health and Domestic Violence against Women: Initial Results on Prevalence, Health Outcomes and Women's Responses* (Geneva: World Health Organization, 2005), available at www.who.int; and UN Secretary-General's 'In-Depth Study of Violence Against Women' (New York: UN, 2006).
22. Antrobus, *The Global Women's Movement*, 81. See also UNIFEM, *Putting Gender on the Agenda: A Guide to Participating in UN World Conferences* (New York: UN Development Fund for Women, 1995).
23. *Report of the Economic and Social Council for 1997*, UN document A/52/3, 18 September 1997, ch. 4.
24. Jain, *Women, Development, and the UN*, 2; and Arvonne S. Fraser and Irene Tinker, eds., *Developing Power: How Women Transformed International Development* (New York: Feminist Press, 2004).
25. Ester Boserup, *Woman's Role in Economic Development* (New York: St. Martin's Press, 1970).
26. See *Women Go Global*; and Lourdes Beneria, 'Accounting for Women's Work: The Progress of Two Decades,' *World Development* 20, no. 11 (1992): 1546–1560.

27. Caroline O. N. Moser, *Gender Planning and Development: Theory, Practice and Training* (London: Routledge, 1993); and Marilyn Waring, *If Women Counted: A New Feminist Economics* (San Francisco: Harper and Row, 1988).

28. Antrobus, *The Global Women's Movement*, 86; Women's Environment and Development Organization, *Women's Action Agenda for a Healthy and Peaceful Planet 2015* (New York: Women's Environment and Development Organization, 2002); and Martha Chen, 'Engendering World Conferences: The International Women's Movement and the UN,' in *NGOs, the UN and Global Governance*, ed. Thomas G. Weiss and Leon Gordenker (Boulder, Colo.: Lynne Rienner, 1996).

29. Boutros-Ghali, *The United Nations and the Advancement of Women, 1945–1995*, 27.

30. UNDP, *Human Development Report 1995* (New York: Oxford University Press, 1995).

31. Gender Monitoring Group of the World Summit, 'What's At Stake for Women in the World Summit' and 'UN 2005 World Summit Outcomes,' available at www.beijingandbeyond.org.

32. Pietilä, *Engendering the Global Agenda*, 32; and *Women Go Global*.

33. Rosalind Petchesky, *Global Prescriptions: Gendering Health and Human Rights* (London: Zed Books with UNRISD, 2003), 34–35; see also Sonia Corrêa, with Rebecca Reichmann, *Population and Reproductive Rights: Feminist Perspectives from the South* (London: Zed Books, 1994).

34. Cynthia Rothschild with Scott Long and Susana Fried, *Written Out: How Sexuality is Used to Attack Women's Organizing* (New York: International Gay and Lesbian Human Rights Commision (IGLHRC), 2005), 83–120; Pinar Ilkkaracan, ed., *Women and Sexuality in Muslim Societies* (Istanbul: Women for Women's Human Rights, 2000); and Jennifer Butler, *Born Again: The Christian Right Globalized* (Ann Arbor: University of Michigan Press, 2006).

35. Charlotte Bunch and Niamh Reilly, *Demanding Accountability: The Global Campaign and Vienna Tribunal for Women's Human Rights* (New York: UNIFEM, 1994); Florence Butegwa, Everjoice Win and Bokani Moyo, *The World Conference on Human Rights: The WiLDAF Experience* (Harare: Women in Law and Development in Africa (WiLDAF), 1993).

36. Reports of the Special Rapporteur on violence against women, its causes and consequences, United Nations Office of the High Commissioner for Human Rights, 1995–2006, available at www.ohchr.org.

37. Human Rights Committee, *Equality of rights between men and women (Article 3)*, General Comment 28, UN document CCPR/C/21/Rev.1/Add.10, 2000, available at www.umn.edu; for ongoing commentary on human rights and women, see www.whrnet.org.

38. These reports are available at www.ohchr.org.

39. *Convention for the Suppression of the Traffic in Persons and of the Exploitation of the Prostitution of Others*, approved by General Assembly resolution 317 (IV), 2 December 1949, 271, see www.unhchr.ch; *Protocol to Prevent, Suppress and Punish Trafficking in Persons, Especially Women and Children, Supplementing the United Nations Convention Against Transnational Organized Crime*, 2000, http://untreaty.un.org; *Report of the Special Rapporteur on Violence Against Women, Its Causes and Consequences, Ms. Radhika Coomaraswamy, on Trafficking in Women, Women's Migration and Violence Against Women, Submitted in Accordance with Commission on Human Rights Resolution 1997/44*, UN document E/CN.4/2000/68, 29 February 2000; see www.ohchr.org for reports of the Special Rapporteur on Trafficking in Persons, Especially in Women and Children.

40. *The Vienna Declaration and Programme of Action: Note by the Secretariat*, UN document A/CONF.157/23, 12 July 1993; and *Report of the Fourth World Conference on Women (Beijing, 4–15 September 1995)*—'The Beijing Declaration and Platform for Action,' UN document A/CONF.177/20, 17 October 1995. For discussion of these concepts, see Mahnaz Afkhami,

'Gender Apartheid and the Discourse of Relativity of Rights in Muslim Societies', in *Religious Fundamentalisms and the Human Rights of Women*, ed. Courtney W. Howland (New York: Palgrave, 1999) and Radhika Coomaraswamy, 'Are Women's Rights Universal? Re-Engaging the Local,' in *Meridians: Feminism, Race, Transnationalism* 3, no. 1 (2002): 1–18.

41. Rhonda Copelon, 'Rape and Gender Violence: From Impunity to Accountability in International Law,' *Human Rights Dialogue* 2, no. 10 (2003), available at www. carnegie-council.org. See also Kelly D. Askin, 'A Decade in Human Rights Law: A Decade of the Development of Gender Crimes in International Courts and Tribunals: 1993 to 2003,' *Human Rights Brief* 11 (Spring 2004): 16–19; and Indai Lourdes Sajor, ed., *Common Grounds: Violence Against Women in War and Armed Conflict Situations* (Quezon City, Philippines: Asian Center for Women's Human Rights, 1998).

42. See Kofi Annan, *Women, Peace, and Security—Report of the Secretary-General*, UN document S/2004/814, 13 October 2004; Elisabeth Rehn and Ellen Johnson Sirleaf, *Women, War, Peace: The Independent Experts' Assessment of the Impact of Armed Conflict on Women and Women's Role in Peace-building* (New York: UNIFEM, 2002); for an overview of ongoing work in this area, see: www. peacewomen.org.

43. *A comprehensive strategy to eliminate future sexual exploitation and abuse in United Nations peacekeeping operations*, General Assembly document A/59/710, 24 March 2005.

44. See Office of the Focal Point for Women in the United Nations in the Office of the Special Adviser on Gender Issues and Advancement of Women (OSAGI), www.un.org; and Kristen Timothy, 'Equality for Women in the United Nations Secretariat,' in Winslow, *Women, Politics, and the United Nations*, 117–135. For information on numbers of women in parliaments compiled by the Inter-Parliamentary Union, see www.ipu.org.

CHAPTER 29

CHILDREN

YVES BEIGBEDER

ACCORDING to the 1959 United Nations Declaration of the Rights of the Child, 'the child, by reason of his physical and mental immaturity, needs special safeguards and care, including appropriate legal protection.' The gender insensitive language of the time nonetheless makes clear that children are vulnerable. More than adults, they are exposed to and suffer from poverty, under-development, ill health, and lack of education. Many suffer hardship and abuse. Governments, with appropriate international support, are responsible for creating the conditions under which children can develop their full potential.

Children are the future citizens of their states. While the proportion of people under the age of fourteen in the industrialized world was 18 percent in 2000 and declining, the proportion in developing countries was 33 percent and rising. In some of these countries, the proportion is even higher—for instance, 44 percent in Algeria. The number of children in developing countries has grown by 500 million during the past quarter-century so that 86 percent of children now live in the global South.[1] There is a growing need for governments in those countries to pay more attention to children's rights and welfare, and for international organizations to expand their work and advocacy on these issues.

This essay begins with a brief summary of the origins of the international children's movement and a review of the growing international legal framework of children's rights, including the landmark 1989 Convention on the Rights of the Child (CRC) and accompanying monitoring work. A second section examines the world summits, resolutions, movements, and reports that have increased the awareness of political leaders and mass publics of children's issues. The next section deals with the role of UN bodies and other intergovernmental organizations in the promotion of children's rights, and is followed by a review of selected operational issues before the conclusion.

THE INTERNATIONAL PROTECTION
OF CHILDREN'S RIGHTS

The sorry fate of children caused by wars and the failures of governments to provide proper health care, education, and protection, along with unfair economic practices and parents' neglect, has inspired some to advocate for child protection norms at the global level. In 1913 a young English woman, Eglantyne Jebb, was on a relief mission to Macedonia and was shocked by the suffering of children following the Balkan wars. She founded Save the Children in 1919, which organized campaigns to feed and clothe children of European countries after World War I. Jebb played a key role in drafting and promoting the 1923 Declaration of Geneva, that recognized that 'Mankind owes to the Child the best it has to give' and set a number of obligations which 'men and women of all nations' had to meet. In 1924, the declaration was adopted by the League of Nations as the Charter of Child Welfare of the League of Nations.[2]

Following the widespread horrors and suffering of World War II, the United Nations created the first intergovernmental agency concerned exclusively with children: on 11 December 1946, the General Assembly adopted resolution 57 (I) setting up the International Children's Emergency Fund, later called the UN Children's Fund and far more widely known now by its acronym, UNICEF.

The General Assembly has created an international human rights regime, which is the foundation and reference for the programs and work on behalf of children by intergovernmental organizations (IGOs) and nongovernmental organizations (NGOs).[3] The 1948 Universal Declaration of Human Rights recognized that the child must be the subject of special care and attention. The 1951 Convention relating to the Status of Refugees and its 1967 Protocol define the rights and duties of refugees, an essential piece of international law because typically more than half of refugees are children. In 1959 the General Assembly adopted resolution 1386 (XIV), a non-binding Declaration of the Rights of the Child, which affirmed that the child should enjoy all the rights set forth in the declaration as well as special protection. The International Covenant on Civil and Political Rights and the International Covenant on Economic, Social and Cultural Rights were adopted in 1966 in resolution 2200 A (XXI), which confirmed the need to pay particular attention to the needs of children. The General Assembly also adopted the Convention on the Elimination of All Forms of Discrimination against Women in 1979, which among other things proclaims that provisions for maternity protection and child care are essential rights.

The Convention on the Rights
of the Child

At the initiative of the Polish delegation and with the full support of NGOs, the General Assembly unanimously adopted the binding Convention on the Rights of the Child on 20 November 1989 in resolution A/44/25.[4] The convention broke all records for ratification and entered into force on 2 September 1990; and by early 2007, 193 countries had ratified it. Somalia (a failed state) and the United States are the only exceptions to this most widely ratified convention.[5]

It is also the most comprehensive statement of children's rights and is the first to back such rights with international law. The convention affirms that both parents have the primary responsibility for the upbringing and development of their children; but it makes states parties responsible for giving assistance to parents and taking appropriate legislative, administrative, social, and educational measures to ensure the respect of children's rights. The convention is innovative in establishing the right of children to be actors in their own development and to participate in decisions affecting their own lives and their communities and societies. This constitutes a legal revolution because the child is no longer an 'object,' a tool in the hands of the parent, but a 'subject' in law.[6] The main rights are to life, healthcare, free and compulsory education, and protection from physical and mental harm and from economic exploitation. The General Assembly adopted resolution A/54/263 on 25 May 2000, which contains two optional protocols to the convention, one on the sale of children, child prostitution, and child pornography, and the other on the involvement of children in armed conflict, which entered into force respectively on 18 January 2002 and 12 February 2002.

The governmental control mechanism for the implementation of the Convention on the Rights of the Child is the Committee on the Rights of the Child (spelled out in Articles 43, 44, and 45). The committee's purpose is to examine the progress made by states parties in achieving the realization of the obligations undertaken in the convention. It is composed of 'eighteen experts of high moral standing and recognized competence in the field covered by this Convention,' who are elected by states parties. They serve in their personal capacities (not as state representatives) and, like other UN settings, are selected with due regard to equitable geographical distribution and to the world's main legal systems.

States parties submit reports to the committee on the measures that they have adopted to give effect to the rights recognized by the convention and on the progress made on the enjoyment of those rights. Every two years, the committee submits reports on its activities to the General Assembly, through the Economic and Social Council.

Almost all countries that have submitted reports to the committee have amended their legal systems to conform to the convention's standards and requirements. Several countries have established an ombudsman for children or other similar structures to monitor independently the treatment of children. Many governments and international organizations have focused on vulnerable groups such as child laborers, child prostitutes, and child soldiers.

OTHER INTERNATIONAL LEGAL INSTRUMENTS

The Hague Convention on the Protection of Children and Co-operation in Respect of Intercountry Adoption was adopted in 1993 and the Hague Convention on Jurisdiction, Applicable Law, Recognition, Enforcement and Co-operation in Respect of Parental Responsibility and Measures for the Protection of Children, in 1996. In 1999, the International Labour Organization adopted the Worst Forms of Child Labour Convention and associated recommendation no. 190.

In 2000, two relevant UN protocols were adopted, supplementing the UN Convention against Transnational Organized Crime: the Protocol to Prevent, Suppress and Punish Trafficking in Persons, Especially Women and Children, and the Protocol against the Smuggling of Migrants by Land, Sea and Air.

International humanitarian law and international criminal law are another basis for the international protection of children. The 1949 Geneva Conventions and the Additional Protocols of 1977 spell out the basis for monitoring by the International Committee of the Red Cross (ICRC). Also relevant are the statutes of the various ad hoc international criminal tribunals and the 1998 Statute of the International Criminal Court.

At the regional level, human rights conventions include references to children's rights: for the Council of Europe, the 1950 Convention for the Protection of Human Rights and Fundamental Freedoms and Protocols, and the European Social Charter of 1961 (revised in 1996); for the Organization of American States, the American Convention on Human Rights of 1969; and for the Organization of African Unity and its successor the African Union, the African Charter on Human and Peoples' Rights of 1981. The Charter of Fundamental Rights of the European Union of 2000 has integrated children's rights as defined in the CRC in several of its articles, and it stresses the child's best interests as a primary consideration in all actions relating to children. Other child-related instruments include the 1989 Inter-American Convention on the International Return of Children and the 1996 European Convention on the Exercise of Children's Rights.

INTERNATIONAL FOCUS ON CHILDREN

In addition to and in parallel with the conventions and protocols related wholly or in part to children, the United Nations has played an important role in calling the attention of world leaders and public opinion to children through summit meetings, resolutions and declarations, reports, and a special session of the General Assembly. The Global Movement for Children, a network of NGOs and people, has similar objectives.

The World Summit for Children, held at UN headquarters in New York on 29–30 September 1990, saw the unprecedented participation of 159 countries, including seventy-one heads of state or government and forty-five NGOs, to promote the well-being of children.[7] Participants jointly signed the World Declaration on the Survival, Protection and Development of Children and the Plan of Action for Implementing the World Declaration on the Survival, Protection and Development of Children in the 1990s. One hundred eighty-one countries are now signatories of these documents, which comprise a detailed set of child-related human development goals. These include targeted reductions in infant and maternal mortality, child malnutrition, and illiteracy, and targeted increases in access to basic services for health and family planning, education, water, and sanitation. The summit created new partnerships between governments, NGOs, donors, the media, civil society, and international organizations concerned with children's welfare. Moreover, with its involvement of world leaders and setting of time-bound, measurable goals, the 1990 children's summit served as an organizational model for the 1992 UN World Conference on Environment and Development in Rio de Janeiro, the 1995 World Summit for Social Development in Copenhagen, and later ones, including the 2005 World Summit in New York.

In 1996, Graça Machel, the former minister for education in Mozambique, submitted her *Study of the Impact of Armed Conflict on Children* to the General Assembly.[8] The Assembly approved in December 1996 the appointment of a special representative on the topic. Also in 1996, the first World Congress against Commercial Sexual Exploitation of Children was held in Stockholm, Sweden; and a follow-up was held in 2001 in Yokohama, Japan.

The Global Movement for Children, a worldwide movement of organizations and people, was launched in 2000 by former South African president Nelson Mandela and Graça Machel. The movement aims at uniting efforts to 'build a world fit for children' by promoting the rights of children.

The movement initiated the Say Yes for Children Campaign, which has rallied people worldwide behind ten key principles to improve and protect the lives of children. Already by 2002, some 95 million pledges had been received. The campaign allows adults and children all over the world to express their views and claims, which will help NGOs in their own campaigns.

Several of the Millennium Development Goals (MDGs) growing from the Millennium Declaration of September 2000—with quantifiable benchmarks in order to determine whether they are achieved by 2015 as targeted—are relevant to the promotion of children's rights. The importance of the MDGs was reaffirmed when the 2005 World Summit endorsed them.

In May 2001, Kofi Annan released *We, the Children: End-decade Review of the Follow-up to the World Summit for Children, Report of the Secretary-General.*[9] The assessment gave a mixed picture. Striking progress was noted in polio eradication, salt iodization, vitamin A supplementation, guinea worm eradication, and in some regions, school enrollment. Maternal mortality, poor hygiene and sanitation, HIV/AIDS, and endemic violence remained 'intractable problems.' The resources provided by the governments of both the industrialized and developing worlds were still insufficient.

In May 2002, the UN General Assembly Special Session on Children attracted sixty-nine heads of state among the 190 national delegations, along with the leadership of UN agencies and leading figures of civil society, NGOs from 117 countries and, for the first time in UN meetings, more than 400 children as delegates and active participants.[10]

On 9 March 2004, the General Assembly adopted resolution 58/157 on the 'Rights of the Child,' which urged states that had not yet done so to sign and ratify the Convention on the Rights of the Child, and states parties to implement it fully. States were called upon to ensure adequate protection of children's rights and prevent discrimination in such areas as poverty, health, the girl child, education, refugees, child labor, sale of children, and children in armed conflict.

On 1 December 2005, World AIDS Day, at the initiative of the Global Movement for Children, millions of children around the world took part in a 'Lesson for Life 2005,' a 'lesson' on HIV, AIDS, and the effect of the pandemic on children.[11]

THE ROLE OF THE UN AND OTHER IGOS

Many states do not have the resources, capacity, or will to give proper assistance to parents and children. Many countries are torn apart by wars or civil strife, or suffer from widespread poverty, and children are among the most obvious victims. International support, through both global and regional IGOs, is necessary to assist and guide governments and national institutions. The major global IGOs concerned with children's rights, and the ICRC, are reviewed here. Their involvement in specific issues is described in the next section.

The role of IGOs is generally to survey and provide facts at the global, regional, and country levels; publicize these facts; set standards; initiate international conventions on child welfare and protection; encourage countries to ratify and apply these conventions; monitor implementation of conventions; help countries review and amend their laws; promote bilateral and regional agreements; set up pilot projects; launch global campaigns; and raise funds. Fact-finding, norm-setting, monitoring and advocacy, at the initiative, or with the support, of such NGOs as NetAid, Oxfam, Save the Children, and World Vision International, are also important.

UNICEF is the key UN organization devoted solely to children, a development agency that also provides substantial emergency relief. Created in 1946 against the wishes of the major specialized agencies of the UN, which feared competition and duplication, it is now a highly visible and universally recognized organization. It is financed mainly by voluntary contributions from governments, and it is unusual in that it also raises funds from private sources. UNICEF's work in health includes the promotion of breastfeeding, the global immunization of children, the ongoing program for the eradication of poliomyelitis, the provision of community water supplies, and participation in the Joint UN Programme on HIV/AIDS.[12]

The agency also deals with nutrition, education, sanitation, gender, and labor issues as well as emergency humanitarian operations. All executive directors have, so far, been US citizens, a recognition of the large portion of funding provided by both US public and private sources. Among its recent past executive directors, James P. Grant (1980–1995) was a well-known dynamic innovator who launched several successful campaigns,[13] and Carol Bellamy, an outspoken advocate for children's rights. Ann Veneman succeeded Bellamy in May 2005.

Other UN agencies have an active role to play in relation to children, in association with UNICEF, in meeting the MDGs. The World Health Organization (WHO) is a major actor in trying to reduce maternal and child mortality and combating HIV/AIDS, malaria, and other diseases. Together with UNICEF, it promotes breastfeeding, oral rehydration therapy, and immunization. WHO, along with the Food and Agriculture Organization (FAO), is also concerned with nutrition and food standards and safety. The UN Educational, Social and Cultural Organization (UNESCO) is the major international actor engaged in one of the most essential of tasks for children—education. The ILO is concerned with regulating child labor; especially pertinent is its 1973 convention no. 138 on the minimum age for admission to employment.

The UN High Commissioner for Refugees (UNHCR) is committed to improving the lives and rights of refugee children. In 1997, UNHCR developed a follow-up strategy to the recommendations of the Machel study. The agency adopted five global priority issues: separation; sexual exploitation, abuse, and violence; military recruitment; education; and the special needs of adolescents.[14]

The Office of the UN High Commissioner for Human Rights (OHCHR) supports human rights education and training initiatives. Its program on Eliminating Trafficking and Protecting the Rights of Trafficked Persons, which includes children, is carried out in close cooperation with the ILO, International Organization for Migration (IOM), and UNHCR, with the support of the Contact Group on Trafficking and Migrant Smuggling.

The UN Development Programme (UNDP) acts as scorekeeper and campaign manager for progress towards achieving the MDGs. It promotes mainstreaming gender into poverty reduction policies and interventions, and works to combat HIV/ AIDS with UNICEF, UNAIDS, WHO, and the World Bank. The United Nations Development Fund for Women (UNIFEM) provides financial and technical assistance to programs to foster women's empowerment and gender equality. Its focus is on reducing women's poverty, ending violence against women, reversing the spread of HIV/AIDS among women and girls, and achieving gender equality in peace and war. The World Bank finances partnerships with other UN organizations for programs to address a host of children's issues.

The IOM deals with rapid humanitarian responses to sudden migration flows, gives assistance to migrants, assists member states in the prevention of trafficking in human beings (especially women and children), and provides assistance and protection to victims. While not a UN agency, IOM works closely with UN bodies and operational agencies, as well as government agencies and NGOs.

The ICRC provides protection to children in war and child refugees. It campaigns against the recruitment of child soldiers and reminds all parties to the Geneva Conventions of their obligations towards children. The ICRC tries to ensure that children in war have adequate access to medical care, food and water, and, when possible, reunites them with their families.

Initiatives at the regional level to implement the UN Convention on the Rights of the Child have to date been few. The European Union (EU) only included children on its agenda in 2000. In October 2005, the European Commission presented its communication 'Fighting trafficking in human beings—an integrated approach and proposals for an action plan,' recommending that its institutions and member states ensure that the EU anti-trafficking policy reflected a child rights approach. The Council of Europe has set up a program for the promotion of children's rights and the protection of children against all forms of violence, following the Third Summit of Heads of State and Governments in Warsaw in 2005. The Inter-American Commission on Human Rights convened an expert meeting on violence against children in March 2005.

Selected Operational Issues

Targets have been set in international conventions, resolutions, meetings, and reports. The problems faced in trying to meet these goals, the work of IGOs and other actors in selected, important areas of children's rights, and possible remedies are summarized below. The challenges include the issues of poverty, hunger, education, gender equality, child mortality, immunization, HIV/AIDS, malaria, child labor, child trafficking, and the child soldier. These inform the MDGs pertaining to children, and have relevance for a selection of children's rights contained in the Convention on the Rights of the Child. Progress has been recorded in some areas, but considerable obstacles remain. It should be noted that global figures often hide important regional and country differences.

Children living in poverty face deprivations in many of their rights, including survival, health and nutrition, education, and protection from harm, exploitation, and discrimination. Over one billion are severely deprived of at least one of the essential goods and services on which they depend to survive, grow, and develop.

All UN organizations are committed to fighting poverty. The FAO has reported that the number of hungry people increased to 852 million in 2000–2002, although the goal set in 1996 was to reduce the world's approximately 800 million hungry people to 400 million by 2015. On the positive side, thirty countries, with a total population of over 2.2 billion, have reduced the prevalence of undernourishment by 25 percent and have made progress in reducing hunger.[15]

Following the World Declaration on Education for All, adopted in 1990 in Jomtien, Thailand, and the adoption of the Dakar Framework for Action in 2000, UNESCO launched the International Education for All Strategy in 2001. Its targets for 2015, in line with the MDGs, include: ensuring that all children have access to, and complete, free and compulsory primary education (particularly girls, children in difficult circumstances, and those belonging to ethnic minorities); and achieving gender equality in education, with a focus on ensuring girls' full, equal access to basic education of good quality.

About 121 million children, mostly girls, do not attend school. Seventy-five million children—70 percent in sub-Saharan Africa—are likely to be denied their right to a primary education by 2015.[16] UNESCO has estimated that seventy-six countries were unlikely to reach gender parity at primary and secondary school levels by 2005. Based on current trends, parity will not be met in fifty-four countries by 2015.

At the initiative of the Working Group on Girls, formed in 1993 at the Vienna World Conference on Human Rights, the need to promote the rights of 'the girl child' was emphasized. Part of the Platform of Action adopted at the Fourth World Conference of Women, held in Beijing in 1995, urged governments, agencies, and the private sector to eliminate all forms of discrimination against the girl child, including negative cultural attitudes and practices, and discrimination in education, health, and nutrition; eliminate the economic exploitation of child labor, providing protection for girls at work; eradicate violence against the girl child; and promote the girl child's awareness of and participation in social, economic, and political life.

UNICEF is the lead agency for the UN Girls' Education Initiative, launched in 2000. The goal of the ten-year initiative is to ensure that, by 2015, all children complete primary schooling, with girls and boys having equal access to all levels of education.[17]

Globally, an estimated 10.6 million children under the age of five die every year—mostly of preventable causes—in spite of the relative success of the global immunization program.[18] In the 1980s, immunization coverage against diphtheria, pertussis (whooping cough), and tetanus rose from less than 20 percent of the global population to more than 70 percent. In the 1990s, deaths from measles and tetanus declined sharply. The eradication of poliomyelitis was progressing until 2004–2005 when a reemergence of the disease struck several African countries. More than 30 million children are not immunized either because vaccines are not available, or health services are poor or inaccessible, or because families are uninformed or misinformed about the value of immunization and when to bring their children in for immunization.

UNICEF, WHO, the World Bank, donor governments, NGOs, foundations, and the pharmaceutical industry are active in immunization programs. Progress in reducing child mortality requires appropriate legislation, the strengthening of public health services, better access to health care and medicines, the education of mothers, and increased resources at national and international levels.[19]

Worldwide, AIDS is responsible for an increasing number of deaths each year. Of the 3.1 million AIDS deaths in 2004, over half a million were children. At the end of 2004, an estimated 2.2 million children were living with HIV. Also in 2004, an estimated 640,000 children worldwide were newly infected with HIV, over 80 percent of whom live in sub-Saharan Africa, with Asia and the Caribbean also experiencing increases. Approximately 90 percent of these children acquired the infection from their mothers during pregnancy, at birth, or from breastfeeding.[20]

UNAIDS, UNICEF, and other partners support the WHO '3 by 5 Initiative,' launched in 2003, which aimed to ensure that 3 million people had access to antiretroviral treatment by the end of 2005. The new target is to move towards universal access to treatment by 2010.

Antiretrovirals are also key to programs to prevent mother-to-child transmission of HIV/AIDS: providing antiretroviral prophylaxis to pregnant women and babies at birth can reduce the risk of transmission by half. UNICEF is supporting such programs in seventy countries. UNICEF, its national committees, and other partners have launched the Global Campaign for Orphans and Children Made Vulnerable by HIV/AIDS, in order to mobilize partnerships and the necessary resources.[21]

Malaria claims more than one million lives each year: 90 percent of deaths are in Africa, where malaria accounts for one in five of all childhood deaths. Anemia, low birth-weight, epilepsy, and neurological problems are frequent consequences of malaria that compromise the health and development of millions of children in developing countries. UNICEF, UNDP, and the World Bank joined WHO in October 1998 to create the global partnership to 'Roll Back Malaria,' with the objective of halving the global burden of malaria by 2010. The Global Fund to Fight AIDS, Tuberculosis and Malaria finances both preventive and curative tools, such as insecticide-treated nets and artemisinin-based combination therapy.[22]

In 1992 the ILO initiated the International Programme on the Elimination of Child Labour, the aim of which is the progressive elimination of child labor worldwide, with the eradication of the worst forms an urgent priority. Since the 2000–2001 biennium, the program has promoted the development of time-bound programs for the elimination of the worst forms of child labor, such as the Networking Initiative, which covers development policy and hazardous child labor.

According to the 2005 ILO report, *The End of Child Labour: Within Reach*, the actual number of child laborers worldwide fell by 11 percent between 2000 and 2004, from 246 million to 218 million.[23] The number of children and youth aged 5–17 in hazardous work, as defined in ILO Labour Convention no. 138, decreased by 26 percent to reach 126 million in 2004, against 171 million in 2000. Among younger child laborers, aged 5–14, there was a 33 percent decrease. The report attributed the reduction in child labor to increased political will and awareness and concrete action, particularly in the field of poverty reduction and mass education.

Trafficking is defined as the illegal transport of human beings, in particular women and children, for the purpose of selling them or exploiting their labor. Worldwide, it is estimated that 1.2 million children are trafficked each year, mostly in commercial sexual exploitation.[24] They are also trafficked for other forms of labor exploitation such as domestic service, services industries, and armed conflict.

Among the many factors that encourage trafficking in children are: poverty and the need or desire to support the family; lack of education and training; civil or foreign war with forced conscription; economic or natural disasters that devastate local economies; cultural attitudes toward children and girls in particular; inadequate laws; and lack of enforcement. Remedial policies include poverty reduction, government prioritization of education, awareness campaigns, lawmaking and enforcement, and reintegration.

There are over 300,000 child soldiers, some as young as eight, exploited in armed conflict in more than thirty countries.[25] Easy prey for guerilla leaders because they are mired in poverty and without access to schools, young children are often eager to engage in combat alongside adult soldiers. Girl soldiers are also used as cooks and sexual slaves, and represent up to 30 percent of some nonstate armed groups.

In 2005 the Security Council adopted resolution 1612 which established a monitoring system for grave violations and crimes against children in armed conflict, attempting thereby to publicly shame organizations that exploit children as soldiers or sex slaves. The Council has also specified that it will 'consider imposing, through country-specific resolutions, targeted and graduated measures,' that is sanctions, against parties to an armed conflict in violation of applicable international law relating to the rights and protection of children in armed conflict.

Organizations involved in this area are UNICEF, the ILO, UNDP, the UN Office on Drugs and Crime, OHCHR, and UNIFEM, as well as the IOM and NGOs.[26]

CONCLUSION

While the League of Nations created the first elements, the children's rights movement emerged with the UN human rights regime created in the wake of World War II and subsequent armed conflicts. NGOs have been essential partners from the beginning. The creation of UNICEF as part of the UN system, the active role of the ILO, UNESCO, WHO, and other UN bodies, the growing influence of national and international NGOs, and the adoption of the CRC have set the stage for building structures, strengthening institutions, setting standards, and initiating global and national programs for the protection and welfare of the world's children. The Committee on the Rights of the Child plays a key role in monitoring the implementation of the convention's measures; it records progress made on the enjoyment of these rights and gives technical advice or assistance to countries.

Despite some progress, many governments are not yet meeting the basic needs of vulnerable children, and few guarantee respect for their rights. Governments and international organizations are, however, increasingly aware of the numerous problems and obstacles to the implementation of the global standards of children's rights. Future efforts should focus on the following issues. Primary healthcare and basic health services should be reinforced and equitable access assured. Communicable diseases should be prevented and controlled more efficiently. Potable drinking water should become more widely available and environmental sanitation should be improved. Starvation and deaths caused by famine should be eliminated, chronic hunger and malnutrition reduced, and the major nutritional deficiency diseases eradicated. Compulsory primary education should be universalized, adult illiteracy combated, and more equitable access to schools achieved, especially for girls. Hazardous, unhealthy, and forced child labor should be ended. Cultural, ethnic, geographic, rural/urban, income, and gender disparities need to be addressed. And measures should be taken to alleviate poverty.

These issues are on the agendas of UN organizations and international NGOs, but political will of governments is, as for other issue areas, lacking. Are governments prepared to allocate sufficient funds for their country's children? Are they genuinely committed to implementing the convention that they have ratified?

There are general approaches to implementation that should be considered. First, the sensible starting point is the law—international conventions, resolutions, and recommendations require better national legislation and target-setting. The implementation of conventions should be monitored and publicized. Laws should be strictly enforced, with sanctions for violators. Second, information and awareness campaigns, both at the international and national levels, play a key role in publicizing children's rights and combating traditional prejudices; such campaigns could influence the behavior of parents and help institutions. Third, more resources for education and health are required—these are often neglected when national budgets are prepared.

In view of the size of the obstacles and the inadequacy of available resources at both national and international levels, it would be unrealistic to expect rapid progress in all the areas where children are at risk. Although governments are primarily responsible and accountable for the welfare and rights of children in their own countries, the complementary work of the UN system and NGOs remains essential. The achievements of UN bodies and NGOs in such areas as immunization, polio eradication, girls' education, the fight against AIDS, and emergency assistance are impressive. Their continuing action is needed to prod governments into action and monitor their performance.

NOTES

1. United Nations Population Division, *World Population Prospects: The 2000 Revision, Population Ageing* (New York: UN Department of Economic and Social Affairs, 2002), 14.
2. See Yves Beigbeder, *New Challenges for UNICEF, Children, Women and Human Rights* (Houndsmill, Basingstoke, UK: Palgrave, 2001), 4–7.
3. See F. J. Hampson, *Legal Protection Afforded to Children Under International Humanitarian Law* (Colchester, UK: University of Essex, 1990).
4. On the Convention, see James R. Himes, ed., *Implementing the Convention on the Rights of the Child, Resource Mobilization in Low-Income Countries* (The Hague: Martinus Nijhoff Publishers, 1995); Rachel Hodgin and Peter Hewell, *Implementation Handbook for the Convention on the Rights of the Child* (New York: UNICEF, 1998); and David A. Balton, 'The Convention on the Rights of the Child: Prospects for International Enforcement,' *Human Rights Quarterly* 12, no. 1 (1990): 120–129.
5. There are several declared reasons for the US refusal to ratify the convention. One is the contradiction between the prohibition of the death penalty for offences committed before the age of eighteen: twenty US states allowed the execution of juvenile offenders before the US Supreme Court in Roper v. Simmons in March 2005 abolished the death penalty for juveniles. Another reason is that many of the issues addressed by the convention lie primarily within the jurisdiction of the individual US states.
6. Recommendation No. 874 of the Parliamentary Assembly of the Council of Europe, adopted on 4 October 1979, states: 'Children must no longer be regarded as parents' property, but must be recognized as individuals with their own rights and needs.'
7. World Summit for Children, New York, 29–30 September 1990, www.un.org.
8. Later published as Graça Machel, *The Impact of War On Children* (New York: Palgrave, 2001).
9. Kofi Annan, *We, the Children: End-decade Review of the Follow-up to the World Summit for Children, Report of the Secretary-General*, UN document A/S-27/3, 4 May 2001.
10. UN General Assembly's Special Session on Children, May 2002: UNICEF *Special Session on Children: Highlights*, www.unicef.org.
11. The Global Movement for Children, *Lesson for Life 2005*, www.gmfc.org.
12. Co-sponsors of UNAIDS are UNICEF, UNDP, UNFPA, UNESCO, WHO, UNHCR, the ILO, WFP, UNODC, and the World Bank.
13. See Richard Jolly, ed., *Jim Grant: UNICEF Visionary* (Florence: Tipografia Giuntina, 2001). Preceding Grant were Maurice Pate (1947–1965) and Henry R. Labouisse (1965–1979).
14. UNHCR, *Refugee Children: Guidelines on Protection and Care* (Geneva: UNHCR, 1994). See also *Refugee Survey Quarterly* 23, no. 2 (2004), Special Issue on 'Refugee Children.'
15. See Urban Jonsson, *Nutrition and the United Nations Convention on the Rights of the Child*, Innocenti occasional papers, Child Rights Series, no. 5 (Florence: International Child Development Centre, 1993); FAO, *The State of Food Insecurity in the World 2004* (Rome: Food and Agriculture Organization of the United Nations, 2004); and 'Worldwide Hunger Kills One Child Every Five Seconds,' *Popline, World Population News Service* 27 (January–February 2005): 3.
16. UNICEF, *The State of the World's Children 2005: Childhood Under Threat* (New York: UNICEF, 2005), 15, 96–97. Global figures often hide important regional and country differences: they are estimates, and observers have questioned the reliability and meaning of some of these. See also Frank Dall, *Education and the United Nations Convention on the Rights of the Child: The Challenge of Implementation*, Innocenti occasional papers, Child Rights Series, no. 4 (Florence: International Child Development Centre, 1993).

17. UNICEF, *Annual Report 2004* (New York: UNICEF, June 2005), 4–9.
18. See Joao Yunes, César Chelala and Nora Blainstein 'Children's Health in the Developing World: Much Remains to be Done,' *World Health Forum* 15, no. 1 (1994): 73–76; World Health Organization, Regional Office for South-East Asia, *Towards a Better Tomorrow: Child Rights and Health* (New Delhi: WHO, Regional Office for South-East Asia, 2001); and Paolo C. Belli, 'Investing in Children's Health: What are the Economic Benefits?', *Bulletin of the World Health Organization: the International Journal of Public Health* 83, no. 10 (2005): 777–784.
19. See 'Facts on Children: Immunization,' UNICEF Press Center, www.unicef.org.
20. 'Children, HIV & AIDS,' AVERT, www.avert.org.
21. UNICEF, *The State of the World's Children 2005*, 75, 81.
22. WHO, *Children and Malaria*, Roll Back Malaria: A Global Partnership, http://rbm.who.int and UNICEF in Action, www.unicef.org.
23. See Alec Fyfe, *All Work and No Play: Child Labour Today* (London: Trade Unions Congress, 1985); Nelien Haspels and Michele Jankanish, eds., *Action against Child Labour* (Geneva: ILO, 2000); and 'New ILO Report shows marked decline in child labour worldwide,' *Press Release ILO/06/15*, 4 May 2006.
24. See Ove Narvesen, *The Sexual Exploitation of Children in Developing Countries* (Oslo: Redd Barna (Save the Children Norway), 1989); Vitit Muntarbhorn, *Sexual Exploitation of Children*, Human Rights Study Series no. 8 (New York: United Nations Centre for Human Rights, 1996); and Roger J. R. Levesque, *Sexual Abuse of Children: A Human Rights Perspective* (Bloomington: Indiana University Press, 1999).
25. See C. and P. M. Shah, *The Impact of Armed Conflict on Children: A Threat to Public Health* (Geneva: WHO, 1996); United Nations Centre for Human Rights, *The Impact of Armed Conflict on Children: A Survey of Existing Standards and their Relevance and Adequacy* (Geneva: United Nations Centre for Human Rights, 1996); Rachel Brett and Irma Specht, *Young Soldiers: Why They Choose to Fight* (Boulder, Colo.: Lynne Rienner, 2004); and Peter W. Singer, *Children at War* (New York: Pantheon Books, 2005).
26. 'Facts on Children: Child Protection,' UNICEF Press Center, www.unicef.org, and 'Factsheet: Trafficking,' UNICEF (undated); and Panudda Boonpala and June Kane, *Unbearable to the Human Heart: Child Trafficking and Action to Eliminate It* (Geneva: ILO, International Programme on the Elimination of Child Labour, 2002).

CHAPTER 30

MINORITIES AND INDIGENOUS PEOPLES

MAIVÂN CLECH LÂM

JUDGE Thomas Buergenthal of the International Court of Justice defines the international law of human rights as 'the law that deals with the protection of individuals and groups against violations of their internationally guaranteed rights, and with the promotion of these rights.'[1] The individual and collective dimensions of human existence being ineluctably co-dependent, this definition has the advantage of clearly indicating that international human rights law responds to both personal and collective vulnerability. Indeed, two human rights regimes now taking shape at the United Nations, for the protection and promotion of the rights of minorities and of indigenous peoples, respectively, take particular account of this co-dependency. While the two regimes follow distinctive paths, they also generate enough mutual impact and interrogation as to warrant their parallel consideration here.[2]

The present examination of the two regimes proceeds in five sections. The first traces current concerns regarding the political vulnerability of minorities and other marginalized groups, as well as the destabilizing potential that this vulnerability poses in international relations. The ethno-nationalist ferment that gripped Europe in the nineteenth century, for example, fueled World War I and underwrote the allies' subsequent dismemberment of the defeated Ottoman and Austro-Hungarian empires. The second section notes the initial muting of the international discourse of group rights following the founding of the UN in 1945 when, reeling still from the horrors wrought by Nazism's exploitation of ethno-nationalism, the organization's founders decided to address the subject of human vulnerability through a discourse of individual human rights rather than group rights. The third and fourth sections describe specific normative frameworks and related mechanisms that, beginning in the 1960s, the UN developed to protect and promote the rights of minorities and of indigenous peoples respectively. These developments, in turn, indicate that substate group vulnerability and restiveness are once again commanding close attention in an interstate system now also subject, not coincidentally, to suprastate pressures emanating from globalization.[3] Together, these bids for power from above and from below are stressing, perhaps beyond endurance, an interstate system premised, since the 1648 Treaty of Westphalia, on the bedrock concept of state sovereignty and, since the 1789 French Revolution, also on the fanciful conceit of a state's cultural homogeneity. Finally, the last part of the chapter compares the two human rights regimes at issue and assesses how they sustain, modify, or challenge bedrock and fantasy.

THE PRE-CHARTER YEARS

The French Revolution may be seen as perfecting that which the Treaty of Westphalia started: the construction of the modern state. Simply put, where Westphalia 'territorialized' the concept of statehood by de-linking its legitimacy from the approbation of pope or holy Roman emperor, the French Revolution 'nationalized' it by adding another dimension, namely, cultural homogeneity. That is, faced with a multilingual and multicultural France hitherto symbolized by the person of its king, the young and regicidal republic had to come up with a new symbol, or glue, of state. It settled on the culturally unitary nation-state—brought into being by a centralized educational system that spread a single historiography, culture, and language throughout the country; and since maintained by a nationalist ideology that conflated the notions of ethnicity and statehood.[4] Since 1789, this zealously reductionist discourse of nationalism swept through not only France, but also the rest of Europe, Latin America, and, somewhat later, Asia, Africa, and Oceania. Left in its wake today is a confection of 192 modern states that now make up the United Nations and that, to this day, strive to paper over the age-old cultural seams that, prior to the dawn of modernity, typically crisscrossed their territories and organized the lives of their multiethnic populations.[5]

The ideology of nationalism contributed in no small measure to the outbreak of World War I. Keen to avoid another such cataclysm, and also to consolidate their hegemony, the allied powers at the end of the so-called Great War decided to break up Germany, Austria-Hungary, and the Ottoman Empire into their presumed ethnic parts, which were then by and large accorded the right to self-determination, understood at the time as a ticket to independent statehood. Where, however, demographic or political factors made this approach unworkable, the League of Nations, established at the end of World War I by its victors, stepped in with a mechanism to protect minorities enclosed within the borders of vanquished multiethnic states.

The mechanism came to be known as the Minority Treaties System. Under it, the League concluded separate treaties with targeted states by which the latter guaranteed citizenship and equal treatment to members of their minority communities; undertook to respect the latter's religions, languages, and schools; and also accepted the League's supervision of their compliance with treaty terms.[6]

Eighteen such treaties were signed between 1919 and 1924.[7] The system, nevertheless, soon fell apart from multiple stresses. These included: its selective application to defeated states, which understandably undermined its legitimacy; its denial of a generalized *locus standi* to affected minorities who, as a result, could access the League's mechanism only with the assistance of willing member states; and, finally, the rise of Nazism which rendered member states increasingly wary of ethnically framed claims. It should be noted that the League of Nations, under the pressure of Western colonial powers, at no time recognized that the right of self-determination applied to the colonized peoples of Asia, Africa, and Oceania or, for that matter, to the indigenous peoples of the settler states of the Americas, Australia, and New Zealand.

FOUNDATIONAL TEXTS

The discourse of collective or group rights is notably underdeveloped in, if not absent from, the UN's three foundational human rights texts.[8] Known collectively as the 'International Bill of Human Rights,' they comprise: the 1948 Universal Declaration of Human Rights (UDHR); the 1966 International Covenant on Economic, Social and Cultural Rights (ICESCR); and the companion 1966 International Covenant on Civil and Political Rights (ICCPR). The 1945 UN Charter, likewise, hardly belabors collective human rights. At the same time, it is not devoid of human rights discourse, nor even of the discourse of collective rights. Indeed, member states themselves are collective entities whose basic rights and duties vis-à-vis one another, and vis-à-vis other collectivities such as non-self-governing peoples, are mapped out in the Charter. Moreover, the document opens with the famous phrase 'We the Peoples of the United Nations,' a set of collectivities arguably distinctive from the states that created and now sustain the world body. Finally, the Charter does in fact directly engage in recognized human rights parlance, however cursorily, in phrases that command respect 'for the principle of equal rights and self-determination of peoples,' as in Article 1 (2), and 'for human rights and for fundamental freedoms for all without distinction as to race, sex, language, or religion,' as in Article 1 (3).

Charter discourse notwithstanding, the San Francisco conference of 1945 by no means sought to create anything resembling a human rights regime. Thomas Buergenthal suggests why: 'That was to be expected, for each of the principal victorious powers had troublesome human rights problems of its own. The Soviet Union had its *Gulag*, the United States its *de jure* racial discrimination, France and Great Britain their colonial empires.'[9] Nevertheless, today's proponents of human rights protection for minorities and for indigenous peoples locate the normative foundations of the regimes that they respectively espouse in the Charter itself, among other sources. In the case of minorities, the relevant Charter phrase is that found in Article 1 (3), quoted above, which bars discrimination. Where indigenous peoples are concerned, the applicable language consists of both this phrase and that found in Article 1 (2), also quoted above, which mandates respect for the self-determination of peoples.

Therein lies the key conceptual difference between the two emerging regimes. The first demands equal treatment for individuals belonging to vulnerable minorities; the second also demands that but simultaneously seeks the right of self-determination for the indigenous collectivity so that it may remain culturally distinctive as well as territorially connected to its ancestral lands even as it participates, along with its members, in the life of the multiethnic state. The shock that the latter discourse imparts to the habits of political modernity cannot be overemphasized. The discourse, in effect, reinscribes a political legitimacy, albeit postmodern rather than premodern, for ethnic groups whose physical and cultural survival in their ancestral territories is endangered by the intrusive and assimilative motor of the state, revved up by the demands of globalization. At the same time, indigenous peoples typically project that their exercise of self-determination will result in, not their separation from enclosing states, but rather a consensual partnership with it. However, many states continue to regard this potentially promising notion of a consensual partnership with constituent entities as something of a mystery, if not threat.

Whether most states will in due course read the foundational human rights texts broadly enough to glimpse the creative vision that is being proposed by indigenous peoples in international forums remains to be seen. The 1948 UDHR, which expands on the Charter's universe of the vulnerable, clearly prohibits discrimination on the bases of 'race, colour, sex, language, religion, political or other opinion, national or social origin, property, birth or other status.' The UDHR thus explicitly anticipates the equality thrust of the 1992 Declaration of the Rights of Persons Belonging to National or Ethnic, Religious and Linguistic Minorities (Minorities Declaration), which presently figures as the centerpiece of a coalescing UN minorities regime. The difficult question is whether the UDHR, while supporting the right to equal treatment for individuals belonging to marginalized groups, concurrently supports, prohibits, or is silent vis-à-vis groups' claims to collective rights, including the right to a social distinctiveness that is seen as necessary to the maintenance of cultural distinctiveness.

The UDHR clearly aims to benefit 'all members of the human family,' 'the human person,' 'all human beings,' and 'everyone.' At the same time, the text recognizes, in several provisions, that some of the individual rights that it protects are realized 'in association with others,' 'in community,' 'through national and international co-operation,' within 'trade unions,' and in 'the family.' Indeed, the latter is explicitly recognized as a rights-bearing collective entity in Article 16 (3): 'The family is the natural and fundamental group unit of society and is entitled to protection by society and the State.' The family, however, remains the only collective entity that the UDHR explicitly recognizes as rights-bearing. As for distinctiveness, it is neither recognized nor repudiated in this most foundational of human rights instruments. Culture itself is referred to only twice, in language that makes no provision for cultural diversity, let alone social distinctiveness. Article 22, for example, arguably references a socially cohesive society or state: 'Everyone, as a member of society, has ... cultural rights'; Article 27, thereafter, anticipates a monocultural society: 'Everyone has the right freely to participate in the cultural life of the community.'

The twin covenants of 1966, for their part, elaborate and concretize the individual rights broadly set out in the UDHR. More to the point, they also expand the reach of human rights law in two significant ways. Common Article 1 of the two covenants recognizes, for the first time in a human rights instrument, 'peoples' as rights-bearing entities:

1. All peoples have the right of self-determination. By virtue of that right they freely determine their political status and freely pursue their economic, social and cultural development.

2. All peoples may, for their own ends, freely dispose of their natural wealth and resources without prejudice to any obligations arising out of international economic co-operation, based upon the principle of mutual benefit, and international law. In no case may a people be deprived of its own means of subsistence.

3. The States Parties to the present Covenant, including those having responsibility for the administration of Non-Self-Governing and Trust Territories, shall promote the realization of the right of self-determination, and shall respect that right, in conformity with the provisions of the Charter of the United Nations.

Finally, Article 27 of the ICCPR recognizes, most significantly, that the rights to culture, religion, and language need to be exercised collectively:

In those States in which ethnic, religious or linguistic minorities exist, persons belonging to such minorities shall not be denied the right, in community with the other members of their group, to enjoy their own culture, to profess and practise their own religion, or to use their own language.

Partisans of the idea of collective human rights thus regularly invoke both common Article 1 of the two covenants and Article 27 of the ICCPR to assert that the concept is inscribed in the UN's foundational human rights texts and hence merits development. Finally, these two articles, taken together, would appear to allow collective entities not only to bear rights, but also to preserve distinctiveness—political, economic, social, and cultural.

Of the three foundational texts, the ICCPR alone provides for its beneficiaries to enforce its terms through a treaty body called the Human Rights Committee, which is composed of independent experts. The Committee was initially mandated to administer two processes: the reporting system by which states were required to report their compliance initiatives to the Committee; and the interstate complaint procedure. The adoption of the First Optional Protocol to the ICCPR then additionally required the Committee to accept and investigate individual complaints. However, the Protocol sets up a serious quandary in relation to Article 1: an individual may not lodge a grievance under Article 1 because the right of self-determination belongs to the collective only. On the other hand, the Protocol only allows individuals, not groups, to file complaints. The Committee, nevertheless, has acted on occasion to bridge the individual and collective dimensions of human existence. In 1994, for example, the Committee, using the device of its General Comments, now widely regarded as legally authoritative, stated in General Comment No. 23 that culture, under Article 27, may involve a way of life that is closely associated with territory, especially in the case of persons belonging to indigenous communities.

In sum, then, the UDHR, ICESCR, and ICCPR focus on the protection and promotion of individual human rights; together they sparingly anticipate the collective exercise of some of these rights. They recognize two collective entities as rights-bearing: the 'family,' described as 'the natural and fundamental group unit of society,' and the 'people,' which has never been defined in any UN instrument.[10] Nowhere, however, do the foundational texts offer a mechanism of redress to a collective entity. The absence of such a mechanism has been keenly felt by minorities and indigenous peoples, and decried by human right advocates.[11]

THE RIGHTS OF PERSONS BELONGING TO MINORITIES

A patchwork-like minorities regime, applicable to about 10–20 percent of the world's population,[12] got off to an earlier start in the United Nations than the regime for indigenous peoples.[13] States' familiarity with the interwar Minority Treaties System, the long shadow cast by the Holocaust on the Charter, the 1948 Convention on the Prevention and Punishment of the Crime of Genocide, the unassailable virtue of the nondiscrimination principle enshrined in both the international bill of human rights and the 1966 Convention on the Elimination of All Forms of Racial Discrimination (CERD), all paved the way for the General Assembly to formalize the rights of minorities in its 1992 Minorities Declaration. Furthermore, as early as 1969 when CERD entered into force, persons discriminated against on the basis of race—broadly interpreted to include color, descent, and national or ethnic origin— could already bring claims to its treaty body, the Committee on the Elimination of Racial Discrimination. The latter, indeed, has proved to be singularly elastic in its conception of its class of beneficiaries. Interpreting its mandate creatively, the CERD committee has issued findings in favor of persons who could be seen as victimized on the bases of, variously, their racial or minority or indigenous status.[14]

Nevertheless, while the beneficiary classes under CERD and under the Minorities Declaration overlap, they are not identical. CERD protects persons rendered vulnerable by virtue of their race, or other aspects of presumed descent, even when they belong to majorities as was true in the case of blacks in apartheid South Africa, the spectacle of which promoted the birth of CERD. The Minorities Declaration, fueled instead by the violence that attended the dissolution of the former Yugoslavia, protects persons rendered vulnerable by virtue of their minority status with respect to cultural, that is behavioral, rather than racial, indices. These include national or ethnic origin (protected in both instruments since it variously denotes descent and/ or behavior), religion, and language. In recognition of its complex genealogy, the declaration's preamble recites its kinship with the instruments listed at the beginning of this section, and with the 1981 Declaration on the Elimination of All Forms of Intolerance and of Discrimination Based on Religion or Belief, as well as the Convention on the Rights of the Child (CRC).

Given that much had already been said against discrimination in prior UN instruments, the Minorities Declaration consists of a mere nine articles—a number that constrasts sharply with the forty-five that make up the 1994 Draft Declaration on the Rights of Indigenous Peoples. The nine articles provide, in essence, that states shall protect the existence and identities of minorities; the latter's members shall enjoy rights to their own culture, religion, language, associations, and cross-border contacts while participating in the civic life of the state; they enjoy such rights individually and/or in concert with others depending on the circumstances; their human rights and fundamental freedoms shall not be infringed; and states shall show due regard for and cooperate with them.

The Minorities Declaration neither creates a new rights-bearing entity nor a new collective right but principally expands the areas where individuals have the right to act in concert with others in their minority group. The instrument does not even define the term 'minority' other than to specify in its title that it is concerned with 'National or Ethnic, Religious and Linguistic Minorities.' The Declaration's most useful feature, then, may be its recruitment of culturally, as opposed to biologically, defined groups into the universe of the vulnerable, where members are accorded human rights protection. Contained in a General Assembly declaration that is not per se enforceable, however, this innovation initiates a normative, but not yet legal, change in the human rights domain. The CERD committee and the Human Rights Committee, then, remain the prime UN mechanisms available to minority and indigenous persons who wish to legally assert human rights claims.

It should be noted, however, that treaty bodies like the CERD committee are not the only human rights mechanisms available at the UN for the promotion and protection of the rights of vulnerable groups. The disbanded Commission of Human Rights (CHR) (replaced by the Human Rights Council (HRC), in June 2006)—with its working groups composed of states, its Sub-Commission on the

Promotion and Protection of Human Rights composed of independent experts and their subsidiary working groups, its special rapporteurs entrusted with investigating specific human rights topics—and the Office of the High Commissioner for Human Rights (OHCHR), together with victims, NGOs, and states that participate in the various meetings and workshops organized by the UN in Geneva, all interactively shape the substance, direction, and impact of the international human rights endeavor.

In brief, a single instrument does not constitute a regime. While the reach and force of any human rights regime depends greatly on the quality of its core instrument and mechanism—in this case the Minorities Declaration—any such regime also expands or contracts in synergy with the several other regimes that comprise the human rights universe.

THE RIGHTS OF INDIGENOUS PEOPLES

As stated, the regime on the rights of persons belonging to minorities began informally at the UN when the Charter enjoined discrimination. Yet, to this day, the regime lacks a core binding instrument and consists instead of normative and procedural 'shreds and patches' that are culled from other regimes and stitched onto the non-binding and barebones Minorities Declaration. The indigenous regime, on the other hand, emerged later but now appears better defined and more robust.[15] While statistics on the number of the regime's beneficiaries vary widely, the OHCHR estimates the world's indigenous peoples to total over 300 million, a figure that many consider far too low.[16]

The regime of indigenous peoples' rights was born, interestingly, not in the Commission on Human Rights but in a specialized UN agency: the tripartite International Labour Organization (ILO) where states, employer associations, and trade unions are represented and vote on an equal basis. In 1952 the ILO organized an interdisciplinary Andean Indian Program to investigate the situation of the concerned subject peoples. A mere five years later, the agency had in place an enforceable treaty pertaining to all indigenous and tribal peoples that was subsequently ratified by twenty-seven states: the 1957 Convention Concerning the Protection and Integration of Indigenous and Other Tribal and Semi-Tribal Populations in Independent Countries, otherwise known as ILO Convention 107. Because the long-standing raison d'être of the ILO is the adoption and enforcement of treaties rather than the formulation of declarations, this first-ever international instrument to concern itself with indigenous peoples arrived complete with an enforcement mechanism.

A second normative development that came to exert significant influence on the development of an overall indigenous regime was the General Assembly's 1960 Declaration on the Granting of Independence to Colonial Countries and Peoples.

This instrument notably converted the Charter's recognition of the 'principle' of self-determination into a 'right' that is vested in peoples; a move that, as seen earlier, was reproduced in common Article 1 of the two 1966 covenants. Responding to pressure from civil society, the UN in 1971 appointed a special rapporteur, José R. Martínez Cobo, to undertake a study of the problems and prospects facing indigenous peoples. He identified the unavailability of the right to self-determination to them as the fundamental impediment to their progress.[17]

Cobo's study produced other important consequences including an influential working definition of indigenous peoples that he intended to be globally applicable:[18]

Indigenous communities, peoples and nations are those which, having a historical continuity with pre-invasion and pre-colonial societies that developed on their territories, consider themselves distinct from other sectors of the societies now prevailing in those territories, or parts of them. They form at present non-dominant sectors of society and are determined to preserve, develop and transmit to future generations their ancestral territories, and their ethnic identity, as the basis of their continued existence as peoples, in accordance with their own cultural patterns, social institutions and legal systems.[19]

As may be seen, Cobo advanced four criteria to mark a group as indigenous: an ancestral tie to a particular geography; a cultural distinctiveness relative to other sectors of society; a desire to maintain said geography and distinctiveness; and a status of vulnerability vis-à-vis the dominant population. Cobo's study also provided the UN with a rationale for establishing, in 1982, the Working Group on Indigenous Populations (WGIP) to monitor disturbing developments in the indigenous world and to develop standards to govern indigenous/state relations.

From 1984 until 1994, the five independent experts appointed to the WGIP worked on its standard-setting mandate by gradually constructing a Draft Declaration on the Rights of Indigenous Peoples which they completed in 1994 and unanimously recommended to the twenty-some independent experts on the then Sub-Commission on Prevention of Discrimination and Protection of Minorities. These, in turn, unanimously recommended it to the states-composed Commission on Human Rights (CHR). The latter, in 1995, turned over the document for review to its own states-composed Working Group on the Draft Declaration (WGDD). This body, which met in two-week annual sessions, by early 2006 succeeded in provisionally adopting only about half of the text's forty-five operative articles due to an impasse that developed early on between indigenous negotiators and a number of state representatives. The deadlock revolved around three main issues: whether indigenous peoples had the right to self-determination; whether they were entitled to restitution for lost territories and other resources; whether they could exercise the right of free, prior, and informed consent regarding matters that affect their lands, territories, and resources.

Faced with the impasse, the chair of the WGDD presented to the CHR, at its final session in March 2006, a chair's text that reproduces consensus language agreed to by states and indigenous representatives, but otherwise advances wording that, in the chair's view, comes closest to conciliating remaining disparate viewpoints. Regarding the three key issues identified above, the chair's text incorporates the classic formulation of the right of self-determination contained in common Article 1 of the 1966 covenants but follows it up with an article that leaves some ambiguity as to whether its content has been reduced to internal self-government. The text elsewhere incorporates, with some nuance, the rights to restitution and to free, prior, and informed consent. At its dissolution in spring 2006, the CHR handed over the current text of the Declaration to its successor body, the Human Rights Council. At its first session in June 2006, the new Council voted to adopt the text and to recommend its adoption by the General Assembly. The latter referred the Declaration to its Third Committee (Human Rights) which, in a controversial vote that pitted 'immediate adoption' against 'deferral' states, recommended that the General Assembly defer action on the Declaration to permit further consultations that are to be completed by the end of the Assembly's 61st session.

The ILO, in the meanwhile, replaced Convention 107, which was avowedly integrationist, with its 1989 Convention Concerning Indigenous and Tribal Peoples in Independent Countries, commonly known as ILO Convention 169. The Convention supports and protects the goal of distinctiveness, which is sought by indigenous peoples. Its provisions relating to the lands of indigenous peoples, for example, command respect for their customary land tenure systems. They further enjoin states to recognize indigenous territories and safeguard their resources. The treaty also advances a description of indigenous and tribal peoples that resembles Cobo's and applies worldwide. While Convention 169 speaks of indigenous 'peoples,' instead of 'populations' as was the case in its predecessor document, it takes no position on whether such peoples have the right to self-determination. Some twenty states, primarily in Latin America, have ratified the convention. As the only enforceable treaty regarding the rights of indigenous peoples, however, its influence extends beyond the ratifying states and informs debates in fora as diverse as the UN, OAS, World Bank, and even the domestic legislatures of nonratifying states.

Like its predecessor, ILO Convention 169 lays out an enforcement process. States parties are obliged to submit compliance reports every one to five years; and the ILO itself is empowered to submit direct requests for information and issue observations. The annual June International Labour Conference, and its tripartite Committee on the Application of Standards, typically discusses about fifty cases a year in public sessions. Any delegate to the annual conference, or member of its tripartite governing body committee, may file a complaint or 'representation' alleging violations of the Convention. A Commission of Inquiry holds hearings in Geneva, visits the relevant country, and issues findings. Convention 169, however, does not provide for indigenous individuals or communities to file formal complaints.

In 2002 the United Nations established a mechanism that, perhaps more than any other, will advance the protection and promotion of the rights and interests of the world's indigenous peoples. That mechanism is the Permanent Forum on Indigenous Issues, which reports directly to ECOSOC and which, to date, has met in plenary session every spring in New York. The PF is composed of sixteen independent experts chosen via a formula that seeks to render the group as a whole acceptable to both states and indigenous peoples. Its mandate is political and administrative, rather than legal. In essence, it is asked to function as a proactive liaison body that links the indigenous peoples of the world to the UN system. The PF receives reports, requests, and recommendations on which it may act; it also identifies goals for itself and for international agencies, and initiates studies and programs that advance them. Unlike human rights institutions and mechanisms in Geneva that pursue more narrowly defined agendas, the PF looks at, and acts on, the big picture. It is for now the most visible transnational mouthpiece of the world's indigenous peoples, capable of effecting an amelioration of their circumstances, not through law, but through political and cultural persuasion.

A number of other UN initiatives and mechanisms contribute to the promotion and protection of the rights of indigenous peoples and minorities. These include, in each case, a Voluntary Fund that supports their participation in several UN forums, special rapporteurs to produce specific studies to guide law and policy or to investigate reports of systemic wrongs, topical seminars and workshops for concerned parties to explore difficult issues, conferences to explore new initiatives like the PF, and special events like dedicated years or decades to focus the world's attention on the subject groups. These mechanisms round out the domains of the evolving regimes discussed and contribute to legal change as well as, undoubtedly, political transformation.

CONCLUSION

The two human rights regimes examined here respond to two distinctive, if not alternative, ways in which the individual and collective dimensions of human existence are experienced.[20] In the case of the minorities regime, its beneficiaries are first and foremost individuals who have experienced vulnerability as a result of their membership in groups that the majority society has, at best, disfavored and, at worst, persecuted. What these beneficiaries need most is the legal assurance that they will not continue to be discriminated against by the dominant society but will enjoy individual rights on a par with members of the majority population. The beneficiaries also require that their set of individual rights includes the right to express their cultural identity—in the form of language, religion, and education—without fear of discrimination or persecution.

In the case of the regime for indigenous peoples, the primary beneficiary is the collectivity that the dominant society in many cases has reduced to virtual nonexistence, whether physically or culturally. Its members, who in other contexts also demand equal individual rights, in this context demand the reconstitution and protection of a collectivity that has been ravaged, if not obliterated. The collectivity longed for is a sociocultural matrix that individuals belonging to the dominant sector exist within and enjoy as a matter of course, without perhaps even being aware of their privilege. For indigenous peoples, paradoxically, because their collectivity is endangered, it is ever visible; for nonindigenous peoples, the collectivity, being effortlessly present, is invisible, as water is to fish.

All persons need to exist on both individual and collective planes in order to thrive. For historical reasons having to do with victors and vanquished as well as power and powerlessness, however, not all persons are positioned to have access to the two dimensions equally, or as needed. As a result, not all persons are equally, or similarly, vulnerable. Human rights law and regimes, which respond to vulnerability, must consequently be tailored to the vulnerabilities at issue. Unfortunately, some regimes disturb the prevailing political and legal habits of states more than others. A regime that protects the rights of persons belonging to minorities challenges the reductionist Jacobin construction of the nation-state but nevertheless appears to fit in well enough with its evolving norms when they accommodate diversity. A regime that protects the collective rights of indigenous peoples, that questions the monopolistic jurisdiction of the state, and that directly rejects its culturally unitary conceit is perceived as more threatening. It must either wait for a postmodern world to arrive, or help to usher it in.[21]

Serendipitously, the UN's practice in the development of human rights instruments is ideally suited to gently ushering in change. Typically, a nonbinding declaration is first generated after a long process during which stakeholders, typically guided by independent experts, key in on main concerns, explore solutions, and settle on a normative yet nonbinding framework that launches an experiment in improved relationships between them. Only later, when controversies lapse into the quotidian, when tolerability replaces unease, does the process turn to the task of generating a binding convention that builds upon the lessons garnered in the experimental phase. The two regimes discussed here are still at this incipient stage.

NOTES

1. Thomas Buergenthal, Dinah Shelton, and David P. Stewart, *International Human Rights in a Nutshell*, 3rd edn. (St. Paul, Minn.: West Group, 2002), 1.
2. For comparative works on the two regimes, see Gudmundur Alfredsson and Peter Macalister-Smith, eds., *The Living Law of Nations: Essays on Refugees, Minorities, Indigenous Peoples, and the Human Rights of other Vulnerable Groups* (Arlington: N. P. Engel, 1996); Catherine Brölmann, Rene Lefeber, and Marjoleine Zieck, eds., *Peoples and Minorities in International Law* (Boston: Martinus Nijhoff Publishers, 1993); Nazila Ghanea-Hercock and Alexandra Xanthaki, eds., *Minorities, Peoples and Self-Determination: Essays in Honour of Patrick Thornberry* (Leiden, Netherlands: Martinus Nijhoff Publishers, 2005); and Thomas Musgrave, *Self-Determination and National Minorities* (Oxford: Oxford University Press, 2000).
3. Studies attentive to the relationship between globalization and human rights include: Robert J. Beck and Thomas Ambrosio, eds., *International Law and the Rise of Nations: The State System and the Challenge for Human Rights* (New York: Chatham House Publishers, 2002); Jean-Marc Coicaud, Michael W. Doyle and Anne-Marie Gardner, eds., *The Globalization of Human Rights: The United Nations System in the Twenty-first Century* (Tokyo: United Nations University Press, 2003); Richard Falk, *Human Rights Horizons:*

The Pursuit of Justice in a Globalizing World (New York: Routledge, 2000); and Gene
Martin Lyons and James Mayall, eds., *International Human Rights in the 21st Century:
Protecting the Rights of Groups* (Lanham, Md.: Rowman & Littlefield, 2003).

4. For a highly influential account of the construction of the culturally unitary nation-state,
see Benedict Anderson, *Imagined Communities: Reflections on the Origin and Spread of
Nationalism* (London: Verso, 1991).

5. For a rich critique of the flattening and homogenizing agenda of the state, see Stanley
Diamond, *In Search of the Primitive: A Critique of Civilization* (New Brunswick, NJ:
Transaction Books, 1981).

6. See Manfred F. Boemeke, Gerald Feldman and Elizabeth Gläser, eds., *The Treaty of Versailles:
a Reassessment after 75 Years* (New York: Cambridge University Press, 1998); Carole Fink,
*Defending the Rights of Others: The Great Powers, the Jews, and International Minority
Protection 1878–1938* (Cambridge: Cambridge University Press, 2004); and Mark Mazower,
'Minorities and the League of Nations in Interwar Europe,' *Daedalus* 126 (1997): 47–63.

7. Richard B. Bilder, 'Can Minorities Treaties Work?', *Israel Yearbook on Human Rights*, 20,
no. 71 (1990): 9.

8. For the view that human rights are rightfully individual and universal, see Jack Donnelly,
Universal Human Rights in Theory and Practice (Ithaca, NY: Cornell University Press,
1989). For works that highlight the tension between universality and culture, see Abdul-
lahi Ahmed An-Na'im and Francis Deng, eds., *Human Rights in Africa: Cross-Cultural
Perspectives* (Washington, DC: Brookings Institution Press, 1990); Joanne R. Bauer and
Daniel A. Bell, eds., *The East Asian Challenge for Human Rights* (Cambridge: Cambridge
University Press, 1999); and Charles Taylor and Amy Gutman, eds., *Multiculturalism:
Examining the Politics of Recognition* (Princeton, NJ: Princeton University Press, 1994).

9. Buergenthal, *Nutshell*, 28.

10. See, however, the International Court of Justice's 'Western Sahara' advisory opinion of 16
October 1975 for intriguing comments on what constitutes a people for purposes of self-
determination. *ICJ Reports 1975*.

11. The author has proposed the establishment of a mechanism to oversee, as needed, the
resolution of indigenous-state conflicts or disputes. See Maivân Clech Lâm, *At the Edge of
the State: Indigenous Peoples and Self-Determination* (Ardsley, NY: Transnational Publishers, 2000), 196–201.

12. Minority Rights Group International, ed., *World Directory of Minorities* (London: Minority
Rights Group International, 1997).

13. The academic literature on the postwar development of minority rights, at international as
well as regional levels, precedes by some two decades that on indigenous peoples' rights. See
Yoram Dinstein and Mala Tabory, eds., *The Protection of Minorities and Human Rights*
(London: Martinus Nijhoff, 1992); Will Kymlicka, ed., *The Rights of Minority Cultures*
(Oxford: Oxford University Press, 1995); John Packer and Kristian Myntti, *Protection of
Ethnic And Linguistic Minorities in Europe* (Turko/Åbo, Finland: Institute for Human
Rights, Åbo Akademi University, 1993); Gaetano Pentassuglia, *Minorities in International
Law: An Introductory Study* (Strasbourg: Council of Europe, 2002); Nalini Rajan, *Democracy
and the Limits of Minority Rights* (New York: Russell Sage Foundation, 2000); Patrick
Thornberry, *International Law and the Rights of Minorities* (Oxford: Clarendon Press, 1991).

14. In spring 2006, for example, the CERD committee formally expressed its concerns and
recommendations to the United States regarding: the latter's assertion 'that Western
Shoshone peoples' legal rights to ancestral lands have been extinguished through gradual
encroachment'; government initiatives to privatize and transfer such lands to mining and
energy concerns; reported plans to resume underground nuclear testing in said lands;

prohibition of tribal activities therein; failure to consult with the Western Shoshone; and the latter's lack of meaningful access to domestic courts. See Committee for the Elimination of Racial Discrimination, *Early Warning and Urgent Action Procedure Decision 1 (68)— United States of America* (Sixty-eighth session, Geneva, 20 February–10 March 2006).

15. The international indigenous movement together with its claim to rights has received considerable academic attention of late. See Pekka Aikio and Martin Scheinin, eds., *Operationalizing the Right of Indigenous Peoples to Self-Determination* (Turku/Åbo, Finland: Åbo Akademi University, Institute for Human Rights, 2000); S. James Anaya, *Indigenous Peoples and International Law*, 2nd edn. (New York: Oxford University Press, 2004); Cynthia Price Cohen, ed., *Human Rights of Indigenous Peoples* (Ardsley, NY: Transnational Publishers, 1998); Bartholomew Dean and Jerome M. Levi, eds., *At the Risk of Being Heard: Identity, Indigenous Rights, and Postcolonial States* (Ann Arbor: University of Michigan Press, 2003); Svein Jentoft, Henry Minde, and Ragnar Nilsen, eds., *Indigenous Peoples: Resource Management and Global Rights* (Delft, Netherlands: Eburon Academic Publishers, 2003); Lâm, *At the Edge of the State* (n. 11, *supra*); Ronald Niezen, *The Origins of Indigenism: Human Rights and The Politics of Identity* (Berkeley: University of California Press, 2003); Patrick Thornberry, *Indigenous Peoples and Human Rights* (Manchester, UK: Manchester University Press, 2002); and Siegfried Wiessner, 'Rights and Status of Indigenous Peoples: A Global Comparative and International Legal Analysis,' *Harvard Human Rights Journal* 12 (1999): 57–128.

16. See 'Indigenous People and the United Nations System: An overview,' Leaflet no. 1, www.unhchr.ch.

17. José R. Martinez Cobo, *Study of the Problem of Discrimination against Indigenous Peoples: Conclusions and Recommendations*, vol. 5 (New York: United Nations, 1987), articles 386–412 and 578–581.

18. Ibid., articles 19–20.

19. Ibid., article 379.

20. The multicultural challenge to liberal states remains a rich subject of debate in academia and elsewhere. See Kwame Anthony Appiah, *The Ethics of Identity* (Princeton, NJ: Princeton University Press, 2005); Michael Herzfeld, *Cultural Intimacy: Social Poetics in the Nation-State* (New York: Routledge, 1997); Timo Makkonen, *Identity, Difference and Otherness: the Concept of 'People,' 'Indigenous People' and 'Minority' in International Law* (Helsinki: Helsinki University Press, 2000); Stephen May, Tariq Modood, and Judith Squires, eds., *Ethnicity, Nationalism and Minority Rights* (Cambridge: Cambridge University Press, 2004); Oliver Mendelsohn and Upendra Baxi, eds., *The Rights of Subordinated Peoples* (Delhi: Oxford University Press, 1994); Lola Romanucci-Ross and George DeVos, eds., *Ethnic Identity: Creation, Conflict, and Accommodation*, 3rd edn. (Walnut Creek, Calif.: AltaMira Press, 1995); Richard A. Shweder, Martha Minow, and Hazel Rose Markus, eds., *Engaging Cultural Differences: The Multicultural Challenge in Liberal Democracies* (New York: Russell Sage Foundation, 2002).

21. For reflections on how a world driven by both power and human rights norms might appear, see Henry Steiner and Philip Alston, *International Human Rights in Context: Law, Politics, Morals: Texts and Materials*, 2nd edn. (Oxford: Oxford University Press, 2000); and Christian Tomuschat, *Human Rights: Between Idealism and Realism* (New York: Oxford University Press, 2003).

CHAPTER 31

....

HUMAN SECURITY

....

FEN O. HAMPSON
CHRISTOPHER K. PENNY

HUMAN security is now firmly entrenched in the language and policy of international affairs. That it is so is in no small measure due to the existence of the United Nations, which has played a key role in advancing and enforcing new international norms that place the individual—rather than the state—at the core of modern understandings of international security. The UN has helped champion the idea that although human beings may be divided by various differences—notably language, culture, ethnicity, religion, and political beliefs—they also share many fundamental aspirations. These include a desire for physical security, economic opportunities that go beyond mere survival, the right to express and practice their own religion, and fair and equitable treatment, including the right of due process in courts of law. While the UN's primary purpose is the maintenance of international peace and security, the world organization rests on an understanding that a world involving widespread and systematic frustration of these individual aspirations will never truly be at peace.

This chapter explores the UN's role and influence in promoting human security, both through norm development and enforcement. Although there has been considerable debate about the content, meaning, and relevance of human security to international relations, it is readily apparent that the concept is now firmly entrenched in both political and academic circles.[1] This widespread acceptance is in no small part due to the work of the UN and, in particular, key international commissions which have articulated its various definitions.[2] While some aspects of human security predate the world organization's founding, the UN has given meaning and expression to the idea that state sovereignty is limited and that in some circumstances the rights and interests of the individual trump state interests. In doing so, the UN has served to advance, both in theory and in practice, three broad conceptions of human security: basic human rights, providing physical, legal, and political protections for individuals and, at times, groups; rights of individuals and communities during war and other situations of acute, violent conflict (sometimes referred to as 'freedom from fear'); and rights of individuals and communities experiencing severe privation and hardship because of natural disasters, disease, or other factors outside of their control that threaten their basic survival (also known as 'freedom from want').

This chapter provides an overview of the UN's role in developing, promoting, and enforcing norms within each of these three broad understandings of human security. While there is obvious overlap, the three conceptions establish a useful framework within which to detail the various human security achievements of the world organization. Following an overview of historical norm development, the achievements of the UN within each understanding of human security are detailed, illustrating in each case the world organization's fundamental role in furthering security for individuals. While this chapter focuses on the substantial accomplishments of the UN, the final section briefly acknowledges that major challenges remain for the world organization to contribute to the realization of these human security ideals.

HUMAN RIGHTS AND HUMAN SECURITY

The 'rights' and 'rule of law' conception of human security has its origins in liberal democratic theory and the foundations of the modern democratic state. It is a view of security that locates the main threats to human well-being in the denial of fundamental human rights, in particular civil and political rights, including the right of self-determination, and the absence of the rule of law.[3] Over the course of its history, and often dramatically, the UN has furthered international understandings of, and respect for, basic human rights.

Historical Background

The belief that respect for human rights is linked to international peace and security can be traced back at least as far as the Peace of Westphalia in 1648. The resulting treaty arrangements not only ended the religious wars of Europe and established the principle of state sovereignty, but also sought to guarantee for some religious minorities the right to practice their own religions. Parties to these treaties agreed to respect minority religious rights in exchange for territorial control (or sovereignty), with the understanding that breach of these protections might provide a legitimate basis for intervention by other states.[4]

In the American and French revolutions of the eighteenth century, the 'rights of man' were given political and legal effect, albeit for a limited cross-section of state inhabitants. Although there was no immediate universal acknowledgment of these rights, this established a significant precedent for the future evolution of the modern international human rights regime. While universal conceptions of human rights would have to wait until after World War II, in the late nineteenth and early twentieth centuries international recognition of minority rights grew, expanding upon this precedent and even resulting in sporadic cross-border norm enforcement.[5]

With the end of World War I, minority rights were equated with the concept of self-determination through American President Woodrow Wilson's 'Fourteen Points,' outlined in his address to the US Congress on 8 January 1918.[6] Although Wilson tried to secure formal protection of minority rights in the Covenant of the League of Nations, this approach was rejected in favor of a series of individual, minority treaties that legally obligated a number of countries in Central and Eastern Europe and the Balkans, though pointedly not the colonial powers, to respect the collective rights of minorities living within their borders. The mechanisms of protection included the right of minorities to petition the League if they felt their rights under the treaties were being violated, the establishment of special Minorities Committees in the League to oversee these disputes, and jurisdiction of the Permanent Court of International Justice on issues pertaining to the interpretation or application of the treaties. The League of Nations was to ensure compliance with these treaties, but its record of protection after an auspicious start in the 1920s worsened in the 1930s as those countries that were bound by the treaties rejected the double standard that forced a distinction between them and the colonial powers.

The Versailles conference in 1919 also saw an attempt to secure rights to religious freedom and racial equality in the League's Covenant. However, Wilson himself strongly opposed any mention of race in this treaty, such that the proposal to include these additional rights was withdrawn. There was a second attempt in the 1930s, led by France and Poland, to develop an international agreement on human rights, but this too came to naught because of international opposition as well as fear of antagonizing Nazi Germany. Prior to World War II, principles of human rights had begun to evolve, including recognition of the need for internal minority protections, yet the international legal and political order remained focused on the principle of state sovereignty.

UN Experience

The experience with fascism in the 1930s, coupled with Nazi and Japanese atrocities during World War II, underscored the need to pay much greater attention to human rights, challenging historical notions upholding the primacy of state sovereignty. This recognition directly influenced the negotiations to establish the UN and its structure, and it continues to shape the world organization's role in international affairs.

Although the Charter does not define the content of human rights, it suggests a link to international peace and security. This relationship is found in various places.

The Preamble 'reaffirm[s] faith in fundamental human rights, in the dignity and worth of the person, in the equal rights of men and women and of nations large and small,' and Article 1 (2) expressly provides that one of the main purposes is '[t]o develop friendly relations among nations based on respect for the principle of equal rights and self-determination of peoples.' Article 1 (3) establishes a further goal to encourage 'respect for human rights and for fundamental freedoms for all without distinction as to race, sex, language, or religion.' Building upon these basic principles, Articles 55 and 56 commit all member states to promote the 'conditions of stability and well-being which are necessary for peaceful and friendly relations among nations based on respect for the principle of equal rights and self-determin-ation of peoples' and to further 'universal respect for, and observance of, human rights and fundamental freedoms for all without distinction as to race, sex, language, or religion.'

Although stated broadly, the direct recognition of these principles within the Charter constituted a dramatic evolution from the prewar League of Nations. So too did the establishment of the Economic and Social Council (ECOSOC) as one of the new world organization's primary organs. In addition, the qualified recognition of state sovereignty found in Article 2 (7) provided expressly for limitations on its exercise in any case characterized by the Security Council as a 'threat to the peace, breach of the peace or act of aggression.' Given the implicit link between human rights and international peace in Article 1, this provision would come to play an important role in UN activity supporting basic human rights inside sovereign states.

Efforts to codify and specify the content of human rights within the world organization began in earnest with the General Assembly's adoption of the Universal Declaration of Human Rights in 1948. The Universal Declaration proclaimed some thirty human rights principles, falling within the following broad themes: personal rights; legal, or procedural, rights; civil liberties; subsistence rights; economic rights; and political rights.[7] While not itself establishing binding international legal obliga-tions, many of the rights enunciated in the Universal Declaration have since crystal-lized as principles of customary international law binding all states.[8]

In addition, many principles have found formal expression in subsequent legally binding treaty regimes. The UN played a crucial role establishing many of these regimes, both directly and indirectly, although the resulting obligations are generally of a state-to-state nature. Indeed, the UN continues to play a direct and significant role in norm enunciation through the drafting work of various entities, including in particular the Sixth Committee of the General Assembly. Indirectly, the world organization provides a necessary and unique forum for interstate negotiations, and the Secretariat and many other subsidiary bodies and specialized agencies remain powerful and independent advocates for human rights and human security, propelling and supporting state participation in such negotiations.

Since its establishment, the UN has played a role in the adoption of numerous multilateral human rights treaty regimes providing additional content and meaning to the rights enunciated in the Universal Declaration. In particular, two treaties were drafted within the United Nations system with the express intention of giving these rights binding legal effect: the International Covenant on Civil and Political Rights (opened for signature, 1966; in force, 1976) and the International Covenant on Economic, Social and Cultural Rights (1966; 1976). UN involvement in the codification of other more specific legal obligations has also resulted in: the Convention on the Prevention and Punishment of the Crime of Genocide (1948; 1951); the Convention relating to the Status of Refugees (1951; 1954); the International Convention on the Elimination of All Forms of Racial Discrimination (1965; 1969); the Convention on the Elimination of All Forms of Discrimination against Women (1979; 1981); the Convention against Torture and Other Cruel, Inhuman, or Degrading Treatment and Punishment (1984; 1987); and the Convention on the Rights of the Child (1989; 1990).[9] Many of the resulting treaty regimes have enshrined a further formal role for the UN in ensuring state compliance, often through the receipt of state reports or complaints by specialized subsidiary committees, and sometimes through receipt of individual complaints. These oversight bodies encourage state transparency and compliance, though generally without the exercise of direct enforcement authority.

When addressing recalcitrant states, the UN has tended to rely on three specific kinds of instruments to promote human rights/rule of law conceptions of human security. Setting aside the authorization of military force, which is discussed below, the two major instruments used by the UN for enforcing domestic protection of human rights are 'shaming' and sanctions, both of which are aimed at altering the political calculations of governments so as to deepen and entrench human rights norms and principles in national legislation, policy, and practice.

Shaming works on public opinion by focusing international attention on policies and practices within states that are detrimental to human rights and at variance with established international norms, principles, and rules. This process can be instigated through the close monitoring of human rights by international oversight bodies, many within the UN system, either with their dissemination of resulting information or through the publicity given to individuals and groups whose rights have been violated or denied. A well-mounted international campaign may, over a period of time, tip the domestic balance of power in favor of greater protection of human rights, or force governments fearful of the impact of continuing negative publicity on their international political reputations to change their domestic human rights policies and practices. Such pressure can also be generated by mobilized constituencies and groups within states, such as business associations or NGOs.

Historically, the Commission on Human Rights had the power to investigate complaints involving alleged gross and systematic human rights abuses, but, in practice, its various subordinate bodies, in particular the Sub-Commission on the Promotion and Protection of Human Rights, were more active and effective.[10] Commission and subcommission reports provided a solid basis for international 'shaming' of human rights violators, whether by the United Nations itself or other international actors.[11] Similarly, since 1993, the UN High Commissioner for Human Rights has played an active role not only advocating state compliance with human rights norms but also directing international attention to persistent state violators. Ongoing UN reform efforts have sought to bolster the effectiveness of its human rights oversight, with General Assembly support for, and subsequent establishment of, a Human Rights Council to replace the commission, and increased funding for the High Commissioner's office, as enunciated at the World Summit in September 2005.[12]

Although international organizations are important instruments of shaming, NGOs have had an equal if not greater impact in a wide variety of countries through well-orchestrated and internationally publicized human rights campaigns; however, the UN will almost certainly have played a fundamental role in the enunciation of the human rights norms underlying this shaming process. In addition, the work of the world organization has often helped to establish domestic conditions favorable to the emergence and flourishing of local human rights groups.

In contrast, sanctions seek to promote respect for human rights by denying domestic groups access to foreign goods, services, markets, and capital. When the instrument is effective, domestic elites will change policies in favor of greater protection of human rights. Though a blunt instrument, examples of UN-authorized sanctions regimes with positive human rights effects may include those directed against: Rhodesia (later, Zimbabwe), following a bid by the white-led government of the time to unilaterally declare independence and disenfranchise the local black community (1966–1979); South Africa, during the apartheid era; and Haiti, following the overthrow of President Bertrand Artistide's democratically elected government (1993–1994).[13] Particularly since the end of the Cold War, the Security Council has shown itself willing to address essentially domestic human rights abuses as 'threats to international peace and security' sufficient to warrant the invocation of its Chapter VII authority and override state sovereignty.[14]

The UN is also frequently involved in fostering adherence to human rights norms in post-conflict societies through other mechanisms. Indeed, some of its most important work has related to the administration of human rights in the implementation of internationally negotiated peace agreements. Over the years, human rights teams have been deployed in El Salvador, Cambodia, Haiti, Mozambique, East Timor, and other conflict and post-conflict zones.[15] These teams have reviewed human rights cases and abuses and monitored violations by state security forces and rebel groups. In addition, the United Nations has helped support the establishment of truth commissions in countries like El Salvador, building on local desires for reconciliation and closure.

In recent years, the UN has taken an active interest in international criminal justice, developing and promoting legal institutions to address gross violations of international human rights and humanitarian law, in particular genocide, crimes against humanity and war crimes. Invoking its Chapter VII authority, the Security Council established international criminal tribunals for the former Yugoslavia in 1993 and Rwanda in 1994, expressly linking the need to address gross human rights violations with international peace and security.[16] Individuals tried before these tribunals have included national political and military leaders, some of whom are currently serving lengthy criminal sentences. Building on these precedents, the United Nations actively supported multilateral treaty negotiations resulting in the adoption of the Rome Statute of the International Criminal Court in 1998, which entered into force for its states parties in July 2002, establishing a permanent court with effective jurisdiction over genocide, crimes against humanity, and war crimes. The Rome Statute also expressly recognizes the authority of the Security Council to refer cases relating to nonstates parties to the Court, pursuant to its Chapter VII enforcement authority.

THE HUMANITARIAN DIMENSION OF HUMAN SECURITY

The humanitarian conception of human security has traditionally focused on securing the moral and legal rights of individuals directly affected by war or other situations of violent conflict, and on providing emergency assistance to those in dire need as an indirect result of hostilities. In contrast to our previous discussion, this narrower view of human security is focused on the security needs and rights of individuals in times of armed conflict, recognizing that specialized instruments may be required to protect human security in violent situations.

Historical Background

The idea that the conduct of war should be subjected to moral and legal restraints has a lengthy historical pedigree. Throughout recorded history, armed forces have frequently accepted humanitarian limitations on their wartime conduct.[17] However, the scope and beneficiaries of these limitations often varied dramatically, and in many circumstances unrestricted conflict was considered legitimate. But as conflict evolved, in particular with the rise of mercenary and professional armies, not discriminating between combatants and noncombatants became harder to sustain. As norms of conflict changed toward the end of the nineteenth century, not only was it considered immoral and illegal to deliberately inflict injury and death on innocent civilians and other noncombatants, it also became increasingly accepted that such harm should be expressly avoided, or at least minimized.

Although pre-dated by ad hoc arrangements between combatants in particular conflicts, along with military codes of conduct adopted unilaterally by particular states, formal codification of multilateral legal regimes governing the conduct of hostilities in general began in the mid-nineteenth century, in particular with the adoption of the Geneva Convention for the Amelioration of the Condition of the Wounded in Armies in the Field in 1864. This treaty, and its subsequent iterations in the late nineteenth and early twentiety centuries, which expanded its scope to also include sailors and prisoners of war, sought to mitigate the worst humanitarian effects of conflict for former combatants no longer participating in hostilities due to injury, disease, or capture. Specific, albeit limited, multilateral legal protections for civilians affected by armed conflict emerged in a concurrent process, in particular through conferences held in the Hague in 1899 and 1907 that resulted in codified rules of land warfare.

Norms also emerged to protect combatants themselves, along with civilians, from unnecessary suffering resulting from the conduct of hostilities. Humanitarian concerns for the life and sufferings of human beings exposed to ravages of war led to various prohibitions on producing, stockpiling, and using certain kinds of indiscriminate or unnecessarily injurious weapons, including, for example, early prohibitions on the use of exploding and expanding (or 'dum-dum') bullets in 1868 and 1899. Perhaps most importantly, the first Hague conference adopted a general humanitarian provision, known as the Martens Clause, in the preamble to the 1899 Hague Convention (II) with respect to the laws and customs of war on land, providing that in all cases, in the absence of specific regulations, 'populations and belligerents remain under the protection and empire of the principles of international law, as they result from the usages established between civilized nations, from the laws of humanity and the requirements of the public conscience.'

In addition, the 'safety of peoples' approach to human security also led to the strengthening of international institutional mechanisms providing emergency assistance and humanitarian relief to peoples in armed conflicts. This historical process was exemplified by the establishment of the International Committee of the Red Cross (ICRC) in the nineteenth century, an organization which continues to act as the 'guarantor' of the Geneva Conventions regime.

Building upon these efforts to mitigate the worst effects of war, a growing international consciousness in the early twentieth century sought to limit recourse to interstate violence in the first place. This changing attitude towards war itself resulted in the Hague Peace Conferences, the establishment of the League of Nations, and the Kellogg–Briand Pact in 1928 that sought to outlaw 'aggressive war.' However, none of these developments prevented the outbreak of World War II, or its ultimate descent into a 'total war.'

UN Experience

The term 'United Nations' referred originally to the Allied forces in World War II but was extended with the formal establishment of the United Nations as an international organization in 1945, focusing on maintaining postwar international peace and security. Recognizing the weaknesses of prewar norms and institutions, Charter Article 2 (3) established an obligation for the peaceful settlement of disputes, bolstered by Article 2 (4) and its general prohibition on the use of force, which is now accepted as a principle of customary international law binding all states.[18] The only express exceptions to this prohibition established in the Charter are self-defense and enforcement action authorized by the Security Council under Chapter VII.

Throughout its history, the UN has been actively engaged in conflict prevention and the enforcement of this basic prohibition, and its Charter spells out numerous mechanisms for the peaceful settlement of disputes, from negotiation and mediation through to the binding, albeit limited, dispute settlement authority of the International Court of Justice. Further, the 'good offices' of the Secretary-General have been used frequently to forestall the outbreak of conflict, or limit its spread, as has the enforcement authority of the Security Council.

The establishment of peacekeeping was one of the most important human security innovations in the history of the United Nations, permitting it to assist former warring parties to monitor and strengthen peace agreements, preventing the reemergence of violent conflict and, at times, offering direct protection for noncombatants. While innovative, peacekeeping is now accepted as falling squarely within the authority of the world organization.[19] Premised on the importance of reestablishing peace following the outbreak of violent conflict, and resting on three traditional pillars of consent, impartiality and the limited use of force, the institution of peacekeeping is perhaps the most visible and recognizable UN human security activity. Peacekeeping has continued to evolve, particularly since the end of the Cold War, with the emergence of violent internal ethnic conflicts and the corresponding need for and authorization of more robust UN responses to protect vulnerable civilian populations.[20]

In addition to consent-based peacekeeping operations, the Security Council has also authorized more forceful measures to respond directly to clear violations of Article 2 (4). Increasingly, and particularly since the end of the Cold War, the Security Council has also applied its enforcement authority to override the exercise of state sovereignty and impose remedial measures to respond to, and mitigate the humanitarian effects of, intrastate conflict and other internal violence.

Despite its increasing interventionism, responding to violent humanitarian catastrophes occurring in the territory of sovereign states continues to pose an ongoing challenge to the UN. Some instances have led to Security Council authorizations of force, but many have not. In particular, the world organization continues to grapple with the ramifications of international inaction in the face of the 1994 Rwandan genocide. In other circumstances, incremental but non-forceful responses by the UN have resulted in more robust 'unilateral' military intervention undertaken by states or regional organizations without prior express Security Council authorization. In some of these cases the UN has played an important post-intervention legitimating role, for example by the *ex post facto* authorization of intervention, as occurred in relation to interventions by the Military Observer Group of the Economic Community of West African States (ECOMOG) in Liberia and Sierra Leone in the 1990s.

Military intervention by the North Atlantic Treaty Organization (NATO) in the former Yugoslavia in 1999 propelled an international and organizational reassessment of the issue of humanitarian intervention. Despite its 1998 characterization of the crisis in Kosovo as an 'impending humanitarian catastrophe,' the UN had not expressly authorized the use of remedial military force. Nonetheless, following a Yugoslavian refusal to accept an internationally imposed peace settlement, NATO launched a 78-day bombing campaign that forced Yugoslav military and paramilitary forces out of Kosovo. Despite the absence of express UN authorization, NATO states argued that the Security Council had implicitly supported their military action through its characterization of the situation as an impending catastrophe. Ambiguities highlighted by NATO's intervention led Secretary-General Kofi Annan to call on states to redefine and clarify the framework for responding to internal humanitarian crises using military force, a quintessential human security task.

As a result, the Canadian government established the International Commission on Intervention and State Sovereignty (ICISS) in 2000 with an announcement in the General Assembly. Its 2001 report, entitled *The Responsibility to Protect*,[21] reiterates that individuals must be protected from mass killing, even when it occurs within the territory of a single sovereign state, redefining the concept of humanitarian intervention to focus more directly on the rights of threatened individuals, rather than those of intervening states. It emphasizes prevention but notes that some egregious domestic situations—defined as 'large-scale loss of life, actual or apprehended' or 'ethnic cleansing'—may require international military responses. In such cases, it recognizes the preeminent role that the Security Council can and should take in authorizing remedial action (right authority) and offers a principled framework for this human security task—right intention, last resort, proportional means, and reasonable prospects. Humanitarian conceptions of human security have been strengthened with the adoption by the 2005 World Summit of many of the principles outlined in *The Responsibility to Protect* seeking to ensure the responsible exercise of Security Council authority in the face of internal atrocities.[22]

In spite of robust norms restricting the use of force, international and intrastate violence has continued and will continue. As a result, much of the UN's important humanitarian work has concerned the protection of victims of armed conflict, while working towards the ultimate but longer-term goal of eliminating conflict altogether.

The first intergovernmental mechanism to help victims of war established under the UN banner was the United Nations Relief and Rehabilitation Administration, founded in 1943 to give aid to countries that were ravaged by war, and continuing until 1947. Other longer-lived UN organizations have also been created to address these humanitarian concerns. For example, the Office of the High Commissioner for Refugees (UNHCR) began formal operations in 1951 and has protected and assisted victims of armed conflict ever since, working alongside NGOs. Under the 1951 Convention relating to the Status of Refugees, its states parties are obligated to protect refugees and to cooperate with the UNHCR. Other main UN agencies involved in helping the victims of armed conflict include the United Nations Relief and Works Agency (UNRWA), the UN Children's Fund (UNICEF), the World Food Programme (WFP), and the UN Development Programme (UNDP), although these agencies clearly have a much wider mandate than the provision of emergency assistance and humanitarian relief alone.[23]

In the late 1980s and 1990s, there was growing awareness that these humanitarian approaches to human security were inadequate, and that something more forceful was called for. Critics argued that human security requires more than 'good works' in armed conflicts, noting that 'in the post-Cold War intra-societal conflicts that mark a number of societies, NGO interventions—even when they are effective in humanitarian, development, or human terms—very often exacerbate the local tensions and suspicions that underlie the violence of the societies they seek to help.'[24] Within the UN itself there was a growing sense that a more strategic approach was needed to prevent those conflicts which had just ended (usually as the result of a negotiated peace settlement) from reigniting after the withdrawal of peacekeeping forces and the end of humanitarian relief. Many senior officials and academics argued for a broader conceptual approach as well as the creation of new strategies and tools to promote human security.[25]

The UN has been instrumental in redefining appropriate longer-term international responses to interstate and internal conflict. In the 1990s, peacebuilding and conflict prevention came to be viewed as vital new instruments of human security, particularly in those settings where a fragile peace accord had been negotiated but the peace process had not yet been consolidated. In his *Agenda for Peace*, Secretary-General Boutros Boutros-Ghali defined peacebuilding as a broad set of activities that 'tend to consolidate peace and advance a sense of confidence and well-being among people.' He also argued that beyond peacekeeping the list of peacebuilding activities should include a broad range of activities and suggested that the 'United Nations has an obligation to develop and provide...support for the transformation of deficient national structures and capabilities, and for strengthening democratic institutions.'[26] A major recognition of the importance of these tasks was the General Assembly's establishment of a Peacebuilding Commission following the 2005 World Summit.[27]

What distinguishes peacebuilding from more conventional peacekeeping and humanitarian assistance is its focus on causes of conflict and the use of a wide range of multifunctional instruments to consolidate and entrench peace processes. Peacebuilding therefore tries to transform the social and political context of conflict so that human beings can live in a stable and secure social, political, and economic environment. It recognizes that unless the peace process addresses the underlying causes of violence, human security will be threatened—a direct expression of the link between human rights and peace and security, as implied in the Charter.

The UN thus has helped redefine modern understandings of the causes of conflict, a major development in furthering humanitarian conceptions of human security. Through the peacebuilding frame of reference, ethnic and intercommunal conflict are seen less in terms of strategic security dilemmas and more in terms of causal relationships in which the key variables are poverty, socioeconomic inequalities, and the denial of human rights, due process of law, and liberal pluralist forms of democracy. Horizontal inequalities resulting from deliberate strategies by elites to hoard resources are also recognized as contributing to a culture of social and political intolerance among different groups in society. Secretary-General Kofi Annan summarized, 'countries that are afflicted by war typically also suffer from inequality among domestic social groups. And it is this, rather than poverty, that seems to be the critical factor. The inequality may be based on ethnicity, religion, national identity or economic class, but it tends to be reflected in unequal access to power that too often forecloses paths to peaceful change.'[28] Although establishing a respect for human rights and legal due process are critical elements of the peacebuilding enterprise, these activities have to be complemented by a wide range of military, nonmilitary, economic, social and political measures, which can help people in war-torn societies rehabilitate themselves. While offering increased humanitarian protection, these UN efforts to redefine understandings of the causes of conflict also clearly apply to and strengthen human rights and 'freedom from want' conceptions of human security, illustrating the interrelated and mutually-reinforcing nature of these concepts.

The UN has also contributed to the development of specific legal norms limiting the impact of armed conflict on noncombatants. Thus, many of the treaty regimes identified in the preceding human rights section have obvious relevance and direct application to limiting the humanitarian impact of hostilities, including, for example, the 1948 Genocide Convention. And although, building on existing historical processes, many specific international humanitarian law protections have also continued their development outside of the formal UN system, nonetheless, the UN has had a significant impact on the implementation and evolution of this body of law as well. For example, the Security Council has frequently called upon states to comply with these legal obligations and established international tribunals as discussed above, thereby helping to strengthen the substantive content and observance of international humanitarian law protecting victims of armed conflict and governing the conduct of hostilities. This process will no doubt continue within the ICC.

In addition, the world organization has had a direct role in the legal and practical regulation of weapons production, proliferation, and use, through its various disarmament forums, including, for example, the Conference on Disarmament, the Department for Disarmament Affairs, and the nonproliferation work of specialized and related agencies such as the International Atomic Energy Agency (IAEA). Over the years multilateral conventions prohibiting the production, stockpiling, and use of chemical and biological weapons have been negotiated with the UN's logistical and technical assistance, as have a number of treaties dealing with the testing, development, production, and use of nuclear weapons. UN organizations have been actively involved in facilitating and ensuring state compliance with these regimes, through mechanisms including, in some circumstances, highly intrusive weapons inspections, such as those imposed upon Iraq by the Security Council in the 1990s. In addition, the United Nations has played an active role responding to, and in some cases leading, a continuing and growing interest in controlling the production, sale, and use of conventional weapons that have the capacity to harm or maim civilians, or cause unnecessary suffering to combatants. UN support for conventional weapons negotiations, for example its ongoing efforts to broaden the scope of the Convention on Certain Conventional Weapons, has helped to limit the humanitarian impact of these weapons. Recent UN endorsement of negotiations towards a comprehensive Arms Trade Treaty exemplifies this ongoing normative role. More directly, arms embargoes restricting the spread of conventional weapons to war zones have frequently been imposed by the Security Council.[29]

'Freedom from Want' and Human Security

The third variant of the human security template focuses on nonmilitary threats that originate from a wide variety of problems such as unchecked global population growth, migration, disparities in economic opportunities, in particular the widening income gap between the world's rich and poor, ecological destruction, and the rise of pandemic and infectious diseases such as HIV/AIDS and SARS. Although often the result of human activity, the threats addressed in this conception of human security typically fall outside of the control of individuals. As a result, this broad view stresses the distributive aspects of development and identifies the principal cause of human security threats in socioeconomic inequalities and lack of social justice.

Historical Background

Unlike the first two conceptions of human security, 'freedom from want' has a much less developed history, and most international principles have evolved primarily within the UN system itself. Indeed, a major failing of the League of Nations was the absence of effective authority in this field. Historically, measures addressing 'freedom from want' typically developed and were implemented at the national level, if at all, though some multinational measures to address these issues existed in discrete subject areas, for example with respect to health and labor issues.

UN Experience

The UN has enunciated and given content to broad-based conceptions of human security premised on freedom from want. This evolution has occurred both through the work of primary organs, in particular ECOSOC, the General Assembly, and the Secretariat, as well as through its numerous and diverse specialized and related organizations.

Although since 1990 the UNDP's annual *Human Development Report* has provided the most coherent articulation of this enlarged concept of security, its origins date back to the early years of the world organization. The Universal Declaration of Human Rights enunciated not only civil and political rights, but also economic, social, and cultural principles. These later found more concrete expression, notably in the International Covenant on Economic, Social and Cultural Rights, which further specified the link between 'fear and want' initiated with the Universal Declaration. With these documents, economic development came to be seen as a right, and crucially, a right of the person, albeit defined in broad and general terms. 'Security of the person' came to include 'social security,' as explicitly provided in Article 9 of the Covenant. Security or its absence became part of the development agenda.

A further broadening of the concept of security occurred at the beginning of the 1970s, when the FAO began to use the term 'food security,' by which it meant access by all people at all times to the food needed for a healthy and active life. Similarly, a broad conception of security was adopted by the Independent Commission on International Development Issues, chaired by former West German Chancellor Willy Brandt, whose 1980 report argued that '[o]ur survival depends not only on military balance, but on global cooperation to ensure a sustainable biological environment, and sustainable prosperity based on equitably shared resources.' The Brandt Commission explicitly identified poor countries as one of the keys to international security, arguing that '[m]uch of the security in the world is connected with the divisions between rich and poor countries—grave injustice and mass starvation causing additional instability.'[30]

Academic and policy reflections on the implications of environmental degradation have also helped move the security agenda away from solely territorial-based definitions of security, in particular nuclear weapons and deterrence. Increased risks of conflict were associated with environmental degradation, both with the exhaustion of nonrenewable resources (e.g., oil) and with the destruction of renewable ones (e.g., water). One of the catalysts in the growing debate about the role of the environment in human conflict was the World Commission on the Environment and Development, chaired by former Norwegian Prime Minister Gro Harlem Brundtland, whose 1987 report coined the expression 'sustainable development,' which placed sustainability, primarily if not exclusively environmental, at the core of the agenda. Conflict was seen as a key factor in that sustainability, and the report devoted a whole chapter to the linkages between peace, security, development, and the environment, arguing that 'environmental stress is both a cause and an effect of political tension and military conflict.'[31]

The 1992 UN Conference on the Environment and Development recognized these changes and defined the sustainable development agenda for the twenty-first century. This huge gathering in Rio de Janiero ushered in a new age of international politics, with the largest ever participation by NGOs and the civil society they claimed to represent.[32] The successful assertion of legitimacy distinct from and sometimes superior to that of governments is a lasting legacy of this process, at least as much as its resulting plan of action, dubbed Agenda 21.

During the 1980s and into the 1990s, there were calls both from within and from outside the United Nations to widen the security agenda to include more issues, to detach it from a narrow, state-centered outlook, to break the link between security and conflict, and to expand the number and types of players legitimately given voice in security debates. These varied calls for a redefinition of the very meaning of security, however, failed initially to develop a new, shared definition of this term.

This logical next step would occur with the emergence of the concept of human security, arising in large part from the UNDP's *Human Development Report 1994*, which put the argument baldly: 'The world can never be at peace unless people have security in their daily lives.' With this report, the concept of security was framed in terms of ordinary people and their day-to-day security concerns:

For most people, a feeling of insecurity arises more from worries about their daily life than from the dread of a cataclysmic world event. Will they and their families have enough to eat? Will they lose their jobs? Will their streets and neighbourhoods be safe from crime? Will they be tortured by a repressive state? Will they become the victim of violence because of their gender? Will their religion or ethnic origin target them for persecution?[33]

While this conception of security clearly includes issues falling within the two more-limited notions of human security discussed earlier, it also encompassed two basic conceptual shifts: away from territorial security to a much greater stress on people's security, and from armaments to sustainable development. The report suggested a clear link between human security and a strategy of sustainable human development, arguing that '[i]t will not be possible for the community of nations to achieve any of its major goals—not peace, environmental protection, not human rights, not democratization, not fertility reduction, not social integration—except in the context of sustainable development that leads to human security.'[34] Thus, human security is viewed as the result, not the cause, of a successful development process that is attentive to equity and social justice considerations. Although more broadly stated, this conception also builds on the implicit linkage between human rights and international security found in the Charter. But the scope of the new concept could hardly be wider, and includes economic, food, health, environmental, personal, community, and political security. Moreover, the threats to these different aspects of human security, such as HIV/AIDS, terrorism, pollution, poverty, and environmental problems, are global in scope and transcend national borders.

The policy implications exceeded UNDP's reach and were explicitly framed as the agenda for the World Summit on Social Development in Copenhagen in 1995. The summit, however, refrained from endorsing the entire human security agenda, reaching a consensus on the issue of investment of the so-called 'peace dividend.'[35] The radical marginalization of military issues was challenged by a growing sense that global chaos and disorder were the real legacies of the Cold War. While recognizing the need for, and importance of, broader conceptions of human security, the Commission on Global Governance gave military issues a renewed emphasis in its diagnosis of the security situation while offering an additional perspective relating to global threats: 'The most pressing security challenge of the twenty-first century [is] preserving and extending the progress made in securing states against the threat of war while finding ways to safeguard people against domestic threats of brutalization and gross deprivation and ensuring the integrity and viability of the life-support systems on which all life depends.'[36]

The notion of human security was explicitly broadened again by the Human Security Commission, whose co-chairs covered the narrower and broader perspectives: former UN High Commissioner for Refugees Sadako Ogata and Nobel laureate Amartya Sen. The 2003 report carries a provocative title—*Human Security Now: Protecting and Empowering People*—but is in many ways indistinguishable from UNDP's 1994 report. Nonetheless, much of *Human Security Now* seeks to bridge the conflict and socioeconomic dimensions of human security, including privations in the realms of poverty, health and education. It also argues that much greater attention has to be paid to the most vulnerable and adversely affected groups in society—women, children, the elderly, the disabled, and the indigenous—with an emphasis on protection and empowerment strategies that are informed by an appreciation of human rights and the need for social and economic development, especially in the areas of health and education.

The broader human security norms relating to 'freedom from want' continue to find practical expression in ongoing work of the United Nations—for example, they provided a strong philosophical foundation for the MDGs and find policy relevance in the capacity-building and monitoring functions of UNEP. Increasingly, the Security Council is showing itself willing to consider non-traditional security challenges, such as HIV/AIDS, as falling within its Chapter VII enforcement authority. Indeed, the UN as a truly universal organization is in a unique position to respond to the global nature of these human security challenges.

CONCLUSION

The UN has played an instrumental role in norm development relating to all three broad conceptions of human security, at times building on existing but inadequate historical precedents. The world organization also has facilitated state compliance with these norms, through a wide variety of mechanisms including the provision of capacity-building assistance, negotiating forums, 'good offices,' and the provision of neutral information sources and monitoring bodies to verify compliance. The Security Council has also on occasion enforced compliance with human security norms through economic sanctions and military force.

Despite these successes, significant gaps remain between the promise of each of these various conceptions of human security and their actual realization. While global acceptance of international human rights norms has increased dramatically in the past half century, many states continue to face implementation challenges, while some continue to actively oppose extension of basic human rights to their citizens. Similarly, even with substantial, and often successful, UN efforts to limit the use of violence by states and rebel groups, armed conflicts continue to rage across various regions of the world. Further, despite growing recognition of the need to consider broader security threats, 'freedom from want' remains an elusive and long-term human security goal.

The United Nations evolved in response to massive and tangible human security challenges, and it must continue to do so, building upon its success by fostering the further development and internalization of norms, and facilitating and enforcing state compliance. Without greater state support for this endeavor, the world organization is faced with a daunting task. However, even in the face of its limitations, it has played a profound role in promoting and building state compliance with human security norms. Despite its relatively modest resources, the human security successes of the world organization are unparalleled. While substantial challenges remain, individual human security—however defined—has been strengthened beyond recognition through the work of the United Nations over the first six decades of its existence.

NOTES

1. See, e.g., Fen Osler Hampson and Jean Daudelin, *Madness in the Multitude: Human Security and World Disorder* (Don Mills, Ont.: Oxford University Press, 2002); S. Neil MacFarlane and Yuen Foong Khong, eds. *Human Security and the UN: A Critical History* (Bloomington: Indiana University Press, 2006); Robert G. MacRae and Don Hubert, eds., *Human Security and The New Diplomacy: Protecting People, Promoting Peace* (Montreal: McGill-Queens University Press, 2001); Keith Krause, 'Is Human Security More than Just a Good Idea?,' in Brief 30, *Promoting Security: But How, and for Whom? Contributions to BICC's Ten Year Anniversary Conference*, ed. Michael Brzoska and Peter J. Croll (Bonn: Bonn International Center for Conversion, 2004); and Roland Paris, 'Human Security: Paradigm Shift or Hot Air?,' *International Security* 26, no. 2 (2001): 87–102. See also United Nations Office for the Coordination of Humanitarian Affairs, Digital Library of Human Security available under the Humanitarian Issues subheading at http://ochaonline.un.org.

2. The following definitions of 'human security' are presented in *Empowering People at Risk: Human Security Priorities for the 21st Century*, Working Paper for the Helsinki Process, Report of the Track on 'Human Security' (Helsinki: Finnish Ministry for Foreign Affairs, 2005), 11:

   • 'Human security in its broadest sense embraces far more than the absence of violent conflict. It encompasses human rights, good governance, access to education and health care and ensuring that each individual has opportunities and choices to fulfill his or her own potential.' Kofi Annan, United Nations Press Release SG/SM/7382, 8 May 2000, www.un.org/News.

   • 'Human security means the security of people—their physical safety, their economic and social well-being, respect for their dignity and worth as human beings, and the protection of their human rights and fundamental freedoms.' International Commission on Intervention and State Sovereignty, *The Responsibility to Protect*, 2001.

   • 'The Commission on Human Security's definition of human security: to protect the vital core of all human lives in ways that enhance human freedoms and human fulfilment.' Commission on Human Security, *Human Security Now*, 2003.

   • 'Human security means freedom from pervasive threats to people's rights, their safety or even their lives.' Human Security Network, www.humansecuritynetwork.org.

3. See Jack Donnelly, 'International Human Rights: A Regime Analysis,' *International Organization* 40, no. 3 (1986): 599–642; Jack Donnelly, *International Human Rights: Dilemmas in World Politics* (Boulder, Colo.: Westview Press, 1993); and Paul Gordon Lauren, *The Evolution of Human International Rights: Visions Seen* (Philadelphia: University of Pennsylvania Press, 1998).

4. Stephen J. Krasner, *Sovereignty: Organized Hypocrisy* (Princeton, NJ: Princeton University Press, 1999).

5. For example, French forces intervened in Turkey in 1860 to protect the local Christian population in Lebanon from massacre, while Russia also intervened in Bulgaria in the 1870s, for similar reasons.

6. Daniel Patrick Moynihan, *Pandaemonium: Ethnicity in International Politics* (New York: Oxford University Press, 1993), 78.

7. Johannes Morsink, *The Universal Declaration of Human Rights: Origins, Drafting and Intent* (Philadelphia: University of Pennsylvania Press, 1998).

8. See, e.g., Oscar Schachter, *International Law in Theory and Practice* (Boston: Martinus Nijhoff, 1991), 85 ff. See also Charles Norchi, 'Human Rights: A Global Common Interest,' in *The United Nations: Confronting the Challenges of a Global Society*, ed. Jean E. Krasno (Boulder, Colo.: Lynne Rienner, 2004), 79–114, for an overview of the substantial human rights accomplishments of the UN.

9. Philip Alston, ed., *The United Nations and Human Rights: A Critical Appraisal* (New York: Oxford University Press, 1992); Paul Gordon Lauren, *The Evolution of Human International Rights: Visions Seen* (Philadelphia: University of Pennsylvania Press, 1998).

10. The commission only began to deal with human rights violations in the 1960s, focusing almost exclusively on South Africa, Chile, and Israel.

11. Donnelly, 'International Human Rights: A Regime Analysis'; Thomas J. Farer and Felice Gaer, 'The UN and Human Rights: At the End of the Beginning,' in Adam Roberts and Benedict Kingsbury, eds., *United Nations, Divided World*, 2nd edn. (New York: Oxford University Press, 1993).

12. *2005 World Summit Outcome*, UN document A/Res/60/1, 24 October 2005, paras. 124 and 157. While concerns remain regarding the size and composition of the new council, its establishment suggests an increasing UN human rights focus.

13. Margaret P. Doxey, *International Sanctions in Contemporary Perspective*, 2nd edn. (Basingstoke, UK: Macmillan, 1996). Recognizing the potential negative humanitarian implications of sanctions regimes, the UN is engaged in ongoing reform efforts to refine this enforcement method. See, e.g., David Cortright and George A. Lopez, 'Reforming Sanctions,' in David M. Malone, ed., *The UN Security Council: From the Cold War to the 21st Century* (Boulder, Colo.: Lynne Rienner, 2004), 167–179.

14. See, e.g., Joanna Weschler, 'Human Rights,' in ed. Malone, *The UN Security Council: From the Cold War to the 21st Century*, 55–68, for an overview of evolving Security Council approaches to human rights.

15. Neil J. Kritz, ed., *Transitional Justice: How Emerging Democracies Reckon with Former Regimes*, vol. 1 (Washington, DC: United States Institute of Peace, 1995); Fen Osler Hampson, *Nurturing Peace: Why Peace Settlements Succeed or Fail* (Washington, DC: United States Institute of Peace Press, 1996).

16. See, e.g., Security Council resolution 827, 25 May 1993.

17. Leslie C. Green, *The Contemporary Law of Armed Conflict*, 2nd edn. (Manchester, UK: Manchester University Press, 2000), 20–29.

18. See, e.g., *Case concerning the Military and Paramilitary Activities in and against Nicaragua (Nicaragua v. United States of America)*, Judgement of 27 June 1986, ICJ Rep 1986, paras. 188 ff.

19. *Certain Expenses of the United Nations*, Advisory Opinion of 20 July 1962, ICJ Rep 1962.

20. See, e.g., *Report of the Panel on United Nations Peace Operations*, UN document A/55/305–S/2000/809, 21 August 2000.

21. International Commission on Intervention and State Sovereignty, *The Responsibility to Protect* (Ottawa: International Development Research Centre, 2001).

22. *2005 World Summit Outcome*, paras. 138–9. The document does not address the issue of unilateral intervention, focusing instead on ensuring responsible UN reactions.

23. Jonathan Moore, *The UN and Complex Emergencies: Rehabilitation in Third World Transitions* (Geneva: UNRISD, 1996).

24. Mary B. Anderson, 'Humanitarian NGOs in Conflict Intervention,' in *Managing Global Chaos: Sources of and Responses to International Conflict*, ed. Chester A. Crocker, Fen Osler Hampson, and Pamela Aall (Washington, DC: United States Institute of Peace Press, 1996), 347.

25. Boutros Boutros-Ghali, *An Agenda for Peace—Preventive Diplomacy, Peacemaking and Peacekeeping: Report of the Secretary-General* (New York: United Nations Department of Public Information, 1992); Moore, *The UN and Complex Emergencies*; United Nations, *The Copenhagen Declaration and Programme of Action, World Summit for Social Development* (New York: UN, 1995); United Nations (DESIPA), 'An Inventory of Post-Conflict Peace-Building Activities,' UN document ST/ESA/246; UNDP, *Building Bridges Between Relief and Development: A Compendium of the UNDP Record in Crisis Countries* (New York: UNDP, 1997).

26. Boutros-Ghali, *An Agenda for Peace*, 55 and 59.

27. *2005 World Summit Outcome*, para. 97.

28. Kofi A. Annan, *Facing the Humanitarian Challenge: Towards a Culture of Prevention* (New York: UN, 1999).

29. See, e.g., Derek Boothby, 'Disarmament: Successes and Failures,' in *The United Nations: Confronting the Challenges of a Global Society*, ed. Jean E. Krasno (Boulder, Colo.: Lynne Rienner, 2004), 193–223, for a discussion of the UN's achievements and remaining challenges in this field.

30. Independent Commission on International Development Issues, North–South, *A Programme for Survival: Report of the Independent Commission on International Development* (Cambridge, Mass.: MIT Press, 1980), 24.

31. World Commission on Environment and Development, *Our Common Future* (New York: Oxford University Press, 1987), 24 and 290.

32. Peter Timmerman, 'Breathing Room: Negotiations on Climate Change,' in ed. Fen Osler Hampson and Judith V. Reppy, *Earthly Goods: Environmental Change and Social Justice* (Ithaca, NY: Cornell University Press, 1996), 221–243.

33. UNDP, *Human Development Report 1994* (New York: Oxford University Press, 1994), 22.

34. UNDP, *Human Development Report 1994*, 1.

35. Österreichisches Institut für Friedensforschung und Friedenserziehung; United Nations, Department for Development Support and Management Services, Reconstruction Unit, and Austria, Bundesministerium für Auswärtige Angelegenheiten, *International Colloquium on Post-Conflict Reconstruction Strategies* (Stadtschlaining: Austrian Centre for Peace and Conflict Resolution, 1995).

36. Commission on Global Governance, *Our Global Neighbourhood* (Oxford: Oxford University Press, 1995), 80.

PART VII

DEVELOPMENT

COORDINATING ECONOMIC AND SOCIAL AFFAIRS

JACQUES FOMERAND
DENNIS DIJKZEUL

THE UN 'system' is highly fragmented, rife with competition, and certainly not a harmonious cooperative whole in which the parts work towards a common purpose. Not surprisingly, there have been many calls for better coordination within the UN system. The exact meaning and results of such coordination, however, remain vague. In common parlance, 'coordination' means to place or arrange things in proper position relative to each other and to the system of which they are constituent parts. One definition of coordination is found in Secretary-General Boutros Boutros-Ghali's report, *An Agenda for Development*:

Coordination means a clear allocation of responsibilities, an effective division of labour among the many actors involved in development, and a commitment by each of those actors to work towards common and compatible goals and objectives. Individual development actors must strive to make their efforts complementary and contributory, rather than isolated or competing. Coordination, so viewed, must guide the actions of each of these actors and the interactions among them.[1]

Bearing in mind this definition, this chapter explains the UN 'non' system and its elaborate coordination machinery, as well as the many attempts to improve coordination in the economic and social sectors. It shows that the UN does not fully live up to its own definition of coordination. It identifies recurring coordination issues and draws attention to recent developments in the praxis of coordination, which might be viewed as a source of guarded optimism concerning the future prospects for better coordination.

THE UN SYSTEM IN BRIEF

While there is much talk about 'one United Nations' and the need for 'holistic' and 'integrated' approaches to the maintenance of international peace and security, it is useful to recall that the drafters of the Charter understood the links between peace and security and economic and social development. The demise of democracies, rise of totalitarian regimes, and denial of human rights in Europe and the Far East were consequences of the worldwide socioeconomic dislocations of the 1930s. The postwar multilateral regime that the Charter prescribed, therefore, rested on the twin notions that international order would be achieved through policing by the powerful and nurtured by a system of international cooperation and an expanding world economy. In the words of the Charter Article 1, the United Nations should be 'a center for harmonizing the actions of nations in the attainment of... common ends.' One such end was 'to maintain international peace and security,' and another to solve 'international problems of an economic, social, cultural or humanitarian character and to promote and encourage respect for human rights.'

However, the institutional prescriptions that eventually emerged from the 1944 Dumbarton Oaks meetings and the 1945 UN founding conference in San Francisco can hardly be described as 'holistic.' The edifice that the founders constructed was a compromise between democratic ideals and state-based *realpolitik*. The primary purpose of the Security Council was to prevent and deter aggression. Economic and social questions were first and foremost the province of the Bretton Woods institutions and other 'specialized agencies' and, only secondarily so, of the General Assembly and the Economic and Social Council (ECOSOC), which were given the more circumscribed role of standard setters and 'town meetings of the world.'

As the UN's role expanded from policy and analytical work to norm- and standard-setting, to advocacy, and then to technical cooperation activities in support of national development efforts, UN structures carrying out these multifaceted tasks became increasingly more complex. The 'system' now includes the General Assembly (and its Second and Third Committees, which deal with economic and social issues and humanitarian questions respectively).[2] Over the years, the Assembly has established a number of distinct 'funds' and 'programs,' which report to the Assembly and carry out cross-sectoral work in areas like children, refugees, the environment, and humanitarian assistance. The funds and programs have their own budget and governing bodies but their executive heads are appointed by the Secretary-General. These organizations include the UN's Conference on Trade and Development (UNCTAD), Development Programme (UNDP), Environment Programme (UNEP), High Commissioner for Refugees (UNHCR), Relief and Works Agency (UNRWA), Children's Fund (UNICEF), Population Fund (UNFPA), World Food Programme (WFP), International Drug Control Programme (UNDCP), and Human Settlements Programme (Habitat).

Under the authority of the General Assembly, ECOSOC serves as an arena for policy deliberation and coordination on economic, social, and humanitarian issues and the governance of the UN's operational activities in these areas. Eight 'functional commissions' (social development, human rights, narcotic drugs, crime prevention and criminal justice, women, population, statistics, and sustainable development), five regional commissions (Latin America and the Caribbean, Europe, Asia and the Pacific, Africa, and Western Asia), and a number of session-specific and standing committees and expert ad hoc bodies also report to ECOSOC.

The UN development system further comprises a set of organizations based on separate intergovernmental treaties that fulfill a wide variety of functions in such key socioeconomic sectors as health, employment, agriculture, and education. Some actually date back to the nineteenth century or the League of Nations. Those with agreements with ECOSOC also are known as 'specialized agencies.' The fourteen autonomous agencies with their own constitutions, governing bodies, budgets, and secretariats are: the International Labour Organization (ILO), Food and Agriculture Organization (FAO), Educational, Social and Cultural Organization (UNESCO), International Civil Aviation Organization (ICAO), World Health Organization (WHO), Universal Postal Union (UPU), International Telecommunication Union (ITU), World Meteorological Organization (WMO), International Maritime Organization (IMO), World Intellectual Property Organization (WIPO), International Fund for Agricultural Development (IFAD), Industrial Development Organization (UNIDO), World Tourism Organization (UNWTO), and International Atomic Energy Agency (IAEA). The World Bank (formally the International Bank for Reconstruction and Development, or IBRD, and the International Development Association, or IDA) and International Monetary Fund (IMF) are also technically part of the UN system but operate separately. The World Trade Organization (WTO) also operates independently but is not part of the UN system. Together with the UN proper (i.e., its principal organs and funds and programs), the specialized agencies constitute the so-called UN system.

In such a functionally decentralized system, avoiding duplication and redundancies while bringing together organizations into working relationships has become an increasingly important requirement to ensure the viability of the system. Such coordination is achieved only through voluntary arrangements and practices; there is no top-down control or hierarchy. The need for 'harmonization' has become ever more pressing as the 'system' has rapidly expanded and development thinking moved away from the narrow confines of 'economic growth' into the vague contours of 'sustainable development' and 'human security.'

For a minority of observers, the UN's structural complexity is a source of strength as it enables the world organization and its constituent parts, individually or in concert, to respond flexibly and from different perspectives to the evolving international environment and the changing requirements of member states. For the majority of commentators, however, it is a major stumbling block in the way of substantive coordination and a cause of costly overlaps leading to inefficiency and ineffectiveness. This chapter does not settle this raging debate, which started virtually at the outset of the UN era. As a step toward understanding the debate, however, the next section provides a brief history of coordination at the international policy level.

A Brief History of Attempts to Improve UN Coordination

In March 1945, when Latin American countries met with the United States in Mexico City to discuss issues of postwar cooperation, two conceptions of the UN's role in development emerged. Washington did not envisage giving the UN any regulatory or legislative powers in this arena. The governance of the world economy and international cooperation for development properly belonged with the Bretton Woods institutions whose activities were designed to strengthen market-oriented solutions to under-development. Conversely, for Latin American countries, development policies required regulatory national and international mechanisms to tame the vagaries of markets. For them, the world organization stood as the embodiment of a compact among equal and sovereign states. Accordingly, it should have authoritative decision-making powers in the management of the development system and exert oversight functions with regard to the World Bank and IMF. The Latin American countries, however, did not succeed in putting the World Bank and IMF under General Assembly control.

As the UN's membership expanded with the independence of African and Asian states, the organization came under increasing pressure to engage in new activities. On the peace and security side, peacekeeping was invented; but operations in the 1960s, in the Congo and Middle East in particular, already had prompted the Soviet Union and some other member states to refuse paying their UN dues in full. In subsequent years, the UN's financial difficulties increased, as only a handful of member states paid their assessed contributions in full and on time.

Simultaneously, the East–West standoff provided developing countries with the necessary political leverage to create new organizations that would meet their specific requirements for enhanced development activities. Dissatisfied with ECOSOC's response to their demands and objecting to its lack of representation, they bypassed it and relied on the General Assembly. Thus came into existence such organizations as UNDP, UNCTAD, and UNIDO, which assumed functions traditionally considered as falling within ECOSOC's purview. ECOSOC's expansion in 1965 and 1973 hardly improved its status or performance. In fact, these Charter amendments further damaged the body's political credibility, as they compounded visible problems of duplication with the General Assembly. The Assembly's role continued to expand well into the 1980s, while ECOSOC's status steadily declined.[3]

Not surprisingly, concerns about better cooperation, interaction, synergy, coherence, and consistency within the UN system became the fodder for would-be reformers as well as UN-bashers. There is no dearth of reports, blueprints, and concepts by 'commissions' and other eminent persons whose recommendations tend to fall into oblivion but still ring remarkably true.[4] For example, the 1969 Pearson report, *Partners in Development*, prepared by the Commission on International Development addressed the linkages between trade, debt, financing, and technology and proposed that the World Bank hold a conference to discuss the creation of improved machinery for coordination.[5]

A comprehensive review of the UN's operational activities, carried out at the request of UNDP under the direction of Robert Jackson in 1969, bluntly criticized the UN system's incapacity to handle technical assistance resources. *A Study of the Capacity of the United Nations System*, more widely known as the Jackson report, highlighted the absence of an effective system for the control of the resources entrusted to the UN, the diffusion of responsibility throughout the system, and the general reluctance of the specialized agencies to cohere. Warning that the UN development system was 'becoming slower and more unwieldy, like some prehistoric monster,' Jackson called for a complete restructuring of UN development operations with a central financial and coordinating role for UNDP backed up by organizational, managerial, and administrative changes.[6] UNDP implemented some of the suggestions, but other UN institutions and member states ignored most of the recommendations pertaining to system-wide reform. UNDP never succeeded in obtaining a central funding role; indeed, agencies pursued separate fund-raising strategies for voluntary funds from donors.

In 1975, another report emerged from the Group of Experts on the Structure of the United Nations System bemoaning the decentralization of the system and calling for the creation of a centralized UN Development Authority.[7] In the same year, the Secretary-General also established the Negotiating Committee on the Financial Emergency of the UN. One year later, the committee reported that 'no common approach could be found. The socialist and Western countries became concerned at the rapid growth of the UN budget. These countries ... view restraint or a cut in expenditure as a requirement for financial viability. The developing countries held a different view—they looked to a strong and growing UN to support their demands' to establish a New International Economic Order.[8]

In 1979, the Independent Commission on International Development Issues under the chairmanship of German chancellor Willy Brandt also voiced concerns on the fragmentation of UN development bodies.[9] After his inauguration, Secretary-General Javier Pérez de Cuéllar initiated several administrative changes, which centered on programming and budgeting, as well as monitoring these processes. Within the Secretariat, he established 'the Program Planning and Budgeting Board, an internal senior-level board to review and approve program budget issues, and the Central

Monitoring Unit to monitor program performance.'[10] In the following decade, Secretariat reform remained high on the agenda, often because member states could only agree to debate these issues. They frequently clashed on financial contributions and different ideas for development.

In 1992, newly elected Secretary-General Boutros Boutros-Ghali merged the office of the Director-General for Development and International Economic Cooperation, which was supposed to play an important coordinating role, 'into the Department of Social and Economic Development, which was dissolved ten months later. Subsequently, the Department for Policy Coordination and Sustainable Development (DPCSD) was established as the main source of support to the Secretary-General for the provision of overall coordination of the UN System in the economic and social fields and for the provision of policy guidance to operational programs and field offices.' In 1994, he entrusted the UNDP administrator with the responsibility to improve the coordination of operational activities, including the resident coordinator system.[11] In addition, through global conferences and his *An Agenda for Peace* and *An Agenda for Development*, the Secretary-General attempted to strengthen UN responses to new challenges in the interrelated areas of security and development, quintessential tasks for the system.[12]

In 1991, the Nordic countries—always a pillar of multilateralism—put forward reports deploring the fragmentation of the system that prevented it from reaching a critical mass in terms of its financial, staff, and research capabilities.[13] A year later, the South Centre put on the table a clear Third World view advocating better funding and a stronger role for the UN system in development.[14]

The 1997 reform under Kofi Annan was the brainchild of Maurice Strong, who had been influenced by his role in the 1972 UN Conference on the Human Environment held in Stockholm and the 1992 UN Conference on Environment and Development held in Rio, his experience as head of UNEP, and his participation in the Commission on Global Governance. Under his draft proposals, the UN Centre for Human Settlements would have been incorporated into a restructured UNEP, humanitarian activities would have been centralized, and the UN's overall development programmatic would have been guided by the executive board of UNDP. None of these proposals was approved, but several parts of the Secretariat were merged into the new Department of Economic and Social Affairs (DESA).

The 2000 Millennium Summit and the 2002 International Conference on Financing for Development in Monterrey and their follow-up further underlined the importance of the Secretary-General's leadership in structuring the debate about coordination by identifying areas of remedial intervention. The Secretary-General has no authority over the specialized agencies and many funds and programs—he is *primus inter pares* but does not really exert top-down control over the members of the system.

The protracted negotiations that took place prior to the September 2005 World Summit demonstrated again differences among governments. Some viewed the Millennium Development Goals (MDGs) as overly simplistic goals that failed to address the structural roots of poverty and deprivation. Others believe that they unduly focus on the problems of the least developed countries and pay too little attention to the needed reforms in international economic governance. And when the discussions moved from such broad normative principles as poverty eradication to the trade and financial policies to achieve them, North–South cleavages resurfaced.

In February 2006, the Secretary-General set up a fifteen-member High-level Panel on UN System-wide Coherence in the areas of development, humanitarian aid, and the environment (see page 579).[15] Coordination initiatives have thus become an integral and ongoing component of UN reform. Restructuring measures have sought to develop clearer lines of authority, responsibility, accountability, and communication. Efforts have been made to enhance the consistency of UN messages, avoid duplication, and ensure that its actions are mutually reinforcing. Yet, despite these cycles of reform and a series of handsomely presented reports, member states have different priorities and different definitions of such terms. Continuing concerns about inefficient operations, fragmentation, duplication, and the proliferation of mandates go side-by-side with a collective unwillingness to fund and implement radical restructuring.

CURRENT COORDINATION MACHINERY

The coordination of United Nations activities in the economic and social areas takes place at several levels. At the intergovernmental level, the main purpose of coordination is the development of consistent, complementary, and mutually supportive broad policy objectives. This function is vested in ECOSOC under the authority of the General Assembly. Coordination between the UN and the specialized agencies is the responsibility of the Chief Executives Board for Coordination. Within the UN itself, program planning, development, and implementation is orchestrated through a variety of bodies arising from the 1997 reforms. In addition, there are a number of separate mechanisms involved in the coordination of developmental work at the field level.

Coordination by States: ECOSOC

Under Charter Articles 62, 63, 64, 65, and 66, ECOSOC is assigned the role of promoting higher standards of living, full employment, and economic and social progress. The council is also expected to identify solutions to international economic, social, and health problems, facilitate international cultural and educational cooperation, and encourage universal respect for human rights and fundamental freedoms. ECOSOC thus has two main responsibilities: to develop international policies in the economic and social fields—through studies, reports, conventions, and international conferences—and to coordinate UN activities in these areas. Charter Article 63 provides that the council may enter into agreements 'defining the terms on which the agency concerned shall be brought into relationship with the United Nations.' ECOSOC could also 'coordinate the activities of the specialized agencies through consultation with and recommendations to such agencies and through recommendations to the General Assembly and to the Members of the United Nations.'

Much uncertainty has existed over the years about the exact modalities of this coordinating function. In San Francisco, there was considerable discussion as to how the council could carry out its mandate. Ruth Russell's definitive volume on Charter negotiations states: 'The basic decision made at Dumbarton Oaks and confirmed at San Francisco was that the relationship to be established between the organization and the agencies would be one of coordination and cooperation rather than one of centralization and direction.'[16] The Charter notes that ECOSOC can obtain regular reports from the specialized agencies and also request progress reports from them about steps taken to give effect to its own recommendations. It could also coordinate agency activities through recommendations to them directly, to the Assembly, or to member states. The Charter was, however, silent about ways to enforce recommendations.

Throughout its existence, ECOSOC has sought to come to grips with the coordination problems unaddressed in 1945. The council has passed resolutions giving specific guidance to the agencies as to what should be included in their annual reports. It has also repeatedly sought to establish program priorities for the entire system. As things stand now, ECOSOC's coordinating work is tailored to the provisions of 1991 General Assembly resolution 45/264, which spelled out the 'basic principles and guidelines, goals and measures . . . for the revitalization of the United Nations in the economic, social and related fields.' Among such measures were those intended to enable the council 'to discharge the responsibilities entrusted to it by the Charter of the United Nations by enhancing its role as a central forum for major economic, social, and related issues and policies and its coordinating functions relating to the United Nations system' in these areas.

ECOSOC meets once a year for four to five weeks, alternating between New York and Geneva. Until 1991, it met twice a year. Its sessions typically unfold sequentially along 'segments,' the first being a 'high-level' one devoted to the consideration of major economic or social themes determined a year earlier.[17] The high-level segment includes a one-day policy 'dialog and discussion' on important developments in the world economy and international economic cooperation. The purpose of the high-level segment is to create an action-oriented political consensus among member states over issues of international economic and social cooperation. Recent topics, for example, range from rural development to employment and the empowerment of women, from the contributions of human resources to market access by developing countries in the context of globalization and liberalization, and from the UN's role in Africa to resource mobilization for poverty eradication in the least developed countries.

Next is a four-to five-day 'coordination segment' devoted to the coordination of policies and activities of the specialized agencies, organs, organizations, and bodies. Again, discussions are structured around preselected themes, which provide the basis for broad system-wide assessments of and recommendations on the status of coordination addressed to various parts of the UN system. An essential topic during this segment has been the contribution of the UN system to the follow-up to UN global conferences and summits.

The last 'segment' of relevance here concerns 'operational activities,' which concerns the coordination of field work across the UN system. The volume of such activity has grown from roughly $6 billion in 1992 to over $10 billion in 2003.[18] A key focus of this coordination exercise is ECOSOC's triennial review of operations shared with the General Assembly and, in particular, its examination of their 'management process.'

Coordinating through the Executive Heads

The Chief Executives Board for Coordination (CEB) is the main interagency forum that brings together the executive heads of organizations in the UN system. It is the successor body of the Administrative Committee on Coordination (ACC), which was established in 1946 at the request of ECOSOC in resolution 13 (III). Chaired by the Secretary-General, the main purpose of the ACC was originally to supervise the implementation of agreements between the UN and the specialized agencies. Over the following decades, as the system expanded, ACC evolved into the central body for coordination of the UN organizations in implementing the goals of member states in a wide range of substantive and management issues.

In 2000, the transformation of ACC into the CEB underlined the collective steering of the system's work. Another concern was to streamline the ACC subsidiary machinery, which had ballooned into five main committees that reported to the ACC and dealt with particular aspects of coordination (organizational, administrative, sustainable development, program and operational questions, and gender equality). In turn, these committees had apportioned their work to a flurry of subsidiary bodies dealing with a wide range of issues extending from information systems, staff training, and personnel issues to questions related to water, the oceans, statistics, demographic projection, nutrition, drug control, and operational activities training.[19]

From the original four ACC members (the UN, the ILO, the FAO, and UNESCO), the CEB has expanded into a 28-member body that meets twice a year and is comprised of the UN funds and programs and the specialized agencies along with the Bretton Woods institutions and the WTO. The CEB seeks to advance cooperation among its members and focuses on broad common objectives mainly through its High-level Committee on Programmes and the High-level Committee on Management. In a deliberate move away from the idea of 'permanent subsidiary bodies,' the bulk of the CEB's coordination work is carried out through informal arrangements. These mechanisms consist of working groups and networks of managers, focal points, and experts in such different areas of interagency work as the Inter-Agency Network on Women and Gender Equality, the United Nations Communications Group, and the Network on Rural Development and Food Security. Only a handful of standing bodies have survived the 2000 reforms as expert bodies rather than as 'subsidiary bodies' like the Sub-Committee on Statistical Activities or the United Nations System Standing Committee on Nutrition. None of the technical bodies has decision-making authority for the participating entities.[20]

This less formal network builds on previous trends as the CEB has focused its work on broad intersectoral themes, for instance, the implications of globalization for development, the economic and social causes of conflict and humanitarian crisis in Africa, the digital divide, financing for development, the Doha development agenda, transnational crime, the campaign to combat HIV/AIDS, and the follow-up to UN global conferences held in the 1990s on sustainable development, population, human rights, and women. The CEB's agenda also devotes considerable attention to the implementation of the Millennium Declaration.

Coordination with the Bretton Woods Institutions

With their widely differing governance structures, political constituencies, and development philosophies, the UN and the Bretton Woods institutions operated for a long time on separate tracks. They occasionally crossed on highly formal and brief occasions such as the annual joint meetings of the World Bank and the IMF where the United Nations has observer status. This overall pattern was long criticized by many observers, including the Joint Inspection Unit.[21]

Yet, some improvement has occurred since the late 1990s. At the prodding of the General Assembly in resolution 50/227, ECOSOC has held 'special high-level meetings' with the Bank and the IMF. Representatives of the WTO and UNCTAD, as well as civil society and the private sector, now participate in such meetings, which take place every year immediately after the spring gatherings of the international financial institutions (IFIs). Their intent is to facilitate a policy dialogue between ministers of cooperation and foreign affairs and to address issues of coherence, coordination, and cooperation between the UN and the Washington-based international financial institutions. For instance, the 1998 and 1999 meetings addressed the functioning of international financial markets against the background of the Asian financial crisis. International financial arrangements and poverty eradication were discussed in 2000 and 2001. The 2002 International Conference on Financing for Development has given further impetus to this political dialogue between the UN and IFIs, which has focused on the impact of private investment and trade-related issues on financing for development, the role of multilateral institutions in reaching the MDGs, debt sustainability, and other questions related to the 'Monterrey Consensus' and the Millennium Declaration.

The 2002 Monterrey Consensus established an intergovernmental follow-up process in the General Assembly and ECOSOC. In addition to considering different financing issues on the annual agenda of the Second Committee, the Assembly every two years now hosts a two-day High-level Dialogue on Financing for Development. ECOSOC also holds an annual high-level meeting in the spring on different aspects of the Monterrey Consensus with the leadership of the Bank, IMF, WTO, and since 2004 UNCTAD.

Interagency support involves collaboration among concerned institutions and systematic outreach. The Financing for Development Office of DESA, the World Bank, the IMF, the WTO, UNCTAD, UNDP, and the regional commissions cooperate closely in preparing the follow-up reports for the Assembly. Within their respective mandates, they also organize multi-stakeholder consultations on conference follow-up. These consultations are open to member states, civil society, and business organizations.

Coordination in the Secretariat

Among the reforms initiated by the General Assembly and the Secretary-General in 1997 was the establishment of a number of structures that simplified institutional arrangements within the Secretariat. These structures were intended to lead to greater information-sharing, better definition of responsibility and timelines of implementation, and more effective decision-making.

At the end of 1997, the Assembly established the post of deputy secretary-general (DSG) 'to help manage Secretariat operations and to ensure coherence of activities and programs.' One of the stated purposes was to ensure that this new senior post, the second highest-ranking member of the international civil service, would assist the Secretary-General in the full range of his responsibilities. In March 1998, a Canadian, Louise Fréchette, became the first person to hold the post. Her office orchestrated the reforms of 2002. In 2005, she played a role in the development of further management, oversight, and accountability changes in the Secretariat in response to the criticism of the Iraq oil-for-food inquiry. She resigned and was replaced as deputy secretary-general by a Briton, Mark Malloch Brown.

Another important component of the 1997 reforms was the establishment of four 'executive committees' overseeing the organization's main areas of work. Each committee (peace and security, economic and social affairs, development operations, and humanitarian affairs) has its own 'convener' who brings together the heads of the major UN units active in these areas. The executive committees were designed to identify possible manners of pooling resources and services in order to maximize program impact and minimize administrative costs, reduce duplication, and facilitate greater complementarity and coherence. As such, they were intended to function as instruments of policy development, joint strategic planning and decision-making, and management. Each executive committee has a small staff at its disposal.

The 1997 reforms set up a Senior Management Group (SMG), chaired by the Secretary-General. This group is the functional equivalent of a 'cabinet.'

Coordination in the Field: The Resident Coordinators

The wide array of activities in developing countries nominally takes place under UNDP's aegis. Those in charge of the activities are variously known as 'country representatives,' 'resident coordinators,' or 'resident representatives' who coordinate the UN's operational activities at the country level and act as team leaders representing the UN system on issues of common concern.[22]

The exact modalities of representation and coordination through the resident coordinators vary from country to country. Broadly speaking, in each country where the UN has development assistance activities, the resident coordinator is the designated representative of the Secretary-General for development cooperation and is considered the leader of the UN country team. Resident coordinators work in tandem with and lead 'thematic groups' and 'country management teams.' Both bodies comprise representatives of all UN agencies present with a country, but the resident coordinator seeks to consolidate and coordinate UN assistance in individual sectors in consultation with the government, major bilateral and multilateral donors, NGOs, and the private sector. The actions of resident coordinators are structured and facilitated by two key management tools: the United Nations Development Assistance Framework (UNDAF) and the Common Country Assessment (CCA).

UNDAF, prepared by all UN agencies in collaboration with recipient governments, serves as a common framework for UN activities and defines the strategic areas of collective effort taking into account the goals and objectives of UN global conferences and most particularly the MDGs. UNDAF thus provides overall guidance to the UN system's field work by defining common goals, objectives, priorities, indicators, monitoring and reporting mechanisms, and a UN resource framework agreed to by all agencies and endorsed by the recipient government.

All UN organizations in a country are involved in the preparation of CCAs. They identify trends related to national development goals and suggest strategic issues to be considered for UNDAF. In addition, they define the roles which each UN agency is expected to play.

COORDINATION, A REPORT CARD

The UN's current coordination machinery seems impressive on paper. To what extent has it actually brought unity and coherence in purpose and modalities of action to the 'system?' This section aims to answer that question by examining the extent to which theory matches practice in each of the five areas discussed above: coordination by states, through executive heads, with the Bretton Woods institutions, by the Secretariat, and in the field.

Coordination by States: ECOSOC

Donor countries took too long to recognize that unsustainable levels of indebtedness were canceling out much of public and private investments in many developing countries. The practice of tied aid—that is, requiring that grant monies be used in a specific way—also deprived recipient countries of the possibility of obtaining goods and services at the best possible cost or developing indigenous production capacities. It took the AIDS pandemic to drive home the point that without greater flexibility in implementing patent protection, most developing country victims of the disease would never be able to afford treatment. And there is, at long last, serious public debate on the detrimental impact on developing countries of farm subsidies—thanks in part to UN advocacy and NGO campaigns.

Developing countries also face their own coherence challenges concerning social and economic policies. The issue is not only to achieve an optimum allocation of scarce resources but also to tackle the policies and practices that discourage investors and undermine the confidence of the donor community. In addition, many recipient countries lack the capacity to coordinate the diverse development actors on their soil.

Frequently, donor and recipient governments do not coordinate among themselves so that, for example, the ministry of agriculture and the ministry of foreign affairs may propose different policies in different UN forums. The organizational fragmentation of the UN system is then exacerbated by conflicting instructions and priorities. Similarly, late payments of assessed contributions, as well as inadequate commitments in the first place, create UN cash-flow problems and inhibit long-term planning and smooth execution. In addition, with their voluntary contributions donors 'often tend to favour funding for high-visibility projects, which is in contradiction with the call that United Nations organizations should work more... together, and join forces in programme implementation which necessarily results in lessened visibility and lowering of individual agency profile.'[23]

The lack of policy coherence also influences policymaking and execution in the UN system. 'The Economic and Social Council had never fully lived up to its central responsibilities under the Charter for overall policy formulation and implementation and coordination, in the economic and social fields,'[24] noted a perceptive insider back in 1981. ECOSOC has given considerable attention to the question of priorities over the years. But the wide variety of interests of member states, the complexity of social and economic questions, and an overloaded agenda have precluded any meaningful definition of priorities—thus undermining any determination of program priorities. Even the overarching goal of 'poverty eradication,' which seems to be prevalent in most policy discussions, is an elusive tool for priority-setting, especially when eight MDGs are being translated into concrete national and international policy measures.

Some delegations are more pointed in their assessment drawing attention to the need to bring about greater thematic coherence to the various segments of ECOSOC sessions and to encourage greater synergies among its functional commissions. Others underline the necessity to pursue more vigorously the reform of the UN funds, programs, and specialized agencies in order to 'ensure system-wide coherence.' Still others highlight the fact that the UN environmental governance structures should be more 'integrated.'[25]

The sheer number of bodies formally reporting to ECOSOC increased steadily at least until the mid-1980s. Without denying the quality of the work produced by the Statistical Commission or the Population and Development Commission, for example, this vast machinery required constant monitoring, which exceeded ECOSOC's limited capacity. During the 1990s and early 2000s, the council seems to have recovered at least partially as it underwent a drastic reorganization of its agenda and working methods, which was spearheaded through Secretariat-inspired resolutions passed by the General Assembly.

Past debates in both the General Assembly and ECOSOC acknowledge progress in enhancing policy coordination within the UN system. Officially, all national delegations agree that ECOSOC should play a central role in the follow-up and implementation of the outcomes of major UN conferences and summits as well as in the achievements of the MDGs. They also stress that ECOSOC is well placed to serve as a platform for global policy dialogue and guidance and as an instrument for the comprehensive monitoring of the UN development agenda. Nevertheless, the political message is that the council is not yet performing these functions adequately. The basic political cleavages that have traditionally hampered ECOSOC's capacity to be more proactive are very much still in evidence.

Coordinating the System through the Executive Heads

Despite the lack of consensus among member states, the 2000 Millennium Summit may constitute the beginning of a new phase in the UN's long quest for coordination. The Millennium Declaration articulated an overarching policy framework for the system's organizations. Because they are concrete, quantified, and time-bound, the MDGs have demonstrated their usefulness as tools for the mobilization of the system.[26]

Against this background, the CEB has expanded its focus from narrow sectoral concerns to broader strategic issues of system-wide concern. Since 2001, it has organized its work around the themes identified by the Secretary-General in his *Road map towards the implementation of the United Nations Millennium Declaration.*[27] Its main concern has been to devise and promote common strategies to achieve a 'coordinated follow-up to the Declaration and related outcomes of other UN global conferences.' More pointedly, the CEB has attempted to frame these strategies and policies around a common set of goals, and individual agencies of the wider UN system, including the World Bank and the IMF, have adopted a multi-year 'strategic framework.' Concurrently, UN organizations have focused on mainstreaming the MDGs into their field activities in an attempt to maximize the coherence and effectiveness of the system's support for the recipient countries' implementation of the Millennium Declaration.

Coordination with the Bretton Woods Institutions

Have the yearly meetings of ECOSOC with the IFIs and WTO brought about greater coherence, coordination, and cooperation? Undoubtedly, they pull together an impressive number of 'stakeholders'—representatives of the governing bodies of the IFIs and WTO, senior officials of the Organisation for Economic Co-operation and Development and the UN (notably UNDP and UNCTAD), ministers of finance and development cooperation, governors of central banks, NGOs, and private sector organizations. Neither the novelty nor the limitations of this policy dialogue should be underestimated. The fact that the General Assembly's Second Committee still hosts its own 'High-level Dialogue on Financing for Development' is a stark reminder of the duplication that still hangs over the authority and credibility of ECOSOC.[28]

The Bretton Woods institutions have embraced the MDGs and are integrating them, often together with other UN organizations, into country-level planning instruments, including in the poverty reduction strategy papers (PRSPs). Programmatic priorities are reviewed to ensure that they support the MDG targets. The Secretary-General's reports to the General Assembly form a system of monitoring to track global, regional, and national progress towards attaining the MDGs. Interagency and expert groups on MDG indicators coordinated by DESA and country-level monitoring by UNDP are complemented by a wide array of reports produced by individual organizations, while Bank and Fund annual 'global monitoring reports' provide an integrated assessment of progress on policies and actions needed to achieve MDGs and related conference outcomes.

Coordination by the Secretariat

The internal structures put in place in 1997 show a similar pattern of 'work in progress.' That the growth of membership had made the Senior Management Group unwieldy as a policy formulation and coordination organ was acknowledged in May 2005 when the Group established two executive decision-making committees. The SMG now meets every two weeks (at first, weekly) serving as a vehicle for information and experience sharing among all senior managers and to provide guidance on cross-cutting issues. The two new committees, chaired by the Secretary-General, have a restricted membership limited to twelve members for the Policy Committee and seven members for the Management Committee and supersede several single-issue coordination mechanisms. The Policy Committee meets once a week to consider issues requiring strategic guidance and decisions and identify emerging policy issues, while the Management Committee convenes once a month to implement internal management reform recommendations.[29] Whether these new bodies will really reinforce the ability of the world body's Secretariat to face new challenges remains to be seen.

The deputy secretary-general has since 1998 served as an additional high-profile advocate for UN ideas and activities. Not infrequently, the DSG has acted as a trouble shooter for the Secretary-General, for example by strengthening the impression that the UN would not tolerate sexual abuses in its peacekeeping operations. As chair of a Steering Committee on Reform and Management Policy, the DSG also oversaw the 2002 reforms and measures to counteract the oil-for-food scandal. The DSG also chaired a Management Performance Board to advise the Secretary-General on whether individual managers carry out their duties and properly discharge their responsibilities.

With a proliferation of seemingly unconnected tasks, the DSG's role in enhancing the 'coherence' of the UN's activities in economic and social areas received mixed reviews. The prevailing view emanating from the 'substantive' departments of the Secretariat is that the office of the DSG is yet another bureaucratic layer. The added value of the functions relative to other mechanisms established in the 1997 reform, notably the executive committees, is widely perceived as low, as well as a source of uncertainty with regard to lines of authority and coordination.

The nebulous nature of the DSG's mandate relates to the lack of political consensus that presided over its creation. The Group of 77 made it plain in 1997 that development questions should be the priority tasks of the deputy secretary-general.[30] Most industrialized countries took the opposite stand arguing that the incumbent of the new post should primarily assist the Secretary-General in the performance of his administrative functions. These irreconcilable differences resulted in an ill-defined mandate for the DSG. In this regard, the story of the DSG is reminiscent of the problems that plagued the director-general for international economic cooperation, a post that was created in 1977 by the Assembly in its resolution 32/197 as a result of Southern pressures to enhance the role of the United Nations in international cooperation for development. The incumbents were never provided with the financial, political, and institutional means to exert leadership and achieve coordination; Boutros-Ghali quietly abolished the post in 1992 as part of his reform of the Secretariat.[31]

While the UN Development Group is generally credited with having helped create a more cohesive and unified leadership at the operational level,[32] the same cannot be said for the Executive Committee on Economic and Social Affairs. The heterogeneity of its large membership and irregular meetings make it a less than satisfactory instrument for strategic planning and policy development. From its proceedings, only a handful of policy papers reflecting the common views of its members have emerged on the international financial architecture, debt problems of developing countries, official development assistance, and the social dimensions of macroeconomic policy. Laboriously put together and considerably watered down to reconcile the positions of individual organizations, these papers were issued in June 2001 after over a year of institutional quarrelling over their contents. By the time of their publication, their prescriptions had by and large been overtaken by events.

Field Coordination

The resident coordinator system has developed further since 1997 and resulted in some cost-savings, contributed to the emergence of a more cohesive and unified leadership, and begun to reduce competition among UN agencies. Nevertheless, if coordination and information sharing have significantly improved at the highest levels, they are less evident at the operational level. Practical management issues and clashing organizational cultures continue to place obstacles to a fuller integration of country-level activities. It is not rare that CCAs are delayed inordinately because particular agencies seek to emphasize development indicators in line with their own mandates and programming, no matter what the government's view. Country team working groups are sometimes inactive because officials are reluctant to spend time working on issues not directly related to their own agencies' priorities.

In brief, like many bureaucracies everywhere, UN agencies in the field tend to put their separate organizational interests above overall UN systemic ones. The prevalence of this competitive environment explains why field projects, whether or not they fall within agreed system-wide priorities, can still be initiated and developed directly with the approval of government officials. The dual functions of the resident coordinator—who is often both a UNDP official accountable to the UNDP administrator and supposedly also a representative and advocate of the entire system—casts doubt on the resident coordinator's reputation as an impartial and neutral broker of the system with partner governments. UN organizations, as well as the member states, frequently argue that there are not enough high-quality resident coordinators.

Another illustration of the system's parochialism is the difficulties encountered in setting up 'UN houses.' The idea was to consolidate under the authority of a single official and in a single location all UN activities. A single blue flag was to fly in front of a dedicated UN facility. The objective remains to provide common premises to create closer ties among UN staff and promote a more unified presence at the country level in a cost effective manner. There are about sixty UN houses: seventeen in Africa, five in Arab states, ten in Asia and the Pacific, sixteen in Europe and Commonwealth of Independent States, and ten in Latin America and the Caribbean.[33]

The UN Development Group has played a critical role in the steady expansion of the networks leading to economies of scale and, to a certain extent, 'better working relations...which affect in turn the cohesion and unified image of the United Nations system at the country level.'[34] But numerous obstacles have slowed this expansion, including, as the UNDP administrator noted in a 2004 report to ECOSOC, 'insufficient staff time and resources; lack of common premises; differing procedures and the need for further agency cooperation and commitment.'[35] Progress in harmonization and simplification of programming, monitoring, and evaluation procedures has been slow at the field level, for example with synchronized program cycles to facilitate joint assessments and programming activities.

In a growing number of countries, UN organizations also cooperate with formulating the World Bank's poverty reduction strategy papers. If these papers become more multisectoral—for example, by integrating human rights, gender, and environmental perspectives—they may provide a comprehensive framework for policy dialog, national ownership, aid coordination, and donor cooperation. They may also engage NGOs and private corporations to a larger extent. Ultimately, PRSPs, UNDAF, and CCA, as well as individual organization reports, may be integrated further, which would save time and resources, but such an effort would require sustained CEB attention.[36]

CONCLUSION

In the functionally decentralized UN system, with sovereign members holding conflicting views about the proper role of the organization in the process of development, coordination is bound to become problematic. Overall, UN coordination shows a mixed picture of slow progress within the system and continued complaints and lack of support from most member states.

Appearances notwithstanding, organizational processes have changed substantially since 1945. The system's approach to coordination used to be an *ex post facto* ritualistic exercise overshadowed by 'territorial' concerns and mutual suspicions. The stated goal was to clarify the division of responsibilities of each organization, develop synergies building on their comparative advantages, and maximize resource mobilization and utilization. In effect, the purpose was primarily to delimit and legitimize discrete 'mandates' and responsibilities. Since then, a substantial shift has taken place towards greater consultation at the programming stage.

UN global conferences, especially those of the 1990s, gave a crucial impetus to this shift. While concentrating on different dimensions of development, they also underlined the connections among the development challenges and highlighted the need for global as well as multisectoral approaches. In this sense, these conference processes and the Millennium Summit provided the system with a broad set of policy objectives around which it could mobilize, paving the way toward a greater sense of common ownership and commitment within the system.

Whether ECOSOC has been revitalized enough remains to be seen, but it has moved away from its former rituals. Official proceedings are now supplemented by a flurry of useful 'side events' and activities, including 'policy dialogs,' sponsored by individual agencies, and special briefings by officials from the UN, World Bank, and IMF as well as business leaders, academics, and civil society representatives. Attendees can also participate in 'roundtable discussions' on cross-cutting themes. Another example is the 1994 ECOSOC decision to authorize the creation of a new joint and co-sponsored UN program on HIV/AIDS, which brought together the existing AIDS-related resources and expertise of WHO, UNICEF, UNDP, UNFPA, UNESCO, and the World Bank into a consolidated program, thus eliminating duplication of effort and enhancing the ability of member states to cope with the AIDS pandemic.

These changes have been accompanied by greater informality throughout the UN system. Information and communications technology, in particular, has facilitated a proliferation of informal bodies with coordination functions across thematic lines and locations—variously known as task forces, coordination groups, framework teams for coordination, and steering committees.

Such incremental innovations have contributed to more extensive joint planning and programming, pooled resources, and strengthened resident coordinators; and they have contributed to the emergence of a more cohesive and unified leadership for the world organization. They should neither be underestimated nor overlooked. At the same time, ongoing complaints within the system and among member states, not to mention the recent report of the High-level Panel on UN System-wide Coherence in the Areas of Development, Humanitarian Assistance and the Environment, suggest plenty of room for improvement. The report proposes to establish by 2012 one integrated UN Country Team (with a strengthened resident coordinator, one unified country program, one budgetary framework, and where appropriate one office), one board for the main UN funds and programs, and one funding mechanism. However, without continuous support from the member states, this proposal is likely to go the way of other proposals and its full implementation may run into great resistance.

This is mainly because UN coordination is only partially an organizational question. It is also a deeply divisive political issue hinging on the views of member states about the organization's priorities. The absence of a political consensus on the desirable nature and functions of the system has proved to be a long-term debilitating pattern yielding a series of reform rounds amounting, in the final analysis, to circular argumentation and marginal change. Viewed in the context of recurring critiques of the system, obvious flaws can be attributed less to a lack of intrinsic merits of reform ideas than to the existence of deep-seated and enduring structural defects. Strengthening the United Nations to fulfill its economic and social mandates, and more specifically enhancing ECOSOC's role, will undoubtedly remain a challenge. In addition, avoiding intractable structural issues—for instance, the autonomy of the specialized agencies and especially of the Bretton Woods institutions, or non-payment of assessed contributions— inevitably will limit the scope of change.

As member states complain about inefficiency, fragmentation, duplication, and proliferation, the main leverage for change is the leadership of reformers within and outside the system. Against the odds, some Secretaries-General and other key individuals have demonstrated leadership in headquarters and the field and improved coordination. But, personal qualities cannot overcome a decentralized structure, limited resources, and a lack of political will. We should thus expect the issue of coordination to continue as an integral part of the development debate and to overshadow the 'system.'

NOTES

1. Boutros Boutros-Ghali, *An Agenda for Development* (New York: UN, 1994), para. 213.
2. The Advisory Committee on Administrative and Budgetary Questions (ACABQ) essentially fulfills an external reviewer's function. It advises the Fifth Committee of the General Assembly on budget and management questions.
3. See Gert Rosenthal, *The Economic and Social Council of the United Nations: An Issues Paper*, Occasional Paper 15 (Berlin: Friedrich Ebert Stiftung, 2005).
4. See Joachim W. Mueller, *The Reform of the United Nations*, 2 vols. (London: Oceana Publications, 1992). For an early and probing expression of concern about coordination, see Martin Hill, *The United Nations System: Coordinating Its Economic and Social Work* (Cambridge: Cambridge University Press, 1978).
5. Lester B. Pearson, chairman, *Partners in Development* (New York: Praeger, 1969). For a discussion of such groups, see Ramesh Thakur, Andrew F. Cooper, and John English, eds., *International Commissions and the Power of Ideas* (Tokyo: United Nations University Press, 2005).
6. Robert Jackson, *A Study of the Capacity of the United Nations Development System* (Geneva: United Nations, 1969), iii.
7. *A New United Nations Structure for Global Economic Cooperation. Report of the Group of Experts on the Structure of the United Nations System* (New York: UN, 1975).
8. Mueller, *The Reform*, 27. See also Douglas Williams, *The Specialized Agencies and the United Nations: The System in Crisis* (New York: St. Martin's Press, 1987).
9. Independent Commission on International Development Issues, *North-South: A Programme for Survival* (Cambridge, Mass.: MIT Press, 1980).
10. Mueller, *The Reform*, 28.
11. *Role and Functions of Resident Coordinators of the UN System's Operational Activities for Development: Arrangements for the Exercise of the Functions of Resident Coordinator*, ACC/1994/POQ/CRP.19/Annex.
12. See Michael G. Schechter, *United Nations Global Conferences* (London: Routledge, 2005); and Boutros Boutros-Ghali, *An Agenda for Peace* (New York: United Nations, 1992) and *An Agenda for Development* (New York: UN, 1994).
13. Nordic UN Reform Project, *The United Nations in Development: Reform Issues in the Economic and Social Fields: A Nordic perspective: Final Report* (Stockholm: Almqvist & Wiksell International, 1991).
14. The South Centre, *The Economic Role of the United Nations* (Geneva: The South Centre, 1992).
15. CEB/2006/4 of 24 March 2006, paras. 2–21.
16. Ruth Russell assisted by Jeannette E. Muther, *A History of the United Nations Charter: The Role of the United States* (Washington, DC: The Brookings Institution, 1958), 797.
17. The Council's sessions also include a 'humanitarian' segment that is omitted here and treated in a separate chapter. Readers may consult Antonio Donini, *The Policies of Mercy: UN Coordination in Afghanistan, Mozambique and Rwanda*, Occasional Paper no. 22 (Providence, RI: Watson Institute, 1996); Marc Sommers, *The Dynamics of Coordination*, Occasional Paper no. 40 (Providence, RI: Watson Institute, 2000); Jonathan Moore, *Independent Study of UN Coordination Mechanisms in Crisis and Post-Conflict Situations* (New York: UNDP/Emergency Response Division, 2000); and Nicola Reindorp and Peter Wiles, *Humanitarian Coordination: Lessons from Recent Field Experience* (New York: UNOCHA, 2001).
18. See *Comprehensive Statistical Data on Operational Activities for Development for 2003: Report of the Secretary-General*, UN document A/60/74–E/2005/57, 6 May 2005.

19. For details, see Francesco Mezzalama, Khalil Issa Othman, and Louis Dominique Oue-draogo, *Review of the Administrative Committee on Coordination and its Machinery*, JIU/REP/99/1 (Geneva: Joint Inspection Unit, 1999), 19.
20. For details, see http://ceb.unsystem.org.
21. R. V. Hennes and S. Schumm, *United Nations System Co-operation with Multilateral Financial Institutions–Performance and Innovation Challenges*, JIU/REP/92/1 Part I, and *United Nations System Co-operation with Multilateral Financial Institutions - Examples of Fresh Approaches*, JIU/REP/92/1 Part II (Geneva: Joint Inspection Unit, 1992).
22. The origins of the system can be traced back to the establishment in the early 1950s of a network of 'resident representatives' of the Expanded Programme of Technical Assistance (EPTA) in countries receiving technical assistance to oversee projects. These individuals acted as contact points between EPTA, recipient governments, and the specialized agencies.
23. Doris Bertrand, *Some Measures to Improve Overall Performance of the United Nations System at the Country Level*, JIU/REP/2005/2, Part II (Geneva: Joint Inspection Unit, 2005), para. 115.
24. Cited in John Renninger *ECOSOC: Options for Reform* (New York: UN Institute for Training and Research, 1981), viii.
25. See Steinar Andresen, 'Global Environmental Governance: UN Fragmentation and Coordination,' in *Yearbook of International Co-operation on Environment and Development 2001/2002*, ed. Olav Schram Stokke and Øystein B. Thommessen (London: Earthscan, 2001), 19–26.
26. Chief Executive Board, *One United Nations. Catalyst for Progress and Change: How the Millennium Declaration is Changing the Way the UN System Works* (New York: UN, 2005). See also Sakiko Fukuda-Parr, 'Millennium Development Goals: Why They Matter,' *Global Governance* 10, no. 4 (2004): 395–402.
27. *Road Map towards the Implementation of the United Nations Millennium Declaration, Report of the Secretary-General*, UN document A/56/326, 6 September 2001.
28. The decision by the Assembly in December 2005 to create a Peacebuilding Commission also suggests that ECOSOC is still not sufficiently engaged in the coordination of UN system activities in countries emerging from conflict. This decision could be viewed as another slap in the face of ECOSOC, which could have been assigned these functions.
29. 'Ethics and Accountability Reform Measures,' Reform at the United Nations: Reference Reports and Materials, www.un.org.
30. *Preliminary Position of the Group of 77 and China on the Report of the Secretary-General: Renewing the United Nations: A Program for Reform*, UN document A/51/950, 14 October 1997. See www.g77.org.
31. For a useful analysis of the 1977 'restructuring' of the economic and social activities and governance of the United Nations, see Ronald I. Meltzer, 'Restructuring the United Nations System: Institutional Reform Efforts in the Context of North-South Relations,' *International Organization* 32, no. 4 (1978): 993–1018.
32. See, e.g., the qualified endorsement of this view by Bertrand, *Some Measures*, paras. 45–67.
33. United Nations Development Group, UN Houses by Region, www.undg.org.
34. Bertrand, *Some Measures*, para. 93.
35. Ibid., para. 95.
36. This may cause a dilemma between finding agency specific expression in some sectors and avoiding duplication and transaction costs. For more detail, see ibid., paras. 1–19.

CHAPTER 33

....

HEALTH AND INFECTIOUS DISEASE

....

GIAN LUCA BURCI

SINCE time immemorial, governments and populations have confronted the prevention and control of infectious diseases, which have an inherently international dimension. Pathogens do not stop at national boundaries. International flows of persons, animals, and goods carry an implicit risk that communicable diseases will spread, rendering every country vulnerable. For these reasons, the control of infectious diseases was one of the first areas of institutionalized international cooperation in the nineteenth century, first within Western Europe and then progressively in other regions.

The growing realization of the inherently cross-cutting nature of health and its interactions with other areas of international law and relations have recently led to the development of innovative forms of international cooperation and governance. This chapter reviews the main institutional and international legal aspects of cooperation in the fight against the scourge of infectious diseases, with particular reference to the role of the World Health Organization (WHO) and other agencies of the United Nations system.

The opinions expressed in this chapter are those of the author and do not necessarily reflect the views of the World Health Organization.

INTERNATIONAL COOPERATION
ON INFECTIOUS DISEASES AND WHO's ROLE

International cooperation began in earnest with the 1851 First International Sanitary Conference held in Paris, which aimed to adopt a convention to control the spread of cholera, plague, and yellow fever through maritime traffic. This event signaled the beginning of a century of intense diplomatic activity in the field of infectious diseases, marked by a large number of diplomatic conferences and an increasing number of regional or international conventions and regulations.[1] The main purpose of such activity was initially to protect European states from the importation of 'Asiatic' diseases through maritime travel and traffic. The sanitary cordon was largely based on the application of quarantine and other control measures, which by their nature affected and could disrupt international traffic. The balance between protecting health and maintaining open trade has been and still remains a central feature of the system of international control. The balance was pursued in the nineteenth and early twentieth centuries through the harmonization of quarantine measures and the setting of maximum measures that states could adopt with regard to specific diseases, thus creating a more level playing field from a commercial point of view. Another very important feature was the establishment of an international system of surveillance to generate knowledge and crucial information on the epidemiological situation of the areas exporting diseases.

The development of this rather uncoordinated system soon led to the establishment of permanent international institutions that would perform a number of tasks requiring a more centralized approach: coordinating the harmonization of quarantine and surveillance; providing assistance to countries; encouraging research; and facilitating the development of international treaties by offering a permanent negotiating forum. The patchwork nature of international cooperation actually led to the creation of three organizations before WHO—namely, the Pan-American Sanitary Bureau in 1905; the Office International d'Hygiène Publique in 1907; and the Health Organization of the League of Nations in 1919.

Thus, the establishment of WHO in 1948 represented continuity in the international approach to the control of infectious diseases, which continued to be based on the principles developed in preceding decades. The real change was twofold. The first was the centralization into a single universal agency of the functions previously exercised by a number of international bureaux. Second, striking normative powers were entrusted to WHO. Articles 21 and 22 of the organization's constitution empower the World Health Assembly (WHA) to adopt legally binding regulations in a number of areas, including on 'sanitary and quarantine requirements and other procedures designed to prevent the international spread of disease.'

Regulations enter into force at a given date for all member states, except those that object or file a reservation. The traditional treaty-based normative system could thus be replaced by a more vertical approach, under which state sovereignty could only be safeguarded by 'opting out' of the regulations. Another fundamental shift was that control of infectious diseases became part of a broader institutional mandate to pursue the most diverse aspects of public health, with particular regard to poorer countries which traditionally have been exporters of infectious diseases and have suffered from a lack of proper health systems and resources.

WHO has historically tackled infectious diseases in a variety of ways, but mainly through policy, technical, and normative approaches. WHO's policy approach has focused on using intergovernmental mechanisms to garner consensus among member states on the organization's broad lines of action. This has meant, first of all, agreeing on the particular strategy to follow with regard to specific diseases, for example through a holistic global health-sector strategy for HIV/AIDS (resolution WHA 56.30 of 28 May 2003); or through directly observed treatment as the strategy to combat tuberculosis (resolution WHA 53.1 of 19 May 2000). Most importantly, it has meant framing the core function of fighting infectious diseases within a broader vision of health governance.

In this context, the most important and long-lasting contribution of WHO has arguably been the 'health for all' (HFA) process launched at the WHO–UNICEF (UN Children's Fund) 1978 Alma-Ata conference on primary health care, as well as the reorientation of WHO's activities and priorities underscoring that process. Even though the initial ambitious goal of health for all 'by the year 2000' has proved unachievable, the policy was revised and reaffirmed in 1998 to serve as one of the main principles inspiring WHO's activities.[2] In short, HFA emerged from the growing dissatisfaction of developing countries about the fragmented, vertical, and technology-based approach to health care that WHO had promoted until then. HFA was based on the primary health care approach, rooted in the concept of affordable and socially acceptable methods and technologies, as well as a strong sense of social equity and empowerment of individuals and communities. Primary health care was, in turn, based on a number of main components, including some which are crucial for the control of infectious diseases such as safe water and basic sanitation, immunization, and the prevention and control of locally endemic diseases.

From a technical point of view, WHO focused at an early date on coordinating and catalyzing campaigns to eradicate or manage a number of infectious diseases, from influenza to poliomyelitis and from childhood disease such as measles and whooping cough to a range of neglected tropical diseases such as onchocerciasis and leishmaniasis. WHO's early success in controlling yaws induced a generalized but ill-founded optimism that the advances in medical sciences were heralding the end of epidemic diseases as a serious public health threat. The first decades of WHO's history were thus marked by successive campaigns against the most important infectious diseases, in particular tuberculosis, malaria, and smallpox, with mixed success. The eradication of smallpox by 1980 undoubtedly was the major achievement of WHO to date, and poliomyelitis will probably be eradicated within the next few years. At the same time, the organization's campaigns have not effectively controlled malaria and tuberculosis; and, together with the rest of the UN system,

WHO has been powerless to slow down the relentless worldwide progression of the HIV/AIDS pandemic.

With the specific purpose of controlling the spread of disease while avoiding unnecessary interference with international travel and trade, the International Health Regulations (IHR) were adopted by the World Health Assembly in 1951 under Article 21 of its constitution and revised in 1969.[3] The IHR represent the international response to the inadequacy of the pre-WHO legal regime, by replacing that system with a single legal instrument managed by a universal international agency. The IHR are based on principles similar to the conventions that these regulations replaced. They only apply to specific diseases—cholera, plague, and yellow fever in the current version—down from an initial list of six diseases. States parties are under an obligation to report any case of a listed disease to WHO, which circulates the case to the entire membership.[4] Besides the publication of such reports, however, WHO does not have substantial powers to interact with states parties to ensure effective international control. The IHR were still premised on the principle of the maximum measures applicable in general as well as for specific diseases, including the disinfection and removal of insects and rodents from ships and aircraft; the performance of medical examinations or other measures on travelers and conveyances; and the presentation of health documents as a requirement for travellers to enter a state.

The IHR initially provided a useful legal reference for routine measures but became increasingly marginal. States by and large stopped complying with the regulations for three reasons. First, the disease-specific approach made the IHR inapplicable to the growing number of emerging or reemerging diseases that have characterized the late twentieth century. Second, the regulations did not protect reporting countries from excessive and damaging reactions from other countries, while the lack of credible monitoring and enforcement mechanisms did not deter many countries from applying more intrusive measures than those authorized in the IHR. Third, the approach of maximum measures was not compatible with the science-based approach embodied in a number of General Agreement on Trade and Tariffs (GATT) and later World Trade Organization (WTO) treaties, such as those on sanitary and phytosanitary measures (SPS) and on technical barriers to trade (TBT).[5] These agreements in practice partly replaced the IHR as the guiding instruments to balance trade and health protection.

The international community has, since the 1990s, been confronted with a growing problem of emerging and reemerging diseases and of their increasing resistance to available drugs (as in the case of malaria and tuberculosis). In some ways, countries may feel as vulnerable as they did at the end of the nineteenth century. This is due partly to failures in the eradication or control of some crucial diseases, as noted above, partly to the emergence of new and potentially catastrophic diseases such as SARS, avian flu, and hemorrhagic fevers, and partly to the state of neglect of many national health systems that are unable to act as the primary barriers against the international spread of disease. The increasing speed and volume of international travel and trade create the conditions for the rapid spread of such diseases, while the growing fears of a terrorist attack using biological or chemical agents has blurred the lines between public health action and national security and injected heightened political urgency into the former.

This sense of vulnerability culminated in the SARS epidemic of 2003, which caught the world by surprise but was successfully controlled through WHO's decisive coordination and guidance, a role that fell completely outside the legal framework of the IHR. By using approaches developed during the previous decade, WHO relied on information mostly received from nongovernmental sources. It also collaborated with other institutions to define policies and measures which, through a heavy reliance on the internet, were communicated not only to governments but also to economic operators and the public at large.[6]

Confronted with this complex situation, the World Health Assembly launched a major revision process of the IHR, which was successfully completed with the adoption in May 2005 of a drastically revised instrument.[7] The list of diseases is replaced by the open concept of 'event,'[8] which can be of biological, chemical, or nuclear source and of any origin (i.e., natural, accidental, or intentional). This allows WHO to go beyond 'traditional' infectious diseases and cooperate with several international agencies to avoid overlaps or gaps (e.g., the International Atomic Energy Agency, World Meteorological Organization, UN Environment Programme, and Organization for the Prohibition of Chemical Weapons). States must assess all unusual health events in accordance with an algorithm and notify WHO of all events that may constitute 'public health emergencies of international concern' (PHEIC). WHO is a central actor in the implementation of the 2005 IHR; it may, among other things, consider information from nonstate sources, and the WHO's director-general has the authority to declare a PHEIC and to issue recommendations for the management of the emergency. States have a number of new obligations with regard not only to surveillance, verification, cooperation, and information sharing but also to strengthen their own domestic capacities.

The current IHR reflect a science-based approach that should render them largely compatible with the GATT, SPS, and TBT. And, for the first time, the regulations contain express provisions for the respect of human rights and the protection of personal data. The implementation of such a complex regime, which pulls together under a health protection framework elements deriving from other international regimes, will be a major challenge for the international community, in particular for the UN and other international agencies, since it cuts across areas falling within their competence. While the newly revised IHR entered into force in June 2007, the risk of a flu pandemic in 2005–2006 led WHO's member states to agree in May 2006 on immediate and voluntary compliance with some of the new provisions contained in the regulations with specific regard to avian and pandemic flu (resolution WHA 59.2 of 26 May 2006).

Even though this chapter focuses on WHO's leadership in infectious disease control, the cross-cutting nature of this issue has led to the involvement of many other UN bodies, both in their own right and in cooperation with WHO. The UN program with the most intense involvement in infectious diseases has traditionally been UNICEF because of the institution's focus on childhood diseases.[9] WHO and UNICEF have been cooperating since their inception, first in eradication campaigns against yaws, tuberculosis, and malaria, then increasingly in the development of basic health services and child immunization. As mentioned earlier, UNICEF also co-sponsored the 1978 Alma-Ata conference and the HFA process,[10] and is one of the initial co-sponsors of the Joint UN Programme on HIV/AIDS (UNAIDS). More recently, UNICEF was one of the initiators of the Global Alliance for Vaccines and Immunization, a public–private partnership established in 2000 to channel financial resources to countries to purchase vaccines and other supplies and to support the operational costs of immunization.

While UNDP has financed some of WHO's health programs since the mid-1960s, their relations have been characterized by the search for a balance between WHO's assertion of 'independence' from UNDP's attempts to centralize the system of technical cooperation around the lead of the resident coordinator, and on the other hand an effort to cooperate with UNDP for the integration of health programs in overall development activities. Most importantly, UNDP is co-sponsoring with WHO and the World Bank the Special Programme for Research and Training in Tropical Diseases. Established in 1978, this co-sponsored effort seeks to facilitate research in the prevention and treatment of the major tropical diseases in the face of a relative lack of interest by the pharmaceutical industry towards the so-called diseases of the poor.[11]

The growing dissatisfaction at the yawning gap between the mortality and morbidity engendered by infectious diseases in developing countries (affecting almost 90 percent of the world's population) and the research and pharmaceutical resources spent on them—estimated at no more than 10 percent—have also led since the 1990s to the establishment of numerous public-private partnerships to generate additional financial resources, develop new medicines, and try to correct the inadequacies of the market. The initiatives have taken the form of long-term collaborative mechanisms to address a specific public health problem, encompassing a diverse array of partners both private and public, with an agreed division of labor and contribution of resources. Most of these partnerships are not established as separate international agencies or private law entities; rather they are unincorporated groups of stakeholders, and are normally 'hosted' by an existing international organization that provides their secretariat. WHO has been particularly active in this effort, hosting more than thirty such initiatives.[12]

INFECTIOUS DISEASES AND SECURITY

The link between health and security was underscored as early as 1946 in the preamble to the WHO's constitution, which states that 'the health of all peoples is fundamental to the attainment of peace and security.' A similar tone can be found in Article 55 of the UN Charter, which links the attainment of peaceful and friendly relations among nations with, among others, 'solutions of international, economic, social, health and related problems.' That link, however, was largely lost in both political and scholarly discourse during the Cold War; security was conceptualized in military terms while public health focused on vertical programs for the eradication of diseases.

The linkage between infectious diseases and a broader vision of security reemerges during the 1990s, mainly due to the developments summarized in the previous section. These developments also coincided with the emergence of the concept of human security within the UN system.[13] The WHA adopted in 1995 a resolution on new, emerging, or re-emerging infectious diseases (resolution WHA 48.13), while various US agencies analyzed with growing alarm the security and foreign policy threats posed by the resurgence of infectious diseases.[14]

The growing attention to the health/security paradigm has been developing along two main lines. The first concerns the impact of naturally occurring diseases on national and international security. A high level of political attention, for example, has been given to the spread of HIV/AIDS in developing countries, predominantly through heterosexual transmission. The decimation of the productive segments of society in many countries may lead to their economic and social collapse and political destabilization, and consequently affect the security of their neighbors.

In January 2000, the Security Council devoted a day-long session to AIDS in Africa, the first time that a public health situation was discussed in that forum and specifically framed as a threat to international peace and security.[15] Even though the Council did not adopt a formal decision, there was a consensus that the AIDS pandemic posed a security threat of the greatest magnitude and that a broader security agenda had to encompass new pandemics as well as the emergence of resistant strains of old diseases. This was followed by similar statements at the Group of 8 summits of Okinawa and Genoa and the 2001 General Assembly special session on HIV/AIDS. The social and economic consequences of the spread of SARS in 2003 and the H5N1 strain of avian flu in 2005–2006, and the growing fear of a human flu pandemic, represent other major examples of this trend.

The second main line concerns the growing fear of bioterrorism, especially since the terrorist attacks and the anthrax scare in the United States in late 2001. International action against biological weapons is not new, and the 1925 Geneva Protocol as well as the 1972 Biological and Toxin Weapons Convention represent the normative response to this particular form of warfare. At the same time, the lack of an internationally agreed verification or early warning mechanism along with the fear of terrorist groups spreading biological agents or contaminating the food or water supply have exacerbated the sense of vulnerability of Western countries and the political urgency of strengthening national and international preparedness.

The common thread between these two developments is that national and international public health surveillance and response mechanisms inevitably become instrumental to a 'security paradigm.' The prevention and control of diseases such as HIV/AIDS and pandemic flu may be crucial as a security measure in preventing the destabilization of entire regions. Moreover, since the deliberate release of a biological agent would in most cases be initially considered as a natural event, public health systems would be the first line not only of response but also of early warning in the event of a bioterrorist act.

These considerations pose many challenges to a technical agency such as WHO, which has been trying, since its unsuccessful 1996 attempt to obtain an advisory opinion on the health effects of nuclear weapons from the International Court of Justice, to strictly adhere to its public health mandate without getting too close to the politics of arms control or the fight against terrorism.[16] The WHA in 2002 adopted a balanced decision (resolution WHA 55.16), which urged member states to treat any deliberate release of biological and chemical agents as a global public health threat, while at the same time clearly limiting the role of the organization to public health guidance and support. In 2004 the WHO's secretariat thoroughly revised its technical guidance on public health responses to biological and chemical weapons.[17] Moreover, it has generally strengthened since the mid-1990s its capacities for international surveillance and response to disease outbreaks, including within the overarching context of the revised IHR. At the same time, overtly including WHO in an international security framework risks creating growing divisions between Western and developing countries. It also may divert resources from diseases with heavy public health impact but lower security relevance, such as many tropical diseases or non-communicable conditions such as cardio-vascular diseases.

The on-going debate has been made more complex by UN reports and decisions that clearly include infectious diseases among interconnected security threats of social and economic origin. The UN consequently advocates a closer and complementary relationship between WHO and the Security Council. The report of the High-level Panel on Threats, Challenges and Change,[18] for example, calls for a second Security Council special session on HIV/AIDS aiming at a long-term strategy against this threat to international peace and security. Most significantly, the panel envisages Security Council cooperation with WHO in enforcing effective quarantine measures, supporting the work of WHO 'investigators,' and mandating greater access for WHO personnel in extreme cases of disease outbreaks of natural or deliberate origin. The Secretary-General's 2005 report *In Larger Freedom*[19] and the 2005 World Summit Outcome[20] do not go so far, but they still call for a full implementation of the IHR and strengthening WHO's Global Outbreak Alert and Response Network and national health systems to tackle the double challenges of naturally occurring infectious diseases as well as human-made outbreaks. While these developments may generate more attention and resources towards crucial areas of public health, they also raise concerns for the possible political implications and expectations with regard to WHO's involvement in infectious disease control.

The normative lynch-pin in this increasingly complex area is the revised IHR. The broadening of their scope and of the definition of disease, as noted above, means that intentional release of biological, chemical, or radiological agents falls within the purview of the instrument and WHO's responsibilities. This became the most contentious issue during the revision process for the IHR and was only solved a few days before their adoption in May 2005. As a result of this compromise, deliberate release is not mentioned explicitly but is indirectly alluded to through the expression 'unexpected or unusual public health event.' At the same time, the IHR carefully restrict WHO to perform exclusively public health functions in case of a deliberate release and request it to coordinate its activities with other international agencies. This means, for example, that WHO would play no role in determining whether a state has violated its international obligations or in enforcement measures. WHO has also consistently held this position with regard to its possible participation in a UN investigation of alleged use of biological or chemical weapons envisaged in resolutions of the Security Council and General Assembly.[21]

CONCLUSION

While the scope of this chapter does not allow full elaboration of the evolution of international cooperation in the fight against infectious diseases, it nonetheless underscores the intrinsically international dimension of this problem and the realization since the nineteenth century of the essential importance of international cooperation. The principles underlying such cooperation have undergone significant changes since the days of sanitary cordons and quarantines, even though recent developments concerning bioterrorism and emerging diseases show how easily governments may be led by public opinion or sheer fear to fall back on unilateral measures. As such, they affect international traffic and individual rights while proving sometimes of limited effectiveness in preventing the international spread of disease.

Still, it can be argued that the generally accepted need for accountability of states in this area—together with the importance of centralized coordination, guidance, and policymaking—are leading to the development of a system of 'global health governance.' The WHO and other UN agencies are playing an increasingly visible role for the pursuit of 'global health security.'

NOTES

1. See the data reported in David Fidler, *International Law and Infectious Diseases* (Oxford: Clarendon Press, 1999), 22–23.
2. For a summary of the policy and its implications, see Gian Luca Burci and Claude-Henri Vignes, *World Health Organization* (The Hague: Kluwer Law International, 2004), 160–165.
3. World Health Organization, *International Health Regulations (1969)*, 3rd edn. (Geneva: WHO, 1983). For a general overview of the IHR (1969), Fidler, *International Law and Infectious Diseases*, 58–80.

4. They are customarily reported in the publication *Weekly Epidemiological Record*, available at www.who.int/wer/en.

5. For a broader analysis of the collapse of the 'classical regime' for infectious disease control, see David Fidler, 'From International Sanitary Conventions to Global Health Security: The New International Health Regulations,' *Chinese Journal of International Law* 4, no. 2 (2005): 325–392.

6. Gian Luca Burci, 'L'impatto della SARS e la politica sanitaria mondiale,' in *L'Italia e la politica internazionale*, ed. Alessandro Colombo and Natalino Ronzitti (Bologna: il Mulino, 2004), 213–224.

7. Available at www.who.int.

8. Defined in Article 1 of the regulations as 'a manifestation of disease or an occurrence that creates a potential for disease.'

9. See Yves Beigbeder, *New Challenges for UNICEF: Children, Women and Human Rights* (Houndmills, Basingstoke, UK: Palgrave, 2001), esp. 61–100.

10. Burci and Vignes, *World Health Organization*, 76–78.

11. Ibid., 79–80.

12. The NGO Global Forum for Health Research has created an online database of public-private partnerships for health, available at www.ippph.org.

13. See S. Neil MacFarlane and Yuen Foong Khong, *Human Security and the UN: A Critical History* (Bloomington: Indiana University Press, 2006).

14. David Fidler, 'Caught Between Paradise and Power: Public Health, Pathogenic Threats, and the Axis of Illness,' *McGeorge Law Review* 35, no. 45 (2004): 65.

15. Security Council 4087th meeting 'The impact of AIDS on peace and security in Africa,' UN document S/PV.4087, 10 January 2000.

16. The International Court of Justice, on 8 July 1996, refused to render an advisory opinion to the World Health Assembly on the legality of the use by a state of nuclear weapons in the light of their health and environmental effects, as the request fell outside the competence of WHO. *ICJ Reports* (1996), 66–84. See Burci and Vignes, *World Health Organization*, 114–118.

17. World Health Organization, *Public Health Response to Biological and Chemical Weapons: WHO Guidance*, 2nd edn. (Geneva: WHO, 2004).

18. High-level Panel on Threats, Challenges and Change, *A More Secure World: Our Shared Responsibility—Report of the High-level Panel on Threats, Challenges and Change*, UN document A/59/565, 2 December 2004, 26–27, 30, 44–45.

19. Kofi Annan, *In Larger Freedom: Towards Development, Security and Human Rights for All—Report of the Secretary-General*, UN document A/59/2005, 21 March 2005, 20, 27.

20. *Resolution adopted by the General Assemby 60/1: 2005 World Summit Outcome*, UN document A/RES/60/1, 24 October 2005.

21. World Health Organization, *Deliberate Use of Biological and Chemical Agents to Cause Harm, Public Health Response, Report by the Secretariat*, WHO document A55/20, 16 April 2002.

CHAPTER 34

NATURAL RESOURCE MANAGEMENT AND SUSTAINABLE DEVELOPMENT

NICO SCHRIJVER

THE management of natural resources and the environment is not an issue featured in the UN Charter, yet the United Nations has, since 1945, had a profound impact on how natural resources are viewed and how they are used. This chapter begins by identifying four themes in the development of natural resource management, and then outlines eight phases in the evolution of the UN's resource management policy. The chapter then turns to a discussion of the principal actors within the UN system involved in resource management, before summarizing the conceptual contribution of the UN to international approaches to natural resource management.

THEMES IN RESOURCE MANAGEMENT

Over the course of the evolution of natural resource management since 1945, four themes or trends can be distinguished. The first is the post-World War II concern over the security of supply of and access to natural resources. Consequently, in the early years of the world organization, several UN bodies were engaged in securing resource supplies: the Food and Agriculture Organization (FAO), for example, undertook forestry projects as a means of reconstructing natural resource bases destroyed during the war; the Economic and Social Council (ECOSOC) was engaged in promoting the effective utilization of natural resources; and the General Assembly debated how natural resources could be more effectively harnessed in support of global economic interests.

A second theme—tied to the concept of 'resource sovereignty'—became apparent during the push for decolonization. Using the UN as an arena to voice their right to self-determination, newly independent states also claimed the right to benefit fully from the exploitation of their own natural resources and to review, where appropriate, 'inequitable' legal arrangements with other states or foreign companies.

The third theme—a growing concern about the sustainable use of natural resources—emerged in the 1960s but took firmer root after the 1972 United Nations Conference on the Human Environment (UNCHE) held in Stockholm. It was not until the 1992 United Nations Conference on Environment and Development (UNCED) at Rio de Janeiro that this concept became integrated into international law, as exemplified by the incorporation into treaties of provisions on sustainable development[1] and by international jurisprudence.[2]

The fourth theme is a shift in thinking about the role of natural resources in stability and development. While it seems logical that plentiful natural resources should engender prosperity, the record of instability and violence in countries like Angola, Sierra Leone, and the Democratic Republic of the Congo (DRC) suggests, in fact, a correlation between resource abundance and conflict—the so-called 'resource curse.'

THE UN'S EVOLVING ROLE

The themes identified above, and the changes in perception they encompass, have influenced the way in which the UN and its bodies have approached natural resource management. It is possible to discern eight phases in the UN's resource management policies; these are outlined below.

Early Ideas about the International Management of Natural Resources

The postwar preoccupation about the security of supply of and access to natural resources had been articulated as early as 1941, in the Atlantic Charter, in which the allies agreed to 'endeavour, with due respect for their existing obligations, to further the enjoyment by all States, great or small, victor and vanquished, of access, on equal terms, to the trade and to the raw materials of the world which are needed for their economic prosperity.'[3]

This concern also served as a leitmotif both in the establishment in the mid-1940s of the Bretton Woods institutions and in the conclusion in 1947 of the General Agreement on Tariffs and Trade (GATT). The opening words in the articles of agreement of both the International Bank for Reconstruction and Development (IBRD) and the International Monetary Fund (IMF) refer to the aim of developing 'the productive resources of all members,' while the GATT preamble includes among its objectives 'the full use of the resources of the world.'

In the late 1940s, a concern arose in the UN about the conservation and effective utilization of natural resources. Timber shortages, especially in Europe, formed one of the initial concerns of the newly established FAO. Hence, the Rome-based institution convened an international timber conference in 1947, which stressed the need for a satisfactory distribution of timber supplies and the imperative of identifying and implementing long-term measures to restore forests as a part of European reconstruction.

In addition, pursuant to a US proposal in 1946, ECOSOC organized in 1949 a UN Scientific Conference on the Conservation and Effective Utilization of Natural Resources. The primary goal was to exchange ideas and experiences in the field of resource management and explore the human use of resources. Discussions focused on the world resource situation, including resource depletion, critical shortages, use and conservation, and resource exploitation techniques suitable for what were then called less-developed countries. The central question was how to meet growing demand. Although the conference did not adopt specific recommendations, it stated that 'scientific knowledge can discover and create new resources and husband better those already in use, so that a new era of prosperity awaited mankind' on the condition that war and the wasteful depletion of resources associated with it would be eliminated.[4]

These early postwar projects and initiatives reflected the wartime problems of the allied powers in gaining access to and properly managing scarce natural resources. Initially such proposals were made in an optimistic spirit of international cooperation. However, rivalry between the East and the West soon emerged, and tensions arose as less-developed countries struggled to assert control over their own natural resources.

The Rise of Economic Nationalism

From the early 1950s various efforts were made to strengthen national control over natural resources. In 1951 a Polish proposal led to General Assembly resolution 523 (VI) on integrated economic development and long-term trade agreements.[5] The Polish draft stipulated that the 'under-developed countries have the full right to determine freely the use of their natural resources.' The United States subsequently submitted an amendment proposing the insertion of a reference to 'the interests of an expanding world economy.' Finally, a compromise was reached, following an Egyptian proposal, and the final resolution encouraged 'the development of natural resources which can be utilised for the domestic needs of the under-developed countries and also for the needs of international trade.'

In 1951, the then socialist government of Iran, led by Prime Minister Mohammed Mossadegh, announced the decision to nationalize the oil industry and to terminate the 1933 concession agreement with the Anglo-Iranian Oil Company, which had been granted exclusive rights, over a sixty-year period, to the extraction and processing of petroleum in a specified area. Perceiving its oil supplies to be jeopardized, the United Kingdom instituted proceedings at the International Court of Justice (ICJ).[6] The ICJ, however, concluded in 1952 that it lacked jurisdiction over the case; nor did the Security Council take a definitive view. The resource dispute ended only with the 1953 coup that brought Mohammad Reza Pahlavi to power in Teheran (and in which allegedly the British and American secret services played an instrumental role). In 1954 an international consortium of oil companies was established, which signed an agreement with the new government.

Meanwhile, in November 1952 Uruguay had submitted a draft resolution under the item 'Economic Development of Under-Developed Countries.'[7] This draft resolution advocated strengthening the hand of economically weak nations in the exploitation of their natural resources. Member states were called upon to recognize the right of each country to nationalize and exploit freely its natural wealth, as an essential factor of independence. Following strong protests, especially from the West, the explicit reference to the right to nationalize was replaced by the right to use and exploit natural wealth and resources. The draft resolution led to heated debate. Last-minute amendments tabled by India were adopted; they referred to 'the need for maintaining mutual confidence and economic co-operation among nations' and 'the need for maintaining the flow of capital in conditions of security.' However, such phrases could not prevent the stigmatization of General Assembly resolution 626 (VII) as the 'nationalization resolution.'

Self-determination and Resource Sovereignty

From the early 1950s natural resource management began to figure in debates about human rights. In 1952, the General Assembly included in the draft international human rights covenants an article on the right to political and economic self-determination. In an early stage of the negotiations, Chile proposed to add to this article the following wording: 'The right of the peoples to self-determination shall also include permanent sovereignty over their natural wealth and resources. In no case may a people be deprived of its own means of subsistence on the grounds of any rights that may be claimed by other States.'[8]

This proposal came under a severe attack by the West. It was argued that such a provision—one which reaffirmed the principle of national sovereignty—would be out of place in an article promoting self-determination and human rights; opponents of the proposed provision claimed, furthermore, that it could be interpreted to question the validity of treaties, contracts, and concession agreements. France stated that it would not 'legalize the autarchic practices of certain States which had a virtual monopoly of the raw materials indispensable to the international community,' and asserted that 'some sovereignty would have to be surrendered to international organizations, such as the Schumann Plan.'[9] In response to this dissension, a nine-member working party was established which recommended a substantial change to the earlier text proclaiming permanent sovereignty over natural resources.[10] This text was maintained and features prominently in Article 1 of the two human rights covenants, finally adopted in 1966.[11]

Deepening Resource Sovereignty

Following discussions in the Commission on Human Rights (CHR), ECOSOC, and the Third Committee of the General Assembly in 1954 and 1955, the General Assembly passed resolution 1314 (XIII), establishing a nine-member Commission on Permanent Sovereignty over Natural Resources. After vigorous debate and many amendments, the group's work led to resolution 1803 (XVII) and the 1962 Declaration on Permanent Sovereignty over Natural Resources—widely considered a landmark agreement, and often described as the economic equivalent of the Decolonization Declaration of 1960.

From the 1960s developing countries continued to use the UN as a forum to assert permanent sovereignty over natural resources, believing this to constitute a fundamental basis for economic development and a means of more equitably distributing wealth and power among industrialized and developing countries. Initially, the UN's political organs worked towards consolidating and elaborating the 1962 declaration and, as follow-up to the first meeting of the United Nations Conference on Trade and Development (UNCTAD I) in 1964, the UN also sought to establish a link between resource sovereignty and the promotion of development. Building upon the 1962 declaration's foreign investment provisions, the General Assembly identified some problems in the relationship between foreign investors and developing host countries, such as an asymmetrical share in the administration and in the profits of wholly or partly foreign-operated enterprises. In resolution 2158 (XXI), the Assembly emphasized that developing countries themselves should undertake the exploitation and marketing of their natural resources, so that the profits could help stimulate development.[12] The developmental dimension of the debate thus became more pronounced, and the efforts of developing countries to assert control over resource exploitation gained currency.

From Confrontation to Cooperation

The debate over resources effectively sparked the 1970s confrontation over a New International Economic Order (NIEO). In response to the Yom Kippur war of 1973, the Organization of the Petroleum Exporting Countries (OPEC) wielded oil as a political weapon, levying a temporary oil embargo against the United States and the Netherlands in response to their allegedly pro-Israeli policies, and pursuing a cartel policy that quadrupled oil prices. OPEC's initial success bolstered the assertiveness of developing countries in international affairs, and consultations were undertaken with a view to establishing various producers' associations, including for copper, bauxite, tea, and bananas.[13] Large-scale nationalizations took place in a number of developing countries, including Chile (1971), Iraq (1972), Peru (1974), Libya (1971 and 1973), and Venezuela (1976).[14] Direct clashes between developing countries and transnational corporations occurred often, with those countries carrying out nationalizations seeking international support and legitimization through UN organs, and through the call for the NIEO.

The Sixth Special Session of the General Assembly in 1974 made the permanent sovereignty over natural resources applicable to all economic activities. Nationalization—or even the transfer to nationals of ownership over resources—was claimed to be a legitimate way of exercising such sovereignty 'in order to safeguard these resources.'[15] In a similar vein, restitution and full compensation were claimed for the exploitation and depletion of the natural resources of states and peoples under foreign occupation, alien and colonial domination, or apartheid. Furthermore, the session reaffirmed the right to establish producers' associations, as well as the need for price indexation between industrialized products and raw materials.

Meanwhile, following a 1972 initiative launched by Mexican President Luís Echeverría during UNCTAD III in Santiago, a deeply-divided General Assembly adopted in 1974 resolution 3281 (XXIX), a Charter of Economic Rights and Duties of States (CERDS). Alongside the 120 votes in favor of the resolution were six negative votes and ten abstentions: the sixteen states that had not approved the resolution were all members of the Organization for Economic Co-operation and Development. The main point of contention was Article 2, which addressed permanent sovereignty over natural resources, the regulation of foreign investment, expropriation, nationalization, and dispute settlement.[16] Similarly, Article 16 includes the principle of restitution ('making good injustices') for depriving a nation and oppressed peoples of the natural resources that could otherwise have contributed to their development. Article 5 confirms the right of all states to associate in organizations of primary commodity producers such as OPEC.

However, CERDS also contains a number of resource-related provisions that provoked less confrontation between developing countries and industrialized countries. Article 6, for instance, deals with the duty of states to contribute to the development of international trade, particularly by the conclusion of long-term multilateral commodity agreements, taking into account the interests of producers and consumers. Article 31 records the duty of each state to contribute to the balanced expansion of the world economy, and Article 30 calls upon states to preserve the environment. Both articles feature in the final chapter of the economic charter, entitled 'Common responsibilities towards the international community.'

In subsequent years, the basic conceptual differences between industrialized and developing countries narrowed. While echoes of the NIEO resolutions could still be heard during the second conference of the UN Industrial Development Organization (UNIDO) held in 1975 in Lima, during the negotiations on a Draft Code of Conduct on Transnational Corporations and, occasionally, at debates in the General Assembly, a new spirit of constructive engagement became apparent after 1975. This cooperative trend was reflected in the unanimous approval of the final document at the Seventh Special Session of the 1975 General Assembly on Development and International Economic Co-operation; in the UNCTAD IV Integrated Programme for Commodities (1976); and at the Third UN Conference on the Law of the Sea (1973–82). In 1980 UNCTAD realized its aim of a global commodity policy through individual agreements and the establishment of an umbrella Common Fund for Commodities, although the requisite funding never materialized.[17]

In short, the international debate over resource sovereignty had shifted. The original question of how to demarcate the parameters for foreign participation in the exploitation of natural resources (i.e., establishing conditions for foreign investment, foreign participation in management and profits, the training by foreigners of national personnel and the transfer of technology) was reoriented to how international cooperation could contribute to the exploration, exploitation, processing, and marketing of the natural resources of developing countries to mutual benefit.

Broadening Resource Sovereignty: Extending Control over Marine Resources

The UN has played a pivotal role in the management of marine resources. For centuries the law of the sea had been based on customary international law, especially on the notion of *mare liberum* as advocated by Hugo Grotius in the early seventeenth century. In essence this meant that everyone could fish and otherwise exploit marine resources, as long as the rights of others were not infringed upon. The notion of sovereignty occupied only a modest place in the classical law of the sea, its applicability restricted to a narrow belt of territorial sea, not exceeding a three-mile limit.[18]

After 1945 there was increasing pressure to bring a wider area of the sea and its natural resources under coastal state jurisdiction, as emphasis shifted from the sea 'as an avenue of transportation and communication' to the sea as an important economic zone for the exploitation of natural resources.[19] Latin American countries and newly independent countries in Asia and Africa in particular pushed for a wider territorial sea and an exclusive fishery zone. In addition, following the Truman

Proclamation of 1945, coastal states began to claim exclusive resource jurisdiction over their respective continental shelves.[20]

Building on the work of the UN International Law Commission, the UN adopted at the 1958 Conference on the Law of the Sea four conventions—on the territorial sea, the continental shelf, the high seas, and fisheries.[21] However, this conference, and a subsequent one in 1960, failed to reach agreement on the width of the territorial sea. As a result, coastal states followed Iceland's lead and proclaimed, in the absence of wider agreement, a twelve-mile territorial sea and beyond it an exclusive fishery zone. Chile, El Salvador, and Panama went further, claiming a 200-mile zone.[22] Latin American countries in particular asserted the right of developing countries to the full utilization of the natural resources in 'their adjacent seas,' identified in the preamble to Assembly resolution 2692 (XXV). UNCTAD III (Santiago, Chile, 1972) confirmed the right of coastal states to marine resources, within the limits of national jurisdiction, in support of the development and welfare needs of their peoples.[23] However, these resolutions were controversial. The increasing uncertainty about the extent of the limits of national economic jurisdiction at sea served as one of the reasons to convene a Third UN Conference on the Law of the Sea (UNCLOS III). Another reason was to find answers to comparatively novel questions over the deep seabed. As a result of developments in technology and perceived resource scarcity, exploitation of the deep seabed (especially manganese or polymetallic nodules) became both a technical possibility and a seeming necessity. However, the existing legal framework—elaborated in the seventeenth century and based on the principle of the freedom of the high seas and the concept of the ocean being open for common use (*res communis*)—clearly could not accommodate the deep seabed and the right to exploit its resources.

In 1967, Ambassador Arvid Pardo of Malta proposed that the General Assembly pronounce the seabed and the ocean floor beyond the limits of national jurisdiction as 'the common heritage of mankind,' echoing the Assembly's declaration earlier that same year christening outer space—including the moon and other celestial bodies—'the province of all mankind.'[24] In 1970, the Assembly adopted resolution 2749 (XXV), the 'Declaration of Principles Governing the Sea-bed and the Ocean Floor, and the Subsoil Thereof, Beyond the Limits of National Jurisdiction,' in which the principle of the common heritage of humankind features prominently. On the same day, the General Assembly decided in resolution 2750 (XXV) to convene UNCLOS III, which opened in 1973. The conference eventually resulted in the 1982 UN Convention on the Law of the Sea, a landmark achievement labeled by the conference president, Singapore's Ambassador Tommy Koh, 'a Constitution for the Oceans.'

Agreement was reached on the fractious issue of the territorial sea, the width of which was limited to twelve nautical miles; the agreement also affirmed the full sovereignty of the coastal state over the natural resources located within this zone. The 1982 convention also substantially extended the continental shelf and set out rules for the exploitation of the oil and gas resources found there.

An innovation of the 1982 UN regime was the official introduction of a 200-mile Exclusive Economic Zone (EEZ). As in the case of the extended continental shelf, a coastal state does not enjoy full sovereignty over the EEZ, but only sovereign rights to the natural resources, whether living or nonliving, of the seabed and subsoil and the superjacent waters. The EEZ regime, furthermore, does not only confer rights, but imposes duties and responsibilities also. The coastal state is under a general duty to conserve the resources within its EEZ and to avoid overexploitation, specifically to implement measures to maintain or restore the so-called maximum sustainable yield. In addition, states are obliged to protect and preserve the marine environment and to take all kinds of measures to control pollution.[25]

Part XI of the 1982 convention contains an extensive framework for regulating future deep seabed mining. While the agreement to proclaim the deep seabed and its natural resources 'the common heritage of mankind' is enshrined in Article 136, not all controversies over the deep seabed mining regime had faded, with the result that several industrializing states did not ratify the convention. However, soon after the conclusion of the 1982 convention, it became clear that commercial deep seabed mining was unlikely in the near future. Following a series of informal consultations, a so-called Supplementary Agreement was concluded in 1994 that substantially accommodated the objections of the United States and other Western countries to Part XI. The Supplementary Agreement eliminated major stumbling blocks—among them proposed limits to production that would have favored land-based producers of minerals; provisions making mandatory the transfer of technology to developing countries; and the perceived overempowerment of the envisaged supranational mining company, the UN Enterprise. The 1994 agreement also responded in important ways to political and economic changes that occurred after 1982, in particular 'a growing reliance on market principles' and 'the growing concern for the global environment.'[26] The modifications put forward in the Supplementary Agreement widened support for the 1982 convention: in December 2006, 152 states had ratified the UN Convention on the Law of the Sea.

Sustainable Use of Natural Resources

Shortly after the 1962 Declaration on Permanent Sovereignty over Natural Resources, the General Assembly approved resolution 1831 (XVII) on 'Economic Development and the Conservation of Nature,' highlighting the tension created by the need both to preserve natural resources and to harness them for the purposes of economic development. Upon Sweden's initiative, the Assembly in 1968 approved resolution 2398 (XXIII), which led to UNCHE, held at Stockholm in 1972. At the conference, the friction between environmental and developmental concerns was apparent.[27] Early drafts were severely criticized for dissociating environmental problems from developmental issues and for not putting at 'the forefront the basic principle that each State has inalienable sovereignty over its environment and over its natural resources.'[28]

In June 1972, the twenty-six-principle Declaration of the United Nations Conference on the Human Environment was adopted. From the perspective of natural resource management, the Stockholm declaration expresses a number of interesting precepts. Principle 2 declares that careful planning and management are required for safeguarding natural resources. Principle 3 stipulates that 'the capacity of the earth to produce vital renewable resources must be maintained and, wherever practical, restored or improved.' Nonrenewable resources, the declaration states, must be employed in such a way 'as to guard against the danger of their future exhaustion and to ensure that benefits of such employment are shared by all mankind.' Principles 13 and 14 link integrated and coordinated planning to the rational use of resources and compatibility between environmental preservation and development.

The Stockholm declaration also situates resource sovereignty in an environmental context. Principle 21 confers upon states 'the responsibility to ensure that activities within their jurisdiction or control do not cause damage to the environment of other States or of areas beyond the limits of national jurisdiction,' drawing from the international legal principles as good neighborliness, diligence, and due care. Although Principle 21 was exclusively concerned with preventing the spillover of resource mismanagement from one country to others, it paved the way for the General Assembly to call later upon member states to pursue and apply effective management and conservation policies within the domestic sphere.

For example General Assembly resolution 37/7 approved the 1982 World Charter for Nature, which had been initiated by the International Union for the Conservation of Nature. This charter proclaims five principles of conservation for living natural resources and notes the view that, while competition for scarce resources foments conflict, the conservation of nature and natural resources promotes justice and peace.

In 1987, the World Commission on Environment and Development—commonly known as the Brundtland Commission after its chair, Gro Harlem Brundtland, Norway's then prime minister—published *Our Common Future*. A key contribution of the report was a new intellectual framework for development: 'sustainable development,' according to the commission, is 'development that meets the needs of the present without compromising the ability of future generations to meet their own needs.'[29] In 1987 the General Assembly welcomed the report—albeit without committing itself to its contents—and in 1989 decided in resolution 44/228 to convene the UN Conference on Environment and Development, in view of 'the continuing deterioration of the state of the environment and the serious degradation of the global life-support systems' that could result in 'an ecological catastrophe.'

UNCED's most notable outcome was the 1992 Rio Declaration on Environment and Development. Somewhat less centered on the environment than the 1972 UNCHE declaration and the 1982 World Charter for Nature, the Rio Declaration seeks to strike a balance between the protection of the environment and the need to promote growth in developing countries. Principle 5 links environmental preservation to poverty eradication and Principle 6 calls for the prioritization of the needs of developing countries, particularly the least developed and those which are the most environmentally vulnerable.

Another achievement of the 1992 Rio conference was the opening for signature of the UN Framework Convention on Climate Change (UNFCCC) and the Convention on Biological Diversity. UNCED also produced a Statement on Forestry Principles;[30] 'Agenda 21,' an international action program presenting concrete measures to protect the environment; and a new coordinating organ, the Commission on Sustainable Development.[31]

Ten years later, on the basis of General Assembly resolution 55/199 of 2000, the World Summit on Sustainable Development took place in Johannesburg; its mandate was to take stock of the implementation of the measures agreed in Rio and 'to reinvigorate the global commitment to sustainable development.' UN Secretary-General Kofi Annan urged the summit to concentrate upon five specific issues which are often grouped under the abbreviation WEHAB: that is, water and sanitation, energy, healthcare, agriculture, and biological diversity. The Johannesburg Summit in 2002 attracted less international attention, perhaps, than the meetings in Stockholm and Rio, but the main protagonists remained the United States, the European Union, and the Group of 77.[32]

Those who took part included not only member states and officials from international organizations but also a colorful array of representatives from nongovernmental, scientific, women, youth, environmental, indigenous peoples, and developmental organizations as well as from the corporate world. The summit adopted two policy documents.[33] First, a political declaration—the Johannesburg Declaration on Sustainable Development—reconfirmed collective responsibility for the living environment and the welfare of all people, both now and in the future. Second, a comprehensive international action program, the Johannesburg Plan of Implementation, outlined the steps which needed to be taken at the international and national levels. This implementation plan proposes, among other things, sustainable strategies for food production; ways of changing unsustainable consumption and production patterns; mechanisms for the protection and management of natural resources (including sustainable fishing); and the introduction of new public–private partnerships.[34]

The themes of the Johannesburg documents were evident again during the September 2005 UN World Summit in New York. World leaders endorsed steps towards the implementation of sustainable resource policies—essentially through improving the protection and management of natural resources, initiating schemes for changing production and consumption patterns to produce less pollution, developing renewable energy resources, and undertaking integrated ecosystem management.[35]

The 'Curse' of Natural Resources

The proliferation of civil war in the 1990s, and the concentration of such conflicts in resource-abundant countries, called into question the relationship between natural resources and stability, with the availability of natural resources increasingly viewed as both a political and societal evil and an economic blessing. The conflicts in Angola, Liberia, and Sierra Leone, to mention just a few, were caused or fueled by access to natural resources. Furthermore, rivalry over natural resources characterized several interstate wars: for instance, the Iraqi invasion of Kuwait was sparked because of the disputed transboundary Rumaila oil field, and a principal reason for Rwandan and Ugandan aggression against the DRC was to gain access to its extensive natural resources. The relationship between natural resources and armed conflict has thus received increasing attention from practitioners and social scientists.[36]

The Security Council, too, has given its attention to the nexus of instability and natural resources, attempting to prevent the illicit trafficking of 'conflict goods,' such as diamonds and timber. A key aspect of the Council's work in this area has been to establish a regime for the certification of origin of certain precious natural resources, with a particular view to banning the trade in 'blood diamonds,' which has been so central to the perpetuation of conflict in West Africa.[37]

The growth of environmental awareness has been paralleled by a greater appreciation of the directly negative impact of armed conflict on the physical environment. This is reflected in a comparison of the Stockholm and Rio declarations. While Principle 26 of the UNCHE Declaration states, 'Man and his environment must be spared the effects of nuclear weapons and all other means of mass destruction,' the 1992 Rio Declaration is more explicit: 'Warfare is inherently destructive of sustainable development. States shall therefore respect international law providing protection for the environment in times of armed conflict and cooperate in its further development, as necessary.'

MAIN UN INSTITUTIONS

The debate over the UN's natural resource management policies has spanned a period of nearly sixty years and involved all six principal organs. Initially, ECOSOC and the General Assembly played the key roles. ECOSOC was the first to address the postwar concerns over the scarcity, and in particular the effective utilization, of natural resources. To this end, it organized conferences and was instrumental in data collection and disseminating findings to the relevant specialized agencies, for example the FAO and the World Bank. In acting as the coordinating agency within the UN system, ECOSOC performed the role envisaged for it in Article 62 of the UN Charter. ECOSOC also established the ad hoc Committee on the Survey Programme for the Development of Natural Resources, a forerunner of the Standing Committee on Natural Resources. Established in 1970, the Standing Committee was intended to assist ECOSOC in planning and coordinating activities within the UN system for the management of natural resources and in making recommendations to governments and UN bodies such as the UN Development Programme (UNDP) about priorities for exploration and exploitation.

The Standing Committee on Natural Resources played a role in assessing the implementation of the principle of sovereignty over natural resources and in conducting fact-finding on trends in national legislation, joint ventures, service agreements, government ownership of natural resource ventures, transfer of technology and technical cooperation among developing countries. It always generated solid information. However, its functions were ultimately absorbed into the CSD.

The relationship between natural resources and human rights has also figured in the Commission on Human Rights, one of ECOSOC's main functional commissions and a body that UN member states agreed, at the 2005 World Summit, to replace with the Human Rights Council. During the 1950s, the principles of economic self-determination and permanent sovereignty over natural resources as elements of human rights, in particular the rights of peoples, were hotly debated. However, with the virtual end of decolonization, the primary forum for discussing these issues became the economic wings of the General Assembly (Second Committee and UNCTAD); as we have already seen, the Assembly has, over the course of the post-World War II period, approved several resolutions and declarations that have sought to clarify and to assert sovereignty over natural resources and to enhance the role of developing countries in the processing, marketing, and distribution of their natural resources.

As noted, the Security Council has also sought to input into effective natural resource management, for example through its involvement in attempting to stem the trade in conflict goods. In addition the Council, through resolution 687 of 1991, held Iraq liable for the environmental damage and depletion of natural resources caused by its invasion and occupation of Kuwait. The Security Council has also occasionally employed Chapter VII to impose trade embargoes on states where natural resources fueled or sustained violence. It has also empowered several expert panels to look into specific situations; for example the Porter Commission's mandate was the plundering of the DRC's natural resources.[38] Furthermore, with a view to strengthening its effectiveness in conflict prevention, particularly in Africa, the Security Council in September 2005 passed resolution 1625, expressing the Council's determination 'to take action against illegal exploitation and trafficking of natural resources and high-value commodities in areas where it contributes to the outbreak, escalation or continuation of armed conflict.' This policy was reaffirmed in 2006 in resolution 1653 about the Great Lakes region.

The ICJ has similarly been involved in natural resource management, specifically through its settlement of various border and maritime boundary disputes in which natural resources were at stake. Examples of land boundary disputes before the Court include *Libya v. Chad* (1992), *Namibia v. Botswana* (1998), and *Cameroon v. Nigeria* (2002). Maritime delimitation disputes, which have appeared more frequently before the Court, include the *North Sea Continental Shelf Cases* (1969), *Fisheries Jurisdiction Cases* (1974), *Gulf of Maine Case (Canada v. United States,* 1984), *Libya v. Malta* (1985), *Jan Mayen Island (Denmark v. Norway,* 1993), *Qatar v. Bahrain* (2001), and *Cameroon v. Nigeria* (2002).

The ICJ has more recently also taken up the issue of the relationship between natural resources and armed conflict. Its *Advisory Opinion on the Legality of the Threat or Use of Nuclear Weapons* (1996) declared that states have 'the responsibility to ensure that activities within their jurisdiction or control do not cause damage to the environment of other States or of areas beyond the limits of national jurisdiction.' It went on to argue that this obligation was 'now part of the corpus of international law relating to the environment.' More specifically, the ICJ decided in the *Case concerning Armed Activities on the Territory of the Congo (Democratic Republic of the Congo v. Uganda,* 2005*)* that the looting, plundering, and exploitation of natural resources by Ugandan military forces constituted a violation of *jus in bello,* in reference to the Hague Regulation of 1907 and Geneva Convention IV relating to the Protection of Civilians in Times of Armed Conflict.[39] The World Court also confirmed the customary international law status of the principle of permanent sovereignty over natural resources.

Though not a principal UN organ, the UN Environment Programme (UNEP) merits special attention.[40] Established after the Stockholm conference, with its head office in Nairobi, UNEP became the first UN body whose headquarters were located in a developing country. Originally, it was to act as a coordinator and catalyst of environmental policy within the UN system, but UNEP has also undertaken a variety of operational activities. Important examples of UNEP's accomplishments include the Regional Seas Program (which now involves ten regions and as many as 120 countries); integrated environment and development programs for the catchment areas of large river systems (such as the Zambezi and Mekong); and the groundwork for various multilateral and regional environment treaties, including those relating to the ozone layer (1985), dangerous waste products (1989), and biological diversity (1992). UNEP's achievements have been notable, not least given its modest resources and influence. UNEP has nevertheless attracted its share of criticism and, in light of its insufficient clout, there have been calls for UNEP to be upgraded to a more powerful UN Environmental Organization.

The World Bank is today a crucial source of finance for sustainable development initiatives, and has had some involvement in global natural resource management. Critics have often accused the Bank of sacrificing environmental imperatives in the pursuit of developmental objectives.[41] There are indications, however, that the World Bank has grown more sensitive to environmental issues and more attuned to the impact of its policies on the environment, particularly following a few major failures—for example in constructing huge hydroelectric dams in India and China. The Global Environment Facility, set up under the stewardship of the World Bank, in cooperation with UNEP and UNDP, provides a useful example of interinstitutional environmental cooperation.

In conclusion, a wide array of organs and agencies within the UN system are involved, to varying degrees, in the natural resource sector. The roles of the Assembly and ECOSOC have withered somewhat, while those of the specialized agencies (including the World Bank, the FAO, and UNESCO), the Security Council, and the ICJ have grown. As in so many fields of UN activity, no particular principal organ or specialized agency is firmly in control. To encourage effective cooperation among these various bodies, the Secretary-General in February 2006 set up a fifteen-member High-level Panel on UN System-wide Coherence in the areas of development, humanitarian aid, and the environment.

THE UN'S CONCEPTUAL CONTRIBUTION

Multilateral processes taking place at the United Nations have generated a number of new concepts which have had important and lasting implications for international law and international relations, and which have, in turn, influenced trends in natural resource management. First and foremost among these innovations is the principle of resource sovereignty. While sovereignty over natural resources could be seen as a corollary of the traditional concepts of territorial jurisdiction and national sovereignty, state practice during the colonial era and the immediate post-colonial years suggested otherwise.

Initially, in elaborating resource sovereignty the emphasis was on deepening the potential application of the principle, both by claiming as many resource-related rights as possible—including the right to regulate foreign investment and the right to establish producers' associations—and by extending it to cover natural wealth (e.g., forests, fauna and flora, and biological diversity) and marine resources.

Gradually, the rights conferred by resource sovereignty became qualified by the formulation of accompanying duties and obligations. These include the duty to use natural resources for national economic development and the well-being of the entire population; the obligation to respect the rights and interests of indigenous peoples; the duty to grant foreign investors fair treatment and to provide for a due process of law; and the responsibility for conserving the environment. The latter responsibility, at present more commonly understood as the 'sustainable use of natural resources,' constitutes not only the origin but probably also the hallmark of the concept of sustainable development.

Sustainability is closely related to two other key concepts that are both offsprings of negotiations and deliberations at the UN: the 'common heritage of humankind' and the 'common concern of humankind.' The former emerged in the context of the natural resource regimes for outer space and the celestial bodies (see in particular the Moon Treaty of 1979) and for the earth's deep seabed and mineral resources. These remote areas served as the laboratory for this new principle of common heritage, a principle that implies not only non-appropriation but also the distribution of benefits across countries, as well as the obligation to preserve the environment for future generations.[42]

The notion of the 'common concern of humankind' emerged as a compromise in light of state-level apprehension over the internationalization of resource management and the environmental regime. The 'common concern of humankind' thus informs the conventions on climate change, biological diversity, and antidesertification. This concept avoids the creation of an international regime yet still conveys the global scope of the problems at stake and takes into account the rights of future generations.

Most difficult proved to be the management of transboundary resources, also called shared resources, about which fervent nationalism was never far below the surface. The UNEP Guidelines of 1978 remained guidelines and without compliance mechanisms. The Brundtland group's set of principles, rights, and obligations concerning transboundary natural resources and environmental interference got no endorsement (not even by the commission itself). The Rio Declaration calls merely for 'prior and timely notification and relevant information to potentially affected States.' Nevertheless, the UN has put the issue of cooperation with respect to management of transboundary resources firmly on the international agenda and has been instrumental in generating practical schemes of cooperation, such as the Zambezi River Plan and the Mekong Delta Treaty.

Another conceptual contribution of the UN has been to help expose and formulate policies to address the nexus between armed conflict and natural resource exploitation, especially regarding 'blood diamonds.' This began in May 1999, when the Security Council established a panel of experts to investigate the diamonds-for-arms linkages in Angola and continued in 2000 when the Council banned the purchase of all non-government-purchased diamonds from Sierra Leone and set up another panel of experts to monitor the sanctions. Other actions included sanctions in Liberia and the DRC. The UN's naming and shaming panels complement the setting up of a certification regime requiring diamonds to be traceable to the country of origin, and shed light on the interface between international economic activity and instability. The issue also brought urgency to the need to formulate responsible, accountable strategies for natural resource management, so that a country's natural wealth, rather than being used to finance war, is harnessed for the benefit of that country's development.

CONCLUSION

The UN has been instrumental in generating widespread interest in natural resource management, taking into account developmental, environmental, and social dimensions. UN organs as well as specialized agencies have made intellectual investments and undertaken numerous operational activities to foster economic development. Moreover, the political debates in various UN forums and conferences have resulted in new concepts for resource management, such as resource sovereignty (on land and in the sea), the global commons, and sustainable development.

At first glance considerable tensions, if not contradictions, exist among these various concepts. However, the UN has arguably been able to help interested parties to strike a viable balance among these interests. Hence, national resource sovereignty has been complemented with duties concerning proper resource management, while environmental and developmental issues have been married within the comprehensive concept of sustainable development. Furthermore, functional, rather than strictly territorial, arrangements have been negotiated that facilitate the sharing of the world's resources through cooperative regimes for prudent natural resource management, combating climate change, preserving biological diversity, and promoting sustainable fisheries and forestry.

These are considerable achievements but, at the same time, current concepts are incomplete and existing institutions insufficiently equipped to curb the alarming rates of resource degradation and to provide functional rather than territorial regimes aimed at an integrated ecosystem approach for sustainable development.

Notes

1. Examples include not only the United Nations Framework Convention on Climate Change and the Convention on Biological Diversity but also the Agreement Establishing the World Trade Organization.
2. A prime example is the *Case Concerning the Gabčíkovo-Nagymaros Project*, 1997 ICJ Report 7, para. 140, in which the Court observed: 'This need to reconcile economic development with protection of the environment is aptly expressed in the concept of sustainable development.'
3. *Documents on American Foreign Relations* (1941–42), vol. IV (Boston: World Peace Foundation, 1943), 10.
4. *Yearbook of the United Nations 1948–9* (New York: UN, 1950), 482.
5. *Yearbook of the United Nations 1951* (New York: UN, 1952), 417–419.
6. See ICJ Reports (1952).
7. *Yearbook of the United Nations 1952* (New York: UN, 1953), 387.
8. UN document E/CN.4/L.24, 16 April 1952.
9. UN document E/CN.4/SR.260, 6 May 1952, 9.
10. See *Yearbook of the United Nations 1955* (New York: UN, 1956), 154–156.
11. It now reads: 'All peoples may, for their own ends, freely dispose of their natural wealth and resources without prejudice to any obligations arising out of international economic co-operation, based upon the principle of mutual benefit, and international law. In no case may a people be deprived of its own means of subsistence.' In 1966, the Third Committee decided, upon a proposal of African, Asian, and Latin American countries, to insert an additional article in both covenants. This reads: 'Nothing in the present Covenant shall be interpreted as impairing the inherent right of all peoples to enjoy and utilize fully and freely their natural wealth and resources.' See *United Nations Yearbook 1966* (New York: UN, 1968), 419, 422.
12. *Yearbook of the United Nations 1966* (New York: UN, 1968).
13. L. N. Rangarajan, *Commodity Conflict: the Political Economy of International Commodity Negotiation* (London: Croom Helm, 1978).
14. Adeoye A. Akinsanya, *The Expropriation of Multinational Property in the Third World* (New York: Praeger, 1980).
15. See UN document A/9556, 30 April 1974.
16. For an extensive review Robert F. Meagher, *An International Redistribution of Wealth and Power: A Study of the Charter of Economic Rights and Duties of States* (New York: Pergamon Press, 1979); and Nico Schrijver, *Sovereignty over Natural Resources: Balancing Rights and Duties* (Cambridge: Cambridge University Press, 1997), 102–111.

17. See Abdelaziz Megzari, 'Negotiating the Common Fund for Commodities,' in *Effective Negotiation: Case Studies in Conference Diplomacy*, ed. Johan Kaufmann (Dordrecht, Netherlands: Martinus Nijhoff, 1989), 205–230.

18. See Robin R. Churchill and Alan V. Lowe, *The Law of the Sea*, 3rd edn. (Manchester, UK: Manchester University Press, 1999), 78.

19. René-Jean Dupuy, *The Law of the Sea: Current Problems* (Leiden, Netherlands: Sijthoff, 1974), 9.

20. Text in *American Journal of International Law* 40, no. 1 (1946), Supplement of Documents, 45.

21. See UN Conference on the Law of the Sea, UN document A/CONF.13, *Geneva Conference Reports*, 1958.

22. See Karin Hjertonsson, *The New Law of the Sea: Influence of the Latin American States on recent developments of the Law of the Sea* (Leiden, Netherlands: Sijthoff, 1973). See also Nasila S. Rembe, *Africa and the International Law of the Sea: A Study of the Contribution of the African States to the Third United Nations Conference on the Law of the Sea* (Alphen aan den Rijn, Netherlands: Sijthoff & Noordhoff, 1980) and R. P. Anand, *Studies in International Law and History: An Asian Perspective* (Leiden, Netherlands: Martinus Nijhoff, 2004).

23. Principle XI of Resolution 46 (III), adopted by UNCTAD III.

24. See *Yearbook of the United Nations 1967* (New York: UN, 1969), 43; and UN document A/C.1/PV.1515.

25. See also Part XII of the 1982 Convention, entitled 'Protection of the Marine Environment,' www.un.org.

26. See Yuwen Li, *Transfer of Technology for Deep Sea-Bed Mining: the 1982 Convention and Beyond* (Dordrecht, Netherlands: Martinus Nijhoff, 1995).

27. See the in-depth report by Louis B. Sohn, 'The Stockholm Declaration on the Human Environment,' in *Harvard International Law Journal* 14, no. 3 (1973): 423–515.

28. UN document A/CNF.48/PC.12, Annex II, paras. 3 and 58.

29. World Commission on Environment and Development, *Our Common Future* (Oxford: Oxford University Press, 1987), 8.

30. The official name is 'A Non-Legally Binding Authoritative Statement of Principles for a Global Consensus on the Management, Conservation and Sustainable Development of All Types of Forests.'

31. *Report of the United Nations Conference on Environment and Development: Volume I— Resolutions Adopted by the Conference*, UN document A/CONF.151/26, 1993. See also *Yearbook of the United Nations 1992* (Dordrecht, Netherlands: Martinus Nijhoff, 1993), 670–681.

32. For a discussion of the dynamics of these gatherings, see Michael G. Schechter, *United Nations Global Conferences* (London: Routledge, 2005). For the politics over the years, see Pamela S. Chasek, David L. Downie, and Janet Welsh Brown, *Global Environmental Politics*, 4th edn. (Boulder, Colo.: Westview Press, 2006); and Pamela S. Chasek, *Earth Negotiations: Analyzing Thirty Years of Environmental Diplomacy* (Tokyo: United Nations University Press, 2001).

33. For a discussion of the Johannesburg World Summit see V. Barral, 'Johannesburg 2002: quoi de neuf pour le développement durable?' *Revue Générale de Droit International Public* 107, no. 2 (2003): 415–432; M. K. S. Hussain, 'World Summit on Sustainable Development, Johannesburg: An Appraisal,' *Indian Journal of International Law* 42 no. 3 (2002): 348–369; K. R. Gray, 'World Summit on Sustainable Development: Accomplishments and New Directions?', *International and Comparative Law Quarterly* 52 (2003): 256–268; Paul Wapner, 'World Summit on Sustainable Development: Toward a Post Johannesburg Environmentalism,', *Global Environmental Politics* 3, no. 1 (2003): 1.

34. The Johannesburg Declaration on Sustainable Development and the Johannesburg Plan of Implementation were both adopted by consensus and published in *Report of the World Summit on Sustainable Development*, UN document A/CONF. 199/20, 2002.

35. See *2005 World Summit Outcome*, UN document A/RES/60/1, 24 October 2005, paras. 48–56.

36. See, e.g., Paul Collier et al., *Breaking the Conflict Trap: Civil War and Development Policy* (New York: Oxford University Press, 2003); Roland Paris, *At War's End: Building Peace after Civil* Wars (Cambridge: Cambridge University Press, 2004); and Michael T. Klare, *Resource Wars: the New Landscape of Global Conflict* (New York: Metropolitan Books, 2001).

37. See Lansana Gberie, Ralph Hazelton, and Ian Smillie, *Heart of the Matter: Sierra Leone, Diamonds, and Human Security* (Ottawa: Partnership Africa Canada, 2000); and Greg Campbell, *Blood Diamonds: Tracing the Deadly Path of the World's Most Precious Stones* (Boulder, Colo.: Westview Press, 2004).

38. Judicial Commission of Inquiry into Allegations of Illegal Exploitation of Natural Resources and Other Forms of Wealth in the Democratic Republic of the Congo set up by the Ugandan Government and headed by Justice David Porter.

39. *International Court of Justice Reports 2005*, 77, para. 245.

40. For discussions, see Elizabeth R. DeSombre, *Global Environmental Institutions* (London: Routledge, 2006); Mostafa K. Tolba with Iwona Rummel-Bulska, *Global Environmental Diplomacy: Negotiating Environmental Agreements for the World, 1973–1992* (Cambridge, Mass.: MIT Press, 1998); Regina S. Axelrod, David Leonard Downie, and Norman J. Vig, eds., *The Global Environment: Institutions, Law and Policy*, 2nd edn. (Washington, DC: CQ Press, 2005); Frank Biermann and Steffen Bauer, eds., *A World Environment Organization: Solution or threat for effective international environmental governance?* (Aldershot, UK: Ashgate, 2005); and Bradnee W. Chambers and Jessica F. Green, eds., *Reforming International Environmental Governance: From Institutional Limits to Innovative Reforms* (Tokyo: United Nations University Press, 2005).

41. For a discussion, see Robert Wade, 'Greening the Bank: The Struggle over the Environment, 1970–1995,' in *The World Bank: Its First Half Century*, vol. 2, ed. Devesh Kapur, John P. Lewis, and Richard C. Webb (Washington, DC: Brookings Institution, 1997), 611–734.

42. See Edith D. Brown-Weiss, *In Fairness to Future Generations: International Law, Common Patrimony and Intergenerational Equity* (Tokyo: United Nations University Press, 1989) and Catherine Redgwell, *Intergenerational Trusts and Environmental Protection* (Manchester, UK: Manchester University Press, 1999).

CHAPTER 35

ORGANIZED CRIME

FRANK G. MADSEN

THIS chapter consists of two parts. In the first the role of the United Nations in combating transnational organized crime (TOC) is considered, while the second part is concerned with the particulars of TOC and with some of its many aspects, including illicit traffic in drugs and trafficking in humans.

THE ROLE OF THE UNITED NATIONS

The UN has been involved in the fight against organized crime from the inception of the organization in 1945. Its mandate for this activity stems from Article 1 of the Charter and Articles 28 and 29 of the Universal Declaration of Human Rights. From the very beginning, it has interpreted organized crime as a threat to the social and economic well-being of the world's population.

The UN conventions against crime, including drug trafficking, are crucial in today's world where speed of communications and ease of transportation increasingly place judicial authorities in situations involving intractable practical and juridical difficulties. Major criminal cases already pose serious problems on a national level; these assume extreme complexity when one has to deal with different criminal laws and different legal systems.

The UN cannot and does not perceive its role as one of imposing a uniform penal code throughout the world. Instead, the organization seeks to provide a global legal framework consisting of a set of agreed rules, which may assist countries in international law enforcement and judicial cooperation. Consequently, the UN has played a key role in the development of international criminal law, an area in which member states are typically extremely reluctant to relinquish sovereignty as they often interpret criminal law as if it were the visual emanation of regal power. Furthermore, public opinion takes a dim view of crimes that cannot be prosecuted because of jurisdictional problems, while the same public at the same time remains intuitively attached to territoriality. In view of these fundamental difficulties, the work and aspirations of the world organization are all the more admirable.

One of the principal ways that the world organization has confronted international crime is through the United Nations Office on Drugs and Crime (UNODC). Established in 2003 through the merger of existing UN bodies dealing with drugs and crime, UNODC, which has its headquarters in Vienna, is mandated to assist member states in their struggle against illicit drugs and crime. The Security Council has also decided upon several enforcement measures under Chapter VII to combat terrorism. Some of the most notable efforts include the establishment of its resolution 1267, 1373, and 1540 committees.

On a pragmatic level, one may observe the UN system at work in its battle against organized crime. For instance, the Fifth UN Congress on the Prevention of Crime and the Treatment of Offenders, in Geneva in 1975, tried to conceptualize crime on the international level by subdividing it into Organized Crime and Corporate Crime,[1] or crime *as* business and crime *in* business. The United Nations concentrated on the purely commercial aspect—taking it to be the core of organized crime.

In 1988, one of the most important steps forward was taken; namely the adoption of the UN Convention against Illicit Traffic in Narcotic Drugs and Psychotropic Substances, commonly known as the 'Vienna Convention.' The negotiations leading to its adoption and the convention itself were essential in the development of international thinking on drugs, crime and money laundering. The Vienna Convention, for example, stipulates that drug and money laundering offences are extraditable offences. Where no bilateral or regional extradition regime exists, the Convention itself acts as an extradition treaty—an important improvement on previous practice, which in such cases reposed on comity. The year 1992 saw the creation of the United Nations Commission on Crime Prevention and Criminal Justice in Vienna.

In December 2000, in Palermo, Italy, a Convention against Transnational Organized Crime was opened for signature along with two protocols, viz. the Protocol to Prevent, Suppress and Punish Trafficking in Persons, Especially Women and Children and the Protocol against the Smuggling of Migrants by Land, Air and Sea. A third protocol, the Protocol against the Illicit Manufacturing of and Trafficking in Firearms, Their Parts and Components and Ammunition was opened for signature in July 2001.

The first session of the Conference of the Parties to the United Nations Convention against Corruption took place in December 2006. Addressing corruption has become an increasingly important aspect of the UN's efforts to combat organized crime, as a means of facilitating progress towards the MDGs, and as a principle of the UN's Global Compact with business.

TRANSNATIONAL ORGANIZED CRIME

There is no commonly accepted definition of organized crime; but an important characteristic of this type of criminality could lead one to see it as a commercial structure that provides goods and services which are otherwise prohibited or restricted.

The concept of organized crime was born in the United States at the end of the nineteenth century; it was fully developed in the 1930s. Unfortunately, the general perceptual outcome of this development is the view of organized crime as a closed ethnic group, i.e., 'foreign.'[2] This so-called Sicilian Syndrome or Alien Conspiracy Theory has gravely impeded scholarship.[3] This model does not conform to the actual characteristics of organized crime, with different societal problems as well as policies.

More modern views construe organized crime as an informal, loosely structured, open system that is reactive to fluctuations in the economic, political, and legal environment. This view stresses symbiosis between the 'upperworld' and the underworld, making it very difficult to distinguish the corrupter from the corrupted.

The concept of the 'economics of crime' has been developed typically to refer to two major issues, the disputed questions of the profits that organized crime may generate and of organized crime as an economic actor. Estimates of the total yearly 'Gross Criminal Product' are based on assumptions, which most scholars reject. There is, however, an ongoing debate between those scholars who think that the alleged profits of crime are overestimated and those who take a more alarmist view of the role of 'criminal' profits in the world economy.[4] A second debate is between those who are worried about the reach of crime, that is, crime as a global phenomenon or international crime as a security issue, and those who do not see TOC as a security issue.

As regards the more crucial question of organized crime as an economic actor,[5] Mark Findlay quite rightly observes that as international treaties are becoming identified with the management problems of global economic interdependence, 'so too . . . the internationalisation of crime control is being promoted as a reaction to the assumed expansion of crime in a global economic context.'[6] At the same time, 'crime as economy' emphasizes the need to view crime as a process of interconnected relationships working toward the maximization of profit.

Since intensive terrorist activity marked the passage from the twentieth to the twenty-first century, the question remains: is there a relationship between organized crime and terrorism? For this discussion, terrorism is to be viewed as the triangular and communicative usage of illegal acts: the originator (the terrorist) sends a message via the transmitter (the victim) to the receiver (an authority) with a view to influencing the outcome of the latter's administrative, judicial, or political processes. Terrorism and organized crime have little in common on an intellectual level, since the former is based on ideological, religious, or political motives while the latter is based on profit. It is clear, nevertheless, that one may use the methodology of the other, so that terrorists will engage in common crime to fund their operations, while organized crime may use 'terrorist methodology' to 'send messages.' Furthermore, terrorists and organized criminals may cooperate. Such cooperation or interchange of methodologies cannot but influence the development of the respective organizations; in particular terrorist organizations have tended to glide, insidiously, toward organized crime. Indeed, one might perceive the 'terrorist—organized crime spectrum' as a continuum in perpetual movement.

Counterfeiting

Violation of intellectual property rights, i.e., the counterfeiting of merchandise, has become a major source of income not only for organized crime but also for terrorist groups. An additional risk is that some of these products are substandard and can represent a danger to the public, for example counterfeit automobile and aircraft spare parts, and also counterfeit human and veterinarian medicinal products. In its 1998 report *The Economic Impact of Counterfeiting*, OECD estimated that the global trade in counterfeit goods was $450 billion or 5–7 percent of the value of global trade. Most observers agree that the volume and value of counterfeiting have since been growing rapidly. There is little doubt of the involvement of organized crime, in particular from the Far East, as the very organization of the manufacture and distribution of counterfeit products demands excellent managerial skills: namely organized crime.

One of the UN's specialized agencies, the World Intellectual Property Organization (WIPO), drafts model legislation and prepares international treaties in this area and thus it complements the anti-organized crime work done by the other parts of the UN system.

Narcotics

One of the most noxious subsets of transnational organized crime is the illicit traffic in narcotic substances.[7] International cooperation in drug control began in 1909 at the International Opium Commission meeting in Shanghai, China, which led to the signing in 1912 in The Hague of the first international convention to attempt the control of a narcotic, namely the International Opium Convention.

Man-made substances were outside the scope of the various pre-World War II conventions, but they were brought under international law and control by a 1948 Protocol. The importance of the evolution of the manufacture of man-made narcotic substances can easily be gauged from Table 35.1.

Three treaties now govern the international drug control system, and they require that governments exercise control over such items as production and distribution and drug abuse. The Single Convention on Narcotic Drugs, 1961, replaced the drugs treaties that had been concluded before World War II. It was amended by the 1972 Protocol, which deals with the treatment and rehabilitation of drug addicts. The Convention on Psychotropic Substances was adopted in 1971, while the newest treaty is the 1988 UN Convention against Illicit Traffic in Narcotic Drugs and Psychotropic Substances. This very comprehensive convention includes money laundering and illicit traffic in precursor and essential chemicals within the ambit of drug trafficking activities.

Table 35.1 Number of drugs and substances under international control, 1912–1995

	1912	1925	1931	1948	1961	1971	1988	1995
Synthetic	0	0	0	12	53	98	187	245
Natural	4	7	17	24	32	32	33	37

Source: Istvan Bayer and Hamid Ghodse, 'Evolution of International Drug Control 1945–1995,' *Bulletin on Narcotics* LI, nos. 1 and 2 (1999): 1–18.

The UN system for narcotic drugs repression now rests on three main pillars. The Commission on Narcotic Drugs (CND), established in 1946, consists of fifty-three members; it is a subsidiary body of ECOSOC and is the UN system's main policymaking organ for international drug control. The thirteen-member International Narcotics Control Board (INCB), created in 1961, is the independent and quasi-judicial control organ for the implementation of UN drug conventions; it began its work in 1968. The INCB strives to restrict the availability of drugs to medical and scientific purposes. Finally, UNODC coordinates the organization's drug control activities.

The value of the global illicit drug market for the year 2003 was estimated by the United Nations at $13 billion at production level; $94 billion at wholesale level (taking seizures into account); and $322 billion at retail level (based on retail prices and taking seizures and other losses into account).

Most informed observers realize that the UN's work cannot by itself defeat the illicit international traffic in narcotic drugs. Since the 1980s, when consumer countries were very aggressive in their attitude to supplier states, they have slowly come to accept an increasing responsibility for the drug problem; and they have realized that an illicit market has never been defeated on the supply side.[8] Easy availability remains, however, a major element of concern. The increasing demand for synthetic drugs manufactured in the consumer countries, e.g., ATS (amphetamine-type stimulants), has also tended to blur the always somewhat artificial borderline between producer and consumer countries.

People Trafficking

Two issues concerning the movements of human beings across borders are of major concern, trafficking in persons and smuggling of migrants.[9] The former is distinct from the latter, in particular because it involves elements of force and coercion, which do not generally apply in the case of smuggling of migrants. A further difference is that the smuggling of migrants generates a one-time profit, whereas trafficking in persons may, and indeed often does, include long-term exploitation thus attracting continuous profits for the criminal organizations.

Research from the late 1990s is fairly consistent in its indication that approximately one half of migrants in the world are being smuggled by organized crime. The crime is often linked with modern-day indenture, whereby migrants, once they have arrived at the destination country, work off their debt—often under appalling conditions.

The trafficking in persons protocol has two main purposes—halting forced labor and sexual exploitation. The UN has worked assiduously on the issue of trafficking in persons all through its history culminating in the 2000 Protocol to Prevent, Suppress and Punish Trafficking in Persons, Especially Women and Children. Trafficking in persons is believed to be the third-largest source of income for organized crime—after illicit traffic in drugs and arms—and it is growing.

Commercial Sexual Exploitation of Children

A particular aspect of such trafficking is the Commercial Sexual Exploitation of Children (CSEC.) In her 1995 report on Sale of Children, Child Prostitution and Child Pornography, the UN's special rapporteur defines child prostitution as 'the act of engaging or offering the services of a child to perform sexual acts for money or other consideration with that person or any other person.' She thus points out that children cannot prostitute themselves, they can only *be* prostituted; they are victims, not actors. CSEC is perhaps the most international of crimes—apart from the illicit traffic in narcotics—and it has three major international aspects: transborder sale of children for sexual exploitation, 'sex tourism,' and international dissemination of child pornography. Children are routinely sold to brothel owners in other countries; but also a certain number of adoptions, international transfers into shelters for street children and into orphanages are, in reality, camouflage for sexual exploitation. Two groups typically sexually exploit children. First, indigenous clients abuse children, some giving as justification the myth prevalent in some countries that intercourse with prepubescent children carries a lesser risk of HIV/AIDS infection. Second, sex tourists also engage children to perform sexual acts, seeking to avoid the legal consequences and social opprobrium such activity would entail in their home countries.

With the use of modern means of communication, child pornography has taken on a decidedly international aspect. The film footage may be shot in one country, production done in another, and distribution, be it in the form of video cassettes, DVDs, or electronically via the internet, from yet a third country. An alarming development is the involvement of organized crime in this sphere. It has been firmly established that from web sites based in Eastern Europe organized crime distributes child pornography worldwide. Links with child trafficking and child prostitution are an obvious danger and in many cases a certainty.

It is very difficult to be very precise as regards the number of persons involved and profits obtained. The UN estimates that there are approximately two million children in the world who are part of the prostitution industry and who generate income, worldwide, of approximately $5 billion. CSEC does not take place in developing countries alone: US studies show that approximately 1.2 million children in the United States are sexually exploited; 150,000 of these are regularly prostituted.

Trafficking Radioactive Materials

That organized crime might involve itself in the illicit traffic in radioactive material is most worrying.[10] If organized crime were interested in this market, it would, presumably, assume the role of intermediaries selling to governments eager to undertake a nuclear weapons program or to terrorist organizations, though such materials could also be used for other purposes. The UN's 1980 Convention on the Physical Protection of Nuclear Material does provide the framework for the security of stockpiling nuclear materials; weapons-grade substances can, nevertheless, be obtained on

Table 35.2 A nuclear glossary

Name	Licit Use	Illicit Use
Americum 214	Alpha-particle source for smoke detectors and other devices	Fraud (Substitute for more desirable elements)
Beryllium	Neutron reflector in reactors or bombs	Illicit reactors Nuclear weapons
Cesium 137	Radiation source for industrial or medical applications; present in radioactive waste from reactors	Fraud Murder by radiation
Cobalt 60	Gamma-radiation source for industrial or medical applications	Fraud Murder by radiation
Lithium 6	Thermonuclear weapons	Thermonuclear weapons
Plutonium	Alpha-particle source for smoke detectors; nuclear weapons; nuclear reactor fuel	Fraud Nuclear weapons
Polonium 210	Alpha-particle and neutron source for industrial applications	Nuclear weapons Murder by radiation
Uranium	Nuclear reactor fuel; nuclear weapons	Fraud Nuclear weapons
Zirconium	Structural material for nuclear reactors	Illicit reactors

Source: Phil Williams and Paul N. Woessner, 'The real threat of nuclear smuggling,' *Scientific American* 274 (January 1996): 28.

the grey market. They are easy to smuggle because of their small size; a kilogram of plutonium fills up one seventh of the volume of a standard aluminum soft-drink can. Several of the most dangerous isotopes are only weakly radioactive and they cannot easily be picked up by a Geiger counter at border check points. A number of radioactive isotopes, apart from uranium and plutonium, are of interest in this context; some of these with their licit as well as illicit uses are indicated in Table 35.2. Criminals or terrorists may not be able to obtain enough material to produce a 'nuclear' bomb or, indeed, the expertise to do so. Yet experts expect that they could also create a 'dirty bomb' by mixing unstable isotopes with ordinary explosives, thus killing thousands and rendering a large part of, say, a city uninhabitable. Also, radioactive material has been used for murder; Polonium 210 was used in November 2006 to kill a former KGB operative in London.

Most uncontrolled or insufficiently controlled radioactive materials are to be found in the former Soviet Union, over the course of the transformation of which indigenous criminal groups have been very active domestically and internationally. In the ten-year period from 1992 to 2002, small quantities of radioactive material were trafficked, in particular into Germany and Austria. Scholars are not in agreement as regards the role of organized crime in such traffic. Some argue that the illicit traffic in radioactive materials is so risky because of the law enforcement attention it would attract, and that the risks outweigh the gains. Others, however, claim that if the price offered is high enough, organized crime will not hesitate. A third group maintains that organized crime already has been involved in assisting the transfer of nuclear weapons technology. It is possible that the market for illicit radioactive materials has not firmed up enough. It would be naïve to believe that this state of affairs can continue; with this in mind the UN established the 2005 International Convention for the Suppression of Acts of Nuclear Terrorism.

Traffic in Natural Resources

The natural resources of the earth are restricted commodities and they are therefore coveted and traded by organized crime. Diamonds and in particular so-called 'conflict diamonds' constitute an example, as does coltan (used for electronic devices). As a response to the problem of conflict diamonds, in December 2000, the Assembly adopted resolution 55/56 supporting the creation of international verification arrangements for rough diamonds. What resulted almost two years later was the Kimberley Process Certification Scheme—regulatory mechanisms designed to keep conflict diamonds out of the legitimate diamond trade.

Even more insidious, however, is the involvement of organized crime in the illicit trade in timber, since deforestation deprives a local population not only of primary resources, but more importantly of its livelihood.[11] Hardwood in particular has become a restricted commodity as more and more producer countries are attempting to manage the remaining stock. This has led to timber entering into the category of 'conflict commodities,' both in the normally accepted sense of a commodity generating profits to sustain conflict (e.g., war, civil war, or terrorism), as well as in the sense of a commodity causing conflict regarding its ownership and control. In the first sense, West African timber is bartered directly against arms or the funds obtained from its sale are disbursed for the purchase of arms. In the second sense, conflicts, leading to violence and unlawful killings, arise between local populations and other persons or groups of persons claiming ownership. Such disagreements can almost always be traced back to a disharmony between long-established tribal law and more recent national law.

The illicit traffic in timber lies, however, first and foremost within the ambit of organized crime, since this can apply requisite pressure on the local population—in conjunction with extensive corruption of police or military forces—and provide the managerial expertise to have the trees felled, transported internationally by ship, and sold in another country, often with false documentation as to the timber's origin. In Southeast Asia, where most of the world's remaining high-value hardwood grows, the 'organizers' pay $11 to the local population per cubic meter of illegally logged hardwood and they resell the same logs in another country in the region for up to $270 (factory gate price). The logs are then cut and used (especially for floorboards) at a mark-up on the factory gate price of approximately 500 percent. The profits accruing to organized crime are staggering, even considering that they pay an average of $200,000 in corruption payments for each shipload. Apart from the societal damages usually connected with organized crime (corruption, lack of respect for the rule of law, etc.), this particular commodity also entails revenue losses and environmental costs to the producer countries, generally estimated for Southeast Asia at $15 billion per year.

CONCLUSION

Globalization presents the UN system with the transnational phenomena of crime, terrorism, and drugs. The complexity of globalization will undoubtedly continue to offer new opportunities for organized crime; for example in providing organs for transplantation from unwilling donors, treatment of toxic waste, counterfeiting of cutting-edge medicinal products, etc. Addressing such problems is intrinsic to, not additional to, the work of the United Nations. And it should be seen against the backcloth of the overarching aim of the United Nations, namely human security.[12]

NOTES

1. See Sally S. Simpson, *Corporate Crime, Law and Social Control* (Cambridge: Cambridge University Press, 2002).
2. The best known exponent for this concept (ethnic relationship, world conspiracy of organized crime, etc.) is Claire Sterling; see, e.g., *Octopus: The Long Reach of the International Sicilian Mafia* (New York: W. W. Norton, 1990) and *Thieves' World: The Threat of the New Global Network of Organized Crime* (New York: Simon and Schuster, 1994).
3. See Boronia Halstead, 'The Use of Models in the Analysis of Organized Crime and Development of Policy,' *Transnational Organized Crime* 4, no. 1 (1998): 1–24.
4. Guilhem Fabre, *Les Prospérités du crime* (Paris: Editions de l'Aube, 1999).
5. See Gary S. Becker, 'Nobel Lecture: The Economic Way of Looking at Behavior,' *The Journal of Political Economy* 101, no. 3 (1993): 385–409.
6. Mark Findlay, *The Globalization of Crime* (Cambridge: Cambridge University Press 1999), 138.
7. UN Office on Drugs and Crime, *World Drug Report, 2005*, 2 vols. (New York: United Nations, 2005).
8. Robin Thomas Naylor, *Wages of Crime: Black Markets, Illegal Finance, and the Underworld Economy*, 2nd edn. (Ithaca, NY: Cornell University Press, 2002), 11.
9. See Amy O'Neill Richard, *International Trafficking in Women to the United States: A Contemporary Manifestation of Slavery and Organized Crime* (Washington, DC: Center for the Study of Intelligence, 2000); Lin Lean Lim, *The Sex Sector: The Economic and Social Bases of Prostitution in Southeast Asia* (Geneva: International Labour Office, 1998); and Max Taylor and Ethel Quale, *Child Pornography: An Internet Crime* (New York: Brunner-Routledge, 2003). See also the 2004 film *Promised Land* by Amos Gitaï.
10. Center for Strategic and International Studies, *The Nuclear Black Market* (Washington, DC: Center for Strategic and International Studies, 1996); Phil Williams and Paul N. Woessner, 'The Real Threat of Nuclear Smuggling,' *Scientific American* 274, no. 1 (1996): 26–30.
11. See Julian Newman and Arbi Valentinus, *The Last Frontier* (London: EIA/Telapak, 2005); and Murl Baker, Robert Clausen, Ramzy Kanaan, Michel N'Goma, Trifin Roule, James Jarvie, Michael Malley, and Jamie Thomson, *Conflict Timber: The Dimensions of the Problem in Africa and Asia*, 3 vols. (Washington, DC: ARD/USAID, 2003).
12. Sam Daws, 'The United Nations in the Twenty-First Century' in Colin Jennings and Nicholas Hopkinson, *Current Issues in International Diplomacy and Foreign Policy*, vol. 1, (London: The Stationery Office, 1999), 405–406.

CHAPTER 36

DEMOCRACY AND GOOD GOVERNANCE

W. ANDY KNIGHT

As recently as the late 1970s, there were only forty countries whose governments were democratic. But with the end of the Cold War came a global shift towards democratic governance. Indeed, the final two decades of the last century witnessed a significant increase in efforts to promote democracy and good governance globally. 'In the formal sense of civilian, constitutional, multiparty regimes,' Larry Diamond writes, 'there are more democracies in the world than ever before.'[1]

As a result of this 'third wave,'[2] over 120 countries, representing roughly two-thirds of the global population, are today engaged in the process of building democratic systems of governance. The United Nations has been at the center of this activity, but it has discovered that the transition to democracy in many countries can be fleeting, imperiled, insecure, and fragile.[3] Based on Freedom House criteria, one third of the so-called democracies are not really 'free' because their elected leaders are constrained by non-elected and unaccountable groups within their jurisdiction, such as rebel forces and other irregular militia; political, ethnic, or religious violence limits individual freedom in those polities and thus undermines or inhibits political competition; or the elected leaders suppress the media, engage in corruption, and stifle political opposition.[4]

Indeed, Marina Ottaway reminds us that in the last decade of the twentieth century there was a rise in semi-authoritarian regimes—i.e., regimes that displayed

The author thanks Greg Bereza for research assistance and Stina Larserud of International IDEA for help in locating key primary documents on democratization movements.

characteristics of both democracy and authoritarianism. 'They are ambiguous systems that combine rhetorical acceptance of liberal democracy, the existence of some formal democratic institutions, and respect for a limited sphere of civil and political liberties with essentially illiberal or even authoritarian traits.'[5] These regimes are, in fact, threatened by democracy and simply go through the motions of elections and erecting certain institutions while resisting the kind of change that could threaten their power base.

Democratic governance is also threatened by emerging theocratic regimes, secessionists, terrorists, drug traffickers, organized criminals, state decay and failures, as well as by the effects of footloose transnational capital and untamed globalization. More than any other contemporary observer of the democratization phenomenon, David Held has warned of the disjuncture between formal state authority and the realities of the emerging global system.[6] The erosion of state autonomy by the global activities of transnational corporations (TNCs) combined with the nature of porous national borders raise the serious question of whether democracy and good governance should be the concern of regional and global intergovernmental organizations as well as states. Decisions that affect citizens are often made in some of these regional and global bodies.

In this context the UN system has devoted much time and energy to the issue of democratic governance. The importance of this theme was stressed at the turn of the century in the Millennium Development Goals (MDGs). At the Millennium Summit, it became evident that democratic governance was seen by most world leaders as central to the achievement of the goals. It was felt by these leaders that faced with crime, corruption, weak administrative structures, unaccountable leadership, and the social and political exclusion of minorities, several of the fledgling democracies would quickly regress into undemocratic practices and result in the MDGs becoming even more elusive. Thus, the spread of democracy and good governance is expected to provide an 'enabling environment' for achieving the MDGs. In fact, the Millennium Declaration represents at this stage the most explicit statement to date by member states in support of democratic and participatory governance. General Assembly resolution 55/2 approved that declaration, by which world leaders promised to spare no effort in promoting democracy, strengthening the rule of law, and recognizing human rights and fundamental freedoms, including the right to development.

This chapter examines the UN's role in promoting and encouraging democracy and good governance. The overall argument is that the UN is in a position to help promote and strengthen a new global norm which posits that democracy validates governance in the contemporary world; and, that in order to be considered 'democratic,' governments should not only engage in running periodic free and fair elections but also demonstrate the ability to govern inclusively and humanely, and to respect human rights and the rule of law.[7] Thus, it is not sufficient for the UN to establish democracy simply as a process, in the Schumpeterian sense. The world body must also ensure that any state that considers itself a 'democracy' is adhering to certain normative governance principles and specific requirements of democracy, including constitutionally guaranteed rights so as to prevent erosion of liberty, the abuse of power, ethnic and internecine strife, and even the outbreak of violence.[8] In addition, the UN must practice what it preaches and address its own democratic deficit. The chapter concludes by evaluating the extent to which the UN is succeeding in accomplishing the above.

DEFINING DEMOCRACY AND GOOD GOVERNANCE

Although we use the word 'democracy' often, its meaning is contested. Michael Saward points out that the word is a 'signifier' that evokes particular meanings in different people. Governments, dissidents, and dictators all claim it for their actions.

Saward presents the example of General Pervez Musharraf who overthrew the corrupt, but elected, leadership of Pakistan's Prime Minister, Nawaz Sharif, in October 1999. After the coup, Musharraf is quoted as saying that he was in fact instituting 'not martial law, only another path towards democracy. The armed forces have no intention to stay in charge any longer than is absolutely necessary to pave the way for true democracy to flourish in Pakistan.' He went on to say that under his leadership he would take Pakistan from 'the era of sham democracy' to 'a true one'[9] and institute a rolling series of local elections with the stipulation that six out of twenty-one seats in all local councils be reserved for women candidates. He claims to have introduced democracy at the grassroots level and argued, quite convincingly, that democracy was not simply about elected government, but rather about how an elected government behaves, 'whether it is democratic in its disposition.'[10] Just when President Musharraf seemed about to introduce nationwide elections, 9/11 occurred. On 30 April 2002, President Musharraf sought from Pakistanis five more years in power, 'deploying the most democratic of mechanism'—the referendum.[11] The new mandate has allowed him to become a key player in the US-led global fight against terrorism. But clearly, Musharraf's democracy model is quite different from say that of the United States. Does this make Pakistan's version less democratic than the American one?

The United States is commonly regarded as a beacon of democracy. The US Declaration of Independence was not only about the right to self-determination but also about the establishment of a democracy. But the US form was quite different from classical notions of democracy. James Madison, the fourth president, in the *Federalist Papers No. 10*, clarified the nature of US democracy and made a distinction between a strictly 'democratic Athenian-style state' and a republic. Whereas the former would consist of a society of a small number of citizens who assemble to administer the government in person, the latter would be a government in which the scheme of representation was paramount. And, being a republic was considered necessary for the United States because of its vast land expanse. Madison's objective was to create a governance system that could control a country with continental proportions.

Such a system would not allow individual citizens to play a direct political role in running the country. Instead, an Electoral College was developed that allowed citizens periodically to elect representatives to carry out the nation's business in Washington. In this system, a presidential candidate can get the most popular votes nationally and still lose the election on account of having fewer electoral college votes. This in fact happened in the 2000 Presidential race in which Albert Gore was able to gather more popular votes nationally than George W. Bush but still lose the presidency. The race boiled down to the results in Florida where serious questions existed about the fairness and equality of the vote. In the end, the Supreme Court decided the outcome.

Noam Chomsky reminds us that the US form of democracy was based on protecting the opulent minority from the tyranny of the majority. He quotes James Madison as saying that political power ought to be in the hands of 'the wealth of the nation,' that is, those men who can be trusted to 'secure the permanent interests of the country' (the rights of the propertied), and to defend these interests against the 'levelling spirit' of those who 'labour under all the hardships of life, and secretly sigh for a more equal distribution of its blessings.'[12]

Democracy thus has different meanings, and such factors as 'local language, history, knowledge, levels of trust, [and] religion' condition and shape the meaning conveyed by the term 'democracy.'[13] But according to the Greek origin of the term, democracy means rule of the people—*demos* means 'people' and *kratos* means 'authority' or 'power.' It is a system of government in which supreme authority lies with the people. The governance in a democracy can be direct or indirect, but the governors can only rule with the consent of the governed.

The UN's operational definition has the following characteristics: government decisions made in consultation with a country's citizens or via elected representatives; frequent and fair elections of representatives who exercise their constitutional powers without violent opposition from unelected officials; universal adult suffrage; all adults have the right to run for public office; freedom of expression without the risk of state punishment; free access to alternative sources of information that are protected by law; freedom of association; and all citizens have the right to form independent associations and organizations, including independent political parties and interest groups. Amartya Sen provides a snapshot of the current status of this form of governance:

While democracy is not yet universally practiced, nor indeed uniformly accepted, in the general climate of world opinion democratic governance has now achieved the status of being taken to be generally right. The ball is very much in the court of those who want to rubbish democracy to provide justification for that rejection.[14]

The term 'governance' has been long associated with democracy—coming from the Greek word meaning 'to steer,' which can be for either good or evil ends.

Major donors and international financial institutions (IFIs) have been increasingly conditioning their aid and loans on 'good governance.' As argued below, African states and states in transition have more often than not been the main targets for implementing such good governance measures.

The term 'good governance' is often used to refer to the promotion of the rule of law and equal justice under the law, and to a governing process that ensures that political, social, and economic priorities of a state are based on a broad consensus within its civil society. In addition, good governance is now generally accepted to mean a process through which governments actively address socioeconomic problems facing their citizens. As Kofi Annan has noted, 'Good governance is perhaps the single most important factor in eradicating poverty and promoting development.'[15]

Another take on good governance can be found in Article 9 (3) of the Cotonou Partnership Agreement between the European Union (EU) and seventy-seven countries from sub-Saharan Africa, the Caribbean and the Pacific. This article specifies that good governance is:

The transparent and accountable management of human, natural, economic and financial resources for the purposes of equitable and sustainable development, in the context of a political and institutional environment that upholds human rights, democratic principles and the rule of law.[16]

Other definitions of good governance focus on social and political concerns while yet others reveal a more technical economic side. A brief overview of donors' definitions illustrates this well. For example, in the IMF good governance refers generally to the technical economic aspects of governance—the transparency of government accounts, the effectiveness of public resources management, and the stability of the regulatory environment for private sector activity. In the Organization for Security and Co-operation in Europe (OSCE), the term focuses on the social dimension—to build, strengthen and promote democratic institutions as well as tolerance throughout society; whereas the Organisation for Economic Co-operation and Development (OECD) stresses the politico-legal dimension of good governance—the legitimacy of government, the accountability of the political elements of government, and respect for human rights and the rule of law.

By good governance, therefore, is meant a process of decision-making that is participatory, inclusive, transparent, accountable, responsive, effective, and efficient. These elements are closely interrelated, and ideally all six aspects would be expected to work in synergy for good governance to exist.

THE UN AND DEMOCRATIC GOVERNANCE

Lawrence Finkelstein reminds us that 'democracy' does not appear in the Charter either as a condition of membership or as a goal of the United Nations.[17] Neither is it mentioned in the International Covenant on Civil and Political Rights or in the

Universal Declaration of Human Rights, although there is reference in the latter document to human freedom, including freedom of religion and assembly. The word is also not to be found anywhere in the Charter of the IMF or in the Articles of Agreement for the five institutions comprising the World Bank Group.

Yet, the ideal of democratic governance underpins much of the UN's contemporary work. When the world body was founded, in addition to being an alliance against aggression, it was premised on the belief that stable, peaceful conditions within states would underpin peaceful and stable relations between them. But when did the UN become preoccupied with advancing and promoting democracy?

It began in December 1989 when the General Assembly in its resolution 44/146 finally took the stand that political legitimacy required democracy. This text underscores the significance of both the Universal Declaration of Human Rights and the International Covenant on Civil and Political Rights, which had established earlier that the authority to govern shall be based on the will of the people, as expressed in periodic and genuine elections. With the fall of the Berlin Wall a month earlier, a surge in democratic entitlement began and democracy started to acquire the status of a global norm. That same year, the UN supervised the Namibian elections in its transition from trusteeship to independence—the first time that the organization became engaged in democratic interventionism that combined traditional peacekeeping and observer tasks with actual institutional development. In February of the following year, the UN launched its first electoral observation mission within a member state, Nicaragua, and followed this up later in that same year with another such mission in Haiti.

In 1991 the Assembly took a major step in adopting resolution 46/137 to enhance the robustness of the global democracy norm. This text reaffirmed principles stated in the Universal Declaration of Human Rights and noted what would enhance the effectiveness of the principle of periodic and genuine elections: everyone should have the right to take part in the government of her/his country, either directly or through freely chosen representatives; everyone has the right of equal access to public service in her/his country; the will of the people should be the basis of the authority of government; the people's will shall be expressed in periodic and genuine elections which should be held by secret ballot; and universal and equal suffrage shall be accepted as the norm.

This resolution also referred to the provision in the International Covenant on Civil and Political Rights for 'every citizen' to take part in the conduct of public affairs, 'without distinction of any kind, such as race, colour, sex, language, religion, political or other opinion, national or social origin, property, birth or other status.' It used this principle to condemn apartheid in South Africa and Rhodesia's systematic denial of the right of black people to vote. The Assembly also recognized that there was no single political system or electoral method equally suited to every country. Therefore, any attempt to assist in the implementation of periodic and genuine elections 'should not call into question each State's sovereign right to choose and develop its own unique political, socio-economic and cultural systems.'

Already by 1991, the UN was providing advisory services and technical assistance through the Centre for Human Rights to states that asked for help in the transition to democracy. In addition, technical assistance was being provided by the Department of Technical Co-operation for Development (DTCD) and the United Nations Development Programme (UNDP). The UN gave direct technical electoral assistance to over eighty countries between 1989 and 1999.

Before the UN can provide any type of electoral assistance, it first does an evaluation of the preelection conditions in the country requesting assistance. The following procedure is then followed for a government to obtain help. First, the state must send an official written request for assistance to the UN Focal Point for Electoral Assistance Activities at least three months before the election is to be held, to allow for meaningful involvement. Usually those making the country request are from the national electoral authorities, the Office of the President, or the Ministry of Foreign Affairs. Second, the Electoral Assistance Division will then consult with the relevant regional division of the Department of Political Affairs (DPA) and the UNDP Resident Representative, among others, about whether preelection conditions in the requesting country satisfy the established criteria for UN electoral assistance. Third, if the Focal Point determines that an in-depth assessment of the preelection conditions is required before deciding whether to provide assistance, the Electoral Assistance Division (EAD) in cooperation with UNDP will then dispatch a needs assessment mission to evaluate the political, material, institutional, and security situation in the requesting country. Fourth, the mission will also assess the appropriateness, necessity, and potential impact of UN assistance to ascertain whether the main contesting political parties and civil society representatives support the organization's involvement.

Over thirty of those states asking for UN technical assistance between 1989 and 1999 were from sub-Saharan Africa. To assist the states that could not finance the electoral verification mission, a voluntary trust fund was created by the Secretary-General. And, due to the increase in demand for assistance in the transition process to democracy, the Secretary-General designated his under-secretary-general for political affairs as the Focal Point for Electoral Assistance Activities.

The democratization norm became even more robust in 1992 when Secretary-General Boutros Boutros-Ghali published his *An Agenda for Peace*. He asserted that democracy within nations 'requires respect for human rights and fundamental freedoms,' as set forth in the Charter. He continued by saying that democracy 'requires as well a deeper understanding and respect for the rights of minorities and respect for the needs of the more vulnerable groups of society, especially women and children.' For Boutros-Ghali, this was not simply a political matter. As he put it:

The social stability needed for productive growth is nurtured by conditions in which people can readily express their will. For this, strong domestic institutions of participation are essential. Promoting such institutions means promoting the empowerment of the unorganized, the poor, the marginalized. To this end, the focus of the United Nations should be on the 'field', the locations where economic, social and political decisions take effect.[18]

But the Secretary-General did not limit the application of this democratization norm to states. In fact, he argued that the application of the relevant principles should also be taken seriously within the Secretariat. By this he meant that decision-making at the UN ought to be based on attaining 'the fullest consultation, participation and engagement of all States, large and small.' It also meant applying the principles of the Charter consistently so that the moral authority of the organization would be sustained and the level of trust in the organization would increase. Boutros-Ghali was the first UN Secretary-General to assert that democracy at all levels was essential to attaining peace, prosperity and justice within the international system.[19] Increasing demand by member states for assistance in running elections led the world body to systematize and institutionalize its electoral assistance missions, and to this end the EAD was created in April 1992.

This new unit was responsible for: coordinating the electoral assistance activities of the UN system; reviewing requests for UN electoral assistance; undertaking needs assessment missions; developing operational strategies for the electoral components of peacekeeping operations; providing support to the activities of international observers; supporting the development of in-country capacity to monitor elections; providing substantive advice and guidance to member states; maintaining a roster of international experts who could provide technical advice; advising and assisting the Focal Point of trust funds for UN electoral assistance activities; maintaining contact with regional, intergovernmental and nongovernmental organizations; supporting regional networks; preparing the Secretary-General's annual report to the General Assembly on elections; establishing an internal information system; and organizing international conferences, workshops, seminars, and training courses on election-related subjects with other organizations.

The ability of the EAD was soon tested with major electoral assistance missions in El Salvador, Eritrea, Cambodia, Angola, and the Western Sahara. The Angola mission was an utter failure due to the inadequate level of human and financial resources devoted to it. Civil conflict broke out in Angola immediately after the UN-supervised elections in September 1992. However, the El Salvador Mission (ONUSAL) whose tasks included a combination of human rights monitoring, the monitoring of a ceasefire, peacekeeping, and civilian policing, helped bring to an end an ongoing civil war and bringing rebels into the constitutional process was considered successful. Another relatively successful mission was the UN Transitional Authority in Cambodia (UNTAC). This electoral assistance mission was instrumental in bringing about a peaceful transition to a multiparty system in that country. The UN spent over $2 billion in this effort and for a while literally ran the country and its bureaucracy. In UNTAC we saw the beginnings of what is now called post-conflict peace-building.[20]

Over the years since 1989, the UN has developed two main types of electoral assistance. The first is standard electoral assistance, and the second consists of major electoral missions usually conducted alongside extended peacekeeping/peacebuilding operations.

Standard Electoral Assistance Activities

Since its establishment, the EAD has learned to tailor electoral assistance to meet particular needs of requesting states. Although much of the literature has been devoted to examining the UN's role in supporting the election components of peacekeeping operations, the majority of the electoral assistance provided by the organization is relatively small-scale, technical assistance activities that hardly require a specific mandate from the General Assembly or the Security Council.

There are at least four such small-scale electoral assistance activities that deserve mention here. The first is the coordination and support of international observers— an activity utilized when a requesting member state invites several governments and organizations to observe an election. In such cases, the EAD generally establishes a small secretariat in the requesting country, with the assistance of UNDP. This secretariat coordinates and provides logistical support to international election observers (from other states, IGOs, and NGOs) that together make up the joint international observer group (JIOG). Throughout the operation of these missions, the UN is expected to maintain a public position of neutrality. The JIOG normally issues a joint statement of its findings in the pre- and immediate post-election period, in addition to issuing their own reports. The costs of this type of assistance are generally offset by direct financing from member states that sponsor the observers. Such assistance activity allows the UN to retain a low profile and is one of the least intrusive on national sovereignty. This kind of electoral assistance was tried in Ethiopia and Kenya (1992), Niger (1993), Lesotho (1993), Malawi (1993 and 1994), Tanzania (1995), Armenia (1995), Azerbaijan (1995), Sierra Leone (1996), Mali (1997), and Algeria (1997).

The second set of UN electoral assistance activities fall under the rubric of 'technical assistance.' This is the most frequently requested type of electoral assistance and covers a broad range of both short-term and long-term assistance to national election authorities who are responsible for running elections in their countries. In such cases, the UN provides advice and assistance to electoral authorities in electoral administration and planning, voter registration, election budgeting, electoral laws review and regulations, the training of election officials, logistics, voter and civic education, procurement of election materials, coordination of international donor assistance, electoral dispute resolution, computerization of electoral rolls, boundary delimitation, among others.

The third UN electoral assistance activity falls under the heading of support for national election monitors, which focuses on building the domestic observation capacity by providing support to civil society groups that are monitoring elections on a non-partisan basis. This type of assistance is usually provided to countries that are relatively well developed, pluralistic, and with a viable community of civic organizations that are able to undertake national election observation. Such support was provided, for example, in Mexico in 1994 and 1997.

The final electoral assistance activity is usually composed of UN political affairs officers who are sent to a country to do a follow-up of the final phase of an electoral process. These officers then prepare internal reports for the Secretary-General.

Major Electoral Missions

Major electoral missions must have a General Assembly or a Security Council mandate and are only considered in exceptional cases. They are normally a core part of a comprehensive peacekeeping operation. The following three types of electoral assistance activities fall in this category of major electoral missions.

The first is the organization and actual conduct of an election. When the UN is mandated to organize and conduct an election or referendum, it becomes a surrogate for national electoral authorities. To fulfill these missions, the world organization is usually required to establish a system of laws, procedures, and administrative measures that can be used in the holding of free and fair elections. The UN is also responsible for the administration of the electoral process, e.g., establishing a legal framework, registering voters, and conducting elections in accordance with international norms. These types of assistance missions are very costly and are unlikely except in extraordinary circumstances (e.g., in the case of failing or failed states). Typical examples of such major electoral missions include UNTAC, the UN Transitional Authority in Eastern Slavonia, Baranja and Western Sirmium (UNTAES), and the UN Mission for the Referendum in Western Sahara (MINURSO).

The second major electoral mission is also seldom undertaken by the UN and involves the supervision of an electoral process usually in the context of decolonization or trusteeship. In such cases, a special representative of the Secretary-General is normally appointed to certify the results as well as to report on the fairness and appropriateness of the entire process. Examples of this kind of activity include the 1989 UN Transition Assistance Group (UNTAG) that supervised the elections leading to independence for Namibia.

The final major electoral activity is the verification of an electoral process. This is a more common type of electoral assistance that is provided in the context of a 'major mission.' It requires authorization by the Security Council or the General Assembly, but the requesting government remains responsible for the organization and conduct of elections. The results of UN verification missions are not legally binding, but they can lend legitimacy to an electoral process and help ensure compliance from the national electoral authorities with electoral regulations. On these missions, international observers are deployed throughout the country to scrutinize all aspects of the electoral process. Such verification missions have been undertaken in Angola (UNAVEM II), El Salvador (ONUSAL), Eritrea (UNOVER), Haiti (ONUVEH), Mozambique (UNOMOZ), Nicaragua (ONUVEN), South Africa (UNOMSA), and Liberia (UNOMIL).

The UN electoral assistance work is normally supported by several organizations of the UN system. With respect to technical assistance, the EAD works closely with UNDP, the Department of Economic and Social Affairs (DESA) and the United

Nations Office for Project Services (UNOPS). At times, support is provided by the Centre for Human Rights and the United Nations Volunteers programme (UNV). Additionally, the Bretton Woods system has become involved in electoral monitoring and assistance activity particularly as it pertains to 'good governance.'

THE INTERNATIONAL FINANCIAL INSTITUTIONS AND GOOD GOVERNANCE

Good governance and political liberalization as desirable ends were imposed on African governments by external actors. Disappointment with Africa's economic failure was compounded by corruption almost three decades after independence of several African countries from Western colonial rule. At the same time Central and Eastern European countries were breaking loose from the Soviet model, and for Western countries the search for a new foreign policy thrust to replace anti-communism took on added urgency.[21]

This eventually resulted in the transformation by the major Western industrial democracies of the fairly innocuous term 'governance' into a contentious political conditionality having as its focus the promotion of democracy. For many African governments and leaders, this new conditionality on top of other conditionalities associated with the Structural Adjustment Programs (SAPs) of the IMF was nothing short of a ticking time bomb. Even those African leaders who were genuinely committed to economic reform in their countries were dubious of the consequences of the political conditionality being imposed from outside. The conditionality promised to increase their dependence on external benefactors even as it encouraged home-grown opposition to authoritarian regimes. The majority of these leaders resisted this program while others introduced cosmetic changes to their constitutions and organized 'sham' elections designed to preserve the political status quo while giving the appearance of adherence to the terms of conditionality.

The lukewarm reception that the campaign for good governance and democratization received from its African hosts raises the following question: can Africa's political leadership, in good faith, be expected to produce and guarantee the political reforms necessary for good governance to flourish? Because African leaders were reluctant at best and hostile at worst to governance and democratization reform, their commitment was, at best, questionable. It is therefore unlikely that they can be counted on to implement the necessary reforms that will lead to good governance on the continent.

Governance linked to democracy has become 'the new political conditionality for the distribution of both bilateral and multilateral assistance to developing African countries,' according to one African analyst. 'Henceforth, financial aid and loans would be given only to countries tending toward pluralism, public accountability and human rights, and market principles. The test of democratization would be based on the presence of multiparty systems, free elections, press freedom, and an independent judiciary.'[22]

CONCLUSION

To date, almost half of the UN's 192 member states have requested assistance in conducting elections.[23] As of July 2002, ninety-two states had requested some form of electoral assistance. Some states made more than one request for help with presidential and parliamentary elections. There were ninety-eight cases of states asking for technical assistance. In some cases they needed help with electoral commissions or with drafting electoral laws. In other cases, they needed the UN to provide technical assistance in the planning of referendums or parliamentary elections. Certain requests were for broader support and actual coordination of elections. There were at least thirty-eight such cases since 2002. During that time about nine states requested only needs assessment. There were at least fifty-one cases in which the UN was simply unable to fulfill the request of the state that was asking for assistance. The reasons for this varied from 'lack of funds' to 'insufficient lead time.' Finally, there were a few cases in which states withdrew their requests, and at least one case (Togo) in which the UN's technical assistance was suspended because an election was postponed.[24]

However, we are becoming increasingly aware that an election does not necessarily resolve many of the deep-seated problems that plague states in transition to democracy, such as Kosovo, Afghanistan, Haiti, and Iraq. While the range of democracy assistance activities is wide, as indicated earlier, the primary focus of the EAD is essentially on getting the 'process' of democracy right.

Secretary-General Kofi Annan is correct to state that democracy is now more widely accepted and practiced than at any other time in our history.[25] There is no doubt that the UN has helped to shore up this new global democratization norm. The Millennium Declaration provides the strongest and most unanimous statement to date from member states about the importance of democratic and participatory governance. Indeed, the MDGs are supposed to be achieved through good governance within all countries. The declaration calls on governments to spare no effort to 'promote democracy and strengthen the rule of law.' But democracy is about far more than elections. Boutros-Ghali back in 1994 saw democracy as much more than creating conditions for free and fair elections. He felt that democratic development should be linked directly to good governance, to the promotion of adherence to human rights, and to rebuilding the rule of law and state institutions, particularly in war-torn countries.[26]

Democracy can be described as the only form of government that creates the space within which individuals can fully enjoy human rights. Only in a democracy can human rights truly be respected, and without human rights, there can be no genuine democracy. Because democracy generally delivers accountability, representative governments are far less likely to resolve disputes by armed conflict, and far more likely to ensure that resources are managed equitably. Thus, democracies can contribute to the preservation of peace and security. As human rights are respected in democracies, representative governments are far more likely to address the needs of those in society that often suffer lack of respect of their rights, including women, the poor, and minorities. The UN is helping to strengthen not only the norm of democracy but also the norm of good governance.

Global democracy has to 'move in two different directions simultaneously. It must deepen democratic participation at the lower levels (local, national, regional), while broadening it at the higher level of global decision-making.'[27] In assisting states that are in need of consolidating their democratic processes, and in insisting that such processes be linked to good governance, the UN system has been making an important contribution to the deepening of democratic participation. Democratic practices can be further broadened at the global level if the UN succeeds in eliminating the democratic deficits within its various bodies.

NOTES

1. Larry Diamond, *Promoting Democracy in the 1990s: Actors and Instruments, Issues and Imperatives: a Report to the Carnegie Commission on Preventing Deadly Conflict* (Washington, DC: Carnegie Corporation of New York, 1995), 1.
2. See Samuel P. Huntington, *The Third Wave: Democratization in the Late Twentieth Century* (Norman: University of Oklahoma Press, 1991).
3. On this point see UNDP, *Human Development Report 2000: Overcoming Human Poverty* (New York: Oxford University Press, 2000), 56.
4. Adrian Karatnycky, Charles Graybow, Douglas W. Payne et al., *Freedom in the World: The Annual Survey of Political Rights and Civil Liberties, 1994–1995* (New York: Freedom House, 1995), 3.
5. Marina Ottaway, *Democracy Challenged: The Rise of Semi-Authoritarianism* (Washington, DC: Carnegie Endowment for International Peace, 2003), 3.
6. David Held, 'Democracy, the Nation State and the Global System,' in *Political Theory Today*, ed. David Held (Cambridge: Polity, 1991), 214–218.
7. See Thomas M. Franck, 'The Emerging Right to Democratic Governance,' *The American Journal of International Law* 86, no. 1 (1992): 46–91.
8. See Fareed Zakaria, 'The Rise of Illiberal Democracies,' *Foreign Affairs* 76, no. 6 (1997): 42; and Jack L. Snyder, *From Voting to Violence: Democratization and Nationalist Conflict* (New York: Norton, 2000).
9. Quoted in Michael Saward, *Democracy* (Cambridge: Polity Press, 2003), 2–3.
10. Rory McCarthy and Luke Harding, 'Interview with General Pervez Musharraf (Special report on Pakistan),' *The Guardian Unlimited*, 16 May 2001.

11. Saward, *Democracy*, 5.
12. Noam Chomsky, 'How US Democracy Triumphed Again,' *The Independent*, 14 January 2001.
13. Michael Saward, *Democracy*, p. 4.
14. Amartya Sen, 'Democracy as a Universal Value,' *Journal of Democracy* 10, no. 3 (1999): 5.
15. Kofi Annan, 'Concept Paper on State of Governance in LDCs Report,' 1, available at www.unpan.org.
16. The European Commission, The Cotonou Agreement: 'Partnership agreement between the members of the African, Caribbean and Pacific groups of states on the one part, and the European Community and its member states, on the other part,' available at www. europa.eu.int.
17. See Lawrence Finkelstein, 'Essay: From Seeds to System—The United Nations Charter', *the UN Chronicle Online* 42, no. 3, (2005), available at www.un.org.
18. Boutros Boutros-Ghali, *An Agenda for Peace: Preventive Diplomacy, Peacemaking and Peacekeeping*, UN document, A/47/277–S/24111, 17 June 1992, para. 81. Also see Boutros Boutros-Ghali, *An Agenda for Development*, UN document A/48/935, 6 May 1994.
19. Ibid., para. 82.
20. See Thomas F. Keating and W. Andy Knight, eds., *Building Sustainable Peace* (Tokyo: United Nations University Press, 2004).
21. Thomas M. Callaghy, 'Political Passions and Economic Interests: Economic Reform and Political Structure in Africa,' in *Hemmed In: Responses to Africa's Economic Decline*, ed. Thomas M. Callaghy and John Ravenhill (New York: Columbia University Press, 1993).
22. Ndiva Kofele Kale, 'Good Governance as Political Conditionality,' Democracy and Good Governance, Management Of Social Transformation (MOST) Project, Ethno Net Africa, ICASSRT, UNESCO 1999, available at www.ethnonet-africa.org.
23. For a list of UN electoral assistance by country, see UNDP, 'Member States Requests for Electoral Assistance to the United Nations,' in Alphabetical Order since 1989 (As of July 2002), www.un.org.
24. For a more detailed breakdown of states' requests for electoral assistance see the United Nations, Department of Political Affairs, Electoral Assistance Division, 'Member States' Requests for Electoral Assistance to the United Nations System,' www.un.org.
25. Kofi Annan, 'In Larger Freedom: Decision Time at the UN,' *Foreign Affairs* 84 no. 3, (2005): 63–74.
26. Boutros-Ghali, *An Agenda for Development*, para. 21. Also see Boutros Boutros-Ghali, *Support by the United Nations System of the Efforts of Governments to Promote and Consolidate New or Restored Democracies (An Agenda for Democratization)*, UN document A/51/761, 20 December 1996.
27. Majid Tehranian, 'Democratizing Governance,' in *Democratizing Global Governance*, ed. Eşref Aksu and Joseph A. Camilleri (Houndmills, Basingstoke, UK: Palgrave Macmillan, 2002), 56.

CHAPTER 37

....

HUMAN DEVELOPMENT

....

RICHARD JOLLY

A focus on people as the central concern of economic and social development has been a hallmark of the UN's approach almost from the beginning.[1] The ILO, for example, was founded to be concerned with the conditions of employment and the mandates of FAO deal with food supply and the ending of hunger, WHO with health and human well-being, and UNESCO with education, science and culture. The funds and agencies of the UN have also long had a human focus—UNICEF on children, WFP on supplying food for people in emergencies, UNFPA and UNIFEM on women. The UN Human Settlements Programme (Habitat) focuses on people in urban communities and many of the smaller UN agencies or divisions are concerned with migrants, older persons, and other special groups. The UN Development Programme (UNDP) has a broader mandate, but its coordinating role for all UN field operations has inevitably put human concerns at the center. All this has meant that the UN has followed a multidisciplinary approach to development as opposed to the primarily economic approach which has been more characteristic of the World Bank and the IMF.

In 1990, the UN's focus on human concerns was given conceptual depth and broad application by the creation of UNDP's *Human Development Report (HDR)*.[2] Since that time, the *HDR* has been issued annually, each edition applying the human development approach to specific issues of development policy. Especially innovative and important in terms of critical thinking have been the *HDRs* linking human development to human security, gender, poverty and deprivation, globalization, human rights, the Millennium Development Goals (MDGs), and culture. Largely in response to these global reports, over 130 developing countries have produced their own *National Human Development Reports* (*NHDRs*), using human development methodology to analyze issues within their own borders and to reach conclusions for national policy. Over 550 of these *NHDRs* have now been produced, many countries issuing a number of reports over different years, focused on different themes.

The human development approach should be set in the context of the UN's wider contributions. The UN was founded on four great principles: peace and negotiation in place of war and aggression; sovereign independence for all countries; economic and social development to raise living standards worldwide; and human rights for all. Initially these four principles were mostly pursued in parallel and often by different parts of the world organization. But beginning in the 1980s, the four concerns have increasingly been brought together and seen to be interrelated parts of a broader and more balanced process of human development, combining peace and security, democratic governance, sustainable and equitable development, and human rights. The human development approach has provided the framework that brings these issues together and shows their conceptual and operational links.

Human development is, however, only one of many UN contributions to ideas, analysis, measurement and policy making in the area of economic and social development. In the 1950s, the UN argued the need for concessional loans for poorer countries which, though opposed by the World Bank for most of the 1950s, led eventually to the creation of the IDA. In the 1960s, the UN took up the idea of a Decade for Development with quantitative goals for growth and aid. UNCTAD was created in 1964 as a forum for negotiating changes in trade, technology, and other relations between developed and developing countries. In the 1970s, the ILO led the way with work on employment strategies, the informal sector, and basic needs. At the end of the 1970s, UNCTAD underlined the special needs of the least developed countries and the impact of growing debt on the developing countries more generally. In the 1980s, UNICEF, ECA, and the ILO drew attention to the human costs of structural adjustment policies and the need for 'adjustment with a human face.' As the independent and multi-volume UN Intellectual History Project (UNIHP) has shown,[3] much of this work has been pioneering and influential. The UN has often been 'ahead of the curve,' in the sense that its contributions have led the way among international organizations and even sometimes within the academic community. Many of the ideas developed by the UN have made the implementation of human development more effective and rapid.

Notwithstanding these positive contributions and achievements, since the early 1980s, the balance of international funding and leadership for economic and social development shifted from the UN to the World Bank, the International Monetary Fund (IMF), and the World Trade Organization (WTO). (Though formally specialized agencies of the UN, the different voting structure of the Bank and the IMF means that in approach and operations they have largely operated separately. Thus in this chapter, references to the UN are to be read as excluding the Bretton Woods institutions.) This often left the UN in the role of dissenter on economic and social matters, operating from the periphery of global policy. The consequences meant the serious neglect of many of the important issues pioneered by the UN, including priorities for issues of human development, especially in the poorest and least developed countries.

Following the Millennium Summit in 2000 and the adoption of the Millennium Declaration and the Millennium Development Goals (MDGs), a new emphasis has been given to cooperation between the Bretton Woods institutions and the UN, but more time is needed to assess how successful this cooperation will be. Moreover, the World Bank uses the term human development to mean support for education and health, which is important but far narrower and more limited than the pursuit of a human development approach as set out in the series of *Human Development Reports*. This broader agenda still remains a challenge for development in most countries and internationally.

HUMAN DEVELOPMENT: CONCEPTS AND ORIGINS

A formal definition of human development is set out in the first *Human Development Report*:

Human development is a process of enlarging people's choices. The most critical ones are to lead a long and healthy life, to be educated and to enjoy a decent standard of living. Additional choices include political freedom, guaranteed human rights and self-respect—what Adam Smith called the ability to mix with others without being 'ashamed to appear in publick.'

The enlargement of choices goes beyond traditional liberalism by emphasizing the need for actions to 'strengthen human capabilities' for all of a country's population as an essential component of human development strategy. As that first report puts it:

Human development has two sides: the formation of human capabilities such as improved health, knowledge and skills—and the use people make of their acquired capabilities—for leisure, productive purposes or being active in cultural, social and political affairs. If the scales of human development do not finely balance the two sides, considerable frustration will result.[4]

Human development draws enormously on the thought and writings of Amartya Sen, the distinguished economist and philosopher who won the Nobel Prize in Economic Sciences in 1998. Sen traces the origins of human development thinking back to Aristotle, who argued for seeing the difference between a good political arrangement and a bad one in terms of its successes and failures in enabling people to lead flourishing lives. 'Wealth is evidently not the good we are seeking, for it is merely useful and for the sake of something else.' Sen himself has summarized his thinking in *Development as Freedom*, described by Secretary-General Kofi Annan as 'revolutionizing the theory and practice of development.'[5]

The founder of the *Human Development Report* was Mahbub ul Haq, a visionary economist and former Minister of Finance in Pakistan, who led the work for the first six years, subsequently returning to Pakistan where he established a regional Human

Development Centre for South Asia. Mahbub ul Haq had the insight to promote the concept of human development by developing a series of human development indicators by which all countries could be ranked in their performance in human development. This ensured widespread media attention to the concept from the beginning and also introduced a sense of competition between countries.

HUMAN DEVELOPMENT INDICATORS

The main indicator of human development is the HDI—the Human Development Index. This is a composite indicator comprising for each country three components: the average length of life of the country's population, their 'knowledge,' and their access to a range of choices sufficient for a decent standard of living. For HDI, the first component is measured as life expectancy at birth for the population as a whole; the second component is a measure of educational achievement based on a country's adult literacy rate and the percentage of its school-aged population enrolled in the educational system as a proxy for 'knowledge'; and the third is an adjusted measure of per capita income. The latter is incorporated as a proxy indicator of the extent to which people in the country can make consumption choices in relation to their needs and wishes. The third component of the HDI is based on a logarithmic adjustment of per capita income (i.e., purchasing power parity), that gives decreasing weight to each addition to per capita income as per capita income rises, with the weight falling off rapidly after a level of about $10,000, which is about the average of global per capita income. Purchasing Power Parity in US dollars ($PPP) is a measure that provides an estimate of the equivalent spending power of the per capita income of each country in US dollars.[6]

The HDI is now available for over 175 countries, covering both developing and developed countries. Although all indices have weaknesses and limitations, the advantages of the HDI is that its components—length of life, access to knowledge and access to sufficient income for a reasonable standard of living—relate to some of the most basic elements for human life. The arbitrary weighting of these three components had aroused technical controversy. Nonetheless, if the focus of concern is the situation of a country's population, the HDI remains a better measure than GNP per capita.

There are three other human development indices: the Gender-related Development Index (GDI), the Gender Empowerment Measure (GEM), and the Human Poverty Index (HPI), each designed to emphasize a different aspect of human development. The first two focus on the situation of women and girls and reflect the inequalities between women and men in keeping with the human and egalitarian approach under-lying human development. The GDI includes the same measures as the HDI, but for women and girls separately and combined in a measure that penalizes countries with differences in achievement between men and women. The GEM focuses on women's opportunities rather than their capabilities, capturing gender inequality in three key areas: political participation and decision-making power, as measured by the percentage share of women and men in parliamentary seats; economic participation and decision-making, as measured by their percentage shares in positions as legislators, senior professionals, and managers; and women's earned income compared with that of men.

The Human Poverty Index is an indicator of deprivation, measuring the proportion of a country's population failing to reach minimum standards in each dimension of human development. Thus, for developing countries the indicator combines the percentage of the population whose life expectancy at birth is below 40 years, who are illiterate and who lack access to a decent standard of living—as indicated by lack of sustainable access to an improved water source and the proportion of children who are underweight for their age. The HPI is thus a combined measure of the proportion of a country's population who are deprived of the basic choices and capabilities—just as the income standard for poverty is the proportion of a country's population living below some specified measure of income.

For industrialized countries, more stringent standards for assessing deprivation are used in keeping with their higher average standard of living as a point of departure. Thus, HPI-2 combines the percentage of the population whose life expectancy at birth is less than 60 years; the percentage who are *functionally* illiterate; the proportion living below the income poverty line and the proportion socially excluded, as indicated by the rate of long-term unemployment. The difference in components between the HPI-2 (for industrialized countries) and HPI-1 (for developing countries) reflects both the belief that a higher standard for measuring deprivation is appropriate in richer countries and the availability of more reliable data.

The ranking of most countries of the world by HDI and for many countries by the other three indicators can be found in the *Human Development Reports* and on the UNDP website for human development.[7] Table 37.1 includes the indicators for the five highest countries ranked by HDI, and for a selection of other countries, including most of the largest countries as well as the richest in terms of per capita income. Recent *Human Development Reports* also provide data on the changes in human development indicators since 1975.

The picture summarized by the overall human development indicators reveals some important features that apply to the other categories as well. Most importantly, achievement in human development is often different from achievement of high levels of per capita income. Indeed, the countries classed as high human development include several with relatively low levels of per capita income. Similarly, some countries which are relatively poor in terms of per capita income—like Costa Rica, Cuba, Sri Lanka, Bangladesh and some countries of the former Soviet Union now in transition—score relatively well in terms of HDI indicators. Moreover, as the *HDR 1996* showed, it is possible for a country to make relatively rapid improvements in human development even while making only slow advances in terms of economic growth—though as the same report showed, it is difficult to sustain the human development advances for a long period without economic expansion.

Table 37.1 Human development indicators for selected countries, 2003

	HDI ranking	HDI	GDI[a] ranking	GEM[b] (%)	HPI[c] (%)	GDP $ per capita (PPP)
	(1)	(2)	(3)	(4)	(5)	(6)
Norway	1	0.963	1	38	7	37,700
Iceland	2	0.956	3	30	–	31,200
Australia	3	0.955	2	28	13	29,600
Luxembourg	4	0.949	7	23	11	62,300
Canada	5	0.949	5	25	11	30,700
USA	10	0.944	8	15	15	37,600
Japan	11	0.943	14	9	12	28,000
UK	15	0.939	15	18	15	27,200
France	16	0.938	16	14	11	27,700
Germany	20	0.930	20	31	10	27,800
Russian Federation	62	0.795	–	8	32	9,200
Brazil	63	0.792	52	9	10	7,800
China	85	0.755	64	20	12	5,000
India	127	0.602	98	9	31	2,900
Nigeria	158	0.453	123	6	39	1,100

[a] Since GDI is only available for 140 countries, the rankings at lower levels provide a somewhat over-optimistic impression.
[b] Since GEM is only available for 80 countries, that column shows the percentage of seats held by women in parliament.
[c] For OECD and CIS countries, the human poverty measure HPI-2 uses a more stringent standard than HPI-1, used for developing countries.
– not available

Source: UNDP, *Human Development Report 2005: International Cooperation at a Crossroads* (New York: Oxford University Press, 2005), Table 1, 3, 4, 25, and 26.

THEMES AND PERSPECTIVES

The range and influence of the human development approach has been demonstrated in a succession of intellectually stimulating reports. Each has focused on a different theme, analyzing it from a human development perspective and presenting conclusions for national and international policy. The perspectives and the policies have raised important questions about alternatives to conventional thinking about development, as can be seen from the subtitles of the reports from 1990 to 2006:

Concept and Measurement of Human Development
Financing Human Development

Global Dimensions of Human Development
People's Participation
New Dimensions of Human Security
Gender and Human Development
Economic Growth and Human Development
Human Development to Eradicate Poverty
Consumption for Human Development
Globalization with a Human Face
Human Rights and Human Development
Making New Technologies Work for Human Development
Deepening Democracy in a Fragmented World
The Millennium Development Goals: A Compact Among Nations to End Human Poverty
Cultural Liberty in Today's Diverse World
International Cooperation at a Crossroads: Aid, Trade and Security in an Unequal World
Beyond Scarcity: Power, Poverty and the Global Water Crisis

It may be useful to elaborate four of the important themes: human rights, gender, human security, and globalization.[8] Over the 1990s, the rights-based approach to development received much attention, not only within the UN system but also among associated NGOs.[9] Indeed, issues of human rights and human development became so intertwined that the *HDR 2000*'s focus on human rights and human development clarified the differences as well as the areas of overlap. This was done by analyzing what human rights added to human development and what human development added to human rights.

As regards the first, human rights bring to human development international legitimacy, legal specifics, clarification of duties and obligations, and, in many countries, depending on the extent to which rights have been codified into national law, formal commitments which can be called upon in the courts and in public opinion. In a different way, human development brings added value to human rights: a tradition of quantitative and qualitative social science analysis of human development which can help complement legal approaches to human rights. In this respect, human development can also help the assessment of how different policy choices will affect the prospects for fulfilling human rights, in the future as well as at present. While human rights are ultimately matters of individual entitlement, their fulfillment depends on appropriate social conditions. Human development can use the tools of economics and social science to explore the dynamics of how these conditions can change and be changed. In this way, progression in the fulfillment of human rights over time—a process of human development sensitive to human rights—can be incorporated.

The *HDR 1995*'s focus on gender and human development not only elaborated many of the ways in which gender inequalities affected women but showed, with rough quantification, how the perception of women's roles in national economies were often misrepresented by conventional economic indicators. Thus work in the home, by men as well as women, is not counted in conventional national accounts—and much other work 'outside the market' is generally uncounted or greatly underestimated.

This report presented estimates of time use showing that these omissions meant that about two-thirds of women's work was uncounted. The inclusion of all work, paid and unpaid, would show that women carry 53 percent of the total burden of work in developing countries and 51 percent in developed countries. Making estimates of the value of the unpaid work of women and men would raise the value of national income by a staggering 70 percent, just under one-third of which represents the uncounted contribution of men and just over two-thirds the uncounted, and often invisible, contribution of women.

The *Human Development Report* on gender made many proposals for policy and action. In a phrase, this argued that human development if not engendered was endangered. The proposed policy measures ranged widely, from implementation of equal rights for women, ensuring in each country programs for universal education, improved reproductive health, and more credit for women, to the opening of opportunities for women so that they can become agents as well as beneficiaries of change, with 30 percent adopted as the critical minimum threshold for women in decision-making positions at the national level. The report also took a strong stand against violence against women, with proposals to tackle gender violence in the home and community as well as at national and international level.

The *Human Development Report* on human security, issued in 1994, emerging in the aftermath of the Cold War, represented a major reinterpretation of security issues.[10] Instead of the traditional approach to national security—the protection of a nation's borders by military means—this report argued that the protection of people from a wide range of new threats must be central. These threats range from disease to urban crime, from food insecurity to environmental degradation, from unemployment to terrorism. The new perspective is to focus on the threats to a country's people and to set priorities for the state to minimize the impact of the risks of these threats to people.

A human development approach to security does not ignore the military dimensions of security, but it proposes that there be a better balance between activities and expenditures based on the military and armaments, and on non-military activities and actions which contribute to human security. This would help, for example, to diminish other threats to security by making resources available for police forces to tackle urban crime, health personnel to prevent international disease transmission, and national and international investments to ensure food security and to guard against natural and man-made disasters. *HDR 1994* gave particular attention to measures to control the international flow of arms and to provide for the demobilization of soldiers, including teenage soldiers, in post-conflict situations. It proposed a Global Demobilization Fund, drawing on initiatives by Oscar Arias, the former President of Costa Rica and winner of the Nobel Peace Prize. The Demobilization Fund would be financed by reductions in military budgets, with reallocations going to disarming and demobilizing armed forces in developing countries with retraining and reeducation programs to reintegrate military personnel into civilian jobs and society. Although it is easy to dismiss such proposals as impractical, some $500 billion had already been trimmed worldwide from military budgets in the first half-decade of the post-Cold War period, 1988–1993. Conflicts in many developing countries over the 1990s might have been greatly diminished if such proposals had been given more serious attention.

Although much of human development has focused on state policy within nations, international issues have never been absent, and globalization has remained an essential theme. The first *Human Development Report* recognized the need for global targets for human development, foreshadowing the MDGs of a decade later. It also recognized that, 'although the battle for human development must be fought in the developing countries, a favourable external environment can help considerably.'[11] The report commented that 'Never before have the developing countries faced such difficult external circumstances as those in the 1980s.'[12] That first effort already identified the need for various actions to tackle problems: a new debt-refinancing facility; concerted international action to tackle obstacles and ensure a liberal and expanding trade environment; and a revitalization of aid and technical assistance to provide more support for national strategies of human development.

The *HDR 1999* concentrated on globalization and the new challenges to ensure that it acted to strengthen and incorporate the poorer and weaker countries, rather than marginalize them further. It called for reinventing global governance by harmonizing global competition and free market approaches with steady and expanding support for human development and human rights in all countries, developing and developed. This would require a new perspective, a new global ethic, a new approach to globalization. And it would require a range of actions from the broad to the specific.[13]

HUMAN DEVELOPMENT AND THE MDGS

The focus of human development, especially its normative concerns with strengthening human capabilities, established from the beginning a close relationship between goals for improving life expectancy and educational attainment, and those for reducing malnutrition and illiteracy and other indicators of human deprivation. The very first report elaborated the importance of setting global goals for human development and illustrated this by reference to quantified global targets for reduction of child mortality and adult literacy, increases in primary school enrolment, and access to safe water. Goals for these had already been set for the 1990s at the World Summit for Children in 1990 and other global conferences.[14] The *HDR 1990* emphasized the need for incorporating these into national plans of action, adapting the global goals to the national context, setting national priorities, ensuring cost effectiveness, and adequate budget support.[15]

Over the 1990s (and before, during the 1980s) many developing countries adopted such goals and pursued them vigorously, encouraged by various UN agencies, especially UNICEF and WHO. Notwithstanding the economic difficulties of the 1980s, there was considerable success in this pursuit of goals—for example, most countries rapidly expanded immunization and some seventy developing countries achieved the goal of immunizing at least 80 percent of young children against measles, tetanus, polio, and other major threats for which low-cost preventive vaccines were available. It was this achievement which encouraged more attention to goals in the 1990s and which led, in September 2000, to the formulation of the MDGs following the Millennium Declaration, agreed by the heads of state and government present at the Millennium Summit. There are eight major goals and eighteen targets. The eight MDGs are to:

1. Eradicate extreme poverty and hunger
2. Achieve universal primary education
3. Promote gender equality and empower women
4. Reduce child mortality
5. Improve maternal health
6. Combat HIV/AIDS, malaria and other diseases
7. Ensure environmental sustainability
8. Develop a global partnership for development

The eighteen targets are more specific, quantified as to exactly what should be achieved by the year 2015—for the first goal, for instance, to reduce by half the proportion of people living on less than a dollar per day and to reduce by half the proportion of people who suffer from hunger. Each of the first seven goals relating to developing countries had quantified targets attached to them, the sole exception being the eighth goal, which related to the formation of a global partnership for development, and which thus might have incorporated obligations from the developed countries. The targets in this case encompassed broad generalizations such as the development of an open trading and financial system, addressing the special needs of the least developed countries and of small island states with tariff- and quota-free access for their exports and more generous official development assistance, comprehensive action to deal with debt problems of developing countries, and to make available affordable essential drugs and the benefits of new technologies.

Over the first five years of the new millennium, support for the goals became a consensus among donor countries and a focus for a growing proportion of development aid, with the World Bank providing coordination at the global level and country-level coordination being the responsibility of the Bank and UNDP working with the government concerned. The *Human Development Reports* of 2002 and 2003 focused on strategies towards the implementation of the goals, including calling for a global compact for their achievement. The reinforcement of the MDGs was a major theme at the September 2005 World Summit, the largest-ever gathering of heads of state and government.[16]

Misunderstandings of Human Development

With ever more attention to the MDGs, 'human development' is increasingly used as a positive term for investment in education and health or as a phrase for all sorts of actions which vaguely have human concerns in mind. It is important to distinguish these from human development as used in the series of *Human Development Reports* and as defined in the beginning of this chapter. Human development embraces much more than expanding education and health and in particular involves strengthening the capacity of individuals and communities to make choices about their lives and the opportunities to do so. Human development is thus a concept that is deeply democratic and closely linked with human rights. It is a serious failure of understanding and practice for this not to be recognized.

The UN's Wider Contributions to Economic and Social Development

However important, human development is only one of a very large number of wide-ranging contributions of the United Nations to thinking and practice in the field of economic and social development. This is hardly surprising. The world organization has a wide range of responsibilities for the oversight of the planet's economic and social systems, with concerns ranging from international relations in trade and finance, law and intellectual property, civil aviation and communications, meteorology and maritime relations, environmental protection, protection of refugees and other minority groups, and human rights. About four-fifths of the UN system's budget is in support of such activities, but the bulk of this is focused on the support of development in developing countries. Although the World Bank and donor agencies now provide by far the largest share of financial resources for development, the various bodies of the United Nations still provide more than $5 billion in grant aid each year as well as a wide range of policy advice, technical assistance, and other resources in the major areas of health, education, water and sanitation, population, social integration, and urban policy.

The UN system also provides policy advice, technical assistance, and small amounts of financial support for agriculture, industry, services and other economic areas, including those related to international economic relationships relating to trade, foreign investment, debt, etc. The UN takes initiatives and often has the mandate for leadership in many more specialist fields—with respect to children, women and gender issues, the needs of older persons, support for immigrants, refugees, indigenous peoples, and such vulnerable groups as children in war. In these areas, the financial support from the UN system is essential. Finally, the UN takes positions of international leadership and action in key areas of conflict prevention and control with respect to illicit drugs, crime, and terrorism.

In matters of economic and social development, the UN's many contributions can be conveniently placed in three categories: development objectives and assistance with policymaking; the provision of finance and technical assistance; and support for monitoring and evaluation.

Development Objectives and Support for Policymaking

Compared to other international organizations, in particular the World Bank, the IMF, and the WTO, the UN has always approached development within a broad, multidisciplinary perspective and encouraged such an approach to the framing of development objectives. Much of this reflects the sectoral objectives and disciplinary professionalisms of the specialized agencies (ILO, FAO, WHO, UNESCO, and UNIDO) as well as the specialized focus of the UN funds (UNDP, WFP, UNICEF, UNFPA, and IFAD). These funds provide a substantive lead to a sectoral group or a dimension of development, backed up by the provision of resources: WFP for the use of food aid for emergency relief and for support in other sectors of development, such as for school feeding; UNICEF for children; UNFPA for population activities and more recently for women's empowerment; and IFAD for small-scale agriculture and poor farmers. UNDP has a broader mandate but in addition to taking the lead in coordination at country level has specialist concerns and funds in support of such key areas as women and gender, environment, and democratic governance. As indicated, it has also led the way with human development.

All this has meant that the UN's approach to development has long had human concerns at the center—in contrast to the Bretton Woods institutions whose focus traditionally has been more directly on more narrowly defined economic and financial issues. Over the years, the UN's broad objectives have become more carefully defined and more closely integrated. Initially, the UN tended to emphasize development as an economic and social process. In parallel and largely separate was the UN's political work with respect to the maintenance of peace and conflict resolution, together with political work on countries in trusteeship or colonial status, focused on assistance in the process towards sovereign independence. And in parallel but again largely separate was the UN's work on human rights.

Over the years, these parallel activities have increasingly been brought together, especially after the Cold War—though, in fact, beginning a decade or two before this. The issue of women and gender is a helpful illustration of a larger reality. In 1975, most notably, the first World Conference on Women was held in Mexico and concluded with agreements to bring concerns for women more directly into development planning as well as to promote more actively human rights for women, by changing the Declaration for the Elimination of all forms of Discrimination Against Women into a convention, CEDAW. This started a process of integrating rights with development. This approach was carried further in the 1980s with the Declaration on the Right to Development in 1986 and the Convention on the Rights of the Child in 1989. Later, in 2000, came resolution 1325 of the Security Council, which urges member states to increase the participation of women at all levels and stages of the peacemaking process. This path-breaking resolution shifted the Security Council from being a gender-neutral body to one which is committed to work for women's involvement at all levels of conflict prevention and peace building.[17]

In the 1970s, the other global conferences of the decade broadened the UN's approach to development by introducing concerns for the environment, population, food and hunger, employment and basic needs, and urban settlements. Each of these conferences concluded with resolutions and programs of work bringing these issues ever more into the mainstream of development objectives and policy. Countries were recognized to have the main responsibility for follow up but the UN itself often provided technical assistance to support national efforts of policymaking and implementation. Thus increasingly and formally, the UN's view of development objectives was broadened, made more multidisciplinary, and carried into country application.

Ironically, the broadening of development concerns in the 1970s occurred in parallel with massive oil price increases in 1973/4 and 1979, which led to rising deficits and debt in many developing countries. By about 1980, these Third World countries had to confront the political and economic shift to neoliberal economic orthodoxy in the United States and other major economic powers. The international result was a shift of power, finance, and donor support away from the UN and toward the World Bank and the International Monetary Fund. With little initial opposition, the Bretton Woods institutions took the lead in promoting tough structural adjustment policies for developing countries to deal with the debt and deficits. These in turn forced most developing countries to adopt neoliberal economic policies—freeing markets, extending privatization, and pursuing liberalization more generally—which became known as the 'Washington consensus.' Many of the broader human and social policy concerns of the 1970s were abandoned.

The various development agencies of the UN which had the courage to disagree and to present alternatives moved toward what has been characterized as the 'New York dissent,' still presenting human concerns and objectives at the center of development objectives but struggling to promote these in a much more difficult international economic environment. For most of Africa and Latin America, the 1980s and 1990s became lost decades for development. The major exception to these economic failures was in Asia where countries like Korea, Taiwan, Malaysia, China, and later India had the economic strength and independence to pursue policies which often contrasted sharply with Washington orthodoxy.

Notwithstanding these constraints and the limitations in its resources, the UN has continued to exert considerable influence on development thinking, both through its own activities and, notably, through the world summits and other global and regional conferences which have done much to set the agenda for development priorities. Indeed, a review of the UN's role has concluded that the world organization's contributions to ideas and innovative action in economic and social development may be among its most important effects on development over the last sixty years.[18]

Such ideas and innovative leadership have covered many fields—often initially neglected by bilateral donors and other multilateral funding agencies. The UN has provided pioneering leadership and support in such areas as priority programs for children, the special needs of least developed countries, sustainable development and environmental protection, human rights, and democracy as part of development. As mentioned earlier, the UN has also taken the lead in matters of women and gender, social development, population, and food and hunger. The sixty-year record shows that the UN has often been ahead of the curve in all these areas.

Financial Support

In recent years, the main UN funds and specialized agencies together have been providing about $5 billion from their core funds and another $5 billion from supplementary funds; about 6 to 12 percent of total aid to developing countries. Financial support covers both finance and resources provided in kind—both technical assistance and supplies. In the case of WFP, much of the support is in the form of food. In the case of the other UN funds, technical assistance and supplies account for about a third of the total; for the specialized agencies, this generally accounts for over three-quarters.

Three important features of past and ongoing support from the world organization are salient. As a share of total world aid, that provided by the UN funds and specialized agencies amounts to about a quarter of that provided by the World Bank and regional development banks. However, most of this UN aid is provided on grant terms, as opposed to being provided as loans, a feature which adds to the relative attractiveness of UN support. Moreover, stringent conditionality has never been a feature of UN aid, further reinforcing its relative attractiveness. Finally, much of the financial assistance provided through the UN is in addition to the core or regular budgets of the agencies concerned. This adds a degree of uncertainty to all the parties concerned—by limiting the capacity of the UN agencies to make long-term plans with confidence and for the recipient government, whose access to non-core resources now depends on the decisions of both the UN agency and the government providing the extra resources. Moreover, most funding to the UN system is provided as part of annual or biennial budgets, again limiting the possibility of long-term planning.

Monitoring and Evaluation

As part of its focus on goals and its more general work on regulation, the UN plays an important role in monitoring progress in many fields. With respect to the MDGs, for instance, the UN has been given the lead in ensuring that every country produces data to track progress. UNDP assembles the data for the human development indicators as already described and publishes the results annually. All this is in line with the role of the UN Statistics Division and the Statistical Commission which from the beginning of the UN had the mandate for developing international data systems to make possible what today would be termed improved global governance.[19]

Most of the data is collected by countries themselves, though mostly working within guidelines and statistical frameworks agreed at international level. Thus the quality of the resulting data reflects the resources available and the organization and efficiency of the national statistical offices in each country. The inevitable result is that most poor countries generally produce poor quality data. This has led to additional resources often being provided by the UN system to improve the data available and sometimes to support special additional efforts. One noteworthy example that suggests the kind of efforts mounted across the UN system is the MICS—the Multiple Indicator Cluster Surveys, pioneered by UNICEF to produce data on child mortality and on the coverage of measures such as immunization designed to reduce child deaths. The MICS involve mounting a low-cost sample survey, often using medical students as enumerators in the rural areas. The use of medical students reduces the costs of enumeration but also gives them an opportunity to see first hand the health conditions of poorer people in rural and peri-urban areas, an experience often missing in their normal training.

CONCLUSION

Human development is increasingly recognized to be central to development and to poverty reduction. It is also central to the work and objectives of many parts of the world organization—and an area where many UN agencies have pioneered new thinking and new approaches. In spite of this, attention and development resources have increasingly been channelled to and through the World Bank, notably since the 1980s.

With the MDGs now widely accepted, the time seems ripe for a better balance between the UN and the Bretton Woods institutions. Some increase in the proportion of international financial resources available to the UN would provide more opportunity for the UN to support directly the goals and policies that it has developed. Such a change in financing would strengthen international action and partnership and legitimacy at country level—and could help speed the progress towards the implementation of global goals and poverty reduction.

NOTES

1. See, e.g., Louis Emmerij, Richard Jolly, and Thomas G. Weiss, *Ahead of the Curve? UN Ideas and Global Challenges* (Bloomington: Indiana University Press, 2001); and Richard Jolly, Louis Emmerij, Dharam Ghai, and Frédéric Lapeyre, *UN Contributions to Development Thinking and Practice* (Bloomington: Indiana University Press, 2004).

2. For overviews of many of these issues, see Sakiko Fukada-Parr and A. K. Shiva Kumar, eds., *Readings in Human Development* (Oxford: Oxford University Press, 2003).

3. Details can be found at www.unhistory.org.

4. UNDP, *Human Development Report 1990* (New York: Oxford University Press, 1990), 10.

5. Amartya Sen, *Development as Freedom* (Oxford: Oxford University Press, 1999), back cover.

6. Over the years, a number of improvements have been made in the HDI and other indices. This exposition concentrates on the most recent versions of the indicators, as found in UNDP, *Human Development Report 2005* (New York: United Nations Development Programme, 2005).

7. See http://hdr.undp.org/.

8. See David Held and Anthony McGrew, with David Goldblatt and Jonathan Perraton, *Global Transformations: Politics, Economics, and Culture* (Palo Alto, Calif.: Stanford University Press, 1999).

9. See Sarah Zaidi and Roger Norman, *The UN and Human Rights Ideas: The Unfinished Revolution* (Bloomington: Indiana University Press, 2007 forthcoming).

10. For a critical examination, see S. Neil MacFarlane and Yuen Foong Khong, *Human Security and the UN: A Critical History* (Bloomington: Indiana University Press, 2006).

11. UNDP, *Human Development Report 1990*, 78.

12. Ibid.

13. UNDP, *Human Development Report 1999* (New York: Oxford University Press, 1999), 97.

14. See Michael G. Schechter, *United Nations Global Conferences* (London: Routledge, 2005).

15. UNDP, *Human Development Report 1990*, 61–84.

16. United Nations, *2005 World Summit Outcome*, UN document A/60/L.1, 15 September 2005. See also Millennium Project, *Investing in Development: A Practical Plan to Achieve the Millennium Development Goals*, ed. Jeffrey D. Sachs (New York: United Nations Development Programme, 2005); and Jeffrey D. Sachs, *The End of Poverty: Economic Possibilities for Our Time* (New York: Penguin Books, 2005).

17. Devaki Jain, *Women, Development and the UN: A Sixty-year Quest for Equality and Justice* (Bloomington: Indiana University Press, 2005), 154–155.

18. See Louis Emmerij, Richard Jolly, and Thomas G. Weiss, *The Power of UN Ideas: Lessons from the First 60 Years* (New York: UN Intellectual History Project, 2005).

19. See Michael Ward, *Quantifying the World: The UN and Statistics* (Bloomington: Indiana University Press, 2004).

PART VIII

....

PROSPECTS FOR
REFORM

....

CHAPTER 38

PRINCIPAL ORGANS

EDWARD C. LUCK

At the United Nations, reform has been a constant refrain. For more than six decades, one wave of reform efforts has followed another, each crashing into the hard shore of political realities and bureaucratic inertia. Yet, for all of the frustration this agonizingly slow process engenders, each cycle of reform does manage to leave its mark on the organization. Each wave's residue of unsettled issues, moreover, forms the nucleus of the next chapter of the unending and slow moving UN reform saga. Never finished, never perfected, the world body is ever a work in progress.

At no point, either in its inception or in its operation, has the UN been above controversy and criticism. It has lurched from crisis to crisis not only in the agendas of world problems it seeks to ameliorate, but also in terms of recurrent questioning of its orientation and priorities, of the fairness and efficacy of its decision-making structures, of its funding and fiscal management, of its operational techniques and readiness, and of the quality and integrity of its Secretariat and leadership. The UN has yet to experience its salad days. Conceived and born in the midst of the most destructive global conflagration in history, the world body's blueprint was largely dictated by the leaders—the United States, Soviet Union, and United Kingdom—of the winning wartime alliance. Indeed, at US President Franklin D. Roosevelt's insistence, the new organization adopted the alliance's mantle, derived from the Declaration of the United Nations agreed by the twenty-six allies gathered in Washington, DC the first day of 1942. In the late summer and early fall of 1944, the Big Three, with a modest input from Chiang Kai-shek's China, met at the elegant Dumbarton Oaks estate in Georgetown to craft the essential provisions of what was to become the United Nations Charter.[1] Even at the height of their wartime collaboration, however, the Big Three found it difficult to agree on some of the essential dimensions of postwar organization. At several points, it appeared as if the Soviet delegation was prepared to return to Moscow empty handed.

The following spring, the Big Four, now including China, presented their blueprint to the other forty-seven members of the alliance in San Francisco.[2] The debate there, mostly between the four convening powers and the rest, made the testy exchanges at Dumbarton Oaks appear relatively tame and tempered. To a remarkable extent, the struggles in San Francisco over the scope, even existence, of the veto, over the prerogatives of the Security Council's permanent members, over the size and composition of the Council, over its relationship to the General Assembly, over how to address economic and social issues, and over a range of management and budgetary questions are echoed in the divisiveness of the current UN reform debates.

To placate the restless majority, the convening powers agreed to add Article 109 to the Charter, which opened the possibility of holding 'a General Conference of the Members of the United Nations for the purpose of reviewing the present Charter' by the Assembly's tenth session in 1955.[3] Cold War tensions intervened, however, casting a shadow over much of the organization's first decade. By its end, the Assembly in resolution 992 (X) reaffirmed the desirability of convening such a review conference, but only 'under auspicious international circumstances.' An open-ended committee was formed on 'fixing a time and place for the Conference, and its organization and procedures.' Needless to say, the committee has never identified a suitable time for such a review.

While the major powers did consent at San Francisco to at least opening the door slightly to the option of a general Charter review, they insisted on keeping the hurdles to amending the Charter at a high level. None of them was eager for the lesser powers to tamper with the handiwork they produced at Dumbarton Oaks, particularly their special privileges. The Soviet Union, recognizing the likelihood that initially it would be outnumbered in the new Assembly, was the most adamant about keeping the brakes on the change process. Whatever the outcome of a review conference, it would still need to be confirmed by the arduous Charter amendment process outlined in Article 108:

Amendments to the present Charter shall come into force for all Members of the United Nations when they have been adopted by a vote of two thirds of the members of the General Assembly and ratified in accordance with their respective constitutional processes by two thirds of the Members of the United Nations, including all the permanent members of the Security Council.

Each of the five permanent members of the Security Council—the four convening powers plus France—would therefore have a veto over any amendments to the Charter, including, of course, any diminution of their exclusive veto power.

Achieving a two-thirds vote in the Assembly for Charter change is no easy task in such a large and diverse intergovernmental body. All four occasions when this has proven possible have related, not surprisingly, to the enlargement of select membership bodies (twice with the Economic and Social Council (ECOSOC) and once with the Security Council).[4] Though most member states see an advantage in expanding intergovernmental organs to increase their chance of serving on them, they have nevertheless been cautious about pushing this agenda because of differences over the course and shape of any enlargement, reluctance to risk a late veto in one of the five permanent member capitals, or concern that too large an expansion could hinder the performance and effectiveness of the body in question. As discussed more fully below, these hesitancies could be seen in the Assembly's failure to endorse any plans for expanding the Security Council in 1997 and 2005, as well as in the eight-year delay before the Assembly voted in December 1963 to enlarge the Council from eleven to fifteen.

Below the level of Charter amendment, the intergovernmental bodies have proven far readier to endorse some kinds of change than others. Again, they have demonstrated a much more pronounced penchant for adding mandates, tasks, and subsidiary machinery than for eliminating outdated or ineffective ones. The politically inspired inertia that makes Charter amendment so rare conspires as well to discourage trimming marginal items or recasting agendas and priorities. Since the mid-1980s, this tendency has been magnified by a strong preference for making change decisions by consensus in the now 192-member Assembly. As will become apparent in the review below of reform efforts organ by organ, it has generally proven true that the larger the intergovernmental body, the slower it has been to adopt significant reforms in the way it organizes and goes about its work. The most recent illustration was the September 2005 World Summit, which produced a 178-paragraph Outcome Document with only a handful of vaguely worded paragraphs about the need to strengthen the UN's six principal organs.[5] Follow-up on even the agreed innovations—a Peacebuilding Commission, a Human Rights Council, and management reforms—has proven slow and arduous despite their modest scope.

As the organ-by-organ review below confirms, grand and ambitious reform campaigns have invariably stumbled, while more focused and subtle change processes have yielded more progressive and sustainable results. As a general rule, broad, ambitious, and interrelated packages, such as that proposed by Secretary-General Kofi Annan in March 2005, do not fare well.[6] At best, some of their component parts may find fertile soil. The Charter may be hard to amend, but it has repeatedly been reinterpreted in light of changing conditions and policy challenges. It has proven to be a remarkably flexible and adaptable instrument, even as its core purposes, principles, and structures have largely stood the test of time. While the major intergovernmental bodies have resisted radical reform, they have proven more innovative in terms of their working methods, the scope of their work, and the range and activities of their subsidiary bodies.

Beneath the surface, too often out of the public eye, change does occur, year after year, in what the world body does, in how it goes about it, and in the players shaping the organization's decisions and output. As this author has argued elsewhere, the UN has proven to be as adaptable to changing demands, needs, and circumstances as it has been resistant to formal structural and Charter reform.[7] Otherwise, it long ago would have followed the path of its ill-fated predecessor, the League of Nations, which, unlike the UN, did fade away as it became progressively irrelevant. Today, the very commotion about the need to reform the world body and the depth of the struggles over the course changes should take testify to the organization's enduring role in international affairs.

This chapter considers the interdependent change process, involving both reform and adaptation, in the UN's four principal intergovernmental organs. As related in Article 7 (1), the UN was to have the following principal organs: a General Assembly, a Security Council, an Economic and Social Council, a Trusteeship Council, an International Court of Justice (ICJ), and a Secretariat. The first four are addressed below in order. The ICJ was established as 'the principal judicial organ of the United Nations' under Article 92 and as an integral component of the new world body, unlike the more autonomous status of its predecessor, the Permanent Court of International Justice.[8] However, to preserve a degree of independence from the UN's political bodies, the workings and structure of the Court traditionally have not been addressed in past UN reform efforts. Reforming the Secretariat has been, of course, a perennial preoccupation of many member states. To cover the topic adequately would be beyond the space and scope of this chapter. The politics and dynamics of Secretariat reform, moreover, are of a distinct nature, while a parallel examination of efforts to reform the four principal intergovernmental bodies may yield cross-cutting lessons and insights.

THE GENERAL ASSEMBLY

One of the least controversial acts at Dumbarton Oaks and San Francisco was the establishment of the General Assembly. The convening powers appreciated that a universal membership body would be needed not only to carry out much of the day-to-day political and oversight work of the world body, but also to reassure the larger membership that they would have a substantial voice in the organization's affairs even in the face of the special roles and prerogatives given to the five permanent members of the Security Council. Though the League of Nations also had an assembly and a council, the Covenant gave them precisely the same mandate and failed to differentiate clearly between their relative compositions, procedures, and powers. Making these distinctions between the two principal political bodies proved to be an arduous but ultimately achievable task at San Francisco. Basically, the Assembly may discuss any matter and make recommendations on all except those matters of peace and security being addressed by the Council. It can make binding decisions, however, only on financial and budgetary questions, the election of nonpermanent members of the Security Council and the members of ECOSOC, and, upon the Security Council's recommendation, the appointment of the Secretary-General and the admission, suspension, and expulsion of member states. Like the Council, the Assembly sets its rules and procedures and establishes its subsidiary bodies.

On the whole, these Charter-based provisions have stood up quite well and the Council and Assembly have worked out a reasonably efficient and sustainable division of labor. Nevertheless, as the debates in San Francisco anticipated, these arrangements have not precluded recurrent sniping between the two bodies, particularly as the more powerful Council gained ascendancy in terms of public and governmental attention in the post-Cold War years. At times, it has seemed as if some members of the General Assembly have been more concerned with correcting the perceived imbalance between the Council and Assembly than in working to reform and strengthen the Assembly itself. Their concerns have related chiefly to making the Council's working methods more transparent and inclusive and its annual reporting to the Assembly more analytical and substantive.[9]

The Assembly's core strength, of course, lies in the virtual universality of its membership. But its strength has also been its weakness. In terms of the efficiency and coherence of its decision-making, its universality has proven to be a very difficult hurdle to overcome. With size comes inertia. Probably more than any of the other principal organs, the Assembly has proven unable to set priorities or make choices. It has something for everyone, but rather little for anyone.

The progressive enlargement of the Assembly from 51 to 192 members inevitably placed enormous strains on its structures, procedures, and working methods. In a one-nation, one-vote forum, whose very purpose was entwined with the principle of giving all member states at least the appearance of an equal say in its affairs, there was no possibility of developing a hierarchical or subdivided framework for decision-making or even for deliberations.[10] From its earliest days, the Assembly chose to employ regional groups to put forward member state candidacies for service on the Security Council, ECOSOC, and other limited membership intergovernmental bodies. While this practice has facilitated a more coherent and streamlined decision-making process, it has also, in the eyes of critics, distorted the politics of the Assembly and allowed intra- and inter-regional group dynamics to dominate its proceedings to the chagrin of the United States and others wielding independent power and less tied to a regional group. For smaller states, on the other hand, regional solidarity provides one way of sidestepping the pressures of larger countries outside of the region.

As would be expected in such a large, diverse, and substantively open-ended body, the girth of its mandates and membership has been reflected in the large number of subsidiary bodies, resolutions, and agenda items it produces. In each case, the Assembly has proven far more adept at addition than subtraction. A General Committee, composed of the president and twenty-one vice presidents of the Assembly and the chairmen of its six main committees, attempts to bring some order to the agenda for each annual session.[11] Through the years, the Assembly has adopted several techniques to try to reduce the quantity of resolutions, including clustering, omnibus resolutions, biennialization, triennialization, and informal restraint and consultation.[12] There have also been efforts to strengthen the office of Assembly president. These initiatives appear to be having a modest positive effect, though they clearly have not eliminated the problem, as the number of resolutions continues to hover between 250 and 300 annually, almost three-quarters of which are adopted by consensus.[13]

The politics and process that produce Assembly resolutions conspire to keep their number large.[14] Once a member state introduces a resolution for a given topic, it tends to become an advocate for its renewal year after year. To drop a resolution, even for a year or two, is seen by many as an indication that that issue is of declining priority for the member states. There is also built-in redundancy in the process. Customarily, in plenary session the Assembly votes to affirm the decisions already adopted by its main committees. Since this is done by rote and habit, some member states claim that the practice soaks up relatively little time and is not worth revising, even if it adds to the impression that much of the Assembly's work is duplicative and wasteful. More troubling is the tendency of the Assembly's Second and Third Committees to repeat the work of ECOSOC. Once a position is worked out in the form of a resolution of the 54-member ECOSOC, generally delegations will then seek its endorsement in these main committees of the Assembly, and then by the Assembly plenary, in the vain hope that repetition by these universal bodies will bolster the authority carried by the redundant resolutions. A radical solution proposed by outside studies—the universalization of ECOSOC, topped by a relatively compact ministerial board of representative member states, along with the elimination of the Second and Third Committees—has never gained much momentum.[15]

Member states have complained as often about the quality of resolutions as about their number. Too often, they are too vague to be of much use for affecting either policy decisions in capitals or public opinion. This tendency has been encouraged by the largely successful drive over the past two decades to take as many Assembly decisions as possible by consensus. Indeed, the reform process itself has been slowed by the assumption that each step should have consensus support. The strong preference for consensus reflects, in part, the results of the major reform campaign of the mid-1980s, which sought to institute consensus-based decision-making in the Assembly on budgetary issues.[16] While few with long memories would trade any perceived obsession today with consensus for the divisive voting patterns of the 1970s and 1980s, it needs to be recognized that every reform measure has a downside as well as an upside.

Recognizing that Assembly decisions on political matters are just recommendations that may or may not have policy impact in the larger world outside of UN meeting halls, those initiating resolutions often add clauses calling for reports, reviews, or the creation of some sort of a mechanism to monitor implementation and to report back to the Assembly on progress achieved. As a result, there has been a proliferation of papers, mandates, and entities purporting to follow up on Assembly (as well as ECOSOC and Security Council) resolutions. While member states frequently fret about this general tendency, they rarely offer to eliminate the particular reports or units that their pet resolutions have mandated. At the September 2005 summit-level meeting of the Assembly, however, the heads of state and government called for a sweeping review 'by the General Assembly and other relevant organs' of the thousands of existing mandates more than five years old in order to 'strengthen and update the programme of work of the United Nations so as to respond to the contemporary requirements of Member States.'[17] As a first step, the UN Secretariat prepared the requested 'analysis and recommendations' to facilitate this review.[18] In the meantime, the outcomes and results of the review remain to be seen.

Another stubborn problem has been the complexity and incoherent growth of the Assembly's subsidiary machinery.[19] Under Article 22, the Assembly, like the other principal intergovernmental organs, 'may establish such subsidiary organs as it deems necessary for the performance of its functions.' In 1996–1997, the Assembly's Strengthening Working Group compiled the first unofficial roster of the scores of subsidiary organs and briefly reviewed the purposes and functioning of each in turn. Because this open-ended Working Group was operating under consensus rules, however, it was unable to eliminate, merge, or rationalize any of the scores of subsidiary bodies.[20] While there has been little movement toward eliminating outdated or under-performing units, now the UN at least publishes the list of the Assembly's subsidiary bodies, which currently number fifty-seven (plus the six Main Committees).

The slow pace of General Assembly reform appears to reflect the inherent inertia in trying to move such a large, disparate, ungainly body, not a fundamental political divide among the member states. Indeed, the perennial debates on Assembly reform suggest, if anything, a remarkably broad agreement on what is wrong with the Assembly. Though observers often characterize the Assembly as a forum dominated by small states, the latter are usually the first to complain about how fecklessly it operates. More powerful states generally share these apprehensions, but are unwilling to invest major political capital in trying to fix a body that produces far more talk than action. The intricacies of the workings of the Assembly, moreover, are known to relatively few policymakers or experts outside of those diplomats and Secretariat officials who toil in its myriad debates and committees. Even the Assembly's two global summits of this century—in 2000 and 2005—simply reaffirmed 'the central position of the General Assembly as the chief deliberative, policymaking and representative organ of the United Nations' without offering any prescriptions for improving its performance.[21] For all its widely acknowledged flaws, the assembled heads of state and government were not prepared, on either occasion, to declare the Assembly to be dysfunctional or in need of the kind of radical surgery Secretary-General Kofi Annan prescribed for the Security Council.

THE SECURITY COUNCIL

At San Francisco and ever since, no reform issue has attracted nearly the high-level attention, public interest, or partisan passion as the matter of changing the composition, decision-making rules, and working methods of the Security Council. This testifies, of course, to the importance, both symbolically and operationally, that member states and publics alike attach to the work of the Council. The core of the debate, in essence, has revolved around two competing contentions that have proven exceedingly difficult to reconcile. On the one hand, it is claimed today, as it was vociferously in San Francisco, that the two-tiered structure and voting rules of the Council are grossly inequitable. Of that, there is little doubt. On the other hand, it is argued by others with equal conviction that these perceived inequities of permanent membership and veto power for five big powers are precisely the qualities that have allowed the Security Council not only to survive four decades of Cold War but to accumulate a record of achievement and relevance unmatched either by other UN intergovernmental bodies or by its less distinguished predecessor, the Council of the League of Nations.[22]

Because the stakes are high, both the demand for Council reform, especially by member states wanting a seat at the Council table, and the level of resistance, especially by the five permanent members, have been much higher than in the cases of the other principal organs. Change came at a particularly glacial pace during the Cold War years.[23] Yet in 1965 it was possible—ironically in part because of the Cold War competition—to accomplish something that has proven elusive ever since: the enlargement of the Council's membership, in that case from eleven to fifteen members. While relations between Moscow and Washington refused to thaw during the first two decades of the Cold War, UN membership as a whole was heating up with the influx of scores of newly independent countries from Asia and Africa, parts of the world markedly underrepresented at San Francisco.

By 1963, the organization's membership had swelled from 51 to 114, as had demands for making the composition of the Council more reflective of the new look of the Assembly. Calls for Council expansion, in fact, had been escalating since 1956, following the admission of a score of new members over the two previous years. Though the Charter is silent on the geographical distribution of the nonpermanent seats, an unwritten East-West 'gentlemen's agreement' on this matter had held over the intervening years. But to the newly independent countries of the South, as well as the socialist bloc, it looked as if Western Europe and Latin America, both groups that tended to vote with the United States, were overrepresented. Rather than accepting calls for redistributing the nonpermanent seats or agreeing to amend the Charter to expand their number, Washington preferred to accept, for a few years at least, the questionable, though expedient, practice of splitting the two-year terms between countries from different regions for some of the seats. The Soviet Union, meanwhile, vehemently opposed Security Council expansion while the Chinese communists continued to be blocked by the General Assembly from occupying the Chinese seat on the Security Council.

The long-simmering issue finally came to a boil in December 1963. Over the objections of four of the five permanent members (the nationalist Chinese favoring Security Council expansion), the developing country majority pushed for a vote on a two-part resolution, 1991 (XVIII), to enlarge both the Security Council, from eleven to fifteen, and the Economic and Social Council, from 18 to 27.[24] Though none of the permanent members voted for both parts of the resolution, it passed the Assembly easily (97–11–4).[25] Yet the proposed Charter amendment could not come into force until two-thirds of the member states, including all five permanent members, had acted in capitals to ratify it by the deadline of 1 September 1965, as specified in the resolution. The fact that all the permanent members eventually accepted the will of the majority may tell us more about the tenor of the times than about the likely validity of this episode as a precedent for the future.

Moscow, normally home to strict constructionists when it comes to questioning the founders' product, was the first to give in. It seems likely, though further research would be required, that the Soviets, engaged with the West in a contest for influence in the developing world, calculated that it made sense to let the United States and/or its allies bear the onus for frustrating the longstanding quest of the African and Asian states. Taipei, already highly exposed by the even longer-standing debate over who should properly be representing China in the world body, was the next to go. Paris and London followed, no doubt under pressure from their former colonies. In a classic example of free-riding, they decided to let Washington take the heat. Left standing alone and faced with a UN in the midst of a deep financial and political crisis following Soviet and French refusal to pay their peacekeeping arrears, the Johnson Administration decided that expanding the Council to fifteen was not such a bad idea after all.[26] It had proposed an expansion to thirteen in any case, and two more nonpermanent seats would hardly challenge its dominance of the Council.[27] Administration officials dutifully presented the case for the long-overdue enlargement to the Senate with such enthusiasm that one would have thought it was their idea. With little debate, the Senate voted overwhelmingly to give its consent and the Charter's first amendment was accomplished in good order and on schedule.

Pressures for Council expansion did not disappear with the 1965 Charter amendment, as the UN's membership continued to grow. Only a relatively modest portion of the larger membership, of course, could serve at any point in time even on the enlarged Council. Just eight years after its first expansion, ECOSOC's membership was doubled, from twenty-seven to fifty-four, in 1973. No parallel growth in its effectiveness, however, was observed. Nor were the remaining years of the Cold War especially productive ones for the enlarged Security Council either, as it was routinely bypassed in major crises. Ironically, there were only sporadic calls for reform during these lean years for Council activism. It was only after the Council found new life with the end of the Cold War that the chorus demanding Council reform reached a crescendo in the 1990s. As resolutions, Chapter VII references, and peacekeeping missions soared and the use of vetoes ebbed, the queue of countries seeking an enlarged Council and a place at the table grew apace. In late 1993, the General Assembly decided to convene an open-ended working group on Security Council reform, including both expansion and working methods. Now widely dubbed the never-ending working group, the General Assembly's Open-Ended Working Group on the Question of Equitable Representation On and Increase in the Membership of the Security Council and Other Matters Related to the Security Council is still seeking a widely acceptable answer to its quest.

The 1996–1997 President of the General Assembly, Razali Ismail of Malaysia, tried his best. After consulting with scores of member states, on 20 March 1997 he offered a proposal that he believed had the support of some two-thirds of the membership. It would have added nine more places at the table, five permanent and four nonpermanent, though the former without veto power, eliminated the enemy states clauses from the Charter, convened a review conference after a decade to assess how the implementation was progressing, and urged the introduction of no less than eighteen modifications of the Council's working methods aimed at improving transparency, accountability, and inclusiveness.[28] Whatever private assurances he had received, when Razali presented his proposal to the Working Group the tentative response suggested that the Assembly remained unprepared to commit to any specific reform formula. To a significant extent, this was due to the determined opposition of what was then nicknamed the 'Coffee Club,' a group of geographically diverse middle powers that believed that the elevation of another group of big powers to permanent status would be to their—and the Council's—disadvantage.

The story opened differently, then followed much the same course, for the next round, though a decade and a millennium later. This time, however, Kofi Annan, rather than the president of the Assembly, sought to be the first Secretary-General to seek to be the catalyst for Council change. In September 2003, following the polarized and ultimately ineffectual debate in the Council over the use of force in Iraq, the Secretary-General warned member states that 'we have come to a fork in the road. This may be a moment no less decisive than 1945 itself, when the United Nations was founded.'[29] In his view, the time had come for a 'radical' revision of the UN's intergovernmental bodies. There was an 'urgent need,' in particular, to make the Council 'more broadly representative of the international community as a whole, as well as the geopolitical realities of today.' With more hope than analysis, like some delegations, the Secretary-General asserted that the member states had come to agree on all but 'the details' of an expansion package. He failed to understand that the fact that the Assembly Working Group was still at it after a decade of deliberations was an indication of just how stubborn the differences were proving to be, not that the member states must have been close to wrapping up their seemingly endless labors.[30] The core historical lesson had not been learned. For reform of the Security Council, like so many other aspects of UN reform, the political ripeness of the issue is not a factor of the length of time it has been under consideration.

The Secretary-General delegated the task of developing proposals for expanding the Council and for addressing a host of other security challenges not to the member states, but to a High-level Panel composed of sixteen notables from around the world.[31] Yet even his hand-selected group of independent experts could not agree on a single approach to expansion, offering two possible models instead. Moreover, they had little to say about the Council's working methods, other than that considerable progress had already been made on that front. Their December 2004 report offered two model plans for enlarging the Council to twenty-four members, one by adding six permanent and three nonpermanent seats, the other by creating a new category of eight four-year, renewable seats and a ninth two-year, nonrenewable seat. Like Razali, they did not foresee veto power for the new permanent members and urged the current ones to exercise restraint in its use.[32] Once again, however, member states had their own ideas and preferences.

Over the first half of 2005, UN meeting halls were filled with a shrill rhetorical struggle between two camps, one favoring additional permanent seats and one opposing them, with many member states caught in the middle because they saw little advantage and/or some potential harm in a large expansion.[33] The G-4—Brazil, Germany, India, and Japan—had long pined for permanent seats and hoped to add two African candidates to become a powerful G-6 coalition.[34] The old Coffee Club, which had done so much to derail the Razali plan, reappeared as the 'Uniting for Consensus' group, contending that five permanent seats were more than enough.[35] Though the contest about who should sit around the Council table dominated both official and unofficial commentary, Switzerland and other smaller countries tried to point out that, whichever enlargement option was chosen, it was important not to neglect the equally important question of the Council's working methods, i.e., how those on the Council would relate to the much larger membership outside.[36] If all of this was not complex enough, the Africans, unable to decide which of their members should be candidates for the two proposed permanent seats, offered their own draft to bring the Council to 26 members, giving Africa two new nonpermanent seats as well as two permanent ones. They also insisted on having full veto power.[37]

Though the Secretary-General had proclaimed the existence of 'a new San Francisco moment,' the proliferation of competing proposals and the decidedly negative tone of the ensuing debate suggested quite the opposite.[38] Indeed, he had chosen a particularly unpropitious point to launch his wide-ranging reform effort: when member states were divided both over the use of force in Iraq and, more fundamentally, over the enormous strategic disparities between the United States and the rest in terms of disposable military and economic power. Unlike the Razali round, this time both the current superpower, the United States, and its potential contender, China, were decidedly unenthusiastic about the proposals on the table. Early in the game, China let its feelings about a permanent seat for Japan be known not only through diplomatic channels, but through anti-Japanese street demonstrations as well.[39] The United States, sensing an effort to dilute its influence through the addition of so many new permanent members and fretting that a big Council would be an unwieldy and ineffective one, suggested that an expansion to nineteen or twenty would be plenty.[40] It continued to favor a permanent seat for Japan, but openly opposed one for Germany and was silent on the other candidates.[41] True to the tenor of the times, none of the draft resolutions appeared to have the support of the requisite two-thirds majority in the Assembly, much less the blessing of the five permanent members. Therefore, none has been put to a vote as of the end of 2006.

Less in the public eye, the Council has over the past decade adopted a number of innovations in its working methods. While as much adaptations to changing circumstances and escalating demands for its services as formal reforms, these steps have tended to make the Council a somewhat more accountable, transparent, and inclusive body. Among the measures have been the following:[42]

- Under the Arria formula, a member of the Council invites the others to meet, outside of the Council Chamber, with one or more independent experts for a candid exchange of views on a pressing issue before the Council. This practice, which permits more direct input from civil society and encourages Council members to reflect on the complexities of the choices facing them, was once considered to be quite innovative, but has now become standard operating behavior. Now there are frequent informal and formal meetings with agency heads and others with knowledge of developments in the field.

- The Council has also participated in a number of retreats, away from headquarters, with the Secretary-General, other UN officials, and sometimes leading independent experts. For the last four years, for example, the Finnish Mission has sponsored a 'Hitting the Ground Running' workshop at which the fifteen current and five incoming members of the Council discuss the Council's work, working methods, and plans off site.[43]

- The Council members have undertaken a number of missions to visit areas where developments are of particular interest or concern to the Council. This has allowed much more extensive contact with government officials, nongovernmental groups, and UN personnel on the ground in regions of crisis. Some of these have been co-sponsored by ECOSOC.

- The Council has met a number of times since the end of the Cold War at either the foreign minister or summit level, including to discuss counter-terrorism at the time of the September 2005 global summit.

- To assist transparency and accountability, it has become common practice for the president of the Council to brief nonmembers, and often the press, on the results of informal (private) consultations.

- Tentative monthly forecasts and the provisional agendas for the Council's upcoming work are now provided regularly to nonmembers, as are provisional draft resolutions.[44]

- Consultations among Security Council members and troop contributors, along with key Secretariat officials, are now held on a more regular basis.

- As the Council's agenda and responsibilities have grown, so has its reliance on subsidiary bodies. Mostly chaired by nonpermanent members and operating by consensus, several of the currently twenty-eight subsidiary bodies have developed expert staffs, receive reports from member states, and undertake fact-finding, monitoring, and capacity-building missions around the world.

- Through the work of its subsidiary bodies, as well as in plenary, the Council has begun to include nonmembers in its work on a more regular and substantive basis.

These are incremental steps, of course, and are unlikely to satiate the demands for greater openness and responsiveness made regularly by the 177 nonmembers of the Council. The demands for Council reform, whether through enlargement or the modification of working methods, reflect its high level of activity, its penchant for interventionist and enforcement measures, and its tendency to adopt thematic resolutions on a range of issues.[45] Should the push for Council reform subside, it would most likely be a worrying sign of its fading energy, engagement, and relevance. So, paradoxically enough, the current clamor over Council reform may be a good sign in disguise.

ECOSOC

ECOSOC is no stranger to reform. Indeed, according to Gert Rosenthal, a former permanent representative of Guatemala and ECOSOC president in 2003, it 'has been the subject of more reform proposals than any of the other intergovernmental bodies of the United Nations.' It is the only principal organ to be enlarged twice, now with triple its original eighteen members. Yet, as Rosenthal acknowledges, in terms of the 'real or perceived weaknesses of ECOSOC. Those perceptions have changed little over the fifty-year period covered by the various reform proposals.'[46] The Secretary-General's High-level Panel lamented that, because international economic decision-making 'has long left the United Nations' and even the UN's specialized agencies are 'independent of the principal United Nations organs,' the role of ECOSOC has been reduced 'to one of coordination.'[47] In response, the Secretary-General agreed that 'the Economic and Social Council has been too often relegated to the margins of global economic and social governance.' In his view, 'it has not as yet done justice' to the unique functions it does have.[48] At the 2005 World Summit, the assembled heads of state and government underlined 'the need for a more effective Economic and Social Council as a principal body for coordination, policy review, policy dialogue and recommendations on issues of economic and social development.'[49]

Its two expansions have left ECOSOC in something of a political and institutional limbo: too large for efficient or coherent decision-making, but too small to be as inclusive and representative as its Second and Third Committee cousins (as noted above). While the increments have clearly not resolved ECOSOC's identity deficits, it would be equally unfair to suggest that they have caused them. As Rosenthal noted, while the smaller ECOSOC in the early days 'was more agile and less bureaucratic,' its record of accomplishment then, as now, was quite modest.[50]

Unlike the Security Council, ECOSOC was conceived in a blur of ambivalence. At Dumbarton Oaks, the Soviet delegates even resisted the American notion that the proposed world body should address economic and social matters.[51] At San Francisco, on the other hand, Washington joined the other convening powers in preferring that ECOSOC be kept small, be given few powers, and have a limited agenda.[52] Though it too is a principal organ, ECOSOC's members are elected by the General Assembly (Article 61 (1)), it reports to the Assembly on a number of matters (Articles 6 (1), 62 (3), 63 (1), 63 (2), and 64 (2)), it needs the Assembly's approval to perform more services (Article 66 (2)), and the Assembly may assign it unspecified functions (Article 66 (3)). According to Article 60, responsibility for economic and social

666   EDWARD C. LUCK

cooperation 'shall be vested in the General Assembly and, under the authority of the General Assembly, in the Economic and Social Council.' Neither body makes binding decisions on the vast array of substantive issues that come before it, nor do they have enforcement powers. The Assembly, however, does have the power of the purse and whatever legitimacy can be derived from universal membership.

Some would-be reformers have sought to make ECOSOC into something that neither its pedigree nor its limited powers would permit: a major player in global finance, trade, and monetary matters. Some of the grander schemes have called for an Economic Security Council, an Economic and Social Security Council, or dividing ECOSOC into an Economic Council and a Social Council with enhanced powers.[53] None of these ambitious proposals has gained much traction. At San Francisco, moreover, the convening powers had rejected any such models of global economic governance, just as most developed countries do today. They prefer to address such big-ticket items in places that have weighted voting, such as the Bretton Woods institutions, that rely on reciprocity to enforce the rules, as in the World Trade Organization (WTO), or that have been developed in an ad hoc fashion to deal with specific policy concerns. In that sense, the enlargement of ECOSOC has made it a less attractive place to do such business from their perspective, hence compounding its worries about relevancy. With developed and developing countries often pulling in opposite directions, it has been hard to develop and sustain a vision of what ECOSOC could be that is consistent with its limited powers and authority.

Though some criticize ECOSOC for not being what it cannot and was not meant to be, the more telling concerns have related to its inability to perform satisfactorily the tasks assigned to it in the Charter. Particularly vexing has been the stubborn problem of coordinating the disparate activities of the specialized agencies and related UN programs, funds, and departments. ECOSOC somehow is to coordinate the independent-minded specialized agencies through consultation and recommendations (Article 63 (2)), its only Charter-given tools. If, on the other hand, deliberations in ECOSOC can manage to convince those states that are members both of ECOSOC and of the governing boards of the agencies to make a concerted effort to follow-up on the former's decisions, then ECOSOC could be said to be making a difference in this regard. Any number of the reform drives and ECOSOC resolutions have identified the urgency of bringing greater coherence to the UN system, beginning with complaints from the US Senate as early as 1945 to 1948.[54] Yet implementing the obvious first step of fostering greater policy coherence within capitals has often proven to be a bridge too far.[55] As with many of the other reform issues, the roots of the dilemma lie, as well, with the assumptions and priorities that guided the UN's founding architecture. The functionalist doctrine popular at the time, as well as later during the Cold War years, sought to keep some distance between the practical and humanitarian work of the agencies and the presumably tainted politics of the UN's principal intergovernmental bodies, ECOSOC included. Some of the more important agencies, such as the International Labour Organization (ILO), pre-dated the UN in any case and ECOSOC had to negotiate—not dictate—arrangements with them (Articles 63 (1), 57, and 58).

Through the years, there has come to be a keener appreciation that ECOSOC's value and potential need not be limited to its dual roles as a place for states to meet and as a bridge to the agencies. Secretary-General Annan, for example, pointed out that the Charter assigns ECOSOC not only the task of coordination, but also those of 'policy review and policy dialogue.'[56] To those ends, ECOSOC offers, as well, windows through which the UN can relate—at least within the areas of ECOSOC's competence—with nongovernmental organizations (NGOs), research centers, and other sources of independent information and ideas. Article 71, in fact, makes the Charter's only reference to NGOs and names ECOSOC as their only Charter-based point of entry (though in practice access can also be gained through the UN Department of Public Information). Under Article 62 (1), the first function assigned to ECOSOC is to 'make or initiate studies and reports with respect to international economic, social, cultural, educational, health and related matters.' Clearly, the Charter places greater priority on ECOSOC's intellectual and institutional bridge-building functions than on its subsidiary role as a resolution-producing machine. It is assigned neither implementation nor enforcement tasks. Thus the key to ECOSOC reform may lie in its rediscovery, not its reinvention.

The heads of state and government at the September 2005 summit likewise concluded that 'the Council should serve as a quality platform for high-level engagement among Member States and with the international financial institutions, the private sector and civil society on emerging global trends, policies and action.' They called on ECOSOC to hold a biennial high-level Development Cooperation Forum, to ensure follow-up of the outcomes of the major UN conferences and summits, to promote an improved, coordinated UN response to humanitarian emergencies, and, of course, to facilitate coherence and coordination of the funds, programs, and agencies.[57] On the other hand, the summit decided two other matters in a way that reflects ECOSOC's somewhat junior status among the principal organs.

Article 68 gave ECOSOC the responsibility to set up a commission 'for the promotion of human rights.' For many years, the Commission on Human Rights did serve as one of the key vehicles for promoting human rights around the world. But, in Kofi Annan's words, as 'States have sought membership of the Commission not to strengthen human rights but to protect themselves against criticism or to criticize others...a credibility gap has developed, which casts a shadow on the reputation of the United Nations system as a whole.' He urged the creation of 'a smaller standing Human Rights Council.'[58] The summit agreed in principle[59] and, after much wrangling, the General Assembly established the new council as a subsidiary body of the General Assembly, not ECOSOC.[60] The theory is that this shift will enhance the new body's status and, by having its members elected directly by the larger Assembly, make it less likely that gross violators of human rights will gain entry to the Human Rights Council.[61]

A second major institutional innovation endorsed by the summit—the establishment of a Peacebuilding Commission—also involves ECOSOC. The High-level Panel had offered an innovative way to handle the institutional dilemmas posed by efforts to assist countries sliding into or emerging from intrastate or transnational conflict.

Because these situations cannot be addressed adequately with traditional military or even peacekeeping tools alone, given their economic, social, and human rights dimensions, they were stretching the capacity and the authority of the Security Council. These unstable transition periods, in the Panel's view, should be considered by a Peacebuilding Commission capable of drawing the advice and participation of a wide range of actors, including the Bretton Woods institutions and regional and subregional organizations. They recommended that it be established by the Security Council, as a subsidiary body under Article 29, in consultation with ECOSOC.[62] The Secretary-General, reflecting pressures from some developing countries, suggested that it report to the two Councils in sequence and dropped the notion that it could have 'an early warning or monitoring function.'[63]

Though the summit agreed that the new commission should focus on post-conflict, not pre-conflict, cases, it could not resolve the sticky institutional question of how the commission should relate to the two Councils.[64] It is instructive that, when this was resolved a few months later, ECOSOC had faded a bit from the picture, as the Assembly in resolution 60/180 and Council in resolution 1645 established it through concurrent and identical resolutions. The Peacebuilding Commission is to submit an annual report to the General Assembly and, when the Security Council is 'actively seized' of a matter, 'the main purpose of the Commission will be to provide advice to the Council at its request.' Seven slots on the 31-member state Organizational Committee are to be reserved for ECOSOC members, but its prescribed role—once again—pales to that of its fellow principal organs. Nevertheless, this step does give ECOSOC an institutional foothold, however modest, for considering the critical economic and social dimensions of peace and security. Perhaps it is a sign of greater relevance in the days ahead.

THE TRUSTEESHIP COUNCIL

The Trusteeship Council is one of those rarities in governmental and intergovernmental affairs: it did its job so well that it put itself out of business. None of the other principal organs is likely to follow suit anytime soon. These days, it is easy to forget that the Charter devotes three full chapters to the problem of non-self-governing territories and trusteeship. Composed of the five permanent members of the Security Council and those member states administering trust territories (Article 86), even the formula for the composition of the Trusteeship Council sounds distinctly archaic. Reformers have been of two minds about what to do with the Trusteeship Council: eliminate it or give it something new to do. Of the last two former Secretaries-General, Boutros Boutros-Ghali favored the former and Kofi Annan, at least initially, the latter.

In his 1994 report on the work of the organization, Boutros-Ghali reminded the members that the last of the eleven such territories had held a plebiscite that favored independence.[65] Since a 'smooth transition to Palau's new status is under way,' he urged the Assembly to 'proceed with steps to eliminate' the Trusteeship Council through the Charter amendment process. The following year, he regretted 'that no decision to abolish the Trusteeship Council has been taken,' while noting that Malta had proposed a metamorphosis for the Council to become a 'guardian and trustee of the global commons' and 'the common heritage of mankind.'[66] As the UN's fiftieth commemoration of its founding approached in 1995, a number of independent observers were drawn to the notion of developing bold new tasks for the Council.[67] The Assembly in its December 1995 resolution 50/55 asked the member states for their views on the issue. Most of the nineteen that replied agreed that elimination was the best option.[68]

Nevertheless, in his first major reform plan, the new Secretary-General, Kofi Annan, indicated in July 1997 his readiness to take a different tack than his predecessor on this symbolic issue. Despite the results of the 1996 survey, he concluded that the 'Member States appear to have decided to retain the Trusteeship Council.' Therefore, much like Malta, he suggested that 'it be reconstituted as the forum through which Member States exercise their collective trusteeship for the integrity of the global environment and common areas such as the oceans, atmosphere, and outer space.'[69] In 1998, the Secretary-General asked a task force addressing environmental and human settlement issues to consider his proposal, but that group thought it best to leave the issue for the Millennium Assembly and Millennium Forum.[70] While the proposal to transform the Trusteeship Council never gained momentum, a number of members seemed reluctant to formally close it down, since that would open the Pandora's box of Charter reform. The latter would be a risky step as the debate over Security Council expansion was heating up.

In 2003, a flurry of editorials and newspaper columns raised a variation: using the Trusteeship Council for dealing with failed or failing states.[71] But, again, the member states seemed to prefer to leave the Council in an institutional limbo. It receives no staff or administrative support and never meets, while its grand chamber is a fine place for any number of intergovernmental meetings, including, ironically, on UN reform. Finally seeking to put the Trusteeship Council out of its misery, the High-level Panel, a chastened Secretary-General, and the September 2005 summit have all declared its demise. Yet, given the reluctance to open the Charter amendment process until there is agreement on what to do about the Security Council, action has yet to be taken in the Assembly itself on a motion to actually amend the Charter.

CONCLUSION

Once again, a negative linkage has been established by which movement on the reform of one intergovernmental body is held hostage to progress on another one. In each of the four fronts surveyed here, there has been progress. In each, however, it has been measured in inches, not miles and in years of patient effort, not in grand leaps forward. It is no wonder, then, that UN reform is often called a process, not an event.[72] It is a lesson each generation of big-vision reformers has had to learn, usually the hard way. The institution evolves and adapts to changing circumstances and needs more rapidly than it adopts structural reform. In the final analysis, that is the way the founders wanted it. In all probability, they would be pleased. Their invention, at the very least, has demonstrated staying power.

Notes

1. For the fullest account of the two-part Dumbarton Oaks meeting, see Robert C. Hilderbrand, *Dumbarton Oaks: The Origins of the United Nations and the Search for Postwar Security* (Chapel Hill: University of North Carolina Press, 1990).

2. With only a provisional government, France did not join the other leading allies to form the Big Five until the San Francisco Conference was already underway.

3. See Ruth B. Russell, *A History of the United Nations Charter: The Role of the United States 1940–1945* (Washington, DC: Brookings Institution, 1958), 742–749.

4. As discussed in greater detail below, ECOSOC was enlarged from 18 to 27 in 1965 and from 27 to 54 in 1973, and the Security Council from 11 to 15 in 1965. The fourth amendment modified the first paragraph of Article 109 regarding a review conference to take account of the enlargement of the Security Council. It came into force in 1968.

5. For a critique of the timing, content, and management of the 2003–2006 reform process see Edward C. Luck, 'How Not to Reform the United Nations,' *Global Governance* 11, no. 4 (2005): 407–414.

6. Kofi Annan, *In Larger Freedom: Towards Development, Security and Human Rights for All*, UN document A/59/2005, 21 March 2005 and his speech to the General Assembly presenting the report, UN document GA/10335, 21 March 2005.

7. Edward C. Luck, *Reforming the United Nations: Lessons from a History in Progress*, Occasional Paper No. 1 (New Haven, Conn.: The Academic Council on the United Nations System, 2003).

8. For a history of the deliberations establishing the ICJ, see Russell, *A History of the United Nations Charter*, 277, 282–284, 289–290, 379–386, and 864–896.

9. Draft General Assembly resolution on Security Council working methods, 10 November 2005, www.eda.admin.ch.

10. Assembly voting rules are not based on the principle of sovereign equality. As was decided at San Francisco, the latter principle related to equal status before the law, not to political matters, such as the one-nation, one-vote formula. See Russell, *A History of the United Nations Charter*, 672.

11. *Rules of Procedure of the General Assembly*, A/520/Rev. 15, (New York: United Nations, 1985), Rule 38 and Rule 40.

12. See, e.g., resolutions 45/45, 48/264, 51/241, 55/285, 58/126, 58/316, and A/58/L.66.

13. Only 256 resolutions were adopted in 2005, one of the lowest totals in recent years. The delegations' preoccupation with a range of reform matters during the Fall of 2005 may have reduced the time and attention available for introducing new resolutions on other subjects, www.un.org.

14. Some of the observations in this section are drawn from a paper by the Mission of the Netherlands to the United Nations, 'General Assembly Reform: The Role and Impact of Resolutions,' 26 October 2003, to which this author contributed substantially, www.pvnewyork.org.

15. See Peter Fromuth, ed., *A Successor Vision: The United Nations of Tomorrow* (New York: United Nations Association of the United States of America, 1988) and *The United Nations in Development: Reform Issues in the Economic and Social Fields, A Nordic Perspective* (Stockholm: The Nordic UN Project, 1991).

16. Luck, *Reforming the United Nations*, 35–41.

17. *2005 World Summit Outcome*, UN document A/RES/60/1, 15 September 2005, para. 163 (b).

18. *Mandating and Delivering: Analysis and Recommendations to Facilitate the Review of Mandates, Report of the Secretary-General*, UN document A/60/733, 30 March 2006.

19. There have been pressures to enlarge the size, not just the number, of subsidiary bodies. See M. J. Peterson, *The UN General Assembly* (London: Routledge, 2006), 109–110.

20. The proceedings of the Working Group were closed, but its report can be found in *Strengthening of the United Nations System, Annex*, UN document A/RES/51/241, 31 July 1997.

21. See, respectively, the *United Nations Millennium Declaration*, UN document A/RES/55/2, 18 September 2000, para. 30 and the *2005 World Summit Outcome*, para. 149.

22. These themes are developed at greater length in Edward C. Luck, *The Life and Times of the UN Security Council: Practice and Promise* (London: Routledge, 2006).

23. Dimitris Bourantonis, *The History and Politics of UN Security Council Reform* (London: Routledge, 2005), 12–31.

24. For key points in the Assembly debate, see UN document A/PV.1285, 17 December 1963, 6–17. For the report of the Committee on Arrangements for a Conference for the Purpose of Reviewing the Charter, see UN document A/5487, 4 September 1963, 1–7. A summary of Security Council resolutions from the preceding years on these issues can be found in Report of the Security Council, 16 July 1962–15 July 1963, UN document A/5502, 95–96. For a summary of the events of this period, see Luck, *Reforming the United Nations*, 8–10.

25. China, then represented by the Taipei government of the Republic of China and under considerable pressure, ended up voting for the Security Council part of the resolution, though it had, like the rest of the five, called for a postponement.

26. For a fuller outline of this Article 19 crisis, see Edward C. Luck, *Mixed Messages: American Politics and International Organization, 1919–1999* (Washington, DC: Brookings Institution Press, 1999), 233–238.

27. The United States stated on 14 December 1963, for instance, that it could go along with a 'modest' expansion of the Council from 11 to 13 members (and of ECOSOC, the Economic and Social Council, from 18 to 24 members), as had been suggested by the Latin American and Caribbean countries.

28. Though the Razali Plan was in the form of a draft Assembly resolution, it was presented as a conference room paper to the Working Group. Since the sessions of the group were closed, there is no UN number assigned to the paper and it cannot be found among the UN's public papers. It can be found, however, through the website of the Global Policy Forum, www.globalpolicy.org. This author served as an advisor to President Razali in the development of his plan.

29. Address to the General Assembly, UN document SG/SM/8891–GA/10157, 23 September 2003. Also see his press conference, UN document SG/SM/8855, 8 September 2003.

30. For explanations for the hurdles to be overcome in attempting to expand the Council, see Thomas G. Weiss, *Overcoming the Security Council Reform Impasse: The Implausible versus the Plausible*, Occasional Paper no. 14 (Berlin: Friedrich-Ebert-Stiftung, 2005); Edward C. Luck, 'How Not to Reform the United Nations,' *Global Governance* 11, no. 4 (2005): 407–414; and Luck, 'The UN Security Council: Reform or Enlarge?' in Paul Heinbecker and Patricia Goff ed., *Irrelevant or Indispensable? The United Nations in the 21st Century* (Waterloo, Canada: Wilfrid Laurier University Press, 2005).

31. For the panel's final report, see *A More Secure World: Our Shared Responsibility, Report of the High-level Panel on Threats, Challenges and Change*, UN document A/59/565, 2 December 2004. For thoughtful critiques, see Ernesto Zedillo, ed., *Reforming the United Nations for Peace and Security* (New Haven, Conn.: Yale Center for the Study of Globalization, 2005); Michael J. Glennon, 'Idealism at the U.N.,' *Policy Review*, no. 129 (February–March 2005): 3–13; and Mats Berdal, 'The UN's Unnecessary Crisis,' *Survival* 70, no. 3 (2005): 7–32.

32. The Secretary-General's March 2005 report, *In Larger Freedom: Towards Development, Security and Human Rights for All*, simply echoed the panel's findings on Council reform. It added, however, the novel theory that the founders had created the Security Council, the Trusteeship Council, and ECOSOC on a par, but that the unity and energy of the Security Council had outstripped the other two. Thus, he claimed, 'we need to restore the balance.' Whether this would entail enlarging and slowing the Security Council so that it could be more like ECOSOC, he did not say. See *In Larger Freedom*, paras. 165 and 166.

33. For an overview of the broad-based reform efforts of 2005, see Thomas G. Weiss and Barbara Crossette, 'The United Nations: The Post-Summit Outlook,' in *Great Decisions: 2006 edition* (New York: Foreign Policy Association, 2006): 9–20.

34. For the G-4 draft resolution, see *Security Council Reform*, UN document A/59/L.64, 6 July 2005.

35. For the Uniting for Consensus draft resolution, see *Reform of the Security Council*, UN document, A/59/L.68, 21 July 2005.

36. In the Spring of 2005, the Swiss Mission to the United Nations convened a series of informal roundtable meetings of member states to discuss further steps toward working methods reform based on a background paper prepared by this author, 'Reforming the Security Council—Step One: Improving Working Methods,' 25 April 2005. Some of the discussion in this subsection draws on that paper. More recently, the so-called S-5 (Switzerland, Costa Rica, Jordan, Lichtenstein, and Singapore) have prepared a draft resolution on working methods. This took the form of an Annex to a letter of 3 November 2005 signed by the five Permanent Representatives, www.reformtheun.org.

37. For the African draft resolution, see *Reform of the Security Council*, UN document A/59/L.67, 14 July 2005.

38. UN document SG/SM/8891, and Kofi Annan, '"In Larger Freedom": Decision Time at the UN,' *Foreign Affairs* 84, no. 3 (2005): 63–74.

39. See, e.g., Press Release, People's Republic of China Mission to the United Nations, 11 July 2005; Robert Marquand, 'Anti-Japan Protests Jar an Uneasy Asia,' *Christian Science Monitor*, 11 April 2005; Norimitsu Onishi, 'Tokyo Protests Anti-Japan Rallies in China,' *New York Times*, 11 April 2005; and Chris Buckley, 'Anti-Japan Protests Sweep Across China' *International Herald Tribune*, 18 April 2005. On Japan's campaign, see Edward C. Luck, 'Tokyo's Quixotic Quest for Acceptance,' *Far Eastern Economic Review* 168, no. 5 (2005): 5–10.

40. US Department of State, 'On United Nations Reform,' Testimony of R. Nicholas Burns, Under Secretary for Political Affairs, to the Senate Foreign Relations Committee, Washington, DC, 21 July 2005, www.state.gov.

41. Steven R. Weisman, 'US Rebuffs Germans Anew on Bid for Security Council,' *New York Times*, 9 June 2005 and Nicholas Kralev, 'US Declines to Back German Bid,' *The Washington Times*, 9 June 2005.

42. This list is drawn from Luck, *The UN Security Council: Practice and Promise*, 123–124. See also Sydney D. Bailey and Sam Daws, *The Procedure of the UN Security Council*, 3rd edn. (New York: Oxford University Press, 1998).

43. For summaries of the first two workshops, see *'Hitting the ground running': workshop for newly elected members of the Security Council*, UN documents S/2004/135, 20 February 2004, *'Hitting the ground running': second annual workshop for newly elected members of the Security Council*, UN document S/2005/228, 6 April 2005, and *'Hitting the ground running': third annual workshop for newly elected members of the Security Council* UN document S/2006/483, 30 June 2006.

44. For an independent monthly account of the Council's deliberations and activities, see the Security Council Report, available at www.securitycouncilreport.org.

45. On thematic resolutions and the appropriateness of the Council attempting to play a law-making or legislative role, see José E. Alvarez, Review Essay, 'Between Law and Power,' *American Journal of International Law* 99, no. 4 (2005): 926–932; and Erika de Wet, *The Chapter VII Powers of the United Nations Security Council* (Oxford: Hart Publishing, 2004).

46. Gert Rosenthal, *The Economic and Social Council of the United Nations: an issue paper*, Occasional Paper no. 15 (Berlin: Friedrich-Ebert Stiftung, 2005), 4 and 25.

47. *A More Secure World*, para. 274.

48. *In Larger Freedom*, 62, paras. 165 and 171.

49. *2005 World Summit Outcome*, para. 155.

50. Rosenthal, *The Economic and Social Council*, 10–11.

51. Hilderbrand, *Dumbarton Oaks*, 86–93.

52. Russell, *A History of the United Nations Charter*, 777–807.

53. See, e.g., The South Centre, *For A Strong and Democratic United Nations: A South Perspective on UN Reform* (Geneva: The South Centre, 1996) and *Enhancing the Economic Role of the United Nations* (Geneva: The South Centre, 1992); Erskine Childers and Brian Urquhart, *Renewing the United Nations* (Uppsala, Sweden: Dag Hammarskjöld Foundation, 1994); Commission on Global Governance, *Our Global Neighbourhood* (Oxford: Oxford University Press, 1995); The Independent Working Group on the Future of the United Nations, *The United Nations in Its Second Half Century: The Report of the Independent Working Group on the Future of the United Nations* (New York: Ford Foundation, 1995); and Mahbub ul Haq, 'The Case for an Economic Security Council in the United Nations,' in Albert J. Paolini, Anthony P. Jarvis and Christian Reus-Smit eds., *Between Sovereignty and Global Governance: The United Nations, the State and Civil Society* (Houndmills, Basingstoke, UK: MacMillan Press, 1998), 228–243.

54. Luck, *Reforming the United Nations*, 17–27.

55. For the most recent effort, see the Report of the Secretary-General's High-level Panel on System-wide Coherence, *Delivering as One*, UN document A/61/583, 9 November 2006.

56. *In Larger Freedom*, para. 171.

57. *2005 World Summit Outcome*, paras. 155.

58. *In Larger Freedom*, paras. 182 and 183.

59. *2005 World Summit Outcome*, paras. 157–160.

60. UN General Assembly resolution A/RES/60/251, 3 April 2006. The vote was not unanimous, as the United States and three smaller countries voted against the new Human Rights Council, arguing that it did not represent a sufficiently deep reform of the old Commission on Human Rights.

61. In practice, the first election of members of the new Human Rights Council produced mixed results. See *General Assembly Elects 47 Members of New Human Rights Council*,

Marks 'New Beginning' for Human Rights Promotion Protection, UN document GA/10459, 9 May 2006.

62. *A More Secure World*, paras. 261–269.

63. *In Larger Freedom*, paras, 115–116.

64. *2005 World Summit Outcome*, paras. 97–105.

65. *Report of the Secretary-General on the Work of the Organization* (advance version), UN document A/49/1, 2 September 1994, paras. 43–46. Later that year, Palau became the 185th member of the United Nations.

66. For the Secretary-General's report, see *Report of the Secretary-General on the work of the Organization*, UN document A/50/1, 22 August 1995, paras. 67–69. For the Malta proposal, see *Review of the Role of the Trusteeship Council*, UN document A/50/142, 16 June 1995.

67. See, for example, Thomas G. Weiss, 'The United Nations at Fifty: Recent Lessons,' *Current History*, 1 May 1995, 227 and *Our Global Neighborhood*, 251–253.

68. *Review of the Role of the Trusteeship Council, Report of the Secretary-General*, UN document A/50/1011, 1 August 1996.

69. *Renewing the United Nations: A Programme for Reform, Report of the Secretary-General*, UN document A/51/950, 14 July 1997, para. 85. Also see para. 282.

70. *United Nations Reform: Measures and Proposals, Note by the Secretary-General*, UN document A/52/849, 31 March 1998, and *Environment and Human Settlements, Report of the Secretary-General*, UN document A/53/463, 6 October 1998.

71. See, e.g., Suzanne Nossel, 'A Trustee for Crippled States,' *Washington Post*, 25 August 2003; Stephen Handelman, 'U.N. as Colonial Power? Why Not?' *Toronto Star*, 2 September 2003; and Paul Kennedy, 'UN Trusteeship Council Could Find Role in Postwar Iraq,' *Daily Yomiuri*, 9 May 2003.

72. 'Transcript of Press Conference by Secretary-General Kofi Annan, at the United Nations headquarters, 13 September 2005,' UN document SG/SM/10089, 13 September 2005.

CHAPTER 39

....

FINANCING

....

JEFFREY LAURENTI

COMPARED to its soaring mandates to maintain international security, promote better standards of life in larger freedom, achieve self-determination of peoples, and strengthen universal peace, UN financing would seem mere housekeeping, a dry and specialized detail of administration of scant intrinsic interest or political import. Yet some of the most contentious political struggles that have wracked and at times imperiled the organization have swirled around its financing.

Finances are a fundamental metric of power—the wherewithal that gives tangible effect to the verbal intentions that political authorities solemnly proclaim. The viability and performance of any political unit depends on the financial resources it can muster. Moreover, in any political system, the allocation of the burden of providing revenue, on the one hand, and of the expenditure of resources, on the other, provides a vivid demonstration of that system's power relationships and political values.

In the UN's case, arguably the most immediately consequential of the General Assembly's six standing committees is the one dealing with budget and finance, because the resolutions it shapes—prescribing how much is to be spent and where, and levying assessments on member states to pay for it—are virtually the only ones that the Assembly adopts with binding effect. People are hired and paid; goods and services are delivered around the globe; governments forward money to pay for it.

The key to the financing of this political unit, however, depends on the member states: while governments extract revenue by taxing people and activities within their jurisdiction, the UN—like nearly all international organizations—must rely on the contributions its member governments provide. Some of those contributions are assessed, with their payment an obligation of membership; others are voluntary, with governments deciding whether and how much they wish to donate for activities they deem worthy or expedient.

Battles over assessments and expenditures have punctuated the world organization's history and highlight the interplay between the Charter's asserted values and the projection of power within the UN: by what criteria should the financial burden be spread among states, which vary enormously in wealth and size, and toward what purposes should the organization's resources be spent? These battles have also underscored the tension between power within the formal political process, under the ostensibly democratic rules for decision-making by equally sovereign states, and power grounded in realities outside the house. In the case of voluntary contributions, of course, power rests overwhelmingly with the decision-makers of states with the resources to give—they decide amount and purpose. But in the case of assessed budgets, those with substantial financial power are expected to share decision-making with the far more numerous participants in the system who have little. Since the mid-1980s, larger contributors to the system, above all the United States, have parried the 'parliamentary' power over budgetary policy of the General Assembly's poorer majority with financial pressures.

By the late twentieth and early twenty-first centuries, UN finances were chronically precarious, a result of consistently late payments and outright non-payment by its largest contributor, which coincided with the ascendancy in American politics of assertively nationalist and unilateralist conservatism. In many ways, the recurrent struggles over finances reflect a persistent challenge to the UN's legitimacy, and the notion it embodies of a global political community, in the world organization's most powerful member state.

DEVELOPING A CHARTER FRAMEWORK

As in so many other respects, the League of Nations provided a trial run for its successor. Article 6 of the League Covenant had a single sentence: 'The expenses of the League shall be borne by the Members of the League in the proportion decided by the Assembly.' This became one of the Covenant's contentious provisions for conservatives in the US Senate who were determined to avoid binding obligations from a supranational political association. The ninth of the fourteen reservations that Senate Foreign Relations Committee chairman Henry Cabot Lodge required for US ratification of the League Covenant aimed directly at the nascent institution's financing:

The United States shall not be obligated to contribute to any expenses of the League of Nations, or of the Secretariat, or of any commission, or committee, or conference, or other agency organized under the League of Nations or under the treaty or for the purpose of carrying out the treaty provisions, unless and until an appropriation of funds available for such expenses shall have been made by the Congress of the United States.

President Wilson rejected this and Lodge's other reservations, warning the Senate their adoption would 'not provide for ratification but, rather, for the nullification of the treaty.'[1] The Senate rejected ratification, and the League experiment unfolded without US participation.

The League was wobbly even before an emerging axis of belligerent major powers triggered the crises of the 1930s. States withdrew and reentered depending on political convenience—of the sixty-three countries that were members at one time or another, only twenty-eight were members continuously from its inception to its end. Revolving-door membership inevitably meant recurrent problems of collections. Still, the League established important precedents, in particular apportioning expenses in rough correspondence to an ability to pay.

By its tenth year—the midpoint between the League's creation and the start of World War II it had been established to prevent, and coincidentally the midpoint of Germany's seven-year membership—the League's total budget of $5.2 million covered its own operations ($3.1 million) and those of the International Labour Office and the Permanent Court. Britain (assessed 10.6 percent of the League budget), France and Germany (8 percent), and Italy and Japan (6.1 percent), along with British-ruled India, strife-torn China, and Spain paid over half of the League's expenses.[2] The defection of Japan and Germany in 1933, Italy in 1937, and then ten smaller countries led to significant reductions in the League's budget and, of course, the most destructive war in human history.

The League's experience guided the UN's architects. Article 17 of the UN Charter entrusted to the General Assembly the responsibility to approve the organization's budget and to apportion expenses among the members. While the League's Covenant established a general requirement of unanimity for decisions in its Assembly, Charter Article 18 specified budgetary questions as among the 'important questions' that 'shall be made by a two-thirds majority of the members present and voting.' A US proposal for weighted voting on budgetary matters in accordance with each state's contribution was, however, turned aside by its principal wartime allies at the four-power Dumbarton Oaks preparatory conference.[3]

In San Francisco, delegations from states such as Norway, the Netherlands, and India recalled the League's financial stresses caused by members' dilatory payments, pressing the Charter's drafters to impose penalties on financially delinquent members. They finally agreed on an enforcement mechanism in Article 19:

A Member of the United Nations which is in arrears in the payment of its financial contributions to the Organization shall have no vote in the General Assembly if the amount of its arrears equals or exceeds the amount of the contributions due from it for the preceding two full years. The General Assembly may, nevertheless, permit such a Member to vote if it is satisfied that the failure to pay is due to conditions beyond the control of the Member.

Automatic enforcement has been key to the provision's success. The Secretary-General certifies every January which member states are in arrears on dues equal to their assessments for at least the two immediately preceding years, and those states are unable to vote in the Assembly until either they pay just enough to reduce their arrears below the threshold of the two prior years' assessments, or the General

Assembly adopts a resolution waiving the penalty in that particular country's case because of exceptional circumstances.[4]

The enforcement mechanism would not affect a delinquent member's vote in other principal organs. Indeed, when American arrears at the century's end threatened forfeiture of Washington's vote, fervent opponents of paying UN dues argued that the loss of a vote in the jaw-boning Assembly would be inconsequential, since the US would still have its veto in the Security Council. But vote forfeiture has carried enough political risks that most delinquent states have, at the very least, sought to pay just enough to stay below the 'two full years' threshold for suspension of voting privileges.[5] The states that have surrendered their vote by continued and determined nonpayment have almost always been pariah governments under UN sanctions, including apartheid South Africa, Saddam Hussein's Iraq, and Slobodan Milošević's Yugoslavia. In such cases, a successor government has often been permitted to resume the country's voting rights before the arrears have been cleared.

Fixing a Scale

At the first session of the General Assembly in 1946 no country could have accumulated two years of arrears, but this gathering promptly found itself mired in controversy over the apportionment of budgetary expenses among the member states—a controversy that would continue to divide the Assembly for decades, long after the good will that facilitated compromise in the founding session had evaporated.

Allocation of a revenue burden occasions bitter battles within every organization. In systems where voting power reflects share of the budget—a feature, for example, of the International Monetary Fund and the World Bank—members may actually jockey to pay more than what a general formula would require. More commonly, influence in a political organization bears little relation to the revenue a member is obliged to contribute, and members often seek to limit their own liability at the expense of others in the system. In local governments that rely on property taxes, for example, politics are often roiled by disputes on how to assess 'value'; when to reassess as values change; whether to discount value of residential relative to commercial property; how to insulate the low-income homeowner; what circumstances may warrant tax abatements; whether to grant a community's large corporate taxpayer a reduced assessment lest it leave the community. Similar tensions have marked the UN system for apportioning expenses from its outset.

One of the first actions of the first General Assembly was the creation of a Committee on Contributions, a panel that would periodically review extant economic data and possible formulas for determining each member's appropriate share of expenses in accordance with the principle of 'capacity to pay.' In 1946, the committee devised a formula that weighed 'relative national incomes, temporary dislocations of national economies and increases in capacity to pay arising out of the war, availability of foreign exchange and relative per capita national incomes.'[6]

Under the committee's calculation (based largely on pre-war data), for 1946–1947 the five largest contributors would together pay 75 percent of the budget, with 3.73 percent from India, 5.50 percent from France, 6.00 percent from the Soviet Union, 10.50 percent from the United Kingdom—and 49.89 percent from the United States.[7] While not disputing that its economic product was roughly half of the world's immediately after the war, Washington was adamant that it should not bear so large a share of the fledgling organization's expenses. The ranking Republican on the Senate Foreign Relations Committee, Arthur Vandenberg of Michigan, speaking as a US representative to the first General Assembly, couched the American objections as consistent with the global interest in avoiding 'special rights':

The few [who would pay so outsized a share of the organization's budget], in sheer self-defence, would probably insist upon special rights of audit and control which are at variance with the 'sovereign equality' to which we are indispensably devoted....

Neither we nor any other nation, in some other day, should be allowed a greater privilege in our councils than is measured by a maximum contribution of 25 percent per annum—far short of what, in common parlance, might be called 'fiscal control.'

The US call for a 'ceiling' of 25 percent drew the most vocal opposition from some of America's nearest and dearest partners. Mexico warned that the ceiling would violate the principle of capacity to pay. Canada argued that the ceiling Washington was demanding would halve Americans' per-capita contribution, while forcing a one-third increase in the per-capita contributions of other countries. Britain called the ceiling proposal illogical and a dangerous departure from capacity to pay.[8] But after months of bargaining, they acquiesced in an eventual 25 percent cap on the largest contributor, and Washington agreed to pay in the meantime at a rate closer to its share of world income (39.89 percent) that would drop in stages—to 33.33 percent in seven years as war-ravaged economies recovered, and eventually to 25 percent. The admission of new states—in particular the former Axis powers, Italy (1955), Japan (1956), and Germany (with two states admitted in 1973)—provided crucial occasions to achieve the promised reduction in the US ceiling without significantly raising assessments on the rest of the membership.

Over time, the UN Statistical Office was able to secure current economic data of reliable quality from most member states, and struggled to integrate income data from radically divergent systems of economic accounting. For its part, the Committee on Contributions faced growing pressures over time to make allowance for the low per-capita incomes of many of its member states. For instance, India and the Netherlands by 2000 had roughly the same national income, but it was spread out over nearly a billion Indians and barely 16 million Dutch respectively; by the standards of progressive revenue built into most states' tax codes, the former might justifiably be assessed less than the latter. The UN apportionment scales came to effect such relief by a discount for low per-capita incomes. The assessments on states whose per-capita income is less than the average per-capita gross economic product worldwide (calculated at $5,099 for the 2004 scale) are discounted by a factor reflecting how far short of that global per-capita average is each state's per-capita

Table 39.1 Rates of assessment for selected countries

	Proposed 1946	Adopted 1946	1953	1964	1974	1984	1995	2000	2005
Brazil	1.2	1.94	1.45	1.03	0.77	1.39	1.62	1.47	1.523
Canada	3.10	3.35	3.30	3.12	3.18	3.08	3.07	2.73	2.81
China	2.75	6.30	5.62	4.57	5.50	0.88	0.72	1.00	2.05
Egypt	0.70	0.81	0.50	a	0.12	0.07	0.07	0.07	0.12
Ethiopia	0.07	0.08	0.10	0.05	0.02	0.01	0.01	0.01	0.00
France	5.50	6.30	5.75	5.94	5.86	6.51	6.32	6.55	6.03
Germany (Federal Republic)[b]	–	–	–	–	7.10[b]	8.54[b]	8.94	9.86	8.66
India	3.08[c]	3.35[c]	3.45	2.03	1.20	0.36	0.31	0.30	0.42
Italy	–	–	–	2.24	3.60	3.74	4.79	5.44	4.89
Japan	–	–	–	2.27	7.15	10.32	13.95	20.57	19.47
Mexico	0.54	0.66	0.70	0.74	0.86	0.88	0.78	1.00	1.88
Netherlands	1.40	1.47	1.25	1.01	1.24	1.78	1.58	1.63	1.69
Saudi Arabia	0.07	0.08	0.07	0.07	0.06	0.86	0.80	0.56	0.71
USSR/Russia	6.00	6.62	12.28	14.97	12.97	10.54	5.68[d]	1.08[d]	1.1[d]
United Kingdom	10.50	11.98	10.38	7.58	5.31	4.67	5.27	5.09	6.13
United States	49.89	39.89	35.12	32.02	25.00	25.00	25.00	25.00	22.00

Source: UN Document ST/ADM/SER.B/666 (10 November 2005)

[a] In 1964, Egypt and Syria were federated in the United Arab Republic.
[b] The Federal Republic of Germany represented only the western Länder until 1991. Till that year, Germany's eastern länder were represented by the German Democratic Republic (the Communist-ruled East Germany), which was assessed separately at a rate of 1.22% in 1974 and 1.39% in 1984.
[c] Pro-rated, based on the allocation between India and Pakistan after partition in 1947. The rates proposed and adopted for the entire Dominion of India in 1946 were 3.73% and 4.09%, respectively.
[d] Figures for 1995 et seq. are for Russian Federation only. To compare with figures for the Union of Soviet Socialist Republics, add 1.33% (the total of the other 12 former Soviet republics admitted to UN membership in 1991–92) for 1995, 0.167% for 2000, and 0.108% for 2005.

income. In total, the low-income discount shifts 9.4 percentage points on the assessment scale from poorer to wealthier countries—and almost half of that, 4.1 percent, is transferred from just two countries, China and India, that have hundreds of millions of impoverished people. In addition, there is a much smaller offset granted as an adjustment for heavy external indebtedness.

Periodically, countries with surging economies or fast-growing oil revenues have sought to put a brake on paying higher rates of assessments, and—over the opposition of the Committee on Contributions—the General Assembly attached a 'scheme of limits' to the assessment formula in 1985 to limit the rise or fall of assessments from one assessment period to the next. Just as the committee had predicted, the scheme had perverse effects—primarily slowing the increase in Japan's assessment during its

1980s boom, while preventing a fall in assessments on ex-Soviet states as their economies contracted in the 1990s. Reformers finally succeeded in killing the scheme of limits in the assessment scale adopted for the 2001–2003 triennium, but by 2005 some developing countries with fast-growing economies were beginning once again to clamor for putting brakes on commensurate growth in their assessments.

The largest distortion from a scale built on capacity to pay, in the view of many diplomats and observers, is the ceiling that has capped the American contribution at below the US share of world income since the UN's founding. In the climax to bitter battles over dues delinquency in the 1990s, the General Assembly in 2000 agreed to lower the US assessment to 22 percent (the US Congress had demanded 20 percent) tied to a package of reforms that included elimination of the scheme of limits and rationalization of the special assessment scale for peacekeeping expenses. By 2006, the dropped ceiling raised the assessments of other wealthy countries by 21 percent.

Even when the apportionment formula has been weighted, stretched, and capped to yield desired results, individual states may still seek to negotiate a special rate that no generally applicable formula provision could achieve.[9] In the first years of the twenty-first century, the most striking case of a country voluntarily assuming a larger apportionment than any general formula would produce was Russia. The once mighty superpower that was paying nearly 13 percent of the UN budget in the mid-1970s could generate scarcely 0.8 percent of global income by 2003, and its embarrassing eligibility for the low-income discount would have trimmed further its assessment down to less than half of one percent. A Russian contribution level of 0.466 percent—just behind Portugal's and equal to Poland's—would have highlighted humiliatingly the country's faded claim to great power permanency on the Security Council, especially in comparison with China. China's great leap forward led, even with its low-income discount, to a tripling of its assessment level in just a decade to nearly 2.1 percent of UN assessed costs in 2005. So Moscow insisted on an assessment of 1.10 percent, more than double its formula apportionment, and rushed to make full payment of its assessed contribution in early January, weeks before it was due—in sharp contrast to Washington, which since 1982 has wreaked havoc with international organization budgets by making payment of its contributions in the last three months of the year.

The due date for member states to make payment of their assessments for the UN regular budget is 31 January—a month after official notice to members of assessments for the calendar-year budget. The early payment date was a measure of fiscal prudence, to ensure enough cash on hand to meet obligations throughout the year—and provide the capacity to respond immediately to emergencies, since supplemental assessments inevitably take time to collect. In fact, the first General Assembly also created a working capital fund 'to meet unforeseen or extraordinary expenses' without having to go back to member states for supplemental assessments.[10] The system worked efficiently—until the United States abruptly stopped paying its contribution in 1982 when due and unilaterally postponed its payment till the end of the year.[11] The UN would consequently be able to cover all its expenses for the year's first three quarters only if every other state paid its assessment by summer. Not all members do.

Table 39.2 UN assessment adjustments for selected countries

Country	Gross National Income	Debt Adjustment	Low Per Capita Income Adjustment[a]	Floor Rate[b]	Least Developed Countries[c]	Ceiling rate (Machine Scale)[d]	2005 Scale of Assessments[e]
Argentina	0.723	0.671	0.741	0.741	0.741	0.900	0.956
Australia	1.179	1.191	1.314	1.314	1.315	1.596	1.592
Bangladesh	0.157	0.152	0.039	0.039	0.010	0.010	0.010
Brazil	1.718	1.639	1.078	1.077	1.078	1.237	1.523
Canada	2.162	2.184	2.410	2.409	2.410	2.926	2.813
China	4.939	4.925	1.897	1.896	1.897	2.177	2.053
Cuba	0.086	0.077	0.041	0.041	0.041	0.047	0.043
Egypt	0.289	0.280	0.112	0.112	0.112	0.128	0.120
Ethiopia	0.020	0.018	0.004	0.004	0.004	0.004	0.004
France	4.415	4.460	4.921	4.920	4.923	5.976	6.030
Germany	6.251	6.315	6.968	6.967	6.970	8.461	8.662
India	1.464	1.439	0.385	0.385	0.385	0.442	0.421
Iran	0.319	0.318	0.137	0.137	0.137	0.157	0.157
Israel	0.354	0.358	0.395	0.394	0.395	0.479	0.467
Italy	3.586	3.623	3.997	3.996	3.998	4.854	4.885
Japan	14.671	14.821	16.354	16.350	16.359	19.858	19.468
Korea (Republic of)	1.384	1.348	1.487	1.487	1.487	1.806	1.796
Mexico	1.770	1.722	1.900	1.899	1.900	2.307	1.883
Netherlands	1.249	1.261	1.392	1.391	1.392	1.690	1.690
Nigeria	0.129	0.117	0.029	0.029	0.029	0.034	0.042
Russia	0.804	0.746	0.333	0.333	0.333	0.382	1.100
Saudi Arabia	0.563	0.553	0.610	0.610	0.611	0.741	0.713
Singapore	0.285	0.288	0.318	0.318	0.318	0.386	0.388
South Africa	0.392	0.386	0.239	0.239	0.239	0.275	0.292
Sweden	0.728	0.735	0.811	0.811	0.811	0.985	0.998
United Kingdom	4.679	4.727	5.216	5.215	5.217	6.334	6.127
United States	31.690	32.014	35.324	35.317	35.334	22.000	22.000

Sources: UN Document A/58/11 (2–27 June 2003); UN Document ST/ADM/SER.B/666 (10 November 2005)

[a] Low per capita income threshold—based on global average per capita income—is $5,099, and the gradient—the percentage by which the lower-income state's assessed share is discounted—is limited to 80% of its shortfall from the global per capita average.
[b] 'Floor rate' is a minimum assessment required for membership, even if in excess of a small or impoverished state's share of world income; as of 2001 it was 0.001%.
[c] Least developed countries have a maximum rate of 0.01%.
[d] Ceiling rate is 22%.
[e] Scale figures are derived by averaging the results of the scale methodology with base periods of 3 and 6 years. All adjustments in this table have a 3 year base period (1999–2001).

By 2005, only twenty-nine member states paid in full their assessments by the 31 January deadline. With no authority to impose a late penalty, the UN was reduced to publishing an 'honor roll' of timely contributors.[12] These countries' payments amounted to barely 22 percent of the budget, with only two of the UN's ten largest contributors among them (Canada and France); by the end of the first quarter, an additional 27 states had made full payment, including large contributors Britain, Italy, and Spain. Japan's large cash infusion arrived in April, Germany's in June, and with partial or full payments by other states the UN had 68 percent of assessments by mid-year. China—now the ninth largest contributor—completed its payment in July, and Mexico—the tenth largest contributor—paid the final third of its 2005 assessment in August.

The last (but largest) of the top ten contributors, the United States, made $73 million in payments in 2005 by the end of its fiscal year on September 30—but these were for its assessment for the *2004* budget, more than a third of which remained unpaid as the United States began fiscal year 2006. But while the United States was responsible for the lion's share of delinquent contributions toward the regular budget, its equally large unpaid assessments for UN peacekeeping operations in the first years of the twenty-first century were increasingly matched by delinquencies by Japan and other contributors.[13]

PAYING FOR PEACE

The earliest peace operations—such as mediation in Palestine and truce observation along ceasefire lines in Kashmir and Jerusalem—were relatively small and accommodated within the organization's regular budget. The development of more costly peacekeeping operations after the Suez crisis of 1956 led to the creation of separate accounts for each such mission funded by separate assessments. Peacekeeping operations respond to largely unforeseen crises, and most governments make scant provision for security emergencies when they adopt their national budgets. The financial burden of the controversial Congo operation of the early 1960s was more than that of the UN regular budget, and with the proliferation of increasingly complex peace operations after the Cold War, assessments for peacekeeping rapidly outraced those for the regular budget.

Developing countries with threadbare treasuries protested that their limited national budgets could not absorb the escalating costs of unforeseen peacekeeping operations. As early as 1961, many newly independent countries responded to the rapidly mounting assessments for the Congo operation with delinquency, prompting the General Assembly to reduce peacekeeping assessments on small developing countries by 80 percent from their regular budget rate, and those on larger developing countries by 50 percent. The hope that wealthier members would cover the resulting shortfall by voluntary contributions proved illusory, and the Assembly experimented in succeeding years with different formulas for easing the peacekeeping burden on poorer members until the issue was temporarily rendered moot by the end of the Congo operation in 1964 and Egypt's fateful expulsion in 1967 of UN peacekeepers in the Sinai.

The two Arab–Israeli wars that followed led to the creation of new peacekeeping forces and haggling over how to finance them. Under a 'provisional' formula that lasted till the century's end, linked in broad terms to the rates for the regular budget and assessed contribution rates, developing countries would be divided into two classes—the presumptively and the desperately needy. Instead of a statistical formula to define need, the Assembly simply specified by name the poorest countries—mostly in sub-Saharan Africa, but also including Afghanistan, Haiti, and Yemen—that would constitute 'Category D,' assessed at a peacekeeping rate that was one-tenth of their regular budget assessment (i.e., a 90 percent discount from their regular rate). Accordingly, Afghanistan—which paid in 1973 the then-minimum regular assessment of 0.02 percent of the UN budget—would be assessed 0.002 percent of the cost of Sinai and Golan peacekeepers. The peacekeeping assessment on all other developing countries ('Category C') would be one-fifth of their regular assessment; thus Mexico, then paying 0.86 percent of the regular budget, would be assessed 0.172 percent for the disengagement forces. The twenty-three developed countries, mostly in Europe, were assigned to Category B, paying the same rate for the peacekeeping force as for the regular budget. It fell to the five permanent members of the Security Council, in recognition of their 'special responsibilities for the maintenance of peace and security'—a euphemism for their veto power—to pick up the share of expenses shed by the developing countries, which amounted in 1973 to 8.5 percentage points on the assessment scale. And within this Category A, the amount shifted from the poor would be pro-rated among the five based on their respective regular assessments.

The United States, Britain, and France reluctantly agreed to the formula because they were anxious to insert a peacekeeping force quickly lest the Middle East suffer a third explosion, but they insisted that the resolution establishing the new peacekeeping scale describe it as 'ad hoc,' to last only a year. Inevitably, the scale was renewed each year. In 1978, Israel's invasion of Lebanon triggered a new crisis in the region, and the Carter administration readily accepted application of the same peacekeeping scale in order to get UN peacekeepers into, and Israeli forces out of, Lebanon as quickly as possible. A decade later, the Reagan administration did not even think to question the apportionment scale when peacekeeping missions were established to monitor the ceasefire ending the Iran–Iraq war, achieve Namibia's independence from South African rule, and oversee Cuban troops' departure from Angola.

But the three peacekeeping operations the Security Council established in the waning days of the Reagan administration were just the first in an exponential growth of the number, scope, and cost of UN peace operations after the end of the Cold War. Moreover, a shift in the relative assessment burden of the five permanent members made the skyrocketing assessments for peacekeeping seem even more onerous to Washington. As discounts on the regular scale for low per-capita incomes deepened in the mid-1970s, China's regular assessment, which had been 5.50 percent in 1974, shrank to just 0.72 percent in 1995; as a result, China picked up virtually none of the Category A 'premium' as peacekeeping costs soared. The breakup of the Soviet Union and the rapid downward spiral of the Russian economy halved Moscow's share as well. Britain and France, like all developed countries save the ceiling-insulated United States, had to absorb a compensatory share of the declining assessments for the Chinese and Russians on the regular scale. Then, for peacekeeping, London, Paris, and Washington had to split the difference in the permanent members' premium.

Washington pushed back. It was tolerable, when total peacekeeping bills came to $30 million, for the US to take on roughly two-fifths of an 8.5 percent redistribution from those considered poor in 1973. When the United States was billed for nearly three-fifths of a twelve-point redistribution on bills nearing $1 billion, resistance mounted in the Congress, where hostility to the UN had in any event become increasingly overt in the 1980s. The fact that the peacekeeping formula had locked even high-growth developing countries—like Kuwait, Singapore, and the United Arab Emirates—into the 80 percent discount of Category C exacerbated Washington's discontent.

One stratagem was simply to refuse to approve new peacekeeping operations. Stung by congressional criticism of the relentless rise in peacekeeping bills, the Bush administration in April 1992 drew the line at Somalia. The United States would not approve any peacekeeping mission there funded by assessments; if the UN was to dispatch peacekeepers there at all, they would have to be funded by voluntary contributions, just as the costs of the previous year's enforcement action to drive Iraqi forces from Kuwait had been voluntarily funded. Unfortunately, such funding was hard to secure in a situation where powerful countries had little interest, and the financier that Washington volunteered to pay for the mission, Saudi Arabia, declined to reach deep into its purse. By year's end, a large and costly US intervention was deemed necessary to protect food deliveries to Somalis threatened with massive starvation, soon accompanied by a major UN peace operation funded by assessments.[14]

With voluntary funding of peacekeeping apparently discredited, leading states on the Security Council experimented with other alternatives in the 1990s—involving the delegation of peacekeeping to regional organizations or ad hoc 'coalitions of the willing.' As with voluntary financing, these proved workable mainly in areas, such as the former Yugoslavia after the Dayton peace settlement, where Western powers had a strong interest and were willing to carry the load with troops as well as money. The experience in Africa was far less encouraging, and regionally led military missions in Sierra Leone and Liberia were finally superseded by UN assessed peace operations. By early 2006 the African Union force in troubled Darfur was proving financially unsustainable, leading to calls for its handover to the UN and the relative reliability of its assessments.

The increasing costs of missions to Kosovo, East Timor, and Sierra Leone in 1999 intensified demands in Washington for an overhaul of the peacekeeping assessment scale, which occurred as part of a larger UN financing deal negotiated late in 2000. The reform abolished discounts on the peacekeeping scale based on an arbitrary listing of 'developing' countries. Instead, reductions from the regular rate would be tied to per capita income. The discount was still a full 90 percent off the regular assessment rate for the least developed countries, while those with per capita incomes roughly between $500 and $9,600 were spread among six categories based on a

Table 39.3 UN peacekeeping and regular assessments for selected countries

Member State	2000		2005	
	Regular Scale Assessment	Peacekeeping Assessment	Peacekeeping Assessment	Regular Scale Assessment
Argentina	1.103	0.2206	0.2868	0.956
Australia	1.483	1.4829	1.5920	1.592
Bangladesh	0.010	0.0010	0.0010	0.010
Brazil	1.471	0.2941	0.3046	1.523
Canada	2.732	2.7319	2.8130	2.813
China	0.995	1.2052	2.4714	2.053
Cuba	0.024	0.0048	0.0086	0.043
Egypt	0.065	0.0130	0.0240	0.120
Ethiopia	0.006	0.0006	0.0004	0.004
France	6.545	7.9277	7.2590	6.030
Germany	9.857	9.8567	8.6620	8.662
India	0.299	0.0598	0.0842	0.421
Iran	0.161	0.0322	0.0314	0.157
Israel	0.350	0.0700	0.4670	0.467
Italy	5.437	5.4368	4.8850	4.885
Japan	20.573	20.5724	19.4680	19.468
Korea (Republic of)	1.006	0.2012	1.7960	1.796
Mexico	0.995	0.1990	0.3766	1.883
Netherlands	1.632	1.6319	1.6900	1.690
Nigeria	0.032	0.0064	0.0084	0.042
Russia	1.077	1.3045	1.3242	1.100
Saudi Arabia	0.562	0.1124	0.2852	0.713
Singapore	0.179	0.0358	0.3589	0.388
South Africa	0.366	0.3660	0.0584	0.292
Sweden	1.079	1.0790	0.9980	0.998
United Kingdom	5.092	6.1678	7.3757	6.127
United States	25.000	30.2816	26.4838	22.000

Sources: UN Document ST/ADM/SER.B/565 (6 October 2000); UN Document ST/ADM/SER.B/666 (10 November 2005).

sliding income scale. The wealthy 'developing' countries that had enjoyed an 80 percent discount from their regular assessment in the old Category C—Brunei, Kuwait, Qatar, Singapore, and United Arab Emirates—were now held to a merely token reduction of 7.5 percent from their regular rate of assessment.

The 2000 reform of the peacekeeping assessment scale was a remarkable achievement in the UN's easily immobilized politics, but the fact that the US assessment for peace operations fell from 30.4 percent to 26.5 percent was not enough to satisfy conservative politicians in Washington who had legislated their own 25 percent cap on American peacekeeping assessments. By mid-decade, they reimposed a policy barring payment of peacekeeping assessments beyond their unilaterally determined 25 percent ceiling.

The refusal by the largest member states to pay assessed contributions whose level or purpose displeases them has become a recurrent feature of funding politics at the UN. The consequent fragility of its financial base is one of the UN's fundamental weaknesses.

CRISES OF FINANCE

Although the United States is now the member state most readily associated with the use of nonpayment to bend the UN to its will, it was actually the Soviet Union that triggered the organization's first financial crisis in the early 1960s. The Soviet Union at that time was assessed nearly 15 percent of the UN budget (Ukraine and Byelorussia paid additionally)—a share large enough that its nonpayment could seriously disrupt the organization. In a political crisis, the Soviets determined to use their power of the purse to force the organization to accommodate their interests. Others were just as determined to show that a willful government could not use its financial leverage to extort its will from the world body.

The issue was, in Moscow's view, constitutional as well as political. The Security Council, with Soviet support, established a peacekeeping mission as the Congo began to unravel within days of independence. But instead of shoring up the authority of Congo's elected and left-leaning prime minister, Patrice Lumumba, the mission increasingly seemed to treat him as part of the problem, and the Soviets soon blocked follow-up resolutions in the Council to strengthen the mission's mandate. When Secretary-General Dag Hammarskjöld turned, under the 1950 'Uniting for Peace' resolution, to the General Assembly to bypass the Soviet veto in the Security Council, an enraged Moscow branded the operation illegal, arguing that the Charter entrusted 'primary responsibility for the maintenance of international peace and security' to the Council and allowed the Assembly only to make 'recommendations.' After the Soviets simply refused to pay any peacekeeping assessments, the General Assembly sought an advisory opinion from the International Court of Justice, which ruled in 1962 that Assembly-approved costs of peacekeeping operations were indeed 'expenses of the Organization' that member states were obliged to pay.[15]

The Soviet government adamantly refused to pay these peacekeeping assessments and was joined in its rejection by its Communist allies and France. When the Congo operation was concluded in June 1964, its accounts had a gaping hole—a quarter of its $332 million cumulative cost—and the unpaid peacekeeping assessments of the recalcitrant states exceeded their total assessments for the previous two years, thus crossing the Article 19 threshold for forfeiture of vote. The Soviets warned that they would pull out of the UN if disfranchised, while the United States insisted on either Soviet payment of enough funds to avert application of Article 19 or their loss of vote.[16] To buy time for a solution, member states agreed to go through the Assembly session with no contested item coming to a vote; competing candidates for Assembly offices and elections to UN bodies were pressured to withdraw their candidacies so that essential business could be transacted by consensus without a single roll call.

In 1965, facing ebbing support in the Assembly for confronting the Soviets, the United States acquiesced in a resolution of the crisis that consigned the unpaid Congo arrears to a special account that would not be counted toward Article 19; the Soviets and French made 'voluntary' UN contributions (which almost certainly never made up for the unpaid contributions) and recognized prospectively that peacekeeping assessments approved by the Assembly were obligatory expenses. The US representative advised the special peacekeeping committee that hammered out the arrangement, however, that 'if any Member can insist on making an exception to the principle of collective financial responsibility with respect to certain activities of the Organization, the United States reserves the same option to make exceptions if, in our view, strong and compelling reasons exist for doing so.'[17]

By the mid-1980s, in Washington's judgment, such 'strong and compelling reasons' had arisen. The first warning shot had already been fired in 1978, as resentment grew in Washington against the domination of the UN agenda by a swollen Third World majority. Freshman senator Jesse Helms of North Carolina targeted the proliferation of 'technical assistance' funds in UN agencies' assessed budgets—this technical assistance, he argued, was just a covert way of extorting from wealthy countries ever rising levels of development aid that should be exclusively funded by voluntary contributions. He won adoption of an appropriations amendment barring payment of the US contribution to any UN organization that included such technical assistance programs in its assessed budget.

The General Assembly and specialized agency assemblies refused to eliminate the technical funds, and the Carter administration finally persuaded the Congress to rescind the Helms amendment. But Jimmy Carter would be the last US president of the century to make payment of US assessments on time, in full, and without conditions.

The administration of Ronald Reagan was determined to subject international organization spending to the same constraints it was imposing on nonmilitary domestic spending at home, and it launched a campaign to rein in assessed budgets across the UN system and subject them to 'zero real growth'—a campaign supported enthusiastically by the hard currency-starved Soviet bloc. After withdrawing from UNESCO in 1984, citing its 'excessive' budgetary growth as one reason, the administration stepped up the pressure in New York. The goal was to achieve what the

Roosevelt administration had failed to secure at Dumbarton Oaks, namely budgetary voting based on each state's share of assessed contributions. The weapon would be massive US withholding of its assessed contribution.

The Johnson administration had discreetly but unsuccessfully tried to interest the Soviets in supporting weighted voting on budgetary matters as part of a package to entice them to pay the Congo assessments.[18] By 1985, US officials warned that unless the General Assembly adopted a system of weighted voting, the United States would hold back a fifth of its contribution. The Congress needed no prodding to up the ante, sharply reducing the appropriation for assessments to international organizations and allowing only $100 million to be paid to the UN on its 1986 assessment of $210 million. Tellingly, opponents targeted assessed and not voluntary contributions. It is not just that voluntarily funded programs have domestic constituencies, which assessments for UN 'bureaucracy' do not; for some architects of withholding, the point was to challenge the very notion of a legally binding assessment—the same objection Henry Cabot Lodge had leveled against the financing provision of the League.[19]

American nonpayment brought the UN to the brink of insolvency. Its reserve and capital accounts were drained to pay current expenses, and peacekeeping operations limped along as the regular budget borrowed from peacekeeping accounts, postponing reimbursements to troop-contributing countries till the promised US payments would arrive. By 1987, member states reached agreement on a budgetary package that reduced UN staffing, cut and froze overall spending, and established a new process for budgetary decision-making based on *consensus*—like the old League of Nations. The new process gave Washington more budgetary leverage, though not the weighted voting it had sought.

Washington made only desultory payments on the arrears it wracked up in that two-year crisis. Indeed, the number of conditions it attached to its dues payments only multiplied. The Congress reduced its payments for its imputed share of the costs for the UN's office on Palestinian rights, a cause that was anathema in 1980s Washington; it attached withholding provisions to force the organization to create an independent inspector-general's office and to expel a coalition of gay and lesbian groups from UN-recognized nongovernmental status; it prohibited the US from approving any new peacekeeping mission in the Security Council until congressional leaders had had two weeks' notice to scrutinize the proposal. When a shift in party control catapulted UN foes into the chairmanships of key congressional committees in early 1995, the Congress simply refused to appropriate funds for major peacekeeping operations, and US arrears quintupled in just two years.

Resentment at alleged high-handedness about financing spread throughout the membership, even in the Western group. American candidacies—guaranteed of election in the UN's first half-century—were defeated in contests for the key budget advisory panel, the narcotics control board, and other bodies. The overhang of delinquency disabled US diplomats in nearly all UN negotiations. The Clinton administration struck a deal with its most intransigent foe, Senate foreign relations chairman Jesse Helms, to pay a portion of US arrears if the General Assembly would approve a reduction in the American assessment and dozens of other conditions, including budgetary restrictions (such as continuing 'zero nominal growth,' with no allowance for inflation); a bar to creation of a 'UN standing army'; and prohibition of any discussion by UN political bodies of international 'taxes.' In the last days of the Clinton administration, a hard-won deal was struck in the General Assembly that gave Senate conservatives much of what they wanted—in particular, a reduction in the regular assessment ceiling to 22 percent and a reduction in America's peacekeeping assessment to not quite 27 percent.[20]

What neither Clinton nor his successor George W. Bush would concede was an explicit acknowledgment that assessed contributions constitute a legally binding international obligation. Nor could the Europeans—whose share of the regular budget was as a result of the dues deal further inflated to 35.5 percent, despite a share of world income virtually equal to that of the United States[21]—extract a pledge during the negotiations that Washington would not withhold in the future. Indeed, in June 2005 congressional conservatives—citing allegations of UN malfeasance in the Iraqi Oil-for-Food Programme—raced legislation through the House of Representatives that would bar substantial dues payments until member states acquiesced in new 'reform' demands. In this climate, the prospects for renewed reliability of the assessment-based system of UN financing in the early twenty-first century seem uncertain.

APPROVING A BUDGET

In 1946 the General Assembly approved a budget of US$18.9 million for the fledgling organization's first year. Six decades later, its regular budget totaled $1.4 billion—the financial cornerstone of a far-flung system that by the early twenty-first century accounted for $15 billion annually. Beyond that UN regular budget, the General Assembly assessed its members for peacekeeping operations and war crimes tribunals that in 2005 cost $4 billion, and the specialized agencies levied another $2.3 billion in assessments to support their own regular budgets. This system-wide total of $7.7 billion in assessed and budgeted expenditures is reinforced by voluntary contributions of a similar order of magnitude.[22] All told, the entire system spends in a year about half the budget of the American state of New Jersey (population of 8 million)—or more than one and a half times the budget of the Asian nation of Bangladesh (population: 120 million).

The membership of the General Assembly collectively controls the expenditure only of the UN regular budget and of assessed peacekeeping operations. The Secretary-General is theoretically free to request whatever amounts he deems necessary, but his discretion is constrained by political realities. For instance, both Boutros Boutros-Ghali, in requesting funds for troops to establish 'safe havens' in Bosnia, and Kofi Annan, in requesting a force for eastern Congo, bowed to pressure from leading contributors to keep budget requests for these missions low even at risk of an inadequate military contingent. That major contributors influence Secretariat budget recommendations is widely taken for granted, prompting many developing countries to resist reform proposals in the 60th General Assembly that would free the Secretary-General from the Assembly's minute scrutiny over budgets and administration.

Until 1973 the General Assembly approved budgets annually, and since then it has adopted biennial budgets. The Secretary-General's budget requests go first to the Advisory Committee on Administrative and Budgetary Questions (ACABQ), a sixteen-member panel of budgetary 'experts' who are elected by the Assembly with exquisite regard for geographical distribution. The ACABQ has developed a keen attention to detail, carefully weighing not only budgeted amounts but the number of staff posts to be dedicated to each program activity. Even though its determinations are technically 'advisory'—it is the member states of the General Assembly that formally make the policy decisions, not the handful of 'experts' on the ACABQ—the committee's proposals for rearranging Secretariat priorities command considerable weight. Indeed, when the Assembly grants lump-sum spending authority to the Secretary-General, it routinely requires the ACABQ to approve the specific allocation before the expenditure can be made.

The fact that the committee is not technically an intergovernmental body, but a panel of elected individuals, makes its power over expenditures all the more remarkable. Many representatives of developing countries, which hold the majority of seats on the ACABQ, are convinced that Western (and particularly American) pressures to free the Secretariat from stringent accountability to the committee really aim at loosening their chokehold on spending priorities. Developing countries have also been the principal defenders of another layer of budgetary review, the Committee for Programme and Coordination, which was established in the 1970s to coordinate programs and spending across the UN system. Its lack of power over the agencies has made the coordination more rhetorical than real, but despite calls for its abolition, review by the committee is obligatory.

The Assembly's Fifth Committee is composed of all member states and is the intergovernmental body responsible for approving UN expenditures. Like the other principal committees of the Assembly, all member states have a vote in its deliberations, though a large number of delegations from small countries are unable to dedicate a delegate to Fifth Committee issues and show up mainly for votes, relying on a handful of active Group of 77 delegates for guidance.

The revision in budgetary procedures approved in 1987 established a presumption that the committee should obtain consensus on its budgetary recommendations. Through the early 1980s, decision-making pitted developing countries, which could comfortably marshal the required two-thirds majorities to approve budgets, against those in the Soviet bloc and the West that opposed budget increases. The consensus-based procedures enhanced Western leverage in the budget process, and the impact is clear in the budgetary trend line. In the decade from 1960 to 1970, the regular budget grew 167 percent in current dollars, and from 1970 to 1980 it grew 267 percent. But in the 1980s the decade-long growth in the regular budget was held to 57 percent, and

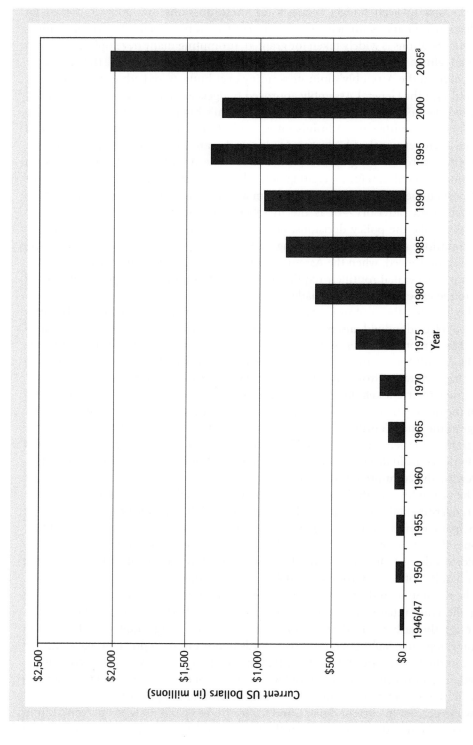

Figure 39.1 United Nations Organization Regular Budget Appropriations

[a] 2005 budget includes a $429 million supplemental appropriation approved with UN Resolution A/RES/59/277 A–C (9 March 2005).

between 1990 and 2000 the increase was just 31 percent—below the rate of inflation. Indeed, between 1995 and 2000 the regular budget actually *shrank* in current dollars by 5 percent.

The contraction of expenditures reflected strong Washington pressure. With a hostile Congress at its back, the Clinton administration held rigidly to a target of 'zero nominal growth'—no accommodation at all for inflation, with supposedly urgent new priorities funded by reducing existing program accounts. This goal became politically unsustainable after 2000 as the Europeans defected. EU countries had supported the budget straitjacket to avoid exacerbating congressional distemper toward the UN in the 1990s but—confident that a Republican administration could better control congressional obstreperousness—they broke ranks to permit a 3.5 percent increase for 2002–2003, followed by a 20 percent spike for 2004–2005 and a 19 percent increase for 2006–2007.[23] Japan shared American preferences for a no-growth budget but deserted once the EU shifted position.

The Americans themselves began to doubt the wisdom of zero nominal growth after confronting resistance to their strong support for substantial increases in UN peacekeeping staff capacity in 2000. The major expansion of staff recommended by a peacekeeping reform panel headed by Lakhdar Brahimi simply could not be accommodated by equally deep reductions in other program staff, nor would developing countries budge on their decision in 1997 to banish the military staff seconded by wealthy Western governments to the Department of Peacekeeping Operations. If they wanted stronger peacekeeping, the Americans would have to acknowledge it had to be additional to the existing budget.

While the relaxation in budgetary stringency reflected a victory by the poorer countries on the point of principle, the priorities to which the added funding was actually applied were quite compatible with those of the West. While the overall budget grew by 25 percent in the four years after 2001, funds allocated for human rights protection jumped by 38 percent, and those for political affairs and peacekeeping preparedness by 51 percent. On the other hand, support for development cooperation rose by 20 percent, and for the Department of Public Information by 8.5 percent. Regular budget funding for economic and social programs was twice the allocation for political-security activities in 2004–2005; twenty years earlier, the respective ratio had been almost four-to-one.[24]

Peacekeeping operations in areas of conflict are separately assessed, and it was these that showed the most explosive growth at the very moment that US pressures were forcing painful reductions in the regular budget. In 1985 the UN's two peacekeeping missions financed by special assessment cost $130 million, a sixth the size of the regular budget. Twenty years later, the $4 billion in peacekeeping assessments was more than twice the regular budget and rising. The large expansion of peace operations tilted assessed program expenditure in the UN system as a whole perceptibly toward security in the early twenty-first century, a marked reversal of emphasis in two decades. In 2005, spending for peacekeeping operations, the International Atomic Energy Agency, and the UN's political and security activities constituted 52 percent of system-wide assessed expenditure.[25] It was only through states' voluntary contributions to the system that the economic and social fields clung to their traditional status as the predominant focus of the UN's work.

Voluntary Contributions

From its inception, the United Nations has filled out the flesh of program activities in the field with voluntary contributions. In 2003, funds provided by willing donor governments to implement specific programs beyond the levels that member states collectively agreed to pay as common expenses amounted to $6.2 billion—with another $1.3 billion furnished to specialized agencies. The largest share of voluntary contributions traditionally go to UN programs for food (WFP at $2.5 billion), children (UNICEF at $1.1 billion), refugees (UNHCR at $824 million), and development (UNDP at $770 million). Aside from a few senior positions that are funded from the UN regular budget, the expenditures of these programs and funds escape the budget-making scrutiny of the General Assembly.

The agencies' own governing bodies, which are elected by the Assembly, approve their expenditure plans. However, in this process donor governments have vastly greater leverage than in the Assembly, since they can simply refuse to fund programs they deem ineffective or politically irritating. Thus, the General Assembly could include in the regular UN budget an office of Palestinian rights that angered American supporters of Israel for promoting Palestinian claims to independence and sovereignty. But the agency providing relief services for the hundreds of thousands of Palestinian refugees, UNRWA, is financed by voluntary contributions ($313 million in 2003, of which 43 percent came from the United States)—and it scrupulously avoids promotion of Palestinians' political goals.

A voluntarily funded program offers other advantages to donors. It allows them to escape long-term budgetary commitments, so when domestic politics demand budgetary belt-tightening, voluntary funds for the international programs can be one more notch on the belt; or when domestic political interests shift, the voluntary funding can be promptly switched to other priorities. By contrast, consensus-building in the General Assembly for a change in regular budget priorities proceeds at a glacial pace. Voluntary pledges are subject to normal appropriations scrutiny by finance ministries and legislators back home, in contrast to assessed contributions. Voluntary contributions to the entire UN system dropped steadily from $7.1 billion in 1994 to $5.4 billion in 1997, then rose modestly to $6.2 billion in 1999, fell again to $5.9 billion by 2002, and hit $7.5 billion in 2003.[26]

Voluntary financing entitles the larger donors to seats on the boards that control the recipient agency's program, and allows them quickly to penalize poor program performance. Thus, two major donors to the UN International Drug Control Program, Britain and the Netherlands, suspended their contributions in 2001 after press exposés suggested inefficiency and waste in the program, precipitating the departure

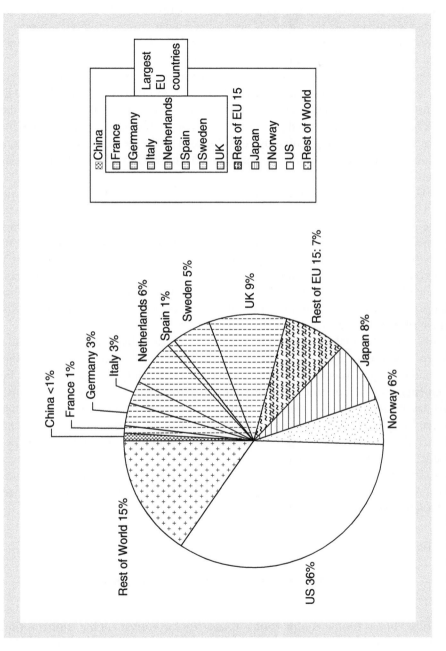

Fig. 39.2 United Nations Organization Voluntary Contributions, 2002–2003

of its director. But donor control is not absolute. Since the early 1980s, when America's right-to-life movement launched a major campaign against China's abortion policies, presidents allied with the movement have cut off contributions to UNFPA to force it to suspend cooperation with China's family planning program. But other countries on the agency's governing board closed ranks in support of UNFPA's work, accepting the loss of US funding (which was reversed for the eight years of the Clinton administration) rather than a *diktat* from Washington.

Sometimes donor governments rely on UN programs to serve as the executing agency for what is really a bilaterally agreed, or 'tied,' grant. This is often the case for UN trust funds established with Assembly approval on the initiative of a member state to accomplish a designated purpose. In this regard, the Bush administration had unusual success in drawing matching contributions to the Democracy Fund in 2005. Trust funds as vehicles to support new program initiatives have, however, historically been hard to sustain.

The United States is the largest single government contributor of voluntary funds to the UN system, but it has given way to the Europeans in many agencies and has lost the presumption to nominate the program heads as a result. US development assistance, bilateral as well as multilateral, dropped dramatically as soon as the global competition with the Soviets subsided, falling from 0.21 percent of GNP in 1990 to 0.11 percent in 1999, and voluntary contributions to UN agencies were similarly hard hit. When US contributions to UNDP sank from $140 million in 1993 to $78 million in 2000, continued American leadership of the agency became politically impossible; the post of Administrator went next to a European.

Other countries make strategic choices to concentrate their voluntary contributions on a handful of agencies. Japan provided UNHCR with 16 percent of its budget when Sadako Ogata was High Commissioner (and let it slide to 11 percent after her retirement), and became the lead voluntary contributor to UNESCO after Kenichi Matsuura became Director-General; Italy was the main benefactor for the International Drug Control Program so long as its nationals ran it. Some governments feel responsibility to give extra support to a UN agency headquartered on their territory; the Japanese regularly provide over half the budget of the Tokyo-based UN University, and the Italians are consistently the first or second largest voluntary contributor to the FAO, headquartered in Rome. The French, by contrast, feel no such sentimental obligation to Paris-based UNESCO.

ALTERNATIVE FINANCING

The United States has been a mainstay of another form of financing, contributions from the private sector. Such grassroots fundraising was pioneered for UNICEF, which now receives a fairly steady $93 million a year in small donations from individuals. American philanthropists intervened to provide the land on which the

UN was built (the Rockefeller family), $1 billion for UN programs on children's health, women's rights, and environmentally sustainable development (Ted Turner), and support for Global Fund initiatives against AIDS, malaria, and other diseases (Gates Foundation). The Global Fund has also drawn pledges of contributions from the corporate sector, including Swiss insurer Winterthur and US pharmaceutical maker Pfizer—triggering some anguished debate among traditional UN supporters about corporate interests and influence, although Secretary-General Annan encouraged UN cooperation with the private sector.

The weaknesses in the assessment system and vagaries of voluntary funding have led to calls for establishing revenue sources dedicated to international activities. Advocates have suggested that states agree to earmark revenues for purposes like security and development from levies on international trade in petroleum (a 'carbon tax'), or on airline tickets, or international arms transfers, or currency transactions (this last often called the 'Tobin Tax' after the late Nobel economics prize winner James Tobin, who proposed it).[27] French President François Mitterrand had called for a Tobin-style tax at the 1995 Copenhagen Summit for Social Development, asserting it would dampen currency speculation as well as generate resources from the wealthy for development in poor countries.[28] A decade later, Mitterrand's successor, Jacques Chirac, joined with Brazilian President Luiz Ignácio Lula Da Silva to propose, on the eve of the 2005 General Assembly debate, 'a solidarity contribution levied on air tickets for global sustainable development.'

While the French National Assembly in December 2005 became the first legislature to adopt such a levy,[29] the prospects overall for international agreement on commonly assessed taxes to be dedicated to specific international causes did not seem promising in the first years of the twenty-first century—even if revenue-starved states were to claim a large share of the receipts for their own treasuries. When Secretary-General Boutros Boutros-Ghali warned in early 1996 that the failure of states to honor the assessment system had rendered the UN insolvent and suggested some form of international tax, Clinton administration officials competed with Republican congressmen in the intensity of their denunciations of the idea. The Congress promptly voted to bar payment of US dues to the UN so long as officials or even member states proposed 'global taxes.' While the issue has receded from the Washington debate, revival of serious discussion of shared global levies is likely in the near term to reawaken conservative suspicions of a creeping, unaccountable world government threatening national sovereignty. Although the Carter administration had suggested in 1978 that the United States was prepared to consider alternative revenue suggestions, the strain in American politics that had motivated Senator Lodge's 1919 reservation against dues obligations also runs deep.

NOTES

1. *Letter Dated 18 November 1919 from the President Addressed to Senator G. M. Hitchcock.*
2. *The League of Nations: A Pictorial Survey* (Geneva: League of Nations, 1929), 30–31. Posted at www.indiana.edu.

3. Reprinted in Ruth B. Russell, *A History of the United Nations Charter: The Role of the United States 1940–1945* (Washington, DC: Brookings Institution, 1958), 998.

4. When cumulative arrears on peacekeeping assessments brought it within the scope of Article 19 in the early 1960s, the Soviet Union contested the automaticity of vote forfeiture, arguing that Article 18 requires a two-thirds vote of the General Assembly for 'suspension of the rights and privileges of membership.' The Soviet delinquency crisis was defused in 1965 without explicitly addressing the Soviet claim. In 1968, when the names of the Dominican Republic and Haiti were simply skipped in Assembly roll calls because of their dues delinquency, the Soviets made a desultory objection; the Secretary-General's legal counsel ruled that vote forfeiture under Article 19 was indeed automatic, with affirmative action by the Assembly required not to apply the sanction but to exempt a state from it; the Soviets acquiesced. Automaticity thus became settled law—demonstrating afresh that binding precedents of principle and equity are more readily applied to the weak than the strong. See Christian Schricke, 'Article 19,' in Jean-Pierre Cot and Alain Pellet, eds., *La Charte des Nations Unies: commentaire, article par article* (Paris: Economica, 1985), 401–403.

5. Even when the US Congress was most aggressively mandating the withholding of assessed UN contributions in the late 1990s, concern about the domestic and international repercussions of US vote forfeiture led Republican congressional leaders to include discreet language in omnibus budget resolutions directing that, notwithstanding specifically legislated withholdings, the United States should pay just enough to avoid falling under the Article 19 penalty.

6. UN, *Yearbook of the United Nations, 1946–47* (New York: UN Department of Public Information, 1947), 217.

7. Ibid., 217–218. In 1946, British-ruled India included today's Bangladesh, India, and Pakistan. As members of the United Nations in their own right, the Soviet republics of Ukraine and Byelorussia were assessed an additional one percent between them, distinct from Moscow's 6.00 percent.

8. Ibid., 218.

9. See *Report of the Committee on Contributions—Sixty-third session*, UN document A/58/11, 2–27 June 2003, 32–47.

10. Appropriation Resolution, Financial Year 1947, in *Yearbook 1946–47*, 216.

11. President Ronald Reagan proposed the delay in payment of contributions to international organizations in 1981, and Washington treated it as a harmless way to effect a one-time saving in the State Department budget. Since the US federal budget year runs from 1 October to 30 September, Washington could 'save' one fiscal year's contributions to international organizations for fiscal year 1982 by making its 1982 payment on October 1—out of fiscal year 1983 appropriations—rather than by January 31.

12. The 'Honor Roll' is posted at www.un.org.

13. The United States was responsible for 28.1 percent of the total $2.5 billion of unpaid prior-year assessments for UN peacekeeping operations when 2005 opened, slightly behind Japan's 28.6 percent. The third largest outstanding peacekeeping bill was Ukraine's, representing 6.1 percent of assessments unpaid from prior years. *Status of contributions as at 30 September 2005*, UN document ST/ADM/SER.B/666, 10 November 2005.

14. The fragility of voluntary financing of peacekeeping operations was underscored in 1993 when the General Assembly agreed to an assessment to cover $8.8 million of the costs of the long-running force in Cyprus, which the USSR agreed in 1964 to permit if the funding were strictly voluntary. NATO governments provided the funding for three decades, but donor fatigue took its toll. By 2005, assessments were covering roughly a third of the UN's

$46 million total cost; 'voluntary' contributions were required of Cyprus (to cover a third of the UN mission's costs) and Greece ($6.5 million). See *Status of contributions as at 30 September 2005*, UN document ST/ADM/SER.B/666, 10 November 2005, 79. The principle that the country hosting a UN peacekeeping operation should contribute substantially toward its costs has not proved replicable elsewhere.

15. *Certain Expenses of the United Nations (Article 17, Paragraph 2, of the Charter)*, International Court of Justice, Advisory Opinion of 20 July 1962, ICJ Rep 1962.

16. If Article 19 were not applied, US representative Adlai Stevenson told Secretary-General U Thant, 'all assessments would be put on a voluntary basis where everyone would pick and choose what he wished to support.' See 'Telegram From the Mission to the United Nations to the Department of State,' document 327, 13 January 1965 in *Foreign Relations of the United States, 1964–1968, Volume XXXIII, Organization and Management of Foreign Policy; United Nations*, ed. David C. Humphrey and James E. Miller (Washington, DC: Department of State, 2004).

17. Ibid., document 365, 16 August 1965. In the internal Johnson administration debate about the issue, some saw a 'silver lining' in the Afro-Asian group's pushing a compromise that undermined the principle of state obligation to pay assessed contributions: 'a voluntary system will allow us to avoid paying for a UN operation to which we fundamentally object.' Ibid., document 337, 12 February 1965.

18. US Secretary of State Dean Rusk raised the prospect of financially weighted voting in a meeting with Soviet foreign minister Andrei Gromyko in late 1964, noting that 'there were some members today who contributed as little as 0.04 percent of the total UN budget. Indeed, one could construct a hypothetical two-thirds majority in the General Assembly whose total contribution to the UN budget would amount to something like 5 percent. For these reasons, we believed that those who carried a larger financial burden should have a greater voice in financial decisions.' Ibid., document 365, 'Memorandum of Conversation,' 2 December 1964.

19. Tellingly, when Congress enacted the 'Gramm–Rudman' deficit control measure in 1987 imposing automatic across-the-board reductions in all 'discretionary' accounts, it refused to exempt UN assessed contributions with other legal mandates, treating dues to international organizations as discretionary.

20. The Senate quickly passed legislation in early 2001 accepting the compromise negotiated in the General Assembly and permitting disbursement of the funds reserved for partial payment of arrears. Conservative leaders in the House of Representatives blocked its passage, however, until the World Trade Center attack on 11 September 2001 heightened pressures on Washington to promote cooperation with the international community.

21. These figures, using 2005 assessment levels, are for the fifteen states that were members of the European Union in 2000. The same 'EU 15' paid an aggregate 38 percent of peacekeeping costs in 2005.

22. See *Budgetary and financial situation of organizations of the United Nations system*, UN document A/59/315, 1 September 2004, Tables 1 and 8.

23. To gain leverage in the negotiations over UN administrative reform after the 2005 World Summit, the United States insisted that it would accept the biennial budget for 2006-2007 only if the authorization to spend from the appropriated amounts was suspended on 30 June 2006—allowing another round of budget brinkmanship in the reform battle.

24. See *Programme budget for the biennium 2004-2005*, UN document A/Res/58/271 A, 23 December 2003. The four-year comparisons are based on the last 'zero-growth' spending plan, the *Programme budget for the biennium 2000–2001*, A/Res/54/250 A, 9 February 2000. In the 1984–85 biennium, funds appropriated for economic and social program

functions totaled $503.4 million, while those for political-security functions amounted to $144.4 million. *Programme budget for the biennium 1984–1985*, UN document A/Res/39/237 A, December 18, 1984. These direct program functions (both economic-social and political-military) totaled 40 percent of regular budget expenditures in 1985 and 42 percent in 2005, with the balance going to support of the policymaking bodies, administration and management, capital construction, and public information—a small but not insignificant result of two decades of pressure for budget 'concentration.'

25. See *Budgetary and financial situation of organizations of the United Nations system*, UN document A/59/315, 1 September 2004, Table 2. The relative shares between political/security activities (31.6 percent in 2005) and economic/social activities (68.4 percent) assume a pro-rata allocation between them of the central management, policymaking, and public information elements of the regular budget.

26. See reports of the Administrative Committee on Coordination (and, since 2000, of the United Nations System Chief Executives Board for Coordination), *Budgetary and financial situation of organizations of the United Nations system*: UN documents A/51/505, 6 December 1996; A/53/647, 6 November 1998; A/55/525, 26 October 2000; and A/59/315, 1 September 2004.

27. Pressed by advocates of a revenue stream dedicated to global purposes, Secretary-General Kofi Annan submitted to the preparatory committee for the 2002 Monterrey Summit on Financing for Development an analysis of these and other proposals for 'innovative sources of finance.' See Technical note no. 3: Existing proposals for innovative sources of finance, UN document A/AC.257/27/Add.3, 20 September 2001.

28. Tobin himself acknowledged that 'The tax would have to be worldwide, at the same rate in all markets. Otherwise it could be evaded by executing transactions in jurisdictions with no tax or lower tax.' UNDP, *Human Development Report 1994* (New York: Oxford University Press, 1994), 70.

29. 'Le Sénat a adopté la taxe de solidarité sur les billets d'avion,' *Le Monde*, 19 December 2005.

CHAPTER 40

WIDENING PARTICIPATION

CHADWICK F. ALGER

THIS volume reveals the extent to which multilateralism has evolved throughout the history of the United Nations and suggests that this process will continue well into the future. This persisting dynamism is not surprising given that technology is constantly developing, which enables people to engage in travel, trade, and communication at ever greater distances and with ever more rapidity. It is perhaps equally natural that these expanding opportunities have been accompanied by the emergence of a new range of problems, themselves constantly expanding and traversing borders. To meet these challenges effectively, it will be necessary both to develop new organizations and adapt existing ones.

A defining feature of this process has been the involvement of new actors—even within the quintessentially *intergovernmental* forums of the UN system—alongside those officials traditionally tasked with carrying out a state's foreign policies. Virtually all government departments now have a foreign policy agenda. At the same time, civil society organizations, business organizations, and local and provincial governments within states have become increasingly involved in activities that stretch beyond their state borders. Given the wide array of actors now linked via diverse networks, multilateralism has become more complex.

Relatively recent developments have changed popular perceptions of the long-term goal of multilateralism. In the past, many saw the eventual goal as 'world government,' the replication of state-level institutions at the international level. But increasingly the present multilateral process is referred to as 'global governance,' with governance referring to 'governing styles in which boundaries between and within public and private sectors have become blurred.'[1] Furthermore, many observers now tend to perceive present global governance as a 'laboratory' in which a unique form of governance is being created for the world.

Virtually all of the world's peoples—as a result of what they consume and the air that they breathe—live their daily lives linked to others around the world. Given the push and pull that they themselves exert on this web of connections and their own personal stake in the global good, citizens should be empowered to understand the nature of evolving multilateralism.

This chapter begins with a recent history of multilateralism, highlighting the impact of nonstate voices and activities. It then gives an overview of efforts, both past and ongoing, to expand participation in the UN system. In recognition of the fact that all reforms at the UN ultimately depend on the political and financial support of member states, the discussion then explores some proposals for finding alternative sources of more predictable and substantial financing for the UN. The chapter concludes with some forward-looking remarks about citizen input into the UN system.

MULTILATERALISM'S ROOTS

The issues that the UN is addressing today have deep roots. The contemporary challenge of 'failed states' provides a vivid example. Beginning with a phenomenon christened by William McNeill the 'closure of the global ecumene,' the surge in long-distance European exploration between 1500 and 1650 laid the foundations for the colonial era.[2] Eventually efforts to set standards for the governance of colonies, followed by the movement to abolish colonial rule altogether, became a multilateral endeavor producing a litany of outcomes, including the League of Nations Mandate Commission, the Trusteeship Council, the Declaration Regarding Non-Self-Governing Territories in the UN Charter, the General Assembly's 1960 Declaration on the Granting of Independence to Colonial Countries and Peoples, and almost a fourfold increase in UN membership. Furthermore, many of the states that are unstable or disintegrating are former colonies, demonstrating the impact of historical legacies as well as multilateral strategies.

While pondering the future direction of these strategies, it is important to bear in mind the effects of social structures and time frames. The processes leading to the UN's founding at San Francisco in 1945 and the establishment of the specialized agencies and other bodies, for example, were lengthy and complex. The treaties that created these organizations emerged from multilateral processes that long preceded the 'founding' conferences.

For example, Inis Claude points to the Concert of Europe, which emerged out of the 1815 Congress of Vienna, as a prototypical instrument of modern international organization—an 'executive council of the great powers.'[3] Thus the Concert of

Europe can be viewed as the forerunner of the League of Nations Council, whose experiences, both positive and negative, in turn have influenced the composition, practice, and reality of the UN Security Council.

In the nineteenth century, international conferences focused on identifying means of managing the increasing linkages among people across political borders—through, for example, the establishment of postal and telecommunications systems, the facilitation and regulation of trade, and the containment of communicable disease.[4] Meetings to cope with these problems became permanent conferences called 'public international unions;' at the outbreak of World War I there were thirty such unions, each with a permanent administrative office. In a book first published in 1911, Paul Reinsch divides these international associations into five categories: communication, economic interests, sanitation and prison reform, police powers, and scientific.[5] A number of these organizations created precedents for the specialized agencies of the current UN system; some remain more or less unchanged since their establishment (e.g., the Universal Postal Union and the International Telecommunication Union), while others replaced predecessors (e.g., the World Health Organization and the Food and Agriculture Organization).

The 1899 and 1907 International Peace Conferences held in The Hague started the movement toward universal participation in international political conferences by including both small European states as well as non-European states. 'Thus,' concludes Claude, 'the world achieved in 1907 its first General Assembly.'[6]

High on the agenda of The Hague conferences was the creation of international judicial institutions. The Permanent Court of Arbitration, a product of these meetings, served as the precursor to both the League's Permanent Court of International Justice and the UN's International Court of Justice and laid the foundation for contemporary ad hoc tribunals and the International Criminal Court.

Spearheaded by the International Association for Labor Legislation, an NGO created in 1900, multilateral concern for 'fair and humane conditions of labor' grew more rapidly than did zeal for securing other human rights. In April 1919, the draft constitution for the International Labour Organization (ILO) became Part XIII of the Treaty of Versailles.[7] The ILO soon began developing treaties to formulate a comprehensive framework of labor standards and, in parallel, set out guidelines for states parties to file reports on the fulfillment of their treaty obligations. In 1926, special machinery was created to assist and strengthen the treaty monitoring process. A committee of independent experts was mandated to evaluate state reports and then submit their assessments to the Conference Committee on the Application of Standards, an intergovernmental body.[8] So again we find that modern procedures—in this instance the UN human rights treaty bodies that track compliance and expose treaty contraventions—have their origin in much earlier developments.

Since 1919 the tripartite structure of the ILO—based on government, labor, and employer representation—has also offered potential answers to a question posed often by the twenty-first century multilateralist: how can the nascent role of nonstate actors in global governance be reflected within the deliberative processes of interstate organizations? In the ILO General Conference, every member state has four delegates—two that represent the state, and one each for employers' and workers' organizations. The executive committee has twenty-eight state representatives, fourteen employer members, and fourteen worker members. It is indeed significant that, after eighty-five years, no other agency in the UN system has adopted a similar type of representation although numerous proposals have emerged, as we see below, for pluralizing intergovernmental deliberations.

Finally, the UN Charter's designation of the Economic and Social Council (ECOSOC) as a principal organ of the UN brought to fruition a trend underway at the League of Nations towards the development of an economic and social council, again demonstrating how the previous experiences can shed light on new paths for multilateralism.[9] ECOSOC emerged, in part, because multilateral collaboration in solving economic and social problems was not only valuable in itself and relatively uncontroversial, but also because the UN's founding members believed that development could prevent serious armed conflicts and violence. David Mitrany referred to this process as 'functionalism,'[10] while recently we are inclined to refer to it as prevention or peacebuilding.

EXPANDING PARTICIPATION
IN THE UN SYSTEM

Framers of the Charter in San Francisco would probably be very surprised that the organization's membership has swelled from fifty-one at its founding to 192 today, and that the stakeholders in the UN system have grown so diverse and encompass officials from many governmental departments in addition to those from foreign ministries; nongovernmental organizations (NGOs); local government authorities; and business organizations.

As a result of the expansion of the world organization's agenda and array of bodies operating both within and in close proximity to the UN system, virtually all governmental departments in member states have incorporated into their respective mandates a foreign policy perspective and have created administrative units to promote this perspective. Similarly, officials from these wide-ranging departments are now more involved in formulating national policies for global issues and participating in UN debates. This suggests that multilateral approaches are gradually being 'mainstreamed.'

Article 71 of the Charter provides for consultations between NGOs and ECOSOC; this form of dialog has expanded widely at the UN headquarters and elsewhere throughout the system.[11] These consultations have in turn provided other opportunities for NGO participation.

NGO involvement in public decision-making within UN bodies has deepened so that it extends well beyond mere observation. Opportunities for NGOs to address public sessions also have spread beyond ECOSOC to include committees of the General Assembly and, through the Arria formula, to meet informally but regularly with members of the most closed of forums, the Security Council. They have also participated in what have been labeled 'formal' and 'informal panels' of General Assembly committees.

At the same time, the relationship of NGOs to UN-system secretariats has developed. Addressing NGO representatives at the UN in September 1994, Secretary-General Boutros Boutros-Ghali said, 'I want you to consider this your home.'[12] While this could be dismissed as a public relations exercise, the thrust of the statement is none-theless significant. NGO contact with the Secretariat includes regularly scheduled meetings and annual consultation meetings; representation on committees; sympo-siums; and participation in national steering committees. UN policy papers are fur-thermore posted on the web for NGO comment, and NGOs often receive training and financial backing. The UN-system secretariats often award NGOs subcontracts, and collaboration is undertaken on research. There are also NGO liaison offices stationed at the headquarters of many UN agencies. It is worth noting that the surge in NGO cooperation with UN bodies has been effected through informal mechanisms and has been accompanied by marginal changes to the formal rules first established for NGO access to the UN in 1950.[13]

Convening UN conferences on specific global issues around the world builds on a tradition that reaches back to the 1932 World Disarmament Conference.[14] These conferences were especially important in framing issues in the 1970s and again in the 1990s[15] and have had an impact on evolving NGO involvement in the UN system in at least two respects. First, NGO conferences running parallel to these governmental meetings have fostered collaboration among NGOs to formulate policy on specific issues. Second, ad hoc procedures employed for NGO participation at these confer-ences have led to demands for wider NGO access at permanent headquarters.[16]

Conferences for drafting treaties have provided yet another avenue for NGO participation in interstate decision-making. For instance, the International Campaign to Ban Landmines (ICBL), an international network of one thousand NGOs in sixty countries, played a leading role in galvanizing agreement behind the 1997 Convention on the Prohibition of the Use, Stockpiling, Production and Transfer of Anti-Personnel Mines and on Their Destruction, also known as the Ottawa Convention; the ICBL and its coordinator were in fact jointly awarded the Nobel Peace Prize for their efforts.[17] The success of the campaign, which relied heavily on electronic communication, arose in part out of a marriage between NGOs and like-minded states.

During negotiations on the International Criminal Court, 'NGOs participated, informally, alongside governments in a high-level negotiating process. They spoke, circulated documents, met frequently with delegations and had a major impact on the outcome.'[18] In preparation for the conference, the NGO Coalition for an Inter-national Criminal Court brought together a broad-based network of NGOs and international legal experts to foster awareness and develop viable strategies. The input of these actors played an important part in bringing about the eventual signature of the Rome Statute of the International Criminal Court in 1998.

Attracting increasing attention has been the role of NGOs as a force for securing the implementation of treaties, in particular those concerned with human rights and the environment. The UN Convention to Combat Desertification (CCD), for example, places unusually strong emphasis on the contribution of NGOs toward the implementation of treaty provisions; the text of the CCD in fact contains twenty-two references to the role of NGOs.

NGO activity at UN conferences has engendered broadly four formats for NGO engagement in international decision-making processes. First, NGOs have convened a number of conferences to follow up on issue-specific UN world conferences. For example, the NGO Forum on Social Development provides NGOs a platform for discussing their role in implementing the recommendations produced by the 1995 World Summit for Social Development in Copenhagen.

Second, a number of broad-agenda, free-standing NGO conferences have been held which have built upon the tradition of convening nongovernmental meetings in parallel with issue-specific world conferences held under the auspices of the UN. These are often referred to as 'people's assemblies.'

Third, there has been support for the establishment of NGO assemblies as 'companions' to specific meetings of the General Assembly. In December 1998, the General Assembly adopted resolution A/53L.73, which designated the fifty-fifth session of the General Assembly the 'Millennium Assembly.' At the time, UN Secretary-General Kofi Annan, in his 1997 report on renewing the United Nations, joined the call for a 'People's Millennium Assembly' to be convened.[19] In May 2000 the People's Millennium Forum convened, gathering some 1,350 representatives from over one thousand NGOs based in more than one hundred countries.

Fourth, for several decades there have been several calls for the establishment of a 'second' General Assembly. These proposals have differed with respect to membership, with varying ideas about the representation of state legislatures and NGOs and about directly elected members. More recent recommendations include the 1994 proposal put forward by Erskine Childers and Brian Urquhart for a UN Parliamentary Assembly; the call for an annual Forum of Civil Society set out in the 1995 Report of the Commission on Global Governance; and the 'Proposal for a UN Second Assembly, 1987–8 edition,' of the International Network for a UN Second Assembly.[20]

Some supporting the People's Millennium Forum saw it as a one-off event, while others hoped it would evolve into an annual people's forum that would offer NGOs an opportunity to make highly publicized recommendations to the UN General Assembly. There were some, too, who saw it as a building-block toward creation of a permanent, directly-elected second UN assembly. However, the creation of such a forum would require an amendment to the Charter and is thus unlikely given the inherent difficulty of this process. Nonetheless, all of these proposals indicate the growing pressure to pluralize and diversify participation within the UN system.[21]

Before focusing on growing involvement by local authorities in the UN system proper, it is useful to review numerous efforts by local groups to influence international relations. Many communities, particularly just after World War II, participated in exchange programs intended to 'internationalize' the community in order to facilitate understanding and peaceful relations. In many places, these exchanges evolved into 'sister-city' relationships featuring cooperative programs for exchanges between local officials and individuals sharing common professions, as well as dialog among the citizens of the respective cities.

Sister-city relationships have also evolved into locally based initiatives, which can be seen to supplement—or indeed replace—the foreign policy of states. Prominent here are efforts by cities in rich countries to facilitate the economic development of sister cities in the impoverished South. Another example of local engagement in foreign policy processes is the mobilization of communities in support of local immigrants declared 'illegals' by the state government, and local efforts to block the government from deporting these immigrants. Local campaigns—in both the North and South—against apartheid rule in South Africa constituted yet another challenge to the traditional monopoly of the state over influence within the international system.

Governments of cities throughout the world have joined together to create international partnerships that are both global and regional, with some having general purposes and some more limited concerns. The first such global organization, the International Union of Local Authorities, was founded in 1913. Today, these associations are often comprised of larger cities and focus on specific issues such as the environment and peace. Border regions in Europe have been particularly active in the development of cross-state border associations of local and regional authorities. In addition, regions in different states that share a common problem have developed transregional functional associations. There are now over thirty in Europe alone.[22] They include the Working Group of Traditional Industrial Regions and the Conference of Peripheral Maritime Regions.

The rise in local activism within global processes has been accompanied by an increase in the involvement of local governments in the UN system. The UN Environment Programme (UNEP), the UN Development Programme (UNDP), the UN Children's Fund (UNICEF), the World Bank, and UNCHS (Habitat) each undertake projects to assist the economic development of cities. A World Urban Forum was held in the run-up to the 1992 UN Conference on Environment and Development, and a Colloquium of Mayors was held before the World Summit for Social Development in 1995.

With a view to establishing a means to project their concerns onto the UN system's agendas, international organizations of local authorities joined together in 1996 to form the World Association of Cities and Local Authorities, which played an important role in the creation of a UN Advisory Committee of Local Authorities. In his 2005 address to the United Cities and Local Governments, an international advocacy group for local governments, Secretary-General Kofi Annan noted that 'forums such as the UN Advisory Committee of Local Authorities are also proving valuable in raising the international profile of local authorities.'[23]

When pondering the possible futures for the participation of local authorities in global governance, the Council of Europe's creation of the Congress of Local and Regional Authorities of Europe (CLRAE) in 1994 is very evocative. As a consultative body its responsibilities include helping new member states to make progress in establishing effective local and regional self-government. CLRAE has two chambers, the Chamber of Local Authorities and the Chamber of Regions, comprised of 291 members and 291 substitute members that represent more than 200,000 European local and regional authorities. The members of CLRAE, composed of only elected local and regional officials, are representative of the various types of authority in each member state. Although advisory, CLRAE is a third pillar, along with the Parliamentary Assembly and the Committee of Ministers, in the Council of Europe.

Local government input is an important aspect of both formulating and implementing regional and global legislation. While the exact impact of efforts by local authorities to influence international decision-making is unknown, the push for enhanced access to the UN and other forums challenges us to think creatively about the potential contribution by local communities and their citizens to a better, more equitable system of global governance.[24]

There is a vast literature about the widespread influence of transnational business corporations on world affairs, and they too enter into the contemporary notion of a UN system more open to a broader variety of perspectives.[25] For our purposes, what is significant is the UN's effort to make partners of these corporations in the quest to secure human rights, high labor standards, and respect for the environment. This endeavor to establish a more cooperative relationship with the private sector was initiated in Secretary-General Annan's 1999 address to the World Economic Forum in Davos, Switzerland. He called for a 'Global Compact' to be set up, urging business to join forces with UN agencies, labor, and civil society to help realize common, long-term interests in enhancing human rights, environmental protection, and peace and stability—all of which, though beneficial in themselves, are also fundamental components of a fertile business climate. In July 2000, shortly before the Millennium Summit later that year, more than fifty corporation heads met with the Secretary-General to launch the Global Compact.

In 2006, some 2,500 companies from ninety countries, as well as international labor and civil society organizations, were engaged—on a strictly voluntary basis—in furthering the aims of the Global Compact, which are summarized in a list of ten universal principles.[26] The Compact's self-description is important: 'The Global Compact is a purely voluntary initiative. It does not police or enforce the behavior or actions of companies. Rather, it is designed to stimulate change and to promote good corporate citizenship and encourage innovative solutions and partnerships.'[27] Six UN agencies are involved in this 'learning exercise' with the Global Compact office: the Office of the High Commissioner for Human Rights, UNEP, ILO, UNDP, the UN Industrial Development Organization, and the UN Office on Drugs and Crime.

POSSIBLE FUTURE GOVERNANCE OPTIONS

In recognition of the need to adapt the UN to the changes that have occurred within the international system since 1945, former Secretary-General Kofi Annan said, 'The United Nations exists not as a static memorial to the aspirations of an earlier age, but as a work in progress—imperfect, as all human endeavours must be, but capable of adaptation and improvement.'[28] To this end, and with a view to harnessing nonstate energies and reflecting nonstate views, Annan spearheaded a UN reform agenda. His vision of change is reflected particularly in four major documents issued since 2000: the Millennium Declaration, passed as a resolution by the General Assembly at the Millennium Summit in September 2000; the December 2004 report of the UN Secretary-General's High-level Panel on Threats, Challenges and Change (HLP); the Secretary-General's own report, *In Larger Freedom: Towards development, security and human rights for all*, published in March 2005 in advance of the World Summit later that year; and the June 2004 report of the UN Secretary-General's Panel of Eminent Persons on UN–Civil Society Relations.[29] The key contributions of these reports are set out below, with emphasis given to the last report because of its specific mandate to put forward recommendations for widening participation at the UN.

The Millennium Assembly of September 2000 issued a broad ranging Millennium Declaration, which led to the enumeration of eight Millennium Development Goals (MDGs) with quantifiable targets to be met by 2015. The MDGs represent a crucial advance within international development as they reflect an unprecedented level of consensus about multilateral development strategy, one in which NGO involvement in eradicating poverty and achieving economic justice is considered vital.[30]

The report of the HLP, entitled *A More Secure World: Our Shared Responsibility*, provides a comprehensive overview of the post-9/11, post-Iraq international security landscape and 'sets out a bold new vision of collective security for the 21st century.' The panel identified six clusters of new and enduring threats to international security that reflect the broadening of the collective security agenda: war between states; violence within states; poverty, infectious disease, and environmental degradation; nuclear, radiological, chemical, and biological weapons; terrorism; and transnational organized crime.[31] Again, this perspective makes room for the priorities and perspectives and inputs from nonstate actors.

In Larger Freedom constitutes the Secretary-General's reply to the HLP's recommendations. Indeed, the report endorses the bulk of the panel's proposals for the future direction of collective security and also voices strong support for *Investing in Development*, produced in January 2005 at Annan's request. Importantly, *In Larger Freedom* 'gives equal weight and attention to three purposes of the UN: development, security and human rights, all of which must be underpinned by the rule of law,' thereby articulating the emerging recognition of the interdependence of the UN's objectives, and giving impetus to the formulation of policies that reflect these linkages. As in the Millennium

Declaration and the HLP's report, nonstate participation in identifying and implementing these policies is judged essential.

For the purposes of this chapter, the most germane of these recent overviews is that
of the Panel of Eminent Persons on UN–Civil Society Relations—commonly known
as the Cardoso report after its chair, former Brazilian president Henrique Fernando
Cardoso. It expresses the growing realization, even among member states, that
nonstate actors are effective and indeed essential actors within the search for and
implementation of multilateral solutions to global challenges. The report recommends that the UN foster wider-ranging multilateral partnerships within what are
described as 'multi-constituency processes.' The Cardoso report's twenty-nine proposals are important because they match a vision of more inclusive and effective
participation in the UN with concrete steps.

The first recommendation captures the overall spirit of future governance options: In exercising its convening power, the United Nations should emphasize the inclusion of all constituencies relevant to the issue, recognize that the key actors are different for different issues
and foster multi-stakeholder partnerships to pioneer solutions and empower a range of global
policy networks to innovate and build momentum on policy options. Member States need
opportunities for collective decision-making, but they should signal their preparedness to
engage other actors in deliberative processes.[32]

Toward this end, the report advises the UN to employ an array of forums, including high-level roundtables, global conferences, multi-stakeholder partnerships, and
multi-stakeholder hearings to 'monitor compliance, review experience and revise
strategies.' This would include 'carefully planned participation of actors besides
central governments' in the General Assembly. The Secretary-General is also urged
to create a Partnership Development Unit within the Secretariat itself as a means of
supporting this process.

The UN is furthermore called upon to foster the 'multi-constituency process'
within states; the UN Development Group, composed of twenty-five UN organizations, is asked to ensure that 'all constituencies' within states 'contribute to the goals
of the United Nations.' The Security Council is urged to strengthen its dialog with
civil society, including the development of 'an experimental series of Security
Council seminars to discuss issues of emerging importance to the Council.' This
would include presentations by civil society, members of other constituencies, and
experts. In addition, the Council is urged to convene independent commissions of
inquiry linked to national foreign affairs committees to review Council-mandated
operations.

The UN is urged to engage with elected government representatives by encouraging national parliaments to hold debates on major issues coming up in the world
organization and by making relevant documents available to parliaments. The
Secretary-General is, moreover, encouraged to seek the cooperation of the Inter-
Parliamentary Union and other parliamentarian associations, and to form a small
Elected Representatives Liaison Unit. The Cardoso panel envisages that the unit
would provide an information service for parliaments, urge parliaments to increase

their attention to the UN, enhance opportunities for members of parliaments to take part in UN forums, and organize global public policy committees to work closely with national parliaments, the Inter-Parliamentary Union, specialized agencies, and other relevant organizations.

In order to open up participation to as many civil society organizations as possible, recommendations are also put forward to streamline and depoliticize the process through which UN accreditation is awarded to civil society organizations. This would involve merging procedures now spread across ECOSOC, the Department of Public Information (DPI), and UN conferences. This responsibility would be assumed by a committee of the General Assembly. In December 2005, there were 2,719 NGOs in consultative status with ECOSOC, and some 400 NGOs accredited to the Commission on Sustainable Development. About 1,500 NGOs with a specific interest in public information on issues of relevance to the UN are associated with DPI.

The Secretary-General is also asked to appoint an under-secretary-general to oversee a new Office of Constituency Engagement and Partnerships. 'Responsible for formulating and implementing the strategy for United Nations engagement with all constituencies beyond the formal membership of central Governments, it would have units on civil society partnership development, elected representatives liaison, the Global Compact (business organizations), and indigenous issues.'

The panel's final proposal asks the Secretary-General to 'assert global leadership by using his capacity as chairman of the UN system coordination mechanism to encourage all agencies, including the Bretton Woods institutions, to enhance their engagement with civil society and other actors and to cooperate with one another across the system to promote this aim, with periodic progress reviews.' It also suggests that 'Member states should encourage, through the forums of the UN, an enabling policy environment for civil society throughout the world and expanded dialogue and partnership opportunities in development processes.'

FINANCIAL CHALLENGES: THINKING OUTSIDE THE BOX

The extension of multilateral capacity advocated in the Millennium Declaration, *A More Secure World*, *In Larger Freedom*, and the Cardoso report cannot be achieved without substantial increases in the UN's financial resources and more assurances about their availability. Current limitations are vividly demonstrated by comparing the UN system's $12 billion annual budget with yearly world military expenditures of some $800 billion—a sum that could finance the UN system as it currently stands for a period of sixty-five years. Indeed, the UN's yearly budget is less than 3 percent of US annual military expenditures. This imbalance challenges the UN system in two ways.

First, it spreads tools of violence and thus undermines conflict management. Second, it starves both states and the UN system of resources that could have otherwise been directed to conflict prevention and longer-term peacebuilding. An additional and related challenge is that less than half of the system's total finances come from guaranteed sources—that is, assessed contributions from member states—the other half coming from voluntary contributions. This places limits on the capacity of UN organizations to undertake long-term planning of programs and staffing, and throws into stark relief the extent of the UN's dependence on the goodwill of its member states.

With a view to lessening this reliance and enhancing the predictability of the UN's financial resources, a number of proposals have been put forward for alternative funding, including the introduction of varying types of global taxes.'[33] In addition to providing a source of revenue for the pursuit of global objectives, these taxes are also envisioned as potential policy instruments to steer international and national activities away from undesirable consequences. Several types are under discussion. Perhaps the most prominent and longstanding proposal is the scheme, put forward in 1978 by Nobel Prize-winning economist James Tobin, advocating the taxation of international monetary transactions, to be applied uniformly by all major member states. Proponents of the Tobin Tax argue that even a tiny amount could deter speculation on currency fluctuations and raise international revenues. The logic is that the rate would be low enough to avoid adversely affecting longer-term investment where yield is higher but would be able to cut into the yields of speculators moving massive amounts of currency. According to the theory, even a 0.25 percent tax on international monetary transactions could generate over $300 billion per year.

A second tax proposal targets e-mail or internet activity. Under this scheme, each person sending one hundred e-mails a day, with each e-mail containing a ten-kilobyte document, would pay a tax of just 1 cent; it is estimated that globally in 1996, such a tax would have yielded $70 billion.[34] A third possibility is an arms sales tax; given the volume of these transactions, a 1 percent arms sales tax each year paid into a global fund administered by the UN would raise hundreds of millions of dollars. A carbon/energy use tax is a fourth option, with advocates arguing that economic activity, in particular the combustion of fossil fuels, imposes costs on society, including damage to the climate system from carbon dioxide emissions. A fifth option is a tax on the extraction of natural resources. A Brussels-based NGO that monitors the world's fifty poorest states has proposed a 'polluter pays' tax for extracting natural resources, again another way of simultaneously raising resources and affecting social policy. An aviation fuel tax is a sixth proposal. Although airplane travel currently accounts for only 3 percent of global carbon emissions, it is also the fastest-growing source; the Intergovernmental Panel on Climate Change, a joint venture of UNEP and the World Meteorological Organization, expects airplane travel to account for 15 percent of all carbon emissions by the mid-twenty-first century. An airline ticket tax and increases in landing fees have also been floated as means of generating revenues for the provision of global public goods.

These alternative sources for financing the UN system could be instituted without prohibitive disruption to the activities targeted for taxation. However, the implementation of these schemes could alter fundamentally the control currently exerted over the activities of the UN by member states, and member states are very protective of this control. The very limited and quite precarious financial support provided to the UN system is therefore arguably no accident: member states can choose to support activities that tally with national interests and reject others which do not.

This explains why it is the powerful member states, and most notably the United States, that are the most intransigent about finding alternative financing for the UN. In 1996 Senators Jesse Helms and Judd Gregg asked the Government Accounting Office to give its opinion on the UN's ability to raise revenue outside of members' assessments. The response was not enthusiastic; noting that alterations to the UN's financial base would require a Charter amendment and that any proposals were thus subject to the veto power of the Security Council's permanent members. The opinion of the Government Accounting Office was that the US government would veto any proposal for such an amendment. As one NGO group has summarized, 'Since 1994, discussions on this subject have drawn increasing interest and support, although the obstinacy of the US has blocked all discussion in inter-governmental fora.'[35]

CONCLUSION

Those making decisions about the future of multilateralism confront complex challenges, including how to organize enhanced roles for NGOs and civil society, local authorities, business organizations, and representatives of legislatures in member states. How should involvement in decision-making be shared across this array of participants? In particular, how should citizens aspiring to fulfill their participatory responsibilities distribute their efforts across these involved parties?

Although the challenges emerging from the 'messiness' of global governance may seem more overwhelming than those confronted in the simpler model of multilateralism in which states are the only actors, this complexity also comes with advantages: when participation in multilateralism is extended to NGOs, business organizations, local governments, and even members of state legislatures, it necessarily widens input to and interest in overcoming global problems. Indeed, this widening of participation is consistent with a conclusion reached by Johan Galtung, a Norwegian peace researcher, over a quarter of a century ago: '[A] social theory that designates only a limited category of the inhabitants of society as the carriers of the new (and better) times to come is a dangerous theory, regardless of how well it may have corresponded with facts in the past... Hence, the answer lies rather in having tasks for everybody.'[36]

This challenges everybody, particularly those residing in democracies, to examine the effects of their actions on the planet, in recognition of the reality that, today, people throughout the world are linked through the 'foreign policies' of their daily lives. At the same time, the actions of the UN and its constituent organizations exert a tangible impact on the lives of individuals—for instance, when a letter is received, a flight taken, or a health concern alleviated.

Thus, the nature of emerging global governance challenges individuals to examine the relevance of organizations in which they are or could be involved. Those who respond will be transformed, from unconscious to conscious participants, in the perennial effort to enhance the capacity of the UN system to respond to an ever more challenging global agenda.

NOTES

1. Gerry Stoker, 'Governance as Theory: Five Propositions,' *International Social Science Journal* 50 (March 1998): 17.
2. William McNeill, *The Rise of the West: A History of the Human Community* (Chicago: University of Chicago Press, 1963), 766–777.
3. Inis Claude, *Swords Into Ploughshares: The Problems and Progress of International Organizations*, 4th edn. (New York: Random House, 1971), 28.
4. See Craig N. Murphy, *International Organization and Industrial Change: Global Governance since 1850* (Cambridge: Polity Press, 1994).
5. Paul Reinsch, *Public International Unions; Their Work and Organization: A Study in International Administrative Law*, 2nd edn. (Boston: World Peace Foundation, 1916).
6. Claude, *Swords*, 29.
7. L. Larry Leonard, *International Organization* (New York: McGraw-Hill, 1951), 448–450.
8. Walter Galenson, *The International Labour Organization: An American View* (Madison: University of Wisconsin Press, 1981), 197–251.
9. See, for example, Ernst B. Haas, *When Knowledge Is Power: Three Models of Change in International Institutions* (Berkeley: University of California Press, 1990).
10. David Mitrany, *A Working Peace System: An Argument for the Functional Development of International Organization* (London: Royal Institute of International Affairs, 1944).
11. Chadwick F. Alger, 'Evolving roles of NGOs in member state decision-making in the UN system,' *Human Rights Review* 2, no. 3 (2003): 407–424.
12. 'Statement by the Secretary-General on the Occasion of the Forty-Seventh Conference of Non-Governmental Organisations,' London, UN Information Centre, 20 September 1994, 1. See also Boutros Boutros-Ghali, 'Democracy: A Newly Recognized Imperative,' *Global Governance* 1, no. 1 (1995): 3–11.
13. Chadwick F. Alger, 'Searching for Democratic Potential in Emerging Global Governance,' in Bruce Morrison, ed., *Transnational Democracy in Critical and Comparative Perspective* (Aldershot, UK: Ashgate, 2003), 90–92.
14. Peter J. Spiro, 'New Global Communities: Nongovernmental Organizations in International Decision-making Institutions,' *Washington Quarterly* 18, no. 1 (1995): 49.
15. See Michael G. Schechter, *United Nations Global Conferences* (London: Routledge, 2005).
16. Alger, 'Searching,' 93–94.
17. See, e.g., Don Hubert, *The Landmine Ban: A Case Study in Humanitarian Advocacy*, Occasional Paper no. 42 (Providence, RI: Thomas J. Watson Jr. Institute for International

Studies, 2000); and Richard Price, 'From Politics to Law: Emerging Customary Norms and Anti-Personnel Landmines,' in *The Politics of International Law*, ed. Christian Reus-Smit (Cambridge: Cambridge University Press, 2004), 106–130.

18. J. A. Paul, *NGOs and the United Nations: Comments for the Report of the Secretary General* (New York: Global Policy Forum, 1999), 3, www.globalpolicy.org.

19. *Renewing the United Nations: A Programme for Reform—Report of the Secretary-General*, UN document A/51/950, 14 July 1997.

20. See Erskine Childers and Brian Urquhart, *Renewing the United Nations System* (Uppsala, Sweden: Dag Hammarskjöld Foundation, 1994) and Commission on Global Governance, *Our Global Neighbourhood, The Report of the Commission on Global Governance* (Oxford: Oxford University Press, 1995).

21. See Leon Gordenker and Thomas G. Weiss, 'Pluralizing Global Governance: Analytical Approaches and Dimensions,' in *NGOs, the UN, and Global Governance*, ed. Thomas G. Weiss and Leon Gordenker (Boulder, Colo.: Lynne Rienner, 1996), 17–47.

22. Aygen Aykac, 'Transborder Regionalisation: An Analysis of Transborder Cooperation Structures in Western Europe Within the Context of European Integration and Decentralization Toward Regional and Local Governments,' *Libertas Paper 13* (Sindelfingen, Germany: Europäisches Institut GmbH, 1994).

23. *In Remarks to 'United Cities and Local Governments' Secretary-General says Local Action Needed to Achieve Global Goals*, UN document SG/SM/10081, 9 August 2005.

24. Chadwick F. Alger, 'The Future of Democracy and Global Governance Depends on Widespread Public Knowledge about Local Links to the World,' *Cities* 16, no. 3 (1999): 203–206.

25. Sorcha Macleod and Douglas Lewis, 'Transnational Corporations: Power, Influence and Responsibility,' *Global Social Policy* 4, no.1, (2004): 77–98.

26. For details, see www.unglobalcompact.org. See also John Gerard Ruggie, 'global_governance.net: The Global Compact as a Learning Network,' *Global Governance* 7, no. 4 (2001): 371–378.

27. See www.unglobalcompact.org.

28. Kofi Annan, *Strengthening of the United Nations: an agenda for further change, Report of the Secretary-General*, UN document A/57/387, 9 September 2002.

29. See *United Nations Millennium Declaration*, UN document A/55/L.2, 8 September 2000; *Report of the Panel on United Nations Peace Operations*, UN document A/55/305-S/2000/809, 21 August 2000; *A More Secure World: Our Shared Responsibility, Report of the Secretary-General's High-level Panel on Threats, Challenges and Change*, UN document A/59/565, 2 December 2004; *In Larger Freedom: Towards Development, Security and Human Rights for All*, UN document A/59/2005, 21 March 2005; *We the Peoples: Civil Society, the United Nations and Global Governance, Report of the Panel of Eminent Persons on United Nations–Civil Society Relations*, UN document A/58/817, 11 June 2004.

30. For more details, see www.un.org/millenniumgoals.

31. *A More Secure World*, www.un.org.

32. *We the Peoples: Civil Society, the United Nations and Global Governance, Report of the Panel of Eminent Persons on United Nations–Civil Society Relations*, UN document A/58/817, 11 June 2004.

33. Global Policy Forum, 'Alternative Financing for the UN,' www.globalpolicy.org.

34. See UNDP, *Human Development Report 1999* (New York: Oxford University Press, 1999), 66.

35. Global Policy Forum, 'Alternative Financing for the UN,' www.globalpolicy.org.

36. Johan Galtung, *The True Worlds: A Transnational Perspective* (New York: The Free Press, 1980), 396.

APPENDIX 1: SUGGESTED FURTHER READING

Any brief selection of readings is necessarily subjective. Moreover, many of the topics in this *Handbook* overlap and are mutually reinforcing; and we list sources here under one heading when, in fact, they inform several topics. The endnotes for each chapter, however, contain more authoritative recommendations about specialized readings for each topic. Here, as editors, we select a handful of more general works that should be readily available in most research libraries. In this regard, we steer clear of electronic sources because they often change. Moreover, we avoid a comprehensive list of 'classics'—which would have been too lengthy and many of them dated—and instead we emphasize recent treatments that we ourselves judge to be up-to-date overviews of the subject matter. This list has the additional advantage that we are not bashful about citing the work of our contributors, who might be reluctant to do so.

Part II: Theoretical Frameworks

2. Political Approaches

Baldwin, David, ed. 1993. *Neorealism and Neoliberalism: The Contemporary Debate.* New York: Columbia University Press.

Barnett, Michael, and Martha Finnemore. 2005. *Rules for the World: International Organizations in Global Politics.* Ithaca, NY: Cornell University Press.

Bull, Hedley. 1977. *The Anarchical Society.* New York: Columbia University Press.

Holsti, Kalevi J. 2004. *Taming the Sovereigns: Institutional Change in International Politics.* Cambridge: Cambridge University Press.

Karns, Margaret P., and Karen A. Mingst. 2004. *International Organizations: The Politics and Processes of Global Governance.* Boulder, Colo.: Lynne Rienner.

Krasner, Stephen D., ed. 1983. *International Regimes.* Ithaca, NY: Cornell University Press.

——1999. *Sovereignty: Organized Hypocrisy.* Princeton, NJ: Princeton University Press.

Pearson, Frederic S., and J. Martin Rochester, 1997. *International Relations: The Global Condition in the Twenty-First Century,* 4th edn. New York: McGraw-Hill.

Rosenau, James N., and Ernst-Otto Czempiel. 1992. *Governance without Government: Order and Change in World Politics.* Cambridge: Cambridge University Press.

Ruggie, John Gerard, ed. 1993. *Multilateralism Matters: The Theory and Praxis of an Institutional Form.* New York: Columbia University Press.

Wendt, Alexander. 1999. *Social Theory of International Politics.* Cambridge: Cambridge University Press.

3. Legal Perspectives

Alvarez, José E. 2005. *International Organizations as Lawmakers.* Oxford: Oxford University Press.

Byers, Michael, ed. 2000. *The Role of Law in International Politics: Essays in International Relations and International Law.* Oxford: Oxford University Press, 2000.

Cassese, Antonio. 2004. *International Law*. Oxford: Oxford University Press.

Franck, Thomas M. 1995. *Fairness in International Law and Institutions*. Oxford: Oxford University Press.

Goldsmith, Jack L., and Eric A. Posner. 2004. *The Limits of International Law*. Oxford: Oxford University Press.

Higgins, Rosalyn 1994. *Problems and Process: International Law and How We Use It*. Oxford: Oxford University Press.

Joyner, Christopher C., ed. 1997. *The United Nations and International Law*. Cambridge: Cambridge University Press.

Kirgis, Frederic L. Jr., 1993. *International Organizations in Their Legal Setting*. 2nd edn. St. Paul: West.

Reus-Smit, Christian, ed. 2004. *The Politics of International Law*. Cambridge: Cambridge University Press.

Rochester, J. Martin. 2006. *Between Peril and Promise: The Politics of International Law*. Washington, DC: CQ Press.

Sands, Philippe, and Philippe Klein, eds. 2001. *Bowett's Law of International Institutions*. 5th edn. London: Sweet & Maxwell.

Simma, Bruno, ed. 2002. *The Charter of the United Nations: A Commentary*. 2nd edn. Oxford: Oxford University Press.

White, N. D. 1996. *The Law of International Organisations*. Manchester: Manchester University Press.

4. *Evolution in Knowledge*

Global Governance: A Review of Multilateralism and International Organizations, published quarterly, since 1995.

Haas, Ernst B. 1990. *When Knowledge Is Power: Three Models of Change in International Organization*. Los Angeles: University of California Press.

Hajnal, Peter I., ed. 1997–2001. *International Information: Documents, Publications and Electronic Information of International Governmental Organizations*. Engelwood, Colo.: Libraries Unlimited, 2 vols.

International Organization, published quarterly, since 1947.

Jackson, Robert. 2000. *The Global Covenant: Human Conduct in a World of States*. Oxford: Oxford University Press.

Kennedy, Paul. 2006. *The Parliament of Man: The Past, Present, and Future of the United Nations*. New York: Random House.

Philpott, Daniel. 2001. *Revolutions in Sovereignty: How Ideas Shaped Modern International Relations*. Princeton: Princeton University Press.

Part III: Principal Organs

5. *General Assembly*

Alker, Hayward R. Jr., and Bruce M. Russett. 1965. *World Politics in the General Assembly*. New Haven: Yale University Press.

Bailey, Sydney D. 1964. *The General Assembly of the United Nations*. Dunmow: Pall Mall Press.

Kaufmann, Johan. 1988. *Conference Diplomacy: An Introductory Analysis*. 2nd rev. edn. Dordrecht: Nijhoff.

Moynihan, Daniel Patrick. 1990. *On the Law of Nations*. Cambridge: Harvard University Press.

Peterson, M. J. 2005. *The UN General Assembly*. London: Routledge.

Schechter, Michael G. 2005. *United Nations Global Conferences*. London: Routledge.

UN Association of the USA, *A Global Agenda: Issues before the General Assembly of the United Nations*. New York: UNA–USA, published annually in September.

6. *Security Council*

Bailey, Sydney D., and Sam Daws. 1998. *The Procedure of the UN Security Council.* 3rd edn. Oxford: Oxford University Press.

Blokker, Niels, and Nico Schrijver, eds. 2005. *The Security Council and the Use of Force: Theory and Reality—A Need for Change?* Leiden: Martinus Nijhoff.

De Wet, Erika. 2004. *The Chapter VII Powers of the Security Council.* Oxford: Oxford University Press.

Finnemore, Martha. 2003. *The Purpose of Intervention: Changing Beliefs about the Use of Force.* Ithaca, NY: Cornell University Press.

Luck, Edward C. 2006. *The UN Security Council: Practice and Promise.* London: Routledge.

—— and Michael W. Doyle, eds. 2004. *International Law and Organization: Closing the Compliance Gap.* Lanham, Md.: Rowman and Littlefield Publishers.

Malone, David M., ed. 2004. *The UN Security Council: From the Cold War to the 21st Century.* Boulder, Colo.: Lynne Rienner.

Price, Richard M., and Mark W. Zacher, eds. 2004. *The United Nations and Global Security.* New York: Palgrave MacMillan, 2004.

Weiss, Thomas G. 2005. *Overcoming the Security Council Impasse: The Implausible Versus the Plausible,* Occasional Paper No. 14. Berlin: Friedrich–Ebert–Stiftung.

7. *Economic and Social Council*

Arnold, Tim. 1995. *Reforming the UN: Its Economic Role.* London: The Royal Institute of International Affairs.

Fromuth, Peter, ed. 1988. *A Successor Vision: The United Nations of Tomorrow.* Lanham, Md: University Press of America, Inc.

Independent Working Group on the Future of the United Nations. 1995. *Agenda for Change: New Tasks for the United Nations.* New York: Ford Foundation.

Jolly, Richard, L. Emmerij, Dharam Ghai, and Frédéric Lapeyre. 2004. *UN Contributions to Development Thinking and Practice.* Bloomington: Indiana University Press.

Nordic UN Reform Project. 1996. *The United Nations in Development: Strengthening the UN Through Change: Fulfilling its Economic and Social Mandate.* Stockholm: The Nordic UN Reform Project.

Rosenthal, Gert. 2005. *The Economic and Social Council of the United Nations,* Occasional Paper No. 15. Berlin: Friedrich–Ebert–Stiftung.

8. *Trusteeship Council*

Chesterman, Simon. 2004. *You, The People: The United Nations, Transitional Administration and State-Building.* Oxford: Oxford University Press.

Chowdhuri, Ramendra N. 1955. *International Mandates and Trusteeship System: A Comparative Study.* The Hague: Martinus Nijhoff.

Crawford, James. 2006. *The Creation of States in International Law,* 2nd edn. Oxford: Oxford University Press.

Hall, H. Duncan. 1948. *Mandates, Dependencies and Trusteeship.* Dordrecht: Martinus Nijhoff.

Narayan, C. V. L. 1951. *United Nations' Trusteeship of Non-Self-Governing Territories.* Paris: Imprimeries populaires.

9. *Secretariat: Independence and Reform*

Ameri, Houshang. 2003. *Fraud, Wastes and Abuse: Aspects of UN Management and Personnel Policies.* New York: University Press of America.

Beigbeder, Yves. 1997. *The Internal Management of United Nations Organizations: the Long Quest for Reform.* Houndmills, Basingstoke, UK: Macmillan Press.

Dijkzeul, Dennis. 1997. *The Management of Multilateral Organizations*. The Hague: Kluwer.

Gordenker, Leon. 2005. *The Secretary-General and Secretariat*. London: Routledge.

Graham, Norman A., and Robert S. Jordan, eds. 1980. *The International Civil Service: Changing Role and Concepts*. New York: Pergamon.

Langrod, George. 1963. *The International Civil Service: Its Origins, Its Nature, Its Evolution*. New York: Oceana Publications Inc.

Mathiason, John. 2007. *Invisible Governance: International Secretariats in Global Politics*. Bloomfield, Conn.: Kumarian Press, Inc.

Meyer, Jeffrey A., and Mark G. Califano. 2006. *Good Intentions Corrupted: The Oil-for-Food Scandal and the Threat to the UN*. New York: Public Affairs.

Mouritzen, Hans. 1990. *The International Civil Service: A Study of Bureaucracy—International Organizations*. Aldershot, NH: Dartmouth.

Ranshofen-Wertheimer, Egon. 1945. *The International Secretariat: A Great Experiment in International Administration*. Washington, DC: Carnegie Endowment.

Weiss, Thomas G. 1975. *International Bureaucracy: An Analysis of the Operation of Functional and Global International Secretariats*. Lexington, Mass.: DC Heath and Company.

10. *Secretary-General*

Chesterman, Simon, ed. 2007. *Secretary or General? The UN Secretary-General in World Politics*. Cambridge: Cambridge University Press.

Newman, Edward. 1998. *The UN Secretary-General from the Cold War to the New Era: A Global Peace and Security Mandate?* London: Macmillan.

Rivlin, Benjamin J., and Leon Gordenker, eds. 1993. *The Challenging Role of the UN Secretary-General: Making the 'Most Impossible Job in the World' Possible*. Westport, Conn.: Praeger.

Urquhart, Brian, and Erskine Childers. 1990. *A World in Need of Leadership: Tomorrow's United Nations*. Uppsala: *Hammarskjöld* Foundation.

Vance, Cyrus R., and David A. Hamburg. 1997. *Pathfinders for Peace: A Report to the UN Secretary-General on the Role of Special Representatives and Personal Envoys*. Washington, DC: Carnegie Commission on Preventing Deadly Conflict.

11. *International Court of Justice*

Boisson de Chazournes, and Philippe Sands, eds. 1999. *International Law, the International Court of Justice and Nuclear Weapons*. Cambridge: Cambridge University Press.

Damrosch, Lori Fisler. 1987. *The International Court of Justice at a Crossroads*. Dobbs Ferry, NY: Transnational Publishers.

Eyffinger, Arthur. 1996. *The International Court of Justice 1946–1996*. The Hague: Kluwer Law International.

Lowe, Vaughan, and Malgosia Fitzmaurice, eds. 1996. *Fifty Years of the International Court of Justice: Essays in Honour of Sir Robert Jennings*. New York: Cambridge University Press.

Rosenne, Shabtai. 1983. *Procedure in the International Court: A Commentary on the 1978 Rules of the International Court of Justice*. The Hague: Nijhoff.

Schachter, Oscar, and Christopher C. Joyner, eds. 1995. *United Nations Legal Order*. Cambridge, Mass.: Harvard University Press.

Shahabuddeen, Mohamed. 1996. *Precedent in the World Court*. Cambridge: Cambridge University Press.

Part IV: Relationships with Other Actors

12. *Regional Groups and Alliances*

Boulden, Jane, ed. 2003. *Dealing With Conflict in Africa: The United Nations and Regional Organizations*. London: Palgrave.

Challenges Project. 2005. *Meeting the Challenges of Peace Operations: Cooperation and Coordination.* Stockholm, Elanders Gotab.

Fawcett, Louise, and Andrew Hurrell, eds. 1995. *Regionalism in World Politics: Regional Organizations and World Order.* Oxford: Oxford University Press.

Pugh, Michael, and Waheguru Pal Singh Sidhu, eds. 2003. *The United Nations and Regional Security: Europe and Beyond.* Boulder, Colo.: Lynne Rienner.

Weiss, Thomas G., ed. 1998. *Beyond UN Subcontracting: Task-Sharing with Regional Security Arrangements and Service-Providing NGOs.* London: Macmillan.

13. *Bretton Woods Institutions*

Birdsall, Nancy, and John Williamson. 2002. *Delivering on Debt Relief: From IMF Gold to a New Aid Architecture.* Washington, DC: Institute of International Economics.

Boughton, James. 2001. *The Silent Revolution: The IMF 1979–1989.* Washington, DC: International Monetary Fund.

Blustein, Paul. 2001. *The Chastening: Inside the Crisis that Rocked the Global Financial System and Humbled the IMF.* New York: Public Affairs.

Bøås, Morten, and Desmond McNeill. 2004. *Global Institutions and Development: Framing the World?* London: Routledge.

Caufield, Catherine. 1997. *Masters of Illusion: the World Bank and the Poverty of Nations.* New York: Henry Holt.

Haq, Mahbub ul, Richard Jolly, Paul Streeten, and Khadija Haq, eds. 1995. *The UN and the Bretton Woods Institutions: New Challenges for the Twenty-First Century.* London: Macmillan.

Harold, James. 1996. *International Monetary Cooperation since Bretton Woods.* Oxford: Oxford University Press.

Hoekman, Bernard, and Petros Mavroidis. 2007. *The World Trade Organization: Law, Economics and Politics.* London: Routledge.

Jackson, John H. 1998. *The World Trade Organization: Constitution and Jurisprudence.* London: Royal Institute of International Affairs.

Kapur, Devesh, John P. Lewis, and Richard Webb. 1997. *The World Bank: Its First Half Century.* 2 vols. Washington, DC: Brookings.

Rahman, Maahfuzur. 2002. *World Economic Issues at the United Nations: Half a Century of Debate.* Dordrecht: Kluwer.

Stiglitz, Joseph. 2002. *Globalization and its Discontents.* New York: Norton.

Toye, John, and Richard Toye. 2004. *The UN and Global Political Economy: Trade, Finance, and Development.* Bloomington: Indiana University Press.

Truman, Edwin M. 2006. *A Strategy for IMF Reform.* Washington, DC: Institute for International Economics.

Vreeland, James. 2007. *The International Monetary Fund: Politics of Conditional Lending.* London: Routledge.

Woods, Ngaire. 2006. *The Globalizers: The IMF, the World Bank, and their Borrowers.* Ithaca, NY: Cornell University Press.

14. *Civil Society*

Charnovitz, Steve. 1997. *Two Centuries of Participation: NGOs and International Governance,* special issue of *Michigan Journal of International Law* 18.2.

Eberly, Don, ed. 2000. *The Essential Civil Society Reader: The Classical Essays.* Lanham, Md.: Rowman & Littlefield.

Edwards, Michael, and David Hulme, eds. 1992. *Making a Difference: NGOs and Development in a Changing World*. London: Earthscan.

Finnemore, Martha, and Kathryn Sikkink. 1998. *Activists Beyond Borders: Advocacy Networks in International Politics*. Ithaca, NY: Cornell University Press.

Florini, Ann, ed. 2000. *The Third Force: The Rise of Transnational Civil Society*. Washington, DC: Carnegie Endowment for International Peace.

Glasius, Marlies, Mary Kaldor, and Helmut Anheier, eds. 2003. *Global Civil Society 2003*. Oxford: Oxford University Press.

Martens, Kersten. 2005. *NGOs and the United Nations: Institutionalization, Professionalization and Adaptation*. Houndmills, Basingstoke, UK: Palgrave Macmillan.

Panel of Eminent Persons on United Nations-Civil Society Relations. 2004. *We the People: Civil Society, the United Nations and Global Governance*, UN document A/58/817.

Singer, Peter. 2004. *One World: The Ethics of Globalization*. New Haven, Conn.: Yale University Press, 2nd ed.

Wapner, Paul. 1996. *Environmental Activism and World Civic Politics*. Albany, NY: State University Press.

Weiss, Thomas G., and Leon Gordenker, eds. 1996. *NGOs, the UN, and Global Governance*. Boulder, Colo.: Lynne Rienner Publishers.

15. *Private Sector*

Bruce Hall, Rodney, and Thomas J. Biersteker, eds. 2002. *The Emergence of Private Authority in Global Governance*. Cambridge: Cambridge University Press.

Dunning, John H., ed. 2003. *Making Globalization Good: The Moral Challenge of Global Capitalism*. Oxford: Oxford University Press.

Murphy, Craig N. 1994. *International Organization and Industrial Change: Global Governance since 1850*. Cambridge: Polity Press.

Murphy, Dale D. 2004. *The Structure of Regulatory Competition: Corporations and Public Policy in a Global Economy*. Oxford: Oxford University Press.

Nelson, Jane. 2002. *Building Partnerships between the United Nations System and the Private Sector*. New York: United Nations.

Preston, Lee E., and Duane Windsor. 1997. *The Rules of the Game in the Global Economy: Policy Regimes for International Business*, 2nd edition. Dordrecht: Kluwer Academic Publishers.

Robinson, William I. 2004. *A Theory of Global Capitalism: Production, Class, and the State in a Transnational World*. Baltimore, Md.: Johns Hopkins University Press.

Sagafi-Nejad, Tagi, with John Dunning. 2008 (forthcoming). *The UN and Transnationals, from Code to Compact*. Bloomington: Indiana University Press.

Schmidheiny, Stephan. 1992. *Changing Course: A Global Perspective on Business and the Environment*. Cambridge, Mass.: MIT Press.

Wilkinson, Rorden. 2006. *The WTO: Crisis and the Governance of Global Trade*. London: Routledge.

16. *Media*

Alleyne, Mark D. 2003. *Global Lies? Propaganda, the UN and World Order*. Houndmills, Basingstoke, UK: Palgrave Macmillan.

Eckhard, Frederic, ed. 2005. *Speaking for the Secretary General—A History of the UN Spokesman's Office*. New York: United Nations.

Gowing, Nik. 1997. *Media Coverage: Help or Hindrance in Conflict Prevention?* New York: Carnegie Commission on the Prevention of Deadly Conflict.

Lehmann, Ingrid. 1999. *Peacekeeping and Public Information: Caught in the Crossfire.* London: Frank Cass Series on Peacekeeping.

Minear, Larry, Colin Scott, and Thomas G. Weiss. 1996. *The News Media, Civil War, and Humanitarian Action.* Boulder, Colo.: Lynne Rienner Publishers.

Strobel, Warren. 1997. *Late Breaking Foreign Policy: The News Media's Influence on Peace Operations.* Washington, DC: United States Institute for Peace Press.

Part V: International Peace and Security

17. Disarmament

Boothby, Derek. 2002. The United Nations and Disarmament. New Haven, Conn.: Academic Council on the UN System.

Burns, Richard Dean, ed. 1993. *Encyclopedia of Arms Control and Disarmament.* New York: Charles Scribner's Sons.

Butler, Richard. 2000. *The Greatest Threat: Iraq, Weapons of Mass Destruction, and the Crisis of Global Security.* New York: Public Affairs.

Fischer, David. 1997. *History of the International Atomic Energy Agency: The First Forty Years.* Vienna: IAEA.

Krasno, Jean E., and James S. Sutterlin. 2003. *The United Nations and Iraq: Defanging the Viper.* Westport, Conn: Praeger.

18. Peaceful Settlement of Disputes and Conflict Prevention

Axelrod, Robert. 1984. *The Evolution of Cooperation.* New York: Basic Books.

Bercovitch, Jacob, ed. 1996. *Resolving International Conflicts: The Theory and Practice of Mediation.* Boulder, Colo.: Lynne Rienner.

Carnegie Commission on the Prevention of Deadly Conflict. 1997. *Preventing Deadly Conflict.* New York: Carnegie Corporation.

Crocker, Chester A., Fen O. Hampson, and Pamela R. Aall, eds. 1999. *Herding Cats: Multiparty Mediation in a Complex World.* Washington, DC: United States Institute for Peace Press.

Darby, John, and R. Macginty, eds. 2003. *Contemporary Peacemaking: Conflict, Violence and Peace Processes.* Houndmills, Basingstoke, UK: Palgrave-Macmillan.

Evans, Gareth. 1993. *Cooperation for Peace: The Global Agenda for the 1990s and Beyond.* St. Leonards: Allen and Unwin.

Hampson, Fen Osler. 1996. *Nurturing Peace: Why Peace Settlements Succeed or Fail.* Washington, DC: US Institute of Peace Press.

Hampson, Fen Osler, and David M. Malone, eds. 2002. *From Reaction to Conflict Prevention: Opportunities for the UN System.* Boulder, Colo: Lynne Rienner.

Hauss, Charles. 2001. *InternationalCconflict Resolution: International Relations for the 21st Century.* New York: Continuum.

Merrills, J. G. 2005. *International Dispute Settlement.* 4th edn. Cambridge: Cambridge University Press.

Miall, Hugh. 1992. *The Peacemakers: Peaceful Settlement of Disputes since 1945.* New York: St. Martin's Press.

Oye, Kenneth, ed. 1986. *Cooperation under Anarchy.* Princeton, NJ: Princeton University Press.

Peck, Connie. 1998. *Sustainable Peace: The Role of the UN and Regional Organizations in Preventing Conflict.* Lanham, Md.: Rowman & Littlefield.

Ramcharan, Bertrand G. 2008 (forthcoming). *Preventive Diplomacy at the UN: A Journey of an Idea.* Bloomington: Indiana University Press.

Rubin, Barnett R. 2002. *Blood on the Doorstep: The Politics of Preventive Action*. Washington, DC: The Brookings Press.

Sriram, Chandra Lekha, and Karin Wermester, eds. 2003. *From Promise to Practice: Strengthening UN Capacities for the Prevention of Violent Conflict*. Boulder, Colo.: Lynne Rienner.

Stedman, Stephen John, Donal Rothchild, and Elizabeth M. Cousens, eds. 2002. *Ending Civil Wars: The Implementation of Peace Agreements*. Boulder, Colo.: Lynne Rienner.

Williams, Abiodun, ed. 1992. *Many Voices: Multilateral Negotiations in the World Arena*. Boulder, Colo.: Westview Press.

Zartman, I. William, and J. Lewis Rasmussen, eds. 1997. *Peacemaking in International Conflict: Methods and Techniques*. Washington, DC: United States Institute of Peace Press.

19. *Peacekeeping Operations*

Alan, James. *Peacekeeping in International Politics*. 1990. London: Macmillan.

Center on International Cooperation. *Annual Review of Global Peace Operations*. Boulder, Colo.: Lynne Rienner, published annually, since 2006.

Diehl, Paul F. 1993. *International Peacekeeping*. Baltimore, Md.: Johns Hopkins University Press.

Doyle, Michael W., and Nicholas Sambanis. 2006. *Making War and Building Peace: United Nations Peace Operations*. Princeton, NJ: Princeton University Press.

Durch, William J., ed. 1996. *Peacekeeping, American Policy, and the Uncivil Wars of the 1990s*. New York: St. Martins.

Higgins, Rosalyn. 1969. *United Nations Peacekeeping 1946–1967: Documents and Commentary*. London: Oxford University Press.

International Peacekeeping, published quarterly, since 1994.

Ramsbotham, Oliver, and Tom Woodhouse. 1999. *Encyclopedia of International Peacekeeping Operations*. Santa Barbara, Calif.: ABC-CLIO.

Ruggie, John Gerard. 1993. *The United Nations Stuck in a Fog Between Peacekeeping and Peace Enforcement*, McNair Paper 25. Washington, DC: National Defense University.

20. *Sanctions*

Baldwin, David. 1985. *Economic Statecraft*. Princeton, NJ: Princeton University Press.

Brzoska, Michael, ed. 2001. *Design and Implementation of the Arms Embargoes and Travel and Aviation Related Sanctions: Results of the 'Bonn-Berlin Process.'* Bonn: Bonn International Center for Conversion.

Conlon, Paul. 2000. *United Nations Sanctions Management: A Case Study of the Iraq Sanctions Committee, 1990–1994*. Ardsley, NY: Transnational Publishers.

Cortright, David, and George A. Lopez, eds. 2002. *Smart Sanctions: Targeting Economic Statecraft*. Lanham, Md.: Rowman & Littlefield.

Cortright, David, and George A. Lopez, eds. 2000. *The Sanctions Decade: Assessing UN Strategies in the 1990s*. Boulder, Colo.: Lynne Rienner.

Doxey, Margaret P. 1987. *International Sanctions in Contemporary Perspective*. New York: St. Martin's Press.

Growlland-Debbas, Vera, ed. 2001. *United Nations Sanctions and International Law*. The Hague: Kluwer Law International.

Hufbauer, Gary C., Jeffrey J. Schott, and Kimberly A. Elliott. 1990. *Economic Sanctions Reconsidered: History and Current Policy*. 2nd edn. Washington, DC: Institute for International Economics.

Martin, Lisa. 1992. *Coercive Cooperation: Explaining Multilateral Economic Sanctions*. Princeton, NJ: Princeton University Press.

Wallensteen, Peter, and C. Staibano, eds. 2005. *International Sanctions: Between Words and Wars in the Global System*. New York: Frank Cass.

—— —— and Mikael Eriksson, eds. 2003. *Making Targeted Sanctions Effective: Guidelines for the Implementation of UN Policy Options*. Uppsala, Sweden: Department of Peace and Conflict Research, Uppsala University.

21. *Peace Enforcement*

Adebajo, Adekeye, and Chandra L. Sriram, eds. 2001. *Managing Armed Conflicts in the 21st Century*. London: Frank Cass.

Bellamy, Alex J., and Paul Williams, eds. 2004. *Peace Operations and Global Order*. London: Frank Cass.

Dallaire, Roméo A. 2003. *Shake Hands with the Devil. The Failure of Humanity in Rwanda*. Toronto: Random House.

Debrix, François. 1997. *(Re)Envisioning Peacekeeping: The United Nations and the Mobilization of Ideology*. Minneapolis: University of Minnesota Press Borderlines Series.

Holt, Victoria K., and Tobias C. Berkman, 2007. *The Impossible Mandate? Military Preparedness, the Responsibility to Protect, and Modern Peace Operations*. Washington, D.C.: The Henry L. Stimson Center.

Huldt, Bo, Annika Hilding, and Arita Eriksson. 1998. *Challenges of Peace Support into the 21st Century*. Stockholm: Försvarshögskolans ACTA B9, Strategic Institute, Swedish National Defence College.

Malone, David M. 2006. *The International Struggle over Iraq: Politics and the UN Security Council 1980–2005*. Oxford: Oxford University Press.

Sarooshi, Danesh. 1999. *The United Nations and the Development of Collective Security: The Delegation by the Security Council of its Chapter VII Powers*. Oxford: Clarendon University Press.

22. *Humanitarian Intervention*

Annan, Kofi A. 1999. *The Question of Intervention: Statements by the Secretary-General*. New York: United Nations Department of Public Information.

Chesterman, Simon. 2001. *Just War? Just Peace? Humanitarian Intervention and International Law*. Oxford: Oxford University Press.

Crawford, Neta. 2002. *Argument and Change in World Politics: Ethics, Decolonization and Humanitarian Intervention*. New York: Cambridge University Press.

International Commission on Intervention and State Sovereignty. 2001. *The Responsibility to Protect*. Ottawa: ICISS.

Lepard, Brian D. 2002. *Rethinking Humanitarian Intervention*. University Park: Pennsylvania State University Press.

Moore, Jonathan, ed. 1998. *Hard Choices: Moral Dilemmas in Humanitarian Intervention*. Lanham, Md.: Rowman & Littlefield Publishers.

Murphy, Sean D. 1996. *Humanitarian Intervention: The United Nations in an Evolving World Order*. Philadelphia: University of Pennsylvania Press.

Tesón Fernando. 2005. *Humanitarian Intervention: An Inquiry into Law and Morality*. 3rd edn. Ardsley, NY: Transaction Publishers.

Thakur, Ramesh. 2006. *The United Nations, Peace and Security: From Collective Security to the Responsibility to Protect*. Cambridge: Cambridge University Press.

Weiss, Thomas G. 2007. *Humanitarian Intervention: Ideas in Action*. Cambridge: Polity Press.

—— 2005. *Military–Civilian Interactions: Humanitarian Crises and the Responsibility to Protect*. Lanham, Md.: Rowman & Littlefield.

—— and Don Hubert. 2001. *The Responsibility to Protect: Research, Bibliography, and Background*. Ottawa: International Development Research Centre.

Welsh, Jennifer M., ed. 2004. *Humanitarian Intervention and International Relations*. Oxford: Oxford University Press.

Wheeler, Nicholas J. 2000. *Saving Strangers: Humanitarian Intervention in International Society*. Oxford: Oxford University Press.

23. *Post-Conflict Peacebuilding*

Berger, Mark T., ed. 2006. *From Nation-Building to State-Building*. Special issue of *Third World Quarterly* 27, no 1.

Call, Charles T., with Vanessa Hawkins Wyeth, eds. 2006 forthcoming. *Building States to Build Peace*. Boulder, Colo.: Lynne Rienner.

Caplan, Richard. 2005. *International Governance of War-Torn Territories: Rule and Reconstruction*. New York: Oxford University Press.

Chesterman, Simon, ed. 2004. *Civilians in War*. Boulder, Colo.: Lynne Rienner.

—— 2004. *You, the People: The United Nations, Transitional Administration, and Statebuilding*. New York: Oxford University Press.

—— Michael Ignatieff, and Ramesh Thakur, eds. 2005. *State Failure and the Crisis of Governance: Making States Work*. Tokyo: UN University Press.

Collier, Paul, Lance Elliot, Håvard Hegre, Anke Hoeffler, Marta Reynal-Querol, and N. Sambanis. 2003. *Breaking the Conflict Trap: Civil War and Development Policy*. Washington, DC: World Bank.

Cousens, Elizabeth M., Krishna Kumar, and Karin Wermester, eds. 2000. *Peacebuilding as Politics*. Boulder, Colo.: Lynne Rienner.

Dobbins, James, et al. 2005. *The UN's Role in Nation Building: From the Congo to Iraq*. Santa Monica, Calif.: RAND Corporation.

Donini, Antonio, Norah Niland, and Karen Wermester. 2004. *Nation-Building Unraveled? Aid, Peace and Justice in Afghanistan*. Bloomfield, Conn.: Kumarian.

Forman, Shepard, and Stewart Patrick, eds. 2000. *Good Intentions: Pledges of Aid for Postconflict Recovery*. Boulder, Colo.: Lynne Rienner.

Hoffman, Peter J., and Thomas G. Weiss. 2006. *Sword & Salve: Confronting New Wars and Humanitarian Crises*. Lanham, Md.: Rowman & Littlefield.

Jeong, Ho-Won. 2005. *Peacebuilding in Postconflict Societies*. Boulder, Colo.: Lynne Rienner.

Keating, Tom, and W. Andy Knight, eds. 2004. *Building Sustainable Peace*. Tokyo: United Nations University Press.

Kumar, Krishna, ed. 1997. *Rebuilding Societies after Civil War: Critical Roles for International Assistance*. Boulder, Colo.: Lynne Rienner.

Paris, Roland. 2004. *At War's End: Building Peace After Civil Conflict*. Cambridge: Cambridge University Press.

Roeder, Philip, and Donald Rothchild, eds. 2005. *Sustainable Peace: Power and Deomcracy after Civil Wars*. Ithaca, NY: Cornell University Press.

Stedman, Stephen John, Donald Rothchild, and Elizabeth M. Cousens, eds. 2002. *Ending Civil Wars: The Implementation of Peace Agreements*. Boulder, Colo.: Lynne Rienner Publishers.

Stiefel, Mattias. 1999. *Rebuilding After War: Lessons From WSP*. Geneva: War-torn Societies Project.

Tschirgi, Neclâ. 2004. *Post-Conflict Peacebuilding Revisited: Achievements, Limitations, Challenges*. New York: International Peace Academy.

24. *Terrorism*

Boulden Jane, and Thomas G. Weiss, eds. 2003. *The UN and Terrorism: Before and After September 11.* Bloomington: Indiana University Press.

Cortright, David, George A. Lopez, Alistair Miller, and Linda Gerber. 2004. *An Action Agenda for Enhancing the United Nations Program on Counter-Terrorism.* Goshen, Ind.: Fourth Freedom Forum.

Crenshaw, Martha, ed. 1983. *Terrorism, Legitimacy, and Power: The Consequences of Political Violence.* Middletown, Conn.: Wesleyan University Press.

O'Sullivan, Meghan. 2003. *Shrewd Sanctions: Statecraft and State Sponsors of Terrorism.* Washington, DC: Brookings Institution Press.

Talbott, Strobe, and Nayan Chanda, eds. *An Age of Terror: America and the World After September 11.* New York: Basic Books.

Wilkinson, Paul. 2000. *Terrorism versus Democracy: The Liberal State Response.* London: Frank Cass.

Part VI: Human Rights

25. *Norms and Machinery*

Alston, Philip, and Frederic Megret, eds. 2005. *The United Nations and Human Rights: A Critical Appraisal.* 2nd edn. Oxford: Oxford University Press.

Bailey, Sydney D. 1994. *The UN Security Council and Human Rights.* New York: St. Martin's Press.

Coicaud, Jean-Marc, Michael W. Doyle, and Anne-Marie Gardner, eds. 2003. T*he Globalization of Human Rights: The United Nations System in the Twenty-first Century.* Tokyo: United Nations University Press.

Donnelly, Jack. 1989. *Universal Human Rights in Theory and Practice.* Ithaca, NY: Cornell University Press.

Dunne, Tim, and Nicholas J. Wheeler, eds. 1999. *Human Rights in Global Politics.* Cambridge: Cambridge University Press.

Falk, Richard. 2000. *Human Rights Horizons: Tthe Pursuit of Justice in a Globalizing World.* New York: Routledge.

Lauren, Paul Gordon. 2003. *The Evolution of International Human Rights: Visions Seen.* Philadelphia: University of Pennsylvania Press.

Mertus, Julie. 2005. *The United Nations and Human Rights: A Guide for a New Era.* London: Routledge.

Ramcharan, Bertrand G. 2002. *The UN High Commissioner for Human Rights: The Challenges of International Protection.* Leiden: Martinus Nijhoff.

——— ed. 2006. *Human Rights Protection in the Field.* Leiden: Martinus Nijhoff.

Risse, Thomas, Stephen C. Ropp, and Kathryn Sikkink, eds. 1999. *The Power of Human Rights: International Norms and Domestic Change.* Cambridge: Cambridge University Press.

Steiner, Henry and Philip Alston, eds. 2000. *International Human Rights in Context: Law, Politics, Morals.* 2nd edn. Oxford: Oxford University Press.

Tomuschat, Christian. 2003. *Human Rights: Between Idealism and Realism.* New York: Oxford University Press.

Zaidi, Sarah, and Roger Norman. 2007 (forthcoming). *Human Rights Ideas at the United Nations: The Political History of Universal Justice.* Bloomington: Indiana University Press.

26. *International Criminal Court and Ad Hoc Tribunals*

Bass, Gary Jonathan. 2000. *Stay the Hand of Vengeance: The Politics of War Crimes Tribunals.* Princeton, NJ: Princeton University Press.

Bouchet-Saulnier, Françoise. 2002. *The Practical Guide to Humanitarian Law*. Lanham, Md.: Rowman & Littlefield.

Broomhall, Bruce. 2003. *International Justice & The International Criminal Court; Between Sovereignty & the Rule of Law*. Oxford: Oxford University Press.

Macedo, Stephen, ed. 2001. *The Princeton Principles on Universal Jurisdiction*. Princeton, NJ: Princeton University Press.

Minow, Martha. 1998. *Between Vengeance and Forgiveness: Facing History after Genocide and Mass Violence*. Boston: Beacon Press.

Ratner, Steven R., and James L. Bischoff, eds. 2004. *International War Crimes Trials: Making a Difference?* Austin: University of Texas Law School.

Roberts, Adam, and Richard Guelff, eds. 2000. *Documents on the Laws of War*. 3rd edn. Oxford: Oxford University Press.

Stover, Eric and Harvey M. Weinstein, eds. 2004. *My Neighbor, My Enemy: Justice and Community in the Aftermath of Mass Atrocity*. New York: Cambridge University Press.

27. *Humanitarian Action and Coordination*

Barnett, Michael, and Thomas G. Weiss, eds. 2008 (forthcoming). *Humanitarianism in Question: Politics, Power, Ethics*. Ithaca, NY: Cornell University Press.

Byers, Michael. 2005. *War Law: Understanding International Law and Armed Conflict*. New York: Grove Press.

Cronin, Bruce. 2003. *Institutions for the Common Good: International Protection Regimes in International Society*. Cambridge: Cambridge University Press.

Forsythe, David P. 2005. *The Humanitarians: The International Committee of the Red Cross*. Cambridge: Cambridge University Press.

Helton, Arthur. 2002. *The Price of Indifference: Refugees and Humanitarian Action in the New Century*. New York: Oxford University Press.

Kennedy, David. 2004. *The Dark Sides of Virtue: Reassessing International Humanitarianism*. Princeton, NJ: Princeton University Press.

Loescher, Gil. 2001. *The UNHCR and World Politics: A Perilous Path*. Oxford: Oxford University Press.

Minear, Larry. 2002. *The Humanitarian Enterprise: Dilemmas & Discoveries*. Bloomfield, Conn.: Kumarian.

Office for the Coordination of Humanitarian Affairs. 2004. *The Humanitarian Decade: Challenges for Humanitarian Assistance in the Last Decade and into the Future*. 2 vols. New York: UN.

Rieff, David. 2002. *A Bed for the Night: Humanitarianism in Crisis*. New York: Simon & Schuster.

Smillie, Ian, and Larry Minear. 2004. *The Charity of Nations: Humanitarian Action in a Changing World*. Bloomfield, Conn.: Kumarian.

Terry, Fiona. 2002. *Condemned to Repeat? The Paradox of Humanitarian Action*. Ithaca, NY: Cornell University Press.

UNHCR. *The State of the World's Refugees*. Oxford: Oxford University Press, published in 1993, 1995, and 2000.

Weiss, Thomas G., and David A. Korn. 2006. *Internal Displacement: Conceptualization and its Consequences*. London: Routledge.

28. *Women and Gender*

Antrobus, Peggy. 2004. *The Global Women's Movement: Origins, Issues and Strategies*. London: Zed Books.

Basu, Amrita. 1995. *The Challenge of Local Feminisms: Women's Movements in Global Perspectives.* Boulder, Colo.: Westview Press.

Center for the Study of Human Rights. 1996. *Women and Human Rights: The Basic Documents.* New York: Columbia University Press.

Jain, Devaki. 2005. *Women, Development, and the United Nations: A Sixty-Year Quest for Equality and Justice.* Bloomington: Indiana University Press.

Meillon, Cynthia, with Charlotte Bunch. 2001. *Holding On to the Promise: Women's Human Rights and the Beijing +5 Review.* New Brunswick, NJ: Center for Women's Global Leadership.

Petchesky, Rosalind. 2003. *Global Prescriptions: Gendering Health and Human Rights.* London: Zed Books.

Peterson, V. Spike, and A. Sisson Runyan. 1993. *Global Gender Issues.* Boulder, Colo.: Westview.

Pietila, Hilkka. 2002. *Engendering the Global Agenda: The Story of Women and the United Nations.* New York: UN Non-governmental Liaison Service.

Sajor, Indai Lourdes, ed. 1998. *Common Grounds: Violence Against Women in War and Armed Conflict Situations.* Quezon City, Phillippines: ASCENT.

United Nations. 2003. *Women Go Global: The United Nations and the International Women's Movement, 1945–2000.* New York: UN. CD-ROM developed in collaboration with the National Council for Research on Women.

Winslow, Anne, ed. 1995. *Women, Politics, and the United Nations.* Westport, Conn.: Praeger.

29. *Children*

Beigbeder, Yves. 2001. *New Challenges for UNICEF: Children, Women and Human Rights.* Houndmills, Basingtoke, UK: Palgrave.

Brett, Rachel, and Irma Specht. 2004. *Young Soldiers: Why They Choose to Fight.* Boulder, Colo.: Lynne Rienner Publishers.

Hampson, F. J. 1990. *Legal Protection Afforded to Children Under International Humanitarian Law.* Colchester, UK: University of Essex.

Himes, James R., ed. 1995. *Implementing the Convention on the Rights of the Child, Resource Mobilization in Low-Income Countries.* The Hague: Martinus Nijhoff.

Levesque, Roger. 1999. *Sexual Abuse of Children: A Human Rights Perspective.* Bloomington: University of Indiana Press.

Machel, Graça. 2001. *The Impact of War On Children.* New York: Palgrave.

Singer, P. W. 2005. *Children at War.* New York: Pantheon.

UNICEF. *The State of the World's Children.* New York: UNICEF, published annually, since 1980.

30. *Minorities and Indigenous Peoples*

Aikio, Pekka, and Martin Scheini, eds. 2000. *Operationalizing the Right of Indigenous Peoples to Self-Determination.* Turku: Abo Akademi University Institute for Human Rights.

Anaya, S. James. 2004. *Indigenous Peoples and International Law.* New York: Oxford University Press.

Cohen, Cynthia Price, ed. 1998. *Human Rights of Indigenous Peoples.* Ardsley, NY: Transnational Publishers.

Crawford, James, ed. 1988. *The Rights of Peoples.* Oxford: Oxford University Press.

Dean, Bartholomew, and Jerome M. Levi, eds. 2003. *At the Risk of Being Heard: Identity, Indigenous Rights, and Postcolonial States.* Ann Arbor: University of Michigan Press.

Jentoft, Svein, Henry Minde, and Ragnar Nilsen, eds. 2003. *Indigenous Peoples: Resource Management and Global Rights.* Delft: Eburon Academic Publishers.

Kymlicka, Will, ed. 1995. *The Rights of Minority Cultures.* Oxford: Oxford University Press.

Lâm, Maivân Clech. 2000. *At the Edge of the State: Indigenous Peoples and Self-Determination.* Ardsley, NY: Transnational Publishers.

Minority Rights Group International. 1997. *World Directory of Minorities.* London: Minority Rights Group International.

Niezen, Ronald. 2003. *The Origins of Indigenism: Human Rights and the Politics of Identity.* Berkeley: University of California Press.

Rajan, Nalini. 2000. *Democracy and the Limits of Minority Rights.* New York: Russell Sage Foundation.

Redgwell, Catherine. 1999. *Intergenerational Trusts and Environmental Protection.* Manchester: Manchester University Press.

Thornberry, Patrick. 2002. *Indigenous Peoples and Human Rights.* Manchester: Manchester University Press.

31. *Human Security*

Commission on Human Security. 2003. *Human Security Now.* New York: Commission on Human Security.

Hampson, Fen Osler, with contributions by others. 2002. *Madness in the Multitude: Human Security and World Disorder.* Toronto: Oxford University Press.

MacFarlane, S. Neil, and Yuen Foong-Khong. 2006. *Human Security and the UN: A Critical History.* Bloomington: Indiana University Press.

Mack, Andrew, and others. 2005. *Human Security Report 2005: War and Peace in the 21st Century.* Oxford: Oxford University Press.

McRae, Rob, and Don Hubert, eds. 2001. *Human Security and the New Diplomacy.* Montreal: McGill-Queen's University Press.

Neack, Laura. 2007. *Elusive Security: States First, People Last.* Lanham, Md.: Rowman & Littlefield.

Newman, Edward, and Ramesh Thakur, eds. 2001. *The United Nations and Human Security.* London: Palgrave.

Part VII: Development

32. *Coordinating Economic and Social Affairs*

Alger, Chadwick F. 2006. The *United Nations System: A Reference Handbook.* Santa Barbara, Calif.: ABC-CLIO.

Childers, Erskine, and Brian Urquhart. 1994. *Renewing the United Nations System.* Uppsala, Sweden: Dag Hammarskjöld Foundation.

Glassner, Martin Ira, ed. 1998. *The United Nations at Work.* Westport, Conn.: Praeger.

Hill, Martin. 1978. *The United Nations System: Coordinating Its Economic and Social Work.* Cambridge: Cambridge University Press.

Muldoon, James P., Jr. and others, eds. 1999. *Multilateral Diplomacy and the United Nations Today.* Boulder, Colo.: Westview.

Murphy, Craig N. 2006. *The United Nations Development Programme: A Better Way?* Cambridge: Cambridge University Press.

Nordic UN Reform Project. 1991. *The United Nations in Development: Reform Issues in the Economic and Social Fields: A Nordic perspective: Final Report.* Stockholm: Almqvist & Wiksell International.

Roberts, Adam, and Benedict Kingsbury, eds. 1993. *United Nations: Divided World.* 2nd edn. Oxford: Oxford University Press.

South Centre. 1992. *The Economic Role of the United Nations.* Geneva: The South Centre.

United Nations High-level Panel on UN System-Wide Coherence in the Areas of Development, Humanitarian Assistance, and the Environment. 2006. *Delivering as One*. New York: UN.

Ward, Michael. 2004. *Quantifying the World: UN Contributions to Statistics*. Bloomington: Indiana University Press.

Weiss, Thomas G., David P. Forsythe, Roger A. Coate, and Kelly-Kate Pease. 2007. *The United Nations and Changing World Politics*. 5th edn. Boulder, Colo.: Westview.

Williams, Douglas. 1987. *The Specialized Agencies and the United Nations: The System in Crisis*. New York: St. Martin's Press.

33. *Health and Infectious Disease*

Burci, Gian Luca, and Claude-Henri Vignes. 2004. *World Health Organization*. The Hague: Kluwer Law International.

Fidler, David. 1999. *International Law and Infectious Diseases*. Oxford: Oxford University Press.

Gordenker, Leon, and Roger A. Coate, Christer Jönsson, and Peter Söderholm. 1995. *International Cooperation in Response to AIDS*. London: Pinter.

34. *Natural Resource Management and Sustainable Development*

Axelrod, Regina S., David Leonard Downie, and Norman J. Vig, eds. 2005. *The Global Environment: Institutions, Law and Policy*. Washington, DC: CQ Press.

Biermann, Frank, and Steffen Bauer, ed. 2005. *A World Environment Organization*. Aldershot, UK: Ashgate.

Chambers, Bradnee W., and Jessica F. Green, eds. 2005. *Reforming International Environmental Governance: From Institutional Limits to Innovative Reforms*. Tokyo: United Nations University Press.

Chasek Pamela S. 2001. *Earth Negotiations: Analyzing Thirty Years of Environmental Diplomacy*. Tokyo, New York, and Paris: United Nations University Press.

——— David L. Downie, and Janet Welsh Brown. 2006. *Global Environmental Politics*, 4th edn. Boulder, Colo: Westview Press.

DeSombre, Elizabeth R. 2006. *Global Environmental Institutions*. London: Routledge.

Haas, Peter M., Robert O. Keohane, and Marc A. Levy, eds. 1993. *Institutions for the Earth: Sources of Effective International Environmental Protection*. Cambridge, Mass.: MIT Press.

Rosenne, Shabtai. 2005. *Provisional Measures in International Law: The International Court of Justice and the International Tribunal for the Law of the Sea*. Oxford: Oxford University Press.

Schrijver, Nico. 2008 (forthcoming). *The UN and the Global Commons: Development Without Destruction*. Bloomington, Ind.: Indiana University Press.

Tolba, Mostafa K., with Iwona Rummel-Bulska. 1998. *Global Environmental Diplomacy: Negotiating Environmental Agreements for the World, 1973–1992*. Cambridge, Mass: MIT Press.

Weiss, Edith Brown, ed. 1992. *Environmental Change and International Law: New Challenges and Dimensions*. Tokyo: UN University Press.

World Commission on Environment and Development. 1987. *Our Common Future*. Oxford: Oxford University Press.

35. *Organized Crime*

Findlay, Mark. 1999. *The Globalisation of Crime*. Cambridge: Cambridge University Press.

Naylor, Robin Thomas. 2002. *Wages of Crime: Black Markets, Illegal Finance, and the Underworld Economy*. Ithaca, NY: Cornell University Press.

Simpson, Sally. 2002. *Corporate Crime, Law and Social Control*. Cambridge: Cambridge University Press.

Sterling, Claire. 1994. *Thieves' World: The Threat of the New Global Network of Organized Crime*. New York: Simon and Schuster.

UN Office on Drugs and Crime. *World Drug Report*. New York: United Nations, published annually.

36. *Democracy and Good Governance*

Aksu, Esref, and Joseph A. Camilleri. 2002. *Democratizing Global Governance*. Houndmills, Basingstoke, UK: Palgrave Macmillan.

Diamond, Larry. 1995. *Promoting Democracy in the 1990s: Actors and Instruments, Issues and Imperatives*. Washington, DC: Carnegie Corporation.

Freedom House. *Freedom in the World: The Annual Survey of Political Rights and Civil Liberties*. New York: Freedom House.

Huntington, Samuel P. 1991. *The Third Wave: Democratization in the Late Twentieth Century*. Norman: University of Oklahoma Press.

Zakaria, Fareed. 2003. *The Future of Freedom: Illiberal Democracy at Home and Abroad*. New York: W. W. Norton.

37. *Human Development*

Emmerij, Louis, Richard Jolly, and Thomas G. Weiss. 2001. *Ahead of the Curve? UN Ideas and Global Challenges*. Bloomington: Indiana University Press.

Fukada-Parr, Sakiko, and A. K. Shiva Kumar, eds. 2003. *Readings in Human Development*. Oxford: Oxford University Press.

Journal of Human Development: Alternative Economics in Action, published three times a year since 2000.

Sachs, Jeffrey D. 2006. *The End of Poverty: Economic Possibilities for Our Time*. New York: Penguin.

Sen, Amartya. 1999. *Development as Freedom*. Oxford: Oxford University Press.

UNDP. *Human Development Report*. New York: Oxford University Press, published annually, since 1990.

Weiss, Thomas G., Tatiana Carayannis, Louis Emmerij, and Richard Jolly. 2005. *UN Voices: The Struggle for Development and Social Justice*. Bloomington, Ind.: Indiana University Press.

Part VIII: Prospects for Reform

38. *Principal Organs*

Annan, Kofi A. 2000. *'We the Peoples': The Role of the United Nations in the 21st Century*. New York: UN.

—— 2005. *In Larger Freedom: Towards Development, Security and Human Rights for All*. New York: UN.

Fassbender, Bardo. 1998. *UN Security Council Reform and the Right of Veto: A Constitutional Perspective*. The Hague: Kluwer Law International.

Fawcett, Eric, and Hanna Newcombe, eds. 1995. *United Nations Reform: Looking Ahead after Fifty Years*. Toronto: University of Toronto Press.

Heinbecker, Paul, and Patricia Goff, eds. 2005. *Irrelevant or Indispensable? The United Nations in the 21st Century*. Waterloo, Ontario: Wilfred Laurier University Press.

High-level Panel on Threats, Challenges and Change. 2004. *A More Secure World: Our Shared Responsibility*. New York: UN.

Luck, Edward C. 2003. *Reforming the United Nations: Lessons from a History in Progress*, Occasional Paper 1. New Haven, Conn.: The Academic Council on the United Nations System.

39. *Financing*

Haq, Mahbub ul, and Inge Kaul, with Isabelle Grunberg. 1996. *The Tobin Tax: Coping with Financial Volatility*. Oxford: Oxford University Press.

Kanninen, Tapio. 1995. *Leadership and Reform: The Secretary-General and the UN Financial Crisis of the Late 1980s*. London: Kluwer Law International.

Laurenti, Jeffrey. 2001. *Financing the United Nations*. New Haven, Conn.: Academic Council on the UN System.

McDermott, Anthony. 1994. *United Nations Financing Problems and the New Generation of Peacekeeping and Peace Enforcement*. Providence, RI: Watson Institute.

Ogata, Shijuro, and Paul Volcker. 1993. *Financing an Effective United Nations*. New York, Ford Foundation.

40. *Widening Participation*

Alger, Chadwick F., ed. 1998. *The Future of the United Nations System: Potential for the Twenty-first Century*. Tokyo: United Nations University Press.

Chadwick, Andrew. 2006. *Internet Politics: States, Citizens, and New Communications Techologies*. New York: Oxford University Press.

Commission on Global Governance. 1995. *Our Global Neighbourhood*. Oxford: Oxford University Press.

Dijkzeul, Dennis, and Yves Beigbeder. 2003. *Rethinking International Organizations*. New York: Berghahn Books.

Edwards, Michael. 2000. *Future Positive: International Co-operation in the 21st Century*. London: Earthscan.

Held, David, and Anthony McGrew, with David Goldblatt and Jonathan Perraton. 1999. *Global Transformations: Politics, Economics, and Culture*. Stanford: Stanford University Press.

Jacobson, Harold K. 1979. *Networks of Interdependence: International Organizations and the Global Political System*. New York: McGraw-Hill.

Newman, Edward, Ramesh Thakur, and John Tirman. 2006. *Multilateralism Under Challenge? Power, International Order, and Structural Change*. Tokyo: United Nations University Press.

Slaughter, Anne-Marie. 2004. *A New World Order*. Princeton, NJ: Princeton University Press.

Thakur, Ramesh, and Thomas G. Weiss. 2008 (forthcoming). *The UN and Global Governance: An Idea and its Prospects*. Bloomington: Indiana University Press.

The United Nations System

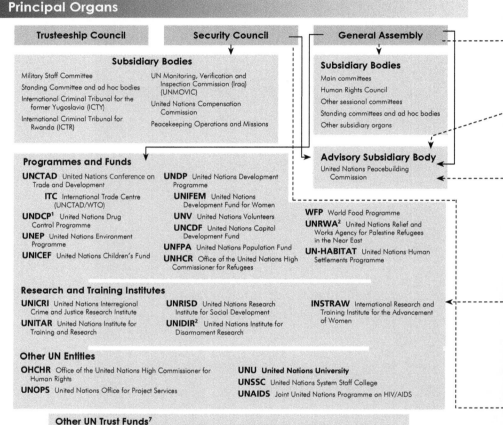

Principal Organs

Trusteeship Council

Security Council

General Assembly

Subsidiary Bodies

Military Staff Committee

Standing Committee and ad hoc bodies

International Criminal Tribunal for the former Yugoslavia (ICTY)

International Criminal Tribunal for Rwanda (ICTR)

UN Monitoring, Verification and Inspection Commission (Iraq) (UNMOVIC)

United Nations Compensation Commission

Peacekeeping Operations and Missions

Subsidiary Bodies

Main committees

Human Rights Council

Other sessional committees

Standing committees and ad hoc bodies

Other subsidiary organs

Programmes and Funds

UNCTAD United Nations Conference on Trade and Development

　　ITC International Trade Centre (UNCTAD/WTO)

UNDCP[1] United Nations Drug Control Programme

UNEP United Nations Environment Programme

UNICEF United Nations Children's Fund

UNDP United Nations Development Programme

　　UNIFEM United Nations Development Fund for Women

　　UNV United Nations Volunteers

　　UNCDF United Nations Capital Development Fund

UNFPA United Nations Population Fund

UNHCR Office of the United Nations High Commissioner for Refugees

Advisory Subsidiary Body

United Nations Peacebuilding Commission

WFP World Food Programme

UNRWA[2] United Nations Relief and Works Agency for Palestine Refugees in the Near East

UN-HABITAT United Nations Human Settlements Programme

Research and Training Institutes

UNICRI United Nations Interregional Crime and Justice Research Institute

UNITAR United Nations Institute for Training and Research

UNRISD United Nations Research Institute for Social Development

UNIDIR[2] United Nations Institute for Disarmament Research

INSTRAW International Research and Training Institute for the Advancement of Women

Other UN Entities

OHCHR Office of the United Nations High Commissioner for Human Rights

UNOPS United Nations Office for Project Services

UNU United Nations University

UNSSC United Nations System Staff College

UNAIDS Joint United Nations Programme on HIV/AIDS

Other UN Trust Funds[7]

UNFIP United Nations Fund for International Partnerships

UNDEF United Nations Democracy Fund

NOTES: Solid lines from a Principal Organ indicate a direct reporting relationship; dashes indicate a non-subsidiary relationship.
1 The UN Drug Control Programme is part of the UN Office on Drugs and Crime
2 UNRWA and UNIDIR report only to the GA
3 The United Nations Ethics Office and the United Nations Ombudsman's Office report directly to the Secretary-General
4 IAEA reports to the Security Council and the General Assembly (GA)
5 The CTBTO Prep.Com and OPCW report to the GA
6 Specialized agencies are autonomous organizations working with the UN and each other through the coordinating machinery of the ECOSOC at the intergovernmental level, and through the Chief Executives Board for coordination (CEB) at the inter-secretariat level
7 UNFIP is an autonomous trust fund operating under the leadership of the United Nations Deputy Secretary-General. UNDEF's advisory board recommends funding proposals for approval by the Secretary-General.

Economic and Social Council

International Court of Justice

Secretariat

Functional Commissions

Commissions on:
 Narcotic Drugs
 Crime Prevention and Criminal Justice
 Science and Technology for
  Development
 Sustainable Development
 Status of Women
 Population and Development
Commission for Social Development
Statistical Commission

Regional Commissions

Economic Commission for Africa (ECA)

Economic Commission for Europe (ECE)

Economic Commission for Latin
 America and the Caribbean (ECLAC)

Economic and Social Commission for
 Asia and the Pacific (ESCAP)

Economic and Social Commission for
 Western Asia (ESCWA)

Other Bodies

Permanent Forum on Indigenous Issues
 (PFII)

United Nations Forum on Forests

Sessional and standing committees

Expert, ad hoc and related bodies

Related Organizations

WTO World Trade Organization

IAEA[4] International Atomic Energy
 Agency

CTBTO Prep.Com[5] PrepCom for the
 Nuclear-Test-Ban-Treaty Organization

OPCW[5] Organization for the
 Prohibition of Chemical Weapons

Specialized Agencies[6]

ILO International Labour
 Organization

FAO Food and Agriculture
 Organization of the United Nations

UNESCO United Nations
 Educational, Scientific and Cultural
 Organization

WHO World Health Organization

World Bank Group

IBRD International Bank
 for Reconstruction and
 Development

IDA International Development
 Association

IFC International Finance
 Corporation

MIGA Multilateral Investment
 Guarantee Agency

ICSID International Centre for
 Settlement of Investment
 Disputes

IMF International Monetary Fund

ICAO International Civil Aviation
 Organization

IMO International Maritime
 Organization

ITU International Telecommunication
 Union

UPU Universal Postal Union

WMO World Meteorological
 Organization

WIPO World Intellectual Property
 Organization

IFAD International Fund for
 Agricultural Development

UNIDO United Nations Industrial
 Development Organization

UNWTO World Tourism
 Organization

Departments and Offices

OSG[3] Office of the
 Secretary-General

OIOS Office of Internal Oversight
 Services

OLA Office of Legal Affairs

DPA Department of Political Affairs

DDA Department for Disarmament
 Affairs

DPKO Department of Peacekeeping
 Operations

OCHA Office for the Coordination of
 Humanitarian Affairs

DESA Department of Economic and
 Social Affairs

DGACM Department for General
 Assembly and Conference
 Management

DPI Department of Public Information

DM Department of Management

OHRLLS Office of the High
 Representative for the Least
 Developed Countries, Landlocked
 Developing Countries and Small
 Island Developing States

DSS Department of Safety and
 Security

UNODC United Nations Office on
 Drugs and Crime

UNO UN Office at Geneva

UNOV UN Office at Vienna

UNON UN Office at Nairobi

August 2006

APPENDIX 3: THE CHARTER OF THE UNITED NATIONS

Preamble

WE THE PEOPLES OF THE UNITED NATIONS DETERMINED

to save succeeding generations from the scourge of war, which twice in our lifetime has brought untold sorrow to mankind, and

to reaffirm faith in fundamental human rights, in the dignity and worth of the human person, in the equal rights of men and women and of nations large and small, and

to establish conditions under which justice and respect for the obligations arising from treaties and other sources of international law can be maintained, and
to promote social progress and better standards of life in larger freedom,

AND FOR THESE ENDS

to practice tolerance and live together in peace with one another as good neighbors, and
to unite our strength to maintain international peace and security, and

to ensure by the acceptance of principles and the institution of methods, that armed force shall not be used, save in the common interest, and

to employ international machinery for the promotion of the economic and social advancement of all peoples,

HAVE RESOLVED TO COMBINE OUR EFFORTS TO ACCOMPLISH THESE AIMS

Accordingly, our respective Governments, through representatives assembled in the city of San Francisco, who have exhibited their full powers found to be in good and due form, have agreed to the present Charter of the United Nations and do hereby establish an international organization to be known as the United Nations.

Chapter I. Purposes and Principles

ARTICLE 1

The Purposes of the United Nations are:

1. To maintain international peace and security, and to that end: to take effective collective measures for the prevention and removal of threats to the peace, and for the suppression of acts of aggression or other breaches of the peace, and to bring about by peaceful means, and in conformity with the principles of justice and international law, adjustment or settlement of international disputes or situations which might lead to a breach of the peace;
2. To develop friendly relations among nations based on respect for the principle of equal rights and self-determination of peoples, and to take other appropriate measures to strengthen universal peace;
3. To achieve international co-operation in solving international problems of an economic, social, cultural, or humanitarian character, and in promoting and encouraging respect for

human rights and for fundamental freedoms for all without distinction as to race, sex, language, or religion; and

4. To be a center for harmonizing the actions of nations in the attainment of these common ends.

ARTICLE 2

The Organization and its Members, in pursuit of the Purposes stated in Article 1, shall act in accordance with the following Principles.

1. The Organization is based on the principle of the sovereign equality of all its Members.
2. All Members, in order to ensure to all of them the rights and benefits resulting from membership, shall fulfill in good faith the obligations assumed by them in accordance with the present Charter.
3. All Members shall settle their international disputes by peaceful means in such a manner that international peace and security, and justice, are not endangered.
4. All Members shall refrain in their international relations from the threat or use of force against the territorial integrity or political independence of any state, or in any other manner inconsistent with the Purposes of the United Nations.
5. All Members shall give the United Nations every assistance in any action it takes in accordance with the present Charter, and shall refrain from giving assistance to any state against which the United Nations is taking preventive or enforcement action.
6. The Organization shall ensure that states which are not Members of the United Nations act in accordance with these Principles so far as may be necessary for the maintenance of international peace and security.
7. Nothing contained in the present Charter shall authorize the United Nations to intervene in matters which are essentially within the domestic jurisdiction of any state or shall require the Members to submit such matters to settlement under the present Charter; but this principle shall not prejudice the application of enforcement measures under Chapter VII.

Chapter II. Membership

ARTICLE 3

The original Members of the United Nations shall be the states which, having participated in the United Nations Conference on International Organization at San Francisco, or having previously signed the Declaration by United Nations of 1 January 1942, sign the present Charter and ratify it in accordance with Article 110.

ARTICLE 4

1. Membership in the United Nations is open to all other peace-loving states which accept the obligations contained in the present Charter and, in the judgment of the Organization, are able and willing to carry out these obligations.
2. The admission of any such state to membership in the United Nations will be effected by a decision of the General Assembly upon the recommendation of the Security Council.

ARTICLE 5

A Member of the United Nations against which preventive or enforcement action has been taken by the Security Council may be suspended from the exercise of the rights and privileges of membership by the General Assembly upon the recommendation of the Security Council. The exercise of these rights and privileges may be restored by the Security Council.

ARTICLE 6

A Member of the United Nations which has persistently violated the Principles contained in the present Charter may be expelled from the Organization by the General Assembly upon the recommendation of the Security Council.

Chapter III. Organs

ARTICLE 7

1. There are established as the principal organs of the United Nations: a General Assembly, a Security Council, an Economic and Social Council, a Trusteeship Council, an International Court of Justice, and a Secretariat.
2. Such subsidiary organs as may be found necessary may be established in accordance with the present Charter.

ARTICLE 8

The United Nations shall place no restrictions on the eligibility of men and women to participate in any capacity and under conditions of equality in its principal and subsidiary organs.

Chapter IV. The General Assembly

Composition

ARTICLE 9

1. The General Assembly shall consist of all the Members of the United Nations.
2. Each member shall have not more than five representatives in the General Assembly.

Functions and Powers

ARTICLE 10

The General Assembly may discuss any questions or any matters within the scope of the present Charter or relating to the powers and functions of any organs provided for in the present Charter, and, except as provided in Article 12, may make recommendations to the Members of the United Nations or to the Security Council or to both on any such questions or matters.

ARTICLE 11

1. The General Assembly may consider the general principles of co-operation in the maintenance of international peace and security, including the principles governing disarmament and the regulation of armaments, and may make recommendations with regard to such principles to the Members or to the Security Council or to both.
2. The General Assembly may discuss any questions relating to the maintenance of international peace and security brought before it by any Member of the United Nations, or by the Security Council, or by a state which is not a Member of the United Nations in accordance with Article 35, paragraph 2, and, except as provided in Article 12, may make recommendations with regard to any such questions to the state or states concerned or to the Security Council or to both. Any such question on which action is necessary shall be referred to the Security Council by the General Assembly either before or after discussion.
3. The General Assembly may call the attention of the Security Council to situations which are likely to endanger international peace and security.
4. The powers of the General Assembly set forth in this Article shall not limit the general scope of Article 10.

ARTICLE 12

1. While the Security Council is exercising in respect of any dispute or situation the functions assigned to it in the present Charter, the General Assembly shall not make any recommendation with regard to that dispute or situation unless the Security Council so requests.

2. The Secretary-General, with the consent of the Security Council, shall notify the General Assembly at each session of any matters relative to the maintenance of international peace and security which are being dealt with by the Security Council and shall similarly notify the General Assembly, or the Members of the United Nations if the General Assembly is not in session, immediately the Security Council ceases to deal with such matters.

ARTICLE 13

1. 1. The General Assembly shall initiate studies and make recommendations for the purpose of:

(*a*) promoting international co-operation in the political field and encouraging the progressive development of international law and its codification;

(*b*) promoting international co-operation in the economic, social, cultural, educational, and health fields, and assisting in the realization of human rights and fundamental freedoms for all without distinction as to race, sex, language, or religion.

2. The further responsibilities, functions and powers of the General Assembly with respect to matters mentioned in paragraph 1(*b*) above are set forth in Chapters IX and X.

ARTICLE 14

Subject to the provisions of Article 12, the General Assembly may recommend measures for the peaceful adjustment of any situation, regardless of origin, which it deems likely to impair the general welfare or friendly relations among nations, including situations resulting from a violation of the provisions of the present Charter setting forth the Purposes and Principles of the United Nations.

ARTICLE 15

1. The General Assembly shall receive and consider annual and special reports from the Security Council; these reports shall include an account of the measures that the Security Council has decided upon or taken to maintain international peace and security.

2. The General Assembly shall receive and consider reports from the other organs of the United Nations.

ARTICLE 16

The General Assembly shall perform such functions with respect to the international trustee-ship system as are assigned to it under Chapters XII and XIII, including the approval of the trusteeship agreements for areas not designated as strategic.

ARTICLE 17

1. The General Assembly shall consider and approve the budget of the Organization.

2. The expenses of the Organization shall be borne by the Members as apportioned by the General Assembly.

3. The General Assembly shall consider and approve any financial and budgetary arrangements with specialized agencies referred to in Article 57 and shall examine the administrative budgets of such specialized agencies with a view to making recommendations to the agencies concerned.

Voting

ARTICLE 18

1. Each member of the General Assembly shall have one vote.

2. Decisions of the General Assembly on important questions shall be made by a two-thirds majority of the members present and voting. These questions shall include: recommendations

with respect to the maintenance of international peace and security, the election of the non-permanent members of the Security Council, the election of the members of the Economic and Social Council, the election of members of the Trusteeship Council in accordance with paragraph 1(c) of Article 86, the admission of new Members to the United Nations, the suspension of the rights and privileges of membership, the expulsion of Members, questions relating to the operation of the trusteeship system, and budgetary questions.

3. Decisions on other questions, including the determination of additional categories of questions to be decided by a two-thirds majority, shall be made by a majority of the members present and voting.

ARTICLE 19

A Member of the United Nations which is in arrears in the payment of its financial contributions to the Organization shall have no vote in the General Assembly if the amount of its arrears equals or exceeds the amount of the contributions due from it for the preceding two full years. The General Assembly may, nevertheless, permit such a Member to vote if it is satisfied that the failure to pay is due to conditions beyond the control of the Member.

Procedure

ARTICLE 20

The General Assembly shall meet in regular annual sessions and in such special sessions as occasion may require. Special sessions shall be convoked by the Secretary-General at the request of the Security Council or of a majority of the Members of the United Nations.

ARTICLE 21

The General Assembly shall adopt its own rules of procedure. It shall elect its President for each session.

ARTICLE 22

The General Assembly may establish such subsidiary organs as it deems necessary for the performance of its functions.

Chapter V. The Security Council

ARTICLE 23

1. The Security Council shall consist of fifteen Members of the United Nations. The Republic of China, France, the Union of Soviet Socialist Republics, the United Kingdom of Great Britain and Northern Ireland, and the United States of America shall be permanent members of the Security Council. The General Assembly shall elect ten other Members of the United Nations to be non-permanent members of the Security Council, due regard being specially paid, in the first instance to the contribution of Members of the United Nations to the maintenance of international peace and security and to the other purposes of the Organization, and also to equitable geographical distribution.

2. The non-permanent members of the Security Council shall be elected for a term of two years. In the first election of the non-permanent members after the increase of the membership of the Security Council from eleven to fifteen, two of the four additional members shall be chosen for a term of one year. A retiring member shall not be eligible for immediate re-election.

3. Each member of the Security Council shall have one representative.

Functions and Powers

ARTICLE 24

1. In order to ensure prompt and effective action by the United Nations, its Members confer on the Security Council primary responsibility for the maintenance of international peace and security, and agree that in carrying out its duties under this responsibility the Security Council acts on their behalf.
2. In discharging these duties the Security Council shall act in accordance with the Purposes and Principles of the United Nations. The specific powers granted to the Security Council for the discharge of these duties are laid down in Chapters VI, VII, VIII, and XII.
3. The Security Council shall submit annual and, when necessary, special reports to the General Assembly for its consideration.

ARTICLE 25

The Members of the United Nations agree to accept and carry out the decisions of the Security Council in accordance with the present Charter.

ARTICLE 26

In order to promote the establishment and maintenance of international peace and security with the least diversion for armaments of the world's human and economic resources, the Security Council shall be responsible for formulating, with the assistance of the Military Staff Committee referred to in Article 47, plans to be submitted to the Members of the United Nations for the establishment of a system for the regulation of armaments.

Voting

ARTICLE 27

1. Each member of the Security Council shall have one vote.
2. Decisions of the Security Council on procedural matters shall be made by an affirmative vote of nine members.
3. Decisions of the Security Council on all other matters shall be made by an affirmative vote of nine members including the concurring votes of the permanent members; provided that, in decisions under Chapter VI, and under paragraph 3 of Article 52, a party to a dispute shall abstain from voting.

Procedure

ARTICLE 28

1. The Security Council shall be so organized as to be able to function continuously. Each member of the Security Council shall for this purpose be represented at all times at the seat of the Organization.
2. The Security Council shall hold periodic meetings at which each of its members may, if it so desires, be represented by a member of the government or by some other specially designated representative.
3. The Security Council may hold meetings at such places other than the seat of the Organization as in its judgment will best facilitate its work.

ARTICLE 29

The Security Council may establish such subsidiary organs as it deems necessary for the performance of its functions.

ARTICLE 30

The Security Council shall adopt its own rules of procedure, including the method of selecting its President.

ARTICLE 31

Any Member of the United Nations which is not a member of the Security Council may participate, without vote, in the discussion of any question brought before the Security Council whenever the latter considers that the interests of that Member are specially affected.

ARTICLE 32

Any Member of the United Nations which is not a member of the Security Council or any state which is not a Member of the United Nations, if it is a party to a dispute under consideration by the Security Council, shall be invited to participate, without vote, in the discussion relating to the dispute. The Security Council shall lay down such conditions as it deems just for the participation of a state which is not a Member of the United Nations.

Chapter VI. Pacific Settlement of Disputes

ARTICLE 33

1. The parties to any dispute, the continuance of which is likely to endanger the maintenance of international peace and security, shall, first of all, seek a solution by negotiation, enquiry, mediation, conciliation, arbitration, judicial settlement, resort to regional agencies or arrangements, or other peaceful means of their own choice.
2. The Security Council shall, when it deems necessary, call upon the parties to settle their dispute by such means.

ARTICLE 34

The Security Council may investigate any dispute, or any situation which might lead to international friction or give rise to a dispute, in order to determine whether the continuance of the dispute or situation is likely to endanger the maintenance of international peace and security.

ARTICLE 35

1. Any Member of the United Nations may bring any dispute, or any situation of the nature referred to in Article 34, to the attention of the Security Council or of the General Assembly.
2. A state which is not a Member of the United Nations may bring to the attention of the Security Council or of the General Assembly any dispute to which it is a party if it accepts in advance, for the purposes of the dispute, the obligations of pacific settlement provided in the present Charter.
3. The proceedings of the General Assembly in respect of matters brought to its attention under this Article will be subject to the provisions of Articles 11 and 12.

ARTICLE 36

1. The Security Council may, at any stage of a dispute of the nature referred to in Article 33 or of a situation of like nature, recommend appropriate procedures or methods of adjustment.
2. The Security Council should take into consideration any procedures for the settlement of the dispute which have already been adopted by the parties.
3. In making recommendations under this Article the Security Council should also take into consideration that legal disputes should as a general rule be referred by the parties to the International Court of Justice in accordance with the provisions of the Statute of the Court.

ARTICLE 37

1. Should the parties to a dispute of the nature referred to in Article 33 fail to settle it by the means indicated in that Article, they shall refer it to the Security Council.
2. If the Security Council deems that the continuance of the dispute is in fact likely to endanger the maintenance of international peace and security, it shall decide whether to take action under Article 36 or to recommend such terms of settlement as it may consider appropriate.

ARTICLE 38

Without prejudice to the provisions of Articles 33 to 37, the Security Council may, if all the parties to any dispute so request, make recommendations to the parties with a view to a pacific settlement of the dispute.

Chapter VII. Action with Respect to Threats to the Peace, Breaches of the Peace, and Acts of Aggression

ARTICLE 39

The Security Council shall determine the existence of any threat to the peace, breach of the peace, or act of aggression and shall make recommendations, or decide what measures shall be taken in accordance with Articles 41 and 42, to maintain or restore international peace and security.

ARTICLE 40

In order to prevent an aggravation of the situation, the Security Council may, before making the recommendations or deciding upon the measures provided for in Article 39, call upon the parties concerned to comply with such provisional measures as it deems necessary or desirable. Such provisional measures shall be without prejudice to the rights, claims, or position of the parties concerned. The Security Council shall duly take account of failure to comply with such provisional measures.

ARTICLE 41

The Security Council may decide what measures not involving the use of armed force are to be employed to give effect to its decisions, and it may call upon the Members of the United Nations to apply such measures. These may include complete or partial interruption of economic relations and of rail, sea, air, postal, telegraphic, radio, and other means of communication, and the severance of diplomatic relations.

ARTICLE 42

Should the Security Council consider that measures provided for in Article 41 would be inadequate or have proved to be inadequate, it may take such action by air, sea, or land forces as may be necessary to maintain or restore international peace and security. Such action may include demonstrations, blockade, and other operations by air, sea, or land forces of Members of the United Nations.

ARTICLE 43

1. All Members of the United Nations, in order to contribute to the maintenance of inter-national peace and security, undertake to make available to the Security Council, on its call and in accordance with a special agreement or agreements, armed forces, assistance, and facilities, including rights of passage, necessary for the purpose of maintaining inter-national peace and security.

2. Such agreement or agreements shall govern the numbers and types of forces. their degree of readiness and general location, and the nature of the facilities and assistance to be provided.

3. The agreement or agreements shall be negotiated as soon as possible on the initiative of the Security Council. They shall be concluded between the Security Council and Members or between the Security Council and groups of Members and shall be subject to ratification by the signatory states in accordance with their respective constitutional processes.

ARTICLE 44

When the Security Council has decided to use force it shall, before calling upon a Member not represented on it to provide armed forces in fulfillment of the obligations assumed under Article 43, invite that Member, if the Member so desires, to participate in the decisions of the Security Council concerning the employment of contingents of that Member's armed forces.

ARTICLE 45

In order to enable the United Nations to take urgent military measures Members shall hold immediately available national air-force contingents for combined international enforcement action. The strength and degree of readiness of these contingents and plans for their combined action shall be determined, within the limits laid down in the special agreement or agreements referred to in Article 43, by the Security Council with the assistance of the Military Staff Committee.

ARTICLE 46

Plans for the application of armed force shall be made by the Security Council with the assistance of the Military Staff Committee.

ARTICLE 47

1. There shall be established a Military Staff Committee to advise and assist the Security Council on all questions relating to the Security Council's military requirements for the maintenance of international peace and security, the employment and command of forces placed at its disposal, the regulation of armaments, and possible disarmament.

2. The Military Staff Committee shall consist of the Chiefs of Staff of the permanent members of the Security Council or their representatives. Any Member of the United Nations not permanently represented on the Committee shall be invited by the Committee to be associated with it when the efficient discharge of the Committee's responsibilities requires the participation of that Member in its work.

3. The Military Staff Committee shall be responsible under the Security Council for the strategic direction of any armed forces placed at the disposal of the Security Council. Questions relating to the command of such forces shall be worked out subsequently.

4. The Military Staff Committee, with the authorization of the Security Council and after consultation with appropriate regional agencies, may establish regional sub-committees.

ARTICLE 48

1. The action required to carry out the decisions of the Security Council for the maintenance of international peace and security shall be taken by all the Members of the United Nations or by some of them, as the Security Council may determine.

2. Such decisions shall be carried out by the Members of the United Nations directly and through their action in the appropriate international agencies of which they are members.

ARTICLE 49

The Members of the United Nations shall join in affording mutual assistance in carrying out the measures decided upon by the Security Council.

ARTICLE 50

If preventive or enforcement measures against any state are taken by the Security Council, any other state, whether a Member of the United Nations or not, which finds itself confronted with special economic problems arising from the carrying out of those measures shall have the right to consult the Security Council with regard to a solution of those problems.

ARTICLE 51

Nothing in the present Charter shall impair the inherent right of individual or collective self-defense if an armed attack occurs against a Member of the United Nations, until the Security Council has taken measures necessary to maintain international peace and security. Measures taken by Members in the exercise of this right of self-defense shall be immediately reported to the Security Council and shall not in any way affect the authority and responsibility of the Security Council under the present Charter to take at any time such action as it deems necessary in order to maintain or restore international peace and security.

Chapter VIII. Regional Arrangements

ARTICLE 52

1. Nothing in the present Charter precludes the existence of regional arrangements or agencies for dealing with such matters relating to the maintenance of international peace and security as are appropriate for regional action, provided that such arrangements or agencies and their activities are consistent with the Purposes and Principles of the United Nations.
2. The Members of the United Nations entering into such arrangements or constituting such agencies shall make every effort to achieve pacific settlement of local disputes through such regional arrangements or by such regional agencies before referring them to the Security Council.
3. The Security Council shall encourage the development of pacific settlement of local disputes through such regional arrangements or by such regional agencies either on the initiative of the states concerned or by reference from the Security Council.
4. This Article in no way impairs the application of Articles 34 and 35.

ARTICLE 53

1. The Security Council shall, where appropriate, utilize such regional arrangements or agencies for enforcement action under its authority. But no enforcement action shall be taken under regional arrangements or by regional agencies without the authorization of the Security Council, with the exception of measures against any enemy state, as defined in paragraph 2 of this Article, provided for pursuant to Article 107 or in regional arrangements directed against renewal of aggressive policy on the part of any such state, until such time as the Organization may, on request of the Governments concerned, be charged with the responsibility for preventing further aggression by such a state.
2. The term enemy state as used in paragraph 1 of this Article applies to any state which during the Second World War has been an enemy of any signatory of the present Charter.

ARTICLE 54

The Security Council shall at all times be kept fully informed of activities undertaken or in contemplation under regional arrangements or by regional agencies for the maintenance of international peace and security.

Chapter IX. International Economic and Social Co-operation

ARTICLE 55

With a view to the creation of conditions of stability and well-being which are necessary for peaceful and friendly relations among nations based on respect for the principle of equal rights and self-determination of peoples, the United Nations shall promote:

(a) higher standards of living, full employment, and conditions of economic and social progress and development;

(b) solutions of international economic, social, health, and related problems; and international cultural and educational co-operation; and

(c) universal respect for, and observance of, human rights and fundamental freedoms for all without distinction as to race, sex, language, or religion.

ARTICLE 56

All Members pledge themselves to take joint and separate action in co-operation with the Organization for the achievement of the purposes set forth in Article 55.

ARTICLE 57

1. The various specialized agencies, established by intergovernmental agreement and having wide international responsibilities, as defined in their basic instruments, in economic, social, cultural, educational, health, and related fields, shall be brought into relationship with the United Nations in accordance with the provisions of Article 63.

2. Such agencies thus brought into relationship with the United Nations are hereinafter referred to as specialized agencies.

ARTICLE 58

The Organization shall make recommendations for the co-ordination of the policies and activities of the specialized agencies.

ARTICLE 59

The Organization shall, where appropriate, initiate negotiations among the states concerned for the creation of any new specialized agencies required for the accomplishment of the purposes set forth in Article 55.

ARTICLE 60

Responsibility for the discharge of the functions of the Organization set forth in this Chapter shall be vested in the General Assembly and, under the authority of the General Assembly, in the Economic and Social Council, which shall have for this purpose the powers set forth in Chapter X.

Chapter X. The Economic and Social Council

Composition

ARTICLE 61

1. The Economic and Social Council shall consist of fifty-four Members of the United Nations elected by the General Assembly.

2. Subject to the provisions of paragraph 3, eighteen members of the Economic and Social Council shall be elected each year for a term of three years. A retiring member shall be eligible for immediate re-election.

3. At the first election after the increase in the membership of the Economic and Social Council from twenty-seven to fifty-four members, in addition to the members elected in place of the nine members whose term of office expires at the end of that year, twenty-seven additional

members shall be elected. Of these twenty-seven additional members, the term of office of nine members so elected shall expire at the end of one year, and of nine other members at the end of two years, in accordance with arrangements made by the General Assembly.

4. Each member of the Economic and Social Council shall have one representative.

Functions and Powers

ARTICLE 62

1. The Economic and Social Council may make or initiate studies and reports with respect to international economic, social, cultural, educational, health, and related matters and may make recommendations with respect to any such matters to the General Assembly, to the Members of the United Nations, and to the specialized agencies concerned.

2. It may make recommendations for the purpose of promoting respect for, and observance of, human rights and fundamental freedoms for all.

3. It may prepare draft conventions for submission to the General Assembly, with respect to matters falling within its competence.

4. It may call, in accordance with the rules prescribed by the United Nations, international conferences on matters falling within its competence.

ARTICLE 63

1. The Economic and Social Council may enter into agreements with any of the agencies referred to in Article 57, defining the terms on which the agency concerned shall be brought into relationship with the United Nations. Such agreements shall be subject to approval by the General Assembly.

2. It may co-ordinate the activities of the specialized agencies through consultation with and recommendations to such agencies and through recommendations to the General Assembly and to the Members of the United Nations.

ARTICLE 64

1. The Economic and Social Council may take appropriate steps to obtain regular reports from the specialized agencies. It may make arrangements with the Members of the United Nations and with the specialized agencies to obtain reports on the steps taken to give effect to its own recommendations and to recommendations on matters falling within its competence made by the General Assembly.

2. It may communicate its observations on these reports to the General Assembly.

ARTICLE 65

The Economic and Social Council may furnish information to the Security Council and shall assist the Security Council upon its request.

ARTICLE 66

1. The Economic and Social Council shall perform such functions as fall within its competence in connection with the carrying out of the recommendations of the General Assembly.

2. It may, with the approval of the General Assembly, perform services at the request of Members of the United Nations and at the request of specialized agencies.

3. It shall perform such other functions as are specified elsewhere in the present Charter or as may be assigned to it by the General Assembly.

ARTICLE 67

1. Each member of the Economic and Social Council shall have one vote.

2. Decisions of the Economic and Social Council shall be made by a majority of the members present and voting.

Procedure

ARTICLE 68

The Economic and Social Council shall set up commissions in economic and social fields and for the promotion of human rights, and such other commissions as may be required for the performance of its functions.

ARTICLE 69

The Economic and Social Council shall invite any Member of the United Nations to participate, without vote, in its deliberations on any matter of particular concern to that Member.

ARTICLE 70

The Economic and Social Council may make arrangements for representatives of the specialized agencies to participate, without vote, in its deliberations and in those of the commissions established by it, and for its representatives to participate in the deliberations of the specialized agencies.

ARTICLE 71

The Economic and Social Council may make suitable arrangements for consultation with non-governmental organizations which are concerned with matters within its competence. Such arrangements may be made with international organizations and, where appropriate, with national organizations after consultation with the Member of the United Nations concerned.

ARTICLE 72

1. The Economic and Social Council shall adopt its own rules of procedure, including the method of selecting its President.
2. The Economic and Social Council shall meet as required in accordance with its rules, which shall include provision for the convening of meetings on the request of a majority of its members.

Chapter XI. Declaration Regarding Non-Self-Governing Territories

ARTICLE 73

Members of the United Nations which have or assume responsibilities for the administration of territories whose peoples have not yet attained a full measure of self-government recognize the principle that the interests of the inhabitants of these territories are paramount, and accept as a sacred trust the obligation to promote to the utmost, within the system of international peace and security established by the present Charter, the well-being of the inhabitants of these territories, and, to this end:

(a) to ensure, with due respect for the culture of the peoples concerned, their political, economic, social, and educational advancement, their just treatment, and their protection against abuses;

(b) to develop self-government, to take due account of the political aspirations of the peoples, and to assist them in the progressive development of their free political institutions, according to the particular circumstances of each territory and its peoples and their varying stages of advancement;

(c) to further international peace and security;

(d) to promote constructive measures of development, to encourage research, and to co-operate with one another and, when and where appropriate, with specialized international bodies with a view to the practical achievement of the social, economic, and scientific purposes set forth in this Article; and

(*e*) to transmit regularly to the Secretary-General for information purposes, subject to such limitation as security and constitutional considerations may require, statistical and other information of a technical nature relating to economic, social, and educational conditions in the territories for which they are respectively responsible other than those territories to which Chapters XII and XIII apply.

ARTICLE 74

Members of the United Nations also agree that their policy in respect of the territories to which this Chapter applies, no less than in respect of their metropolitan areas, must be based on the general principle of good-neighbourliness, due account being taken of the interests and well-being of the rest of the world, in social, economic, and commercial matters.

Chapter XII. International Trusteeship System

ARTICLE 75

The United Nations shall establish under its authority an international trusteeship system for the administration and supervision of such territories as may be placed thereunder by subsequent individual agreements. These territories are hereinafter referred to as trust territories.

ARTICLE 76

The basic objectives of the trusteeship system, in accordance with the Purposes of the United Nations laid down in Article 1 of the present Charter, shall be:

(*a*) to further international peace and security;

(*b*) to promote the political, economic, social, and educational advancement of the inhabitants of the trust territories, and their progressive development towards self-government or independence as may be appropriate to the particular circumstances of each territory and its peoples and the freely expressed wishes of the peoples concerned, and as may be provided by the terms of each trusteeship agreement;

(*c*) to encourage respect for human rights and for fundamental freedoms for all without distinction as to race, sex, language, or religion, and to encourage recognition of the interdependence of the peoples of the world; and

(*d*) to ensure equal treatment in social, economic, and commercial matters for all Members of the United Nations and their nationals and also equal treatment for the latter in the administration of justice without prejudice to the attainment of the foregoing objectives and subject to the provisions of Article 80.

ARTICLE 77

1. The trusteeship system shall apply to such territories in the following categories as may be placed thereunder by means of trusteeship agreements:

(*a*) territories now held under mandate;

(*b*) territories which may be detached from enemy states as a result of the Second World War; and

(*c*) territories voluntarily placed under the system by states responsible for their administration.

2. It will be a matter for subsequent agreement as to which territories in the foregoing categories will be brought under the trusteeship system and upon what terms.

ARTICLE 78

The trusteeship system shall not apply to territories which have become Members of the United Nations, relationship among which shall be based on respect for the principle of sovereign equality.

ARTICLE 79

The terms of trusteeship for each territory to be placed under the trusteeship system, including any alteration or amendment, shall be agreed upon by the states directly concerned, including the mandatory power in the case of territories held under mandate by a Member of the United Nations, and shall be approved as provided for in Articles 83 and 85.

ARTICLE 80

1. Except as may be agreed upon in individual trusteeship agreements, made under Articles 77, 79, and 81, placing each territory under the trusteeship system, and until such agreements have been concluded, nothing in this Chapter shall be construed in or of itself to alter in any manner the rights whatsoever of any states or any peoples or the terms of existing international instruments to which Members of the United Nations may respectively be parties.
2. Paragraph 1 of this Article shall not be interpreted as giving grounds for delay or postponement of the negotiation and conclusion of agreements for placing mandated and other territories under the trusteeship system as provided for in Article 77.

ARTICLE 81

The trusteeship agreement shall in each case include the terms under which the trust territory will be administered and designate the authority which will exercise the administration of the trust territory. Such authority, hereinafter called the administering authority, may be one or more states or the Organization itself.

ARTICLE 82

There may be designated, in any trusteeship agreement, a strategic area or areas which may include part or all of the trust territory to which the agreement applies, without prejudice to any special agreement or agreements made under Article 43.

ARTICLE 83

1. All functions of the United Nations relating to strategic areas, including the approval of the terms of the trusteeship agreements and of their alteration or amendment, shall be exercised by the Security Council.
2. The basic objectives set forth in Article 76 shall be applicable to the people of each strategic area.
3. The Security Council shall, subject to the provisions of the trusteeship agreements and without prejudice to security considerations, avail itself of the assistance of the Trusteeship Council to perform those functions of the United Nations under the trusteeship system relating to political. economic, social, and educational matters in the strategic areas.

ARTICLE 84

It shall be the duty of the administering authority to ensure that the trust territory shall play its part in the maintenance of international peace and security. To this end the administering authority may make use of volunteer forces, facilities, and assistance from the trust territory in carrying out the obligations towards the Security Council undertaken in this regard by the administering authority, as well as for local defence and the maintenance of law and order within the trust territory.

ARTICLE 85

1. The functions of the United Nations with regard to trusteeship agreements for all areas not designated as strategic, including the approval of the terms of the trusteeship agreements and of their alteration or amendment, shall be exercised by the General Assembly.
2. The Trusteeship Council, operating under the authority of the General Assembly, shall assist the General Assembly in carrying out these functions.

Chapter XIII. The Trusteeship Council

Composition

ARTICLE 86

1. The Trusteeship Council shall consist of the following Members of the United Nations:
   (*a*) those Members administering trust territories;
   (*b*) such of those Members mentioned by name in Article 23 as are not administering trust territories; and
   (*c*) as many other Members elected for three-year terms by the General Assembly as may be necessary to ensure that the total number of members of the Trusteeship Council is equally divided between those Members of the United Nations which administer trust territories and those which do not.
2. Each member of the Trusteeship Council shall designate one specially qualified person to represent it therein.

Functions and Powers

ARTICLE 87

The General Assembly and, under its authority, the Trusteeship Council, in carrying out their functions, may:
   (*a*) consider reports submitted by the administering authority;
   (*b*) accept petitions and examine them in consultation with the administering authority;
   (*c*) provide for periodic visits to the respective trust territories at times agreed upon with the administering authority; and
   (*d*) take these and other actions in conformity with the terms of the trusteeship agreements.

ARTICLE 88

The Trusteeship Council shall formulate a questionnaire on the political, economic, social, and educational advancement of the inhabitants of each trust territory, and the administering authority for each trust territory within the competence of the General Assembly shall make an annual report to the General Assembly upon the basis of such questionnaire.

Voting

ARTICLE 89

1. Each member of the Trusteeship Council shall have one vote.
2. Decisions of the Trusteeship Council shall be made by a majority of the members present and voting.

Procedure

ARTICLE 90

1. The Trusteeship Council shall adopt its own rules of procedure, including the method of selecting its President.
2. The Trusteeship Council shall meet as required in accordance with its rules, which shall include provision for the convening of meetings on the request of a majority of its members.

ARTICLE 91

The Trusteeship Council shall, when appropriate, avail itself of the assistance of the Economic and Social Council and of the specialized agencies in regard to matters with which they are respectively concerned.

Chapter XIV. The International Court of Justice

ARTICLE 92

The International Court of Justice shall be the principal judicial organ of the United Nations. It shall function in accordance with the annexed Statute which is based upon the Statute of the Permanent Court of International Justice and forms an integral part of the present Charter.

ARTICLE 93

1. All Members of the United Nations are *ipso facto* parties to the Statute of the International Court of Justice.
2. A state which is not a Member of the United Nations may become a party to the Statute of the International Court of Justice on conditions to be determined in each case by the General Assembly upon the recommendation of the Security Council.

ARTICLE 94

1. Each Member of the United Nations undertakes to comply with the decision of the International Court of Justice in any case to which it is a party.
2. If any party to a case fails to perform the obligations incumbent upon it under a judgment rendered by the Court, the other party may have recourse to the Security Council, which may, if it deems necessary, make recommendations or decide upon measures to be taken to give effect to the judgment.

ARTICLE 95

Nothing in the present Charter shall prevent Members of the United Nations from entrusting the solution of their differences to other tribunals by virtue of agreements already in existence or which may be concluded in the future.

ARTICLE 96

1. The General Assembly or the Security Council may request the International Court of Justice to give an advisory opinion on any legal question.
2. Other organs of the United Nations and specialized agencies, which may at any time be so authorized by the General Assembly, may also request advisory opinions of the Court on legal questions arising within the scope of their activities.

Chapter XV. The Secretariat

ARTICLE 97

The Secretariat shall comprise a Secretary-General and such staff as the Organization may require. The Secretary-General shall be appointed by the General Assembly upon the recommendation of the Security Council. He shall be the chief administrative officer of the Organization.

ARTICLE 98

The Secretary-General shall act in that capacity in all meetings of the General Assembly, of the Security Council, of the Economic and Social Council, and of the Trusteeship Council, and shall perform such other functions as are entrusted to him by these organs. The Secretary-General shall make an annual report to the General Assembly on the work of the Organization.

ARTICLE 99

The Secretary-General may bring to the attention of the Security Council any matter which in his opinion may threaten the maintenance of international peace and security.

ARTICLE 100

1. In the performance of their duties the Secretary-General and the staff shall not seek or receive instructions from any government or from any other authority external to the Organization. They shall refrain from any action which might reflect on their position as international officials responsible only to the Organization.
2. Each Member of the United Nations undertakes to respect the exclusively international character of the responsibilities of the Secretary-General and the staff and not to seek to influence them in the discharge of their responsibilities.

ARTICLE 101

1. The staff shall be appointed by the Secretary-General under regulations established by the General Assembly.
2. Appropriate staffs shall be permanently assigned to the Economic and Social Council, the Trusteeship Council, and, as required, to other organs of the United Nations. These staffs shall form a part of the Secretariat.
3. The paramount consideration in the employment of the staff and in the determination of the conditions of service shall be the necessity of securing the highest standards of efficiency, competence, and integrity. Due regard shall be paid to the importance of recruiting the staff on as wide a geographical basis as possible.

Chapter XVI. Miscellaneous Provisions

ARTICLE 102

1. Every treaty and every international agreement entered into by any Member of the United Nations after the present Charter comes into force shall as soon as possible be registered with the Secretariat and published by it.
2. No party to any such treaty or international agreement which has not been registered in accordance with the provisions of paragraph I of this Article may invoke that treaty or agreement before any organ of the United Nations.

ARTICLE 103

In the event of a conflict between the obligations of the Members of the United Nations under the present Charter and their obligations under any other international agreement, their obligations under the present Charter shall prevail.

ARTICLE 104

The Organization shall enjoy in the territory of each of its Members such legal capacity as may be necessary for the exercise of its functions and the fulfillment of its purposes.

ARTICLE 105

1. The Organization shall enjoy in the territory of each of its Members such privileges and immunities as are necessary for the fulfillment of its purposes.
2. Representatives of the Members of the United Nations and officials of the Organization shall similarly enjoy such privileges and immunities as are necessary for the independent exercise of their functions in connection with the Organization.
3. The General Assembly may make recommendations with a view to determining the details of the application of paragraphs 1 and 2 of this Article or may propose conventions to the Members of the United Nations for this purpose.

Chapter XVII. Transitional Security Arrangements

ARTICLE 106

Pending the coming into force of such special agreements referred to in Article 43 as in the opinion of the Security Council enable it to begin the exercise of its responsibilities under Article 42, the parties to the Four-Nation Declaration, signed at Moscow, 30 October 1943, and France, shall, in accordance with the provisions of paragraph 5 of that Declaration, consult with one another and as occasion requires with other Members of the United Nations with a view to such joint action on behalf of the Organization as may be necessary for the purpose of maintaining international peace and security.

ARTICLE 107

Nothing in the present Charter shall invalidate or preclude action, in relation to any state which during the Second World War has been an enemy of any signatory to the present Charter, taken or authorized as a result of that war by the Governments having responsibility for such action.

Chapter XVIII. Amendments

ARTICLE 108

Amendments to the present Charter shall come into force for all Members of the United Nations when they have been adopted by a vote of two-thirds of the members of the General Assembly and ratified in accordance with their respective constitutional processes by two-thirds of the Members of the United Nations, including all the permanent members of the Security Council.

ARTICLE 109

1. A General Conference of the Members of the United Nations for the purpose of reviewing the present Charter may be held at a date and place to be fixed by a two-thirds vote of the members of the General Assembly and by a vote of any seven members of the Security Council. Each Member of the United Nations shall have one vote in the conference.
2. Any alteration of the present Charter recommended by a two-thirds vote of the conference shall take effect when ratified in accordance with their respective constitutional processes by two-thirds of the Members of the United Nations including all the permanent members of the Security Council.

3. If such a conference has not been held before the tenth annual session of the General Assembly following the coming into force of the present Charter, the proposal to call such a conference shall be placed on the agenda of that session of the General Assembly, and the conference shall be held if so decided by a majority vote of the members of the General Assembly and by a vote of any seven members of the Security Council.

Chapter XIX. Ratification and Signature

ARTICLE 110

1. The present Charter shall be ratified by the signatory states in accordance with their respective constitutional processes.
2. The ratifications shall be deposited with the Government of the United States of America, which shall notify all the signatory states of each deposit as well as the Secretary-General of the Organization when he has been appointed.
3. The present Charter shall come into force upon the deposit of ratifications by the Republic of China, France, the Union of Soviet Socialist Republics, the United Kingdom of Great Britain and Northern Ireland, and the United States of America, and by a majority of the other signatory states. A protocol of the ratifications deposited shall thereupon be drawn up by the Government of the United States of America which shall communicate copies thereof to all the signatory states.
4. The states signatory to the present Charter which ratify it after it has come into force will become original Members of the United Nations on the date of the deposit of their respective ratifications.

ARTICLE 111

The present Charter, of which the Chinese, French, Russian, English, and Spanish texts are equally authentic, shall remain deposited in the archives of the Government of the United States of America. Duly certified copies thereof shall be transmitted by that Government to the Governments of the other signatory states.

IN FAITH WHEREOF the representatives of the Governments of the United Nations have signed the present Charter.

DONE at the city of San Francisco the twenty-sixth day of June, one thousand nine hundred and forty-five.

APPENDIX 4: STATUTE OF THE INTERNATIONAL COURT OF JUSTICE

Article 1

The International Court of Justice established by the Charter of the United Nations as the principal judicial organ of the United Nations shall be constituted and shall function in accordance with the provisions of the present Statute.

Chapter I. Organization of the Court

Article 2

The Court shall be composed of a body of independent judges, elected regardless of their nationality from among persons of high moral character, who possess the qualifications required in their respective countries for appointment to the highest judicial offices, or are jurisconsults of recognized competence in international law.

Article 3

1. The Court shall consist of fifteen members, no two of whom may be nationals of the same state.
2. A person who for the purposes of membership in the Court could be regarded as a national of more than one state shall be deemed to be a national of the one in which he ordinarily exercises civil and political rights.

Article 4

1. The members of the Court shall be elected by the General Assembly and by the Security Council from a list of persons nominated by the national groups in the Permanent Court of Arbitration, in accordance with the following provisions.
2. In the case of Members of the United Nations not represented in the Permanent Court of Arbitration, candidates shall be nominated by national groups appointed for this purpose by their governments under the same conditions as those prescribed for members of the Permanent Court of Arbitration by Article 44 of the Convention of The Hague of 1907 for the pacific settlement of international disputes.
3. The conditions under which a state which is a party to the present Statute but is not a Member of the United Nations may participate in electing the members of the Court shall, in the absence of a special agreement, be laid down by the General Assembly upon recommendation of the Security Council.

Article 5

1. At least three months before the date of the election, the Secretary-General of the United Nations shall address a written request to the members of the Permanent Court of Arbitration belonging to the states which are parties to the present Statute, and to the members of the national groups appointed under Article 4, paragraph 2, inviting them to

undertake, within a given time, by national groups, the nomination of persons in a position to accept the duties of a member of the Court.

2. No group may nominate more than four persons, not more than two of whom shall be of their own nationality. In no case may the number of candidates nominated by a group be more than double the number of seats to be filled.

Article 6

Before making these nominations, each national group is recommended to consult its highest court of justice, its legal faculties and schools of law, and its national academies and national sections of international academies devoted to the study of law.

Article 7

1. The Secretary-General shall prepare a list in alphabetical order of all the persons thus nominated. Save as provided in Article 12, paragraph 2, these shall be the only persons eligible.
2. The Secretary-General shall submit this list to the General Assembly and to the Security Council.

Article 8

The General Assembly and the Security Council shall proceed independently of one another to elect the members of the Court.

Article 9

At every election, the electors shall bear in mind not only that the persons to be elected should individually possess the qualifications required, but also that in the body as a whole the representation of the main forms of civilization and of the principal legal systems of the world should be assured.

Article 10

1. Those candidates who obtain an absolute majority of votes in the General Assembly and in the Security Council shall be considered as elected.
2. Any vote of the Security Council, whether for the election of judges or for the appointment of members of the conference envisaged in Article 12, shall be taken without any distinction between permanent and non-permanent members of the Security Council.
3. In the event of more than one national of the same state obtaining an absolute majority of the votes both of the General Assembly and of the Security Council, the eldest of these only shall be considered as elected.

Article 11

If, after the first meeting held for the purpose of the election, one or more seats remain to be filled, a second and, if necessary, a third meeting shall take place.

Article 12

1. If, after the third meeting, one or more seats still remain unfilled, a joint conference consisting of six members, three appointed by the General Assembly and three by the Security Council, may be formed at any time at the request of either the General Assembly or the Security Council, for the purpose of choosing by the vote of an absolute majority one name for each seat still vacant, to submit to the General Assembly and the Security Council for their respective acceptance.

2. If the joint conference is unanimously agreed upon any person who fulfills the required conditions, he may be included in its list, even though he was not included in the list of nominations referred to in Article 7.

3. If the joint conference is satisfied that it will not be successful in procuring an election, those members of the Court who have already been elected shall, within a period to be fixed by the Security Council, proceed to fill the vacant seats by selection from among those candidates who have obtained votes either in the General Assembly or in the Security Council.

4. In the event of an equality of votes among the judges, the eldest judge shall have a casting vote.

Article 13

1. The members of the Court shall be elected for nine years and may be re-elected; provided, however, that of the judges elected at the first election, the terms of five judges shall expire at the end of three years and the terms of five more judges shall expire at the end of six years.

2. The judges whose terms are to expire at the end of the above-mentioned initial periods of three and six years shall be chosen by lot to be drawn by the Secretary-General immediately after the first election has been completed.

3. The members of the Court shall continue to discharge their duties until their places have been filled. Though replaced, they shall finish any cases which they may have begun.

4. In the case of the resignation of a member of the Court, the resignation shall be addressed to the President of the Court for transmission to the Secretary-General. This last notification makes the place vacant.

Article 14

Vacancies shall be filled by the same method as that laid down for the first election subject to the following provision: the Secretary-General shall, within one month of the occurrence of the vacancy, proceed to issue the invitations provided for in Article 5, and the date of the election shall be fixed by the Security Council.

Article 15

A member of the Court elected to replace a member whose term of office has not expired shall hold office for the remainder of his predecessor's term.

Article 16

1. No member of the Court may exercise any political or administrative function, or engage in any other occupation of a professional nature.

2. Any doubt on this point shall be settled by the decision of the Court.

Article 17

1. No member of the Court may act as agent, counsel, or advocate in any case.

2. No member may participate in the decision of any case in which he has previously taken part as agent, counsel, or advocate for one of the parties, or as a member of a national or international court, or of a commission of enquiry, or in any other capacity.

3. Any doubt on this point shall be settled by the decision of the Court.

Article 18

1. No member of the Court can be dismissed unless, in the unanimous opinion of the other members, he has ceased to fulfill the required conditions.

2. Formal notification thereof shall be made to the Secretary-General by the Registrar.

3. This notification makes the place vacant.

Article 19

The members of the Court, when engaged on the business of the Court, shall enjoy diplomatic privileges and immunities.

Article 20

Every member of the Court shall, before taking up his duties, make a solemn declaration in open court that he will exercise his powers impartially and conscientiously.

Article 21

1. The Court shall elect its President and Vice-President for three years; they may be re-elected.
2. The Court shall appoint its Registrar and may provide for the appointment of such other officers as may be necessary.

Article 22

1. The seat of the Court shall be established at The Hague. This, however, shall not prevent the Court from sitting and exercising its functions elsewhere whenever the Court considers it desirable.
2. The President and the Registrar shall reside at the seat of the Court.

Article 23

1. The Court shall remain permanently in session, except during the judicial vacations, the dates and duration of which shall be fixed by the Court.
2. Members of the Court are entitled to periodic leave, the dates and duration of which shall be fixed by the Court, having in mind the distance between The Hague and the home of each judge.
3. Members of the Court shall be bound, unless they are on leave or prevented from attending by illness or other serious reasons duly explained to the President, to hold themselves permanently at the disposal of the Court.

Article 24

1. If, for some special reason, a member of the Court considers that he should not take part in the decision of a particular case, he shall so inform the President.
2. If the President considers that for some special reason one of the members of the Court should not sit in a particular case, he shall give him notice accordingly.
3. If in any such case the member Court and the President disagree, the matter shall be settled by the decision of the Court.

Article 25

1. The full Court shall sit except when it is expressly provided otherwise in the present Statute.
2. Subject to the condition that the number of judges available to constitute the Court is not thereby reduced below eleven, the Rules of the Court may provide for allowing one or more judges, according to circumstances and in rotation, to be dispensed from sitting.
3. A quorum of nine judges shall suffice to constitute the Court.

Article 26

1. The Court may from time to time form one or more chambers, composed of three or more judges as the Court may determine, for dealing with particular categories of cases; for example, labour cases and cases relating to transit and communications.

2. The Court may at any time form a chamber for dealing with a particular case. The number of judges to constitute such a chamber shall be determined by the Court with the approval of the parties.
3. Cases shall be heard and determined by the chambers provided for in this article if the parties so request.

Article 27

A judgment given by any of the chambers provided for in Articles 26 and 29 shall be considered as rendered by the Court.

Article 28

The chambers provided for in Articles 26 and 29 may, with the consent of the parties, sit and exercise their functions elsewhere than at The Hague.

Article 29

With a view to the speedy dispatch of business, the Court shall form annually a chamber composed of five judges which, at the request of the parties, may hear and determine cases by summary procedure. In addition, two judges shall be selected for the purpose of replacing judges who find it impossible to sit.

Article 30

1. The Court shall frame rules for carrying out its functions. In particular, it shall lay down rules of procedure.
2. The Rules of the Court may provide for assessors to sit with the Court or with any of its chambers, without the right to vote.

Article 31

1. Judges of the nationality of each of the parties shall retain their right to sit in the case before the Court.
2. If the Court includes upon the Bench a judge of the nationality of one of the parties, any other party may choose a person to sit as judge. Such person shall be chosen preferably from among those persons who have been nominated as candidates as provided in Articles 4 and 5.
3. If the Court includes upon the Bench no judge of the nationality of the parties, each of these parties may proceed to choose a judge as provided in paragraph 2 of this Article.
4. The provisions of this Article shall apply to the case of Articles 26 and 29. In such cases, the President shall request one or, if necessary, two of the members of the Court forming the chamber to give place to the members of the Court of the nationality of the parties concerned, and, failing such, or if they are unable to be present, to the judges specially chosen by the parties.
5. Should there be several parties in the same interest, they shall, for the purpose of the preceding provisions, be reckoned as one party only. Any doubt upon this point shall be settled by the decision of the Court.
6. Judges chosen as laid down in paragraphs 2, 3, and 4 of this Article shall fulfill the conditions required by Articles 2, 17 (paragraph 2), 20, and 24 of the present Statute. They shall take part in the decision on terms of complete equality with their colleagues.

Article 32

1. Each member of the Court shall receive an annual salary.
2. The President shall receive a special annual allowance.

3. The Vice-President shall receive a special allowance for every day on which he acts as President.
4. The judges chosen under Article 31, other than members of the Court, shall receive compensation for each day on which they exercise their functions.
5. These salaries, allowances, and compensation shall be fixed by the General Assembly. They may not be decreased during the term of office.
6. The salary of the Registrar shall be fixed by the General Assembly on the proposal of the Court.
7. Regulations made by the General Assembly shall fix the conditions under which retirement pensions may be given to members of the Court and to the Registrar, and the conditions under which members of the Court and the Registrar shall have their travelling expenses refunded.
8. The above salaries, allowances, and compensation shall be free of all taxation.

Article 33

The expenses of the Court shall be borne by the United Nations in such a manner as shall be decided by the General Assembly.

Chapter II. Competence of the Court

Article 34

1. Only states may be parties in cases before the Court.
2. The Court, subject to and in conformity with its Rules, may request of public international organizations information relevant to cases before it, and shall receive such information presented by such organizations on their own initiative.
3. Whenever the construction of the constituent instrument of a public international organization or of an international convention adopted thereunder is in question in a case before the Court, the Registrar shall so notify the public international organization concerned and shall communicate to it copies of all the written proceedings.

Article 35

1. The Court shall be open to the states parties to the present Statute.
2. The conditions under which the Court shall be open to other states shall, subject to the special provisions contained in treaties in force, be laid down by the Security Council, but in no case shall such conditions place the parties in a position of inequality before the Court.
3. When a state which is not a Member of the United Nations is a party to a case, the Court shall fix the amount which that party is to contribute towards the expenses of the Court. This provision shall not apply if such state is bearing a share of the expenses of the Court.

Article 36

1. The jurisdiction of the Court comprises all cases which the parties refer to it and all matters specially provided for in the Charter of the United Nations or in treaties and conventions in force.
2. The states parties to the present Statute may at any time declare that they recognize as compulsory *ipso facto* and without special agreement, in relation to any other state accepting the same obligation, the jurisdiction of the Court in all legal disputes concerning:
   (*a*) the interpretation of a treaty;
   (*b*) any question of international law;
   (*c*) the existence of any fact which, if established, would constitute a breach of an international obligation;

(*d*) the nature or extent of the reparation to be made for the breach of an international obligation.

3. The declarations referred to above may be made unconditionally or on condition of reciprocity on the part of several or certain states, or for a certain time.

4. Such declarations shall be deposited with the Secretary-General of the United Nations, who shall transmit copies thereof to the parties to the Statute and to the Registrar of the Court.

5. Declarations made under Article 36 of the Statute of the Permanent Court of International Justice and which are still in force shall be deemed, as between the parties to the present Statute, to be acceptances of the compulsory jurisdiction of the International Court of Justice for the period which they still have to run and in accordance with their terms.

6. In the event of a dispute as to whether the Court has jurisdiction, the matter shall be settled by the decision of the Court.

Article 37

Whenever a treaty or convention in force provides for reference of a matter to a tribunal to have been instituted by the League of Nations, or to the Permanent Court of International Justice, the matter shall, as between the parties to the present Statute, be referred to the International Court of Justice.

Article 38

1. The Court, whose function is to decide in accordance with international law such disputes as are submitted to it, shall apply:

   (*a*) international conventions, whether general or particular, establishing rules expressly recognized by the contesting states;

   (*b*) international custom, as evidence of a general practice accepted as law;

   (*c*) the general principles of law recognized by civilized nations;

   (*d*) subject to the provisions of Article 59, judicial decisions and the teachings of the most highly qualified publicists of the various nations, as subsidiary means for the determination of rules of law.

2. This provision shall not prejudice the power of the Court to decide a case *ex aequo et bono*, if the parties agree thereto.

Chapter III. Procedure

Article 39

1. The official languages of the Court shall be French and English. If the parties agree that the case shall be conducted in French, the judgment shall be delivered in French. If the parties agree that the case shall be conducted in English, the judgment shall be delivered in English.

2. In the absence of an agreement as to which language shall be employed, each party may, in the pleadings, use the language which it prefers; the decision of the Court shall be given in French and English. In this case the Court shall at the same time determine which of the two texts shall be considered as authoritative.

3. The Court shall, at the request of any party, authorize a language other than French or English to be used by that party.

Article 40

1. Cases are brought before the Court, as the case may be, either by the notification of the special agreement or by a written application addressed to the Registrar. In either case the subject of the dispute and the parties shall be indicated.
2. The Registrar shall forthwith communicate the application to all concerned.
3. He shall also notify the Members of the United Nations through the Secretary-General, and also any other states entitled to appear before the Court.

Article 41

1. The Court shall have the power to indicate, if it considers that circumstances so require, any provisional measures which ought to be taken to preserve the respective rights of either party.
2. Pending the final decision, notice of the measures suggested shall forthwith be given to the parties and to the Security Council.

Article 42

1. The parties shall be represented by agents.
2. They may have the assistance of counsel or advocates before the Court.
3. The agents, counsel, and advocates of parties before the Court shall enjoy the privileges and immunities necessary to the independent exercise of their duties.

Article 43

1. The procedure shall consist of two parts: written and oral.
2. The written proceedings shall consist of the communication to the Court and to the parties of memorials, counter-memorials and, if necessary, replies; also all papers and documents in support.
3. These communications shall be made through the Registrar, in the order and within the time fixed by the Court.
4. A certified copy of every document produced by one party shall be communicated to the other party.
5. The oral proceedings shall consist of the hearing by the Court of witnesses, experts, agents, counsel, and advocates.

Article 44

1. For the service of all notices upon persons other than the agents, counsel, and advocates, the Court shall apply direct to the government of the state upon whose territory the notice has to be served.
2. The same provision shall apply whenever steps are to be taken to procure evidence on the spot.

Article 45

The hearing shall be under the control of the President or, if he is unable to preside, of the Vice-President; if neither is able to preside, the senior judge present shall preside.

Article 46

The hearing in Court shall be public, unless the Court shall decide otherwise, or unless the parties demand that the public be not admitted.

Article 47

1. Minutes shall be made at each hearing and signed by the Registrar and the President.
2. These minutes alone shall be authentic.

Article 48

The Court shall make orders for the conduct of the case, shall decide the form and time in which each party must conclude its arguments, and make all arrangements connected with the taking of evidence.

Article 49

The Court may, even before the hearing begins, call upon the agents to produce any document or to supply any explanations. Formal note shall be taken of any refusal.

Article 50

The Court may, at any time, entrust any individual, body, bureau, commission, or other organization that it may select, with the task of carrying out an enquiry or giving an expert opinion.

Article 51

During the hearing any relevant questions are to be put to the witnesses and experts under the conditions laid down by the Court in the rules of procedure referred to in Article 30.

Article 52

After the Court has received the proofs and evidence within the time specified for the purpose, it may refuse to accept any further oral or written evidence that one party may desire to present unless the other side consents.

Article 53

1. Whenever one of the parties does not appear before the Court, or fails to defend its case, the other party may call upon the Court to decide in favour of its claim.
2. The Court must, before doing so, satisfy itself, not only that it has jurisdiction in accordance with Articles 36 and 37, but also that the claim is well founded in fact and law.

Article 54

1. When, subject to the control of the Court, the agents, counsel, and advocates have completed their presentation of the case, the President shall declare the hearing closed.
2. The Court shall withdraw to consider the judgment.
3. The deliberations of the Court shall take place in private and remain secret.

Article 55

1. All questions shall be decided by a majority of the judges present.
2. In the event of an equality of votes, the President or the judge who acts in his place shall have a casting vote.

Article 56

1. The judgment shall state the reasons on which it is based.
2. It shall contain the names of the judges who have taken part in the decision.

Article 57

If the judgment does not represent in whole or in part the unanimous opinion of the judges, any judge shall be entitled to deliver a separate opinion.

Article 58

The judgment shall be signed by the President and by the Registrar. It shall be read in open court, due notice having been given to the agents.

Article 59

The decision of the Court has no binding force except between the parties and in respect of that particular case.

Article 60

The judgment is final and without appeal. In the event of dispute as to the meaning or scope of the judgment, the Court shall construe it upon the request of any party.

Article 61

1. An application for revision of a judgment may be made only when it is based upon the discovery of some fact of such a nature as to be a decisive factor, which fact was, when the judgment was given, unknown to the Court and also to the party claiming revision, always provided that such ignorance was not due to negligence.
2. The proceedings for revision shall be opened by a judgment of the Court expressly recording the existence of the new fact, recognizing that it has such a character as to lay the case open to revision, and declaring the application admissible on this ground.
3. The Court may require previous compliance with the terms of the judgment before it admits proceedings in revision.
4. The application for revision must be made at latest within six months of the discovery of the new fact.
5. No application for revision may be made after the lapse of ten years from the date of the judgment.

Article 62

1. Should a state consider that it has an interest of a legal nature which may be affected by the decision in the case, it may submit a request to the Court to be permitted to intervene.
2. It shall be for the Court to decide upon this request.

Article 63

1. Whenever the construction of a convention to which states other than those concerned in the case are parties is in question, the Registrar shall notify all such states forthwith.
2. Every state so notified has the right to intervene in the proceedings; but if it uses this right, the construction given by the judgment will be equally binding upon it.

Article 64

Unless otherwise decided by the Court, each party shall bear its own costs.

Chapter IV. Advisory Opinions

Article 65

1. The Court may give an advisory opinion on any legal question at the request of whatever body may be authorized by or in accordance with the Charter of the United Nations to make such a request.
2. Questions upon which the advisory opinion of the Court is asked shall be laid before the Court by means of a written request containing an exact statement of the question upon

which an opinion is required, and accompanied by all documents likely to throw light upon the question.

Article 66

1. The Registrar shall forthwith give notice of the request for an advisory opinion to all states entitled to appear before the Court.
2. The Registrar shall also, by means of a special and direct communication, notify any state entitled to appear before the Court or international organization considered by the Court, or, should it not be sitting, by the President, as likely to be able to furnish information on the question, that the Court will be prepared to receive, within a time limit to be fixed by the President, written statements, or to hear, at a public sitting to be held for the purpose, oral statements relating to the question.
3. Should any such state entitled to appear before the Court have failed to receive the special communication referred to in paragraph 2 of this Article, such state may express a desire to submit a written statement or to be heard; and the Court will decide.
4. States and organizations having presented written or oral statements or both shall be permitted to comment on the statements made by other states or organizations in the form, to the extent, and within the time limits which the Court, or, should it not be sitting, the President, shall decide in each particular case. Accordingly, the Registrar shall in due time communicate any such written statements to states and organizations having submitted similar statements.

Article 67

The Court shall deliver its advisory opinions in open court, notice having been given to the Secretary-General and to the representatives of Members of the United Nations, of other states and of international organizations immediately concerned.

Article 68

In the exercise of its advisory functions the Court shall further be guided by the provisions of the present Statute which apply in contentious cases to the extent to which it recognizes them to be applicable.

Chapter V. Amendment

Article 69

Amendments to the present Statute shall be effected by the same procedure as is provided by the Charter of the United Nations for amendments to that Charter, subject however to any provisions which the General Assembly upon recommendation of the Security Council may adopt concerning the participation of states which are parties to the present Statute but are not Members of the United Nations.

Article 70

The Court shall have power to propose such amendments to the present Statute as it may deem necessary, through written communications to the Secretary-General, for consideration in conformity with the provisions of Article 69.

APPENDIX 5: UNIVERSAL DECLARATION OF HUMAN RIGHTS

Preamble

Whereas recognition of the inherent dignity and of the equal and inalienable rights of all members of the human family is the foundation of freedom, justice, and peace in the world,

Whereas disregard and contempt for human rights have resulted in barbarous acts which have outraged the conscience of mankind, and the advent of a world in which human beings shall enjoy freedom of speech and belief and freedom from fear and want has been proclaimed as the highest aspiration of the common people,

Whereas it is essential, if man is not to be compelled to have recourse, as a last resort, to rebellion against tyranny and oppression, that human rights should be protected by the rule of law,

Whereas it is essential to promote the development of friendly relations between nations,

Whereas the peoples of the United Nations have in the Charter reaffirmed their faith in fundamental human rights, in the dignity and worth of the human person and in the equal rights of men and women and have determined to promote social progress and better standards of life in larger freedom,

Whereas Member States have pledged themselves to achieve, in cooperation with the United Nations, the promotion of universal respect for and observance of human rights and fundamental freedoms,

Whereas a common understanding of these rights and freedoms is of the greatest importance for the full realization of this pledge,

Now, therefore THE GENERAL ASSEMBLY proclaims THIS UNIVERSAL DECLARATION OF HUMAN RIGHTS as a common standard of achievement for all peoples and all nations, to the end that every individual and every organ of society, keeping this Declaration constantly in mind, shall strive by teaching and education to promote respect for these rights and freedoms and by progressive measures, national and international, to secure their universal and effective recognition and observance, both among the peoples of Member States themselves and among the peoples of territories under their jurisdiction.

Article 1

All human beings are born free and equal in dignity and rights. They are endowed with reason and conscience and should act towards one another in a spirit of brotherhood.

Article 2

Everyone is entitled to all the rights and freedoms set forth in this Declaration, without distinction of any kind, such as race, colour, sex, language, religion, political or other opinion, national or social origin, property, birth or other status. Furthermore, no distinction shall be made on the basis of the political, jurisdictional or international status of the country or territory to which a person belongs, whether it be independent, trust, non-self-governing or under any other limitation of sovereignty.

Article 3
Everyone has the right to life, liberty and security of person.

Article 4
No one shall be held in slavery or servitude; slavery and the slave trade shall be prohibited in all their forms.

Article 5
No one shall be subjected to torture or to cruel, inhuman or degrading treatment or punishment.

Article 6
Everyone has the right to recognition everywhere as a person before the law.

Article 7
All are equal before the law and are entitled without any discrimination to equal protection of the law. All are entitled to equal protection against any discrimination in violation of this Declaration and against any incitement to such discrimination.

Article 8
Everyone has the right to an effective remedy by the competent national tribunals for acts violating the fundamental rights granted him by the constitution or by law.

Article 9
No one shall be subjected to arbitrary arrest, detention or exile.

Article 10
Everyone is entitled in full equality to a fair and public hearing by an independent and impartial tribunal, in the determination of his rights and obligations and of any criminal charge against him.

Article 11
1. Everyone charged with a penal offense has the right to be presumed innocent until proved guilty according to law in a public trial at which he has had all the guarantees necessary for his defense.
2. No one shall be held guilty of any penal offence on account of any act or omission which did not constitute a penal offense, under national or international law, at the time when it was committed. Nor shall a heavier penalty be imposed than the one that was applicable at the time the penal offence was committed.

Article 12
No one shall be subjected to arbitrary interference with his privacy, family, home, or correspondence, nor to attacks upon his honour and reputation. Everyone has the right to the protection of the law against such interference or attacks.

Article 13

1. Everyone has the right to freedom of movement and residence within the borders of each state.
2. Everyone has the right to leave any country, including his own, and to return to his country.

Article 14

1. Everyone has the right to seek and to enjoy in other countries asylum from persecution.
2. This right may not be invoked in the case of prosecutions genuinely arising from non-political crimes or from acts contrary to the purposes and principles of the United Nations.

Article 15

1. Everyone has the right to a nationality.
2. No one shall be arbitrarily deprived of his nationality nor denied the right to change his nationality.

Article 16

1. Men and women of full age, without any limitation due to race, nationality or religion, have the right to marry and to found a family. They are entitled to equal rights as to marriage, during marriage and at its dissolution.
2. Marriage shall be entered into only with the free and full consent of the intending spouses.
3. The family is the natural and fundamental group unit of society and is entitled to protection by society and the State.

Article 17

1. Everyone has the right to own property alone as well as in association with others.
2. No one shall be arbitrarily deprived of his property.

Article 18

Everyone has the right to freedom of thought, conscience, and religion; this right includes freedom to change his religion or belief, and freedom, either alone or in community with others and in public or private, to manifest his religion or belief in teaching, practice, worship, and observance.

Article 19

Everyone has the right to freedom of opinion and expression; this right includes freedom to hold opinions without interference and to seek, receive, and impart information and ideas through any media and regardless of frontiers.

Article 20

1. Everyone has the right to freedom of peaceful assembly and association.
2. No one may be compelled to belong to an association.

Article 21

1. Everyone has the right to take part in the government of his country, directly or through freely chosen representatives.
2. Everyone has the right of equal access to public service in his country.
3. The will of the people shall be the basis of the authority of government; this will shall be expressed in periodic and genuine elections which shall be by universal and equal suffrage and shall be held by secret vote or by equivalent free voting procedures.

Article 22

Everyone, as a member of society, has the right to social security and is entitled to realization, through national effort and international cooperation and in accordance with the organization and resources of each State, of the economic, social, and cultural rights indispensable for his dignity and the free development of his personality.

Article 23

1. Everyone has the right to work, to free choice of employment, to just and favourable conditions of work, and to protection against unemployment.
2. Everyone, without any discrimination, has the right to equal pay for equal work.
3. Everyone who works has the right to just and favourable remuneration ensuring for himself and his family an existence worthy of human dignity, and supplemented, if necessary, by other means of social protection.
4. Everyone has the right to form and to join trade unions for the protection of his interests.

Article 24

Everyone has the right to rest and leisure, including reasonable limitation of working hours and periodic holidays with pay.

Article 25

1. Everyone has the right to a standard of living adequate for the health and well-being of himself and of his family, including food, clothing, housing and medical care and necessary social services, and the right to security in the event of unemployment, sickness, disability, widowhood, old age, or other lack of livelihood in circumstances beyond his control.
2. Motherhood and childhood are entitled to special care and assistance. All children, whether born in or out of wedlock, shall enjoy the same social protection.

Article 26

1. Everyone has the right to education. Education shall be free, at least in the elementary and fundamental stages. Elementary education shall be compulsory. Technical and professional education shall be made generally available and higher education shall be equally accessible to all on the basis of merit.
2. Education shall be directed to the full development of the human personality and to the strengthening of respect for human rights and fundamental freedoms. It shall promote understanding, tolerance and friendship among all nations, racial or religious groups, and shall further the activities of the United Nations for the maintenance of peace.
3. Parents have a prior right to choose the kind of education that shall be given to their children.

Article 27

1. Everyone has the right freely to participate in the cultural life of the community, to enjoy the arts, and to share in scientific advancement and its benefits.
2. Everyone has the right to the protection of the moral and material interests resulting from any scientific, literary, or artistic production of which he is the author.

Article 28

Everyone is entitled to a social and international order in which the rights and freedoms set forth in this Declaration can be fully realized.

Article 29

1. Everyone has duties to the community in which alone the free and full development of his personality is possible.
2. In the exercise of his rights and freedoms, everyone shall be subject only to such limitations as are determined by law solely for the purpose of securing due recognition and respect for the rights and freedoms of others and of meeting the just requirements of morality, public order, and the general welfare in a democratic society.
3. These rights and freedoms may in no case be exercised contrary to the purposes and principles of the United Nations.

Article 30

Nothing in this Declaration may be interpreted as implying for any State, group, or person any right to engage in any activity or to perform any act aimed at the destruction of any of the rights and freedoms set forth herein.

SUBJECT INDEX

Abu Ghraib prison 130, 434
Academic Council on the United Nations
    System (ACUNS) 89
accountability:
    and Bretton Woods institutions 252
    and democratic governance 632
    and international organizations 204–6
    and nongovernmental organizations 261
    and peacebuilding 422–3
    and United Nations 261
Administrative Committee on Coordination
    (ACC) 569
Advisory Committee on Administrative and
    Budgetary Questions (ACABQ) 691
Afghanistan 121
    and International Security Assistance Force
    124
    and peace enforcement 372, 380
    and peacebuilding 410–11, 416
    and sanctions 128, 357, 429
        monitoring and implementation 362
        targeted sanctions 358, 359
    and Soviet Union 393
    and United States 410
Africa:
    and electoral assistance to 626
    and good governance 630–1
    and HIV/AIDS 588
    and peacekeeping operations 222, 228, 229
    and regional organizations 125
    see also individual countries
African Charter on Human and Peoples'
    Rights (1981) 514
African Commission on Human Rights 451,
    455
African Court of Human Rights 456
African National Congress (ANC) 435
African Standby Force 230
African Union (AU) 125, 227, 381
    and capacity building 229
    and children's rights 514
    and Darfur 229, 377
    and peacebuilding 407, 419
    and peaceful settlement of disputes 307
Agence France-Presse 276
Agenda 21 552, 602

Al Jazeera 276
Al Qaeda 128, 410, 427
Alabama Claims arbitration (1872) 193
Albania 379
Algeria:
    and electoral assistance to 628
    and Non-Aligned Movement 130
alliances, and United Nations 53
American Convention on Human Rights
    (1969) 514
Amnesty International 256
anarchy 4, 44
Anglo-Iranian Oil Company 595
Angola 121, 122, 186
    and electoral assistance to 627, 629
    and natural resources 593, 602, 607
    and peacebuilding 413, 415
    and peacekeeping operations 405
    and sanctions 124, 352, 357
        commodity-specific 359–60
        monitoring of 362
        targeted sanctions 358, 359
anti-globalization movement 239
Aouzou Strip 119
apartheid 453
    and Security Council 121
Arab Charter on Human Rights 455, 456
Arab League 218–19
    and peaceful settlement of disputes 307
Arab–Israeli War (1967), and General
    Assembly 104
arbitration, and peaceful settlement of
    disputes 306
Argentina, and financial crisis 238
Armenia, and electoral assistance to 628
arms embargoes, and sanctions 359
Asian–African Conference (Bandung, 1955)
    108
Assembly of States Parties (ASP), and
    International Criminal Court 474
Associated Press 276
Association of Southeast Asian Nations
    (ASEAN) 227
Atlantic Charter (1941) 593–4
Atlantic City Conference (1916) 266
Australia 380

autonomy 56 n19
    and United Nations 53
avian flu 588
Azerbaijan, and electoral assistance to 628

Bangladesh 393
Baruch Plan 289
BBC 276
Berlin Blockade 120
Biafra war (1967–1970) 482, 483
Biological and Toxin Weapons Convention
    (BTWC) 294, 588
bioterrorism 588–9
Bloomberg News 278
Bolivia, and International Court of Justice
    195
Bonn International Center for Conversion
    363
Bonn–Berlin Process 363
Bosnia and Herzegovina 41, 122, 127, 332
    and foreign administration 155
    and Implementation Force 123
    and institutional coordination 240
    and 'mixed' courts 472
    and peace enforcement 380, 406
    and peacebuilding 415
    and peacekeeping operations 184
    and regional organizations 125
    and Stabilisation Force 123
Bougainville 380
Brahimi report, see Report of the Panel on
    United Nations Peace Operations
    (2000)
Brandt Commission 552
    see also Partners in Development: Report of
    the Commission on International
    Development
Brazil:
    and financial crisis 238
    and Global Compact 271
    and International Court of Justice 195
Bretton Woods institutions 140, 233, 562
    and coordination of economic and social
        affairs 570–1
        assessment of 575
    and Economic and Social Council 138, 139
    and natural resources 594
    and structural adjustment 646
    see also international financial institutions;
        International Monetary Fund;
        World Bank
British Committee on the Theory of
    International Politics 47
Brundtland Commission 552, 601, 607
Burundi 154
    and Boutros-Ghali 187
    and peace enforcement 222

and peacebuilding 407, 411, 416
business, see private sector
Business Council for Sustainable
    Development (BCSD) 270
Businessman's Peace Movement 265

Cambodia 41, 122, 127, 393
    and criminal tribunal 129
    and electoral assistance to 627
    and 'mixed' courts 472, 473
    and peace enforcement 373
    and peacebuilding 414, 627
    and peacekeeping operations 327, 405
    and UN administration 155
Cameroon 154
Cameroons 154
    as Trust Territory 151
Canada:
    and financing of United Nations 679, 683
    and influence in United Nations 52–3
capital investment, and 'soft' intervention
    399
capitalism, and United Nations 51–2
Cardoso report, see Report of the Panel of
    Eminent Persons on United
    Nations–Civil Society Relations
    (2004)
CARE 481
Carnegie Commission on Preventing
    Deadly Conflict 312, 314
Carnegie Endowment for International
    Peace 88–9
Central African Republic 123
Chad 8, 119
change, and United Nations:
    and qualitative changes 15–16
    and quantitative changes 13–15
Charter of Child Welfare of the League of
    Nations 512
Charter of Economic Rights and Duties of
    States (CERDS) 597–8
Charter of the United Nations:
    and amendment process 654–5
    and collective rights 527
    and conflict prevention 300–1, 313
    and disarmament 288–9
    and Economic and Social Council 568
    and economic and social development 562
    and finance provisions 677–8
    and General Assembly 58
    and human rights 441–2, 541–2
    and humanitarian action 481
    and humanitarian intervention 391, 397,
        401
    and international criminal courts 465–6
    and international law 59
    and legal positivism 59

and legal powers 58–9
and obligations under 58
and peace enforcement 332
and peaceful settlement of disputes 300, 301
    Article 2 301–2
    Article 2 (3) 302–3
    Article 33 303–4
and provisions of 58–9
and sanctions 349
and Secretary-General 176–8
and state sovereignty 8, 58, 389, 395
and use of force 394
and women 496
see also United Nations Conference on
    International Organization (San
    Francisco, 1945)
Chechnya 381
Chief Executives Board for Coordination
    (CEB) 569–70, 574
children:
and armed conflict 515
and child labor 520–1
and child mortality 12, 519–20
and child pornography 616
and child soldiers 521
and Committee on the Rights of the
    Child 513, 522
and Convention on the Rights of the
    Child 513–14, 516
    implementation 522
and conventions relating to 514
and developing countries 511
and education 519
and gender equality 519
and HIV/AIDS 520
and human rights 512
and hunger 519
and immunization programs 520
and intergovernmental organizations
    516–17
and international focus on 515–16
and international law 514
and malaria 520
and nongovernmental organizations
    515, 517
and origins of international children's
    movement 512, 521
and poverty 519
as refugees 512, 517
and regional organizations 514, 518
and trafficking 521, 615
    sexual exploitation 616
and United Nations agencies 517–18
and United Nations Children's Fund 517
and vulnerability of 511
and World Summit for Children (1990)
    515

Chile 595
China 8, 599
and Comprehensive Test Ban Treaty 295
and financing of United Nations 681, 683,
    684–5
and International Court of Justice 196
and International Criminal Court 130, 473
and landmine convention 296
and North Vietnam 393
and responsibility to protect 398
and Security Council 120, 660,
    661, 663
cholera, and International Health Regulations
    585
cities, and international relations 707
civil society:
and definition of 256
and global civil society 6
    nongovernmental organizations 256,
        257–8, 261
    robustness of 256
and nature of 255–6
and political relevance of 256
and the state 255–6
and United Nations 262, 711
    attempts to influence 258–9
    global deliberations 257–9
    global partnerships 259–60
    reciprocity 257
    relationship between 254, 262
    as target of 256
    see also nongovernmental organizations;
        nonstate actors
civilians, and deaths in wars 5, 129, 395
CNN 276
'coalitions of the willing':
and humanitarian intervention 400
and peace enforcement 123–4, 222, 371
Cold War:
and General Assembly 103–4, 107–9
and humanitarian action 483
and peacekeeping operations 405
and regional organizations 218–20
and Secretary-General's role 179–82
    under Hammarskjöld 180–1
    under Lie 180
    under Pérez de Cuéllar 182
    under U Thant 181–2
    under Waldheim 182
and Security Council 117, 120–1, 219
collective security, and peace enforcement
    371–3
colonialism, and trusteeship 150
Columbia University, and oral history
    archive 87
commercial sexual exploitation of children
    (CSEC) 616

Commission for Conventional Armaments (CCA) 289–90
Commission for Relief in Belgium 480
Commission for Social Development (CSD) 502
Commission on Global Governance 142, 566
    and *Our Global Neighbourhood* 10
    and security 553
    see also global governance
Commission on Human Rights (CHR) 138, 439, 447–50, 531–2, 543, 667
    and establishment of 441–2
    and indigenous peoples 533–4
    and international bill of human rights 442–3
    and natural resource management 596, 604
    and reform of 440–1
    and responding to violations 453–4
    see also Human Rights Council
Commission on International Development 565
Commission on Narcotic Drugs (CND) 615
Commission on Sustainable Development 258
Commission on the Private Sector and Development 271
Commission on the Status of Women (CSW) 497–8
Committee for Programme and Coordination 691
Committee on the Elimination of Racial Discrimination 530–1
Common Country Assessment (CCA) 572, 577
Commonwealth of Independent States (CIS) 227
    and Georgia 125, 380
    and human rights 456
conciliation commissions, and peaceful settlement of disputes 305–6
Conference of the Committee on Disarmament (CCD) 291
Conference on Disarmament (CD) 291–2, 550
Conference on Security and Co-operation in Europe 360
    see also Organization for Security and Co-operation in Europe
    and peaceful settlement of disputes 307
conflict commodities, and organized crime 618
conflict prevention:
    and *An Agenda for Peace* 311
    and analysis of 301
    and apprehension towards 313

and approaches to 314
    operational prevention 314–15
    structural prevention 315–16
    and Carnegie Commission on Preventing Deadly Conflict 312, 314
    and challenges of:
        classification problems 317
        invisibility of 317
        systemic prevention 317
    and Charter of the United Nations 300–1, 313
    and Economic and Social Council 315–16
    and General Assembly 315, 317–18
    and impact of Rwandan genocide 312
    and increased focus on 311
    and International Criminal Court 312
    and key principles 314
    and mandate for:
        development of 311–13
        sources of 313–14
    and Peacebuilding Commission 313
    and *Prevention of Armed Conflict* 311
    and preventive diplomacy 312, 406
    and Secretary-General 315, 316
    and Security Council 312, 315, 318
    and states 318
    see also peaceful settlement of disputes
Congo crisis 181, 310, 373
    and financing of United Nations 683–4, 687–8
Congress of Local and Regional Authorities of Europe (CLRAE) 708
constructivism:
    and international law 72
    and role of United Nations 48–50, 51
        autonomy 53
    and study of United Nations 86
Convention against Genocide (1948) 443, 453, 455, 465, 543
Convention against Torture 454, 455, 543
Convention against Transnational Organized Crime 612
Convention Concerning Indigenous and Tribal Peoples in Independent Countries 534
Convention Concerning the Protection and Integration of Indigenous and Other Tribal and Semi-Tribal Populations in Independent Countries 532
Convention on Biological Diversity 601–2
Convention on Conventional Weapons 550
Convention on Psychotropic Substances (1971) 614
Convention on the Elimination of All Forms of Discrimination against Women (CEDAW) 12, 454, 500–1, 512, 543, 645

Convention on the Elimination of All
    Forms of Racial Discrimination
    (1965) 443, 454, 455, 530–1, 543
Convention on the Physical Protection of
    Nuclear Material (1980) 616
Convention on the Prohibition of the
    Development, Production, Stockpiling
    and Use of Chemical Weapons
    (CWC) 293–4
Convention on the Prohibition of the Use,
    Stockpiling, Production and Transfer
    of Anti-Personnel Mines and Their
    Destruction (1997) 9, 296, 705
Convention on the Rights of the Child (1989)
    511, 513–14, 516, 543, 645
Convention on International Trade in
    Endangered Species of Wild Fauna
    and Flora (CITES) 260
Convention relating to the Status of Refugees
    (1951) 512, 543, 548
conventional weapons 550
    and disarmament 289–90, 295–6
    see also disarmament
coordination:
    and humanitarian action 483, 484, 485–6,
        488–9
    and peacekeeping operations 335–6, 420–2
    and United Nations 561–2
    see also coordination of economic and
        social affairs
coordination of economic and social affairs
        561–2, 578–9
    and assessment of 572–3
        Bretton Woods institutions 575
        Economic and Social Council 573–4
        executive heads 574–5
        field coordination 577
        Secretariat 575–6
    and attempts to improve 564–7
        Annan's reforms 566
        Boutros-Ghali's reforms 566
        High-level Panel on UN System-wide
            Coherence 567
        Millennium Development Goals 566–7
        A New United Nations Structure for
            Global Economic Co-operation (1975)
            565
        Partners in Development (1969) 565
        Pérez de Cuéllar's reforms 565
        A Study of the Capacity of the United
            Nations Development System (1969)
            565
    as divisive issue 579
    and Economic and Social Council 563,
        567–9, 578–9, 665
    and machinery of 567
        Bretton Woods institutions 570–1

Economic and Social Council 567–9
    executive heads 569–70
    field coordination 572
    Secretariat 571–2
    and outline of 562–4
        autonomous agencies 563
        Charter of the United Nations 562
        complexity of 563–4
        decentralized nature of 563
        Economic and Social Council 563
        General Assembly 562–3
        United Nations Conference on
            International Organization (San
            Francisco, 1945) 562
corruption, and peacekeeping procurement
        170
Côte d'Ivoire 125
    and peace enforcement 222
    and peacebuilding 411, 416
    and sanctions 357, 358–9
        monitoring and implementation 362
Cotonou Partnership Agreement 624
Council of Europe:
    and Bosnia and Herzegovina 125
    and children's rights 514, 518
    and human rights 455, 456
    and local authorities 708
    and peaceful settlement of disputes 307
counterfeiting, and organized crime 613–14
counter-terrorism, and sanctions 359
Counter-Terrorism Committee (CTC) of
        the UN Security Council 128, 430
Counter-Terrorism Executive Directorate
        (CTED) 431
crime, see organized crime
crimes against humanity 399
    and Nuremberg trials 465
    see also International Criminal Court;
        international criminal tribunals
crisis management, and peace enforcement 373
Croatia 406, 407, 413
Cuba:
    and Non-Aligned Movement 130
    and Nuclear Non-Proliferation Treaty 293
Cuban Missile Crisis 120
cultural homogeneity, and statehood 526
custom, and international law 66
Cyprus 120, 373
Czechoslovakia 393

Dag Hammarskjöld Foundation 163
Dag Hammarskjöld Library 278–9
Dakar Framework for Action (2000) 519
Darfur 125, 490
    and African Union 229, 377
    and humanitarian action 491
    and peacebuilding 416

Dayton Peace Accords 357, 413, 415, 472
Declaration of Geneva (1923) 512
Declaration of the Rights of the Child (1959)
    512
Declaration of the United Nations Conference
    on the Human Environment 600–1
Declaration on Permanent Sovereignty over
    Natural Resources 596, 600
Declaration on the Elimination of Violence
    against Women (DEVAW) 501
Declaration on the Granting of
    Independence to Colonial
    Countries and Peoples (1960)
    532–3
Declaration on the Protection of Women
    and Children in Emergency and
    Armed Conflict 505
Declaration on the Right to Development
    645
Declaration on the Rights of Persons
    Belonging to National, Ethnic,
    Religious and Linguistic Minorities
    (1992) 528, 530, 531, 532
decolonization 7, 12, 21, 22, 482
    and General Assembly 108
    and resource sovereignty 593
    and United Nations 47
democratic deficit, and international law
    75–6
democratic governance:
    and donors' definition 624
    and human rights 632
    and international financial institutions
        630–1
    and meaning of democracy 622, 623
        Pakistan 622
        United Nations' definition 623
        United States 622–3
    and meaning of governance 623–4
    and Millennium Development Goals
        621, 631
    and recent expansion of 620
    and regional organizations 621
    and requirements of 621–2
    and restraints on 620
    and semi-authoritarian regimes 620–1
    and threats to 621
    and transnational corporations 621
    and United Nations 624–7
        electoral assistance 625–631
        General Assembly 625
    see also global governance; governance
Democratic Republic of the Congo (DRC)
    120
    and natural resources 593, 604

and peace enforcement 222, 377, 380
and peacebuilding 406, 407, 416
and sanctions 357, 607
    monitoring and implementation 362
    targeted sanctions 358–9
democratization:
    and peacebuilding 418
    and Security Council 127
    see also democratic governance
Department for Policy Coordination and
        Sustainable Development (DPCSD)
        566
Department of Disarmament Affairs 427
Department of Economic and Social Affairs
        (DESA) 566, 629
Department of Humanitarian Affairs
        (DHA) 358, 486
    and weaknesses of 489
Department of Peacekeeping Operations
        (DPKO) 165, 166, 220, 222, 226, 229
    and peace enforcement 370–1
Department of Political Affairs (DPA) 221,
        310
    and conflict prevention 315
Department of Public Information (DPI)
        83, 276–9
Department of Social and Economic
        Development 566
Department of Technical Co-operation for
        Development (DTCD) 626
deputy secretary-general (DSG) 576
developing countries:
    and children in 511
    and financing of United Nations 683–4
    and human rights 440, 442, 444
    and media 283
    and resource sovereignty 595–600
        marine resources 599
    and right to development 456–7
Development Alternatives with Women
        for a New Era (DAWN) 499
Development Cooperation Forum 145
diamonds:
    and natural resource management 607
    and organized crime 618
    and sanctions 359–60
disarmament 287–8
    and achievements in:
        Biological and Toxin Weapons
            Convention 294, 588
        Chemical Weapons Convention 293–4
        Comprehensive Test Ban Treaty 295
        land mines 296
        Nuclear Non-Proliferation Treaty
            291–2

Partial Test Ban Treaty 294–5
and Charter of the United Nations 288–9
and Conference of the Committee on
    Disarmament 291
and Conference on Disarmament 291–2
and conventional weapons 289–90, 295–6
and Disarmament Commission 290, 291
and great power consensus 297
and human security 550
and implementation 297
and joint Soviet–American statement
    (1961) 290–1
and League of Nations failure 287, 288
and multilateral disarmament 290
and normative framework for 290, 296
and nuclear weapons 289
    Baruch Plan 289
and postwar concern with 287
and role of 296
and weapons of mass destruction 289
Disarmament Commission 290, 291
disaster relief, see humanitarian action
discrimination, and definition of 446–7
disputes, see peaceful settlement of disputes
Division for the Advancement of Women
    (UN Secretariat) 498
Dominican Republic 120
Draft Declaration on the Rights of Indigenous
    Peoples 533–4
drugs, and organized crime 612, 614–15
Dumbarton Oaks 139, 161, 562, 653

East Asian financial crisis 238
East Timor 122
    and election monitoring 127
    and humanitarian crisis 396
    and International Force in East Timor 123–4
    and 'mixed' courts 471
    and peace enforcement 377, 380
    and peacebuilding 406, 413
    and UN Transitional Administration
        118–19, 155
Eastern Slovenia:
    and peacekeeping operations 327
    and UN Transitional Administration 155
Economic and Social Council (ECOSOC) of
    the United Nations 704
    and assessment of 141–3, 573–4, 665
    and Bretton Woods institutions 138, 139,
        570–1
    and conflict prevention 315–16
    and coordination of economic and social
        affairs 563, 567–9, 578–9, 665
    and decline of 138, 564–5, 664
    and expansion of 660, 661, 664
    and functions of 136, 568

and future of 145–6
and General Assembly 98–9, 104, 105, 138,
    140, 658
and history and development of 139–41
and human rights 138, 667
and International Court of Justice 138
and international financial institutions
    138, 139
and membership of 138, 140
and natural resource management 593,
    594, 596, 603
and nongovernmental organizations 136,
    146, 257, 667
and reform efforts 143–5, 664–8
and Secretariat 138
and Security Council 118, 138, 146
and subsidiary bodies of 137–8
and transnational corporations 268
and Trusteeship Council 138
and United Nations conferences 138
and women's rights 498
and working methods 138–9, 568–9
and World Summit Outcome (2005) 145–6
economic and social development 644
    and development objectives 644–5
    and financial support 646–7
    and monitoring and evaluation 647–8
    and support for policymaking 646
    and women and gender 645
    see also human development
Economic Community of West African
    States (ECOWAS) 125
    and Liberia 220, 380, 381, 414, 547
    and Military Observer Group of 124
    and peacebuilding 407
    and peaceful settlement of disputes 307
    and Sierra Leone 547
economic development, see coordination
        of economic and social affairs;
        economic and social development;
        human development
economics, and international law 71
education 12
    and children 519
    and Human Development Index 637
    see also human development
EFE (Spanish-language news agency) 276
Egypt:
    and Chemical Weapons Convention 293
    and Comprehensive Test Ban Treaty 295
    and landmine convention 296
    and Non-Aligned Movement 131
El Salvador 41, 599
    and electoral assistance to 627, 629
    and human rights 126
    and International Court of Justice 203

El Salvador (*cont.*)
  and peacebuilding 413–14
  and peacekeeping operations 327, 405
Elected Representative Liaison Unit 710–11
election assistance 127, 628–30
  see also individual country cases
Electoral Assistance Division (EAD) 626, 627
  and major electoral missions 629–30
  and standard electoral assistance activities 628–29
emergency relief coordinator 486
English School, and role of United Nations 47–8
environmental degradation 4–5
  and human security 552
  and women and gender 502
environmental issues, and business 270
Equatorial Guinea 204
Eritrea:
  and electoral assistance to 627, 629
  and peace enforcement 222
  and sanctions 357
    arms embargoes 359
Ethics Office 170
Ethiopia:
  and electoral assistance to 628
  and peace enforcement 222
  and sanctions 357
    arms embargoes 359
European Convention on the Exercise of
    Children's Rights (1996) 514
European Convention on the Prevention of
    Torture 455
European Court of Human Rights 451, 456
European Union (EU) 4, 227
  and Bosnia and Herzegovina 125
  and children's rights 514, 518
  and financing of United Nations 693
  and peace enforcement 380
  and peacebuilding 407
  and peaceful settlement of disputes 307
  and peacekeeping operations 228, 229
  and sanctions 360
  and Security Council 125–6
  and state sovereignty 7
European Union Force (EUFOR) 380
Exclusive Economic Zone (EEZ), and marine
    resources 599–600
Executive Committee on Humanitarian
    Affairs (ECHA) 489
Executive Outcomes 407

fact-finding, and peaceful settlement of
    disputes 304–5
failed states:
  and historical legacies 702
  and state sovereignty 8
  and terrorism 410
  and trusteeship 155

family, and human rights 529
Federal Bureau of Investigation 162
Federal Republic of Yugoslavia (Serbia and
    Montenegro) 372
feminism 497
  see also women and gender
feminist theory, and international law 74
finances of United Nations:
  and alternative financing 711–13
    arms sales tax 712
    aviation fuel tax 712
    carbon energy tax 712
    dedicated taxes 697, 712
    Internet activity/e-mail tax 712
    natural resources extraction tax 712
    private sector 696–7
    Tobin Tax 697, 712
  and assessed budgets 676
  and assessment of contributions 678–81
  and budget approval 690–4
  and centrality of 675
  and Charter of the United Nations 677–8
  and conflicts over 676
  and crises in:
    Soviet Union 687–8
    United States 688–90
  and expenditure 14, 15
  and late payments 681–3
  and League of Nations precedent 676–7
  and member state contributions 675
  and peacekeeping operations 683–7, 693–4
    assessment of contributions 684
    developing countries 683–4
    reform of assessment 685–7
    regional organizations 685
    United States 685, 687
    voluntary contributions 685
  and penalties for nonpayment 677–8
  and precarious state of 676
  and United States 676, 679, 681, 683, 684,
    685, 693, 696, 713
  and voluntary contributions 676, 684, 685,
    693–6
First International Sanitary Conference
    (Paris, 1851) 583
flu pandemic 588
Food and Agriculture Organization (FAO) 265,
    481, 503, 517, 519, 563, 593, 634, 703
  and natural resource management 594
food security, and human security 552
Ford Foundation 142, 163
foreign aid, and 'soft' intervention 399
Fourth UN World Conference on Women
    (Beijing, 1995) 498, 499–500, 519
France:
  and financing of United Nations 679, 683,
    684, 685, 688, 697

and former Yugoslavia 375
and human rights 441, 443–4, 528
and International Court of Justice 196
and International Criminal Court 130
and Rwanda 375
and sanctions 364, 365
and Security Council 661
and Sudan 377
Freedom House 620
French Revolution 526
functionalism 704
  and study of United Nations 85–6

Gardner report, see *A New United Nations*
    Structure for Global Economic
    Co-operation (1975)
Gates Foundation 272, 697
gender, see women and gender
Gender Empowerment Measure (GEM) 637
Gender-related Development Index (GDI)
    503, 637
General Agreement on Tariffs and Trade
    (GATT) 139, 267
  and control of infectious diseases 585
  and natural resources 594
General Assembly of the United Nations:
  and authority of:
    appointments 102
    colonial affairs 104–5
    overshadowing of 105–6
    peace and security issues 103–4, 118
    powers of 103
    relations with member states 103
    resolution 377 ('Uniting for Peace', 1950)
        104, 118, 309, 372
  and basic character of 98–9
    domination by weak states 98
    multilateral traditions 98
    parliamentary practices 98
    relationship with other UN organs 98–9
    sovereign equality of states 98
  and budget approval 690–4
  and Charter amendment 654–5
  and children's rights 512, 513, 515, 516
  and complexity of subsidiary machinery 659
  and conflict prevention 315, 317–18
  and democratic governance 625
    major electoral missions 629
  and disarmament 288, 289, 291
  and Economic and Social Council 98–9,
      104, 105, 138, 140, 658
  and economic and social development
      562–3
  and expansion of 657
  and finances 675
    assessing contributions 678–81
  and functions of 97, 656

and future of 112–13
and General Committee of 100
and HIV/AIDS 588
and human rights 453, 454
and humanitarian action 486
and inertia of 659
and institutional decline 97
and International Court of Justice 99, 197
and International Criminal Court 473
and legal powers 61
and natural resource management 593,
    596, 604
  marine resources 599
and natural resource sovereignty 597
and nongovernmental organizations 705
and Peacebuilding Commission 668
and peaceful settlement of disputes 302,
    309, 317–18
and political balance within 106–10
  Third World majority 105, 108–9
  Third World/European 'coalition' 109–10
  United States 107, 109
and reform of 656–9
and regional organizations 657
and Secretary-General, appointment
    process 176
and Security Council 98, 103–4, 118, 656–7
  reform of 661–2
and strengths and weaknesses of 657
and terrorism 428–9
  Ad Hoc Committee on 429
  definitional difficulties 428
  resolutions and conventions 428–9
and Trusteeship Council 98–9, 104–5
and working methods 99–102, 657–8
  agenda setting 100
  assessing support for resolutions 102
  committee system 100–1, 658
  consensus decision-making 658
  deliberative process 100–1
  gaining support for resolutions 101–2
  informal consultations 101
  regular sessions 99
  resolution production 657–8
  resolution quality 658
  scope of discussions 99
  special sessions 99
  time pressures 99–100, 105
  votes 102
and writings on 97
  purposes 110
  roll-call analyses 112
  scholarly 111–12
  United States' foreign policy 110–11
Geneva Conventions 465, 480
  and children 514
  and humanitarian law 445

Geneva Conventions (*cont.*)
  and laws of war 464, 545–6
  and war crimes 399
Georgia 125
  and peace enforcement 222, 380
Germany 683
Ghana 154
Ghana Aluminium Products 269
Global Alliance for Vaccines and
      Immunization 587
Global Campaign for Orphans and Children
      Made Vulnerable by HIV/AIDS 520
global civil society, *see* civil society
Global Compact 67, 256, 260, 264,
      270–1, 708
Global Demobilization Fund 641
Global Environment Facility 605
Global Fund to Fight AIDS, Tuberculosis
      and Malaria 520, 697
global governance 10–11, 254
  and challenges facing 713–14
  and General Assembly 112–13
  and 'global ruling class' 264–5, 272
  and local authorities 706, 707–8
  and multilateralism 701–2
  and United Nations 41, 257
    global deliberations 257–9
    global partnerships 259–60
  see also Commission on Global Governance;
      democratic governance; governance
Global Governance (journal) 10
Global Movement for Children 515, 516
Global Partnership for Conflict Prevention 312
globalization:
  and human development 642
  and organized crime 619
  and state sovereignty 7
Gold Coast 154
good offices, and peaceful settlement of
      disputes 305
governance:
  and human rights 459
  and international financial institutions 630–1
  and meaning of 623–4
  and United Nations, possible options 709–11
  see also democratic governance; global
      governance
Grameen Bank 502
Grenada 393
Group of '77', 105, 107, 130, 576
Group of 8, and health and security 588
Group of Experts on the Structure of the
      United Nations System 565
'groups of friends,' and Security Council 128–9
Guantánamo Bay 434
Guatemala:
  and human rights 126

and International Court of Justice 195
  and peace enforcement 406
  and peacebuilding 413–14
Guinea-Bissau 118
Gulf War (1991) 17
  and peace enforcement 372
  and Secretary-General 183
  and Security Council 123

Habitat, *see* United Nations Centre for Human
      Settlements (UNCHS, Habitat)
Hague Conventions 193, 306, 464
  and children 514
  and Martens Clause 546
Hague Peace Conferences 546, 703
Haiti 118
  and electoral assistance to 625, 629
  and naval blockade 124
  and Operation Uphold Democracy 123
  and peace enforcement 222, 375–6
  and sanctions 124, 352, 358, 544
    commodity-specific 359
Hamas 435
health:
  and children 519–20
  and public–private partnerships 587
  and security 587–90
  and women and gender 503–4
  see also HIV/AIDS; infectious diseases;
      World Health Organization
health for all (HFA), and World Health
      Organization 584
Health Organization of the League of
      Nations 583
heavily indebted poor countries (HIPC) initiative,
      and Bretton Woods institutions 239–40
Helsinki Accords 67
Heritage Foundation 89
High-level Panel on Threats, Challenges and
      Change (HLP) 18, 87, 118
  and establishment of 145, 432
  and HIV/AIDS 589
  and *A More Secure World* 229, 709
  and Peacebuilding Commission 157, 313
  and responsibility to protect 398
  and terrorism 432
High-level Panel on UN System-wide
      Coherence 567, 579
HIV/AIDS 5
  and children 520
  and human security 588
  and Joint UN Programme on HIV/AIDS
      503, 587
  and Security Council 588
  and women and gender 503
  and World AIDS Day (2005) 516
  and World Health Organization 584–5

hot pursuit, and military intervention 393
human development 5, 12
  and centrality of 634–5, 648
  and concepts of 636
    origin of 636
  and definition of 636
  and gender 640–1
  and Gender-Empowerment Measure 637
  and Gender-Related Development Index
    637
  and globalization 642
  and Human Development Index 636–9
  and Human Development Reports 12, 142,
    634–5, 639–42
  and Human Poverty Index 637
  and human rights 640
  and human security 641
  and Millennium Development Goals 456–7,
    642–3
  and misunderstandings of 643
  and natural resource sovereignty 596
    marine resources 598–600
  and right to development 456–7
  and security 301
  and sustainable development 600–2
  and women and gender 502–3
  see also coordination of economic and
    social affairs
Human Poverty Index (HPI) 637
human rights:
  and challenges facing:
    preventing government violation of 439
    upholding international protection 440
  and Charter of the United Nations 441–2,
    527–8
  and children 512
  and collective rights 527–30
  and Commission on Human Rights 138, 439
    establishment of 441–2
    international bill of human rights 442–3
    reform of 440–1
  and definition of international human
    rights law 525
  and democratic governance 632
  and developing countries 440, 442
  and development of international norms 12,
    439, 443–4
  and Economic and Social Council 138, 667
  and enforcement of 543–6
    international criminal tribunals 544–5
    sanctions 544
    shaming 543–4
    strategies for dealing with 455–6
  and human development 640
  and human security 539–40
    Charter of the United Nations 541–2
    enforcement 543–5

  historical background 540–1
  treaty regimes 542–3
  Universal Declaration of Human Rights
    (1948) 542
and humanitarian intervention 400
and implementation 453–4
  apartheid 453
  Commission on Human Rights 453–4
  General Assembly 454
  International Criminal Court 454
  Security Council 454
  treaty monitoring 454
and indigenous peoples 525–6, 532–6
  Charter of the United Nations 528
  definition of 533
  Draft Declaration on the Rights of
    Indigenous Peoples 533–4
  International Labour Organization
    conventions 532, 534
  League of Nations 527
  Permanent Forum on Indigenous
    Issues 534–5
  self-determination 532–4
  Universal Declaration of Human Rights
    (1948) 528–9
and machinery of:
  Commission on Human Rights 447–50
  Human Rights Council 450–1
  Office of the High Commissioner for
    Human Rights 452–3
  treaty bodies 451–2
and market capitalism 440
and Millennium Development Goals 457
and minorities 525–6, 530–2, 535, 536, 540–1
  Charter of the United Nations 528
  League of Nations 526–7
  Minorities Declaration (1992) 528, 530,
    531, 532
  Minority Treaties System 526–7
  Universal Declaration of Human Rights
    (1948) 528–9
and natural resource management 595, 604
and nongovernmental organizations 544
and principles of international human
    rights law 444–7
  humanitarian law 445
  international public policy 445
and responsibility to protect 397–8, 401,
    440, 458, 548
and right to development 456–7
and risk assessment 458–60
and United Nations Conference on
    International Organization (San
    Francisco, 1945) 441–2, 527
and Security Council 126–7
and sexual rights 503–4
and state sovereignty 8, 391

human rights (*cont.*)
  and states 391, 400
  and terrorism 434
  and violations of 5, 125, 439, 450, 453, 458, 483, 490
  and women and gender 504–5
Human Rights Centre (Geneva) 532
Human Rights Committee 446–7, 529–30
  and minorities and indigenous peoples
    529–30, 531
Human Rights Council 138, 440, 447–8, 450–1,
    531–2, 544, 604, 667
  and creation of 146
  and Draft Declaration on the Rights of
    Indigenous Peoples 534
human security 5, 539–40, 554–5
  and broadening agenda of 552–4
  and debate over 539
  and definition of 555 n2
  and freedom from fear 540
  and freedom from want 540, 551
    breadth of agenda 552–4
    economic development 301, 551
    environmental degradation 552
    food security 552
    historical background 551
    inequality 552
    sustainable development 552, 553
  and human development 641
  and human rights 539–40
    Charter of the United Nations 541–2
    enforcement of 543–5
    historical background 540–1
    treaty regimes 542–3
    Universal Declaration of Human Rights
      (1948) 542
  and humanitarian conception of 545
    armaments regulation 550
    Charter of the United Nations 546
    historical background 545–6
    legal norm development 550
    peacebuilding 548–50
    peacekeeping operations 547
    responsibility to protect 548
    use of force 547–8
    victims of war 548
  and the individual 539
  and infectious diseases 587–90
    surveillance and response mechanisms 588–9
  and origin of concept 552–3
Human Security Commission 553–4
Human Security Report 2005 12
humanitarian action 492–3
  and calls for reform 490–2
    consolidation and centralization 492–3
    system upgrade 491–2
  and centrality of 479
  and changing humanitarian landscape 487–9

  and Charter of the United Nations 481
  and collaborative approach 490, 491
  and constraints on 481–2
  and coordination problems 480, 483–6,
    488–9
  and criticisms of 479–80, 484, 491
  and Darfur 491
  and definition of 479
  and Department of Humanitarian Affairs
    486
  and Executive Committee on Humanitarian
    Affairs 489
  and gender awareness 506
  and human security:
    Charter of the United Nations 546
    historical background 545–6
    peacekeeping operations 547
    use of force 547–8
    victims of war 548
  and internally displaced persons 490
    Darfur 491
  and nongovernmental organizations 481,
    482, 483–4
  and Office for the Coordination of
    Humanitarian Affairs 489
  and post-Cold War era 485–7
    emergency relief coordinator 486
    expectations 485
    norms and principles 486–7
    Persian Gulf crisis (1991) 485
    reorganization of 486
  and postwar development of 481–2
  and pre-1945 period 480–1
  and refugees 482
    growth of 483
  and United Nations Disaster Relief
    Coordinator 482–4
    agency competition 483, 484
    Cold War 483
    funding 483
  see also humanitarian intervention
humanitarian changes, and qualitative
    change 15–16
humanitarian intervention:
  and abuse of 400
  and anti-colonialism 392
  and authorizing agents for 394
  and debate over 387, 388, 391, 396, 401
    Kosovo 396
    opposition to 397
    rejected by Non-Aligned Movement 396–7
    Rwanda 396
  and definition of 388
  and end of Cold War 391
  and history of 392
  and human security 547–8
  and illegality 392

and impact of media 126
and International Commission on
    Intervention and State Sovereignty
    397–8
and interpretation of phrase 397
and justifications for 388
    civil war 394
    human rights 400
    self-determination 394
and legitimacy of 387
    criteria for 398, 399
and nonintervention 389, 390, 395
and paradox of 387
and peace enforcement 378
and responsibility to protect 397–8, 401,
    458, 548
and Security Council 126, 391
and 'soft' intervention 399
and state sovereignty 8, 389–90
    and use of force 388, 392–4, 398
see also humanitarian action; International
    Commission on Intervention and State
    Sovereignty
Humanitarian Response Review (HRR) 491

Iceland 599
ideas:
    and constructivism 49
    and role of United Nations 49–50
impartiality:
    and peace enforcement 381–2
    and peacekeeping operations
        325–6
Implementation Force (IFOR) 380
income levels, and Human Development
    Index (HDI) 637
Independent Commission on International
    Development Issues 552, 565
India:
    and Comprehensive Test Ban Treaty 295
    and financing of United Nations 679
    and International Court of Justice 196
    and landmine convention 296
    and military intervention 393, 395, 400
    and Nuclear Non-Proliferation Treaty 293
indigenous peoples:
    and Charter of the United Nations 528
    and definition of 533
    and Draft Declaration on the Rights of
        Indigenous Peoples 533–4
    and estimate of population size 532
    and human rights 525–6, 532–6
    and International Covenant on Civil and
        Political Rights 529–30
    and International Labour Organization
        conventions 532, 534
    and League of Nations 526–7

and Permanent Forum on Indigenous
    Issues 534–5
and protection of 444
and self-determination 528, 532–4
and Universal Declaration of Human
    Rights 528–9
and Working Group on Indigenous
    Populations 533
see also minorities
inequality 5
    and conflict 317, 318, 549–50
    and human security 552
infant formula campaign 268
infectious diseases 582
    and bioterrorism 588–9
    and growing problem of 585–6
    and human security 588–9
    and international cooperation on 583–7
    and public–private partnerships 587
    and security 587–90
    and Special Program for Research and
        Training in Tropical Diseases 587
    and surveillance and response
        mechanisms 588–9
    and United Nations Children's Fund 586–7
    and World Health Organization 583–7
information about United Nations:
    and Department of Public Information
        276–9
    and public accessibility 83–4
    and use of 84
    see also knowledge of United Nations
Institute of International Law 204, 463–4
institutionalism, and international law 72
intellectual property rights, and
        counterfeiting 613–14
Inter Press Service 276, 283
Inter-African Mission to Monitor the Bangui
    Agreements (MISAB) 123
Inter-Agency Network on Women and Gender
    Equality 570
Inter-Agency Standing Committee (IASC)
    486
Inter-Agency Trust Fund on the Elimination
    of Violence against Women 501
Inter-American Commission on Human
    Rights 451, 455, 518
Inter-American Commission on Women 456
Inter-American Convention on the
    International Return of Children
    (1989) 514
Inter-American Convention on the Prevention
    of Violence against Women 455
Inter-American Court of Human Rights 451, 456
interdependence, and study of United Nations 86
Intergovernmental Authority on
    Development 125

Intergovernmental Panel on Climate Change 712
Interlaken process (1998-9) 124, 363
internally displaced persons (IDPs) 490
    and Darfur 491
    see also refugees
International Association for Labor
    Legislation 703
International Atomic Energy Agency (IAEA)
    297, 550, 563
    and monitoring role of 46
    and World Health Organization 586
International Bank for Reconstruction and
    Development (IBRD) 139, 236, 247,
    249, 563
    and natural resources 594
    see also Bretton Woods institutions;
    international financial institutions;
    World Bank
International Campaign to Ban Landmines
    (ICBL) 705
International Centre for Settlement of
    Investment Disputes (ICSID) 67
International Chamber of Commerce (ICC)
    265
International Civil Aviation Organization
    (ICAO) 63, 563
international civil service:
    and League of Nations 160-1
    and origins of concept 160
    see also Secretariat of the United Nations
International Civil Service Commission
    (ICSC) 167
International Commission on Intervention
    and State Sovereignty (ICISS) 8, 126,
    397-8, 446, 548
    see also humanitarian action; humanitarian
    intervention
International Committee of the Red Cross
    (ICRC) 480, 514, 546
    and children's issues 518
international community, meaning of term
    6-7
International Conference on Financing for
    Development (Monterrey, 2002) 138, 566
International Conference on Population and
    Development (Cairo, 1994) 503
International Convention for the Suppression
    of Acts of Nuclear Terrorism 428, 618
International Court of Justice (ICJ) 206-7, 703
    and advisory opinions 196-7
    and appointments to 198-9
    and cases/opinions:
        Administrative Tribunal of the ILO 201
        Cameroon v. Nigeria 203-4, 604
        Case concerning Armed Activities on the
            Territory of the Congo 605

Corfu Channel 200
Diplomatic and Consular Staff in Tehran
    200
East Timor 196
El Salvador v. Honduras 203
Fisheries Jurisdiction Cases 604
Gabčíkovo-Nagymaros 200
Gulf of Maine 201, 604
Interpretation of Peace Treaties 197
Jan Mayen Island 604
Legal Consequences of the Construction
    of a Wall in the Occupied Palestinian
    Territory (Advisory Opinion) 197, 201, 316
Legality of the Threat or Use of Nuclear
    Weapons (Advisory Opinion) 604
Legality of the Use by a State of Nuclear
    Weapons in Armed Conflict (Advisory
    Opinion) 196-7, 201
Libya v. Chad 604
Libya v. Malta 604
Lockerbie 205
Monetary Gold 196, 204
Namibia v. Botswana 604
Nauru 203, 204
Nicaragua 200, 203, 204, 392, 394, 445
North Sea Continental Shelf Cases 604
Nuclear Tests 204
Qatar v. Bahrain 604
Reparations for Injuries Suffered in the
    Service of the United Nations 60-1, 204
South West Africa 200, 202
Western Sahara 197
and composition of 198-9
and contentious cases 195-6
and deliberations of 201-2
and dissenting opinions 201-2
and Economic and Social Council 138
and expansion of subject matter considered 203
and finance of 202
and financing of peacekeeping operations 687
and functions of 194
and General Assembly 99, 197
and humanitarian intervention 392
and inactivity of 202
and influence on international law 202
and international organizations 204-6
and international rule of law 205
and Iran's nationalization of oil companies 595
and Israel 119
and jurisdiction of 58-9, 195-6
and law applied by 197-8
and legal positivism 59
and location of 200
and Mandate System 150
and multilateral cases 203-4
and natural resource
    management 604-5

and Nicaragua 119
and nonstate actors 206
and obligations of states 445
and origins and development of 193–4
and peaceful settlement of disputes 303–4,
    306–7, 311, 316
and procedures of 199–201
and reform proposals 202–3
and role of 99
and Security Council 119, 194, 198
and standing before 198
and state sovereignty 389
and Statute of (1945) 194
and third-state intervention 203–4
International Covenant on Civil and Political
    Rights (ICCPR) 12, 444, 446, 447, 454,
    455, 504, 512, 543
and collective rights 529–30
International Covenant on Economic, Social
    and Cultural Rights (ICESCR) 12, 443,
    444, 512, 543, 551
International Criminal Court (ICC) 9, 312, 399,
    446, 464, 473–6, 545, 703
and administrative body for 474
and appointments to 474
and Assembly of States Parties 474
and cases of:
    referral by Central African Republic 475
    referral by Democratic Republic of the
        Congo 475
    referral by Uganda 474
    Sudan/Darfur 475
and establishment of 473–4
and human rights 454
and jurisdiction of 474
and nongovernmental organizations 705
and opposition to 130
and relationship with states 475
and safeguards of 475–6
and sexual and gender crimes 505
and support for 476–7
and treaty negotiations 63
and United Nations 474
and United States 130, 454, 473,
    475–6
see also international criminal tribunals
International Criminal Tribunal for the
    former Yugoslavia (ICTY) 465–7, 505
and completion strategies 468–70
and successes and failures of 467–8
International Criminal Tribunal for Rwanda
    (ICTR) 465–7, 505
and completion strategies 468, 469–70
and successes and failures of 467–8
international criminal tribunals 129–30, 465–7,
    544–5
and completion strategies 468–70

and impact on peace and justice 476
and 'mixed' courts 470–3
    Bosnia and Herzegovina 472
    Cambodia 472, 473
    East Timor 471
    Kosovo 471–2
    Sierra Leone 472–3
and 'soft' intervention 399
and successes and failures of 467–8
see also International Criminal Court;
    International Criminal Tribunal for
    the former Yugoslavia; International
    Criminal Tribunal for Rwanda
International Development Association
    (IDA) 236, 246, 248
and United States 248
International Finance Corporation (IFC) 236,
    267
international financial institutions (IFIs):
    and Economic and Social Council 138, 139
    and good governance 630–1
    and Security Council 120
    see also Bretton Woods institutions;
        International Bank for Reconstruction and
        Development; International Monetary
        Fund; World Bank
International Force for East Timor
    (INTERFET) 123–4, 226
International Fund for Agricultural
    Development (IFAD) 563
International Gay and Lesbian Association
    257
International Health Regulations (IHR) 585,
    586, 589–90
international humanitarian law:
    and children 514
    and development of 463–4
    and international customary law 464
    see also international law
International Labour Office 677
International Labour Organization (ILO) 63,
    65, 265, 269, 455, 498, 517, 563, 634,
    703, 704
    and child labor 520
    and indigenous peoples 532, 534
    and Worst Forms of Child Labour
        Convention 514
international law:
    and agents of 68
    and children 514
    and critical analyses of 73, 75
    and custom 66
    and democratic deficit 75–6
    and economics 71
    and feminist theory 74
    and General Assembly 111
    and general principles 66

international law (*cont.*)
    and human rights 444–7
        international public policy 445
            and humanitarian law 445
    and influence of International Court of
        Justice 202
    and international legal processes school 70
    and international organizations 59–60
        legal personality 61
    and international relations 72
    and interstate cooperation 46
    and legal positivism 41, 59
        changes in 69
        tenets of 59, 62–3
        United Nations' challenges to 62–3
    and nongovernmental organizations 68
    and nonstate actors 68
    and obligations of states 445
    and Security Council 129–30
    and 'soft law' 66–8
    and United Nations 59
        establishment of legal personality 60–1
        as lawmaker 60–8
        political organs 61–2
        significance of interpretations by 62
        treaties 63–6
    and Yale School view of 69–70
    see also international humanitarian law
International Law Commission (ILC) 63, 473,
        599
    and Rules of State Responsibility 67–8
international legal processes, and international
        law 70
International Management Institute 266
International Maritime Organization (IMO) 563
International Monetary Fund (IMF) 14, 42,
        139, 563
    and accountability of 252
    and 'Anglo-Saxon' character of 234
    and autonomy of 235
    and conditionality 237
    and conflict sensitive adjustment policies
        418
    and criticisms of 235, 251
    and debt crisis (1980s) 237–8
    and effectiveness of 251
    and finance of 234, 245–6
    and financial crises (1990s) 238–9
    and functions of 233
    and good governance 624
    and governance of 234, 242–5
        United States' influence 243–5
    and heavily indebted poor countries 239–40
    and human rights 451
    and Independent Evaluation Office 241
    and information collection 46
    and legitimacy of 251

    and loan policy and practices 249–51
    and measuring success/failure 241–2
    and membership of 234
    and natural resources 594
    and origins and development of 235–7
    and post-conflict reconstruction 240–1
    and realist view of 44
    and resources of 246–7
    and Special Drawing Right 236
    and staff of 234
    and transition economies 238
    and United Nations 234
        relationship with 235
    and weighted voting 140, 234, 243
        veto powers 243–4
    and World Bank 233–4
    see also Bretton Woods institutions; World
        Bank
International Narcotics Control Board
        (INCB) 615
International Opium Commission 614
International Opium Convention 614
International Organization for Migration
        (IOM) 486, 490, 517, 518
International Organization for Standardization
        (ISO) 267–8
International Organization (journal) 84
international organizations (IOs):
    and accountability of 204–6
    and coordination problems 240, 241
    and International Court of Justice 204–6
    and international law 59–60
    and intrastate wars, critical analyses of 73
    and legal personality 61
    and treaty negotiations 63–6
        negotiation forums 65–6
International Peace Academy 89
International Police Task Force
        (IPTF) 380
International Refugee Organization 481
international relations:
    and General Assembly 111–12
    and international law 72
    and research agendas on United Nations:
        autonomy 53, 56 n19
        influence of states 52–3
        international civil service 53–4
        social networks 54
        voting blocs and alliance patterns 53
    and role of United Nations 42–3
        as agent of change 50
        as constructor of social world 48–50
        as facilitator of interstate cooperation
            45–7
        as governor of society of states 47–8
        as structure of legitimation 50–2
        as tool of great powers 43–5

and theories of 41
  constructivism 49–50, 51
  English School 47–8
  Gramscian perspectives 51–2
  principal–agent analysis 46
  rationalist 45–7
  realism 43–5, 51
International Relief Union (IRU) 480
International Rescue Committee 260, 481
International Research and Training Institute
    for the Advancement of Women
    (INSTRAW) 500
International Security Assistance Force
    (ISAF) 124, 226, 380
international society, and role of United
    Nations 48–50
International Telecommunication Union
    (ITU) 563, 703
International Trade Organization
    (ITO) 139
international treaties, see treaties
International Union for the Conservation of
    Nature 601
International Union of Local Authorities 707
International Women's Year (1975) 498
Inter-Parliamentary Union 710, 711
Iran:
  and Comprehensive Test Ban Treaty 295
  and landmine convention 296
  and nationalization of oil companies 595
  and nuclear weapons 293
Iran Khodro 269
Iran–Iraq war 129
  and Security Council 117, 121
Iraq:
  and Coalition Provisional Authority (CPA)
    156
  and invasion of Kuwait 123
  and military intervention 395–6
  and naval blockade 124
  and Oil-for-Food Programme 351
  and peacebuilding 411, 416
  and sanctions 124, 349, 350–2
    arms embargoes 359
    commodity-specific 359
    humanitarian impact of 357
    targeted sanctions 358
  and United Nations Special Commission
    288, 297
Iraq war (2003) 372
  and humanitarian intervention 400
  and Secretary-General 183
  and Security Council 124, 132, 133
  and United Nations 17–18, 45
Irish Republican Army (IRA) 435

Israel 119
  and Boutros-Ghali 185
  and International Court of
    Justice 196
  and military intervention 393
  and Nuclear Non-Proliferation Treaty 293
Italy 683, 696
Ivory Coast, see Côte d'Ivoire

Jackson report, see A Study of the Capacity
    of the United Nations Development
    System
Japan 683
  and financing of United Nations 680–1, 696
Johannesburg Declaration 602
Johannesburg Plan of Implementation 602
Joint UN Programme on HIV/AIDS
    (UNAIDS) 503, 587
Jubilee 2000 239

Kellogg–Briand Pact (1928) 392, 546
Kenya, and electoral assistance to 628
Kimberley Process 360, 618
knowledge of United Nations 82
  and academic scholarship 84–5, 110–12
    constructivism 86
    functionalist approach 85–6
    institutional approach 84–5
    interdependence approach 86
    network analysis 86–7
    realist approach 85
    regimes theory 86
  and economic development
    publications 88
  and historical studies 87
  and memoirs 87
  and oral history archives 87
  and popular knowledge:
    media coverage 90–1
    opinion surveys 90, 94 n35
  and publicly accessible information 83–4
  and research institutions 88–90
  and use of information 84
Korean War:
  and General Assembly 104, 309
  and peace enforcement 372
  and release of American prisoners-of-war
    180–1
  and Secretary-General 180
  and Security Council 120
Kosovo 122
  and humanitarian intervention 396, 400
  and 'mixed' courts 471–2
  and NATO campaign 131
  and peace enforcement 222

Kosovo (*cont.*)
  and peacebuilding
  and UN Transitional Administration 118–19, 155
Kurdistan 17
Kuwait 123

land mines, and Convention on (1997) 9, 296, 705
Latin America, and military intervention 394
  see also individual countries
League of Nations 3, 82, 546
  and Assembly of 98
  and children 512, 521
  and Covenant of 392
  and disarmament 287, 288
  and failure of 11
  and financing of 676–7
  and Health Organization of 583
  and humanitarian action 480–1
  and indigenous peoples 526–7
  and international civil service 160–1
  and Mandate System 150–1
    administration 152
    duration of 151–2
  and minority protection 526–7, 541
  and Permanent Court of International
      Justice 194
  and refugees 481
Lebanon 120
legal positivism:
  and Charter of the United Nations 59
  and international law 41
    changes in 69
  and tenets of 59, 62–3
  see also international law
legitimation, and role of United Nations 50–2
Lesotho 381
  and electoral assistance to 628
liberalism, and international law 72
liberalization:
  and conflict 317
  and governance 630–1
  and peacebuilding 418–19
  and structural adjustment 646
Liberia 124, 125, 220
  and electoral assistance to 629
  and natural resources 602
  and peace enforcement 222, 380, 381
  and peacebuilding 411, 413, 414
  and sanctions 357, 607
    commodity-specific 359, 360
    monitoring and implementation 362
    targeted sanctions 359
Libya 119
  and sanctions 124, 128, 357, 429
    targeted sanctions 358

Lieber Code 463
life expectancy 12
  and Human Development Index 636, 637
literacy 12
local authorities, and global governance 706, 707–8
local groups, and international relations 706–7
Lomé Peace Accord 376
Lord's Resistance Army (LRA, Uganda) 467
Lutheran World Federation 481

Macedonia 380
malaria:
  and children 520
  and World Health Organization 584
  see also infectious diseases
Malawi, and electoral assistance to 628
Mali, and electoral assistance to 628
malnutrition 12
Mandate System 150–1
  and administration 152
  and duration of 151–2
  and UN Trusteeship System 151
  see also Trusteeship Council of the United
      Nations
Manila Declaration on the Peaceful Settlement
    of International Disputes 302
Mariana Islands 155
market capitalism, and human rights 440
Marshall Islands 155
Marshall Plan 236
Médecins sans Frontières (MSF) 483
media, and United Nations 6, 83, 84, 90–1, 275, 284
  and attitudes towards 281
  and broadcast media 276
  and celebrity/human-interest stories 282–3
  and 'CNN effect' 126
  and critical coverage 280
  and Department of Public Information 276–9
  and developing countries 283
  and focus on Security Council 283
  and humanitarian intervention 126
  and nature of coverage by 275
  and news agencies 276, 283
  and newspapers 276
  and nongovernmental organizations 278
  and Office of the Spokesman of the
      Secretary-General 280–1
  and role of editors and producers 282
  and Secretary-General's influence 280–1
  and United Nations Information
      Centres 278
  and United Nations News Centre 277
  and United Nations Radio 278
  and United Nations TV 278

mediation, and peaceful settlement of
disputes 305
Meetings of the Parties (MOPs), and
multilateral treaties 64
Mekong Delta Treaty 607
memoirs, and knowledge of United Nations
87
Mexico:
and electoral assistance to 628
and financial crisis 238
and financing of United Nations 679, 683
Micronesia 155
Middle East, and General Assembly 118
see also individual countries
military expenditure 711
and global levels 297
and United States 9
military intervention, and justification of 392–5
see also humanitarian intervention
Military Professional Resources Incorporated,
and peacebuilding 407
Millennium Declaration (2000) 574, 642, 709
and democratic governance 621, 631
Millennium Development Goals (MDGs) 42,
45, 145, 234, 574, 648, 709
and attitudes towards 566–7
and children's rights 516
and democratic governance 621, 631
and education 519
and human development 456–7, 642–3
and human rights 457
and human security 554
and monitoring and evaluation 647
and women and gender 503
Millennium Summit (2000) 503, 574
minorities:
and Charter of the United Nations 528
and human rights 525–6, 530–2, 535, 536,
540–1
and International Covenant on Civil and
Political Rights 529–30
and League of Nations 526–7
and Minorities Declaration (1992) 528, 530,
531, 532
and Minority Treaties System 526–7
and protection of 444
and Universal Declaration of Human
Rights 528–9
see also indigenous peoples
Minority Treaties System 526–7, 530, 541
Monterrey Consensus 138, 571
Montevideo Convention on the Rights and
Duties of States (1934) 8, 389
Montreal Protocol on Substances that Deplete
the Ozone Layer 258, 270
mortality rates 12
Mostar, and EU administration 155

Mozambique 122
and electoral assistance to 629
and peacebuilding 413
and peacekeeping operations 327, 405
Multiple Indicator Cluster Surveys (MICS) 648
Multilateral Investment Guarantee Agency
(MIGA) 236
multilateralism:
and challenges facing 713–14
and complexity of 701
and evolution of 701
and expanding participation in
UN 704–8
and financing of United Nations 711–13
and popular perceptions of goal of 701–2
and possible governance options 709–11
and roots of 702–4
multinational corporations 268
see also transnational corporations

Namibia 41, 118, 121, 122
and electoral assistance to 625, 629
and peacebuilding 413
and peacekeeping operations 327, 405
and South Africa 153–4
narcotics, and organized crime 612, 614–15
National Union for the Total Independence
of Angola (UNITA) 124, 187, 349, 352,
357, 359, 360
nationalism 526
nationalization, and resource sovereignty 595,
597
natural resource management 607–8
and access 592–4
and Charter of Economic Rights and Duties
of States 597–8
and 'common concern of humankind' 606
and 'common heritage of humankind' 606
and early postwar thinking 593–4
and economic nationalism 593, 594–5
and human rights 595, 604
and main institutions:
Commission on Human Rights 604
Economic and Social Council 603
General Assembly 604
International Court of Justice 604–5
Security Council 604
Standing Committee on Natural
Resources 603–4
United Nations Development
Programme 605
World Bank 605
and organized crime 618
and resource sovereignty 593, 595–600, 606
marine resources 598–600
and security of supply 592–4
and self-determination 595–6

natural resource management (*cont.*)
  and stability and development 593, 607
    'curse' of natural resources 602–3
  and sustainable development 593, 600–2, 606
    Brundtland Commission 601
    Johannesburg Declaration 602
    Johannesburg Plan of Implementation 602
    Rio Declaration 601
    Stockholm Declaration 600–1
    World Charter for Nature 601
  and transboundary resources 606–7
Nature Conservancy 256
Nauru 154
  as Trust Territory 151
naval blockades 372
  and peace enforcement 124
negotiation, and peaceful settlement of
    disputes 304
neoconservatives, and United States' foreign
    policy 111
neoliberal institutionalism 45, 55 n4, 85
Nestlé 268
NetAid 517
Netherlands 679, 694–6
Network on Rural Development and Food
    Security 570
networks, and study of United Nations 86–7
neutrality, and peacekeeping operations 325–6
New Guinea 154
  as Trust Territory 151
New International Economic Order (NIEO) 52,
    65, 88, 108, 268, 597
New International Information Order 281
New Internationalist (magazine) 268
New Partnership for Africa's Development
    (NEPAD) 455
*A New United Nations Structure for Global
    Economic Co-operation* (1975) 565
New Zealand, and Bougainville 380
news agencies, and United Nations 276, 283
newspapers, and United Nations 276
Nicaragua 119
  and electoral assistance to 625, 629
  and International Court of Justice 203
  and peacebuilding 413–14
Niger, and electoral assistance to 628
Nigeria 154
Non-Aligned Movement (NAM) 107
  and humanitarian intervention 396–7
  and Security Council 130–1
nongovernmental organizations (NGOs) 6
  and accountability of 261
  and children's rights 515, 517
  and conference participation 705
  and conflict prevention 312
  and consultative role 258
  and criticisms of 261

  and Economic and Social Council 136, 146,
    257, 667
  and expansion of 256
  and General Assembly 705
  and global civil society 256, 261
  and human rights 544
  and humanitarian action 481, 482, 483–4
  and influence on United Nations 258–9
  and International Criminal Court 705
  and international decision-making 706
  and international law 68
  and interstate organizations 703–4
  and partnerships with United
    Nations 259–60
  and peacebuilding 407–10
  and People's Millennium Forum 706
  and Persian Gulf crisis (1991) 486
  and Secretariat 705
  and Security Council 130, 705
  and treaty implementation 706
  and treaty negotiations 63–4
  and United Nations 704–6
  and women and gender 501
  see also nonstate actors
nonstate actors 701
  and International Court of Justice 206
  and international law 68
  and interstate organizations 703–4
  and *Report of the Panel of Eminent Persons
    on United Nations–Civil Society
    Relations* (2004) 710
  and treaty negotiations 63–4
  and world politics 6–7
  see also nongovernmental organizations
Nordic countries 142, 566
  and influence in United Nations 52–3
norms, and role of United Nations:
  and constructivist view of 48–50
  and English School view of 47–8
  as legitimator of 50–1
North American Free Trade Agreement
    (NAFTA) 68
North Atlantic Treaty Organization (NATO):
  and Afghanistan 380
  and Bosnia and Herzegovina 125, 228
  and former Yugoslavia 375, 378, 547–8
  and humanitarian intervention 396, 400
  and peacebuilding 407
  and Response Force 230
  and sanctions enforcement 361
  and Security Council 125–6
  and United Nations 219–20
North Korea:
  and Chemical Weapons Convention 293
  and Comprehensive Test Ban Treaty 295
  and landmine convention 296
  and Nuclear Non-Proliferation Treaty 293

Novum Nieuws 278
Nuclear Non-Proliferation Treaty (NPT) 291–2
nuclear weapons:
    and Baruch Plan 289
    and Comprehensive Test Ban Treaty 295
    and disarmament 289
    and Nuclear Non-Proliferation Treaty 291–2
    and Partial Test Ban Treaty 294–5
    see also disarmament
Nuremberg trials 464–5

Office for Emergency Operations in Africa
        (OEOA) 484
Office for the Coordination of Humanitarian
        Affairs (OCHA) 358, 489
    and Humanitarian Response Review 491
    and internally displaced persons 490
Office international d'hygiène publique 583
Office of Internal Oversight Services (OIOS) 168, 170
Office of the High Representative (OHR) in
        Bosnia and Herzegovina 155
Office of the Special Adviser to the Secretary-
        General on Gender Issues and
        Advancement of Women (OSAGI) 500
Office of the United Nations Disaster Relief
        Coordinator (UNDRO) 482–4
Oil-for-Food Programme 351
    and Volcker report 89–90, 124, 133, 169–70,
        188–9, 351
opinion polls 94 n35
    and knowledge of United Nations 90
oral history, and United Nations 87
Organisation for Economic Co-operation and
        Development (OECD) 67, 106, 423
    and business regulation 268
    and counterfeiting 614
    and good governance 624
Organization for Security and Co-operation in
        Europe (OSCE) 125, 155
    and good governance 624
    and human rights 455
    and peacebuilding 407
    see also Conference on Security and Co-
        operation in Europe
Organization for the Prohibition of Chemical
        Weapons (OPCW) 294
    and World Health Organization 586
Organization of African Unity (OAU) 381, 514
    and peacebuilding 407
    and peaceful settlement of disputes 307
    and Security Council 125
    see also African Union
Organization of American States (OAS) 70, 219
    and children's rights 514
    and Haiti 376
    and peacebuilding 406
    and peaceful settlement of disputes 307

and Security Council 125
Organization of Eastern Caribbean States 393
Organization of the Petroleum Exporting
        Countries (OPEC) 108, 237, 597
organizational behavior, and United Nations 53–4
organized crime:
    and concept of 612–13
    and counterfeiting 613–14
    and drugs 612, 614–15
    and economics of crime 613
    and globalization 619
    and natural resources 618
        timber 618
    and people trafficking 615
        sexual exploitation of children 616
    and role of United Nations 611–12
    and terrorism 613
    and trafficking radioactive materials 616–18
Ottawa Convention 9, 296, 705
Oxfam 260, 481, 517

Packages Limited 269
Pakistan:
    and Comprehensive Test Ban Treaty 295
    and democracy 622
    and landmine convention 296
    and Non-Aligned Movement 131
    and Nuclear Non-Proliferation Treaty 293
Palau 118, 149, 155, 669
Palermo Protocol 505
Palestine, and Boutros-Ghali 185
Palestine Liberation Organization (PLO) 435
Palestinian–Israeli conflict, and General
        Assembly 104
Panama 599
Pan-American Sanitary Bureau 583
Pan-American Union 218
Panel of Eminent Persons on United Nations–Civil
        Society Relations 709, 710–11
    see also Report of the Panel of Eminent Persons on
        United Nations–Civil Society Relations
Papua 154
Papua New Guinea 154
Partners in Development: Report of the
        Commission on International
        Development (1969) 565
peace enforcement 370–1, 383–4, 405
    and basis in interests 370
    and bias 381–2
    as blunt instrument 383
    and 'coalitions of the willing' 123–4, 222, 371
    and ideological framing of 384
    and impartiality 381–2
    and key developments:
        Democratic Republic of the Congo 377
        East Timor 377
        former Yugoslavia 374–5

peace enforcement (*cont.*)
    Haiti 375–6
    Rwanda 375
    Sierra Leone 376–7
    Somalia 374
    Sudan 377
  and meaning of 371
    collective security 371–3
    crisis management 373
  and military doctrine 382
  and 'mission creep' 379
  and norms governing 383–4
  and operational issues 382–3
  and politics of 377–9
    delegation and decentralization 379–81
    humanitarian justification 378
    norms governing 383–4
    representation of 379
    self-interest 378–9
  and regional organizations 380–1
  and Security Council 123–4
  and strategic function 370
  and targets of 370
  and third-generation peacekeeping 327–33
  see also peacebuilding; peaceful settlement
    of disputes; peacekeeping operations
peacebuilding 404–5, 423–4
  and evaluating record of 411, 416
    African 416
    Angola 415
    Cambodia 414, 627
    Central America 413–14
    Côte d'Ivoire 416
    durable peace 413–14
    former Yugoslavia 415
    Liberia 414
    methodological challenges 411–12
    resumption of violence 412–13
    Rwanda 415
    Sierra Leone 415–16
  and evolution of 405
    defining 405–6
    growth during 1990s 406–10
    post-9/11 period 410–11
  and human security 548–50
  and lessons learned:
    building effective states 423
    care in democratization 418
    importance of security 417–18
    legitimacy problem 422
    need for accountability 422–3
    need for local participation 422
    need for long-term commitment 416–17
    sensitive liberalization policies 418–19
    sensitivity to local/regional
      conditions 419–20
  and mandate/trusteeship systems 410

  and nongovernmental organizations 407–10
  and regional organizations 406–7
  and *Report of the Panel on United Nations
    Peace Operations* (2000) 420
  and terrorism 410
  see also peace enforcement; peacekeeping
    operations
Peacebuilding Commission (PBC) 157, 229, 313,
    420, 422, 423–4, 549, 667–8
Peacebuilding Support Office (PBSO) 229
peaceful settlement of disputes:
  and challenges of 316
  and Charter of the United Nations:
    Article 2 301–2
    Article 2 (3) 302–3
    Article 33 303–4
  and 'Friendly Relations Declaration' 302
  and General Assembly resolutions 302
  and International Court of Justice 303–4,
    306–7, 311, 316
  and international disputes 302–3
  and literature on 301
  and Manila Declaration on 302
  and means of 303–4
    arbitration 306
    conciliation 305–6
    inquiry/fact-finding 304–5
    international tribunals 306–7
    mediation/good offices 305
    negotiation 304
    'other peaceful means' 307–8
    regional agencies/arrangements 307
  and need for 300
  and responsibility for 302, 303, 308
    General Assembly 309, 317–18
    International Court of Justice 311
    parties to the conflict 308
    Secretary-General 309–10, 316
    Security Council 303, 308–9, 318
    special envoys/representatives of
      Secretary-General 310
  and states 318
  see also conflict prevention; peace
    enforcement; peacebuilding;
    peacekeeping operations
peacekeeping operations:
  and *An Agenda for Peace* 220–1, 323, 324
    Supplement to 221, 333
  and assessment of 226
  and budget for 333
  and capacity for 226–7
  and Cold War period 405
  and consent 326–7
  and coordination problems 420–2
  and cost of 226
  and enforcement operations 327–33
    Charter basis of 332

and evolution of doctrine 324, 333–4
  first-generation peacekeeping 324–7
  fourth-generation peacekeeping 334
  retrenchment 333–4
  second-generation peacekeeping 325, 327
  strategic peacekeeping 334–8
  third-generation peacekeeping 325,
    327–33
and expansion of 13–14, 41, 123, 220, 226, 333
and funding of 683–7, 693–4
and General Assembly 104
and *Handbook on Multi-dimensional Peace
    Operations* 229
and human security 547
and impartiality 325–6
and increase in 12
and monitoring role of 46, 326
and multidimensional peacekeeping 327
and nature of contemporary 323
and neutrality 325–6
and *No Exit Without Strategy* 323, 334
and peacekeeping triangle:
  hostility of factions 323, 338, 339–40, 341
  international assistance 323–4, 338, 339–40,
    341
  local capacity 323, 338, 339, 340–1
  modelling determinants of success
    341–4
  participatory peace 341–4
  reconstruction 340
and peacemaking 326
and principles of 220
and regionalization of 217–18, 334
  benefits and risks of 227–8
  categories of operations 222–6
  critical theory approach 217
  expansion of 228
  future of 228–30
  managerialist approach 217
  post-Cold War era 220–7
and *Report of the Panel on United Nations
    Peace Operations* (2000) 221–2, 323,
    334, 420
and Security Council 120, 222
  difficulties faced by 122–3
  expanded role of 122
  internal conflicts 122
and strategic peacekeeping 334–8
  cooperation problems 335–6
  coordination problems 335–6
  facilitative strategies 335–6
  identifying conflict type 337
  role of peace treaties 337
  spoiler problems 336–8
  transformative strategies 335–6
  transitional strategy 338
  types of conflict 334–5

and strategic reserve for 229–30
and sustainable peace 323
and troop-contributing countries 128, 222,
    333
  see also Troop Contributing Nations
and United Nations' role 324
and use of force 326, 333
  see also peace enforcement; peacebuilding
Pearson report, see *Partners in Development:
    Report of the Commission on
    International Development* (1969)
People's Millennium Forum 706
Permanent Court of Arbitration (PCA) 193,
    306, 703
Permanent Court of International Justice
    (PCIJ) 194, 541, 677, 703
  and *Eastern Carelia* case 197
Permanent Forum on Indigenous Issues
    (PF) 534–5
Persian Gulf crisis (1991), and humanitarian
    action 485–6
Pfizer 697
plague, and International Health Regulations
    585
  see also infectious diseases
polio 260
population growth 4–5
Porter Commission 604
post-conflict peacebuilding, see peacebuilding
poverty 5
  and children 519
  and Human Poverty Index 637
poverty reduction, and Bretton Woods
    institutions 239–40
Prague Spring 120
precautionary principle 67
Preparatory Commission of the United
    Nations (London, 1945) 161
Press Trust of India 276
principal–agent theory, and United Nations 46
  and autonomy 53
  and international civil service 53–4
principles, and role of United Nations 47–8
private sector:
  and civil society 256
  and financing of United Nations 696–7
  and Global Compact 67, 256, 260, 264,
    270–1
  and international organization 265–6
  and United Nations 6, 260, 708
    in Annan era 270–2
    changed attitude of 269–70
    early postwar period 266–7
    regulation issues 267–9
    relationship between 264–5, 272
public–private partnerships,
    and health 587

racism, and Security Council 121
radioactive materials, and organized crime
    616–18
rationalist theory, and role of United
    Nations 45–7
realism:
    and role of United Nations 43–5, 51
    and study of United Nations 85
Red Cross movement 445, 480, 482, 486
Red Cross Treaty (1864) 463
reform, and United Nations 669–70
    and adaptation 655
    and Charter amendment process 654–5
    and Commission on Human Rights 440–1
    as constant process 653
    and coordination of economic and social
        affairs 565, 566
    and Economic and Social Council 143–5,
        664–8
    and financing of United Nations 685–7
    and General Assembly 656–9
    and humanitarian action 490–3
    and intergovernmental bodies 655
    and International Court of Justice 202–3
    and possible governance options 709–11
    and proposed review conference 654
    and sanctions 350, 362–3, 364–6
    and Secretariat 165–7
    and Security Council 131–2, 659–65
    and Trusteeship Council 156, 668–9
    and unlikelihood of radical reform 655
    and veto power 654
refugees 260, 548
    and children 512, 517
    and growth of 483
    and League of Nations 481
    and postwar definition of 482
    and Security Council 126
    see also internally displaced persons
regimes theory, and study of United Nations
    86
regional organizations:
    and An Agenda for Peace 220–1
        Supplement to 221
    and children's rights 514, 518
    and Cold War 218–20
    and democratic governance 621
    and financing of United Nations 685
    and future relations with UN 228–30
    and General Assembly 657
    and human rights 455–6
    and peace enforcement 380–1
    and peacebuilding 406–7, 419
    and peaceful settlement of disputes 307
    and peacekeeping operations 217–18, 334
        benefits and risks of involvement 227–8
        categories of 222–6

critical theory approach 217
    expanded role in 228
    managerialist approach 217
    post-Cold War era 220–7
    Report of the Panel on United Nations
        Peace Operations (2000) 221–2
    and Security Council 119–20, 122, 125–6, 219
        veto powers 219
regulation, and business 267–9
Report of the Panel of Eminent Persons on
        United Nations–Civil Society Relations
        (2004) 257, 709, 710–11
Report of the Panel on United Nations Peace
        Operations (2000) 131, 221–2, 323, 334,
        391, 420, 693
reproductive rights, and women and gender
        503–4
reputation, and influence in United Nations
        52–3
research institutions 88–90
Reuters 276
Revolutionary United Front (RUF, Sierra
        Leone) 360, 376
Rhodesia 121, 124, 391
    and sanctions 349, 372, 544
    see also Zimbabwe
Rio Declaration 601, 607
risk assessment, and human rights 458–60
Rome Statute (1998) 9, 63, 64, 130, 312, 464,
        473–4, 505, 514, 544–5
    see also International Criminal Court
Rotary International 260
Ruanda-Urundi 154
    as Trust Territory 151
Russia:
    and Chechnya 381
    and financial crisis 238
    and financing of United Nations 681
    and International Criminal Court 130
    and landmine convention 296
    and Nuclear Non-Proliferation Treaty 292–3
    and sanctions 365
    see also Soviet Union
Rwanda 17, 41, 123, 185
    and failure to intervene 396
    and formation of 154
    and genocide 312
    and human rights 126–7
    and humanitarian crisis 396
    and International Criminal Tribunal for
        Rwanda 129, 465–7
        successes and failures of 467–8
    and peace enforcement 375
    and peacebuilding 413, 415
    and peacekeeping operations 373
    and sanctions 357, 362
        arms embargoes 359

Sahel, and famine 482–3
St. Petersburg Declaration (1868) 463
Samoa 154
sanctions:
  and arms embargoes 359
  and Bonn–Berlin Process 363
  and commodity-specific 359–60, 607
  and counter-terrorism 359, 429
  and decision-making procedures 364–5
  and enforcement of 360–1
    independent expert panels 361–2
    monitoring improvements 362
  and former Yugoslavia 360–1
  and human rights 544
  and humanitarian impact of 357–8
  and Interlaken process (1998–9) 124, 363
  and Iraq 349, 350–2
    humanitarian impact of 357
  and legal authority for 349
  and purpose of 349
  and reasons for using 349–50
  and reform of 350, 362–3
  and sanctions assistance missions 360–1
  and Security Council 124
  and Stockholm Process 363
  and targeted sanctions 358–9
  and time limits 364
  and unanticipated consequences of 350
  and use of (1990–2005) 352–7
    effectiveness 357
  and working group on reform 364–6
SARS epidemic 586, 588
Save the Children 512, 517
Say Yes for Children Campaign 515
Secretariat of the United Nations:
  and coordination of economic and social
      affairs 571–2
    assessment of 575–6
  and Deputy Secretary-General 576
  and Division for the Advancement of
      Women 498
  and Economic and Social Council 138
  and Ethics Office 170
  and Focal Point for Women in the
      Secretariat 500
  and future prospects of 171–2
  and General Assembly 99
  and human resources management 163–4
    administrative justice 168–9
    aims of reforms 167
    geographical recruitment 166
    Integrity Survey (2004) 165
    International Civil Service Commission
      167
    management reform 165–6, 167
    Office of Human Resources Management
      165

  permanent staff contracts 163–4
  recruitment 165–6
  salaries 167–8
  staff secondments 164, 166–7
  whistle-blower program 167
  and Management Committee 576
  and nongovernmental organizations 705
  and Office of the Ombudsman 169
  and Oil-for-Food Programme 169–70
  and origins and development of 160–3
    Secretary-General's role 161–3
  and Panel on the Strengthening of the
      International Civil Service 164
  and peacekeeping procurement 170
  and Policy Committee 575–6
  and role of 99
  and Secretary-General, appointment
      process 170–1
  and Senior Management Group 575
  and staff numbers 166
Secretary-General of the United Nations
  and annual reports of 177
  and appointment process 170–1, 176–7
  and budget requests 690–1
  and conflict prevention 315, 316
  and evolution of office:
    under Annan 188–9
    under Boutros-Ghali 183, 184–8
    Cold War era 179–82
    under Hammarskjöld 180–1
    under Lie 180
    under Pérez de Cuéllar 182
    post-Cold War era 182–9
    under U Thant 181–2
    under Waldheim 182
  and functions of 177–8
  and Gulf War (1991) 183
  and humanitarian action 479
  and independence of 178
  and Iraq war 183
  and legal powers 61
  and media 280–1
  as mediator 305
  and Office of the Spokesman of the
      Secretary-General 280–1
  and Oil-for-Food Programme 188–9
    Volcker report 169–70
  and peace and security issues 119, 177–8
  and peaceful settlement of disputes 309–10,
      316
  and role of 177–8, 189–90
    constraints on 175–6, 179, 189
    impact of personality 178–9
    potential influence of 175, 190
  and Secretariat:
    disciplinary powers 169
    historical development of 161–3

Secretary-General of the United Nations (*cont.*)
  and Security Council 119
    impact on 129
    referral of issues to (Article 99) 177–8
  and terrorism 432–3
    Policy Working Group 432
    strategy for combating 433
  see also individual Secretaries-General
Security Council of the United Nations:
  and authorization of force 124
  and children in armed conflict 521
  and coercive measures 122
  and Cold War 117, 120–1, 219
  and conflict prevention 312, 313, 315, 318
  and Counter-Terrorism Committee 128
  and decision-making:
    changes in drivers of 126–8
    changes in nature of 122–6
  and democratization 127
  and disarmament 288
  and Economic and Social Council 118, 138,
    146
  and electoral assistance 629
  and enlargement of 660–3
  and General Assembly 98, 118, 656–7
    peace and security issues 103–4
    reform attempts 661–2
  and Gulf War (1991) 123
  and HIV/AIDS 588
  and human rights 126–7, 454, 544
  and human security 554
  and humanitarian action 479
  and humanitarian intervention 126, 391,
    547–8
  and increased activism of 121–2
  and institutional developments:
    activist Secretaries-General 129
    'groups of friends' 128–9
    International Criminal Court 130
    international criminal law 129–30
    Non-Aligned Movement 130–1
    nongovernmental organizations 130, 705
    North–South divisions 130–1
    transparency 128
  and International Court of Justice 119, 194, 198
  and international criminal tribunals 465–6
  and international financial institutions 120
  and Iraq war 124, 132, 133
  and legal powers 61
  and membership of 117, 128
  and natural resource management 603, 604
  and peace enforcement 123–4, 332
  and peacebuilding 406
  and Peacebuilding Commission 668
  and peaceful settlement of disputes 303,
    308–9, 318
  and peacekeeping operations 120, 222

  difficulties faced in 122–3
    expansion of 122, 123
    internal conflicts 122
  and post-Cold War era 117, 121–2, 123
  and preventive diplomacy 406
  and reform of 131–2, 659–65
  and regional organizations 119–20, 122,
    125–6, 219
    veto powers 219
  and resolutions passed by 14
  and responsibilities of 117
  and sanctions 124
    arms embargoes 359
    Bonn–Berlin Process 363
    commodity-specific 359–60
    counter-terrorism 359
    decision-making procedures 364–5
    effectiveness 357
    former Yugoslavia 360–1
    humanitarian impact of 357–8
    Interlaken process (1998-9) 124, 363
    Iraq 349, 350–2
    monitoring and implementation 361–3
    reasons for using 349–50
    reform of 350, 362–3
    Stockholm Process 363
    targeted sanctions 358–9
    time limits 364
    unanticipated consequences of 350
    use of (1990-2005) 352–7
    working group on reform 364–6
  and Secretary-General 119
    appointment process 170–1, 176
  and state sovereignty 117
  and terrorism 127–8, 429–31
    condemnation of 430
    Counter-Terrorism Committee 430–1
    nuclear, biological, and chemical weapons 431
    reports from member states 431
    requirements of states 430, 431
    resolution 1269 430
    resolution 1373 430
    resolution 1540 431
    sanctions 429–30
  and Trusteeship Council 118–19
  and United States 132
  and use of force 59, 547–8
  and vetoes 14, 654
  and Women, Peace and Security resolution
    506, 645
  and working methods 663–4
  and World Health Organization 589
self-defense:
  and military intervention 393, 400
  and terrorism 433–4
self-determination 5, 22, 526
  and Charter of the United Nations 7, 441

and indigenous peoples 528, 532–4
and intervention 394
and natural resource management 595–6
and Trusteeship System 154
and United Nations 47
self-interest, and peace enforcement 378–9
September 11 terrorist attacks 128, 410, 430
sex tourism, and sexual exploitation of
    children 616
sexual rights, and women and gender 503–4
shaming, and human rights enforcement 543–4
Sierra Leone 124, 125
    and electoral assistance to 628
    and human rights 127
    and 'mixed' courts 472–3
    and natural resources 593, 602, 607
    and peace enforcement 376–7
    and peacebuilding 406, 407, 415–16
    and sanctions:
        commodity-specific 359, 360
        monitoring and implementation 362
        targeted sanctions 359
    and Special Court 129
    and Truth and Reconciliation Commission
        473
Singapore 266
Single Convention of Narcotic Drugs (1961)
    614
smallpox 12
    and World Health Organization 584
    see also infectious diseases
social affairs, see coordination of economic
    and social affairs; economic and social
    development; human development
society of states, and role of United Nations
    47–8
Somalia 8, 122, 123, 185, 332, 513
    and deaths of US soldiers 123, 132
    and formation of 154
    and humanitarian crisis 396
    and peace enforcement 373, 374,
        390, 406
    and peacekeeping operations 184, 185
    and sanctions 359
    and UN administration 155
Somaliland 154
    as Trust Territory 151
Soros Foundation 272
South Africa 121, 391
    and electoral assistance to 629
    and International Court of Justice 196
    and Lesotho 381
    and military intervention 393, 394
    and Namibia 153–4
    and sanctions 349, 544
South Asian Association for Regional
    Cooperation (SAARC) 227

South Centre 142–3
South West Africa, and South African
    Mandate 153
    see also Namibia
Southern African Development Community 125
sovereignty, see state sovereignty
Soviet Union:
    and Afghanistan 393
    and collapse of 109
    and Czechoslovakia 393
    and disarmament 290–1
    and financing of United Nations 679, 685,
        687–8
    and human rights 441, 528
    and North Vietnam 393
    and Nuclear Non-Proliferation Treaty 292–3
    and radioactive materials 617
    and Secretariat 161, 162, 163
    and Secretary-General 181
    and Security Council 660, 661
    see also Russia
Spain 683
Special Program for Research and Training in
    Tropical Diseases 587
special representative of the Secretary-General
    (SRSG) 119
    and peacekeeping operations 122
Srebrenica 44, 375
    and humanitarian crisis 396
Stabilization Force (SFOR) 123, 380
Stanley Foundation 89
state sovereignty 389–90
    and centrality of 4
    and challenges to 390–1
    and changing conception of 378, 389–90
    and Charter of the United Nations 58
    and human rights 391
    and humanitarian intervention 126
    and the International Commission on
        Intervention and State Sovereignty 8, 126,
        312, 397, 446, 548
    and international legal processes school 70
    and natural resource management 595–6
    and nonintervention 389, 390, 395
    and reformulation of 7–9
        failed states 8
        human rights 8
        impact of globalization 7
    and resource sovereignty 595–600, 606
        marine resources 598–600
    and responsibility to protect 440
    and Security Council 117
    and Trusteeship System 152
    and United Nations 47
    see also states
states:
    and centrality of 3, 4

states: (*cont.*)
  and conflict prevention 318
  and construction of modern state 526
  and human rights 391
  and humanitarian intervention 401
  and influence in United Nations 52–3
  and international organizations 68
  and obligations of 445
  and peaceful settlement of disputes 318
  and responsibilities of 390, 397, 398–9
  and responsibility to protect 397–8, 401, 458, 548
  and role of United Nations:
    constructivist view of 48–50, 51
    English School view of 47–8
    rationalist view of 45–7
    realist view of 43–5, 51
  and Rules of State Responsibility 67–8
  see also International Commission on
    Intervention and State Sovereignty;
    state sovereignty
Statistical Commission 647
Stockholm Conference on the Human
    Environment (1972) 259
Stockholm Declaration:
  and natural resource management 600–1
  and precautionary principle 67
Stockholm International Peace Research
    Institute 412
Stockholm Process, and sanctions 363
Strategic Trust Territory of the Pacific Islands
    151, 154–5
structural adjustment programs:
  and Bretton Woods institutions 646
  and governance 630–1
*A Study of the Capacity of the United Nations
    Development System* (1969) 565
Sudan:
  and peace enforcement 222, 377
  and peacebuilding 411, 416
  and sanctions 124, 128, 357, 429
    monitoring and implementation 362
    targeted sanctions 359
Suez crisis (1956) 325, 683
  and General Assembly 104, 118
  and Security Council 120
Summit of the Americas 455
Suriname, and International Court of Justice 196
sustainable development 552
  and human security 553
  and natural resource management 593,
    600–2, 606
  see also Bruntland Commission
Syria, and Chemical Weapons Convention 293

Taiwan, and Security Council 120
Tajikistan 380
Tanganyika 154

  as Trust Territory 151
Tanzania 154, 393, 400
  and electoral assistance to 628
terrorism 5, 427
  and bioterrorism 588–9
  and definitional difficulties 428, 432, 433, 434
    motivation issues 434–5
  and dilemma posed by 427
  and failed states 410
  and General Assembly 428–9
    Ad Hoc Committee on 429
    definitional difficulties 428
    resolutions and conventions 428–9
  and human rights 434
  and multidimensional nature of 427
  and organized crime 613
  and Secretary-General 432–3
    Policy Working Group 432
    strategy for combating 433
  and Security Council 127–8, 429–31
    condemnation by 430
    Counter-Terrorism Committee 430–1
    nuclear, biological, and chemical
      weapons 431
    reports from member states 431
    requirements of states 430, 431
    resolution 1269 430
    resolution 1373 430
    resolution 1540 431
    sanctions 429–30
  and self-defense 433–4
  and threat of 427, 435
  and use of force 433–4
Thailand, and International Court of Justice
    195
Third World Approaches to International
    Law (TWAIL) 73
Third World countries, and General
    Assembly 105, 108–9
timber, and organized crime 618
Tobacco Framework Convention 64
Tobin Tax 697, 712
Togo 154
Togoland 154
  as Trust Territory 151
torture, and United Nations 62
trafficking of people:
  and children 521
  and organized crime 615
    sexual exploitation of children 616
  and women and gender 504–5
  see also organized crime
transition economies, and Bretton Woods
    institutions 234, 238
transnational corporations 268
  and state autonomy 621
  and world affairs 708

transparency:
    and Security Council 128
    and United Nations 83–4
treaties:
    and increase in 14
    and international law 63–6
    and legal positivism 59
    and negotiation forums 65–6
    and nongovernmental organizations 706
Treaty on Conventional Armed Forces in
        Europe (CFE) 295
Tribune (NGO) 499
Troop Contributing Nations (TCNs) 128, 222,
        333
    see also troop-contributing countries
Truman Proclamation (1945) 599
trust, and concept of 150
trusteeship 150
    and failed states 155
    and Peacebuilding Commission 157
    and revival of idea 155–6
Trusteeship Council of the United Nations:
    and abolition of 156–7
    and concept of 'trust' 150
    and dormancy of 156
    and Economic and Social Council 138
    and functions of 149
    and General Assembly 98–9, 104–5
    and League of Nations Mandate System
        150–1
        administration 152
        duration of 151–2
    and reform proposals 156, 668–9
    and Security Council 118–19
    and self-determination 154
    and South West Africa/Namibia
        controversy 153–4
    and suspension of 149, 155
    and Trusteeship System 149, 151
        administration of territories 153
        legal status 152
        objectives of 152
        territories covered 151
    see also trusteeship
Trusteeship System, see Trusteeship Council
tuberculosis, and World Health Organization
        584
Turkey:
    and financial crisis 238
    and International Court of Justice 195

Uganda 393, 400
    and Lord's Resistance Army 467
Ukraine 272
UNAIDS, see Joint UN Programme on
        HIV/AIDS (UNAIDS)
Unified Task Force (UNITAF) 226, 374

unilateralism, and United States 9
Union of International Associations 6
United Kingdom:
    and Afghanistan 380
    and Bretton Woods conference 235
    and financing of United Nations 679, 683,
        684, 685, 694–6
    and former Yugoslavia 375
    and human rights 441, 443–4, 528
    and International Court of Justice 196, 208 n17
    and International Criminal Court 130
    and Iran's nationalization of oil companies 595
    and Iraq:
        military intervention 396
        sanctions 364
    and Rwanda 375
    and sanctions 364–5
    and Security Council 661
    and Sierra Leone 376, 415
    and Sudan 377
United Nations Advisory Committee on
        Local Authorities 707
United Nations Aouzou Strip Observer
        Group (UNASOG) 119
United Nations Assistance Mission for
        Rwanda (UNAMIR) 375
United Nations Assistance Mission in
        Afghanistan (UNAMA) 226
United Nations Association of the United
        States of America 90, 141–2
United Nations Atomic Energy Commission
        (UNAEC) 289
United Nations Centre for Human Settlements
        (UNCHS, Habitat) 563, 566, 634
United Nations Centre on Transnational
        Corporations 65
United Nations Children's Fund (UNICEF) 260,
        268, 479, 481, 503, 512, 548, 563, 634
    and control of infectious diseases 586–7
    and Multiple Indicator Cluster Surveys 648
    and origins and work of 517
United Nations Commission on Crime
        Prevention and Criminal Justice 612
United Nations Commission on International
        Trade Law (UNCITRAL) 63
United Nations Commission on Transnational
        Corporations 268
United Nations Communications Group 570
United Nations Conference on Environment
        and Development (UNCED) (Rio de
        Janeiro, 1992) 258, 259, 264, 270, 502,
        515, 552, 566, 593, 601, 707
United Nations Conference on Human Rights
        (Teheran, 1968) 503
United Nations Conference on the Human
        Environment (Stockholm, 1972) 566,
        593, 600

United Nations Conference on International
    Organization (San Francisco, 1945) 11, 562
  and amendment process 654
  and disagreements at 654
  and Economic and Social Council 139, 664,
    665
  and General Assembly 656
  and historical roots of 702–3
  and human rights 441–2, 527
  and international bill of human rights 442
  and international disputes 302
  and open deliberations 83
  and proposed review conference 654
  and Secretariat 161
  and women 496
United Nations Conference on the Law of
    the Sea (UNCLOS) 598, 599
United Nations Conference on Trade and
    Development (UNCTAD) 65, 88, 105,
    139, 562, 596
  and commodity policy 598
  and New International Economic Order 52
  and transnational corporations 268
United Nations Congress on Crime Prevention
    and Criminal Justice 427
United Nations Congress on the Prevention of
    Crime and the Treatment of Offenders
    (1975) 612
United Nations Convention against Illicit Traffic
    in Narcotic Drugs and Psychotropic
    Substances 612, 614
United Nations Convention Against
    Transnational Organized Crime 505, 514
United Nations Convention on the Law of the
    Sea 600
United Nations Convention to Combat
    Desertification (CCD) 706
United Nations Crime Commission 505
United Nations Declaration of the Rights of
    the Child 511
United Nations Development Assistance
    Framework (UNDAF) 572
United Nations Development Decade 108
United Nations Development Fund for
    Women (UNIFEM) 500, 518, 634
United Nations Development Group 576, 577
United Nations Development Programme
    (UNDP) 266, 479, 548, 562
  and business 269–70
  and children 517–18
  and democratic governance 626
  and field coordination 572
    assessment of 577
  and Global Compact 271
  and governance 10
  and Human Development Reports 12, 142,
    634–5, 639–42

and human security 551, 552–3
and humanitarian action 483
and Millennium Development Goals 643
and monitoring and evaluation 647
and natural resource management 605
and nongovernmental organizations 260
and World Health Organization 587
and establishment of 482
United Nations Educational, Scientific and
    Cultural Organization (UNESCO) 68,
    281, 455, 498, 517, 519, 563, 634
  and American withdrawal from 688
United Nations Emergency Force (UNEF) 120,
    325
United Nations Environment Programme
    (UNEP) 712
  and human security 554
  and World Health Organization 586
United Nations Focal Point for Electoral
    Assistance Activities 626
United Nations Foundation 89
United Nations Framework Convention on
    Climate Change (UNFCCC) 258, 601–2
United Nations Girls' Education Initiative 519
United Nations High Commissioner for
    Human Rights 452–3, 455
  and children 517
  and gender integration 504
  and human rights violations 543
United Nations High Commissioner for
    Refugees (UNHCR) 155, 260, 479, 481,
    482, 548, 562–3
  and children 517
  and Department of Humanitarian Affairs
    489
  and humanitarian action 485
  and Persian Gulf crisis (1991) 485
United Nations Implementation Force
    (IFOR) 123, 226, 333
United Nations Independent Commission of
    Inquiry (UNICOI) 362
United Nations Industrial Development
    Organization (UNIDO) 563, 598
United Nations Information Centre (UNIC)
    278
United Nations Information Organization
    (UNIO) 276–7
United Nations Institute for Training and
    Research (UNITAR) 89
United Nations Intellectual History Project
    (UNIHP) 635
United Nations Interim Administration Mission
    in Kosovo (UNMIK) 226, 471
United Nations International Drug Control
    Programme (UNDCP) 563, 694
United Nations Legal Office, and peaceful
    settlement of disputes

and inquiry/fact-finding 305
and mediation/good offices 305
and negotiation 304
United Nations Military Observer Group in
    India and Pakistan (UNMOGIP) 120
United Nations Mission in East Timor
    (UNAMET) 226
United Nations Mission in Kosovo 380
United Nations Mission in
    Sierra Leone (UNAMSIL) 376
United Nations Mission in the Democratic
    Republic of the Congo (MONUC) 377
United Nations News Centre 277
United Nations Observer Mission in Sierra Leone
    (UNOMSIL) 226
United Nations Office for Project Services
    (UNOPS) 629–30
United Nations Office on Drugs and Crime
    (UNODC) 427, 612
United Nations Operation in Somalia
    (UNOSOM) 123, 226, 374
United Nations Operation in the Congo
    (ONUC) 333
United Nations Population Fund (UNFPA)
    503, 634, 696
United Nations Protection Force
    (UNPROFOR) 185, 226, 333, 374–5
United Nations Radio 278
United Nations Relief and Rehabilitation
    Administration (UNRRA) 481, 548
United Nations Relief and Works Agency
    (UNRWA) 548, 563, 694
United Nations Special Commission
    (UNSCOM) 288, 297
United Nations Special Committee on
    Peacekeeping Operations 378
United Nations Stabilization Mission in Haiti
    (MINUSTAH) 376
United Nations Staff Council 169
United Nations Statistical Office 647, 679
United Nations Transition Assistance Group
    (UNTAG) 154, 629
United Nations Transitional Administration in
    East Timor (UNTAET) 226, 377, 471
United Nations Transitional Authority in
    Cambodia (UNTAC) 627, 629
United Nations Transitional Authority in
    Eastern Slovenia (UNTAES) 333, 629
United Nations Truce Supervision Organization
    (UNTSO) 120
United Nations TV 278
United Nations University (UNU) 89, 696
United Nations Volunteers Programme
    (UNV) 630
United Nations World Tourism Organization
    (UNWTO) 563
United Somali Congress 374

United States:
    and Afghanistan 410–11
    and blocks Boutros-Ghali's
        reappointment 184–5
    and Bosnia and Herzegovina 240
    and Bretton Woods conference 235
    and Comprehensive Test Ban Treaty 295
    and Convention on the Rights of the Child
        513
    and democracy 622–3
    and development assistance 696
    and disarmament 290–1
    and financing of United Nations 676, 679,
        681, 683, 684, 685, 687, 688–90, 693,
        696, 713
    and former Yugoslavia 375, 379
    and General Assembly 107, 109
    and Gulf War (1991) 123
    and Haiti 376
    and human rights 441, 444, 459, 528
    and humanitarian intervention:
        opposition to 397
        responsibility to protect 398
    and International Court of Justice 196
    and International Criminal Court 130, 454,
        473, 475–6
    and international criminal tribunals 129
    and International Development
        Association 248
    and International Monetary Fund:
        capital subscriptions to 246
        influence on 243–5
        quota increase debates 247
    and landmine convention 296
    and Marshall Plan 236
    and military expenditure 9
    and military intervention 393, 394
        Iraq 45, 396
        Kosovo 396
    and National Security Strategy (2002) 410
    and natural resource management 595
    and Nuclear Non-Proliferation Treaty
        292–3
    and peace enforcement 382, 383
    and peacebuilding 410–11
        Afghanistan 410–11
        Iraq 411, 416
    and pre-eminence of 9
    and Rwanda 375
    and sanctions:
        decision-making procedures 364–5
        Iraq 351, 352, 364
    and Security Council 132, 660, 661, 663
    and Somalia 374
    and Sudan 377
    and terrorism 410
    and unilateralism 9

United States (*cont.*)
  and United Nations 132
    debates over 110–11
    foreign policy debates over 110–11
    realist view of 44
  and World Bank:
    capital subscriptions to 248
    influence on 243–5, 248
United States Agency for International
    Development (USAID) 244
United States Centers for Disease Control and
    Prevention 260
United States Federal Reserve 237
Uniting for Peace (1950) 104, 118, 309, 372
Universal Declaration of Human Rights (1948)
    12, 67, 443, 444, 446, 447, 453, 459, 465,
    496, 512, 542
Universal Postal Union (UPU) 563, 703
University for Peace 89
Uruguay 595

values, and role of United Nations 47–8
Vanuatu 8
Venezuela 8
Versailles conference (1919) 541
Vienna Convention on the Law of Treaties
    (1969) 306
Vietnam, and military intervention 393, 394,
    395, 400
Vietnam War 120
violence against women (VAW) 501, 504, 505
Voice of America 276
voting blocs, and United Nations 53

war:
  and deaths from 11
    civilians 5, 395
  and intrastate wars 5
  and laws of 463–4, 545–6
  and proscriptions on 392
war crimes 399
  and Nuremberg trials 465
  see also International Criminal Court;
    international criminal tribunals
Warsaw Pact 219
Washington consensus 250, 646
Wassenaar Agreement 363
weapons of mass destruction (WMDs) 5
  and Biological and Toxin Weapons
    Convention 294, 588
  and Chemical Weapons Convention 293–4
  and disarmament 289
  and Nuclear Non-Proliferation Treaty 292–3
  see also disarmament
Western European Union (WEU) 361
Western Sahara 629
  and electoral assistance to 627

  and peace enforcement 222
  and peacekeeping operations 405
Western Samoa 154
  as Trust Territory 151
Westphalia, Peace of (1648) 389, 526, 540
Winterthur 697
Women 2000: Gender Equality, Development
    and Peace for the Twenty-first Century
    (New York, 2000), 259
women and gender 4–5, 506–7
  and awareness-raising 499
  and children 519
  and Decade for Women (1976-85) 498–9
  and development 502–3
  and gender mainstreaming 502
  and Gender-Empowerment Measure 637
  and Gender-Related Development Index
    503, 637
  and health issues 503–4
  and human development 640–1
  and human rights 504–5
  and humanitarian action 506
  and International Women's Year (1975) 498
  and meaning of terms 496–7
  and Millennium Development Goals 503
  and nongovernmental organizations 501
  and peace issues 505–6
  and United Nations Conference on
    International Organization (San
    Francisco, 1945) 496
  and social and economic development 645
  and standards setting 498, 500–1
  and strategies 497
  and violence against women 501, 504, 505
  and women's contribution 497
  and women-specific conferences 498–500
  and women-specific institutions 497–8, 500
  and work 502
  see also Convention on the Elimination of
    All Forms of Discrimination against
    Women
Women's Agenda 21 502
Women's Caucus for Gender Justice 505
Women's International Democratic
    Federation 498
Women's World Banking 502
Working Group on Indigenous Populations
    (WGIP) 533
World AIDS Day (2005) 516
World Association of Cities and Local
    Authorities 707
World Bank 14, 42, 563
  and accountability of 252
  and 'Anglo-Saxon' character of 234
  and autonomy of 235
  and behavior of staff 54
  and children's issues 518

World Bank: (cont.)
  and Comprehensive Development
    Framework 241
  and conflict sensitive adjustment policies
    418
  and control of infectious diseases 587
  and criticisms of 235, 251
  and debt crisis (1980s) 237–8
  and effectiveness of 251
  and *Equity and Development* (2006) 317
  and finance of 234, 245–6
  and financial crises (1990s) 238–9
  and functions of 233
  and governance of 234, 242–5
    United States' influence 243–5, 248
  and heavily indebted poor countries
    239–40
  and human development 635
  and human rights 451
  and Independent Evaluation Group
    241–2
  and International Monetary Fund 233–4
  and legitimacy of 251
  and loan policy and practices 249–51
  and measuring success/failure 241–2
  and membership of 234
  and Millennium Development Goals 643
  and natural resource management 605
  and origins and development of 235–6
  and post-conflict reconstruction 240–1
  and poverty reduction strategy papers 239,
    577–8
  and realist view of 44
  and resources of 247–9
  and Security Council 120
  and staff of 234
  and structural adjustment 237–8
  and transition economies 238
  and United Nations 234
    relationship with 235
  and weighted voting 140, 234, 243
    veto powers 243–4
  see also Bretton Woods institutions;
    international financial institutions;
    International Monetary Fund;
    International Bank for Reconstruction
    and Development
World Charter for Nature 601
World Commission on Environment and
  Development 552, 601
World Conference on Human Rights (Vienna,
  1993) 445, 446, 504, 519
World Conference of the International Women's
  Year (Mexico City, 1975) 498, 499, 503, 645
World Conference to Review and Appraise the
  Achievements of the UN Decade for
  Women (Nairobi, 1985) 498, 499

World Conference of the UN Decade for
  Women (Copenhagen, 1980) 498, 499
World Congress against Commercial Sexual
  Exploitation of Children (Stockholm,
  1996) 515
World Declaration on Education for All (1990) 519
World Declaration on the Survival, Protection
  and Development of Children (1990) 515
World Disarmament Conference (1932) 705
World Economic Forum 266, 708
World Food Programme (WFP) 479, 482, 548,
  563, 634
world government 10
  and General Assembly 113
  see also global governance
World Health Assembly (WHA) 268, 583, 588
  and human security 589
  and International Health Regulations 585,
    586, 589–90
  see also World Health Organization
World Health Organization (WHO) 260, 268,
  481, 563, 634, 703
  see also World Health Assembly
  and children 517
  and control of infectious diseases 583–7
    approach to 584
    campaigns 584–5
    growing problem of 585–6
    inter-agency cooperation 586–7
    International Health Regulations 585
    SARS epidemic 586
  and establishment of 583
  and Global Outbreak Alert and Response
    Network 589
  and health for all (HFA) process 584
  and HIV/AIDS, '3 by 5 Initiative' 520
  and human security 589
  and International Health Regulations 586,
    589–90
  and powers of 583
  and public health response and surveillance
    589
  and Security Council 589
  and violence against women 501, 503
World Intellectual Property Organization
  (WIPO) 563, 614
World Meteorological Organization (WMO)
  563, 712
  and World Health Organization 586
world politics:
  and global governance 10–11
  and new threats 4–5
  and nonstate actors 6–7
  and state sovereignty 3–4, 7–9
    failed states 8
    impact of globalization 7
    impact of human rights 8

world politics: (*cont.*)
    and United Nations' changing fortunes
        17–18
    and United States' pre-eminence 9
    see also international relations
World Population Conference (Bucharest,
        1974) 503
World Summit (2005) 18, 301, 310, 566
    and conflict prevention 312–13
    and Economic and Social Council 664, 667
    and human rights 440
    and Human Rights Council 440, 450
    and Peacebuilding Commission 667–8
    and peaceful settlement of disputes 316
    and responsibility to protect 398, 440, 548
    and sustainable development 602
World Summit for Children (1990) 515
World Summit for Social Development
        (Copenhagen, 1995) 259, 271, 502, 515,
        553
World Summit on Sustainable Development
        (Johannesburg, 2002) 259, 602
World Summit Outcome (2005) 229, 589, 655
    and Economic and Social Council 145–6
    and peaceful settlement of disputes 302
World Trade Organization (WTO) 563
    and control of infectious diseases 585
    and Economic and Social Council 138, 139
World Urban Forum 707

World Vision International 517
World Wide Fund for Nature (WWF) 260

Xinhua 276

Yale School, and international law 69–70
Yale University, and oral history archive 87
yellow fever, and International Health
        Regulations 585
    see also infectious diseases
Yom Kippur war (1973) 597
Yugoslavia, former 8, 122, 123
    and humanitarian intervention 547–8
    and International Criminal Tribunal for the
        former Yugoslavia 129, 465–7
    successes and failures of 467–8
    and naval blockade 124
    and peace enforcement 332–3, 374–5
    and peacekeeping operations 185–6, 373
    and sanctions 352, 357, 360–1
        arms embargoes 359
        commodity-specific 359
        targeted sanctions 358
    see also individual countries

Zambezi River Plan 607
Zanzibar 154
Zimbabwe 125
    see also Rhodesia

PERSONAL NAME INDEX

Abbott, Kenneth 72
Adams, Gerry 435
Aideed, Mohammed Farah 374, 382
Albright, Madeleine 132, 170, 281, 374
Alexander II, Tsar 463
Amin, Idi 393
Anghie, Tony 73
Annan, Kofi 119
   and administrative changes 566
   and assessment of 129
   and change in UN 16, 709
   and Commission on the Private Sector and
      Development 271
   and conflict prevention 26, 301, 311–12, 313–16
   and democracy 631
   and Economic and Social Council 667
   and 'fork in the road' speech 18, 87, 145, 662
   and Global Compact initiative 6, 260, 270–1
   and good governance 624
   and Human Rights Council 450, 454
   and humanitarian intervention 378, 396, 548
   and *In Larger Freedom* 229, 589, 709–10
   and inequality 549–50
   and *Interim Report of the Secretary-General
      on the Prevention of Armed Conflict* 312
   and Kosovo 131
   and local authorities 707
   and media 280, 281
   and Oil-for-Food Programme 169–70, 188–9
   and peacebuilding 412
   and peaceful settlement of disputes 310
   and *Prevention of Armed Conflict* 311, 313–16
   and private sector 264, 270–2, 708
   and reform proposals 655
   and requests for finance 690–1
   and responsibility to protect 398
   and Secretariat 163, 164
   and Secretary-General's role 188–9
   and Security Council reform 662, 663
   on Sen's *Development as Freedom* 636
   and sovereignty 8, 395, 396
   and sustainable development 602
   and terrorism 432
   and Trusteeship Council 156, 668, 669
   and *We, the Children* 516
Antrobus, Peggy 499, 501–2

Arbour, Louise 127, 452
Arias, Oscar 641
Aristide, Jean-Bertrand 376, 544
Aristotle 636
Augustine, Saint 27
Avenol, Joseph 161, 164
Axworthy, Lloyd 364

Ball, Nicole 419
Ban Ki-moon 23, 172, 177, 190, 310
Barros, James 179
Begtrup, Bodil 498
Bellamy, Carol 517
Bernadotte, Count Folke 429
Boserup, Ester 502
Bouteflika, Abdelaziz 131
Boutros-Ghali, Boutros 119
   and administrative changes 566
   and *An Agenda for Development* 561
   and *An Agenda for Peace* 129, 220–1, 301,
      302, 310, 311–12, 323, 324, 327, 379, 405,
      488, 549, 626
   and Angola 187
   and appointment of 170, 171
   and conflict prevention 26
   and coordination 561
   and declaratory activism 186
   and democracy 626–7, 631
   and enforcement operations 123
   and financing of United Nations 697
   and former Yugoslavia 185–6
   and Israel 186
   and media 23–4, 281
   and *No Exit without Strategy* 323, 334
   and nongovernmental organizations 705
   and peace enforcement 378
   and peacebuilding 406, 412, 549
   and peaceful settlement of disputes 310
   and political activism 187
   and preventive diplomacy 178, 406
   and reappointment blocked 184–5
   and requests for finance 690–1
   and Rwanda 186
   and Secretariat 163
   as Secretary-General 183, 184–8
   and Somalia 185, 374

Boutros-Ghali, Boutros (*cont.*)
    and sovereignty 8
    and *Supplement to an Agenda for Peace* 221, 333
    and Trusteeship Council 668–9
Brahimi, Lakhdar 221–2, 334, 693
Braithwaite, John 267
Brandt, Willy 552, 565
Brownlie, Ian 445
Brundtland, Gro Harlem 552, 599
Buergenthal, Thomas 525, 528
Bull, Hedley 4
Bunche, Ralph 163
Bush, George H. W. 184, 685
    and Iraqi sanctions 351
Bush, George W. 9, 111, 623, 690
    and Millennium Development Goals 283

Cardoso, Fernando Henrique 257, 710
Carr, E. H. 11, 266
Carter, Jimmy 127, 684, 688, 697
Chamie, Joseph 281–2
Chiang Kai-shek 653
Charlesworth, Hilary 74
Chayes, Abram 70, 72
Chayes, Antonia 72
Chesterman, Simon 422
Childers, Erskine 14–15, 143, 706
    and Secretariat 163
Chinkin, Christine 74
Chirac, Jacques 375, 697
Chomsky, Noam 623
Chowdhury, Anwarul 364
Churchill, Winston 218
Claude, Inis L., Jr. 5, 51, 178, 702, 703
Clinton, Bill 334, 688, 690, 693, 697
    and Haiti 376
    and Iraqi sanctions 351
    and Kosovo 379
Cobo, José R. Martínez 533
Cohen, Roberta 8
Czempiel, Ernst 10

Dallaire, Roméo 396
Deen, Thalif 283
Deng, Frances M.8, 390
Diamond, Larry 620
Djindjic, Zoran 475
Doe, Samuel 414
Downs, George 412
Doyle, Michael 133
Drahos, Peter 267
Draper, William A., III 269
Drummond, Eric 161, 164, 177
Dujarric, Stéphane 284

Echeverría, Luís 597
Eckhard, Frederic 279

Ehrlich, Thomas 70
Ekéus, Rolf 351
Evans, Gareth 312

Filene, Edward 265, 272
Findlay, Mark 613
Finger, Seymour Maxwell 182
Finkelstein, Lawrence 624–5
Fitzmaurice, Gerald 201–2
Forman, Shepard 420
Franco, Francisco 388
Fréchette, Louise 571

Galtung, Johan 371, 713
Gardner, Richard N. 441
Gates, Bill 270, 697
Gorbachev, Mikhail 121
Gordenker, Leon 178, 179
Gore, Al 623
Goulding, Marrack 182–3
Gramsci, Antonio 51–2
Grant, James P. 517
Greenstock, Jeremy 133
Gregg, Judd 713
Grotius, Hugo 27, 598
Guillaume, Gilbert 203

Haas, Ernst 7
Hammarskjöld, Dag 22, 119, 687
    and annual report 177
    and appointment of 171
    and media 280–1
    and peaceful settlement of disputes 310
    and peacekeeping 325
    and release of American prisoners-of-war 180–1
    on role of UN 18
    and Secretariat 162, 163–4, 165, 171
    and Secretary-General's role 177, 178, 180–1
Hampson, Fen O. 412
Haq, Mahbub ul 142, 269, 636
Held, David 621
Helman, Gerald 155
Helms, Jesse 688, 689, 713
Helton, Arthur 493
Hoffman, Paul 266, 267, 269
Holsti, Kalevi 13, 15
Howe, Jonathan 374
Hubert, Don 400
Hun Sen 414
Hussein, Saddam 18, 124, 132, 351, 352, 678

Ismail, Razali 662

Jackson, Robert 484, 565
Jacobson, Harold 10
Jain, Devaki 497, 502
James, Harold 235

Jebb, Eglantyne 512
Jennings, Robert 202
Johnson, Lyndon B 689
Johnstone, Ian 51
Jordan, Robert S. 181, 190

Karadžić, Radovan 467, 476
Kelly, Grace 267
Kennedy, David 73
Keynes, John Maynard 235, 266
Khan, A. Q. 431
Khrushchev, Nikita 162
Kingsbury, Benedict 4
Koh, Tommy 599
Koskenniemi, Martti 73
Krasner, Stephen 7

Lasso, José Ayala 452
Lasswell, Harold 69
Lewis, W. Arthur 266
Lie, Trygve 23
    and media 280
    and peaceful settlement of disputes 310
    and Secretariat 161
    and Secretary-General's role 180
Lindbaek, Jannik 271
Liu, F. T. 325
Lodge, Henry Cabot 676, 689, 697
Lowenfeld, Andreas 70
Lubanga, Thomas 475
Lubin, David 265
Luck, Edward C. 493
Lumumba, Patrice 687
Lund, Michael 317

McDougal, Myres 69
Machel, Graça 515
McNair, Arnold 152
McNamara, Robert 236
McNeill, William 702
Madison, James 622–3
Malloch Brown, Mark 271, 280, 571
Mandela, Nelson 435, 515
Martin, Paul 271
Martin, Susan 493
Matsuura, Kenichi 696
Mikesell, Raymond 243
Milošević, Slobodan 396, 466, 468, 475, 476, 678
Mitrany, David 704
Mitterand, François 697
Mladić, Ratko 467, 476
Montgomery, Thomas 374
Morgenthau, Hans 72
Morse, Bradford 484
Mortimer, Edward 282
Mossadegh, Mohammed 595
Mubarak, Hosni 124, 128, 429

Musharraf, Pervez 622
Myint-U, Thant 280

Naim, Moises 54
Nansen, Fridtjof 481
Nasser, Gamal Abdel 310
Nassif, Ramses 280
Ndimbati, Aloys 467

O'Brien, Conor Cruise 16–17
Ogata, Sadako 553, 696
Okabe, Marie 284
Ottaway, Marina 620–1
Owen, David (British diplomat) 266
Owen, David (British politician) 185

Page Fortna, Virginia 412
Pahlavi, Mohammad Reze 595
Pardo, Arvid 599
Paulus, Andreas L. 69
Pearson, Lester B. 565
    and peacekeeping 325
Peck, Connie 313
Pérez de Cuéllar, Javier 119, 176
    and administrative changes 565
    and annual report 177
    and Iran–Iraq war 121, 129
    and media 281
    and peaceful settlement
        of disputes 310
Petchesky, Rosalind 503
Petrén, S. 201
Pianim, Kwame 271
Pol Pot 393, 414
Pugh, Michael 227

Ramcharan, Bertrand G. 452
Ranshofen-Wertheimer, Egon 179
Ratner, Steven 155
Reagan, Ronald 109, 269, 376, 684, 688
    and military intervention 394
Reinsch, Paul 703
Rhodes, Cecil 150
Roberts, Adam 4
Robinson, Edward G. 267
Robinson, Mary 127, 452
Rockefeller, John D. 265, 272
Roosevelt, Eleanor 442
Roosevelt, Franklin D. 243, 653
Rose, Michael 375
Rosenau, James 10, 255
Rosenthal, Gert 665
Rowntree, Joseph 272
Rubin, Barnett 317
Rubin, Robert 271
Rusk, Dean 699 n18
Russell, Ruth 568

Saltzman, Arnold A. 182
Sankoh, Foday 472
Savimbi, Jonas 187, 415
Saward, Michael 622
Schwabel, Stephen 178
Scoon, Paul 393
Sen, Amartya 553, 623, 636
Sharif, Nawaz 622
Sharp, Walter R. 140
Sikubwabo, Charles 467
Sills, Joe 281
Silva, Luiz Inácio da 697
Simma, Bruno 69, 302, 304
Singer, Hans 266
Sipilä, Helvi 503
Smuts, Jan 150
Snidal, Duncan 72
Stedman, Stephen 337, 412
Strong, Maurice 270, 566

Taylor, Charles 357, 362, 414, 473
Tharoor, Shashi 282
Thatcher, Margaret 109
Tobin, James 697, 712
Turner, Ted 89, 270, 697

U Thant:
    and media 280
    and peaceful settlement of disputes 310
    and Secretariat 163, 165

and Secretary-General's role 181–2
Urquhart, Brian 14–15, 143, 277, 706
    and appointment of Secretaries-General 176
    on Hammarskjöld 280–1
    and Secretariat 163

Vandenberg, Arthur 679
Védrine, Hubert 9
Veneman, Ann 517
Vieira de Mello, Sérgio 127, 452
Vittachi, Tarzie 283
Volcker, Paul 124, 351
    and Oil-for-Food Programme 169–70

Waldheim, Kurt:
    and media 281
    and peaceful settlement of disputes 310
    and Secretariat 163
    and Secretary-General's role 182
    and terrorism 428
Watson, Thomas J. 265, 272
Weiss, Thomas G. 400, 492–3
Wells, H. G. 150
Wendt, Alexander 10
White, Harry Dexter 266
Wilson, Woodrow 82, 541, 676–7
Winsemius, Albert 266
Wiranto, General 471

Zedillo, Ernesto 271